Monumentality in Early Chinese Art and Architecture

英汉对照

中国古代艺术与建筑中的“纪念碑性”（上）

（美）巫鸿 著　李清泉 郑岩 等译

外语教学与研究出版社
FOREIGN LANGUAGE TEACHING AND RESEARCH PRESS
北京 BEIJING

图书在版编目（CIP）数据

中国古代艺术与建筑中的“纪念碑性”. 上 ：英汉对照 /（美）巫鸿著 ；李清泉等译. -- 北京 ：外语教学与研究出版社，2024. 8. -- ISBN 978-7-5213-5366-2
I. J120.92；TU-092.2
中国国家版本馆 CIP 数据核字第 2024V197D1 号

出 版 人 王 芳
系列策划 吴 浩
责任编辑 仲志兰
责任校对 易 璐
封面设计 潘振宇
出版发行 外语教学与研究出版社
社 址 北京市西三环北路 19 号（100089）
网 址 https://www.fltrp.com
印 刷 北京尚唐印装包装有限公司
开 本 710×1000 1/16
印 张 62
字 数 1030 千字
版 次 2024 年 8 月第 1 版
印 次 2024 年 8 月第 1 次印刷
书 号 ISBN 978-7-5213-5366-2
定 价 258.00 元

如有图书采购需求，图书内容或印刷装订等问题，侵权、盗版书籍等线索，请拨打以下电话或关注官方服务号：
客服电话：400 898 7008
官方服务号：微信搜索并关注公众号“外研社官方服务号”
外研社购书网址：https://fltrp.tmall.com

物料号：353660001

“博雅双语名家名作”出版说明

1840年鸦片战争以降，在深重的民族危机面前，中华民族精英“放眼看世界”，向世界寻求古老中国走向现代、走向世界的灵丹妙药，涌现出一大批中国主题的经典著述。我们今天阅读这些中文著述的时候，仍然深为字里行间所蕴藏的缜密的考据、深刻的学理、世界的视野和济世的情怀所感动，但往往会忽略：这些著述最初是用英文写就，我们耳熟能详的中文文本是原初英文文本的译本，这些英文作品在海外学术界和文化界同样享有崇高的声誉。

比如，林语堂的 *My Country and My People*（《吾国与吾民》）以幽默风趣的笔调和睿智流畅的语言，将中国人的道德精神、生活情趣和中国社会文化的方方面面娓娓道来，在美国引起巨大反响——林语堂也以其中国主题系列作品赢得世界文坛的尊重，并获得诺贝尔文学奖的提名。再比如，梁思成在抗战的烽火中写就的英文版《图像中国建筑史》文稿（*A Pictorial History of Chinese Architecture*），经其挚友费慰梅女士（Wilma C. Fairbank）等人多年的奔走和努力，于1984年由麻省理工学院出版社（MIT Press）出版，并获得美国出版联合会颁发的“专业暨学术书籍金奖”。又比如，1939年，费孝通在伦敦政治经济学院的博士论文以 *Peasant Life in China—A Field Study of Country Life in the Yangtze Valley* 为名在英国劳特利奇书局（Routledge）出版，后以《江村经济》作为中译本书名——《江村经济》使得靠桑蚕为生的“开弦弓村”获得了世界性的声誉，成为国际社会学界研究中国农村的首选之地。

此外，一些中国主题的经典人文社科作品经海外汉学家和中国学者的如椽译笔，在英语世界也深受读者喜爱。比如，艾恺（Guy S. Alitto）将他1980年用中文访问梁漱溟的《这个世界会好吗——梁漱溟晚年口述》一书译成英文（*Has Man a Future? —Dialogues with the Last Confucian*），备受海内外读者关注；

此类作品还有徐中约英译的梁启超著作《清代学术概论》(*Intellectual Trends in the Ch'ing Period*)、狄百瑞(W. T. de Bary)英译的黄宗羲著作《明夷待访录》(*Waiting for the Dawn: A Plan for the Prince*),等等。

有鉴于此,外语教学与研究出版社推出"博雅双语名家名作"系列。

博雅,乃是该系列的出版立意。博雅教育(Liberal Education)早在古希腊时代就得以提倡,旨在培养具有广博知识和优雅气质的人,提高人文素质,培养健康人格,中国儒家六艺"礼、乐、射、御、书、数"亦有此功用。

双语,乃是该系列的出版形式。英汉双语对照的形式,既同时满足了英语学习者和汉语学习者通过阅读中国主题博雅读物提高英语和汉语能力的需求,又以中英双语思维、构架和写作的形式予后世学人以启迪——维特根斯坦有云:"语言的边界,乃是世界的边界",诚哉斯言。

名家,乃是该系列的作者群体,广涉文学、史学、哲学、政治学、经济学、考古学、人类学、建筑学等领域,皆海内外一时之选。

名作,乃是该系列的入选标准。系列中的各部作品都是经过时间的积淀、市场的检验和读者的鉴别而呈现的经典,正如卡尔维诺对"经典"的定义:经典并非你正在读的书,而是你正在重读的书。

胡适在《新思潮的意义》(1919年12月1日,《新青年》第7卷第1号)一文中提出了"研究问题、输入学理、整理国故、再造文明"的范式。秉着"记载人类文明、沟通世界文化"的出版理念,我们推出"博雅双语名家名作"系列,既希望能够在中国人创作的和以中国为主题的博雅英文文献领域"整理国故",亦希望在和平发展、改革开放的新时代为"再造文明"、为"向世界说明中国"略尽绵薄之力。

外语教学与研究出版社

双语版序

《中国古代艺术与建筑中的“纪念碑性”》英文版于1995年问世，至今已近三十载。中文版于2009年出炉，也已有十五年之久。此次能够以双语形式再版，一方面说明这本书仍然持续着它的生命力，一方面也要衷心感谢北京外国语大学外语教学与研究出版社，投入大量人力对原译本进行逐字校对，加强了文字和图版的精确性，同时也替换了一些图片，提高了全书的质量。此外，吴浩、郑岩等同事和友人的鼓励和协助，以及北京大学艺术学院博士研究生吴宛妮所做的资料查对，也都是新版得以完成的重要条件。

现在回头看这本书，使我特别感到高兴的是，它在上世纪90年代提出的一些史学概念和研究方向，现在已被学界普遍接受并发展为中国美术史研究中的重要领域。比如书中第四章“丧葬纪念碑的声音”，以墓地、享堂和墓葬作为分析和理解汉代美术的一个相互依存、环环相扣的对象，从家庭、赞助人、工匠和死者四个角度探寻墓葬建筑和画像的内容、动机和意义。这种对“原境”（context）的重构和解释隐含了我此后提出的“墓葬美术”概念，在国内外学者的共同努力下，在以往十几年中已经发展成为中国美术史研究和教学中的一个耳熟能详的领域。

又如本书第三章“纪念碑式城市——长安”中对西汉长安城的研究，在方法论上扭转了根据静态平面形态将古代城市进行分类比较的做法，强调城市作为社会活体的性质，从其形态和结构的历史变迁入手进行层累式的历史重构，进而发掘造成其不断变化的“人”的因素。对于美术史研究者来说，长安城中持续叠加的关键性建筑体——从汉高祖营造的未央宫到汉惠帝兴建的长安城墙，从汉武帝开辟的上林苑到王莽创立的明堂辟雍——都不断重新定义了这个城市的重心和边界，同时也引起大众心理的转移和社会风尚的流变。在本书首版后的近三十年里，这种强调历史纵深维度的动态观念，已经越来越深入地内化到对古代中国城市和物质文化的研究之中。

本书第一章“礼制艺术的时代”与第二章“宗庙、宫殿与墓葬”互为表里，重构和讨论了史前、三代到秦汉的礼制艺术，一方面以“礼器”为线索，发掘这种特殊器物在中国古代文化和艺术中的重要意义，另一方面将礼仪器具放到礼制建筑的环境中，观察祖先崇拜中心从“庙”到“墓”的转变以及中国人对“石材”作为建筑和雕刻媒材的发现。这种将艺术品和建筑环境结合起来的研究方法，目前已被许多学者采用。另一值得特别提出的方面是，本书提出了中国古代礼器的大宗，不论是史前时期产生的精美玉器，还是夏商周三代盛行的青铜彝器，都与特殊的材质和制作技术密不可分。这可以说是我最近提出的“中国材质艺术”的源头，属于一个方兴未艾的学术潮流，值得多说几句。

以古代玉器和青铜器为例，“材质”同时指涉着“材”和“质”：前者是制作艺术品的物质材料 (material)，后者指不同材料在意识形态和审美层次上的质量 (quality)。因此这个概念包含了物质和精神两个维度，一方面引导我们探究艺术创作中对物质材料的选择标准和使用方式，同时也促使我们思考这些材料所承载的历史、文化、宗教，政治、性别和思想上的含义。从这两个角度出发，我们可以更加自觉地探索艺术创造与物质文化、技术发展之间的关系，也可以把中国美术的品种和特性与中国文化传统的多元性更加紧密地连接起来。由于任何艺术品都由具体材料制成，“材质”观念超越了时代和地区的限制，可以应用于对不同时期中国美术的分析，甚至可以设想把中国和世界上的各类“材质艺术”联系起来讨论，扩展出更为宏观的视野。

以此为例证，我希望这本书不仅是学术史中的一份材料，而且能够继续在当下的学术研究和知识生产中发挥作用。我也希望它能够不断吸引越来越多的中外读者，引发人们对于古代中国美术的更大兴趣和更深思考。

巫　鸿

2024 年 4 月于芝加哥

中文版序

值本书中译本即将出版之际，译者嘱我写一篇序言。想了一想，感到回顾一下这本书的成书背景和动因，或许有利于国内读者了解它的内容和切入点。因为大家知道，每一本书、每一篇文章，都是一次无声对话的一部分。不管著者自觉与否，都有其特定的文化、学术环境和预先设想的读者。对话的对象不同，立论的角度、叙述的简繁，甚至行文的风格也会有所不同。当一本书被翻译，它获得了一批新的“实际读者”（actual readers）。但是一个忠实的译本并不致力于改变原书所隐含的“假想读者”（assumed reader 或 implied reader）——他仍然体现在书的结构、概念和语言之中。

这本书是在 1990 年至 1993 年间写成的。当时，我对中国美术史写作的思考有过一次较大的变化，变化的原因大致有三点：一是《武梁祠：中国古代画像艺术的思想性》于 1989 年出版了，该书基本上是我的博士论文，因此可以说是我以往学习过程的一份最后答卷。目前该书的中文版已由三联书店翻译出版，读过这本书的人不难获知，其主旨是把这个著名的汉代祠堂放入“两个历史”中加以讨论。这两个历史，一是汉代社会、思想和文化的历史，一是宋代以来对汉代美术的研究史。《武梁祠》所体现的因此是一种结合了考据学、图像学和原境分析（contextual analysis）等方法的“内向”型研究，希望通过对一个特定个案的分析来探索汉代美术的深度。答卷交出去了，思想上无甚牵挂。虽然个案研究还不断在做，但内心却希望能在下一本书中换一个角度，以展现古代中国美术史中的另一种视野。

第二个原因是知识环境的变化。到 1989 年秋，我在哈佛大学美术史系已经教了两年书，和系里其他教授的学术交流也逐渐展开。如同其他欧美大学一样，哈佛美术史系的基本学术方向，可以说既是跨地域的，又是以西方为中心的。大部分教授的研究领域是从古典到当代的西方美术史，其余少数几位教授专门负责美洲、亚洲和非洲艺术。我则是该系唯一的中国美术史教员。这种学术环境，自然而然地促使我对世界各地美术的历史经验进行比较，特别是对中、西艺术之异同进行思考。本书“纪念碑性”（monumentality）这个概念，就是从这种思考中产生的。这里我想顺带地提一下，我并不喜欢这个生造的中文词，如果是在国内学术环境中直接写这本书的话，我大概也不会采取这样的字眼。但是如果放在“比较”的语境中，这个概念却能够最直接、最迅速地引导读者反思古代艺术的本质，以及不同艺术传统间的共性和特性。这是因为纪念碑（monument）一直是古代西方艺术史的核心：从埃及的金字塔到希腊的雅典卫城，从罗马的万神殿到中世纪教堂，这些体积庞大的集建筑、雕塑和绘画于一身的宗教性和纪念性建构，最集中地反映出当时人们对视觉形式的追求和为此付出的代价。这个传统在欧洲美术和知识系统中是如此根深蒂固，以至于大部分西方美术史家，甚至连一些成就斐然的饱学之士，都难以想象其他不同的历史逻辑。对他们来说，一个博大辉煌的古代文明必然会创造出雄伟的纪念碑，因而对古代文明的理解也就必然会以人类的这种创造物为主轴。

反思这种西方历史经验的普遍性，探索中国古代艺术的特殊形态和历史逻辑，是我写这本书时的期望之一，也是当时我在哈佛所教的一门名为“中国古代艺术与宗教”课程的一个主要目的。这门课属于为本科生设置的“外国文化基本课程”（foreign culture core course），选修者来自不同专业，但他们对中国美术和文化大都鲜有所闻。面对着坐满赛克勒美术馆讲演厅的这些来自各国的年轻人（这门课在1990年代初吸引了很多学生，有两年达到每次近300人，教室也移到了这个讲演厅），我所面临的最大挑战，是如何使他们理解那些看起来并不那么令人震撼的中国古代玉器、铜器和蛋壳陶器，实际上有着堪与高耸入云的埃及金字塔相比拟的政治、宗教和美学意义。我希望告诉他们为什么这些英文中称作“可携器物”（portable objects）的东西不仅仅是一些装饰品或盆盆罐罐，而是具有强烈“纪念碑性”的礼器，以其特殊的视觉和物质形式强化了当时的权力概念，成为最有威力的宗教、礼仪和社会地位的象征。我也希望使他们懂得为什么古代中国人“浪费”了如许众多的人力和先进技术，去制造那些没有实际用途的玉斧和玉琮（正如古代埃及人“浪费”了如许众多的人力和先进技术去制造那些没有实际用途的金字塔）；为什么他们不以坚硬的青铜去制造农具和其他用具以提高生产的效率；为什么三代宫庙强调深邃的空间和二维的延伸，而不强调突兀的三维视觉震撼；为什么这个古代建筑传统在东周和秦汉时期出现了重大变化，表现为高台建筑和巨大坟丘的出现。

我为这门课所写的讲稿逐渐演变成本书部分章节的初稿；其他一些章节则汇集、发展了当时所做的一些讲演和发言。记得也是在 1990 年左右，系里组织了一项教授之间定期交流研究成果的学术讨论活动，每次讨论由一人介绍正在进行的学术项目。我所讲的题目是著名的九鼎传说，以此为例讨论了中国古代礼器艺术中的“话语”和实践的关系。这次研讨会，使得我和专攻现代德国艺术和美学理论的恰普利茨卡教授开始就有关“纪念碑性”的理论著作进行持续的阅读和对话；而我在那次会上的发言也成为本书导论的最早雏形。

最后，这本书的产生还反映了我对当时一个重大学术动向的回应。受到后现代思潮的影响，一些学者视“宏观叙事”为蛇蝎，或在实际运作上把历史研究定位于狭窄的“地方”或时段，或在理论上把中国文化的历史延续性看成是后世的构建，提倡对这种延续性（或称传统）进行解构。我对这个潮流的态度是既有赞同的一面，也有保留的一面。一方面，我同意“新史学”对以往美术史写作中流行的进化论模式的批评，其原因是这种模式假定艺术形式具有独立于人类思想和活动的内在生命力和普遍意义，在这个前提下构造出一部部没有文化属性和社会功能的风格演化史，实际上是把世界上的不同艺术传统描述成一种特定西方史学观念的外化。但另一方面，我又不赞同对宏观叙事的全然否定。在我看来，“宏观”和“微观”意味着观察、解释历史的不同视点和层面，二者具有不同的学术功能和目标。历史研究者不但不应该把它们对立起来，而且必须通过二者之间的互补和配合，以揭示历史的深度和广度。在宏观层面上，我认为要使美术史研究真正摆脱进化论模式，研究者需要发掘艺术创作中具有文化特殊性的真实历史环节，首要的切入点应该是那些被进化论模式所排斥（因此也就被以往的美术史叙述所忽略）的重大现象。这类现象中的一个极为突出的例子，是三代铜器（以及玉器、陶器、漆器等器物）与汉代画像（以墓室壁画、画像石和画像砖为大宗）之间的断裂：中国古代美术的研究和写作常常围绕着这两个领域或中心展开，但对二者之间的关系却鲜有涉及。其结果是一部中国古代美术史被分割成若干封闭的单元。虽然每个单元之内的风格演变和类型发展可以梳理得井井有条，但是单元之间的断沟却使得宏观的历史发展脉络无迹可循。这些反思促使我抛弃了以往那种以媒材和艺术门类为基础的分类路径，转而从不同种类的礼器和礼制建筑的复杂历史关系中寻找中国古代美术的脉络。

回顾了本书的成书背景和写作动机，这篇序言本来可以就此打住了。可是，由于这本书在几年前曾经引起过一场“辩论”，我感到有必要在这里澄清一下这个辩论所反映的学术观点中的一些根本分歧。在我和国内学者和学生的接触中，我感到许多人对美术史方法论有着浓厚的兴趣。通过揭示潜藏在这个辩论背后的不同史学观念，我可以就本书的研究和叙事方法做一些补充说明，也可以进一步明确它的学术定位。这个辩论起因于美国普林斯顿大学教授罗伯特·巴格利（Robert Bagley）在《哈佛东亚学刊》（*Harvard Journal of Asiatic Studies*）第 58 卷第 1 期上发表的一篇书评，对本书做了近乎从头到尾的否定，其尖刻的口吻与冷嘲热讽的态度在美国的学术评论中也是十分罕见的。我对巴格利的回应刊布于 1999 年的《亚洲艺术档案》（*Archives of Asian Art*）。其后，北京大学李零教授注意到巴格利书评所反映的西方汉学中的沙文主义倾向，组织了一批文章发表在《中国学术》2000 年第 2 期上，其中包括一篇对本书内容的综述、巴格利的书评和我的答复的中译本，以及美国学者夏含夷（Edward Shaughnessy）和李零本人的评论。这个讨论在《中国学术》2001 年第 2 期中仍有持续：哈佛大学中国文学教授田晓菲的题为《学术“三岔口”——身份、立场和巴比伦塔的惩罚》的评论，指出已发表文章中种种有意无意的“误读”，实际上反映了不同作者的自我文化认同。

在此我不打算一一绍述各位学者的观点，对此有兴趣的读者可以直接阅读他们的文章并做出自己的判断。我个人对这一辩论的总体看法是：虽然参与讨论的学者都旗帜鲜明地表明了自己的立场，但是由于讨论的焦点一下子集中在研究者和评论者的身份问题上，与本书内容直接有关的一些有争议的学术问题，反而没有得到充分的注意。需要说明的是，这些争议并不是由本书首次引发的，而是在西方中国美术史学界和考古学界渊源有自，甚至在本书出版以前就已经导致我和巴格利之间的若干重要分歧。

这些分歧中的最重要的一个牵涉到美术史是否应该研究古代艺术的“意义”。许多读者可能会觉得这是个不成问题的问题，但是，了解美国的中国青铜器研究的人都知道，在这个领域中一直存在着围绕这一问题的两种不同观点：一种观点认为，青铜纹样，特别是兽面等动物纹和人物形象，肯定具有社会、文化和宗教的含义；而另一种意见则坚持这些纹样并无这些意义，其形状和风格是由艺术发展的自身逻辑所决定的。绝大多数学者认同前一种意见，其中有些人试图从古文献中寻找青铜纹样的图像志根据，另一些人则把青铜器纹饰的意义定位于更广泛的象征性和礼仪功能。对“无意义”理论提倡最力的是原哈佛大学美术史系教授罗樾（Max Loehr），其师承可以追溯到著名的奥地利形式主义美术史家海因里希·沃尔夫林（Heinrich Wolfflin）。巴格利是罗樾的学生，虽然他的研究重点与其老师不尽相同，将注意力从青铜器艺术风格的演化转移到铸造技术对形式的影响，但在青铜器纹饰有无意义这一点上，他完全秉承了形式主义学派的理论，否定青铜器装饰的宗教礼仪功能和象征性，也拒绝社会和文化因素在形式演变中的作用。

需要指出的是，当前西方学界同意这第二种观点的人已为数甚少，因此巴格利对青铜纹饰无意义的坚持可以说是体现了一种学术信念。这种信念的核心是：美术史必须排除对形式以外因素的过多探索，否则就会失去这个学科的纯粹性和必要性。了解这个基本立场，便不难看到巴格利对本书的否定之所以如此坚决和彻底，原因在于本书从头到尾都在讨论艺术形式（包括质地、形状、纹饰、铭文等因素）与社会、宗教及思想的关系；也在于“纪念碑性”这一概念的首要意义就是把艺术与政治和社会生活紧紧地联系在一起。许多读者知道，在学术史上，这种结合美术史、人类学和社会学的跨学科解释方法，在 20 世纪中晚期构成了对形式主义美术史学派的一个重大逆反和挑战。我与巴格利在 20 世纪末期的分歧是这两种学术观念的延续。

由此出发，大家也便不难理解为什么我们二人之间又出现了另外两点更为具体的分歧——一点关系到古代美术史研究能否参照传世文献，另一点牵涉到讨论秦汉以前的美术时可否使用“中国”这个概念。巴格利在书评中对这两个问题都有十分明确的表态。对于第一个问题，他把传世文献说成是历史上“汉族作家”的作品，认为早期美术史是这些“汉族作家并不了解也无法记载的过去”，因此使用传世文献去研究早期美术是严重的学术犯规。以他的话来说就是：“用《周礼》和《礼记》解释商代的青铜器和新石器时代的玉器是中国传统学术最司空见惯的做法，它在科学考古的年代已经名誉扫地。”（除特别注明以外，此处和下文中的引文均出于其书评。）这种对文献和文献使用者的武断裁判成为巴格利的一项重要“方法论”基础。由此，他可以在商代和史前艺术的研究中不考虑古代文献，也不需要参考任何运用这些文献的现代学术著作；他可以坚持形式主义学派的自我纯洁性，把研究对象牢牢地限制在实物的范围里。他还可以十分方便地对学者进行归类：使用传统文献解释古代美术的，是“中国传统学术最司空见惯的做法”；而对传统文献表示拒绝的，则体现了“科学考古”的思维。

与此类似，他认为“中国”是一个后起的概念，因此需要从“前帝国时期”的美术史研究和叙述中消失。他在书评中写道：“我们不能心安理得地把同一个‘中国’的标签加在良渚、大汶口、红山、龙山、石岭下、马家窑和庙底沟等有着显著特色的考古文化所代表的人群身上。而这只不过是众多考古文化中可以举出的几个例子……”“尽管因为有语言方面的强有力的证据，我们把公元前 1500—前 1000 年的安阳人叫‘中国人’还说得过去，但我们并不知道他们的哪些邻国人或有多少邻国人是说同一种语言。”由此，他质疑考古学家和美术史家把地区之间的文化交往和互动作为主要研究课题，特别反对追溯这种互动在中国文明形成过程中所起的作用。在他看来，这种研究不过是“对‘Chineseness’（中国性）的编造”，而他自己对“地方”的专注，则是对这种虚构的中国性的解构。

我在这两个方面都和巴格利有着重要分歧。首先，我认为美术史家应该最大限度地发掘和使用材料，包括考古材料、传世器物和文献材料，也包括民俗调查和口头文学提供的信息。这是因为现代美术史已经发展成为一个非常广阔的领域，所研究的对象不仅仅是作品，而且包括艺术家和制作者、赞助人和观众、收藏和流通、视觉方式与环境，以及与艺术有关的各种社会机构、文化潮流和思想理论。即使研究的对象是实际作品，所需要解释的也不仅仅是形式和风格，而且包括它们的名称和用途、内容和象征性、创作过程和目的，以及在流传过程中的意义变化，等等。这些研究项目中的绝大部分需要多种材料的支持。实际上，要想把一项研究做得深入和富有新意，最首要的条件是开发研究资料，包括各种各样的文献材料。和所有研究资料的运用一样，引证文献有其一定的方法，对传世文献的使用更需要特殊的训练。但是如果因为某些文献有"年代错乱"和内容"不可靠"的情况而全盘否定这类材料的潜在价值，那就不免太过偏颇，最终只能被视为缺少辨识、驾驭文献的必要水准。

巴格利把文献的用途限定为对历史事实的直接记录，因此极度简化了一个复杂的学术问题。实际上，即便考古发现的"当时记载"，也向来具有其尤其特殊的主体性和目的性，不能被看作是对历史的纯客观描述。所以，现代美术史对文献的使用，已经远远不止于对简单事实的考证。实际上，文献记述的事件、礼仪、景观以及人的生活环境和思想感情等方面的信息，通常是考古材料所难于保存的。通过合理地运用这些文献材料，美术史家往往可以重构出特定的视觉环境，使孤立的艺术品成为社会生活的有机部分。而且，文献的重要性还体现在它为研究古代艺术的"话语"（discourse）提供了第一手材料。"话语"的一个定义是"处理人类非文献活动的文献主体"，波洛克（Griselda Pollock）因此认为美术史本身就是关于美术创造的历史话语。中国古籍中保留了极为丰富的解释艺术和视觉文化的这种"文献主体"。虽然这些文献并不是对特殊史实的记录，但是它们把实践上升到概念的层次，为理解中国古代艺术提供了本土的术语和逻辑。正是从这个角度，我在本书中讨论了"三礼"中包含的极为重要的关于"礼器"艺术的系统话语，也从班固和张衡的文学作品中发掘出东汉人对西汉长安的不同描述，大量的铭文材料进而引导我去倾听东汉时期墓葬艺术中的不同"声音"。可以说，对中国古代艺术话语的发掘和讨论是本书的一个重要组成部分。但巴格利对这种有关"话语"的历史研究似乎毫无兴趣或全然不解。对他来说，讨论玉器和青铜器时只要提到《礼记》或《仪礼》，就足以令一部著作"名誉扫地"了。

关于秦汉以前美术中的"中国"概念问题，我的态度与绝大多数考古学家、历史学家和美术史家一样，一方面注意不同地区、不同时期的文化差异性，另一方面也尽力发掘不同文化之间的渊源与互动。这个辩证的观念可以说是所有关于中国文明起源的重要理论的共同基础。许多杰出的考古学家和历史学家，包括苏秉琦、张光直、吉德炜（David Keightley）等，都对这些理论的形成有过重要贡献。“中国”无疑是这些理论中的一个基本概念，但这并不是那种铁板一块的、所谓后世“汉族作者”心目中的华夏概念，而是一个既具有复杂文化内涵、又具有强烈的互动性和延续性、在变化中不断形成的文化共同体。如前所述，本书的主要目的是在宏观层面上重新思考早期中国美术史的叙述问题，因此我把讨论的重点放在了中国古代美术发展中的延续和断裂上，以时间为轴，重新界定这一艺术传统的主线。所说的“中国”或“中国美术传统”也就决不是巴格利所谴责的那种强加于古代的现代政治理念，而是一个被讨论和研究的历史对象。还需要加以说明的是，我一向认为这种宏观叙述只是美术史写作的一种模式；对地区文化和考古遗址的“近距离”分析代表了另外的模式，业已反映在我的其他著述中（见《礼仪中的美术》中的多篇文章）。总的说来，我认为美术史家不但可以选择不同的研究对象和研究方法，而且也应该发展不同的史学概念和解释模式。这些选择不应该是对立和互相排斥的，而应该可以交流和互补。唯其如此，才能不断推进美术史这个学科的发展。

遗憾的是，这种合作的态度与巴格利所强调的美术史的“纯洁性”又产生了矛盾。他在对本书的评价和其他一些著作中都显示了一种强烈的排他性，其主要的批评对象是他称为“中国考古学家”（Chinese archaeologists）的一群人，其中既包括国内的考古学家和美术史家，也包括在西方从事研究的华人学者。据我所知，他从未从学术史的角度对这个集合体进行界定，但他的批评显示出这些学者在他心目当中的三个共性：一是他们的民族主义立场；二是他们对传统史学的坚持；三是他们对文献的执着。从某些特定的角度和场合来看，巴格利所批评的现象是有着一定的事实基础的，但他的总的倾向是把个别现象本质化，把学术问题政治化。在他的笔下，这些中国考古学家的“研究目的总是为了牵合文献记载，宁肯无视或搪塞与此抵牾不合的证据”；他们总是“维护国家的尊严”和“坚持传统的可靠性”，不惜通过对考古资料的曲解去达到这种目的；他们对传统文献的钟爱不但表明了他们的守旧立场，而且还赋予自己以“文化当局者的权威”（引文见书评和他写作的《商代考古》一章，载于《剑桥中国上古史》）。他以这些武断的词句，一方面为众多中国或中国出生的学者塑造了一个漫画式的群像，另一方面又赋予自己一个“文化局外人”的客观、科学的身份。诚然，任何学术研究都不可能完美无缺，面面俱到，严肃的批评和商榷因此对学术的发展具有非常重要的意义。但是巴格利的这种“学术批评”，可以说是已经滑到了种族主义的边缘。

田晓菲教授在她的评论中指出，巴格利并不能代表西方考古学家，更遑论“先锋”。同样，我需要声明这本书绝不是任何“中国学派”的代言，它记录的只是我个人在探索中国古代美术传统中的一些心得体会。“传统”在这里不是某种一成不变的形式或内容，而是指一个文化体中多种艺术形式和内容之间变化着的历史联系。上文对本书写作初衷的回顾已显示出，我对中国古代美术传统的界定是沿循着两个线索进行的。一个是文化比较的线索，即通过“纪念碑性”在中国古代美术中的特殊表现来确定这个艺术传统的一些基本特性；另一个是历史演变的线索——通过对一个波澜壮阔的历史过程的观察去发掘中国古代美术内部的连续性和凝聚力。正是这样一种特殊的研究目的和方法，使我把目光集中到那些我认为是中国古代美术最本质的因素上去，而把对细节的描述和分析留给更具体的历史研究。因此，我希望读者们能把这本书看作重构中国古代美术宏观叙述的一种尝试，而不把它当成提供研究材料和最终结论的教科书或个案分析。对我来说，这本书的意义在于它反映了一个探索和思考的过程。十多年后的今日，我希望它所提出的问题和回答这些问题的角度仍能对研究和理解古代中国美术的发展有所裨益。

巫　鸿

2007 年 8 月于北京

To K. C. Chang

献给张光直

ACKNOWLEDGMENTS

Clearly, a study such as this must rely on previous scholarship on early Chinese art and architecture and must address many questions posed by that scholarship. Indeed, this book grew from six years of dialogues, lectures, and seminars with scholars and students, and it is meant to continue this process of communication. The project began to take shape in conversations with my colleagues at Harvard, in particular John Czaplicka, a scholar learned in the history and theory of monuments. But it was my teaching on both graduate and undergraduate levels that offered me the chance to pursue a systematic reinterpretation of early Chinese art. My lecture notes gradually grew into writings, conceptualized as sections in this volume but presented as individual papers in more than twenty symposia, conferences, and colloquia. On all these occasions I benefited from many inspiring comments and suggestions. A number of scholars read the first draft of this book, among whom Martin Powers offered detailed comments important to my revision. John R. Ziemer and Helen Tartar, editors at Stanford University Press, have been two major supporters of this project from its beginning; they are also responsible for the book's fine form. Finally and most of all, my wife, Judith Zeitlin, has always been the first reader of every section and chapter, and her critical reading contributed not only to the book's arguments but also to its conceptualization.

W. H.

鸣 谢

很显然，像本书这样的一项研究必须建立在前人对中国古代艺术和建筑的多项学术贡献上，必须回应在此之前提出的许多学术问题。实际上，这本书产生于六年来我与诸多学者和学生的对话、演讲及讨论，它的写作也是这种交流过程的延续。这项计划是从我与哈佛的同事们——特别是以研究纪念碑历史与理论而著称的约翰·恰普利茨卡——交谈时开始成形的。但是，直至就此题目给本科生和研究生们授课时，我才有机会着手对中国古代艺术重新做系统的解释。我的演讲笔记逐渐发展成为文字，作为单篇文稿在二十多次座谈、讨论会和报告会中发表，随即逐渐条理成为本书的各个部分。在所有这些场合中，我都获得了许多富有启发性的评论和建议。许多学者审读了本书的初稿，其中包华石提出了诸多详细的建议，对于我后来的修改极为重要。从这个项目启动时，斯坦福大学的两位编辑约翰·R. 齐默和海伦·塔塔尔就是两位主要支持者，本书雅致的设计也归功于他们二位。最后，也是最重要的，我的妻子蔡九迪总是每个章节的第一读者，她批评性的阅读不仅对于本书观点的形成，而且对于其理论化有着重要贡献。

巫 鸿

导论　九鼎传说与中国古代的『纪念碑性』

Figures 插图

INTRODUCTION THE NINE TRIPODS AND TRADITIONAL CHINESE CONCEPTS OF MONUMENTALITY

001 My use of *monumentality* as the organizing concept of this study calls for some explanation. I chose it, rather than the more common word *monument,* because its relative abstractness offers flexibility for interpretation and because it is not overburdened with preexisting connotations. The word *monument,* as so often encountered in tourist guides and other writings, is frequently associated with giant, durable, solemn structures in public places—the Arc de Triomphe, the Lincoln Memorial, the Statue of Liberty, the Mount Rushmore National Memorial, and the Monument to the People's Heroes in Tiananmen Square (Figs. I.1a-d). Such associations imply a conventional understanding of the monument based on size, material, topology, and location—anyone passing a granite obelisk or a bronze statue would call it a "monument" without knowing anything about it. This common wisdom is shared by artists and art historians. Many scholars, for example, consider the art of monuments synonymous with "monumental architecture" or "public sculpture," an unspecified equivalence underlying their discussion of monuments.[1] Some avant-garde artists who attack traditional "official" art also focus on conventional monumental images. Claes Oldenburg thus designed a series of "anti-monuments," including a pair of scissors that parodies the Washington Monument (Fig. I.2): "The scissors are an obvious morphological equivalent to the obelisk, with interesting differences—metal for stone, humble and modern for ancient, movement for monumentality."[2] The quintessential official monument is once again defined in terms of permanence, grandiosity, and stillness.

It remains questionable, however, whether this seemingly universal understanding sums up every sort of "monument" from every time and place, or whether it is itself a historical construct conditioned by its cultural origin. Indeed, it has been challenged by some writers even in the

West. For example, in “The Modern Cult of Monuments: Its Character and Its Origin” (1902), the Austrian art historian and theoretician Alois Riegl attributed monumentality not only to “intentional” commemorative

导论　九鼎传说与中国古代的“纪念碑性”

首先有必要对本文所使用的“纪念碑性”这一基本概念做若干解释。我之所以用这个词而不是更为常见的“纪念碑”一词，是因为前者相对的抽象性使得在对它进行解释时可以有更大的弹性，同时也可以减少一些先入为主的概念。正如在诸如旅行指南之类的文献中常常可以见到的那样，纪念碑经常是和公共场所中那些巨大、耐久而庄严的建筑物或雕像联系在一起的。巴黎小凯旋门、林肯纪念堂、拉什莫尔山国家纪念碑、自由女神像，以及天安门广场上的人民英雄纪念碑等，是这类作品的代表［图 I.1］。这种联系反映了传统上依据尺寸、质地、形状和地点对于纪念碑的理解：任何人在经过一座大理石方尖塔或者一座青铜雕像时总会称其为“纪念碑”，尽管他对于这些雕像和建筑物的意义可能一无所知。艺术家和艺术史家们沿袭了同一思维方式，很多学者把纪念碑艺术和纪念性建筑或公共雕塑等量齐观。这种未经说明的等同来源于对纪念碑的传统理解。[1] 一些叛逆“正统”艺术的前卫艺术家以传统纪念碑作为攻击对象，美国现代艺术家克拉斯·奥尔登堡因此设计了一系列“反纪念碑”，包括模仿华盛顿纪念碑的一把大剪刀［图 I.2］，并解释说：“显而易见，这把剪刀在形态上是模仿华盛顿纪念碑的，但同时也表现出一些饶有趣味的差异，如金属和石质的区别，现代之粗鄙和古意之盎然的不同，变动和恒定的对立。”[2] 因此，在这种“反纪念碑”的话语系统中，纪念碑的定义再次与永恒、宏伟和静止等观念相通。

然而，这种似乎“普遍”的理解是否能够概括不同时期、不同地点的各种纪念碑呢？或者说，这种理解本身是否即是一个由其自身文化渊源所决定的历史建构？事实上，即使在西方，许多学者已经对此观念的普遍性提出质疑。如奥地利艺术史家、理论家李格尔在其《纪念碑的现代崇拜：它的性质和起源》（1902）一书中就认为，纪念碑性不仅仅存在于“有意而为”的庆典式纪念建筑或雕塑中，

Fig. I.1. (a) Arc de Triomphe du Carrousel, Paris. (b) Mount Rushmore National Memorial, South Dakota. (c) Statue of Liberty, New York. (d) Monument to the People's Heroes, Beijing.

图 I.1 （a）法国巴黎小凯旋门。（b）美国南达科他州拉什莫尔山国家纪念碑。（c）美国纽约自由女神像。（d）中国北京天安门广场人民英雄纪念碑。

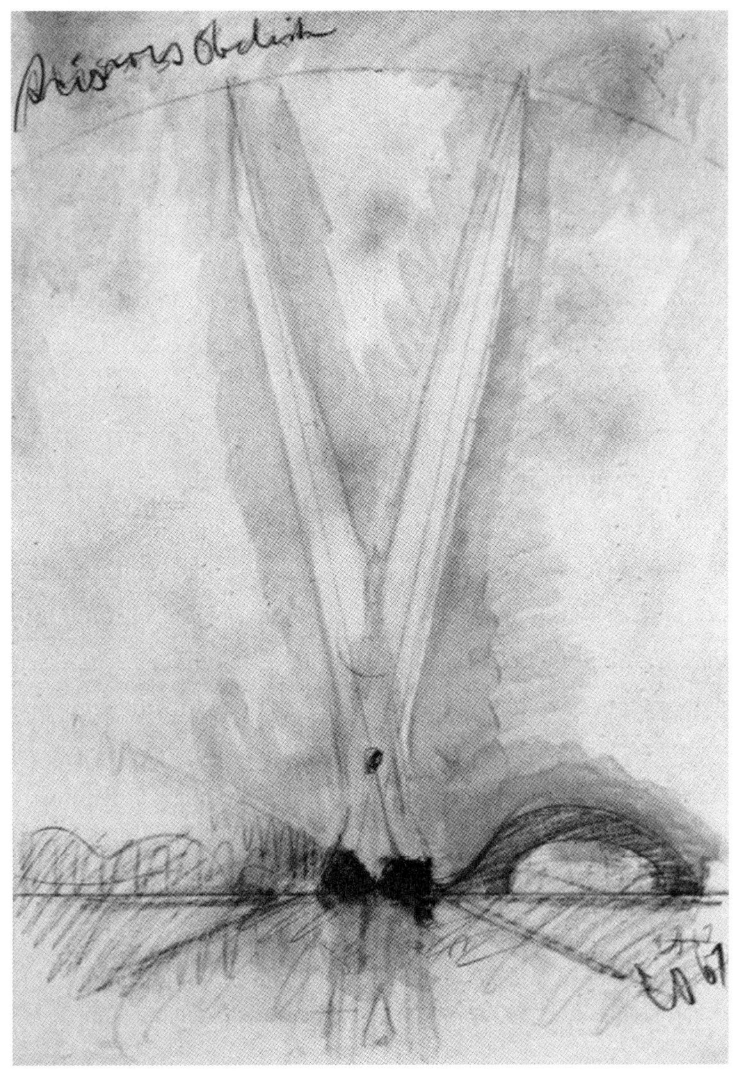

Fig. I.2. Claes Oldenburg, "Giant Scissors," 1965-69. Watercolor on paper.
图 I.2 克拉斯·奥尔登堡《巨剪》，1965—1969 年，纸本水粉。

monuments, but also to those "unintentional" ones (such as ruins) and
003 any object possessing "age value."[3] A yellowed historical document would readily fall into this last category. Following a different line, the American scholar John Brinckerhoff Jackson noticed the widespread desire after the Civil War to declare the Gettysburg battlefield a "monument": "This was something unheard of: an immense, populated landscape of thousands of acres of fields and roads and farmhouses becoming a monument to an event which had taken place there." Such reflections led him to conclude that a monument can take any form. It certainly does not have to be an intimidating structure and does not even have to be a manufactured object—"A monument can be nothing more than a rough stone, a fragment of ruined wall as at Jerusalem, a tree, or a cross."[4]

Riegl's and Jackson's views oppose the conventional understanding of the monument. To them, topology and physical appearance count little in identifying a monument; what makes a thing a monument is its essential ability to memorialize and commemorate. As thought-provoking as this assertion is, it fails to account fully for individual monuments, especially their tangible forms. It lends itself to abstract discourses on memory and history but contributes only indirectly to analyses of art and architecture. Historians who deal with concrete forms (these would include art, architectural, and cultural historians) have to find a third position between empiricism and metaphysics. Their observation of a monument must take into account its function as well as its visual properties. Thus the following questions were posed at a 1992 conference at the University of Washington, entitled straightforwardly "The Monument": "What is a monument? What are the common denominators that constitute monumentality? Is it inherent in size, in power, in mood, in specific temporality, in perdurability, in place, in immortalization? Are concepts of the monumental transhistorical, or have they evolved or radically shifted in the modern period?"[5]

The organizers of the conference felt it necessary to raise these questions because, according to them, “no common ground has been established to account for the phenomenon of the monument in a cross-disciplinary and broadly theoretical way.”[6] But if one believes (as this author does) that the phenomenon of the monument (or the phenomenon

所涵盖对象应当同时包括“无意而为”的东西（如遗址）以及任何具有“年代价值”的物件，如一本发黄的古代文献就无疑属于后者。[3] 从另外一个角度，美国学者约翰·布林克霍夫·杰克逊注意到在美国内战后，出现了一种日渐高涨的声音，要求将葛底斯堡战场宣布为“纪念碑”：“这是一件前所未闻的事：一片数千英亩、遍布着农庄和道路的土地，成了发生在这里的一件历史事件的纪念碑。”这一事实使他得出，“纪念碑可以是任何形式”的结论。它绝对不必是一座使人敬畏的建筑，甚至不必是一件人造物：“一座纪念碑可以是一块未经加工的粗糙石头，可以是诸如耶路撒冷断墙的残块，可以是一棵树，或是一个十字架。”[4]

李格尔和杰克逊的观点与对纪念碑的传统理解大相径庭。对他们来说，类型学和物质体态不是判定纪念碑的主要因素；真正使一个物体成为纪念碑的是其内在的纪念性和礼仪功能。但是，虽然这种观点非常具有启发性，它却难于帮助人们解释纪念碑的个例，尤其是它们真实生动的形式。他们的论述引导我们对回忆和历史做抽象的哲学性反思，但对分析艺术和建筑的形式或美学特征只有间接的贡献。研究具体形式的历史学家们（包括艺术、建筑和文化史家）不得不在经验主义和抽象思辨间寻找第三种位置。他们对于一座纪念碑的观察要兼顾它的功能和外在的特征。因此在 1992 年华盛顿大学召开的一个以“纪念碑”这一直截了当的词为名的学术讨论会上就提出了这样一些问题：“什么是纪念碑？构成纪念碑性的普遍特征是什么？它是否和尺度、权力、氛围、特定的时间性、持久、地点以及不朽观念相关？纪念碑的概念是跨越历史的，还是在现代时期有了变化或已被彻底改变？”[5]

会议的组织者之所以觉得有必要提出这些问题，据他们所言，是因为“还没有建立起一种在交叉原则和多种方法论的基础上来解释纪念碑现象的普遍理论”。[6] 但是如果有人相信（我本人即属于

of anything) is never "transhistorical" and "transcultural," then one must describe and interpret such phenomena historically and culturally. Rather than attempting to find another universal "common ground" that accounts for various kinds of monuments in a "broadly theoretical way," a more urgent and plausible goal is to historicize the phenomenon of the monument—to explore indigenous concepts and forms within well-defined cultural and political traditions, to contextualize these concepts and forms, and to observe conflicting notions and manifestations of the monumental in specific situations. Such case studies, not general abstractions or syntheses, will broaden our knowledge of the monument
004 and will prevent culturally biased theoretical formulations. This is why I propose to treat the monument strictly as a historical issue, and why I need first to define the geographical, chronological, and cultural scope of my study: in the following pages, I examine the concepts of monumentality and the forms of monuments in the specific context of ancient China from prehistorical times to the period known as the Northern and Southern Dynasties.

Here I use the two concepts—*monumentality* and *monument*—to indicate two interrelated levels in my discussion. Both terms derive from the Latin word *monumentum*, meaning to remind and to admonish. But in my usage, *monumentality* (defined in *Webster's New International Dictionary* as a "monumental state and quality"[7]) sustains such functions of a "monument": a physical monument can survive even after it has lost its commemorative and instructive significance. The relationship of monumentality to monument is thus close to that of *content* and *form*. This explains why only an object possessing a definite monumentality is a functional monument. *Monumentality* thus denotes memory, continuity, and political, ethical, or religious obligations to a tradition. This primary meaning underlies a monument's manifold social, political, and ideological significance. As scholars have repeatedly stated, a monument, no matter what shape or material, serves to preserve memory, to structure history, to immortalize a figure, event, or institution, to consolidate a community or a public, to define a center for political gatherings or ritual communication, to relate the living to the dead, and to connect the present with the future. All these concepts

这种人）纪念碑现象（或其他任何受时空限制的现象）从不可能“跨历史”和“跨文化”的话，那他就必须从历史和文化角度来描述和解释这些现象。与其试图寻求另一种广泛的、多方法论基础上的“普遍理论”来解释纪念碑的多样性，倒不如将纪念碑现象历史化更为迫切和合理。这也就是说，我们应该在特定的文化和政治传统中来探索纪念碑的当地概念及表现形式，研究这些概念和形式的原境，并观察在特定条件下不同的纪念碑性及其物化形态的多样性和冲突。这些专案研究并非宽泛的抽象概念或综合体，将拓宽我们有关纪念碑的知识，也会防止含有文化偏见的理论模式的产生。这就是我为什么坚持把纪念碑严格地看成是一种历史事物，以及为什么在研究中首先要界定地域、时间和文化范畴的原因：在本书中，我将在中国的史前到南北朝时期这一特定背景下来探索纪念碑的概念和形式。

这里我使用了“纪念碑性”和“纪念碑”这两个概念，来指示本书中所讨论的两个互相联系的层次。这两个词都源于拉丁文monumentum，本意是提醒和告诫。但在我的讨论中，“纪念碑性”（在《新韦伯斯特国际英文词典》中被定义为“纪念的状态和内涵”）[7]是指纪念碑的纪念功能及其延续；一座“纪念碑”即使在丧失了这种功能和教育意义后，仍然可以在物质形式上存在。因此，“纪念碑性”和“纪念碑”之间的关系类似于“内容”和“形式”间的联系。由此可以认为，只有一座具备明确“纪念性”的纪念碑才是有内容和功能的纪念碑。因此，“纪念碑性”和回忆、延续以及政治、种族或宗教义务有关。“纪念碑性”的具体内涵决定了纪念碑的社会、政治和意识形态等多方面的意义。正如学者们所反复强调的那样，一座有功能的纪念碑，不管它的形状和质地如何，总要承担保存记忆、构造历史的功能，总力图使某位人物、某个事件或某种制度不朽，总要巩固某种社会关系或某个共同体的纽带，总要成为界定某个政治活动或礼制行为的中心，总要实现生者与死者的交通或是现在和未来的联系。对于理解作为社会和文化产物的

are obviously important for any understanding of art and architecture as social and cultural products. But these are nevertheless empty words until they are historically defined. Moreover, even when a particular type of monumentality is defined, it remains an isolated phenomenon until it is linked with other kinds of monumentality into a dynamic historical sequence. I call this sequence a "history of monumentality"; it reflects the changing notion of memory and history.

This transformation in meaning is reflected and expressed by the development of monuments—physical entities that embody and realize historical monumentality. Like the concepts and notions they signify, the tangible properties of a monument—shape, structure, medium, decoration, inscription, and location—constantly change; there is absolutely nothing we can categorically label a standard "Chinese monument." In other words, my identification of various forms of ancient Chinese monuments and their historical relationship is supported by my discussion of different conceptions of monumentality and their historical relationship. These forms may or may not agree with our conventional idea of monumental images. In either case, their qualification as monuments must be justified by their function and symbolism in ancient Chinese society. More important, they must not be viewed as isolated types of monuments but as products of a continuous development of symbolic forms, which I call a "history of monuments."

By combining the history of monumentality and the history of monuments into a single narrative, I hope in this book to discover the essential developmental logic of ancient Chinese art and architecture up to the appearance of educated artists and private works of art. Before this moment, all three major traditions of Chinese art and architecture—the ancestral temple and ritual vessels, the capital city and palaces, the tomb and funerary paraphernalia—resulted from large religious or political projects. Instead of pleasing a sensitive viewer, they reminded the public of what it should believe and how it should act. All can be qualified as monuments or components of monumental complexes. By identifying their monumentality, we may find a new way to interpret these traditions and thereby to reconstruct early Chinese art history. To demonstrate this, let us begin by exploring perhaps the oldest Chinese concept of

艺术品和建筑物，所有这些概念无疑都是十分重要的。但在对其进行历史的界定前，这些概念无一例外都是空话。进而言之，即使某种特定的纪念碑性得到定义，但在把它和历史中其他类型的纪念碑性相互联系、形成一个有机的序列以前，它仍然只是一个孤立的现象。我把这种序列称为“纪念碑性的历史”，它反映了不断变化的对历史和回忆的概念。

思想的转变外化为实物的发展——物质的纪念碑体现出历史的纪念碑性。和它们所包含的概念和含义一样，纪念碑可视可触的特性如形状、结构、质地、装饰、铭文和地点等，都是在不断变化的；这里根本不存在一个我们可以明确称为标准式的“中国纪念碑”的东西。换言之，我对纪念碑性的不同概念及其历史联系的有关讨论，有助于我对中国古代纪念碑多样性的判定。这些多样性可能与人们对纪念碑的传统理解相符，但也可能不符。不论是哪种情形，我们判定一件事物是否是纪念碑，必须着眼于它们在古代中国社会中的功能和象征意义。更重要的是，它们不能单纯地被视为纪念碑的各种孤立类型，而必须看成是一个象征形式发展过程的产物，这个过程就构成了“纪念碑的历史”。

通过把这两个历史——“纪念碑性的历史”和“纪念碑的历史”——综合入一个统一叙事，我希望在本书中描述中国艺术和建筑从其发生到知识型艺术家及私人艺术品出现之间的基本发展逻辑。在独立艺术家和私人艺术作品出现之前，中国艺术和建筑的三个主要传统——宗庙和礼器，都城和宫殿，墓葬和随葬品——均具有重要的宗教和政治内涵。它们告诉人们应该相信什么以及如何去相信和实践，而不是纯粹为了感官上的赏心悦目。这些建筑和艺术形式都有资格被称为纪念碑或者是纪念碑群体的组成部分。通过对它们纪念碑性的确定，我们或可找到一条解释这些传统以及重建中国古代艺术史的新路。为了证明这一点，我将从中国最早的有关纪念碑

monumentality, a concept revealed most clearly in an ancient myth about a set of legendary bronze tripods.

In the year 605 B.C., an ambitious lord of the southern state of Chu went on an expedition near the Zhou capital at Luoyang. The campaign was not aimed to show his loyalty toward the Zhou royal house, which had been reduced to puppet status and was constantly threatened by the feudal princes' increasing demands for political power. In this case, the
005 lord's disloyalty was first shown by his holding military maneuvers near the capital. The submissive Zhou king sent a minister named Wangsun Man to bring "greetings" and gifts to the troops. The lord of Chu immediately questioned the minister: "Could you tell me how large and heavy are the Nine Tripods?" This seemingly innocent question aroused Wangsun Man's famous speech recorded in *Master Zuo's Commentaries on the Spring and Autumn Annals* (*Chunqiu Zuo zhuan*):

> The Tripods do not matter; virtue does. In the past when the Xia dynasty was distinguished for its virtue, the distant regions put their *things* [*wu*] into pictures and the nine provinces sent in copper as tribute. The Tripods were cast to present those *things*. One hundred different *things* were presented, so that the people could distinguish divine from evil. . . . Hereby a harmony was secured between the high and the low, and all enjoyed the blessing of Heaven.
>
> When the virtue of Jie [the last king of the Xia] was all-obscured, the Tripods were transferred to the Shang dynasty, and for six hundred years the Shang enjoyed its ruling status. Finally King Zhou of the Shang proved cruel and oppressive, and the Tripods were transferred to the Zhou dynasty.
>
> When virtue is commendable and brilliant, those which are small will be heavy; when things come to be crafty and decrepit, those which are large will be light. Heaven blessed intelligent virtue, and on this its favor rests. King Cheng [of the Zhou] fixed the Tripods in the Zhou capital[8] and divined that the Zhou dynasty should last for thirty reigns,

over seven hundred years. This is the Zhou's mandate from Heaven. Though now the Zhou has lost its past glory, the decree of Heaven is not yet changed. The weight of the tripods cannot yet be inquired about![9]

This passage has been frequently quoted as a valuable source for the "meaning" of ancient Chinese bronze art. Scholars have often focused their attention on the term *things* and have interpreted and translated it as "totems," "emblems," "symbols," "decoration," or "animal sacrifices" to suit their various arguments, but I suggest that the significance of this record goes far beyond an iconographic reference. What this passage

性的概念着手，这一概念十分清楚地反映在关于一组列鼎的传说中。

公元前605年，一位雄心勃勃的楚王挥师至东周都城洛阳附近。这一行动的目的并非为了表现他对周王室的忠诚：此时的周王室已经成为傀儡，并不时受到那些政治权欲日益膨胀的地方诸侯的威胁。这一情形下，在国都附近挥师首先就表明了楚王的叛心。周王派大臣王孙满前去劳师，楚王则张口就问“鼎之大小轻重”。这一看似漫不经心的提问引发出王孙满一段非常著名的回答，见载于《左传》：

> 在德不在鼎。昔夏之方有德也，远方图物，贡金九牧，铸鼎象物，百物而为之备，使民知神奸。……
>
> 用能协于上下，以承天休。
>
> 桀有昏德，鼎迁于商，载祀六百。商纣暴虐，鼎迁于周。
>
> 德之休明，虽小，重也。其奸回昏乱，虽大，轻也。天祚明德，有所厎止。成王定鼎于郏鄏[8]，卜世三十，卜年七百，天所命也。周德虽衰，天命未改。鼎之轻重，未可问也。[9]

王孙满的这一段话经常被用来解释中国古代青铜艺术的意义，但学者们多关注于文中所说的“铸鼎象物”的“物”，并根据各自理论的需要将其解释为图腾、族徽、符号、纹饰或动物祭祀等。但在我看来，这段话的意义远远超出了图像学研究的范畴，它所揭示

implies is, above all, an ancient *monumentality* in Chinese culture, and the essence of an entire artistic genre called *liqi* or "ritual art."

The implications of the Tripods exist on three different levels corresponding to the three paragraphs of this passage. First, the Nine Tripods as a collective monument were made to commemorate the most important political event in ancient China: the establishment of the Xia, which initiated a series of "dynasties" and separated traditional Chinese history into two broad periods. Before this moment, it was thought, various regional groups fought for political dominance; after this moment, a centralized power appeared and assumed a position to give orders to subsidiary authorities. The Nine Tripods thus fall into Riegl's general category of an *intentional monument*, which is commemorative in nature. On the other hand, the Nine Tripods not only commemorated a past event but also legitimated and consolidated the consequence of the event—the implementation of a centralized political power over the whole country. Wangsun Man expressed this idea symbolically. According to him, the tripods bore the *things* of various regions. These regions were Xia's allies. The act of sending their *things* to the Xia demonstrated their submission to Xia authority. The engraving of their *things* on the tripods meant that they had entered into a single political entity. Wangsun Man stated this idea even more clearly when he said that after the Tripods were made, "people could distinguish divine from evil": all the tribes and kingdoms belonging to the Xia alliance were identified (by the Tripods) as "divine," whereas all enemy tribes and kingdoms (whose *things* were absent from the Tripods) were considered "evil."

This may have been the original impulse behind the creation of the Tripods. But as soon as these ritual objects came into being, their significance, or monumentality, changed. They became something that could be possessed, and indeed this new theme dominates the next part of Wangsun Man's political rhetoric. Here we find the second symbolism of the Tripods: these objects had become a symbol not only of a

particular political power (the Xia) but of Power itself. It was thought that any dynasty would inevitably perish (as Wangsun Man asserted, the Zhou was mandated to last no longer than thirty reigns), but the centralization of political power—hence the Tripods—would persist. Correspondingly, the changing possession and location of the Tripods indicated the 006
transmission of political power from one dynasty to another. (Thus,

的首先是中国文化中一种古老的纪念碑性，以及一个叫作“礼器”的宏大、完整的艺术传统。

这段文献中的三段话显示了“九鼎”在三个不同层次上的意义。首先，作为一种集合性的“纪念碑”，九鼎的主要作用是纪念中国古代最重要的政治事件——夏代的建立。这一事件标志了“王朝”的肇始，因此把中国古代史分成两大阶段。在此之前，各地方部落混战争夺政治权力；在此以后，产生的中央政权对下属分封地发号施令。因此，我们可以把九鼎划入李格尔所说的“有意而为”的纪念碑的范畴。但另一方面，九鼎不仅仅是为了纪念过去的某一事件，同时也是对这一事件后果的巩固和合法化——即国家形态意义上的中央权力的实现和实施。王孙满形象地表达了这一观点。从他的话中可以看出，九鼎上铸有不同地域的“物”。这些地域是夏的盟国，贡“物”于夏就是表示臣服于夏。“铸鼎象物”也就意味着，这些地域进入了以夏为中心的同一政治实体。王孙满所说的九鼎可“使民知神奸”的意味是：进入夏联盟的所有部落和方国都被看成是“神”，而所有的敌对部落和方国（它们的“物”不见于九鼎之上）则被认为是“奸”。

这层意义也许是铸造九鼎的最初动机。但是当这些礼器铸成之后，它们的意义或者说纪念碑性马上发生了变化。首先，这些器物成为某种可以被拥有的东西，而这种“拥有”的观念也就成为王孙满下一段话的基础。这里我们发现九鼎的第二种象征意义：这些器物不仅仅标志某一特殊政治权力（夏），同时也象征了政治权力本身。王孙满这段话的中心思想是，任何王朝都不可避免地要灭亡（如他所言，周王朝的统治也将不会超过三十代），但政治集权——也就是九鼎——将超越王朝而存在。因此，九鼎的迁徙指明了王朝

Wangsun Man said: "When the virtue of Jie was all-obscured, the Tripods were transferred to the Shang dynasty, and for six hundred years the Shang enjoyed its ruling status. Finally King Zhou of the Shang proved cruel and oppressive, and the Tripods were transferred to the Zhou dynasty.") From the Xia to the Shang and then to the Zhou, possession of the Nine Tripods coincided exactly with the succession of the Three Dynasties. The transmission of the Tripods thus became synonymous with the progression of History.

The broadening symbolism of the Tripods leads finally to the third significance of these objects: they and their transmission were not so much the *consequence* of historical events as the *prerequisite* for historical events. Theoretically, the distinguished virtue of a dynasty led to its mandate, which was then demonstrated by its creation or possession of the Tripods. In actuality, however, this logic was reversed: because a ruler possessed the Tripods, he was certainly virtuous and ought to enjoy Heaven's favor. This is why the ambitious lord asked about (in fact, asked *for*) the Tripods, and this is also why Wangsun Man answered: "Though now the Zhou has lost its past glory, the decree of Heaven is not yet changed. The weight of the Tripods cannot yet be inquired about!" His argument may be summarized this way: although the Zhou is declining, it is still the possessor of the Nine Tripods; hence it is still the legitimate ruler of China, hence it still retains Heaven's mandate, and hence it is virtuous and morally unshakable. The Zhou's control of the Tripods had become the sole prop for its survival; for the ambitious lord, obtaining the Tripods would be the first step toward dynastic power.

As a collective political monument, the physical properties of the Nine Tripods both agree with and differ from those of a monument in a conventional, modern understanding. As mentioned earlier, a monument, or more precisely an "intentional" monument, is usually considered a manufactured form of durable materials that bears signs "to preserve a moment in the consciousness of later generations, and therefore to remain alive and present in perpetuity."[10] The legendary Nine Tripods conform to this basic definition: they were made of the most durable material available at the time, and their engraved signs registered the establishment of the First Chinese dynasty. But beyond this, the Nine Tripods were perhaps unique. First, the material of the Tripods was not only the most durable but was also the most prized. During the Three Dynasties, only the ruling classes possessed bronze. Moreover,

的更替。所以王孙满说："桀有昏德，鼎迁于商，载祀六百。商纣暴虐，鼎迁于周。"从夏到商再到周，九鼎的归属正好和三代的更替吻合，九鼎的迁徙因此成为历史进程的同义词。

九鼎逐渐扩大的象征意义最终引申出这些器物的第三层含义：九鼎以及九鼎的变迁在很大程度上不再是历史事件的结果，而是这些事件的先决条件。理论上来讲，一个王朝的明德使其获得天命，铸造九鼎或拥有九鼎则表现出这种天命。但事实上，这一逻辑被逆转，因为一个统治者拥有了九鼎，他理所当然地是天命的所有者。这也就是为什么雄心勃勃的楚王要问（事实上是"求"）九鼎的缘故，这也是为什么王孙满回答"周德虽衰，天命未改。鼎之轻重，未可问也"的原因。王孙满的理由或可以这样来概括：尽管周德衰落了，但它仍然是九鼎的拥有者，因此它还是王朝的合法统治者，因此它还拥有天命，因此它仍有德，在道义上不可动摇。在其辩解中，周王朝对九鼎的拥有成为它继续存在的唯一理由。而对于楚王来讲，夺取九鼎则是获得王朝权力的第一步。

作为集合式的政治性纪念碑，九鼎的特征与对纪念碑的约定俗成的现代理解既有相同又有不同之处。如上文所说，一座纪念碑，或更准确地讲，一座"有意而为"的纪念碑通常被看成是用耐久材料所制造出来的某种形式，它所带有的符号是"为了在后来者的意识当中保留某一瞬间，并以期获得生命和永恒"[10]。传说中的九鼎符合这一基本概念：它们不但是用当时最为耐久的材料铸造的，而且所镌刻的符号（物）表明了中国第一个王朝的建立。但除此之外，九鼎还有其独特之处。首先，铸鼎所用的青铜不仅是当时最耐久的材料，同时也是最宝贵的材料：夏商周三代只有统治阶层才拥有青铜。

Wangsun Man especially emphasized that people from China's nine provinces had presented the bronze used to make Tripods. This implies that the symbolism of bronze lay not only in its solidity, durability, and preciousness but also in its origins and in the process of the Tripods' manufacture. When bronze from various places was mixed and cast into a single set of ritual vessels, it was understood that those who presented the material were assimilated into a single unity. As we have noted, the same logic also underlay the practice of engraving the *things* of these places on the Tripods.

Second, the word *monument* is often associated with colossal constructions whose giant size dominates public view. But as bronze vessels, the Nine Tripods could not possibly have been taller than two meters, and they were transportable from one location to another to correspond with a change in the dynastic succession (Fig. I.3).[11] We
007 may say that their condensed form and their portability made the Tripods important; it was not their imposing size that made the ideas they represented grandiose. As Wangsun Man attested, "When virtue is commendable and brilliant, those which are small will be heavy; when things come to be crafty and decrepit, those which are large will be light." This is also why in ancient China all ritual bronzes were called "heavy vessels" (*zhongqi*), a term referring to their political and psychological importance, not to their physical size and weight. We read in the *Book of Rites* (*Li ji*) that "when one is holding a ritual article belonging to his lord, though it may be light, he should seem unable to sustain it."[12]

Third, the form of a monument is often related to the characteristics of permanence and stillness. The Nine Tripods, however, were believed to have an "animate" nature. The last part of Wangsun Man's speech has been translated: "When the virtue of Jie was all-obscured, the Tripods were transferred to the Shang. . . . Finally King Zhou of the Shang proved cruel and oppressive, and the Tripods were transferred to the Zhou." But the meaning of the original text is by no means so definite. In particular, the verb *qian* can be interpreted both as "to be transferred" and "to transfer itself"; and in fact the syntax of the sentences seems to encourage the second reading (a word-by-word translation of the two sentences, *ding qian yu Shang* and *ding qian yu Zhou* would be "the tripods move to Shang/Zhou").

王孙满特别强调九鼎的材料来源是"贡金九牧"，这说明青铜的象征性不仅在于其坚固、耐久和珍贵，还包括它的来源以及器物的铸造过程。当来自不同地域的青铜原料被熔化在一起从而铸造成一套礼器时，这个过程也象征了不同地区的贡金者融合于同一个政治集合体当中。如上文所说的那样，这也是把各地的"物"铸在鼎上的意义之所在。

其次，现代概念中的"纪念碑"一词经常是和巨大的建筑物联系在一起的，其宏伟的外观非常抢眼。但作为青铜容器，九鼎的高度不会超过两米，随着王朝的更替，它们还要从一地搬迁到另外一地［图 I.3］。[11] 我们可以认为，正是这种简洁的造型和可移动性使九鼎显示出它们的重要性；其意义和内涵并非通过外形的巨大而体现。因此王孙满说："德之休明，虽小，重也。其奸回昏乱，虽大，轻也。"这也就是为什么中国古代青铜礼器被称为"重器"的原因：这里的"重"指的是器物在政治和精神意义上的重要性，而不是其物质的尺寸和重量。《礼记》规定"凡执主器，执轻如不克。"[12]

第三，纪念碑的形式经常和永恒、静止等特性密切相连，但九鼎却被认为是"有生命"的神物。在王孙满的话中有这么一句："桀有昏德，鼎迁于商……商纣暴虐，鼎迁于周。"在英文翻译中，"鼎迁"一词被译成"鼎被迁"，但原文的含义并非如此明确。"迁"既可以解释为"被迁"，也可以理解为"自迁"。事实上，根据句子的语法，后一种理解更符合原意。因此，"鼎迁于商"和"鼎迁于周"可以解释为"鼎自迁于商 / 周"。

Fig. I.3. *Ding* tripod. Bronze. Early Western Zhou. 10th century B.C. H. 122 cm. Excavated in 1979 at Chunhua, Shaanxi province. Chunhua County Cultural House.
图 I.3 鼎。青铜。西周早期，前 10 世纪。高 122 厘米。1979 年陕西淳化出土。淳化县文化馆藏。

Another version of the Tripod legend makes this even more explicit: it is recorded in the *Mozi* that a divination was made before casting the Tripods and a divine message appeared on the tortoise shell: "Let the Tripods, when completed, have a square body and four legs. Let them be able to boil without kindling, to hide themselves without being lifted, and to move themselves without being carried so that they will be used for the sacrifice at the field of Kunwu." The diviner, whose name was Wengnan Yi, then interpreted the oracle: "Oh! like those luxuriant clouds that float to the four directions, after their completion the Nine Tripods will move to three kingdoms: when the Xia clan loses them, the people of Yin [[i.e., Shang]] will possess them, and when the people of Yin lose them, the people of Zhou will have them."[13] Comparing the Nine Tripods to drifting clouds, Yi's metaphor clearly *suggests* that these divine objects generated their own movement (or transmission)—that the various dynasties could possess them only because the Tripods were willing to be possessed by these legitimate owners.

This "animate" quality of the Nine Tripods was even further mystified during the Han dynasty: people began to think that they could not only generate their own movement but also possess consciousness (Figs. 1.4, 5): "The Tripods are the essence of both substance [*zhi*] and refinement [*wen*]. They know the auspicious and the inauspicious and what continues and what perishes. They can be heavy or light; they can be at rest or in motion. Without fire they cook, and without drawing water they are naturally full. . . . The divine tripods appear when a ruler rises and disappear when a ruler falls."[14] As I discuss later in this book, this "animate" 008

这个意义在另一个有关九鼎的传说中表达得更为明确。《墨子·耕柱篇》记载夏后开铸鼎，使翁难乙卜于白若之龟，曰："鼎成四足而方，不炊而自烹，不举而自藏，不迁而自行，以祭于昆吾之墟，上飨。" 翁难乙释卜兆曰："飨矣！逢逢白云，一南一北，一西一东，九鼎既成，迁于三国。夏后氏失之，殷人受之。殷人失之，周人受之。"[13] 翁难乙将九鼎和流云相比拟，显然意在说明九鼎有"不迁而自行"的自身运动能力，不同王朝之所以拥有九鼎，是因为这些神秘的器物愿意被这些合法所有者所拥有。

九鼎的这种"生命性"在汉代被进一步神秘化：人们开始相信，九鼎不仅能自行迁移，而且还具有意识［图 I.4，图 I.5］。如孙柔之《瑞应图》中说："神鼎者，质文精也。知吉凶存亡，能轻能重，能息能行，不灼而沸，不汲自盈……王者兴则出。衰则去。"[14] 下文中我将进一步说明，九鼎的"生命性"并不完全是一种抽象的概念，

Fig. I.4. Divine tripod. Carving on the ceiling of the Wu Liang Shrine. A.D. 151. Jiaxiang, Shandong province. Woodblock reconstruction.

图 I.4 神鼎。刻于武梁祠顶部。东汉晚期，151 年。山东嘉祥。木板摹刻。

Fig. I.5. Divine tripod. Stone carving. Eastern Han. 2nd century A.D. Excavated in 1954 at Suining, Jiangsu province. Xuzhou Museum. Ink rubbing.

图 I.5 神鼎。画像石。东汉晚期，2 世纪。1954 年江苏睢宁出土。徐州博物馆藏。拓片。

quality was not a metaphysical conception but a visual one. This quality is directly related, on the one hand, to the general idea of "metamorphosis" in early Chinese ritual art, and on the other hand, to actual decoration on bronzes, which favors protean images.

Fourth, it seems surprising that the Nine Tripods, the most important political monument in ancient China, were actually a set of vessels. Unlike a conventional monument, which often fulfills no practical function, the Nine Tripods were used for cooking in sacrifices. They were therefore functional objects in religious communication with certain divine beings, most likely the spirits of deceased ancestors.[15] The Tripods commemorated not only the ancestors who originally created and acquired these ritual objects (i.e., their establishment of the Three

Dynasties) but also all previous kings who had successfully maintained the Tripods in the royal temple (and had thus proved a dynasty's continuing mandate from Heaven). The political symbolism of the Tripods could be sustained over the several hundred years of a dynasty precisely because the *memory* of these ancestral kings was constantly renewed through ancestral sacrifices. Since only royal descendents could hold such sacrifices, any *user* of the Tripods was self-evidently the inheritor of political power.

Finally, unlike a conventional monument, whose grandeur is often displayed on public occasions, the Nine Tripods were concealed in darkness. In fact, many ancient writings, including Wangsun Man's statement, suggest that only because the Tripods were hidden and unseen

而是在艺术中得到了视觉的表现。这种表现在广义上与中国古代礼制艺术中一贯的“变形”原理有关，具体说来则在强调不断变异的铜器装饰中获得明显的体现。

第四，一个现代人可能会吃惊：作为中国古代最为重要的政治性纪念物，九鼎竟是一套实用器物。虽然一般概念中的纪念碑多不具备实用功能，但九鼎在祭祀时却用作炊器。因此，它们成为宗教活动中沟通人神，尤其是与已逝祖先沟通的礼器。[15] 它们的意义不仅仅在于纪念那些最早创造和获得这些神器的祖先（即他们建立了夏商周三代），同时也在于纪念所有继承过九鼎的先王们（因此而证明一个王朝“天命”的延续）。九鼎的政治象征意义之所以能够在一朝内数百年流传下来，正是在于通过祭祀祖先，可以不断充实和更新对以往先王的回忆。由于只有王室成员才能主持这样的祭祀，九鼎的使用者因此也自然是政权的继承者。

最后，一般意义上的纪念碑总是在公共场合中展现其宏伟壮丽，但九鼎却秘藏在黑暗之处。事实上，很多的古文献，包括王孙满的那一段论述，都表明正因为九鼎被如此秘藏，不为外人所见，

could they maintain their power. We know that during the Shang and Zhou, ritual bronzes were kept in ancestral temples at the center of cities where the ruling clan held all important ceremonies. As I discuss in Chapter 2 of this book, such a temple, described in ancient texts as "deep" and "dark," functioned to structure a ritual process leading toward the ritual bronzes concealed deep inside, where only the male members of the ruling clan were allowed to enter. Outsiders were firmly forbidden to approach these vessels because this would have implied access to political power. This is why the Nine Tripods remained silent symbols of authority during the Xia, Shang, and Western Zhou, and why they suddenly became the focus of public interest during the Spring and Autumn and the Warring States periods after the Zhou royal house had declined and local kingdoms were competing for political dominance. The Chu lord's inquiry about the Tripods' "weight" in 605 B.C. initiated a series of similar events.[16] In 290 B.C., for example, Zhang Yi, the prime minister of Qin, proposed an attack on two towns in central China: "Once this is done, our troops will reach the outskirts of the Zhou capital. . . . The Zhou's only way to survive would be to submit its secret Nine Tripods and other precious symbols. With the Nine Tripods in our control, official maps
009 and documents in our possession, and the Zhou King himself as hostage,
the Qin can thereby give orders to all under Heaven and no one would dare disobey."[17]

But according to the *Intrigues of the Warring States* (*Zhanguo ce*), the Zhou did manage to survive without losing its treasures. This was again accomplished through a clever minister's eloquence on the mysterious Tripods. It is said that not only the Qin but other powerful kingdoms such as the Qi, the Chu, and the Liang cast covetous eyes on the Tripods. The Zhou minister Yan Shuai first made use of Qi's desire for the vessels to upset Qin's plan. He then traveled to the east, persuading the king of Qi to believe that even if he could have the Tripods (as the Zhou had promised him), it would be impossible for him to move these monumental objects to his kingdom in Shandong:

> The Tripods are not something like a vinegar bottle or a bean-paste jar, which you can bring home in your hand. . . . In the past, when the Zhou king conquered the Shang and obtained the Nine Tripods, he ordered 90,000 people to draw each of them [to the Zhou capital]. Altogether 810,000 people, including officials, soldiers, master workers, and apprentices, were involved, and all kinds of tools and instruments were employed. People thus take this event as a most thoughtful and well-prepared undertaking. Now, even assuming that

它们才能保持其威力。我们知道，商周时期的青铜礼器常保存在位于城中心的宗庙之中，而宗庙是统治者家族举行重要祭祀活动的法定场所。如我将在本书第二章讨论的那样，在古文献中宗庙常被描述成“深邃”和“幽暗”的地方，其建筑形态赋予庙中举行的礼仪活动以特定的时空结构。这些礼仪活动引导人们，特别是男性成员接近和使用深藏于宗庙中的礼器。外人不得靠近这些宗庙重器，因为这就意味着接近政治权力。这就是为什么九鼎在夏、商、西周时期只是沉默的权力象征，直到春秋、战国时期，随着周王室的式微，它们突然成为纷争中列国的兴趣焦点。公元前 605 年的楚王问鼎引发出一系列类似的事件。[16] 如公元前 290 年，秦相张仪向秦惠王建议，“秦攻新城、宜阳，以临二周之郊……周自知不能救，九鼎宝器必出。据九鼎，按图籍，挟天子以令于天下，天下莫敢不听。”[17]

据《战国策》记载，周王室所采取的措施最后使其不至失去九鼎，这同样归功于一位大臣机智的应辩。当时不仅是秦，其他强国如齐、楚、梁等也都垂涎九鼎。周大臣颜率首先利用齐国对九鼎的贪婪而克制了秦的野心，随后又东行至齐，告诉齐王即使齐得到九鼎，他也不可能将这些重器迁到山东：

> 夫鼎者，非效醯壶酱甀耳，可怀挟提挈以至齐者……昔周之伐殷，得九鼎，凡一鼎而九万人挽之，九九八十一万人，士卒师徒器械被具，所以备者称此。今大王纵有其人，

> Your Majesty could gather enough men to pull the Tripods, which route could you take to bring them home? [The country is divided and all the kingdoms located between the Zhou and the Qi are eager to possess the Tripods; their lords would certainly not allow you to ship the Tripods through their land.] I worry that your desire will only bring trouble.[18]

In retrospect, we realize that in his defense of the Zhou possession of the Tripods, Wangsun Man of the late seventh century B.C. was still relying on the Zhou's mandate and moral authority; Yan Shuai of the early third century B.C., however, resorted to a physical exaggeration of the size of the secret Tripods. His words remind us of other instances in which the lack of empirical experience with an object helps confound any real sense of its size and proportions. For example, Barbara Rose has observed in her study of modern Western artworks:

> Our idea of the monumentality of Picasso's works is not dependent on actual scale; in fact, in my case an appreciation of their monumentality was largely a result of never having seen the originals, but of having experienced them as slides or photographs. In this way, the comparison with the human body never came up, so that the epoch-making 1928-29 *Construction in Wire*, although a scant twenty inches high in actuality, was as large as the imagination cared to make it.[19]

Unlike Picasso's masterpiece, only verbal descriptions of the Tripods were available, allowing even freer exaggeration of these mysterious objects in imagination and expression. Also unlike the modern case, access to the Tripods was tightly controlled by law; an insider's knowledge of these secret objects thus became his means of possessing and exercising power. This is perhaps why Yan Shuai's account, though obviously fictional, still helped stop the king of Qi's plan to obtain the Tripods. On the other hand, Yan's emphasis on the Tripods' physicality was something new and alien to the traditional concept of the vessels' monumentality: he no longer described them as self-animated divine beings but as immobile, stupendous physical entities, each of which had to be drawn by an army of 90,000 people. The Tripods were now literally "heavy vessels," an expression originally denoting their extraordinary political significance invested in a limited material form. Likewise,

> 何途之从而出？臣窃为大王私忧之。[18]

我们回过头去看公元前 7 世纪末年的情况，当时王孙满为周王室对九鼎所有权的辩解还依赖于周室的天命和道德权威。但到了公元前 3 世纪早期，颜率就只能通过夸大九鼎的体积来欺骗齐王了。颜率的话令我们想到其他的例证，表明对于某一物体感性经验的缺乏就会搞错它的真实尺寸和比例。芭芭拉·罗丝在她对当代西方艺术品的研究中指出：

> 人们对于毕加索作品纪念碑性的概念并不是依据其实际的大小。事实上，就我而言，对于它们的纪念碑性的欣赏在相当大程度上是因为从来没有看到过原作，而只是借助于幻灯片或照片。在这种情况下，也就不存在作品和人体自身尺度的比较，因此事实上仅仅 20 英寸（合 50.8 厘米）高的《金属线结构》却给人以巨大到难以置信的感觉。[19]

和毕加索作品不同的是，有关九鼎只有文字上的描述，这就使得想象和表达这些神秘的宗庙重器更加夸张。此外，与观赏现代艺术作品不同，接近九鼎有着严格的限制，局内人士对于九鼎的了解也因此成了他们拥有和行使权力的手段。这也可能就是颜率虚构的描述竟能够阻止齐王迁鼎的原因。另一方面，颜率对于九鼎物体特征的强调也不同于先前对于这些礼器纪念碑性的理解：他不再把九鼎描述成有生命的神器，而是无法自动、巨大笨重的东西，要搬动其中一件竟需动用九万人众。此时的九鼎真是成了直意的“重器”，而非原意上的“重器”，即具有超强政治意义的有限物质形体。

whereas Wangsun Man was still confident enough to refuse the Chu lord's inquiry about the "weight" of the Tripods ("The weight of the Tripods cannot yet be inquired about"), Yan Shuai volunteered information about the Tripods' "weight" and based his whole rhetoric on exaggerating it. As we will see, such differences reflect a crucial change in the concept of monumentality during the Eastern Zhou, when China was undergoing a transition from the archaic Three Dynasties to the imperial era. In fact, Yan Shuai's account represented a final effort to save the Tripods by supplying these old political symbols with the symbolism and forms of new types of monuments. In this sense, the original monumentality of the Nine Tripods had been rejected, and they, as material monuments, would soon disappear: when the Zhou dynasty finally fell, they also vanished into a river.[20]

010 The story of the Nine Tripods is probably sheer legend: although many ancient writers recorded and discussed the Tripods, no one ever claimed to have seen them and could thus describe them in detail. Nothing seems more unsuitable for an art-historical inquiry than such elusive objects. But to me, their value as historical evidence lies not in their physical form, not even in their existence, but in the myth surrounding them. Instead of informing us what the Nine Tripods were, the ancient authors told us what they were supposed to be. They were supposed to commemorate an important historical event and to symbolize political unity and its public. Concealed in the royal temple, their location defined the center of the capital and the country; the common knowledge of their location made them a focus of social attention. They could change hands, and their possession by different owners, or their "movement" from one place to another, indicated the course of history. They took the form of a cooking utensil but exceeded the utilitarian usage and productive requirements of any ordinary vessel. Most important to an art-historical inquiry, they demonstrated their unique status through physical attributes including material, shape, and surface patterns. Since all these implications of

the Nine Tripods are crucial to our understanding of extant ancient bronzes and other ritual objects, these legendary objects help us discover not only a forgotten concept of monumentality in ancient China, but also a new perspective in interpreting the whole tradition of *liqi* (ritual paraphernalia) or *zhongqi* ("heavy" vessels), which dominated Chinese art from late Neolithic times to the end of the Three Dynasties.

同样，公元前 7 世纪的王孙满尚可有自信拒绝告诉楚王鼎之轻重（“鼎之轻重，未可问也”），此时的颜率只能夸大其词，主动将鼎之轻重告知齐王。这里我们可以发现，在东周时期对于九鼎的纪念碑性的理解已发生了一个根本变化，而此时正是古代中国从三代向帝国时代的过渡期。事实上，颜率通过赋予九鼎以新的形式和象征意义，对维护这些古老政治象征物做出了最后的努力。从这一点上说，九鼎原有的纪念碑性被摒弃了，而作为物质存在的这些器物本身不久之后也将消失：当周王朝最终灭亡时，九鼎也沉于河中。[20]

有关九鼎的记载可能纯属传说，尽管古人对此有不少记载和讨论，但没有人说他亲眼见过九鼎，也没有人对其做过详细描述。对于艺术史研究而言，九鼎可能是最不理想的材料了。但对我说来，九鼎的价值不在于它们的物质形态，甚至不在于它们是否真实存在过，而恰恰在于围绕它们而产生的传说。这些古代传说的作者没有告诉我们何为九鼎，而是告诉我们九鼎应为何物。九鼎应纪念重要的历史事件并代表政体及其公众。珍藏九鼎的宗庙同时也是国都和国家的中心；知道了它们的藏地便使其成为人们关注的焦点。九鼎可以易主；不同人对九鼎的拥有，或者说九鼎的迁移反映了历史的变迁。九鼎的造型虽为炊器，但它们远远超出了其他任何日常用器的功用和目的。对于艺术史研究而言，九鼎的独特地位体现于其具体形象特征，如质地、形状和装饰图案。由于所有这些牵涉到的方面对我们理解“礼器”非常重要，这些器物不仅帮助我们发掘出中国古代一种被遗忘的纪念碑性，同时也为我们提供了一条解释礼器或重器传统的新思路，正是这个传统决定了自新石器时代晚期到三代晚期中国艺术的主流。

This interpretation is pursued in Chapter 1 of this book, "The Age of Ritual Art." As the earliest artistic tradition in China, ritual art divorced itself from the principle of "least effort" associated with crafts and introduced the concept of "conspicuous consumption."[21] Thorstein Veblen's idea, that wasteful spending can enhance social prestige and power,[22] has enabled anthropologists to find an essential feature of monumental architecture: its vast scale requires an extraordinarily large amount of human energy.[23] But to the ancient Chinese, who did not pursue colossal buildings until the end of the Three Dynasties, conspicuous ritual objects signified the power to control and "squander" human labor. The earliest works of ritual art were therefore "expensive" imitations and variations of ordinary tools and utensils: an axe made of extremely hard jade or a clay jar with paper-thin walls. The distinction between *liqi* and *yongqi* (practical utensil) began to emerge through conscious choices of *material* and *shape*; surface patterns then appeared as additional signifiers of *liqi* and developed into *decoration* and *inscription*.

The conspicuous principle of ritual art also implies that during this early period, whenever a new medium was discovered or a new technology invented, it would be absorbed into the *liqi* tradition to become its exclusive properties. The amazing development of bronze art in ancient China best demonstrates this theory. The concept of a Bronze Age is conventionally understood as a period in human history characterized by the intensive production and utilization of bronze implements; the Chinese Bronze Age, however, must be defined as a specific stage of ritual art. Bronze vessels and other ceremonial paraphernalia became the major representatives of this art tradition; practical tools were rarely, if at all, made of this "precious" material. The course of ritual art thus conforms to a traditional Chinese evolutionary theory that places the Bronze Age after a Jade Age. In this scheme, jade is distinguished from stone just as bronze is differentiated from iron: stone and iron are "ugly" materials for practical tools, whereas jade and bronze are "fine" media for ritual art.

This and other observations lead me to depart from two standard methods of studying early Chinese art. First, instead of classifying ancient objects into individual material categories (such as jade, pottery, and bronze) and observing their relatively independent evolution, I pay special attention to the historical and conceptual relationship between works in different media. Second, rather than taking "shape" and "decor"

这一观点在本书第一章"礼制艺术的时代"中得到进一步阐述。作为中国最早的艺术传统，礼制艺术背离了"最少致力"的制作原理，而引进了"奢侈消费"的原则。[21]凡勃仑认为"浪费可以提高消费者的社会声誉和权力"[22]，这个观点使人类学家得以确定纪念碑建筑的一个基本特征，即它们巨大的造型需要庞大的人力资源。[23]但在中国古代，对巨型建筑的追求直到三代晚期才出现，显著的礼器体现了对权力的控制和对人工的"浪费"。因此，对普通工具和用器的"贵重"模仿——硬质玉做成的玉斧或薄如蛋壳的陶器——标志了礼制艺术的开端。礼器和用器的区别首先表现为对"质地"和"形状"的有意识选择；"纹饰"随之成为礼器的另一个符号，并进而产生了装饰和铭文。

礼制艺术另一重要的特点是，在中国古代，每当有一种新材料或新技术出现，它总是毫无例外地被吸收到礼器传统中来，成为其专有的"财产"。中国古代极度发达的青铜艺术就有力地证明了这一点。社会学中"青铜时代"这一概念，一般指人类历史上广泛制造和使用青铜工具的时代；但中国的青铜时代应该被定义为礼制艺术的特定阶段，这是因为青铜容器和其他礼仪用器在这个时期成为这一艺术传统最主要的代表，实用工具即使有，也很少采用这种"贵重"材料。因此，礼制艺术的发展符合青铜时代延承玉器时代这一传统的中国进化理论。在这一理论中，玉和石的差别正如铜和铁的区别：石和铁都是用来制作实用工具的"恶"材，而玉和铜则是服务于礼制艺术的"美"材。

鉴于这种观察以及相关研究，我摒弃了对中国早期艺术研究的两个通行模式。第一，我没有按照质地把古代遗物进行分类（如玉器、陶器和青铜器）来研究其相对独立的线性演变过程，而是倾向于探讨不同质地的器物间历史的和概念的联系与互动；第二，我没有

as the major criteria for an artistic or semiotic analysis, I assume that the four basic attributes of ritual art—*material, shape, decoration,* and *inscription*—all possessed meaning and could separately play the leading role in developing a new stage of this art. Although these two approaches
011 are by no means entirely new, I hope not only to *propose* but also to *practice* them in a reconstruction of the history of ritual art, which will integrate and further develop many important discoveries and ingenious observations by individual scholars in art history, architectural history, archaeology, anthropology, metallurgy, religion, and history.

If we take the course of bronze art as an example, the late Xia plain cups from Erlitou (see Fig. 1.34)—the earliest known Chinese bronze vessels—have been considered "primitive" because they lack surface decoration. But in my view they represented a major advance in ritual symbols by transforming ceremonial pottery into metal; their meaning, or monumentality, was conveyed primarily by the newly discovered art medium. Decoration appeared during the early and middle Shang and soon became the locomotive of bronze art (see Figs. 1.37-46). The study of decoration usually falls into the domains of iconography and formal analysis; the former classifies and identifies motifs, and the latter focuses on the evolution of style. My investigation, however, shows that Shang bronze decoration is deliberately "metamorphic" in both style and motif. This fundamental characteristic challenges the premises of iconography and stylistic analysis and demands a new interpretation of the development of bronze art. Scholars have frequently noticed that Western Zhou bronze decor developed in the direction of abstraction and simplification. This process, in my view, did not necessarily reflect a formal evolution. Rather, the decline in decoration resulted from the increasing dominance of inscription: now that it bore a long commemorative text, a bronze became an object of "reading," not of "viewing" (see Fig. 1.65).

Interestingly, Wangsun Man seems to have encapsulated this dynamic process of bronze art into the single set of Nine Tripods. His emphasis on the symbolism of the bronze material could have been shared by the maker of the Erlitou cups (Fig. 1.34). He said that the Tripods bore things, most likely emblems of local regions, and such emblems only appeared on bronzes after the early Shang (see Fig. 1.47). His belief in the

把形状和装饰看成艺术或符号分析的主要标准，而是认为礼制艺术的四个基本要素——质料、形状、装饰和铭文——都有其含义，并能够分别在这一艺术的不同发展阶段中扮演领先角色。尽管这两个观点并非没有人谈到过，我希望的不仅是提出这些观点，而是对这些观念进行实践以重构中国礼制艺术的发展史。这个发展史将综合并进一步发展个人学者在艺术史、建筑史、考古学、人类学、冶金学、宗教和历史等领域中的重要发现和独立研究。

这里可以用青铜艺术的发展来简单地说明。已知最早的中国古代青铜容器——二里头遗址出土的夏代晚期平底爵［见图 1.34］——通常因为器表没有装饰纹样而被认为“原始”。但我认为，它们实际上代表了古代礼器从陶器向金器过渡的重大变革。它们的含义，或者说它们的纪念碑性，主要是由新出现的青铜媒介来实现的。丰富的纹饰在商代早中期青铜礼器上出现，并很快成为青铜艺术中领先的形式因素［见图 1.37—1.46］。以往对铜器装饰艺术的研究多在图像学和形式分析的范畴内进行：前者对主题纹样加以分类和定名，后者则关注风格的演变。我的研究没有沿循这两个通行方式，而是提出商代铜器的装饰在形式和主题上都强调不断的“变形”。这一基本特征对图像学和形式分析的研究前提提出挑战，要求对商代青铜艺术的发展过程进行新的解说。学者们经常注意到西周铜器装饰趋向抽象和简练，但在本书的叙事中，这一变化并非必定是形式上的变革，反而是铭文在青铜器上的逐渐普及导致了装饰的衰落：西周青铜礼器通常带有长铭，这些器物成为“读”而非“看”的对象［见图 1.65］。

有意思的是，王孙满似乎把青铜艺术的这一长期发展演变的过程凝聚到了九鼎之上。他强调青铜质料的象征意义，似乎反映了夏代二里头铜爵［见图 1.34］制造者的观点。他所说的鼎上的“物”很可能是族徽，而族徽只是到了商代早中期才出现在青铜器上［见

Fig. I.6. Five *ding* tripods and four *gui* vessels from Yu Bo's tomb. Mid-Western Zhou dynasty. *Ca.* 9th century B.C. Excavated at Rujiazhuang, Baoji, Shaanxi province. Drawing.
图 I.6 強伯墓出土的五鼎四簋。西周中期，约前 9 世纪。陕西宝鸡茹家庄出土。线图。

supernatural qualities of the Tripods—their "intelligence" and ability to generate their own movement—seems to have been related to late Shang bronze decoration, whose metamorphic imagery gave a vessel an air of animation (see Figs. 1.45-46). The number of the Tripods, however, must have reflected a Western Zhou convention that a set of "nine tripods" symbolized the Son of Heaven (Fig. I.6). As mentioned earlier, ancient writers recorded that the Tripods disappeared into a river some time after the Western Zhou. When the fierce Qin First Emperor unified the country in the third century B.C., the Tripods exposed themselves in the river. The emperor was overjoyed and immediately ordered several thousand men to seek these divine objects. The men had secured the Tripods with ropes and were about to haul them out when a dragon suddenly appeared and bit the ropes to pieces. The Tripods vanished, never to appear again (Fig. I.7).[24] Significantly, the "life" of the Tripods coincided exactly with the duration of the pre-imperial Three Dynasties.

With the disappearance of the Nine Tripods, the age of ritual art ended. The monuments of the new historical era were no longer secret "heavy vessels" but enormous palaces and funerary buildings, whose imposing images dazzled the eye. This historical transformation is the topic of Chapter 2, which also tackles the unanswered questions of why murals and bas-relief carvings became the main forms of Han art and

why pictorial images came to dominate the artist's imagination. My survey again begins from the Three Dynasties, but with a new focus on architectural forms that housed *liqi*. These were ancestral temples established at the center of large and small cities and towns. Their 012
name, *zongmiao* or "lineage temple," most clearly points to their social and political significance: as K. C. Chang and other scholars have convincingly demonstrated, the society of the Three Dynasties was fundamentally a hierarchy of patrilineages, and the temples (or, more precisely, the ancestors worshipped in them) identified these lineages' status and interrelationship in the overall sociopolitical network.[25]

图 1.47］。他相信九鼎具有自我意识和“自迁”等超自然能力，这似乎和商代晚期的铜器装饰相关，其不断变化的像生造型赋予器皿一种动态生命的感觉［见图 1.45，图 1.46］。九鼎之数进而反映了西周的一个新概念，即以“九”象征天子至高无上的地位［图 I.6］。上文已经提到，据文献记载，西周灭亡后不久九鼎就沉没于河。公元前 3 世纪秦始皇统一六国后，九鼎又现于河。始皇大喜过望，命令数千人下河寻找九鼎。但当他们找到了九鼎，正用绳子准备拉上来的时候，突然出现了一条龙将绳子咬断，九鼎又一次消失，再也没有出现［图 I.7］。[24] 重要的是，九鼎的“生命”历程正好和三代的历史吻合。

礼制艺术的时代随着九鼎的消失而结束。新历史时期的纪念碑不再是神秘的“重器”，取而代之的是宏伟庞大的宫殿和陵墓建筑。这一历史转变是本书第二章讨论的主题，该章同时也涉及一些尚未解决的艺术史中的重要问题，如为什么壁画和画像砖石成为汉代艺术的主要形式，为什么图像性艺术表现越来越吸引艺术家的想象力。我在这一章中的讨论仍然是从三代开始，但关注的不再是礼器本身，而是存放礼器的建筑形式，即建在大小城市中心的宗庙。“宗庙”这一名称最清楚不过地揭示了这种建筑的社会和政治功能。张光直和其他学者已经令人信服地证明，三代社会从根本上讲是父系宗族构成的统治集团，宗庙（更准确地讲是宗庙中祭祀的祖先们）则反映了各宗族的地位及其在整个社会政治体系中的相互关系。[25]

Fig. I.7. The First Emperor's unsuccessful search for the divine tripods. Carving on the Left Wu Family Shrine. Late Eastern Han. 2nd half of 2nd century A.D. Jiaxiang, Shandong. Ink rubbing.

图 I.7　秦始皇泗水升鼎。刻于武氏祠左石室。东汉晚期，2 世纪后半叶。山东嘉祥。拓片。

Ancient hymns, documents, and ritual canons reveal the overwhelming importance of a temple: a "noble man" was supposed to erect this building before he made any structure for the living, just as ritual vessels were supposed to be made before any cooking or eating utensil. Such statements identify *liqi* and the temple as the two basic components of a Three Dynasties monumental complex: the former defined the locus of power, and the latter provided a ritual site.

Excavated Three Dynasties temples further enable us to understand how a temple embodied social and political values in its architectural form. A flat courtyard structure surrounded by walls, a temple created an enclosed space, separating itself from the surrounding mundane world (see Figs. 2.4, 6). Never pursuing the third dimension, the evolution of this architectural type was characterized by extending the central axis and by adding more layers of gates and walls—the two principal features of a temple that punctuated a ritual journey. This journey began with the worship of recent ancestors in the shrines near a temple's entrance, and ended at the last shrine, which honored the Original Ancestor or the founder of a lineage. What we find here is the essence of ancestral worship during the Three Dynasties: "to go back to the Origin, maintain the ancient, and not forget those to whom the living owe their being."[26]

The royal temple in the capital—the temple with the highest status—housed both sacrifices to former kings and all important state ceremonies. In this sense, it combined the functions of a religious center and a political center. But when the archaic social system based on a lineage hierarchy fell apart after the Western Zhou, the palace gained

古代的颂歌、文献和礼书都强调宗庙无与伦比的重要性：对一位贵族而言，他应该在为生者兴建其他任何建筑之前修建宗庙，正如他应该在制作任何“用器”之前制作礼器。这一观点肯定了礼器和宗庙是三代纪念碑体系中最基本的两个部分：前者界定了权力的地点，后者则提供了礼仪场所。

考古发掘的三代宗庙遗址使我们了解到，宗庙是如何通过建筑形式体现其社会和政治价值的。高墙重门的宗庙形成了一个封闭的平面院落，把它和周围的世俗世界隔开［见图 2.4，图 2.6］。宗庙建筑并未向三维发展，其发展主要表现为中轴线的延伸以及门、墙的复加。中轴线和坐落在中轴线上的门、墙是宗庙建筑的两个主要特点，其隐含作用是规范礼仪活动的过程和段落。祭祀仪式通常是从祭祀靠近宗庙入口处享堂内的晚近祖先开始，而以祭祀坐落于宗庙最内部享堂内的始祖告终。这里我们可以发现三代祖先崇拜的本质：“教民反古复始，不忘其所由生。”[26]

在这个宗教系统里，都城中王室宗庙的地位最为崇高，对先王的祭祀以及所有重要的国家庆典仪式都在此举行。在这个意义上，王室宗庙同时充当着政治中心和宗教中心的角色。但是，这种以宗法为基础的古代社会体系在西周之后逐渐瓦解，作为政治中心的

independence and became the chief political symbol of powerful feudal lords. Tall *tai* platforms and terrace-buildings—new types of palatial architecture—emerged to suit the needs of the new social elite (see Fig. 2.18). We are told that some of these structures, more than a hundred meters high, helped their owners intimidate and even terrorize political opponents. These palatial buildings contradicted the old ancestral temple in every respect: no longer a deep, walled compound concealing secrecy, an Eastern Zhou and Qin palatial platform soared into the sky. It did not guide people back to the Origin through a temporal ritual sequence but displayed the immediate power of the current ruler.

The appearance of terrace-buildings in graveyards indicated another aspect of the Eastern Zhou social transformation: in the religious sphere, the center of ancestral worship gradually shifted from temple to tomb (see Fig. 2.27). This development originated in the divergent symbolism of these two kinds of architecture: even during the Shang and the Western Zhou, a temple honored generations of ancestors, among whom the founder of a lineage was the most venerated; a tomb, on the other hand, was built for one's late father or close relatives. As the ambition of individuals skyrocketed during the Eastern Zhou, the grandeur
013 of funerary structures rapidly increased. Feudal lords considered an enormous mausoleum a personal monument; they constructed their "funerary parks" and issued laws to guarantee their completion. This architectural movement gained additional momentum during the Han: nuclear families replaced large lineages as the basic social unit; popular religions supported by the Liu imperial family prevailed, and irregular royal successions caused difficulties in maintaining traditional temple worship. This last factor led Emperor Ming, the second ruler of the Eastern Han, to abolish all temple services and to transfer them to graveyards. The next two centuries emerged as the golden age of funerary art in Chinese history. This instance also teaches us that the development of monuments was not a teleologic process but was affected by chance

accidents. Sometimes the needs of a particular group of patrons could dramatically change the form and function of monuments and could reorient the direction of artistic creation. An art-historical study should not only describe a general evolution but also explore such accidents and determine their impact on the general development of art and architecture.

宫殿就逐渐独立出来并成为封建统治者权力的象征。高台建筑和楼阁建筑获得长足发展，以满足新兴的统治阶层的需求［见图 2.18］。据文献记载，这类建筑有的高度超过 100 米，其惊人的高度帮助其所有者慑服甚至恐吓政治对手。这些宫殿式建筑和传统的宗庙建筑截然不同，东周和秦代的高台建筑不再是高墙环绕、深邃隐秘的封闭结构，而是高耸入云的“摩天大厦”。它们的作用不再是通过程序化的宗庙礼仪来“教民反古复始”，而是直截了当地展示当前统治者的世俗权力。

墓地中高台建筑的出现体现了东周社会变革的另一侧面：在宗教领域里，祖先崇拜的中心逐渐从宗庙转移到墓地［见图 2.27］。这一变化渊源于这两类建筑不同的象征意义：即使在商和西周时期，历代祖先均供奉在宗庙中，地位最高的是家族的始祖；墓葬则是为生者的先父或者近亲而建。在个人野心蓬勃高涨的东周时期，丧葬建筑的宏伟程度迅速增加。诸侯把高大的陵墓看成是个人的纪念碑；他们为自己修建陵园，并颁行法令以确保它们的竣工。这一发展趋向在汉代又因新的社会、宗教因素而增加了势头：小规模的核心家庭代替大型宗族成为社会的基本单位；皇族刘氏所支持的民间宗教广泛流行；皇位继承中的不延续性给传统宗庙祭祀带来了困难。最后这一因素致使东汉的第二个皇帝汉明帝废除了所有的宗庙祭祀，而以墓祭取代之。此后的两个世纪成为中国古代丧葬艺术的黄金时代。这一例子也证明：纪念碑的发展不是受目的论支配的一个先决历史过程，而是不断地受到偶然事件的影响。有时，某一特殊社会集团的需求能够戏剧性地改变纪念碑的形式、功能及艺术创造的方向。艺术史研究不仅要描述一个总体上的演变过程，同时也要研究这些突发事件并确定它们对美术和建筑总体发展的影响。

Unlike wooden-framed palaces, many Eastern Han funerary monuments were made of stone—a material the ancient Chinese had never favored (see Figs. 4.2-5). I investigate this sudden "discovery" of stone and conclude that the Han Chinese learned this medium from the ancient Indians, who had been building stone monuments for centuries. My principal goal, however, is not simply to suggest *what* happened but to show *how* and *why* this cultural exchange took place. The alien material became "meaningful" to the Chinese only because it became associated with intrinsic Chinese concepts. Three interrelated concepts in the Han immortality cult and funerary art—death, immortality, and the West—became associated with stone. Such conceptual correlations enable me to explain many puzzling phenomena. Why, for example, did Prince Liu Sheng's tomb have a wooden house built in his underground "audience hall" but a stone house in his burial chamber? Why did Emperor Wu construct his mausoleum due west of the capital Chang'an? Why was a temple of the Queen Mother of the West a stone structure? Why did Emperor Ming, the first Chinese ruler to send envoys to seek Buddhism in India, build the first imperial stone funerary shrine for himself? Finally, why did stone become the proper medium for funerary monuments that also bore many "Buddhist" motifs?

Chapter 2, therefore, describes and explains the transition from Shang-Zhou ritual art to Qin-Han palatial and funerary monuments. In this way, it introduces the next two chapters, which focus on the palace and the tomb, respectively. The topic of Chapter 3 is the Western Han capital Chang'an. Although scholars have tried repeatedly to reconstruct this important historical city, they tend to offer a static image reduced to a two-dimensional plan: a Chang'an with city walls, twelve gates, thirteen imperial mausoleums, and a certain number of palaces (see Figs. 3.1-4). My reconstruction of the city takes a different route: instead of synthesizing all literary and archaeological evidence into a single, timeless image, I try to use this evidence to illustrate crucial changes in Chang'an's history. We find that Emperor Gaozu, the founder of the Han, built an individual palace as the supreme symbol of the new regime. The city walls came into being only under his son, and their construction, guided by an old city plan, reveals the power of tradition in early Han politics. The fifth Han emperor, Wu, turned his eyes to the city's outskirts, where

与木构的宫室不同，东汉时期很多丧葬建筑是石制的［见图4.2—图4.5］，而石头是在汉代以前少有使用的建筑材料。本书认为对石料的“发现”，与有长期建造石质建筑和雕刻历史的印度文化有关。但我的主要目的不是简单地追溯文化影响的来源，而是希望解释中国建筑中这一演变的内部原因以及演变的具体发生过程。石头这种陌生的质料之所以在汉代变得“有意义”，只是因为它和当时中国文化中的某些相当本质性的概念发生了联系。汉代丧葬艺术和神仙崇拜中的三个相互关联的概念——死、成仙、西方——都和石头发生了联系。这种多边的概念联系解释了一些令人困惑的现象，如为什么中山王刘胜要在其地宫的中室内建造一座木构房屋，但在后室中建一石屋？为什么汉武帝要把他的陵墓建在都城长安正西面？为什么《汉书》中记载的西王母祠是石构的建筑？为什么中国第一位遣使到印度取经的皇帝汉明帝也是最早为自己建造石祠的皇帝？最后，为什么石头成为丧葬建筑的适当原料，不少佛教题材也出现于这些丧葬建筑中？

本书第二章描述和解释了商周时期礼制艺术向秦汉时期宫殿和丧葬建筑的转变，由此又引出下文有关宫殿和墓葬的两章。第三章的主题是西汉都城长安。尽管学者们对复原这一历史名城进行了反复的尝试，但通行的方法是以静止、二维的观点来复原：长安有几重城墙、12座城门、13座皇陵和诸多宫殿［见图3.1—图3.4］。本书中对长安城的复原采取了另一种办法。我没有把分散的文献和考古材料糅合到一座孤立的、没有时间性的“纸面”城市中，而是试图利用这些证据来勾画出长安城的变化。我们发现，汉代开国皇帝汉高祖仅建造了一座宏伟的宫殿用作新政权的象征，而长安城城墙的建造则是在他的儿子惠帝时完成的。惠帝对长安的改造按照周代传统城市规划进行，反映出传统在这一时期政治的影响。到了汉武帝时，这位雄才大略、醉心于求仙的君主把视线从长安城内转移到

he built a fantastic garden and a replica of the Heavenly Palace. Finally, Wang Mang, who took over the Han throne and founded the short-lived Xin dynasty, destroyed Emperor Wu's garden and reused its material to build a group of Confucian monuments to legitimate his mandate from Heaven. What I hope to show is Chang'an as a dynamic historical process, shaped by a series of changes that reflected divergent concepts of monumentality.

A different strategy is employed in my discussion of Han funerary monuments in Chapter 4. Instead of tracing the general evolution of this art, I limit my observation to a single region in present-day western Shandong and to the two decades from A.D. 150 to 170. This narrow scope helps me uncover different intentions behind establishing and decorating funerary monuments. I thus share the basic approach of Martin Powers and other scholars that a Han funerary complex
014 represented a cross section of society: it was not only a center of ancestral worship within the family but was also a focus of social relationships; its monuments not only were the property of the dead but also bore witness to the various concerns of the living.[27] Instead of dividing patrons of funerary monuments into different social groups or classes, however, my discussion shows that the construction of an Eastern Han funerary site often combined the efforts of four groups of people: the deceased, his family, his former friends and colleagues, and the builders. I try to uncover their different concerns—the "voices" of Han funerary monuments—by reconstructing a number of historical scenarios based on existing funerary inscriptions and carvings.

Chapter 5 ends this book by discussing what may be the most important event in Chinese art history: the appearance of individual artists during the post-Han era who transformed public monumental art into their private idiom. Before this moment, what we call works of art, whether a bronze vessel or a stone shrine, served a direct function in religious and political life; their creation was generally mobilized by the desire to make religious and political concepts concrete. They were made by anonymous craftsmen through collective efforts, and major changes in subject matter and style were determined, first of all, by broad social and religious movements. Unlike later scroll paintings that can be appreciated individually, the various forms of early Chinese art were integral parts of

长安郊区，修建了规模宏大的上林苑和象征天堂的建章宫。最后，王莽篡汉，建立了为时不久的新。他拆毁了武帝的上林苑，利用其原料修建了明堂和辟雍等儒家建筑，借此表示他对汉代天命的合法继承。我希望所展示的长安，是一个动态的历史过程，一个包含一系列变化的复杂过程，而这些变化反映了各个时期不同的纪念碑性的概念。

随后的第四章是对汉代丧葬纪念碑的一项研究。这里我采用了另一种方法，不再去探讨这一类型纪念碑总的发展脉络，而是着重分析公元 150—170 年这 20 年间山东西部的一些遗存范例。这种小范围的研究有助于了解在当时当地建立和装饰丧葬纪念碑的动机。在这里我同意包华石以及其他学者的基本观点，即汉代丧葬建筑是当时社会的缩影：那不仅仅是家族内部祖先崇拜的中心，同时也是社会关系的焦点；丧葬纪念碑不仅是死者的财产，同时也是生者各种考虑的见证。[27] 在这里我不把丧葬纪念碑的制作者分成不同的社会群体或等级，而是证明东汉墓园的建造通常涉及四种人群：死者本人、他的家庭成员、他的生前好友和同事，以及墓葬的建造者。我试图通过考证丧葬铭文和画像来复原若干“场景”，进而揭示出这些人在建造丧葬建筑时的不同考虑。可以说，这些考虑就是丧葬纪念碑所凝固的人的“声音”。

在本书的结尾第五章中，我讨论了或可称得上是中国古代艺术史中最为重要的事件，即汉代以后独立艺术家的出现，公共性的纪念碑艺术通过这些人的努力被转化为个人行为。在此之前，我们所说的艺术品，不论是一件青铜器还是一座石享堂，都在人们的政治和宗教生活中起着直接的作用；它们的制作从总体上讲是把政治和宗教概念具体化；它们凝聚着无名工匠们的集体努力；它们在主题和风格上的变化首先是由社会和宗教演变的大趋势决定的。和后世那些供个人欣赏的书画作品不一样，早期中国艺术的种种形式是

larger monumental complexes; an individual form gained significance both through its intrinsic attributes and in conjunction with other forms. These essential features of early Chinese art determine the scope of this book.

This study, therefore, is essentially a historical inquiry rather than a theoretical abstraction. The theme of monumentality enables me to pursue a systematical reconstruction and reinterpretation of early Chinese art history. Instead of a single Chinese concept of the monumental, we find multiple ones, whose divergent ideals highlight different art traditions and whose historical relationship reveals a major thread running through the course of early Chinese art and architecture. We find this thread in the shifting focus of artistic creation from ritual paraphernalia to palatial and funerary structures. Decorative, pictorial, and architectural forms, often approached and described as separate histories, appear to be interrelated and subordinated to a broad artistic movement. It is my hope that a reconstruction of this movement will lead to a better understanding of how art and architecture evolved and functioned in a changing society—how forms were selected and employed in ritual and religious contexts, how they oriented people both physically and mentally, how they exemplified common moral or value systems, how they supported and affected the constitution of collective identities and specific political discourses, and how they suited individual ambitions and needs.

In terms of methodology, the theme of monumentality helps me bring some current scholarly concerns in early Chinese art history into a single focus. The first of these concerns is to "revolutionize" traditional formal analysis by broadening the scope of observation, by studying the relationship and interaction between different types of signs, and by investigating the technological determinants of styles. The second concern emphasizes the interaction between the viewer and objects; it is argued that such interaction—rather than the "objective" attributes of a work of art—determines the work's value and meaning in the observer's perceptual system. The third concern focuses on various "contexts": by placing and observing a work of art in its physical, ritual, religious, ideological, and political environment, scholars hope to determine more accurately its position, significance, and function in a given society. Related to such contextual research is a fourth trend of ten termed "patronage studies,"

更为广泛的纪念碑艺术的有机部分；每一种形式通过它自身的特点以及与其他形式的联系实现其意义。早期中国艺术的这些最本质的特征决定了本书的范围。

本书的研究因此在本质上是一种历史学的探索，而非纯理论的抽象演绎。纪念碑性这一主题使我可以对中国古代艺术史做一个系统的解释和重构。我们发现了多种而不是孤立的中国的纪念碑概念，它们的不同理想突出了不同的艺术传统，它们的历史关系帮助我们发现古代中国艺术和建筑发展的主线。这条主线显现于艺术创作焦点从宗庙礼器到宫室墓葬建筑的变换过程中。在这一历史演变中，美术史研究中经常被分割开的艺术门类——如装饰艺术、图像艺术和建筑艺术——显示出它们的内在联系，并都从属于更大范围的艺术运动。我希望通过对这种运动的复原，使我们能够更好地了解在一个变化的社会中，艺术和建筑是如何发展并发挥功能的——在礼制和宗教的背景下，形式是如何被选择运用的，这些形式如何决定人们的精神和物质生活的方向，如何表现道德或价值体系，如何支持和影响社会群体和特殊政治话语，以及如何满足个人的野心和需求。

从方法论的角度来看，纪念碑性这个主题使我将现有的中国古代艺术史研究中的不同学术观念融合为一。第一个观念是，对传统的形式分析方法进行更新，更新的手段是不断拓展观察范围，研究不同符号间的相互联系和相互作用，考察各种风格的技术性决定因素。第二个观念是，强调观者和作品间的相互作用，这种相互作用——而不仅是艺术品的“客观”特征——决定着作品在观者感知系统中的价值和含义。第三个观念是不同的“原境”：通过审视一件艺术品的物质、礼制、宗教、思想和政治环境，学者们希望能够更准确地确定它在某一特定社会中的地位、意义和功能。和这种“原境”研究相关的是第四种方法论，即所谓的对艺术“赞助”的研究。

which concentrate on the sociological aspect of art and explore the direct impact of patrons upon subject matter and style. Finally, a fifth trend called "cultural history" focuses neither on individual objects nor on their contexts but utilizes all sorts of visual and textual materials to reconstruct the past in all its vividness.

I believe that these methods are not contradictory but can be used complementarily either to show various aspects of early Chinese art or to conform to the available data. The five chapters of this book deliberately
015 employ these different methods. Chapter 1 on *liqi* tries to reconstruct the history of ritual art based primarily on its intrinsic visual properties. I select the mode of a broad historical narrative partly because of the lack of detailed information about artisans, workshops, and patrons, and about the design and manufacture of specific objects. Chapter 2 locates ritual paraphernalia in their architectural, ritual, and political contexts; the decline of *liqi* and the independence of architectural monuments signifies, then, an important historical transformation. Chapters 3 and 4 share the goal of cultural history in portraying a broad social and historical spectrum, but my reconstruction of Chang'an follows a chronological order whereas my discussion of funerary monuments explores a cross section of society. Both chapters consider patrons' roles but with different focuses: I relate Chang'an's changes directly to the ambitions and political agenda of individual rulers; the patrons of funerary monuments, on the other hand, included petty officials, local scholars, and commoners, whose concerns often reflected prevailing social and moral values. Chapter 5 describes the transition from early Chinese art to later Chinese art. Instead of reconstructing specific historical situations, I hope to employ various kinds of evidence to illustrate a "revolution" in visual perception and representation: when educated artists and writers began to dominate the art scene, they viewed public monuments in a new light and transformed them into a private art.

这类研究强调从社会学角度来研究艺术创造，探索赞助者对艺术作品主题和风格的直接影响。最后，我也将运用文化史研究的方法。这种方法不针对单个的作品和它们的历史背景，而是利用视觉和文献材料尽可能地复原一个宏观而生动的“过去”。

我相信这些研究方法并不矛盾，而是可以互补，或用以说明中国古代艺术的不同方面，或与现有资料相吻合。本书的五章有意识地使用了以上提到的五种研究方法。第一章讲礼器，主要依据礼器的内在视觉特征重构了礼制艺术。由于记载这些器物具体设计制作、资助人及工匠和作坊等情况的文献资料鲜有遗存，我选择了宏观的历史叙述方式。第二章着眼于礼器的建筑、礼制和政治背景（即“原境”研究）；礼器的衰落和建筑性纪念碑的兴起反映出一个关键性的历史转变。第三章和第四章重在文化史研究，表现出广阔的历史和社会视野。但第三章对长安城的复原遵循年代顺序；第四章对丧葬纪念碑的研究则着眼于社会的一个剖面。这两章都讨论了赞助人的作用，但又有不同侧重：长安城的变迁与最高统治者的个人野心和政治目的直接关联；所讨论的丧葬纪念碑的赞助人则主要是地方官吏、学者以及普通百姓，他们的关注往往反映了当时流行的一般性社会道德。第五章讨论了中国早期艺术向后期艺术的过渡。这里我未对某种具体历史情境进行重构，而是希望通过各种证据来勾画出一个视觉感知和艺术再现中的“革命”：当文人式的艺术家和作家开始统治艺术领域，他们以一种崭新的眼光来审视公众性纪念碑并把它们转化为一种个人艺术。

CHAPTER ONE THE AGE OF RITUAL ART

017 When Heaven gave birth to the multitudes of people,
There came images and words.
Holding up ritual vessels [that bore them],
People could appreciate fundamental virtue.

These lines open a famous Zhou dynasty ode in the *Book of Songs*. But I doubt that readers, even learned sinologists, could immediately identify the original Chinese source. This is because this English translation rejects the ode's orthodox exegesis and follows a reinterpretation proposed by Liu Jie fifty years ago. Although largely unknown or forgotten, this reinterpretation, in my opinion, "rediscovered" the poem, which had been buried underneath thick layers of Confucian commentaries.[1] To appreciate the freshness of Liu's reading we need only compare it with James Legge's 1871 translation of the same stanza:

Heaven, in giving birth to the multitudes of the people,
To every faculty and relationship annexed its law.
The people possess this normal nature,
And they [consequently] love its normal virtue.[2]

Here Legge closely followed a Confucian exegetical tradition, first established by Mencius and then elaborated by two Han Confucian masters, Mao Heng (2nd c. B.C.) and Zheng Xuan (A.D. 127-200).[3] Mencius cited the lines to support his view of human nature. Mao and Zheng focused on individual terms; in itself the need for annotation implies that the original meaning of these lines had become obscure by Han times. Without citing philological or textual evidence, they defined three characters in the verse as three key concepts in Confucian ideology: *wu*, as general human faculties and relations; *ze*, as common laws and principles that govern or guide these faculties and relations;

and *yi*, as the "constancy" (*chang*) in human nature. They thus followed Mencius in viewing the ode as an abstract Confucian philosophical discourse, and their commentaries transformed the lines into such a discourse.

壹 礼制艺术的时代

当上天孕育万民，
图像和文字也一同降临。
人们高擎［载有它们的］礼器，
便可感戴基本的道德。

这些诗行出自《诗经》中一首著名的周代颂诗。但是我怀疑，诸位读者乃至那些饱学的汉学家能否立刻说出它的出处。因为英译本的依据并不是原诗的传统注疏，而是 50 年前刘节的新解释。刘注鲜为人知，甚至已被遗忘，但是在我看来，它"重新发现"了被历代儒生的重重注释所淹没的原诗。[1] 对比一下 1871 年理雅各对该诗的翻译，我们就能体会到刘节的解释是如何清新。

在上天孕育万民之时，
它也孕育了与人类原则有关的各种能力和关系。
人有其常情，
他们［因而］喜好其规范的道德。[2]

理雅各译文的依据是儒家的传统注疏。注疏经典的传统由孟子开创，汉代大儒毛亨（前 2 世纪）和郑玄（127—200）又加以发展。[3] 孟子引征这些诗句用来支持他有关人性的论点，毛亨与郑玄则侧重于对字意的诠释。这首诗之所以需要诠释，说明其原初的意义到了汉代已经十分模糊。注疏家没有引用文献学或上下文的证据，而将其中的三个字眼看作儒家思想的三个关键概念："物"指一般的人类能力和关系；"则"是统领或引导这些能力和关系的一般规律与原则；"彝"的意思是"常"或人性的一致性。跟随孟子所开的先例，汉儒把这首颂诗看作一种抽象的儒家哲学话语，而其注释也确确实实地将这些诗句转换成了这种话语。

This Confucian exegesis remained the basis for all discussions of the ode until it was challenged when China entered the modern era. Liu Jie, an advocate of New Historical Studies (*xin shixue*) in the May Fourth tradition, wrote an article in 1941 redefining the three terms. Citing evidence from a comparative textual analysis, he argued that *ze* means "inscription" or "to inscribe" instead of "laws" or "principles." His identification of *wu* as "totem" is less successful (largely because of the
018 vagueness of the Western concept "totem").[4] But his basic assumption, that *wu* are images symbolizing groups of people, threw much light on this and other ancient passages, including the one about "distant regions" sending the pictures of their *wu* to the Xia and having them represented on the Nine Tripods. Finally, he pointed out that *yi* is a collective term for ritual vessels; this definition was still well remembered during the Han. With this explanation, Liu Jie allowed students of Classical literature to read the lines from the *Book of Songs* anew. The ode seems to present an idea much older than that of Mencius, Mao Heng, or Zheng Xuan. It teaches that when Chinese civilization had just appeared, what supported it were not abstract laws but concrete ritual vessels engraved with images and words; only by treasuring these ritual objects could people "appreciate fundamental virtue."

These lines thus convey to us an authentic voice from the Age of Ritual Art, the subject of this chapter. Equally important to my discussion, the rediscovery of these lines in modern scholarship attests to the power of interpretation. It sets an excellent example for my study of archaic monumentality in China, a study that also aims to restore to their original cultural context some well-known examples of early Chinese art and architecture.

❶ The Concept of *Liqi*

At the bottom of each branch of human knowledge rests a classification. Before the world can be explained, it must be ordered; a mass of undifferentiated phenomena must be divided into manageable groups or classes. Members of a single group are considered to share certain common characteristics, either physical or conceptual. Since criteria essential for a classification are selected (though not always consciously) from the myriad features of the objects being classified, a classification

作为长期以来研究该诗的基础，这种儒家注疏传统直到近代才受到挑战。刘节是五四运动“新史学”的一位倡导者。当他在 1941 年著文重新解释这三个字的时候，他引征可资比较的语篇分析，认为“则”的意思是“铭文”或“题写”，而不是“规律”或“准则”。虽然他将“物”认定为“图腾”不一定恰当（这在很大程度上是由于当时对西方“图腾”概念的认识模糊），[4] 但他提出的“物”代表人类族群的图像的这个基本看法，使得这段文字和其他古代文献的意义变得更为明了，如夏代将“远方”进贡的“物”铸在九鼎上。最后，刘节指出“彝”是礼器的总称，汉代人对于这个定义记忆犹新。刘节的解释使古代经典的研究者们得以重新体会《诗经》中这些句子的含义。这首颂诗所表达的似乎是一种远比孟子、毛亨和郑玄的思想更为古老的观念，即当中国文明刚刚出现的时候，支持这种文明的并不是抽象的法则，而是铸刻着图像和文字的有形礼器；只有通过珍视它们，人们才得以“懂得基本的道德”。

这些诗行给我们传达了一种来自礼制艺术时代的真实声音，发掘这种声音也正是本章的主题。就我的讨论来说，同样重要的是，现代学术研究对于这些诗句本意的再发现证实了“解释”的力量。这为研究中国古代纪念碑性提供了一个绝好的例证，因为这一研究的目的也在于通过复原文化原境而对早期中国艺术和建筑中一些为人熟知的实例提出新的解释。

一、“礼器”的概念

人类知识的每一分支都建立在分类的基础之上。必须先建立某种秩序，世界才能够被解释；混乱无序的现象必须分成可以把握的组或类。一个组或类的成员应在物质上或概念上具有某种相同的特征。由于最重要的分类标准总是从被分类对象的诸多特征中选择出来的（尽管不一定总是有意识地），所以分类的结果常常由分类者

is always determined by the position of the classifier and thus always appears as a historical phenomenon, temporal and purposeful.

Generally speaking, there are two basic ways in which social phenomena are classified: the "internal classification" or "natural order position," made by contemporary members of the society, and the "external classification" or "artificial order position," pursued by people outside the society, either from alien cultures or from later periods.[5] These two systems both reflect and index the cognitive and cultural structures of the classifiers, but the latter is often viewed as an objective system and is often imposed on the original society.

The classification at the bottom of the study of early Chinese art is a typical external classification. It displaces ancient works of art and transfers them from their original contexts into the structure of a later social science. When antiquarians first cast their eyes on ancient artifacts, they were dealing with random assemblages of old objects whose natural orders had largely been forgotten. It is these antiquarians—collectors and cataloguers—who first overcame this chaos by re-establishing a new order.[6] Even the Chinese term for antiquarianism, *jinshi xue*, suggests a basic classification. *Jin* and *shi* mean, respectively, "metal" and "stone," and *xue* means "discipline." The term can properly be translated into English as "the study of [ancient] metal and stone works."[7] This system, established during the Song, has been continuously refined ever since. The number of medium-oriented categories has constantly increased; Zhao Ruzhen's early twentieth-century *Guide to Antiques (Guwan zhinan)* alone introduces 30 kinds of ancient artifacts of different materials.[8]

The classification of research materials further led to the classification of the researchers themselves. As data proliferated and scholarship became increasingly sophisticated, no one individual could deal with the vast array of ancient works in an encyclopedic manner. Collectors and researchers began to concentrate on one particular class of objects, and their expertise in their own field made them acknowledged scholars and connoisseurs. The medium-oriented division of professionals thus rests firmly on a medium-oriented classification of materials. Consequently, the belief emerged that each medium-based branch was an independent artistic "genre" with its own life. True, there have been efforts to reunite these separated branches into a coherent narrative, but until recently the boundaries separating categories were rarely crossed.

的立场观点所决定，因而必然是具有时间性和目的性的历史现象。

总的说来，对社会现象进行分类有两种基本途径：一种是由当时的社会成员所做的“内部分类”或“自然归位”；另一种是由社会外部的人——包括他文化或后世的人——所做的“外部分类”或“人为归位”。[5] 这两个系统都反映了分类者本身的认知与文化结构，但后者却往往被看作一个客观体系，强加于原来的社会之上。

早期中国艺术研究中的基础性分类方法是一种典型的外部分类法。它使古代艺术作品脱离原境，将其转移到后来的社会科学中。当古物学家们把目光落到古代遗存上时，他们最先看到的是杂乱无章的古代物品的集合，其原来的“自然归位”在很大程度上已被遗忘。正是这些古物学家——包括收藏者和著述家——开始去凿空这种混乱，重新建立起一种新的次序。[6] 甚至中国古物学的名称“金石学”也可以被看成是一种基本的分类：“金”和“石”分别指“金属”和“石头”，而“学”意思是“学科”。这个术语因此可以确切地译成 the study of (ancient) metal and stone works。[7] 这一体系创建于宋代，以后得到不断发展完善。以材质分类的艺术品数量不断增加，如 20 世纪初赵汝珍《古玩指南》一书就介绍了 30 种不同材质的古董。[8]

对古董材质的分类进一步导致了研究者自身的分类。资料日益丰富，学术研究也日益复杂化，没有哪一个人能以百科全书式的学识来应对浩如烟海的古物。收藏家和研究者开始专注于某一特别的种类，在各自领域内的特长给他们带来了学者和鉴赏家的声名。这样，以材质划分的专家就牢固地建立在以材质划分的器物基础上。其结果是，人们开始相信每一种基于材质的分支都是一个独立的艺术“类别”并有着自己的发展逻辑。虽然近年来一些学者尝试着把这些单独的门类整合为一个整体，但总的说来，很少能突破这种分类的界限。

Thus, when at the beginning of the twentieth century the British
019 Board of Education commissioned Stephen W. Bushell to write the first comprehensive English-language introduction to Chinese art, one of his major tasks was the organization of his material (and hence the structure of his book). A learned sinologist who had lived in Beijing for some thirty years, Bushell described himself as "a diligent collector of Chinese books relating to antiquities and art industries [who has] tried to gain a desultory knowledge of their scope."[9] In establishing the basic descriptive categories for his book, he combined the Chinese antiquarian tradition with a Western classification of "collectible objects" popular in his day. The twelve chapters of the book survey the histories of twelve branches of Chinese art, including bronzes, carved jades, pottery and ceramics, and lacquer wares, with "typical" examples selected from the Victoria and Albert Museum. As Bushell wrote in his preface, "These have been the lines followed here as far as the brief space assigned to each branch of art has allowed."[10] Many other scholars of early Chinese art and archaeology shared Bushell's strategy for studying the whole span of Chinese art history, though their "material categories" were often fewer. When the prominent historian Liang Qichao delivered a talk entitled "Archaeology in China" before the crown prince of Sweden in 1926, he began: "If we classify the objects that have been treated by the archaeologists [a term also referring to traditional antiquarians and art historians] of the last 150 years, we get four kinds: (1) Stone, (2) Bronze, (3) Pottery, and (4) Bones and Tortoise Shells."[11]

Although such a classification has the obvious advantage of arranging the vast and often chaotic collection of ancient objects into comprehensible units, it has disadvantages. As Stephen Owen points out in a discussion of Chinese poetry:

> There are dimensions of the poetic art, often those of the "greatest force," which lie beyond the reach of our usual discourse on literature. When that "greatest force" is felt to move in poems, there is no reason

to meddle with it or to seek to expose its workings. But when an art is displaced—by transfer to another civilization, by time's long spans, or by the disruption of its continuity—then we must discover a way to give voice to those very dimensions of the poetic art which are usually left in tactful silence.[12]

这样，当 20 世纪初英国国家教育委员会委托卜士礼编写一本综合介绍中国艺术的英文著作时，他面对的主要挑战之一是如何组织他的材料，也就是如何确立书的结构。卜士礼曾在北京生活三十年，是一位博学的汉学家。他说自己是"一位收藏家，尽力搜集有关中国古董和艺术品的书籍，试图获得各个领域的驳杂知识"。[9] 在建构其著作的基本描述性类别时，他综合了中国古董学的传统与当时流行的西方对"可收藏物品"的分类。他的著作分为十二章，概述了中国艺术十二个门类的发展历史，包括青铜器、玉器、陶瓷和漆器，并以维多利亚和艾伯特博物馆的"典型"藏品作为例证。正如卜士礼在该书序言中所说的那样，"这是对于每一艺术门类最简明的介绍"。[10] 其他许多研究中国早期艺术和考古学的学者运用了同样的方法来研究整个中国艺术史，尽管他们以"材质"所分的类别通常会少一些。比如，1926 年著名历史学家梁启超旅行至瑞典，在一个有瑞典皇太子参加的集会上介绍"中国考古学"，他开宗明义地说："我把他们所研究的对象，用来做分类的标准，大概可分四大类。甲石类，乙金类，丙陶类，丁骨甲及其他。"[11]

虽然这种分类方式的优点在于可将众多混乱的古董梳理为容易被理解的单位，但是它也有其致命的弱点。宇文所安在讨论中国诗歌时说过：

> 诗的艺术有其维度，即通常所谓其"宏大的力量"，这类维度存在于我们一般的文学研究范围之外。当我们感知到这种"宏大的力量"在诗中游移时，我们没有理由去干预它，或者去寻找、去探索其运行。但是当一种艺术被移植时——或被转化为另一种文明，或通过时间的流转，或其连续性被中断——我们就必须找到一种方法，使诗的艺术的这些通常缄默无语的方面重新发出声音。[12]

The question confronting a student of early Chinese art is, therefore, where and how to "discover a way to give voice" to the silent force that once governed the original working of this art but has largely been neglected in later "external classifications." More specifically, how can we explore the ancient Chinese concept of monumentality if it is conveyed by unfamiliar forms? To pursue this goal, I suggest that we try to discover the "internal classification" of early artworks or, more practically, to find ancient classification systems closer to the original classification than our own.[13] This proposal has led me to the *Three Ritual Canons* (*San li—Li ji*; *Yi li*, or *Ceremonies and Rites*; *Zhou li*, or *Rites of Zhou*). Compiled at the end of the Bronze Age, these records were written by ritual specialists who attempted to revitalize (by systematization and idealization) earlier ritual procedures and institutions. These are not art-historical or historical studies, and their authors treated bronzes or carved jades as contemporary, functional objects rather than as relics of the remote past. Differing from later medium-oriented scholarship, which often isolates works of art from their contexts, these books always situate manufactured objects in groups and in specific ritual occasions. In terms of both chronology and ideology, therefore, these records are close to the period during which ancient bronzes and jades were produced and used, and they preserve important clues for a proper understanding of early Chinese art.

The most fundamental classification of manufactured forms proposed by the authors of these books is that between "ritual paraphernalia" and "daily utensils." This distinction, which is closely related to the ancient Chinese conceptualization of art, craft, and monumentality, is clearly stated in the following passages:

> When a nobleman is about to prepare things for his lineage, the vessels of sacrifice should have the first place; the offerings, the next; and the vessels for use at meals, the last.[14]
>
> Not until [a Grand Officer] has made sacrificial vessels is he

permitted to make vessels for his own private use.[15]

The [jade] *gui* tablets, *bi* disks, and the gilt libation cups are not allowed to be sold in the marketplace [where utensils are sold]; nor 020
are the official robes and chariots, the gifts of the king, or vessels of an ancestral temple.[16]

因此，摆在研究中国早期艺术的学者面前的问题就是：从何处以及如何“找到一种方式”，使曾经统御原生艺术运行、后来却被“外部分类”大大忽略了的沉默力量“发出声音”？更具体地说，如果中国古代纪念碑性的概念表现为某种我们所不熟悉的形式，那么我们如何才能发现它？要达到这个目的，我建议我们应该去努力探索古代作品的“内部分类”，或者更可行一些，去探索一种比我们自己的分类更接近于原始分类的古代分类体系。[13] 这个提议引导我注意到“三礼”——《礼记》《仪礼》和《周礼》。这些文献出现于青铜时代晚期，是由一些试图（通过系统化和理想化）恢复早期礼仪程序和制度的礼家编纂的。它们并非艺术史或历史学著作，其作者把青铜器或玉器看作礼仪中的实用器，而非遥远的古代遗物。上文说到后代的学者以材质进行分类，常常割裂作品的原境，孤立地看待作品。这些著作则不同，其对器物的分组总是根据特定的礼仪场合。因此，在年代和思想体系上，这些著作更接近于制造和使用古代青铜器和玉器的时期，为我们理解中国早期艺术的原意保存了重要线索。

这些书的作者对器物最基本的分类是将其分为“礼仪用品”（称为“礼器”或“祭器”）和“日常生活用品”（称为“用器”“养器”或“燕器”）。这种区分与中国古代艺术、工艺以及纪念碑性的概念密切相关，在以下几段文献中表现得十分清楚：

> 君子……凡家造，祭器为先，牺赋为次，养器为后。[14]
>
> 大夫……祭器未成，不造燕器。[15]
>
> 有圭璧金璋，不粥于市。命服命车，不粥于市。宗庙之器，不粥于市。[16]

The last passage suggests more detailed categorizations based on material, form, and precise usage within the general class of "ritual paraphernalia." In fact, large portions of the ritual books are devoted to regulating the combinations of such objects to be used on different ritual occasions. Thus, we read in the *Rites of Zhou* that the senior and junior *zongbo*, the two chief ceremonial officials of the royal lineage (*zong*), are responsible for "the rituals for the heavenly deities, human ghosts, and earthly spirits of the state." All the articles they administer are ritual objects and include "six types of ritual jades, " "six types of bronze vessels for presenting sacrificial food," "six types of bronze vessels for presenting sacrificial wine," and many others.[17] The production of daily utensils is not their business.

The standard Chinese term for "ritual paraphernalia" is *liqi* (*jiqi*, or "vessels for ancestral sacrifices," is sometimes used interchangeably). The meaning of *li* is close to "ritual" or "rite, " and *qi*, to "vessel" or "implement." Although this composite term itself draws a rough boundary for the genre, it is far from adequate for defining its actual content, since the two characters of the term—*li* and *qi*—refer to innumerable things and concepts. The nineteenth-century French sinologist Joseph Marie Callery summarized the usages of the character *li* in Classical Chinese writings:

> As far as possible, I have translated *li* by the word "rite," whose meaning has the greatest range; but it must be acknowledged that according to the circumstances in which it is employed it can signify ceremonial, ceremonies, ceremonial practices, etiquette, politeness, urbanity, courtesy, honesty, good manners, respect, good education, good breeding, the proprieties, convention, *savoir-vivre*, decorum, decency, personal dignity, moral conduct, social order, social duties, social laws, duties, rights, morality, laws of hierarchy, sacrifice, mores, and customs.[18]

Callery's list is by no means a compact definition, but it does make clear two major aspects of human lives to which the concept of *li* is applied: ceremonies and related practices, and the social conventions—primarily those of law, morality, and propriety—that govern the working of society at large. These two aspects overlap: in the ritualized society of the Three Dynasties, ceremonies both reflected and regulated human relationships and thus determined legal and moral standards; correct

最后一段文献根据材料、形式和使用方式对"礼器"进行了较为详细的划分。实际上，礼书中屡屡对不同礼仪场合中所用器物的组合进行规范。如我们在《周礼》中读到，周代王室世系（"宗"）的两个主要礼官，即大小宗伯，其首要职能是"掌建邦之天神、人鬼、地祇之礼"和"掌建国之神位"。他们所司掌的器物均为礼器，包括用玉制作的"六器"、盛祭品的青铜"六尊"和盛酒的青铜"六彝"，等等。[17] 日常生活用品的制作与他们无关。

"礼仪用具"一词标准的中国术语是"礼器"（或"祭器"）。"礼"的含义接近于英文的 ritual 或 rite，"器"则常常翻译成 vessel 或 implement。尽管这个合成词的字面本身对其含义作了大致的界定，但是远不足以说明其真正的内涵，因为"礼"和"器"两个字可以涉指无数的事物和概念。19 世纪法国汉学家范尚人归纳了中国古典文献中"礼"字的用法：

> 我尽可能地将"礼"字译为 rite，其含义十分广泛。但必须指出，根据其使用的环境，这个字可以指礼节、仪式、典礼、礼仪、彬彬有礼、文雅、谦恭、诚实、良好的举止、尊敬、有学识、有教养、礼仪礼节、常规、有礼貌、高雅、体面、个人尊严、德行、社会秩序、社会职责、社会规则、责任、权利、道德、等级规范、祭祀、习俗和风俗等。[18]

范尚人所开的这个单子不能说是一个简洁的定义，但它指出了人类生活中运用"礼"的两个主要方面：一是仪式和与仪式有关的行为；二是制约着社会运行的普遍社会规范——主要指法律、道德和礼节。这两个方面彼此交叉：在三代的礼制社会，礼仪反映和规范着人际关系，因此也决定了法律和道德的标准；正确的"礼仪

"ritual behavior" could hardly be distinguished from "propriety" or "good manners."[19] If we must explain *li* in a short formulation, we may say that it means the principles and forms of both secular and sacred relations and communications.[20]

Li, therefore, seems to have embodied general social principles shared by everyone, and indeed many writings on ancient Chinese ideology have created an impression that *li* was universally applicable to all members of society.[21] This may have been the dream of later philosophers, but it was certainly not a reality, for the whole system of *li* depended on and also guaranteed social stratifications and distinctions. It is stated plainly in the *Book of Rites*: "*Li* does not extend down to the commoners, nor does *xing* [punishment] extend to the noble."[22] *Li* became meaningful and functional only within this polar structure. It provided reasons for the king to be a king, a lord to be a lord, and so on down to the lowest level of the aristocratic hierarchy. It forced an individual of the aristocratic class to behave according to his inherited and assigned status; otherwise he would be accused of being *feili* ("against *li*"), a severe denunciation implying "unlawful" and "immoral." *Li*, therefore, was the manus of the ruling machine, and both its fundamental premise and its primary function were "to distinguish." This role of *li* was explained explicitly by the ancient Chinese themselves: "It is *li* that clarifies the dubious and distinguishes [things] to the minute, and thus it can serve as dykes for the people. Because of *li*, there are the grades of the noble and the mean; there are the distinctions of dresses [as symbols of social ranks]; the court has its proper position; and people all yield their places."[23] A more elaborate paean glorifies *li* to almost godlike proportions:

> Of all things by which men live, *li* is the greatest. Without *li*, there would be no means of regulating the services paid to the spirits of heaven and earth; without *li*, there would be no means of distinguishing the positions of ruler and subject, superior and inferior, old and young;

without *li*, there would be no means of maintaining the separate relations between men and women, father and son, elder and younger brothers, and of conducting the intercourse between families related in marriage, and the frequency and infrequency [of the reciprocities between friends].[24] 021

This quotation provides an explanation for the origins of *li*. Here, two hierarchical systems, one political and the other genealogical,

行为”无法与“礼节”和“良好的举止”分开。[19] 如果我们一定要为“礼”做一个简洁的解释，我们可以说，它指的既是世俗性也是宗教性的人类关系和交往的原则与形式。[20]

因此，“礼”似乎体现了人人必须遵守的一般社会准则。许多关于中国古代思想的著作确实也留给我们一个印象，即“礼”广泛地适用于所有社会成员。[21] 这可能是后代思想家的一个梦想，但却并非三代的事实，因为在那个时期里，礼的整个体系依赖于并维护着社会的等级和差别。《礼记》明确指出：“礼不下庶人，刑不上大夫。”[22] 礼只有在这个两极结构中才有其意义和作用。礼是君王之所以为君王、贵族之所以为贵族的理由之所在，以至贵族统治集团最底层。它要求贵族阶层中个人的行为必须与其世袭的和被授予的身份相一致，否则将被指为“非礼”，这一严厉的谴责意味着“非法”和“无德”。因此，礼是统治机器的手，其基本前提和主要功能是进行“分别”。中国古人对礼的这个职责作了清楚的解释：“夫礼者，所以章疑别微，以为民坊者也。故贵贱有等，衣服有别，朝廷有位，则民有所让。”[23]《礼记》中的一段颂词更把礼抬高到神一样的地位：

> 民之所由生，礼为大。非礼无以节事天地之神也，非礼无以辨君臣、上下、长幼之位也，非礼无以别男女、父子、兄弟之亲、昏姻疏数之交也。[24]

对于礼的起源，这段文献提供了一种解释。在这里，两个等级系统——一个是政治的，另一个是世系的——在礼的作用下糅合在

become entangled as the result of *li's* operation. These systems were two dimensions of a single network that unified the aristocratic society of the Three Dynasties. Among modern scholars, K. C. Chang has argued most forcefully that the basic elements of pre-Qin society were patrilineages fragmented from a number of clans.[25] Theoretically, all members of the ruling group, from the king down to the lowest-ranking official, were related by blood or marriage. A person's social and political status was primarily determined by seniority in the overall genealogical structure. For instance, a king had the right to be a king because he was a direct descendent of the founder of the clan that dominated the country; his younger brothers could only be lords of principalities. Following this pattern of fragmentation, direct descendents of a lord carried on their ancestor's duty under the same official title; other branches of the lineage were set up with descending ranks and fiefs.

This is, of course, much too simplistic a summary of the social and political structure of archaic China and the Zhou system, but it may help us understand the most important component and expression of *li*—*ji*, or ancestral sacrifices. The *Book of Rites* states: "Of all the methods for the good ordering of men, there is none more urgent than the use of *li*. *Li* are of five kinds [i.e., sacrificial, mourning, greeting, military, and festive], and there is none of them more important than *ji*."[26] We may add another layer to this statement: of the many ways available to the living to show their respect to their ancestors, none was more important than offering food and drink. Year after year, members of a lineage gathered in the ancestral temple and placed food and wine before the symbols of the dead. As I discuss in Chapter 2, the design of the temple reflected the lineage's genealogy, with its founder worshipped at the innermost location in the compound and more recent ancestors worshipped nearer the entrance.[27] This architectural form thus became a metaphor for the social structure, and the ancestral ritual held in it defined the social hierarchy. As the ritual of ancestral sacrifice identified a person's status in the clan-lineage framework with clarity and repetition, his position in the political framework was regulated. Any attempt to break these bonds was "against *li*."

To Shang and Zhou people, ancestors were not abstract concepts but concrete beings. Although believing the departed kin had become spirits with whom one could communicate only through secret means, they also

了一起。这是统一三代贵族社会网络的两个方面。在当代学者中，张光直最明确地指出，先秦社会的基本元素是从许多氏族中裂变出来的父系宗族。[25]从理论上讲，从君王到最底层的官员，统治集团中所有的成员都是由血缘和婚姻联系在一起的。人的社会和政治地位首先由他在整个家族结构中的地位所决定。比如说，君王之所以有权成为君王，是因为他是统治这一国家的氏族创立者的直系后代，他的弟弟只能做封邑的公侯。遵循这种分支模式，公侯的直系后代在同样的名分下履行其祖先的职责。非直系分支亦建立起来，等级和封地递降。

这当然只是对于远古中国（主要是对周代）社会与政治结构极度简化的归纳，但这一归纳也许有助于我们理解礼的最重要的成分与表现——祭。《礼记》中写道："凡治人之道，莫急于礼，礼有五经（即吉礼、凶礼、宾礼、军礼和嘉礼），莫重于祭。"[26]我们可以再加上一层意思：生者有许多途径对其祖先表达敬意，但最重要的莫过于为其提供酒食。年复一年，家族成员集合在祖庙中，将酒食陈列在死者的象征物前。我在本书第二章将谈到，宗庙的设计反映了宗族的世系，其远祖被供奉在最里面的位置，晚近的祖先则被供奉在靠近入口的地方。[27]这样，宗庙的建筑形式就是对社会结构的隐喻，而里面举行的祭祖仪式则规范着社会的等级。由于祭祖仪式在家族世系框架中毫不含糊而且一再重复地对一个人进行了定位，他在政治框架中的位置也由此确定了。任何企图打破这种规范的企图都被视作"非礼"。

对商人和周人来说，祖先并不是抽象的概念，而是具体的存在。尽管他们相信死去的亲族已经变为通过神秘方式才能沟通的灵魂，

insisted that these invisible beings retained all human desires, especially that for food. This mortal attachment divulges a kind of intimacy beyond political calculation. Descendents kept recalling the hardships their remote ancestors had experienced; the accuracy of their reminiscences often surprises a modern anthropologist.

> In the past, our former kings had no palaces and houses. In winter they excavated caves and lived in them, and in summer they framed nests and stayed in them. They knew nothing about fire and cooking; they ate the fruits of plants and trees, as well as the flesh of birds and beasts. They drank the blood of animals and swallowed their hair. They were ignorant of flax and silk and clothed themselves with feathers and skins.
>
> Later, sages arose and invented and utilized fire. They moulded the metals and fashioned clay, and they built towered pavilions and houses with windows and doors. They toasted, grilled, boiled, and roasted. They produced must and sauces, and they made linen and silken fabric from flax and silk. They were thus able to nourish the living, to carry out mourning for the dead, and to serve the spirits of the departed and the Lord on High: in all these things we must follow their examples.[28]

The history of Chinese civilization is thus viewed as the creation and elaboration of *li* or *ji*; the later generations must follow *li* and *ji* diligently because these are the foundation of the whole civilization:

> Thus, [in our sacrifices] the dark liquor is offered in the inner
> 022 chamber [of the temple]; the vessels containing must are placed near its entrance; the reddish liquor is offered in the main hall; and the clear, in a place below. Animal victims are displayed, and the tripods and stands are prepared. The lutes and citherns are arranged in rows, with the flutes, sonorous stones, bells, and drums. The prayers and the benedictions are framed. All of these aim to bring down the Lord on High, as well as ancestral deities, from above.

> The relation between the ruler and ministers is then rectified; generous feeling between father and son is maintained; elder and younger brothers are harmonized; the high and low find their own positions; and the proper relationship between husband and wife is established. This is what is called "securing the blessing of Heaven."[29]

As suggested by this passage, in the course of history the quality of offerings was gradually refined and newly discovered materials and techniques were employed to make ritual paraphernalia. But the function

他们仍坚信这些看不见的存在依然保留着人类的所有欲望，尤其是对食物的欲望。这种对世间的依恋透露出一种超乎政治算计的亲情。后人回忆着其远祖所经历的磨难，其记忆的准确程度可以让一个现代人类学家吃惊：

> 昔者先王未有宫室，冬则居营窟，夏则居橧巢。未有火化，食草木之实、鸟兽之肉，饮其血，茹其毛。未有麻丝，衣其羽皮。
>
> 后圣有作，然后修火之利。范金，合土，以为台榭宫室牖户。以炮，以燔，以亨，以炙。以为醴酪。治其麻丝以为布帛。以养生送死，以事神鬼上帝。皆从其朔。[28]

根据这种逻辑，中华文明的历史也就是“礼”或“祭”产生与完善的过程。后代必须认真地遵循“礼”和“祭”，因为它们是整个文明的基础之所在：

> 故玄酒在室，醴醆在户，粢醍在堂，澄酒在下，陈其牺牲，备其鼎俎，列其琴瑟管磬钟鼓，修其祝嘏，以降上神与其先祖。
>
> 以正君臣，以笃父子，以睦兄弟，以齐上下，夫妇有所，是谓承天之祜。[29]

这些文字指出，祭品的质量在历史的进程中逐渐完善，新发现的材料和技术也不断用来制作祭器。但是，“祭”的功能却没有改变，

of *ji* or ancestral sacrifices remained without change: they maintained the social structure by drawing distinctions, because proper distinctions meant a good order. The same logic can be reversed: although the ancestral sacrifices supported social organizations throughout ancient Chinese history, their paraphernalia was subject to constant change, and from these changes emerged a history of ritual art centered on sacrificial vessels.

An idea repeatedly emphasized in the ritual books is that "*li* began from meat and drink [of sacrifices]."[30] To students of art, this means that *li* began with the use of vessels and other ritual implements. In fact, this implication of *li* is suggested by the character itself, which consists of two pictograms; one (see character *a* to right) represents an ancestral tablet, and the other (*b*) shows a bowl containing offerings, perhaps two strings of jades.[31] This image, therefore, defines *li* by presenting its most tangible form—offerings presented to spirits.

示 a

豊 b

But the same image can also be understood as a representation of a ritual action—to *place* offerings before spirits, as explained in the earliest Chinese dictionary, the *Shuo wen*: "The character *li* means 'one step in an act'; whereby we serve spiritual beings and obtain happiness."[32] This twofold meaning of the character corresponds to two visual aspects of a rite: on the one hand, a ritual employs numerous individual symbols—vessels, musical instruments, banners, insignia, ornaments—that we call *liqi*, or ritual paraphernalia, whose functions and meanings are signified by their material, shape, decoration, and inscription. On the other hand, a ritual is always a sequence of actions, and an individual symbol is always an integral element of a larger ritual complex and realizes its function and meaning in the ritual sequence. Such sequences may be discovered from ancient texts, but to art historians a ritual sequence must be defined according to the spatial conjunctions of individual symbols.[33] These two aspects of a ritual presentation thus determine the two levels of our investigation of ritual art: on the first level we study *liqi* as individual symbols, and on the second level we observe their spatio-temporal structure in relation to their architectural context.

The present chapter focuses on the first aspect, and its central question is What are *liqi*? The most convenient answer to this question is that *liqi* are objects used in ritual practices; thus the Qing scholar

因为恰当的界限意味着良好的秩序，所以这些功能通过划定界限来保持社会结构。同样的逻辑反之亦然，尽管祖先祭祀在整个中国历史中支持着社会的组织，但其用具却不断变化，从这些变化中衍生出了以礼器为中心的礼仪美术的早期历史。

礼书中反复强调的一个思想是“夫礼之初，始诸饮食”[30]。对一个美术史学者来说，其含义是礼始于对祭器以及其他礼仪用具的使用。实际上，“礼”（禮）字本身也能说明其含义，它包括两个象形的部分。其左侧的偏旁（示）表示祖先的灵位，其右边的部分（豊）是一个器皿中盛有或许是两串玉器的祭品。[31]这个字通过明确的形象——向神灵奉献的祭品——说明了礼的含义。但是，这一图像也可以理解为动态的“礼仪行为”的表现——在神灵面前陈列祭品，与此对应的解释可以在中国最古老的字典《说文解字》中找到：“礼，履也，所以事神致福也。”[32]因此，“礼”字的双重含义表达了一项礼仪活动的两种视觉表现：一方面，礼仪活动要使用我们称之为“礼器”的多种多样的象征物，包括容器、乐器、旗帜、徽章、饰物等，其材质、形状、装饰和铭文显示了它们的功能和意义。另一方面，礼仪总是由一连串的行为构成的，一个单独的象征物总是组成更大的礼仪体系的一个元素，其功能和意义只有在礼仪的过程中才能得到体现。这个过程或可在古代文献中读到，但是对美术史家来说，一个礼仪的过程必须根据单独的象征物的空间联系来确定。[33]由此，礼仪的这两个方面就决定了我们观察礼仪美术的两个层面：在第一个层面上，我们将礼器作为单独的象征物来研究；在第二个层面上，我们综合礼仪行为的建筑原境来考察礼器的时空框架。

本章讨论第一个层面，其中心的问题是：什么是礼器？对这个问题最简单的回答是，礼器是举行礼仪活动时所使用的器物。清代

Gong Zizhen enumerated as many as nineteen different usages of *liqi* in a learned article entitled "On Temple Vessels" ("Shuo zongyi").[34] This understanding of *liqi* is still dominant in scholarly writings, largely because it fits well with a functional classification of ancient objects: the *ding* tripod is a type of ritual bronze because it was *used* to cook sacrificial meat, and the *gui* bowl is another type because it was *used* to contain sacrificial rice. These interpretations or identifications are important but not sufficient for our understanding of *liqi*, because they do not answer the question: What is the art of ritual paraphernalia? By using the word art, we assume that these ancient ritual objects, in addition to their use as cooking pots or food containers in religious ceremonies, possess other kinds of values. What are these values, and how can we explore and identify these values? These much neglected questions are of crucial importance to early Chinese art history.

I explore these values and see how they change over time in the next section. But before throwing readers into an ocean of works of art, I need to examine the concept of *liqi* more closely and to relate it to the concepts of monuments and monumentality. As a conceptual
023 entity, *liqi* are characterized by a deliberate ambiguity that results from the multiple meanings of the term *qi*. The standard and narrowest dictionary definition of *qi* is "vessel," as in the *Shuo wen* dictionary: "*qi* means containers."[35] But the character was often employed in a broader sense, referring to all kinds of artifacts, including vessels, implements, and insignia; thus Duan Yucai, a Qing dynasty authority on ancient ritual books, argued that "*qi* is the general term for all manmade objects."[36] The concept *qi* was sometimes further broadened; The *Yellow Emperor's Inner Classic* (*Huangdi neijing*), an ancient medical book, defines it as "all forms that are empty inside and thus able to contain things."[37] In accord with this definition, the term is used in the book not for pottery or bronze jars but for the human body, which "contains" vital energy. This generalization finally leads to the broadest usage of the term, in the *Book of Changes* (*Yi*

jing): "Form is called *qi*."[38]

The character *qi* was thus used and understood by the ancient Chinese both literally and metaphysically. As the former, a *qi* is a physical object distinctive in its function; as the latter, it is close to an "embodiment" or "prosopopeia"—a physical entity "containing" meaning

学者龚自珍在《说宗彝》一文中归纳了礼器多达十九种的用途。[34] 这种对礼器的理解在学术研究中仍占主导地位，很大程度上是因为它与对古代器物功能的分类相一致：鼎是一种青铜礼器，是因为它被用来煮祭祀的肉食；簋也是一种礼器，是因为它被用来盛放祭祀的饭食。这种解释或界定对于我们理解礼器的含义虽然重要，但还不够充分，因为它们并没有回答什么是礼器艺术。当我们用"艺术"这个词来谈礼器的时候，我们假设这些古代的礼仪用品除了在仪式中用作炊煮器和盛食器外，还应当具有其他方面的价值。这些价值是什么？我们如何来探索和确定这些价值？这些被忽视的问题对于中国早期艺术史的研究来说至关重要。

我将在下面一节讨论这些价值及其变迁的过程。但是在将读者投入艺术品的汪洋大海之前，我们需要对礼器的概念做更进一步的考察，并将它和纪念碑及纪念碑性联系起来。作为一个概念实体，"礼器"这一概念有一个特征，就是它的有意的模糊性，这是因为"器"这个字有着多重含义。这个字的标准的狭义定义是"器具"。《说文解字》云："器，皿也。"[35] 但是它常在更广泛的意义上使用，用来指所有类型的器物，像容器、工具和徽章等等。以研究古代礼书著称的清代学者段玉裁因此指出，"器乃凡器统称。"[36] "器"的概念有时更为宽泛。中国古代医书《黄帝内经》中说，"故器者，生化之宇。"[37] 根据这个定义，这里所说的"器"并不指那些陶罐铜壶，而是"容纳"能量的人体。"器"的这种含义的扩大化在《易经》中达到了顶点："形而下者谓之器"（即一切有形的、物质的东西都可以被称为"器"）。[38]

因此，中国古人对"器"字的理解既有字面上的意义，也有形而上的意义。在前一种意义上，器是以其功用为特征的实体；在后一种意义上，它的含义近乎"体现"或"拟人法"，即一种"容纳"

and typifying an abstraction. The range of the changing concept of *qi* is demonstrated by the following quotations from the Chinese Classics, which are extremely important to a final definition of *liqi*:

1. *Qi* are [things] that can be handled and used.[39]

2. The round and square food containers *fu* and *gui*, the stand *zu*, and the tall dish *dou*, with their regulated [forms] and surface decoration, are the *qi* embodying *li*.[40]

3. The grand ceremonial bells and *ding* tripods, these are beautiful *qi* of extraordinary importance.[41]

4. It is only the *qi* and the title of a ruler that cannot be granted to others, because these are what enable him to govern. It is by his title that he secures the confidence [of the people]; it is by that confidence that he preserves the *qi*; it is these *qi* that conceal *li*; it is *li* that is essential to the practice of righteousness; it is righteousness that contributes to the advantage [of his state]; and it is that advantage which secures the quiet of the people. These are the principles of politics.[42]

5. What is above Form is called Principle; what is within Form is called *qi*; what transforms things and fits them together is called Change; what stimulates them and sets them in motion is called Continuity; what raises them up and sets them forth before all people on earth is called Action. Therefore, with respect to Symbols: the sages were able to see those hidden in all the things under heaven; they provided them with forms to present their manifestations. These are called Symbols.[43]

6. [The sages] made *qi* to present Symbols.[44]

Thus, *qi* are vessels and objects in general, and *liqi* are ceremonial paraphernalia for specific ritual purposes. Utensils—*yongqi* or *yangqi*—are used in daily life and could be sold in the marketplace, whereas *liqi*—which embody essential ritual codes and political power—cannot be sold or granted to others. This understanding, in turn, leads us to another paradox of *liqi*: on the one hand, as a symbol, a *liqi* must be physically distinguishable from a utensil (also called a *qi*) in material, shape, decoration, and inscription so the concepts that it typifies can be clearly recognized and conceived. On the other hand, it is still a *qi*—a vessel or an implement comparable with a utensil in typology. In other words, a *liqi* is an axe, a pot, or a bowl, but it should not be an "ordinary" axe, pot, or bowl. This seemingly paradoxical feature of *liqi*, in fact, lies at the heart of the artistic genre, and its importance was clearly recognized by the ancient Chinese themselves:

含义和代表抽象的实体。下面所引的几段古代文献反映了"器"的演变的概念范围，对于我们最后确定礼器的定义非常重要：

1. 可执而用曰器也。[39]
2. 簠簋俎豆，制度文章，礼之器也。[40]
3. 大钟鼎，美重器。[41]
4. 唯器与名，不可以假人，君之所司也。名以出信，信以守器，器以藏礼，礼以行义，义以生利，利以平民，政之大节也。[42]
5. 形而上者谓之道，形而下者谓之器。化而裁之谓之变，推而行之谓之通。举而措之，天下之民谓之事业。是故夫象，圣人有以见天下赜，而拟诸其形容，象其物宜，是故谓之象。[43]
6.（圣人）制器者尚其象。[44]

因此，"器"指一般意义上的容器和物品，"礼器"则指有特定礼仪功用的器具。"用器"或"养器"用于日常生活，可以在市场上出售，而体现着重要礼仪意义和政治权力的礼器是不能出售或赠予他人的。这种理解使我们注意到有关"礼器"的一个悖论：一方面，作为一种象征物，礼器必须在材质、形状、装饰和铭文等物质形态上和实用器区别开来，人们因此可以清楚地识别和认识它所代表的概念。另一方面，礼器仍是"器"，在类型上与日常用器一致。换言之，礼器是一把斧头、一个壶、一只碗，但它不是"普通的"斧头、壶或碗。这个看似矛盾的特征实际上是礼器艺术的核心，其重要性也早已被中国古人清楚地认识到：

> The offerings to ancestral kings serve as food but do not minister to the pleasures of the palate. The ceremonial cap and the grand carriage serve for display but do not awaken a fondness for their use. The ceremonial Wu dance is characterized by its gravity but does not awaken the emotion of delight. The ancestral temple is majestic but does not dispose one to rest in it. The ritual vessels may be of use but are never made for people's convenience. The idea is that those used to communicate with spirits should not be identical with those for rest and pleasure.[45]

Significantly, the author of this passage speaks about the appearance and perception of *liqi*: the *forms* of the ceremonial cap, the chariot, the dance, the ancestral temple, and the temple vessels should not be "identical" with their counterparts as utensils, and the *feeling* and
024 *thoughts* they arouse should be distinguished from those aroused by ordinary utensils. There are interesting parallels between such ancient Chinese writings and modern discussions of monuments. According to these discussions, a monument, though taking the basic shape of a hall, gate, or tower, distinguishes itself from an "ordinary" hall, gate, or tower in material, form, and implication. In other words, broadly speaking, these modern monuments are also *liqi*—physical embodiments (*qi*) of principles or monumentality (*li*). I have cited ancient Chinese descriptions of *li*, which "clarifies the dubious and distinguishes [things] to the minute, and thus it can serve as dykes for the people." Similar admonitions abound in official rhetoric on modern monuments, which, without exception, identify a marble memorial hall or a stone obelisk as an embodiment of fundamental social codes and moral value: "Thus monuments are lasting incentives, to those who view them, to imitate the virtues they commemorate, and attain, by their life and spirit, glory and honor."[46] In Georges Bataille's critical view, "[Monumental] architecture, formerly the image of social order, now guarantees and even imposes this order. From being a simple symbol it has now become master."[47] The

same words can be said of the ancient Chinese tradition of *liqi*.

Not every modern monument commemorates a definite figure or event. In fact, the numerous statues of anonymous figures in the United States, starting from the statue of the Minute Man erected on Lexington Green in 1900, has led Jackson to propose an interesting theory: "This

> 先王之荐，可食也，而不可似耆也。卷冕路车，可陈也，而不可好也。武壮，而不可乐也。宗庙之威，而不可安也。宗庙之器，可用也，而不可便其利也。所以交于神明者，不可以同于所安乐之义也。[45]

耐人寻味的是，这段文字所说的是礼器的外形以及人对礼器的感知。作者所强调的是卷冕、路车、武舞、宗庙及彝器应该在形式上和日常的器物和建筑区别开来，它们带给人的感觉和想法也要与一般器物带来的感觉和想法区分开来。有意思的是，中国古人所写的文字与现代学者对纪念碑的讨论有许多相似之处。根据这些论者的观点，一座纪念碑尽管也具备殿堂、拱门、塔刹等基本形状，但它们本身的材质、形式和内涵却不同于"普通的"殿堂、拱门、塔刹。换言之，在更广泛的意义上讲，这些现代的纪念碑也可称作"礼器"——即对原则和纪念碑性（礼）的具体体现（器）。我已经引证了中国古代对于礼的表述，即"所以章疑别微，以为民坊者也"。类似的箴言充满晚近时代官方对现代纪念碑的阐释，往往将一座大理石修建的纪念堂或方尖碑说成是对基本社会准则和道德价值的体现。因此"对于那些瞻仰的人，纪念碑有一种持久的激励作用。人们通过仿效所纪念的德行，在生活和精神方面获得荣耀。"[46] 乔治·巴塔耶指出："（纪念性）建筑最初是社会秩序的反映，现在则成为这种秩序的保证，甚至强迫人们接受这种秩序。原来不过是一种简单的象征物，现在却变成了主宰。"[47] 同样的话也适用于中国的礼器传统。

并不是每一座现代纪念碑都是为纪念特定的人物或事件而建造的。实际上，从 1900 年竖立于列克星敦绿地的民兵雕像开始，在美国出现了许许多多的"无名纪念像"。对此，杰克逊提出了一种颇有

kind of monument is celebrating a different past, not the past which history books describe, but a vernacular past, a golden age where there are no dates or names, simply a sense of the way it *used to be*, history as the chronicle of everyday existence."[48] We can approach many *liqi* from ancient China in a similar light: without inscriptions identifying their specific causes and purposes, these objects commemorated a nameless past through rituals rather than through records. They realized their monumentality in constantly refreshing the memories of bygone ages ("in the past, our former kings had no palaces and houses") and in transferring these memories into the ritual behavior of the living generation ("in all these things we must follow their examples"). On this level, all *liqi*, from a tiny ritual jade to a grand bronze sacrificial vessel, can be identified as commemorative objects in a specific ritual context. Some *liqi* did refer to a specific figure and event, however. In addition to their basic function as ritual paraphernalia, they were reminders of such figures and events, and contributed to the formation of a written history. The Nine Tripods were the epitome of this type of *liqi* and could thus be singled out as the most important monument in archaic China.

In the discussion that follows, I shift to a more concrete level to examine the physical features of *liqi*: most important, their specific materials, shapes, decorations, and inscriptions as signifiers of *li* or monumentality. These features were gradually invented, enriched, and formulated over the course of a long process. Having attempted to define the concept of *liqi* based on textual sources, I therefore hope to reconstruct the history of *liqi*—as Arnold Isenberg has said, "those which have no simple names, are revealed, if at all, in acquaintance."[49]

❷ The Legacy of Ritual Art

"COSTLY ART"

In Chinese art history, the notion of distinguishing *liqi* from *yongqi* (or ritual paraphernalia from utilitarian objects) emerged during the fourth millennium B.C. in the East Coast cultural tradition.[50] The first clear sign of this movement was the appearance of "costly" imitations of "cheap" tools, daily wares, and ornaments. I use the word *costly* to describe an object that is made of precious material and/or requires specialized craftsmanship and an unusual amount of human labor. Two early types of

意味的理论："这种纪念碑所纪念的是一种不同的'过去'——不是书本上所描写的那种历史，而是一种日常的'过去'，是一个没有日期和名字的黄金时代，是曾经有过的一种感觉，是历史作为一种日常存在的纪事。"[48] 我们可以用类似的眼光来看待许多中国古代礼器：这类器物并无铭文来说明特定的制作原因和目的，它们通过礼仪而非文字来纪念一种无可名状的过去。它们通过不断地追溯对以往的记忆（"昔者先王，未有宫室"），将这种记忆迁移到活着的一代人的礼仪行为当中（"皆从其朔"），以实现其纪念碑性的功用。在这个层面上，从一件小型玉器到一件大型的青铜祭器，所有的礼器都可以被看作是在特定的礼仪语境中的纪念物。然而，有的礼器的确指涉具体的人和事。除了发挥礼器的基本功用外，它们令人们想起那具体的人和事，为见诸文字的历史记载提供了材料。九鼎是这类礼器的极致，因此也可以被看作中国古代最重要的纪念碑。

在下面的讨论中，我将转移到一个更具体的层面上去考察礼器的物质特征，最首要的是表现礼或纪念碑性的器物材质、形状、装饰和铭文。这些特征是在一个漫长的过程中逐步创造、丰富和制定的。我已经在文献资料的基础上探讨了礼器的概念，接下来想重构礼器的历史，正如阿诺德·伊森伯格所言："对于那些没有简单名称的东西，只能通过对它的了解显示出来。"[49]

二、礼仪美术的遗产

1. "昂贵美术"

在中国美术史上，礼器与用器相区别的观念产生于公元前 4000—前 3000 年东部沿海的文化传统中。[50] 这个趋向的最初标志是出现了对"低廉的"工具、日用器皿和装饰品的"昂贵的"仿造。这里，"昂贵"一词形容以贵重材料和（或）特殊工艺制作的器物。

such work are jade axes and rings from the Dawenkou culture in present-day Shandong.[51] Like a stone axe, a jade axe is roughly rectangular in shape, with a sharpened edge and a perforation at one end (Figs. 1.1a, b). Similarly, jade rings (Fig. 1.2) appear to be faithful copies of pottery ornaments. At first sight, the lack of originality in these carvings seems almost astonishing: no decoration, no surface engraving, no innovation in shape. What is unusual is the medium: jade.

025 Ancient Chinese used the term *yu*, or "jade," for a hard stone noted for its fine texture and rich color.[52] Jade is difficult to work because of its extraordinary hardness. It is so tough that steel makes no impression on it, and it can be cut and polished only by using semiliquid abrasives mixed with a powdered material harder than jade itself. Ethnologists report that the Maori of New Zealand, who until recently lived at a neolithic level of material culture, cut jade with a piece of sandstone or slate, while constantly applying an abrasive made from powdered quartz and water to the edge of the "saw." It took a month of ceaseless work for a Maori craftsman to cut a piece of raw jade measuring less than 1.5

这类作品的两个早期类型是今山东地区大汶口文化的玉铲和串饰。[51] 玉铲的形状和石铲基本一样，大致呈长方形，一端有刃，另一端穿孔［图 1.1］。同样，玉串饰［图 1.2］也忠实地模仿了陶串饰的形式。乍看上去，这些物品缺乏创意，几乎令人吃惊：它们没有装饰和表面雕刻，外形也毫无新奇之处。唯一与众不同的是其质地——玉。

在中国古代，"玉"指的是肌理细腻、色泽丰富、质地坚硬的石头。[52] 玉因为异常坚硬而难以加工，即使用铁器擦划，其表面也难以留下痕迹。只有利用混合着比玉还坚硬的矿物粉末的半流体磨料，才能对玉进行切割和磨光。据民族学者报告，在近代仍处在新石器时代发展阶段的新西兰毛利人，以砂岩或板岩为"锯"，往"锯"刃上不断加入石英末和水进行研磨来切割玉料。将一块八开纸大小、不到 3.8 厘米厚的玉料大体加工成长方形，一个毛利匠师须不停地

Fig. 1.1. (a) Stone axe. Dawenkou culture. 5th-4th millennia B.C. L. 16.8 cm. Excavated in 1959 from Tomb no. 59 at Dawenkou, Shandong. Shandong Provincial Museum. (b) Jade axe. Dawenkou culture. 4th-3rd millennia B.C. L. 17.8 cm. Excavated in 1957 from Tomb no. 117 at Dawenkou. Shandong Provincial Museum.

图 1.1 （a）石斧。大汶口文化，前 5000—前 4000 年。长 16.8 厘米。1959 年山东泰安大汶口 59 号墓出土。山东博物馆藏。（b）玉铲。大汶口文化，前 4000—前 3000 年。长 17.8 厘米。1957 年山东泰安大汶口 117 号墓出土。山东博物馆藏。

inches thick and the size of an octavo book into a roughly triangular slab.[53] Though simple in shape, a Dawenkou jade axe or ring required a more complex manufacturing process that must have consisted of at least five steps: (1) splitting the jade boulder and wearing away the rough surface, (2) cutting the raw material roughly into the desired shape, (3) elaborating the shape and sharpening the edge, (4) boring the hole, and (5) polishing the surface to make it smooth and shiny. Judging from the Maori example, one can imagine that the whole process must have been extremely slow and tedious. On the other hand, working jade does not require advanced technology. In fact, to carve a piece of jade, a metal knife is no more useful than a block of stone, a piece of bamboo, or a linen string. Generally speaking, in jade carving the tool is less important than human hands and patience.

What the Dawenkou jade axes and rings pose, therefore, is a puzzling question. A stone axe or a pottery ring could be produced with far less time and energy than the months or even years it took to carve and polish a piece of hard jade. What led the Dawenkou people to create jade axes and rings that resembled stone and pottery objects but involved over a thousand times the cost in human labor?

The secret of these jade artifacts is that they imitated stone and pottery objects but were not intended to be the same. Although similar in shape, the differences between a jade axe and its humble stone prototype are obvious (Figs. 1.1a, b). Rich in color, the surface of a polished jade glistens with changing reflections. There is a physical delight in it, for it is simultaneously smooth, moist, and unyielding. A jade's formal or typological resemblance to a stone or pottery work, therefore, became symbolic and rhetorical: it looked like an ordinary thing, but it was not. To people familiar with the difficulty of carving a jade work, it meant a prodigious amount of human energy frozen in a small object. Consequently, the jades signified the ability of their owner to control and "squander" such a huge amount of human energy. The same rhetoric underlies a modern advertisement for a wine goblet: "At Waterford we take 1,120 times longer than necessary to create a glass." The goblet is expensive and thus precious not because of its shape or function (which are no different from those of "cheap" glass goblets) but because of its crystal material and the excessive labor involved in its manufacture. The advertisement is aimed not at people who want to buy a glass for drinking

工作一个月。[53] 大汶口文化的玉铲或串饰的形制看似简单，但其制作实际上更为复杂，包括至少五个生产工序：（1）从玉石原料上切割下玉材并去掉粗糙的表面，（2）将玉材大体切割成所设计的形状，（3）精心修整外形并磨出刃部，（4）钻孔，（5）抛光。从毛利人的例子我们可以想象，这一过程是极为缓慢和乏味的。但是从另一方面看，制作玉器并不需要先进的技术。实际上，要切割一片玉料，一把金属刀并不比一块砂岩、一段竹筒或一根麻绳更为有用。总的说来，在加工玉器时，人的双手和耐心比工具更重要。

大汶口文化的玉铲和玉串饰因此提出了一个令人迷惑的问题：切割和磨光一块坚硬的玉材要用数月甚至数年的劳作，制作一柄石铲或一个陶环所用的时间和精力则少得多。是什么原因使得大汶口人花费上千百倍的劳动，来制造这些在器物类型上与石器和陶器没有差异的玉铲或玉饰？

这些玉器的秘密在于：它们模仿了石器或陶器，意图却不相同。虽然玉铲和粗陋的石铲外形相同，但二者的差异也显而易见［图 1.1］。玉器色泽丰富，磨亮的表面熠熠生辉，它平滑、润泽、坚硬，令人赏心悦目。因此，一件玉器在外形上与一件石器或陶器的相似就有了象征和修辞的意义。它看似普通，但实际上却不寻常。对于那些了解攻玉之难的人来说，这些小器物实际上凝聚了巨量的人工。因此，这些玉器意味着其所有者拥有控制和"浪费"这些人工的能力。一则兜售酒杯的现代广告利用了同样的修辞："在沃特福德，我们花费 1200 倍于所需的时间来制作一只酒杯。"这只酒杯之所以贵重，并不是由于其独特的外形和功能（看上去与"廉价"酒杯毫无二致），而是因为它以水晶玻璃制作，并花费了令人惊异的大量人力。这则广告并不是给那些想买一只杯子喝酒的人看的，

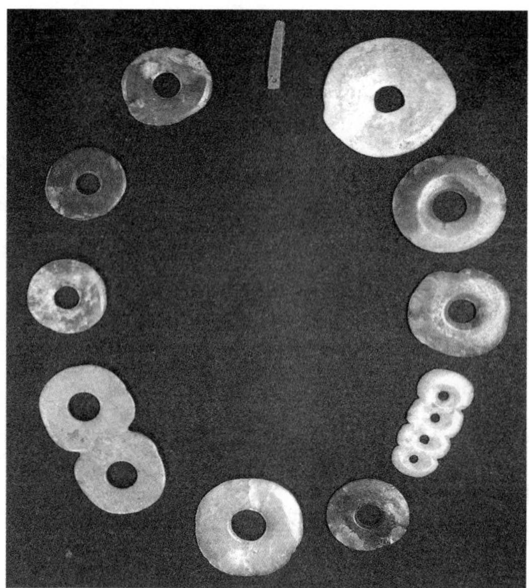

Fig. 1.2. Jade rings and other ornaments. Dawenkou culture. 4th-3rd millennia B.C. L. 3-6.8 cm. Excavated in 1971 at Zouxian, Shandong. Shandong Provincial Museum.

图 1.2 玉饰品。大汶口文化，前 4000—前 3000 年。长 3—6.8 厘米。1971 年山东邹县野店出土。山东博物馆藏。

Fig. 1.3. (a) Dawenkou Tomb no. 128.4th-3rd millennia B.C. (b) Dawenkou Tomb no. 10.4th-3rd millennia B.C.

图 1.3 （a）大汶口 128 号墓。前 4000—前 3000 年。（b）大汶口 10 号墓。前 4000—前 3000 年。

but at potential customers eager to prove and parade their wealth to their honored guests. In both the ancient and modern cases, the objects, with their "conventional" shape and huge investment of labor, become concrete symbols of power.

It is no accident that the appearance of the Dawenkou jade carvings 026
coincided with a profound social transformation. It was during this period that the differentiation of the wealthy and the poor, as well as concepts of privilege and power, emerged. This social stratification and polarization are most clearly reflected in Dawenkou burials: the majority of tombs were unfurnished or poorly furnished (Fig. 1.3a), but a few graves contained hundreds of fine objects (Fig. 1.3b). Without exception, jade carvings were found only in the largest tombs that were also richly furnished with other objects of value.[54] What these objects demonstrate is a historical stage of seeking a political symbol, which in this case found expression in the medium of jade.[55]

In *What Is Art For?*, Ellen Dissanayake argues that one of the major ingredients of artistic creativity is the desire to "make things special":

而是给那些热衷于向尊贵的客人证明和炫耀其财富的潜在顾客。在这两个古代和现代的例子中，器物以其“常规”的形状和巨大的人力投入，成为了权力的具体象征。

玉器产生于大汶口文化时代并非偶然，它的产生和当时发生的深刻社会变革同时发生。正是在这一时期出现了贫富分化，以及特权和权力的观念。社会分层和两极化的现象最清楚地反映在大汶口墓葬中：大汶口墓地中的大部分墓葬没有或仅有少量的随葬品［图 1.3a］，但少数死者则随葬有数以百计精美的器物［图 1.3b］。[54] 玉器无一例外地发现在规模最大、包含大量其他精美随葬品的墓葬中。这些随葬品所见证的是一个寻求政治象征物的历史阶段，而玉成为表达这种欲望的媒介。[55]

在《艺术是为什么的？》这本书中，埃伦·迪萨纳亚克提出，艺术创作的一个主要因素是“使物品与众不同”的欲望：

> From an ethnological perspective, art, like making things special, will embrace a domain extending from the greatest to the most prosaic results. Still, mere making or creating is neither making special nor art. A chipped stone tool is simply that, unless it is somehow made special in some way, worked longer than necessary, or worked so that an
> 027 embedded fossil is displayed to advantage. A purely functional bowl may be beautiful, to our eyes, but not having been made special it is not the product of a behavior of art. As soon as the bowl is fluted, or painted, or otherwise handled using considerations apart from its utility, its maker is displaying artistic behavior.[56]

Here Dissanayake is speaking about a general characteristic of art. The Dawenkou jade carvings, however, emerged from a specific stage in Chinese art history. In particular, they signify the beginning of the tradition of *liqi* or ritual paraphernalia, which, as I argue in the preceding section, both resemble and distinguish themselves from ordinary implements. It is the visual properties of jade—its unusual color and texture—that define the specific status of a *liqi*. In this way, "forms" could "conceal ritual codes" and become political symbols.

The divorce of *liqi* from *yongqi*, or "art" from "crafts," also occurred in pottery production. The problem faced by the Dawenkou potter was the same as that faced by the jadesmith: how to transform a utilitarian object into a symbol? Vessels of special colors (mostly white or black) were made, but the key was found in altering shape. A small group of pottery wares began to exhibit a delicacy of style. The legs or the stem of a vessel were gradually elongated, and openwork patterns were added. A complex silhouette became the point of departure in design. Deliberately rejected were the functional aspects of the vessel as a food or water container and the sense of volume.[57] An early example of this type of pottery is a cup dated to the fourth millennium B.C. (Fig. 1.4). The cup is slender and angular, with an extremely elongated foot, but the bowl of the cup is comparatively insignificant—it is disproportionally small and shallow.

One wonders how someone could drink from its much attenuated and flaring mouth without the liquid pouring out, or whether the vessel would stand firmly when it was full.

> 从民族学角度来看，如同使物品与众不同一样，艺术可以含括相当广阔的幅度，产生从最伟大到最平庸的结果。但仅仅是制作或创作本身既没有使物品与众不同也没有创造艺术。一把豁口的石头工具只不过是个石头工具，除非是利用某些手段使它变得特殊，或是投入比正常需要更多的加工时间，或是把嵌入的化石更好地衬托出来。一只纯粹功能性的碗或许在我们的眼中并不难看，但由于没有被特殊化，因此并不是艺术品。一旦在上面刻槽、彩绘或进行其他非实用目的的处理，其制造者就正在展示一种艺术行为。[56]

这里，迪萨纳亚克所谈的是艺术的一般特征。但是，大汶口文化的玉器产生于中国美术史上的一个特殊阶段。更具体地说，它们标志着礼器传统的开端。如我在上节中所述，这种特殊器物既与普通的器物相似，又有所不同。玉的视觉因素——它的不同寻常的色彩和质感——被用来表现礼器的特殊身份。“形式”因此得以“藏礼”而成为政治性的象征符号。

礼器和用器的分离，或者说“艺术”与“工艺”的分离，也表现在陶器制作上。大汶口文化的陶工和玉工面临着同样的问题：如何将一件实用器转变成一种符号？为这个目的，他们制作了特殊色彩的陶器（主要是白陶和黑陶），但关键是对器物形制的改造。一小组陶器开始显露出一种精细纤弱的风格：容器的足或颈逐渐拉长，还出现了镂孔的装饰方法。这些器物的设计起点是追求复杂的外轮廓，而有意摒弃了作为容器及体积感的功能。[57] 这类陶器的一个早期例子是一件约公元前 3000 年的陶觚［图 1.4］。它高挑秀颀，有尖角，足部尤长，但杯部小而浅，不成比例，显得无足轻重。我们就纳闷，如何能从它那平敞的喇叭口喝酒而不洒出来，或者里面盛满酒时是否能站稳。

The impression of delicacy and fragility was also emphasized by reducing a vessel's thickness. A white pottery *gui* (Fig. 1.5), whose shape is the most complicated among all discovered Dawenkou wares, has three sharply pointed legs, an arched handle, and a superfluous complex built above the mouth. With such a complex shape and an extreme thinness, the vessel resembles a paper construction rather than a clay product. I have been informed that it would be impossible to raise the *gui* by holding its handle: the paper-thin handle would break if the vessel were even half full of water. The particular aesthetics exemplified by this *gui* culminated in the pottery industry of the succeeding Longshan culture in the Shandong peninsula. A group of extremely thin black vessels "represented the highest achievement of pottery-making at the time."[58] A number of special features of these vessels have led the Chinese archaeologist Wu Ruzuo to identify them as *liqi*: (1) they have been found only in tombs, not in residential sites; (2) they have only appeared in the richest tombs, not in small- or even medium-sized burials; (3) in such tombs they have been found beside the arms of the dead, separated from "ordinary pottery vessels" but grouped together with other "ceremonial insignia" such as jade axes; and (4) they cannot have been used in daily life due to their peculiar shapes and extreme thinness.[59] We are thus again reminded of the passage in the ritual books: "The ritual vessels may be of use but are never made for people's convenience. The idea is that those which serve to communicate with spirits should not be identical with those for rest and pleasure."[60]

对器壁厚度的减薄进一步突出了精致和纤弱的印象。图 1.5 中的白陶鬶有着尖细的三足，弧形的把手，以及口部上的一个“帽”状装饰，是大汶口文化陶器中形状最复杂的一件。由于外形复杂，器壁薄巧，这件器物看上去像是用纸做的而不是陶制的。有人告诉过我，这件陶鬶是不能抓着把手拿起的，因为即使盛上一半的水，当提起来的时候，像纸一样薄的把手也会断掉。这只鬶所代表的

Fig. 1.4. Pottery *gu* cup. Dawenkou culture. 4th millennium B.C. H. 28 cm. Excavated in 1978 at Yanzhou, Shandong province. Yanzhou Museum.

图 1.4　陶觚形杯。大汶口文化，前 4000—前 3000 年。高 28 厘米。1978 年山东兖州西吴寺出土。兖州博物馆藏。

特殊审美观在随后山东龙山文化的陶器制造业中达到了顶点。一组器壁极薄的黑陶器“代表了当时陶器制造的最高水平”。[58] 中国考古学家吴汝祚根据这些器物的多种特征将它们认定为礼器，这些特征包括：（1）它们只出土于墓葬，而不见于居址中；（2）它们只见于随葬品丰富的墓葬，而不见于小型甚至中型的墓葬；（3）在墓葬中，这些器物放置在死者的胳膊旁，与日用器皿分开，但与玉斧等其他礼仪象征物放在一起；（4）从其特别的形状和极薄的器壁来看，这些器物不可能用于日常生活。[59] 因此，这些器物再次使我们想起了礼书中的话：“宗庙之器，可用也，而不可便其利也。所以交于神明者，不可以同于所安乐之义也。”[60]

"DECORATION" AND "EMBLEM"

028 The *gui* mentioned above was made close to the end of the Dawenkou period in the early third millennium B.C. Around the same time, jade art was flourishing in the Liangzhu culture, another regional variant of the East Coast cultural tradition centered on the lower Yangzi River valley. Liangzhu jades were known even before modern archaeology began in China: the *Illustrated Examination of Ancient Jades* (*Guyu tukao*) by the Qing antiquarian Wu Dacheng (1835-1902) contains at least six examples identifiable as Liangzhu products (Fig. 1.6).[61] The earliest excavation of a Liangzhu site took place in 1936, and the report came out two years later.[62] But until the publication of the first group of radiocarbon dates for Liangzhu remains in 1977, carved jades from this prehistorical coastal culture had generally been considered Zhou or even Han works.[63] An archaeological boom followed the new dating and attribution of Liangzhu jades: in the next decade, an amazing number of rich Liangzhu burials were found in the three adjacent provinces of Zhejiang, Jiangsu, and Anhui.[64] The special term *jade-furnished burial* (*yulianzang*) was invented for tombs with an extraordinary number of jades. One such burial is Tomb no. M3 at Sidun in Jiangsu. Excavated in 1982, this small rectangular grave contained more than a hundred jade carvings, including 33 short or long tubular *cong* encircling the corpse of a young male (Fig. 1.7).[65] Entire Liangzhu cemeteries were subsequently discovered in 1986 and 1987: the eleven tombs in the Fanshan cemetery in Zhejiang yielded some 1,200 jades or groups of jades, and more than 700 jades or groups of jades came from the twelve tombs in a nearby cemetery at Yaoshan (Figs. 1.8a, b).[66] More discoveries followed the Yaoshan excavation: 21 jade-furnished tombs at Fuquanshan near Shanghai included human sacrifices; large Liangzhu tombs are distributed not only in the Yangzi Delta and around the Hangzhou Bay but also along the Jiangsu-Shandong border in the north; a survey in Changming village near Yuhang in Zhejiang has located Liangzhu cemeteries that are "even larger than those

at Fanshan and Yaoshan."[67] Finally a large architectural site, 450 meters north-south and 670 meters east-west, was found in 1992 at Mojiaoshan 030
near Hangzhou. Surrounded by Fanshan, Yaoshan, and other Liangzhu cemeteries and sacrificial sites, it may have been the center of a large religious network.[68]

2. “装饰”与“徽志”

上文谈到的陶鬶属于大汶口文化晚期，年代约为公元前 3000 年左右。大致在同一时期，玉器艺术在良渚文化流行开来。这一文化分布在以长江下游为中心的东部沿海地区。良渚文化玉器在中国现代考古学产生之前已为人所知，清代金石学家吴大澂（1835—1902 年）的《古玉图考》一书著录了至少 6 件可断定属于良渚文化的玉器［图 1.6］。[61] 良渚遗址的首次发掘在 1936 年，两年后报告发表。[62] 但在 1977 年第一组良渚文化碳十四测年数据发表之前，一般都认为这些沿海地区史前文化中的玉器是周代至汉代的遗物。[63] 碳十四年代数据的确定和对良渚文化玉器新的断代，引发了考古热：在过去的十年内，大批良渚文化的墓葬在苏浙皖交接地区发现。[64] 研究者称随葬有大量玉器的墓葬为“玉敛葬”。一个典型的例子是 1982 年发掘的江苏寺墩 3 号墓。这座小型的长方形墓葬竟随葬了上百件玉器，包括年轻男性死者周围的 33 件长短不一的玉琮［图 1.7］。[65] 随后在 1986 和 1987 年又发现了完整的良渚文化墓地，浙江反山墓地的 11 座墓葬中随葬了大约 1200 件（组）玉器，距其不远的瑶山墓地的 12 座墓中出土了 700 件（组）玉器［图 1.8］。[66] 瑶山墓地发掘之后又有一系列发现：上海附近福泉山发现的 21 座玉敛葬中有人殉现象；良渚文化大墓不仅发现于长江三角洲和杭州湾地区，而且也见于北部的山东江苏交界处；浙江余杭长名村所发现的良渚文化墓地“甚至比瑶山和反山墓地更大。”[67]1992 年在杭州附近的莫角山还发现了一处南北 450 米、东西 670 米的建筑遗址，为反山、瑶山以及其他良渚文化墓地和祭祀遗址所环绕，可能是一个巨大的宗教祭祀网络的中心。[68]

Fig. 1.5. Pottery *gui* tripod. Dawenkou culture. 4th millennium B.C. H. 37.2 cm. Excavated in 1977 at Linyi, Shandong province. Linyi Museum.

图 1.5 陶鬶。大汶口文化，前 4000—前 3000 年。高 37.2 厘米。1977 年山东临沂大范庄出土。临沂市博物馆藏。

攷工記玉人云大琮十有二寸射四
寸厚寸是謂內鎮宗后守之鄭
注云如王之鎮圭也右琮二器大澂
得自都門為三十二琮之冠其一
樸素無文與鎮圭第一器尺寸同
其一有駔刻者與鎮圭第二器尺寸
同皆十有二寸之大琮蓋時代有先後
制器之尺稍有出入耳按瑋與琮皆

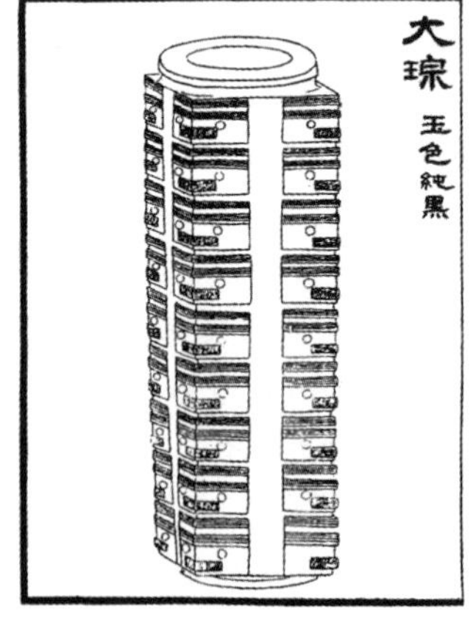

Fig. 1.6. Liangzhu *cong*, as recorded by Wu Dacheng

图 1.6 吴大澂著录的良渚文化玉琮

Fig. 1.7. Sidun Tomb no. 3. Liangzhu culture. 3rd millenium B.C. Excavated in 1979 at Sidun, Wujin, Jiangsu province.

图 1.7 寺墩 3 号墓。良渚文化，前 3000—前 2000 年。1979 年江苏武进寺墩出土。

a

Fig. 1.8. (a) Yaoshan cemetery. Liangzhu culture. 3rd millennium B.C. Excavated in 1987 at Yaoshan, Yuhang, Zhejiang province. (b) Plan of the cemetery.

图 1.8 （a）瑶山墓地。良渚文化，前 3000—前 2000 年。1987 年浙江余杭瑶山出土。（b）墓地平面图。

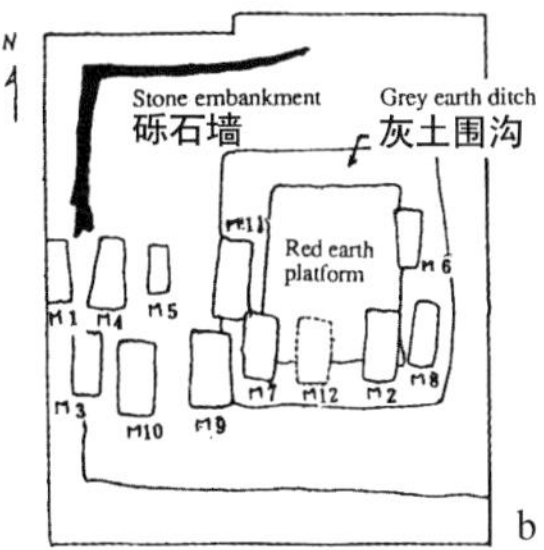

b

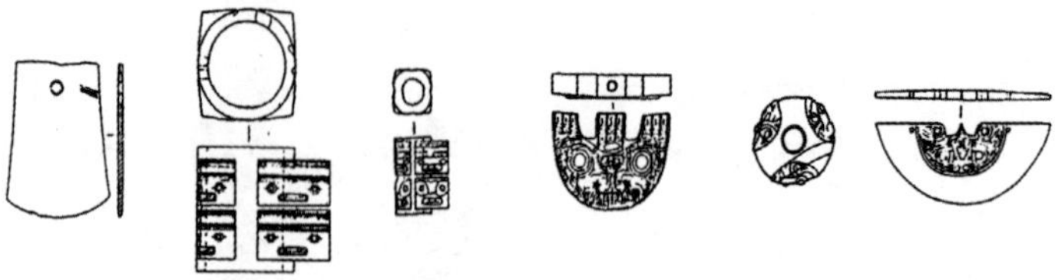

	jade axe 玉钺	large *cong* 大型琮	small *cong* 小型琮	three-pointed crown ornament 三齿冠状器	round plaque 璧	*huang* pendant 璜
Tomb no. 8 8号墓	1 1	yes 有		1 1		
Tomb no. 2 2号墓	1 1	yes 有	yes 有	1 1	1 1	
Tomb no. 12 12号墓	1 1	7 7	yes 有	1 1		
Tomb no. 7 7号墓	1 1	yes 有	yes 有	1 1		
Tomb no. 9 9号墓	1 1	yes 有	yes 有	1 1		
Tomb no. 10 10号墓	1 1	yes 有		1 1		
Tomb no. 3 3号墓	1 1	yes 有		1 1		
(northern row)（北列）						
Tomb no. 6 6号墓					yes 有	1 1
Tomb no. 11 11号墓					13 13	4 4
Tomb no. 5 5号墓					yes 有	
Tomb no. 4 4号墓					8 8	2 2
Tomb no. 1 1号墓					6 6	2 2

Fig. 1.9. Classification of Yaoshan jades

图 1.9 瑶山玉器的分类

Serious research on Liangzhu culture must be postponed until the publication and analyses of this rich archaeological data. Indeed, although the available "preliminary" excavation reports reveal important and sometimes unexpected features of this prehistorical culture, they often pose more questions than we are able to answer. For example, it was extremely exciting to learn that the graves in two separate tiers in the Yaoshan cemetery belonged to males and females, respectively.[69] But who were these deceased? Were they priests and priestesses, shamans and shamanesses, or chieftains and their wives—as some writers have suggested?[70] The excavators of this site noted that jades buried with males and females also differ: axes, *cong*, and three-pronged objects only accompanied men, whereas women possessed arched *huang* pendants, round plaques, and "spinning wheels" (Fig. 1.9).[71] What, however, were the exact symbolism and uses of these jade objects? Were they purely religious and social symbols or paraphernalia for certain rituals? The differences between the Yaoshan and Fanshan cemeteries are puzzling. Merely five kilometers apart, they seem to reflect quite different burial customs: the furnishings of the Fanshan tombs included 125 large *bi* disks (41 from Tomb no. M20 alone), but none of the Yaoshan graves contained this type of object. What do such differences imply?

对良渚文化更深入的研究还有待于这些丰富的考古资料的发表和分析。的确，尽管发掘简报已揭示出该史前文化一些重要和出人意料的特征，但是仍有许多问题我们无法回答。例如，瑶山墓地中的墓葬分属两排，分别埋葬男性和女性，这一发现实在令人惊异。[69] 但是这些死者是什么人？他们是不是真像有的研究者所说的那样，是男女祭司、男女巫师，或是首领与其妻属？[70] 该遗址的发掘者指出，男女死者所随葬的玉器种类不同。钺、琮和三齿冠状器只见于男性的墓葬中，女性的墓葬中则是璜、璧和"纺轮"[图 1.9]。[71] 然而，这些玉器具体的象征意义和用途是什么？它们是纯粹的宗教或社会象征物，还是某种礼仪的用具？瑶山和反山墓地之间的差异也令人迷惑，二者仅仅相距 5 公里，却反映出十分不同的习俗：反山墓地的随葬品包括 125 件大型的璧（其中 41 件出自 20 号墓），而瑶山墓地却不见这种器物。这种差异意味着什么？

A recognition of our inability to answer these questions, however, should caution us against making premature generalizations but should not prevent all discussion. Certain aspects of Liangzhu culture are better known, and at certain levels interpretation can be pursued with greater confidence. Hundreds of published Liangzhu jade carvings, including both previously known and recently excavated examples, constitute a large enough corpus of research material. Although these tell us little about the patrons, makers, and precise use of individual types, and although reconstruction of a developmental pattern and symbolic system
031 of Liangzhu jades is still beyond our reach,[72] known Liangzhu jade works do allow us to observe their basic formal and semiotic features. These features, in turn, indicate the position of this art in the general development of ancient Chinese *liqi*.

Unlike earlier Dawenkou jades, Liangzhu jades are not direct copies of stone and pottery objects. The *bi* disk may have developed from ornamental rings, but the Liangzhu *bi* are so large and heavy that they could not function as personal ornaments. Similarly, the axes are so thin that it would have been impossible to use them in any practical way. These two types of Liangzhu jades, therefore, may be considered a second generation of imitated forms; their form still attests to their connection with earlier implements and ornaments, but dysfunctional aspects have been accentuated by formal characteristics. A more important development in Liangzhu jade art (in fact, the most important Liangzhu contribution to ancient Chinese ritual art), however, is the invention and proliferation of surface engravings: all Dawenkou jade works are plain, but the Liangzhu jades are richly decorated with zoomorphic patterns and other signs.

In a paper on the semiotics of visual art, Meyer Schapiro argues that the appearance of manufactured objects and architectural forms was preceded by a period during which people had no idea of a well-defined picture surface and no sense of regularity in design. Paleolithic cave paintings appear on an unprepared and unlimited ground, and the primitive artist worked on a field with no set boundaries and thought very little of the "surface" as a distinct pictorial plane.

> The smooth prepared field of the surface is an invention of a later stage of humanity. It accompanies the development of polished tools in the Neolithic and Bronze Ages and the creation of pottery and an

我们没有充分的条件来回答这些问题，因此不能妄做不成熟的归纳，但是我们仍可进行一定程度的讨论。良渚文化的某些方面我们已经了解得较多，因此可以较有把握地在一定层面上做一些解释。早年出土和新近发现的玉器已公布了数百件，这是一批数量很大的研究材料。尽管我们对于赞助人、制作者、某些器物的用途知之甚少，尽管复原良渚文化玉器的发展形态和象征体系仍十分困难，[72] 但已知的良渚文化玉器的确可以使我们观察其形式规律和符号特征。这些特征进而显示出这些器物艺术在中国古代礼器总体发展过程中的地位。

与较早的大汶口文化玉器不同，良渚文化玉器并不直接模仿石器和陶器的外形。璧或许是从装饰性的环形物发展而来的，但是良渚文化玉璧既大又重，不可能有装饰人体的功能。同样，钺的器身越来越薄，也不可能有实际用途。因此，这两种类型的玉器可以被看作第二代的模仿形式；它们的外形仍显示出与早期工具和装饰品的联系，但是也突出了非功能性的特性。然而，良渚文化玉器更重要的一个演进（实际上是良渚文化玉器对于中国礼仪美术最重要的贡献）是表面雕刻的发明与发展：所有的大汶口文化玉器都是素面的，但良渚文化玉器则装饰有丰富的动物形图案和其他母题。

在一篇探讨视觉符号学的文章中，迈耶·夏皮罗指出，在很长一段时间内，古代的人们对于图画性装饰和设计的“面”的规范化一无所知，此后人们才意识到人工制品和建筑上表面的存在。旧石器时代的洞穴壁画绘制在未经加工的窟壁上，原始艺术家在漫无边界的墙上作画，很少想到作为绘画平台的“表面”的存在。

> 平滑的经过处理的表面是人类发展较晚阶段的发明。与之相伴的是新石器时代和青铜时代的磨制工具的发展、

> architecture with regular courses of jointed masonry. It might have come about through the use of these artifacts as sign-bearing objects. The inventive imagination recognized their value as grounds, and in time gave to pictures and writing on smoothed and symmetrical supports a corresponding regularity of direction, spacing and grouping,
> 032 in harmony with the form of the object like the associated ornament of the neighboring parts.[73]

Although thought-provoking, Schapiro's statement implies the predominance of a "picture ground" over the images it bears. Applied to decorative art, this theory means that decoration "fills" a visual field defined by shape, a basic assumption shared by many scholars who interpret the function of ornamentation as framing, filling, and linking.[74] It may be argued, however, that the relationship between shape and decoration is dialectical: surface patterns not only embellish a shape but also redefine it. A particular formation of patterns can reorient viewing, blur or reinforce the silhouette of an object, or provide a geometric shape with symbolic or mimetic meaning. As Oleg Grabar has observed: "It is possible for an ornament to be *the* subject of the design. . . . There is a difference between 'filling' a space with a design and transforming an object by covering all or parts of its surfaces with that design. In the first instance, the filling design has no other purpose than to partake of whatever uses its carrier has; in the second one, it can transform the very purpose of its carrier."[75]

This argument about the function of ornamentation provides a basis for analyzing Liangzhu jade carvings. Many Liangzhu jades are flat, thin plaques (Figs. 1.10a-d); holes drilled along the edges or on the backs allowed them to be attached to clothing or stands, or to be used as pendants. The mask motifs embellishing these flat objects may have developed from a local tradition, which can be traced back to the Hemudu period of the fourth millennium B.C. A mask engraved on a Hemudu black pottery basin consists of a pair of round eyes and a curved headdress with a trapezoid ornament in the center and is further flanked by two crudely depicted birds (Figs. 1.11a, b). All these pictorial elements, as well as their symmetrical arrangement, survived in Liangzhu jade decoration. The relationship between mask and the objects that bear

> 制陶术的发明和使用规整石材接缝技术的建筑。表面的概念可能是由于把这些人工制品作为符号载体而出现的。人类富于创造性的想象力认识到它们作为背景的价值，逐渐给予那些图写在平滑和对称的器表上的图画和文字相应的方向、空间和组合上的规律感，以与物品的形式——如周围有关的装饰物——相协调。[73]

尽管夏皮罗的观点发人深思，其中却隐含了“图画背景”比所承载的图像本身更为重要的意味。当这一观点被用来讨论装饰艺术时，就意味着装饰“填充”了一个被形状限定了的视觉范围。许多学者赞同这一基本假设，因此将装饰的功能解释为设计外框、填充和连接。[74] 但是这一观点仍值得商榷，形状和装饰的关系应当是辩证的：表面的图案不仅修饰形状，同时也重新界定形状的意义。一种特殊的图案构成能够决定视线的方向，模糊或强调物体的轮廓，或者赋予物体的抽象形状以象征或模拟意义。正如奥莱格·格拉巴尔所观察到的：“装饰纹样的本身可以是设计的主体……以某种装饰设计‘填充’一个空间的概念，与用这种装饰覆盖物体表面各个部分而使之转化的概念是不相同的。在第一种情况里，作为填充物的装饰设计只是共享承载物体本身的意义；在第二种情况里，装饰可以改变载体最终的功能。”[75]

这个关于装饰艺术功能的观点为分析良渚文化玉器提供了一个基础。许多良渚文化玉器为平整光滑的片状［图 1.10］；其边缘或背面钻孔，估计原来可能是附于衣物或支架上，或是垂挂的饰物。器表的兽面纹可能源于东南地区的传统，因为这种装饰母题可以上溯到公元前 4000—前 3000 年间的河姆渡文化：一件河姆渡文化黑陶盆上刻画有两个圆形的眼，其上有一拱形头饰，头饰中央有一梯形，两侧各有一刻画粗疏的鸟［图 1.11］。所有这些元素及其整体的对称形式都被良渚文化玉器继承了下来，但是兽面纹和承载它的

a

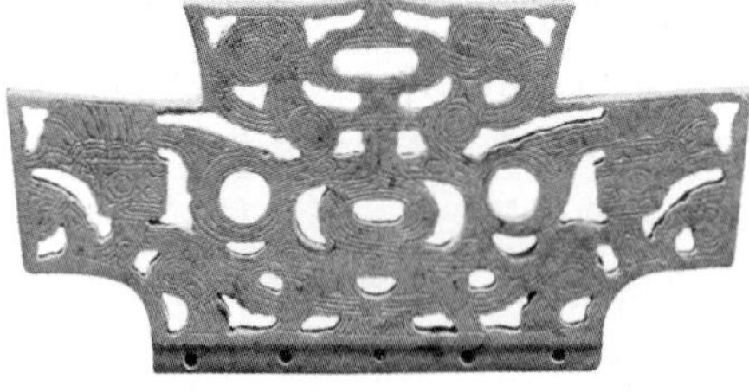

b

c

d

Fig. 1.10. Jade ornaments. Liangzhu culture. 3rd millennium B.C. (a) H. 5.6 cm. Excavated in 1986 from Fanshan Tomb no. 22 at Yuhang, Zhejiang province. Zhejiang Provincial Institute of Archaeology. (b) H. 5.2 cm. Excavated in 1986 from Fanshan Tomb no. 16. Zhejiang Provincial Institute of Archaeology. (c) H. 6.2 cm. Excavated in 1987 from Yaoshan Tomb no. 10. Zhejiang Provincial Institute of Archaeology. (d) H. 5.4 cm. Minneapolis Institute of Art.

图 1.10 玉饰品。良渚文化，前 3000—前 2000 年。（a）高 5.6 厘米。1986 年浙江余杭反山 22 号墓出土。浙江省考古研究所藏。（b）高 5.2 厘米。1986 年浙江余杭反山 16 号墓出土。浙江省考古研究所藏。（c）高 6.2 厘米。1987 年瑶山 10 号墓出土。浙江省考古研究所藏。（d）高 5.4 厘米。明尼阿波利斯艺术学院藏。

them, however, changed markedly. Unlike the Hemudu mask, which forms part of a continuous decorative band on the exterior of the basin, a Liangzhu mask at the center of a two-dimensional plaque defines a fixed visual focus. The silhouette of the object—either semicircular, three-pronged, or trapezoidal—then becomes the boundary of the image and

Fig. 1.11. (a) Pottery basin with incised decoration. Hemudu culture. 4th millennium B.C. H. 16.2 cm. Excavated in 1973 at Hemudu, Zhejiang province. Museum of Chinese History, Beijing. (b) Decoration. Ink rubbing.

图 1.11 （a）刻纹陶盆。河姆渡文化，前 4000—前 3000 年。高 16.2 厘米。1973 年浙江余姚河姆渡出土。中国国家博物馆藏。（b）装饰纹样。拓片。

sometimes even appears as the "face" of a zoomorph. In other words, the mask has become "the subject of design" and supplements the meaning of an otherwise geometric or abstract shape.

Such a centralized mask motif seems to reflect a desire to forge a nonrepresentational icon. A Liangzhu mask does not portray a real animal or human figure. It is an artificial image whose most prominent feature is a pair of large eyes formed by concentric circles.

器物之间的关系却有了很大变化。河姆渡文化陶盆外壁的兽面是连续性花纹带的一部分，但良渚文化兽面纹则位于二维平面的中央，形成一个固定的视觉焦点。器物的轮廓——无论是半圆形、三齿形或梯形的——因此成为图像的边界，有时甚至变成兽面的轮廓。换言之，这里的兽面纹已经变成“设计的主题”，并为几何的或抽象的外形增添了意义。

这种焦点性的兽面纹母题似乎反映了创造抽象性偶像的愿望。良渚文化兽面纹并不是对于真正的动物或人物的刻画。它是一种人为的形象，其最突出的特点是一对同心圆式的眼睛。兽面全然正面

Perfectly frontal and symmetrical, this mask on a flat plaque directly faces the viewer, demanding his visual and mental
033 concentration. The implication of this form can be understood in the light of other religious iconic representations, as B. A. Uspensky has observed:

> Medieval painting, and in particular icon painting, was oriented primarily toward an INTERNAL viewer's position, that is, towards the point of view of an observer imagined to be within the depicted reality and to be facing the spectator of the picture. (Renaissance painting, on the contrary, was understood as 'a window on the world' and hence was oriented towards an EXTERNAL viewer's position, that is, towards the position of the spectator of the picture who is, in principle, a non-participant in this world.)[76]

He suggests that similar iconic representations existed in many different religious arts from antiquity to the Middle Ages. Such an image always embodies an "internal observer" who is "looking out" at the viewer from an imaginary world.[77] These features on a two-dimensional Liangzhu mask establish a direct conjunction between the mask and the spectator and between this world and the supernatural. The modern Chinese scholar Zhang Minghua has proposed that some of these flat jades were originally fixed on stands as cult objects.[78] His reconstruction of these objects helps explain their "iconic" decoration—as commonly understood, establishing a direct conjunction between a deity and a devotee is essential to religious worship. Similar masks on pendants and headdresses may have also functioned to identify the person wearing them. Interestingly, a Fanshan *huang*-pendant bears an upside-down
034 mask (Fig. 1.12). Its unique decorative position implies that the

Fig. 1.12. Jade necklace. Liangzhu culture. 3rd millennium B.C. H. 7.6 cm (*huang* pendant only). Excavated in 1986 from Fanshan Tomb no. 22. Zhejiang Provincial Institute of Archaeology.

图 1.12 玉项饰。良渚文化，前 3000 —前 2000 年。璜高 7.6 厘米。1986 年浙江余杭反山 22 号墓出土。浙江省考古研究所藏。

和对称，它正视观者，强调视线和精神的集中。我们可以通过和其他类型宗教偶像的比较来理解这种形式的含义。正如乌司潘斯基所指出的：

> 中世纪的绘画，特别是宗教偶像画，主要是采取了一个内在观者的位置。也就是说，所绘的偶像朝向一个想象的、存在于被描绘的本体之中的，面对看画人的观察者。（与之相反，文艺复兴时期的绘画则被理解成是“通向另一世界的窗口”，因此是朝向一个外在观者的地位。也就是说，从原则上讲，朝向存在于此世界之外的一个观者。）[76]

乌司潘斯基认为，类似的偶像表现存在于从上古到中世纪许多不同的宗教艺术中。这种表现形式中的主体形象总是体现为从一个想象的世界面对观者“向外看”的“内在观察者”。[77] 二维的良渚文化兽面纹的特征，可说是在兽面纹本身和观者之间、在这个世界和超自然之间建立起了直接联系。中国当代学者张明华认为，这些扁平的玉器有的原是安装在架子上的礼拜对象。[78] 他的推测有助于解释其“偶像性的”装饰——众所周知，在神祇和崇拜者之间建立直接联系对于宗教崇拜本身来说极为重要。此外，佩饰和头饰上类似的兽面纹也可能有助于标志佩戴者的身份。有趣的是，反山出土的一件璜上装饰了一个倒置的兽面［图 1.12］。其独特的装饰方位暗

expected viewer was none other than the owner and bearer of the jade. Looking down at the mask hanging on her chest, she would find herself confronting a "mirror image," which, however, distorted and mystified reality.[79]

Fig. 1.13. (a, b) Two views of a jade *cong*. Liangzhu culture. 3rd millennium B.C. H. 7.2 cm. Excavated in 1982 from Sidun Tomb no. 4 at Wujin, Jiangsu province. Nanjing Museum.

图 1.13 （a, b）玉琮（两个角度）。良渚文化，前 3000—前 2000 年。高 7.2 厘米。1982 年江苏武进寺墩 4 号墓出土。南京博物院藏。

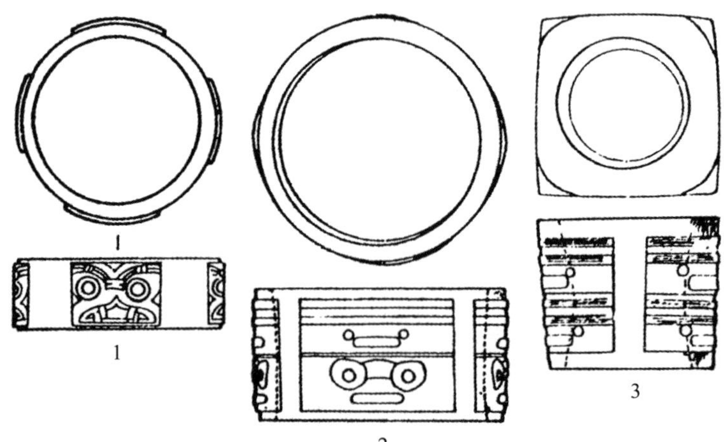

Fig. 1.14. Developmental stages of Liangzhu *cong*

图 1.14 良渚文化玉琮演变的三个主要阶段

These two-dimensional jades differ from the tubular *cong* not only in shape but also in decor. Although similar mask motifs appear on both kinds of jades, their application follows divergent principles. The exterior of a typical *cong* is modified into a truncated, square prism, on which masks are placed along the four corners (Figs. 1.13a, b). This design thus completely destroys the concept of a two-dimensional visual field: each flat side of a *cong* is both terminated with two half-masks and open-ended. In order to comprehend a whole image, the viewer must shift his gaze to an adjacent side to find the other half of the face. This peculiar decorative scheme of a *cong*, most likely a Liangzhu invention, signifies the second orientation of Liangzhu art: "decomposing" a static icon. The essence of this design, that an image has to consist of two identical halves, identifies it as an important early example of the "dualistic phenomena" that, according to K. C. Chang, characterized early Chinese civilization.[80] Separated on two adjacent sides of a square *cong*, a mask appears as a

示着观者不是外人，而是其所有者和佩戴者。当她低头看到自己胸前的兽面时，她会发现自己面对着一个“镜像”，尽管这个镜像是已变形和神秘化了的现实。[79]

这些二维玉器与管状玉琮在外形和装饰上都很不相同。虽然二者都具有相似的兽面纹，但其装饰方式却遵循了不同的原则。典型的玉琮外形是一段方形棱柱，兽面装饰在转角处［图 1.13］。这样的一种设计完全打破了二维视觉艺术的观念：玉琮每一个平面的边缘都停顿在半个兽面上，图案在这个平面上未到尽头。为了看到整个形象，观者必须转到相邻的平面上去寻找兽面的另外半张脸。这一特殊的装饰模式很有可能是良渚文化的发明，它表现出了良渚艺术的第二种倾向性：将一个静态的偶像进行“分解”。张光直曾提出，中国早期文明的一个重要特征是“二元现象”。[80] 良渚文化玉琮上一个形象由两个相同部分组成的设计，可以被看作这种“二元现象”一个重要的早期例证。把一个兽面分置于两个相连的平面上，

perfect profile when viewed from the side, and as a whole face when seen from a corner. This pattern thus represents an abrupt change in image making: a single image could and ought to be viewed in two ways—both frontally and in profile—and an artificial image could and ought to represent various dimensions of a single subject.[81] Unlike a two-dimensional mask that stresses the confrontation between the image and the viewer, this new decorative formula emphasizes the interplay between the individual parts of an image.

Rudolf Arnheim has observed in his study of visual psychology that "as soon as we split the compositional space down the middle, its structure changes. It now consists of two halves, each organized around its own center. The pattern represents the two symmetrical partners in dialogue, balanced along the interface."[82] This theoretical formulation can be historicized in the development of the *cong*; the Chinese scholar Liu Bin proposes that the Liangzhu mask motif "developed in parallel

Fig. 1.15. Jade *cong*. Liangzhu culture. 3rd millennium B.C. H. 16.2 cm (two sections). Excavated in 1984 from Fuquanshan Tomb no. 40 at Qingpu, Shanghai. Shanghai Cultural Relics Administration.

图 1.15 玉琮。良渚文化，前 3000—前 2000 年。高 16.2 厘米（两部分）。1984 年上海青浦福泉山 40 号墓出土。上海市文物管理委员会藏。

with the transformation of the shape of the *cong*: "A mask originally on a curved surface [on a bracelet] was later divided into two halves on two flat surfaces along the raised vertical axis."[83] According to archaeologist Wang Wei, the three major stages in this evolution are exemplified by the examples in Fig. 1.14: (1) four rectangular picture fields containing identical masks were defined on tall rings; (2) slight angles then emerged along the vertical axis of each mask; and (3) these angles became increasingly sharper, finally transforming a circular ring into a square prism, with masks centered on its corners.[84] These observations point to two fundamental impulses in Liangzhu artistic creation—the multiplication of a motif (Fig. 1.15) and the formation of composite

其结果是两种视觉形象：对着琮的侧面看到的是兽面完美的侧面，对着琮的转角看到的则是一个完整的正面兽面形象。这种图案设计因此表现出形象创作中的一个突变：即一种形象可以也应当从两个方向——既从正面又从侧面——来看；一种人为的形象可以并且也应当表现出同一主题的不同方面。[81] 和二维兽面纹强调图像与观者直面相对的静止状态不同，这种新的装饰程式着力表现图像内部因素之间的相互作用。

鲁道夫·阿恩海姆在其关于视觉心理学的研究中指出："我们一旦将一个组合的空间从中央分开，其结构就改变了。这时它就包括了两个部分，每一部分围绕中心点进行组织。该式样表现了相互对话的两个对称的部分，彼此沿着其分界线求得和谐。"[82] 这一理论性阐述也可以用来描述琮的发展历史；中国学者刘斌认为，良渚文化兽面纹的发展"与琮体的演变保持了同步"："原来在一弧面上的兽面纹，就以这条脊为中轴，被从中间分置于两个平面上了。"[83] 根据考古学家王巍的研究，玉琮演变的三个主要阶段可以用图 1.14 来表示：（1）四个装饰有同样兽面纹的矩形排列在较宽的玉环上；（2）每个兽面的中线上出现了微微凸起的棱；（3）这些凸起的棱变得越来越尖，最后使圆环变成了一个四角装饰兽面纹的方柱体。[84] 这些看法涉及良渚艺术创作的两个基本趋向：一是装饰纹样在数量上的递增［图 1.15］，二是组合型和二元的图像构成

and dual motifs (Fig. 1.13); the former creates visual repetitions resembling a verbal charm, and the latter leads to metamorphosis and dynamism.

As defined earlier, a composite mask has its two identical halves placed on two picture planes left and right. Dual masks, on the other hand, consist of two varying zoomorphs one above the other. The surface of a *cong* is frequently separated into upper and lower registers, each containing a mask (Fig. 1.13). The similarity between these two masks is evident: they both have circular eyes, and their mouths or noses are both represented by a short bar. But the divergences between them are also unmistaken: the upper mask is relatively simple and topped with a tripartite horizontal band, which may stand for a crown; the lower one has a sunken nose, and its oval eyes are connected by a "bridge." The upper one is plain, while the lower one is embellished with fine spiral incisions. Significantly, each of dual masks is also a composite mask. When these two compositions are combined, they attest to a single underlying dualistic structure in Liangzhu decorative art. Varieties of dual images are found on Liangzhu jade, not only on the corners of a *cong* but also on plaques (Figs. 1.10c-d). On some jades from Fanshan and Yaoshan, a frontal anthropomorphic image with a huge feathered headdress replaces the upper, simplified mask in a more conventional design (Figs. 1.17-19). On other jades from the same sites, this image is represented by its profiles flanking a large, frontal mask (Fig. 1.10a).

Although the multiplication of a single motif and the formation of composite and dual masks are based on different principles, they are by no means contradictory. Most important, both types of decoration negate a single dominant icon. Moreover, as soon as a composite mask or a dual-mask motif was invented, it immediately became the subject of repetition (Fig. 1.16). Although these complex decorative patterns

Fig. 1.16. Jade *cong*. Liangzhu culture. 3rd millennium B.C. H. 9.6 cm. Excavated in 1986 from Fanshan Tomb no. 20. Zhejiang Provincial Institute of Archaeology.

图 1.16　玉琮。良渚文化，前 3000—前 2000 年。高 9.6 厘米。1986 年浙江余杭反山 20 号墓出土。浙江省考古研究所藏。

方式［图 1.13］；前者创造出一种视觉上的反复，类似咒语的魔力，后者则导致形式的变异与物力论。

如上所述，一个“组合型”的兽面是由左右两个镜像组成的。其所根据的二元设计原理又演化为上下图像的对照。一种良渚文化短琮的表面分为上下两层，每层有一个兽面纹［图 1.13］。上下面纹的相似点很明显：二者都有一对圆眼，嘴或鼻也都以短的横带来表现。但是二者的差异也不能忽略：上层的面纹相对比较简单，顶部三排水平条带可能代表王冠；下层面纹鼻子下凹，卵形的双眼以一桥状纹样相连。上层的面纹为素面，下层的面纹则饰有许多精细的螺旋线条。有意义的是，这种双层设计中的每一个兽面同时也是组合式的。当这两个构图放置在一起的时候，它们所见证的是一个单一的基础性的二元结构。良渚文化玉器中有多种二元的形象，不仅出现在琮的转角处，也出现在徽志上［图 1.10c, d］。在反山和瑶山出土的一些玉器上，一个正面、头戴华丽羽冠的神人形象取代了玉琮上部常见的简化面纹［图 1.17—图 1.19］。在这两个遗址出土的其他一些玉器上，这个形象又被表现为夹持大型兽面的侧面形象［图 1.10a］。

单个母题的递增与纹样的二元组合遵循了不同的原则，但是二者绝不矛盾。最为重要的是，这两种类型的目的都不是构成一个孤立独尊的偶像。而且一旦组合式的和二元的纹样被发明，就立刻会变成被递增的主题［图 1.16］。尽管这些复杂的图案是从更早的偶像

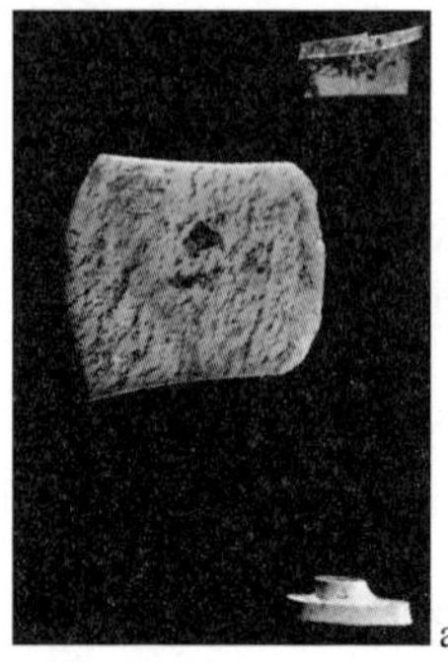

Fig. 1.17. (a) Jade axe. Liangzhu culture. 3rd millennium B.C. H. 17.9 cm. Excavated in 1986 from Fanshan Tomb no. 12. Zhejiang Provincial Institute of Archaeology. (b) Emblem on the axe.

图 1.17 （a）玉钺。良渚文化，前 3000—前 2000 年。高 17.6 厘米。1986 年浙江余杭反山 12 号墓出土。浙江省考古研究所藏。（b）玉钺上的神徽。

developed from the earlier iconic image, they never replaced it. In fact, the most striking feature of Liangzhu jade art is the coexistence of many kinds of imagery and the increasing richness of the visual vocabulary. I would argue that the Liangzhu jade mask, like later bronze decoration, is characterized by its protean shapes and incessant permutations, not by a "standard" iconography. As an example, no two of the 700 jades from the Yaoshan cemetery bear identical masks. It is unlikely that all these
037 variations were subject to stylistic or iconographic evolution. A more plausible assumption is that the divergences are deliberate and that the "metamorphosis" of styles and images, a concept which I explore more deeply in my discussion of bronze decoration, was itself a fundamental goal of Liangzhu ritual art.

Liangzhu art, however, also demonstrates another tendency opposed to metamorphosis and even to decoration. To define this tendency, let us return to a dual-mask motif consisting of an anthropomorphic figure and a large mask (Figs. 1.10a, c, 12, 17-19). Following the general decorative principle of Liangzhu art, this motif appears in various forms and styles:

a

b

Fig. 1.18. (a) Jade *cong*. Liangzhu culture. 3rd millennium B.C. H. 8.8 cm. Excavated in 1986 from Fanshan Tomb no. 12. Zhejiang Provincial Institute of Archaeology. (b) Emblem on the cong.

图 1.18 （a）玉琮。良渚文化，前 3000—前 2000 年。高 8.8 厘米。1986 年浙江余杭反山 12 号墓出土。浙江省考古研究所藏。（b）玉琮上的神徽。

发展而来的，但是它们并没有取代原有的形式。实际上，良渚文化玉器艺术最突出的特征，便是多种形象的并存以及视觉语汇的不断丰富。在我看来，如同后来的青铜纹样一样，良渚文化玉器的兽面并不是一种“标准化”的偶像，而是以其形状的多样性和非固定性为主要特征的。例如，瑶山墓地出土的 700 件玉器中没有任何两件的兽面完全相同。这种多样性不应看成是风格或图像志演变的结果。一个更为合理的推测是，这种多样性是有意造成的。风格与形象的“变异”——这一概念我将在讨论青铜装饰时做深入的探索——本身就是良渚文化礼仪美术的基本目标。

然而，良渚美术还显露出与装饰变异原理，甚至与装饰本身背道而驰的另外一种倾向。为了说清楚这种倾向，让我们再回到包含神人形象和一个大兽面的二元纹样［图 1.10a，c，图 1.12，图 1.17—图 1.19］。根据良渚美术总的装饰原则，这种纹样有着不同的形式和风格：

it is rendered in either relief, sunken lines, or openwork patterns, and its anthropomorphic figure shows either frontal or profile images. All these variations, however, correspond closely to the shape of a given object: they fit the shapes and also provide these shapes with meaning. In this sense, we call such designs "decoration."

One of these variations on a large axe from Tomb no. M12 at Fanshan, however, violates this principle (Figs. 1.17a, b). Although still consisting of the anthropomorphic figure and the front mask, it is a tiny image against a plain background at an upper corner of the axe. Its small size greatly limits its decorative role, and its design and placement have little to do with the overall shape of the object. Moreover, unlike the metamorphic decoration on most Liangzhu jades, this particular image is duplicated on other objects with minute precision. It recurs on a *cong* and a round column, both from Tomb no. M12 (Figs. 1.18-19), and can also be observed on a *huang* pendant from M22 at the same site (Fig. 1.12). The objects bearing this "standardized" twin image are themselves extraordinary: the axe, 16.8 centimeters across the blade, is the largest ever discovered in Liangzhu burials; the *cong*, 17.6 centimeters wide and 6.5 kilograms in weight, is the largest and heaviest Liangzhu *cong*; and the column has not been seen in any other place. Not coincidentally, Tomb no. M12, where

它们或是浅浮雕，或是阴线刻，或是透雕，其中的神人或是正面，或是侧面。然而，所有这些变化都与器物的形制密切结合在一起：纹样适合器物的形体，同时也赋予器物形体以新的意义。在这种情况下，我们可以把这种设计称为“装饰”。

反山 12 号墓出土的一件玉钺上的装饰则背离了这一原则［图 1.17］。尽管这一纹样也是由一位神人和一个兽面组成，但却只是玉钺上角的一个微型形象，与周围的大片空白背景形成鲜明对比。其微小的尺度限制了其装饰的作用，其设计和位置也与器物的整体外形没有多少关系。不仅如此，与大部分良渚文化玉器上多变的神人装饰不同，

Fig. 1.19. Jade column. Liangzhu culture. 3rd millennium B.C. H. 10.5 cm. Excavated in 1986 from Fanshan Tomb no. 12. Zhejiang Provincial Institute of Archaeology.

图 1.19　玉圆柱。良渚文化，前3000—前 2000 年。高 10.5 厘米。1986 年浙江余杭反山 12 号墓出土。浙江省考古研究所藏。

这一特殊的形象还被精细地复制到其他器物上：同墓出土的一件玉琮和一件圆柱状玉器［图 1.18，图 1.19］，以及该遗址 22 号墓出土的一套项饰中的璜上都有这个形象［图 1.12］。刻有这种“标准化”图像的器物本身也十分独特：钺，刃部宽 16.8 厘米，是良渚文化墓葬中迄今所见的最大的一件钺；琮，边长 17.6 厘米，重 6.5 千克，也是良渚文化玉琮中最大最重的一件；圆柱状玉器在其他遗址中从未出土过。出土这三件玉器的 12 号墓是反山

these three objects were found, was the most prominent Fanshan grave, located at the center of the cemetery and furnished with 511 carved jades. M22, which yielded the *huang* pendant, was next to M20. It has been suggested that axes and *cong* were buried with
038 Liangzhu noblemen and *huang* with Liangzhu noblewomen. Jean James thus concludes that "the use of a very similar image on jades from both M20 (male) and M22 (female) could indicate a close relationship between the two occupants."[85] In other words, this "very similar image"—the highly formulated and duplicated dual-mask motif—now functioned to identify the status and relationship of their owners. It is not simply a decorative motif that could be manipulated at will, but a fixed symbol for identification.

To date, this particular dual-mask image has been found only in these two tombs at Fanshan. But bird signs rendered in similar fashion are distributed in a broad area along the eastern coast and may shed more light on the meaning of this type of prehistoric jade engraving. In 1963, Alfred Salmony reported on incisions on three *bi* disks in the Freer collection.[86] These pictorial marks share a number of elements (Figs. 1.20a-c, 29a-c) : an altar or a "mountain" whose top arches in steps toward the center, a bird standing on the top of this altar, and a circle—most likely representing the sun—on the front side of the altar. On the other hand, the visible minor compositional and stylistic differences may indicate different dates for these engravings. The incisions shown in Figs. 1.20a and 1.29a are the most complete and "picture-like": the bird is almost realistically drawn, with a round spot on its shoulder. An additional crescent halved by a median line and placed below the sun represents the new moon.[87] In the next design (Figs. 1.20b, 29b), the altar has duplicated contours. A bird's tail is added to the sun motif along with, in Salmony's words, "two flanking birds' heads, which have hooked beaks and

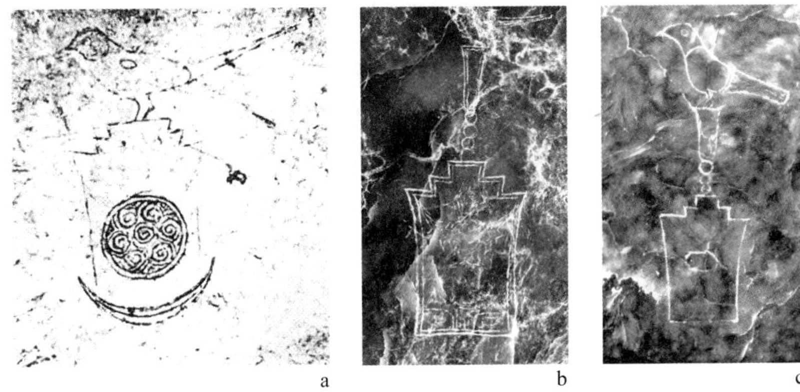

Fig. 1.20. (a-c) Bird emblems on three Liangzhu *bi* disks. 3rd millennium B.C. Freer Gallery of Art, Washington, D.C.

图 1.20 （a—c）良渚文化玉璧上的鸟。前 3000—前 2000 年。华盛顿，弗利尔美术馆藏。

最重要的一座墓葬，它位于整个墓地的中心，随葬的玉器多达 511 件，这里出土的重要玉器带有这个形象因此绝非偶然。出土玉璜的 22 号墓靠近 12 号墓。有人指出，钺和琮是良渚文化贵族男子的随葬品，璜则是良渚文化贵族妇女的随葬品。金 · 詹姆斯认为，“由于 12 号墓（男）和 22 号墓（女）所出土的玉器上有着相似的纹饰，这两座墓的墓主之间应存在着密切的关系。”[85] 换言之，这种“相似的纹饰”——反复出现、高度程式化的二元兽面纹——标志着其拥有者的身份和相互关系。这不是一个一般的装饰纹样，而应该是身份的固定象征物。

迄今为止，这种独特的二元兽面形象只发现于反山的这两座墓。但是，具有同样风格的鸟的符号却分布于东部沿海更为广大的区域内，这些符号或许更能揭示出史前玉雕的意义。1963 年，苏蒙尼报道了弗利尔美术馆所藏三件玉璧上的雕刻。[86] 这些绘画性的符号包含着一些共同的元素［图 1.20，图 1.29a—c］：一座上部有台阶通向中央高起的祭坛或“山”，祭坛上站着的一只鸟，祭坛正中的一个圆形，可能表示太阳。但是这些图像的构图和雕刻风格也有细微的差别，或反映其时代的不同。图 1.20a 的雕刻最为完整［又见图 1.29a］，也最具有图画性：鸟的形象几乎是写实的，其肩部有一圆点。太阳下部附加的一个月牙状物被一弧线中分，代表一弯新月。[87] 在另一例中［图 1.20b，图 1.29b］，祭坛的轮廓为双线，太阳旁边增加了鸟尾，用苏蒙尼的话说，是“两侧各有一鸟头，带勾喙，

long pointing crests,"[88] thus transforming the circle motif into a sun-bird combination. The crescent moon, however, disappears. This incision becomes somewhat simplified and abstracted in the third image (Figs. 1.20c, 29c) drawn in coherent and fluent lines. An oval formation replaces the earlier sun motif; a vertical band in the middle further transforms this shape into the pictograph of the sun in Chinese writing.

Lacking reliable comparative data, Salmony dated these three images, as well as the disks bearing them, to the Shang dynasty.[89] But in the
039 1970's, Chinese archaeologists found three similar incisions on large pottery jars of ceremonial use from Dawenkou sites in Shandong (Fig. 1.21).[90] One vessel bears sun and moon images (Fig. 1.22c); the incisions on the other two vessels (Figs. 1.22a, d) are more complicated—a five-peaked "mountain," akin to the "altar" motif on the three Freer *bi*, is added to support the sun-moon cluster.[91] More Dawenkou engravings of both kinds have been reported (Figs. 1.22b, e, f),[92] and similar marks have increasingly been found on carved jades. Among these jade objects, a tall ring in the Freer Gallery has the sun-moon combination on one side and an "abstract" bird on the opposite side (Figs. 1.23a-b, 29h);[93] a large

Fig. 1.21. Pottery jar. Dawenkou culture. 4th-3rd millennia B.C. H. 59.5cm. Excavated at Lingyanghe, Juxian, Shandong province. Museum of Chinese History, Beijing.
图 1.21 陶尊。大汶口文化，前 4000—前 2000 年。高 59.5 厘米。山东莒县陵阳河出土。中国国家博物馆藏。

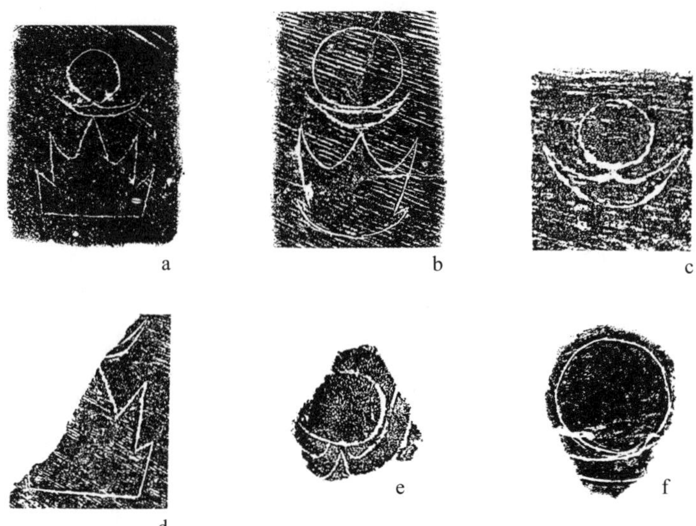

Fig. 1.22. Emblems on pottery vessels. Dawenkou culture. 4th-3rd millennia B.C. (a, c, e-f) Excavated at Lingyanghe, Juxian, Shandong province. (b) Excavated at Qianzhai, Zhucheng, Shandong province. (d) Excavated at Dazhucun, Juxian. Ink rubbings.

图 1.22　陶尊上的符号。大汶口文化，前 4000—前 3000 年。(a, c, e, f) 山东莒县陵阳河出土。(b) 山东诸城前寨出土。(d) 山东莒县大朱村出土。拓片。

有长而尖的羽冠”，[88] 因此，其原型就变成了太阳和鸟的组合，但是月牙消失了。第三个图形的线条更为连贯流畅，形象则变得有些简化和抽象［图 1.20c，图 1.29c］：一个椭圆形代替了原来的太阳，其中央的竖线进一步将这一图形转化为汉字中象形的“日”字。

由于缺少可资类比的材料，苏蒙尼将这三个图形及玉璧的年代确定为商代。[89] 但到了 20 世纪 70 年代，中国的考古工作者在山东的大汶口文化遗址中发现了三种类似的刻画符号，均刻在用于礼仪的陶尊上［图 1.21］。[90] 其中一件刻有太阳和月亮［图 1.22c］；另外两件陶尊上的符号更为复杂［图 1.22 a，d］——日月以下有一座五峰“山”形，与弗利尔玉璧上的“祭坛”类似。[91] 这两类大汶口文化的刻画符号在近年又有更多的发现［图 1.22 b，e，f］，[92] 带有类似刻符的玉器也被越来越多发现，如弗利尔美术馆收藏的一件宽环或镯的外壁上一侧刻日月图案，另一侧刻一“抽象的”鸟［图 1.23，

cong in the Museum of Chinese History in Beijing also bears the sun-moon motif (Figs. 1.24, 29i);[94] a *cong* in the Museé Guimet is engraved with a sign combining a sun-altar and a crescent moon (Fig. 1.29f); another *cong* in the Capital Museum in Beijing (Figs. 1.25a-b, 29d) and a *bi* disk in the Palace Museum in Taipei (Figs. 1.26a-b, 29e) are engraved with images identical in both form and style with the incisions on the Freer *bi*.[95] Deng Shuping has recently discussed all these pieces in a learned article and, based on a newly excavated example from Anxi (Figs. 1.27a-b, 29d),[96] has identified them as Liangzhu products.[97]

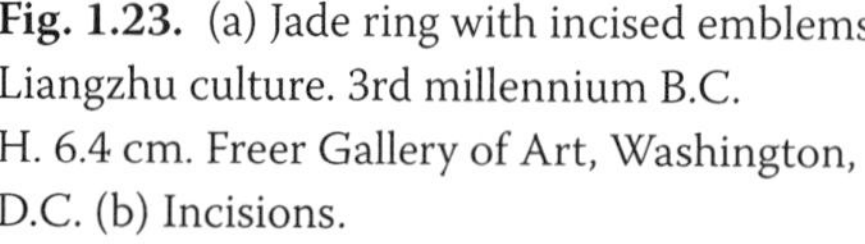

Fig. 1.23. (a) Jade ring with incised emblems. Liangzhu culture. 3rd millennium B.C. H. 6.4 cm. Freer Gallery of Art, Washington, D.C. (b) Incisions.

图 1.23 （a）带线刻符号的玉环。良渚文化，前 3000—前 2000 年。高 6.4 厘米。华盛顿，弗利尔美术馆藏。（b）线刻符号。

Fig. 1.24. Jade *cong*. Liangzhu culture. 3rd millennium B.C. H. 49.2 cm. Museum of Chinese History, Beijing.

图 1.24 玉琮。良渚文化，前 3000—前 2000 年。高 49.2 厘米。中国国家博物馆藏。

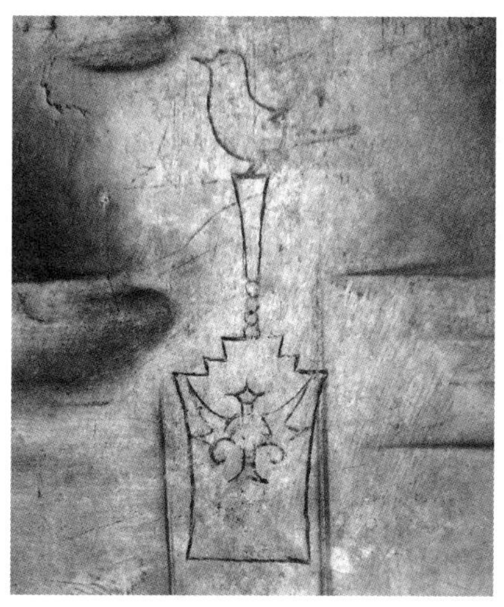

Fig. 1.25. (a) Jade *cong*. Liangzhu culture. 3rd millennium B.C. H. 38.2 cm. Capital Museum, Beijing. (b) Emblem on the *cong*.
图 1.25 （a）玉琮。良渚文化，前 3000—前 2000 年。高 38.2 厘米。北京，首都博物馆藏。（b）琮上的符号。

图 1.29h］。[93] 北京中国国家博物馆收藏的一件高大的琮也刻有日月图案［图 1.24，图 1.29i］；[94] 集美博物馆收藏的一件琮刻有太阳—祭坛以及月牙［图 1.29f］；北京首都博物馆收藏的另一件琮［图 1.25，图 1.29d］和台北故宫博物院收藏的一件璧［图 1.26，图 1.29e］上的刻符与弗利尔璧上的刻符无论在形式还是风格都如出一辙。[95] 邓淑苹最近在一篇论文中根据安溪的新发现［图 1.27，图 1.29d］[96] 集中讨论了上述诸例，将它们确定为良渚文化的遗物。[97]

040 A number of significant features of these engravings reject any attempt to identify them as "decoration." First, these engravings are small, sometimes so tiny that they can hardly be seen, and thus their decorative function is deliberately negated (Fig. 1.28). Second, these images are formed by thin, incised lines; this means that they were added after the completion of the works. Third, these and other bird images are always shown in silhouette. George Rowley has called such a simple profile "ideational," that is, an image representing a concept, reduced to its essence.[98] Call to mind the abstract idea of "bird"; instantly it will appear in profile in the mind's eye. Finally, the incisions appear in isolation, without obvious relationship with the shapes of the objects. These isolated, tiny images call for the viewer's concentration, but the more attention one pays to them, the less attention one pays to the object as a whole.

On the other hand, all these features suggest interesting parallels between these engravings and certain pictographs in early Chinese writing. We can even find direct evidence for this relationship. The circular motif on the first Freer *bi* (Fig. 1.20a), for example, is filled with spirals and thus resembles the character shown in the margin, meaning "sun-brightness" in Shang oracle bone inscriptions. When this motif is further simplified on the third Freer *bi*, it resembles the Chinese character *ri*, or sun (Fig. 1.20c). This form also appears independently on another *bi* disk, and this confirms its use as a graph.[99] Significantly, incisions belonging to this group have been observed in a broad area along China's east coast from the lower Yellow River valley to the lower Yangzi River region. Although the various cultures in this region developed distinctive decorative art motifs and styles, they seem to have shared these "pictographs" for a considerable period.[100] Moreover, we find that some bronze ritual vessels of the Shang dynasty bear similar "bird-altar" signs (Fig. 1.30), which scholars have considered symbols of a certain clan.

This last observation leads us to identify these incisions not only as "pictographs" but also as "pictorial emblems" (Fig. 1.29), which Paul Ekman and Wallace V. Friesen define as follows: "Emblems are those nonverbal acts which have a direct verbal translation, or dictionary definition. This verbal definition or translation of the emblem is well 043

这些刻符的许多重要特征使我们不能将其看作"装饰"。第一，这些雕刻的图像都很细小，有时小到几乎看不见，因此在雕刻这些图像的时候，古人有意地否定了它们的装饰功能［图 1.28］。第二，这些图像皆以很细的阴文构成，这说明它们是在器物完成后加刻的。第三，这些图像中鸟和其他形象总是以侧面轮廓的形式出现。罗丽将这种简单的轮廓表述称作"概念型"图像。就是说形象只表现绘画对象的概念，简化到它的本质。[98] 比如，当人们想到"鸟"的抽象概念时，眼前便会立刻呈现出这种轮廓。第四，这些刻符都是孤立的，与器物的外形没有明显的联系。这种孤立的、微小的刻符唤起了观者的注意力，但人们越注意它们，就越失去了对器物的整体关注。

从另一方面看，所有这些特征都显示出这些符号与早期汉字特有的象形性之间的共性。我们甚至可以发现这种联系之间的确切证据。例如弗利尔第一件玉璧上［图 1.20a］的圆形中有一些螺旋状的线，与商代甲骨文中的"炯"（即"阳光"）字十分接近。当这一主题在弗利尔第三件璧上出现时［图 1.20c］，则与汉字中的"日"近似。这一形式还独立出现在另一件璧上，证明它有类似字符的功能。[99]

一个重要的现象是，这组刻符在中国东部沿海北到黄河下游，南到长江下游的广大区域内都有发现。尽管这一区域内不同的文化各有其独特的装饰艺术题材和风格，但是它们在相当长的一段时间内似乎都在使用着这些"图画文字"。[100] 我们甚至在一些商代青铜礼器铭文中仍可发现类似"鸟－祭坛"的符号［图 1.30］，学者们将这样的符号认定为族徽。

从这最后一点我们可以推测，这些符号不仅是一种"图画文字"，而且是一种"图形徽志"［图 1.29］。保罗·埃克曼和瓦列斯·弗里森对于徽志做了如下定义："徽志是具有一种直接的语译或词典式定义功能的非文字行为。一个群体、阶级或文化中的所有成员

known by all members of a group, class or culture. . . . People are almost aware of their use of emblems; that is, they know when they are using an emblem, can repeat it if asked to do so, and will take communicational responsibility for it."[101] The identification of the bird motifs as emblems is supported by ancient legends and myths.[102] It was a widespread belief in ancient China that the God of the East named Jun had a bird's head with a sharp beak. Jun lived in Heaven, but two altars were dedicated to him on earth and were administered by his "earthly friends," who were multicolored birds. Lord Jun supervised Four Birds, and one of his two wives gave birth to ten sun-birds, the other to twelve moons.[103] Many versions of this legend exist, but no matter how elaborated or abridged, all versions share four basic elements—the bird, the sun, the moon, and the east. The *Classic of Mountains and Seas* (*Shanhai jing*) mentions yet another element—a great mountain: "In the Eastern Wilderness there is a mountain known as Heming. It is the origin of Jun's clan and the place whence the sun and moon emerge."[104]

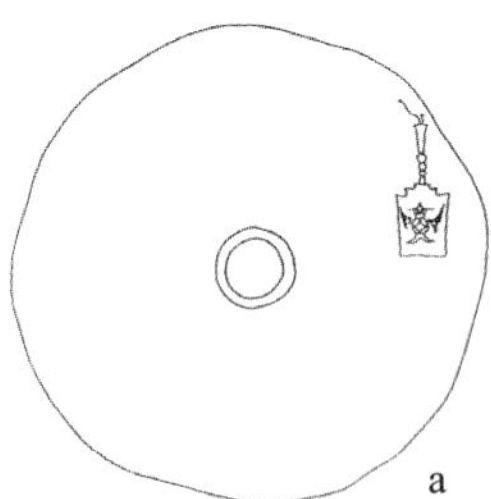

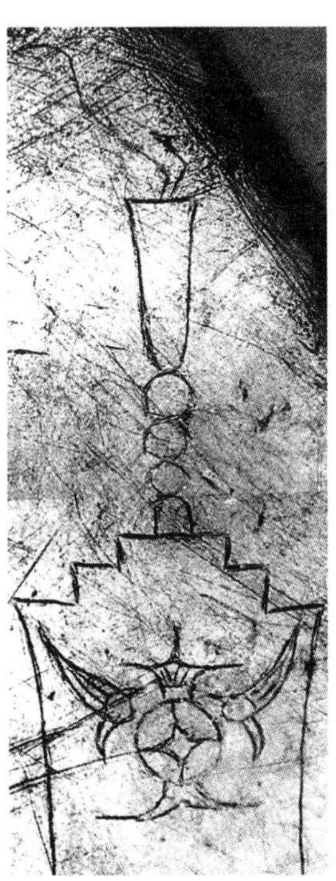

Fig. 1.26. (a) Jade *bi* disk. Liangzhu culture. 3rd millennium B.C. Diameter 13.17-13.44 cm. Palace Museum in Taipei. (b) Emblem on the *bi*.

图1.26 （a）玉璧。良渚文化，前3000—前2000年。直径13.17—13.44厘米。台北故宫博物院藏。（b）玉璧上的符号。

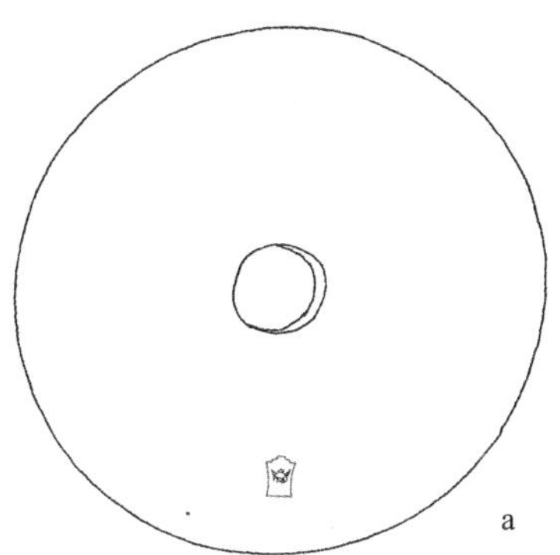

Fig. 1.27. (a) Jade *bi* disk. Liangzhu culture. 3rd millennium B.C. Diameter 26.2 cm. Excavated in 1989 at Anxi in Yuhang, Zhejiang province. Zhejiang Provincial Examination Committee of Cultural Relics. (b) Emblems on the *bi*.

图 1.27 （a）玉璧。良渚文化，前 3000—前 2000 年。直径 26.2 厘米。1989 年浙江余杭安溪出土。浙江省文物鉴定委员会藏。（b）玉璧上的符号。

均熟悉这种语译或词典式定义功能……人们几乎都了解徽志的用途；或者说，他们知道何时使用徽志，如果有所要求的话还可以重复使用它，可以为其承担交流的责任。"[101] 将良渚文化玉器上鸟的图像认定为徽志也可以在古代传说和神话中找到证据。[102] 如中国古人普遍相信东方之帝名俊，鸟首尖喙。俊住在天上，但在世界上有属于他的两座祭坛，由他在地上的"友"五采鸟管理。俊役使四鸟，他的一位妻子生了十只阳鸟，另一位则生了十二个月亮。[103] 这个传说有多种版本，但是不管是简是繁，它们都含有四个基本元素——鸟、日、月、东方。《山海经》一书提到了另一个元素——山："东荒之中，有山名曰壑明俊疾，日月所出。"[104]

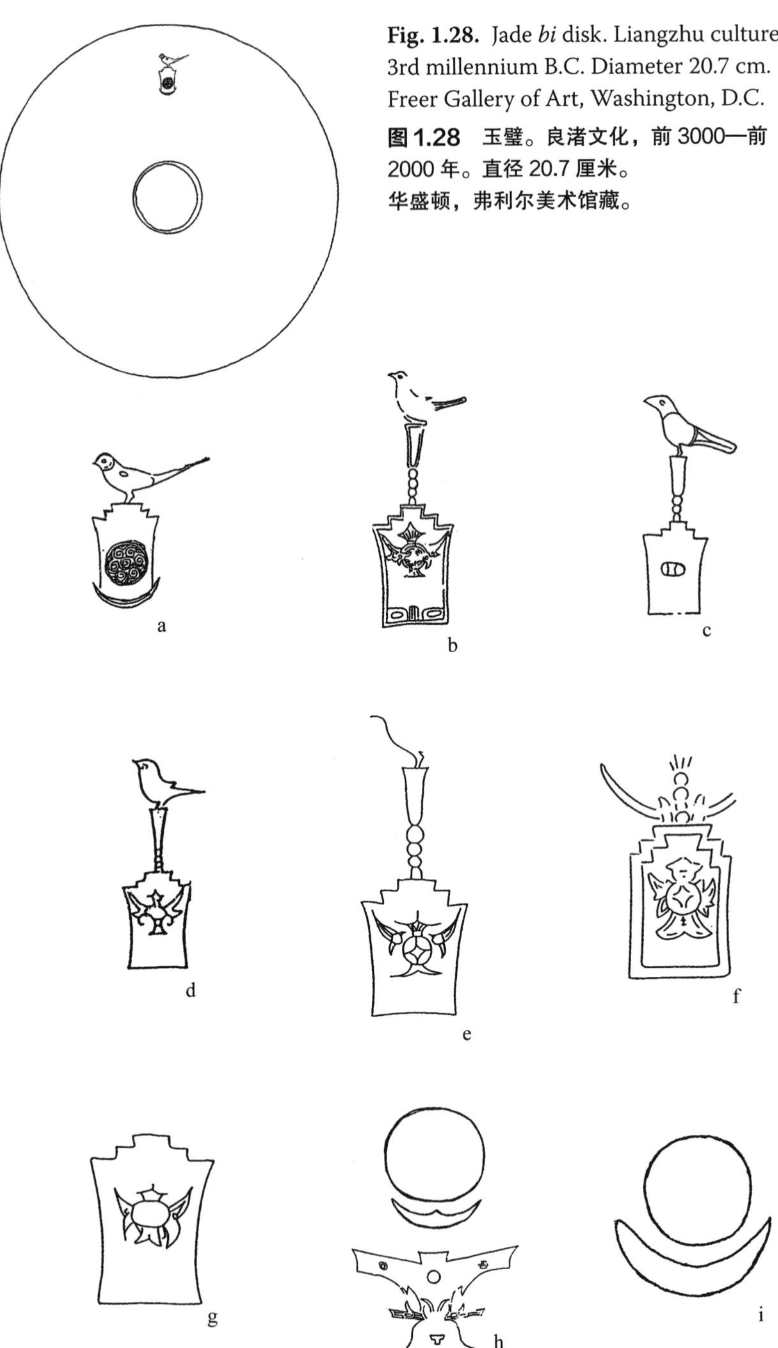

Fig. 1.28. Jade *bi* disk. Liangzhu culture. 3rd millennium B.C. Diameter 20.7 cm. Freer Gallery of Art, Washington, D.C.

图 1.28 玉璧。良渚文化，前 3000—前 2000 年。直径 20.7 厘米。华盛顿，弗利尔美术馆藏。

Fig. 1.29. Incised emblems on Liangzhu ritual jades

图 1.29 良渚文化玉礼器上的符号

This last reference seems less "legendary" in nature. It neither offers a creation myth nor glorifies Jun as a supreme god, but simply identifies the origin of Jun's clan. In the earliest Chinese geographic text, "The Tribute of Yu" ("Yu gong"), various groups of people on the east coast are given the designation Yi or Bird Yi, and their "precious things" include "beautiful stones" or jades.[105] Even more fascinating, this text contains the following passage concerning the area between the Yellow and Yangzi rivers:"The Huai and the sea formed the boundaries of Yangzhou. The lake of Pengli was confined to its proper limits; and the 'Sun Birds' [*yangniao*] had a place to settle in. . . . [The area's] articles of tribute were. . . elephants' teeth, hides, feathers, fur, and timber. The wild bird-men brought garments of grass."[106]

Here the term *Sun Birds* is clearly the name of a group of people who settled in the region. These people, also called "wild bird-men," treasured certain goods including bird feathers. Not incidentally, the ritual jades from the places where they lived are engraved with the emblem "Sun Bird."[107] The modern

Fig. 1.30. Bird inscriptions on late Shang dynasty ritual bronze vessels
图 1.30　晚商青铜礼器上的鸟形铭文

最后这条文献似乎缺少"神话色彩"。它既没有提供一种造物的神话，也没有将俊提升为一位至高无上的神明，而是说明了俊的地望。在中国最早的地理学著作《禹贡》一书中，东方的各方先民被说成是夷或"鸟夷"，他们的"宝"包括"怪石"，可能和玉石有关。[105]尤为引人注目的是，该文献在谈到黄河长江之间的地区时说："淮海惟扬州。彭蠡既潴，阳鸟攸居。……厥贡……齿革羽毛惟木。岛夷卉服。"[106]

这里的"阳鸟"一词显然代表居于长江下游的一人类群体，这些人也叫作"岛夷"（即"鸟夷"），其珍宝中包括鸟羽。因此，在这一民族所活动的地区出土的玉礼器上刻画有"阳鸟"恐非偶然。[107]中国

Chinese scholar Xu Xusheng has suggested that the myth about Jun's giving birth to the ten suns and twelve moons and his employment of groups of "birds" reflect the structure and fragmentation of an eastern cultural complex during prehistoric times. He also compared this legend with an episode in ancient Egyptian history in which Menes integrated the symbols of the tribes that he had conquered into his own royal emblem.[108] His discussion prompts a reexamination of the composition of various Dawenkou-Liangzhu emblems (Figs. 1.22, 29). The main element of the Dawenkou incisions is the sun-moon unit, sometimes combined with the five-peaked mountain. The Liangzhu emblems, on the
044 other hand, emphasize a bird standing on the mountain embellished with the sun; a crescent moon is sometimes present. Possibly these various signs identified different branches of a pan-eastern cultural complex, as Xu Xusheng has argued based on textual sources.[109]

The identification of these Dawenkou-Liangzhu incisions as emblems suggests that during this early stage, engravings on ritual objects were of two kinds: *decoration* favoring protean imagery, and *emblems* identifying the ownership of objects. Decoration is primarily a visual expression, and an emblem is fundamentally a verbal expression. These two types of signs, however, could be transformed into one another, as we have observed in a variety of examples. The properties and determinants of *liqi* thus not only consisted of *material* and *shape* but now also included *decoration* and *inscription*. As we shall see, the interplay of these four elements determined the course of ritual art during the following Bronze Age.

FROM IMITATION TO SYNTHESIS

By the beginning of the Bronze Age around 2000 B.C., a set of formal characteristics defining a symbolic art had emerged. These characteristics reveal a conscious effort to separate ritual paraphernalia from ordinary utensils and reflect a tendency to supply visual forms with written expressions, exemplified in the beginning by emblems.

This artistic tradition culminated in the Shandong Longshan culture: the wall of a pottery vessel (Figs. 1.31a, b) was reduced to a critical point, 2 to 3 millimeters in thickness; the subtle curves of its contours were meticulously calculated; and its monochrome color exaggerates the sharpness of its silhouette. Some jade works are ground so thin that they become literally semitransparent (Fig. 1.32); fragility seems to have

学者徐旭生认为，俊生十个太阳和十二个月亮以及他役使众“鸟”的神话，反映了史前时期东方文化体系的结构与裂变。他还比较了古埃及神话中关于美尼斯将所征服的部落整合到自己帝国的徽志下的情节。[108] 这一讨论促使我们重新观察各种大汶口文化和良渚文化徽志的结构［图 1.22，图 1.29］。大汶口文化符号的主要元素是日月，有时与五峰山形组合在一起。而良渚文化的徽志则突出了鸟站在有太阳标志的山上，有时也刻画月亮。正像徐旭生根据文献资料所指出的那样，这些不同的符号或许标志着东方文化体系中不同的分支及其变化的组合。[109]

将大汶口文化和良渚文化的刻符认定为徽志，说明早期阶段礼器上的雕刻可以分为两类，一类是千变万化的图像装饰，另一类是标志着所有权的图像徽志。装饰主要是一种视觉性的表现方式，而徽志基本属于文字性的表现方式。然而，正如我们在上述不同的例证中所见，这两种符号可以互相转换。礼器的基本特性和决定因素中不仅包括材质和形状，而且包括装饰与铭文。我们将会看到，正是这四种因素的交互作用，决定了接下来青铜时代中礼仪美术的发展进程。

3. 从模仿到综合

中国大约在公元前 2000 年前后进入青铜时代，在此以前，一整套规范的象征性艺术的特征已经出现。这些特征包括，人们有意识地将礼器和日常用器加以区分，采用徽志来为文字表达提供一种视觉形式。这种艺术传统在山东龙山文化中达到顶峰：陶器的器壁薄到了极点［图 1.31］，只有 2—3 毫米的厚度；器物轮廓的曲线极尽微妙，显然经过了精心的设计；单一的色彩使得器物轮廓更为突出。许多玉器制作得非常薄，甚至变得半透明［图 1.32］，纤薄

Fig. 1.31. Pottery cups. Shandong Longshan culture. 3rd millennium B.C. Excavated in 1960 at Yaoguanzhuang, Weifang, Shandong province. Shandong Provincial Museum, Ji'nan. (a) H. 26.5 cm. (b) H. 17.5 cm.

图 1.31 陶高柄杯。龙山文化，前 3000—前 2000 年。（a）高 26.5 厘米。山东日照东海峪出土。山东省文物考古研究所藏。（b）高 17.5 厘米。1960 年山东潍坊姚官庄出土。山东博物馆藏。

been the highest artistic goal. On other jades, pairs of masks and birds are executed in fine fillets in various forms (Fig. 1.33).[110] It is against this background that the Chinese Bronze Age began.

Like painting, bronze art is not a single artistic genre. When bronze first appeared as a "precious" art medium, it was employed to express values of ritual art previously conveyed by clay and jade. Our earliest Chinese bronze vessels—seven *jue* cups excavated at the late Xia capital site in Erlitou[111]—can be studied from precisely this perspective. The best Erlitou *jue* (Figs. 1.34 a, b) has been described as showing "an exaggerated fragility: the waist is sharply constricted; spout and tail are drawn out to an extreme slenderness; and the top-heavy superstructure is delicately balanced on three long and elegant legs, faintly curved to continue the profile of the skirt. These graceful, mannered proportions, in a vessel type already curiously contrived, bear witness to the Erlitou founder's conscious concern for formal, aesthetic matters."[112] The "graceful" shape of this *jue*, however, cannot be attributed entirely to its maker. It represents, in fact, the apex of a long development that extended back to pre-historical times. Dawenkou or Longshan pottery wares (Figs. 1.4-5, 31) may have different shapes, but they display the same emphasis on thinness, slenderness, and delicacy, and the same pursuit of a complex silhouette by vitiating volume and usefulness. One can hardly believe that the Longshan cup was made of soft clay or that the Erlitou bronze emerged from fitted molds. In both cases the materials have been

似乎成为艺术创作的目标。在另一些玉器上，对应的兽面纹和鸟纹以精细的线条和不同的形式刻画出来［图 1.33］。[110] 中国青铜时代开始时，所承袭的就是这样一个背景。

如同绘画一样，青铜艺术也不是一个单一的艺术类型。青铜以一种“贵重的”艺术媒介出现，被用来传达在此之前陶和玉所承载的礼仪美术的价值。我们可以从这个角度来考察迄今所知年代最早的一批中国青铜器，即夏晚期都城二里头遗址出土的 7 件青铜爵 [111]。二里头爵中最精美的一件［图 1.34］具有“一种夸张的脆弱性：腰部纤细；流与尾长长地伸出；三足修长而雅致，平稳地承托着较重的器身，其下部微微外侈的线条像是垂下的裙裾。这些优雅适度的比例用在这样一件刻意设计的容器上，反映出二里头青铜铸造者在形式与审美上自觉的考虑”。[112] 但是，这件爵的“优雅”并不能完全归功于其制造者。实际上，它代表了自史前时代以来长期发展过程的一个顶峰。大汶口文化或龙山文化陶器［图 1.4，图 1.5，图 1.31］的形状和这件青铜器可能有所不同，但是它们同样背离了器物的容量和功用，而在轮廓上表现出对于微薄、轻巧和精致的追求。人们难以相信龙山文化的高柄杯是用陶土制作的，也同样难以相信二里头的铜爵是模具铸造的。在这两个例子中，材料都

"conquered" and the normal production of a thick, durable utensil has been replaced by a painstaking process aimed at "fragility"—a traditional quality of ritual art.

Evidence for a genealogy stretching from Longshan pottery to Erlitou bronzes can be derived from other sources. First, both the Erlitou bronze vessels and Longshan black pottery neglect decoration: six of the seven Erlitou *jue* have no embellishment, and the decorated one bears only six faint dots on its waist. The Erlitou artisan seems to have shared the Longshan approach that excessive surface pattern would increase the impression of volume and thus was uncalled for.[113] Second, the dualism of Erlitou art seems to continue a prehistorical convention: decoration is reduced to a minimum on bronze vessels, but jades and inlaid works from the same site bear elaborate mask designs.[114] One of the Erlitou jades (Figs. 1.35a, b) is covered with masks on parallel registers, and each mask is centered on a corner; the decorative formula is apparently derived from the Liangzhu *cong* design (Figs. 1.13-16).

This dualism, however, diminished during the mid-Shang period (*ca.*
046 1500-1300 B.C.).[115] Mid-Shang bronze art appears to have synthesized the two most powerful preceding art traditions—pottery and jade. Almost all mid-Shang bronze vessels derived their shapes from pottery types (Fig. 1.36), but the masks that had been previously monopolized by jade art were now transplanted onto them. In this respect, mid-Shang bronzes differ fundamentally from the earlier *jue* from Erlitou, which are aesthetically homogeneous with Longshan black ritual pottery. Rather than following any one tradition, mid-Shang bronze art utilized the available artistic vocabulary from divergent sources to create new conventions. In this way, these works announced the independence of bronze art, which then dominated Chinese art for a thousand years. The transformation in bronze art from the early Shang to mid-Shang thus supports Susanne K. Langer's assertion that "almost every technical advance is first felt to be the discovery of a better means of imitation, and only later is recognized as a new form, a stylistic convention."[116] Earlier

I proposed that the first jade *liqi* faithfully imitated stone and pottery objects (Fig. 1.1). Only during the following period did the gradual formulation of the distinctive formal characteristics of jade carvings 047
establish jade art as an independent artistic genre (Figs. 1.10, 12-20). The evolution of bronze art during the Shang followed the same path.

被"征服"，旨在获得"脆弱性"的艰苦工序——这是早期礼仪美术的一个传统品质——取代了以厚重、实用为目的的一般性生产。

龙山文化陶器和二里头文化青铜器之间的传承关系还可以从其他方面找到证据。首先，二里头青铜器和龙山文化黑陶都没有装饰，二里头 7 件爵中的 6 件没有任何纹饰，另一件只在腰部有 6 个圆点。二里头文化的艺术家们似乎有着与龙山人同样的观念，即认为过多的表面装饰将使体量感增强，因而不予采用。[113] 其次，二里头艺术中的一个二元现象似乎也延续了史前的惯例，青铜器上的装饰被减少到最低限度，但是同一遗址出土的玉器和镶嵌品却有着复杂的兽面纹。[114] 二里头的一件玉器周身装饰着成排的兽面纹［图 1.35］，每个兽面都以转角为轴心；这种装饰方式显然来自良渚文化的玉琮［图 1.13—图 1.16］。

但是，这种二元分化到了商代早中期（约前 1500—前 1300 年）便减弱了。[115] 商代中期青铜器艺术似乎综合了先前陶器和玉器这两种最有影响力的传统：几乎所有的商代中期青铜器的造型都继承于陶器［图 1.36］，但是原来由玉器垄断的兽面纹现在转移到了青铜器上。从这个角度看，商代中期青铜器与二里头出土的早期青铜爵有着根本的差别。二里头铜器在审美上更接近龙山文化黑陶礼器，商代中期青铜艺术则并非单一地继承任何一种传统，而是从不同的渠道选取可以运用的艺术语汇，来创造新的形式。这时期的作品就是通过这样的途径宣告了统治中国艺术长达千年之久的青铜艺术的独立。青铜艺术从商代早期到商代中期的转变支持了苏珊·朗格的论断："几乎所有技术的演进都首先是从找到一种较好的模仿手段开始，新形式、新风格只是到了后来才被承认。"[116] 我在前文指出，最早的玉礼器忠实地模仿了石器和陶器［图 1.1］。只是到了后来，逐渐出现的一系列鲜明的玉器雕刻特征才使得玉器艺术成为独立的艺术类型［图 1.10，图 1.12—图 1.20］。商代青铜艺术的发展也遵循了同样的途径。

Fig. 1.32. Jade blade. Longshan culture. Late 3rd millennium B.C.

图 1.32 玉刀。龙山文化，前 3 千纪晚期。

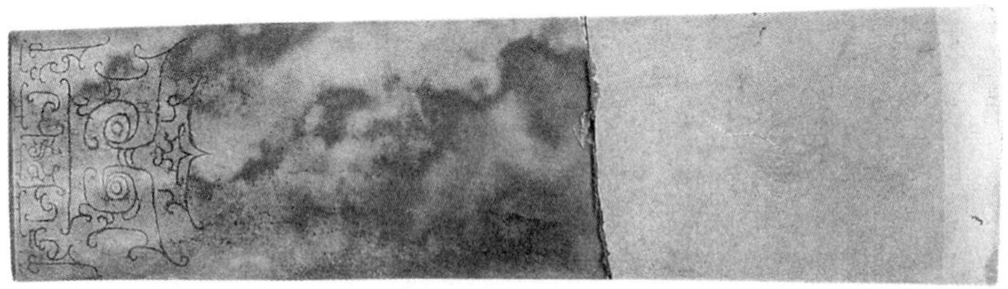

Fig. 1.33. Ceremonial jade adz. Shandong Longshan culture. Late 3rd millennium B.C. L. 18 cm. Found in 1963 at Liangchengzhen, Rizhao, Shandong province. Shandong Provincial Museum, Ji'nan.

图 1.33 玉圭。龙山文化，前 3 千纪晚期。长 18 厘米。1963 年发现于山东日照两城镇。山东博物馆藏。

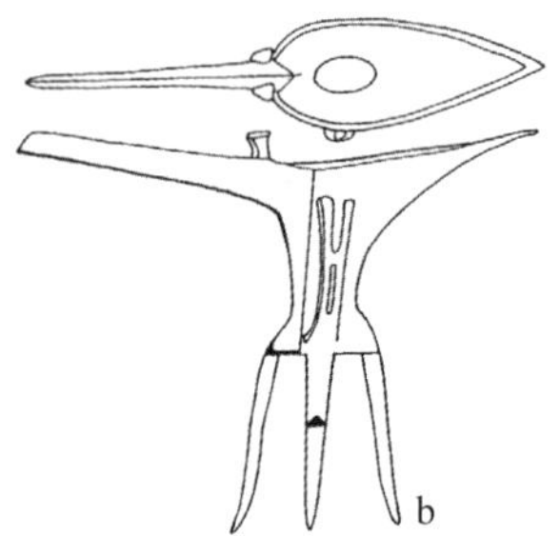

Fig. 1.34. (a) Bronze *jue* vessel. Late Xia dynasty. 2nd millennium B.C. H. 22.5 cm. Excavated in 1975 at Erlitou, Yanshi, Henan province. Yanshi County Cultural House. (b) Drawing.

图 1.34 （a）青铜爵。夏代晚期，前 2000—前 1000 年。高 22.5 厘米。1975 年河南偃师二里头出土。偃师县文化馆藏。（b）线图。

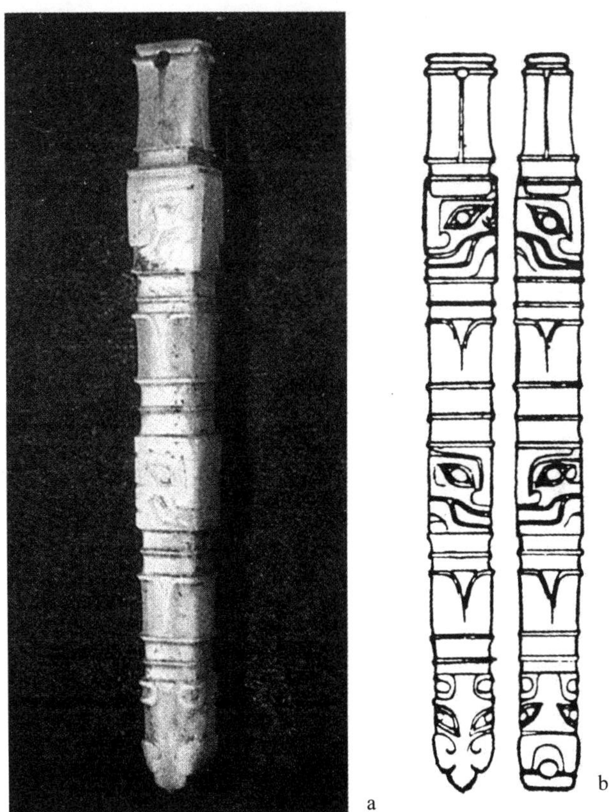

Fig. 1.35. (a) Jade "handle." Late Xia dynasty. 2nd millennium B.C. L. 17.1 cm. Excavated in 1975 at Erlitou, Yanshi, Henan province. Institute of Archaeology, CASS. (b) Drawing.

图 1.35 （a）玉柄形器。夏代晚期，前 2000—前 1000 年。高 17.1 厘米。1975 年河南偃师二里头出土。中国社会科学院考古研究所藏。（b）线图。

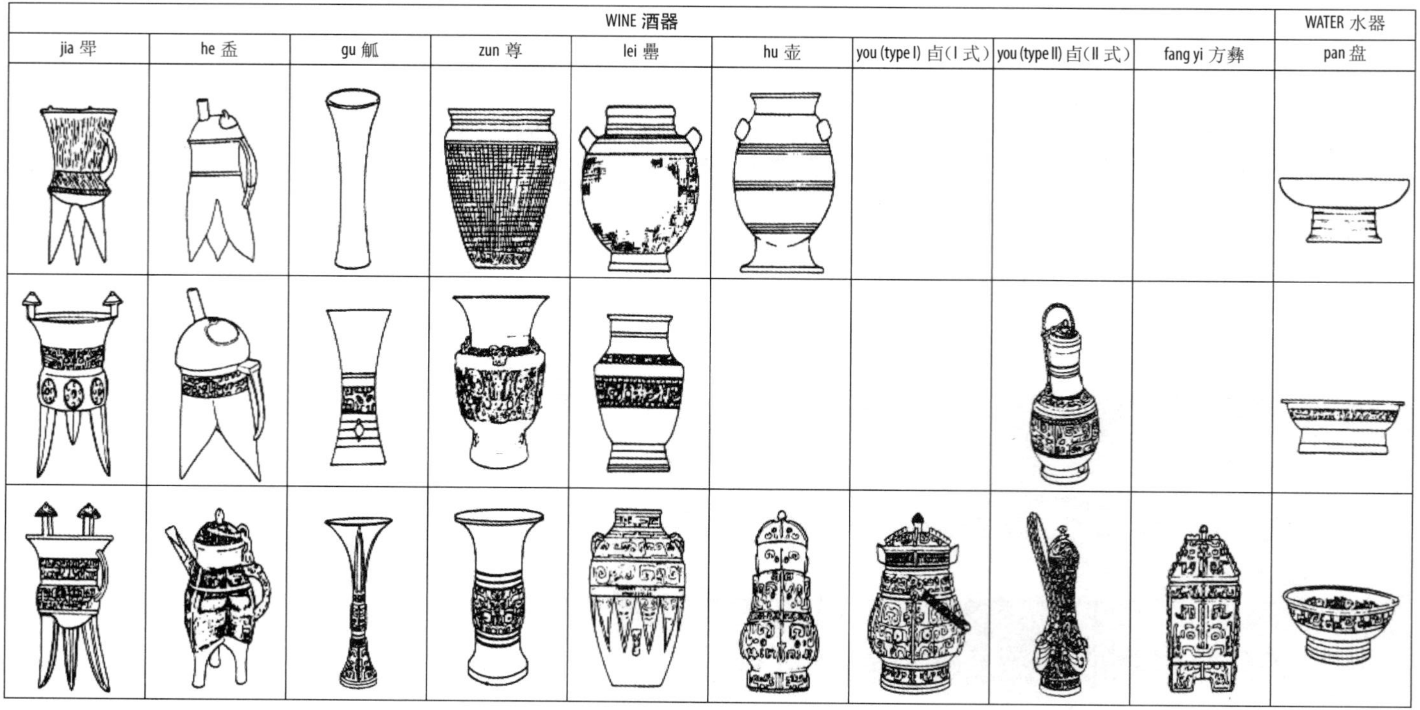

WINE 酒器									WATER 水器
jia 斝	he 盉	gu 觚	zun 尊	lei 罍	hu 壶	you (type I) 卣（I 式）	you (type II) 卣（II 式）	fang yi 方彝	pan 盘

Fig. 1.36. Typological relationship between prehistoric pottery vessels and Shang bronze vessels

图 1.36 史前陶器和商代青铜器的类型关系

FUNCTION 功用	FOOD 食器							
NAME OF VESSEL TYPE 器物名称 / STAGE OF DEVELOPMENT 发展阶段	ding 鼎	fang ding 方鼎	ge 鬲	li 甗	gui 簋	yu 盂	dou 豆	jue 爵
POTTERY PROTOTYPE 陶器原型		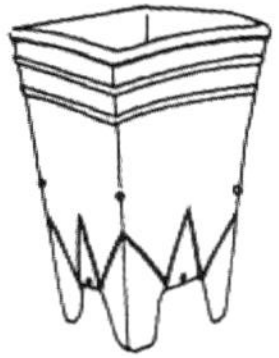	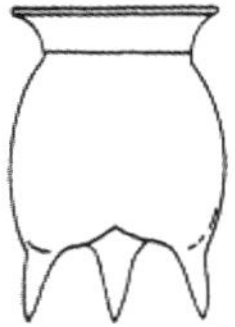	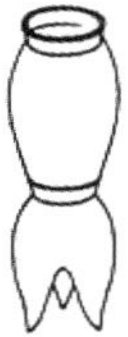	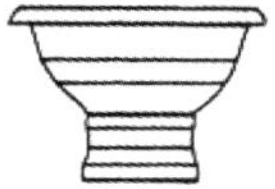	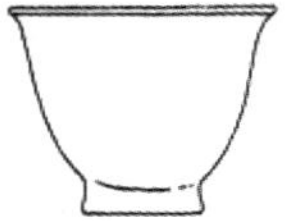	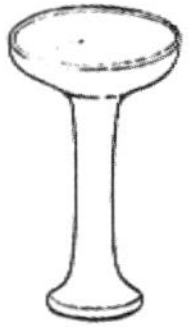	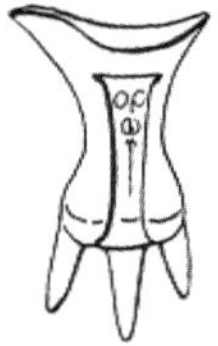
EARLY SHANG 早商	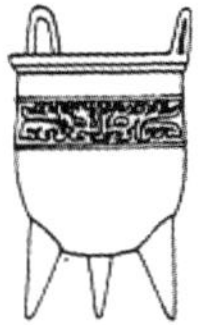			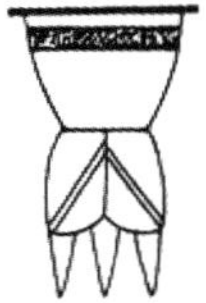				
LATE SHANG 晚商			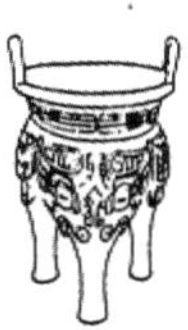					

Fig. 1.37. Bronze square *ding*. Mid-Shang dynasty. Mid-2nd millennium B.C. H. 100 cm. Excavated in 1974 at Zhangzhai, Zhengzhou, Henan province. Museum of Chinese History, Beijing.

图 1.37 青铜方鼎。商代中期，前 2 千纪中期。高 100 厘米。1974 年河南郑州张寨出土。中国国家博物馆藏。

The most popular decorative motif on middle and late Shang bronzes is the zoomorphic mask traditionally called the *taotie* (Fig. 1.38). In Eleanor von Erdberg Consten's words:

> The term *taotie* denotes mask-like animal faces in frontal view, which lie flat on the surface of the vessel. . . with legs, tails, and the intimation of a body added to the sides of the face. Except for inconspicuous variation in the linear pattern fillings, the two halves of the face are symmetrical to both sides of a line—either imaginary or stressed by flange or ridge—that runs down from the forehead to the nose.[117]

Consten points out a distinctive feature of a *taotie*: the zoomorph is often composed as a pair of profile "dragons" standing nose to nose to form a frontal mask. This iconography long puzzled scholars; as Jordan
048 Paper wrote in 1978: "The origin of the t'ao-t'ie [*taotie*] is still a mystery. It has not been found on extant objects from the neolithic culture."[118] But recent archaeological discoveries help clarify both the *taotie's* origin and its peculiar imagery.[119] On Liangzhu *cong* (Figs. 1.13a, b) and the Erlitou

jade (Figs. 1.35a, b), a mask is centered on a corner so that it appears as a perfect profile viewed from the side, and as a whole face viewed frontally. The mid-Shang people inherited this convention and pursued it further: they not only applied a mask to a corner of a bronze but also stretched it open to fill a frieze (Fig. 1.37). As the three-dimensional mask became two-dimensional, it still combined both frontal and profile aspects.[120] We should not overlook the importance of this transformation: it represents an abrupt advance in image-making. A mask on Liangzhu and Erlitou jades exhibits its full face and profile only when viewed from different angles. The depiction, therefore, is still conditioned by ordinary visual

商代中后期最流行的青铜器装饰母题是原来称作饕餮的兽面纹［图 1.38］。康时登是这样描述饕餮的：

> 饕餮一词指平展地装饰在器物表面面具般的动物形象……它的腿、尾和示意性的身体分列在面部两侧。除了填充在图案中的线条有一些变化外，兽面的两部分左右对称，从额部到鼻子为其轴线，这条轴线有时不太明显，有时则形成一条中脊。[117]

康时登指出了饕餮的一个显著的特征：其动物性的形象常常表现为两只相对的侧面的“龙”纹，两“龙”共同形成一个正面的兽面。这一图像特征使学者们长期迷惑不解，如裴玄德在 1978 年写道：“饕餮的起源仍是一个谜。在现存的新石器时代器物中尚未见到这类题材。”[118] 但是最近的考古发现可以帮助我们弄清饕餮的起源及其奇特的意象。[119] 在良渚文化玉琮［图 1.13］和二里头文化玉器［图 1.35］上，兽面纹以转角为轴线，这样，当从一侧看时，它所显示的是一个侧面像，当从正面看时，则是一张完整的脸。商代中期的人们继承了这一传统并加以发扬：他们不仅将兽面用在铜器转角处，而且还将兽面展开，填充在平面横带里［图 1.37］。当兽面由三维变成二维时，正面和侧面都保留了下来。[120] 我们不应忽略这种转变的重要性：它表现了图像创作过程中的一个质的变化。在观看良渚文化和二里头文化玉器时，我们只有从不同角度才能看到其兽面纹的正面和侧面。这种表现手法因此仍然受到人们日常视觉

experience in viewing a three-dimensional entity. The two-dimensional and "split" *taotie* on Shang bronzes, however, is an entirely artificial image since it shows its full face and two sides at the same time. William Watson once commented: "It is impossible to see the *t'ao-t'ieh* simultaneously as a single mask *and* as two dragons standing nose to nose. An awareness of these two possible readings of the shapes disturbs a viewer as soon as they are pointed out to him."[121] But achieving such visual ambiguity and departing radically from naturalism may have been the aims of early Chinese art.

METAMORPHOSIS OF DECORATION

Shang *taotie* imagery suggests that important prehistorical decorative codes—*multiplication, dualism,* and *metamorphosis*—continued to play fundamental roles in Shang bronze art. This contention both requires and leads to a reexamination of the most widely used theory in analyzing Shang bronzes in the West—the Five Styles sequence that Max Loehr proposed in 1953.[122] Various scholars have summarized and interpreted this sequence;[123] here is Loehr's own abstraction (see Fig. 1.38):

Style I: Thin relief lines; simple forms; light, airy effect.

Style II: Relief ribbons; harsh, heavy forms; incised appearance.

Style III: Dense, fluent, more curvilinear figurations developed from the preceding style.

Style IV: First separation of motifs proper from spirals, which now become small and function as ground pattern. Motifs and spirals are flush.

Style V: First appearance of motifs in relief: the motifs rise above the ground spirals, which may be eliminated altogether.[124]

经验的局限。而商代青铜器上二维的“合成式”的饕餮则完全是一种人为的形象，因为它同时显示出了一张完整的脸和侧面。华威廉曾经说:“几乎不可能既把饕餮看成是一个单独的兽面又看成两条相对的龙。一旦观者被告知这个形象有着这两种认读的可能性，这一认知立刻使他的视觉产生混乱。”[121] 但是，获得这种视觉上的歧义，从自然主义中挣脱出来，或许正是中国早期青铜艺术的目的。

I

II

III

IV

V

Fig. 1.38. Five bronze decorative bands representing the Five Styles of Max Loehr (Styles I-V, top to bottom). Ink rubbing.

图 1.38　罗樾所划分的五种青铜器装饰类型的举例（从上到下，I—V 式）。拓片。

4. 装饰的变形

商代饕餮的构思表明，史前装饰的许多重要原则，如递增、二元性和变异，在商代青铜艺术中仍然扮演着基本的角色。这一观念要求我们重新思考西方在研究商代青铜器时最普遍采用的一种理论，即 1953 年罗樾提出的五种连续性风格的理论。[122] 已有许多学者对此进行了总结和阐释；[123] 以下是罗樾本人的表述［图 1.38］：

> I 式：细凸线图案，形式简单，轻松明快。
>
> II 式：浮雕的带状图案，形式粗疏厚重，阴刻的形象。
>
> III 式：从前一种风格发展成由繁密、流畅、婉转的线条构成的图案。
>
> IV 式：主体图案与螺旋形云雷纹首次分离，后者变得非常细密，构成地纹。主体图案与地纹在一个平面上。
>
> V 式：首次出现浮雕的主体图案，即主体图案从螺旋地纹上凸起，有时螺旋形地纹甚至被省略。[124]

Loehr's identification of Styles I and II as early types of Shang decoration has been proved by subsequent archaeological discoveries.
049 His characterizations of the five individual styles have provided scholars, including this writer, with standards in categorizing and describing the forms of Shang bronze decor. But his basic theoretical assumption, that the five styles constituted a consecutive sequence and each dominated a particular period in the course of Shang bronze art, is based on an evolutionary pattern that is not supported by excavated materials.[125] New archaeological evidence reveals that the development of Shang bronze art was far more complex: the five styles did not occupy equal segments of time during the Shang dynasty, nor did they replace one another in a linear progression. Rather, all five styles were invented during a relatively short period from approximately 1400 to 1300 B.C.[126] Many instances indicate the wide coexistence of divergent styles in a given period. There are mid-Shang vessels decorated with both Style I and II patterns (Figs. 1.39a, b);[127] some even have Style III designs and a cast-on handle (Fig. 1.40). A set of bronzes from a mid-Shang tomb or hoard often consists of vessels bearing designs of various styles (Figs. 1.41a, b).[128] There are late Shang bronzes covered with both Style IV and V patterns,[129] and vessels with Style IV or Style V patterns appear together in a single tomb.[130] Moreover, after the invention of Style V, Shang bronze art continued to develop, and earlier styles remained in use. Louisa G. Fitzgerald Huber has identified a number of new styles that emerged toward the end of the Shang, including an "archaic" style reminiscent of Styles I and II of the mid-Shang period (Fig. 1.58).[131]

罗樾对于商代早期 I 式和 II 式风格装饰的界定为后来的考古发现所证实。他对这五种风格特征的表述，为包括本书作者在内的学者提供了一种对商代装饰形式进行分类和描述的标准。但是他认为这五种风格构成了一种前后的序列关系，每种风格在商代青铜艺术发展的一个特定阶段起着支配性作用，这一观点的基本理论前提是

Fig. 1.39. Mid-Shang bronzes with Styles I and II decoration.
(a) *Jue* vessel. H. 17.2 cm. Said to be from Huixian, Henan province. Royal Ontario Museum, Toronto. (b) *Jia* vessel. H. 26.7 cm. Shanghai Museum.

图 1.39　装饰 I 式和 II 式纹样的商代中期青铜器。（a）爵。高 17.2 厘米。传出河南辉县。多伦多，安大略皇家博物馆藏。（b）斝。高 26.7 厘米。上海博物馆藏。

基于一种进化论模式，并没有得到考古资料的支持。[125] 新的考古发现证明，商代青铜艺术的发展实际上更为复杂：五种风格在商代既没有占据同样长的时段，也不存在着线性的依次更替的关系。实际上，这五种风格在大约公元前 1400—前 1300 年这一相对较短的时期内就都被发明了。[126] 而且许多例子可以证明，在一个特定的时期内不同的装饰风格可以并行不悖。如在商代中期的青铜器上，可以同时看到 I 式和 II 式的图案［图 1.39］；[127] 有的甚至装饰有 III 式图案并带有分铸的把手［图 1.40］。商代中期墓葬或窖藏内出土的一组青铜器往往包含有各种装饰风格的器物［图 1.41］。[128] 有的晚商青铜器同时装饰着 IV 式或 V 式的图案；[129] 饰有 IV 式或 V 式图案的器物也同时出土于一座墓葬中。[130] 甚至当 V 式图案出现后，青铜艺术仍继续发展，早期的风格也继续被沿用。胡博指出，在商末出现的一些新风格中包括一种“古风”装饰［图 1.58］，使人回想起商代早中期的 I 式和 II 式风格。[131]

From a strict evolutionary approach, these situations must be viewed as "exceptions," and the coexistence of different styles must be interpreted as the survival (or revival) of older ones after new ones had come into being.[132] But the frequency of such "exceptions" may in fact indicate
050 important "norms" in Shang artistic creation.[133] The key to understanding these norms, I suggest, is not a straight stylistic sequence or a revision of such a sequence, but the concept of *metamorphosis*, which helps explain a series of problems unsolved by an evolutionary interpretation and allows us to discover the dynamic nature of Shang ritual art. The term *metamorphosis* is used here in its dictionary meaning to refer to deliberate alteration, transformation, or transmutation of form, structure, or substance. In art, the effort toward metamorphosis rejects monotony and invites variation and permutation. Instead of a "standard" or "dominant" style or iconography, it favors protean styles and motifs. The combining of complementary or even contradictory styles and motifs in the decoration of a single object creates visual ambiguity and dynamism that contribute to the sense of *animation*. E. H. Gombrich has contrasted the principle of "animation" in design with that of "stylization": "The latter imposes order and approximates the living form to geometric shapes, the former imbues the shapes with life and therefore with movement and expression."[134] Interestingly, a second century B.C. Chinese author appreciated ancient bronze *liqi* exactly for their seemingly puzzling ability to evoke a sense of life and movement.

从严格意义的进化论观点来看，这种情况都被视作“例外”，不同风格的共存被解释为新风格诞生后旧风格的残存（或再生）。[132]但是如果这类“例外”不断出现的话，就可能说明这些现象实际上是商代艺术创作中的重要“定制”。[133]在我看来，这些定制的关键并不是一种直线发展的风格序列或对这种序列的局部修订，而是变形这个概念，因为这个概念可以帮助我们解答进化论所不能解决的一系列问题，引领我们去发现商代礼仪美术充满活力的机能。此处所使用的变形一词取其字典上的意义，表示形式、结构或物质方面

Fig. 1.40. Bronze *you* vessel. Mid-Shang dynasty. Mid-2nd millennium B.C. H. 31 cm. Excavated in 1974 at Panlongcheng, Huangpi, Hubei province. Hubei Provincial Museum, Wuhan.

图 1.40　青铜卣。商代中期，前 2 千纪中期。高 31 厘米。1974 年湖北黄陂盘龙城出土。湖北省博物馆藏。

有意识的变更、转化或嬗变。艺术上的变形不是单调枯燥的，而是变幻不定的。它鼓励千变万化的风格和主题，而不是某种“标准化”或“统治性”的风格或图像学。在一件器物的装饰上，互补的甚至是彼此矛盾的风格和主题结合在一起，其结果是视觉上的多义性和活力论，进而产生出勃勃的生机感。贡布里希曾对比设计中的“生机”与“风格化”这两个原理，指出：“后者赋予几何形体以秩序性和直接性的存在形式，前者则为形体注入了生命，使之具有动感和表现力。”[134] 有趣的是，一位公元前 2 世纪的中国学者在谈到古代青铜礼器时，也正是被它富有生命力和动感的迷人外表所吸引：

> The grand ceremonial bells and *ding* tripods, these are beautiful *qi* of extraordinary importance. They are engraved with elaborate birds of intertwining bodies, crouching rhinoceros, stealthy tigers, and coiling dragons whose interlocking forms resemble a textile design. Their shining color dazzles people's eyes; ablaze with lights, they radiate even more brilliantly. Flexible and intricate, their spiral decoration comprises complex patterns. Further inlaid with tin and iron, they change their appearance as if the sky were now darkened, now brightened.[135]

Since metamorphosis does not reject the concepts of "style" and "iconography" but creates and integrates stylistic and iconographic variations, the study of Shang bronze art can utilize the result of previous formal analyses. In other words, Loehr's basic identifications of the five styles may still be valid, but the intent behind the creation of these styles and the relationships among them must be reconsidered. Such a reconsideration reveals that two essential modes—a *metamorphosis* in "style," or the way of presentation, and a *metamorphosis* in "image," or the subject of presentation—characterize mid-Shang and late Shang bronze decoration, respectively.

The deliberate stylistic variation during the mid-Shang is most apparent in the wide coexistence of Style I and II patterns, designs that are contradictory and complementary in visual effect. The main motif executed in thin threads in Style I is expressed by thick ribbons in Style II; correspondingly, the ground left empty in the former becomes thin sunken "lines" in the latter. In fact, the "mirroring" effects[136] of these two styles was best described by Loehr himself: the first style is light, airy, and in relief; the second is harsh and heavy and has an incised appearance.[137] The depiction of the *taotie* in these two styles on a single vessel (Figs. 1.39a, b) or on different vessels in a single set (Figs. 1.41a, b) must, therefore, signify the Shang people's fascination with the possibility of rendering a single image in various ways.[138] The same fascination is
051 apparent in the decoration of Liangzhu ritual jades: the two masks in

a pair are sometimes distinguished not only in iconography but also in carving style (Figs. 1.17b, 18b).

Bagley rightly suggests that "it is important to note that they [i.e., Style I and II designs] retain precisely the same non-pictorial character. The raised areas of Style II do not outline or embody a creature any more than did the thread-relief designs of Style I."[139] The mid-Shang

> 大钟鼎，美重器。华虫疏镂，以相缪紾，寝兕伏虎，蟠龙连组。焜昱错眩，照燿辉煌，偃蹇寥纠，曲成文章。雕琢之饰，锻锡文铙，乍晦乍明。[135]

装饰形象的变异并不排斥"风格"和"图像学"的概念，而是创造和融汇了风格和图像学上的新变化，所以对于商代青铜艺术的研究可以利用原有分析的结论。这也就是说，罗樾关于五种风格的分类仍有其意义，但是我们在使用这个理论的同时应该考量这些风格背后的创作动机以及蕴藏在其中的各种关系。这种考量揭示出两个重要方面，一是"风格"（或者说表现方式）的变形，二是"形象"（或者说所表现的主题）的变形，这两方面分别是商代中期和晚期青铜装饰艺术的主要特征。

商代中期青铜器风格中有意识的形象变异最明显地反映在I式和II式两种纹样和设计普遍共存，显示出既矛盾又互补的视觉效果。以细阳文构成的I式主体纹样转变为II式所特有的厚重的带状纹样；前者留出的空白背景也相应地变为后者凹入的细"线"。实际上，罗樾本人已经非常精当地描述了这两种风格的"镜像"效果[136]：第一种风格轻松明快，线条凸起；第二种风格粗疏厚重，表面有刻画的阴线。[137] 因此，在同一件器物上［图 1.39］或属于同一组的不同器物上［图 1.41］用这两种风格刻画饕餮，意味着其制造者对利用不同方式演绎同一形象的可能性的兴趣。[138] 这种兴趣在良渚文化玉礼器上已经表现得十分明显：一对兽面的区别有时不仅体现在图像学上，而且也体现在雕刻风格上［图 1.17b，图 1.18b］。

贝格利正确地指出："重要的是要注意到它们（指I式和II式纹样）准确地保留着同样的非图画性特征。在勾画或表现一种动物形象方面，II式纹样凸起的块面并不比I式纹样凸起的线条更有效。"[139]

Fig. 1.41. Sets of bronzes with decor of different styles. Mid-Shang dynasty. Mid-2nd millennium B.C. (a) Set consisting of a *ding* (H. 18.0 cm), a *jia* (H. 24.3 cm), and a *gu* (H. 15.3 cm). Excavated in 1950 from Liulige Tomb no. 110, Huixian, Henan province. (b) Set consisting of a *jue* (H. 17.0 cm) and a *gu* (H. 12.6 cm). Excavated in 1950 from Liulige Tomb no. 148, Huixian.

图 1.41 装饰不同样式纹样的青铜器，商代中期。前 2 千纪中期。（a）鼎（高 18 厘米）、斝（高 24.3 厘米）、觚（高 15.3 厘米）。1950 年河南辉县琉璃阁 110 号墓出土。（b）爵（高 17 厘米）、觚（高 12.6 厘米）。1950 年河南辉县琉璃阁 148 号墓出土。

taotie imitated and, to some extent, distorted earlier mask motifs on jades. In many cases the *taotie* consists of little more than a pair of eyes, surrounded by abstract linear patterns that can hardly be conceived as the "body" of any real or imaginary creature. Even though details were gradually added, the *taotie* generally remained an elusive image with an ambiguous contour. The tendency toward visual complexity rather than organic imagery is especially evident in Style III, which is characterized by repetitions of abstract elements. The fine, slender, feather-like extensions projecting from various parts of a *taotie*—the trademark of this style—create a disciplined rhythm but at the same time further blur the *taotie's* outline.

The best examples of mid-Shang stylistic *metamorphosis* are the thirteen bronze vessels unearthed in 1982 from a Zhengzhou hoard (H1; Fig. 1.42).[140] The largest bronzes in this group are two imposing square *ding* (Figs. 1.43a, b). These apparently formed a pair, to judge from their identical decorative scheme and measurements (both 81 cm high and 53 cm wide), but they differ in using Styles I and II, respectively.

商代中期的饕餮在某种程度上简化了早期玉器上的兽面。在许多例子中，饕餮只有一对眼睛，周围的抽象线条很难被看作任何真实的或想象中动物的“躯体”。尽管一些细节逐渐加入进来，但饕餮各部分的轮廓却依旧模糊，总体上难以捉摸。III 式纹样尤为明显地反映出饕餮在视觉上的复杂化，而不是要清晰地表现具体器官的特征。这一风格最主要的特征是某些抽象元素的重复。例如从饕餮不同部位延展开来的羽毛般的精细线条——如同是这种风格的商标——形成一种编排有致的韵律，但同时又进一步模糊了饕餮的轮廓。

体现商代中期风格变异的最好例子是 1982 年出土于郑州一个窖藏内的 13 件青铜器［图 1.42–H1］。[140] 这组青铜器中最大的是两件气势雄伟的方鼎［图 1.43］。从其相同的设计思路和体量（均高 81 厘米，宽 53 厘米）来看，这两个鼎显然是成对的，其差别则在于分别采用了 I 式和 II 式风格的装饰。同样重要的是，这两个大鼎

Significantly, these two vessels were placed in the hoard side by side but in opposite directions (Fig. 1.42). In other words, they seem to "invert" each other in both decoration and placement. The same dualistic convention may also underlie the decoration of two other vessels in the group—a *lei* and a *you* (Figs. 1.44a, b). Although the *lei* has an angular shoulder and the *you* is equipped with a lid and a handle, they are similar in size and their bodies are covered with large *taotie* of similar shapes. The dense "quill" motifs surrounding the *taotie* identify the masks as Style III designs, but the pattern on the *lei* is "positive"—the *taotie* is

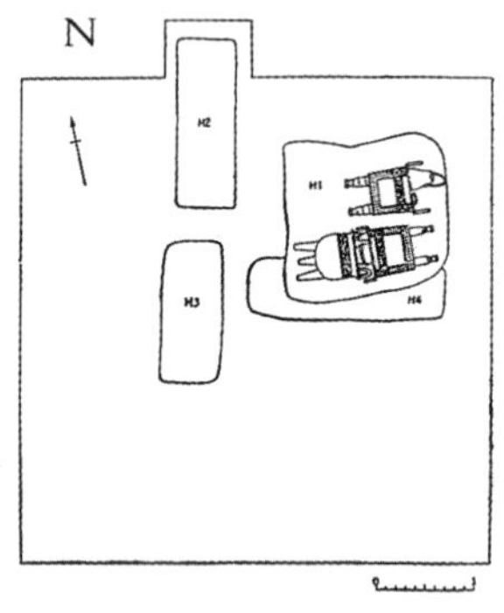

Fig. 1.42. Zhengzhou Hoard no. 1. Mid-Shang dynasty. Mid-2nd millennium B.C. Excavated in 1982 at Zhengzhou, Henan province. Drawing.

图1.42 郑州 1 号窖藏。商代中期，前 2 千纪中期。1982 年河南郑州出土。线图。

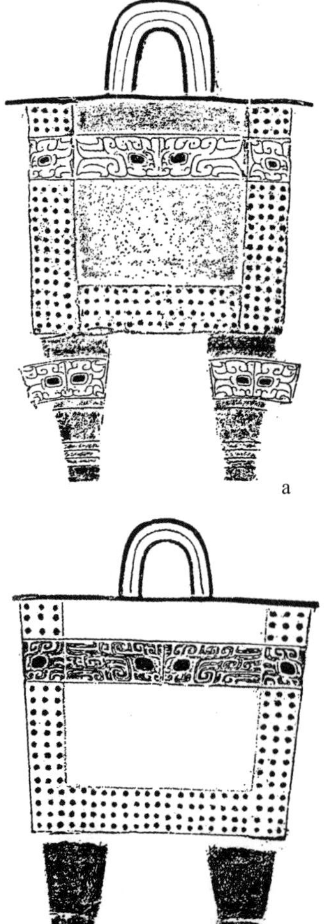

Fig. 1.43. (a, b) Two bronze square *ding* from Zhengzhou Hoard no. 1. Mid-Shang dynasty. Mid-2nd millennium B.C. Both H. 81 cm. Zhengzhou Museum. Ink rubbing.

图1.43 （a, b）郑州 1 号窖藏出土的两件青铜方鼎。商代中期，前 2 千纪中期。高均为 81 厘米。郑州博物馆藏。拓片。

represented by thick ribbons above the ground—whereas the pattern on the *you* is "negative"—the *taotie* is a "hollowed" image defined by the raised ground.[141] The group of bronzes from this hoard not only exhibit 052
the first three of Loehr's five styles, but high-relief *taotie* also appear on vessels otherwise decorated with more "primitive" patterns.

The movement toward protean and complementary styles, however, was altered during the late Shang. The emphasis was now on *metamorphic images* represented by various *taotie* rendered in a uniform style. The precise date of the change is uncertain, but available evidence places it close to or around 1200 B.C.[142] The strong interest in images, first revealed by the conscious effort to distinguish organic *taotie* (and other animals and birds) from the ground covered with geometric spirals (i.e., Style IV), was furthered by the overwhelming popularity of relief *taotie* (Style V). Loehr has described such phenomena as the "'growth' from rudimentary and vaguely suggested, semi-geometric forms to neatly

在窖藏中并列放置而方向相反［图 1.42］。换言之，在方向和布局上，两个鼎似乎都是互相“反转”。类似的对偶现象在成组的一件罍和一件卣上也可见到［图 1.44］。尽管二者造型不同，罍为折肩，卣有盖和提梁，但是二者的体量相近，也都装饰有形状近似的大片饕餮纹。饕餮周围均有密集的羽状平行纹，说明属于 III 式风格。但罍上的图案是阳纹——饕餮由凸起的宽线构成，而卣上的图案是阴纹——饕餮由凹入的“虚”的形象组成。[141] 该窖藏内出土的铜器不仅展现了罗樾五种风格中的前三种，而且也出现了高浮雕的饕餮，有的则装饰着较为“原始”的图案。

然而，这种向多变和互补发展的运动在商代晚期却出现了转向。此时所强调的是同一风格的饕餮纹组成变异形象。我们不太清楚这一转变的准确时刻，但许多线索说明可能在公元前 1200 年左右。[142] 对形象的强烈兴趣首先显现于，有意识地把整体性的饕餮（以及其他鸟兽）从云雷纹覆盖的背景上区别出来（即 IV 式纹样）。这种兴趣进一步由浮雕式饕餮（即 V 式纹样）的流行而得到明证。罗樾将这一现象描述为“从尚未充分展开的、模糊暗含的几何形式

Fig. 1.44. Two bronze vessels from Zhengzhou Hoard no. 1. Mid-Shang dynasty. Mid-2nd millennium B.C. (a) *You* vessel. H. 50 cm. (b) *Lei* vessel. H. 33 cm. Zhengzhou Museum. Drawing and ink rubbing.

图 1.44 郑州 1 号窖藏出土的两件青铜器。商代中期，前 2 千纪中期。（a）卣。高 50 厘米。（b）罍。高 33 厘米。郑州博物馆藏。线图和拓片。

defined, fully zoomorphic forms."[143] Bagley has interpreted the invention of Style IV as "a major innovation, and one that makes an abrupt break with the earlier trend toward ever more complex designs."[144] Although these statements still reflect an evolutionary theory, the two authors imply that the five styles are not equal phases in a smooth evolution but that the first three styles and the last two differ fundamentally in intention and visual quality and that they should be redefined as representing two essential decorative "modes."[145]

The problem of dating Styles IV and V has been partially resolved by the discovery of Tomb no. 5 at Anyang—the only known Shang royal burial to have escaped robbers. Belonging to Fu Hao, a consort of King Wu Ding (*ca.* 1200-1181 B.C.),[146] the tomb yielded hundreds of bronze vessels decorated with large *taotie*, many of which are relief images that surface from a densely incised ground with force and vividness (Fig. 1.45).[147] The effort to create tangible plastic images was coupled with the wide application of vertical flanges that protrude from the surfaces of a bronze.[148] The visual psychology behind this device was apparently to create a kind of picture frame. With the help of flanges, even a round vessel appears as an assemblage of rectangular units containing masks and half-masks as the foci of the viewer's concentration (Fig. 1.46).[149] Bronze vessels have become bearers of images and were sometimes even transformed into three-dimensional images (Fig. 1.47).

中‘生长’出整齐划一的动物性形式”。[143] 贝格利将 IV 式纹样的发明解释为“一个大创新，它利用原有的趋势造成一次突破，使之发展为更为复杂的装饰”。[144] 尽管这些陈述仍然局限于进化论，但两位学者都暗指五种风格并不是等距离地平缓演进，其中前三种和后两种在意图和视觉效果上都有根本的差别。在我看来，这种差别应当被重新认定为表现了两种不同性质装饰的“样式”。[145]

安阳小屯殷墟 5 号墓的发现，部分地解释了 IV 和 V 式纹样的断代问题。该墓是目前所见唯一没有被盗掘的商王室墓葬，其墓主为商王武丁（约前 1200—前 1181 年）的配偶妇好。[146] 墓中出土了数以百计的装饰有巨型饕餮纹的青铜器，其中许多是从细密的地纹上突起的鲜明有力的浮雕形象［图 1.45］。[147] 在创造这些强有力且富有立体感的形象的同时，从器表突起的扉棱也被广泛采用。[148] 这种设计背后的视觉心理，显然是要制作一种“画框”。有了这些扉棱，即便是一个圆形器物的表面也被转化为多个矩形的集合体，而矩形中的兽面和半兽面也正是观者目光的焦点［图 1.46］。[149] 到这一步，青铜器已经成为动物形象的载体，有时器物本身甚至转化为三维的动物形象［图 1.47］。

Fig. 1.45. Bronze square *yi* vessel. Late Shang dynasty. Late 2nd millennium B.C.

H. 36.6 cm. Excavated in Yinxu Tomb no. 5 at Anyang, Henan province.

Museum of Chinese History, Beijing.

图 1.45 青铜方彝。商代晚期，前 2 千纪晚期。高 36.6 厘米。河南安阳殷墟 5 号墓出土。中国国家博物馆藏。

Fig. 1.46. Bronze *bu* vessel. Late Shang dynasty. Late 2nd millennium B.C.

H. 42.5 cm. Excavated in 1959 at Zhaizishan, Ningxiang, Hunan province.

Hunan Provincial Museum.

图 1.46 青铜瓿。商代晚期，前 2 千纪晚期。高 42.5 厘米。1959 年湖南宁乡出土。湖南省博物馆藏。

Fig. 1.47. Bronze *gong* vessel. Late Shang dynasty. Late 2nd millennium B.C. H. 24.8 cm. Harvard Art Museums, Cambridge, Mass.

图 1.47 青铜觥。商代晚期，前 2 千纪晚期。高 24.8 厘米。麻省剑桥，哈佛大学美术馆藏。

a

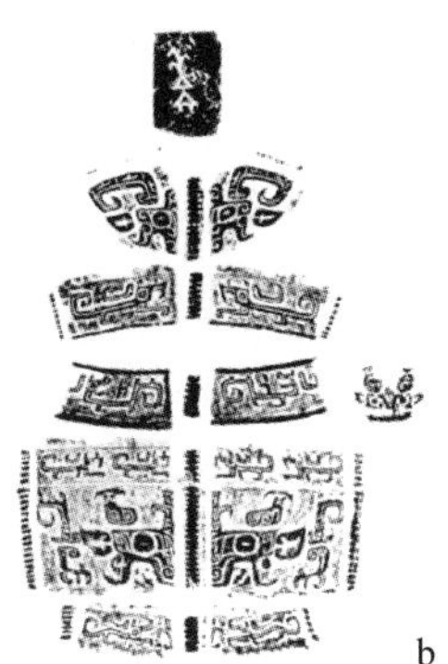

b

Fig. 1.48. (a) Bronze *you* vessel. Late Shang dynasty. Late 2nd millennium B.C. H. 24.6 cm. Palace Museum in Taipei. (b) Decoration and inscription. Ink rubbing.

图 1.48 （a）青铜卣。商代晚期，前 2 千纪晚期。高 24.6 厘米。台北故宫博物院藏。（b）装饰纹样与铭文。拓片。

There has been a persistent scholarly impulse to attempt to define or identify the *taotie*. But in my opinion, late Shang art never recognized a "standard" *taotie*, only endless variations. However forceful and demanding, late Shang zoomorphs are not static symbols. They combine
features from different animal species but never become naturalistic 053
representations or formulated icons. Even on a single vessel, the *taotie* assume different forms and are shown from various angles (Figs. 1.48a, b);[150] and even pairs of vessels never bear identical decoration. In analyzing the bronzes from Fu Hao's tomb, the Chinese archaeologist

许多学者一直抱有认定或识别“饕餮”的愿望。但我认为晚商艺术中从未有过一个“标准的”饕餮，而只有无穷无尽的变体。不管多么威严有力，晚商的动物形象从来不是一种固定的符号。它们集合了各种动物的特征，但从未流于一种自然主义的描写或定型化的偶像。即使在单独一件器物上，饕餮也呈现出不同的形式，展示着其多变的角度［图 1.48］；[150] 甚至成对的器物也装饰着不同的纹样。

Zheng Zhenxiang was puzzled by what she considered a peculiar phenomenon: "In the pairs and sets of vessels. . . the overall body of decoration is basically the same, but there are always slight differences of detail in the decor and the background designs. [But] the forms of the characters in the inscriptions on the paired vessels are similar, as if written by one person. . . . The question of why the decorative designs manifest differences still requires further investigation."[151]

The answer to Zheng's question is found in the metamorphic nature of Shang decorative art. What distinguishes late Shang bronze decoration from the previous stage is that the *metamorphosis* now occurs primarily in iconography, not in style. In other words, it is the form of an image that is protean and constantly changing, although all the variations may be rendered in a single style. It is likely that these metamorphic images—not only molded on bronzes but also painted and carved everywhere in a "sacred" place—functioned to "animate" inanimate material—a piece of metal or wood.[152] Similar beliefs existed in many traditions in the ancient world, along with a universal belief in the magic power of eyes or masks.[153] These varying images seem to attest to a painstaking effort to create metaphors for an intermediate state between the supernatural and reality—something that one could depict but not portray.

THE TRIUMPH OF WORDS

We have seen that three basic elements of a monument—material, shape, and decor—in turn played important roles in the development of bronze art. This art again changed orientation from the end of the Shang through the Western Zhou: symbolic imagery gradually declined, and the literary values of ritual bronzes were heightened. The fourth and last signifier of *liqi*, inscription, now became the most important marker of monumentality in bronze art.

055 As mentioned earlier, the "emblem" as a primitive form of inscription had appeared on Liangzhu ritual jades (Fig. 1.29). Inscriptions on mid-Shang bronze vessels are also emblems in animal shapes (Fig. 1.49a, b);

as an emblem, such an inscription identifies the clan or lineage that owned the ritual object.[154] By the early thirteenth century B.C., however, a person's name could be added to specify an attribution further.[155] This seemingly minor modification testifies to a major change in the significance of a bronze ritual object: instead of being linked to a group of

关于最后这个特性，中国学者郑振香在研究妇好墓青铜器时发现以下值得注意的现象："在成对的或成套的器物中……器身总体的装饰基本上是相同的，但细部的装饰格调和地纹的设计总有些许的差别。（但是）成对器物铭文的字体是相同的，似乎出自同一人之手……装饰设计差异背后的原因仍需要更深入的探讨。"[151]

郑振香提出的问题可以在商代装饰艺术的变形性中找到答案。晚商青铜器装饰与以前时期最大的差别在于，晚商的变形主要发生在图像中，而不是在风格上。换言之，此时的变形表现为形象的千变万化，尽管所有这些变化可以用一种风格来表现。这些变异的形象不仅被铸造在青铜上，而且也被描画和雕刻在所有"神圣"的场合，这些形象很可能为那些没有生命的材料——一块金属或一段木头——灌注了活力。[152] 古代人们普遍相信眼睛和兽面具有神奇的力量，类似的观念也存在于世界其他的许多文化传统中。[153] 商代铜器上变化多端的形象似乎在努力创造出一种隐喻，以代表一个介于超自然世界和现实世界之间的中间层面——一个可以用形象隐喻但却无法具体图绘的层面。

5. 文字的胜利

以上的讨论显示出，在青铜艺术的早期发展过程中，纪念碑的三种基本要素——材料、形状和装饰——依次扮演了重要的角色。从商末至西周，青铜艺术的定位又发生了变化：象征性的形象逐渐衰落，青铜礼器的文学价值不断提高。礼器的最后一个要素——铭文——这时变成了青铜艺术中纪念碑性最重要的标志。

如上所述，作为铭文原始形式的"徽志"早在良渚文化玉礼器上就已出现［图 1.29］。商代中期青铜器上的铭文也呈现为动物的外形［图 1.49］；作为徽志，这种铭文标志着礼器拥有者的氏族和血统。[154] 然而，直到公元前 13 世纪初，个人的名字才被加进来。[155] 这一看似微小的调整却意味着青铜礼器意义上的一次大变化：青铜

people (as indicated by a shared emblem), the bronze was now associated with a specific person (as indicated by his or her name). Such an association could be established by an individual, in which case the "living name" of a person would be inscribed on a vessel, or by descendents, in which case the "temple name" of a person would be inscribed instead. (During the Shang, a noble man or woman had a "living name" while alive; after death, his or her spirit received a "temple name" in ancestral worship.) David N. Keightley explains this second practice:

> It is well-known that some late Shang and early Zhou ancestors were given temple names, such as "Father Jia" and "Grandmother Keng," and that these temple names employed the same "heavenly stems" (*tiangan*) given to the ten days of the Shang week, *jia*, *yi*, *bing*, *ding*, and so forth. Further, we know that Father (Mother, Grandfather, or Grandmother) Jia received cult on a *jia* day, the first day of the week, Father Yi on an *yi* day, the second day of the week, and so on. There were ten *gan* stems available for naming ancestors, just as there were ten days to the Shang week.[156]

a

b

Fig. 1.49. (a) Bronze *lei* vessel. Mid-Shang dynasty. Mid-2nd millennium B.C. H. 25 cm. Excavated at Baijiazhuang, Zhengzhou, Henan province. (b) Emblem on the *lei*. Ink rubbing.

图 1.49 （a）青铜罍。商代中期，前 2 千纪中期。高 25 厘米。河南郑州白家庄出土。（b）罍上的徽志。拓片。

Fig. 1.50. Inscriptions on bronzes from Yinxu Tomb no. 5. Late Shang dynasty. *Ca.* 13th century B.C. (a) "Si Tu Mu." (b) "Si Mu Xin." (c) "Fu Hao." Ink rubbings.

图1.50　殷墟5号墓青铜器上的铭文。商代晚期，约公元前13世纪。（a）"司㚸母"。（b）"司母辛"。（c）"妇好"。拓片。

Inscriptions on bronzes found in Fu Hao's tomb include both types of names: among the 190 inscribed bronzes, 31 bear "temple names"—"Queen Tu Mother" (Si Tu Mu) (Fig. 1.50a) or "Queen Mother Xin" (Si

器在这一时期与一个特定的人（以其名字为标志）而不是一群人（以一个共同的徽志为标志）联系起来。这样的联系有时可以通过其本人建立起来，即把他的"生称"铭刻在青铜器上；有时可以通过其子孙建立起来，即把过世祖先的"庙号"铭刻在青铜器上。吉德炜对后者进行了如下解释：

> 众所周知，一些晚商和周初的祖先有其庙号，如"父甲"和"妣庚"之类。这些庙号都使用同样的"天干"，即商代一旬中的10天，包括甲、乙、丙、丁，等等。另外，我们还知道父甲（或母甲、祖甲、妣甲）在甲日，即一旬的第一天接受祭祀，父乙在乙日，即第二天接受祭祀，依次类推。庙号中的天干有10个字，正如商代一旬有10天一样。[156]

妇好墓所发现的青铜器铭文中包含有两类名字：在190件有铭铜器中，31件有"庙号"——"司㚸母"［图1.50a］或"司母辛"［图1.50b］；

Mu Xin) (Fig. 1.50b); and 109 bear the name Fu Hao (Fig. 1.50c), which is well documented in the oracle-bone inscriptions as the "living name" of a consort of King Wu Ding.[157] The extraordinary number of the Fu Hao bronzes, which include some huge vessels and axes, seems to indicate that around the time of Wu Ding's reign many bronzes were made not
056 for the dead but for living members of the royal house as symbols of their social status and power. Nevertheless, ritual vessels with "temple names" soon became dominant, and this dominance demonstrates that bronzes increasingly served ancestral worship and "commemorative" purposes.[158] The nature of such temple-name inscriptions is unmistakable: the emphasis lies on the person to whom the bronze was dedicated, not on the person who dedicated the bronze.[159] This emphasis is clearly indicated by the omission of the commissioner's name. Even when the verb *zuo* (to make) was added and the inscription became "To make this precious ritual vessel for a certain ancestor (or ancestress)" (Fig. 1.51),[160] the presence of the living person who dedicated the bronze was still implicit.

The inclusion of the dedicator's name in an inscription, therefore, signified another important change in the meaning of the text, the intention behind the commissioning of the ritual object, and

Fig. 1.51. Inscription on Mu Wu *gong*. Late Shang dynasty. 12th-11th centuries B.C. Excavated in 1975 at Xiazhuang, Linxian, Henan province. Linxian County Museum. Ink rubbing.

图 1.51 母戊觥铭文。商代晚期，前 12—前 11 世纪。1975 年河南林县夏庄出土。林州市文物管理所藏。拓片。

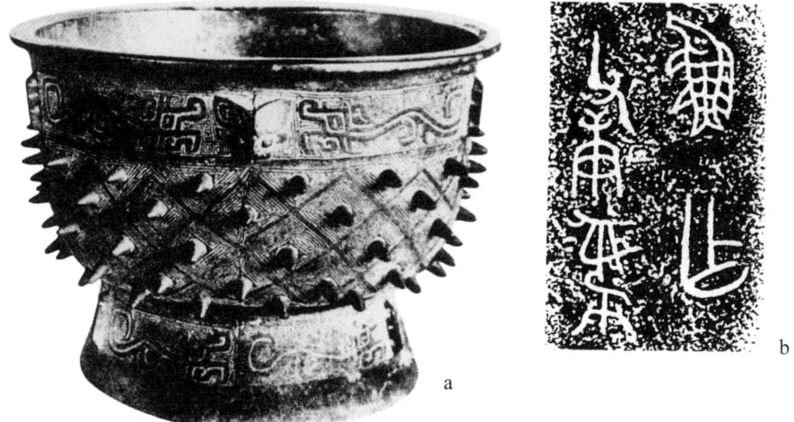

Fig. 1.52. (a) Yu *yu*. Late Shang dynasty. 11th century B.C. (b) Inscription. Ink rubbing.
图 1.52 （a）鱼盂。商代晚期，前 11 世纪。（b）铭文。拓片。

the “monumentality” of the bronze. An inscription reading “[I,] X, commissioned this precious ritual bronze for [my deceased] ancestor Y” (Figs. 1.52a, b) not only states the purpose of the dedication but also

109 件有“妇好”［图 1.50c］。妇好之名见于甲骨文，应是“生称”，她是武丁的配偶。[157] 有妇好铭文的青铜器数量相当多，包括大型的容器和钺，这似乎说明在武丁时代前后，许多青铜器并不是为死者，而是为王室中活着的成员制作的，这些器具是其社会地位和权力的象征。然而，铸有“庙号”的礼器很快成为主流，这种变化说明青铜器越来越多地被用于祖先祭祀，并且具有了纪念的目的。[158] 这种庙号铭文的性质十分清楚：它所强调的是被纪念者，而不是奉献这些铜器的人。[159] 这种强调是通过省略做器者的名字而清楚地表达出来的。即使当动词“作”字加进铭文，形成“作父（或母）× 宝尊彝”［图 1.51］的格式时，[160] 奉献这些铜器的生者仍然隐而不彰。

因此，在铭文中包括奉献者的名字意味着另一个重要变化，涉及文字的含义，制作这些青铜器的意图以及这些青铜礼器的纪念碑性。记载“X 作父 Y 彝”［图 1.52］的铭文不仅表明了奉献的目的，

makes clear that it was X who conducted the dedication. The memory the ritual vessel and its inscription bears thus became double-edged: when used in ancestral rituals, it would remind future generations of X as well as Y.

This change ushered in a type of "narrative" inscription, a practice that became popular toward the end of the Shang dynasty during the reigns of the last two Shang kings (Di Yi and Di Xin).[161] The emphasis of the inscription shifted further to the reason for an ancestral dedication. In most cases this was a courtier's receipt of awards from the king or his superiors. The courtier's worldly achievements thus led to his making the bronze vessel for his ancestors, and the religious event (the ancestral dedication) was the result of a non-religious event (an award to the courtier). A typical example reads: "On the day *guizi* the King awarded [me], *xiaochen* Yi, ten strings of cowries, which [I] then used to make this ritual vessel for [my deceased] mother Gui. It was in the King's sixth *si*, during the *rong* sacrificial cycle, in the fourth month. [Emblem]" (Figs. 1.53a, b).

It is clear that the primary focus of such inscriptions is no longer ancestral dedication, but the commemoration of the worldly glory of its commissioner. This is perhaps why the date of the receipt of the award is always carefully recorded. Moreover, we find that such commemorative bronzes were often related to war and royal sacrifices—the two most important state activities in Bronze Age China.[162] Sometimes awards were conferred on officials during royal sacrifices:[163] "On the day *bingwu* the King awarded [me], Shu Si Zi, twenty strings of cowries at the X Temple, which I then used to make this precious *ding* tripod for [my deceased] father Gui. It was when the King held the X-sacrifice in the Great Hall at the temple in the ninth month. [Emblem]" (Figs. 1.54a, b).[164]

The king mentioned in this inscription is perhaps the last Shang ruler, Di Xin. The same king also frequently conferred awards on his ministers during his unfortunate military expedition to the Ren Fang southeast of the Shang, and these grants consequently led to the casting of commemorative bronzes.[165] But instead of introducing an inscription with a record of the award, these bronze texts often begin by mentioning the military campaign and thus assume a more obvious "archival" quality:[166]

同时也说明这是 X，而不是别人所作的奉献。这样，礼器及其铭文所承载的记忆就变成了两个方面：当这些铜器在祭祖仪式中使用时，它们使家族的子孙在回想 Y 的同时也想起 X。

这一变化导致一种"叙事性"铭文的出现，于晚商最后的两个王（帝乙和帝辛）在位时期流行开来。[161] 这种铭文的重点进而转移到祭祖的原因上，通常的情况是作器者从王或上司那里得到奖赏。如此一来，铭文所记述的是一个朝臣基于他在现世的成就而为祖先制作了青铜礼器，一个宗教性事件（向祖先的奉献）成为一个非宗教性事件（受到奖赏）的结果。一条典型的铭文是："癸子，王易（赐）小臣邑贝十朋，用乍（作）母癸隮（尊）彝。隹（唯）王六祀，肜日才（在）四月。（族徽）"（大意：在癸子这一天，王赏赐了我——小臣邑——十串（朋）贝，我用来为我亡故的母亲癸制作了这件青铜礼器。时在王进行第六祀，在四月肜日。）［图 1.53］

很清楚，这种铭文主要的用意不再是对祖先的奉献，而是对其奉献者现世荣耀的夸赞。这也许就是为何要将受到奖赏的时间写得清清楚楚的原因。不仅如此，我们发现这种有纪念意义的铜器还常常与战争和王室祭祀相关——这两件事正是中国青铜时代国家的头等大事。[162] 不少奖赏是在王室举行祭祀时进行的，[163] 如《戍嗣子鼎》铭载："丙午，王商（赏）戍嗣子贝廿朋，才（在）阑宗，用乍（作）父癸宝（鼎），隹（唯）王䣄阑大室，才（在）九月。（族徽）"（大意：在丙午这天，王在宗庙明堂大室，赏赐给戍嗣子贝二十朋，戍嗣子因受荣宠，作了这件祭祀父亲的宝鼎。）［图 1.54］[164]

这条铭文中提到的王可能是商代最后一个王帝辛。这位商王曾失败地向东南用兵，远征人方，在此过程中，他经常赏赐其臣属，这些事例也被记录在青铜器上。[165] 但是这些青铜铭文开头所提到的总是军事征伐，而不是册命，更具有"历史档案"价值。[166]

"The King came to conquer the Ren Fang. . . . The King awarded [me], archivist Ban, cowries, which I then used to make this sacrificial vessel for
057 [my deceased] father Ji. [Emblem]" (Fig. 1.55).

Fig. 1.53. (a) Yi *jia*. Bronze. Late Shang dynasty. 11th century B.C. H. 45.9 cm. St. Louis Art Museum. (b) Inscription. Ink rubbing.

图 1.53 （a）乙斝。青铜。商代晚期，前 11 世纪。高 45.9 厘米。圣路易斯美术馆藏。（b）铭文。拓片。

Fig. 1.54. (a) Shu Si Zi *ding*. Bronze. Late Shang dynasty. 11th century B.C. H. 48 cm. Excavated in 1959 at Hougang, Anyang, Henan province. Institute of Archaeology, CASS. (b) Inscription. Ink rubbing.

图 1.54 （a）戍嗣子鼎。青铜。商代晚期，前 11 世纪。高 48 厘米。1959 年河南安阳后冈出土。中国社会科学院考古研究所藏。（b）铭文。拓片。

a

b

Fig. 1.55. (a) Zuoce Ban *yan*. Bronze. Late Shang dynasty. 11th century B.C. Museum of Chinese History, Beijing. (b) Inscription. Ink rubbing.
图 1.55 （a）作册班甗。青铜。商代晚期，前 11 世纪。中国国家博物馆藏。（b）铭文。拓片。

The implication of the inscription thus becomes more complex: in addition to recording the courtier's merit and his consequent dedication of the ritual bronze, the king and his activities become a major focus of the inscribed texts. It is understood that the bronze was made only because its commissioner had received an award and that this award was conferred only because the king had held an important ceremony or military campaign. Bronze inscriptions thus developed toward elaborating the causes of the religious dedication. Sometimes these causes even became the sole content of an inscription. The text cast on a rhinoceros-shaped

“王宜人（夷）方……王商（赏）乍（作）册般贝，用乍（作）父己尊。（族徽）”（大意：王征伐人（夷）方……王赏赐了担任作册的般（我）贝，我用来为故去的父亲己制作了这件尊。）[图 1.55]

铭文的含义因此变得更加复杂：除了要体现朝臣的功绩及其随后对死者奉献礼器之举，商王及其活动成为铭文最主要的一个焦点。可以这样理解，这类青铜器之所以被制作是因为它的制作者受到奖赏，而行赏的原因则是因为王举行了一次重要的仪式或者进行了一次军事征伐。青铜铭文因此变得越来越注重于描写宗教奉献背后的原因。有时某种原因甚至变成铭文唯一的内容。如旧金山亚洲美术馆所藏

vessel in the Asian Art Museum of San Francisco records only the king's
058 expedition and the award received by a courtier named Yu: there is no ancestral dedication, and the vessel is purely commemorative: "On the day *dingzi* the King inspected X-place. The King presented [me], *xiaochen* Yu, cowries from that place. It was during the King's expedition against the Ren Fang. It was in the King's fifteenth *si*, a day in the *yu* sacrificial cycle" (Figs. 1.56a, b).

These late Shang inscriptions reveal a crucial change in the monumentality of ritual bronzes. They also pertain to the development of ritual bronzes in two ways. As Virginia Kane has pointed out, they provided "important late Shang precedents for the many similar features subsequently found in the inscriptions of the Early and Middle Western Chou [Zhou] period."[167] Moreover, the change in inscription was associated with important innovations in late Shang bronze decoration, which again strongly influenced the further development of bronze art during the Zhou. The following discussion thus proceeds from two angles: the development of inscription and the stylistic transformation of bronze decoration.

Fig. 1.56. (a) Rhinoceros-shaped *zun* vessel. Bronze. Late Shang dynasty. 11th century B.C. H. 22.9 cm. Said to be from Liangshan, Shandong province. Asian Art Museum of San Francisco, The Avery Brundage Collection (B60 B1+). (b) Inscription. Ink rubbing.

图1.56 （a）犀牛尊。青铜。商代晚期，前 11 世纪。高 22.9 厘米。传出山东梁山。旧金山亚洲美术馆藏，艾弗里·吉德兰布藏品（B60 B1+）。（b）铭文。拓片。

First, although often much longer, Western Zhou inscriptions grew from their Shang precedents. Many early Zhou (*ca.* 1050-975 B.C.) examples focus on political events, among which the most important ones are King Wu's conquest of the Shang, King Cheng's construction of the capital Chengzhou and his military campaigns to suppress rebellions in the east, and King Zhao's military expedition against southern uprisings.[168] Other inscriptions, again following the Shang examples, document royal sacrifices.[169] A majority of lengthy Western Zhou bronze texts, however, record "investiture" ceremonies routinely held in the Zhou royal temple, during which officials were given titles, properties, and status symbols by the king.[170] As the Chinese historian Chen Hanping

犀尊上的铭文仅仅记录了商王的远征和小臣艅受到册命的事，而没有记载对祖先的奉献，这件铜器的意义因此是纯粹记功性质的："丁子，王省夒且，王易（赐）小臣艅夒贝。隹（唯）王来正（征）人方。隹（唯）王十祀又五，肜日。"（大意：在丁子这一天，王巡查了夒且这个地方。王在这里赏赐了我小臣艅贝。这时，王正在征伐人方。时在王进行第十五祀，在肜日。）［图 1.56］

这些晚商铭文显示出青铜礼器纪念碑性一个至关紧要的变化，与青铜器的两种发展途径有关。首先，正如弗吉尼亚·凯恩所指出的那样，这些"晚商铭文为后来许多具有类似特征的西周早中期铭文提供了可以沿用的先例"。[167] 此外，铭文中的这个变化也和晚商青铜器装饰中的重要变革密切相关，而这一变革又深刻影响了周代青铜艺术的进一步发展。因此，我们接下来的讨论将沿着两个方面展开：铭文的发展和青铜装饰风格的转变。

尽管西周铭文通常比商代铭文要长得多，但其来源仍必须追溯到商代。许多周代初年（约前 1050—前 975 年）的铭文往往重点记录政治事件，最重要的是武王征商、成王建都成周以及镇压东方反抗、昭王平定南方叛乱等历史事件。[168] 还有一些铭文因袭商代的先例，记录了王室的祭祀。[169] 然而，大多数西周时期的长篇铭文则是记载了周王室宗庙中举行的"受命"仪式，以及在这类仪式中官员被王授予封号、财物以及身份象征物的实况。[170] 中国学者陈汉平

recently demonstrated in an exhaustive study of such documents, this type of inscription became popular during the middle Western Zhou (*ca.* 975-875 B.C.).[171] The political and ritual events considered important enough to record in earlier inscriptions disappear from such writings, which were now stereotypical in both content and format. The following
059 inscription repeated on three ritual bronzes commissioned by an official named Li (Figs. 1.57a, b) exemplifies the convention:

> In the first quarter of the eighth month, the King arrived at the Temple of Zhou. The Duke of Mu guided me, Li, into the Middle Court, to stand facing north. The King commanded the attendants to present me with scarlet cloth, black jade, and a bridle, saying: "By these tokens, govern the Royal Officers and the Three Ministers—the Seneschal, the Master of Horse, and the Master of Artisans." The King commanded me, saying: "For the time being, take charge of the lieutenants of the Six Regiments [the army of the West] and of the Eight Regiments [the army of the eastern capital, Chengzhou]." I, Li, bowed to the floor and made bold to answer that I would proclaim the King's trust by casting precious vessels for my gentle ancestor Yi Gong. I said, "The Son of Heaven's works defend our empire everlastingly! I prostrate myself before him and vow to be worthy of my forebears' faithful service."[172]

Regulations for such ceremonies can be found in the *Book of Rites*.[173] The author of this text also recorded an exemplary "investiture" inscription and explained the idea behind casting such texts on ritual bronzes: "By casting such a discourse on a ritual vessel, the inscriber makes himself famous and proves that he is entitled to sacrifice to his ancestors. In the celebration of his ancestors he exalts his filial piety. That he himself appears after them is natural. And in the clear showing of all this to future generations, he is giving instruction."[174] This author thus defined "inscription" (*ming*) as *ziming*—"to make oneself known" or "self-identification."[175] As we have seen, this idea of "making oneself known" can be traced back to the personal names in late Shang bronze inscriptions. A major difference in a Zhou "investiture" text, however, is that such a document, with its exhaustive description of the ritual, has become a truly personal record. Shorter inscriptions still existed during the Zhou, but unlike Shang examples of similar length, which

最近详细研究了这类铭文，指出受命铭文在西周中期（约前975—前875年）得到流行，[171] 以前业已出现的记录政治和礼仪事件的铭文在内容和格式上都变得极为程式化。下面的这则铭文重复出现在三件由盠制作的青铜器上［图1.57］，即是这种程式化铭文的一个例子：

> 唯八月初吉王各（格）于周庙。穆公又（佑）盠立（位）于中廷，北鄉（向）。王册令（命）尹易（锡）盠赤市、幽亢（黄）、攸勒，曰：用𤔲（司）六自（师）王行，参有𤔲（司）：𤔲（司）土（徒）、𤔲（司）马、𤔲（司）工（空）。王令（命）盠曰：䵼𤔲（司）六自（师）眔八自（师）埶。盠拜䭫首，敢对䫘（扬）王休，用乍（作）朕文且（祖）益公宝尊彝。盠曰：天子不叚（遐）不（丕）其（基），万年保我万邦。盠敢拜䭫首曰：剌（烈）朕身，（赓）朕先宝事。[172]
>
> （大意：八月初吉，王来到周庙。在穆公的引领下，我［盠］进入中廷，面北而立。王命尹赐给我深红色的布匹、黑色的玉器和攸勒［马具］，说：你用这些作为标志，统领王室的六师以及三有司，即司徒、司马、司空。王命令我说：［今后］你统领六师和八师。我跪拜，斗胆地说：我一定显扬王的信赖。因此我为我尊敬的祖先益公制作了这宝贵的礼器。我说：天子的宏图大业，将保证我们的帝国万年永固！我俯身于他的面前，立誓承担起祖先的忠诚于王室的事业。）

在《礼记》一书中可以读到关于这些仪式规范化的记载。[173] 这些文字的作者也提到了程式化的"册命"铭文并且解释了铭文背后的思想："而酌之祭器，自成其名焉，以祀其先祖者也。显扬先祖，所以崇孝也。身比焉，顺也；明示后世，教也。"[174] 作者将"铭"定义为"自名"——也就是"使自己扬名"或"自我识定"的意思。[175] 上文提到，"扬名"的思想可以追溯到晚商青铜器所铸的人名。但是周代"册命"铭文的一个重要差别在于，这种详细记载了礼仪过程的铭文已经变成一种真正的个人化记录。虽然简短的铭文在周代依然存在，但如果说

a b

Fig. 1.57. (a) Li *fangyi*. Bronze. Late 11th century B.C. H. 22.8 cm. Excavated in 1976 at Lintong, Shaanxi province. Museum of Chinese History. (b) Inscription. Ink rubbing.

图1.57 （a）盠方彝。青铜。西周中期，前 11 世纪。高 22.8 厘米。1976 年陕西临潼县出土。中国国家博物馆藏。（b）铭文。拓片。

emphasize the dedicatee rather than dedicator, they often omit the ancestral dedication and contain only the name of the commissioner of the vessel. Although this may seem to be a return to the ancient practice of inscribing one's "living name" on vessels (as exemplified by the Fu Hao bronzes), short inscriptions during the late Western Zhou resulted from the general decline of ancestor worship.

The development of bronze inscription from the late Shang to the end of the Western Zhou was closely related to, and to a certain extent determined, the appearance of ritual bronzes. Significantly, the innovation of Shang "narrative" inscriptions was coupled with a dramatic change in decorative style: many vessels bearing such texts are not embellished with large, powerful *taotie*. Instead, these vessels are "plain" and "sober," often decorated only with narrow bands reminiscent of mid-Shang designs (Figs. 1.58a, b). The contours of the vessels are smooth and gentle, lacking protruding flanges as image frames. Without ruling out the possibility that this style derived from pottery wares or was associated with a particular group of patrons, I strongly suggest an intimate relationship between inflating inscription and deflating decoration—two phenomena

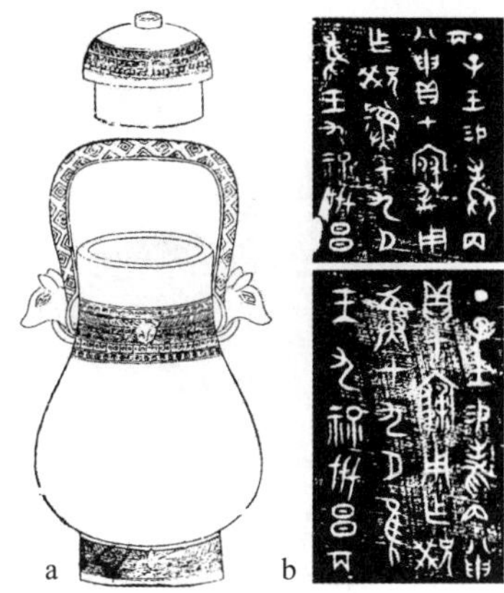

Fig. 1.58. (a) Bronze *you* vessel. Late Shang dynasty. 11th century B.C. (b) Inscription. Woodblock reconstruction.

图 1.58 （a）青铜卣。商代晚期，前 11 世纪。（b）铭文。木版复原。

that together attest to the growing importance of words over images. It is perhaps still too early to estimate the absolute importance and far-reaching influence of this change in the history of Chinese art and
culture in general, but a number of clues may lead us to see its multiple 061
manifestations in art, religion, and literature.

商代短铭的主要目的是突出受奉献者而不是奉献者，那么周代短铭则经常省略对祖先奉献的纪录，而只标出做器者的名字。尽管这种现象可以被看作对在青铜器上铭记“生称”做法（如妇好青铜器所见）的恢复，但是实际上西周晚期短铭是祖先崇拜日渐衰落的结果。

商代晚期到西周末年青铜器铭文的发展与礼器形态和装饰的变化紧密相关，前者甚至在一定程度上决定了后者。值得注意的是，商代“叙事性”铭文的兴起和装饰风格中一种戏剧性的变化同步发生：许多带有这类铭文的青铜器并没有装饰大型、强有力的饕餮，这些器物的外表朴素而庄重，通常只装饰窄长的花纹带［图 1.58］，具有商代中期纹样的风格。器物的轮廓线也是流畅而雅致，不见那些作为图像框格的扉棱。我们不能排除这种风格产生于陶器的影响，或者与某一特殊赞助人集团的可能关系，但是需要特别指出的是，这种渐长的铭文和简缩的装饰（这两种现象证明了文字的重要性日益超过图像）之间的确有着密切的关系。确切估计这种变化对于中国艺术和文化的重要性和深远影响也许还为时过早，但是也有若干线索使我们看到它在中国艺术、宗教和文学等领域多方面的表现。

Fig. 1.59. Bronze *zun* vessel (Huber's Style Va). Late Shang dynasty. 12th-11th centuries B.C. H. 36.8 cm. Freer Gallery of Art, Washington, D.C.

图 1.59 青铜尊（胡博 Va 式风格）。商代晚期，前 11 世纪。高 36.8 厘米。华盛顿，弗利尔美术馆藏。

Fig. 1.60. Bronze *you* vessel (Huber's Classic Style). Late Shang dynasty. 11th century B.C. H. 36.5 cm. Freer Gallery of Art, Washington, D.C.

图 1.60 青铜卣（胡博古典风格）。商代晚期，前 11 世纪。高 36.5 厘米。华盛顿，弗利尔美术馆藏。

Fig. 1.61. Bronze *gong* vessel (Huber's Post-Classic Style). Late Shang dynasty. 11th century B.C. H. 22.9 cm. Asian Art Museum of San Francisco, The Avery Brundage Collection.

图 1.61 青铜觥（胡博后古典风格）。商代晚期，前 11 世纪。高 22.9 厘米。旧金山亚洲美术馆藏，艾弗里・布兰德吉藏品。

In an excellent study of late Shang bronze art, Louisa Huber observes that after the "golden age" of this art during the Wu Ding period, "the inventory of motifs ceases to grow. . . and thereafter becomes relatively conventional and standardized."[176] From this conservative movement appeared what she calls Style V(a) and the Classic Style. In Style V(a), uniform spiral patterns cover both the main zoomorphic motifs and the background, and a *taotie*, now disassembled, loses its sculptured image (Fig. 1.59).[177] The Classic Style, on the other hand, continued to employ large, plastic zoomorphs, but "the designs are neither charged with the energy of the Wu Ding pieces nor can they be considered innovative, insofar as the repertory of designs has become quite restricted" (Fig. 1.60).[178] These two styles anticipated the further patternization of bronze decor toward the end of the Shang: the *taotie* became even more conventional and mannered in a Post-Classic Style (Fig. 1.61); a kind of "plain" bronze appeared with only narrow bands of geometric patterns (Fig. 1.58a); and stark high-relief *taotie* protruded above the plain background (Fig. 1.62).

在一篇关于晚商青铜艺术的精彩论文中，胡博注意到在商代青铜艺术的“黄金时代”武丁时期以后，“(装饰纹样)母题的总量不再增加……而是变得相对因循和定型化”[176]。从这种守旧趋势中出现了她所说的 Va 式风格和古典风格。在 Va 式风格中，旋转的云雷纹覆盖着动物形的主体纹样和地纹，而饕餮却被分解，失去了原来的雕刻性形象［图 1.59］。[177] 另一方面，虽然古典风格持续着大型的具有整体感的动物形象，但是“由于设计题材的范围已经变得备受局限，所以这种风格既没有武丁时代作品的活力，也不具有任何创造性”［图 1.60］。[178] 这两种风格是晚商青铜装饰变得更为定型化的先声：在一种后古典式风格中，饕餮变得更为拘谨和矫饰［图 1.61］。同时，一种只有狭窄几何装饰带的“素面”青铜器也出现了［图 1.58a］；在另一种情况下，拘谨的高浮雕饕餮纹凸现于平素的背景上［图 1.62］。

Fig. 1.62. Bronze *you* vessel. Late Shang dynasty. 12th-11th century B.C. H. 34.8 cm. Museum of Fine Arts, Boston.

图 1.62 青铜卣。商代晚期，前 12—前 11 世纪。高 34.8 厘米。波士顿美术馆藏。

Huber relates this conservative tendency in late Shang art to a contemporary change in ancestor worship summarized by Keightley as follows:

> The whole process of divination has become more artificial, more routine, less spontaneous, less dramatic, less important. . . . The entire scope of Shang divination, in fact, had become constricted remarkably by Period V [i.e., the reigns of the last two Shang kings] so that questions about many problematical matters of Period I [i.e., the Wu Ding period] universe, such as the weather, sickness, dreams, ancestral curses, requests for harvest. . . were rarely divined about, if at all. The bulk of Period V divination was concerned with three topics: the routine execution of the rigid sacrificial schedule, the ten-day period, and the king's hunts. . . . The changes no longer involved specific forecasts about what the ultra-human powers might do to man. The inscriptions record, as it were, the whispering of charms and wishes, a constant

bureaucratic murmur, forming a routine background of invocation to the daily life of the late Shang kings, now talking, perhaps, more to themselves than to the ultra-human powers. Optimistic ritual formula had replaced belief. . . . Man, rather than Ti and the ancestors, was thought to be increasingly capable of handling his own fate.[179]

Not coincidentally, we have found parallel changes in the monumentality of ritual art. As demonstrated earlier, the focus of some late Shang bronze inscriptions gradually shifted from the deity to the devotee, and narratives of worldly events replaced ancestral dedications. This style of inscription,

胡博将晚商艺术中这种守旧趋势与当时祖先崇拜的变化联系起来。吉德炜对这一变化做了如下总结：

> （在这个时期里，）占卜的整个过程变得更为造作，更为程序化，缺乏自发感和戏剧性，不再如以前那么重要……实际上，到第五期（即商代最后两个王在位的时期），商代占卜的范围明显缩小，所以从总体上来看，第一期（即武丁在位的时期）中有关世界和宇宙万物的许多疑问，诸如天气、疾病、梦、祖先的祸咒、对丰收的祈求……都被排除在占卜的范围之外。第五期的大量占卜涉及三个方面：例行公事地完成祭祀的程序、十天一旬的祭祀周期，以及商王的狩猎……通过这个变化，卜辞不再包括关于可能施加于人们头上的极端权力的特别预言。也许在这一时期，卜辞中话语的对象主要是人们自己，而不是那些拥有极端权力的主体。这些文字中似乎是充满了魔力和希望的低低细语，对稳定的官僚政治的窃窃私议，这一切构成了晚商诸王日常占卜的基本背景。乐观的礼仪程式取代了信仰……看来，人——而不是帝或祖先——掌握自身命运的能力正在增强。[179]

无独有偶，我们在礼仪美术的纪念碑性之中，也可以看到与之平行的变化。如上所述，许多晚商青铜器铭文的重心从神明逐步转向信众，关于世俗事件的叙述取代了对祖先的奉献。与晚商的青铜

as well as the late Shang art styles in decoration, continued into the
Zhou. This observation is reminiscent of an approach of ancient writers,
who persistently placed the Shang and Zhou cultures in opposition:
the Shang emphasized *zhi* or "material substance," whereas the Zhou
062 emphasized *wen* or "literary refinement": the Shang worshipped ancestral
ghosts, but the Zhou honored Heaven and people. Sarah Allan recently
suggested that the key to understanding the Shang-Zhou transition is
that the former's "myth tradition" was replaced by the latter's "historical
schemes."[180] In a broader historical scale my discussion agrees with these
interpretations and formulations, but this discussion also reveals that the
rigid separation of the Shang and Zhou may be artificial—many elements
thought to be characteristic of Zhou art and culture had emerged before
the Zhou conquered the Shang.

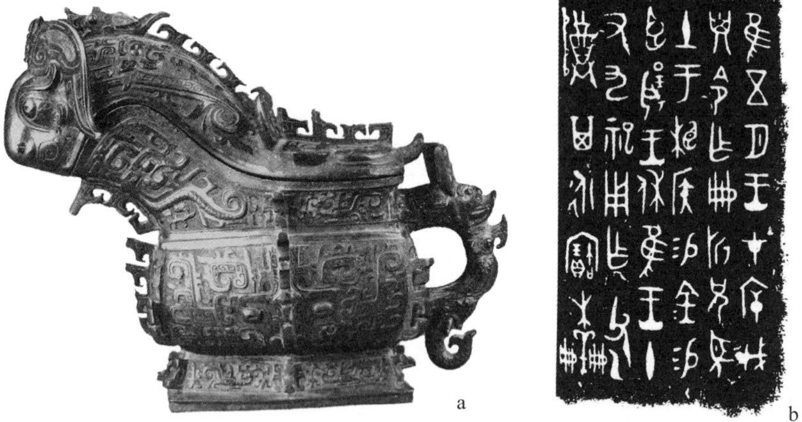

Fig. 1.63. (a) Zhe *gong*. Bronze. Early Western Zhou. 11th-10th centuries B.C. H. 28.7 cm. Excavated in 1976 from Zhuangbai Hoard no. 1, Fufeng, Shaanxi province. Fufeng Cultural Relics Administration. (b) Inscription. Ink rubbing.

图 1.63 （a）折觥。青铜。西周早期，前 11—前 10 世纪。高 28.7 厘米。1976 年陕西扶风庄白 1 号窖藏出土。扶风县文物管理所藏。（b）铭文。拓片。

Fig. 1.64. (a) Yanhou *yu*. Bronze. Early Western Zhou. Early 10th century B.C. H. 24 cm. Excavated in 1955 at Kezuo, Liaoning province. Museum of Chinese History, Beijing. (b) Decoration. Ink rubbing.

图 1.64 （a）燕侯盂。青铜。西周早期，前 10 世纪早期。高 24 厘米。1955 年辽宁喀左出土。中国国家博物馆藏。（b）纹样。拓片。

As many art historians have observed, Western Zhou bronze decoration generally evolved toward patternization.[181] This tendency was visible from the beginning of the dynasty: the late Shang "archaic" style prevailed, and a "flamboyant" style (Fig. 1.63a) began to exaggerate the

装饰风格一样，具有这种风格的铭文一直延续到周代。这一现象使人回想起古代学者们的思路，他们坚持将商和周的文化对立起来理解：商强调"质"，而周突出"文"；商尚鬼，而周更尊敬天和人。艾兰最近指出，理解商—周转变的关键在于前者的"神话传统"被后者的"历史系统"所取代。[180] 在一个宽阔的历史范围内，我在本章中的讨论同意此类解释和陈述，但需要补充的是，我的讨论也揭示出对商和周的硬性划分很可能过于人为——因为通常被认为是周的艺术和文化特征的许多典型因素早在周灭商之前就已出现。

正如许多美术史家所指出的那样，西周青铜器装饰逐步向图案化发展。[181] 这种趋势在西周初年就已比较明显：晚商"古风式"风格继续盛行，同时一种"浮华的"风格［图 1.63a］开始将先前动物

ornamental features of earlier zoomorphs. Ornate details were intensively produced; feather-like hooks became a universal vocabulary, added to every image and even reshaping flanges. A more important change was the dismissal of the frontal mask. The two dragons became divorced (Figs. 1.64a, b), and the result is a fundamental change in perception: there is no longer a visual center; instead, profile images guide the viewer's gaze around the surface of a vessel. Consequently, flanges as image frames were abolished. This new formula then provided a structure for the bird motifs popular during the mid-Western Zhou (Fig. 1.65). With their reversed heads, elaborate crests, and large and often detached tails, such birds form smooth S-shaped patterns that echo the carved outlines of the vessels. Both the abolition of a visual focus and the emphasis on ornamental details led to the further abstraction and fragmentation of zoomorphs. Finally, during the late Western Zhou, animal motifs
063 were dismembered into pure "patterns"—quills, eyes, and scales—often applied on a series of vessels of decreasing sizes (Fig. 1.66). The number of bronzes in such a set denoted the rank of its maker or owner.[182]

Fig. 1.65. Geng Ying *you*. Bronze. Mid-Western Zhou. 10th-9th centuries B.C. H. 24.8 cm. Harvard Art Museums.

图 1.65 庚嬴卣。青铜。西周中期，前 10—前 9 世纪。高 24.8 厘米。麻省剑桥，哈佛大学美术馆藏。

Again, the stylistic evolution (or degeneration) sketched here must be understood in relation to the parallel development in inscription. As I have shown, from the end of the Shang the focus of inscription gradually shifted from the ancestral deity to the living devotee. Although most Western Zhou bronzes were still dedicated to deceased ancestors, the dedication appeared as a consequence of an important event in the life of a living descendent. It was these events, mainly court audiences and investitures, that provided the cause for making ritual vessels, and they were elaborately described in a commemorative inscription. Consequently, the meaning and function of a ritual vessel, and hence its monumentality,

纹样的装饰性特征加以夸张。华美的细节被集中发挥；羽毛状的勾纹变成了一种普遍性语汇，用于每一个形象，甚至被施加在扉棱上。一个更为重要的变化是正面的兽面纹被打散。构成兽面的双龙被拆分［图 1.64］，其结果导致了视觉上的一种基本变化：视觉中心不复存在，众多的侧面形象引导观者的视线在器表上移动。作为形象框格的扉棱因此也被取消。这种新的格局为西周中期流行的鸟纹提供了一个结构性的基础［图 1.65］。这种具有华冠的鸟纹头部回转，尾部巨大并回旋展开，形成流畅的 S 形，与器物的流畅轮廓线相呼应。不管是视觉焦点的消除还是对装饰性细节的强调，这些变化都使得动物纹样被进一步抽象和分解。最后，到了西周晚期，动物母题被肢解成纯粹的“图案”——羽纹、目纹和鳞甲——经常装饰于象征其制作者或拥有者身份等级的列鼎上［图 1.66］。[182]

需要再次强调的是，这里所勾画出的装饰风格的演进（或衰退）必须结合铭文的相应变化来理解。正如上文所述，从商末开始，铭文的强调对象逐步从祖先神明转向活着的信众。尽管大多数西周青铜器仍是奉献给死去的祖先的，但是奉献本身成为其在世子孙们生活中重要事件的结果。正是这类事件——主要是宫廷的晋见和授职——构成制作青铜礼器的原因，并被详尽地记录在纪念性的铭文中。因此，青铜礼器的意义和功能——包括其纪念碑性——便发生

Fig. 1.66. Some decorative patterns of late Western Zhou bronze vessels. Ink rubbing.
图1.66 西周晚期青铜器的几种纹样。拓片。

changed: it was no longer an instrument in a ritual communication with deities, but a proof of glory and achievement in this life. Consequently, the symbolic protean imagery lost its vitality and dominance; lengthy documents were painstakingly cast on a poorly decorated plate or a shallow tripod. As monuments, such bronzes demand "reading," not "seeing" (Figs. 1.67a, b, 2.12a, b).

❸ The Chinese Bronze Age

The concept of a "Bronze Age," frequently employed in modern scholarship on early Chinese history and art history, is borrowed from the Western evolutionary theory called the "three-stage technological sequence."[183] Credit for this theory is usually given to two nineteenth-century Danish scholars, Christian Thomsen and Kens Worsaae, although similar sequences had been proposed by Johann von Eckart in the early eighteenth century and can even be found in the writings of Lucretius of ancient Rome.[184] Thomsen defines the Three Ages in his *Guide to Northern Antiquities*:

> The Age of Stone, or that period when weapons and implements were made of stone, wood or bone, or some such material, and during

which very little or nothing at all was known of metals. . . .

The Age of Bronze, in which weapons and cutting implements were made of copper or bronze, and nothing at all, or but very little was known of iron or silver. . . .

The Age of Iron is the third and last period of the heathen times, in which iron was used for those artifacts to which that metal is eminently suited, and in the fabrication of which it came to be used as a substitute for bronze.[185]

了一个重要的转化：这些器物的主要意义不再是在礼仪中与神明交通的器具，而更多地成为展示生者现世荣耀和成就的物证。其结果是，变化多端的象征性形象失去了它的活力和优势；冗长的文献记录被煞费苦心地铸在一件没有多少装饰的盘内或浅腹鼎中。作为纪念性的作品，这样的青铜器要求的是“阅读”而非“观看”［图 1.67，图 2.12］。

三、中国青铜时代

在现代关于中国早期历史和美术史的研究中，学者们经常使用“青铜时代”这个概念。这一概念借自西方进化论中所谓的“技术演进三期说”。[183] 尽管 18 世纪初的约翰·冯·艾科特，甚至是古罗马的卢克莱修就已有了类似的说法，但人们通常将这一理论的发明权归于 19 世纪的丹麦学者克里斯蒂·汤姆森和肯·沃尔索。[184] 汤姆森在其《北欧古物指南》一书中对这个理论做了以下定义：

> 在石器时代，武器和工具以石、木、骨或类似材料制造，人们对金属了解很少，或一无所知……
>
> 在青铜时代，武器或切割类工具以红铜或青铜制造，人们对于铁或银一无所知，或知之甚少……
>
> 铁器时代是野蛮时代的第三个也是最后一个阶段。在这个时期，人们以铁来制造最为适合的器具，铁器的使用取代了青铜。[185]

a

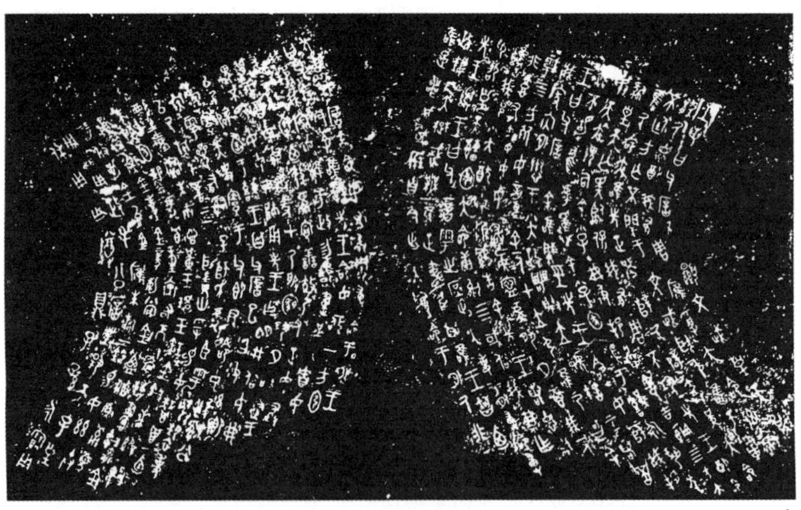

b

Fig. 1.67. (a) Maogong *ding*. Bronze. Late Western Zhou. 9th century B.C. H. 53.8 cm. Said to be from Qishan, Shaanxi province. (b) Ink rubbing of inscription.

图 1.67 （a）毛公鼎。青铜。西周晚期，前 9 世纪。高 53.8 厘米。传出陕西岐山。台北故宫博物院藏。（b）铭文。拓片。

The simplicity of Thomsen's model was not to endure for long; the 064
"three-stage sequence" was greatly elaborated during the second half of the nineteenth century and the beginning of the twentieth century: John Lubbock divided the Stone Age into the Paleolithic and Neolithic periods; the term *Mesolithic* was introduced by Aleen Brown; and Italian archaeologists suggested an Eneolithic period between the Stone Age and the Bronze Age.[186] But it was Gordon Childe who finally integrated these individual discoveries into a coherent theory of cultural evolution consisting of "a series of consecutive stages in technological development." In this general context, the Bronze Age was thought to comprise three subsequent "modes":

> In Mode 1, weapons and ornaments were made from copper and its alloys, but no "mutant" tools and few implements were adapted exclusively for industrial use. Stone tools continued to be made with care. In Mode 2, copper and bronze were regularly used in handicraft, but neither in husbandry nor in rough work. The metal types included knives, saws, and specialized axes, adzes, and chisels. Mode 3 is

汤姆森对该理论的这一简单表述并没有存在很久，因为“三期说”在 19 世纪后半叶和 20 世纪前半叶得到了极大的丰富：约翰·拉博克将石器时代划分为旧石器时代和新石器时代；阿林·布朗提出“中石器时代”的命名；意大利的一些考古学家提出在石器时代和青铜时代之间应该还存在有一个铜石并用的时代，等等。[186] 最后，戈登·柴尔德将这些单项的发现综合成“一系列连续技术演进阶段”的文化发展系统理论。在这种总体的前后关系中，青铜时代被认为有三种更迭的“模式”：

> 在模式 1 中，武器和装饰品以红铜及其合金制成，但是没有专为生产制造的金属工具，石工具仍然在继续认真地制造。在模式 2 中，红铜和青铜通常用来制造工艺品，但既不用于农牧业，也不应用于其他重体力劳动。金属器包括刀、锯、专用的轴、扁斧和凿等。模式 3 的特征是

> characterized by the introduction of metal implements in agriculture and for heavy labor, shown in the archaeological record by metal sickles, hoe blades, and even hammerheads.[187]

The evolution of the Bronze Age itself thus attests to (and results from) the basic assumption of the theory in general—the continuous development of "forces of production" brought about by the invention of advanced tools and their widening employment. Moreover, as a general evolutionary theory, this pattern was thought to have been shared by various cultures in the ancient world.[188] Belief in the universality of the "three-stage technological sequence" led to the free borrowing of the term Bronze Age in the study of early Chinese history to refer to the period traditionally called the Three Dynasties during which the bronze industry reached its zenith.

The problem, as a number of scholars have pointed out, is that although Chinese bronze works are commonly recognized as products of the most advanced bronze technology developed in the ancient world, the Chinese never made advanced bronze agricultural implements and
065 only produced limited handicraft tools.[189] Among them, K. C. Chang tried to redefine the concept of the Bronze Age in the Chinese context in an important article published in 1980: "Since bronze was not widely used for agricultural implements, the Bronze Age [of China] was not achieved primarily through a revolution in productive technology. If there was a revolution, it was in the realm of social organization."[190] This general proposition led him to two further observations. First, since the Chinese Bronze Age coincided with factors such as the state form of government, urbanism, and civilization, this concept "could well serve as a criterion for cultural and social definitions." Second, "the characteristic feature of the Chinese Bronze Age is that the use of that metal was inseparable from ritual and from war. In other words, bronze was political power."[191] These observations provide a basis for my discussion in this section on the symbolism of bronze in relation to the concepts of power and

monumentality. Before I begin, however, it is necessary to survey the basic uses of bronze in ancient China.

Extant bronze objects allow us to reach three preliminary conclusions regarding the function of bronze. First, after the discovery of bronze in China, this new material was used *primarily* for nonproductive purposes. These nonproductive bronze objects fall into two large categories:

> 金属工具在农业和重体力劳动中得到应用，农业中的金属工具有镰刀、锄头，甚至包括锤头。[187]

因此，青铜时代本身的发展证实了（同时也来源于）这种理论在总体上的一种基本假设——即先进工具的发明和不断广泛应用带来了“生产力”的持续发展。作为一般意义上的一种进化论理论，这个范式进而被认为适用于古代社会的不同文化。[188]对“技术演进三期说”的崇尚使得人们在研究早期中国历史时，简单地借用青铜时代一词来指传统上称作三代的历史时期，因为在这一时期内中国的青铜制造业达到其顶峰。

但是许多学者已经指出，这里的问题在于，尽管中国青铜器被公认为古代世界技术最为高超的青铜作品，然而古代中国人从未用青铜制造农业工具，而只是制造了少量的手工工具。[189]这些学者当中，张光直在 1980 年发表的一篇重要文章试图在中国的特殊背景下重新定义青铜时代的概念：“由于青铜并没有广泛地用来制造农业工具，（中国）青铜时代主要不是通过生产技术的革命产生的。如果真的有一次革命，那么它就应该是社会组织领域内的革命。[190]这一基本主张引导他展开了两项更为深入的观察。首先，由于中国青铜时代和诸如国家的形成、城市化以及文明等因素相合，“青铜时代”这一概念“可以用来作为衡量文化和社会的一个标准”。其次，“中国青铜时代的特征是这种金属的使用与礼仪和战争密切联系，换言之，青铜是一种政治权力”。[191]这些观点为我在本节中的讨论提供了一个基础。我所要探讨的是与权力以及纪念碑性等概念相关的青铜器的象征意义问题。然而在开始讨论之前，我们有必要简要地巡视一下中国古代青铜器的基本用途。

从现存的青铜器来观察，我们可以得出有关古代中国青铜器功能三个初步的结论。首先，在青铜发明之后，这种新的金属主要服务于非生产性目的。这些非生产性青铜器分作两大类，一是礼仪中使用的

Fig. 1.68. (a) Spear. Bronze and jade. Late Shang dynasty. 13th-12th centuries B.C. L. 18.4 cm. Palace Museum, Beijing. (b) Yachou axe. Bronze. Late Shang dynasty. 12th-11th centuries B.C. L. 32.7 cm. W. 34.5 cm. Excavated in 1964 at Yidu, Shandong province. Shandong Provincial Museum.

图 1.68 （a）矛。青铜和玉。商代晚期，前 13—前 12 世纪早期。长 18.4 厘米。北京故宫博物院藏。（b）亚醜钺。青铜。商代晚期，前 12—前 11 世纪早期。长 32.7 厘米，宽 34.5 厘米。1964 年山东益都苏埠屯出土。山东博物馆藏。

(1) vessels and musical instruments used in rituals, and (2) weapons and chariot fittings. Some weapons and chariots could have been used in warfare,[192] but a considerable number are exquisitely inlaid and/or oversized and must have also served a ceremonial purpose (Figs. 1.68a, b).

Second, some bronze drills, knives, chisels, and small spades have been found, but it would be dangerous to identify these as utilitarian tools used in daily life. For example, Shang oracle bones—instruments of royal divination—were drilled with holes in order to produce cracks after burning. It was estimated in the early 1960s that some 460,000 Shang oracle bones existed, including 150,000 inscribed ones, and that each

bore five holes on average, so that an astonishing number of 2.3 million
holes should be found on these bones.[193] Most holes, if not all, were
created by using bronze drills; one such tool was found together with
bones and turtle shells in 1952 in Zhengzhou, and another drill found
in 1953 in the same area fits the holes on oracle bones perfectly (Fig. 066
1.69).[194] Based on this evidence, the Chinese archaeologist Guo Baojun
has concluded that a large number of bronze drills must have been made
for religious services controlled by the Shang royal house.[195]

A rich tomb discovered in 1989 at Xin'gan in present-day Jiangxi probably belonged to a ruler of a southern kingdom contemporary with the Shang. Although 127 bronze objects from this tomb have been termed "implements,"[196] many of them are embellished with *taotie* and mystical zoomorphic images (Fig. 1.70). The same feature is shared by

容器和乐器，二是武器和车器。有些武器和车可能用于战争，[192] 但是其数量可观，并且运用了精巧的镶嵌工艺，或者形体巨大，可能也是在礼仪中使用的［图 1.68］。

再者，尽管有一些青铜钻、刀、凿和小型的铲子被发现，但是如果立即将这些东西认定为日常生活中的实用工具却是相当危险的。例如，作为商王室占卜用具的卜骨需要钻孔，以便使卜骨在经过火烤后出现裂纹。20 世纪 60 年代的学者估计，当时所发现的甲骨数量达 46 万片，其中 15 万片有文字，每片甲骨平均钻有五个孔，那么，这些甲骨上的钻孔就多达 230 万个。[193] 大多数的孔——即使不是所有的——是用青铜钻完成的。

1952 年在郑州曾有这种工具和甲骨一同出土；1953 年在同一地区发现的另一件铜钻与卜骨上的钻孔十分吻合［图 1.69］。[194] 基于这种现象，中国考古学家郭宝钧认为，大批青铜钻可能是为商王室所控制的宗教活动制作的。[195]

1989 年在今江西新干发现了一座埋葬丰富的墓葬，墓主可能是与商同时的一个南部方国的统治者。尽管该墓出土的 127 件青铜器被冠以“工具”之名，[196] 但这些器具中有许多装饰着饕餮纹和其他神秘的动物纹样［图 1.70］。传世的一些所谓的青铜“农具”也

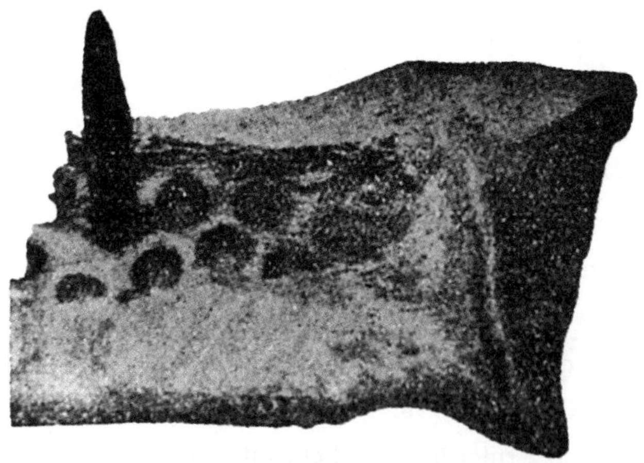

Fig. 1.69. Oracle bone with a bronze drill. Middle to late Shang dynasty. 14th-11th centuries B.C. Excavated in 1952 at Erligang, Zhengzhou.

图 1.69 带有青铜凿的卜骨。商代中晚期，前 14—前 11 世纪。1952 年河南郑州二里岗出土。

some extant bronze "tools" (Figs. 1.71); other extant chisels and axes even bear emblems, titles, and the names of Shang or Zhou aristocratic clans and personages (Figs. 1.72a-d). The appearance of the same inscriptions and patterns on ritual vessels suggests that these so-called tools may have been part of ritual paraphernalia. The Xin'gan tomb provides strong support for this argument: the 127 "tools" were grouped together with ritual vessels, ceremonial weapons, jade carvings, and a half-meter-tall bronze icon. These objects surrounded the dead and were obviously his personal belongings.[197] It is possible that the precious bronze "tools" were *liqi* used in certain agricultural rituals; we read in ritual books that such ceremonies were important duties for a ruler.[198]

In an archaeological discovery in Ningxiang in Hunan predating the excavation of the Xin'gan tomb, bronze "tools" had been found along with other ritual objects: 224 small bronze axes were placed inside a large ceremonial jar.[199] In other finds in the same area, a *you* vessel discovered in 1963 contained more than 1,100 jade tubes and beads, and another *you* unearthed in 1970 held some 320 ritual jades.[200] Most likely, all

Fig. 1.70. Bronze implements. Late Shang dynasty. *Ca.* 13th century B.C. Excavated in 1989 at Dayangzhou, Xin'gan, Jiangxi province. Jiangxi Xin'gan County Museum.

图 1.70　青铜工具。线图。商代晚期，约前 13 世纪。1989 年江西新干大洋洲出土。江西新干县博物馆藏。

four cases present original groupings of different kinds of ritual objects; similar groupings are recorded in ancient ritual books but become unrecognizable when bronzes and jades are studied as individual "tools" or "works of art." It is also significant that when the market economy

具有同样的特征［图 1.71］；其他传世的凿和斧上标有族徽、官职名称，以及商、周贵族或个人的名字［图 1.72］。同样的铭文和纹样也出现在礼仪中所使用的容器上，说明这些所谓的工具可能也是礼仪用具的一部分。新干墓的发现有力地支持了这样一个观点：这 127 件"工具"与同时发现的容器、仪仗用的兵器、玉器和半米高的青铜偶像同属于一个组合。这些器具围绕在死者周围，很显然是其个人的私有财产。[197] 这些珍贵的青铜"工具"很可能是在某种与农业有关的仪式中所使用的礼器；我们从礼书的记载可知，举行这类仪式是统治者重要的职责。[198]

在湖南宁乡一项早于新干墓的考古发现中，青铜"工具"也与礼器相伴出土：224 件小型青铜斧放置在一件礼仪用的大型罐内。[199] 在同一地区的其他发现中，1963 年出土的一件卣中盛有 1100 多件玉管和玉珠，1970 年出土的另一件卣中盛有大约 320 件玉礼器。[200] 这四项发现的共同点在于，它们向我们展示了不同种类的礼器原来的组合关系；在礼书中也记载有同样的组合，但是，当我们将青铜器和玉器分别作为独立的"工具"和"艺术品"加以研究时，就会对这类关系视而不见。同样值得注意的是，随着周晚期市场经济

Fig. 1.71. Bronze adz with *taotie* decoration. L. 29.2 cm. Harvard Art Museums, Cambridge, Mass.

图 1.71 装饰饕餮纹的青铜锛。长 29.2 厘米。麻省剑桥，哈佛大学美术馆藏。

developed during the late Zhou period, bronze coins took the shapes of spades, knives, or rings—objects originally used in ritual and warfare but now invested with commercial value (Figs. 1.73a, b). In fact, scholars have argued that those small and thin "spades" from Shang and Western Zhou burials were in fact "prototypes" of such coins.[201]

Third, excavated Shang and Western Zhou agricultural implements are made of stone. The excavation of the Erlitou site has shown that people continued to employ stone agricultural implements after bronze casting was invented.[202] Among the later Shang examples, 3,640 stone knives or sickles were found between 1928 and 1937 at the last Shang capital, Anyang (Fig. 1.74).[203] This archaeological evidence has led some Chinese scholars to raise questions about the nature of the Chinese Bronze Age. The historian Lei Haizong wrote in 1957: "The [Chinese] Bronze Age
067 was essentially a Stone Age. Tools of production, especially agricultural implements, were still largely made of stone and wood. Productive forces were still very low, and surplus was considerably limited."[204] His opinion was supported by the prominent archaeologists Chen Mengjia and Yu Xingwu.[205] Chen proposed: "When bronze casting became known, this technique was employed in making implements for royal craftsmen, weapons for royal armies, and vessels for royal sacrifices. Individual farmers were unable to make bronze agricultural implements for themselves, and slaves were certainly not allowed to use precious bronzes in farming."[206]

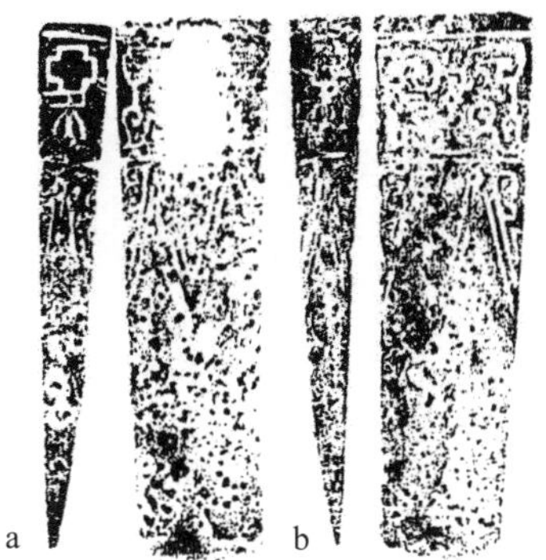

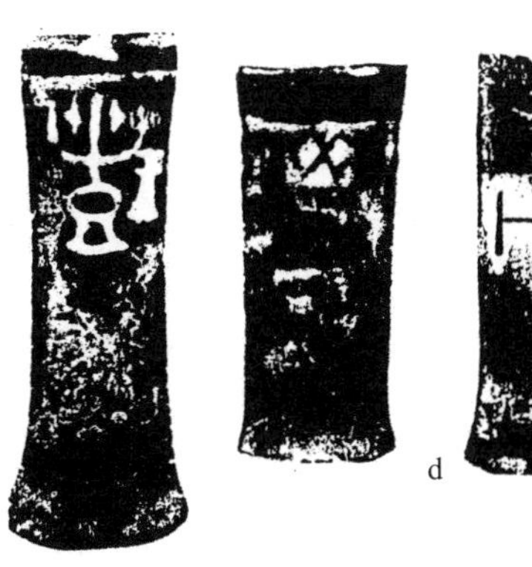

Fig. 1.72. Inscribed bronze implements. (a) Ya Yi adz. Late Shang dynasty. 13th-11th centuries B.C. H. 11.5 cm. (b) Feng adz. Early Western Zhou. 11th-10th centuries B.C. H. 11.5 cm. (c) Gui adz. Western Zhou. 11th-8th centuries B.C. (d) Wang adz. Late Western Zhou. 9th-8th centuries B.C. Ink rubbings.

图 1.72　带铭文的青铜工具。拓片。（a）亚吴锛。青铜。商代晚期，前 13—前 11 世纪。高 11.5 厘米。（b）豐锛。青铜。西周早期，前 11—前 10 世纪。高 11.5 厘米。（c）癸锛。青铜。西周，前 11—前 8 世纪。（d）王锛。青铜。西周晚期。前 9—前 8 世纪。

的发展，青铜铸币出现了，其形态采用了铲、刀或环的外形。这些器物原来被用于礼仪或战争中，而现在却被赋予了商业的价值［图 1.73］。实际上，学者们已经指出，商代和西周墓葬中出土的那些小而薄的“铲”可能就是这类货币的“原型”。[201]

第三，考古发现的商和西周的农业工具主要用石头制作。二里头遗址的发掘证明，在青铜器被发明以后，人们继续使用石质的农业生产工具。[202] 晚商的情况也是如此，1928—1937 年间在安阳晚商都城的发掘中出土了 3640 件石刀或石镰［图 1.74］。[203] 这些考古学材料使许多中国学者对中国青铜时代的性质提出了疑问。如历史学家雷海宗在 1957 年提出，中国的青铜时代实质上是一个石器时代，工具，特别是农业工具，多以石和木制造，生产力水平仍十分低下，剩余产品非常有限。[204] 他的观点得到著名考古学家陈梦家和于省吾的支持。[205] 陈梦家认为，王室的匠师以新出现的青铜铸造技术制造器具，武器用于战争，容器用于王室祭祀，自由民无力为自己制造青铜农具，奴隶当然也不被允许在农业生产中使用贵重的青铜。[206]

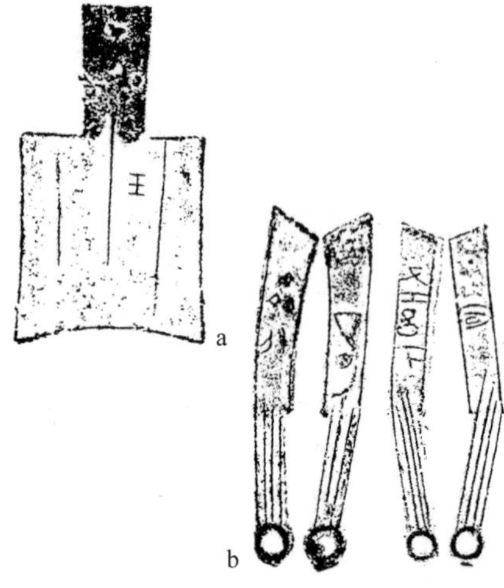

Fig. 1.73. Eastern Zhou coins.
(a) Hollow-headed *bu* coin with the character *wang*.
(b) Ming knife coins. Ink rubbings.
图 1.73 东周货币。青铜。拓片。
（a）带“王”字铭文的空首布。
（b）“明”刀币。

This discussion in the 1950's, however, was soon forced to stop abruptly: an important component of the Chinese Communist Party's doctrine of "historical materialism" was the "three-stage technological sequence" believed to be fundamental in the social evolution of the human race.[207] Any doubt about the existence of bronze tools in Chinese history was considered heretical. Lei Haizong and Chen Mengjia were condemned, labeled counter-revolutionary "rightists," and forced to stop writing. Tang Lan's 1960 article "A Preliminary Study of Problems Concerning the Use of Bronze Agricultural Implements in Ancient Chinese Society" concluded the debate by announcing the victory of the official line.[208]

但是，20 世纪 50 年代的这项讨论不久就被迫中断："历史唯物主义"的一个重要组成部分是，把"技术演进三期说"作为人类社会进化的一项基本原则。[207] 任何怀疑中国历史上曾存在青铜工具的说法都被视为异端。雷海宗和陈梦家受到指责，被冠以"反动学术权威"之名，其写作的权利被剥夺。唐兰 1960 年发表的《中国古代社会使用青铜农器问题的初步研究》一文宣布了官方观点的胜利，为这个争论做出结论。[208]

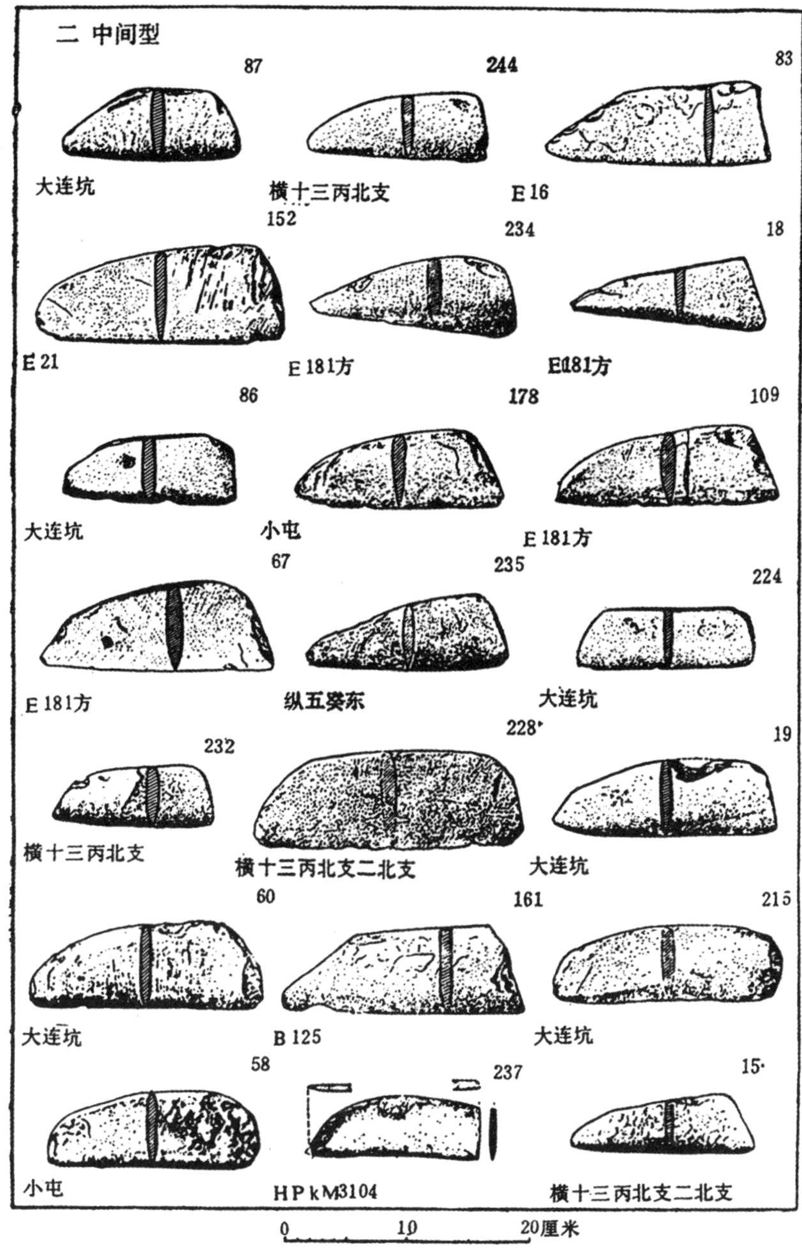

Fig. 1.74. Stone agricultural tools. Late Shang dynasty. 13th-11th centuries B.C. Excavated at Xiaotun, Anyang, Henan province.

图 1.74 石质农业工具。商代晚期，前 13—前 11 世纪。河南安阳小屯出土。

A scholar learned in the Chinese Classics and antiquarianism, Tang found written characters for agricultural tools with "metal" radicals in
068 almost all surviving pre-Qin texts and listed 45 actual bronzes that he claimed were agricultural implements. But ironically, these examples proved the absolute poverty of his evidence: most texts he quoted were written during the Eastern Zhou and their extant versions were compiled even later. The 45 objects were scattered over a broad period of some 1,500 years from Shang to Han. Not only is the limited number of these "tools" incommensurate with the numerous bronze ritual paraphernalia and weapons produced during the same period, but these so-called agricultural implements include small and thin spades, axes and "hoes" with prestigious inscriptions and *taotie* masks, and some weapons.[209] In explaining the poor result of his laborious search, Tang argued—and his argument has been repeated by many scholars who follow the party line—that "precious bronze" had to be reused and that bronze tools must have been melted down to recast other objects.[210] This assumption is, however, self-contradictory: if bronze was "precious," it had to be strictly controlled by the ruling class and had to be used to make "precious" objects.[211]

This last statement leads to a crucial question in studying early Chinese history and art history: Were "precious materials" used to improve production in ancient China? Or, was there a tradition that "precious materials" and advanced technology were persistently employed in nonproductive practices? It is interesting in this regard to see a native Chinese tradition of an evolutionary pattern. Yuan Kang of the first century A.D. stated in his *Yuejue shu* (The distinction of the Yue)[212] that "stone weapons" characterized the utopia of the Three Sovereigns, and jade artifacts (which he called "divine objects") were invented by the
069 Yellow Emperor, a legendary figure responsible for creating statecraft and regulating social ranks.[213] The use of bronze was associated with the first dynasty, Xia, and this was again followed by the Iron Age after the Three

Dynasties. In this scheme, jade is distinguished from stone just as bronze is differentiated from iron. Each of the two general material categories—"stone" and "metal"—thus again contains two subcategories ("stone": ordinary stone and jade; "metal": bronze and iron). In ancient texts, ordinary stone and iron were called "ugly" or "crude" materials (*e*) and

作为一位古代文献和古物知识甚丰的学者，唐兰指出几乎所有现存先秦文献中出现的农具名字都带有"金"字旁。此外，他还列举了他认为可以断定为农器的 45 件存世青铜器。但是具有反讽意味的是，这些例证对于支持他的观点来说实在是太贫乏了：他所引用的文献大多成于东周，现存的版本甚至是在更晚的时期才被编成。而那 45 件器物分散在从商代到汉代大约 1500 年的漫长时期内。这些"工具"与同时期制作的大量青铜礼器和武器相比，不仅在数量上极不相称，而且所谓的农具实际上包括小而薄的铲、斧以及铸有高贵的铭文和饕餮的"锄"，还包括一些武器。[209] 在为这项费力劳神的研究所得的薄弱结论寻找理由时，唐兰指出（他的结论被尊奉"主流"观点的许多学者所重复）"珍贵的青铜"被不断再生利用，青铜工具可能被熔化以铸造其他的器物。[210] 然而这种假设实际上是自相矛盾的：如果青铜确实很"珍贵"的话，那么它就应当被统治阶级严格控制，用来制造"珍贵"的器物。[211]

这最后一点对于中国早期历史和美术史的研究提出了一个至关重要的问题：中国古人是不是真的把"贵重材料"用来推进生产的发展？或者说，中国古代是否存在着一个将"贵重材料"和先进技术不断地用于非生产性活动的传统？在思考这些问题时，观察一下中国本土传统中的一个进化论描述是饶有趣味的。公元 1 世纪的袁康在其《越绝书》中提到，[212]"以石为兵"是上古乌托邦式的三皇时代的特征，而玉器（他称作"神器"）则是创造了国家、规范了社会等级的黄帝的发明。[213] 青铜器的使用与第一个王朝夏相联系，接着便是三代以后的铁器时代。在袁康的系统中，玉比石高贵，铜与铁有别。因此，"石"与"金"两大类质料又分别包含了两个亚类（"石"包括普通的石头和玉；"金"包括青铜和铁）。在古代文献中，普通的石和铁被看作"丑陋"或"粗劣"（"恶"）的材料，

were used to make tools, whereas jade and bronze were called "beautiful" or "fine" materials (*mei*) and were employed to fashion nonproductive artifacts.[214] Yuan's Four-Age theory—if we may call it this—does not testify to a straightforward evolution of productive forces but implies two separated but interrelated developments of *liqi* (ritual paraphernalia) and *yongqi* (utilitarian implements and utensils). The Jade and Bronze ages in this scheme are correlated with the development of ritual art and with the concept of monumentality during the Shang and Western Zhou outlined in the preceding section. As I have shown, carved jades were intensively made from the fourth millennium B.C. on and all physical characteristics of jade were understood in social terms. I have proposed that this phenomenon reflected a desire to forge symbols of privilege and power, a desire that appeared only at a certain stage in human history. Some basic characteristics for *liqi*—the major form of archaic Chinese monuments—were gradually formulated: works of ritual art always required the highest technology available at the time; these works were always made of rare materials and/or demanded an extraordinary amount of labor by skilled and specialized craftsmen; and their forms, while maintaining some basic typological features of implements, deliberately neglected functional aspects. The evidence of these early prestigious artifacts leads to the conclusion that once a new technique was invented and a "precious" material was discovered, they would be absorbed into the *liqi* tradition and used for entirely non-utilitarian purposes. It is only logical that bronze casting was employed to produce religious paraphernalia and status symbols. A major difference between these new prestigious artifacts and the older ones, however, is that they were more effective in legitimating the control of power, as the authors of an excellent study on prehistorical cultures and ideology have observed:

> To those without access to modern scientific explanations, metal working is inherently a magical transformation of aspects of the natural world. By selecting certain stones and heating them in certain

conditions a liquid is produced which can be poured into moulds of varying shapes and forms. Left to cool, the liquid becomes a solid which is at the same time bright, shiny and attractive as well as stronger and more durable than the hardest stone. . . . It is hardly surprising in these circumstances that individuals capable of controlling such processes should have acquired considerable prestige.[215]

通常用来制作工具，而玉和青铜则被看作“美丽”或“优良”（“美”）的材料，用以制作非生产性物品。[214] 袁康的四期说——如果我们可以这样称呼它的话——并没有勾画出一个生产力单线进化的模式，而是包含了礼器和用器这两个既不同又相关的发展系统。在这个系统中，玉器时代和青铜时代的概念与上文所描述的商和西周时期的礼器美术，以及中国古代纪念碑性的发展紧密相关。正如上文所指出的，玉器雕刻从公元前 4000 年后开始集中出现，玉的所有物质性特征都被赋予社会意义。我提出，这种现象反映出一种对创造特权与权力的象征物的渴望，而这是一种在人类历史上某一特定阶段出现的渴望。礼器的某些基本特征——古代中国纪念碑的主要形式——逐渐得到定型化：礼器美术作品总是采用那个时代最高超的技术；这些作品总是使用珍贵的材料来制作，并且 / 或者包含着熟练技工的大量劳动；这些作品在形式上具有工具的基本类型学特征，但同时又故意抹杀实用的功能。这些特征说明，一旦一种新的技术被发明或一种“贵重”的材料被发现，它们就会被吸收纳入礼器的传统中去，被运用于非实用的目的。这种逻辑揭示了为什么青铜铸造技术仅仅被用于制造宗教用品和身份地位的象征物。然而，正像一些研究者在讨论史前文化和思想时所指出的那样，这些新出现的贵重物品和以前的物品的一个重要区别是，前者可以更有效地体现出统治权力的合法性：

> 对于那些缺少现代科学知识的人们来说，金属制品本身即体现了将自然世界的性质加以转换的神奇能力。选取某种特别的石头进行加热，在达到某个特定温度时石头熔化为液态。通过浇注到模具中，这些液浆可以变化成各种形状和形式。冷却之后，液浆变得坚硬，光彩夺目，富有魅力，同时也变得比最坚硬的石头更加持久……在这种情况下，有能力掌控这一过程的个人得以获得崇高的声望，也就绝不出人意料了。[215]

Fig. 1.75. Bronze *gu* vessel. Late Shang dynasty. 13th-11th centuries B.C. Freer Gallery of Art, Washington, D.C.

图 1.75 青铜觚。商代晚期，前 13—前 11 世纪。华盛顿，弗利尔美术馆藏。

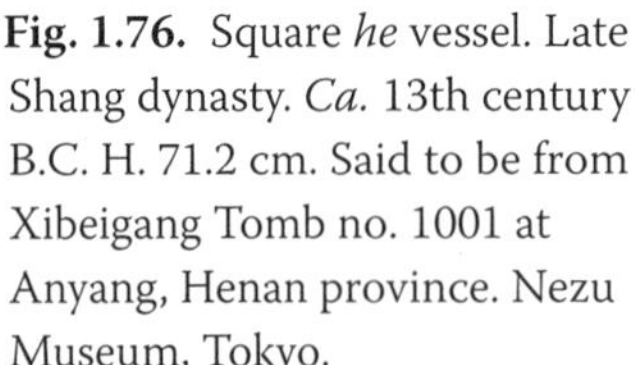

Fig. 1.76. Square *he* vessel. Late Shang dynasty. *Ca.* 13th century B.C. H. 71.2 cm. Said to be from Xibeigang Tomb no. 1001 at Anyang, Henan province. Nezu Museum, Tokyo.

图 1.76 青铜方盉。商代晚期，约前 13 世纪。高 71.2 厘米。据传出于河南安阳西北冈 1001 号墓。东京，根津美术馆藏。

As *liqi*, bronze ritual vessels had to distinguish themselves from
ordinary utensils. A bronze *gu* has a narrow body and a flared mouth
(Fig. 1.75)—what was the point of making a “drinking vessel” into such
an inconvenient shape? A *he* became so ornate and heavy (Fig. 1.76)— 070
can one imagine holding it to pour wine from its narrow spout? A *pan* is covered with such a long commemorative inscription (Figs. 2.12a, b)—is it a plate for a meal or a medium for documentation? It is obvious that the material, the shape, the decoration, and the inscription of these bronzes were meant to attest to something entirely beyond the range of ordinary experience, to demonstrate that the vessels, as *liqi* or ritual paraphernalia, were sacred and unworldly.

According to the “three-stage technological sequence,” bronze functioned to reinforce production. I would argue, however, that ancient Chinese bronze *liqi*, as well as previous ritual jades and pottery, “squandered” and “absorbed” productive forces. Only because these man-made objects were able to “squander” and “absorb” productive force could they have power and gain monumentality.

作为礼器，青铜器必须使自身与日常器具区别开来。一件青铜觚具有细长的身体和外侈的口部［图 1.75］——将“饮器”做成这种极不方便的形状，到底是为了什么？一件作为饮器的盉变得如此华丽而沉重［图 1.76］——如何能够举起它并从其细小的流口向外倒酒？一件盘的内底覆盖着一通长篇大论的纪念性铭文［图 2.12］——它究竟是一个用来盛饭的盘子，还是一种文案的媒介？很显然，这些青铜器的材料、形状、装饰，以及铭文有意地体现出某种完全超乎通常经验的意义，证明这些器具作为礼器所具有神圣的、非尘世的性格。

根据通行的“技术演进三期说”，青铜的功能在于推进生产。然而，我希望强调的是，中国古代的青铜礼器，包括珍贵的礼仪性玉、陶器，实际上都是在“浪费”和“吞并”生产力。而正是因为这些人造的器物能够如此“浪费”和“吞并”生产力，它们才得以具有权力，才能够获得它们的纪念碑性。

But what is "power"? In Marxist historical philosophy the raison d'être and most fundamental determinant of power are located in the economy.[216] Power results from the control of the means and forces of production (tools and labor) and thus appears ultimately "as a concrete possession analogous to a commodity which can be wielded, transferred, seized or alienated."[217] Among the many critics of this theory, Michel Foucault has most effectively attempted to dispel the notion that power is inherently negative or repressive: "Power is not something that is acquired, seized, or shared, something that one holds on to or allows to slip away; power is exercised from innumerable points, in the interplay of nonegalitarian and mobile relations."[218] The first of these two views focuses on the political relationship between antagonistic groups or classes, and the second approaches power as a general force (which is not necessarily "political" in a strict sense) within a single social unity.[219] Since they deal with different situations and interpret power on different levels, these two approaches may not be entirely contradictory, and each may reveal something essential about ancient society.

The strict control of bronze resources and production implies coercion and repression. When an alien tribe or kingdom was conquered, it may have had to surrender its bronze (as the "different regions" sent bronze to the Xia to make the Nine Tripods), and within each of the Three Dynasties such control generated and guaranteed social stratification. It is also clear, however, that in order to bestow raw bronze—the alloy of two natural elements, copper and tin—with social value, this material had to be transformed into a "work." The exercise of power was thus most intimately related to certain bronze forms, and, conversely, these forms reflect different aspects of the exercise of power.

K. C. Chang has pointed out that a famous dictum from ancient China—"The principal affairs of the state are sacrifices and military actions"—explains the exclusive use of bronze in manufacturing ritual paraphernalia and weapons.[220] We may develop this argument even further: the polarity between sacrifices and military actions and between ritual paraphernalia and weapons reflects two kinds of *power*, which M. Benton has termed as *power* to and *power* over.[221] The first concept, *power* to, refers to *power* as a "component of all social interaction and as a feature embedded in all social practices. This *power* draws upon

但是，何为“权力”？在马克思主义的历史哲学中，权力存在的理由和最基本的决定因素存在于经济中：[216] 权力被认为是对生产（工具和劳动）手段和力量进行控制的结果，因此最终表现为“一种具体的占有，就像一种商品那样可以被支配、转移、掌握或转让”。[217] 在对这一理论的许多批评者中，福柯最有力地反驳了权力在本质上是被动的和受压抑的观念：“权力并不是一种可以获取、掌控或分享的东西，也不是一种可以把持或任其脱离的东西。在非平等主义和可变（社会）关系的相互作用下，权力实际上是无数因素的共同运作。”[218] 前一种理论强调对立的集团或阶级之间的政治性关系，后者则将权力视为存在于社会统一体内部的一种（在严格意义上并不必然是“政治性”的）综合力量。[219] 由于这两种理论着眼于不同的情况，同时对权力的解释也不处在同一个层面上，所以它们并不是全然对立的，每种理论都可能揭示出古代社会的一些重要的问题。

对于青铜资源和生产的严格控制自然包含了压制和强迫的机制。当异族或异邦被征服后，它们可能会被迫交出其青铜（如“远方”将它们的青铜献给夏以铸造九鼎）。在三代的每一个朝代中，这种控制导致并保证了社会中的分层。然而，同样明显的是，为了赋予单纯的青铜材料——红铜和锡的合金——以社会价值，这种材料必须被改造为一种“作品”。权力的行使因此与某些特定的青铜形式产生了密切的联系，反过来，这些形式也最有力地反映了权力行使中不同的方面。

张光直曾经提到，中国古代的一句名言——“国之大事，在祀与戎”——说明了青铜专门用于制造礼器和武器。[220] 我们或许可以进一步将这一观点加以发展：祭祀和军事，礼器和武器——这种两分的描述方式反映了权力的两种类型，本顿将其称为植入权力和施加权力。[221] 植入权力的概念指，权力是“社会上所有互动作用中的组成部分，是所有社会实践的内部环节。这种权力利用并创造了资源。

and creates resources. Viewed at perhaps the most abstract level it can be regarded as a dispositional capability, neither possessed nor exercised or controlled by any particular agent or collectivity, but as a structural feature of social systems, which is only manifested through its effects on individuals, groups and institutions."[222] *Power over*, on the other hand, means coercion and control—asymmetrical forms of social domination that involve a "dialectical relationship between the *power* 'holder' and those upon whom *power* is exercised."[223] These two aspects of *power* are thus related, respectively, to the two views offered by Marxists and Foucauldians.

The connection between *power over* and weapons is obvious. The whole history of the Three Dynasties was based on the domination of three clans over other kin and regional groups.[224] The ultimate and most effective form of political domination was military conquest, which was also a major source of wealth and slaves.[225] It is perhaps no coincidence that wars were often directly associated with the rise and decay of a ruling
071 power or a culture. Among many instances, the sudden flourishing of the Shang civilization during King Wu Ding's reign was coupled with endless military campaigns against alien tribes and kingdoms,[226] and the reasons for the Shang's collapse included King Zhou's failure in such campaigns as well as ethnic slave rebellions. It is recorded that facing attack by the Zhou army, this desperate king was forced to recruit soldiers from among his slaves and to equip them with bronze weapons, which were then turned on him. His fall thus appeared as a direct consequence of his losing the means of political domination.

Liqi or ritual paraphernalia, on the other hand, played a very different role in the same society. As discussed earlier, *liqi* embodied *li*, and *li* encompassed the entire repertoire of rules for all sorts of nonviolent social activities and regulations—ceremonial practices and manners, legal and moral codes, and personal behavior and conduct. No one created *li* or could ever "possess" it, but everyone was obliged to practice it. It was in the omnipresent practices of *li* that a social order was achieved. The power of *li*, therefore, did not derive from antagonism or dominance but emerged from mutual conditions and restrictions that characterized all kinds of ritual practices. In other words, this power was not possessed but exercised. Conversely, all individuals and groups who exercised this power were also subject to its exercise.

从可能是最为抽象的层面来看，这种权力可被视作一种心理的潜能，它既不是占有性的，也不是行使性的，更不被任何特殊的中介者或集团所控制。它是社会系统的一种结构性成分，只通过它在个体、集团或组织中所产生的影响体现出来"。[222] 施加权力则意味着社会统治中的高压和控制性——它指的是不对等的形式，包括"权力'拥有者'和权力被施加者之间的辩证关系"。[223] 如果这样理解的话，马克思主义和福柯学说分别提出的权力的两个方面就可以被联系在一起。

施加权力的概念和武器的联系是很明显的。整个三代历史的基础就是三个部族对于其他部族和地域性集团的征服。[224] 政治支配最终极和有效的形式是军事征伐，这也是财富和奴隶的主要来源。[225] 战争常常与统治权力或一种文化的兴起和衰落直接联系在一起。这种例子很多，如商文明在武丁时期的突然兴盛是与对外族和外邦无休止的战役联系在一起的。[226] 商代覆灭的原因也包括了纣在这种战役中的失败以及种族奴隶的暴动。据记载，面对周军的进攻，这位绝望中的商王不得不以奴隶补充军队，并且以青铜兵器来武装他们，而正是这些青铜武器随后成为"倒戈"、攻击他自己的工具。因此，纣的失败可以说是他失去政治统治手段的结果。

另一方面，礼器在社会中扮演了一个十分不同的角色。如上文所述，礼器使"礼"得以具体化，而礼统括了一切非暴力的社会行为和规范的内涵——包括仪式的实施及其具体实施方式、法律和道德的规范、个人的举止和行为，等等。没有人能够创造礼或者"占有"礼，但人人又必须按照礼行事。正是于这种无所不在的礼的实践中，社会秩序得以建立。因此，礼的权力并不产生于对抗或者控制，而是源于人们彼此共存和制约的状态。这样的状态同时也就是各种礼仪行为的特征；反过来说，所有运用礼的权力的个体和集团也都服从于这种权力的运用。

Likewise, the power of *liqi* was not located in physical possession. Even though one could seize the ritual vessels of others through violence, without the necessary justification of *li* such acquisition only proved one's violation of basic social codes. Ritual vessels were neither functional in a practical sense nor static symbols of social status; they became "powerful" only when they were made and used properly by proper persons for proper purposes at proper times in proper places and in proper ways. The sum of this endless "propriety" was *li*, and in this way a ritual vessel could conceal principles. To take a Western Zhou investiture bronze as an example, the inscription records the ritual leading to the bronze's creation as well as rituals initiated by its creation. The investiture ceremony was held in the royal ancestral temple in the early morning and was conducted by the king in person. All participants—the king, the ceremonial officials, and the recipient of the investiture—were dressed in the appropriate ritual costumes, took their appropriate places, moved with the appropriate gestures, and delivered the appropriate speeches. The king praised his own ancestors as well as the ancestors of the recipient. He confirmed the title and privileges previous kings had given to the recipient's family and sometimes conferred additional favors. A set of symbolic gifts was presented to the recipient, who then in his response praised the king, the former kings, and his own ancestors. The bronze that he made after the ceremony not only finalized the investiture, but would be "treasured and used by his sons and grandsons"—a standard expression meaning that the vessel would be installed in his family temple and would be used in sacrifices as long as the family line continued.[227] The significance of this ritual lay in its confirmation of sets of social relationships, including those between the king and his royal ancestors, the minister and his own ancestors, the king's ancestors and the minister's ancestors, the king and the minister, and the minister and his descendents. The monumentality of the ritual bronze, therefore, lay in embodying and consolidating the web of social relationships.

The investiture ceremony was only one of numerous rituals conducted on greater or lesser scales in all spheres of social life. The six general *li* described in ancient ritual books in abundant detail—rituals of capping, marrying, mourning, sacrificing, feasting, and gathering—encompass almost all the activities of a life.[228] *Li* thus became life itself,

与此一致，礼器的力量不存在于物质性占有。尽管一个人可以通过暴力从其他人那里夺取礼器，但是如果没有符合礼的必要理由，这种获取只能证明他违反了基本的社会准则。礼器既不具有实用的功能，也不是社会身份静态的象征；只有当礼器被恰当的人在恰当的时间和恰当的地方以恰当的方式为了恰当的目的来制造和使用时，它们才会变得“有力量”。这一大堆“恰当性”的总和便是礼，通过这样的方式，礼器便可以达到“藏礼”的作用。以西周册命铜器为例，其铭文记录了册命的礼仪，这种礼仪是该青铜器制作的原因，而其制作又导致进一步的礼仪行为。根据铭文和文献记载，周代册命礼仪于清晨在王室的祖庙中由王本人亲自主持举行。所有的参加者——王、礼官以及接受册命者——都穿着符合礼仪的恰当的服装，站在恰当的位置，以恰当的姿势行动，说恰当的、符合于礼仪的话。周王颂扬自己的祖先，也颂扬接受册命者的祖先。他重申先王给予受命者家庭的称号和特权，进而赐给他们新的恩典。他会把一套带有象征性的物品赏赐给受命者，而后者则在他的答复中称颂当前的周王和先王，以及自己的祖先。他在仪式结束后所制作的青铜器不仅是整个册命过程的最后一环，而且会被“子子孙孙永宝用”——这一标准的铭文用语说明，随着家族的延续，这件器物将被存放在受命者的家庙中并用于祭祀。[227] 这个仪式的意义因此在于，确认了包括周王与其祖先、大臣与其祖先、周王的祖先与大臣的祖先、周王与大臣，以及大臣与其子孙在内的诸种社会关系。青铜礼器的纪念碑性实际上也就存在于体现和巩固这种社会关系的网络之中。

册命仪式只是社会生活中或大或小的大量礼仪活动中的一种。古代礼书中详细描述的六礼——冠、昏（婚）、丧、祭、乡（飨）、相见——几乎包含了社会生活中的所有活动。[228] 礼因而成为社会

and its power, masked by reference to the "natural order" of human life, became fundamental, unchangeable, and itself natural. Rather than creating coercive sanctions, *li* in these activities constantly reassured and adjusted social relationships—between senior and junior, husband and wife, the living and the dead, descendent and ancestor, host and guest, and ruler and subject. Although the two parties in each relationship were not equal, no two relationships were overlapping and this means that no single "powerholder" could be in absolute control; even the king had to worship his ancestors and honor his seniors and guests. If there were a single force that dominated this system, it could only be *li* itself, for all
072 individuals and groups who exercised the power of *li* were also subject to its exercise.[229]

But these two aspects of power—*power over* and *power to*—were never separated. Connecting them was the concept of monumentality. On the one hand, even before the Three Dynasties, jade "weapons" had appeared as an important type of *liqi*; the wide existence of oversized and inlaid bronze axes, knives, and spears proves the continuation of this tradition in the Bronze Age. On the other hand, many ritual vessels were made during or after military expeditions; I have cited some inscriptions recording such events in this chapter. Such instances guide us back to the Nine Tripods. This set of monumental bronzes reflects not a single function of power but a dialectical relationship between the two; only in this way could the Tripods become a primary symbol of the Chinese Bronze Age. My earlier investigation of the Tripods has shown (1) that the Tripods attested to political domination since the change in their ownership signified alternating rulership, and (2) that the Tripods were structural features of a given society since they generated and sustained the society's internal system. In other words, the Tripods were "objects whose acquisition conferred status on the individual either within a particular group or vis-à-vis other groups," and which also "act[ed] as the concrete confirmation of acquired power."[230]

This twofold function of the Tripods is best revealed by the transition from the Shang to the Zhou. As soon as King Wu of the Zhou conquered the Shang, he ordered the removal of the Nine Tripods and ritual jades from the Shang capital—a gesture signaling the irretrievable destruction of the older dynasty.[231] Afterward the Tripods were sent to the base of the Zhou clan.[232] But interestingly, the physical seizure of the Tripods did

生活本身。被看成是人类生活的“自然秩序”，礼的权力因此成为最基本的、不变的、天生的东西。与那些强制性的手段不同，在这些社会活动中，礼不断地更新并调整上下之间、夫妇之间、生者与死者之间、祖先与子孙之间、主人与客人之间以及统治者与被统治者之间的各种社会关系。尽管每种关系中的双方并不平等，但是没有任何两种关系可以重叠，这就意味着一位“掌权者”不可能拥有绝对的控制力：即便是王也要尊崇他的祖先，敬重长者和客人。如果说有一种权力可以凌驾于这个系统之上的话，那只能是礼本身，因为所有运用礼的权力的个体和集团都必须屈从于礼的运用。[229]

但是，权力的这两个方面——施加权力和植入权力——又决不分离。将二者连接起来的也就是纪念碑性的概念。一方面，早在三代之前，“玉兵”已作为一种重要的礼器类型出现；青铜时代众多的形体硕大、镶嵌华美的钺、刀、矛是对这一传统的延续。另一方面，军事征伐和胜利导致对大量容器类礼器的制作——前文中已经引述了记载这类事件的青铜铭文。这些例子引导我们再次回到九鼎。这套纪念性的青铜器反映出的不是权力的单一功能，而是两种功能之间辩证的关系；只有通过这种方式，九鼎才成为中国青铜时代政治权力的首要象征。我在上文关于九鼎的讨论表明：（1）九鼎显示了政治的支配权，因为鼎的所有者的改变标志着统治权的改变；（2）九鼎代表着特定的社会结构性特征，因为它们引发并维持着社会的内在系统。换言之，九鼎的“占有既赋予本集团或他集团中的占有者以特殊身份”，也“起到实际证实他们所获得的权力的作用”。[230]

九鼎的这两种功能在从商到周的换代中得到了极明确的体现。有文献记载，当周武王征服了商，他立即下令取走商代都城中的九鼎和玉礼器——这一行为标志着旧王朝的崩溃已无法挽回。[231] 九鼎随后被运送到周的本部。[232] 有意思的是，对九鼎的物质性夺取并

not automatically prove the Zhou their legitimate owner. The transaction had to be ritualized through the act of *dingding*, a term meaning both "to settle the *ding* tripods" and "to establish a new political power." In other words, the Zhou's possession of the Tripods had to be converted from negative proof of the Shang's destruction to positive proof of the Zhou's ruling mandate. In demonstrating the Shang's destruction, the Tripods were still viewed as symbols of the Shang; to legitimate the Zhou's mandate, the Tripods had to become internal elements of the Zhou.

We read in the *Book of Changes*: "*Ge* [overcoming or conquering] means to get rid of the old, and *ding* [settling the Tripods] means to establish the new."[233] Thus, King Wu was given the royal title Wu—"military prowess"—because he had conquered the Shang and captured the Tripods. But it was his son who "established the new" by settling the Tripods in a newly constructed capital; he was thus given the title Cheng or "Accomplishment." Elaborate rituals were conducted: divine oracles were sought to determine the proper location for the Tripods; a city was built to house them; and the Tripods were moved into their new home through a specific entrance called the Tripod Gate.[234] These rituals provided occasions to display the might of the new dynasty, hold court audiences and investitures, and make additional ritual bronzes.[235] In this process, various social and political relationships were established and justified. It can be said that only at that point did the Tripods become a collective monument of the Zhou.

Five hundred years later, the Zhou royal house had degenerated to a puppet government struggling for survival, and the Chu lord held his military maneuvers outside the Zhou capital and impudently inquired about the Tripods. His intention was understood to be the overthrow of the Zhou, and Wangsun Man's speech on the Nine Tripods aimed to demonstrate the Zhou's legitimacy as the central power. This clever minister drew his evidence from King Cheng, who "fixed the Tripods in the Zhou capital and divined that the Zhou dynasty should last for thirty reigns, over seven hundred years." What is omitted from his account is

King Wu's seizure of the Tripods from the Shang, a historical episode that the Chu lord could readily use to justify his ambition.

It is impossible to know whether Wangsun Man had ever seen the Tripods, believed to be housed somewhere deep inside the Zhou royal temple. But the set of Tripods that we learn about from his speech are without doubt a historical fabrication. Significantly, this fabrication condenses and abstracts the whole course of ritual art into a single image. As the most important monument of the Three Dynasties, the Tripods 073

不能自动证明周对其所有权的合法性——所有权的转换必须通过“定鼎”的活动给以礼仪性的确认。“定鼎”这个词的意思既是“把鼎安置下来”，也是“建立一个新政权”。换言之，鼎必须从商代灭亡的负面物证变为周代统治的正面物证，才能成为周人的法定所有物。在证明商的灭亡时，鼎仍被看作商的象征；为了证明周所有权的合法性，鼎必须变成周的内在因素。

《易经》说:“革，去故也;鼎，取新也。”[233] 武王由于征服了商并夺取了鼎而被赋予“武”的谥号。在新建都城中通过定鼎来“取新”的人是其儿子，被称为“成”。一套完备的礼仪在定鼎的过程中被逐渐实现：九鼎的位置通过占卜得以确定，新的城市被建立；九鼎从专门的“鼎门”运送到它的新家。[234] 这些仪式为新王朝展示其威力和合法性提供了大好机会，举行晋见和册命，制作新的礼仪青铜器。[235] 在定鼎的过程中，各种社会性和政治性的关系也被确立和认定。可以说，这些礼仪活动使九鼎真正成为周人的一座集体的纪念碑。

五百年后，周王室已经退化为一个苟延残喘的傀儡政府，楚军兵临城下，楚王使臣口出狂言询问九鼎之轻重，他的意图被认为是要想篡夺王权。王孙满一番谈论九鼎的话则力图证明周作为权力核心的合法性。这位机智善辩的大臣从成王那里找到他的证据：“成王定鼎于郏鄏，卜世三十，卜年七百。”但他回避了武王从商代夺取九鼎的事实——这个历史事件太容易被楚王利用以证明其野心的正当性。

我们无法知道王孙满是否真的见过深藏在周代宗庙中的九鼎，但是他所说的九鼎无疑是一种历史的虚构。耐人寻味的是，这一虚构将整个礼仪美术浓缩和提炼为一个单独形象。作为三代时期最为

apparently had to combine all phases of ritual art and all significant aspects of a dominant concept of monumentality that had developed over a long period of several thousand years.

The history of *liqi* began in at least the fourth millennium B.C. Works of ritual art were created by imitating ordinary objects in "precious" materials. Shapes were then altered, and symbolic decoration and emblems were added. This sequence was replicated in the development of bronze art. Bronze as the new "precious" material was first employed to imitate the fragile imagery of earlier ritual pottery. A new emphasis on metamorphic images then brought about great variations in style and motif. Commemorative inscriptions, in turn, took over, and finally a bronze became a "text" for reading. The changing foci in this evolution—from material to shape to decoration to inscription—suggest the changing signifiers of ritual art from the most concrete to the most abstract, and from natural elements to artificial signs.

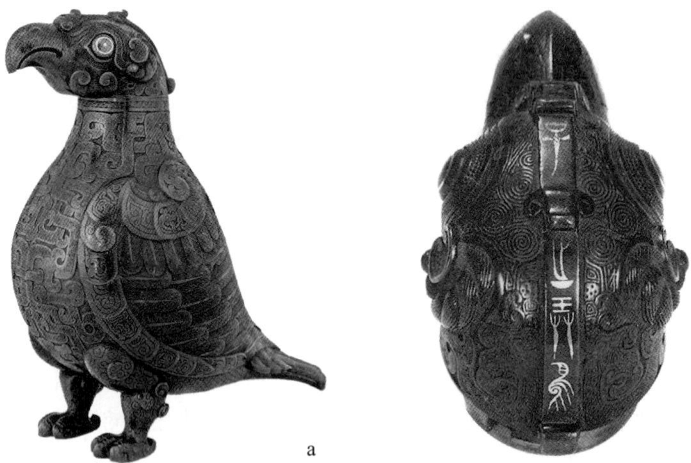

Fig. 1.77. (a) Bird-shaped bronze *zun* vessel, with the gold inlay inscription "The gentlemen commissioned this bird for amusement." Eastern Zhou, *ca*. 5th century B.C. H. 26.5 cm. Freer Gallery of Art, Washington, D.C. (b) Inscription on the bird's head.

图 1.77 （a）鸟形青铜尊。东周，约前 5 世纪。高 26.5 厘米。华盛顿，弗利尔美术馆藏。（b）鸟头部的错金铭文"子作弄鸟"。

All these layers and aspects of ritual art were woven into Wangsun
Man's image of the Nine Tripods. Their material was contributed by
various regions so that the Tripods could symbolize a unified political
power. The same symbolism was also expressed by casting regional
things—most likely emblems of local authorities—onto the Tripods; such
emblems also characterized ritual jades and early bronzes. The belief in
the supernatural qualities of the Tripods—their "intelligence" and their
ability to generate their own movement—seems to have been related
to late Shang metamorphic imagery, which gives a vessel an animated
presence. The number and formation of the Tripods, moreover, attests to 074
the Zhou convention that only the Son of Heaven could possess a set of
nine tripods.[236]

重要的纪念碑，九鼎必须把礼仪美术的所有阶段，以及千年间发展出来的具有支配地位的纪念碑性的所有重要方面综合在一起。

如上所述，礼器的历史至少开始于公元前第四个千年，通过用贵重材料模仿平常物品以创作出礼仪美术的作品。随后，礼器的外形被特殊化，象征性装饰和徽志也被创造出来。这个过程在青铜艺术的发展中重复：青铜首先被用作一种新的贵重材料以仿制早期“脆弱”的陶礼器。对变异形象的重视随即带来了风格和题材的重大变化。接着，纪念性的铭文出现了，并最终使青铜器变为一种用来阅读的“文本”的承载物。从材料到外形，再到装饰和铭文，这一系列演进中的变化焦点展现出礼仪美术特征的变化，即从最实在到最抽象，从自然的因素到人工的标记。

礼仪美术的所有这些层次和方面都被包含在了王孙满论九鼎的那番话中。根据他的说法，九鼎的材料来源于不同的地区，所以这些礼器可以象征政权的统一。同样的象征性还表现于将地域性事物——很可能是地方政权的徽志——铸造在鼎上；我们知道，这些徽志也是玉礼器和早期青铜器的特征。关于鼎有超自然特性的信念——它们的顺应天命和移动自身的能力——似乎与晚商青铜器上具有活力的变形图像有关。此外，鼎的数量和成套排列又体现出一个周代的概念，即只有天子才能拥有九鼎。[236]

Fig. 1.78. A set of bronze *zun* and *pan* vessels. Eastern Zhou. 5th century B.C. H. 33.1 cm (*zun*) ; 24 cm (*pan*). Excavated in 1978 at Leigudun, Suixian, Hubei province. Hubei Provincial Museum, Wuhan.

图 1.78 青铜尊盘。东周，前 5 世纪。尊高 33.1 厘米，盘高 24 厘米。1978 年湖北随县擂鼓墩出土。湖北省博物馆藏。

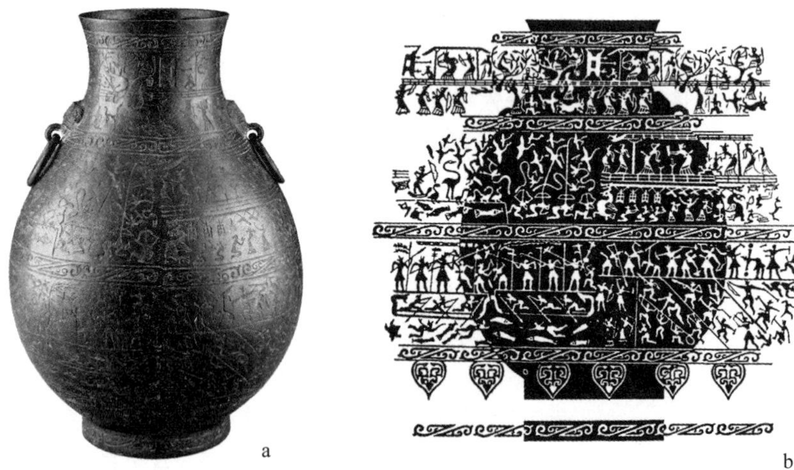

Fig. 1.79. (a) Bronze *hu* vessel with pictorial decoration. Eastern Zhou. *Ca.* 5th century B.C. H. 38.3 cm. Palace Museum, Beijing. (b) Drawing of the decoration.

图 1.79 （a）装饰画像的青铜壶。东周，约前 5 世纪。高 38.3 厘米。故宫博物院藏。（b）画像线图。

It has been suggested that political monuments are most often established when a new power is forming or when an old power is collapsing.[237] The Xia forged the Tripods at the dawn of China's dynastic history; toward the end of the Three Dynasties the Tripods again dominated people's thoughts. But as we have seen, the Tripods conceived in the sixth century B.C. were no longer real vessels, but *memories* of the bygone history of *liqi*. It was on these memories, not on the physical Tripods, that the Zhou's fate depended. Wangsun Man's speech on the Tripods was thus also a lamentation, but what he lamented was not only the Zhou's loss of glory but also the decline of an ancient monumentality and the Chinese Bronze Age. By this time, the production of ritual paraphernalia had been largely replaced by the manufacture of luxury goods. Patronized by powerful lords, an extravagant artistic style had come into vogue.[238] Commemorative inscriptions fell out of fashion; words on bronzes now stated that these were dowries or "playthings" (*nongqi*) (Figs. 1.77a, b). Meaningless decoration conquered substance; intricate designs transformed a solid bronze into a honeycomb (Fig. 1.78). Vessels were also

曾有人指出，政治性的纪念碑常常在一个新政权形成或一个旧政权衰落时被建立。[237] 这个说法和中国古代情况相符：当中国朝代史的黎明到来时，夏铸造了九鼎；当三代即将结束的时候，九鼎又重新占据了人们的思想。但正如我们已经看到的，公元前 6 世纪构想的九鼎已不再是真正的器具，而是对于已逝礼器历史的记忆。正是这些记忆而不是实际的鼎，寄托着周的命运。因此，王孙满关于九鼎的议论也是一种悲叹，所叹息的并不仅仅是周代消逝了的荣耀，而且包括整个古代纪念碑性和中国青铜时代的没落。在这个时期，礼器的制作在很大程度上被奢侈品的制造所替代。在强大的地方统治者的赞助下，一种奢靡的艺术风格成为时尚。[238] 纪念性的铭文不再流行；青铜器上的文字标明这些器具是嫁妆或“弄器”［图 1.77］。缺乏宗教意义的装饰充斥于器物之上；复杂精巧的设计将一件坚实的铜器转化为一个“蜂房”般的构件［图 1.78］。同时，

Fig. 1.80. (a) Human-shaped lamp. Bronze with gold, silver, and turquoise inlay. Eastern Zhou. 4th century B.C. H. 66.4 cm. Excavated in 1966 at Pingshan, Hebei province. Hebei Provincial Museum. (b) Chamber pot. Bronze with gold and silver inlay. Late Eastern Zhou. *Ca.* 4th-3rd centuries B.C. Palace Museum, Beijing.

图 1.80 （a）人形灯。青铜嵌金、银、绿松石。东周，约前 4 世纪。高 66.4 厘米。1966 年河北平山出土。河北省博物馆藏。（b）虎子（溺器）。青铜嵌金、银。东周，约前 4—前 3 世纪。故宫博物院藏。

turned into pictures, illustrating banquets, hunting games, and killing (Figs. 1.79a, b).

The important signifiers of the archaic monumentality—commemorative inscription, symbolic decoration, and shape—were thus, one by one, rejected, and this counter-development finally led to the abandonment of bronzes. About a hundred years after Wangsun Man's speech, in 512 B.C., a reformer from the state of Jin named Zhao Yang "published" a legal document. While this act was in itself a rebellion against the old social system based on *li*, his way of doing it seemed also to parody traditional monumentality: he inscribed the document on a *ding* tripod made of the "ugly and crude" metal iron. When Confucius—an admirer of the traditional Zhou system—heard this, he sighed: "Now that the iron tripod has been made, Order has been abandoned."[239] Iron, however, never became a popular material for vessels. The demands for extravagance were satisfied by inlaid objects of mixed media (Figs. 1.80a, b). These works—sculptures, mirrors, belt hooks, musical instruments, wine and food containers, and even chamber pots—contradicted in every way the solemnity of ritual bronzes. Rich in color, intricate in design, but poor in commemorative content, what they exhibited was the uncontrolled desire for luxury.[240]

This was the end of *liqi* and the Chinese Bronze Age. So the Nine Tripods—the chief monuments of this age—retreated from history: they vanished in 336 B.C. No one was ever able to obtain them again.

器物也被转化成画，来描绘宴饮、竞射以及杀伐等场景［图 1.79］。

古老的纪念碑性的各个重要的方面——纪念性的铭文、象征性的装饰以及外形——就这样被一一抛弃，这种反方向的发展最终导致青铜礼器的衰亡。在公元前 512 年，即在王孙满对楚子问的大约百年后，晋国一位叫作赵鞅的改革家发行了一份“刑书”。这个行动的本身就是对基于礼的旧社会系统的一种反叛，同时他做这件事的方式也像是对于传统的纪念碑性的有意讽刺：他将这个法律文件铸在以“恶金”（铁）制作的一件鼎上。当尊崇传统周礼的孔子听说此事后，他说道：“晋其亡乎，失其度矣！”[239] 然而，铁并没有成为制作容器的流行材料。与之相反，用多种材料制作的精美镶嵌器物满足了当时人们对奢侈的需求［图 1.80］。这些作品——雕塑、镜子、带钩、乐器、饮食器，甚至包括溺器——在各个方面都与庄重的青铜礼器相抵触。色彩绚烂，设计繁复，但纪念性的内容却了无踪影——它们所展示的是对于奢华的毫无约束的渴望。[240]

这就是礼器和中国青铜时代的终结。也就是在这个时候，作为青铜时代纪念碑性的主要代表，九鼎也从历史舞台上退场：它们在公元前 336 年突然消失，再也没有人能够得到它们。

CHAPTER TWO TEMPLE, PALACE, AND TOMB

077 When he built the Spirit Tower,
When he planned it and founded it,
All the people worked at it;
In less than a day they finished it. —*Book of Songs*

Introductions to early Chinese art history often show an alarming discontinuity: zoomorphic patterns on bronze vessels dominate the chapters on Shang-Zhou art; discussions of Qin-Han art focus on figurative images and pictorial scenes. Questions such as how these two distinct phases were linked historically in the cultural tradition, why ritual bronzes died out and were replaced by carvings and paintings, and what caused such a dramatic change, obviously among the most crucial problems in the study of early Chinese art, have drawn only limited attention from scholars, however. Two interrelated factors may be responsible for this neglect. First, the foci and interests of art historians are often restricted by their chosen "field" of either Shang-Zhou bronzes or Han bas-reliefs. Second, in the conventional conceptualization of early Chinese art history, bronze art is a "decorative" tradition and pictorial art a "representational" tradition. The transition from the former to the latter is approached either as a revolution in visual forms or as a consequence of foreign influence from a more vivid "barbarian" world.

This conceptualization is fundamentally misleading because it favors surface patterns over objects and privileges isolated objects over their groupings and context. In other words, it reflects the mentality of an art collector influenced by painting connoisseurship who appreciates examples of early art for their individual aesthetic and historical value. But unlike a later scroll painting, a Shang-Zhou bronze vessel or a Han pictorial slab was never created or viewed as an independent "work of art." Such works were always originally a component of a larger assembly, either a set of ritual paraphernalia or a pictorial program. These assemblies in turn always appeared as integral components of special architectural structures—a temple, a palace, or a tomb. Such a structure constituted a monumental complex in society. As the site of administration and important ceremonies, it focused people's attention and defined a political

 宗庙、宫殿与墓葬

经始灵台，经之营之。
庶民攻之，不日成之。

——《诗经·大雅·灵台》

早期中国美术史的通论经常表现出一种惊人的不连贯性：青铜器上的动物纹样在有关商周艺术的章节中占据了主导地位；而对秦汉艺术的讨论却集中于写实的人物形象和图画场面。这两种迥然不同的艺术风格究竟是怎样在中国文化传统中被历史地联结在一起？青铜礼器又为何衰亡，为雕刻与绘画所取代？是什么因素导致了这一划时代的变化？诸如此类的问题在早期中国艺术中显然十分关键，然而却很少引起学者们的注意。导致这一漠视的内在因素或许有两点。其一，美术史家的注意力和兴趣往往为其既定的研究领域——商周青铜器或汉代画像——所限制。其二，在对早期中国美术史的研究中，青铜艺术被当作一种“装饰性”的艺术传统，而画像艺术被定义为是一种“表现性”的艺术传统。从前者到后者的转变或被解释成一场视觉形式的革命，或被看作受到某种更为“生动”的外来影响的结果。

这些概念从根本上可以说是误导性的，因为它们对表面纹样和画像的强调超过对于负载它们的器物和建筑的兴趣，而对器物和建筑的重视又胜过对它们的组合以及环境的研究。换言之，这反映了收藏家的心理状态。画作鉴赏家欣赏早期艺术独特的美学和历史学价值，而收藏家受到鉴赏家的影响。与后来的卷轴画不同，一件商周青铜彝器或者一块汉画像石从来都不是作为独立的“艺术品”制作出来的，并且也从来不被当成一件独立的“艺术品”使用和看待。这些作品最初总是一个更大的集合体（要么是一组礼器，要么是一套画像）的组成部分，而这些集合体又总是特定建筑物——宗庙、宫殿或坟墓——的内在组成部分。这些建筑物在社会上构成了带有纪念性质的综合体，作为执政和举行重要仪式的场所而引人注目，成为政治中心的特色。

center. It synthesized and organized individual forms of ritual art into a coherent and functional whole, and it provided people with a place and occasions to encounter and utilize these forms—objects and images—in ritual practices. This understanding, first reached by social historians
078 through their study of textual sources,[1] has profound implications for the methodology of early art history. It demands that art historians shift their focus from individual objects and images to large monumental complexes with all their physical, ritual, and ideological components: only at this level of analysis can we discuss the precise historical relationship among art, ritual, social structure, and politics, and explain important changes in early Chinese art, including the decline of ritual bronzes and the flourishing of pictorial images.

This understanding also determines my first task in this chapter: to contextualize *liqi's* monumentality in relation to the structure and symbolism of the ancestral temple, the legitimate place for holding both political and religious ceremonies during the Western Zhou and the most important site for storing and displaying commemorative bronzes, including the Nine Tripods. A dialectic relationship existed between *liqi* and their architectural context: sacred bronzes gave meaning and authority to a temple, but these bronzes became functional and meaningful only during temple rituals. The most important ritual, that of metaphorically "returning" to the Origin of a clan or lineage, was oriented and punctuated by the temple's two-dimensional, layered spatial structure. A temple with its *liqi* thus became a collective monument of a clan or lineage, identifying its political status, preserving memories of its past, and linking it into a large social network through a "temple system" (*miaozhi*).

The temple system gained its most sophisticated form during the Western Zhou, but declined from the Eastern Zhou to the Han as palatial and funerary monuments assumed its political and religious roles. The appearance of these new monuments corresponded to essential changes in the country's social and religious structures. First, following the decline of Zhou rule based on the ancient clan-lineage system, powerful principalities gained independence and a unified political state finally emerged. Consequently, the palace became divorced from the lineage temple and became the chief symbol of political power. Second, this social

它们将各种独立的礼仪形式综合组织为相互关联的功能整体，为人们的礼仪活动提供面对和利用这些形式的机会和场所。这一最先由社会史学家通过研究文献资料而达成的理解，[1] 对研究早期美术有着深远的方法论意义。它要求美术史家将眼光由那些单独的器物和图像转向更大的纪念性综合体，及其所有物质、礼仪和观念性的组成部分：只有在这一层面上进行分析，我们才可以讨论艺术、宗教礼仪、社会结构与政治事件之间的确切历史关系，解释早期中国艺术中的重要转变，包括青铜礼器的衰落和画像的兴盛。

这一理解也决定了本章的首要任务：在与建筑物的关联中去完整地解读礼器的纪念碑性，解读宗庙作为西周时期举行政治与宗教仪式的合法场所、保存和陈列包括九鼎在内的那类具有公共纪念意义的青铜彝器之重地的作用。在礼器及其建筑原境之间存在着一种内在逻辑关系：神圣的青铜器赋予宗庙以权威和意义，而只有在宗庙的礼仪程序中，这些青铜器才能发挥其功能和意义。这些礼仪程序中的最重要者，是由祖庙的二维多重空间结构所引起和强调的、向氏族或宗族起源的隐喻式的“回归”。通过这种礼仪，宗庙及其礼器成为氏族或宗族的集体纪念物，标志着他们的政治地位，保存了他们对过去的记忆，并且通过“庙制”将自己与一个更广大的社会网络连结在一起。

庙制在西周时期获得了最完整的形式。但到了东周至汉代，当宫殿和墓葬取代了宗庙的政治和宗教角色，庙制便随之衰落了。新型纪念物的出现与国家在社会和宗教结构上的一系列重要变革相辅相成。首先，在基于古老宗族血亲体系的周礼式微之后，一些强大的诸侯国获得独立地位，最终导致统一政治帝国的出现。宫殿因而从宗庙中分离了出来，成为政治权力的主要象征。同时，这种社会

and political transformation was coupled with a religious transformation, most clearly signified by the shift of the center for ancestor worship from the collective lineage temple to tombs of families and individuals. Both developments contributed to a new conception of authority and a new symbolic presentation of authority, which took the form of "monumental architecture."

A massive Eastern Zhou tower or a giant Qin tumulus differed from a deep, dark Western Zhou temple not only in visual appearance but also in its essential monumentality. Unlike earlier monuments that guided people back to their clan origin, these new monuments were associated with powerful political entities and personages. A traditional temple relied largely upon the sacred *liqi* inside it to proclaim its monumentality, but palatial and funerary monuments realized their significance mainly through their own architectural form. Important signifiers of monumentality thus shifted from within to without—from objects to architecture, depth to surface, concealment to exhibition. If the development of Chinese art up to this point had been centered on *liqi*, architecture now became the locomotive. The desire for powerful architectural symbols stimulated people's fantasies to create high-rise buildings; architectural decoration—murals and wall-carvings—began to dominate the artistic imagination. The sudden popularity of stone funerary monuments further attests to a new consciousness of the symbolism of building material, just as in the old days special media—jade and bronze—had been employed in making *liqi*. Only at this moment in Chinese history does architecture replace *liqi* to become "the expression of the very soul of societies"—to embody social and political power with the authority to command and prohibit.[2] Following this line of argument, the second and third sections of this chapter reconstruct a historical process that occurred during the Eastern Zhou and Qin, when architectural monuments appeared in China and functioned to express and regulate new social, political, and religious orders. This role of architectural monuments reinforced their further alienation from ordinary architecture:

they had to be "unique" not only in height and volume but also in material. The last section therefore examines the Chinese "discovery" of stone as a major medium for funerary structures. This chapter links the earlier and later chapters in this book and provides a background for my later discussion of Han palatial and funerary monuments.

和政治的变革也伴随着一场宗教的变革，其最突出的表现是祖先崇拜的中心从集体性的宗庙转向家庭和个人的墓葬。这两方面的发展变化共同促成了新的"权威"概念的形成及其象征表达，"纪念性建筑"代替了礼器，成为表达新的政治和宗教权威的法定形式。

一座东周的高台或一座秦朝的陵园不仅在外观上与一座阴暗、幽深的西周宗庙不同，其实质上的纪念碑性也有着巨大差别。这两类新型的纪念性建筑与强大的政治实体和显赫的个人权威直接相关，而不再引导人们寻觅自己宗族的本源。一座传统的宗庙在很大程度上依靠神圣的礼器以获得纪念碑性，而宫殿和墓葬纪念物则主要通过自身的建筑形式来实现它们的意义。这样，纪念碑性的载体就发生了从内到外——从器物到建筑、从核心到表面、从隐匿到展示——的变易。如果说中国艺术的发展曾在一段漫长的时期内重视礼器，那么到这个新的历史阶段，建筑则成了艺术发展的火车头。对强有力的建筑象征符号的欲望刺激了人们营造高大建筑的热情，包括壁画与浮雕等形式的建筑装饰也开始主导人们的艺术想象力。正如此前玉和青铜被用来制作礼器一样，石质墓葬纪念性建筑的突然流行表明了人们对一种新建筑材料的象征性意识的觉醒。只是在中国历史上的这一特定时刻，建筑才取代了礼器，成为当时"社会精神的表达"——成为具有令行禁止权威的社会政治权力的体现。[2] 沿着这一线索，本章的第二节与第三节将重构东周至秦代，当纪念性建筑物在中国出现并且起着表达和调整新的社会、政治与宗教秩序的作用时，所经历的历史过程。纪念性建筑物所扮演的这一角色使其与普通民用建筑进一步拉开距离：它们不仅在高度和体积方面体现其特殊的身份，在对材料的使用方面也不同凡响。因此，本章的最后一节将讨论中国人对东汉以后丧葬建筑的主要材料——石头——的"发现"。本章在全书中起着承前启后的作用，为下文有关汉代宫殿与丧葬纪念性建筑的讨论提供了一个背景。

❶ The Temple

079 When Tan Fu led the members of the Ji clan on a westward march along the Wei River, he was looking for a home for the descendents of Hou Ji, who would eventually conquer the Shang and establish the Zhou dynasty. Tan Fu found this home in the Plain of Zhou (Zhouyuan) at the foot of Mount Qi, a fertile land where "celery and sowthistle were sweet as ricecakes." Tortoise shells were consulted for divine confirmation, and an auspicious prognostication was obtained: "Stop and halt, build your home right here." So Tan Fu stopped and began to build the first Zhou capital.[3] He determined the orientation of the city, drew its boundaries, and entrusted the construction work to the Masters of Works and Multitudes. The first building was an ancestral temple called Jinggong, or the Capital Temple.[4] As recorded in the Zhou ritual hymn "Mian" in the *Book of Songs*,

> Dead straight was the plumb-line,
> The planks were lashed to hold the earth;
> They made the Hall of Ancestors, very venerable.[5]

The poem reveals two principal features of an archaic Chinese capital in terms of its definition and building sequence. First, "a capital [*du*] is a city that has a lineage temple [*zongmiao*] housing ancestral tablets."[6] Second, the construction of Tan Fu's town confirms a regulation later formulated in the *Book of Rites*: "When a nobleman is about to engage in building, the ancestral temple should have his first attention, the stables and arsenal the next, and the residences the last."[7] The function and construction of a town were understood in a hierarchical scheme: ancestor worship first, defense second, living arrangements last. Furthermore, the temple, the heart of a town, provided only a spatial framework for ancestral rites and other ceremonies; its importance lay, to a great extent, in housing ritual vessels dedicated to ancestral spirits. As the same ritual canon continues: "When the head of a lineage is about to prepare things, the vessels of sacrifice should have the first place, the offerings, the next; and the vessels for use at meals, the last."[8] Stated consecutively in the ritual canon, these two passages best demonstrate the intimate relationship between an ancestral temple and its *liqi* as the two basic components of an archaic monumental complex in Shang-Western Zhou society.

一、宗庙

当亶父率领周姓部落成员沿着渭河西行时，他计划为后稷的子孙们寻找一个家园。后来，他们最终征服了商，就在这里建立了周朝。当年，亶父在岐山脚下找到了周原这个地方时，那里的“芹、蓟甜如米糕”。他们以龟甲占卜得一吉兆：“止旅迺密，芮鞫之即。”（定居的人越来越稠密，就居住在这芮水的岸边。）亶父于是停了下来，开始在那里建立第一座周都。[3]他确定了城市的方位，划定了地界，交由司工与众人营建。所建造的第一座建筑是被称作“京宫”的宗庙，用以追溯和崇拜氏族的祖先。[4]正如《诗经·周颂·緜》中所记述的那样：

其绳则直，缩版以载，作庙翼翼。[5]

就其意义和建筑程序而言，这些诗句揭示了古代中国都城的两个主要特征。第一，“凡邑有宗庙、先君之主曰都。”[6]第二，亶父营建都城的基本顺序肯定了以后《礼记》记载下来的一个规矩：“君子将营宫室，宗庙为先，厩库为次，居室为后。”[7]一座都城的建造与功能因此反映为一种等级观念：祭祖在先，城防为次，生活设施在最后。再进一步说，作为都城心脏的宗庙仅仅是为了祭祖和举行其他礼仪活动提供了一个空间架构；它的重要性在很大程度上在于盛放献给先祖的礼器。因此《礼记》继上文又记载道：“凡家造，祭器为先，牺赋为次，养器为后。”[8]接续出现的这两段话有力地证明了三代社会中纪念碑综合体的两个基本组成部分——祖庙与礼器——之间的密切关系。

Tan Fu's town initiated a series of Zhou capitals established by his descendents. Within the three generations from Tan Fu to his grandson King Wen, the Zhou moved their operational center step by step eastward toward the lower streams of the Wei River.[9] Underlying this movement was a persistent Zhou attempt to gain access to China's heartland and to wrest control of the country from the Shang:

> Descendant of Hou Ji was the Great King [i.e., Tan Fu]
> Who lived on the southern slopes of Mount Qi
> And began to trim the Shang.
> Till at last came King Wen and King Wu,
> And continued the Great King's task,
> Fulfilled the wrath of Heaven
> In the field of Mu: "No treachery, no blundering!
> God on high is watching you!"[10]

Although the Zhou defeated the Shang only during King Wu's reign, later Zhou people considered their "dynastic" history to have begun with King Wen and repeatedly praised the merit of this king in their temple hymns:

> 080 Renowned was King Wen,
> Yes, high was his renown.
> He united, he gave peace;
> Manifold were his victories.

Among many factors that contributed to this attitude, an important one was that this king built Feng, a new Zhou capital centered on a new ancestral temple, again called Jinggong. As the same hymn continues:

> He built his city within due boundaries,
> He made Feng according to the ancient plan.
> He did not fulfill his own desires,
> But worked in pious obedience to the dead.[11]

King Wen was thus considered loyal to his ancestors and instrumental in carrying out their plan to conquer the Shang. Because of the new Jinggong in Feng, this capital was also called Zongzhou, meaning the seat of the Zhou lineage.[12]

亶父的都城成为以后一系列周代都城的祖型。在从亶父到其孙文王的三代之间，周一步步将他们的控制中心向东部低洼的渭河流域移动。[9] 这一持续的举动显示出周逐步向中原发展，从商王朝夺取国家控制权的企图。《诗经 · 閟宫》中说：

后稷之孙，实维大王。
居岐之阳，实始翦商。
至于文、武，缵大王之绪，
致天之届，于牧之野。
无贰无虞，上帝临女。[10]

尽管周克商只是发生在武王统治时期，后来的周人却认为其王朝的历史从文王已经开始，并且反复在宗庙颂诗中赞美文王的功绩。《诗经 · 文王有声》中说：

文王有声，
遹骏有声。
遹求厥宁，
遹观厥成。

导致他们如此看待文王的一个最重要原因是文王建邑于丰。这座新都的中央是一处宗庙，仍称“京宫”。同一诗篇继续说道：

筑城伊淢，
作丰伊匹。
匪棘其欲，
遹追来孝。[11]

这些颂歌反映出周人认为文王忠实于他的祖先，为执行先辈伐商的计划做出了贡献。因为丰拥有这座新的京宫，这座都城又被称为宗周，即周宗室所处之地。[12]

King Wen's son and successor, King Wu, expanded the capital to include Hao across the Feng River, but he maintained the temple in Feng and supervised important religious and political matters there.[13] His role in Zhou history was to realize Wen's plan:

> A strong toiler was King Wen;
> Well he opened the way for those that followed him.
> As heir Wu received it,
> Conquered the Yin [i.e., Shang], utterly destroyed them.[14]

After King Wu led an allied army to storm the Shang capital, he immediately abrogated the royal temple and the Land Altar (*she*) of the Shang, obtained the Nine Tripods, and announced that the Zhou had therefore received the mandate from Heaven.[15] In the following days, he communicated this message to his deceased father, Wen, and "set a foundation for administration" (*lizheng*).[16] The king held another series of grand ritual events as soon as he returned to the capital. Wearing the most honored ritual costume and holding a ceremonial scepter, King Wu sacrificed to a series of Zhou ancestors while denouncing the Shang's crimes. He again went to the temple the next day to appoint the ministers of eight major districts.[17] All these rituals functioned to "upgrade" the Zhou lineage to a dynastic level, to establish an administrative system, and to help the king govern the country through this system.

King Wu ended the Shang's political dominance, but the Zhou's final victory over the Shang took place only after his death, when his brother Dan, better known as the Duke of Zhou, helped young King Cheng put down violent disturbances by Shang loyalists. Traditional historiography eulogized this period as that of "accomplishment" (*cheng*): a feudal system (*fengjian*) was established with 71 vassal states "shielding" the Zhou royal house in the center.[18] The beginning of this new era was indicated by founding New Capital (Xinyi), or Chengzhou, near present-day Luoyang in Henan.[19] The city's construction followed the building sequence of Tan Fu's town.[20] The site for the capital was selected by divination, and the city's boundary was then marked out, as recorded in "The Announcement of the Duke of Shao" ("Shao gao"), a Zhou official text now in the *Book of Documents*:

文王的儿子武王将都城的范围扩展到跨过沣水的镐，但他仍将宗庙保留于丰，在那里监管重大的宗教和政治事务。[13] 他在周代历史上发挥的功用首先是实现了文王的计划：

允文文王！
克开厥后。
嗣武受之，
胜殷遏刘。[14]

武王率领其联盟部队攻陷了商都之后，随即废除了商代王室的宗庙和社，获得了九鼎，从而宣布周拥有了天授王权。[15] 在其后的几天里，他将获胜的消息祭告于先父文王，并由此"立政"。[16] 返回自己的都城以后，武王马上主持了一系列重大礼仪活动。身穿礼服，手持王节，他祭祀了周人的列祖列宗，同时声讨了商王的不道。次日，武王又于宗庙任命了八个主要政区的朝臣。[17] 所有这些礼仪活动的作用，在于将周宗室的等级提高到王朝的高度，确立行政体制，进而通过这个体制来治理新建立的国家。

武王伐商结束了商在政治上的统治地位，但是周取得对商的最后胜利却是在武王去世之后。他的弟弟旦，即广为人知的周公，帮助年幼的成王镇压了商代残余势力发动的暴乱。传统史学将这一时期称为有"成"之年：一套分封制度确立了，周王室在周围 71 个诸侯国的屏卫之下，成为政治结构的中心。[18] 位于今河南洛阳附近的新邑（或称成周）的建立，标志着这一新的历史时期的开始。[19] 这座城的结构仿效亶父都城的建筑布局，[20] 城址首先通过占卜选择，城的边界然后得以确定，正如《尚书》中的周代官方文献《召诰》所记：

> In the third quarter of the second month, on the sixth day *yiwei*. . . the Grand Guardian [i.e., the Duke of Shao] preceded the Duke of Zhou to inspect the site. Two days later, on *maoshen*, the Grand Guardian in the morning arrived at Luo and made a tortoise-shell divination about the site. When he had obtained the oracle, he planned and laid out [the city]. On the [next] third day, *gengxu*, the Grand Guardian with all the Yin people started work on the [public] emplacements at the nook of the Luo River; and four days later, on *jiayin*, the emplacements were determined. The next day, *yimao*, the Duke of Zhou arrived at Luo in the morning and again inspected the position of the new city.[21]

Just as Tan Fu had done in the past, the initial selection of Chengzhou's site was reexamined and confirmed by repeated prognostications, which were conducted by the Duke of Zhou, regent for King Cheng.[22] Again like Tan Fu's capital, the first and most important building in Cheng-zhou was an ancestral temple—we know this because the Duke of Zhou instructed young King Cheng to hold a winter sacrifice in the temple as the city's inauguration ceremony. During this ritual, the king sacrificed red bulls to
081 his forebears Kings Wen and Wu. After this, "The king's guests [i.e., the ancestral spirits] all arrived. The king entered Grand Hall [in the temple] and poured out the libation. The king gave investiture to the lineage of the Duke of Zhou, and the archivist Yi made the declaration."[23] The sequence of this ritual seemed to repeat that of King Wu's victory ceremony: sacrifices first and investiture second, both taking place in a royal temple and witnessed by ancestral spirits. A major difference between these two rituals, however, was that at the time of Chengzhou's establishment, King Wu had joined the "former kings" of Zhou; he had become an ancestral spirit worshipped in Chengzhou's temple, a receiver of ritual offerings and a guardian of his son, the living ruler.

Tan Fu's foundation of the Zhou base at Mount Qi, Kings Wen and Wu's conquest of the Shang, and King Cheng's pacification of the country were the three most crucial moments in early Zhou history. All instances were related to the establishment and reestablishment of capitals and royal temples, and all three temples constructed by these Zhou rulers were called Jinggong.[24] But why did new temples have to be built at different stages in Zhou history? What was their internal structure, and who was worshipped in them? What did these subjects of worship signify? There is virtually no evidence for the organization of Tan Fu's temple. Hypothetically, this temple was constructed to worship the Zhou ancestors from Hou Ji down to Tan Fu's father. The temple established

> 惟二月既望，越六日乙未……惟太保先周公相宅……越三日戊申，太保朝至于洛，卜宅。厥既得卜，则经营。越三日庚戌，太保乃以庶殷攻位于洛汭。越五日甲寅，位成。若翼日乙卯，周公朝至于洛，则达观于新邑营。[21]

正如亶父所做的那样，成周城址的选定是由摄政的周公以占卜方式反复验证的。[22]也如亶父的都城一样，成周的第一座，也是最重要的一座建筑，同样是一座祖庙——我们知道这一点，是因为周公曾辅助年幼的成王在这座庙里举行了一次冬祭，作为这个都城的创立典礼。在这次典礼当中，成王以赤牛为牲，祭祀了先祖文王和武王。紧接着，“王宾杀禋咸格，王入太室，祼。王命周公后，作册逸诰。”[23]这次仪式在程序上似乎重复了武王获胜时的庆典仪式：先是祭祀，然后是封赏功臣。两者皆举行于王庙，在祖先神灵的监视下进行。两次仪式的主要不同在于，当成周建立之时，武王业已加入了周的“先王”行列，成为成周祖庙中供奉的对象。作为宗教享祠的接受者，他现在扮演的是保佑其后嗣的守护神角色。

周代早期历史中的三个最为关键时期可说是亶父建周于岐山，文王和武王克商，以及成王之定国安邦。三个时期中的每一中心事件都与都城和王室宗庙的建立和巩固有关，而且三个王室宗庙都叫作“京宫”。[24]但是，为什么周代历史的不同阶段中要建立新的宗庙呢？它们的内在结构如何？其中供奉的是谁？这些供奉对象又意味着什么？我们几乎没有任何关于亶父所建祖庙内部组织的证据，只能估计这个庙中祭拜的是从后稷到亶父父亲的周人祖先。文王所建

by King Wen did not replace this original temple and offered only a place for worshipping a second group of Zhou ancestors. A passage in a document called "The Grand Presentation of Captives" ("Shi fu"), now in the *Leftover Documents from the Zhou* (*Yi Zhou shu*), suggests that during King Wu's reign, those worshipped in the temple at Feng included six ancestors of the four consecutive generations since Tan Fu:[25]

1. Tan Fu
2. Tai Bo (Tan Fu's eldest son, who refused the throne)
3. Yu Zhong (Tan Fu's second son, who refused the throne)
4. Wang Ji (Tan Fu's third son and royal successor)
5. King Wen (Wang Ji's elder son and royal successor)
6. Yi Kao (King Wen's elder son, killed by the Shang)

After King Wu died, his memorial tablet was added to this temple.[26] The temple built by King Cheng, however, differed radically from the previous temples in introducing a new pattern of ancestor worship. It consisted of three ancestral shrines, one for Hou Ji and the other two for King Wen and King Wu.[27] It thus demonstrated three new features that later became crucial for ancestral temples: first, the subjects of worship were restricted to the heads of the royal lineage and did not include indirect ancestors. Second, not all former kings were worshipped in the temple; the chosen ones belonged to two categories: the *yuanzu* (the remote ancestor or the founder of the royal lineage) and the *jinzu* (recent ancestors and direct forebears of the living king). Third, although there was only a single *yuanzu*, the multiple *jinzu* were divided into the *mu* sequence (starting from King Wen) and the *zhao* sequence (starting from King Wu). As time passed and the royal line lengthened, more recent royal ancestors were worshipped in the temple, and Kings Wen and Wu were distinguished from both *yuanzu* and *jinzu*. Because of the extraordinary importance of these two kings in Zhou history, their shrines were kept in the temple and given a special name, *tiao*. This process finally led to a temple consisting of seven shrines to individual ancestors in three groups (Figs. 2.1, 2.2a).[28]

Fig. 2.1. Internal organization of the Zhou royal temple

图 2.1　周王室宗庙的内部组织结构

之庙并未取代这个最初的庙，而是为祭拜第二组周人祖先提供了场所。据《逸周书》中《世俘解》里的一段文字来看，在武王统治时期，被供奉于丰都宗庙中的有自亶父以下四世中的六位祖先，包括：[25]

1. 亶父
2. 太伯（亶父长子，他拒绝了王位）
3. 虞仲（亶父次子，也拒绝了王位）
4. 王季（亶父的第三子，王位继承者）
5. 文王（王季之长子，王位继承者）
6. 邑考（文王之长子，为殷人所杀）

武王死后，他的牌位也被放入这座宗庙。[26] 成王在成周兴建的宗庙与以往的宗庙迥然不同，而是引进了祖先崇拜的一种新模式。这座宗庙由三个祠堂组成，一个为后稷而建，另外两个为文王和武王而建。[27] 这座庙因此显示了对以后周代宗庙发展至关重要的三个新特征：首先，供奉对象限于王室直系的宗子，不包括非直系的祖先。其次，并非所有的先王都供在庙中；被崇拜者包括远祖和近祖两类。最后，虽然所供奉的远祖只有一个，近祖则分为昭（自武王始）穆（自文王始）两个序列。随着时间的推移和王室世系的延长，更多的近祖被供奉在庙中，文王和武王也就获得了既非近祖又非远祖的身份。因为这两个先王在周代历史的特殊重要性，所以宗庙中保留了他们的位置，并给以特别的名称“祧”。通过这个过程，王室宗庙最终包括为不同祖先而设的三组七个祠堂［图 2.1，图 2.2a］。[28]

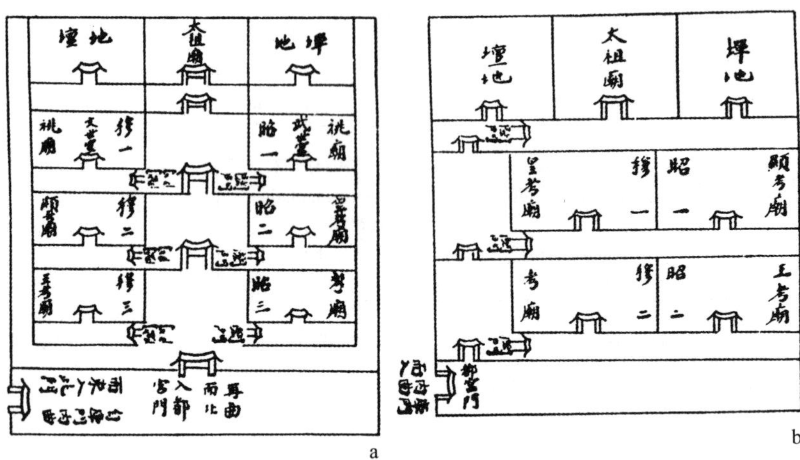

Fig. 2.2 Two levels of ancestral temples. (a) The Zhou royal ancestral temple, with the temple of the founder at the center and three temples of recent ancestors on each side. (b) The temple of a feudal lord, with only two temples of recent ancestors on each side.

图 2.2　宗庙的两种平面布局。（a）周王室宗庙，太祖庙在中间，两侧各置三个近祖庙。（b）侯庙，两侧各有两个近祖庙。

This structure, which must have come into being after King Gong's reign (tenth century B.C.),[29] then became the standard form of the Zhou royal temple. The three shrines of Hou Ji, Wen, and Wu were permanent, but the occupants of the four *zhao* and *mu* shrines changed every generation in order to maintain the fixed number of shrines. When
082 a king died, he would be worshipped in the "father's shrine"; his father, grandfather, and great-grandfather would be moved up; the shrine of his great-great-grandfather would be dismantled, and the tablet of this ancestor would be stored in a *tiao*.

这种“七庙”的建筑结构可能出现于恭王时期（前 10 世纪）之后，[29] 随即成为周王室宗庙的定制：为后稷、文王和武王所设的三个祠堂固定不变，而四个昭、穆祠堂所供奉的对象则每代变更以保持固定的祠堂数目。当一个周王死去时，他被供奉在“考庙”中；他的父亲、祖父和曾祖父将依次上移；其曾祖之父的灵位将被拆除，移存到祧中。

陶鬶，大汶口文化

Pottery *gui* tripod.
Dawenkou culture (p. 88)

玉饰品，良渚文化

Jade ornament.
Liangzhu culture (p. 96)

玉铲，大汶口文化

Jade axe.
Dawenkou culture (p. 77)

玉饰品，良渚文化

Jade ornament.
Liangzhu culture (p. 96)

玉圆柱，良渚文化

Jade column.
Liangzhu culture (p. 109)

青铜爵，夏代晚期

Bronze *jue* vessel.
Late Xia dynasty (p. 128)

青铜罍，商代中期

Bronze *lei* vessel.
Mid-Shang dynasty (p. 152)

矛，商代晚期

Spear.
Late Shang dynasty (p. 180)

亚醜钺，商代晚期

Yachou axe.
Late Shang dynasty (p. 180)

青铜方鼎，商代中期

Bronze square *ding*.
Mid-Shang dynasty (p. 132)

青铜卣，商代晚期

Bronze *you* vessel.
Late Shang dynasty (p. 168)

青铜觥，商代晚期

Bronze *gong* vessel.
Late Shang dynasty (p. 166)

青铜瓿，商代晚期

Bronze *bu* vessel.
Late Shang dynasty (p. 148)

鼎，西周早期

Ding tripod.

Early Western Zhou (p. 20)

燕侯盂，西周早期

Yanhou *yu*.
Early Western Zhou (p. 171)

折觥，西周早期

Zhe *gong*.
Early Western Zhou (p. 170)

庚赢卣，西周中期

Geng Ying *you*.
Mid-Western Zhou (p. 172)

疾十三年壶，西周中后期

13th-year Xing *hu*.
Middle—late Western Zhou (p. 266)

疒四年盨，西周中后期

4th-year Xing *xu*.
Middle—late Western Zhou (p. 265)

史墙盘，西周中期

Shi Qiang *pan*.
Mid-Western Zhou (p. 259)

鸟形青铜尊，东周

Bird-shaped bronze *zun* vessel. Eastern Zhou (p. 204)

Scholars since the Han dynasty have generally agreed about this process. What they have often neglected, however, are the "meaning" of the ancestral groupings and the symbolism of the temple's structure. In my opinion, these two interrelated aspects most clearly disclose the monumentality of the royal temple complex. The three groups of ancestors, which determined the overall organization of this temple and its *liqi*, provided a basic system for organizing fragmentary memories of the Zhou's past into a coherent narrative. In other words, they presented a periodization of Zhou history from the vantage point of the descendents of the royal lineage. Zheng Xuan, a Han commentator on ancient ritual canons, wrote a highly significant passage: "The memorial tablets of the pre-dynastic ancestors [*xiangong*] were stocked in the shrine of the original ancestor, Hou Ji; the tablets of the dynastic ancestors [*xianwang*] were removed and kept in the shrines of King Wen and King Wu."[30] This implies that the three permanent subjects of worship were viewed not merely as individual ancestors but as symbols of two broad stages in Zhou history: Hou Ji initiated the Ji clan and represented the Zhou's pre-dynastic period; Wen and Wu founded the Zhou dynasty and symbolized

汉代以来的学者们大都认可这一程序，然而他们常常忽略祖先神这种组合形式的“意义”和宗庙结构的象征性。在我看来，这两个方面有着重要的内在联系，最为清晰地显示了周代王室宗庙的纪念碑性。总的来说，决定着宗庙结构及其礼器系统的三个祖先群组，为把有关周代的零散历史记忆组织在一起提供了一个基本系统。换言之，这三个祖先群组是从后代角度对周代历史的分期。郑玄在注解“三礼”时写道：“先公之迁主，藏于后稷之庙；先王之迁主，藏于文武之庙。”[30] 这意味着宗庙中的这三个永久性礼拜对象（后稷、文王和武王）不仅仅被看作个体的祖先，而且也被看成周代历史中两个重要阶段的象征：作为姬姓部落的始祖，后稷代表了先周时期；而文王和武王创立了周朝，象征着周代的统一政体。

this political unity. The remaining four ancestors worshipped in the temple testified to the direct ancestry of the living king and linked him to the remote ancestors. This temple in Chengzhou thus incorporated and, to some extent, replaced the old temples of Tan Fu and King Wen; its significance lay in both maintaining the royal lineage's internal order and legitimating its political status. This new Jinggong was the "dynastic temple" of the Zhou and Chengzhou, the "dynastic capital" and the new "seat of the Zhou lineage."[31] Based on documents and bronze inscriptions, the modern scholar Wei Tingsheng has speculated that after conquering the Shang, the Zhou royal house formally moved its capital to Chengzhou and held the most important royal activities there.[32] This movement, in fact, was first planned by King Wu when he moved the Nine Tripods—the symbol of central power—from the Shang capital directly to Luoyang.[33] But it is King Cheng who finally realized this plan: traditional texts record that this king "settled the Tripods" in the new capital,[34] and the inscription on a recently discovered bronze begins with the sentence "King [Cheng] first moved the capital to Chengzhou."[35]

This discussion of the temple's internal organization, however, does not answer an important question concerning the temple's architectural design: Why was the shrine of the founding ancestor, Hou Ji, located deep inside the temple, whereas the recent royal ancestors were worshipped in front halls closer to the outside world? The key to this question is found in the relationship between the temple's spatial system and the temporal sequence of temple rituals. The positions of the individual ancestral shrines in the temple compound implied a chronological order from the present back to the remote past, an order helping to structure ritual events that aimed to refresh people's memory and reconstruct their history. In fact, it is fair to say that a Zhou temple was a temple of the Origin (*shi*), and that the ceremonies performed in the temple followed a uniform pattern of seeking, returning to, and communicating with the Origin. It is stressed more than ten times in the *Book of Rites* that temple

rituals guided people "to go back to their Origin, maintain the ancient, 083
and not forget those to whom they owe their being."[36] The temple hymns of Shang and Zhou survive in the "Daya" section of the *Book of Songs*. Without exception, they trace the origins of specific clans to mythological heroes who emerged from the twilight zone between Heaven and the human world.[37] One of the most famous hymns, for example, commemorates the mysterious birth of Hou Ji. One day Hou Ji's mother, Jiang Yuan, trod on the big toe of God's footprint; she subsequently

庙中崇拜的其余四个祖先表明在位之王的直系血统，并将这个在位之王与他的远祖联系在一起。这样，成周的宗庙就吸收甚至取代了亶父和文王时期的旧式宗庙；其意义既在于维持王室世系的内部秩序，又在于使其政治地位合法化。这种新型的京宫可以说既是周的"宗庙"又是其"王庙"。[31] 当代学者卫挺生根据文献和青铜铭文推测，攻克了商以后，周王室将都城正式移到成周，并且在那里举行了一些最为重要的王室活动。[32] 这一系列行动应该是武王将象征中央政权的九鼎从商都移到洛阳时所计划的。[33] 但最终实现这项计划的是成王：史书记载成王"居九鼎"于洛邑，[34] 新发现的一件青铜器铭文也说"(成)王初移京邑于成周"。[35]

但是，这些关于宗庙内部组织和结构的讨论还没有回答有关宗庙建筑设计的一个重要问题：为什么始祖后稷的祠堂深藏于宗庙的后部，而近祖却被祭祀于靠近外部的享堂？回答这个问题的关键在于发现宗庙的建筑空间与宗庙礼仪程序之间的关系。祖先祠堂在宗庙中的位置隐含着从现时向遥远过去进行回溯的编年顺序；这个顺序帮助确定礼仪程序；而这个礼仪程序又使人们重温历史记忆，赋予自己的历史一个确定的结构。实际上，周代的宗庙可以被认为是一座"始庙"，在庙中举行的仪式活动遵循着一种统一模式，以回归到氏族的初始，并和初始交流。《礼记》中不下十次地强调宗庙礼仪是引导人们"不忘其初""返其所自生"。[36]《诗经·大雅》中所保存的商周时期的宗庙颂诗，无一例外地将人们的始祖追溯到洪荒时期的神话人物。[37] 例如，一首著名的颂诗记录了后稷诞生的神话：一天，后稷之母姜嫄因踩了神人的大脚印而感孕，随后生下一子，

became pregnant and gave birth to a child. The infant, however, was rejected by the mother's family because of his unusual conception:

> Indeed, they put him in a narrow lane;
> But oxen and sheep tenderly cherished him.
> Indeed, they put him in a far-off wood;
> But it chanced that woodcutters came to this wood.
> Indeed, they put him on the cold ice;
> But the birds covered him with their wings.
> The birds at last went away,
> And Hou Ji began to wail.[38]

So Hou Ji survived and "brought down many blessings" to his people:

> Millet for wine, millet for cooking, the early planted and the late planted,
> The early ripening and the late ripening, beans and corn.
> He took possession of all lands below,
> Setting the people to husbandry.[39]

To be sure, the main purpose of such temple hymns was not to glorify individual ancestors; they were composed to specify the common origin of the members of a clan. This is why the poem "Jiang Yuan" begins with the question: "How did she give birth to the people?"[40] This is also why it ends with the stanza:

> Hou Ji founded the sacrifices [to the God],
> And without blemish or flaw
> They have gone on till now.[41]

As long as the song was performed in Zhou temples and the sacrifices were offered to the High Ancestor, the people of Zhou knew their origin and identity. In this tradition, "myth" was conceived as history, and history tied the present to the past.

The essence of temple ceremonies taught in the *Book of Rites*—"to go back to the Origin, maintain the ancient, and not forget those to whom they owe their being"—also provides us with a key to understanding the visual form of the ancestral temple and its relationship with an ancient city. Early examples of Three Dynasties cities include the Shang settlements discovered at Erlitou, Zhengzhou, and Panlongcheng (Fig. 2.3a-b).[42] Though located in different regions, all three share a basic architectural plan: all were roughly rectangular and oriented north-south; all were surrounded by tall thick walls, in which large gates opened to the four directions. Inside each town, a cluster of large buildings, possibly the ritual complex, was constructed in a special area. The Zhou people

然而他母亲的家人拒绝接受这个来路不明的孩子：

诞寘之隘巷，牛羊腓字之；
诞寘之平林，会伐平林；
诞寘之寒冰，鸟覆翼之；
鸟乃去矣，后稷呱矣。[38]

后稷因此活了下来，并为后人带来了种种福祉：

黍稷重穋，稙稺菽麦；奄有下国，俾民稼穑。[39]

确切地说，这类颂诗的主旨并不在于颂扬个别祖先，其创作目的是为了将他们共同的来源告知部落成员。这也就是《姜嫄》一诗为什么以"生民如何"的设问开篇，[40] 又以"后稷肇祀，庶无罪悔，以迄于今"之句作为结语。[41] 当这首诗在周庙中被唱起，祭品在始祖的灵前陈上，祭祀者便可明了自己的身份与由来。在这个礼仪传统中，"神话"被当作历史，而历史又把现在与过去连在一起。

《礼记》所指出的宗庙仪礼的精髓——"不忘其初""返其所自生"——也为我们理解祖庙的视觉形式及其与古代城市的关系提供了一条路径。三代城市的早期例子包括发现于二里头、郑州和盘龙城的夏代到商代的城址［图 2.3］。[42] 尽管所在地点不同，三处城址却具有基本相同的建筑规划：全都略呈矩形，南北向；全都由四面辟门的高大、厚重的城墙所围绕。每座城的内部都在一特定区域内建有一个大型建筑群，或许即是礼仪建筑的群体。周人也是遵循了

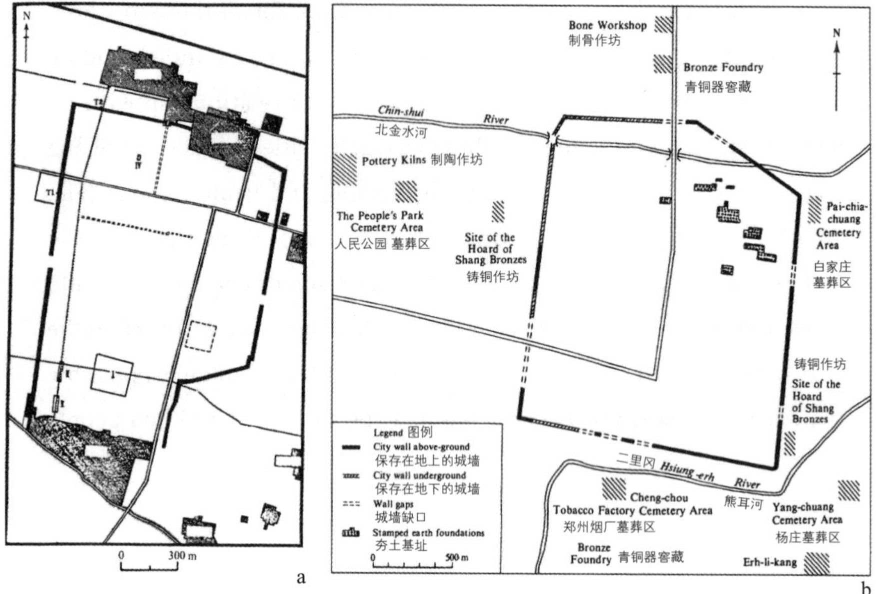

Fig. 2.3. (a) Early Shang city at Yanshi, Henan province. *Ca.* 15th-14th centuries B.C. (b) Mid-Shang city at Zhengzhou, Henan province. *Ca.* 14th-13th centuries B.C.

图 2.3 （a）河南偃师商代早期城址。约前 15—前 14 世纪。（b）河南郑州商代中期城址。约前 14—前 13 世纪。

must have followed this basic plan in constructing their cities. One of the most important cities founded at the beginning of the Zhou was Qufu, the capital of the state of Lu, which was the fief of the famous Duke of Zhou. Excavations of Qufu have continued since the early 1940's, and archaeologists have concluded that although the city was constructed and reconstructed many times from the Zhou to the Han, its basic layout remained basically unaltered.[43] As shown in Fig. 2.4, this rectangular city was encircled by a continuous wall. A well-defined area, 500 meters north-south and 550 meters east-west, occupied the center of the city; its ramped foundation still rises ten meters above the ground. Local people called this area Zhougong *miao*, or the Temple of the Duke of Zhou, a name that suggests the identity of the oldest buildings established there.

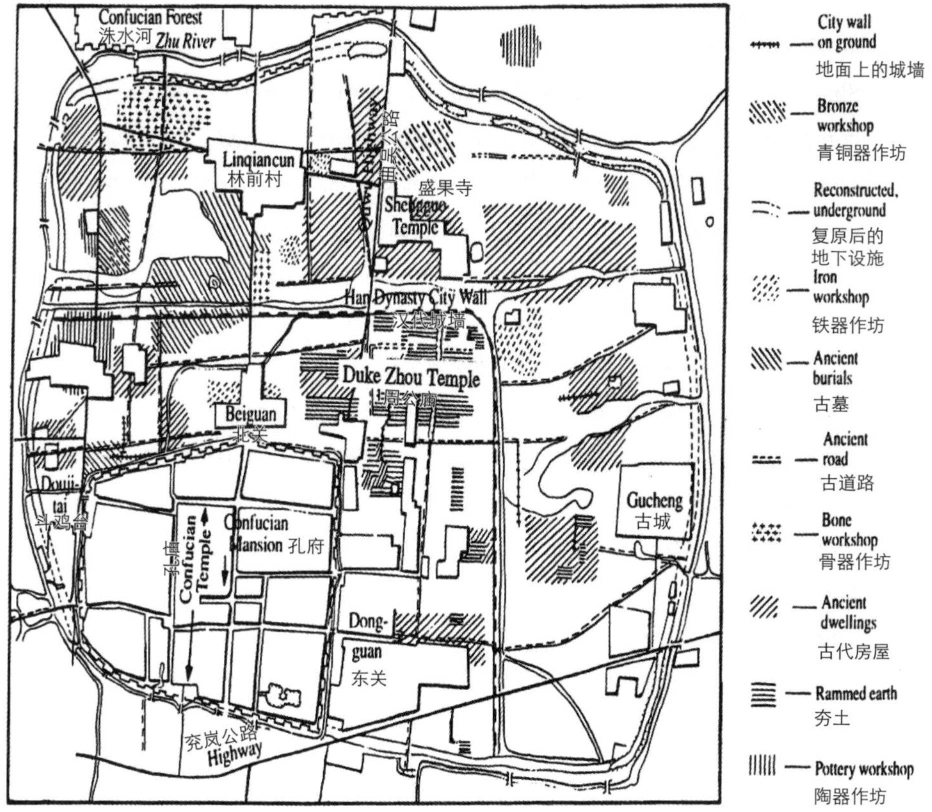

Fig. 2.4. Qufu during the Eastern Zhou. 8th-3rd centuries B.C.

图 2.4 东周时期的曲阜城。约前 8 世纪—前 3 世纪。

这种基本方案来建构他们的城市。创建于周初的最重要的城市之一是作为周公封地和鲁国都城的曲阜。20 世纪 40 年代初开始的对曲阜的考古发掘至今仍在继续，考古学家目前已得出这样的结论：尽管这座城自周至汉已经过多次重修与改建，但它的地面布局基本保持未变。[43] 如图 2.4 所示，这个矩形城址为连绵的城墙所环绕，位于城中央的是一个南北 500 米、东西 550 米的相当规整的区域，那里的夯土台基至今仍高出地面十米以上。当地人称这个地方为周公庙，可证明那里曾经存在过一群古老的礼仪建筑。

Three groups of excavated examples allow us to have a closer look at Three Dynasties temple complexes. These are the late Xia and early Shang structures discovered in Yanshi in present-day Henan and a temple compound found in the Western Zhou capital area, Fengchu, in Shaanxi. Like all timber structures built in ancient China, the aboveground parts of these buildings have long since disappeared. But enough remains are left on their foundations to suggest a consistent plan. Two late Xia
084 structures discovered in Erlitou appear to have been closed compounds surrounded by roofed corridors (Figs. 2.5a-c).[44] An isolated hall was built inside the compound, and an exit opened close to the northeast corner; both show an amazing resemblance to the structure of a Three Dynasties ancestral temple recorded in the *Book of Documents* and the *Ceremonies and Rites* (Fig. 2.6).[45] From an art-historical view, this structure initiated a major architectural principle for constructing an ancient Chinese temple. The corridors create discontinuity in space by separating the "inner" from the "outer," and the enclosed open courtyard then becomes a relatively independent space with its focus in the central hall. Rudolf Arnheim calls such an artificial space "extrinsic space," which "controls the relation

三个考古发掘实例使我们得以进一步对三代时期的宗庙做详细的观察。这三例包括两处位于河南偃师二里头的夏代晚期至商代早期的建筑遗址，以及发现于陕西凤雏的一处西周王室宗庙建筑遗址。与古代中国的所有木构建筑一样，这些建筑物的地上部分早已湮灭不存，但留在建筑基础上的残迹足以表明它们源于同一种建筑类型。发现于二里头的两处夏代晚期建筑遗址皆为由廊庑环绕的封闭院落式建筑体［图 2.5］,[44] 院落中心是孤立的一座堂屋，阙门开在院落的东北角——这些特点与《尚书》和《仪礼》中记载的三代宗庙在结构上具有惊人的相似之处［图 2.6］。[45] 从美术史的角度着眼，这个结构创始了古代中国庙堂建筑的基本格局：廊庑造成了空间的不连续性，把“内部”与“外部”分开。以中央厅堂为焦点的围合式院落随即形成了一个相对独立的空间。鲁道夫·阿恩海姆称这种

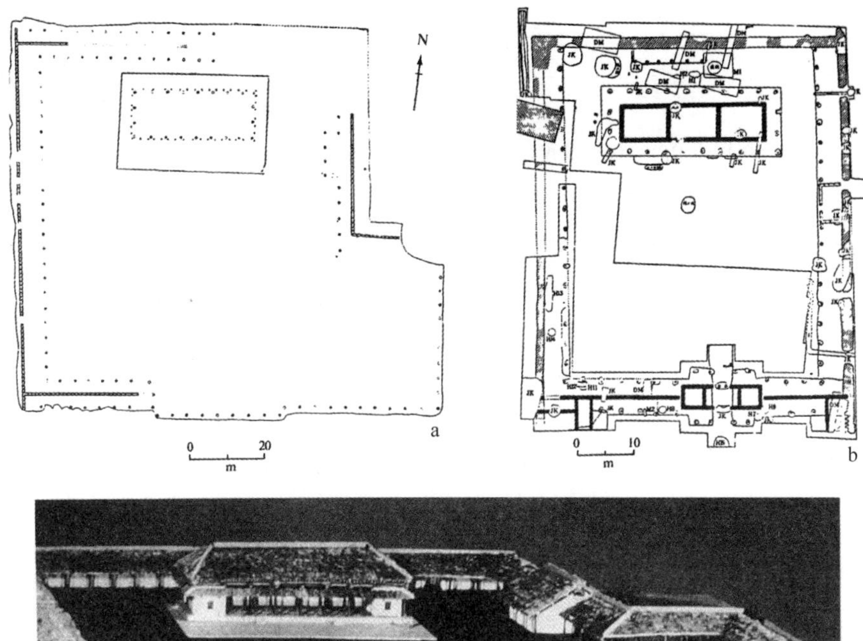

Fig. 2.5. (a, b) Foundations of two late Xia temple-palace structures. *Ca.*16th century B.C. Excavated in 1973-74 (Structure no. 1) and 1977-78 (Structure no. 2) at Erlitou, Yanshi, Henan province. (c) Reconstruction of Structure no. 1.

图 2.5 （a, b）两座庙堂建筑台基。夏代晚期，约前 16 世纪，分别于 1973—1974 年（1 号建筑）、1977—1978 年（2 号建筑）发掘于河南偃师二里头。（c）1 号建筑复原模型。

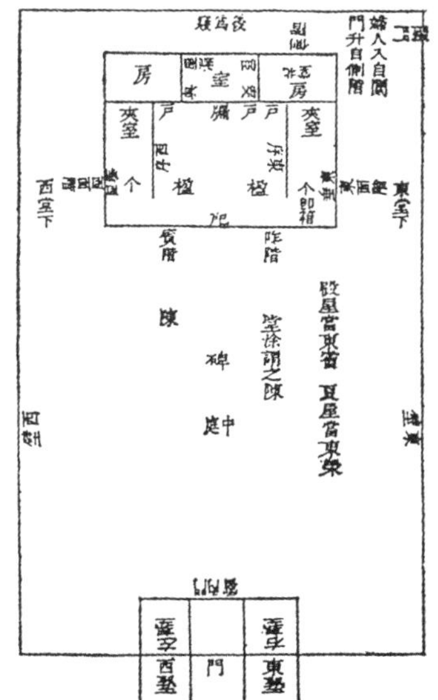

Fig. 2.6. Plan of an ancestral temple during the Three Dynasties as recorded in ancient texts.

图 2.6 古代文献记载的三代宗庙平面图。

between independent object systems and provides them with standards of reference for their perceptual features."[46]

The basic layout of the Xia buildings was shared by early Shang temples and palaces discovered in a nearby site,[47] but the Fengchu building, where divinatory documents of the Western Zhou royal house were found, demonstrated a greater effort to create "extrinsic space" (Figs. 2.7a, b).[48] Compared to the floor plans of earlier ritual buildings, those for
085 this structure are far more complex. The inner hall and courtyard were doubled, so that the whole compound consisted of a series of alternating "open" and "closed" sections. The south-facing halls were connected by two rows of side chambers along the east and west walls; the structure of the compound thus resembled that of a Zhou temple recorded in texts (Fig. 2.2a). A central axis, along which doorways and a corridor were built, now became a prominent architectural feature orienting ritual processions. An earthen screen was erected to shield the front gate. The psychology behind this device and the architectural design of the whole compound was apparently to make the enclosure coherent, closed and "deeper"—to make one cross layers of barriers before reaching the center.

What ideology underlay this architectural form? Before answering this question, let us take an imaginary journey to a Three Dynasties temple. First, we enter the town through gates in tall walls that block off the outside. We then walk toward the center where a palace-temple compound stands, again blocked by walls or corridors. The feeling of secrecy gradually increases as we enter the temple yard and penetrate layers of halls leading to the shrine of the founder of the clan, located at the end of the compound. At last, we enter the shrine; in the dim light,

人造空间为“外在空间”，它“控制着各种独立物象系统之间的关系，并为物象系统的感知特征提供参考标准”。[46]

这两座夏代建筑的平面布局与附近所发现的早商庙堂和宫殿类同，[47] 但出土了西周王室卜辞的凤雏建筑却显示出创造“外在空间”

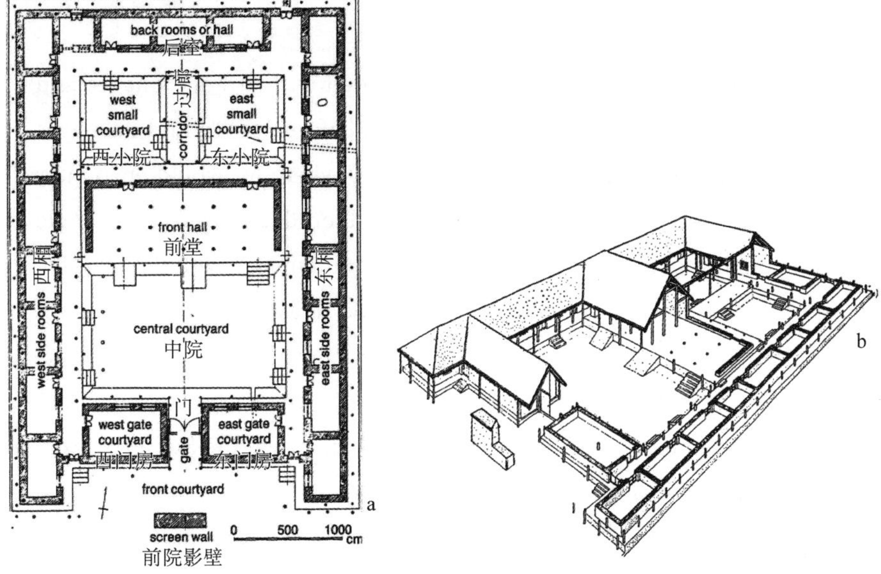

Fig. 2.7. An early Western Zhou temple-palace structure. 11th-10th centuries B.C. 45 by 32.5 m. Excavated in 1976 at Fengchu, Shaanxi province. (a) Floor plan. (b) Reconstruction.

图 2.7　一座西周早期庙堂建筑。前 11—前 10 世纪。长 45 米，宽 32.5 米，1976 年发掘于陕西凤雏。(a) 平面图。(b) 复原图。

的进一步努力［图 2.7］。[48] 与二里头建筑相比，这一建筑的平面规划要复杂得多。堂室和院落都得以倍增，因此围墙内的整个建筑体便包含了一系列交替的“开放”和“封闭”的部分。坐北朝南的堂屋为沿东西墙而建的两列厢房所夹护；所组成的建筑体因此与文献中记载的周代宗庙非常相似［图 2.2a］。台阶与走廊大体沿中轴线而建，显示出中轴线已成为引导礼仪的一个重要建筑特征。大门前方建有一面夯土影壁。这一建筑部件的设计心理以及整个院落的规划显然是为了使其内部更统一、更加隐秘和“幽深”，使人在进入内部时必须穿过一道道屏障。

隐藏在这种建筑形式背后的理念是什么？在回答这个问题之前，让我们做一次前往三代宗庙的虚拟旅行。我们将首先通过城门进城，两旁的高墙隔断了城外的景色。然后我们走向城市中央，那里的宫殿和宗庙又被隔绝于围墙或回廊之内。当我们进入庙堂的院落，穿过层层门阙，步步走近坐落在尽头的始祖祠堂时，神秘之感也在逐渐增加。最后，我们进入祠堂，在幽暗的光线里，各种装饰

numerous shining bronze vessels, decorated with strange images and containing ritual offerings, suddenly loom before us. We find ourselves in a mythical world, the end of our journey where we would encounter the Origin—the *shi*. The ritual vessels hidden deep inside the temple compound provide us with the means to communicate with the invisible spirits of ancestors—to present offerings and to ascertain their will. This final stage is recorded in the *Book of Rites*; following a long list of ritual bronzes (as well as sacrificial food and wine), the passage ends with a crucial statement: " [All of these] aim to bring down the Supreme God,
087 as well as ancestral to bring down the Supreme God, as well as ancestral deities, from above."[49]

We may assume that such a journey was actually undertaken during the Three Dynasties, since the spatial-temporal structure of the ritual sequence is so clearly disclosed by the visual forms of the architecture and objects we can still observe. In fact, the ancient Chinese characterized their temples in similar terms. In the poem "Mian," for example, the construction of the first Zhou temple is described in the following lines:

> Dead straight was the plumb-line,
> The planks were lashed to hold the earth;
> They made the Hall of Ancestors, very venerable.
> They tilted in the earth with a rattling,
> They pounded it with a dull thud,
> They beat the walls with a loud clang,
> They pared and chiseled them with a faint *p'ing p'ing*.
> ...
> They raised the outer gate;
> The outer gate soared high.
> They raised the inner gate;
> The inner gate was very strong.[50]

Instead of focusing on the temple's sacrificial halls, the poet emphasizes its two seemingly less important features: walls and gates. The temple had multiple walls and gates; the result was a layered structure that concealed sacrificial halls and sacred ritual vessels. Such an architectural structure was conceived as "closed," "vast," "hallowed," "solemn," and "mysterious," as we read in two other Zhou hymns:

> Holy is the Closed Temple, 088
> Vast and mysterious;
> Glorious was Jiang Yuan,
> Her power was without flaw.[51]

着诡谲图像、内中盛满供品的闪闪发光的青铜器皿，忽然呈现在我们面前。我们发现自己置身于一个神秘的世界，置身于我们旅行的终点，在那里我们将面对"始"。深藏于宗庙内的礼器为我们提供了与祖先会通的途径——呈献供品以探知他们的意愿。《礼记》中的一段文字描述了这最后一步：在罗列了一长串的礼器（包括祭祀用的酒食）之后，这段文字以一句关键的话语结束："以降上神，与其先祖"。[49]

由于宗庙建筑的视觉形式以及至今可见的实物将礼仪程序的时空结构揭示得如此清晰，所以我们可以推测这种旅行在三代时期确实存在。事实上，古代中国人确曾以类似的方式形容其宗庙的特征。如《诗经》中《緜》这首颂诗就这样描述了周的第一座宗庙：

> 其绳则直，缩版以载；作庙翼翼。
> 捄之陾陾，度之薨薨；筑之登登，削屡冯冯。
> ……
> 迺立皋门，皋门有伉。迺立应门，应门将将。[50]

该诗描述的重点并不是这座庙中的堂室，而是它的两个似乎不甚重要的特征：墙和门。多重的墙和门造成了一种将祠堂和神圣礼器隐匿起来的层叠结构。这种建筑结构被想象为"封闭的""庞大的""空洞的""庄严的""幽暗的"和"神秘的"，如我们在另外两首周代颂诗中读到的那样：

> 閟宫有侐，实实枚枚；
> 赫赫姜嫄，其德不回。[51]

Solemn the hallowed temple,
Awed and silent the participants of the sacrifice,
Well purified the many knights
That handle their sacred task.
There has been an answer in heaven;
Swiftly the spirits flit through the temple,
Very bright, very glorious,
Showing no distaste towards men.[52]

By manipulating space, a temple created a temporal ritual sequence and heightened religious feeling. Instead of exposing its content to the public, it was a "closed" structure—a walled compound that was "solid" outside but "hollow" inside. Separated from the mundane world, its deep courtyards and dark halls became "solemn," "mysterious," and "holy." All its spatial elements led worshippers closer and closer to the center of the secret, but at the same time they created layers of barriers to resist such an effort. Even at the end of the ritual process, what people found was still not a concrete image of the ancestral deity, but ritual bronzes that served as the means to communicate with this invisible being.[53] The whole monumental complex of a temple, therefore, becomes a metaphor of history and the ancestral religion itself: to return to the Origin, maintain the ancient, and not forget those to whom one owed one's being.

❷ From Temple to Palace

Far from being an architectural complex designed and constructed purely for ancestral services, a Western Zhou temple was both a religious and political center.[54] In this sense, the royal temple combined the functions of a temple and a palace—it was the place of both ancestral sacrifices and civil administration. It is impossible and misleading to separate temple ceremonies into "sacred" and "secular" types: a series of ritual events often proceeded from worshipping ancestral spirits to dealing with mundane issues of government. Herrlee Glessner Creel summarizes activities of the latter category: "All of the most important activities of the state took place in the ancestral temple of its ruler. Here the new heir assumed his position. Military expeditions set out from the temple, and returned to it to report and celebrate victory upon their return. The business of diplomacy, and state banquets, took place there. Officials were appointed to office and given rewards, and vassals were invested with territories, in the same hall."[55]

于穆清庙，肃雝显相；
济济多士，秉文之德。
对越在天，骏奔走在庙；
不显不承，无射于人。[52]

依靠对空间的处理，宗庙创造了时间性的礼仪程序，加强了宗教感。它不向公众暴露它的内涵，而是保持着自己的“封闭”结构——一个高墙环绕、外“实”内“虚”的复合建筑体。由于与外部世界隔绝，它那深深的庭院和幽暗的堂室于是变得“庄严”“秘密”和“神圣”。所有的这些空间因素引导着礼拜者步步接近那秘密的中心，但同时也造成重重屏障去抵制这种努力。甚至于在礼仪过程的终点，人们所见到的仍然不是祖先神的实在影像，而是提供与无形神灵沟通之途径的青铜礼器。[53] 作为纪念碑综合体的宗庙因而成为历史和祖先崇拜本身的一种隐喻：返回初始、保存过去、不忘其所自生。

二、从宗庙到宫殿

西周宗庙远非是单纯为供奉祖先而设计、构建的建筑群体，而是一个宗教和政治的双重中心。[54] 从这种意义上说，王室宗庙结合了祖庙和宫殿两种功能——它既是祭祖的场所，也是处理国家政务的重地。将宗庙礼仪分成“宗教性”与“世俗性”的两类是不可能的。实际上，这种二元论本身就是一种概念的误导：当时的礼仪常常从崇拜祖先转化为对国家政务的处理。顾立雅对后者做了这样的概括：“国家所有最重要的活动都在其统治者的祖庙中发生。新的王位继承者在这里宣称就职，军事征伐从这里出发又返回这里报告和庆祝胜利，外交事务与国家的宴会在这里举行，官员的任命、封赏活动也都选择了这一场所。”[55]

Moreover, rather than being a self-contained monument, the royal temple demonstrated and "disseminated" its monumentality through a "temple system" that linked the country into an interrelated network. Scholars have explained this network in terms of the Zhou social and political structure. They have suggested that the basic elements of Zhou society were patrilineages fragmented from a number of clans. Whereas the royal lineage had its seat in Chengzhou, the capital of each vassal state was founded by a lineage sent out by the Zhou king.[56] The establishment of such vassal states is lavishly recorded in inscriptions and ancient texts. A passage from *Zuo's Commentary on the Spring and Autumn Annals* describes King Cheng's *fengjian* (establishing vassal states) at the beginning of the Zhou:

> When King Wu had subdued the Shang, King Cheng completed the establishment of the new dynasty, and chose and appointed [the princes of] intelligent virtue to act as bulwarks and screens to the Zhou. Hence it was the Duke of Zhou that gave his aid to the royal house for the adjustment of all the kingdom, he being most dear and closely related to the Zhou. To him there were given—a grand chariot, a grand flag with dragons on it, the *huang* stone of the sovereigns of the Xia, and the [great bow] called Fangruo of Fengfu. [The heads of] six lineages of the people of the Yin—the Tiao, the Xu, the Xiao, the Suo, the Changshao, and the Weishao—were ordered to lead the chiefs of their kindred, to collect their branches, the remote as well as the near, to conduct the multitude of their connections, and repair with them to the Zhou, to receive the instructions and laws of the Duke of Zhou. They were then charged to perform duty in the Lu principality [of the duke], that thus the brilliant virtue of the Duke of Zhou might be made illustrious.
> 089 Lands [also] were apportioned [to the duke] on an enlarged scale, with priests, superintendents of the ancestral temple, diviners, archivists, all the appendages of State, the tablets of historical records, the various officers and the ordinary instruments of their offices.[57]

Also during the same ceremony, Prince Kangshu, one of the younger brothers of King Wu, received the order to rule the state of Wei in the former Shang territory, and Prince Tangshu was charged to govern the state of Jin in the old land of the Xia.[58] These two princes, as well as the Duke of Zhou, were among the "sixteen sons of King Wen and four children of King Wu" enfeoffed with subsidiary states. Xunzi also stated that of the 71 vassal states established at the time, 53 were given to members of the royal clan and the rest to relatives by marriage and descendents of old privileged clans.[59]

再者，与其说王室宗庙是一个自给自足的独立的纪念碑，倒不如说它是通过一套“庙制”将整个国家联络起来，以证明和“传布”其纪念碑性。有的学者已经将这一网络解释为周的社会政治体制，认为周代社会的基本成分是由若干主要氏族分化出的父系宗族。成周是王室宗族的基地，而诸侯国的都城则由周王分封的宗室和功臣建立。[56] 对这些诸侯国的分封屡屡见于古代文献与铭文，以下是《左传》关于成王于周初实行分封制度的记述：

> 昔武王克商，成王定之，选建明德，以藩屏周，故周公相王室以尹天下，于周为睦。分鲁公以大路大旂、夏后氏之璜，封父之繁弱。殷民六族条氏、徐氏、萧氏、索氏、长勺氏、尾勺氏，使帅其宗氏，辑其分族，将其类丑，以法则周公，用即命于周，是使之职事于鲁，以昭周公之明德。分之土田倍敦，祝宗卜史，备物典策，官司彝器。[57]

也是在同一次典礼活动期间，武王的一个弟弟康叔受命统辖前殷商境内的魏国，唐叔受封位于夏故土的晋国。[58] 康侯、唐侯以及周公，皆在封有采邑的文王十六子及武王四子之列。荀子也提到，封建于当时的 71 个诸侯国中有 53 个属于王室宗族成员，其余的则属于王室姻亲及其他显贵氏族后裔。[59]

Once such vassal states were founded, the segmentation of the clan was continued on another level. With his assigned symbols of authority (including special carriages, scepters, ritual vessels, flags, and especially his ancestral temple), the lord of a state could send out branches of his own lineage to establish secondary territories.[60] These sub-branches would build towns centered on their ancestral temple. The result of this segmentation process was a tightly interrelated hierarchical structure safeguarded by routine ritual practices (see Figs. 2.8a, b). Cho-yun Hsu has characterized the social and political function of this system: "The institutionalization of rank occurred as a consequence of a political authority that relied only in part on force to maintain control. Social order had to be made routine and acceptable in order to sustain political control. The regularization of ritual and status ranking reflected social stability, for privileges and obligations of individual members were known and regulated. Internal conflicts were minimized because everyone's place was known."[61]

Main Line 主线	Branches 分支	Secondary Branches 第二级分支	Tertiary Branches 第三级分支
King 王			
King 王	Dukes 诸侯		
King 王	Dukes 诸侯	Ministers 大夫	
King 王	Dukes 诸侯	Ministers 大夫	Shi 士
King 王	Dukes 诸侯	Ministers 大夫	Shi 士

a

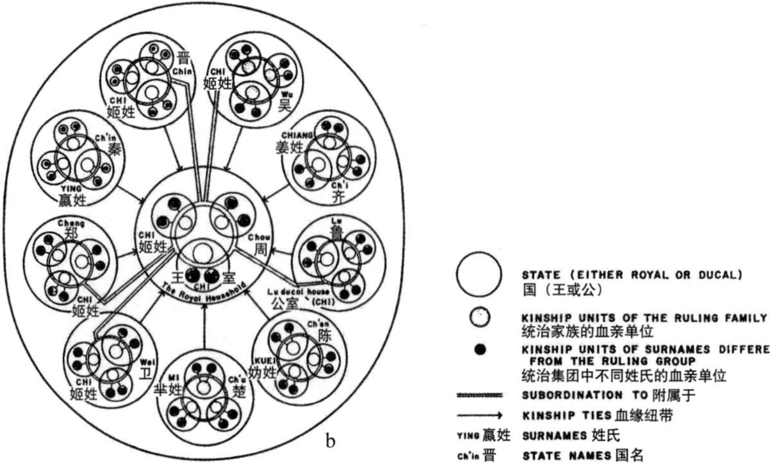

Fig. 2.8. Western Zhou social and political structure. (a) The *zongfa* (lineage-rank) system. (b) The Zhou vassal states.

图 2.8 西周社会政治结构。（a）宗法制度。（b）周的侯国。

Most important to the present study, this sociopolitical structure was indexed and supported by the temple system. An ancestral temple in a city or town was symbolic on three levels: first, it proved the common ancestry and homogeneity of the lineage that owned it. It was understood that as long as lineage members worshipped their ancestors in the temple, they recognized their blood relationship and were united in a basic social group. The *Book of Rites* thus states: "[A nobleman] maintains his ancestral temple and presents sacrifices reverently at proper seasons. This brings order to his lineage and clan."[62] Second, a temple indicated the position of a lineage in a larger social and political hierarchy. As we have seen, the temple of the royal lineage consisted of seven shrines or

一个诸侯国一旦建立，宗族的分化便在另一层面上继续进行。拥有周王赏赐的权力象征（包括专用车马、王节、礼器、徽旗，特别是宗庙）的诸侯可以进而指派自己的宗支去建立二级领地。[60] 这些次级宗支也以其祖庙为中心建立城邑。氏族分化的过程导致了以常规礼仪为保障的具有牢固内在联系的等级体制［见图 2.8］。许倬云对这一体制的社会政治功能曾有过如下描述："等级的制度化作为政治权威的结果出现。这种政治权威只是在一定程度上依赖于保证秩序的暴力。社会秩序必须成为定型化的和为人接受的，以便维持政治统治。礼仪的规律化与身份的等级化反映了社会的稳定性，因为个体成员的权利与义务是众所周知和相对固定的。鉴于每个人都意识到自己和他人的位置，社会内部的冲突也就得到了最大限度的控制。" [61]

对本书目前的讨论最为重要的是，庙制为这种社会政治体制提供了支持和表征。一个城邑中的宗庙在三个不同层面上具有象征意义：其一，它表明庙的所有者同宗同源。只要同一宗族的成员持续在庙中祭拜他们的祖先，他们便会意识到其共同的血缘关系，从而团结在一个基本社会群体中。因此《礼记》说："（君子）修其宗庙，岁时以敬祭祀，以序宗族。"[62] 其二，一座庙体现着某一宗族在一个更大的社会政治等级体系中的位置。一些传统文献记载，王室宗庙中

chambers for seven individual ancestors; the lineage temple of a feudal lord, on the other hand, had only five chambers; and that of a minister, three chambers (see Figs. 2.2a, b).[63] The numbers of the chambers in a temple compound thus signified the different status of the lineages.
090 Third, the "founder" worshipped at the focal point in a temple, which symbolized the beginning of a lineage, also served to remind people of a larger historical context: the existence of a "father lineage" that had sent the ancestor to establish his own sub-branch. A lineage's history was thus always part of a larger historical narrative. The key events in this narrative were a series of "investiture" ceremonies, which made a clan's fragmentation and expansion official.

We thus return to the "investiture" ritual, but with a renewed interest. My earlier discussion of this temple ritual focused on its recording in bronze inscriptions and its relation to the commissioning of bronzes, but it is also crucial to our understanding of the construction and organization of the Western Zhou temple system. In particular, this ritual explains how political power was disseminated within this system and transmitted from one social stratum to another. In fact, this significance is already implied in *ceming*, the original term for the ritual, which means literally "to give and record an order."[64] The pictograph *ce* (see character *a*) illustrates a document written on a set of bamboo splints; *ming* (*c*) shows a figure (*e*) kneeling under a "roof" (*b*) while receiving an order from a "mouth" (*d*). The "roof" symbolizes the ancestral temple or the temple's audience chamber, which was called the Great Hall (Taishi or Dashi); the "mouth" belongs to the king who issues the order. Bronze inscriptions and traditional texts describe *ceming* or investiture ceremonies in a uniform narrative. After providing the date and place of a ceremony, a text often records that the king "assumed his position" (*jiwei*) in front of

the Great Hall, between two stairways ascending from the courtyard. Wearing ritual attire and facing south, he stood before a screen decorated with patterns of ceremonial axes—symbols of royal power. A *bin* ceremonial usher, usually a prominent courtier, then led the receiver of the investiture through the temple gate and positioned him in the courtyard, to the left of the usher and facing the king. When the *ceming* ceremony began, an archivist (*shi*) standing above the east stairway to the

有为七个祖先设置的七所祠堂；诸侯的宗庙中有五所祠堂；而大夫一级的只有三个祠堂［图 2.2］。[63] 庙中祠堂的数目因此意味着其所属宗族的社会地位。其三，供奉于宗庙中最显赫地点的“始祖”提示人们记住一个更大的历史背景，即这个祖先不但属于一个特殊的宗族，而且属于许多由同一氏族分化出去的其他宗族。因此，一个宗族的历史总是一个更大的历史叙事的一部分。这种历史叙事中的关键事件是使氏族分化和扩张的一系列“分封”仪式。

谈到这里，我们带着一种新的兴趣返回到“分封”礼仪上来。在前面关于这种宗庙礼仪的讨论中，我将焦点放在了这种礼仪在青铜器铭文中的记载及其与青铜器铸造的关系上。但是，这些讨论对于理解西周庙制的组织与结构也至关重要。尤其重要的是，通过观察这种礼仪，我们可以看到政治权力如何通过宗庙系统逐渐扩散，又如何从一个社会阶层向另一社会阶层传递。事实上，这种礼仪的名称——“册命”——已经暗示出这层意义。[64] 册命的字面意思是“颁布和记录一道命令”。“册”的字形（a），形象地再现了一组简策的状貌；“命”（c）则显示一个人（e）跪在一个屋顶（b）下方，正在接受由“口”（d）发出的命令。“屋顶”象征着宗庙，或宗庙中称作“太室”“大室”的礼仪建筑；“口”则代表发布命令的君王。青铜器铭文和传统文献以一致的口吻描述册命或分封的过程：在列出举行仪式的地点和场所之后，这些文献往往记载王“即位”于太室前的两列台阶之间。他身穿礼服，面南而立，背后是饰有象征王权的斧钺图案的屏风。典礼官通常由一个显赫大臣担任，他将受封者引入宗庙的大门，立于前庭中靠近左方，面向王。当册命仪式开始

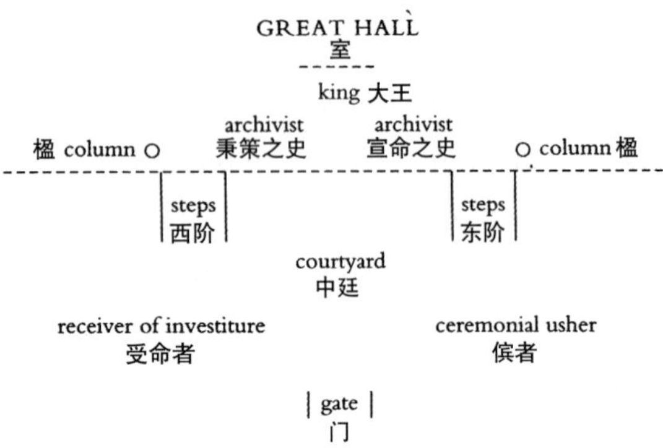

Fig. 2.9. Chen Mengjia's reconstruction of a Zhou investiture ceremony in the royal ancestral temple

图 2.9 陈梦家复原的周王庙中的册命仪式

Great Hall (i.e., to the king's left or east) presented the king with a *ce* document, which recorded the king's order (*ming*). The king then handed the document to another archivist to his right (or west), who read it in a loud voice. After listening to the order and receiving the king's gifts, the official being invested bowed, thanked the king, declared his loyalty, and proclaimed that he would make ritual bronze(s) for his own ancestor(s) which would bear the king's order.[65] The modern Chinese scholar Chen Mengjia has reconstructed the positioning of various participants in such a ceremony (Fig. 2.9).[66]

Chen's reconstruction fits in well with the architectural layout of the Western Zhou royal temple recorded in texts and exemplified by the Fengchu site (Figs. 2.7a, b). But more important is the symbolism of an investiture ritual that it reveals. First, standing in front of the Great Hall and facing south, the king occupied "the host position" (*zhuwei*); he thus presented himself as the master of the temple/palace, a status derived from his royal ancestors, who were worshipped in the ritual structure. The person being invested, on the other hand, was in "the guest position" (*kewei*); he was invited to the temple/palace to receive the king's order. He maintained this submissive position throughout the ceremony—even when leaving the compound after the ritual, he walked backward,

never facing south. Second, during the ritual, the king presented himself as a silent symbol of political and kin authority. He spoke very little, if at all;[67] his order was conveyed by archivists. Two copies were made to record the royal order. One copy was stored in the royal temple/palace as part of the government archive. The other copy was given to the official
being invested, who inscribed the order on the ritual bronze(s) that he 091
made after the ceremony and placed the bronze(s) in his ancestral temple (which also functioned as the palace of a feudal lord or the office of a minister). In this way, power was distributed from the central authority to sub-authorities, and the transmission of power was officialized by transmitting ritual symbols from the royal temple/palace to the temples/offices of the nobility.

时，立在阶上（位于王之左方）的史官向王呈之以册，王遂将这份书有王命的诏书递给立于右方的史官。右史高声宣诵，受封者在聆听了册命，接受了赏赐之后，向王揖拜作谢，表示忠诚，并声明将把册命的过程铸在祭祖的礼器上。[65] 图 2.9 为当代学者陈梦家所复原的“册命”礼仪中不同参与者的位置。[66]

陈氏的复原与文献所记西周王庙的建筑平面布局相合，且为凤雏遗址所证实［图 2.7a，b］。但更重要的是，他的复原揭示出册命礼仪的象征意义。首先，立于太室前面向南方的王占据着“主位”，他的身份因此是宗庙或宫殿的主人以及庙中所供列代先王的继承人。而面向北方的受封者则居于“客位”，被召至庙堂或宫殿领受王命。他在整个册命过程中始终保持恭顺状态——即便在礼仪结束时，他也要倒退着离开，绝不能掉头向南。其次，在礼仪过程中，王的在场似乎是无声地象征了宗族和政治的权威。他即便不是完全沉默，也是说话甚少，[67] 他的命令均由史官来传达。他所颁发的册命通常被复制为两份，一份作为王室档案存之宗庙或宫廷，另一份赐予受封的官员，由他带回铸成礼器上的铭文，存于自己的宗庙（这个宗庙也是一个诸侯国或封邑的施政中心）。权力就以这种方式从中央传播到地方，象征物品从王庙和王宫到贵族宗庙和公署的转移进一步使权力的传播合法化和系统化。

The investiture of an official was only a single link in a long chain of "giving and receiving orders." The Zhou believed that even the king had to receive his mandate from Heaven and from his royal ancestors, and that only then was he able to assign his ministers and relatives noble status and official posts. The absolute importance of *ceming* rituals in Zhou politics explains why they were abundantly recorded in Western Zhou documents, temple songs, and the inscriptions of bronze *liqi*.[68] Based on this written information, the modern Chinese scholar Chen Hanping has classified royal investiture ceremonies into five major kinds.[69] The first is called *shiming*, or "original investitures," during which a prominent official initially received the order to establish a vassal state, along with a noble title, lands, people, and status symbols. Theoretically, the direct descendents of the founders of these states inherited their forefathers' titles and political status. But such succession was supposed to be confirmed by the king through another kind of investiture known as *ximing* (an order to inherit).[70] The "original investiture" could also be altered through *zengming* (an additional order) or *gaiming* (changing an order).[71] The fifth kind of royal investiture was called *chongming*: after a new king ascended the throne, he might hold investiture ceremonies in the royal temple/palace to reconfirm his deceased father's orders.[72] A number of ancient texts explain why all these five types of investiture had to be held in the royal temple: "To invest nobles in a temple means that this is not a private business; to enfeoff feudal lords in a temple means that the king is not despotic. [The location of these rituals thus] demonstrates that the principles of governing were founded by our ancestors, and that the king must thus report all his activities to his ancestors."[73]

Such royal *ceming* ceremonies were duplicated on multiple local levels. After being invested by the king, a feudal lord could then establish his temple/palace; there he ruled his territory and ordered his ministers and relatives to establish their subsidiary fiefs and temples. The chain of events in an investiture thus functioned to construct the state organization, and the formative process of the state organization was mirrored by the expansion of the "temple system" from the center to the periphery and from above to below.

Unfortunately, no temple or office of Western Zhou lords, ministers, and officials has been found.[74] Our chief archaeological evidence for the past existence of these structures, in my opinion, consists of groups of ritual bronzes excavated from large and small storage pits. In 1988, Luo Xizhang reported that he had personally examined 68 such hoards in

对诸侯和官员的册命不过是众多"加封与受封"中的一个环节。周人相信即使是君王也必须从上天和先王那里接受统治的权力。唯其如此，他才能够给予其朝臣与亲族以贵族身份和官职。册命礼仪在周代政治中的这种极端重要性，解释了为什么西周文献、颂诗以及礼器铭文中有如此丰富的册命礼仪记载。[68] 根据这些文字信息，陈汉平将王室册命仪式分作五个主要类别。[69] 一为"始命"，通过这种仪式大臣受封建立一个诸侯国，并获得贵族头衔、土地、人民以及象征其身份的物品。理论上说，这些大臣的直系后代将继承其先辈的官衔与政治地位。但学者也注意到，这类继承须由天子以称作"袭命"的册命加以确认。[70] 同时，"始命"也可以通过"增命"或"改命"而有所变动。[71] 最后一种王室册命是"重命"：当新一代天子登上宝座，他可以在王室宗庙或宫殿中举行册命仪式，确认其先王所做的册命。[72] 不少文献解释了为什么这五种形式的册命都必须在王庙中举行。如《白虎通》中说："爵人于朝者，示不私人以官，与众共之义也。封诸侯于庙者，示不自专也。明法度皆祖之制也，举事必告焉。"[73]

王室的册命仪式在地方层面上被不断重复。诸侯在受封于天子之后，即可兴建自己的宗庙和宫殿，由那里统治自己的领地，并可以进一步命令其臣佐、宗亲建立次级的封邑和宗庙。因而，册命中一环扣一环的事件具有了构建国家体制的功能。反过来说，国家体制的形成与发展过程也反映为"庙制"自上而下、从中央到外围的延伸。

遗憾的是，目前尚没有发现西周公侯的宗庙和宫殿。[74] 以笔者之见，出土于大小"窖藏"中的青铜礼器，可以作为当时这类建筑的一个重要证据。1988 年，罗西章著文总结他研究过的在周原发现

the Plain of Zhou, which had yielded nearly a thousand bronze vessels and musical instruments.[75] Guo Moruo and Huang Shengzhang have contended that an important political event must have caused the burial of such a great number of ritual bronzes. The event that Huang Shengzhang identified took place in 841 B.C., when a group of ministers forced King Li and his followers to leave his capital and go into exile.[76] Guo Moruo, on the other hand, believed that a later event provided a better reason: "In the eleventh year of King You of Zhou [771 B.C.], the invading Quanrong nomads flooded into the Zhouyuan area and destroyed the Zhou capital there. The Zhou royal house decided to move its seat eastward, and noble families hurriedly hid their ritual vessels by burying them. But these nobles never gained an opportunity to return to their homes [and reopen the pits]. The buried bronzes have thus survived for us to discover."[77] Luo Xizhang considered both explanations acceptable, but also pointed out that based on stylistic attributes, some bronzes from the excavated hoards must be dated to periods after King Li and even after King You. He thus proposed that although ritual objects may have been buried during periods of political chaos, the storage pits in Zhouyuan could have also been constructed during peaceful times as a means of storing family treasures.[78]

Instead of following this line of argument, my chief question concerns
092 the origin of the bronzes found in the hoards: Where had these *liqi* been used and displayed *before* their burial? We know that during the Western Zhou, ritual vessels and ceremonial musical instruments were normally housed in ancestral temples. Luo Xizhang has shown that bronzes from one or two hoards often belonged to many generations of a lineage or a family.[79] It seems obvious that these buried *liqi* were removed from temples of Zhou nobles and officials. Thus, although these bronzes and their inscriptions have been studied over and over as important works of art and as historical texts, the approach developed in this study, that *liqi* and temple architecture formed two basic components of a single

monumental complex, suggests that the *relationship* between a group of buried bronzes also supplies evidence for understanding Western Zhou monumentality. By studying the bronzes from a single hoard, we can gain important information regarding the changing significance of a Western Zhou temple, which functioned as the seat of a subordinate political authority and as a "memory site" preserving its owners' history.

的 68 个窖藏，其中出土了上千件包括乐器在内的青铜器。[75] 郭沫若和黄盛璋都认为，如此大量的礼器被埋藏必定由一个重大的政治事件所引发。黄盛璋认为这个事件发生在公元前 841 年，当时一伙大臣逼令厉王及其追随者离开都城流亡异地。[76] 郭沫若则认为稍后的一个事件具有更充分的理由：周幽王十一年（前 771），犬戎游牧部涌进了周原，毁坏了周的都城，周王室因此决定东迁。于是，贵族宗支匆忙地掩埋了他们的礼器。然而，他们再也没有能够回到故土去打开那些窖藏。[77] 罗西章认为这两种解释皆可采纳，但同时又指出，根据其风格特征，窖藏中的部分青铜器应定为厉王甚至幽王以后之物。因此他提出尽管礼器可能埋于政治动荡期间，周原的一些窖藏坑也可能建于和平时期，用以储藏宗族的宝物。[78]

与这些研究有别，这里我所考虑的主要问题是窖藏中青铜器的来源：这些礼器埋藏之前是在哪里使用的？摆放陈列于何处？我们知道，西周时期礼乐器通常放在祖庙里。罗西章也证明了从一个或两个窖藏中出土的青铜器通常属于一个家族中的数代成员。[79] 这些埋藏的礼器明显是从周贵族和命官的宗庙或家庙中移出来的。如果这个推论可以被接受的话，那么对于这些已被当作重要艺术品和历史文献反复研究的铜器及其铭文，我们就可能基于本书所提倡的研究思路——礼器和庙构成一个复合纪念碑的两个基本部分——认识到，窖藏和铜器之间的关系可以为理解西周纪念碑性艺术提供新的依据。通过对同一窖藏中发现的铜器的研究，我们可以获得有关一座西周祖庙意义变动的重要信息，特别是有关它作为政治权力机构中的一级和保存家族历史的“记忆场地”的功能。

a

Fig. 2.10. (a) Zhuangbai Hoard no. 1. Western Zhou. 11th-8th centuries B.C. Excavated in 1976 at Fufeng, Shaanxi province.

图 2.10 （a）庄白 1 号窖藏。西周，前 11 世纪—前 8 世纪。1976 年陕西扶风出土。

Discovered in 1976, Zhuangbai hoard no. 1 provides an excellent opportunity to conduct such a study (Figs. 2.10a, b). The hoard yielded 103 bronze vessels and musical instruments, 74 of them inscribed. The oldest bronzes are of the late Shang—early Zhou, and the latest are in the style of the late Western Zhou.[80] Scholars recognized at once the extraordinary value of this group in reconstructing the evolution of Western Zhou bronze styles; as Jessica Rawson pointed out, it "has proved especially useful to Western Zhou bronze chronology, enabling us to arrange many early Western Zhou bronzes in a firmly based sequence and to date them approximately to certain reigns."[81] Instead of conducting a stylistic analysis, however, I will approach and interpret the Zhuangbai bronzes as integral and cumulative components of a Western Zhou temple, which, in this case, belonged to a branch of the Wei clan.

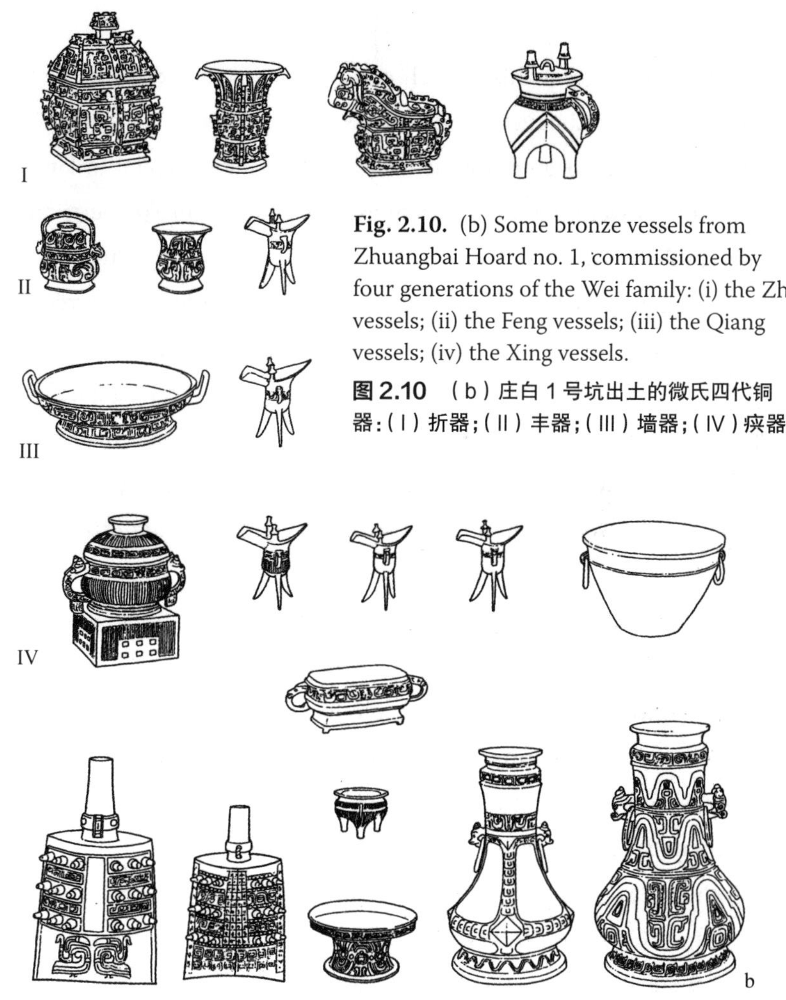

Fig. 2.10. (b) Some bronze vessels from Zhuangbai Hoard no. 1, commissioned by four generations of the Wei family: (i) the Zhe vessels; (ii) the Feng vessels; (iii) the Qiang vessels; (iv) the Xing vessels.

图 2.10 （b）庄白 1 号坑出土的微氏四代铜器：（Ⅰ）折器；（Ⅱ）丰器；（Ⅲ）墙器；（Ⅳ）痶器。

1976 年发现于陕西庄白的 1 号窖藏为这项研究的实施提供了极好的机缘［图 2.10］。这个窖藏共出土了 103 件铜器，其中 74 件有铭文，最早的铜器制作于商末周初，最晚的具有西周晚期特点。[80] 学者们很快就意识到这组铜器对认识西周青铜器风格演变过程的重要价值，正如罗森所指出："事实证明这一材料对西周青铜器的年代学研究特别有帮助，它使我们能够将许多西周早期的青铜器排成一个可靠的基本序列。"[81] 但是我在这里并不打算再一次对青铜器风格进行分析。对我来说，既然庄白窖藏中的这些铜礼器是属于微氏宗族的一个分支，我们就可以把它们当作一所西周家庙中的积累物来对待和解释。

The genealogy of this branch can be reconstructed from the texts inscribed on the Zhuangbai bronzes. Its remote forebear arose from Wei, a place probably located not far from the last Shang capital in Henan.[82] Its members were hereditary archivists or court recordkeepers, and so their emblems included the pictograph *ce* (*a*). When King Wu conquered the Shang, an ancestor of the clan, whom his descendents referred to as their Brilliant Ancestor (Lie Zu), submitted to Zhou rule. He was charged by the new regime to organize court rituals, and he received a fief in the Plain of Zhou. His son, called Ancestor Yi (Yi Zu) in the inscriptions, probably lived during the reigns of Kings Cheng and Kang. His descendents described him as the kings' "henchman" (*fuxin*) but offered no concrete evidence for his achievement. Yi Zu's son Zhe, however, is a very important figure for this study.

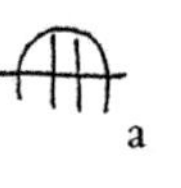

In fact, it is possible that the Zhuangbai bronzes were removed from a temple founded by him, since his temple title (*miaohao*), Ya Zu or Subordinate Ancestor, indicates that he initiated a new lineage within the clan's overall organization.[83] This hypothesis explains why Zhe's great-grandson Xing called him the High Ancestor (Gao Zu), and why bronzes commissioned by him are the oldest made by any identifiable Wei clan member found in the Zhuangbai hoard.[84] These Zhe bronzes, as well as those commissioned by his direct descendents, bear the emblem (*b*), which likely identified this sub-lineage
093 within a larger kin group whose members shared the emblem *ce*.

Zhe, or Ancestor Xin, was also the first Wei clan member whose personal name we know, and he and his son Feng (also called Yi Gong or Lord Yi) continued to serve Zhou kings as court archivists. One of their duties was to participate in royal investiture ceremonies, during which they recorded and announced royal orders. They described such glorious moments in their lives on sacrificial vessels, in the hope that their descendents would remember this tradition always (Figs. 2.11a, b):[85]

Fig. 2.11. (a) Zhe *zun*. Bronze. Early Western Zhou. 11th-10th centuries B.C. H. 32.5 cm. Excavated in 1976 from Zhuangbai Hoard no. 1. (b) Ink rubbing of inscription.

图 2.11 （a）折尊。青铜。西周早期，前 11—前 10 世纪。高 32.5 厘米。1976 年庄白 1 号窖藏出土。（b）铭文拓本。

这个家族的谱系可以从庄白铜器铭文中重构出来，其远祖源于“微”，一个距离商代在河南境内最后一个都城不远的地方。[82] 其家族成员都是世袭史官或是王室档案的保管者，因而其族徽当中包含着“册”的象形文字（a）。当武王克商的时候，该家族中被后世奉为“烈祖”的先人归顺于周，他受到新政权的委任，掌管王室的礼仪活动，并在周原得到一处封地。他的儿子在铭文中被称作“乙祖”，大约生活于成康时期，他的后代将其描述为成王和康王的“腹心”，但并没有提及他有何实际作为。然而，乙祖之子“折”却是本项研究中的一个重要人物。

实际上，我们可以认为庄白青铜器原来储藏于折所创建的家庙中，因为他的庙号“亚祖”表明他在宗族的整体组织中确立了一个新的宗支。[83] 这一推测能够解释为什么折的曾孙称他为“高祖”，以及为什么折所铸的铜器是庄白窖藏中所见由微氏成员制作的最为古老的一批器物。[84] 折的这些铜器及其直系后代所做的铜器都带有一个符号（b），很可能标示着具有“册”这一徽号的宗族集团中的一个分支。

折或祖辛也是我们所知道私名的最早的一位微氏家族成员，他与其子“丰”（乙公或乙侯）继续以书记官的角色服务于周天子，他们的职责之一是参与王室的分封礼仪，于其间记录和宣布王命。他们将一生当中所经历的这类荣耀时刻铭记在祭器上，让后代永远记得这一传统［图 2.11］。[85] 其中一例如下：

> In the fifth month, the king was at Gan. On the day *wuzi*, the king ordered me, Archivist Zhe, to bestow lands on Marquis Xiang; [other gifts from the king included] bronze metal and servitors. I praise the king's beneficence. In the nineteenth year of the king's reign, I make this vessel for [my deceased] Father Yi. May it be treasured forever [by my descendents]. (Lineage emblem.)

Since this and other inscribed bronzes were stored and displayed in the lineage's temple, knowledge about the lineage's ancestors was preserved in the temple and handed down to later generations. Qiang, who followed Feng as head of the lineage and as court archivist, compiled a systematic history of the lineage and recorded it in one of the most important extant Western Zhou bronze inscriptions (Figs. 2.12a, b). The text, inscribed on the vessel known as the Shi Qiang *pan* and roughly rendered into English below, first sets out a chronology of the Zhou royal house from King Wen down to the living ruler, King Gong.[86]

> 唯五月，王才（在）庈。戊子，令乍册折兄望土于相，侯易（赐）金，易（赐）臣。扬王休。唯王十又九祀。用乍父乙尊，其永宝。（族徽）
>
> （大意：五月，周某王在庈。戊子这一天，王命令我——作册折——将土地赐予相侯，王的其他赏赐还包括青铜和仆从。我颂扬王的善行。在王的第十九祀，我为我故去的父亲乙铸造了这件器物。希望子孙们永远珍重它。）

由于这类铭文铜器保存、陈列于祖庙，有关家族祖先的知识也就在宗庙中存留了下来，并且得以传之后世。继丰之后，“墙”成为宗族的领袖和王室史官，他把家族的历史进行了系统的编纂，铭记在一件极为重要的西周铜器上［图 2.12］。这件铜器就是著名的史墙盘，其铭文首先陈述了从文王到当时还在位的共王时期的西周王室年谱：[86]

b

Fig. 2.12. (a) Shi Qiang *pan*. Bronze. Mid-Western Zhou. 10th-9th centuries B.C. H. 16.2 cm. Diameter 47.3 cm. Excavated in 1976 from Zhuangbai Hoard no. 1. (b) Ink rubbing of inscription.

图 2.12 （a）史墙盘。青铜。西周中期，公元前 10 世纪—公元前 9 世纪。高 16.2 厘米，直径 47.3 厘米。1976 年庄白 1 号窖藏坑出土。（b）铭文拓本。

> In antiquity, King Wen first established harmony in government.
> God on High bestowed on him intelligent virtues. He could thus pacify
> [the country], hold fast to the whole world, and assemble and receive
> [tribute delegations] from the ten thousand states. Powerful King Wu
> campaigned in four directions. He took over the people of the Yin
> [Shang], consolidated [the achievements of] his ancestors, and forever
> quelled the troubles with the [nomadic] Di and the [eastern] Yi. The
> wise sage-king Cheng, assisted by strong helpers, governed the country
> with systematic rules. The virtuous King Kang divided the country [by
> 094 enfeoffing feudal lords]. The broad-minded King Zhao campaigned
> southward to the regions of Chu and Jing. The brilliant King Mu set
> a model for the current Son of Heaven, carefully educated him, and
> provided him with a solid dynastic foundation. Our Son of Heaven has
> received a great mandate to continue the long royal line King Wen and
> King Wu began. Our Son of Heaven should enjoy long life and good
> health. He serves the deities well and glorifies the previous kings and
> royal ancestors. God on High blesses him so that he may enjoy good
> harvests and have peoples of all places come to pay their respects.

This dynastic chronology sets a framework for Qiang's narrative of his own lineage's history.

> Our tranquil High Ancestor [Gao Zu] originally resided in Wei. When King Wu had conquered the Shang, our great-great-grandfather, the Brilliant Ancestor [Lie Zu], who had been the archivist of Wei, came to the Zhou court and was received in audience by King Wu. The king commanded the Duke of Zhou to assign him a residence in the Plain of Zhou. Our great-grandfather, Ancestor Yi [Yi Zu], served his king well and enjoyed the king's confidence. Our grandfather, Ancestor Xin [Zu Xin or Zhe, the Subordinate Ancestor], gave birth to many descendents and brought them blessings and happiness. To him we should offer

曰古文王，初𢾊（戾）龢（和）于政，上帝降懿德大甹（甹），匍（敷）有上下，迨受万邦。𩵦圉武王，遹征亖（四）方，达殷畯（畯）民，永不（丕）巩（鞏），狄虘（祖）光（挥）伐尸（夷）童。害（宪）圣成王，ナ（左）右𦀚（绶）𣪕（会），刚（纲）鲧（係），用肇（肇）𢼸（彻）周邦。㳄（渊）悊（哲）康王，分（遂）尹啬（亿）彊（疆）。宖（弘）鲁邵（昭）王，广能（批）楚荆（荆），隹（唯）寏（狩）南行。祗䚄（显）穆王，井（刑）帅宇（于）诲。𤔲（緟）寍天子，天子周屡（纘）文武长剌（烈）。天子𩛥（眉）无匃（害），𡨦（搴）祁（士）上下，亟（极）𤞷（熙）逗（桓）慕（谟），昊𧥝（照）亡（无）𢺦（斁），上帝司（嗣）夏，尢（尫）保受（授）天子𦄅（绾）命：“厚福丰年，方䜌（蛮）亡（无）不𠨘见。”

（大意：在古代，文王初步地做到政事和谐，上帝降给他美德，一切大定，他完全掌握各方面，聚合并接纳了万国。强有力的武王，就征伐四方，达到了殷朝的农民，是永久的。大大地巩固远祖，奋起击伐夷童［指伐纣］。有法度的聪明的成王，在各方面授予概括的治国纲要，用以开始治理周国。渊深明哲的康王，就端正亿万疆土。宏伟的厚重的昭王，大规模地打击楚荆，因为巡狩而到南方。恭敬的显赫的穆王，用型范表率来教诲，继续安定了现在的天子，天子周到地承继了文王武王的绵长的光烈。天子长寿，没有病痛。宣示上下，十分美好，很大的谋划。昊天照临着，没有什么败坏。上帝的后代夏和神巫名保的授予天子以美好的命令：“厚厚的福，丰收的年景，四方以及外族没有不来扬手朝见。”）

这个王朝年谱为墙随后叙述的自己的家族史确立了一个基本年代架构：

青（静）幽高且（祖），才（在）㣲霝（灵）处。雩（越）武王既𢦏殷，㣲（微）史剌（烈）且（祖）迺（乃）来见武王，武王则令（命）周公舍䢔（宇），于周卑（俾）处甬（通）叀（惠）乙且（祖），来匹氏（厥）辟远猷，匌（腹）心子（兹）𠭯（纳）。𢓜（粦）明亚且（祖）且（祖）辛，𢊁（迁）㞢（毓）子孙，𩒹（緐）𡨧（祓）多孷（厘），𢹎（齐）角𤎭（炽）光，义（宜）其𥜈（禋）祀。害（蔼）屖（萋）文考，乙公遽趩

> sincere sacrifices. Our father Lord Yi [Yi Gong or Feng] was wise and virtuous. No one uttered criticism of him. He engaged in farming and managed well, and demonstrated the virtues of loyalty, filial piety, and brotherly love.

The final paragraph of the text describes Qiang's accomplishments.

> I, Qiang the Archivist, work hard all day and night. I dare not neglect court ritual affairs. I praise the brilliant mandate of the Son of Heaven, and for this I make this precious and sacred vessel. It will be used in sacrificing to my Brilliant Ancestor and my fine deceased father, who left me the lineage fief with all its income. May good luck and blessings last until my hair turns white and my skin becomes dry. May I serve my king diligently and well. May this vessel be treasured 10,000 years [by my descendents].

This history of a noble lineage is deliberately interwoven with the history of the Zhou royal house: it was this linkage that legitimated the lineage's status within the Zhou bureaucratic network. Thus, the inscription elaborately narrates how the Brilliant Ancestor received the lineage fief in the capital area from King Wu; and the final paragraph emphasizes that the vessel was made to honor both this ancestor and the Son of Heaven. Once displayed on a bronze vessel in the lineage temple, this text provided later generations of the lineage a standard version of their family history. Not coincidentally, this inscription was partially copied on a set of ceremonial bells (Figs. 2.16a, b) commissioned by Qiang's son and the next lineage head, Xing.[87]

Among the members of the lineage who made ritual bronzes for their temple, Xing was perhaps the last but certainly the most illustrious.[88] The Zhuangbai hoard yielded 43 inscribed bronzes made by him, compared
095 with 13 inscribed vessels commissioned by previous generations. These 43 bronzes, however, still represent only part of Xing's donation to

（爽），㝵（德）屯（纯）无谏（刺），𧀼（农）啬（穑）戉（越）䁠（历）。隹（唯）辟孝䇂（友）。

（大意：安静的隐居的高祖，在微国很好地居住。当武王已经斩伐殷王朝后，微族史官烈祖就来见武王，武王则命令周公安排居住土地，让他住在岐周。通达而惠爱的乙祖，来配他的君长的远大规划，纳入于心腹之臣。善良英明的亚祖祖辛，分立宗支，蕃育子孙，繁多的福，许多喜庆，齐齐整整，焕发光采，应该受到禋祭。竭忠尽力的文考乙公极其明智，德行纯粹，没有人讥刺，耕种收获经营管理。正是君长孝父母，友兄弟。）

铭文的最后一段记述了墙的成就：

史墙夙（夙）夜不彖（坠），其日蔑曆（历），墙弗敢取（叡），对𩁹（扬）天子不（丕）显休令（命），用乍（作）宝障（尊）彝。剌（烈）且（祖）文考卞（淑）寍（贮），受（授）墙尔𪗐（租），福褱（怀）䵋（祓）录（禄）、黄耈弥生（性），龕（钦）事氏（厥）辟，其万年永宝用。

（大意：史墙从早到夜不敢坠失，每天努力做事。墙不敢败坏。对扬天子大的显赫的好命令，用来做宝藏的彝器。烈祖文考好的积蓄，给了墙你的田租。福禄来临，头发由白转黄，脸皮干枯而长寿，恭敬地服事其君长，一万年永久宝用。）

（关于史墙盘铭文的释读和意译，均见唐兰，1978。——译者注）

这里，一个贵族家族的世系被有意地与周王室的历史交织在一起，而正是由于这种联系，这个家族才得以在周王室的官僚政治网络中获得合法地位。由此我们可以了解史墙为什么如此煞费苦心地讲述其烈祖是如何从武王那里得到位于都城的采邑，以及为什么在铭文末尾一段强调这件铜盘的制作为的是光耀这位烈祖和周天子。一旦被铸在礼器上并陈列于祖庙之中，这段文字就为家族的后代提供了一份有关于家族历史的标准版本。并非巧合的是，当墙的儿子和下一个家族首领“𤼈”铸造一套编钟的时候，他把墙盘铭文的一部分复制在了钟的铭文里［图2.16］。[87]

𤼈可能是为微氏祖庙制作礼器的宗族成员中的最后一个，但也是地位最显赫的一个。[88]庄白窖藏出土的带铭铜器中有43件是出自𤼈之手。相比之下，其前代制作的有铭铜器总共只有13件。然而这43件铜器还

the temple: none of his four sets of ceremonial bells from the hoard is complete, and bronzes made by him had been found elsewhere as early as the Song dynasty.[89] Moreover, whereas his close forefathers had served the Zhou kings only as court archivists and attended to investiture rituals in this capacity, Xing was the only lineage member entitled Lord of Wei (Wei Bo) and more than once personally received investiture in the royal temple/palace. The first of these investitures took place in the fourth year of King Xiao's reign.[90] The king gave Xing special chariot fittings as his status symbols, and Xing responded by making a pair of *xu* vessels for his deceased father, Qiang (Figs. 2.13a, b). Nine years later, the same king again invested Xing in the capital Chengzhou. Accompanied by the ceremonial usher Yi Fu, Xing received ritual costumes from the king; he then made a pair of *hu* vessels to commemorate this event (Figs. 2.14a, b). He continued to enjoy favor from the next ruler, King Yi: the inscriptions on two other *hu*, which he made in the third year in the king's reign, record that he twice received bronze vessels from the king during royal rituals and banquets (Figs. 2.15a, b).

只是㾓对宗庙的部分奉献：窖藏中他所铸的四组编钟都不完整，此外早在宋代就在别处发现了由他制作的其他铜器。[89] 而且，他的祖先只是以史官的身份为周天子效力，并以同样的身份出席分封仪式，㾓却是被冠以“微伯”之号的唯一宗族成员，而且不止一次地亲临王宫或王庙受封。其第一次受封是在孝王四年，[90] 孝王赏赐给㾓专用的车马装备，作为他的身份的特殊象征，㾓的回应是特地为其亡父墙制作了一对铜盨［图 2.13］。九年之后，孝王又封㾓于成周，在典礼官夷父的陪同之下，从孝王的手里接受了礼服；他随后铸了一对铜壶纪念其事［图 2.14］。孝王去世之后，他继续得到夷王的恩宠：他于夷王三年铸造的一对铜壶的铭文中，记述了他两次在王室礼仪和宴飨活动中得到夷王赏赐的铜器［图 2.15］。

Fig. 2.13. (a) 4th-year Xing *xu*. Bronze. Middle—late Western Zhou. 10th-9th centuries B.C. H. 13.5 cm. Excavated in 1976 from Zhuangbai Hoard no. 1. (b) Ink rubbing of inscription.

图 2.13 （a）痶四年盨。青铜。西周中后期，前 10 世纪—前 9 世纪。高 13.5 厘米。1976 年庄白 1 号窖藏坑出土。（b）铭文拓本。

a

b

Fig. 2.14. (a) 13th-year Xing *hu*. Bronze. Middle—late Western Zhou. 10th-9th centuries B.C. H. 59.6 cm. Excavated in 1976 from Zhuangbai Hoard no. 1. (b) Ink rubbing of inscription.

图 2.14 （a）痶十三年壶。青铜。西周中后期，前 10 世纪—前 9 世纪。高 59.6 厘米。1976 年庄白 1 号窖藏坑出土。（b）铭文拓本。

a

Fig. 2.15. (a) 3rd-year Xing *hu*. Bronze. Middle—late Western Zhou. 10th-9th centuries B.C. H. 65.4 cm. Excavated in 1976 from Zhuangbai Hoard no. 1. (b) Ink rubbing of inscription.

图 2.15 （a）痶三年壶。青铜。西周中后期，前 10 世纪—前 9 世纪。高 65.4 厘米，1976 年庄白 1 号窖藏坑出土。（b）铭文拓本。

b

In addition to these three groups of bronzes commemorating Xing's investitures, a larger number of bronzes aimed to demonstrate his loyalty and filial piety. This intention is shown most clearly in the following inscriptions, which were cast on two separate sets of ceremonial bells:

In antiquity, King Wen first established harmony in government. God on High bestowed on him intelligent virtues. He could thus pacify [the country], hold fast to the whole world, and assemble and receive [tribute delegations] from the 10,000 states. When King Wu had conquered the Shang, our Brilliant Ancestor [Lie Zu], who had been the archivist of the Wei, came to the Zhou court and was received in audience by King Wu. The king commanded the Duke of Zhou to assign
097 him a residence in the Plain of Zhou, and charged him to organize the 50 kinds of court rituals.

Now I, Xing, work ceaselessly day and night; respectful and reverent, I devote my life [to the royal house]. Thus I make this set of harmonically tuned bells. Use it [so that I may] forever be at ease, [enjoying] ever more ample and manifold fortune. May my awareness be broadly opened up, helping [to obtain] an eternal life-mandate; may I have caringly bestowed upon me abundant good fortune and a good end. May I live for 10,000 years. [My sacrificial bull] has long horns; may I offer them to the Accomplished Spirits according to propriety; may I manifest my good fortune without limit. Use [this set of bells] to make me radiate with glory; forever shall I treasure it. (Figs. 2.16a, b)[91]

I, Xing, am fearful and ceaselessly active from morning to night, always mindful of not losing [my mandate]; striving to practice filial piety toward my High Ancestor Lord Xin, my Accomplished Ancestor Lord Yi, and my august deceased father Lord Ding. I made this set of harmonically tuned chime bells. Use it so as to please and exalt those who arrive in splendor, so as to let the accomplished men of former generations rejoice. Use it to pray for long life, to beg for an eternal life-mandate, [so that I may] extensively command a position of high

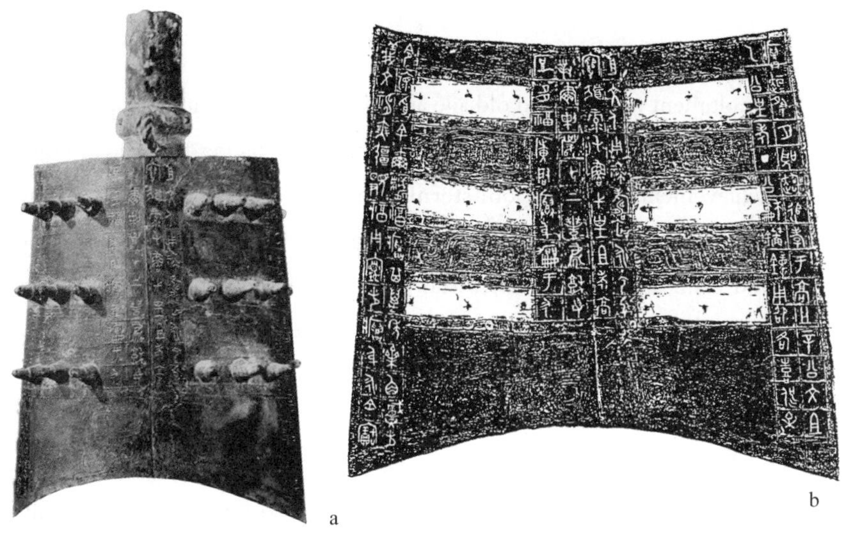

Fig. 2.16. (a) Xing bell. Bronze. Middle-late Western Zhou. 10th-9th centuries B.C. H. 48 cm. Excavated in 1976 from Zhuangbai Hoard no. 1. (b) Ink rubbing of inscription.

图 2.16 （a）瘐钟。青铜。西周中后期，前 10 世纪—前 9 世纪。高 48 厘米。1976 年庄白 1 号窖藏坑出土。（b）铭文拓本。

除了这三组纪念自己受封的铜器，大量由瘐所铸的铜器着意表明他的忠孝。这种意图在下面的两组编钟铭文中表露得最为清楚：

> 曰古文王，初戾龢（和）于政，上帝降懿德大甹，匍有四方，迨受万邦。雩武王既伐殷，敚史剌且，来见武王，武王则令周公舍寓㠯（以）五十颂处。
>
> 今瘐夙夕虔敬、卹氒死事，肇乍龢鑙钟，用䜌妥厚多福，广启瘐身，勵于永令，褱受余尔䵼福霝冬，瘐其万年羊角，义文神无疆，䫉福，用□光瘐身，永余宝。[图 2.16] [91]
>
> （大意：在古代，文王初步地做到政事和谐，上帝降给他美德，一切大定，他完全掌握各方面，聚合并接纳了万国。当强有力的武王斩伐殷王朝后，微族史官烈祖就来见武王，武王则命令周公安排居住周原，任用他来管理五十种王室的礼仪。
>
> 今天，我——瘐，从早到晚每天虔诚恭敬地努力做事，献身于王室。我制作了这套龢钟，从中感受到永远的舒闲，享受到各种福祉。我的身心更为开放，有助于获得永久的使命；让我接受这降临在身上的大量好运和美好的结果，让我长生万年。我所用作祭品的牛有长长的角，让我依礼将它进

emolument in respected old age and [enjoy] unadulterated happiness.

My venerable august ancestors are loftily facing these illustrious achievements, [looking on] sternly from up on high. May they let me be rich and prosperous, forever [enjoying] with ease ever more ample and manifold good fortune. May they broadly open up my awareness, helping [me to obtain] an eternal life-mandate; may they personally bestow upon me that abundant good fortune [of theirs]. May I live for 10,000 years. [My sacrificial bull] has long horns, he is well-fattened, and [his skin] is glistening; sacrificing to the Accomplished Spirits according to propriety, may I manifest my good fortune without limit. Use [this set of bells] to make me radiate with glory, forever shall I treasure it. (Figs. 2.17a, b)[92]

a

b

Fig. 2.17. (a) Xing bell. Bronze. Middle—late Western Zhou. 10th-9th centuries B.C. H. 70 cm. Excavated in 1976 from Zhuangbai Hoard no. 1. (b) Ink rubbing of inscription.

图 2.17 （a）瘐钟。青铜。西周中后期，前 10 世纪—前 9 世纪。高 70 厘米。1976 年庄白 1 号窖藏坑出土。（b）铭文拓本。

These and similar inscriptions on Xing's bronzes reveal a number 098
of changes in the ancestor worship practiced in the Wei lineage temple toward the end of Western Zhou. These changes were related to the attitude toward the deceased ancestors, the intention of preserving past memories, the desire to rewrite history, and the self-esteem of the living generation—all indicative of a new concept of monumentality.

献给文神，表达我无限的祝福。用这套钟来传扬我的荣耀，我将永远宝用它。）

疾趄趄夙夕圣趬，追孝于高且辛公、文且乙公、皇考丁公龢鐂钟，用卲各喜侃乐前文人、用祷寿匄永令，绰绾发录屯鲁。弋皇且考高对尔剌严才（在）上，丰丰㲈㲈，韡受厚多福，广启疾身，勵于永令，裹受余尔黻福，疾其万年，桥角䰛光，义文神无疆，顯福，用□光疾身，永余宝。［图 2.17］[92]

（大意：我——疾，从早到晚每天兢兢业业地努力做事，留心不要失职；努力向我的高祖辛公、文祖乙公、皇考丁公尽孝。我制作了这套龢钟，用它来愉悦和颂扬那些降下了光辉的先祖们，用它来让那些前代有德行的人们感到高兴，用它来祈求长寿，用它来祈求永久的使命。因此我可能获得更高的职位，以礼敬老者，以享受真正的幸福。我的皇考高高在上，威严地俯瞰着这辉煌的成就。让他们佑护我富足多福，让我的身心更为开放，有助于获得永久的使命；让我接受这降临在身上的大量好运和美好的结果，让我长生万年。我所用作祭品的牛有长长的角，让我依礼将它进献给文神，表达我无限的祝福。用这套钟来传扬我的荣耀，我将永远宝用它。）

疾所铸铜器上的这些铭文，揭示了接近西周晚期时微氏家族在祖先崇拜中的几项重要变化，关系到对亡故祖先的态度，保存往昔记忆的动机，重写历史的欲望以及造器者的自我认识。首先，尽管钟铭第一段中的家族史明显依据史墙盘铭文，却略去了先周时期的高祖，而是直接从得到武王封地的烈祖那里开始他的叙述。他因而

First, although the lineage's history recounted in the first inscription was apparently based on the Shi Qiang *pan* inscription, Xing omitted his pre-Zhou High Ancestor and began his narrative from the Brilliant Ancestor, who received the lineage's fief from King Wu. He thus revised his lineage history; the result was a perfect parallel between the history of his family and that of the dynastic Zhou rule. Second, instead of following his father's example of praising every ancestor, Xing restricted his "ancestral models" to three particular personages: his great-grandfather Zhe, his grandfather Feng, and his father Qiang. Moreover, whereas Qiang used the term "High Ancestor" (Gao Zu) in addressing the remote founder of the Wei clan, Xing used the same term for his great-grandfather Zhe, who, as suggested earlier, may have initiated a new branch of the Wei lineage. What we find here is the internal fragmentation of the lineage
099 and the narrowing of a kinship unit. Correspondingly, the focus of ancestor worship gradually shifted from *yuanzu* (remote ancestors) to *jinzu* (close and direct ancestors).

Third, the inscriptions on Xing's bronzes largely served to glorify the donor himself. The description of his ancestry was significantly reduced, and his own worldly achievements laboriously emphasized. Many formulaic sentences convey his hope for longevity and, more frequently, for "good fortune." In the preceding chapter I interpreted this new emphasis in late Western Zhou bronze inscriptions as evidence for the transformation of ritual objects from *liqi* that one devoted to one's ancestral deities to those that one dedicated to oneself. The present discussion, which views these bronzes as an integral component of an ancestral temple, reveals another aspect of the same transformation: as "self-glorifying" bronzes gradually came to dominate the temple, they inevitably created tension between tradition and reality. On the one hand, since the old ritual paraphernalia were still housed in a temple and traditional rituals were still routinely performed there, the temple continued to preserve the past history of a lineage. On the other hand, the living members of the lineage had gradually lost interest in their past and were eager to demonstrate their power straightforwardly by presenting their personal deeds in the temple. In other words, they were eager to transform the temple from a collective lineage monument to a monument to a few illustrious individuals. This contradiction finally led to the division of the traditional temple into twin centers: a temple, which continued to exist as a religious or sacrificial center, and a palace,

改写了家族历史，而改写的结果是微氏的家族史与周的王朝史结合得天衣无缝。其次，没有遵循其父亲对先祖一一加以称颂的遗范，而是将他的“祖先典范”集中在三个特殊人物的身上，即他的曾祖父折、祖父丰和父亲墙。而且，不同于墙把遥远的氏族创立者称为“高祖”，以同样的称谓称呼其曾祖父折。如前所述，折很有可能开启了微氏宗族的一个新分支，我们于此发现的是这个宗族的进一步内部分化和血亲单位的缩小，以及祖先崇拜的焦点逐步由远祖转移到近祖的趋势。

再次，所铸铜器的铭文在很大程度上是为了光耀奉献者本人：他对家族的历史做了显著的简化，但对自己在世上的功绩却做了不遗余力的强调。许多套话也传达出他对长寿，尤其是对“多福”的企盼。我在前一章中将西周晚期青铜器铭文中的这种新变化解释为礼器性质的转变：原来是献给祖先神的神圣器物逐渐变成对作器者本人荣耀的赞颂。现在，当我们将这些青铜器视为祖庙的有机组成部分，我们可以看到同一转变的另一侧面：当“自我荣耀”的铜器渐渐在祖庙中占据优势，它们也就不可避免地造成了传统与现实之间的张力。一方面，由于古老的礼仪用具依然保存在宗庙里，也由于传统礼仪活动仍旧在那里举行，祖庙仍起着保存家族历史的作用。但另一方面，世袭家族在世的成员逐渐失去了对过去的兴趣，而是热衷于以在传统家庙记录其个人功绩的方式直接展现他们的权力。换言之，他们渴望将宗庙由一种对宗族集体的纪念建筑变成一种对少数杰出人物的纪念建筑。这一矛盾的最终结果是传统宗庙分裂为两个中心：一个是继续作为宗教或祭祀中心而存在的祖庙，

which gained its independence as the center of administration. A temple continued to belong to a larger kinship group and worshipped a collective body of ancestors; a palace was the property and symbol of one man and his small family. When the archaic social and political systems based on a large clan-lineage network collapsed after the Western Zhou, princes and lords no longer submitted to the central authority or received their mandate through royal investitures. They had to demonstrate their own worth and strength. Consequently, their palaces became the chief monuments of a new historical era.

This new era lasted some 500 years, from the early eighth to the late third century B.C. In traditional Chinese chronology, it is divided into two stages—the Eastern Zhou (consisting of the Spring and Autumn and the Warring States periods) and the Qin—which witnessed China's transition from a country united by kinship ties to an empire governed by a central government. Scholars have suggested a number of reasons for the devolution of political power from the Zhou kings to the feudal lords during the Eastern Zhou. These include the rapid growth of regional
100 economies and the increasing control of resources and military forces by local rulers, the gradual distancing and detachment of the family lines of these rulers from the central royal lineage, and the internal turmoil and foreign invasions that continuously weakened the Zhou royal house. Jacques Gernet summarized the consequences of this social and political transformation:

> It was no longer the religious and military sovereignty of the [Zhou] kings that was the dominant factor, even if it remained customary to refer to them for arbitration and to lean on their moral authority; ritual practices and the knowledge of precedents formed the foundation of a new order. They governed the relations between these allied yet rival cities, united and also divided by war, vendetta, matrimonial alliances, treaties, and the exchange of goods and services. With the development

of the principalities and the weakening of the royal power a new society and new manners made their appearance: a nobility jealous of its privileges and attentive to questions of protocol, the ideal of the noble warrior, and ethic of honor and prestige.[93]

另一个是独立出来，成为行政中心的宫殿。祖庙继续属于大型血亲集团，用以崇拜宗族或家族的集体的祖先；宫殿则是当权者个人及其家庭的权力象征。西周之后，当建立在宗族网络上的古老社会政治体制逐渐崩溃，地方诸侯们不再归顺于中央政权或通过分封的形式接受王室的委任。他们必须证实其自身的财富和实力，其巍峨壮丽的宫殿于是成为新的历史时期的主要纪念碑。

这一新的历史时期从公元前8世纪初到公元前3世纪末，持续了大约500年。它在传统编年史中被划分为两个阶段——东周（包括春秋与战国时期）和秦，表明了中国正在从一个由血亲纽带缔结而成的国家向一个由中央政体统治管理的国家转变。有学者已经指出东周时期政治权力从周天子向地方诸侯手中转移的诸多原因，包括地方经济的迅速增长和地方统治者对经济资源与军事力量的逐步掌控，地方统治家族与中央王室世系的逐步疏远与脱离，以及各种内乱外侵对周王室的不断动摇。谢和耐对这场社会政治变动的结果做了如下的概述：

> （周）天子在宗教与军事事务中至高无上的地位已不再是主导因素，尽管在习惯上人们仍以天子作为仲裁的参考和道德权威的依靠。礼仪中的实践活动与知识经验构成了新秩序的基础，它们支配着既联合又敌对的城邦之间的关系，使得城邦之间在战争、内讧、联姻、谈判以及商品交换和服务活动中或聚或散。随着诸侯国的壮大发展和王室力量的逐渐衰微，一个新的社会和一套新的行为方式出现了，包括贵族对特权的珍视和对礼节的执著，对“高贵武士”的理想化，以及与荣誉和名望相连的伦理规范。[93]

Struggles between feudal lords for political and territorial dominance further reduced the number of the principalities established previously by Zhou kings through investitures. A handful of "hegemonies" (*ba*)—large, powerful kingdoms able to enforce their will on the Zhou court and the weaker states—appeared; their rulers came to call themselves "kings" (*wang*), a title reflecting their newly gained status and confidence. Political struggles also took place within principalities; often officials of minor lineages and lower positions overpowered their lords. The basic tendency of this historical process, again summarized by Gernet, is that

> political power was trying to free itself from the matrix in which it was imprisoned—that is, from the family and religious context of which it formed an integral part in the ninth to seventh centuries—and that as it gradually broke loose it was conceived more and more clearly as a specific factor. To say that the prince sought to free himself from the weighty tutelage of the families of high dignitaries does not take account of the whole reality: in fact it was power itself that changed its nature during the course of this struggle between tradition and the new demands of the age.[94]

This social transformation is most clearly reflected by the development of Eastern Zhou cities and by the growing importance of the palace, which has now assumed an independent "monumental" status. The divorce of the palace from the lineage temple meant that political power was freeing itself from the "family and religious context" that had imprisoned it; the independence of the palace signified that political power "was conceived more and more clearly as a specific factor"; and the supremacy of the palace over the temple documented the result of "the struggle between tradition and the new demands of the age."

More than twenty Warring States capitals of large and small Eastern Zhou states have been excavated during the past fifty years.[95] Their impressive scale contradicts the traditional building code based on the Western Zhou social hierarchy.[96] We know this code from a statement made by the official Ji Zhong in 722 B.C. In that year, the lord of the state of Zheng gave a large city, Jing, to his younger brother as the latter's fief. Ji Zhong opposed this decision: "According to the rule of the former [Zhou] kings, the larger capital [of a lord?] should be one-third the size of the national capital; the middle capital [of a *qing*-minister?] should be one-fifth the size of the national capital; and the smaller capital [of a *shi*-officer?] should be one-ninth the size of the national capital. Now

诸侯之间因为政治与土地占有权的原因而相互争夺，其结果是先前由周天子分封的诸侯国数目逐渐减少，最后剩下了一些称作“霸”的大国和强国，能够将自己的意愿加于周王室与其他弱小诸侯国之上。这些强国的统治者进而自封为“王”，明显地反映出他们不断增强的地位与野心。政治斗争在诸侯国内部也不断发生，常常是地位较低的家族或下属官吏凌驾于原来的主子之上。对于这段历史时期的基本趋势，谢和耐再次总结道：

> 政治势力试图从其被禁锢的母体中寻求释放——也就是说，从公元前9世纪至前7世纪赖以形成为一股主要势力的家族与宗教背景中寻求释放。当它逐渐挣脱出来的时候，它也就越来越明显地被看作一股特殊的势力。说诸侯企图从其高贵家族的势力监护中挣脱出来并不完全符合事实：实际上是政治力量本身在新旧时代的要求之间的斗争过程中改变了自身的性质。[94]

这一社会变革最清晰地反映在东周城市的发展和宫殿重要性的增长上，后者从这时开始承担独立的纪念碑角色。宫殿与祖庙的分离意味着政治势力正在从禁锢它们的“家族与宗教背景”中获得释放；宫殿的独立表明政治力量“越来越明显地被看作一股特殊的势力”；而宫殿对祖庙原来至尊地位的挑战和超越则证实了“新旧时代的要求之间的斗争”的结果。

过去五十年间的考古调查已发现了二十余座东周时期大小诸侯国的都城，[95]其可观的规模与基于西周等级制度的传统建筑规制明显不合。[96]我们从公元前722年郑国大夫祭仲的一段陈述中可以了解这种传统规制。是年，庄公将京这座大城封与其弟共叔段，祭仲表示反对，说：“先王之制，大都不过三国之一，中五之一，小九之一。

the scale of Jing does not match [your brother's status]; I am afraid that your order is against the established rule."[97] But his protest went in vain; the lord considered the "established rule" no more than a cliché and persevered in his decision.

If the old Western Zhou code was still murmured at the beginning of the Spring and Autumn period, it was completely ignored during the late Eastern Zhou. None of the excavated Warring States cities followed the regulation quoted by Ji Zhong; some of them even surpassed the Zhou Royal City (Wangcheng) in both size and elaborateness.[98] All these new cities contained a special "palace district" (*gongdianqu*). Although the district occupied different positions in the various princely capitals, its presence is indicated by the large remaining foundations enclosed by walls that originally divided a city into areas for the ruler and for his
102 subjects. In the Lower Capital (Xiadu) of the state of Yan (in modern Hebei), this district occupied the city's northern part (Fig. 2.18a). Many large earthen foundations, some still rising 20 meters above the surrounding plain, along with exquisite bronze architectural accessories unearthed there, suggest the splendor of vanished palatial halls and pavilions built on tall terraces (Figs. 2.18b, c).[99] In Linzi, the capital of Qi, in present-day Shandong, the palace district was even more strictly defined: it had become a self-contained "palace town" loosely attached to the city's southwest corner (Fig. 2.19). These and other regional capitals provided the historic basis for an ideal city plan, which emerged during the Warring States period (Fig. 2.20). Recorded in a treatise called "Regulations of Workmanship" ("Kaogongji"), this plan places the palace in the center of a "state capital" (*guo*), flanked by the ancestral temple and the Land Altar, two prominent components of a traditional capital that have become secondary elements of the new city.[100]

This plan, however, only illustrates the "ideal capital" as a flat image and does not show an extremely important development of Warring States cities, which is their rapid vertical growth. For example, near the center of Linzi's palace town is a large mound approached by flights of stairs. Archaeologists have identified it as the remains of a famous terrace building called Huangong tai, the Platform of Duke Huan, where many important historical events took place.[101] Even after more than two thousand years; the oval-shaped foundation of Huangong tai is still 86 meters long. It must have also been of a considerable height:

今京不度，非制也。"[97]（根据先王定下的制度，大型城市的大小不应超过王都的三分之一，中型城市不应超过王都的五分之一，小型都市不应超过王都的九分之一。现在京的尺度不合乎这个规定，因此是违反制度的。）但是他的反对意见全属徒然；庄公视先王之制为陈词滥调，因而固执己见。

如果说古老的西周法典在春秋初期仍然苟延残喘地维持着，那么到了东周晚期，它已经完全不被理睬了。目前发现的战国都城遗址没有一个遵守祭仲引述的传统制度；有的城甚至在规模和精美程度上超过了王城。[98] 所有这些新兴城市都含有一个专门的"宫殿区"。尽管它在不同侯国国都中的位置不同，为围墙所包围的巨大残存建筑基址表明了它的存在，而这些围墙把城市划分为君主和臣民的不同区域。燕下都的宫殿区位于城的北部［图 2.18 b］，那里的许多大型夯土堆有的现在仍高出地表 20 余米，出土的精美青铜建筑附件令人想见昔日立于高台上的殿堂台阁是何等堂皇富丽［2.18 b, c］。[99] 齐国故都临淄的宫殿区甚至被界定得更为严格，成为一个附在大城西南角封闭而独立的"宫城"［图 2.19］。诸如此类的地方性都城为出现于战国时期的一种理想城市规划提供了历史根据［图 2.20］。据《考工记》记载，这个理想城市规划将宫殿安置在都城（国）之中央，位于它两边的是"左祖右社"。这里，传统都城的两个最重要组成部分（祖庙和社）已经变成了新兴城市中的次要元素。[100]

从另一方面说，这一规划仅仅描绘了新型"理想城市"的平面图景，而没有显示战国城市另一个极端重要的发展，那就是它们迅速的纵向发展。例如，靠近临淄宫城的中央就曾有一个以阶梯升降的高大土台，考古学家将它确认为著名的桓公台——许多重要的历史事件在那里发生。[101] 即便经历了两千多年之后，桓公台的椭圆形基础仍有 86 米长，其原来高度想必相当可观：据说当时楚王曾筑

a contemporary *tai* platform constructed by a Chu king was said to have measured 100 *ren* high and reached the floating clouds.[102] A large number of architectural remains surround the Huangong tai, suggesting that it was not an isolated tower but the commanding focus of the palace city. Imposing in appearance, this kind of structure best represents the architectural difference between an Eastern Zhou palace complex and a Western Zhou temple compound. A Western Zhou temple (Figs. 2.2a, b), as discussed earlier, was a walled enclosure that emphasized horizontal expansion; its ritual function lay in gradually guiding visitors to trace their ancestral origin and to re-experience their history. An Eastern Zhou palace, on the other hand, stood on tall terraces or was built around an earthen pyramid; its powerful three-dimensional image had an immediate visual effect (see Fig. 2.21).

It thus becomes understandable why the *tai* platform became fashionable as a new type of monument among Eastern Zhou kings and lords, and why such constructions were extensively recorded in ancient texts. Duke Jing of Qi built the Great Platform (Da tai), Duke Ling of Wei the Juniper Platform (Chonghua tai), Duke Ling of Jin the Nine-Layered Platform (Jiuceng tai), and the kings of Chu the Platform of Qianxi (Qianxi tai), the Platform of Splendid Display (Zhanghua tai), and the Platform of Gold (Huangjin tai), among others.[103] Although these platforms were in different regions, they shared a single political significance: the taller a *tai*, the stronger its patron felt in the contemporary political arena. In the eastern part of the country, when Duke Jing of Qi climbed onto Boqin tai and surveyed his capital, he sighed with satisfaction: "Wonderful! Who in the future will be able to possess a platform like this!"[104] In the north, King Wuling of Zhao built an extremely tall *tai* that allowed him to overlook the neighboring state of Qi; this structure thus demonstrated his strength and intimidated his enemy.[105] In the south, a Chu king constructed an imposing platform as the site for a meeting with other feudal lords. Struck with awe, his guests agreed to join the Chu alliance and made a vow: "How tall this platform! How deep the mind it shows! If I betray my words, let me be punished by other states in this alliance."[106] In the west, Duke Miu of Qin tried to intimidate foreign envoys by showing them his palaces, which "even spirits could not build without exhausting their strength."[107] In the state of Wei in central China, the minister Xu Wan responded as follows to his sovereign's plan to construct the Middle Heaven Platform (Zhongtian tai):

百仞之台，直插云际。[102] 环绕在桓公台周围的大量建筑遗迹表明，这不是一座孤立的建筑，而是整个宫城居高临下的制高点。这种高台建筑恢弘壮丽的外观最能体现出东周宫殿建筑群与西周宗庙建筑群在建筑特征方面的差异。如前文所论，西周的祖庙［图 2.2］是一个为围墙包围的闭合性场所，它强调的是平面的延伸；其礼仪功能在于引导观者回溯其先人的由来，重温其家族的历史。而东周的宫殿则坐落于高台之上或聚于高台建筑四周，其强有力的三维形象造成一种直接的视觉冲击力［见图 2.21］。

我们因此可以理解为什么“台”作为一种新兴的纪念碑性建筑在东周王侯中成为时尚，以及为什么这类建筑物广泛见之于这一时期的文献记载。我们读到齐景公筑大台，卫灵公筑重华台，晋灵公筑九层台；也知道楚王的乾溪台和章华台以及传为燕昭王的黄金台。[103] 虽然这些台分布在不同区域，它们却拥有一种共同而单纯的政治意义：台越高，其建造者便越能在当时的政治舞台上感到自身的强大。在东方，当齐景公登上柏寝台眺望齐国城郭的时刻，他心满意足地感叹道：“美哉，焕乎！后世将孰有之？”[104] 在北方，赵武灵王造了野台以望齐国境内的景况；这个建筑因此成为他的政治实力的证明，也表达了赵国对其邻国的威慑。[105] 在南方，楚王建造了一个五仞之台以会诸侯，与会的诸侯皆向楚王盟誓曰：“将将之台，窅窅其谋，我言而不尚，诸侯伐之。”[106] 在西部，秦缪公为了显示他的威力，请来访使节观看他的“鬼神竭全力而难筑”的宫殿。[107] 在中部，大臣许绾对魏王营建中天台的计划做了如下回应：

I have heard that heaven is 15,000 *li* above the earth. Today Your Majesty wishes to build a platform that will reach half this height; so it must be 7,500 *li* tall with a base of 8,000 *li* on each side. Even all Your Majesty's lands are not enough for its foundation. In antiquity, Yao and Shun established vassal states within a territory of 5,000 *li* on each side.
103 If Your Majesty insists on satisfying your fancy, then you certainly must employ military force to conquer other states. But even if you conquer all the other states, the acquired land will still not be enough for the foundation of your platform. Only when you have conquered the foreign countries in the four directions and have gained an area of total 8,000 *li* on each side, can you begin to think about your building. But still, there will be the questions of building materials and manpower. The construction will also have to be supported by a state granary that can supply billions of bushels of grain. Your Majesty therefore will have to seek such resources 8,000 *li* beyond the nearby foreign lands, and will have to devote all cultivated land for your building.[108]

Fig. 2.18. (a) Bronze door ring. Late Eastern Zhou. 4th-3rd centuries B.C. L. 74.5 cm. W. 36.5 cm. Excavated in 1966 at Laomu tai, Xiadu. Hebei Provincial Institute of Cultural Relics. (b) Plan of Xiadu, capital of the state of Yan. Yixian, Hebei province. Eastern Zhou. 8th-3rd centuries B.C. (c) The remaining foundation of Laomu tai in Xiadu.

图 2.18 （a）青铜铺首门环。东周晚期，前 4 世纪—前 3 世纪。长 74.5 厘米，宽 36.5 厘米。1966 年燕下都老姆台出土。河北省文物研究所藏。（b）河北易县燕下都平面图。东周，前 8 世纪—前 3 世纪。（c）燕下都老姆台遗址。

臣闻天与地相去万五千里，今王因而半之，当立七千五百里高；其趾当方八千里，尽王之地，不足以为台趾。古者尧舜建诸侯五千里，王必愿为台，必其兵伐诸侯，尽有其地犹不足，又伐四夷，得方八千里，乃足以为台趾。材木之积，人徒之众，食廪之输，以千万亿度。八千里之外，当尽农亩之地，足以奉给。王台具者已备，乃可作。[108]

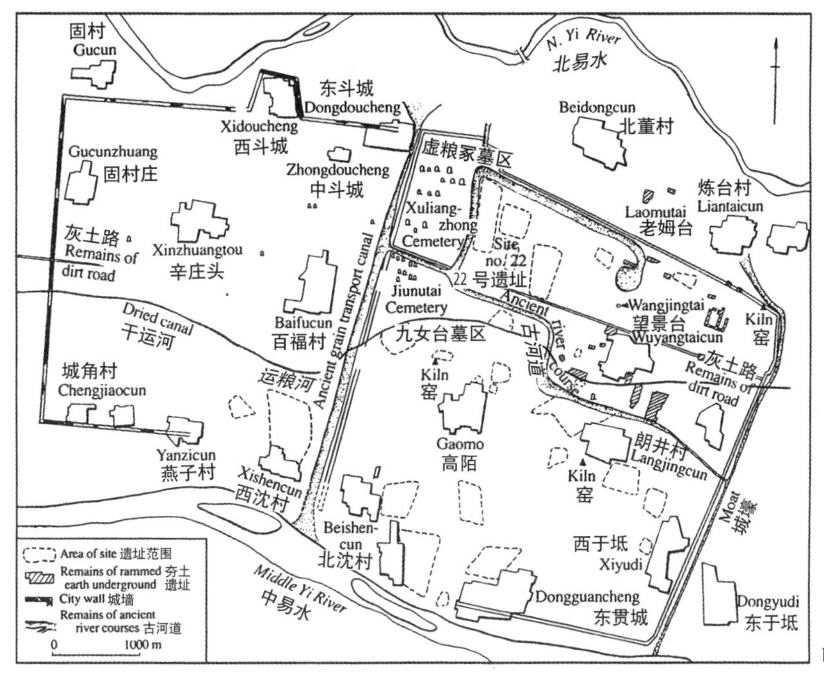

b

c

Xu Wan's fascinating rhetoric most clearly reveals the monumentality
of an Eastern Zhou platform. He seems to have realized the historical
significance of this type of palatial structure: its construction meant the
104 destruction of the feudal system established by ancient sages. To him, the
desire for such a tall building was equivalent to the ambition for political
dominance over the whole nation, even foreign countries—seizing lands
from other states, ruling the entire population, and becoming master of the
world. In Xu Wan's metaphor, the man who achieved this goal would stand
on a giant tower that buried his empire and people underneath. In our
modern historical conception, the process leading to such an empire was
the state of Qin's unification of China, and the man who finally managed to
stand on the tower was Qin Shi Huang, the great First Emperor.

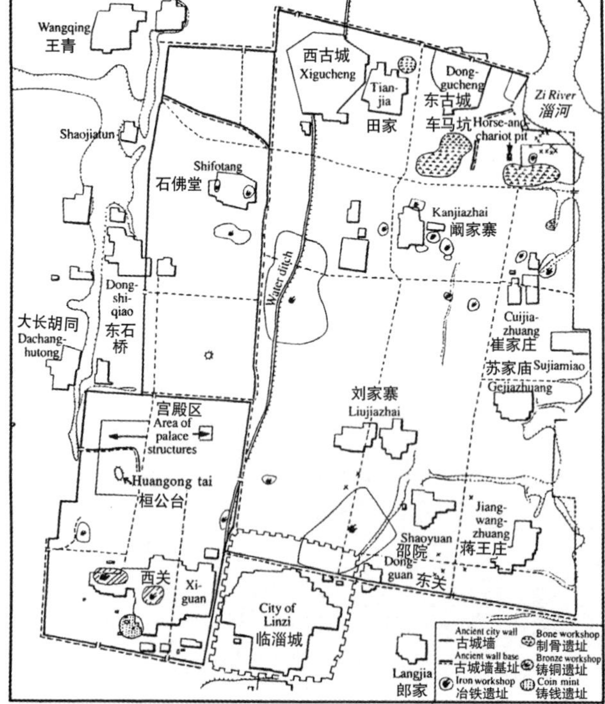

Fig. 2.19. Plan of Linzi, capital of the state of Qi. Shandong province. Eastern Zhou. 8th-3rd centuries B.C.

图 2.19 齐国都城临淄平面图。东周，前 8 世纪—前 3 世纪

许绾这番机智有趣的谏言最清晰地揭示出东周时期高台建筑的纪念碑性质。他似乎已经了解这类富丽宏伟建构的历史意义：它们的建造实际上意味着古代圣贤所确立的分封制度的解体。在他看来，对这样一座高大建筑的追求等于在各国乃至四夷之上建立霸权地位的野心——攫取他国的土地，控制所有的人众，使自己成为天下之主。在许绾的比喻中，这个建筑将把整个帝国和人民埋葬在它的下面，而其建造者将高居于这个宏伟高台之上。在我们当今的历史概念中，通向这样一个帝国的过程是秦国对中国的统一，而秦始皇则是站在这样一座高塔上的第一个统治者。

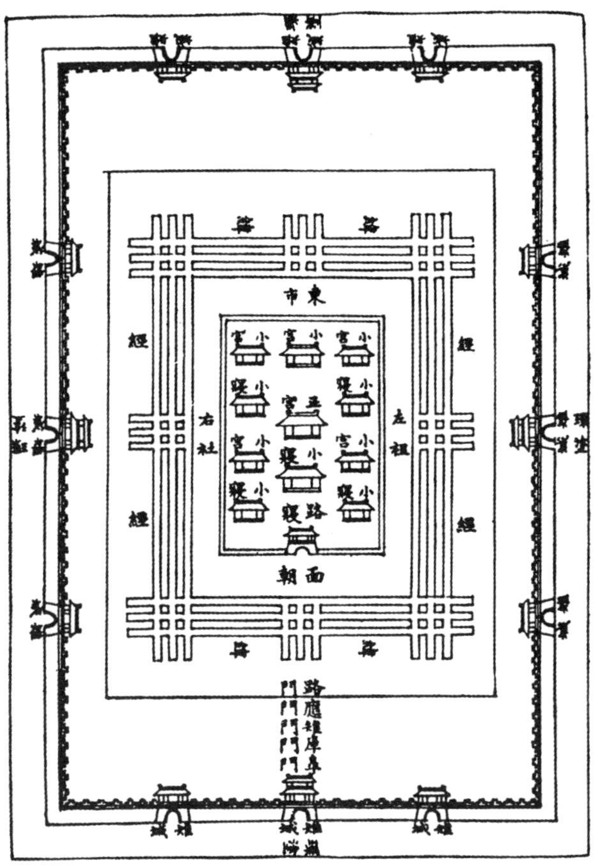

Fig. 2.20. Idealized plan of the Zhou royal capital as recorded in the Eastern Zhou text "Kaogong ji."

图 2.20 东周文献《考工记》所载理想化的周王都平面图

Fig. 2.21. Miniature tower with figures and musicians inside. Bronze. Late Eastern Zhou. 4th-3rd centuries B.C. H. 21.5 cm. W. 9.0 cm. Excavated at Dongguancheng in Xiadu, Yixian, Hebei province. Hebei Provincial Institute of Cultural Relics.

图 2.21 塔楼模型。青铜。东周晚期，前 4 世纪—前 3 世纪。高 21.5 厘米、宽 9.0 厘米，河北易县下都东关城出土。河北省文物研究所藏。

105 The Qin was the most aggressive of the states contending for the imperial seat. Chief credit for its rapid rise to power belongs to Shang Yang, who instituted a series of political reforms from 356 to 338 B.C. A radical Legalist, Shang Yang dedicated his life to transforming an old feudal principality into a "modern" political state. He helped establish the absolute power of the king, forged a centralized administration, reorganized large lineages into small mutual-surveillance family units, converted serfs into taxpaying farmers, and imposed harsh measures on those who broke the law. The old lineages lost their power in this new system; their hereditary status and privilege were abolished, and their members could receive official titles and posts only after making

recognizable contributions to the state. One of Shang Yang's crucial decisions, which also ensured the institutionalization of other new policies, was to move Qin's capital from Yong to Xianyang.[109] Yong, the sacred site of the Qin ancestral temple and the home of many hereditary lineages, represented everything that Shang Yang was trying to abolish. Xianyang, on the other hand, was a new city free from the burden of tradition; its strategic position at the intersection of major rivers and traffic roads allowed the Qin to further influence national politics.

Not coincidentally, when Shang Yang began to construct the new capital, he completely ignored the fundamental precept of traditional architecture that the first building a nobleman erected was his ancestral temple. What he founded first was a pair of palatial halls, which Sima Qian called the Ji que, or the Ji Gate Towers.[110] The modern scholar Wang

秦是列国中争夺帝国宝座的最骁勇好斗者，其势力的迅速上升主要归功于商鞅所发起的变法。商鞅在公元前 356 年到公元前 338 年之间实行了一系列政治改革，这位激进的法家成员以生命为代价，致力于将一个古老的封建侯国转变为一个“现代”的政治大国。他帮助君主确立了绝对权力，打造了一个中央集权制政府，将大宗族重组为相互监督的小型家庭单位，将奴隶改编成赋税农户，对违法者加重徭役。在这个新体制中，旧的世袭贵族失去了他们的传统权力，其世袭地位和特权被废除了，其成员只有在为国家建立相当的功业之后才能获得官衔与职位。商鞅所做最重要的决定之一，同时也是保障其他新政策制度化的决定，是将秦的都城从雍迁到咸阳。[109] 雍是秦人传统祖庙所在的圣地，也是许多世袭贵族的根据地，代表着商鞅试图废止的各种事物。而咸阳是个没有传统负担的新城市，它坐落在主要河流和交通要道的交汇点上，在战略上可以使秦国影响全国的政治形势。

并非偶然的是，当商鞅开始建这座新城时，他全然不顾传统筑城的基本规则，即最先兴建的第一座建筑应是祖庙。他所首先建造的一对有如门阙一样的宫殿，被司马迁称之为冀阙。[110] 当代学者

Xueli interprets Shang Yang's preference for this particular building type as a reflection of the Eastern Zhou custom of posting legal documents and official pronouncements on the *que* gates in front of a palace. The gate-like Qin palace can thus be viewed as an architectural manifestation of Shang Yang's new laws and the imperial authority that he hoped to forge.[111] This interpretation seems convincing, especially because *ji*, the name of the palace, means "to record official orders on a *que* tower."[112] Interestingly, *ji* has a second meaning of "tall and imposing."[113] Indeed, the three-dimensionality of a gate-tower must have inspired the designer of the Qin palace, who wanted to create a new type of monument for his state and ruler.

a

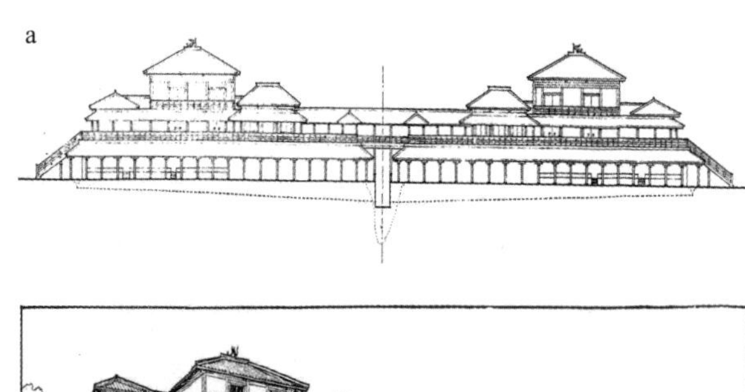

b

Fig. 2.22. (a) Reconstruction of the Jique Palace. (b) The remaining foundation of the Jique Palace. Xianyang, Shaanxi Province. Late Eastern Zhou to Qin. 4th-3rd centuries B.C.

图 2.22 （a）冀阙宫复原图。（b）陕西咸阳冀阙宫基台遗迹。东周末至秦，前 4 世纪—前 3 世纪。

After years of work, Chinese archaeologists finally published their excavation and reconstruction of Shang Yang's building in 1976 (Figs. 2.22a, b).[114] The reconstruction shows an architectural complex consisting of two identical wings, which, like the twin pillars of a *que* gate, were built around solid "earthen cores."[115] Each wing had three stories; the chambers were connected by intricate passages and balconies and were decorated with patterned tiles (Figs. 2.23a, b) and colorful murals (Figs. 2.24a, b). Patterned eave tiles accentuated the outline of each level, and a row of columns 106
surrounding the first level gave the whole structure a stable appearance.

The new interest in the third dimension, which this group of buildings so clearly demonstrates, explains two important developments in Eastern Zhou art and architecture. First, in the images of multilevel structures that frequently decorate Eastern Zhou "pictorial bronzes" (Figs. 2.25a, b), the rituals associated with these structures are no longer ancestral

王学理认为，商鞅对这一特殊建筑类型的偏爱是由于宫殿前面的阙是东周时期张贴法律文书和官方通告的地方，这个像阙一样的秦国宫殿因此可以被看作商鞅所期望打造的新法和皇权在建筑上的体现。[111] 这个解释似乎令人信服，特别是因为这个宫殿的名字“冀”意味着“在阙楼上记录官方命令”。[112] 但值得注意的是，冀还兼有“雄伟壮丽”的意思。[113] 的确，因为这座秦国宫殿的设计意图是为国家和君主创造一种新型纪念碑，一处高耸的阙门必定给设计者带来了启示。

经过数年的工作，考古工作者终于在 1976 年公布了他们对这个建筑的发掘与复原成果［图 2.22］。[114] 复原结果显示出一个建筑群体，其对称的两翼建造在坚实的夯土台周围，看起来就像是一对门阙。[115] 每翼各有三层；每一层上的宫室都以复杂的过道与阳台相连，又以模印砖［图 2.23］和彩色壁画［图 2.24］为装饰。印着花纹的瓦当使每层的轮廓显现得格外清晰，围绕于底层的一圈廊柱也增加了建筑在视觉上的稳定性。

这组建筑清晰地显现出对三维空间的新兴趣，证实了东周时期建筑与艺术中的两项重要发展。第一，多层结构建筑图像在东周画像铜器装饰中频繁出现［图 2.25］。建筑中举行的礼仪活动不再是

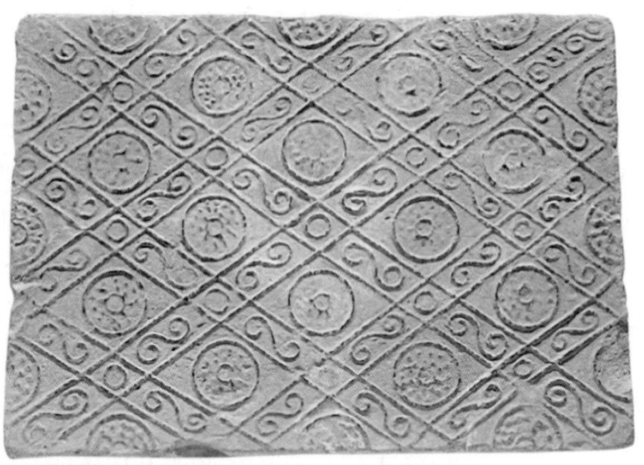

a

b

Fig. 2.23. Decorated tiles from the Jique Palace. Late Eastern Zhou to Qin. 4th-3rd century B.C. Excavated at Xianyang, Shaanxi province. (a) Floor tile with geometric patterns. L. 44 cm. (b) Hollow tile with incised bird images.

图 2.23 冀阙宫印纹砖。东周末至秦，前 4 世纪—前 3 世纪。陕西咸阳出土。（a）几何印纹铺地砖。长 44 厘米。（b）鸟纹空心砖。

sacrifices in a temple but, as the modern scholar Yang Kuan has proved, new kinds of ceremonies—greeting honored guests, for example—which were held during the Eastern Zhou in the palaces of a king or the audience hall of a noble.[116] Instead of representing these structures from a bird's-eye view, the artist depicts their vertical elevation. Second, the emphasis on three-dimensionality must have underlaid the invention and intensive use of the "earthen core" in Eastern Zhou architecture.
Compared with the low foundations of Shang and Western Zhou temple 107
compounds (which rarely exceeded 1 meter in height),[117] the "earthen core" employed by Eastern Zhou architects no longer functioned as the flat base for an entire courtyard structure; rather, it raised a palatial hall toward the third dimension. Its role was mainly visual and symbolic: in an age when techniques for true multistory structures had not yet fully developed, this device allowed people to increase the height and visibility
of a building, although the actual living area in the building remained the 108
same as or even less than that of a single-level structure. I thus disagree with the theory that the "earthen core" in Eastern Zhou architecture

传统庙堂中的祖先祭祀，而是如当代学者杨宽所指出的，表现当时在王宫或贵族的厅堂中举行的新式的仪式，如宾礼等。[116] 艺术家也不再以鸟瞰式的构图来表现这些建筑的平面结构，而是注重于描绘其垂直的立面。第二，对三维空间的强调肯定是东周建筑中夯土台基被发明并得到广泛使用的原因。与商代和西周宗庙建筑低矮的基础（其高度很少超过 1 米）相比，[117] 东周建筑匠师采用的夯土台或"内核"不再为一个完整的庭院式建筑提供统一的基础，而是把一个富丽堂皇的殿堂向垂直于地面的第三空间维度中升高。这种建筑形式的作用主要在于视觉与象征意义：在真正的多层结构建筑技术尚未得到充分发展的时代，虽然这种形式可以增加建筑的高度和可见度，但建筑中的实际可利用空间与单层结构的建筑空间相同或者更少。所以我不同意认为东周的"土核"式建筑是从商和西周的

a

b

Fig. 2.24. Murals in the Qin Palace no. 3. Late Eastern Zhou to Qin. 4th-3rd century B.C. Excavated in 1979 at Xianyang, Shaanxi province. Administration of Cultural Relics from the Qin Capital. (a) Horse-drawn chariot. (b) Palace lady.

图 2.24 秦 3 号宫殿壁画。东周末至秦，前 4 世纪—前 3 世纪。1979 年陕西咸阳出土。(a) 车马。(b) 宫女。

a

b

Fig. 2.25. (a) Bronze vessel with incised pictorial scenes. Mid-Eastern Zhou. *Ca.* 5th century B.C. (b) A terrace building illustrated on the vessel. Drawing.

图 2.25 （a）内壁刻有画像的青铜器。东周中期，约前 5 世纪。（b）该器物上的台阁建筑。线描。

developed smoothly from the leveled foundations of Shang and Western Zhou temple compounds.[118] Although technically the earlier foundation anticipated the later "earthen core," the latter was used for entirely different purposes and, in fact, freed people from the norms of the Shang-Western Zhou ritual architecture. Like a contemporary *tai* platform, Shang Yang's palace derived its meaning from its volume and height, which allowed its owner to "overlook" his subjects and strike them with awe. This is why it was also called a *guan*, a term meaning "to see" or "to be seen."[119]

庙堂建筑的水平台基自然发展而来的说法。[118] 虽说在技术层面上，早先的台基预示着其后“土核”的出现，但后者有着完全不同的目的，而且它实际上把建筑师从商至西周的礼制建筑的规范中解放了出来。与同时代的高台建筑相同，商鞅的宫殿也是从其体量与高度上获得意义，使它的拥有者能够“俯瞰”臣民，也使臣民在“仰望”这座宫殿时心生敬畏。这也正是这类宫殿建筑为什么又被称作“观”（即“看”或“被看”）的原因所在。[119]

Shang Yang's Jique palace was the first in a series of palatial buildings at Xianyang. It is said that King Huiwen "obtained huge amounts of timber from Qi and Yong to create new palaces in a broad area south of the Wei River and beyond the Jing River in the north. The number of individual palaces finally reached 300."[120] These buildings were scattered over a broad region along the Wei River, and no city walls were erected to limit the capital's development. These two features implied that from the very beginning, Xianyang was planned and constructed as an oversized "palace district" that could expand freely to include surrounding areas. Its expansion reached its zenith under Ying Zheng, the future First Emperor. Many palaces, pavilions, and platforms were added. Finally, in one ancient author's words, "North to Jiuzong and Ganquan, south to Changyang and Wuzuo, east to the Yellow River, and west to the intersection of the Yan and Wei Rivers, palaces and imperial villas stood side by side in this region of 800 *li*. There, trees were covered with embroidered silk and earth was painted with the imperial colors red and purple. Even a palace attendant who spent his whole life there could not comprehend the multitude of scenes."[121]

Still, the most crucial development of Xianyang during the First Emperor's reign was not its physical expansion. Rather, under this emperor the palace city Xianyang was finally transformed into the imperial city Xianyang: no longer the capital of a regional kingdom, it became the capital of a unified empire. The definite signs of this development included three groups of monuments. In the *Records of the Historian,* Sima Qian recorded the founding of the first group, the Palaces of the Six Former Kingdoms (Liuguo gongdian):[122]

> The empire extended in the east to the ocean and Chaoxian [part of the present-day Korean Peninsula], in the west to Lintao and Qiangzhong, in the south to Beixianghu, in the north to the fortresses by the Yellow River and along Mount Yinshan to Liaodong. One hundred and twenty thousand wealthy families were brought from all over the

> empire to Xianyang. . . . *Each time the Qin had conquered a state, a replica of its palace was built on the northern bank of the Wei River overlooking the river*, while eastward from Yongmen to the Jing and Wei rivers, in a series of courts, walled-in avenues and pavilions, were kept the beautiful women and musical instruments captured from different states.

Thus, not only were rich families and beautiful women brought from 109
the conquered states, but copies of the palaces of these states were erected in the Qin capital. The most significant aspect of this architectural project

商鞅的冀阙是咸阳宫殿建筑群中的第一座。据说惠文王“初都咸阳，取歧雍巨材，新作宫室。南临渭，北逾泾，至于离宫三百”。[120] 这些建筑分布在渭水沿岸的一个广阔地带，其发展不受城墙的限制。这两点特色暗示出，咸阳从一开始就是被当作一个可以随意扩展乃至囊括周围区域的庞大“宫殿区”来规划和修建的。它的扩展在后来的始皇帝嬴政那里达到了顶点，增加了许多殿阁楼台。用古人的记载来说，最后的结果是“北至九嵕、甘泉，南至长杨、五柞，东至河，西至渭之交，东西八百里，离宫别馆相望属也。木衣绨绣，土被朱紫，宫人不徙。穷年忘归，犹不能遍也”。[121]

尽管如此，咸阳在始皇时期最关键性的发展还不在于其外观上的扩展。更为重要的是，在这段时期里，作为秦国宫城的咸阳最终变成了作为秦代首都的咸阳：它不再是一个区域性诸侯国的都城，而是成为大统一帝国的都城。这一发展变化的明确标志是三组“纪念碑”的建立。司马迁在《史记》中首先记载了最早一组，即“六国宫殿”的营造：[122]

> 地东至海暨朝鲜，西至临洮、羌中，南至北向户，北据河为塞，并阴山至辽东。徙天下豪富于咸阳十二万户……秦每破诸侯，写放其宫室，作之咸阳北阪上，南临渭，自雍门以东至泾、渭，殿屋複道周阁相属。所得诸侯美人钟鼓，以充入之。

由此可见，非但战败国的富足之家和美女被掠到秦国，其宫殿也在秦都中被仿造。这项建筑方案最富意味之处在于它的时间和

was its *timing* and *duration*: whenever a rival state was defeated and its capital razed, its palace was "transplanted" or "relocated" to Xianyang; when the last state disappeared from China's map, the construction of the Palaces of the Six Former Kingdoms was automatically finished. Here we find a fascinating example of monuments that symbolize both the constructive and destructive aspects of a military conquest. First, the monumentality of the duplicated palaces differed radically from that of their models: instead of demonstrating the political power and authority of their original owners, the duplicated palaces became evidence of their fall. Second, the construction of the duplicated palaces echoed the destruction of their models and therefore documented the Qin campaign to unify China. Third, according to Chinese archaeologists, the foundations of these palaces have been found on either side of Xianyang gong, the First Emperor's audience hall. The layout of the whole monumental complex of the emperor's palace thus mirrored the newly established empire, which brought previously fragmented parts of China into a unity dominated by Qin's power.

The *Records of the Historian* also document a second group of Qin monuments:[123]

110 > The emperor divided his empire into 36 provinces, each with a governor, an army commander, and an inspector. Commoners [*min*] were renamed "blackheads" [*qianshou*]. There were great celebrations. *All the weapons in the country were collected and brought to Xianyang. They were melted down to make bronze bells and the "Twelve Golden Men" [*shier jinren*]. These bronze figures, each of which weighed 240,000 catties, were placed in the palace.* All weights and measures were standardized; all carriages had axles of the same width. The script was also standardized.

If the construction of the Palaces of the Six Former Kingdoms coincided with the Qin's military conquests, the Twelve Golden Men fashioned immediately after the completion of these palaces commemorated a single historical moment: Qin's final victory. Sima Qian listed the construction of the Twelve Golden Men among other unification measures that the First Emperor announced the day he assumed the imperial title. The implication of these statues is unmistakable: the country had been pacified and no further wars were necessary. The Six Kingdoms had been destroyed and assimilated into

持续性：当一个敌国被攻克，当它的都城被荡平，它的宫殿就被"移植"或"重置"于咸阳；当最后一个敌国在中国的版图中消失，"六国宫殿"的建造也就自动地完成了。我们在这里所看到的是一个令人深思的建立帝国纪念碑的范例，象征着军事征服的"破坏"和"建设"两个方面。首先，六国宫殿的纪念碑性从根本上不同于其宫殿原型：这些复制的宫殿并不显示其原拥有者的政治力量与权威，相反却是他们覆亡的证明。其次，每一个六国宫殿的建造在呼应其原型的毁灭时也记录了秦统一中国的军事行动的开展。最后，根据中国考古学家的发现研究可知，这些宫殿原来立在咸阳宫——秦宫殿的主殿——的两侧。秦始皇的宫殿区的整体规划因而意在反映新兴政权的崛起，将先前支离破碎的版图统一入由秦之强权所控制的统一帝国。

第二组"纪念碑"是著名的"十二金人"，《史记》对其记载如下：[123]

> 分天下以为三十六郡，郡置守、尉、监。更名民曰"黔首"。大酺。收天下兵，聚之咸阳，销以为钟鐻、金人十二，重各千石，置廷宫中。一法度衡石丈尺。车同轨。书同文字。

如果说"六国宫殿"的建造过程与秦的军事征服首尾一致，每一个宫殿纪念着这个征伐过程中的一个特殊的历史时刻，那么，紧接"六国宫殿"完成之后铸造的十二金人则象征了秦的最后胜利。司马迁把它们的铸造列进了始皇帝登基那天宣布的统一措施中，因此明白无误地表达了这些铜人的政治意义：国家已经太平，不再需要更多的战争；六国已被消灭并被新帝国所吸收，他们的兵器因此

the new empire. Their weapons had to be "melted down" to make new monuments. Standing along the Imperial Way leading to the First Emperor's throne, the Twelve Golden Men formed six pairs of figures that, one may imagine, represented the six defeated kingdoms. These works remind us of the Nine Tripods, which were also made of bronze from different regions and which symbolized the Xia's assimilation of these regions into a political unity.[124] But in the Qin case, the bronze figures were not symbols of the new regime but stood for the conquered states and the bygone feudal society. There exists no better example of the decline of the Bronze Age and the change in the Chinese conception of monumentality.

Ten years later, the First Emperor began the construction of the legendary Epang Palace. Sima Qian again recorded the event:[125]

> The emperor considered that Xianyang was overcrowded and the palaces of the former kings were too small. [He said:] "I have heard that King Wen of Zhou had his capital at Feng, King Wu at Hao. The region between Feng and Hao is fit to be the capital of a great lord." He thus had palaces constructed in the Shanglin Garden south of the Wei River. The front palace, Epang, built first, was 500 paces from east to west and 500 feet from north to south. Ten thousand people could be seated on its terraces; below was room for banners 50 feet tall. One causeway around the palace led to the southern mountains, at the top of which a *que* was erected as Epang's gate; another causeway led across the Wei River to Xianyang, just as the Heavenly Corridor in the sky leads from the Apex of Heaven across the Milky Way to the Royal Chamber.

Unlike the Palaces of the Six Former Kingdoms and the Twelve Golden Men, which denoted the First Emperor's subjugation of rival states, the Epang Palace resulted from his dissatisfaction with "the palaces of the former kings" of the Qin itself. These three groups of monuments thus reflect two main targets of his struggle against the past—the former regional powers and the Qin ancestral tradition. We may also call the Palaces of the Six

Former Kingdoms and the Twelve Golden Men "negative monuments" and the Epang Palace a "positive monument": the former were related directly to the emperor's destruction of his rivals; the latter symbolized his own supremacy. The Epang Palace thus had to be a structure taller and bigger than any building attempted before in Chinese history and to correspond to the Apex of Heaven surrounded by stars and constellations. As I discuss in the following section, the same ambition also led to the construction of

被"熔化"用以制作新的纪念碑。可以设想，立在通向始皇帝宝座的御道两边，这十二尊金人构成了六对，象征着被克灭的六国。它们令我们回想起古老的九鼎，也是用不同地域出产的青铜铸造，以象征夏将这些地域同化入一个政治统一体中。[124] 然而，与九鼎不同的是，对秦始皇来说，这些铜人并非是新政权的象征，而是代表了被他征服的诸侯国以及以往的分封制社会。对于中国青铜时代的衰落和纪念碑性观念变迁来说，这可能是再好不过的例子了。

十年之后，秦始皇开始修造传奇的阿房宫。司马迁对此记述如下：[125]

> 于是始皇以为咸阳人多，先王之宫廷小，吾闻周文王都丰，武王都镐，丰镐之间，帝王之都也。乃营作朝宫渭南上林苑中。先作前殿阿房，东西五百步，南北五十丈，上可以坐万人，下可以建五丈旗。周驰为阁道，自殿下直抵南山。表南山之颠以为阙。为复道，自阿房渡渭，属之咸阳，以象天极阁道绝汉抵营室也。

不同于指示着秦始皇对敌国的征服的六国宫殿和十二金人，阿房宫产生于秦始皇对秦原来的"先王宫殿"的不满足。这三组纪念物因而反映了他所反对的两种主要传统——周代的分封制度和秦国的旧日传统。

我们因此可以称六国宫殿和十二金人为"负面的纪念碑"，而称阿房宫为"正面的纪念碑"：前者直接反映了秦始皇对竞争对手的挫败；后者象征着他个人的至高无上。因此阿房宫必须比中国历史上曾经设想过的任何一座建筑都要高大，乃至高耸天际，为众星所拱。正如下面一章所讨论，同样的野心也导致了宏伟的骊山

the emperor's enormous Lishan mausoleum. This mausoleum, however, resulted from a separate line of development in ancient Chinese monuments and concluded a historical movement in which the center of ancestor worship gradually shifted from temple to tomb.

❸ From Temple to Tomb

The ancient Chinese worshipped many deities, but their religion was "primarily a cult of the ancestors concerned with the relationships between dead and living kin."[126] The ancient Chinese made artworks for many uses, but the major art forms were always closely associated with ancestor worship. All surviving pictorial bricks, stone carvings, and
111 pottery figurines in Han art derive from tombs and funerary shrines, the centers of ancestor worship at the time. All ritual bronzes of the Three Dynasties were likewise paraphernalia associated with ancestor worship; however, they were probably first made for the ancestral temple. I say "probably" because we know nothing about the Xia and very little about Shang ritual practices, but abundant Western Zhou bronze inscriptions and related texts seem to lead to this assumption.[127]

In fact, even during the Shang and Western Zhou, tomb and temple coexisted as twin centers of ancestor worship, but their function and architectural principle were entirely different. An ancestral temple, as discussed in the preceding section, was always a lineage temple, not a family temple or a temple of an individual.[128] A tomb, on the other hand, housed only a single deceased person, as demonstrated by Fu Hao's burial. A lineage temple always formed the nucleus of a walled town; tombs, however, were most frequently built outside the town in an open field. The prominent subject worshipped in a temple was the remote ancestor of the lineage (*yuanzu*), but a tomb was dedicated to a newly deceased (*jinqin*). A temple was a "living monument" of a lineage—its religious content (the ancestors being worshipped) and physical components (ritual vessels) were subject to constant renewal; a tomb was a static symbol of an individual. No living descendents of a lineage ever "created" a temple, which was always constructed by the founder of the lineage, but a tomb was built by oneself or one's heirs. Especially important to my investigation of the architectural symbolism of monuments is that a temple was a walled compound in which shrines of individual ancestors were arranged in a two-dimensional genealogical pattern, whereas a tomb, the alternative center of ancestor worship, assumed a very different form.

陵的建造。不过，这座陵墓来自古老的中国纪念碑艺术中的另外一条发展线索，它预示着祖先崇拜中心渐渐由宗庙转向坟墓的一场历史性运动。

三、从宗庙到墓葬

古代中国人信奉多种神祇，但正如吉德炜所说，其主要宗教形式为体现生者血缘关系的祖先崇拜。[126] 中国古代美术品的用途甚广，然而其主要形式均与祖先崇拜有关。保存至今的汉代画像砖、画像石乃至陶俑都来自墓葬和墓上祠堂，那里是当时祭祖的中心场所。夏商周三代的青铜彝器同样与祭祖有关，它们最初多可能是为祖庙而做的。我说"多可能"，是因为我们对夏还一无所知，对商的礼仪活动也知之甚少，但是大量西周青铜铭文以及相关文献似乎可以帮助我们做出这一推测。[127]

事实上，早在三代时期"庙"和"墓"就同为祖先崇拜的中心，可二者的宗教含义和建筑形式却大相径庭。如前章所论，"庙"总是一个集合性的宗教中心；[128] 而单独的墓葬，比如妇好墓，仅仅属于死者个人或连同其家庭成员。"庙"筑在城内，实际上是城市的核心，而"墓"则多建在城外的旷野。祖庙中祭拜的对象是远祖，而坟墓则奉献给近亲。庙是一个世系的"活纪念碑"——它的宗教内容（被祭拜的祖先）与物质组合（礼器）是可以不断更新的；坟墓则是象征个人的静止符号。"创建"庙的通常不是一个世系宗族的后代，因为那总是宗族开创者的事，而坟墓却是由死者的后人或死者本人建的。对纪念碑的建筑象征研究尤为重要的是，宗庙是一种有围墙的集合建筑，其中的祖先享堂以二维的宗谱形式排列，相反坟墓这一祖先崇拜中心却采取了十分异样的形式。

At Fu Hao's burial site, for example, a small shrine about 5 meters on each side covered the vertical grave pit (Figs. 2.26a, b). Neither walls nor other architectural remains have been observed around this structure; the building seems to have stood in isolation in an open field.[129] The structure of a tomb thus differs essentially from that of a temple: a tomb is "vertical" and a temple is "horizontal"; in a tomb the soul of the deceased traveled along a vertical path to receive offerings, and in a temple the living proceeded along a horizontal axis to worship their ancestors. The only visible part of a tomb—the small shrine—was a landmark, a monument to the deceased individual. Archaeological excavations have revealed that sacrifices, mostly human sacrifices, were made year after year around Shang royal mausoleums (Fig. 2.27).[130] Unlike the temple, the tomb district was the realm of death, not a source from which people derived their knowledge of history and life.

The distinction between temple and tomb is also attested by records in ritual canons. It is recorded that temple sacrifices are "auspicious" in nature (*jili*), since these are dedicated to deities of the country and kingdoms; funerary sacrifices, on the other hand, are "inauspicious rituals" (*xiongli*), which are always associated with death and sorrow.[131] This classification of ancestral sacrifices as well as types of offerings seems to have been related to a unique understanding of the soul. A very significant passage in the *Book of Rites* records a conversation between Confucius and his student Zai Wo. In answering Zai Wo's questions about the nature of *shen* (spirit, divinity) and *gui* (ghost), the master explains that *gui* means the *po* soul that remains underground after one's death, whereas the *shen* flies on high and becomes a divine being.

Fig. 2.26. Fu Hao tomb. Excavated in 1976 at Xiaotun, Anyang, Henan province. Late Shang. *Ca.* 13th-12th centuries B.C. (a) Reconstruction of the structure above the tomb. (b) Floor and section.

图 2.26 妇好墓。商代晚期，约前 13 世纪—前 12 世纪。1976 年发掘于河南安阳小屯。（a）墓上建筑复原。（b）平面图与剖面图。

比如，在妇好墓遗址上，就有一个四边各约 5 米的小祠堂覆盖在竖穴式墓室的上方［图 2.26］。这一构筑的外围既无围墙也无其他建筑遗迹，似乎一直孤独地伫立在空旷的野地中。[129] 这座墓的结构因而与一座庙的结构有着本质上的差别：墓是“垂直的”，而庙是“水平的”；在墓中，死者的灵魂要顺着一条垂直的通道到地上接受供奉；而在庙里，活着的人要沿着水平的轴线前去祭拜他们的祖先。墓葬的唯一可视部分——地上的小祠堂——是一个地界标志，一个为已故个体而设的纪念碑。考古发掘显示，商王室陵墓周围几乎每年都有祭祀活动举行，且祭祀的形式多为人殉［图 2.27］。[130] 与庙不同，墓地是死亡的领域，不是人们可以从中了解宗族历史和其生命由来的场所。

庙与墓的差别亦有文献可资证明。据礼书记载，庙祭为“吉礼”，因为祭祀的对象是乡土和王国之神；而墓祭属于“凶礼”，因为总与死亡和哀伤相连。[131] 祖先祭祀以及供奉类型的这一区分似乎与人们对灵魂的独特理解有关。《礼记》中有一个非常重要的段落，记载了孔子与其门徒宰我之间关于“神”“鬼”性质问题的一段对话。夫子解释说：“众生必死，死必归土，此之为鬼。骨肉毙于下阴为野土，其气发扬于上为昭明。焄蒿悽怆，此百物之精也，神之著也。”又说：

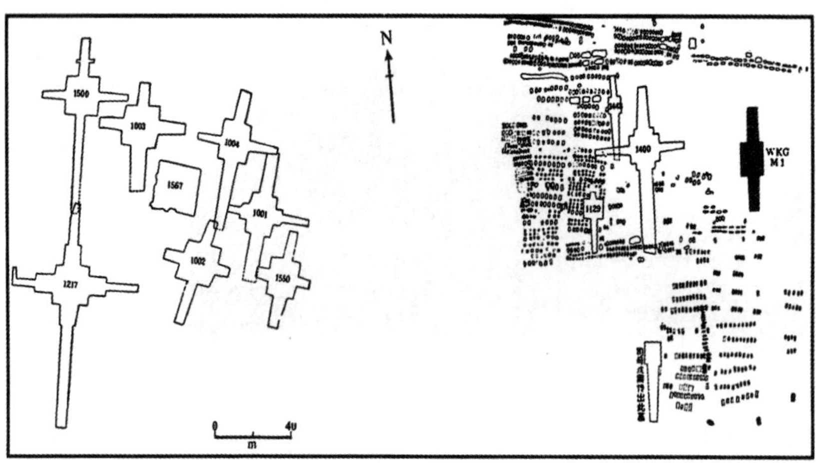

Excavated before 1949
1949 年前发掘

Excavated after 1950
1950 年后发掘

Identified after 1950
but still unexcavated
1950 年后发现，
尚未发掘

Fig. 2.27. Plan of the royal cemetery of the late Shang dynasty at Xibeigang, Anyang, Henan province. 13th-11th centuries B.C.

图 2.27 河南安阳西北岗晚商王室墓地平面图。前 13—前 11 世纪。

112 Once this opposition is established, two kinds of rituals are framed in accordance and [different] sacrifices are regulated. The fat of the innards is burned to bring out its fragrance, which is again mixed with the blaze of dried wood—these serve as a tribute to the spirit [in Heaven], and teach people to go back to their Origin. Millet and rice are presented; the delicacies of the liver, lungs, head, and heart, along with two bowls of liquor and odoriferous wine, are offered—these serve as a tribute to the *po* [in the earth] and teach the people to love one another and cultivate good feeling between high and low.[132]

The humble scale of Fu Hao's shrine cannot be compared with that of the large temple-palace compound inside the capital. Moreover, although descriptions of and regulations for temple rituals fill Shang and Zhou texts, virtually no written record of sacrifices held routinely in graveyards can be found.[133] This lacuna has sparked an extensive debate over whether grave sacrifices were officially practiced and codified during the Three Dynasties.[134] My discussion suggests that the temple system was the religious form that matched the lineage-oriented Shang-Zhou society; the tomb sacrifice for individuals could only be secondary.

This situation, however, changed dramatically during the Eastern Zhou as people began to pay increasing attention to tombs. The *Book of Rites* records that "the ancients made graves only and raised no mounds over them."[135] But now tumuli covered with elaborate terrace pavilions appeared in graveyards. It was said that in his travels Confucius saw some large tomb mounds that were "covered by Summer Palaces."[136] A number of such elaborate funerary structures have been found. A mausoleum of the Zhongshan kingdom is representative. This royal cemetery belonging to King Xi of the fourth century B.C. was never completed; the kingdom

> 二端既立，报以二礼：建设朝（庙）事，燔燎膻芗，见以萧光，以报气也，此教众反始也。荐黍稷羞肝肺首心，见间以侠甒，加以郁鬯，以报魄也。教民相爱，上下用情，礼之至也。[132]

殷墟妇好墓享堂的规模与都城之内的商代宫庙不可同日而语。先秦典籍中有关庙祭的记载很多，但对墓祭的记录却寥寥无几。[133]这一历史空缺曾引起了一场关于三代时期墓祭是否正式实行和有无纳入国家法典的广泛争论。[134]本人认为，庙制是与以血亲世系为导向的商周社会相适应的宗教形态；为个体而设的墓祭，只能是祖先崇拜的次要形式。

然而在东周时期，随着人们对“墓”的兴趣日益增长，这种局面已经发生了戏剧性的变化。《礼记·檀弓上》称：“古也墓而不坟”，[135]但是上方带有华美台阁的坟墓却在这时出现。据说孔子南游时已见到墓葬封土有“若堂”“若夏屋者”。[136]到目前为止，这类精致的丧葬建构已发现了几例，中山王陵即是其中的典型。这座公元前4世纪的墓地系为王而建，墓葬还没来得及建完，其王国就

perished before its completion. But a plan of the mausoleum inlaid on a bronze plate, about a meter long and a half meter wide, was found in the king's tomb (Figs. 2.28a, b). The earliest known architectural drawing from ancient China, it details the placement, dimensions, and measurements of the burial mound and its components. An edict inscribed on the plate warns that anyone not following the design in building the mausoleum will be executed without mercy. The severe tone of this edict, along with the appearance of the architectural plan, signifies important changes in people's psychology: now their central interest was their *own* tomb, not a temple dedicated to their deceased ancestors. The stern edict issued by the king vividly reflects both his desire to build a great mausoleum for himself and his anxiety that his descendents would not share this desire but would devote their time and energy to their own mausoleums.

Based on the design and archaeological excavations, Chinese scholars have reconstructed the Zhongshan mausoleum on paper (Fig. 2.29).[137] The cemetery was originally planned to contain five tombs; the king's tomb is in the center, flanked by two queens' tombs and then by two concubines' tombs. Each grave is covered by an individual ceremonial hall of the terrace pavilion type. The king's hall, about 200 meters square at the base, is built on a three-storied terrace; galleries surround the earthen core at the lowest level, and a free-standing square hall of considerable size stands on top of the pyramid. The five halls are major components of the central area of the mausoleum, the *neigong*, or Inner Palace, which is enclosed by double walls. The outer wall is over 410 meters long and 176 meters wide; the inner wall is 340 meters by 105 meters. Between the two walls and behind the five tombs are four square halls with names
113 identifying them as ceremonial offices. This reconstruction shows three basic features of a large mausoleum of the Warring States period: first, each king had an independent "funerary park" containing the tombs

of himself and his spouses. Second, a funerary park imitated a palace, with double walls (or ditches) defining the king's private domain and his court. Third, each grave in a funerary park was marked by an elaborate ceremonial structure built either above or beside a huge tumulus.

已经灭亡了。然而在这座墓中，却发现了铸在长约 1 米、宽 0.5 米铜板上的一个陵墓建筑方案［图 2.28］。这份目前所知中国最早的建筑图，详细标明了墓葬封土及其各组成部分的尺度与安排。刻在铜板上的一则王命说，若有不依此方案施工者，当斩不赦。王命严厉的语气，连同建筑方案的样貌，意味着人们心理状态的重要变化：此时他们兴趣的焦点已不再是献给祖先的祖庙，而是他们自己的坟墓。中山王所颁布的严酷命令，既反映了他要为自己建一座巨大陵墓的心愿，又折射出他对子嗣只顾建造各人自己的墓葬而不能通力完成这项计划的忧虑。

根据这件图板和现场考古发掘资料，中国学者已经于纸面上对中山王陵作了复原［图 2.29］。[137] 这处陵园最初的设计中含有五座墓；王墓位于中央，其两旁是两王后的墓，再外为两妾的墓，各墓上方皆有一独立的重檐楼阁式享堂。底部方约 200 尺的王堂，上承一三层四阿式屋顶；底层夯土堆为廊道环绕，方尖塔式建筑的顶部，矗立着一个不大不小的独立方堂。这五座享堂亦即“内宫”，是整个陵园中心区域的主要组成部分。环绕着这个区域的是两重围墙，外墙宽 176 米、长 410 米以上；内墙宽 105 米、长 340 米。五座堂后背的两墙之间有四个名称各异的方形宫室，表明是仪式场所。这项复原显示出战国时期大型陵墓的三个特征：一、每个王都有一处自己的“陵园”，其中含有王本人及其配偶的冢茔；二、陵园模仿宫殿，它所拥有的两重围墙（或壕沟），界定着王的私人空间与庭院；三、陵园中的每座坟墓都以建在高冢上方或旁侧的华丽建筑为标志。

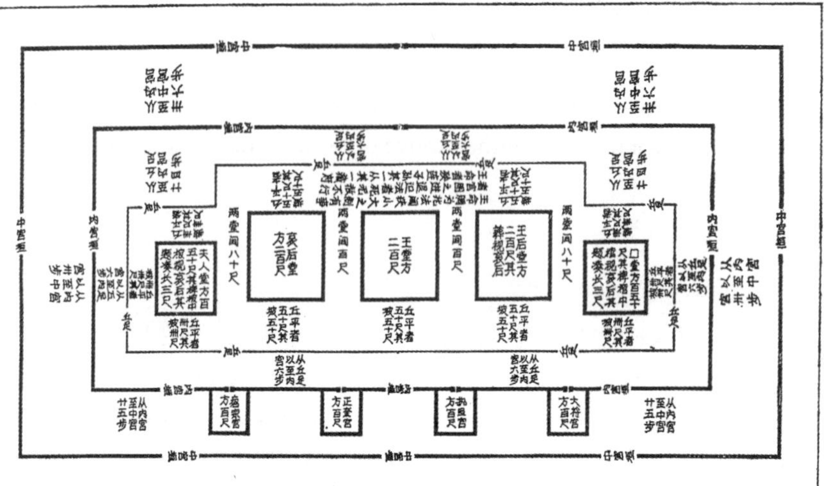

Fig. 2.28. (a) Drawing of the "Design of the Mausoleum District," with the inscriptions transcribed in modern Chinese. (b) "Design of the Mausoleum District" ("Zhaoyu tu"). Bronze with gold inlay. Warring States period. 4th century B.C. L. 94 cm. H. 48 cm. Excavated in 1977 at Pingshan, Hebei province. Hebei Provincial Institute of Cultural Relics.

图 2.28 （a）中山王陵《兆域图》线描，铭文已转写为现代汉字。（b）中山王陵《兆域图》。错金青铜。战国，前 4 世纪。长 94 厘米、宽 48 厘米。1977 年河北平山出土。河北省文物研究所藏。

Like contemporary palaces, this new type of ritual structure in
ancestor worship was related to the social and religious transformation
taking place during the Eastern Zhou. As mentioned in the earlier
discussion, during this period the Zhou royal house gradually declined,
and the society was no longer united in a hierarchical genealogical
structure. Political struggles were waged by families and individuals
who gained power from their control of economic resources and
military forces, not from noble ancestry. The old religious institutions
and symbols could no longer convey political messages and were 114
consequently replaced or complemented by new ones. The lineage-
temple system declined, and tombs belonging to families and individuals
became symbols of the new social elite.

Eastern Zhou texts tell us that during this period an estate system was established to regulate funerary design. The *Rites of Zhou* records that the height of a tomb mound symbolized the rank of the deceased.[138] This system was not an idealized scheme; it was actually practiced in the state of Qin and regulated in the laws of Shang Yang. According to

就像其同时代的宫殿那样，这种与祖先崇拜有关的新型礼仪建构与东周时期社会和宗教的变革有关。如前文所论，周王室在此期间渐趋式微，当时的社会不再以层序系谱结构构成，各强大诸侯的权力地位并非主要来自世袭，而是以其经济和军事势力而定的。旧有的宗教和艺术形式无法反映和支持新的社会结构，从而逐渐为新出现的宗教与艺术形式所取代和补充。其后果则集中表现为宗族祖庙地位的急剧下降和象征家庭、个人权势与身份的“墓”的重要性日益增长。

东周时期的文献告诉我们，为了规范丧葬设计，当时确立了一套等级制度。《周礼·冢人》记载，墓葬封土的高度象征着死者的等级。[138] 这套方案不一定是儒家的虚构，实际反映了东周社会的现实情况，《商君书》中便有类似的规定。值得注意的是，此时死者的

this law, the "rank" of a deceased was determined not by his inherited status but by his achievements in public service.[139] This illustrates the essential difference between a temple and a tomb at that time: a temple represented a person's clan heritage; the tomb demonstrated his personal accomplishments. As individual ambition increased, the size of funerary structures skyrocketed. The following passage from Master Lü's *Spring and Autumn Annals* (*Lüshi chunqiu*), a miscellany compiled near the end of the Eastern Zhou period, vividly describes the consequence of this development.

> Nowadays when people make burials, they erect tumuli tall and huge as mountains and plant trees dense and luxuriant as a forest. They arrange tower-gates and courtyards and build halls and chambers with flights of steps for visitors. Their cemeteries are like towns and cities! This may be a way of making a display of their wealth to the world, but how could they serve the deceased [with such extravagance].[140]

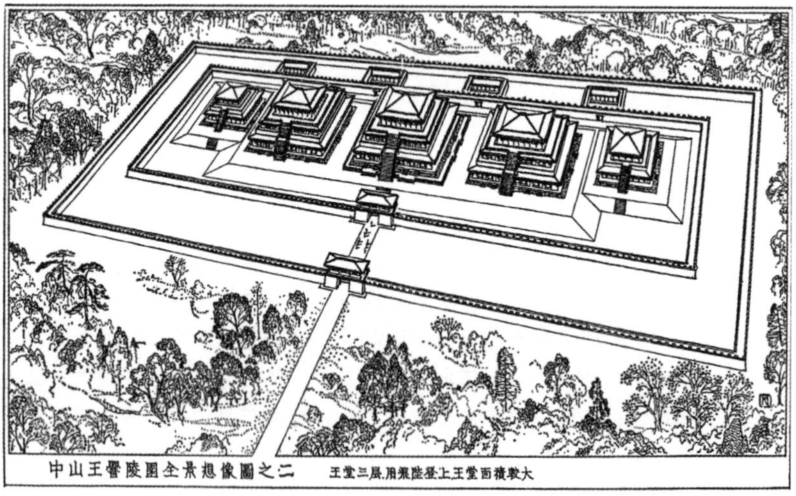

Fig. 2.29. A reconstruction of a Zhongshan royal mausoleum based on the "Design of the Mausoleum District."

图 2.29 根据《兆域图》复原的中山王陵图

The culmination of the inflation of tomb building was the great Lishan mausoleum of the First Emperor (Fig. 2.30).[141] The Qin had ancestral temples in both the old capital of Yong and the new capital of Xianyang, but these temples attracted little of the emperor's attention. Instead, he began building his necropolis the day he mounted the throne. The center of the mausoleum was a huge pyramid. (Only after a long and complex development did the ancient Chinese finally begin to share this monumental architectural design with the ancient Egyptians, who had begun building pyramids thousands of years earlier.) In contrast to the flat, two-dimensional temple compound, an enormous pyramid appears in a vast landscape against an empty sky. No extrinsic space is pursued; the only force with which the structure interacts is nature. The reason for

身份和“爵等”并非由其在宗族内的地位而定，而是取决于他生前的任职和贡献。[139] 从这里我们可以了解东周时期“庙”与“墓”截然不同的社会意义：“庙”代表了宗族的世袭，而“墓”象征着个人在新的官僚系统中的位置和成就。当个人的权势、财富及野心不断膨胀，兆域中建筑的规模也迅速扩长。《吕氏春秋》中的下列记载或可证明东周末期的情况：

> 世之为丘垄也，其高大若山，其树之若林，其设阙庭、为宫室、造宾阼也若都邑。以此观世示富则可矣，以此为死则不可也。[140]

墓葬建筑的膨胀发展，最终导致了秦始皇骊山陵的出现［图2.30］。[141] 秦之初庙原设于雍，但始皇对雍乃至新都咸阳的宗庙并未给予多少重视。与此形成鲜明对照的是，他从登基之始就开始营建骊山陵。这座陵墓的核心部分为一巨大的丘冢。可以说，这一建筑形式的基本原理和象征意义与宗庙建筑全然相反，设计的主题不在于二维空间的纵深扩张，而在于向三维空间发展。在这里，“闭合空间”为“自然空间”取代，矗立在辽阔地平线上的坟丘背衬着青天，数里以外便可望见。值得注意的是，与古埃及、中东地区相比，

the late appearance of this monumental form in China is that only during this stage in Chinese history did such a form become meaningful. As his royal title "Shi Huang Di" signifies, the First Emperor viewed himself as the *shi*, or Origin (*huang di* means a sovereign-emperor). He cast a position for himself in the social and religious hierarchy unequaled by any other being, even his ancestors. This notion, which broke radically with the archaic concept of religious and political authority, is manifested in the monumental design of his tomb.

The pyramid in the Lishan mausoleum was built as a personal monument of the First Emperor, and the underground tomb chamber was transformed into a physical representation of the universe for him. As Sima Qian recorded in the *Records of the Historian*:

> When the First Emperor first ascended the throne, he ordered workers to excavate and construct Lishan. Having just unified the world, he sent over 700,000 convicts to work there. They dug through three springs, stopped their flow, and assembled the chamber there. They carried in [models of?] palaces, pavilions, and the hundred officials, and strange objects and valuables to fill up the tomb. . . . With mercury they made the myriad rivers and the ocean with a mechanism that made them flow about. Above were all the Heavens and below all the Earth.[142]

To students of Chinese art history, the importance of this passage goes far beyond the factual record. It reveals an artistic goal that would have been entirely alien to the Three Dynasties. Shang and Zhou ritual art did not portray worldly phenomena, but aimed to visualize an intermediate stage between the human world and the world beyond it: it thus linked these two separate realms.[143] In the Lishan tomb, however, art imitated things: there was an artificial ocean and flowing rivers, and all images were arranged to create an artificial microcosm of the universe.

Fig. 2.30. Lishan mausoleum of the First Emperor of the Qin. Late 3rd century B.C. Lintong, Shaanxi province.

图 2.30　秦始皇骊山陵。前 3 世纪末。陕西临潼。

这类金字塔式纪念碑建筑物在中国出现得相当晚。其晚出的原因在于，只是在这一特定时期，纪念碑式建筑才成为适当的宗教艺术形式。正如“始皇”这一称号所示，嬴政自视为“始”，给自己确定了一个开天辟地的历史位置，甚至连他的祖先也无法比拟。这一与三代社会、宗教思想截然两立的新观念在他的坟墓设计中得到了具体的表现。

如果说骊山陵中金字塔式坟丘是秦始皇个人绝对权力的象征，那么其地下的墓室则被有意识地建筑成一个宇宙模型。《史记·秦始皇本纪》载：

> 始皇初即位，穿治骊山，及并天下，天下徒送诣七十余万人，穿三泉，下铜而致椁，宫观百官奇器珍怪徙臧满之。……以水银为百川江河大海，机相灌输，上具天文，下具地理。[142]

对于中国美术史研究者来说，这段文献的重要性远远超出了单纯的历史实录，它揭示了一种与三代礼器艺术大异其趣的美学理想。商周礼仪艺术的目的并不在于描绘客观事物，而是企图构建起人神之间的交通渠道，它联系着两个相互分别的领域。[143] 可是骊山陵的墓室结构和装饰则模拟自然：所有这些人工的海洋和河流等等，都是为了造成一个人造宇宙。

Historically speaking, the plan of the Lishan mausoleum combined two major types of mortuary structure current during the Warring States period: one was used in Qin, and the other was popular in certain eastern kingdoms. Two groups of royal burials of pre-dynastic Qin have been found in Fengxiang and Lintong in present-day Shaanxi.[144] According to Chinese archaeologists, the 32 large tombs at Fengxiang may date to the Spring and Autumn and early Warring States period; the three Qin kings buried in Lintong were Zhaoxiang, Xiaowen, and Zhuangxiang, the direct predecessors of the First Emperor.[145] The Lintong tombs share two basic features absent in the mausoleums of the eastern states. First, instead of erecting terrace pavilions over grave pits, wooden-framed architectural complexes were built beside earthen tomb mounds. Second, the Lintong mausoleums, as well as those in Fengxiang, were encircled by two or three rows of ditches, sometimes 7 meters in depth, whereas the royal tombs of the Zhongshan and Wei were surrounded by walls. The Lishan mausoleum appeared to integrate these two designs: it continued the Qin tradition of having a tumulus and a ceremonial structure built separately and adopted the eastern device of replacing ditches with double walls (Fig. 2.31). This combination allowed the First Emperor to develop a well-defined hierarchical structure that distinguished the Lishan mausoleum
116 from its Eastern Zhou predecessors. Its three sections—the district encircled by the inner wall, the area between the inner and outer walls, and the open space surrounding the funerary park—assumed different functions and symbolism. The heart of the mausoleum was the burial and sacrificial area; the area between the inner and outer walls was occupied by ceremonial officials and their departments.[146] An important feature of the Lishan mausoleum was an architectural complex of considerable size, built beside the tumulus in the exact center of the walled funerary park.[147] The Eastern Han scholar Cai Yong identified the model for this building.

An ancient ancestral temple consisted of a ceremonial hall [*miao*] in front and a retiring hall [*qin*] in the rear, just as a ruler had an audience hall in front and a retiring chamber in the rear. The ancestral tablet was set in the ceremonial hall and was worshipped during the seasonal sacrifices. The retiring hall contained royal gowns, caps, armrests, and staffs, like the paraphernalia of the living king, which were used when presenting offerings. The Qin first removed the retiring hall [from the temple] to occupy a position flanking the tomb.[148]

从历史上说，骊山陵的营造方案合并了流行于战国时期的两种主要墓葬建筑体系：一种用于秦，另一种在某些东部国家流行。在今天的陕西凤翔与临潼，已经发现了两批秦代以前的秦王室墓葬。[144] 据中国考古学家的报道，位于凤翔的 32 座大墓大约属于春秋至战国早期；葬于临潼的三个秦王为嬴政的前任：昭襄、孝文和庄襄。[145] 临潼的墓葬都拥有两种不见于东部国家的基本特征：首先，它们不再于墓穴之上建层楼，而将木构建筑建在墓葬封土旁边。其次，临潼以及凤翔的陵墓均掘有两到三重湟濠为陵园界沟，界沟有的深达 7 米；而中山王陵和魏王陵墓却是环以内外宫墙的。骊山陵一方面保持了起享堂于墓侧的做法，另一方面又起内外高墙，从而反映出东西传统的结合［图 2.31］。这一结合使秦始皇得以发展出一套清晰的等级结构，以将他的骊山陵与其东周先人的陵墓区分开来。大体来说，骊山陵包括内、中、外三区，分别承担着不同的功能与象征。内墙之中为墓葬和祭祀区，内外墙之间为礼仪官吏的处所。[146] 骊山陵一个引人注意的特征是，所有有一定规模的建筑物都建在位于陵园中央的冢丘旁侧。[147] 东汉学者蔡邕为这种建筑模式做了注脚：

> 宗庙之制……前制庙以象朝，后制寝以象寝。庙以藏主，列昭穆；寝有衣冠、几杖，象生之具……至秦始皇出寝，起之于墓侧。[148]

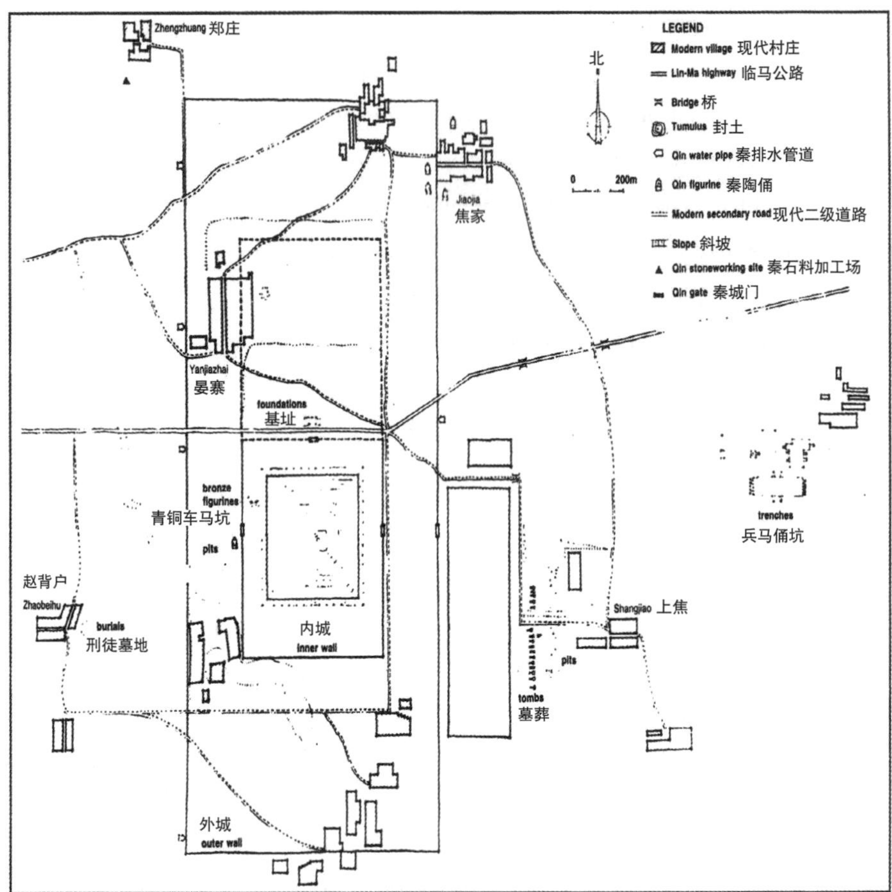

Fig. 2.31. Plan of Lishan mausoleum of the First Emperor of the Qin. Drawing.
图 2.31 秦始皇骊山陵平面图。线描。

117 Based on this passage, scholars have argued that the First Emperor was the first to establish a *qin* hall in a mausoleum. The excavations of the pre-dynastic Qin mausoleums at Lintong, however, have demonstrated that this tradition extended back several generations. Architectural foundations found beside the tomb mounds in the Lintong mausoleums have led excavators to suggest structural similarities between these

buildings and the one in the Lishan mausoleum.[149] A record in the *History of the Latter Han* confirms this: "In ancient times no sacrifices were held in graveyards; the Qin initiated [the custom of] building the *qin* inside the mausoleum. . . . Beginning with Qin, the *qin* was removed [from the temple] and was constructed beside the tomb."[150] Since the name "Qin" in this passage can be understood as the pre-dynastic Qin kingdom, we may contend that the ritual buildings excavated in both the Lintong mausoleums and the Lishan mausoleum were the *qin* halls that were originally part of the traditional ancestral temple.

Unlike the mausoleums of Eastern Zhou kings, the territory of the Lishan necropolis extended to a large area outside the graveyard.[151] To the east, the underground terra-cotta army duplicated the Qin military forces under the First Emperor's command (Fig. 2.32). In the area between the terra-cotta army and the park, nineteen tombs of high officials and members of the royal family, as well as an enormous underground stable, have been found. West of the funerary park lie the

依据这段文献，学者们曾认为秦始皇是最先在陵墓中建寝的人，然而早于秦朝的秦墓发现已经证实，这一传统可以推前好几代。发现于临潼陵墓封土两旁的建筑基础，已经启发发掘者想起这些建筑与骊山陵中的一处建筑在结构上的相似之处。[149]《后汉书》中的一段记载进一步证实："古不墓祭，汉诸陵皆有园寝，承秦所为也……秦始出寝，起于墓侧。"[150] 由于这里所说的"秦"不一定仅指秦代，很可能包括以前的秦国，我们或可认为，发现于临潼陵与骊山陵的礼仪性建筑，皆是原先作为传统宗庙之组成部分的"寝"。

与东周各王的陵墓不同，骊山陵的范围向陵园之外极度扩张。[151] 其东侧，深埋于地下的兵马俑群模拟秦始皇统率之下的秦朝精锐武装［图 2.32］。俑坑与陵园之间发现了 19 座墓和一大型地下马厩。这些墓很可能为高级官员和皇室成员的陵墓。陵西赵家背户村

burials of about seventy convicts, some perhaps buried alive. Thus, while the funerary park itself was constructed as the emperor's "forbidden city," the surrounding area mirrored his empire, with its courtiers, soldiers, servants, and perhaps slaves.

Since the First Emperor had assumed the position of Origin of a great tradition, associating himself with an existing lineage temple became impossible.[152] He thus had a temple dedicated to himself even before his death. This temple, called the Ji miao or the Temple of the Absolute, was built somewhere south of the Wei River; a road was constructed to connect it with the Lishan mausoleum.[153] An important passage from the *Records of the Historian* describes a court meeting held after the emperor's death, during which all ministers agreed upon a new policy concerning ancestor worship:

> In the past, the ancestral temple complex of the Son of Heaven consisted of seven individual temples [for individual ancestors]; that of a lord, five individual temples, and that of a grand official, three individual temples. Such ancestral temple complexes persisted generation after generation. Now the First Emperor has built the Temple of the Absolute, and people within the four seas have sent tribute and offerings. The ritual has been completed and cannot be further elaborated. . . . The Son of Heaven should hold ancestral ceremonies exclusively in this temple of the First Emperor.[154]

The Qin burial system exemplified by the Lishan mausoleum established a basic framework for Han funerary monuments. All pre-Qin burials were vertical earthen pits containing wooden encasements, coffins, and tomb furnishings (Figs. 2.33a, b). This structure was explained by a certain Guozi Gao of the Eastern Zhou: "Burying means hiding away; and this hiding is from a wish that people should not see it. Hence there are clothes sufficient for an elegant covering; the coffin all-around the clothes; the encasement all-around the coffin: and the earth

Fig. 2.32. Terra-cotta "underground army." Pit no. 1 of Lishan mausoleum. Late 3rd century B.C. L. 210 m. W. 62 m. Found in 1974 at Lintong, Shaanxi province.

图 2.32　兵马俑坑，骊山陵 1 号坑。前 3 世纪末。长 210 米，宽 62 米。1974 年出土于陕西临潼。

一带则散布着大约 70 个刑徒葬坑。整个始皇陵因此形成一个整体：陵园本身代表了皇帝的禁城，而陵外的广阔区域则象征了由官僚、军队、仆从、奴隶构成的帝国。

秦嬴政既然为自己确立了"始皇"这一位置，也就无法再附属于集合性的宗庙了。[152] 因此，他生前就在渭河之南给自己造了一座庙，原名"信宫"，后更名为"极庙"。一条通道进而把这座庙与骊山陵连接起来。[153]《史记》记载，秦始皇死后，秦二世召集了一次御前会议讨论祭祀规章，与会群臣皆顿首言曰：

> 古者天子七庙，诸侯五，大夫三，虽万世世不轶毁。今始皇为极庙，四海之内皆献贡职，增牺牲，礼咸备，毋以加……天子仪当独奉酌祠始皇庙。[154]

以骊山陵为代表的秦葬制为汉代丧葬纪念碑确定了一个基本框架。秦代以前的秦墓全部都是竖穴式土坑墓，内中置有木椁、棺及随葬品［图 2.33］。这种墓葬结构被东周的国子高解释为："葬者，藏也；盖藏之所由来，不令人见之也。故有丰衣掩其体，棺掩衣，

118 all-around the encasement."[155] From the mid-Western Han, however, an underground tomb, built of hollow bricks or carved inside a rocky hill, appeared to imitate the deceased's household, with a main hall, a bedroom, and side-chambers (Fig. 2.34).[156] Wooden-framed or stone offering shrines were further erected in front of tomb mounds (Fig. 2.35). Later I discuss pictures on the ceiling, gables, and walls of a shrine that transformed the plain stone structure into a concrete universe, with different sections depicting Heaven, an immortal paradise, and the human world. An inscription on an Eastern Han shrine, dedicated by two brothers to their dead parents, sheds light on the significance of the dualism of the aboveground shrine and the underground tomb in Han ancestor worship: "He [Xiang Wuhuan] and his younger brother worked in the open air in their parents' graveyard, even in the early morning or the heat of summer. They transported soil on their backs to build the tumulus and planted pine and juniper trees in rows. *They erected a stone shrine, hoping that the* hun *souls of their parents would have a place to abide*."[157]

椁护棺，土护椁。"[155] 可是从西汉中期，一座地下墓葬无论是用空心砖墓还是崖墓，都开始模仿死者生前的居所，前有堂，后有寝，两侧还有耳室［图 2.34］，[156] 甚至坟前还有木构或石制享堂［图 2.35］。后面我会讨论一座祠堂的屋顶、山墙和各壁上的画像，以其不同区域描绘天、仙境和人间世界，将素净的石头建筑变成一个真实可感的宇宙。东汉有一对兄弟为其已故的双亲建造了一座祠堂，这个祠堂上的题记，使汉代祖先祭祀中地上祠堂和地下坟墓的二元含义得到了清晰的显现："兄（薌无患）弟暴露在冢，不辟晨夏，负土成墓，列种松柏，起立石祠堂，冀二亲魂灵有所依止。"[157]

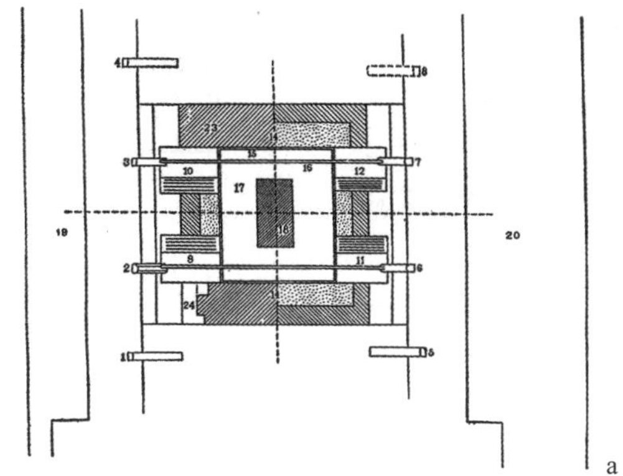

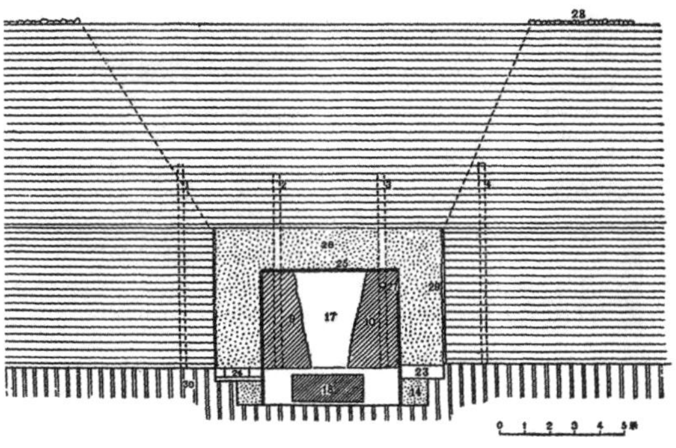

Fig. 2.33. Vertical pit grave, represented by Guweicun Tomb no. 3. Warring States period. 4th century B.C. Excavated in 1950-51 at Huixian, Henan province. (a) Floor plan. (b) Section.

图 2.33 竖穴式墓，以固围村 3 号墓为例。战国，前 4 世纪。1950—1951 年发掘于河南辉县。（a）平面图。（b）剖面图。

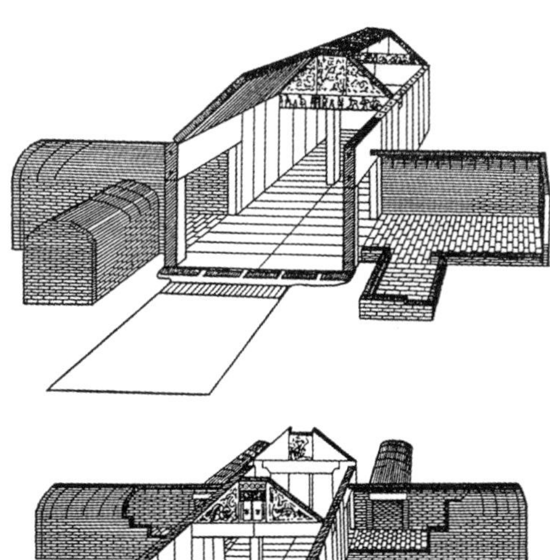

Fig. 2.34. Horizontal pit grave, represented by Luoyang Tomb no. 61. Late Western Han. 1st century B.C. Excavated in 1957 at Shaogou, Luoyang, Henan province.

图 2.34 横穴式墓，以洛阳烧沟 61 号墓为例。西汉晚期，前 1 世纪。1957 年发掘于河南洛阳烧沟。

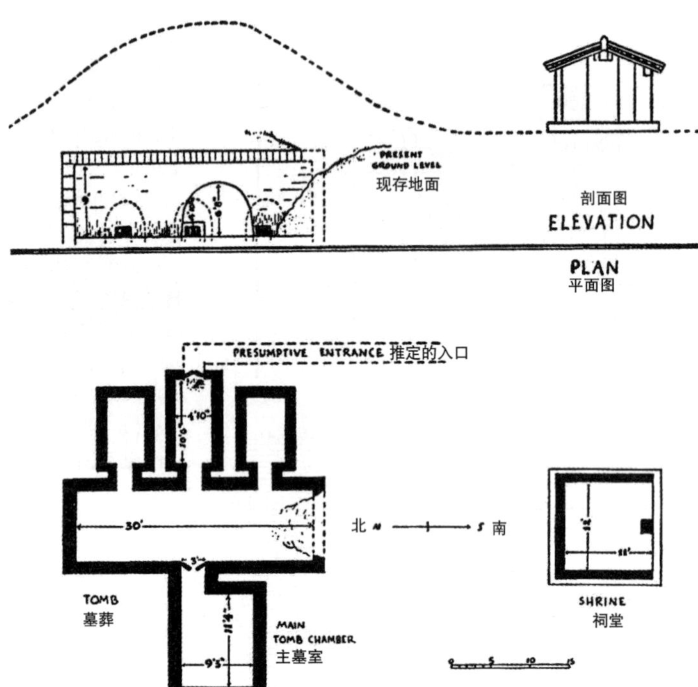

Fig. 2.35. Plan and elevation of Zhu Wei's tomb and offering shrine. Late Eastern Han. 2nd century A.D. Jinxiang, Shandong province. Drawing.

图 2.35 朱鲔墓及其祠堂（剖面图与平面图）。东汉晚期，2 世纪。山东金乡。测绘图。

Likewise, when Kong Dan built a funerary shrine for himself during the second century, he also wrote down his intention: "I realized that even gold and stone would erode and that everything in the world had its beginning and end. I then began to consider the great span of time after this life, and settled on an auspicious shrine that would represent the heavenly kingdom. As I looked at the structure the craftsmen were fashioning, *I rejoiced that I would abide there after this life*."[158]

The idea implied in these two passages was explained by the Ming writer Qiu Qiong: "When a son's parents die, their bodies and *po* souls
119 return to the ground below, and thus the son builds tombs to conceal

them. Their *hun* souls soar into the sky, and thus the son erects a shrine to house them."[159] In a departure from the ancient idea that the temple was the legitimate place for the *hun* soul's visit, it was now believed that the *hun* soul actually dwelled in the funerary shrine. To invoke ancestral deities through a display of ritual paraphernalia and offerings in the temple became less important; the primary ritual practice was to provide the *hun* with housing in a graveyard.

Moreover, the establishment of the Han dynasty greatly reinforced the political and ritual significance of funerary structures. The founder of the Han and his generals arose from commoners who had never had the privilege of holding temple sacrifices.[160] When the Western Han emperors began to construct mausoleums, they had few scruples about deviating from archaic ritual codes. Various components of the palace, including ceremonial halls, rulers' retiring rooms, concubines' quarters, administrative offices, and huge *que* gates, were faithfully copied in funerary parks.[161] Three-dimensional statues, which had still been buried

同样，当 2 世纪的孔耽为自己建墓上祠堂时，他也将自己的意图写了下来："观金石之消，知万物有终始；图千载□洪虑，定吉地于天府。目睹工匠□所营，心欣悦于所处。"[158]

明代邱琼在议论汉代墓葬制度时说："人子于其亲当一于礼而不苟其生也……迨其死也，其体魄之归于地者为宅兆以藏之，其魂气之在乎天者为庙祏以栖之。"[159] 与商周时期以宗庙为"降神"之所的传统观念背道而驰，东汉的祠庙被认为是死者魂灵的居处。这种新的思想直接导致了宗教艺术形式的变化，"降神"的礼器变为"供器"，成为祖先崇拜中的次要因素，给灵魂布置居所则成了主要任务。

汉朝建立以后，丧葬建筑的政治与宗教礼仪含义大大加重了。汉朝皇室和元勋多起于闾巷之中，从未有过设立宗庙的特权，[160] 他们崇拜祖先的方式很有可能为墓祭而非庙祭。"汉承秦制"在陵墓设计中表现得尤其明显。西汉皇帝陵园全仿始皇陵，而且进一步"宫殿化"了，陵园内设有寝殿、便殿、掖庭、官寺。[161] 大型雕塑

underground in the Lishan mausoleum, were erected aboveground to flank the Spirit Path (*shendao*). Satellite burials of members of the royal family and statesmen surrounded an emperor's tomb, as if the ministers and generals were still paying respect to their sovereign.[162]

Following the Qin system, from Emperor Hui's reign on, an ancestral temple, called a *miao*, was dedicated to each deceased emperor and built near his mausoleum.[163] Chinese archaeologists have located the temples of Emperors Jing and Yuan about 400 meters to the south and 300 meters north of their respective tombs.[164] Therefore, the traditional temple dedicated to a single lineage disappeared and dissolved into a number of temples belonging to individual emperors. A special road connected a temple with an emperor's *qin* hall inside the funerary park. Every month, a ceremony was held in the ancestral temple of each deceased ruler, and a ritual procession conveyed the royal crown and costume to lead the soul of the deceased emperor from his tomb to his temple to receive offerings. These roads were therefore named "costume and crown road" (*yiguandao*).[165] Interestingly, the *miao* and *qin* halls were originally two integral sections of an ancestral temple. The Qin extracted the *qin* hall from the temple and reset it in royal mausoleums. The rulers of the Western Han went even further: they attached the *miao* to their mausoleums. Although *qin* were built inside funerary parks and *miao* outside, they were once again united—by the crown and costume road.

A Western Han imperial temple, therefore, differed fundamentally from a Three Dynasties royal temple. As the property of an individual ruler, the Western Han temple no longer signified the genealogical and political tradition of the royal house. The traditional ancestral temple had perished during the Qin and Western Han, and the temple had become firmly wedded to the tomb. Until the Eastern Han, however, the temple was still built outside the funerary park and was still the legitimate place to hold major ancestral sacrifices.[166] The next step was the total independence of the tomb as the center of ancestor worship and the

promotion of funerary structures as the most important monuments
in society. This change, which took place during the mid-first century
A.D., greatly stimulated the development of funerary art and gave it new
significance. The change may have been caused by a number of factors,
including the firm establishment of the family system in society and the 120
heightening of the Confucian virtue of filial piety, but a direct cause is
found in an almost accidental event.

在始皇陵中尚且只埋在地下，可是到武帝时期已开始移到地上，成为神道两旁的护卫。皇亲国戚、勋将功臣的坟墓众星拱月般地围绕着帝陵，仿佛死后仍行君臣之礼。[162]

仍是沿循秦制，自惠帝以降，每个皇帝皆有一庙，并且就建在他的陵墓附近。[163] 这一布局已基本为考古发现所证实。目前，考古学家已经找到了景帝与元帝的庙址，前者位于阳陵南 400 米处，后者位于渭陵南 300 米处。[164] 这样，为一个单独世系而存在的传统宗庙消失了，它化解成一系列仅属于每个帝王个人的庙。庙与陵以甬道相接，每月车骑仪仗将过世皇帝的朝服从陵内寝殿护送到陵外的庙中祭祀一次，这条甬道因而名之为“衣冠道”。[165] 有趣的是，庙堂与寝堂本为一座宗庙的两个不可分割的组成部分，秦从宗庙中萃取了寝，并将其安置在皇陵中。西汉统治者走得更远：他们将庙也变成自己陵墓的附设。虽说寝建在陵园内，庙建在陵园外，可是通过两者之间的那条衣冠道，它们再次连为一个整体。

因此，一座西汉帝庙从根本上不同于三代王庙。作为君主的私有财产，西汉庙不再意味着王室的系谱和政治传统，那种传统宗庙在秦与西汉之间消亡了，庙已经与墓结下了牢固的姻缘。然而直到东汉，庙一直都建在陵园的外面，而且仍然是举行祭祖仪式的主要场所。[166] 紧接其后，墓葬作为祭祖中心获得了完全的独立，丧葬建筑作为社会上最为显著的纪念碑地位得到了充分的提升。公元 1 世纪中期的这一变化，极大地刺激了丧葬艺术的发展，并且为其赋予了新的意义。造成这一变化的原因可能有多种，如家族系统的确立及孝道观念的普及等等，但其最直接的原因却是汉明帝的一项重大礼仪改革。

This event took place at the beginning of the Eastern Han. In A.D. 58, Emperor Ming abolished the temple sacrifice and transferred it to the royal mausoleum.[167] Following this incident, the temple's role was reduced to a minimum, and graveyards became the sole center of ancestor worship. This event has been interpreted in terms of the emperor's devout filial piety;[168] an examination of the historical evidence, however, reveals that the motivation behind this ritual reform was political and aimed at resolving a difficulty in the legitimacy of the Eastern Han regime.

Emperor Ming's father, the Guangwu emperor, was one of many rebel leaders. During his long military struggles against his enemies, he had derived great advantage from two sources: one was his surname, Liu, as evidence of his blood relationship to the Former Han royal house, and the other was his declaration that he would restore orthodox Confucian ideology on the model of Western Zhou ritual. These concerns had led him to establish a lineage temple for the Former Han royal house in A.D. 26, in which tablets of the eleven Western Han emperors were worshipped.[169] But as Guangwu himself understood, perhaps more clearly than anyone else, he was not the legitimate successor of the Western Han royal line. He was from a distant branch of the Liu clan, and in the clan genealogy he was actually two generations senior to the last Western Han emperor. Inevitably, Guangwu faced a dilemma: on the one hand, he had to maintain the newly established Liu royal temple; on the other hand, this temple irked him like "a fishbone in his throat" because it disclosed the irregularity in the royal succession. To resolve this dilemma, he first tried to build a new Eastern Han royal temple, but soon failed because of the resistance of some Confucian ministers.[170] He then made a great effort to transfer temple sacrifices to mausoleums. According to the *History of the Former Han*, no Western Han emperor ever attended a mausoleum sacrifice, for all important ancestral rituals were held in temples. The biography of the Guangwu emperor in the

History of the Latter Han records that the founder of the Eastern Han held ancestral sacrifices 57 times, but only 6 of these were in the temple; the other 51 were held in graveyards.[171] Therefore, even though Guangwu failed to establish a new temple system, he did succeed in shifting the focus of ancestor worship to tombs and thus prepared a way to resolve the problem his successor would eventually face.

公元 58 年，明帝设“上陵礼”，把元旦时百官朝拜这一重大政治典礼移到光武帝的原陵上去举行，随后把最重要的庙祭“酬祭礼”也移到陵墓。[167] 由于这些改革，“庙”在东汉时期的作用下降到最低点，而“墓”终于一跃而为祖先崇拜的绝对中心。东汉皇室为这一改革提供的解释是明帝的“至孝”。[168] 然而，有关历史事相的考证揭示，这次礼仪改革背后的动机是富于政治性的，它的直接指向是化解东汉政权合法性问题中的一个症结。

明帝之父光武帝刘秀崛起于战乱，是历史上造反起家的领袖之一，在长时间的对敌征战过程中，他大大得益于两种资源：一是他的刘姓，这是他与前汉皇室有血缘关系的证据，二是他声称以西周礼仪为典范去恢复正统的儒家社会意识形态。公元 26 年，这两种利害关联促使他为前汉皇室立了一座宗庙，称为“高庙”，于其中供奉了 11 位西汉皇帝的牌位。[169] 但刘秀比谁都清楚，他并非西汉皇室的合法继承人。他的父亲不过是一个县令，出身于刘氏宗室的一个旁支，而且他本人在宗族系谱中实际上与前汉成帝同辈，比西汉末两代皇帝哀、平的辈分都高。因此，一旦一统之业告成，洛阳的高庙既不能废，又如骨鲠在喉，因为这座庙必然会暴露他“继统”说中不可解释的矛盾。为了破除这一两难局面，光武首先试图另立一个“亲庙”，来供奉他自己的直系祖先。但这一举动马上遭到张纯、朱浮等人的激烈反对，这些人上书奏议：“礼为人子事大宗，降其私亲。礼之设施，不授之于自得之异意，当除今亲庙四。”[170] 于是，他又以很大的努力将庙祭移至陵上。据《汉书》可知，西汉帝王皆不曾从事过墓祭，所有重要的祭祖仪式都在庙中举行。

This test appeared immediately after Guangwu's death. The question was where the sacrifice to the founder of the Eastern Han should be held. As we have seen, his son Emperor Ming's solution was to transfer temple ceremonies to the mausoleum. It is said that on the night before an annual ancestral sacrifice, Emperor Ming dreamed of his deceased parents. The emperor was deeply sorrowful and could not fall asleep; the next morning, he led his ministers and courtiers to Guangwu's graveyard and held the sacrifice there. During the ceremony sweet dew fell from Heaven, which the emperor asked his ministers to collect and offer to his deceased father. He became so sad that he crawled forward to the "spirit bed" and began to weep as he examined his mother's dressing articles. "At the time, none of the ministers and attendants present could remain dry-eyed."[172]

We do not know if this story of filial piety is genuine. But the preceding discussion of early Eastern Han politics suggests that Emperor Ming's motives for initiating the "mausoleum sacrifice" (*shanglingli*) were not purely emotional or ethical. Going even further, this emperor ordered in his will that no temple except his funerary shrine be built for him.[173] All later Eastern Han rulers followed this arrangement. Thus, during the next 160 years, the royal temple became nominal. Instead, the graveyard became the focus of ancestor worship. The royal example was in turn imitated by people throughout the country. As the Qing scholar Zhao Yi pointed out: "Taking the imperial 'grave sacrifice' as their model, all officials and scholars erected funerary shrines. Commoners, who could not afford to establish shrines, also customarily held ancestral sacrifices in the family graveyard."[174]

The graveyard was no longer the silent world of the deceased; it
121 became a center of social activities. There yearly, monthly, and daily sacrifices were offered, and large social gatherings were conducted. The royal mausoleums became the political and religious headquarters of the court, and family graveyards provided the common people with a

proper place for banquets, musical performances, and art displays.[175] Pictorial images were not only painted and carved in underground tomb chambers for the deceased, but also in open funerary shrines for the public.[176] Increasing numbers of motifs for educational, memorial, and

《后汉书 · 光武帝本纪》有载，这位东汉的建立者一共主持过57 次祭祖活动，其中只有 6 次于宗庙进行，其余的 51 次全在陵寝举行。[171] 因此，尽管光武另立宗庙的企图没有实现，但他却成功地将人们的注意力从庙祭转移到墓祭，从而为下一代皇帝必将面临的窘境准备了一条出路。

光武一死，马上产生的一个问题是，光武的灵位应供在何处以及对光武的祭祀应在何处举行。正如我们已经看到的那样，其儿子明帝的解决方式是将庙祭“酬祭礼”转移到陵墓。据说就在周年（永平十七年正月）祭祀的前夜，明帝“夜梦先帝、太后如平生欢。既寤，悲不能寐，即案历，明旦日吉，遂率百官及故客上陵。其日，降甘露于陵树，帝令百官采取以荐。会毕，帝从席前伏御床，视太后镜奁中物，感动悲涕，令易脂泽装具。左右皆泣，莫能仰视焉。”[172]

我们不知道这个孝行故事是否真实，但是前面有关东汉早期政治的讨论，暗示着明帝始创“上陵礼”的动机不纯是与情感和伦理有关。比光武有过之而无不及，明帝在其遗诏中表示，除了陵上享堂而外不要为他建庙。[173] 东汉一朝皇帝皆沿循其例。这样，此后的160 年间，王室宗庙名存实亡，而墓地成了祖先崇拜的真正中心。这种皇室典范陆续受到全国各地的效仿，正如清人赵翼所言：“盖又因上陵之制，士大夫仿之皆立祠堂于墓所，庶人之家不能立祠，则祭于墓，相习成俗也。”[174]

墓地不再是死者的寂寞世界了；它成了一种社会活动中心。那里年复一年、月复一月、日复一日地进行着祭供活动和大规模聚会。皇家陵墓成了朝廷的政治宗教策源地，而且家族墓地也为平民阶层提供了一个宴、乐舞和艺术展示的恰当场所。[175] 不仅地下墓室里有为死者刻绘的各种图画形象，开放的墓祠当中还有为公众刻绘的图画形象。[176] 越来越多具有教育功能、纪念功能和娱乐功能的

entertainment purposes entered this art. It is for these reasons that the Eastern Han period appears to have been the golden age of funerary art in Chinese history.

This golden age ended as abruptly as it had begun. In A.D. 222, two years after the fall of the Eastern Han, Emperor Wen of the new dynasty, the Wei, announced that funerary ritual was unorthodox and abolished it. Trying to resume the ancient temple system of the Three Dynasties, he issued an edict to destroy all aboveground funerary structures, including that of his father, the famous warlord Cao Cao.[177] Shrine destruction was apparently not limited to royal mausoleums: Chinese archaeologists have found a number of Wei-Jin tombs in which elaborately engraved stone slabs from destroyed Eastern Han shrines were reused as building materials. In my opinion, these stones, sometimes randomly paved on the floor and sometimes covered with mortar, attest to a nationwide iconoclastic movement and a sweeping shift in the form of ancestor worship.[178] But the advocates of this ritual reform never achieved full success. Rather, from that time until the fall of imperial China, temple and tomb resumed their positions as the twin centers of the ancestor cult. Never again, however, did they attain the political significance they had held during the Three Dynasties and the Eastern Han.

❹ The Chinese Discovery of Stone

In the debate concerning the materials of traditional Chinese architecture, some scholars have noticed and tried to explain the monopoly of wood, which they consider an essential feature of Chinese architecture throughout the ages. Gin Djih Su seeks the solution in economic determinism: "Although wooden-structured buildings easily catch fire, because people's livelihood largely depends on agriculture and the country remains economically underdeveloped, this building type is still the most common even after more than twenty centuries of development."[179] Liu Zhiping, on the other hand, attributes the popularity of timber buildings to China's natural resources: "The earliest Chinese civilization originated in the Central Plain and other loess regions, where trees were abundant but stone was rare. This is why very few stone structures have been built in China."[180] Other scholars, represented by Joseph Needham, argue that the Chinese created not only wooden buildings but also large stone structures comparable to their European

表现题材进入了这一艺术形式。正是因为这些原因，东汉时期才成为中国历史上丧葬艺术的黄金时代。

不过这个黄金时代竟是昙花一现，不久就迅速宣告终结了。造成这一变故的原因又是祖先崇拜中的礼制改革。东汉覆亡后两年，即公元 222 年，魏文帝曹丕下诏废除“上陵礼”。为了恢复古老的三代庙制，他甚至下令将包括其父曹操陵墓在内的地面丧葬构筑悉数毁之。[177] 对祠堂的破坏显然连皇家陵墓也不例外：考古工作者已发现不少魏晋墓以毁掉的东汉祠堂之画像石板为建筑材料。在我看来，这些画像石或被随意地铺在地上，或以灰浆涂盖其画像，表明当时曾经发生过一场全国性的破除旧习运动和一次祭祖形式的彻底转变。[178] 但是，这次礼制改革的提倡者并没有获得完全的成功。确切说，从那时起直到中华帝国的最终衰落，庙和墓再次成为祖先祭祠的一对中心，可是，它们再也没有获得在三代和东汉时期曾经拥有过的政治意义。

四、中国人对石头的发现

在有关中国传统建筑材料的讨论中，一些学者注意到，木质材料的使用是贯穿中国建筑史的一个本质特征，并且试图对木头的这种垄断地位作出解释。如徐敬直试图从经济决定论的立场寻求解答：“尽管木建筑易于失火，但是由于人们的生计在很大程度上依赖于农业，而且国家停留于经济上的相对落后状态，甚至在经历了二十多个世纪的发展之后，木构依然是最普遍的建筑形式。”[179] 刘致平则将木建筑的普及归结于中国的自然资源：“我国最早发祥的地区——中原等黄土地区，多木材而少佳石，所以石建筑甚少。”[180] 以李约瑟为代表的另外一些学者争辩说，中国人不仅创造了木建筑，同时也创造了可以与欧洲和西亚建筑相媲美的大型石建筑，

and Western Asian counterparts. But these stone structures seem to have had distinct religious functions and are mostly "funerary structures, memorial pillars, and monuments."[181]

Although representing a more balanced view, this second observation and explanation is still inadequate for several reasons. First, as we have seen, wood as well as stone was used for funerary structures and other types of monuments in ancient China. Second, timber and stone buildings do not always coexist; the latter appeared far later in Chinese history. Third, rather than purely "natural" materials, wood and stone were given symbolic value and were associated with divergent concepts. Fourth, stone monuments never replaced wooden monuments. As a result, the meaning or monumentality of these two types of structure became interreferential; their coexistence represents a fundamental conceptual opposition or juxtaposition in Chinese culture. These four points imply a methodological proposition, which will direct my discussion in this section. Since the appearance of stone monuments was a specific historical phenomenon, we should try to reconstruct its process and its social, cultural, and religious context. Moreover, since such stone structures marked a distinct stage in the long history of Chinese monuments, we should observe their significance in a larger historical context. In retrospect, we can see that although the ancient Chinese had had a strong interest in the symbolism of art media since prehistorical
122 times, all "special" materials, especially jade and bronze, had been employed in making portable ritual objects (*liqi*).[182] The "discovery" of stone as a special architectural material thus indicated an essential change in psychology; this, in turn, signified the arrival of an age of monumental architecture after the dominance of ritual art for several millennia.

Erecting a stone funerary monument became a common practice during the Eastern Han. All evidence—textual records, extant buildings, and statues, and more than a thousand decorated stone blocks and slabs from abandoned mortuary structures—demonstrates the wide popularity of stone in funerary architecture at the time. A closer examination of the data further indicates that an important change must have taken place some time before the Eastern Han. Prior to the second century B.C., aboveground funerary structures, such as the buildings that once stood above the graves of Fu Hao and the Zhongshan kings, were uniformly

但这些石建筑似乎有着截然不同的宗教功能，多为“丧葬建筑、碑碣和其他类型的纪念碑”。[181]

尽管这第二种观点更为持平，但从某些方面来说仍然不够准确。首先，众所周知，木与石在中国古代都被用于丧葬建筑以及其他类型的纪念性建筑。再者，木建筑与石建筑并非自始至终共存；后者在中国历史上的出现要晚得多。第三，木与石不只是纯粹的“自然”材料，它们还被赋予了象征的内涵，而且分别联系着不同的概念。第四，石制建筑从未取代木制建筑，这两类建筑并行发展的结果是二者具有了相互参照、相互补充的意义或纪念碑性；它们的共存体现了中国文化中的一种基本概念上的对立或并列。这四个方面引导出本节当中讨论的方法论：总的说来，既然石制纪念性建筑的出现是一种特殊的历史现象，我们因此需要重构其出现的过程及其社会、文化、宗教背景。而且，由于石建筑的出现标志着中国纪念碑历史长河中的一个特定阶段，我们应当在一个较大的历史背景上观察它的意义。通过这种回顾我们可以看到，史前时期，中国古人就已经对艺术媒介的象征性产生了强烈兴趣，所有“特殊”材料，特别是玉和青铜，都被用来制作可以移动的礼器。[182] 石头作为一种特殊建筑材料的“发现”因而预示着一种心理层面的实质性变化，意味着在礼器经历数千年优胜地位之后，一个纪念性建筑时代的到来。

建造石质丧葬纪念性建筑在东汉时期成为一种普遍的现象。所有证据——包括文献记载、建筑遗迹、实际存在的雕像，以及来自废弃墓葬和享堂的数以千计的画像石——都表明石头在当时丧葬建筑中的广泛流行。对这些材料的仔细检视进一步表明，在东汉以前的某段时间内必定发生过一次重要的变化。在公元前 2 世纪以前，地面上的丧葬建筑，比如曾经建在妇好墓和中山王墓上的那些地上

timber-framed (Figs. 2.26b, 29). Likewise, no stone stelae or statues have been found in a pre-Han graveyard;[183] even the ambitious First Emperor seemed quite satisfied with his terra-cotta soldiers and bronze chariots. From the first century A.D. on, however, all sorts of funerary monuments—pillar-gates, memorial tablets, offering shrines, and statues in human and animal forms—were customarily made of stone. Inscriptions on these structures often contain a standard statement by the patrons: "We chose excellent stones from south of the southern mountains; we took those of perfect quality with flawless and unyellowed color. In front we established an altar; behind we erected a [stone] offering shrine."[184]

We wonder what caused this dramatic change. The ancient Chinese, who for many centuries had largely ignored stone as an architectural material,[185] suddenly seem to have "discovered" it and bestowed on it fresh meaning. Stone was opposed to wood, and this opposition was understood in symbolic terms. All the natural characteristics of stone—strength, plainness, and especially endurance—became analogous to eternity or immortality; wood, which was relatively fragile and vulnerable to the elements, was associated with temporal, mortal existence. From this dichotomy emerged two kinds of architecture: those of wood used by the living, and those of stone dedicated to the dead, the gods, and immortals.[186] The double connotation of stone with death on the one hand and with immortality on the other implied a further link between death and immortality. Indeed, we find that this link, which was finally established during the second and first centuries B.C., prepared a new ground for imagining and constructing the afterlife, and was responsible for many changes in funerary art and architecture, including the use of stone.

In an excellent introduction to the Han conception of the afterlife, Michael Loewe makes a distinction between several objectives; the first "was a wish to prolong the life of the flesh on earth as long as possible."[187] Indeed, death always inspires fear, and the recognition that life has its limit leads first to the desire to postpone death and then to avoid it altogether. The incessant pursuit of longevity by pre-Han philosophers, necromancers, and princes aimed not at overcoming death but at infinitely prolonging life. This goal, which represented an early belief in immortality, may be characterized as achieving eternal happiness in this world and this life. It might be pursued by internal or external means: longevity might be realized either by transforming oneself into

建筑，一律都是木结构［图 2.26b，图 2.29］。同样，汉代以前的墓地中也没有石碑或石雕；[183] 即便是野心勃勃、好大喜功的秦始皇，似乎也满足于他的陶制兵马俑和青铜车马。然而从公元 1 世纪开始，各种丧葬纪念物——阙、碑、享堂、人和动物形象——通常都以石头制成。有些建筑上的题记还包含着建造者对这种材料的描述："选择名石，南山之阳，擢取妙好，色无斑黄。前设礓砠，后建祠堂。"[184]

是什么导致了这种戏剧性的变化？在漫长岁月中似乎相当忽视石头的建筑材料价值的中国古人，[185] 似乎突然"发现"了石材，并且赋予它新的意义。石与木相对立，而这种对立在象征的层面被理解。石头的所有自然属性——坚硬、素朴，尤其是坚实耐久——使其与"永恒"的概念相连；木头则因其脆弱易损的性质而与"暂时"的概念相关。从这种差异中产生出两类建筑：木构建筑供生者之用，石质建筑则属于神祇、仙人和死者。[186] 石材一方面与死亡有关，另一方面又与不朽和升仙联系。死亡、升仙与石材的共同联系又强化了这二者之间的连接。我们发现死亡和升仙的连接在公元前 2—前 1 世纪时最终在人们的宗教观念中确立，为以图像和建筑表现来世提供了一个新的基础，也与丧葬艺术与建筑的许多变化——包括对石头的使用——密切相关。

鲁惟一在其对汉代生死观的一段精彩介绍中辨明了人们的几种不同企求。第一种是"尽可能延长肉身在世间生命的愿望"。[187] 死亡引起恐惧，生命有其大限——这个思想使得古人渴望尽力延迟以至于完全避免面临这条界限。西汉哲人、方士、王侯所执着探寻的长生之道并不是要征服死亡，而是着眼于无限地延长生命。这个"求仙于生时"的目标，可由内、外两种方式达到：长寿可以由人们

an immortal or by transporting oneself to an immortal land. As early as the Eastern Zhou, people began to think that through certain physical practices, such as purification, starvation, and the breathing exercise called *daoyin* (Fig. 2.36), the practitioner could gradually eliminate his material substance, leaving only the "essence of life." Simultaneously, there emerged the belief in the lands of deathlessness, the most prominent being the Penglai Islands in the Eastern Sea.[188] It was thought that by discovering and reaching such a place, one would cease to age, and death would never occur.

Happy endings for both pursuits were described in ancient literature. Zhuangzi vividly portrayed those ageless men unaffected by time and other natural rules: "There is a Divine Man living on faraway Ku-ye Mountain, with skin like ice or snow, and gentle and shy like a young girl. He doesn't eat the five grains, but sucks the wind and drinks the dew, climbs up on clouds and mists, rides a flying dragon, and wanders beyond
123 the four seas."[189] With similar vividness, the lore of immortal lands was spread by necromancers, whose chief aim was to convince their audience of the existence of a magic land and to arouse the fantasy of such a place through colorful descriptions.[190]

Zhuangzi focused on *man*, and the necromancers on *place*, but in both their accounts, a *divine man* and a *divine place* appear in similar disguise. Both are still found in this world and assume human and natural forms; only their features—unusual shapes, colors, materials, and habits—make them seem unworldly. These extraordinary attributes are thus signs of immortality or longevity: these men and places are no longer governed by the laws of decay and death. Once we understand this train of thought, we can correct a confusion in modern scholarship on early Chinese religion and art, which often equates "immortality" and the "afterlife" without the necessary qualification. In fact, the pre-Han idea of *xian*, or immortal, rested firmly on the hope of escaping death. The notion of an afterlife, however, was based on another premise: as a predestined event, death marked the beginning of a continuous existence in the other world. Indeed, instead of approaching death as the total elimination of living consciousness, the ancient Chinese insisted that it was caused by, and thus testified to, the separation of the body and soul. Yü Ying-shih has demonstrated that this concept appeared long

将自身转化为不食人间烟火的“仙体”而达到，也可以通过把自身转移到一个方外的仙境来实现。至少从周代晚期开始，人们已经开始考虑可否通过某种对身体的训练，如辟谷和称作“导引”的气功［图 2.36］等方式，渐渐脱离其物质的躯壳，仅仅保留其“生命之精髓”了。与此同时，有关“不死之境”的信念也产生了，其中最突出的是位于东海的蓬莱仙岛。[188] 人们相信一旦到达这样的境地，生命的时针就会延缓不前，死亡也就永远不会到来。

古代文学作品对上述两种追求长生的圆满结局多有描述。庄子就曾娓娓勾画过那些不受时间和其他自然规律影响的神人：“藐姑射之山，有神人居焉，肌肤若冰雪，淖约若处子。不食五谷，吸风饮露，乘云气，御飞龙，而游乎四海之外。”[189] 战国秦汉的一些方士也以同样生动的语言大肆扩散着仙境的传说，以激起人们对这种神奇之境的精神幻想。[190]

庄子强调说“人”，而术士侧重说“境”。但是，他们所说的“神人”和“仙境”却拥有同样的特征，都是被改变了面貌的现实。二者都仍然处于此世，也仍保持着人和自然的形貌，只是其非凡的色彩、习性和方位等因素使其显得卓绝人寰。因此，这些奇异非凡的特征也就成为升仙或长生的符号：此“人”或此“境”不再受衰败和死亡法则的制约，“大限”的概念对二者也不再适用。一旦了解了这一连串的思维方式，我们便可以澄清中国早期宗教与艺术研究中常将“成仙”和“来世”混为一谈的模糊认识。实际上，这两种概念并不相同，在汉代以前，“仙”的观念与逃避死亡的愿望密切相关；而“来世”思想则是基于“大限”的另外一种概念，意思是死亡标志着人在另一世界继续存在的开端。确实，中国古人并不把死亡看作生命的完全终结，而相信死亡是由灵魂与肉体的分离而引起的，反过来，死亡又是灵肉分离说的证明。余英时在一篇文章

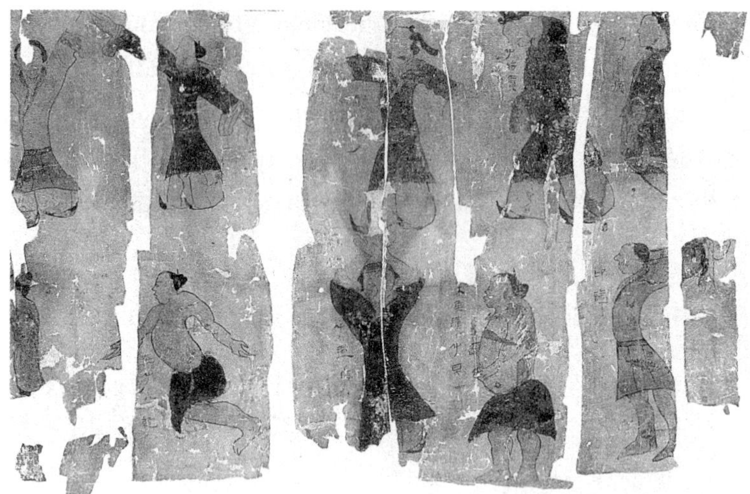

Fig. 2.36. A detail of the "Diagram of Daoyin Exercises" ("Daoyin tu"). Ink and color on silk. Early Western Han. 2nd century B.C. W. 53 cm. L. 110 cm. Excavated in 1973 from Tomb no. 3 at Mawangdui, Changsha, Hunan province. Hunan Provincial Museum, Changsha.

图 2.36 《导引图》局部。墨笔设色帛画。西汉早期，公元前 2 世纪。宽 53 厘米，长 110 厘米。1973 年出土于湖南长沙马王堆 3 号墓。湖南省博物馆藏。

before the desire for immortality: "The notion that the departed soul is as conscious as the living is already implied in Shang-Chou sacrifices."[191] Based on a new archaeological find, we can further date the idea of the autonomous soul to at least the fifth millennium B.C.: a hole was drilled in the wall of a Yangshao pottery coffin to allow the soul to move in and out (Fig. 2.37).

The belief in the posthumous soul naturally led to a simple conception of the afterlife: during pre-Han times, the afterlife in its most ideal form was no more than a mirror image of life.[192] The official hierarchy was projected into the underworld,[193] and the tomb of an aristocrat was arranged as his or her posthumous dwelling, containing luxury goods, food, and drink for a comfortable life. This happy home of the dead was also protected by tomb guardians, first by human sacrifices, then by certain mechanisms as well as sculptured and painted protective

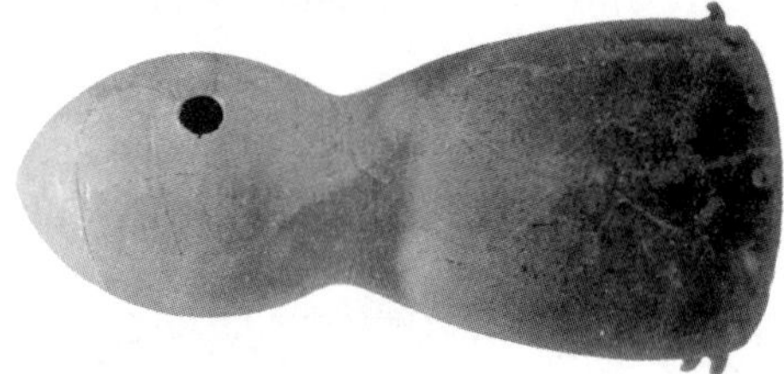

Fig. 2.37. Pottery coffin for a child. Yangshao culture. *Ca.* 3500 B.C. L. 65 cm. Excavated in 1978 at Yancun, Linru, Henan province. Henan Provincial Museum, Zhengzhou.

图 2.37　儿童瓮棺。仰韶文化，约前 3500 年。长 65 厘米。1978 年河南临汝阎村出土。河南省博物馆藏。

deities (Figs. 2.38a, b). The great Lishan mausoleum of the First Emperor, 124
though constructed and considered as a monument of a new historical era, was still based on this traditional approach. As mentioned earlier, its underground chamber was modeled upon the whole universe. This universe, however, cannot be equated with a "paradise" (as some writers have proposed), since all its components—miniature rivers and oceans,

中已经提出，这种观念早在人们企求升仙的热望出现以前就已经存在着，他说："脱离肉体的灵魂具有和活人一般的意识，这一观点早已隐含在商周时期的祭祀活动中了。"[191] 根据新的考古发现，我们可以进一步将灵魂离开身体而独立存在的观念上溯到六七千年以前：仰韶文化陶瓮棺上就钻有一个可供灵魂出入的圆孔［图 2.37］。而曾侯乙墓漆棺上有意绘制和开设的窗户，则表明这种观念在公元前 5 世纪依然存在。

相信死后"灵魂不灭"，自然导致了一种朴素的来世观念：在汉代以前，理想的来世看来不过是生活本身的镜像。[192] 死者的等级身份常常在地下得到反映，[193] 贵族的墓葬被布置得像其生前的居所，其中存储着应有尽有的食物、饮料和各种奢侈品，以保证死后生活得安逸。殉葬的士兵，以及后来以雕塑和绘画形式出现的各种保护神，守护着死者来世中的"幸福家园"［图 2.38］。秦始皇的骊山陵尽管被看作一座划时代的纪念碑，但其基本思想仍然不逾这一传统的藩篱。如前所述，它的地下墓室模仿了整个宇宙。可是，这个宇宙并非某些学者所想象的所谓"天堂"，因为它的所有组成

and other simulations of heavenly and earthly phenomena—were symbols of nature, not of immortality.

a

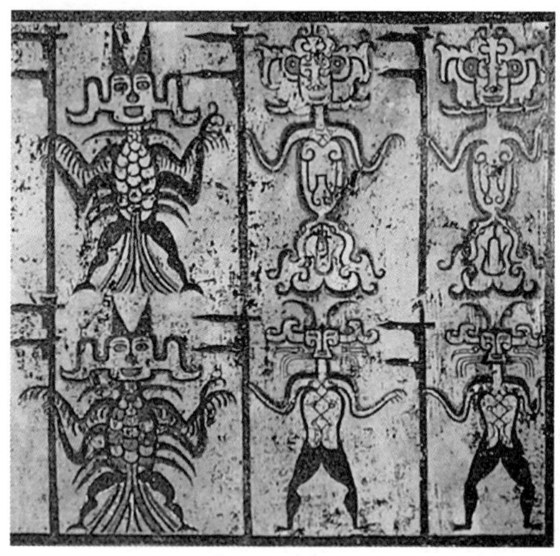

b

Fig. 2.38. (a) Inner coffin of Marquis Yi of the state of Zeng. Wood and lacquer. Early Warring States period. 5th century B.C. L. 250 cm. H. 132 cm. Excavated in 1978 at Leigudun, Suixian, Hubei province. Hubei Provincial Museum, Wuhan. (b) Protective deity painted on the coffin.

图 2.38 （a）曾侯乙内棺。漆木。战国早期，前 5 世纪。长 250 厘米，高 132 厘米。1978 年湖北随县擂鼓墩出土。湖北省博物馆藏。（b）绘在漆棺上的守护神。

The people of the Han inherited and developed both beliefs in a worldly paradise and in an otherworldly happy home. The search for Penglai and other magic lands continued, but now these places were imagined to be occupied by immortals who, having gained the secret of deathlessness, would unselfishly grant mortal beings eternal life.[194] More replicas of immortal mountains were made at this time than at any other time in Chinese history (Figs. 2.39a-c); it was thought that these and other imitations of divine forms would attract immortals with their elixir.[195] At the same time, funerary art also flourished to an unprecedented degree, and it became customary for a person to prepare his or her own tomb.[196] What we find here, therefore, is a heightening inner contradiction in the search for eternal happiness: a tomb would not be necessary if one truly believed that longevity could be achieved, yet the desire to prepare a tomb during one's lifetime must have been based on a certain skepticism toward the search for longevity. This dilemma led to a compromise: the people of the Han increasingly wished to believe that eternal happiness

部分——摹拟的江河、海洋，以及其他天上人间各种现象——都是自然的象征，而不是升仙的符号。

汉代人继承和发展了人间天堂与来世的幸福家园信仰，对蓬莱及其他奇异之境的追求持续不断，但此时这些地方被想象为仙人的居所，仙人掌握着不死的秘密，可以无私地赐给凡人永恒的生命。[194] 这一时期所制造的仙山模型在数量上比历史上任何时期都要多［图 2.39］，因为人们相信这类人工模拟的仙境可以吸引掌有不死之药的神仙降临。[195] 与此同时，尽管看上去有些矛盾，这个时期的丧葬美术也空前繁盛，人们在死前就为自己造墓的做法蔚然成风。[196] 因此，我们在这里看到的是一种高度追求永久幸福时的内心冲突：如果真的相信长生不死，人们就不必营坟造墓，而死前就准备墓葬的愿望又必定出于对追求长生的某种怀疑。这一矛盾局面最终导致了一个折中的选择：人们越来越倾向相信，永久的幸福可以

Fig. 2.39. Immortal mountains. (a, b) Incense burner. Gilded bronze. Western Han. 2nd century B.C. H. 58 cm. Excavated in 1981 at Xingping, Shaanxi province. Mao ling Mausoleum Museum. (c) Clay stand of a "money tree." Late Eastern Han. 2nd century A.D. H. 60.5 cm. Excavated in 1978 near Chengdu, Sichuan province. Chengdu Museum.

图 2.39 仙山。(a, b) 熏炉。青铜鎏金。西汉，前 2 世纪。高 58 厘米。1981 年陕西兴平出土。茂陵博物馆藏。(c) 摇钱树陶座。东汉晚期，2 世纪。高 60.5 厘米。1978 年四川成都近郊出土。成都博物馆藏。

a

b

c

could be realized after death. This idea, which may be called "immortality in the afterlife and the other world," represented a turning point in the ancient Chinese immortality cult and is indicated by both literary and archaeological evidence.

Two instances in the *Records of the Historian* denote the emergence of this new religious trend. After the necromancer Li Shaojun died, Emperor Wu ordered that his tomb be uncovered. Li's corpse could not be found, and only empty clothes remained in the grave chamber. The emperor was thus convinced that the magician had escaped this world through some
posthumous mystical transformation.[197] The same emperor once traveled 126
to the tomb of the Yellow Emperor at Mount Qiao. While offering a sacrifice to the ancient divine ruler, he posed a question to his religious advisers: "I have heard that the Yellow Emperor never died—how is it that he had a tomb?" The advisers told him that the Yellow Emperor had indeed become an immortal and that only his clothes were buried in his grave.[198] The idea implied in these anecdotes would later be developed into a Taoist concept called *shijie*, meaning "the dissolution of the corpse" or "liberation from the corpse." One kind of *shijie* took the form of the

在死后实现。这种或许可以称作"在死后和来世中升仙"的观念，代表着中国古代不死信仰中的一个转折点。这一点业已为现存文献和考古发现所证明。

《史记》中就有两处记载佐证了这一新信仰倾向的出现。方士李少君死后，武帝命人发少君之冢，不见有尸，空棺衣衾而已。武帝于是相信真有一种法术，可以使人通过死后的某种神秘变化脱离人世。[197] 还是武帝，有一次巡幸黄帝所葬的桥山，当致祭黄帝陵时，他向身边的人提了个问题："吾闻黄帝不死，今有冢，何也？"随从的人告诉他：黄帝的确已成神仙，墓中埋的不过是他的衣冠。[198] 这些传闻当中隐含的观念随后发展成道教中的"尸解"概念，意指"尸体的解散"或"自尸体中释放"。有一种"尸解"就是以死者身体

mysterious vanishing of the physical body of the deceased, which was interpreted as the attainment of immortality after death. Integrating various early trends into a coherent theory, the author of the *Canon of Immortality* (*Xianjing*) states: "Gentlemen of the upper rank who can raise their bodies to the air are called Heavenly Immortals. Gentlemen of the middle rank who roam among famous mountains are called Earthly Immortals. Gentlemen of the lower rank cannot avoid death, and they have to shed their physical shells like a cicada; they are called Shijie Immortals."[199]

The design of a burial signified such changes in the conception of the afterlife. It was precisely around the same time in the mid-second century B.C. that rock-cut tombs first appeared in China. Instead of passively imitating a wooden-framed dwelling underground, a tomb carved into a living cliff revealed a new desire to make a person's otherworldly home eternal. This architectural form shared the basic premise of *shijie*, that although death was inevitable, it was a necessary stage in one's achievement of eternity. Emperor Wen of the Western Han, for example, began his testamentary edict of 157 B.C. with the philosophical statement: "Death is a part of the abiding order of heaven and earth and the natural end of all creatures."[200] But the same emperor constructed for himself a mausoleum dug into a rocky mountain, with a special stone sarcophagus intended to last forever. He also carefully planned his own funeral in advance, so that at his death he would safely be transported to his stone palace.[201]

Emperor Wen's mausoleum, Ba ling, is one of the earliest known stone funerary structures in China. Sima Qian recorded that the emperor once led a group of courtiers to this mountain tomb southeast of Chang'an. Confronting his future burial place (and therefore his death), the emperor's heart was full of sorrow, and he began to sing a melancholy song. But his mood soon changed when he began to inspect the arrangement of his otherworldly dwelling: "Oh! Using stone from the Northern Mountains to make my outer coffin, securing it with linen cloth and again gluing the cloth with lacquer, how can the coffin still be shaken!"[202] His desire for an everlasting posthumous home represented a contemporary development in Chinese religious thought, but why did this idea have to be conveyed by stone structures? Until this point the Chinese had rarely, if at all, constructed stone buildings. Were they suddenly able to "discover" this material themselves, or were they, in searching for new symbolic forms to

的神秘消失为征兆的，被说成是死后登仙。在《仙经》当中，作者将各种早期风气整合成一套连贯的理论学说，书中说道："上士举形升虚，谓之天仙；中士游于名山，谓之地仙；下士先死后蜕，谓之尸解仙。"[199]

墓葬的设计体现着来生观念的这些变化。大约在公元前 2 世纪的这段时间里，崖墓开始在中国出现了。一座镌凿于山崖上的墓葬不再是地下木构居所的被动仿效，相反，它透露出一种想要建一个来世永久家园的新愿望。这种建筑形式就有着尸解逻辑的基本前提——死亡固然不可避免，但它也是达致永生的一个必要阶段。公元前 157 年，西汉文帝宣布的遗诏当中就有这样一段富于哲理的话语："死者天地之理，物之自然者，奚可甚哀。"[200] 但正是这位皇帝又在山丘上为自己开凿了一个陵墓，并为自己造了一具特殊石棺以期永固。他还事先仔细规划了自己的葬礼，以确保死亡降临之后能安全地被送往他那石建的宫殿。[201]

文帝的霸陵是目前所知中国最早的石质丧葬建筑之一。司马迁记述这位皇帝曾率领朝臣去到位于长安东南作为墓地的山丘。面对自己将来的葬地（也就是面对死亡），文帝心中充满感伤，吟起一首悲歌。但是当他着手检查为自己死后居所所作的各种安排时，他的情绪很快又转变了回来："嗟乎！以北山石为椁，用纻絮斮陈，蕠漆其间，岂可动哉！"[202] 他对拥有一个身后的永恒家园的期冀反映了中国人的生死观在当时的发展。但是，为什么这种永恒的家园要以石质建筑材料来表现？直到此时，中国人即使不是完全没有，也是很少建造石头建筑。究竟是他们自己突然"发现"了这种材料，还是他们在寻求表达新观念的象征形式的过程中，受到了某种具有

express new ideas, inspired by an outside culture that had a long tradition of stone religious architecture? This question directs attention to the Indian world to the west, where people for centuries had built rock-cut sanctuaries and made stone sculptures. My basic approach to this cultural interaction, however, differs from the old theory of "cultural impact." In my view, instead of passively receiving influences from neighboring countries, the Han Chinese actively sought stimuli from the outside world and, in fact, invented an outside world that provided them with such stimuli.

Wolfgang Bauer has observed that in the ancient Chinese mind, the East and the West were always the places of refuge and immortality.[203] A closer examination reveals that pre-Han searches for immortality were most frequently oriented to the East, as a result of the intense activities of the necromancers from the northeastern states of Qi, Zhao, and Yan, who traveled throughout the country and spread tales about the Penglai Islands off the east coast.[204] From the early and middle Western Han, however, people began to pay increasing attention to the West. This new focus in the immortality search was intimately related to China's unification and its subsequent western-oriented expansion. This expansion process, which may have begun in the early Han,[205]
127 culminated during the reign of Emperor Wu, who made use of the strength accumulated in the early years of the dynasty to double the territory of his empire. By defeating the Huns in a series of brilliant campaigns, the Han armies pushed ever farther across Central Asia until they finally confronted the Roman empire. Two great highways were established; the one north of the Heavenly Mountains (Tianshan) ran through the Gobi Desert to Balkhash, and the one south of the mountains led across the Tarim Basin to Kashgar and Khotan. "Over both roads came Western ideas and art motifs to be incorporated into but never to dominate the Chinese aesthetic canon."[206] Of these ideas and art motifs, many came from the Indian world, which had suddenly

become a neighbor of Han China.

All these activities—expeditions, conquests, travel, trade, geographical investigations, exchanges of ideas and experiences, and the search for immortality—were part of a broad cultural movement characterized, first of all, by a strong attraction to an unfamiliar space as well as an alienation from it.[207] The mysterious West was conceptualized as a geographic

漫长石质宗教建筑传统的外来文化的启发？这个问题将我们的注意力引向西方的印度文化圈，那里的人们早此几个世纪前就开始开凿石窟，雕造石像。但我需要说明：在讨论这种文化交互作用时，我的着眼点与传统的“文化影响”观念不同。在我看来，汉代人并不是被动地接受邻国的影响，而是积极地从外部世界寻求灵感——实际上，他们是为自己创造了一个可以为他们提供这类灵感的外部世界。

鲍吾刚认为，在古代中国人的心目中，遥远的东方和西方总被认为是长生不老的神仙之地和避难之所。[203] 稍做考察我们就会发现，在汉代之前，来自东北地区的齐、赵和燕的方士游行各地，广泛传播有关东海中蓬莱仙岛的神话。[204] 作为他们频繁活动的一个结果，人们对不死之地的求索也多是指向东方。然而，西汉初年到西汉中期的人们开始越来越注意西方。对不死追求中的这一新的焦点与国家的统一，及其随后向西部的扩展密切相关。扩展的进程大约始于西汉初，[205] 至武帝时期达到高潮。武帝凭借自西汉初年起积蓄的人力物力将帝国的疆土扩大了一倍。通过一系列的重要战役，汉代的远征军在挫败匈奴以后推进到中亚，最终逼近罗马帝国。当时所建立的两条交通要道一是天山北道，穿越戈壁沙漠到达巴尔喀什湖，而天山南道则通过塔里木盆地到达喀什与和阗。“沿这两条道路源源而来的西方思想与艺术母题被融会到中国的主流艺术当中，但从来未能占据主导地位。”[206] 这些思想与艺术母题中的许多都来自印度——一个由于汉代疆土的扩张而突然成为中国近邻的外域。

所有这些活动——远征、攻伐、旅行、贸易、地理勘察、思想经验交流，乃至对长生不死的探求——都是一场波澜壮阔的文化运动的组成部分，其首要特征是异域风物的强烈吸引力。[207] 神秘的

territory that expanded from the Han Dynasty proper to the "western limit" of the world, a vast sphere consisting of a number of vaguely divided zones—some actually reached by the Han Chinese, others known only through hearsay. The Near West was occupied by hostile Hun tribes that presented a constant danger. Beyond this barrier were more peaceful states, including Dayuan (Ferghana), Yuezhi (Indo-scythia), Daxia (Bactria), and Kangju (Trans-Oxiana), places that Zhang Qian, Emperor Wu's ambassador to the West, visited during his mission from 138 to 126 B.C.[208] Zhang's report to the emperor, which survives in the *Records of the Historian*, contains amazing factual details;[209] but the farther west the places he describes, the more fantastic his accounts. Tiaozhi (Mesopotamia), for example, is situated several thousand *li* west of Persia; there "great birds lay eggs as large as pots," and one can find the Queen Mother of the West.[210] Gaston Bachelard calls such an imaginary geography a "poetic space," whose objective properties become less important than what it is imagined to be.[211] Edward W. Said further points out that "poetic space" is often associated with distinctive objects that have only a fictional reality (e.g., "the great birds and their huge eggs" frequently mentioned in Han descriptions of western regions), or is viewed as a place outside time (e.g., the realm of the Queen Mother of the West). The attitude toward such a place "shares with magic and with mythology the self-containing, self-reinforcing character of a closed system, in which objects are what they are *because* they are what they are, for once, for all time, for ontological reasons that no empirical material can either dislodge or alter."[212]

We can thus understand why to people of the Han the continually repeated features and tales of this fantastic "West" possessed eternal value. All kinds of suppositions, associations, and fictions related to immortality crowded this alien sphere: a horse from the West was a "heavenly horse," and a tribute elephant, "a passenger of the gods."[213] Both beasts are portrayed as "auspicious omens" and "immortal animals" on a chariot ornament made at the beginning of the first century B.C. (Fig.

2.40).[214] Interestingly, not only was the elephant a foreign tribute, but its image also was derived from a foreign art tradition: almost identical "elephant-tending" motifs are found in India and Pakistan (Figs. 2.41a, b).

"西方"被概念化地想象成从汉朝统治区域一直延伸到世界的"西极"之间的一个广大地域，由若干划分模糊的地区构成。这些地区有些是汉朝人实际到达过的，其他则是通过传闻获知的。根据当时的地理概念，靠近汉朝统治区域的一个地带被持续对汉朝构成威胁的匈奴盘踞，越过这道屏障则是些更为和平友好的国家，包括大宛、月氏、大夏、康居等，都是张骞在公元前 138 至公元前 126 年出使西域期间到过的国家。[208]《史记》载，张骞给武帝的上书中包含着对这些地区非常细致的描述；[209] 但是，所记之处越是靠西，描写的内容也就越具有传说色彩。例如条支被说成是在波斯之西几千里，那里"有大鸟生卵大如罐"，在那里人们还可以见到西王母。[210] 加斯东·巴什拉把这种想象的地理区域称作"诗意的空间"，人们对它的想象比它的客观现实存在更为重要。[211] 萨义德进一步指出，这种"诗意的空间"常常与仅仅具有虚构本体的特殊对象相关（如汉代关于西域记载中频繁提到的"大鸟及巨卵"），或者被看作是一个不受时间控制的空间（如西王母的国度）。对待这种空间的态度"带有巫术和神话所共有的一种自给自足的封闭系统的特征。在这种封闭系统中，事物是它们本身的样子，是因为它们被认为就是那个样子。根源于经验证据无法反驳和修正的本体论原因，它们曾经是如此，也将永远是如此"。[212]

我们因此可以理解为什么对汉代人来说，这个幻想中"西方"的特点和传说被不断重复而具有了永恒的价值。各种各样与"长生"有关的假设、联想和虚构充斥了这个陌生的空间：西方的马是"天马"，一头进贡来的白象成了上帝的使者。[213] 这两种动物在公元前 1 世纪初的一个车饰上以"祥瑞"或"仙兽"的形象出现［图 2.40］。[214] 有意思的是，不仅这件车器上的大象被表现为外国贡品，它的图像同样来自域外艺术传统：几乎同样的"御象"画面屡屡见于印度和巴基斯坦［图 2.41］。

Fig. 2.40. Elephant-tending motif on a bronze chariot ornament. Western Han. Early 1st century B.C. Excavated in 1965 at Sanpanshan, Dingxian, Hebei province. Hebei Provincial Museum, Shijiazhuang. Drawing.

图 2.40 铜车饰上的御象图。西汉，前 1 世纪初期。1965 年河北定县三盘山出土。河北省博物馆藏。线描。

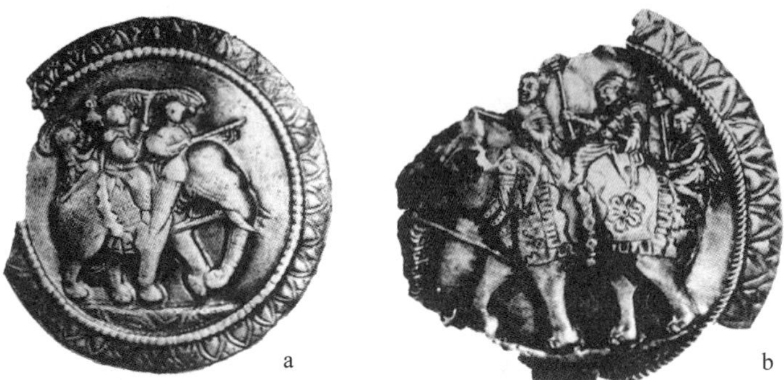

Fig. 2.41. (a, b) Silver disks decorated with elephant-tending motifs. 2nd century A.D. From Rawalpindi. British Museum.

图 2.41 （a, b）装饰御象母题的银盘。2 世纪。出自拉瓦尔品第。大英博物馆藏。

129 This example clinches the argument that at least by the second and first centuries B.C., certain Indian art motifs had been introduced to China and copied there. But such faithful copies of Indian motifs were still rare at that time—they required the importation of foreign art objects

to China. What had greater influence on Chinese culture were vague ideas or "information" about the fantastic West—stories and "reports" spread orally and freely interpreted, modified, and adapted for the sake of their receivers.[215] The reception of western influence in such "twisted" fashion continued into later history: students of Chinese Buddhism are well aware that the early translations of Buddhist canons produced in the third and fourth centuries explained Indian concepts in traditional Chinese terms, and, as I discuss later in this section, during the first and second centuries A.D., the Buddha was viewed in China as nothing more than a foreign *xian* immortal. The people of the Western Han had an even more rudimentary understanding of Indian religion and art. Raised in a culture that had been longing for immortality for centuries, they readily believed the land over the Heavenly Mountains a "paradise," where many "anthropomorphic deities" dwelt. They related Indian Buddhism, which also attempted to provide solutions to the problems of suffering and death, with their own pursuit of eternal happiness; they equated the

最后的这个例子确凿地证实了在公元前 2 至前 1 世纪，某些印度艺术的母题已经传入中国并在当地复制。但是，这类印度题材的忠实摹本在当时还是比较罕见的。一个原因是，这类摹本必须从进口的域外美术品直接仿制，但对汉代文化发生更大影响的则是关于幻想的西方的模糊概念或"信息"，包括口头传播的、为了听众的兴趣而随意解释和增益的故事和传说。[215] 通过这种"扭曲"的方式对西方影响的接受在以后的中国历史中仍然持续：对中国佛教史有所了解的人都知道，三四世纪对佛教经典的翻译习用传统中国术语来解释印度的概念。而且，如我稍后将要谈到的那样，佛在公元 1—2 世纪的汉代不过是被看作一个域外的仙人。在这之前的西汉人对印度宗教和艺术的理解更为粗浅。由于受几百年来始终追求长生的文化的浸淫，他们很自然地想象和相信天山彼岸的世界是众多仙人或神人所居的仙界或天堂。同样，他们把希望解决痛苦和死亡问题的印度佛教和自己对永恒幸福的追求联系在一起。把"涅

concept of Nirvana with their idea of life after death and interpreted the worship of the Buddha's relics as a kind of funerary practice. When they heard about the western rock-cut sanctuaries and stone carvings, they naturally related these foreign forms—not only their design but also their medium—to immortality and eternity, and willingly absorbed such forms into their own religious architecture.

This hypothesis explains the frequent connections among four essential elements in Han religion and religious art, namely, *immortality*, the *West*, *stone*, and *death*. The link between immortality and the West is the most evident. In fact, some scholars attribute Emperor Wu's western-oriented military actions to his desire for longevity: by obtaining the legendary "heavenly horse" in the West he could ride to Heaven.[216] Although this argument may need more evidence,[217] it is true that things in and from the West were customarily considered auspicious or
130 immortal. Most important, Mount Kunlun and the Queen Mother of the West, two primary immortality symbols related to the West, soon overshadowed the older Penglai myth.[218] The *Master Huainan* (*Huainan zi*) composed before 122 B.C., for example, identifies Kunlun as the ultimate designation of the search for immortality: "He who climbs onto the Chilly Wind peak of Kunlun will achieve deathlessness; he who climbs twice as high onto the Hanging Garden will become a spirit and will be able to make wind and rain; he who climbs twice as high again will reach Heaven and will become a god." The same text also locates the Queen Mother of the West at "the edge of the Flowing Sands," possibly the western limit of the Gobi Desert.[219] Sima Xiangru, the court poet of Emperor Wu, described the goddess's attraction in the following lines:

> I went back and forth among the Yin Mountains and soared in great curves; I was able to see the Queen Mother of the West. She, brilliant with her white head and high jade comb, dwells in a cave.[220]

Significantly, here the western goddess is said "to dwell in a cave" (or "to be worshipped in a cave"?). This account may be read together with a passage from the *History of the Former Han*: "To the northwest and beyond the defense line, there is the Stone Chamber of the Queen Mother of the West."[221] It seems that unlike traditional Chinese deities who had always been honored in wooden-framed temples and shrines, western immortals "beyond China's defense line" were associated with alien structures of stone.

槃”等同于他们自己的来世观念，把佛教中对舍利的崇拜解释为一种葬俗。当他们获知西方人在山崖上镌窟造像，也就很自然地将这些域外的做法——不仅是其创意，也还包括其媒介——与不死和永恒联系起来，欣然将这些做法吸收到自己的宗教建筑中去。

我的这个假设可以解释汉代宗教与宗教艺术中四种要素之间的频繁关联，即长生、西方、石头和死亡。长生与西方之间的关联最为明显，实际上，有的学者把汉武帝对西方的用兵归因于他的长生渴望：通过获得传说中的西方“天马”，他可以升天成仙。[216] 尽管这种观点可能还有待更多证据的支持，[217] 西方之物通常和神仙联系起来却是当时的事实。尤其显著的是，昆仑山和西王母这两种与西方相连的重要的仙界象征，很快在西汉时期遮蔽了蓬莱仙岛的神秘光环。[218] 如成书于公元前 122 年之前的《淮南子》已经把昆仑说成是追求不死的最终选择：“昆仑之丘，或上倍之，是谓凉风之山，登之而不死。或上倍之，是谓悬圃，登之乃灵，能使风雨。或上倍之，乃维上天，登之乃神。”该书还说西王母在“流沙之滨”居住，可能位于戈壁滩的西端。[219] 武帝的宫廷诗人司马相如这样地描写了这个女神的魅力：

> 低徊阴山翔以迂曲兮，吾乃今日睹西王母，暠然白首戴胜而穴处兮……[220]

颇有意味的是，这位西方女神在这首诗里被说成是“穴处”(住在山洞里，或者是被供奉于山洞里?)。这个说法可以和《汉书·地理志》中的一段记载对读：“西北至塞外，有西王母石室。”[221] 与传统中国神祇总是被供在木构的庙观中不同，这个远在中国疆域之外的西方仙人似乎和别有异趣的石构建筑有着特殊的关系。

Since immortality might be achieved either during one's lifetime or after one's death, both living people and departed souls could find hope in the Queen Mother and in the West, and structures dedicated to both the goddess and the deceased could be made of stone. Emperor Wu built the Jianzhang Palace—a replica of the Heavenly Court—west of Chang'an. The same emperor also located his mausoleum, quite unconventionally, in a spot directly west of the capital city. Is it possible that the belief in a western paradise determined the sites of both structures? Stone sculptures have been found in the graveyard of General Huo Qubing (140-117 B.C.), a chief commander in Emperor Wu's western expeditionary army. Based on a textual record, scholars commonly believe that this tomb, one of the many satellite burials attached to Emperor Wu's mausoleum, was built to resemble Mount Qilian on the northwest Chinese border. The existing tumulus above Huo's grave, however, is no different from other Han tumuli (Fig. 2.42a). The only unusual feature of this burial is a group of fourteen stone sculptures including the famous "horse trampling a barbarian" (Fig. 2.42b).[222] Standing in Huo's graveyard and covering the tomb mound, these unusual statues must have served a double role: their vivid images reminded people of the general's contribution to the western expansion of the Han empire, yet these images were frozen in stone, an "eternal" material belonging to the "western world" of immortality and death.

Four years after Huo Qubing's death in 117 B.C., Liu Sheng, Prince Jing of Zhongshan, was buried in a rock-cut tomb at Mancheng (Mancheng Tomb no. 1), in present-day Hebei. Other Western Han cave burials found in recent years include the tomb of Liu Sheng's wife Dou Wan (Mancheng Tomb no. 2), a group of five tombs at Jiulongshan near Qufu in Shandong (probably belonging to princes of the Lu principality), and four others near Xuzhou in Jiangsu that have been identified as mausoleums of the princes of Chu.[223] These examples, all dating from the late second century to the first century B.C., demonstrate the popularity of rock-cut tombs among members of the royal family during this period.

The two Mancheng tombs are not the largest in the group (the burial at Beidongshan near Xuzhou, for example, is far grander and consists of a 55-meter-long passageway and nineteen chambers covering an area of 350 square meters; Fig. 2.43), but they are the only ones to have escaped grave robbers. Their dates and occupants can be precisely identified, and their excavations have been thoroughly reported.[224] These factors make these two tombs the best examples for studying Western Han rock-cut burials.

由于升仙可以在人的有生之年或死后实现，活着的人和亡者的灵魂都可以从西方和西王母那里得到希望，因此献给这位女神和死者的建筑也都常常用石头来建造。武帝把模仿天宫的建章宫建在了长安的西边，同时也一反常例地将自己的陵址选在都城的正西。是否有可能是他对西方仙界的信仰决定了这两处建筑的位置呢？汉武帝西征大军的将军霍去病（前 140 —前 117 年）的墓地以其石雕作品著称，学者们根据文献记载普遍相信，这座附栋于武帝陵的墓葬是仿照西北边陲的祁连山而建的。然而，霍去病墓上现存的冢丘与其他汉墓并无明显区别［图 2.42a］，其与众不同的特征是包含著名的“马踏匈奴”在内的 14 件石雕［图 2.42b］。[222] 这些伫立于陵园内或覆盖于墓丘上的非同寻常的雕塑想必曾经担负了双重的角色：它们栩栩如生的形象纪念着当年骠骑大将军霍去病对汉帝国西部拓展的贡献，同时这些形象被凝固在石头里——一种与死亡、不朽以及西方有关的“永恒”材料。

霍去病去世四年之后，中山靖王刘胜被埋葬在位于河北满城的一座崖墓中（满城 1 号汉墓）。近年其他一些西汉崖墓也被陆续发现，其中包括刘胜妻窦绾墓（满城 2 号墓）、山东曲阜九龙山的五座墓（可能属于几代鲁王）和被确定为楚王陵的江苏徐州附近的四座墓。[223] 这些墓葬的年代全都在公元前 2 世纪末至公元前 1 世纪之间，表明这段时期内崖墓在王室成员的中间十分流行。满城的两座崖墓并不是最大的（如徐州北洞山汉墓就大得多，由一个 55 米长的墓道和 19 个墓室构成，占地面积达 350 平方米，［图 2.43］），但它们是唯一没有被盗扰过的这类墓葬，墓葬年代和墓主人身份明确，而且已经出版了发掘报告。[224] 这些特点使得两座墓葬成为研究西汉崖墓的最佳例证。

a

b

Fig. 2.42. (a) Tomb of Huo Qubing at Xingping, Shaanxi province. Western Han. 117 B.C. (b) "Horse trampling a barbarian." Stone statue at Huo Qubing's tomb. H. 168 cm. L. 190 cm.

图 2.42 （a）霍去病墓。陕西兴平。西汉，公元前 117 年。（b）霍去病墓前石雕"马踏匈奴"。高 168 厘米，长 190 厘米。

An often neglected feature of the Mancheng tombs is their site. A
131 topographical map of the area shows that two small hills, like two pillars of a gate, flanked the entrance to the burial ground on Lingshan (the Hill of Spirits). This design recalls Sima Qian's description of the First Emperor's magnificent Epang Palace, which was situated so that "the peaks of southern mountains formed its pillar gate."[225] At Mancheng, the ritual path running east-west through the "mountain gate" extended into the tomb passages, which again led to the underground palaces of Liu Sheng and his wife. At the end of each passage, a vestibule was flanked by two long side chambers (Figs. 2.44a, b). In Liu Sheng's tomb, the chamber on the right (if we assume a position facing inward) was filled with hundreds of jars and large cases containing goods of the sort found in a royal household. The opposite chamber held a tile-roofed and wooden-framed building; four chariots, along with skeletons of eleven horses, were found inside. Apparently this left chamber was supposed to be a royal stable; the right one, a storage room.

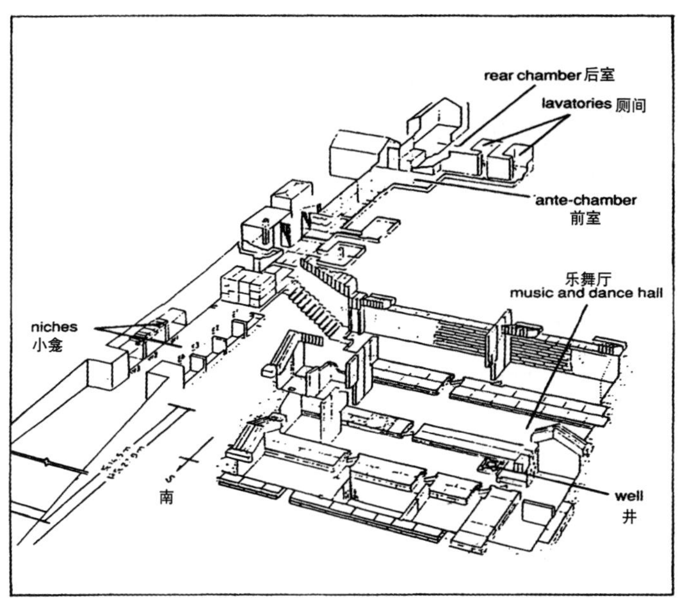

Fig. 2.43. A large Western Han rock-cut tomb at Beidongshan, Xuzhou, Jiangsu province. 2nd century B.C.

图 2.43　江苏徐州北洞山大型崖墓。西汉，前 2 世纪。

研究满城汉墓时经常被忽略的是两墓的位置。墓葬所在区域的地形图显示出两个小山峰如一对门阙，夹峙于通往墓地灵山的入口两侧。这一设计令人想起司马迁对秦始皇宏丽的阿房宫的描述："表南山之颠以为阙。"[225] 在满城，墓葬神道自东而西穿过"山门"通向两墓墓道，再通向刘胜夫妇的地下宫殿，两墓墓道尾端的甬道两旁皆附有一对狭长的耳室［图 2.44］。刘胜墓中，右耳室（假定我们面向墓内）摆满了上百件陶缸和装有王室用物品的大箱子，明显模拟一个库房。对面的左耳室内原有一覆有瓦顶的木构建筑，其中排列着 4 驾马车和 11 具马骨架，显然是模拟王室的马厩。

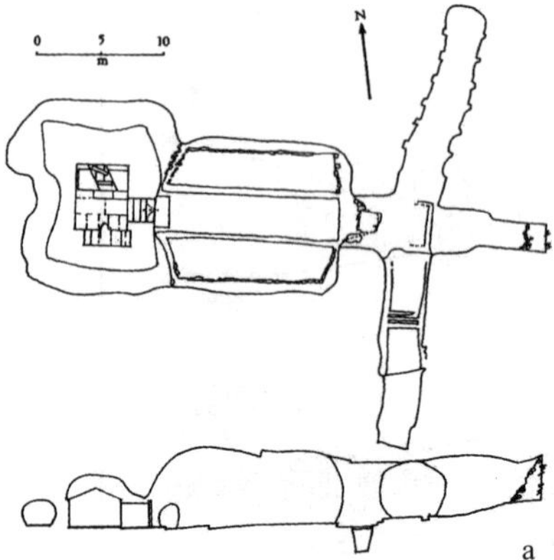

Fig. 2.44. (a) Plan of Liu Sheng's tomb (Tomb no. 1) at Mancheng, Hebei province. Western Han. 113 B.C. (b) Cutaway view showing a tentative reconstruction of Liu Sheng's tomb.

图 2.44 （a）河北满城刘胜墓（1 号墓）（平面与立面图）。西汉，前 113 年。（b）刘胜墓墓内结构复原示意图。

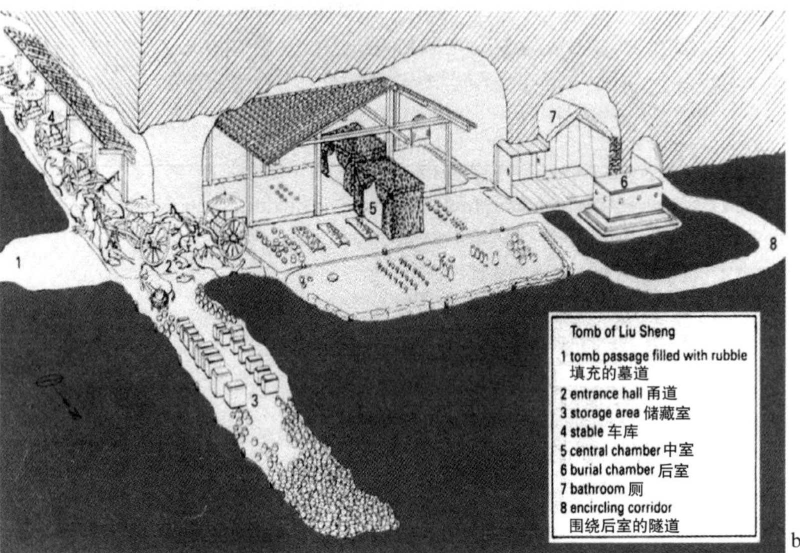

132 Behind the vestibule was a grand cave (Fig. 2.45) that originally contained another wooden-framed structure. Like the stable, it had collapsed long before the excavation; only roof tiles and metal joints scattered on the ground allowed the excavators to speculate on its original form. Inside this building, two seats were originally placed inside two separate wooden-structures covered with silk (Fig. 2.46a). Sacrificial vessels, lamps, incense burners, and figurines were lined up in rows in front of as well as beside the central seat (Fig. 2.44b). A group

Fig. 2.45. The main chamber in Liu Sheng's tomb

图 2.45 刘胜墓中室

of smaller drinking vessels, a miniature chariot, and as many as 2,034 bronze coins, were placed behind this seat and before a thick stone gate that blocked the entrance to the rear chamber—the private space of the deceased prince. This chamber, the last free-standing structure built

甬道的背后是一个宽大的洞穴［图 2.45］，其中原来亦有木构建筑，但与马厩中的木构建筑一样，这一建筑早在发掘前很久就坍塌了，只有散落在地面上的瓦片和金属构件使发掘者可以大略猜测到原来的形式。这个建筑中设有两个座位，原本以丝织帷帐覆盖［图 2.46a］。容器、灯盏、博山炉和俑成排地陈列在中央座位的前方和近旁［图 2.44b］。这个座位的背后，陈列着一组小型器具、车马模型和 2034 枚钱币。再接其后，就是入口有一厚重石门封堵的后室——已故中山靖王刘胜的私人空间。这个后室，是墓中最后一

inside the tomb, housed the corpse dressed in a jade suit. Unlike the stable, the central hall and covered seats, however, it was made of stone, not of wood and tiles (Fig. 2.46b). Four stone figurines, two male and two female, guarded the stone rear chamber, whereas eighteen of the nineteen figurines found in the wooden-framed central chamber were made of clay. All these features indicate the symbolism of the divergent media.
133 There is no doubt that the builders selected different materials for various sections of the tomb: wood and clay suited the front section, which mirrored a "living" household, while the stone chamber and figurines in the rear section constituted the eternal world of the dead.

Two other features of the Mancheng tombs are noteworthy. First, the builders seem to have been carpenters with little knowledge of masonry techniques. In constructing the burial chambers, they first cut and polished stone into thin, narrow panels that resembled wooden boards, and they may have also built a timber frame to support these panels and fix them in their assigned positions.[226] Second, a circular tunnel in Liu Sheng's tomb surrounded the rear burial chamber (Figs. 2.44a, 47a). In an attempt to explain this curious design, the excavators have tentatively suggested that the tunnel may have functioned as a "drainpipe" to protect the rear chamber from underground water.[227] This interpretation is not convincing because the tunnel is not connected with the rear chamber but opens to the central sacrificial hall, and because its scale is far beyond what would be required for drainage. About two meters tall and with an arched ceiling, it was more likely constructed to allow worshippers to walk around the burial chamber. A prototype of this architectural device may be found in an Indian rock-cut temple dating from the mid-second century B.C., in which a stone stupa, the symbol of the Buddha's Nirvana and relics, stood at the rear end of a ceremonial hall and was surrounded by a passageway for the rite of circumambulation (Fig. 2.47b). If this hypothesis contains any truth, the builders of the Mancheng tomb must have thought the stupa was a burial device and replicated its features in Liu Sheng's stone chamber. A Buddhist holy symbol was thus "transplanted" into a Chinese funerary context.

The second and first centuries B.C. were a transitional period, during which the Chinese may have heard about Buddhism and become aware of certain western religious art and architectural forms—possibly rock-cut temples and stone carvings.[228] This knowledge may have contributed to

个搭构了建筑的空间，其内停放着裹以玉衣的尸体。然而，不同于马厩，也不同于主室和上盖帷帐的座位，后室中的建筑既不是木的也不是陶的，而是石头做成的［图 2.46b］。这种差别绝非偶然，因为我们发现在木材建构的中室所出土的 19 个俑中，有 18 个是陶做的，但后室中的两男两女 4 个俑却全部为石质。因此毫无疑问，建筑师在修建该墓不同的部分时，有意采用了不同的材料：木与陶用于包括中厅、马厩和库房在内的前半部，石材用于后面的棺室。

满城汉墓还有两个特征值得注意。其一，建造后室中石屋的人显然是木匠，他们对各种木工活很熟悉，对石工的技术却知之甚少。在建造这个石屋时，他们先把石材切割打磨成又薄又窄的石板，就像一块块木板一样，或许还搭建过木框架来支撑和固定这些石板。[226]其二，刘胜墓后室周围有一环形隧道［图 2.44a，图 2.47a］。发掘者初步推测，这一奇怪的设计可能是为了解决后室的"排水"防潮问题。[227]但这一解释难以令人信服，因为隧道与后室并不相通，而是开口在中央的大厅中，而且隧道的规模也过大，远远超出了排水道的需要。这个隧道约 2 米高，顶部为拱形，它为坚硬的岩石所环绕，更像是为了祭拜者绕室步行而设计的。我们在印度早期石窟寺中见到相似的建筑设计，其中象征着佛舍利的石雕窣堵坡矗立在礼拜堂的后部，周围环绕着供绕塔礼拜所用的通道［图 2.47b］。如果这一假设能够反映一些真实情况的话，那么满城墓的建造者想必曾将窣堵坡误解为一种埋葬方式，并以刘胜的棺室来代替它。这样，一种佛教的神圣符号就被"移植"到中国的丧葬文化背景当中了。

公元前 2 世纪至公元前 1 世纪是一个中国宗教和宗教艺术的转型时期。这个时期的汉代人对佛教已经有所闻，并开始注意某些西方宗教艺术与建筑的样式——石窟与石雕是其中可能的两项。[228]

the creation of rock-cut tombs and stone sculptures in China. A century later, stone was used extensively not only for burial chambers but also for aboveground mortuary monuments, and Buddhist motifs were employed freely in decorating funerary structures. Both developments were strongly encouraged by Emperor Ming who, as noted in the previous section, was also responsible for the final establishment of the tomb district as the most important center of ancestor worship. It is said that this emperor's mausoleum, which was constructed before A.D. 71, contained a "stone palace" (*shidian*),[229] that his tomb bore images of the stupa and the Buddha,[230] and that his dispatch of an envoy to seek Buddhism in India marked the beginning of the official introduction of Buddhism to China.

The mortuary hall of Emperor Ming initiated a series of stone offering shrines (see Fig. 4.4).[231] Stone pillar-gates also appeared in the first century and soon became popular (Fig. 4.2).[232] Also around the same time, stelae bearing commemorative texts began to be made of stone
134 (Fig. 4.5).[233] Stone mortuary statues in animal and human forms, which were extremely rare during the Western Han, now became abundant.[234] The tradition of rock-cut tombs survived in the southwestern part of the country (Figs. 2.48a, b); with an open vestibule and attached cells, their design resembled an Indian vihāra cave (Fig. 2.47b).[235] During the Eastern Han, aboveground stone structures and rock-cut burials were distributed in two distinctive regions: the area stretching from the capital Luoyang to the Shandong-Jiangsu border, and the Sichuan Basin. Not coincidentally, these two regions were also under the strongest Buddhist influence. In Luoyang, Emperor Ming established the first Buddhist temple.[236] His favoritism toward the foreign religion was probably related to the activities of Liu Ying, the prince of Chu, who "observed fasting and performed sacrifices to the Buddha" around the same time.[237] These records have led Erik Zürcher to propose that "around the middle of the
135 first century A.D. Buddhism appears already to have penetrated into the region north of the Huai River, in eastern Henan, southern Shandong and

northern Jiangsu," and that Pengcheng, the seat of the Chu principality, "was situated on the high-way from Luoyang to the South-East which actually formed an eastern extension to the continental silk-route by which foreigners from the West used to arrive."[238]

这种知识或许对汉代艺术中的崖墓与石雕的产生做出了贡献。一个世纪之后，石头在东汉宗教建筑和艺术中的使用已经非常广泛，不仅用来建墓室，也用来构筑地上的丧葬纪念建筑。同时，一些佛教题材也被随意地用来充当丧葬建筑的装饰。这两方面的发展都得益于汉明帝的大力支持。正如我在本章上节中提到的那样，墓地作为祖先崇拜中心的最终确立即与这位皇帝有关。据文献记载，他建于公元 71 年以前的陵墓包括一个“石殿”，[229] 还装饰着佛和佛塔的形象。[230] 此外，他遣使往印度求佛法的事迹标志着佛教通过官方渠道传入中国的开始。

明帝陵墓中的石殿引发了此后的一系列墓葬石构建筑［图 4.4］,[231] 石阙也出现于 1 世纪并迅速得到流行［图 4.2］。[232] 大约在同一时期，刻有纪念性铭文的石碑也应运而生［图 4.5］。[233] 西汉时期罕见的石制丧葬人像和动物像，这时也开始兴盛。[234] 西汉崖墓的传统在西南地区被保存了下来［图 2.48a，b］，其设计往往带有一个开敞的门厅和若干附带墓室的甬道，建筑概念与印度的摩诃罗式石窟不无相似之处［图 2.47b］。[235] 东汉时期，地上石建筑和崖墓集中分布在两个地区，一个是从都城洛阳向东延伸到山东与江苏交界的地区，另一个是四川盆地。并非巧合的是，这两个区域也正是受佛教影响最深的地方。在洛阳，明帝建立了中国历史上的第一座佛教寺院。[236] 他对这个异域宗教的偏爱或许可以与同时期的楚王刘英“学为浮屠，斋戒祭祀”关联起来。[237] 根据这些记载，许理和提出“在东汉，佛教似乎在公元 1 世纪中叶前后就已经渗透到淮河北部，即山东南部与江苏北部地区”。他进而认为，楚国所在地彭城“位于洛阳通往东南道路的要冲，这条道路实际构成了传载西方人来中国的丝绸之路向东部的延伸。”[238]

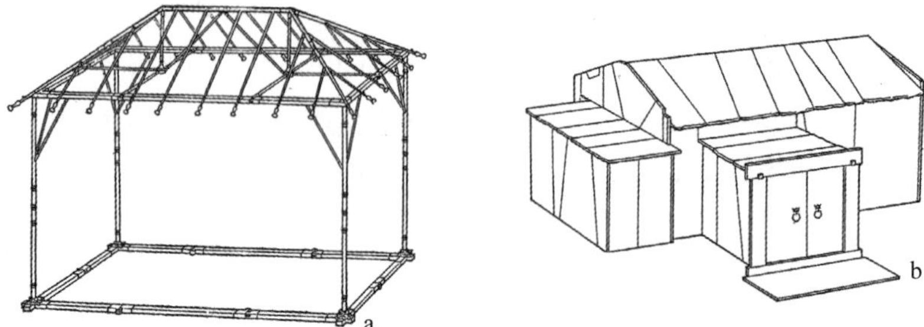

Fig. 2.46. (a) Reconstruction of a wooden structure inside the main chamber in Liu Sheng's tomb. (b) The stone rear chamber in Liu Sheng's tomb.

图 2.46 （a）刘胜墓中室帷帐复原图。（b）刘胜墓后室石屋复原图。

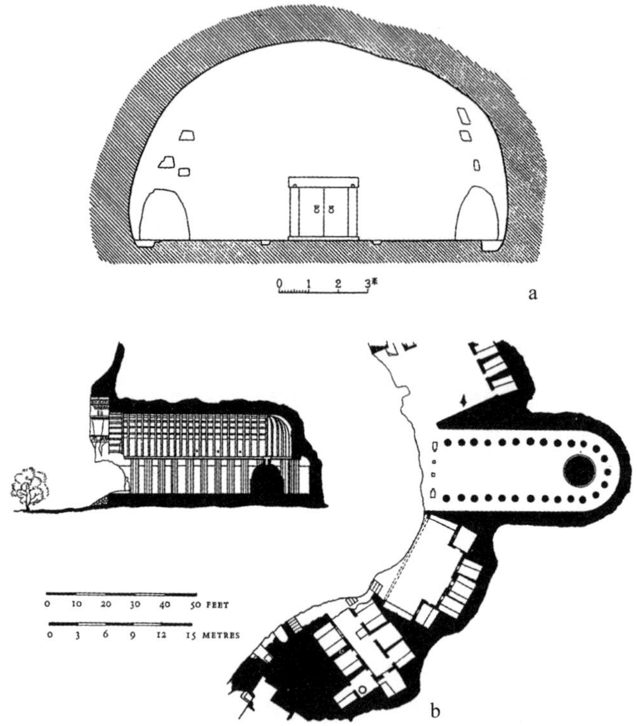

Fig. 2.47. (a) Cross section of Liu Sheng's tomb, showing the entrances to the tunnel and the burial chamber. (b) Plan of the assembly hall and meditation caves at Vat Bhājā, India. 2nd century B.C.

图 2.47 （a）刘胜墓横剖面图，从中可见隧道口与后室石门。（b）印度巴雅塔庙窟剖面图与僧房、塔庙窟平面图。前 2 世纪。

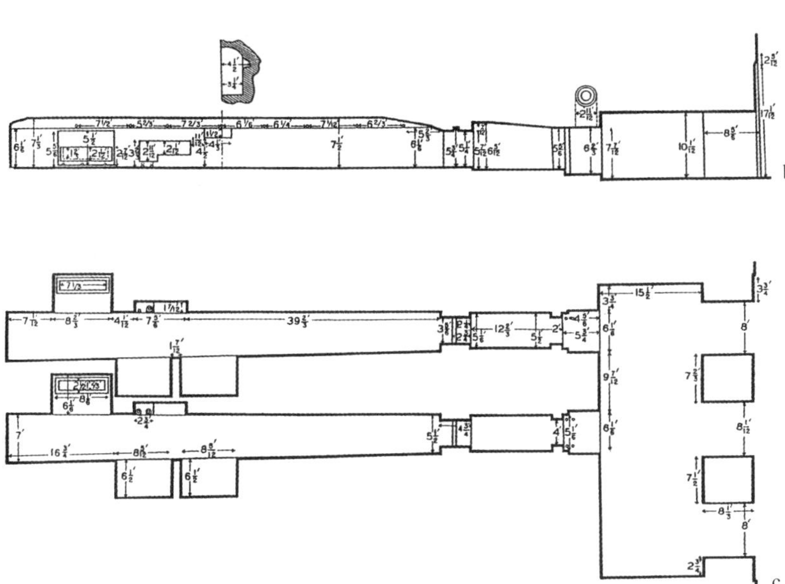

Fig. 2.48. Mahao Cave-Tomb no. 1. Leshan, Sichuan province. Late Eastern Han. 2nd century A.D. (a) Facade. (b) Plan.

图 2.48 四川乐山麻浩 1 号崖墓。东汉晚期，公元 2 世纪。(a) 遗址照片。(b) 剖面图。(c) 平面图。

The Buddhist center in the Luoyang-Pengcheng region continued to develop during the second century. The arrival in 148 of a Parthian missionary, An Shigao, marked the beginning of what has been called "the Buddhist church" at Luoyang;[239] and Emperor Huan (r. 147-67) offered sacrifices to the Yellow Emperor, Laozi, and the Buddha for the sake of peace and prosperity.[240] In the Shandong-Jiangsu area, Xiang Kai from Shiyin submitted a memorial to the throne in 166 in which he quoted a Buddhist script;[241] and in Pengcheng, the notorious warlord Zha Rong erected a large Buddhist temple, made a statue of the Buddha, and held extraordinary ceremonies toward the end of the second century.[242] As for Sichuan, it came under the dominance of religious Daoism during the second century; as I have argued elsewhere, the early Daoist canon and pantheon derived many elements from Buddhist tales and iconography.[243] It is also possible that a route directly linked this southwestern province with the Indian world—a hypothesis supported by both textual sources and artworks that most closely imitated Indian images.[244]

While freely combining Buddhist concepts with Daoist beliefs, the Eastern Han Chinese intensified the practice of absorbing Buddhist motifs into their mortuary art and architecture. This phenomenon was again most visible in the two regions centered on Luoyang-Pengcheng and Sichuan. The connection between stupa worship and funerary practices, only hinted at by the design of Liu Sheng's tomb, became explicit. It is said that a stupa was established (or depicted) in Emperor Ming's graveyard in Luo yang.[245] Whereas this record comes from a later text and is thus open to suspicion, a remarkable scene engraved on one
136 of the famous Wu family shrines in Shandong illustrates two winged figures worshipping a building that looks like a broad-based bottle, with a flying immortal and a bird hovering over it (Fig. 2.49). A comparison of this scene and those of stupa worship in Sānchi and Bhārhut (Fig. 2.50) reveals many similarities in composition, in the basic shape of the central structure, and in the flanked worshippers and celestial beings. A picture

on another shrine portrays a man, possibly the famous filial paragon Yan Wu, kneeling before his father's tomb, a hemisphere on which a vertical shaft supports an umbrella-shaped ornament (Fig. 2.51). The resemblance of this architectural form to an Indian stupa is beyond doubt. What we find here are two interrelated aspects of the stupa in Eastern Han

洛阳至彭城地区的佛教中心在2世纪持续发展。148年安息僧人安世高的到来标志着"佛教教会"在首都洛阳的出现。[239]桓帝（在位时间为147—167年）为祈求平安与繁荣而继续供祭黄帝、老子和佛。[240]至于山东、江苏一带，隰阴人襄楷在公元166年向皇帝呈交的一份奏章中引述了佛经中的文字；[241]在接近2世纪末的时候，声名狼藉的军阀笮融还在彭城修建了一座很大的佛寺，于寺中置佛像，并举行大规模的礼拜仪式。[242]西南地区的四川在2世纪期间被道教所控制。我在另文中曾经讨论了早期道教经典与所崇奉的神灵从佛教传说与圣像系统中汲取的因素。[243]当时可能曾有一条道路将这个西南省份与印度世界直接连在一起——一些文献资料和对印度图像的忠实仿制品为这种可能性提供了证据。[244]

随着佛教观念与道教信仰的自由结合，东汉人在丧葬艺术与建筑的实践活动中强化了对佛教题材的吸收。这一现象再次突出地反映在以洛阳至彭城和四川为中心的两个地区。刘胜墓所暗示的绕塔崇拜与葬俗之间的联系在此时变得显而易见：据说位于洛阳的明帝陵园里就曾建过（或刻画过）一个佛塔。[245]尽管这一记载因出自较晚的文献而不可尽信，但刻在山东武氏祠中的一幅画面十分值得重视。这幅画面描绘了两个有翼的仙人正在膜拜一个瓶状的建筑物，另一飞仙和一只鸟盘旋其上［图2.49］。将这幅画面与在桑奇大塔和巴尔胡特等印度著名佛教遗址发现的拜塔画面［图2.50］做一对照，我们可以清楚地看到二者在构图、中央建筑的基本造型以及拜塔人物等方面的许多相似。一幅东汉祠堂上的画像描绘的可能是颜乌的故事，画中这位孝子跪在父亲的墓前，墓作半圆形，上有竖杆顶着一个伞状装饰物［图2.51］，其建筑形式与印度佛塔极为类似。这里我们所看到的是"佛塔"在东汉丧葬艺术中两方面的意义：

Fig. 2.49. Worshipping the "stupa." Stone carving on the Left Wu Family Shrine at Jiaxiang, Shandong province. Late Eastern Han. 2nd half of the 2nd century A.D. Ink rubbing.

图 2.49 拜"塔"。山东嘉祥武氏祠左石室画像。东汉末，公元 2 世纪后半叶。拓本。

Fig. 2.50. Worshipping the stupa. Stone carving. 2nd century A.D. Bhārhut. Freer Gallery of Art, Washington, D.C.

图 2.50 拜塔。石刻。2 世纪。出自巴尔胡特。华盛顿，弗利尔美术馆藏。

thought: the first picture reflects the (mis)understanding of stupa worship as a kind of immortality cult; the second demonstrates the influence of such worship on Chinese funerary practices.

These examples help us recognize a central characteristic of the early introduction of Buddhism to China: this foreign religion could be accepted because it was largely and willingly misinterpreted. Such misinterpretation is most clearly revealed by the Chinese perception and descriptions of the Buddha. *The Sutra in Forty-two Sections* (*Sishier zhang jing*) records events surrounding Emperor Ming's introduction of

Buddhism: one night in a dream the emperor saw a golden deity flying into his palace and emanating sunlight from the neck. The next day he asked his ministers to identify the image. One of them, Fu Yi, replied that he had heard of a sage in India called "the Buddha," who had attained salvation, was able to fly, and whose body was of a golden hue.[246] Inspired by this report, the emperor sent envoys to seek Buddhism. After they brought back Buddhist scriptures and images, "everyone from the Son of Heaven to the princes and nobles became devotees; they were all attracted by the teaching that *one's spirit did not vanish after death*."[247]

Other early Chinese descriptions of the Buddha were written in a similar vein. According to the *Record of the Latter Han* (*Hou Han ji*), "The Buddha is sixteen feet in height, golden in color, and wears light from the sun and moon on his neck. He can assume countless forms and enter anything at will. Thus, he is able to communicate with a myriad things and help people."[248] The description in Mouzi's *Disputation of Confusion* (*Lihuo lun*) is more detailed:

第一个画面反映了人们把对佛塔的礼拜理解（或误解）为对成仙不死的崇拜；第二个画面表明佛塔这一形式对中国丧葬建筑的影响。

这些例子帮助我们认识到佛教初传到中国时的一个主要特征：这种外来宗教能够被接受，是因为它在很大程度上被自然地曲解了。这一曲解最清楚地表现在汉代人对佛的理解和描述中。《四十二章经》记载了明帝引进佛教的起因：一天夜里他梦见一个金人飞入宫中，其头颈发射着太阳的光芒。第二天他向大臣们询问这个金人的身份来历，一个名叫傅毅的大臣回答说，他曾听说印度有个被称作"佛"的圣人，已入不死的境界，能够飞翔，而且身体是金色的。[246]明帝于是遣使到印度去求佛法。当归来的使者带回佛教的经像之后，"自天子王侯咸敬事之。闻人死精神不灭。莫不惧然自失"。[247]

其他早期中文文献对佛的描述也表现出类似的理解。据《后汉纪》，"佛高十六尺，金色，项戴日月之光，可呈无尽之形，入一切愿中之事，故能通万物而助人伦。"[248] 牟子《理惑论》中的描述更是详细：

137 > "Buddha" is a posthumous title, in the same way that "divine" [*shen*] is the title of the Three Sovereigns [Sanhuang], and that "sage" [*sheng*] is the title of the Five Emperors [Wudi]. The Buddha is the first ancestor of morality and divinity. His words are illuminating. The shape of the Buddha is unpredictable. He can assume endless manifestations. He can be concrete or elusive, large or small, round or square, old or young, emerge or disappear. He is unharmed when walking through fire, and uninjured when standing on a blade. In mud he cannot be tainted. His well-being is never spoiled or damaged by disaster. When he wishes to move, he flies; and when he sits, he emanates brilliant light. That is why he is called the Buddha.[249]

Only by understanding this specific meaning of the Buddha and Buddhism to people of the Eastern Han can we comprehend how they used Buddhist motifs in their art. First, almost all Eastern Han motifs of Buddhist origins appeared in funerary contexts.[250] These include a Buddha-like immortal riding a white elephant (Fig. 2.52), a six-tusked elephant (Fig. 2.53), immortals worshipping a lotus flower (Fig. 2.54), and immortals worshipping the stupa (Fig. 2.49).[251] Together with other immortality symbols, these foreign forms transformed a tomb or a shrine into a paradise for the deceased. Second, iconic images for portraying the Queen Mother of the West appeared in China in the first and second centuries (Figs. 2.55a, b). As I have discussed elsewhere, unlike the traditional Chinese "episodic composition," a frontal iconic image emphasizes a direct relationship between the icon and the viewer (or worshipper), and this new composition can be traced to the Indian imagery of the Buddha (Fig. 2.56).[252] Third, in a funerary context, images of the Queen Mother of the West and the Buddha are either juxtaposed or replace each another.[253] For example, two sides of an octagonal column in the Yi'nan tomb in Shandong bear the images of the Queen Mother of the West and her counterpart deity, the King Father of the East; Buddha-like figures with halos behind their heads occupy the other two main sides (Fig. 2.57). In Sichuan, Buddha images decorate not only tombs (Figs. 2.58a, b) but also a kind of funerary paraphernalia called a "money tree" (Figs. 2.59). In one instance the Buddha appears on a money tree base with dragons, a traditional Chinese symbol, beneath him (Fig. 2.60a); on another example, the Queen Mother is represented in a similar fashion, above an elephant-tending scene originating from India (Fig. 2.60b).

> 佛者，谥号也。犹名三皇"神"五帝"圣"也！佛乃道德之元祖，神明之宗。佛之言，觉也。恍惚变化，分身散体，或存或亡，能小能大，能圆能方，能老能少，能隐能彰。蹈火不烧，履刃不伤，在污不染，在祸无殃。欲行则飞，坐则扬光，故号为佛也。[249]

只有了解东汉人心目中的佛和佛教的这种特殊意义，我们才可能理解他们在艺术作品中使用佛教题材的方式。这些方式可以归纳为四点：首先，几乎所有东汉时期来源于佛教艺术的题材都出现在墓葬当中，[250] 其中包括仙人骑白象［图 2.52］、六牙象［图 2.53］、仙人拜莲花［图 2.54］、仙人拜塔［图 2.49］，等等。[251] 与其他象征长生不死的符号一道，这些外来图像把一座墓葬或祠堂转变成死者的天堂。其二，用于表现西王母的偶像式构图于 1 世纪至 2 世纪间在中国出现［图 2.55］。如我在另文中讨论的，不同于中国传统的"情节式构图"，正面的偶像式构图强调偶像与观者（或礼拜者）之间的直接联系。这种新型构图可以追溯到印度的佛像上［图 2.56］。[252] 其三，在墓葬的建筑环境中，西王母和佛的形象或相互并列或自由置换。[253] 例如山东沂南汉墓中的一个八角形立柱的主要两面上饰有西王母和她的配偶东王公的形象；带有头光的类佛形象则占据了另外两个主要面［图 2.57］。在四川，佛像不仅用来做墓葬的装饰［图 2.58］，而且还用来做随葬用的摇钱树的装饰［图 2.59］。有时佛像出现于摇钱树基座上，佛像下方伴有一对传统中国的象征符号——龙［图 2.60a］。有时以类似方式表现的西王母出现于源于印度的御象画面上方［图 2.60b］。

Fig. 2.51. Worshipping the dead in front of a tumulus. Stone carving. Late Eastern Han. 2nd half of the 2nd century A.D. W. 64 cm. Excavated in 1978 at Songshan, Jiaxiang, Shandong province. Ink rubbing.

图 2.51 冢前祭拜死者。画像石。东汉晚期，2 世纪后半叶。宽 64 厘米。1978 年山东嘉祥宋山出土。拓本。

Fourth and last, the distribution of these "Buddhist" motifs overlaps with that of stone monuments. In retrospect, we realize that in their search for a new art and architectural program, the Han Chinese eagerly
142 absorbed all the major ingredients of a foreign religious art, including its conventional media, composition, and motifs. But these foreign elements only served to enrich and reinforce indigenous Chinese culture. As a result, holy symbols of the Buddha were removed from public sanctuaries to be buried with the dead; and stone was given a particular meaning as a signifier of both longevity and immortality. A Han dynasty folk song goes: "No one is made of gold and stone; /How could one escape death?"[254] But when an entire graveyard has been turned into stone, this premise was reversed, as expressed in another folk song: "At death he has attained the way of holy immortals."[255] Based on this second belief, numerous Han dynasty stone structures, bas-reliefs, and sculptures were made and served as evidence for a new kind of creative energy and imagination in art. The Han "discovery" of stone was thus as significant as the "discovery" of jade in prehistoric times and the "discovery" of bronze in

the Three Dynasties—the consecutive employment of these three media changed the course of Chinese art history. Like the earlier art of *liqi*, Han stone monuments were part of their creators' social and religious lives, providing foci for ritual performances and political activities, and documenting shared beliefs as well as specific concerns, ambitions, desires, and memories. But I will postpone discussion of such specific messages in funerary art until we study one of the most important ancient Chinese cities—the Han capital Chang'an.

其四，也是最后一点，这些“佛教”题材出现的地区刚好与石质纪念建筑的分布区域相吻合。回想一下，我们可以看到在寻求新的艺术与建筑程序的过程中，汉代人急切地吸取了域外宗教艺术的各种主要元素，包括媒介、构图与题材。但是这些外来元素仅仅起到了丰富和加强中国本土文化的作用，以致佛的神圣象征物被从公共崇拜场所中抽取了出来，与死人埋在了一起；而且石材也被赋予了象征长生和不死的特殊内涵。一首汉代民谣这样写道：“人生非金石，岂能长寿考？”[254] 可是当整个一座墓地都以石头制造时，这一前提就被人为地推翻了，就像另外一首民谣所表达的那样：“卒得神仙道，上与天相扶。”[255] 正是基于这第二种信念，大量的汉代石建筑与石雕刻被创造了出来，成为中国艺术中的一种新的创造力与想象力的见证。汉代对石头的“发现”因而也就具有了与史前时期玉的“发现”和三代时青铜的“发现”同样重大的意义——这三种材料的递接运用改变了古代中国美术史的发展路向。如早期的礼器艺术一样，汉代的石造纪念碑是其创造者社会生活与宗教生活的一个部分。它们为人们的礼仪和政治活动提供了焦点，存储了人们共同的信仰以及特殊的关怀、抱负、愿望与记忆。对于丧葬艺术中的这类特殊关怀和抱负的讨论，本书将在我们研究了中国古代最重要城市之一的西汉都城长安之后进行。

Fig. 2.52. Immortal riding a white elephant. Mural in the Helinge'er tomb, Inner Mongolia. Late Eastern Han. Late 2nd century A.D. Drawing.

图 2.52 仙人乘白象。内蒙古和林格尔墓壁画。东汉末，公元 2 世纪末。摹本。

Fig. 2.53. Six-tusked elephant. Stone carving. Late Eastern Han. 2nd half of the 2nd century A.D. From Tengxian, Shandong province.

图 2.53 六牙象。画像石。东汉晚期，2 世纪后半叶。山东滕县出土。

Fig. 2.54. Worshipping the lotus flower. Stone carving on the ceiling of the Wu Liang Shrine at Jiaxiang, Shandong province. A.D. 151. Reconstruction.

图 2.54 拜莲图。山东嘉祥武梁祠天顶画像。东汉，151 年。木板复制品。

a

b

Fig. 2.55. (a) The Queen Mother of the West on the magic mountain Kunlun. Stone carving. Late Eastern Han. 2nd half of the 2nd century A.D. W. 66 cm. Excavated in 1978 at Songshan, Jiaxiang, Shandong province. (b) The Queen Mother of the West and her court. Pictorial tile. Late Eastern Han. 2nd century A.D. Excavated from Qingbaixiang Tomb no. 1 at Xinfan, Chengdu, Sichuan province. Sichuan Provincial Museum.

图 2.55 （a）坐在昆仑山上的西王母。画像石。东汉晚期，2 世纪后半叶。宽 66 厘米。1978 年山东嘉祥宋山出土。（b）西王母及随从。画像砖。东汉晚期，2 世纪。四川新繁清白乡 1 号墓出土。四川省博物馆藏。

Fig. 2.56. The Buddha's first sermon. Kushan dynasty. Late 2nd century A.D. H. 67 cm. From Gandhara, Pakistan. Freer Gallery of Art, Washington, D.C.

图 2.56 佛于鹿野苑初转法轮。贵霜王朝，公元 2 世纪晚期。高 67 厘米。出自巴基斯坦犍陀罗。华盛顿，弗利尔美术馆藏。

Fig. 2.57. Carvings on the central column in the middle chamber of the Yi'nan tomb. Late Eastern Han. Late 2nd century—early 3rd century. Excavated in 1953 at Beizhai, Yi'nan, Shandong province. Drawing.

图 2.57 沂南汉墓中室石柱画像。东汉晚期，2 世纪末至 3 世纪初。1953 年山东沂南北寨村出土。线描。

a

b

Fig. 2.58. (a) Front chamber of Mahao Cave-Tomb no. 1. Leshan, Sichuan province. Eastern Han. 2nd century A.D. (b) The Buddha image in Mahao Cave-Tomb no. 1. H. 37 cm.

图 2.58 （a）四川乐山麻浩 1 号崖墓前室。东汉，2 世纪。（b）麻浩 1 号崖墓中的佛像。高 37 厘米。

Fig. 2.59. Fragment of a bronze "money tree" with a Buddha's image. Eastern Han. 2nd century A.D. Excavated from Hejiashan Cave-Tomb no. 1 at Mianyang, Sichuan province. Mianyang Museum.

图 2.59 带有佛像的青铜摇钱树残片。东汉，2 世纪。四川绵阳何家山 1 号崖墓出土。绵阳市博物馆藏。

a

b

Fig. 2.60. (a) Clay stand of a "money tree," decorated with a Buddha's image. Eastern Han. 2nd century A.D. H. 21 cm. Found at Pengshan, Sichuan province. Nanjing Museum. (b) Clay stand of a "money tree," decorated with the Queen Mother of the West on the upper register and with a procession of elephant chariots on the lower register. Eastern Han. 2nd century A.D. Excavated in 1974 at Santai, Sichuan province. Sichuan Provincial Museum.

图 2.60 （a）饰有佛像的摇钱树陶座。东汉，2 世纪。高 21 厘米。四川彭山出土。南京博物馆藏。（b）摇钱树陶座。基座上部装饰西王母形象，下部装饰象车出行队列。东汉，2 世纪。1974 年四川三台出土。四川省博物馆藏。

143 Withered orchids escort the departing statue along the Xianyang road:
If heaven too had passions even heaven would grow old.
With a plate in hands, the statue comes forth alone under the desolate moon:
The city on the Wei River far back now, quiet the waves.

These lines are from Li He's (790-816) famous "A Bronze Immortal Takes Leave of Han" ("Jintong xianren ci Han ge"), which recounts an event that occurred thirteen years after the Han's fall.[1] In 233, Emperor Ming of the Wei decided to transport a bronze immortal from Chang'an to his new capital at Ye. The statue, which Emperor Wu of the Han had erected in his palace, originally held a plate over its head to catch sweet dew. The plate was broken off in moving the statue. As the immortal was about to be loaded in a cart, tears gushed from the bronze figure's eyes.

Both the story and Li He's melancholy song reflect a later concept of monumentality—a particular sensibility toward ruins as physical remains of the past, whose fragmented and eroded appearance evoked poetic lamentation and artistic admiration. To people of the ninth century, the Han capital Chang'an (the "city on the Wei River") had receded far back into history and memory and was no longer comprehensible as a whole; it had dissolved into disconnected images and tales, told and retold in literature and art. Chang'an's attraction to Tang-Song antiquarians and romantic writers had little to do with its original significance during the Han.

But were there ever objective records, descriptions, representations, or reconstructions of Chang'an? Did the people of the Han share a uniform view of the city and hold the same idea about its history? If not, what were their views and ideas? These questions lead me to add a new dimension to my investigation of ancient Chinese monuments: in addition to interpreting their historical development and significance, I will also consider *discourses* on these monuments. Although focusing on a single object or phenomenon, different authors often had divergent understandings of and criteria for its monumentality; their approaches formed an important aspect of the ancient Chinese conception of monumentality. This is why this chapter focuses on Chang'an alone: this

叁 纪念碑式城市——长安

衰兰送客咸阳道，天若有情天亦老。
携盘独出月荒凉，渭城已远波声小。

这些诗句出自李贺（790 — 816）著名的《金铜仙人辞汉歌》。[1] 该诗叙述了汉灭亡 13 年后的一件事：公元 233 年，魏明帝决定将一尊青铜仙人像从长安运送到其新都邺城。这尊雕像原树立于汉武帝的宫殿中，双手擎盘，高举过顶，以承甘露。承露盘在运送时断裂了。当要被装上车时，仙人的泪水夺眶而出。

这个故事和李贺哀婉的诗篇反映了纪念碑性一个晚期的概念——对于废墟的一种特殊的敏感。废墟是历史的物质性遗存。那些残砖断瓦、败土颓垣往往激发起诗人的嗟叹和艺术家的赏赞。对于 9 世纪的人来说，汉代的长安（渭河上“已远”的一座古城）已经后退到历史和记忆的深处，人们再也不能从整体上把握这座城市。它已破碎为难以拼接的影像和故事，在文学和艺术中被一次次地复述和再复述。唐宋时代的古物学家和浪漫的文学家们固然对于长安的过去十分迷恋，可是这种迷恋已与这座城市在汉代原有的意义没有多少关系。

但是，是不是曾经存在过“客观的”对长安的记录、描述、表现或重构呢？是否汉代人对于这座城市持有一致的看法？对它的历史有着同样的观念？如果他们并不具有这种统一的看法和观念的话，那么各自的观点和想法又是什么？这些问题使我们在探索古代中国的纪念碑时加进一个新的维度：除了说明其历史性的演化和意义，还要考虑到关于纪念碑的各种论述。即使面对同一事物或现象，不同的作者常常会有着对于纪念碑性的不同理解，其判断的标准也会不尽相同；他们不同的思想和论述方法构成了古代中国纪念碑性概念的一个重要维度。这就是本章为什么以长安作为讨论的专题：

Western Han capital was the first large Chinese city whose historical development and physical form can be approximately reconstructed, and whose significance as a "monumental city" ancient writers openly debated.

❶ Two Views of Chang'an

144 The history of Western Han Chang'an began in 202 B.C. when the dynasty's founder, Emperor Gaozu, established his capital in the Wei River valley in present-day southern Shaanxi. It ended in A.D. 25, when "several hundred thousands of its residents had died of hunger; the city itself had become a vast deserted ruin; and most of its splendid temples and mausoleums had been destroyed and plundered." These haunting sentences conclude Ban Gu's *History of the Former Han*.[2]

But Chang'an would continue to fascinate people throughout the next two millennia. Numerous poems, eulogies, and memoirs would be written to commemorate its past glory and to lament its tragic destruction, and abundant field surveys and reconstruction plans would be conducted to trace its vanished image. The present chapter is one such reconstruction. The attempt of undertaking it naturally implies a certain dissatisfaction with previous efforts. Such dissatisfaction, however, should be understood in a historiographic sense, for, in Carl E. Schorske's words, "no man thinks of the city in hermetic isolation. He forms his image of it through a perceptual screen derived from inherited culture and transformed by personal experience."[3] Like previous reconstruction plans, the present one is not free from cultural and intellectual influences. But I hope that as a latecomer, I will have the privilege of pondering the premises and goals of earlier works, the various factors that have shaped an author's thinking, and the traditions and conventions that have both encouraged and restrained an attempt to depict the historical Chang'an.

Such a reflection helps clarify two alternative perspectives or positions in approaching this ancient city. In one view, Chang'an is a changing historical entity with specific causes for its birth, growth, and decay; the purpose of a reconstruction is to trace this process throughout the course of its development. In the other view, Chang'an is the sum of all its historical fragments and is often represented by its culminating stage; the observer tries to depict such an image and to interpret it

这座西汉都城是城市布局及其历史发展过程基本可以被复原的第一座中国都城，而它作为一座“纪念碑式城市”的意义也是古代作家们公开争论的焦点。

一、对长安的两种看法

西汉长安的历史开始于公元前 202 年，这一年，开国皇帝高祖建都于今天陕西南部的渭河谷地。该城的历史结束于公元 25 年，班固在《汉书》中以令人难以忘怀的句子记述了它的终结：“民饥饿相食，死者数十万，长安为虚，城中无人行。宗庙园陵皆发掘。”[2]

但是，长安仍然使人们继续颠倒沉醉了两千年，有无数诗篇、辞赋和追忆的文字纪念其逝去的荣耀，哀悼其悲惨的毁灭。人们在荒野中寻觅它的踪迹，希望重构它的原貌，追回其消逝了的形象。本章也属于这种重构工作，而再次重构的尝试自然包含着对于以往重构的不满足。这种不满足应该从史学史的意义上予以理解。正如舒尔斯克所云：“没有人能在与外界隔绝的情况下来观察一座城市。人们往往通过一道感性的帷幕来形成一座城市的影像，而这道帷幕即产生于被个人经验所转化了的传承性文化。”[3]如同以前的重构方案，本章中的讨论也无法脱离文化和知识的影响。但是我希望，作为一个后来者，我能有一种优势去深入思考前人研究的前提和目标，他们思想背后的各种因素，以及那些既激发又限制着对历史性长安进行描述的种种传统规范。

带着这种思考，我们可以区分出在研究这座古城时两种可选择性的基本观点或立场。一种观点认为，长安的诞生、成长、衰退有着特殊的原因，是一个变化中的历史性实体；重构这座城市的目的在于追踪其发展的全过程。另一种观点认为，长安是其所有历史片断的总和，并且常常在其最后的阶段呈现出来；观察者根据某种

according to some general cultural and ideological principles.[4] Indeed, these two views, both retrospective in nature, emerged in the Eastern Han from two paradigms for interpreting the past. The historian Ban Gu (A.D. 32-92) synthesized old memories of Chang'an into a narrative; the classicist Zhang Heng (A.D. 78-139) transformed Ban Gu's narrative into a still life. Their works, in fact their own remembrances of Chang'an, then became two major sources of later "historical" knowledge. These and other early writings were again fragmented, indexed, integrated, and recomposed into new reconstructions.

Ban Gu and Zhang Heng wrote their pieces in the style of *fu* or rhapsody, the principal poetic form of the Han, which was characterized by florid verbal display and ornamental rhetoric.[5] Ban Gu begins his *Western Capital Rhapsody* (*Xidu fu*) with a conversation between two fictional personages, one (Xidu Bin or the Western Capital Guest) representing the Western Han capital, Chang'an, and the other (Dongdu Zhuren or the Eastern Capital Host) standing for the Eastern Han capital, Luoyang:

The Western Capital Guest questions the Eastern Capital Host, "I have heard that when the great Han first made their plans and surveys, they had the intention of making the He-Luo area the capital. But they halted only briefly and did not settle there. Thus, they moved westward and founded our Supreme Capital. Have you heard of the reasons for this, and have you seen its manner of construction?" The Host said, "I have not. I wish you would

> Unfold your collected thoughts of past recollections,
> Disclose your hidden feelings of old remembrances;
> Broaden my understanding of the imperial way,
> Expand my knowledge of the Han metropolis."[6]

The opening speech of the Western Capital Guest concerns the most important episode in Chang'an's history, namely, the founding of this capital in the Wei River plain. Only because of this initial act could a great metropolis gradually appear in this region. It is said that before this

decision was reached, a heated debate took place within Emperor Gaozu's newly established court. Most of his ministers and generals preferred to locate the capital at Luoyang, the seat of the Eastern Zhou dynasty and
a place not far from Shandong, the homeland of the Liu royal lineage 145
as well as of themselves. For a while their opinion prevailed, and Gaozu held a temporary court at Luoyang until a foot soldier named Lou Jing

文化和思想的一般性原则来描述和解释这一综合形象。[4] 这两类观点的性质都是回顾性的，而且在东汉时期就已经出现了以这两种观念解释长安的范例。历史学家班固（32—92）将以往对长安的记忆综合为叙事性的文字；经学家张衡（78—139）则将班固的叙事转换为一种静态的描述。（虽然张衡以科学发明闻名于世，而且做过太史令；但他的知识根底是“诵《五经》，贯六艺”。）他们的作品实际上是其个人对于长安的回忆，但随即成为后来“历史性”知识的两个主要来源。他们的著作和另外一些早期文献在新的重构中被再次分割、索引、综合和改写。

班固和张衡作品的文体均为赋，这是汉代的一种重要文体，以文字绚丽、注重修辞见长。[5] 班固的《西都赋》以两位虚构人物的对话开篇，“西都宾”代表着西汉都城长安，“东都主人”则是东汉都城洛阳的化身：

> 有西都宾问于东都主人曰：“盖闻皇汉之初经营也，尝有意乎都河洛矣。辍而弗康，寔用西迁，作我上都。主人闻其故而睹其制乎？”主人曰：“未也。愿宾——
> 摅怀旧之蓄念，发思古之幽情。
> 博我以皇道，弘我以汉京。”[6]

西都宾的问题涉及长安历史中最重要的一个篇章，即汉高祖定都于渭河平原的史实。正是由于这一最初的行动，才使得长安这座大都市在这一地区逐渐建立起来。据说在这一决定做出之前，在高祖新建立的宫廷中曾经有过一番激烈的争论。大多数大臣和将军倾向于定都洛阳，这是东周都城的所在地，距离西汉皇族和他们自己的老家山东也比较近。当这一观点盛行时，高祖在洛阳建立了一个

(3rd-2nd centuries B.C.) forced his way into the palace and questioned the emperor to his face: "Your Majesty seems to have settled here—isn't it because you want to be considered as great as the Zhou lords?" When Gaozu admitted this, Lou Jing pointed out a crucial difference between the present dynasty and past dynasties that should determine the whereabouts of the emperor's throne: unlike the Zhou which prospered in peace over centuries, the Han had just gained power through military conquest and would have to secure its rule in the same manner. Chang'an's location and topography, according to Lou Jing, made it the single most important strategic point in China. He ended his argument with an analogy: "When you fight with a man, you have to grip his throat and strike him in the back before you can be sure of your victory. In the same way, if you will now enter the [Hangu] Pass and make your capital there, basing yourself upon the old land of Qin, you will in effect be gripping the throat and striking the back of the empire!" Supported by Gaozu's chief adviser Zhang Liang (?-189 B.C.), Lou Jing convinced the emperor. He rushed to Chang'an that day, and the 200-year-long history of the Supreme Capital began.[7]

The Western Capital Guest only alludes to this event, however, and his question—"Have you heard of the reasons for [the capital's location]?"—is not immediately answered. But Ban Gu's goal is achieved: by introducing his work with this question, he sets up a perceptual framework for the following description. He guides his readers—people of the Eastern Han represented by the Eastern Capital Host—straight back to the first day of the capital. All his later accounts of the city's environment, buildings, avenues, markets, and various activities are then presented as "past recollections" and "old remembrances"—*memories* of bygone scenes. The diachronic structure of his writing is further emphasized by his reminders of the city's chronology. Immediately after the introductory section, the poem describes Chang'an's environment and Gaozu's decision about the capital's location. The first major building to be introduced is the Weiyang Palace, which was also the first imperial hall constructed at the site. Then,

> Beginning with Emperor Gaozu and ending with Ping,
> Each generation added ornament, exalted beauty,
> Through a long succession of twelve reigns.
> Thus, did they carry extravagance to its limit, lavishness to its extreme.[8]

行宫。后来有一位名叫娄敬（前 3—前 2 世纪）的士兵设法见到高祖，劈头问道："陛下都洛阳，岂欲与周室比隆哉？"高祖承认了这一点。娄敬便指出，汉室与周室是很不相同的，因此需要认真考虑都城的位置：周人曾有几百年和平时期的繁荣，而汉室则刚刚通过军事征服取得天下，也必须依靠同样的手段来维护自己的政权。娄敬认为，长安的位置和地形使其成为四海之内最为重要的战略地点。他最后说："夫与人斗，不搤其肮，拊其背，未能全其胜也。今陛下入关而都，按秦之故地，此亦搤天下之肮而拊其背也。"在高祖的谋士张良（？—前 189 年）的支持下，娄敬说服了高祖。当天他便奔赴长安，这个大都市延续了 200 年的历史便由此开端。[7]

但是，西都宾只是间接暗示到这个事件，他对"主人闻其故……乎"这个问题并没有立即回答。可是班固的目的达到了：通过提出这个问题，他为作品以后的铺叙布置了一个感知的框架，引导他的读者——东都主人所代表的东汉人——追忆长安建都的起始。他的文章中的所有内容，包括长安的城市环境、建筑、市场以及各种活动，因此都呈现出"怀旧之蓄念"和"思古之幽情"——对已逝情景的回忆。这一历时性的结构被作品中对城市历史的叙述进一步强化。在序言之后，《西都赋》描述了长安的环境和高祖对都城位置的确定。首先介绍的主要建筑是未央宫，这也是城内第一个被建成的皇宫。接着，

> 肇自高而终平，世增饰以崇丽。
> 历十二之延祚，故穷泰而极侈。[8]

As if afraid that the rhapsody's typically florid language would blur Chang'an's historicity, here Ban Gu steps out and reminds his readers that the city began as a single palace compound, and layers of elaborations were added later. Only after this pause does he proceed to document Chang'an's walls, established by the second Han emperor, the subsequent appearance of "mausoleum towns" and the exciting life in these suburban cities, the expansion of the metropolis into Greater Chang'an, and the many new constructions by Emperor Wu, the fifth ruler of the dynasty, including the divine palace Jianzhang and the fantasy gardens of Shanglin. The last stanza of the rhapsody presents the final stage of this development; it is followed by a speech of the Western Capital Guest that echoes the poem's beginning and completes the perceptual frame of Ban Gu's narrative.

> At this time,
> It was city after city facing one to another;
> Village after village joined one after another.
> The kingdoms relied on a foundation of ten generations;
> The families received a heritage of a hundred years.
>
> . . .
>
> One such as I, having merely beheld the vestiges of old ruins and having heard these things from old men, do not know even one part in ten. Therefore, I cannot offer it to you in detail.[9]

This concluding speech seems to come straight from Ban Gu's mouth. The reader suddenly realizes that all the things the Western Capital Guest has so vividly described are no more than hearsay, and that the whole history of Chang'an narrated in the rhapsody is based on "the vestiges of
146 old ruins" and tales of old men. No one could have actually experienced and witnessed the whole course of Chang'an's development; the fictional Western Capital Guest is actually a personification of "memories" left by the city. It was Ban Gu who, based on the standard chronological structure of *shi* (historical writing), stitched together such fragmentary

memories into a coherent historical narrative. The result was his own remembrance of the destroyed city.

Ban Gu presented his rhapsody to the throne around A.D. 65. Some 40 years later, Zhang Heng composed a work on the same subject and in the same style and titled it the *Western Capital Rhapsody* (*Xijing fu*).[10] Such repetitions were deliberate; we are told that he "slighted and despised Ban Gu's work, and therefore wrote a new one to replace it."[11] This critical attitude must explain the entirely different structure of the

班固似乎担心赋体特有的华丽辞藻会弱化长安的史实性，因此他在这里暂时从迷离的文辞中脱出，以平直的叙述提醒读者该城是从一座宫殿开始的，然后踵事增华。尔后，他紧接着介绍了西汉第二代皇帝所修建的城墙，随后出现的"陵邑"，郊区城郭中活跃的社会生活，长安规模的扩展，以及第五代皇帝武帝所修建的神殿建章宫和皇家苑囿上林苑。赋的最后一节描述了长安建设的最后阶段，以西都宾的一段话呼应文章的起始，从而完成了叙事的框架。

> 于斯之时，都都相望，邑邑相属。国藉十世之基，家承百年之业……若臣者，徒观迹于旧墟，闻之乎故老。十分而未得其一端，故不能遍举也。[9]

这段结束语似乎是班固以自己的口吻说出的。读者突然意识到，西都宾那些鲜活的描写只不过是些传闻，赋中对于整个长安历史的叙述全部基于"观迹于旧墟""闻之乎故老"。并没有人能够真正地体验和证实长安发展的全过程；虚构的西都宾实际上是这座城市留下的"记忆"的化身。是作者班固按照史学标准的年代学结构，将零碎的记忆缀合成一个连续的历史性叙述，其结果是他自己对于这座已经消失的城市的回忆。

班固在公元 65 年将这篇赋进献给宫廷。大约 40 年后，张衡以同样的主题、同样的风格和题目写了一篇《西京赋》。[10] 这种重复是有意的：张衡对班固的《西都赋》"薄而陋之，故更造焉"。[11] 他的这种批评态度可以解释为何张衡给他的作品一个全然不同的结构。[12]

new composition.[12] Although the subject is still the same, Ban Gu's indications of Chang'an's historical growth are gone. Zhang Heng begins with a lengthy description of the city's auspicious location and geomancy. This place, according to him, was favored by Heaven and brought fortune to its occupants. The selection of Chang'an as the Han capital site was thus *predestined* by fate: only because of Heaven's guidance could the founder of the Han have settled in this precious land. Retold in this mystical atmosphere, even the foot soldier Lou Jing becomes an instrument of Heaven's will:

> Anciently, the Great Lord of Heaven was pleased with Duke Miu of Qin, invited him to court, and feted him with the "Great Music of Harmonious Heaven." The Lord, in ecstasy, made a golden tablet, and bestowed on him this land, which was situated under the Quail's Head. At this time, those powerful states who had combined together numbered six. But soon the entire empire came to live in unison under the western Qin. Is that not amazing?
>
> When Our Exalted Ancestor first entered the Pass, the planets of Five Wefts were in mutual accord and thereby lined up with the Eastern Well [the constellation Gemini]. When Lou Jing cast off his cart yoke, he offered a corrective criticism of the emperor's opinion. Heaven opened the founder's mind, and Man taught him the plan. When it came time for the emperor to make his plans, his mind also gave consideration to the spirit of Heaven and Earth, thus making certain it was right for him to establish Chang'an as the Celestial City.[13]

This idealistic approach sets up the basic tone for the whole rhapsody. Zhang Heng reorganizes Ban Gu's recollections of Chang'an's historical development into a new framework by categorizing them into isolated types, which he then describes in a hierarchical sequence: (1) the capital's boundary, (2) the palaces, (3) the walls and suburbs, (4) the imperial park and a hunting game. Described in highly ornate language, the hunting game supposedly held by the grandiose Emperor Wu finalizes Zhang Heng's vision of Chang'an as the epitome of extravagance. He thus contrasts Chang'an with the simpler capital of his own dynasty and praises his master, the Eastern Han emperor, at the end of his work:

> Just now our sage sovereign
> Being equal to Heaven, he is called Lord Radiance,
> He enfolds the Four Seas as his family.
> Of all rich heritages none is greater than ours.

尽管主题没有变化，但是班固对于长安发展史的历史性回顾完全消失了。张衡的赋起始于对这座城市吉祥的方位和占卜的一大段冗长的描述。根据他的说法，上天偏爱这一地区并佑护定都于此的人。因此选择长安为都，是天数注定的：只有在上天的指引下，汉朝的开创者才可定都于这块宝地。在这种神秘的氛围中，甚至士兵娄敬也变成了传达上天意愿的信使：

> 昔者大帝说秦缪公而觐之，飨以钧天广乐。帝有醉焉，乃为金策。锡用此土，而翦诸鹑首。是时也，并为强国者有六，然而四海同宅，西秦岂不诡哉？
>
> 自我高祖之始入也，五纬相汁，以旅于东井。娄敬委辂，干非其议。天启其心，人惎之谋。及帝图时，意亦有虑乎神祇。宜其可定以为天邑。[13]

这种理想主义的态度为整篇赋奠定了一个基调，张衡随即将班固对长安历史发展过程的记忆重新纳入一个新的构架。在这一架构中，他将长安的建设划分为几个孤立的类别，并按照等级次序进行了描述：（1）都城的界限，（2）宫殿，（3）城墙和郊区，（4）皇家苑囿和射猎区。他以华丽的辞藻描写好大喜功的汉武帝所举办的射猎活动，将其作为长安奢靡生活的缩影。由此，在作品结束时他便可以把奢华的长安和自己所属朝代的简朴国都做一对比，以称颂其主人东汉皇帝：

> 方今圣上同天，号于帝皇，掩四海而为家，富有之业，

I only regret that lavish beauty may not serve as the glory of the state.
But mere frugality to the point of niggling and piffling
Ignores what the "Cricket" song [from the Odes] says.
Do we want it but are unable?
Or are we able but do not want it?[14]

We can hardly find better examples of such radically different "accounts" of a city. In the ancient *fu* tradition, a conscious alteration in interpretation only implies the author's intellectual excellence. According to Ban Gu himself, a *fu* writer "is aroused by a circumstance and creates his theme. When his talent and wisdom are profound and excellent, it is possible to consult with him on state affairs."[15] The idea is that a "circumstance"—the stimulus of discourse—may be shared, but the discourse must reveal an author's distinctive "talent and wisdom." Applied to writings on Chang'an, this theory means that memories of this historical city must thus be constantly updated, and the past one
147 knows must be transformed into the past one thinks should have been.[16] The past must also gleam by the light of the present, and the constant re-editing of memories adjusts recollection to current needs.

In the two rhapsodies by Ban Gu and Zhang Heng, each author not only demonstrated his specific apprehension of history through a reflection upon the former capital but also aimed to constitute a different relationship between the past and present.[17] Ban Gu was a professional historian, and to him Chang'an had to be viewed as a dynamic process consisting of a sequence of historical events. Having grown up at the beginning of the Eastern Han, he wrote this work to remind the new ruler of "the old patterns" of the former dynasty.[18] Zhang Heng, on the other hand, was a learned scholar of *jing* or the Confucian classics, which provided his work with a basic model.[19] Instead of compiling chronicles, a writer belonging to this tradition discoursed on fundamental historical, political, and moral principles by interpreting the Classics left by ancient sages. Moreover, when Zhang Heng composed his rhapsody in the early second century, the question faced by the court had become how to sustain its rule. The former capital was no longer a historical issue, but a political and theological one, and its image and history had to be reformulated according to the prevailing theory of the Heavenly Mandate. This changing attitude is most clearly reflected in Zhang Heng's description of Chang'an's founding process. To him, this heavenly endorsed Celestial Capital had to be a "planned city" with a coherent form from the moment of its birth:

> 莫我大也。徒恨不能以靡丽为国华，独俭啬以龌龊，忘蟋蟀之谓何？岂欲之而不能，将能之而不欲欤？[14]

我们几乎难以找到更好的例子，以显示对一个城市如此迥然不同的历史回顾。在古代赋的传统中，在解释层面上做出有意识的变更可以反映作者的才华。据班固自己所说，一首赋的作者应该能够"感物造耑（端），材知深美，可与图事"。[15]"物"——话语的刺激物——可以被不同的作者共享，但是话语则必须展现出某个作者与众不同的"材知"。把这一理论应用于对长安的描写，就意味着关于这座历史性城市的记忆必须被不断地更新，人们对于过去的知识必须被转化为对过去的想象。[16]过去必须笼罩在今日的光芒之下。对回忆持续的再剪辑把往事改编为适应当下需要的新作。

在这两篇赋中，张衡和班固通过对同一座故城的反思表述了各自对历史的理解；也通过这种反思建立起不同的古今关系。[17]班固是一位历史学家，在他的眼中，长安是由一系列历史事件组成的动态过程。他的这篇赋写作于东汉早期，为东汉君主提供了前朝建都的范例。[18]而张衡则是以"通五经"出身，古典经学为其作品提供了一个基本的范式。[19]属于这个传统的学者并不注重对历史作年代学的疏理，而是通过注解古代圣贤遗留下来的经典来表述历史、政治和道德的基本原则。不仅如此，当张衡在公元 2 世纪前期开始写作他的赋时，东汉朝廷面临的问题已变成如何维护其统治。长安这座故城不再是一个历史课题，而是被作为一个政治和理论的项目看待，它的形象和历史必须用流行的天命学说来重新定义。这种转向也表现在张衡对于长安建造过程的叙述中。在他看来，这座上苍佑护下建立的都城在其诞生之初就是一个有完整形式的"规划过的城市"：

Heaven's decree is unvarying;
Who would dare change it?
Thereupon:
He [Gaozu] measured the diameter and circumference,
Reckoned the length and breadth.
He ordered the city walls and moat built
And the outer enclosures constructed.[20]

We will learn later that this report contains little truth: not only did Gaozu not build the city walls, but Chang'an never had "outer enclosures." Zhang Heng's description, in fact, was not based on reality but on literature—more specifically, on passages in the Confucian classics regarding the archaic capitals of the Three Dynasties. His appeal to Heaven echoes a speech in the *Documents*, given by the Duke of Zhou when he began to build the Zhou's royal town: "May the King come and assume the responsibility for the work of God on High and himself serve [in this capacity] at the center of the land."[21] His emphasis on Chang'an's corresponding celestial position is reminiscent of a poem in the *Odes*: "The Ding-star is in the middle of the sky, /We begin to build the palace at Chu."[22] His specifics of Chang'an's planning are derived, quite literally, from another ode that documents the beginning of a pre-dynastic Zhou capital not far from Chang'an:

And so he [the Zhou ancestor Tan Fu] remained quiet, he stopped;
He went to the left, he went to the right,
He made boundaries, he made divisions,
He measured to the cubit, he laid out acres;
From west he went east,
Everywhere he took the task in hand.[23]

Historically speaking, such ancient descriptions were not groundless. As discussed earlier, some Three Dynasties cities, such as the excavated Shang capitals at Erlitou and Zhengzhou, had rectangular shapes and a symmetrical layout—features indicative of an initial design. Western Han

Chang'an, on the other hand, was definitely not a "planned" lineage town but an imperial capital that expanded gradually. This does not mean, however, that such differences would be openly documented in literature. On the contrary, following the canonization of the Confucian classics,[24] empirical experience and memory were forced to conform with these authoritative writings, which made the past intelligible only in their own light. When the Eastern Zhou treatise "Regulations of Workmanship" was

> 天命不滔，畴敢以渝？于是量径轮，考广袤。经城洫，营郭郛。[20]

我们在下文中将会看到，张衡这里所说的并不是历史真实的情况：不仅高祖没有修建城墙，而且长安从来没有修建过“郭”。实际上，张衡这些描述的根据不是事实，而是文献——更明确地说，是儒家经典中有关三代古都的段落。他对上天的诉求呼应着《尚书》所载的周公开始营建周王城时说的一段话：“王来绍上帝，自服于土中。”[21]他强调长安符合天界方位的说法与《诗经》中的句子相合：“定之方中，作于楚宫。”[22]他对于长安规划的详尽叙述则几乎是照搬《诗经》中的另一首颂诗，该诗记述了距离长安不远的一座先周都城开创的历史：

> 古公亶父，……
> 迺慰迺止，迺左迺右，
> 迺疆迺理，迺宣迺亩，
> 自西徂东，周爰执事。[23]

从历史的观点来看，这些上古时期的文字并非毫无根据。如我在上文所讨论的，一些三代时期的城市，如已经发掘的偃师商城和郑州商城，其平面均为布局对称的矩形，说明这些城市在营建之际经过了统一规划。但是，西汉的长安却绝对不属于这种“规划的城市”，而是一座通过逐步扩展而形成的帝都。然而，这并不意味着这种差异会被直截了当地记录在文献中。相反，遵循着儒家学说的经典，[24]生动的历史经验和记忆被加以改造，以符合权威性的文字，使得逝去的历史只能在经典的光辉下被理解。当东周《考工记》一文

integrated into the canonical *Rites of Zhou*, it became a standard model for both literary and visual representations of an imperial capital:

> The official architect [*jiangren*] constructs a state capital. He makes a square nine *li* on each side; each side has three gates. Within the capital are nine streets running north-south and nine streets running east-west.
> 148 The north-south streets are nine carriage tracks in width. On the left is the Ancestral Temple, and to the right are the Altars of Soil and Grain. In the front is the Audience Hall and behind the markets.[25]

From the third century on, this brief passage would become the blueprint for all Chinese capitals. But before that moment, during the Eastern Han, what it offered to scholars like Zhang Heng was the image of an "ideal capital" as well as a method to describe it. Illustrated in Fig. 2.20, this capital appears as a flat silhouette viewed from an imagined vantage point in the sky. In this way it best exhibits all its classical features—the perfect rectangular shape and symmetrical layout reinforced by gates, avenues, and the palace-temple compound. When this image is translated into words, the description proceeds from the city's outermost enclosure to its inner divisions and components—an order taken to be the actual sequence of the city's construction. Based on this "ideal capital," Zhang Heng redrew Chang'an's image and rewrote its history. His Chang'an has no chronology and thus no growth and decay. Like the ancient sovereigns, the great founder of the Han must have first determined his capital's celestial position, ascertained the four cardinal directions, and constructed the city's double walls and moat. Only after this general framework had been laid down did the emperor add other architectural features—palaces, streets, and other buildings—to the empty enclosure. In a way, Zhang Heng rebuilt Chang'an on paper.

The rhapsodies by both Ban Gu and Zhang Heng are retrospective reconstructions from present-minded vantage points. For Ban Gu, however, what is being commemorated and reconstructed are not only events but also their diachronic sequence, whereas in Zhang Heng's work, memories are reorganized according to an overarching, essentially synchronic model. The subject of their reconstructions thus differs fundamentally: Ban Gu's goal was to illustrate the *growth* of Chang'an; Zhang Heng was preoccupied with Chang'an's timeless *image*. These two perspectives, which may be called "historical" and "classical" respectively,

被纳入《周礼》后，这篇文字提供了对都城在文字表述和视觉表现两方面共同的准则：

> 匠人营国，方九里，旁三门。国中九经，九纬，经涂九轨。左祖右社，面朝后市。[25]

从公元 3 世纪起，这段简短的文字成为所有中国都城的蓝图。但在此之前的东汉时期，这段文字为张衡之类的学者所提供的是一个“理想都城”的形象以及描写这样一座城市的方法。如图 2.20 所示，这座“理想都城”显示为从空中某个假想点俯视所见的平面图像。这种特殊描绘方式的长处是，可以完整地展示出这种城市的经典性——完美的长方形外形、对称的城门、规整的街道、排列有序的庙堂。将这张图翻译为文字，叙述的顺序从城市的外轮廓开始，然后是城市内部的空间划分以及各个部分——这种次序随之被认为是该城市建造的实际工序。基于这种“理想都城”的话语，张衡重新勾画出长安的图像，重新书写了它的历史。他笔下的长安不再是一部编年史的主角，也无所谓成长或衰落。根据他的想象，就像上古君王一样，汉帝国英明的开创者首先筹划了其都城神圣的位置，确定四方，构筑城市的两重城墙，开挖城壕。当这些总体性工程结束后，他才在空旷的轮廓内加进了诸如宫殿、街道及其他房屋等建筑。通过这样的叙述，张衡用他的文字重建了长安。

班固和张衡对长安的描写都是基于当时的思想习惯而做的回顾式重构。然而，对于班固来说，被回忆和重构的不仅是历史事件，而且包括了其历史次序；而张衡的作品则根据了一种抽去时间概念的模型，将记忆组织进经学的空间。这两种重构的主题因此有着根本区别：班固的目的在于阐明长安发展演变的历史；张衡则专注于长安永恒的形象。这两种观点可以分别称为“历史性”观点和

have been adopted by all later reconstructors of Chang'an, but the "classical" view has played the leading role. One reason for this result is that to a later observer, Chang'an always appears in *its final* and *total* image. As traces of the city's long evolution become less obvious, what is apparent is a simultaneous assemblage of architectural features: a city whose boundaries are marked by the surviving foundations of its walls and whose components are indicated by ruins of great palaces. As suggested by many drawings made from the Song to the present day (Figs. 3.1-4), efforts to reconstruct Chang'an have been dominated by the desire to bestow on this city a single triumphant image, superimposing walls, gates, palaces, parks, and many other types of buildings at once.[26] Even the most "historical" reconstructions only append dates and other information to individual buildings as secondary evidence (Fig. 3.3). The same method was also employed in literary reconstructions: the city's features are classified into major types (walls, gates, palaces, parks, ritual buildings, and mausoleums) and described in hierarchical sequence, with historical information cited to explain the origin of each structure. This format enabled these authors to merge *jing* (the Classics) and *shi* (history), so that their work could ascribe to the doctrine of traditional learning in which history functioned to illuminate and supplement the Confucian classics.[27]

This idealized image of Chang'an will be dismantled in the following sections. To me, there is not a single Chang'an, but a series of Chang'ans confined in their individual historical strata. According to this understanding, for example, the popular statement that "Chang'an had twelve gates" only reflects the city's image after 190 B.C., because the last city wall was not completed until the last month of this year. Similarly, the commonplace that "eleven royal mausoleums surrounded the city" only implies the view of a post-Han observer, because the last of these tombs was built in A.D. 6 for Emperor Ping (r. A.D. 1-6). In other words, my method is close to Ban Gu's, but rather than compiling a chronology of Chang'an and documenting the physical development of the city, I hope to reveal its changing monumentality—the shifting concerns behind its construction and the logic of its evolution.

The construction of Chang'an underwent four major stages, during the reigns of the first Western Han emperor, Gaozu (r. 206-195 B.C.); 149

"经典性"观点。二者后来都被对长安的各种重构所采纳，但是"经典性"观点却占据了主流。造成这种结果的原因之一是，对于后来的观察者来说，长安的面貌总是以它最后的和总体的形象代表的。城市漫长的进化轨迹已变得模糊不清，但是建筑的遗迹却清晰可辨，并且混在了一起。历历在目的残垣断壁以及宫殿废墟，似乎在证明以往一个"完整城市"的界限和组成部分。如宋代以来许多关于长安的总图［图3.1—图3.4］所示，重构长安的种种努力一直被该城的一个单一和终结的形象所控制，总是把城墙、城门、宫殿、苑囿以及其他各种建筑综合在一起。[26] 即使是最具"历史性"的重构，也仅仅是将修造时间和其他历史信息作为第二级内容添加在这种综合地图中的各个建筑旁边［图3.3］。以文字对长安的重构采取了同样的办法：城市的各项内容被划分为几大类（城墙、城门、宫殿、苑囿、礼制建筑和陵墓），按照等级次序加以描述，只是在注释中才引用历史材料来说明各个建筑的缘起。在这种格式中，"经"和"史"以一种特殊方式结合在一起：历史材料的作用是对儒家经典思维方式作出阐释和补充。[27]

在接下来几部分的讨论中，我将对长安的这种理想化形象进行逐级解构。我的基本观念是历史上从来不存在一个单独的长安——曾经存在的只有被各个历史层次所限定的一系列长安。基于这种理解，一些流行的说法，例如"长安十二城门"，只是反映了这座城市在公元前190年后的形象，因为一直到该年的最后一个月城墙才最终完工。同样，因为最后一个皇帝平帝（1—6年在位）的陵墓建于公元6年，所以俗称的"环城十一陵"也只能是代表了汉以后观察者的看法。换言之，我的想法比较接近班固的观点，但我的着重点不在于编制长安的年表或记录其实际的发展历史，而是希望揭示长安纪念碑性的变化，即在长安的构筑和演进逻辑背后所隐藏的当时人们关注点的改变。

长安的构筑大致可以分为四大阶段，即西汉第一个皇帝高祖

the second emperor, Hui (r. 194-188 B.C.); the fifth emperor, Wu (r. 140-87 B.C.); and Wang Mang who usurped the Western Han throne in A.D. 9. Each of these stages stands out as a period of intensive construction centered on specific projects, and together they narrate the sequence of the city's development. Chang'an's 200-year-long construction was continuously undertaken because of the ambition of individual rulers to establish their own monuments with specific political and religious values. These monuments also reflect the rise and fall of different social forces and attest to changing modes of political rhetoric. The proliferation of political and religious monuments coincided with the social development of the city, since it was around these monuments that a large population gradually concentrated and abundant social activities took place. The construction of a new monument was always a major event in the lives of the city's residents. Once it had appeared, a new monument always reinterpreted the old ones and altered the city's architectural and symbolic structures. In this process, the imperial capital constantly changed its meaning. It is based on this reconstruction of Chang'an's history that I call it a city of monuments or a "monumental city."

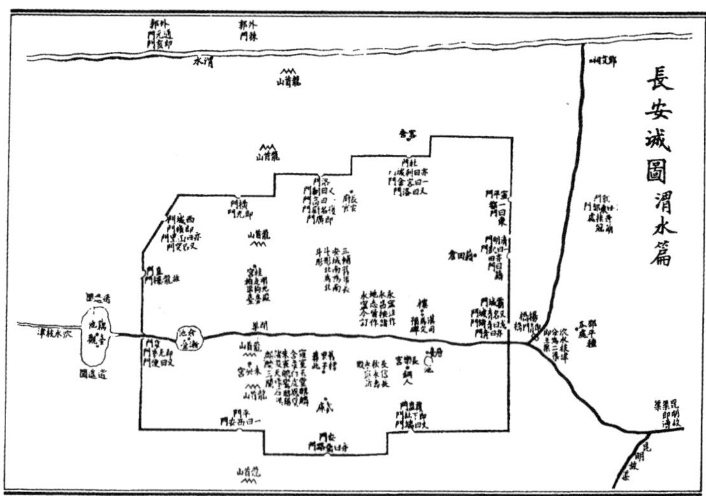

Fig. 3.1. Yang Shoujing's (1839-1915) reconstruction of Western Han Chang'an
图 3.1 杨守敬（1839—1915 年）对西汉长安的复原

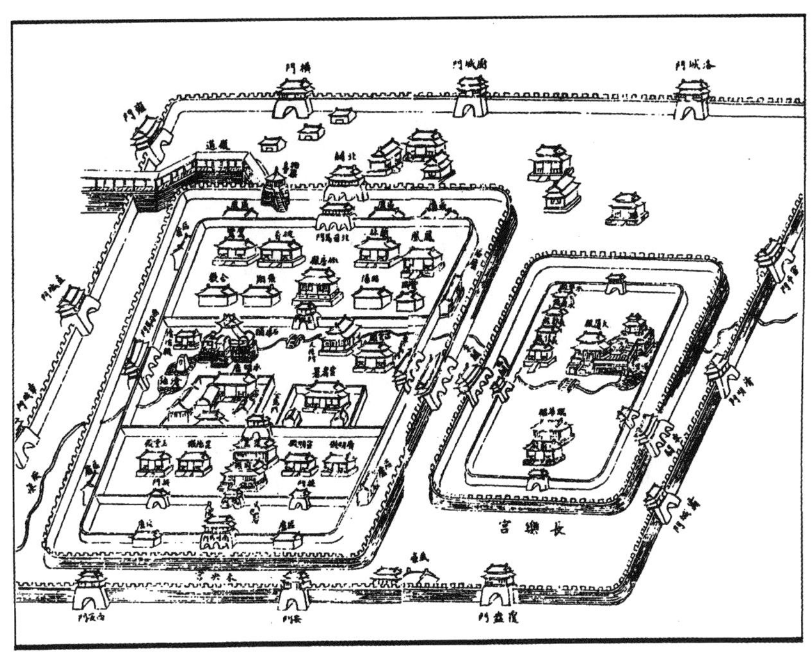

Fig. 3.2. Bi Yuan's (1730-97) reconstruction of Western Han Chang'an

图 3.2　毕沅（1730—1797 年）对西汉长安的复原

（前 206 年称汉王，前 202—前 195 年在位）时期、第二个皇帝惠帝（前 195—前 188 年在位）时期、第五个皇帝武帝（前 141—前 87 年在位）时期和公元 9 年篡权的王莽在位时期。每一个阶段都代表了以特别工程为中心的对长安的集中建设，而这些阶段共同构成了这座城市发展的历史。在这段 200 年之久的历史中，长安的建造既是一个连续的工程，又具有不断变化的中心和目的。每位君主为了表达其特殊的政治和宗教价值观都热衷于建造他们自己的纪念碑。这些纪念碑反映出不同社会力量的兴衰，成为不断变幻的政治策略的见证。这些政治性和宗教性纪念碑的增生又和城市社会的发展一致，因为正是围绕着这些纪念碑聚集起大量的人口，出现了各种各样的社会活动。一座新纪念碑的建立总是城市居民生活中的一件大事。新的纪念碑必然对旧有的纪念碑进行重新解释，城市的建筑结构和象征性格局也都会因之改变。在这一过程中，西汉帝国的首都不断改变着它的意义。正是基于对长安历史的这种重构，我将它称为一座由纪念碑组成的城市或“纪念碑式的城市”。

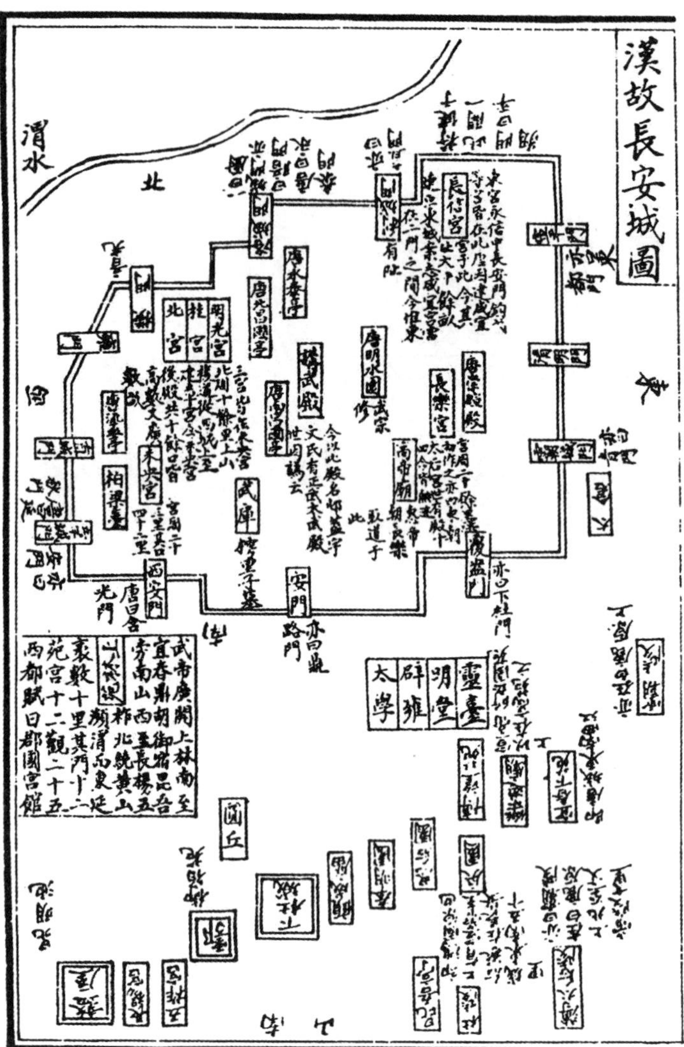

Fig. 3.3. Li Haowen's (14th century) reconstruction of Western Han Chang'an
图 3.3 李好文（14 世纪）对西汉长安的复原

❷ Emperor Gaozu: The Birth of Chang'an

Upon accepting Lou Jing's suggestion to locate the capital in the "heartland of the former Qin dynasty," Emperor Gaozu immediately departed to revisit this area, traditionally called Guanzhong, or the region within the Hangu Pass. What he saw there must have been both shocking and depressing. Just four years earlier in 206 B.C., he had conquered the Qin capital and been amazed by its splendid palaces, and before he had been forced to leave, he had sealed all the palace halls with their treasures inside.[28] But now the whole capital of the former dynasty had literally vanished: General Xiang Yu (232-202 B.C.), Gaozu's chief competitor for the throne, had burned the city. The fire lasted for three months, and the Lishan mausoleum had been looted and some 300 pleasure palaces (*ligong*) of the First Emperor had been reduced to ashes.

Among the few surviving structures was a palace complex south of the 150
Wei River called the Xingle Palace (Palace of Prosperity and Joy). Since the wars continued and the country remained in turmoil, a practical decision was made to turn this summer resort of the previous emperor into the new ruler's throne hall. After Gaozu hurried to join his expeditionary army,[29] his prime minister, Xiao He (?-193 B.C.), took charge of repairing, redecorating, and perhaps also enlarging this group of buildings.[30]

二、高祖：长安的诞生

在接受了娄敬“因秦之故”而定都渭河流域的建议后，高祖立即从洛阳重返关中，即函谷关以内的地区。他之所见想必是满目疮痍、令人目不忍睹的景象。四年前的公元前 206 年，他率领大军攻克秦都咸阳，那时的咸阳到处是豪华壮丽的宫室，令人惊叹。在被迫离开此地之前，他下令将所有财宝密封于各个宫殿中。[28] 但是，现在这座前朝的都城几乎全部被摧毁，与高祖争夺皇位的大将项羽（前 232—前 202 年）一把火焚毁了咸阳。大火整整燃烧了三个月，骊山陵被劫掠，大约 300 座始皇离宫化为灰烬。

仅存的秦宫之一是渭河以南称作兴乐宫的一组宫殿。因为战争仍在持续，各地骚乱未平，高祖便暂借这个前朝基业安置了自己的朝廷。当高祖重归戎旅，[29] 大臣萧何（？—前 193 年）便承担了对这组建筑进行修葺、装饰，或者也包括扩大的任务。[30]

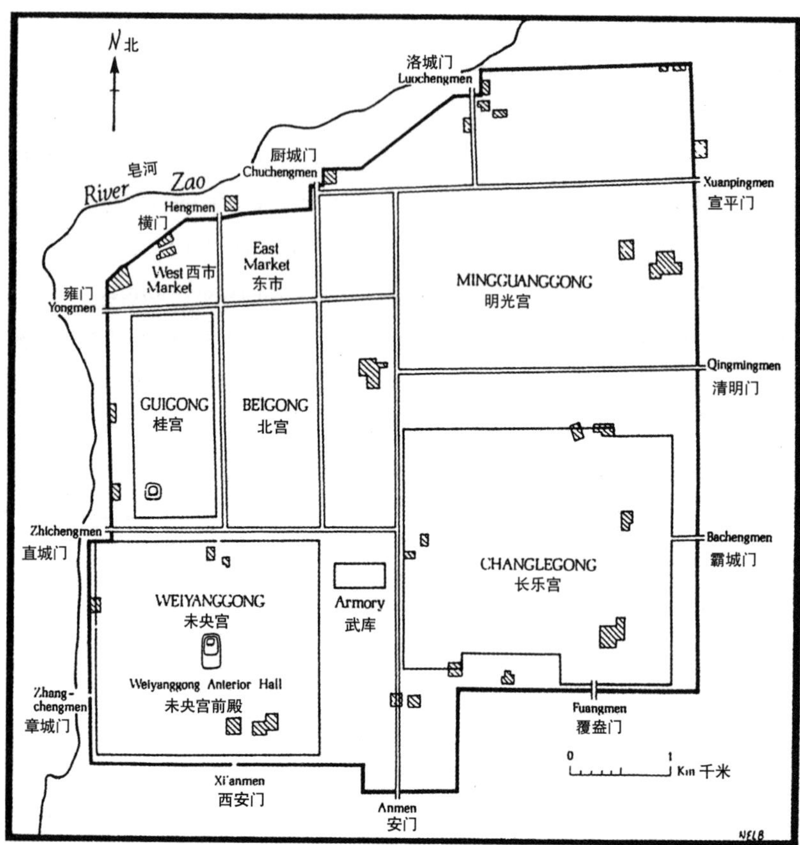

Fig. 3.4. Wang Zhongshu's reconstruction of Western Han Chang'an
图 3.4 王仲殊对西汉长安的复原

No detailed report of this project is available, but the renovation of the Qin palace must have been substantial because the work took one and a half years.[31] The new palace, which was renamed the Changle Palace (Palace of Lasting Joy), was an architectural complex about 10 kilometers in circumference with fourteen halls inside.[32] The main palace, simply called the Anterior Hall (Qiandian), was more than 100 meters long.[33] Ten or twelve huge bronze figures originally made by the First Emperor for his Epang Palace had survived the fire and were repositioned in front of this hall.[34] Not far from the Anterior Hall was an imposing platform called the Wild Goose Terrace (Hong tai), reportedly some 92 meters in height.[35] The palace also retained two artificial lakes from Qin times, one called the Fish Pond and the other the Wine Pond.[36]

Compared with many Chinese palace complexes built before or after the Han, this fourteen-hall compound was modest in scale; however, it was the sole component of Han dynasty Chang'an as the capital first appeared on the map. In fact, in ancient texts this single compound is sometimes referred to as the Imperial City of Chang'an (*Chang'an gongcheng*) or simply the City of Chang'an (*Chang'an cheng*).[37] This explains a puzzling phenomenon during this period: although theoretically Chang'an had assumed the status of the dynasty's capital, the emperor rarely stayed in this "city." Consulting the Han history, we find that Gaozu visited Chang'an in the second month of 200 B.C. when the renovation of Changle Palace was completed, but after holding an 151

文献中并没有记载这一工程的细节，但因为整个工程持续了一年半之久，[31] 应当是对秦代的建筑进行了实质性的重构或扩充。新宫殿区被重新命名为长乐宫，周长大约 10 公里，内部有 14 座殿堂。[32] 其主殿叫作前殿，长度超过 100 米。[33] 原来秦始皇铸造立在阿房宫前的十或十二尊巨大的青铜人像劫后余生，现在也被重新安置在这座殿堂之前。[34] 距离前殿不远处有一个规模宏伟的高台，称为鸿台，据称高度大约 92 米。[35] 秦代所修的两处人工湖泊也在长乐宫中保留下来，其一称为鱼池，另一称为酒池。[36]

与此前此后的许多中国皇宫相比较，这 14 座殿堂组成的宫殿区规模并不大；然而，这个宫殿区却是作为都城而首次出现在地图上的汉代长安的唯一核心元素。实际上，这个宫殿区在文献中被称为“长安宫城”或“长安城”。[37] 这一情况可以解释该时期的一个令人疑惑的现象：尽管从理论上讲，长安已经获得了首都的身份，但是皇帝很少住在这座“城”中。检索汉代历史，我们发现高祖在长乐宫竣工后的公元前 200 年二月到过长安，但在此举行了一个朝会

audience in this palace he soon left for Luoyang in the fourth month.[38] He did not return until two and a half years later, in the tenth month of 198 B.C.[39] Interestingly, this second visit coincided with the inauguration of a new palace (the Weiyang, or Eternal Palace), but again the emperor only stayed a short time and left in the twelfth month of the same year.[40] This pattern, which would continue till the emperor's death, leads me to propose that Chang'an during Gaozu's reign was essentially a political symbol and a ceremonial center, a contention supported by the nature of the rituals held in this "city" and the strong symbolic connotations of new palatial constructions.

The grand ceremony held in the Changle Palace is well documented in both the *Records of the Historian* and *History of the Former Han*.[41] The ceremony was orchestrated by Shusun Tong, a specialist in Confucian rituals from Shandong.[42] Shusun originally served the Qin as an official scholar. After Qin's fall, he went to Gaozu and made a proposal to the new Son of Heaven: "Confucian scholars are not of much use when one is marching to conquest, but they can be of help in keeping what has already been won. I beg to summon the scholars of Lu, who can join with my disciples in drawing up a ritual for the court." Gaozu, who was from a commoner family and had been quite impatient with Confucian jargon, saw no harm in this suggestion but also warned the ritual master: "You may try and see what you can do, but make it easy to learn! Keep in mind that it must be the sort of thing I can perform!" With this permission Shusun went to Lu, the homeland of Confucius, to recruit other ritual specialists. Some thirty scholars agreed to follow him; but two others rejected his offer, blaming his opportunism:

> You have served close to ten different masters, and with each of them you have gained trust and honor simply by flattering them to their faces. Now the world has just been set at peace, the dead have not been properly buried, and the wounded have not risen from their beds, and

yet you wish to set up rites and music for the new dynasty. But rites and music can only be set up after a dynasty has accumulated virtue for a period of a hundred years. We could never bring ourselves to take part in what you are doing, for what you are doing is not in accord with the ways of antiquity.

To this criticism Shusun responded with laughter: "True pigheaded Confucianists you are! You do not know that the times have changed!"

后便于四月离开了长安，去往洛阳。[38] 此后两年半的时间里，他再没有回来过，直到公元前 198 年十月才又返回长安。[39] 值得注意的是，这一次回长安与新建的未央宫的竣工典礼是同一时间，但皇帝仍只是停留了不长的时间，于同年十二月又离开了。[40] 这种状况一直持续到高祖去世。根据这种记载推测，高祖时期的长安实质上是一个政治性符号和礼仪中心，“城”中所举行典礼的性质以及新建筑的强烈的象征性内涵都可以支持这一观点。

《史记》和《汉书》都详细记载了长乐宫盛大的典礼，[41] 由来自山东的儒家礼仪专家叔孙通组织策划。[42] 叔孙通原来以一位学者的身份供职于秦。秦亡以后，他前来晋见高祖并向这位新的天子提出了自己的建议：“夫儒者难与进取，可与守成。臣愿征鲁诸生，与臣弟子共起朝仪。”出身低微的高祖一向对儒生的议论没有什么耐心，此时他却感到叔孙通的建议并无害处。但他也提醒这位礼制专家说：“可试为之，令易知，度吾所能行为之。”在高祖的恩准下，叔孙通去往孔子的故乡鲁地召集其他礼制专家。大约有三十人愿意追随叔孙通，但其他两人拒绝了他的邀请，并且指责他的作为是政治投机：

> 公所事者且十主，皆面谀以得亲贵。今天下初定，死者未葬，伤者未起，又欲起礼乐。礼乐所由起，积德百年而后可兴也。吾不忍为公所为。公所为不合古，吾不行。

对这样的指责叔孙通报以嘲笑：“若真鄙儒也，不知时变。”

The times had indeed changed for both Confucians and the ruler. The former had to modify their tradition in order to become useful, and the latter had to adapt himself to the ancient tradition in order to rule as king. After ascending the throne, Gaozu became increasingly annoyed by the lack of respect from his generals: these men who started their career as bandit leaders "were given to drinking and wrangling over their respective achievements, some shouting wildly in their drunkenness, others drawing their swords and hacking at the pillars of the palace." Their wild behavior and unrestrained manner began to threaten the emperor's authority. This political situation offered Shusun a rare opportunity to realize a scholar's ambition: "Confucius has said that the Xia, Shang, and Zhou dynasties did not merely copy their predecessors. It is my desire to select from a number of ancient codes of ritual, as well as from the ceremonies of Qin, and make a combination of these."[43] He finally managed to organize a group of 100 scholars. After practicing his own version of Confucian rites for a month in the outskirts, he held a rehearsal for the emperor. Gaozu decided that these rites did not seem too difficult to learn and ordered his ministers and generals to study them. The result was the first formal
152 court ceremony of the Han, held in the newly renovated Changle Palace
at the beginning of the seventh year of Gaozu's reign:[44]

> In the seventh year, with the completion of the Xingle Palace, all the nobles and officials came to court to attend the ceremony in the tenth month. Before dawn the master of guests, who was in charge of the ritual, led the participants in order of rank through the gate leading to the hall. Within the courtyard the chariots and cavalry were drawn up. The foot soldiers and palace guards stood with their weapons at attention and their banners and pennants unfurled, passing the order along to the participants to hurry on their side of the stairway, several hundred on each step. The distinguished officials, nobles, generals, and other army officers took their places on the west side of the hall facing east, while the civil officials from the chancellor on down proceeded

to the east side of the hall facing west. The master of ceremonies then appointed men to relay instructions to the nine degree of guests. At this point the emperor, borne on a litter, appeared from the inner rooms, the hundred officials holding banners and announcing his arrival. Then each of the guests, from the nobles and kings down to the officials of 600 piculs' salary, was summoned in turn to come forward and present his congratulations, and from the nobles down every one trembled with awe and reverence. . . . With this, the Emperor Gaozu announced, "Today for the first time I realize how exalted a thing it is to be an emperor!"[45]

确实，不管是对于儒生还是对于统治者而言，时代真的是改变了。儒生们不得不改弦更张，以备重新被录用，统治者也不得不采用古代的礼法，以使自己获得君临天下的威严。登上皇位后，高祖因为感到自己得不到属下足够的尊重而日益烦恼：那些出身于草莽的将军大臣们“饮酒争功，醉或妄呼，拔剑击柱”。他们粗鲁鄙俗的行为威胁到皇帝的权威。这种情况为叔孙通实现一个儒生的抱负提供了难得的机会，他因此进言说：“故夏、殷、周之礼所因损益可知者，谓不相复也。臣愿颇采古礼与秦仪杂就之。”[43] 他最终设法组织了百余名学者和弟子，在郊外对自己重新修订的儒家礼法演练月余，然后邀请高祖前去观看。高祖看到这些礼数并不难学，便下令群臣学习。其成果就是高祖七年年初，在修葺一新的长乐宫里举行的汉代第一次正式的朝仪：[44]

> 汉七年，长乐宫成，诸侯群臣皆朝十月。仪：先平明，谒者治礼，引以次入殿门，廷中陈车步骑卒卫官，设兵张旗志。传言“趋”。殿下郎中侠陛，陛数百人。功臣、列侯、诸将军、军吏以次陈西方，东向。文官丞相以下陈东方，西向。大行设九宾，胪传。于是皇帝辇出房，百官执职，传警，引诸侯王以下至吏六百石以次奉贺。自诸侯王以下莫不振恐肃敬。……于是高帝曰：“吾乃今日知为皇帝之贵也。”[45]

I have quoted this long passage because it illuminates the political psychology behind the establishment of palace rituals in the early Han and hence explains the urgent need for the Changle Palace. But this palace only provided the ritual occasion with a physical setting; its architecture largely derived from the defunct Qin and could hardly be taken as the proper symbol of the new dynasty. This is why Han historians never tried to explain the architectural symbolism of the Changle Palace, and why all such explanations focused on a new palace built exclusively by and for the Han regime. Unlike the *borrowed* Changle Palace standing beside it, this second palace, the Weiyang Palace completed two years later in 198 B.C., was *designed* as an everlasting monument of Han sovereignty.[46]

> In this place,
> One could look out on Qin Mound,
> Catch a glimpse of North Hill,
> Be embraced by the Feng and Ba Rivers,
> And recline on the Dragon Head Hills.
> They planned a foundation of one million years;
> Ah! An immense scale and a grand construction![47]

The Dragon Head Hills, identified here by Ban Gu as the location of the new palace, is explained by Li Daoyuan in his *Annotated Canon of Waterways* (*Shuijing zhu*):

> From east of the Hangu Pass [in Luoyang] Gaozu ordered Xiao He to construct Weiyang. Xiao He then cut the Dragon Head Hills and built the palace [on it]. The hills, more than 60 *li* long, [are shaped like a dragon] whose head rises twenty *zhang* high and reaches the Wei River, and whose tail gradually declines to five or six *zhang* and stretches to the Fan Valley. . . . It is said that in the past a black dragon emerged from the South Mountain to drink in Wei, and as it passed along the hills it left its mark. The head of the dragon [i.e., the top of the hills] provided Weiyang with a natural foundation. Even without additional

construction, it would raise the palace five or six *zhang* above the rest of Chang'an.[48]

Thus, all aspects of the Dragon Head Hills—their shape, height, name, and myth—made them an ideal location for the new imperial palace: standing on top of the hills, this palace overlooked the whole capital area and could be seen from afar. Moreover, the dragon was the general

我之所以引用这一大段文献，是因为它可以说明汉代初年新的宫廷礼仪所隐含的政治性心理状态，也阐明了当时迫切需要建立长乐宫的原因。但是，这座宫殿还只是为朝廷礼仪提供了一个物质性环境；其建筑本身源于亡秦，很难成为新王朝的象征。这就是为什么汉代史家从未试图解释长乐宫建筑象征意义的原因，也是为什么所有这类解释都集中于专门由汉朝廷兴建、为汉朝廷服务的新宫殿——未央宫的原因。与借助前朝基业修葺的长乐宫不同，位于长乐宫旁的这座新宫落成于两年后的公元前 198 年，从起始之日就被作为汉帝国永恒的纪念碑。[46]

如班固所说：

于是睎秦岭，睋北阜。
挟沣灞，据龙首。
图皇基于亿载，度宏规而大起。[47]

班固在此将龙首山认定为这座新宫殿所在的位置，对此郦道元在《水经注》一书中解释说：

高祖在关东（洛阳），令萧何成未央宫。何斩龙首山而营之。山长六十余里，头于渭尾达樊川。头高二十丈，尾渐下五六丈……云昔有黑龙从南山出饮渭水，其行道因山成迹。山即基阙，不假筑，高出长安城。[48]

这样，龙首山所有的特点，包括其形状、高度、名字和传说，都使其成为皇家新宫殿的理想地点：这一宫殿坐落在山顶，一方面可俯瞰整个都城，另一方面也可以被远远望见。不仅如此，龙是任何

symbol of any Chinese emperor, and a "black dragon" was the specific symbol of the founder of the Han. In fact, on one occasion Gaozu had identified himself as the Black Power,[49] and the official astrologer Zhang Cang (256-152 B.C.) "had calculated the movement of the five elements and had determined that the Han possessed the virtue of water and should follow tradition to take black as its proper color."[50]

The remains of the foundation of the Weiyang Palace (Fig. 3.5a) have repeatedly been surveyed by archaeologists. As demonstrated by the drawing of Carl W. Bishop (Fig. 3.5b), the Dragon Head Hills were carved into a series of terraces, measuring 350 by 200 meters overall, gradually ascending to the north where the major structure of the palace, again called the Anterior Hall, was located.[51] Historically speaking, this
153 layout was modeled on the terrace palaces popular before the Han. As discussed in the previous chapter, almost all late Zhou feudal lords, and especially the First Emperor, built such structures.[52] Standing on tall earthen platforms, such palaces formed commanding centers of Eastern Zhou cities, accentuating the growing power and self-esteem of the new social elites. It is no coincidence that the first palatial monument of the Han empire took this architectural form, rather than a two-dimensional temple compound that defined the center of a Shang-Western Zhou city.

There was no reason for Gaozu to disapprove of the Weiyang Palace's location. Elevated by a natural hill, the palace, now destroyed, would have been even more eye-catching than the earlier terrace buildings on manmade platforms. But Gaozu was genuinely shocked by the new palace's scale. Reported by both Sima Qian and Ban Gu, the following exchange between the emperor and Xiao He, the chief architect of the new palace, throws much light on the purpose and function of the Weiyang Palace:

> When Gaozu returned and saw the magnificence of the palace and its tower-gates, he was extremely angry. "The empire is still in great turmoil," he said to Xiao He, "and although we have toiled in battle

these several years, we cannot tell yet whether we will achieve final success. What do you mean by constructing palaces like this on such an extravagant scale?" Xiao He replied, "It is precisely because the fate of the empire is still uncertain that we must build such palaces and halls. A true Son of Heaven takes the whole world within the four seas to be his family. If he does not dwell in magnificence and beauty, he will have no way to manifest his authority, nor will he leave any foundation for his heirs to build upon." With these words, Gaozu's anger turned to delight.[53]

一位中国皇帝的象征，而“黑龙”又是汉代开国者特别的符号：高祖曾自称为“黑帝”，[49] 而官员中擅长律历的张苍（前 256—前 152 年）“推五德之运，以为汉当水德之时，上黑如故”。[50]

考古工作者已经对未央宫的遗址［图 3.5a］做了多次调查。根据毕士博所绘制的线图［图 3.5b］，龙首山上被切出了一个 350 米、长 200 米宽的多层台地，由南向北逐级升高。主殿原来坐落在最北端处，称作前殿。[51] 从建筑史的角度看，这种宫殿的前身是东周时期的台式建筑。正如上一章中所讨论过的，几乎所有先秦统治者，特别是秦始皇本人，都建造过这种形式的宫殿。[52] 矗立于高台之上，这种建筑形成了东周城市中居高临下的中心，凸显了新兴贵族日益增长的权力与自尊。汉代皇帝的第一座纪念碑建筑采取这种形式，而不是依照商—西周城市中心的那种二维殿堂，绝非偶然。

高祖没有理由不赞同未央宫的位置。依托着自然山势，这座如今已经消失的宫殿比早先那些建在人工高台上的建筑更能吸引众人的目光，但他还是实实在在地被这座新宫殿的规模震惊了。司马迁和班固所记载的高祖和萧何关于这座新宫殿的对话明确地体现了未央宫的主旨和功能：

> 高祖还，见宫阙壮甚，怒谓萧何曰：“天下匈匈苦战数岁，成败未可知，是何治宫室过度也？”萧何曰：“天下方未定，故可因遂就宫室。且夫天子以四海为家，非壮丽无以重威，且无令后世有以加也。”高祖乃说（悦）。[53]

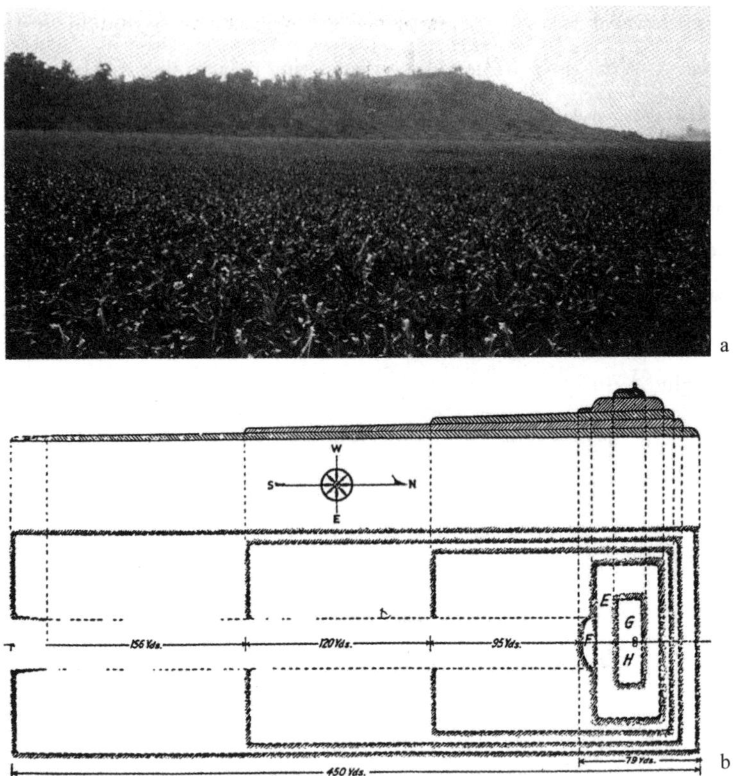

Fig. 3.5. (a) Remaining foundation of the Weiyang Palace. (b) Plan and elevation of the Weiyang Palace foundation.

图 3.5 （a）未央宫遗址。西汉。（b）未央宫基址平、剖面图。

The significance of this conversation is twofold: on the one hand, it reveals the imperial symbolism of the Weiyang Palace; on the other, it demonstrates the crucial role of civil officers represented by Xiao He in constructing this palace and thus signifies the rise of this political group in the Han government. Sima Qian noted that as soon as Gaozu defeated Xiang Yu and ascended the throne, his attitude toward his ministers and generals changed rapidly, Before the construction of the Weiyang Palace, a court meeting was held to discuss the ranking and enfeoffment of the dynasty's founding ministers. To everyone's surprise, the emperor considered that Xiao He won the highest merit. His generals objected:

"Xiao He, who has never campaigned on the sweaty steeds of battle, but only sat here with brush and ink deliberating on questions of state instead of fighting, is awarded a position above us—how can this be?" To this Gaozu answered with a famous analogy: "In a hunt, it is the dog who is sent to pursue and kill the beast. But the one who unleashes the dog and points out the place where the beast is hiding is the huntsman. 154
You, gentlemen, have only succeeded in capturing the beast, and so your achievement is that of hunting dogs. But it is Xiao He who unleashed you and pointed out the place, and his achievement is that of the huntsman."[54]

But once the beast had been caught, the hunting dogs would have become superfluous and even potentially dangerous. Han Xin (?-196 B.C.), the general commander of the Han army, once sighed that "when the cunning hares are dead, the good dogs are boiled; when the soaring birds are gone, men put away the good bow; when the enemy states have been defeated, the ministers who plotted their downfall are doomed. The world is now at peace, and so it is fitting that I be boiled!"[55] Han Xin, as

这段对话具有双重意义：一方面，它揭示了未央宫对新建政权的象征性；另一方面，它表明了萧何所代表的文职官员在建造这一宫殿时所扮演的重要角色，因而也标志着该政治集团在汉朝政府中的崛起。司马迁指出，高祖在打败项羽登上皇帝的宝座之后，对于大臣和将军们的态度立刻发生了转变。在未央宫建造之前，曾召开过一次宫廷会议讨论开国功臣们的官爵和封地问题。令所有人吃惊的是，高祖认为萧何应居头功。其他将领们反对说："今萧何未尝有汗马之劳，徒持文墨议论，不战，顾反居臣等上，何也？"高祖以一个著名的比喻做了答复："夫猎，追杀兽兔者，狗也，而发踪指示兽处者，人也。今诸君徒能得走兽耳，功狗也。至如萧何，发踪指示，功人也。"[54]

但是当野兽已经被捉到，猎狗就变得多余甚至危险了。汉军大将韩信（？—前 196 年）曾因此叹息："'狡兔死，良狗亨（烹）；高鸟尽，良弓藏；敌国破，谋臣亡。'天下已定，我固当亨（烹）！"[55]

well as many other military officers, was indeed executed later; those who were able to consolidate the peaceful state were promoted. One major contribution of this second group of people was to help the founder of the dynasty establish his absolute authority. This role was symbolized by the Weiyang Palace, which they designed and constructed for the emperor. In a way, therefore, this building was also their monument and embodied their power. Xiao He, the chief administrator of the project, remained prime minister until his death, and Yang Chengyan, the actual architect of the palace, advanced from ordinary craftsman to lord.[56]

Later books often describe the huge dimensions of the Weiyang Palace and its many buildings. Such records should be used with great caution because this palace, actually a palace complex, was expanded by various rulers throughout the Western Han. The Weiyang Palace during Gaozu's reign, as attested to by Sima Qian and Ban Gu, consisted of little more than three architectural structures: the imposing Anterior Hall and two pillar-gates to its north and east.[57] According to post-Western Han sources, feudal princes entered the east gate to attend court audiences, and low officials and ordinary people used the north gate for petitions.[58] Such functional identifications, however, may have been based on later history, since there is no evidence that the Weiyang Palace was an administrative center during Gaozu's reign. The emperor's only activity in this palace recorded in Han historical writings is a court meeting at the beginning of the ninth year when the palace was completed.[59] This audience, however, was much more casual than the previous one held in the Changle Palace. The main event was a drinking party, during which the high-spirited Gaozu made a toast and addressed his father, the "Venerable Sire," who had been given the title of the Grand Supreme Emperor (Taishanghuang): "You used to think of me as a rascal unable to look after the family fortunes with only half the industry of my older brother, Zhong. Now how do you compare us by our achievements?" His words won a round of applause.[60]

What we find here, therefore, is an interesting contrast between Gaozu's two palaces: the old palace, Changle, did not possess a distinctive architectural symbolism; its importance was as the site of the first court ceremony. The new palace, Weiyang, on the other hand, was mainly appreciated for its architectural symbolism; the ritual performed inside it became relatively unimportant. Indeed, we find that the significance

韩信和其他许多将领后来的确被诛杀；而那些能够协助皇帝巩固新政权，稳定和平局势的人则得到了重用。这后一集团的一个重要贡献，是帮助高祖建立起绝对的权威。他们为皇帝设计和建设的未央宫是这个集团所扮演的历史角色的见证。因此，从某种程度上说，这一建筑也是文官集团的纪念碑，体现出了他们的政治力量。萧何是这一工程的主要管理者，生前一直担任丞相一职，这座宫殿实际的建筑师阳成延则从一个普通的军匠被提拔为侯。[56]

后世著作常常描写未央宫的雄伟及其众多的宫室。但是，在使用这些文献时必须慎重，因为未央宫实际上是在整个西汉时期由不同皇帝逐步营建和扩展的一个宫殿群。据司马迁和班固的记载，高祖时期的未央宫只包括三组建筑，即宏壮的前殿以及北阙和东阙。[57]根据西汉以后的材料，诸侯王上书奏事时走东阙门，低级的官员和平民则走北阙门。[58]但是，这种功能的区分很可能是以汉初以后的汉代历史为根据的，因为没有迹象表明未央宫在高祖时期是一个实际的行政中心。根据汉代文献来看，高祖在此唯一的活动是九年初未央宫建成时举行的一次宫廷会议。[59]与先前长乐宫的朝会相比，这次会议相当不正式，实际上是一次宫廷宴会。席间得意洋洋的高祖向他的父亲“太公”——太上皇——敬酒，说：“始大人常以臣无赖，不能治产业，不如仲力。今某之业所就孰与仲多？”这一席话赢得殿上群臣的喝彩。[60]

我们在此可以看到高祖的两座宫殿之间有趣的对照：旧的长乐宫并不具有一种特别的建筑象征意义；其重要性在于提供了第一次宫廷典礼的场所。而新建的未央宫被看重的是其建筑的象征意义；其中所举行的仪式则并不那么重要。的确，我们发现未央宫的意义

of the Weiyang Palace lay in itself—in its construction and in its monumental image. As Xiao He stated, it was the construction of the palace that demonstrated Gaozu's mandate, and it was its lasting existence that would signify the regime's immortality. Thus, although this palace was rarely used by Gaozu after its completion and even the yearly audiences—the most important court rituals—were held somewhere else, it laid a "foundation for his heirs to build upon."

These two palaces, along with an arsenal (*wuku*), a granary (*taicang*), and an official market (*dashi*), were among the earliest constructions in Chang'an and formed the core of Gaozu's capital.[61] The founding process of this city thus contrasts sharply with that of a Three Dynasties capital, discussed in the preceding chapter. As recorded in the *Book of Songs*, when the Zhou ancestor Tan Fu began to build his town in the Plain of Zhou, he first "made the *temple* in careful order."[62] This archaic practice, then formulated into the ritual canons,[63] was significantly modified, if not fundamentally violated, by the founder of the Han: what had his first attention was no longer the ancestral temple, but his palace. This change further led to a new definition of a capital. The Eastern Zhou text *Master*
155 *Zuo's Commentaries on the Spring and Autumn Annals* provides an old gloss: "A city with an ancestral temple and the symbols of the ancestors is called a capital."[64] But now it was explained in the Han text *Interpreting Names* (*Shi ming*) that "a capital is the seat of the emperor."[65]

As the emperor's seat, this new type of capital had twin centers: the emperor's palace and his tomb. This dual structure had emerged in Gaozu's Chang'an: the palaces (as well as the market, the arsenal, and the granary) were located south of the Wei River and related to the living; tombs were built north of the river for the dead. Gaozu constructed the first Han royal mausoleum for his father by 198 B.C. near Yueyang.[66] His own mausoleum, Changling, must have been completed by 195 B.C.—he died in the fourth month in this year and was buried merely 23 days later.[67] The location of these two tombs north of the Wei River must not have been a coincidence: a similar pattern seems to have underlaid the plan of the last Shang capital, Yin. In both cases, a river marked the boundary between life and death.

This comparison, however, should not be overemphasized, because the traditional location of graveyards now gained a new significance. In the Shang case, the great mausoleums with their thousands of human

存在于其本身的构筑以及其纪念碑式的形象之中。正如萧何所言，该宫殿的构筑证明了高祖的权力，并以其永恒的形象代表着帝国不朽的名声。因此，尽管该宫殿在建成后很少被高祖使用，甚至每一年的朝会——宫廷最重要的仪式——也在他处举行，但未央宫确实是奠定了“后世有以加”的基础。

这两处宫殿以及武库、太仓、大市，是西汉长安最早的工程，构成了高祖都城的核心。[61] 因此，这座城市的建造过程和前章谈到的三代时期的都城截然不同。《诗经》中说，当周人祖先亶父开始在周原建城时，他首先是“作庙翼翼”。[62] 这一古老的史实随后成为周代礼制的规范。[63] 汉朝的开创者对此即使未有根本性的违背，却也对这个规范做出了耐人寻味的调整：首先引起皇帝关注的不再是祖庙，而是宫殿。这一改变进而为都城带来一个新的定义。东周时期的《左传》提供了一个旧的解释：“凡邑，有宗庙先君之主曰都。”[64] 但是，作于汉代的《释名》却说：“国城曰都者，国君所居。”[65]

作为国君之所居的这种新型国都含有两个并列的中心：皇帝的宫殿和帝王陵墓。这种二元结构在高祖时期的长安已经出现：宫殿（以及大市、武库和太仓）坐落在渭河以南，与生相关；陵墓建在渭河以北，与死相关。公元前 198 年，高祖在栎阳附近为其父建造了汉代第一座皇家陵墓。[66] 高祖自己的陵墓长陵可能完工于公元前 195 年。他死于该年四月，仅仅在 23 天后就举行了葬礼。[67] 这两座陵墓建在渭河以北的格局恐非汉代的发明，晚商的都城殷也有类似的布置。时隔数百年的这两座都城中都有一条河作为生与死的界限。

但是这种共同性也不能被过分强调，因为墓地传统的方位现在具有了新的意义。商代的王陵以及围绕它们的无数杀殉坑构成了

sacrifices literally constituted a realm of death, but during the Western Han, royal mausoleums were accompanied by "mausoleum towns" (*lingyi* or *yuanyi*), which became the nuclei of highly developed—in fact the most developed—residential and cultural centers in the whole country.[68] The first such mausoleum town was Wannian Yi (Town of 10,000 Years), which Gaozu dedicated to his deceased father. This town was located inside Yueyang, the Grand Supreme Emperor's fief. It is said that before his death the old man was unhappy living alone in his empty palaces hundreds of miles away from his hometown of Feng in Shandong. All the ordinary people and street scenes that he had enjoyed most—young butchers, pancake stands, liquor stores, along with cockfighting and football games—were absent there. When Gaozu learned of this, he ordered that these people and scenes be transferred from Feng to Yueyang and that the town's name be changed to New Feng (Xinfeng).[69] After a few years of living in this more comfortable environment, the Grand Supreme Emperor died in 197 B.C. and was buried in the Wannian ling (Mausoleum of 10,000 Years) some 22 *li* north of his city.[70] The city itself, either part of it or as a whole, was then dedicated to the deceased as his mausoleum town.[71] It is said that a thousand rich households were transferred from all over the country to this town.[72] Moreover, the Temple of the Grand Supreme Emperor (Taishanghuang miao) was erected south of the Wei River to hold regular sacrifices.[73]

Gaozu's own mausoleum was built around the same time,[74] and this dating explains some interesting similarities between these two royal tombs.[75] Like his father's tomb, Gaozu's mausoleum was located north of his own "fief," the imperial Chang'an. Again like his father's mausoleum and mausoleum town, which were called Wannian ling and Wannian Yi, respectively, Gaozu's tomb was named Chang ling after Chang'an. In his father's case, the Grand Supreme Emperor's original fief was turned into a mausoleum town; Gaozu never constructed a specific mausoleum town for himself before his death.[76] These parallels may imply that in Gaozu's mind, the palatial city Chang'an south of the Wei River would eventually

be turned into his own mausoleum town after his death, just as his 156
father's fief had been transformed into Wannian Yi.

This plan, however, was never realized: when his son became the master of Chang'an, a smaller mausoleum town was dedicated to the dynastic founder near his tomb. The emperor was dead, and his proper place was north of the Wei River. But the city of Chang'an continued to grow, and it grew in directions quite different from the vision of its founder.

一个死亡的国度，但是西汉皇陵周围伴有陵邑或园邑，成为整个国家中高度发展的——实际上是最高度发展的——居民和文化的中心。[68] 汉代最早的陵邑是高祖为其父亲修建的万年邑，位于太上皇的封地栎阳。据说，太上皇生前厌倦了距故乡山东丰邑数百里之遥的清冷孤独的宫中生活。他平生所喜好的那些平头百姓、市井尘杂——“屠贩少年、酤酒卖饼之业、斗鸡蹴鞠之戏”——在这里都找不到。高祖听说后，便将丰邑的百姓和景物迁徙到栎阳，并将栎阳改名为新丰。[69] 在这种优裕的环境中生活了几年之后，太上皇在公元前 197 年去世，并被安葬在新丰城以北大约 22 里的万年陵。[70] 新丰的一部分或全部在此时被作为“陵邑”奉献给了死者。[71] 据说一千家富户被从全国各地迁徙到了这个陵邑中，[72] 同时在渭河以南还修建了太上皇庙来举行日常的祭祀。[73]

高祖自己的陵墓大约也修建于此时，[74] 相近的修建时间可以解释这两座陵墓之间一些意味深长的相似之处。[75] 与其父亲的陵墓一样，高祖的陵墓也坐落在自己“封地”——长安——以北。父亲的陵墓和陵邑分别称为万年陵和万年邑，高祖的陵墓也根据长安的名字而被称为长陵。太上皇原来的封地被改为陵邑；而高祖在生前从未为自己构筑一座特别的陵邑。[76] 这些相似点很可能说明，在高祖的心目中，正像其父亲的封地被转化为万年邑一样，渭河南岸富丽堂皇的长安将在其死后转化为自己的陵邑。

但是，这一可能的计划并未实现：当他的儿子继他成为长安的主人后，一座奉献给开国皇帝的较小城邑在其陵墓的旁边建立起来。高祖已经死了，他合适的归宿应在渭河以北。但是长安仍在成长，而它成长的方向与其创建者的预想将相去甚远。

❸ Emperor Hui and the Walls of Chang'an

Two months after the renovation of the Changle Palace began, Gaozu issued an edict in the tenth month of 202 B.C. demanding that walls be built around all cities and towns.[77] At that time, the wall of the "city of Chang'an" was identical with that of the palace. According to the Song scholar Cheng Dachang, none of the Qin dynasty pleasure palaces, including the Xingle Palace before it became Gaozu's imperial city, had tall walls; rather, they were surrounded only by short barriers.[78] But a recent survey by Chinese archaeologists shows that the new Changle Palace was encircled by a huge wall some 10 kilometers long; its base was more than 20 meters in cross section, far thicker than the new and more famous "city walls" of Chang'an built after Gaozu's death, during the reign of the second Han ruler, Emperor Hui.[79]

Primary data concerning the construction of Chang-an's new walls can be found in Sima Qian's *Records of the Historian* and Ban Gu's *History of the Former Han*. Both authors, however, seem to have provided inconsistent information. The two relevant passages in Sima Qian's writing read:

> The first year of Emperor Hui [194 B.C.], Spring, the first month: they started work on the northwest part of Chang'an's walls. . . . In the third year [192 B.C.], the construction of Chang'an's walls began.[80]
>
> The construction of Chang'an's walls did not begin till the third year of Emperor Hui; half the walls were finished in the fourth year [191 B.C.]; and the whole enclosure was completed in the fifth and sixth years [190 B.C. and 189 B.C.]. Feudal princes came to attend a court audience, celebrating its completion in the tenth month.[81]

Ban Gu's accounts are more detailed, but again seem contradictory:

> The first year of Emperor Hui. . . Spring, the first month: The city walls of Chang'an were under construction. . . .
>
> The third year, Spring: 146,000 men and women from the area

600 *li* around Chang'an were called out to build the city walls. The construction lasted for 30 days. . . . In the sixth month, 20,000 convicts were called out from the domains of feudal princes and nobles to build the walls of Chang'an.

The fifth year, Spring, the first month: 145,000 men and women from the area 600 *li* around Chang'an were again called out to build the city walls. The construction again lasted for 30 days. . . . In the ninth month, the walls of Chang'an were completed.[82]

三、惠帝和长安城墙

公元前 202 年九月，也就是在长乐宫开始改建后的两个月，高祖颁布了一条敕令，要求在所有的城和邑的周围建筑城墙。[77] 当时，“长安城”的城墙很可能就是长乐宫的宫墙。根据宋人程大昌的观点，秦代的离宫，包括兴乐宫在变成高祖的都城之前，都没有高墙，只是在周围有些低矮的围障。[78] 但是，中国考古工作者最近的调查证明，高祖修葺的长乐宫周围有大约 10 公里长的厚重围墙；墙基的横断面超过 20 米，比高祖死后第二个皇帝惠帝时期新建的更为著名的长安“城墙”还要厚得多。[79]

司马迁的《史记》和班固的《汉书》中都有惠帝建造长安新城墙的记载，但是这两位史学家的记载似乎彼此矛盾。司马迁笔下的两个相关段落如下：

> 孝惠元年（前 194），始作长安城西北方。……三年（前 192），初作长安城。[80]
>
> 三年，方筑长安城，四年（前 191）就半，五年六年（前 190、前 189）城就。诸侯来会。十月，朝贺。[81]

班固的记述较为详细，但似与《史记》的记载不一致：

> 元年……春正月，城长安……
>
> 三年春，发长安六百里内男女十四万六千人城长安，三十日罢……六月，发诸侯王、列侯徒隶二万人城长安。
>
> 五年……春正月，复发长安六百里内男女十四万五千人城长安，三十日罢……九月，长安城成。[82]

> Chang'an was established by Gaozu in his fifth year. The building of its walls commenced in the first year of Emperor Hui, and concluded in the sixth year.[83]

Three confusing points are noticeable; the first two regard the beginning and ending dates of the project, and the third concerns Ban Gu's statement, that the working season of 190 B.C. had ended by the second month, but the city walls were completed in the ninth month. These puzzles, however, can be reasonably resolved. According to my reconstruction of the events, a section of wall was first built northwest of Chang'an in 194 B.C. But the systematic construction of the city walls began only in 192 B.C. and lasted for about three years. During these three years, the labor force used in the construction included peasants living near the capital and convicts sent from various principalities and prefectures. The former worked only during the slack agricultural season in the first month of the year; the latter must have formed a permanent force. Thus, after the peasants returned home, the convicts continued to work and finally finished the whole project. In the early Han calender, a year began with the tenth month. This means that the walls were completed toward the end of 190 B.C., and the celebration took place at the very beginning of 189 B.C. This is why Sima Qian and Ban Gu dated
157 the completion of the project in both years.[84] Moreover, an additional piece of evidence has survived from a lost book called *An Explanation of Han Dynasty Palatial Structures* (*Han gongque shu*): "They built the east city wall in the fourth year, and the north wall in the fifth year."[85] It is possible that the west and south sides were built in the third year.

The walls of Emperor Hui's Chang'an have been a major focus of archaeological investigations since the Song dynasty. The most recent result is summarized by Wang Zhongshu, the director of the PRC archaeological team:[86]

> When archaeologists investigated Chang'an's ruins, they found that most of the wall was still exposed above ground. Many wall sections had

collapsed, but underground the foundations still remained. According to the two surveys of 1957 and 1962, the east wall was 6,000 m. long, the south wall 7,600 m., the west wall 4,900 m., and the north wall 7,200 m. The total length of the four walls was 25,700 m., which corresponds to a little over 63 *li* according to the Han system of measurement. This basically conforms to the recorded 63 *li* in *Han jiuyi*

长安，高帝五年置。惠帝元年初城，六年成。[83]

这里有三点使人困惑之处，前两点是关于工程开始和结束的时间，第三点是班固的记述，即首先说惠帝五年（前 190）正月的工程在三十天后就结束了，但是又说九月城墙完成。然而，这些似是而非的混乱都可以得到合理的解释。根据我对这一事件的重构，公元前 194 年，先在长安西北方修建了一段城墙。但是对城墙的系统修筑要到公元前 192 年才开始，并持续了大约三年的时间。在这三年中，所动用的劳动力包括都城附近的农民以及各诸侯王、列侯封地内的刑徒。前一部分人只在该年正月农闲时来此工作，后者则要服长期的劳役。因此，当附近的农民回家后，刑徒们仍要接着干下去，直到整个工程结束。汉初历法以每年的十月为正月。也就是说，城墙在公元前 190 年底完工，公元前 189 年初即举行了庆祝活动。这就是为何司马迁和班固将完工的时间记到了两年中。[84] 此外，失传的《汉宫阙疏》中还提供了另一条材料："四年筑东面，五年筑北面。"[85] 西面和南面的城墙很可能是在惠帝三年建造的。

自宋代以来，惠帝时期建设的长安城墙就是考古学调查的一个焦点。王仲殊最近总结了近年来的田野考古成果：[86]

考古工作者在长安城遗址勘查时，大部分城墙犹高出地面，虽然有不少断缺之处，但仍有墙基遗留于地下。经 1957 年和 1962 年两次实测，东面城墙长约 6000 米，南面城墙长约 7600 米，西面城墙长约 4900 米，北面城墙长约 7200 米；四面城墙总长约 25700 米，合汉代六十二里强，基本上与《史记·吕后本纪》索引及《续汉书·郡国志》注引《汉旧仪》长安城周围六十三里的记载相符。全城总面

> [The old regulations of the Han]. The total area was about 36 square km. The city wall, which was built of rammed yellow earth, was over 12 m. high, and the width at its base was 12-16 m. . . . . Outside the city wall was a moat, about 8 m. wide and 3 m. deep. The excavations in 1962 of the area outside the Zhangchengmen Gate clarified the shape of the moat outside the city gate and also proved that wooden bridges were built over the moat.

Based on these investigations, Chinese archaeologists have redrawn Chang'an's outline. The result, shown in Fig. 3.4, which Wang Zhongshu published along with his description, differs only in detail from those of investigators since the eleventh century. In all these drawings, Chang'an is an irregular square with three gates on each side. Only the east wall, however, follows a straight line, and the most irregular part is the northwest section, which appears as a diagonal line with a number of sharp bends. Interestingly, according to the construction sequence proposed above, this part of the wall was built first, in 194 B.C., before the systematic construction began. The east wall was built three years later. The relationship between the shape and date of each section is unlikely to be coincidental. It suggests that when the northwest part was built, the builder had not yet developed the notion of shaping Chang'an as a "square" with its four sides corresponding to the four directions. This idea must have only appeared later and then guided the construction of the rest of the walls. The modern scholar Ma Xianxing has also suggested that the northwest section may have been built to stop floods and was then integrated into the whole enclosure.[87] In short, all ancient records and modern investigations lead me to propose that the walls' formal construction began in the third year of Emperor Hui's reign (192 B.C.), and that this date implies an important change in Chang'an's design and monumentality.

Such a chronological view, however, has been largely neglected in traditional studies of Chang'an; a persistent subject in both ancient and modern scholarship has been the design of the walls as a static whole: Was the shape of the city modeled on the Big and Little Dippers (Fig. 3.6), planned according to certain "grid" systems (Fig. 3.7), or simply based on the area's topography? Without ruling out many insightful observations inherent in such speculations, I would start from a perhaps more essential

> 积约 36 平方公里。城墙全部用黄土夯筑而成。其高度在 12 米以上，下部宽度为 12—16 米。……壕沟宽约 8 米，深约 3 米……1962 年在章城门外的发掘，究明了城门前面壕沟的形制，可以判断当时在壕沟上架有木桥，以便出入。

根据这些调查，中国考古学者重新勾画出了长安的轮廓。王仲殊在其著作中所发表的线图［图 3.4］与 11 世纪以来的那些调查只有细节上的差别。在所有这些图中，长安呈现出一个不规则的方形，每面三门。只有东墙是一条直线，而最不规则的部分是西北部，在其倾斜的走向中有多处明显的转折。值得注意的是，根据上述对于长安城建造过程的分析，这部分城墙是于公元前 194 年，在全部工程系统地展开之前首先建成的，而东墙于三年之后才建成。城墙形状和建造时间的这种关系恐非巧合。很可能当筑造西北角落的时候，建造者还没有想到要将整个长安的城墙建成与四方相应的“方形”。这种想法只是在后来才出现，并成为后续工程的指导思想。马先醒也认为西北部的城墙可能是为了防洪而修建的，后来才被纳入整个城圈中。[87] 简单地说，所有古代文献和现代田野调查材料都使我们相信，正式的城墙工程实际上开始于惠帝三年（前 192），而这一年代意味着长安规划和其纪念碑性的一个重要转变。

传统研究在很大程度上忽视了这种年代学的观点，而是长期以来将长安城墙视作一个静态的设计。一旦当我们把城墙的修建看成是一个历史过程，了解到建城思想的变化，我们就可以提出这样的问题：长安城的形状果真是模仿了北斗南斗［图 3.6］，或按照某种“棋盘式”的设计系统［图 3.7］，或是被该地的地形决定的吗？我并不否认这些解释中所包含的富有洞察力的假设，但希望强调我们应该从一个更基本的出发点重新思考长安的营建。首先的一个问题

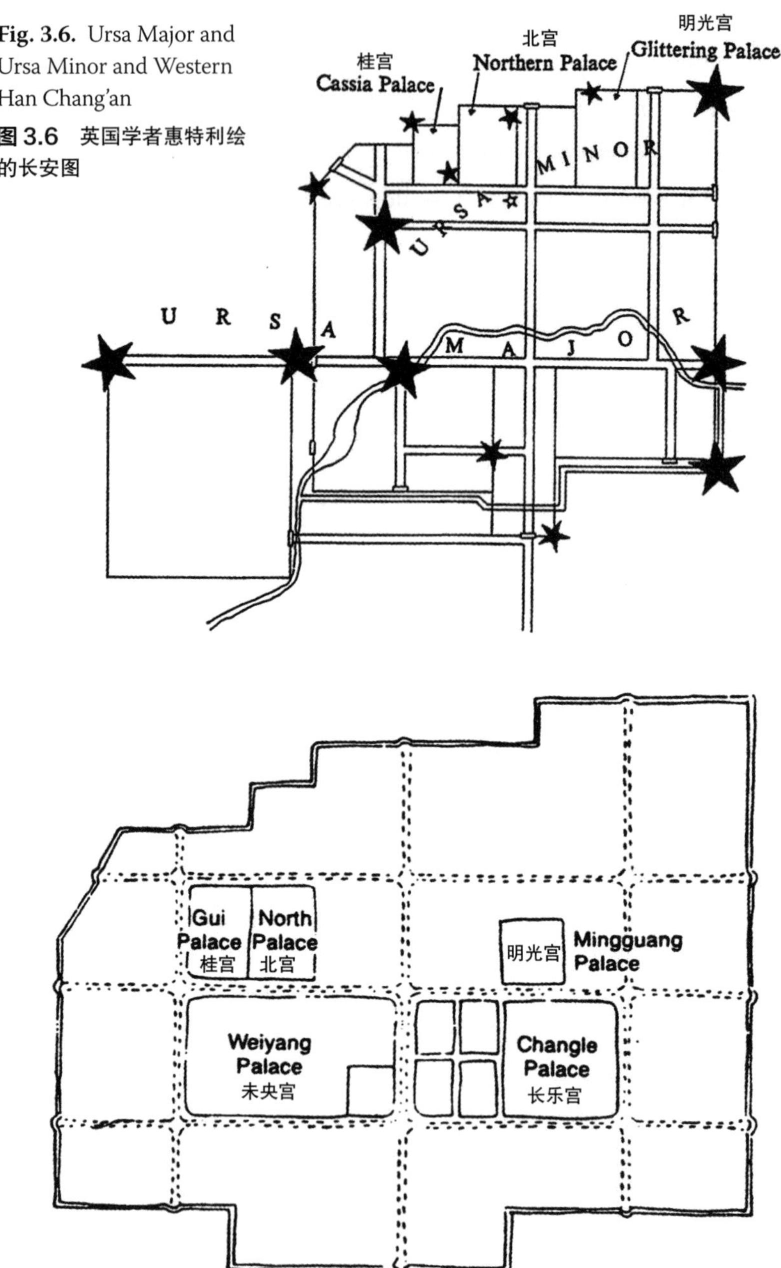

Fig. 3.6. Ursa Major and Ursa Minor and Western Han Chang'an

图 3.6 英国学者惠特利绘的长安图

Fig. 3.7. Reconstruction of Western Han Chang'an based on an idealized grid system

图 3.7 基于理想化的栅格系统而复原的西汉长安

point: Why were these walls built? A common interpretation, that the walls were intended to protect the city residents, seems doubtful. As we have learned, Gaozu's "city of Chang'an" already had much stronger walls, and it is hard to imagine that within two years after Gaozu's death, Chang'an's population would have boomed so suddenly that a much larger city enclosure was needed.[88] I will argue later that in fact walled Chang'an remained an "imperial city" throughout the Western Han, and that the growing population of the capital area was concentrated mainly in the suburbs. 158

The construction of Chang'an's new walls was not an isolated phenomenon. A closer examination of early Han history will disclose that this work was part of a larger project that aimed to give the capital a more traditional and thus more authoritative image. This project, moreover, was related to a profound shift in early Han politics and ideology: namely, that "imperial sovereignty developed from a reliance on force to a dependence on belief and theory; from the seizure of control by armed strength to an initiation of rule backed by religious sanction."[89] This shift had become evident during the later years of Gaozu's reign:

是：为什么在惠帝时期要修建统一的城墙？根据一个通行的解释，筑城墙的目的是为了保护城内的居民，然而这一观点大有疑问。上文说过，高祖的“长安城”已经有了厚重的墙，很难设想仅仅在高祖去世两年后长安就因为人口暴增而需要一个更大的城圈。[88] 而且我在下文还将谈到，实际上，城圈内的长安在整个西汉一朝主要是宫殿区，增加的人口主要集中在郊外。

长安新城墙的修建并不是一个孤立的现象。对汉初历史更为细致的考察可以证明，该工程是一个更大的计划的一部分，其目的在于赋予这座都城一种更为传统的，因而也就更为权威的形象。该计划和汉初政治和思想中的一个深刻变化有密切联系，即“汉帝国正从对武力的依赖转向对信仰和理论的依赖，从以武装夺取政权转向依靠宗教约束力来统治国家”。[89] 这种转变在高祖晚年已经相当明显：

the questions faced by the new regime and posed by it had gradually changed from how to conquer the country to how to rule it. Governing methods were increasingly sought in old traditions, and a symbolic system was demanded to support a hierarchical political structure. The two influential figures in this transition were Lu Jia and Shusun Tong.

These two men differed in two ways from Xiao He, the chief designer of Gaozu's Chang'an. First, Xiao He died a year after Gaozu, but both Lu Jia and Shusun Tong lived through the new reign and played important roles in Emperor Hui's court. Second, unlike Xiao He, who was a practical administrator, Lu and Shusun were Confucian scholars with strong interests in history and ceremony. Both believed that only the Confucian tradition could put the country in order and that the past had to be the model for the present. The following passage from Lu Jia's biography sufficiently illuminates his political approach:

> In his audiences with Gaozu, Lu Jia on numerous occasions expounded and praised the *Songs* and the *Documents*, until one day Gaozu began to rail at him: "All I possess I have won on horseback!" said the emperor. "Why should I bother with the *Songs* and *Documents*?"
>
> "Your Majesty may have won it on horseback, but can you rule it
> on horseback?" asked Lu Jia. "Kings Tang and Wu in ancient times won
> 159 possession of the empire through the principle of revolt, but it was by
> the principle of obedience that they assured the continuance of their
> dynasties. . . . If the Qin, after it had united the world under its rule,
> had practiced benevolence and righteousness and modeled its ways
> upon the sages of antiquity, how would Your Majesty ever have been able
> to win possession of the empire?"
>
> This conversation ended with Gaozu's requesting Lu Jia's writings on "the successes and failures of the states of ancient times." Later, after Lu Jia had presented the twelve chapters of his *New Discourses* (*Xin yu*) to the throne, "the emperor never failed to express his delight and approval."[90]

Lu Jia's rhetoric is reminiscent of Shusun Tong's words quoted earlier in this chapter: "Confucian scholars are not of much use when one is marching to conquest, but they can be of help in keeping what has already been won." As noted earlier, this reasoning led to Gaozu's first court ceremony, in the Changle Palace in 200 B.C. Shusun Tong's influence on the Han court, however, did not stop there.[91] According to his biographers, after 200 B.C. he was given the official title "grand ceremonialist" (*fengchang*) and ordered to take charge of all imperial ritual affairs. He set up the rites for ancestral sacrifices and also composed temple hymns.

他所面对的问题已经从如何征服这个国家转变为如何统治它。统治者越来越多地到旧日的传统中去寻找支持自己统治的手段，寻求一种象征体系以支撑一个等级性的政治架构。在这一转变过程中，两个发挥了重要影响的人物是陆贾和叔孙通。这两人与高祖时期营建长安的主要策划者萧何在两个方面上有差别。首先，萧何在高祖死后一年也去世了，但陆贾和叔孙通一直活到惠帝时期，并在惠帝的朝廷中扮演了重要的角色。再者，与作为行政官员实际参政的萧何不同，陆贾和叔孙通都是儒生。他们对历史和礼仪有着强烈的兴趣，而且都相信只有依靠儒家传统才能建立起国家秩序，相信历史为现实提供了规范。对于陆贾说来，以下出自司马迁所写的《陆贾传》中的这段文字可以充分表现出他的政治取向：

> 陆生时时前说，称《诗》《书》。高帝骂之曰："乃公居马上而得之，安事《诗》《书》！"陆生曰："居马上得之，宁可以马上治之乎？且汤、武逆取而以顺守之……向使秦已并天下，行仁义，法先圣，陛下安得而有之？"
>
> 最后高祖要求陆贾写出"古成败之国"的经验与教训。陆贾于是呈奏了《新语》十二篇，"每奏一篇，高帝未赏（尝）不称善。"[90]

陆贾的进言使我们回想起本章前面所引叔孙通的话"儒者难与进取，可与守成"。如上文所述，这种观点使得高祖于公元前 200 年在长乐宫制订了最早的朝廷礼仪。但是，叔孙通对于汉朝廷的影响并不限于此。[91] 根据其传记，他于公元前 200 年被任命为奉常，负责所有皇室礼仪事务。他制订了宗庙仪法并谱写了宗庙颂歌。

In 198 B.C., he was further named by Gaozu tutor of the crown prince. This new position enabled him to influence the next ruler and to take part in the secret arrangements regarding the royal succession. Partially because of a protest by Shusun, Gaozu gave up the idea of changing his heir, and this must explain Shusun's popularity in Emperor Hui's court.[92] As suggested by a number of instances recorded in his biography, the new ruler adopted all his suggestions regarding ritual affairs; his contribution was considered "to have laid a foundation for the various ceremonial procedures of the dynasty."[93]

Lu Jia and Shusun Tong, therefore, represented a new direction in the transformation of the Han court. Whereas in Gaozu's time this transformation was motivated by the desire to promote the emperor's absolute power, in the period leading up to and during Emperor Hui's reign the focus shifted to establishing a political institution backed by traditional ideology and rites. These successive political agendas found their most concrete manifestations and expressions in the changing forms of the dynasty's capital: Gaozu's imposing but isolated palaces symbolized sovereignty; Emperor Hui's Chang'an, with its various parts enclosed by a unifying wall, embodied a large political organization. Gaozu's palaces were modeled on the terrace buildings of powerful Eastern Zhou lords; Emperor Hui's Chang'an derived its form from China's "classical" architectural tradition exemplified by an idealized Zhou capital. The link between *tradition* and the Western Zhou was not accidental; it had been established long ago by Confucius himself: "Oh! How boundless is its refinement; it is the [Western] Zhou that I am going to follow."[94]

This traditionalistic or "classicist" tendency is evident in many of Emperor Hui's activities designed by his chief advisers. This emperor came to the throne at age fifteen. Three years later in 192 B.C. he reached adulthood and underwent a "capping ceremony" (*guanli*). This rite is regulated in great detail in Confucian ritual books, and the date of the emperor's ceremony agrees with such regulations.[95] In the same year, he also issued an edict to encourage and reward people practicing filial piety and brotherly love—again an unmistakable sign of his adoption of Confucian ideology.[96] This young emperor was a pupil of Shusun Tong, and all his recorded conversations with his teacher are about ritual affairs. Chang'an's new walls and other structures were constructed during the same period and reflected the same tendency—a contention based on the following observations:

公元前 198 年他又被封为太子太傅。这一新的职位使得他能够影响下一位皇帝，并有机会与高祖密谈有关皇位继承的大事。部分地由于叔孙通的抗言，高祖打消了更换继承人的念头，而这也可能就是叔孙通之所以在惠帝朝中更加得势的原因。[92] 叔孙通传记中有很多事例说明，新统治者惠帝采纳了他所有关于仪法的建议，故史书中说"及稍定汉诸仪法，皆叔孙生为太常所论著也"。[93]

因此，陆贾和叔孙通代表着汉朝廷转变中的一个新的方向。这个转变在高祖时期的表现是提升皇帝的绝对权威；在此之后直到惠帝时期，焦点逐渐转向建立一个基于传统意识形态与礼仪上的政治机构。这一系列政治议程在都城长安的变化中得到了最具体的体现和表达：高祖修建的宏伟却孤立的宫殿象征着绝对君权；而惠帝修筑的城墙则把长安城的各部分环绕起来，使其形成一个统一的整体和综合性的政治机构。高祖的宫殿模仿了强大的东周诸侯们的台式高层建筑；惠帝长安的形态则来源于以理想化周代都城为代表的"经典"建筑传统。将传统和西周联系在一起并非偶然；这种联系在很久以前就被孔子本人建立起来："郁郁乎文哉！吾从周。"[94]

惠帝的行动显示了强烈的传统主义或"古典主义"倾向。这些行为大都由其首席顾问所策划。这位皇帝 15 岁登基。三年后的公元前 192 年，他长大成人并举行了"冠礼"。这种礼仪在儒家的礼书中有详细的规定，这位皇帝举行仪式的时间也和这些规定相符。[95] 同一年，他还颁布了一条敕令，鼓励并奖赏人民的孝悌之行，这也是他遵从儒家思想明白无误的宣示。[96] 这位年轻的皇帝是叔孙通的学生，文献所记载的这对师徒之间的所有对话都与礼仪事务有关。长安的新城墙以及其他建筑也在这一时期开工，这些工程反映了同样的倾向，以下几点可以为证：

1. The emperor moved into the Weiyang Palace and had the Temple of Gaozu (Gao miao) built east of the throne hall.[97] The juxtaposition of the palace and the temple thus accords with the plan of the idealized Zhou capital recorded in the "Regulations of Workmanship": "On the left [of the imperial palace] is the Ancestral Temple" ("left" means "east" because the emperor faces south).

2. In 189 B.C., a new official market called the West Market (Xishi) was built north of the Weiyang Palace. Its position again agrees with the "Regulations of Workmanship": "In front is the Hall of Audience and behind the markets."

3. Among Emperor Hui's additions to the old palaces was an
160 icehouse (*lingshi*) inside the Weiyang Palace complex. Such a structure is mentioned in the *Rites of Zhou* as part of the Zhou royal palace.[98]

4. During his reign, Emperor Hui constructed his mausoleum, An ling, to the west (or "right") of Gaozu's mausoleum.[99] This location seems again to have been determined according to the *Rites of Zhou*: "The burial of the dynastic founder should occupy the central position. Those belonging to the *zhao* sequence in the royal lineage should be buried to its left and those belonging to the *mu* sequence to its right."[100] Emperor Hui was the first *mu* emperor of the Han and was thus buried to the right of his father's tomb.

5. According to the "Regulations of Workmanship" as well as the *Songs* and the *Documents*, the palace, the ancestral temple, and the markets are three essential components of a capital and should be enclosed by city walls. The market and the temple of the Grand Supreme Emperor built by Gaozu were located outside his city of Chang'an. Emperor Hui's city walls, however, installed these parts inside the capital. In fact, the orientations of the walls and the size of the new Chang'an were likely determined by these existing structures: the two palaces provided the east, south, and west walls with a fixed reference, but the north wall had to be extended to the south bank of the Wei River in order to enclose the

temple of the Grand Supreme Emperor.

6. The new Chang'an's intended square shape, its twelve gates, and the three openings on each gate were also based on the plan offered by the "Regulations of Workmanship": "The royal architect constructs the state capital [of the Zhou]. He makes a square nine *li* on each side; each side has three gates. Within the capital are nine streets running north-south and nine streets running east-west." In fact, it is these gates that clinch a definite relationship between Emperor Hui's Chang'an and the idealized Zhou capital plan: not only do the number and locations of

1. 惠帝搬进了未央宫，并在其东建立高庙。[97] 皇宫与祖庙的并置遵循了《考工记》所记载的周代都城理想化格局中“左祖”（因为皇帝面南，故东为左）的规定。

2. 公元前 189 年，在未央宫以北建立了一个政府管辖的市场，称作“西市”。其位置也和《考工记》所说的“面朝后市”一致。

3. 惠帝在原未央宫建筑群内新增建的项目中有一处藏冰的“凌室”。这样的设置记载于《周礼》，是周代皇宫的一部分。[98]

4. 惠帝在位时，在高祖陵墓西（右）面修建了自己的未来陵墓安陵。[99] 这一方位似乎也是按照《周礼》来确定的：“先王之葬居中。以昭穆为左右。”[100] 惠帝是汉代第一个属于“穆”的皇帝，所以要葬在其父亲陵墓之右。

5. 根据《考工记》《诗经》和《尚书》等传统文献，宫殿、祖庙和市是都城中的基本组成部分，并且需要有城墙环绕。高祖为太上皇所修建的市和庙位于当时的长安城之外。但是，惠帝的城墙却将所有这几个部分置入都城之中。实际上，城墙的走向和新长安的规模似乎是被这些已存在的建筑决定的：长乐宫和未央宫这两组宫殿确定了东、南和西墙的走向；为了将太上皇庙包括在城里，北墙必须沿着渭河修建。

6. 新长安的平面近于方形，有 12 座城门，每门有三个通道，这种形式也和《考工记》中“匠人营国，方九里，旁三门。国中九经，九纬”的说法相应。实际上，这些城门最有力地证明了惠帝长安和理想化周代都城的格局之间的确定联系：不仅城门的数量和位置

these gates agree with the traditional model, but some of these gates were constructed only for appearance. Most notably, four gates—the Zhangcheng Gate on the west side, the Xi'an Gate and Fu'ang Gate on the south side, and the Bacheng Gate on the east side—were very close to the existing Weiyang and Changle palaces. According to archaeological excavations, the distances between these gates and the palaces were a mere 50 meters,[101] and streets running through these gates would have been blocked by the palaces' tall walls or would have become entryways into the palaces.[102]

7. As many scholars have suggested, Gaozu's palaces faced east. This is because according to an old belief, the west was the most honorable position,[103] and the emperor was supposed to face east toward his ministers during an audience. This convention in architectural planning did not disappear after Gaozu's reign (it especially persisted in the design of individual imperial graveyards), but the orientation of the walled Chang'an was changed to face south to tally with the Zhou plan in the "Regulations of Workmanship." This new orientation, which determined the locations of Gaozu's temple, Emperor Hui's mausoleum, and the new market, was emphasized by the establishment of a major avenue running along the city's north-south axis. The An Gate at the south end of this avenue then became the major entrance of Chang'an, and its specific status was indicated by its placement in a unique U-shaped wall section.

The result of these modifications was a new Chang'an. This new
161 city, however, was modeled on an old architectural plan and restored a traditional sense of monumentality. The towering palaces constructed by Gaozu were now encircled and blocked by double walls; as monuments to sovereignty, they retreated from public sight and again became hidden and secret. With the erection of the walls, Chang'an gained a new measure for its internal structure: an "extrinsic space" was established to control "the relation between independent object systems"

and to provide them "with standards of reference for their perceptual features."[104] No single structure claimed an independent monumentality; Chang'an had been transformed into a "monumental city"—an architectural system that synthesized its various parts into a whole. This new Chang'an is described by Ban Gu in his *Western Capital Rhapsody*:

与传统模式相合，而且有些城门似乎只是为了符合传统格局而修建的。最为明显的是西面的章城门，南面的西安门、覆盎门和东面的霸城门。根据考古发掘，这些城门距离未央宫和长乐宫很近，有的距离仅有 50 米。[101] 进入城门的道路或被宫殿的高墙挡住，或变成进入宫殿的通道。[102]

7. 许多学者认为高祖的宫殿面向东。因为按照一种古老的观念，西是最尊贵的方位，[103] 上朝时皇帝因此应该坐西朝东，大臣背东朝西。虽然这种习俗在高祖时期以后的建筑设计中并没有完全消失（在皇帝陵园的设计中特别明显），但是新建的长安城墙却将整个城市的方向改为坐北朝南，因此与《考工记》中对周式都城的记载吻合。这一改变也决定了高庙、惠帝安陵以及新建的市的方向。南北轴线上主要干道的建立使长安城"面南"的特征更加明确。位于这条大道南端的安门成为长安的主要入口，其特殊地位也由两侧的 U 形城墙表现出来。

这些增建改造的结果是一个"新长安"。但是这座新城却是对旧日建筑规划的模拟并复原了一种传统的纪念碑性的意义。高祖所建造的那些高耸的宫殿现在被包围和遮蔽在双重高墙之中；作为君权的纪念碑，它们又从公众的目光中隐退了，变成一种隐藏起来的私密建筑。由于周围高墙的建立，长安城内的建筑拥有了一个新的衡量尺度："外在空间"被重新确立，控制了"独立物体系统之间的关系"，并赋予它们以"知觉特征的参照标准"。[104] 在这座新的长安城中没有任何一座单体建筑可以被看作一座独立的纪念碑；整个城市变成了一座"纪念碑式城市"——一个将不同部分综合为一体的建筑体系。班固的《西都赋》描写了这座新的汉代都城：

They erected a metal fortress a myriad spans long,
Dredged the surrounding moat to form a gaping chasm,
Cleared broad avenues three lanes wide,
Placed twelve gates for passage in and out.
Within, the city was pierced by roads and streets,
With ward gates and portals nearly a thousand.
In the nine markets they set up bazaars,
Their wares separated by type, their shop rows distinctly divided.[105]

But was Chang'an really turned into a faithful copy of the idealized Zhou capital? The answer is no. Emperor Hui had inherited the old Chang'an, and all he could do was superimpose a traditional structure onto the existing city. The new walls with their twelve gates built by some 320,000 laborers in five years only added a facade to Gaozu's palaces, and the buildings and streets within the enclosure could never be arranged or rearranged satisfactorily to meet the traditional standards. But there is a more profound reason for Chang'an's divergence from an archaic city: China had entered the imperial era, and its capital had to assume new functions and address new needs. Even during Emperor Hui's reign when traditionalism prevailed, it was unmistakably understood that the past could only serve the present; it could never challenge current values. Although a heroic effort was made to give Chang'an a "classical" monumental image, whenever there was a direct confrontation between tradition and a contemporary need, the latter invariably won out.

Immediately after the new Chang'an came into being, its layout had to be altered somewhat in conjunction with the fundamental change in ancestor worship I have described above. Based on the Zhou code, Gaozu's temple was first built east of the Weiyang Palace close to the newly erected south city wall. Every month a ritual procession conveyed Gaozu's royal crown and robes from his mausoleum north of the Wei River to this temple to receive offerings. The road this procession took was the central north-south avenue. This seemingly well-organized ancestral rite, however, soon began to interfere with the living ruler's activities. Since Emperor Hui had moved into the Weiyang Palace and his mother, the powerful Empress Dowager Lü, occupied the Changle Palace, a raised passageway was built over the central avenue to allow the emperor to travel between these two palaces. The young emperor

建金城而万雉，呀周池而成渊。
披三条之广路，立十二之通门。
内则街衢洞达，闾阎且千。
九市开场，货别隧分，
……[105]

但是，长安果真变成理想化周代都城的忠实翻版了吗？答案是否定的。惠帝继承了高祖的长安，他所能做到的只是在已经存在的基础上添加一个传统的框架。动用了 32 万劳力、花了五年时间修成的有 12 个门的新城墙只是为高祖的宫殿加了一个“表面”，城圈内的建筑和街道无法被重新安排，无法与传统标准完全吻合。但是长安和三代城市的差别还有着更深层的原因：中国已经进入了帝国时代，其都城必须具备新的功能，服从于新的需要。即使是在传统主义盛行的惠帝时期，过去也只能服务于现在，而不能挑战现行的价值，这一点是毫无疑问的。尽管当时付出了极大的努力以赋予长安一个“古典式”的纪念碑城市形象，但是每当传统和当下的需要产生直接对抗时，现实总会取得最终的胜利。

比如说，新的长安形成后，其规划必须立即进行某种程度的调整，原因和上文中谈到的汉代祖先崇拜中的基本变化有关。根据周代的模式，高庙建在未央宫以东，靠近新建立的南城墙。每个月里，仪仗队伍将高祖的冠服从渭河以北的陵墓，通过城中的南北大道送到高庙中接受祭祀。这一看来似乎组织完备的祭祀仪式不久便和当朝皇帝的活动发生了矛盾，因为惠帝已经搬进了未央宫，他富有权势的母亲吕后占据着长乐宫，两宫之间有一条跨越中央大道的复道，以便皇帝往返于二者之间。结果是，年轻的皇帝行走于通往

was thus walking *above* the path leading to his father's temple, and the ritual procession carrying Gaozu's relics had to proceed *beneath* his feet. Such disrespect to the dynasty's founder was intolerable. The conflict was resolved not by tearing down the imperial passageway, but by removing the ancestral temple. In making this decision, the Confucian master Shusun Tong once again demonstrated his flexibility:

> The ruler of men never makes a mistake! The walk is already built, and the common people all know about it. Now if Your Majesty were to tear it down, it would be admitting that you had made a mistake in the first place. I beg you instead to set up a second funerary temple north of the Wei River to which the late emperor's robes and caps may be taken each month. To enlarge or increase the number of ancestral temples is after all the beginning of true filial piety![106]

Shusun's message is clear: the Zhou capital plan was not absolute and should be revised according to the demands of realpolitik. The primary criterion for an adjustment was the authority of the living emperor, not tradition. Nevertheless, such an adjustment should still be based
162 on Confucian ideology: since filial piety provided the rationale for the relocation of Gaozu's temple, the revision of tradition was supported by tradition itself.

This event, which marked a crucial step in the transition of the religious and social center from temple to tomb, was related to two other equally important events that took place during or immediately after Emperor Hui's reign. The first was the establishment of the *peiling* (satellite tomb) system; the second, the construction of a series of mausoleum towns. As a result, a new type of imperial mausoleum became the center of religious and secular life and fundamentally changed the structure of the capital city.

Gaozu's prime minister, Xiao He, died in the second year of Emperor Hui's reign (193 B.C.). He was buried immediately outside the main gate of Gaozu's Chang ling mausoleum beside the imperial funerary path.[107] Three years later in 190 B.C., Cao Can, another chief minister of Gaozu, passed away. Like Xiao He, he was from the same town as the dynastic founder, and he succeeded Xiao as prime minister in 193 B.C. His tomb was next to Xiao He's to the east of Chang ling. More founding ministers were buried there during the following years of Emperor Hui's and Empress Dowager Lü's reigns; among them were Zhang Liang, the Marquis of Liu (d. 189 B.C.) and the Right Chief Minister and Grand Tutor Wang Ling (d. 181 B.C.).[108] Such practices contradict

其父亲之庙的道路之上，抬着高祖遗物的队伍不得不从他的脚下走过。这种对于开国皇帝的非礼之举似乎是不能被容忍的。但是，解决这一矛盾的办法却并不是取消复道，而是把高庙迁移到一个新的地点。在做出这一决定时，硕儒叔孙通再次显示了他机变的才能。他说：

> 人主无过举。今已作，百姓皆知之，今坏此，则示有过举。愿陛下原庙渭北，衣冠月出游之，益广多宗庙，大孝之本也。[106]

叔孙通的意思很明白：周城的模式不是绝对的，它必须根据实际的政治需要进行调整。调整的主要依据是当朝皇帝的威信，而不是传统的权威。但是这一调整仍需要以儒家思想为基础：因为“孝”为高庙的迁移提供了理由，传统本身因此支持了对传统的改造。

标志着宗教和社会活动中心从庙向墓的转移中所迈出的重要一步，这一事件又与惠帝时期和此后不久发生的另两件同样重要的事有关。第一件事是陪陵制度的建立，第二件事是陵邑的建设。其结果是一种新型的帝陵成为宗教和世俗生活的中心，从而使得都城结构发生了根本性的变化。

高祖的丞相萧何去世于惠帝二年（前 193），他立刻被安葬在高祖长陵正门外的道旁。[107] 三年后的前 190 年，高祖的另一位重臣曹参也去世了，他是高祖的同乡，在公元前 193 年继萧何之后出任丞相。他的墓葬位于长陵以东萧何的墓旁。在惠帝和吕后时期还有更多的开国功臣葬于此地，其中包括留侯张良（卒于前 189）以及右丞相、太傅王陵（卒于前 181）。[108] 这种做法与传统礼仪相当不同，

Fig. 3.8. Painted clay figurines. Western Han. *Ca.* 179-141 B.C. H. 68.5 cm. Excavated in 1965 at Yangjiawan, Xianyang, Shaanxi province. Xianyang Museum.
图 3.8 彩陶俑。西汉，约前 179—前 141 年。高 68.5 厘米。1965 年陕西咸阳杨家湾出土。咸阳市博物馆藏。

the old tradition, in which the legitimate place of one's tomb was the family graveyard. The change must signify a new belief that emerged simultaneously with the birth of imperial China: to have one's tomb located near a deceased emperor was a great honor, and a minister's relation with the ruler surpassed his relation with his close kin. Supported by this new belief and the corresponding political concept, the number of satellite burials continued to increase throughout the Han. A present-day visitor to Chang ling would find some 63 pyramid-shaped tumuli crowded east of Gaozu's burial, 12 tumuli near Emperor Hui's funerary park, and as many as 72 tombs around Emperor Wu's mausoleum, Mao ling.[109] Some of these satellite tombs have been excavated, and their scale has amazed the excavators. The tomb of General Zhou Bo (d. 169 B.C.) near Chang ling, for example, had an entranceway about 100 meters long, and from the ten sacrificial pits south of the grave chamber alone came 2,400 figurines, including more than 1,800 foot soldiers and 580 horsemen (Fig. 3.8).[110] The recent discovery of similar figurines from sacrificial pits near Emperor Jing's tomb allows us to realize the imperial model of such burial practices (Fig. 3.9). Indeed, accompanying and mirroring an emperor's tomb, each satellite burial was itself a small mausoleum.

As we have observed, Gaozu did not build a specific mausoleum town for either his father or himself. The tradition of constructing such towns began in 182 B.C., when Empress Dowager Lü, Gaozu's widow and Emperor Hui's mother, dedicated Chang Ling Yi (Chang Ling Town) to her departed husband.[111] Located north of the emperor's funerary park, this rectangular walled town was 2,200 meters north-south and 1,245 meters east-west.[112] The town attached to Emperor Hui's mausoleum was similarly situated north of the emperor's funerary park and measured 1,548 meters in its longitudinal dimension.[113] The importance of these and other mausoleum towns, however, lay not in their size but in their

在此之前，一个人死后必须安葬在自己家族的茔地中。陪葬的出现意味着一种新的观念随着中华帝国的诞生而出现了：将一个人的墓葬安置在死去的皇帝旁边是一个极大的荣誉，君臣关系因此凌驾于近亲关系之上。在这一新的观念及相关政治概念的支持下，汉长安附近出现了越来越多的陪葬墓。到长陵的探查者会看到，高祖的陵墓以东大约有 63 座金字塔状的封土，惠帝的陵园中有 12 座封土，武帝茂陵周围的封土多达 72 座。[109] 这些陪葬墓有的已被发掘，其规模之大令发掘者惊异。例如，长陵旁边的周勃（卒于前 169）墓的墓道长约 100 米，单从其南面 10 个丛葬坑中就出土了 2400 件陶俑，包括 1800 件以上的步兵俑和 580 件骑兵俑［图 3.8］。[110] 最近在景帝阳陵的随葬坑中出土的俑，使我们见识到了这种葬俗的皇家模式［图 3.9］。的确，如星罗棋布一般陪伴、映衬于帝陵周围的每一座葬墓，自身即是一座小的陵墓。

我们已经说过，高祖并未给父亲和自己修建特别的陵邑。修建陵邑的传统开始于公元前 182 年，这一年，高祖的夫人，即惠帝的母亲，吕后为其丈夫建造了长陵邑。[111] 邑位于高祖陵园以北，平面呈长方形，四周筑墙，南北 2200 米，东西 1245 米。[112] 惠帝的陵邑也在其陵园以北，纵长 1548 米。[113] 但是，这些陵邑和其他陵邑的

residents. Surprisingly, we find that people living there were not workers,
163 royal servants, or ceremonial officials but members of old provincial clans and new aristocratic families. Those who dwelled in Gaozu's posthumous town were mainly descendents of the Tian clan from the former kingdom of Qi in Shandong, and those in Emperor Hui's town belonged to the Yuan, Ji, Hong, and Ban clans of the former state of Chu in the Yangzi River region.[114] Students of early Chinese history are well acquainted with these names: from Zhou times on these and other powerful clans had dominated the country's various regions and fought one another for local or central power. The establishment of such mausoleum towns near Chang'an, therefore, was not purely a ritual practice but had profound political implications.

Fig. 3.9. Painted clay figurines (originally dressed with clothes made of fabric). Western Han. 143 B.C. H. *ca.* 62 cm. Excavated in 1989 near Emperor Jing's Yang ling mausoleum at Zhangjiawan, Xianyang, Shaanxi province. Shaanxi Provincial Institute of Archaeology, Xi'an.

图 3.9 彩陶俑（原穿有织物所做的衣服）。西汉，前 143 年。高约 62 厘米。1989 年陕西咸阳张家湾景帝阳陵出土。陕西省考古研究所藏。

In fact, the plan to move such powerful clans from the provinces to the capital had been implemented by Gaozu. The designer of this plan was again Lou Jing or Liu Jing (who had been granted the royal surname Liu for suggesting the dynasty's capital be established at Chang'an). Upon the completion of the Weiyang Palace in 198 B.C., Liu Jing gave the emperor another piece of advice:

> Now, although Your Majesty has established the capital within the Pass, there are in fact few people in the area. Close to the north are the barbarian bandits, while in the east live those powerful clans of the Six States of former times, so that if some day trouble should arise somewhere, I fear you could never rest with an easy mind. I beg therefore that you move the various members of the Tian clan of Qi, the Zhao, Qu, and Jing clans of Chu, the descendents of the former royal families of Yan, Zhao, Han, and Wei, and the other powerful and renowned families to the area within the Pass. As long as things are

重要性并不在于其规模，而在于其中的居民。令人惊异的是，我们发现生活在其中的人并非一般的工人、皇家仆从或礼官，而是以往地方上的旧宗族和新兴贵族。如入住高祖陵邑的是原山东地区齐国田氏的后裔，惠帝陵邑的居民则包括长江流域原楚国的爰、籍、闳、班等家族。[114] 研究早期中国史的学者都十分熟悉这些姓氏，从周代起，这些宗族和其他有权势的宗族控制了中国各个地区，为争夺地方或中央权力彼此征伐。因此在长安城旁边设置这些陵邑就不仅仅是一种礼仪行为，同时也具有深刻的政治含义。

实际上，将这些大族从地方迁移到都城的计划在高祖时就已开始实施。这一计划的策划者仍是娄敬，或称刘敬（他因为上奏皇帝，建议建都长安而被赐姓刘）。他在公元前 198 年未央宫完工时向皇帝提出了另一个建议：

> 今陛下虽都关中，实少人。北近胡寇，东有六国之族，宗强，一日有变，陛下亦未得高枕而卧也。臣愿陛下徙齐诸田，楚昭、屈、景，燕、赵、韩、魏后，及豪杰名家居

> going well, they can defend the area against the barbarians, and if there should be disaffection among the feudal lords, they would form an army which could be led east and used in putting down the trouble. This is the type of strategy known as "strengthening the root and weakening the branches" of the empire.[115]

Once more he convinced Gaozu, and the emperor sent him to supervise the relocation of over 100,000 persons to the capital area. When Gaozu and Emperor Hui's mausoleum towns were built, at least part of these immigrants were further transferred there.

The impact of this plan on Han politics is beyond the scope of
the present discussion. Our focus is its profound influence on the
164 development of Chang'an. Gaozu's massive relocations were repeated by
later emperors. As a direct consequence, a large population was gradually concentrated in mausoleum towns in Chang'an's outskirts. By the end of the Western Han, altogether eleven such walled towns had been built near the tombs of deceased emperors and their parents.[116] A national census conducted in A.D. 2 shows that Gaozu's Chang Ling Town had 179,469 residents and that 277,277 people lived in Emperor Wu's Mao Ling Town.[117] Two modern Chinese scholars, Liu Qingzhu and Li Yufang, have suggested that these numbers are conservative, and that Emperor Xuan's Du Ling Town should have had at least 300,000 residents.[118] Significantly, this census also informs us that the walled city of Chang'an had 246,200 residents—even fewer than the mausoleum towns attached to Emperor Wu's and Xuan's tombs.[119]

The residents of these mausoleum towns were from the richest and most renowned families in the country. Many of them were descendents of kings and lords of the previous dynasties and feudal kingdoms. The great concentration of wealth in these towns was further encouraged by Emperor Wu. Following the strategy of "strengthening the root and weakening the branches of the empire," he three times ordered rich provincial families, each possessing over three million cash, to move into his own mausoleum town.[120] It is said that a man named Guo Jie was demanded to move to Maoling. General-in-chief Wei Qing appealed on his behalf that he was quite poor and did not meet the required financial status, but the petition was rejected by Emperor Wu. When Guo finally moved, his rich supporters donated more than ten million cash to help him.[121] Han history records that in the same town the Zhi family was the "richest family under Heaven," that the Ma family possessed billions of cash, and that the Yuan family employed more than a thousand servants. These families were the largest merchants and financial magnates in the country.[122]

关中。无事，可以备胡，诸侯有变，亦足率以东伐。此强本弱末之术也。[115]

刘敬再次说服了高祖，高祖便委派他迁十万人口到关中。当高祖和惠帝的陵邑建成后，至少这些移民中的一部分住到这些城中。

关于这一计划对汉代政治的影响问题，超出此处讨论的范围。我在这里讨论的重点是，这种移民政策对于长安发展所产生的深刻影响。高祖大规模移民的措施为后来的皇帝所继承，其直接结果是，在长安郊外的陵邑中逐渐集中了大量人口。到西汉末年，在已故皇帝及其父母的墓葬附近一共建造了 11 座这类有围墙的城邑。[116] 公元 2 年的人口调查结果显示，高祖长陵邑的人口为 179469，武帝茂陵的人口为 277277。[117] 中国学者刘庆柱和李毓芳感到这些数据仍趋于保守，认为宣帝杜陵邑的人口至少应有 30 万。[118] 值得注意的是，公元 2 年的人口调查表明，当时长安城圈内的人口只有 246200 人，比武帝和宣帝陵邑中的人口还少。[119]

陵邑中的居民均来自全国最富有和最有名望的家族，有些是前代王侯的后裔。武帝继续鼓励将大量财富聚集到这些陵邑中。根据"强本弱末"的战略，他曾三次下令把家产超过三百万钱的地方豪族迁到他自己的陵邑中。[120] 据说有个名叫郭解的人被要求迁往茂陵居住，大将军卫青替他说情，说他家贫不符合迁移标准，但没有得到汉武帝的批准。当郭解迁徙时，送行的富人共出钱一千余万。[121] 史书记载同一邑中的挚家富甲天下，马家则有十亿钱，爰家童仆过千。这些家族都是国内最大的商贾和金融巨头。[122]

The economic strength of the mausoleum towns was matched by their political and cultural influence. During the Western Han, these towns became the main sources of high officials and leading literati. Chang Ling Town yielded two prime ministers, Tian Fen and Che Qianqiu; from An Ling Town came powerful courtiers Ji Ru and Hong Ru, as well as the famous historians Ban Biao, Ban Gu, and Ban Zhao. Three important literary figures—the Confucian theologian Dong Zhongshu, the historian Sima Qian, and the poet Sima Xiangru—lived in Mao Ling Town; and Emperor Zhao's Ping Ling Town produced four prime ministers and a large crowd of scholars. As for Emperor Xuan's Du Ling Town, almost all important officials of the time lived there, and it became a chief political center outside Chang'an. This is the reality behind the following stanza of Ban Gu's *Western Capital Rhapsody*:

> If then
> One gazes upon the surrounding suburbs,
> Travels to the nearby prefectures,
> Then to the south he may gaze on the Du and Ba Mausoleums,
> To the north he may espy the Five Mausoleums,
> Where famous cities face Chang'an's outskirts,
> And village residences connect one to another.
> It is the region of the prime and superior talents,
> Where official sashes and hats flourish,
> 165 Where caps and canopies are as thick as clouds.
> Seven chancellors, five ministers,
> Along with the powerful clans of the provinces and commanderies,
> And the plutocrats of the Five Capitals,
> Those selected from the three categories, transferred to seven locations,
> Were assigned to make offerings at the mausoleum towns.
> This was to strengthen the trunk and weaken the branches,
> To exalt the Supreme Capital and show it off to the myriad states.[123]

What Ban Gu described here certainly had not happened during Emperor Hui's reign. Nevertheless, the establishment of the first two mausoleum towns and the system of satellite burials implied such a far-reaching development. Reviewing Emperor Hui's construction or reconstruction of Chang'an, we find that a new hierarchical structure had begun to emerge. The walled imperial city now symbolized the institutionalization of the Han regime. Inside this city were palaces, government departments, offices of princes, foreign embassies, and sacrificial and commercial centers. Surrounding it were a number of satellite towns attached to the individual emperor's mausoleum. Each of these royal mausoleums formed a secondary political and social center and was accompanied by satellite tombs of high officials and royal

陵邑的经济势力是和它们的政治与文化影响相匹配的。西汉时期，这些陵邑成为高官和高层文人的主要来源。如长陵邑出了两位丞相田蚡和车千秋；安陵邑出了两位重臣籍孺和闳孺，以及著名的史学家班固、班彪和班昭。儒家理论家董仲舒、史学家司马迁和文学家司马相如这三位重要的文人都居住在茂陵邑中；昭帝的平陵邑也产生出四位丞相和一大批学者。至于宣帝的杜陵邑，当时所有重要的官员几乎都居住于其中，使得该邑成为长安以外一个重要的政治中心。这便是班固《西都赋》中下一段文字的背景：

> 若乃观其四郊，浮游近县，则南望杜、霸，北眺五陵。名都对郭，邑居相承。英俊之域，绂冕所兴。冠盖如云，七相五公。与乎州郡之豪杰，五都之货殖。三选七迁，充奉陵邑。盖以强干弱枝，隆上都而观万国也。[123]

班固此处所描写的情况当然并不完全发生在惠帝时期。然而，在这个时期首先建立的两座陵邑和陪葬制度的确影响深远。回顾惠帝对长安的建设或重建，我们发现一种新的等级结构已经开始萌生。城墙环绕的帝都象征着汉王朝制度化的国家机构，其中包括了宫殿、内阁各部、太子府、蛮夷邸和祭祀与商业中心。围绕着它的是附着于每个皇帝陵墓的一批卫星城。每一座皇陵构成一个二级的政治和社会中心，它们的周围又有一些高级官员或皇亲国戚的陪葬墓。

relatives. These satellite tombs again had their own walled enclosures and satellite burials, mirroring descending levels of social organization.

This hierarchical architectural design, which translated the new social and political structures into visual, monumental forms, was never static and always reflected the dynasty's own history. Surrounding the throne-city Chang'an as an embodiment of China's lasting tradition, individual imperial mausoleums with their huge pyramids documented the dynasty's own past. It was understood that as long as the Han's mandate continued, the number of such pyramids would grow, more satellite towns and burials would appear to exalt the Supreme Capital City, and the whole capital would develop "as the 28 constellations revolving about the North Star, and as the 30 spokes of a wheel coming together at the hub, revolving endlessly without stop."[124]

❹ Emperor Wu's Fictional Garden

Emperor Hui and Empress Dowager Lü were followed by Emperors Wen (180-157 B.C.) and Jing (156-141 B.C.). Chang'an's rapid expansion suddenly halted, mainly because of a new economic policy of drastically reducing taxation and government expenses.[125] Indeed, this policy gave these two emperors a reputation as frugal sovereigns ready to sacrifice luxuries for themselves for the good of the public. Emperor Wen, for example, "made no move to increase the size of the palaces or halls, the parks or enclosure, or the number of dogs and horses, vestments and carriages. Whenever a practice proved harmful, he immediately abandoned it in order to ensure benefit to the people." It is said that this emperor once thought of constructing a terrace and called in a builder to discuss the matter. When he was told that the structure would cost 100 catties of gold, he cried out in rage: "A hundred catties of gold is as much as the wealth of ten families of moderate means! Since I inherited the palaces of the former emperors, I have constantly been afraid that I might dishonor them. What business would I have in building such a terrace?"[126]

It is questionable, however, to what extent we can trust this and similar records, which often have a strong flavor of publicity stunts.[127] We do not know whether Emperor Wen indeed forbade any additions to the palace, but we do know about his tomb. His testamentary edict, a public document recorded in both the *Records of the Historian* and *History of the Former Han*, begins with a philosophical statement:

这些陪葬墓也有自己的围墙和陪葬墓，反映出一种逐级递减的社会组织结构。

这种等级性的建筑设计将新的社会和政治结构转变为视觉的和纪念碑式的形式。这些纪念碑不是静态的，而是不断地反映着这个王朝的历史。围绕着皇城长安的帝陵如同一座座巨大的金字塔，体现了皇统的持续，记录着汉王朝的历史。可以说，只要汉祚不绝，这些金字塔的数量就会不断增加下去，同时也将出现更多的卫星城和陪葬墓，使得这座煌煌帝都的规模持续扩展。整个都城的发展因此将如“二十八宿环北辰，三十辐共一毂，运行无穷”。[124]

四、武帝奇幻的苑囿

继惠帝和吕后的两位皇帝是文帝（前 180 —前 157 年）和景帝（前 156—前 141 年）。长安快速扩展的势头在这一时期突然中止，其主要的原因是当时大量削减征税和政府开支的新经济政策。[125] 的确，这一政策为两位皇帝带来了极好的声誉，他们被看作为了公众的利益而舍弃奢华生活的模范帝王。例如，文献记载文帝“宫室、苑囿、狗马、服御无所增益，有不便辄弛以利民”。据说他曾计划建造一座露台，与工匠讨论此事。当他听说需要花费百金时，便大惊而罢：“百金，中民十家之产！吾奉先帝宫室，常恐羞之，何以台为！”[126]

但问题是，我们在多大程度上可以相信这些记载——文献中对此类事情的记述常常带有公共宣传的意味。[127] 我们不知道文帝是否真的曾经阻止增建宫室，但我们却比较清楚地了解其墓葬的情况。《史记》和《汉书》中记载的文帝遗诏以一段富有哲理的话开篇：

> I have heard that of all the countless beings beneath heaven which sprout or are brought to life, there is none which does not have its time of death, for death is a part of the abiding order of heaven and earth and the natural end of all creatures. How then can it be such a sorrowful thing? Yet in the world today, because all men rejoice in life and hate death, they exhaust their wealth in providing lavish burials for the
> 166 departed, and endanger their health by prolonged mourning. I can in no way approve of such practices.[128]

What this edict does not state, however, is that his mausoleum was the only Han imperial tomb dug into a mountain cliff and that he planned his burial rite in great detail before his death. The plan called for the Chief Military Commander Zhou Yafu to be appointed General of Carriage and Cavalry to direct the funerary procession; Director of Dependent States Xu Han to be the General of Encampment to administer the mausoleum town; and Chief of Palace Attendants Zhang Wu to assume the title of the General of Replacing the Grave Earth (in charge of the interment of the emperor's coffin and the excavation and replacement of the rock in the tomb's tunnel). Sixteen thousand soldiers from nearby districts and 15,000 additional soldiers from the whole capital area would serve at the funeral.[129]

Thus, whereas under Emperors Gaozu and Hui the construction of Chang'an was publicly stressed, under Wen and Jing it was deliberately played down. What we find here is that although the establishment of a monumental palace or city could effectively attract public attention, a loud refusal to engage in such "excessive construction" could play a similar role in shaping public opinion toward the emperor and the government. This second strategy, however, had to be presented as the antithesis of the first and required a reinterpretation of the earlier monuments. Its unspoken premise was that a palace or a mausoleum possessed no public, political function and exclusively served a ruler's private desires. Since the professed goal of Wen and Jing was to stabilize the country by practicing thrift, they could gain greater authority by rejecting such desires: in this way they became not only political leaders but also moral exemplars.

These two emperors, therefore, altered the meaning of Chang'an's palatial monuments by *opposing* such buildings to the public good. Once their rhetoric was widely accepted, it led to a new movement in the further construction of the capital: the next ruler, Emperor Wu, erected numerous structures of monumental scale both inside and outside

> 朕闻：盖天下万物之萌生，靡不有死。死者天地之理，物之自然者，奚可甚哀？当今之时，世咸嘉生而恶死，厚葬以破业，重服以伤生，吾甚不取。[128]

但是，这篇遗诏所没有提到的是，文帝的陵墓是汉代唯一开凿在山崖中的帝陵，并且他在生前就详细计划了自己的葬礼。中尉周亚夫为车骑将军，指挥送葬的队伍。属国徐悍为将屯将军，管理陵邑。郎中令张武为复土将军，主管开挖墓圹、瘗埋棺椁和回填墓圹。他的葬礼调动了附近县的16000兵士和京师地区15000兵士。[129]

一个明显的事实是，长安的营建在高祖和惠帝时期被大力宣扬，在文景时期则被故意低调处理。我们在此所看到的是，尽管营建纪念碑式宫殿和城郭可以有效地吸引公众的注意力，而一种反对"大兴土木"的声音也可以左右有关皇帝和政府的公共舆论。然而，后一策略必须作为前者的对立面出现，对以前的纪念碑式建筑进行重新阐释。其隐含的前提是，一座宫殿或陵墓的意义在于它是统治者个人欲望的体现，而不在于它的公共的、政治性的功能。由于文帝和景帝所宣称的目标是通过节俭来稳定国家，因此他们可以通过抛弃这种个人的欲望来获得更高的威信。通过这样一种方式，他们不仅成为政治领袖，同时也成为道德的典范。

通过反对纪念碑式建筑和维护公众利益，这两位皇帝因此改变了长安作为一座宏伟壮丽的纪念碑城市的含义。一旦他们的辩术被广泛接受，就为这座都城的进一步建设奠定了一个新的概念基础：接下来的一位皇帝——武帝——在长安内外建造了大量具有纪念碑

Chang'an, but unlike Gaozu's Weiyang Palace and Emperor Hui's city walls, these buildings were overtly constructed as the emperor's "personal" symbols and property to help fulfill his dream of immortality.

A fascinating figure in Chinese history, Emperor Wu began his career as a young, vigorous, strong-willed, and intelligent ruler. The abundant wealth accumulated during the peaceful reigns of his predecessors[130] and the extraordinary length of his tenure (54 years) provided him with more than enough time and resources to attain his goals. It was during his reign that the Han armies drove across the wastes of Central Asia to the fringes of the Western world, where, on one occasion, Chinese soldiers confronted Roman legions. It was also under his sponsorship that the Confucian Five Classics first gained official recognition at court. Hundreds of Daoist necromancers gathered around him to cultivate methods for achieving immortality, and the emperor left traces on all the sacred mountains throughout his vast empire. The same vigor and ambition are also evident in his construction of Chang'an. The old Weiyang and Changle Palaces were redecorated and rebuilt.[131] Three huge new palace complexes—the Mingguang Palace (Palace of Brilliant Light), the Gui Palace (Cassia Palace), and the Bei Palace (Northern Palace)—finally filled up the interior of walled Chang'an, hithenrto largely empty.[132] The enormous Shanglin Park with its many palatial halls was established west and southwest of the capital city, and the Ganquan Palace (Palace of Sweet Springs), a huge sacrificial center nineteen *li* in circumference, was founded in the northwest.[133] The emperor also built for himself the largest mausoleum and mausoleum town; the pyramid remaining above his tomb is still 46.5 meters tall.[134]

But what was Emperor Wu's exact role in these achievements? Historians have concluded that many of the social and political reforms attributed to the emperor were based on initiatives of people under his patronage.[135] It was Dong Zhongshu (179-104 B.C.) who convinced the emperor to establish Confucianism as the state ideology, Sang Hongyang

(141-80 B.C.) who engineered the emperor's economic policies, and Wei Qing (?-106 B.C.) and Huo Qubing (140-117 B.C.) who led the emperor's army to Central Asia. A similar but subtler situation is also apparent in Emperor Wu's construction of his capital. The numerous architectural projects carried out during his reign shared two essential features. First, the traditional Confucian capital plan had lost its attraction, and Emperor Wu

规模的建筑，但是与高祖的未央宫和惠帝的城墙不同，这些建筑被公然宣称为皇帝的“个人”符号和财富，以帮助他实现成仙的美梦。

武帝是中国历史上一位极富魅力的皇帝，他年富力强，朝气勃勃，意志坚定，充满智慧，以全新的统治者形象出现在历史舞台上。前朝皇帝和平时期所积累的大量财富[130]和他的超长在位时期（54年），为他实现自己的理想提供了充分的时间和资源。正是在这一时期，汉朝的军队横穿中亚大漠，到达了西方世界的边缘，在那里中国士兵甚至得以与罗马军团遭遇。也是在他的支持下，儒家的五经第一次在朝廷获得了官方的认可。数以百计的道家方士围绕着他，提出各自的求仙方法，这位皇帝也在其庞大帝国中的多座神圣山峰上留下了自己的脚印。他的活力和雄心同样在长安的建设中反映出来。以往的未央宫和长乐宫被重新装饰和改建。[131]三组新的宫殿群——明光宫、桂宫和北宫——最终将长安城圈以内空旷的部分填充了起来。[132]在都城以西和西南方向，拥有大批富丽堂皇建筑的上林苑终于修建完成。都城西北方向建造了周长19里的大型祭祀中心甘泉宫。[133]这位皇帝还为自己建造了汉代最大的陵墓和陵邑。2000年后的今天，其陵墓的地面封土仍高达46.5米。[134]

但是，武帝在所有这些成就中到底扮演了什么样的角色？历史学家已经指出，以前归功于武帝的许多社会和政治改革实际上是由辅佐他的人们首先提出的。[135]比如，是董仲舒（前179—前104年）说服了他，将儒家思想尊为国家的意识形态；是桑弘羊（前141—前80年）策划了当时的经济政策；是卫青（？—前106年）和霍去病（前140—前117年）率领帝国的远征军打到中亚。同样的情况存在于武帝对都城的建设中。这个时期所进行的众多建筑工程具有两个基本的特征。首先，儒家传统的都城规划已经失去其吸引

launched a search for new monumental forms. Second, neither practical administrators (like Xiao He) nor Confucian scholars and ceremonialists (like Lu Jia and Shusun Tong) were able to provide inspiration for such new structures; instead, the emperor's vision of Chang'an was strongly influenced by "magicians" —*necromancers* who played at conjuring and writers who played with words. Through the emperor, the fantasies of these two groups of men gained material form.

Necromancer is a loose translation of the Chinese term *fangshi*, which literally means "gentlemen from outlying areas."[136] Since the Eastern Zhou period the region along China's northeast seacoast, notably Yan and Qi around the Bohai Gulf, had been a center of professional diviners, doctors, and magicians who earned a livelihood by practicing exorcism, medicine, and divination.[137] But it was not until Emperor Wu's reign that such men deeply penetrated the central court. Their promises of immortality and longevity gave the emperor the hope of infinitely prolonging his rule, and in helping the emperor achieve this goal they also gained, though often briefly, personal wealth and high official status. Traditional Confucians frequently criticized their learning as "weird and unorthodox" and their search for patrons as "flattery and ingratiation." But such criticism only signifies that these "gentlemen from outlying areas" represented a cultural tradition distinct from orthodox Confucianism. In Kenneth DeWoskin's words, they "dealt most persistently with areas Confucius refused to discuss, namely, strange events, spirits, and fate," and their impact was "a dramatic diffusion of nontraditional knowledge and interests into the highly centralized, literate, and essentially conservative court mainstream."[138]

A number of instances recorded in the *Records of the Historian* enable us to observe these shadowy figures more closely and to detect their influence on Emperor Wu's architectural plans. The first to be favored by the emperor was Li Shaojun from Qi.[139] In his travels to various principalities and finally to the emperor's court, Li Shaojun successfully convinced his audience that he had achieved longevity and possessed the power of driving away death. His secret, he claimed, was that he had once reached the immortal island Penglai in the eastern sea, where Master Anqi (Anqi Sheng) fed him an elixir in the shape of jujubes as big as melons. He told the emperor that "Master Anqi is an immortal who roams about Penglai. If he takes a liking to someone, he will come to meet him, but if not he will hide." Stimulated by these words but too

力，武帝开始着手探索一种新的纪念碑形式。其次，不论是实际的工程管理者（如萧何）还是儒生和礼法专家（如陆贾和叔孙通）都不能够再为新建筑提供灵感，武帝对长安的构思实际上是受到了方士的辩术和文学家的写作的强烈影响。通过皇帝的身体力行，这两种人以不同方式编织出的白日梦具有了物质性的形式。

方士字面上的意思是"来自远方的人士"。[136] 自东周以来，中国东北沿海地区，特别是围绕渤海湾的燕和齐，成为以驱邪、行医、卜策谋生的专业占卜家、医士和术士活动的中心。[137] 但这些人直到武帝时期才成功地渗透到中央朝廷之中。他们对于升仙和长生的种种许诺带给皇帝无限延长其统治的希望。他们声称自己能够帮助皇帝去实现这些理想，以此作为获取财富和官位的手段——尽管这些奖赏往往是暂时的。传统儒生经常批评方士所言"荒诞不经"，认为他们对皇帝"阿谀苟合"。但是，这些批评只意味着，方士们代表了与正统儒学不同的文化传统。用杜志豪的话来说，他们"最顽强地去处理那些孔子拒绝谈论的事情，即所谓怪、力、乱、神"，他们的影响是，"戏剧性地将非传统的知识和兴趣扩散到了高度集中的、知识化、本质上又十分守旧的朝廷主流人物中"。[138]

《史记》记载的许多事例使我们能够近距离地观察这些难以捉摸的人物形象，并分析他们对武帝建筑规划的影响。第一个受到武帝宠爱的方士是来自齐地的李少君。[139] 在游说许多诸侯国之后，他终于来到朝廷，成功地使人们相信他已经获得长生，有永不死亡的本领。根据他的说法，其秘密在于他曾登上过东海中的蓬莱仙山。在那里，安期生给他吃了如瓜一般大的巨枣，这是一种不死之药。他告诉武帝说："安期生，仙者，通蓬莱中，合则见人，不合则隐。"

impatient to wait, the emperor dispatched teams of magicians to search for the island and its inhabitants. But as Li Shaoiun had cleverly hinted, all the searches failed because the immortal was annoyed by this human intrusion.

Sima Qian attested that "after this, any number of strange and dubious magicians from the seacoast of Yan and Qi appeared at court to speak to the emperor about supernatural affairs. Among them was a man from Bo named Miu Ji who instructed the emperor on how to sacrifice to the Great Unity."[140] Following Miu Ji's teaching, Emperor Wu erected a shrine
168 or altar southeast of Chang'an to worship this deity. Around 121 B.C., another necromancer named Shao Weng entered the scene.[141] Emperor Wu had just lost one of his favorite consorts, and Shao Weng promised to make her reappear before the emperor's eyes. The magician then performed, perhaps for the first time in Chinese history, a shadow-puppet play: the emperor was asked to sit behind a curtain, and from there he saw the silhouette of his beloved consort projected onto a curtained screen. The success of this venture brought Shao Weng many gifts from the emperor, along with the title "general of peaceful accomplishments" (*wencheng jiangjun*), and led to another more important proposal, the construction of the Ganquan Palace:

> "I perceive that Your Majesty wishes to commune with the spirits. But unless your palaces and robes are patterned after the shapes of the spirits, they will not consent to come to you." ...[Shao Weng] thus directed the emperor to build the Ganquan Palace, in which was a terrace chamber painted with pictures of Heaven, earth, the Great Unity, and all the other gods and spirits. Here Shao Weng set forth sacrificial vessels in an effort to summon the spirits of Heaven.[142]

It was from this time that the Ganquan Palace, located some 60 km northwest of Chang'an, began to grow into a huge religious center. In 116 B.C., an ancient *ding* tripod was found in Fenyin and was considered an extraordinarily auspicious omen from Heaven. The divine object was brought to Ganquan, where Emperor Wu greeted it in person.[143] In 112 B.C., an altar for worshipping the Great Unity was added to the palace. Modeled on the older one designed by Miu Ji, it had three levels and was surrounded by smaller altars dedicated to the Five Powers.[144] This project, however, was only a prelude to more intensive construction on a far greater scale. According to Sima Qian, "Emperor Wu started

受到这些话的蛊惑，武帝再也没有耐心等待了，他派遣了方士入海去寻求蓬莱和安期生等仙人。但是，正如狡猾的李少君预先说明的那样，仙人们不愿受凡人的打扰而隐藏不显，因此所有的探索都归于失败。

司马迁又记载："海上燕齐怪迂之方士多相效，更言神事矣。亳人薄诱忌（《索隐》："姓谬名忌，居亳，故下称薄忌。此文则衍'薄'字，而'谬'又误作'诱'也。"——译注。）奏祠泰一方。"[140] 根据谬忌的指导，武帝在长安东南郊立祠奉祠泰一。公元前 121 年左右出现了另一位方士少翁。[141] 武帝这时刚刚失去他所宠爱的李夫人，少君说他可以使李夫人重现在武帝眼前。他随后施行的法术可能是中国历史上记载的第一场皮影戏：皇帝按他的要求坐在一顶帷帐中，从那里望见李夫人的轮廓投射在另一顶帷幕的幕壁上。这一冒险表演的成功使少翁得到了皇帝赏赐的许多礼物，并被封为"文成将军"。他还被委任以另一件更重要的工作，即建造甘泉宫：

> "上即欲与神通，宫室被服非象神，神物不至。"……（少翁）又作甘泉宫，中为台室，画天、地、泰一诸神，而置祭具以致天神。[142]

也就是从这时起，坐落在长安西北 60 公里处的甘泉宫发展成为一处大型宗教中心。公元前 116 年，汾阴出土了一件古鼎，被看作来自上天的重大祥瑞。这件神物被运到甘泉宫，武帝在此亲自迎候。[143] 公元前 112 年，甘泉宫内又增建了一座祭祀泰一的祠坛。该坛仿照谬忌所设计的旧坛而造，共有三层，其下环绕着祭祀五帝的小坛。[144] 但是，这些还只是更大规模土木工程的序幕。根据司马迁

to enlarge the various palaces" at Ganquan from 109 B.C.[145] The new buildings included a pair of tall pavilions called Benefiting Life (Yishou) and Prolonging Life (Yanshou), as well as a terrace named Communing with Heaven (Tongtian).[146] It is said that this terrace, more than a hundred *zhang* high, pierced the clouds. During the rituals held there to summon heavenly spirits, 300 eight-year-old boys and girls danced while singing a variety of songs. The building was thus also called Waiting for Divinities (Houshen) or Longing for Immortals (Wangxian).[147] According to historical records, all these new buildings and rituals were inspired by a necromancer from Qi called Gongsun Qing, who had made an important proposal to Emperor Wu earlier that year.

> "It is quite possible to meet with the immortals. It is only that Your Majesty always rushes off in great haste to see them and therefore never succeeds. Now if you would only build some turrets like those on the city wall of Gou [where Gongsun Qing had previously observed the traces of the immortals] and set out dried meat and jujubes, I believe that spirits could be induced to come, for they like to live in towers!"[148]

It is interesting to compare this statement with Xiao He's reasoning for Gaozu's Weiyang Palace, which was also a "terrace building" of unusual height: "A true Son of Heaven takes the whole world within the four seas to be his family. If he does not dwell in magnificence and beauty, he will have no way to manifest his authority." Emperor Wu's imposing terraces and palaces, however, were made not for the human ruler but for supernatural beings who "like to live in towers." Indeed, all the architectural projects promoted by necromancers shared a single premise: compared with the spirits, human beings were infinitely inferior; even the Son of Heaven was no exception. "The immortals do not seek for the ruler of men; it is the ruler who must seek for them!"[149] In order to establish contact with the immortals and to eventually become one of them, the ruler had first to please them—he had to act like a humble student, to learn *their* language, to become familiar with their likings and habits, and to offer *them* suitable dwellings as well as food and drink. The necromancers became extremely powerful because they alone controlled this knowledge; thus Luan Da, another magician from Qi, could even put pressure on the emperor: "My [divine] teacher has no reason to seek for men. It is men who seek for him. If Your Majesty really wishes to summon him, then you must first honor his passenger [i.e., Luan Da himself], making him a member of the imperial family, and treating him as a guest rather than a subject, doing nothing that would humiliate him."[150] Emperor Wu met all his demands.

的记载，从公元前 109 年开始，武帝在甘泉宫“广诸宫室”。[145] 新的建筑包括益寿观、延寿观及通天台。[146] 据说该台高过百丈，直上云霄。在此所举行的迎神仪式中，有三百名八岁的童男童女跳舞唱歌，该建筑因此也被称为候神台或望仙台。[147] 据记载，所有这些新的建筑和礼仪都出自齐地方士公孙卿的主意，他在此前曾向武帝提出过一个重要建议：

> “仙人可见，而上往常遽，以故不见。今陛下可为观，如缑城（公孙卿曾在此见到仙人迹），置脯枣，神人宜可致。且仙人好楼居。”[148]

将这番话与萧何对高祖的陈词比较一下会很有意思。萧何所建的未央宫也是一座高台建筑，其意义是“夫天子以四海为家，非壮丽无以重威”。但是武帝甘泉宫中的高台却不是为了人间的统治者而造，而是为了吸引“好楼居”的超自然神祇。的确，所有这些由方士们提出的建筑项目背后都有同一个前提：与神仙相比，人的地位十分低下，即使天子也不例外。“仙人非有求人主，人主者求之！”[149] 为了和仙人建立联系并最终成为他们中的一员，统治者首先要取悦于他们——他必须像一个谦卑的弟子一样，学习他们的语言，熟悉他们的喜好和习性，为他们提供合适的住所和饮食。方士之所以能够得到权势，是因为他们控制着这些知识，另一位来自齐地的方士栾大甚至向皇帝施加压力：“臣师非有求人，人者求之。陛下必欲致之，则贵其使者，令有亲属，以客礼待之，勿卑。”[150] 武帝满足了栾大所有的要求。

Luan Da's words reveal another important aspect of the necromancers' rhetoric: all claimed acquaintance with the immortal world through intimate personal experience. Li Shaojun claimed to have met Master Anqi at Penglai; Miu Ji possessed a magical formula from the Great Unity; Luan Da was a disciple of an immortal and "frequented the magical island in the ocean"; and Gongsun Qing, among his many miraculous adventures, had encountered a Great Man several *zhang* tall in Eastern Lai. According to them, the immortal paradise was neither an abstract idea nor a fairy tale, but a concrete realm that they had seen and could describe vividly. For example, the immortal island Penglai consisted of three island-mountains; all the birds and animals were pure white, and all palaces and gates were made of gold and silver. From afar, the mountains looked like clouds, but, as one drew closer, they seemed instead to be submerged beneath the water.[151] These and other vivid images became the models for architectural designs and decoration, since in order to induce the spirits, a "likeness" of the immortal world had to be reconstructed and duplicated.

From this we can understand the "nonfictional" nature of the necromancers' teaching. Although their tales would eventually become the material of the post-Han literary genre *zhiguai* (records of oddities),[152] what were perceived later as fictions and marvels were first presented as real things and real events. The "truthfulness" of their reports was supported by the reporters' assertions of the empirical origins of their knowledge, which demanded that their audience not only listen but, more important, believe. "Belief" thus became a central factor in their rhetoric. As Gongsun Qing insisted: "When men discuss spiritual matters, their words are apt to sound wild and irrational, but if these matters are pursued for a sufficient number of years, the spirits can eventually be persuaded to come forth!"[153] Such propositions, however, also put the necromancers themselves at risk, because they had offered what they could not afford to offer. Their assertion, that their tales were nonfictional, had to be confirmed not only by internal proofs but also by real happenings—the arrival of the immortals—which unfortunately never occurred. Consequently, Emperor Wu's necromancers were executed one by one, and their "factual reports" exposed as fabrications; the elaborate halls at Ganquan and other places remained empty, the portrayals of immortals and divinities lifeless.

栾大的话显示出方士辩术的另一个重要方面：即他们自己对于仙界的描述均来自个人经验。李少君声称自己曾在蓬莱见过安期生；谬忌说自己从泰一那里获得了神方；栾大吹嘘自己是仙人的私淑弟子，并且“常往来海中”；公孙卿则声言有过很多神奇的冒险，曾在东莱见过长数丈的“大人”。根据他们的这些说法，仙境既不是一个抽象的概念，也不是虚幻的神话故事，而是一个他们曾亲眼见过并能绘声绘色地加以描述的实实在在的地方。例如他们说，蓬莱仙岛有三座神山，其上禽兽尽白，宫阙皆以金银筑成。远望诸山好像云彩一样，但靠近时则发现三神山在水的下边。[151] 这类的生动描述成为建筑设计和装饰艺术的原型，因为根据方士的说法，要想招致神物就必须重构和复制仙境的形象。

从这里，我们可以懂得方士们说辞的“非虚构性”特征。尽管他们的故事最后将成为汉代以后志怪文学的材料，[152] 但是，这些后来被看作小说和奇迹的事，开始是以真实事物和真实事件的面目出现的。方士们对仙境报道的“真实性”由其切身的体验而得到支持。这些知识需要的不只是听众的倾听，而更重要的是使听众相信。因此，“信”就成为他们辩术成功的中心因素。正像公孙卿所说的那样：“言神事，事如迂诞，积以岁乃可致也。”[153] 但是，这种辩术也将方士自身置于危险的境地，因为他们许下的是无法兑现的诺言。他们对于其故事真实性的声言不仅需要内在的证据，同时最终需要由仙人降临来验证。不幸的是，这种情况永远不会出现。于是，武帝身边的方士们被一一处死，他们“实录性报告”的虚假性被一个一个揭露。精心装饰的甘泉宫以及其他迎神的殿堂空空荡荡，那些对于神仙的描述也黯然褪色。

The modern scholar Kendall Walton has offered a simple but effective formula to distinguish fiction from nonfiction: "What is true is to be believed; what is fictional is to be imagined."[154] It is exactly at this conjunction that necromancers and writers—another inspiration for Emperor Wu's architectural ventures—were set apart. The rhetoric of necromancers, as I have just shown, is based on the principles of truth and belief. The works of writers, on the other hand, aim to construct a fictional world that has no need of external proofs. The main support of this fictional world, according to Walton, is not belief but imagination: "The imagination is meant to explore, to wander at will through our conceptual universe. In this respect imagination appears to contrast sharply with belief. Beliefs, unlike imaginings, are correct or incorrect. Belief aims at truth. What is true and only what is true is to be believed. We are not free to believe as we please. We are free to imagine as we please."[155]

To apply this theory to the Han situation, necromancers constantly failed because their claims could easily be proved groundless. They thus became martyrs of their own propaganda. But this did not mean that the road toward transcendence was entirely blocked, since immortality could be the subject not only of religious belief but of literary imagination. In fact, during the long years of his search for immortality, Emperor Wu never allowed any opportunity to pass by. Even though one necromancer after another failed to help him and all his envoys to Penglai returned empty-handed, he was still willing to "believe" anyone who came with a magic wand. But the failure of this sort of adventure also forced him to pay increasing attention to the alternative and safer path: one might not be able to *encounter* the spirits and receive their elixir, but one could certainly *imagine* such an encounter. Better yet, one could
170 create an immortal world on earth and place oneself at its center. Thus, while searches for the "real" immortal land continued, the creation of a "fictional" paradise was speeded up. Unlike the searches, which demanded passivity and patience, the creation of this manufactured

paradise was exciting and even fun. The difference between the two is similar to that between waiting on the seashore for a mirage and making a sand castle; in Emperor Wu's case, the "castle" required far greater imagination and took him more than 30 years to complete. As in many

当代美国学者肯德尔·沃尔顿曾提出过一个简单但很实用的公式，以区别虚构文学和非虚构文学："真实即信仰，虚构即想象。"[154]的确，方士和文学家也就是在这一点上分道扬镳的。文学家是武帝营造仙境的另一个灵感来源。如我上文所述，方士辩术的概念基础是真实与信仰。而作家写作的目的，则是建构一个不需要外部证实的虚幻世界。沃尔顿认为，这种虚幻世界主要的支柱不是信仰，而是想象力："想象力意味着探索，意味着经由我们概念化的宇宙漫步于意愿之中。对想象力的尊重似乎与信仰有着尖锐的矛盾。与想象不同，信仰所考虑的是正确与否。信仰的目标是真实。真实的事物，只有真实的事物，才可能是被信仰的对象。我们并不享有随意信仰的自由，但我们却可以任我们的喜好去驰骋想象。"[155]

从这个理论来看汉代的史实，可以认为方士最终必然是要失败的，因为他们的诺言可以很容易地被证明为毫无根据的故事，他们因此成为自己谎言的牺牲品。但这并不意味着通往超现实境界的道路因此被阻塞，因为升仙不仅可能依赖于宗教信仰，同时还可能依赖于文学化的想象。实际上，在武帝探索升仙途径的漫长岁月中，他从未放过任何机会。即使一个又一个的方士都无法帮助他，派去寻找蓬莱的一个个使者也都空手而归，但如果又有一位持有魔杖的人士前来对他讲述一个新的求仙故事，武帝仍然乐于"相信"他。但是，这类探险的失败也迫使他对这种不确定并且充满危险的途径倍加警惕：一个人也许不能真的面见神人并获得不死之药，但是他肯定可以想象这种会见。而且，他还可以在地上创造一处仙境，并成为它的主人。这样，在继续探寻"真正"仙境的同时，对于"虚构"天堂的创造也不断升温。对真实仙境的探索是被动的，需要极大的耐心与不懈的努力。与之不同，创造一个人工的天堂则令人兴奋，甚至充满乐趣。这两种行为的差异，就像是坐在海边等待海市蜃楼出现和用沙子建造一座幻想城堡之间的差别。对武帝来说，这座"城堡"需要更多的想象力，甚至要花费他 30 年的时间去完成。

other cases, the imagination was supplied by one of his advisers, who happened to be the most celebrated poet of the Han.

Two events took place shortly after 138 B.C., the year Emperor Wu reached adulthood and was able to exercise his authority in a fuller capacity. First, he re-established the imperial Shanglin Park southwest of Chang'an; and second, he read a *fu* rhapsody describing the great hunting parks of the states of Qi and Chu. In this work (which has fortunately survived), Chu's Cloudy Dream Park (Yunmeng) is said to measure 900 square *li* all sides; a great mountain in the center winds and twists upward and invades the blue clouds. Precious plants and strange animals are found inside the park, and the Chu prince, driving a quad-riga of tamed hippogriffs and riding a chariot of carved jade, holds his hunting parties there. The royal park of Qi, on the other hand, is so large that it could swallow eight or nine of Yunmeng Park, which "would not even be a splinter or straw in its throat."[156] The poem gave the young emperor such a strong impression that upon finishing it he sighed: "What a pity that I could not have lived at the same time as the author of this!" He did not wish to have been born a lord of Chu or Qi—he was the Son of Heaven with far greater power. What he hoped was to know the man who *represented* these fantastic parks in such elaborate words.

To the emperor's astonishment, the author of the rhapsody was a contemporary figure—an imperial dog trainer from Sichuan attested that it was written by a man named Sima Xiangru (179-117 B.C.) from his province. Xiangru was immediately summoned to the capital and received by the eager ruler. To His Majesty's great delight, the poet, who appeared to be a man of unsurpassed elegance, volunteered to compose another rhapsody for the throne. "My earlier piece concerns the affairs of the feudal lords and is not worthy of Your Majesty's attention. If I may be permitted, I would like to compose a new prose poem about your own imperial park." This new composition, entitled *Rhapsody on the Shanglin Park* (*Shanglin fu*), is a sequel to the earlier one: its narrator, Lord No-such (Wangshi Gong),[157] first concludes the debate about the superiority of the Qi and

Chu parks and then begins his discourse on the Han royal garden:[158]

Chu has lost its case, but neither has Qi gained anything to its credit. . . . Have you not seen what is truly great and beautiful? Have you alone not heard of the Imperial Park of the Son of Heaven?

To its left is Verdant Parasol,
To its right is Western Limits;
The Cinnabar River traverses its south,
The Purple Gulf intersects its north.[159]

如同其他事例一样，这种想象力的来源是他的一位谋士，而此人恰巧是汉代最著名的一位诗人。

公元前 138 年，武帝已长大成人，可以行使自己的权力了。在此不久后就发生了两件事。一是他开始在长安西南重建皇家苑囿上林苑；二是他读到一篇赋，描写了齐国和楚国猎苑之盛。在这一幸存至今的作品中，楚国的云梦泽据说是方 900 里，珍禽异木麇集其中。园中央是一座高山，盘桓而上，直逼青云。楚王驾着驯服的四驳（神马），乘坐在雕玉的车中进行围猎活动。而齐国的苑囿则更不得了，能够“吞若云梦者八九，于其胸中曾不蒂芥”。[156] 这篇赋给年轻的皇帝极其深刻的印象，他读毕叹曰：“朕独不得与此人同时哉！”他并不嫉妒往日的楚王或齐王：他贵为天子，自然有更大的权力。他想认识用如此迷人的文字描写了这些神奇的苑囿的诗人。

使他惊讶的是，这篇赋的作者竟然是他的同代人——一位为皇家养狗的蜀人告诉他，这篇赋是其同乡司马相如（前 179 —前 117 年）的作品。相如立刻被召见。令皇帝高兴的是，这位高雅卓越的诗人自愿为皇帝写作另一篇赋：“然此乃诸侯之事，未足观，请为天子游猎之赋。”题为《上林赋》的这篇新作是上篇赋的续篇，其中的讲述者“亡是公”[157] 首先结束了关于齐楚苑囿孰高孰下的争论，随后开始了对汉朝禁苑的描写：[158]

楚则失矣，而齐亦未为得也……君未睹夫巨丽也，独不闻天子之上林乎？左苍梧，右西极，丹水更其南，紫渊径其北。[159]

The park's territory defined here demands some discussion. Verdant Parasol, or Cangwu, is a mountain located on China's east coast;[160] Western Limits, or Xiji, indicates the western terminus of the world. Cinnabar River (Danshui) and Purple Gulf (Ziyuan) are two watercourses found in the mythical text *Classic of Mountains and Seas* (*Shanhai jing*); one flows into the South Sea, and the other originates in the Genqi Mountains in the far north.[161] Within this imaginary enclosure:

> Gazing about the expanse of the park
> At the abundance and variety of its creatures,
> One's eyes are dizzied and enraptured
> By the boundless horizons,
> The borderless vistas.
> The sun rises from the eastern ponds
> And sets among the slopes of the west;
> In the southern part of the park,
> Where grasses grow in the dead of winter
> And the waters leap, unbound by ice,
> Live zebras, yaks, tapirs, and black oxen,
> Water buffalo, elk, and antelope,
> "Red-crowns" and "round-heads."
> 171 Aurochs, elephants, and rhinoceroses.
> In the north, where in the midst of summer
> The ground is cracked and blotched with ice
> And one may walk the frozen streams or wade the rivulets,
> Roam unicorns and boars,
> Wild asses and camels,
> Onagers and mares,
> Swift stallions, donkeys, and mules.

The park thus possesses all manners of beasts from the four quarters of the world; one can similarly find all sorts of fish and birds in its eight swirling rivers and Cinnamon Forests. But the park is certainly not a wild zoo; as the garden of the Son of Heaven, it features the most exquisite buildings for human pleasure.

> Here the country palaces and imperial retreats
> Cover the hills and span the valleys,
> Verandas surrounding their four sides;
> With storied chambers and winding porticoes,
> Painted rafters and jade-studded corbels,
> Interlacing paths for the royal palanquin,
> And arcaded walks stretching such distances
> That their length cannot be traversed in a single day.
> Here the peaks have been leveled for mountain halls,
> Terraces raised, story upon story,

我们需要对这里所说的上林苑的范围做些说明。苍梧是中国东海岸的一座山；[160] 西极指世界最西的终点。丹水和紫渊是神话名著《山海经》中提到的两条水道，一条流入南海，另一条发源于北方遥远的根耆山。[161] 在这个想象中的四至以内：

> 于是乎周览泛观，瞋盼轧沕，芒芒恍忽，视之无端，察之无崖。日出东沼，入于西陂。其南则隆冬生长，踊水跃波；兽则𤜶旄貘犛，沈牛麈麋，赤首圜题，穷奇象犀。其北则盛夏含冻裂地，涉冰揭河；兽则麒麟角𩷑，騊駼橐驼，蛩蛩驒騱，駃騠驴骡。

根据这段描写，上林苑中充斥着来自天下四方的各种各样的动物，人们也可以在园中的河流和树林中发现各种各样的游鱼和飞鸟。但是，上林当然不是一处野生动物园，作为天子的禁苑，其中还有供人享乐的最精美的建筑：

> 于是乎离宫别馆，弥山跨谷，高廊四注，重坐曲阁。华榱璧珰，辇道缅属，步櫚周流。长途中宿。夷嵏筑堂，

> And chambers built in the deep grottoes.
> Peering down into the caves, one cannot spy their end;
> Gazing up at the rafters, one seems to see them brush the heavens;
> So lofty are the palaces that comets stream through their portals
> And rainbows twine about their balustrades.

The reliability of Xiangru's description of the Shanglin Park was questioned by the poet's contemporaries. Sima Qian, who first recorded this work in his *Records of the Historian,* remarked that "the extravagant language of the poet overstepped the bounds of reality and displayed too little respect for the dictates of reason and good sense."[162] Later historians, however, often took the opposite position, either trying to find evidence for the poem's historical credibility or attempting to reconstruct the park based on the rhapsody.[163] In so doing, they have ignored the *fictionality* of this work, which, in my opinion, the Song scholar Cheng Dachang explains best:

> When Lord No-such describes the Shanglin Park, he is actually talking about the whole world within the four seas. In defining the park's boundary, he refers to the Verdant Parasol to the east and Western Limits to the west. In setting the four directions, he says that the sun and moon rise from the eastern ponds and descend among the western slopes. In the south, plants grow in the dead of winter and waters leap and wave, while in the north, the ground is cracked and blotched with ice in the midst of summer, and one can walk the frozen streams and wade the rivulets. When he lists the places where the emperor's hunting team reaches, he tells us that "the Yangzi and Yellow Rivers are the corral and Mount Tai is the lookout tower." All of these are meant to show that the world is within the park of the Son of Heaven, and that Qi and Chu's proud gardens are both encompassed by it. . . . Lord No-such describes this park as real, so how can it be not real? Later people have tried to examine the truthfulness and faultiness of the poem against the actual Shanglin—indeed one cannot talk about a dream in front of idiots![164]

Cheng Dachang also observes in another essay:

When Xiangru was writing his rhapsody on Shanglin, he stated clearly that it came from the mouth of Lord No-such—a name that means there is no such a person. If there is no such a person, how can his words in the poem be other than fictional [*wuyou*]? Knowing the poem is fictional but taking it for real and thus criticizing it—this is the trouble with the previous arguments.[165]

累台增成，岩突洞房。俯杳眇而无见，仰攀橑而扪天；奔星更于闺闼，宛虹拖于楯轩。

与司马相如同时代的司马迁最早在《史记》中记载了这一作品，但作为一个史家，他对司马相如笔下上林苑种种景色的可靠性产生了质疑，认为该赋“侈靡过其实，且非义理所尚”。[162] 但是后来的史学家却往往持相反的观点，或试图寻找证据来证明赋中所记的历史真实性，或试图依靠赋的记载来重构这座禁苑。[163] 在这一过程中，他们忽略了作品的虚构性。在我看来，宋代的程大昌做出了最好的解释：

亡是公赋上林，盖该四海言之。其叙分界，则曰左苍梧右西极。其举四方，则曰日出东沼入乎西陂。南则隆冬生长，涌水跃波。北则盛夏含冻裂地，涉水揭河。至论猎之所及，则曰江河为阹，泰山为橹。此言环四海皆天子苑囿，使齐楚所夸俱在包笼中……叙而置之，何一非实？后世顾以长安上林，核其有无，所谓痴人前不得说梦者也！[164]

在另一篇文章中，程大昌还指出：

相如之赋上林也，固尝明著其指，曰，此为亡是公之言也。亡是公者，明无此人也。夫既本无此人，则凡其所赋之语何往而不为乌有也？知其乌有而以实录责之，故所向驳碍也。[165]

Unlike Sima Qian and other historians who judged the rhapsody in terms of truth and belief, Cheng Dachang read it as a fabrication of the poet's fertile imagination. Someone else who must have shared this view was Emperor Wu, the intended reader of the literary work. All available historical records indicate that when the emperor received the rhapsody, his royal garden was nothing like the one described in Xiangru's ornate lines. It is true that Shanglin had been the site of royal parks since Zhou
172 times and that the First Emperor had built his magnificent Epang Palace there, but this and many other pleasure palaces had been burned down some 65 years earlier by General Xiang Yu. At the beginning of the Han, this former imperial park had been turned into fields and occupied by farmers.[166] In 138 B.C., right before Emperor Wu claimed the park as his personal property, he traveled there incognito and held a hunting party, which was interrupted by a crowd of angry peasants berating the hunters for destroying their crops. Such "inconveniences" led to the emperor's decision to reclaim the park, but in order to do so he had to first purchase the land and to transfer the owners to other places.[167]

与司马迁和其他历史学家不同，程大昌不是从真实和信仰的角度来评判这篇赋，而是将其理解为出自作者丰富想象力的作品。持这一看法的人还包括这一作品的预设读者武帝。所有可信的历史记载都说明，当武帝收到这篇赋时，他的禁苑与相如笔下那些绚丽的描写并不一致。虽然上林的确从周代就已是王室的苑囿，而且秦始皇也曾在此建造富丽堂皇的阿房宫，但是该宫和其他离宫在大约 65 年前就已被项羽付之一炬。汉代初年，原来的皇家苑囿已经变为农田，为乡野村夫所占据。[166] 公元前 138 年，就在武帝将上林宣布为自己的私产之前，他微服出行此地，并举行围猎。这次狩猎活动受到一大群农民愤怒的阻挠，责骂他们毁坏了庄稼。这一“不便”使得皇帝决定收回上林苑，但为了达到这一目的，他仍需要首先买下这片土地，并将其所有者迁往别的地方。[167]

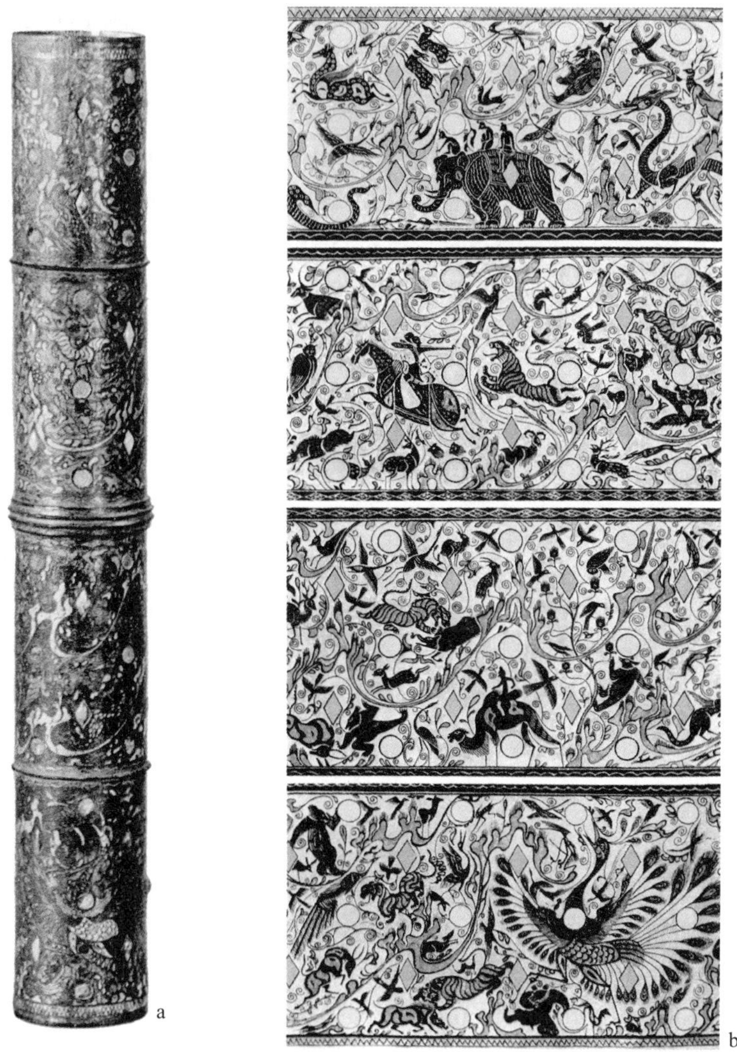

Fig. 3.10. (a) Chariot ornament. Bronze with gold, silver, and stone inlay. Late Western Han. Early 1st century B.C. Excavated in 1965 from Tomb no. 122 at Sanpanshan, Dingxian, Hebei province. (b) Drawing of the decoration.

图 3.10 （a）车饰。青铜嵌金、银、绿松石。西汉晚期，公元前 1 世纪早期。1965 年河北定县三盘山 122 号墓出土。（b）车饰线图。

It is not necessary to list the many pieces of evidence for the fictional nature of Xiangru's work.[168] But it is important to understand that although the rhapsody was well received by Emperor Wu and the poet became one of his personal attendants, it must have also made the emperor consider the real Shanglin Park rather shabby. His subsequent effort was to create an actual park on earth that matched Sima Xiangru's fictional garden, with all its landscape features, strange animals and birds, magnificent palaces and towers, beautiful women and brave warriors. Although no plan or chronicle of this project has survived, by piecing together fragmentary records from various texts and by consulting pictures that may be related to Shanglin Park (Figs. 3.10-13), we can outline the emperor's general vision and goal.

Shortly after 138 B.C., officials all over the country were encouraged to present tributes of unusual plants. Some officials, in order to stress the preciousness and strangeness of their own tributes, labeled their own goods with "beautiful names." More than 3,000 kinds of flowers and trees, as well as some "artificial" plants, found a new home in Shanglin Park.[169] Among the latter was a huge coral tree presented by the prince of South Yue. Planted inside one of the park's ten ponds, its 462 luminous branches emitted light at night.[170] Strange objects were also gained by confiscations. Chang'an financial magnate Yuan Guanghan, for example, owned one of the most beautiful gardens in the country, with manmade rivers and an artificial mountain several *li* long. Yuan had collected "all sorts of unusual plants" and "all kinds of strange animals and precious birds," including white parrots, purple mandarin ducks, yaks, and a black rhinoceros. He had also built multistoried pavilions connected by winding corridors; to travel through them all took hours and hours. "Yuan Guanghan was later executed for certain crimes, and his private garden was confiscated and integrated into the imperial garden. All the birds, beasts, trees, and plants were transferred to Shanglin Park."[171]

Two other sources of "strange and precious goods" were military

conquests and foreign tributes. In 121 B.C., Emperor Wu put down a rebellion in present-day Vietnam. A tropical garden called the Fuli Palace (Palace of Cultivating Lichi Trees) was then built inside Shanglin Park to house the "strange and rare plants" gained from the victory. A surviving 173
inventory lists more than a thousand plants of various kinds.[172] Indeed, during those years the most exciting events in the capital were arrivals

证明相如作品虚构性的证据很多，在此没有必要一一列出。[168] 然而，我们必须理解一个重要的事实，即尽管相如的赋颇受武帝赞赏，并且相如也被擢升为郎，侍奉于皇帝左右，但是相如的赋也一定使得武帝意识到了真实的上林苑是多么不堪入目。他的回应是，在人间创建一处可以与相如虚构的苑囿相媲美的园林，里面充满各种景观和珍禽异兽，宫阙瑰丽，美人如云，兵士英武。尽管历史文献没有保存下该工程的规划和进度设计，但是如果我们把各种来源的零碎记载连接起来，再结合与上林苑可能有关的图像［图 3.10—图 3.13］，我们就能大致地勾画出汉武帝对这个园子的想象和目的。

公元前 138 年稍后，各地的官员受到鼓励，纷纷进贡各种奇草异木。有的官员为了显示其贡品名贵而特殊，往往冠之以“美名”。大约有超过三千种花木包括部分“雕塑性”植物，被汇集到了上林苑。[169] 后者中有南越进献的一株高大的珊瑚树，植于上林苑十个池塘之一，其 462 个枝条在夜间发出璀璨的光芒。[170] 有的奇异物品是通过没收的方式得到的。例如，长安的富人袁广汉有号称国内最精致的一个园子，其中人工的水流和山石绵延数里。袁广汉在其中汇集了种种奇树异草和“奇兽珍禽”，后者中有白鹦鹉、紫鸳鸯、犛牛、青兕，等等。他还修建了多层的楼阁和绵延的长廊，旅行其中需要很长的时间。“广汉后有罪诛，没入为官园。鸟兽草木皆移入上林苑中。”[171]

其他奇物珍品来自战利品和外国贡品。如公元前 121 年，武帝平定了今越南地区的一次反抗，接着便在上林苑建造了一处叫作扶荔宫的亚热带植物园，以盛放胜利后获得的奇草异木。一份保存至今的清单列出了上千件草木。[172] 的确，在这一时期，都城内最令人

of foreign tributes of strange creatures. Following Emperor Wu's military expeditions to the far west and south, exotic animals and birds were sent to Shanglin Park in a steady stream. Ban Gu later recalled that the park contained unicorns from India, heavenly steeds from Turkestan, rhinoceroses from Thailand, and ostriches from Persia: "All the different species of animals and birds were sent to Shanglin Park from various places, some as far away as 30,000 *li*, from beyond the Kunlun Mountains and from the other side of the ocean."[173] Among these foreign tributes were a white elephant and "talking birds," which arrived in 121 B.C.[174] These were interpreted as good omens from Heaven, and Emperor Wu himself wrote a poem in congratulation:

> The elephant, white like jade,
> Comes here from the west.
> It eats the sweet dew from Heaven,
> And drinks luminescent spring water.
> The red geese gather together
> In an unmeasurable number.
> Each has distinctive features on its neck,
> And five-colored patterns on its body.
> They are sent down by the Lord on High;
> Bringing happiness to human beings.
> Oh! It is on the immortal island Penglai,
> Where we reach the infinitude of longevity![175]

The irony of this enterprise, as we can clearly perceive in this poem, is that rather than the emperor visiting the remote Penglai, these wild animals and birds were brought into the fenced imperial garden to make this place a "magical land." The transformation of the park coincided with a transformation in the spectator's eyes and mind: since the object of viewing was no longer an ordinary landscape but a series of strange scenes, the viewer (i.e., Emperor Wu as the master of the garden) was persuaded to forget his earthly existence and to fantasize himself as living in an immortal realm. Many "viewing spots" were then designed for this purpose, including the Pavilion for Viewing the Elephant (Guanxiang guan), the Pavilion of the Albino Deer (Bailu guan), the Pavilion of the Three-legged Crow (Sanque guan), and the Pavilion of the Divine Tripod (Dingjiao guan).[176] The word *pavilion* in these names hardly conveys the meaning of the original Chinese character *guan*, which means both "to view" and "the place from which one views."[177] Each of these *guan* lookouts was oriented toward an individual "stage" with specific

兴奋的事莫过于外国进献的奇异物品。随着武帝对西方和南方边远地区的征伐，来自异域的鸟兽如流水一般输入上林苑中。班固后来回忆说，上林苑"乃有九真之麟，大宛之马。黄支之犀，条支之鸟。踰昆仑，越巨海。殊方异类，至于三万里"。[173] 这些来自国外的物品中，有公元前 121 年获得的白象和"能言鸟"。[174] 这些物品被看作上天所赐的祥瑞，武帝因此撰写了一首颂诗：

象载瑜，白集西。
食甘露，饮荣泉。
赤雁集，六纷员，
殊翁杂，五采文。
神所见，施祉福。
登蓬莱，结无极！[175]

从这首诗中我们可以清楚地感受到一种反讽：与其使皇帝登临遥远的蓬莱，倒不如凭借汇集于禁苑的奇异鸟兽把这个人间花园转化为一处"魔术境界"。这种转化也意味着观者目光和心灵的转化：因为被观看的对象不再是普通的景观，而是一系列奇异的景象，观者（身为禁苑主人的武帝）就可以忘却他所处的现实世界，幻想着自己已在仙境之中。为了这个目的，许多"观景处"被设计出来，包括观象观、白鹿观、三雀观、鼎郊观等。[176] 英文 pavilion（亭、台、榭）一词很难准确地传达中文"观"字的原义，"观"字既表示"观看"，又表示"观看的地方"。[177] 每个"观"都面向一个独立的、

"props"—rare animals, birds, and plants—to stimulate the spectator's imagination.[178] The blueprint for this architectural design, however, had been drawn by Sima Xiangru years ago:

> Green dragons slither from the eastern pavilion;
> Elephant carriages prance from the pure hall of the west,
> Bringing immortals to dine in the peaceful towers
> And bands of fairies to sun themselves beneath the southern eaves.
> . . .
> Such are the scenes of the imperial park,
> A hundred, a thousand settings.[179]

Emperor Wu faithfully realized these lines; and the result was constant additions of "stages" and "settings." According to the *History of the Former Han,* Shanglin Park occupied an area of some 300 square *li* in circumference and contained more than seventy pleasure palaces; each palace was large enough to accommodate thousands of chariots and horsemen.[180] *A Record of the Guanzhong Region* (*Guanzhong ji*) provides a more detailed inventory: "Shanglin Park had 12 gates, 36 individual gardens, 12 palace complexes, and 25 *guan* pavilions."[181] Inside the park, the emperor also created the huge Kunming Lake in 121 B.C. Statues of the Weaving Maid (the star Vega) and the Cowherd (the star Altair) were placed on the opposite shores of the lake to turn it into a replica of the Milky Way, and a big stone whale was placed in the water to identify it as an ocean.[182] All three statues have been found during recent years (Figs. 3.11a, b).

In *Rhapsody on the Shanglin Park,* Sima Xiangru created a microcosm
174 without a focal point. The fantastic park is described from an ever-shifting point of view, and the poet seems to travel in his imaginary landscape without pausing. The real Shanglin Park mimicked this literary structure. Until 104 B.C., the construction of the park was motivated by the desire to create an endless series of individual "scenes"—palaces, pavilions, and ponds embellished with rare creatures and plants. Each scene constituted part of the general environment and atmosphere, never

dominating the whole landscape. But in 104 B.C. an intensive architectural campaign began. All energy was suddenly concentrated on a single group of palatial monuments called Jianzhang Palace (Palace for Establishing the Statutes). The reasons for this development are perhaps complex, but I believe that the central factor must be sought in Emperor Wu's deepening engagement in creating his *fictional* paradise.[183] Most interesting, this new project, which finally provided Shanglin Park with a focus, was

由特殊“道具”——即那些能够激发起观者想象力的稀有鸟兽草木——构成的“舞台”。[178] 司马相如数年前就已经勾画出了这类建筑的蓝图：

> 青龙蚴蟉于东葙，象舆婉僤于西清。灵圄燕于闲馆，偓佺之伦暴于南荣……若此者数百千处。[179]

武帝忠实地再现了赋中描述的这些内容，其结果便是不断地增加这类“舞台”和“场景”。据《汉书》记载，上林苑周袤 300 里，内有 70 多座离宫；每座离宫足以容纳千乘万骑。”[180]《关中记》则提供了一个更详细的目录：“上林苑，门十二，中有苑三十六，宫十二，观二十五。”[181] 公元前 121 年，皇帝还在上林苑中修建了巨大的昆明池。织女像和牛郎像分别安置在相对的两岸，使该池成为对银河的模拟，池中有一巨大的石鲸，把这个人造湖泊转化成一片汪洋大海。[182] 近年来，这三件石雕都已被发现［图 3.11］。

司马相如在《上林赋》中创造了一个没有焦点的缩微宇宙。他对这座离奇禁苑的描写采用了不断移动的视点，诗人似乎在其想象的景色中做着一次不间断的旅行。真实的上林苑模仿了这种文学结构。创造无数单体“景观”的热情在公元前 104 年以前推动着上林苑的建设，这些景观包括宫殿、观以及以稀有动植物装点的池塘湖泊。作为总体环境和氛围的一部分，这些景观从未凌驾于全部景色之上。但在公元前 104 年，一个强化的建筑计划展开了。所有的精力突然集中到一组皇宫纪念性建筑中，这就是建章宫。这一变化的原因可能相当复杂，但我相信主要的缘故必须在武帝不断深化的创造一个虚构天堂的努力中去寻找。[183] 建章宫的建造使得上林苑最终

a b

Fig. 3.11. (a) Cowherd. H. 258 cm. (b) Weaving Maid. H. 228 cm. Stone. Western Han. 2nd-1st centuries B.C. Located at Caotangsi, Chang'an, Shaanxi province.
图 3.11 （a）牛郎。高 258 厘米。（b）织女。高 228 厘米。石雕。西汉，前 2—前 1 世纪。陕西长安县草堂寺。

again inspired by the last rhapsody Sima Xiangru composed before his retirement. Sima Qian documented the context of this work in his *Records of the Historian*:

> Xiangru observed that the emperor desired immortality and took occasion to remark, "My description of the Shanglin Park is hardly deserving of praise. I have something that is still finer. I have begun a rhapsody called *The Mighty One [Daren fu]* but have not completed it yet. I beg to finish it and present it to Your Majesty." [Before Xiangru,] immortals had been pictured as emaciated creatures dwelling among the hills and swamps, but the poet judged that this was not the kind of immortality for great emperors and kings. He finally presented his *Rhapsody on the Mighty One* to the throne, which read as follows:
>
> In this world there lives a Mighty One
> Who dwells in the Middle Continent [i.e., China].

Though his mansion stretches ten thousand miles,
He is not content to remain in it a moment.
But, saddened by the sordid press of the vulgar world,
Nimbly takes his way aloft and soars far away.[184]

In a trance, the Mighty One finds himself traveling in the sky, accompanied by fantastic beasts. His chariot is drawn by winged dragons, with red serpents and green lizards writhing beside it. He snatches a shooting star for a flag and sheathes the flagstaff in a broken rainbow. He crosses to the eastern limit of the universe and then to the west, summoning all the fairies of the Magic Garden to his service. A host of gods ride behind him on the Star of Pure Light, and he orders the Emperors of the Five Directions to be his guides. He surveys the eight dimensions and the four outer wastes, and visits the Nine Rivers and the Five Streams of the world.

有了一个中心，有意思的是，这个工程又是受到司马相如的一篇赋的激发。这是相如在致仕前所写的最后一篇赋。司马迁在《史记》中记载了该赋写作前后的事情：

相如见上好仙道，因曰："上林之事未足美也，尚有靡者。臣尝为《大人赋》，未就，请具而奏之。"相如以为列仙之传居山泽间，形容甚臞，此非帝王之仙意也。乃遂就《大人赋》。其辞曰：

世有大人兮，在于中州。
宅弥万里兮，曾不足以少留。
悲世俗之迫隘兮，朅轻举而远游……[184]

恍惚中，这位称为"大人"的人主发现自己在天上遨游。陪伴他的是各种神兽，为他驾车的是带翼的应龙，旁边是赤螭和青虬。他抓住彗星作为旗帜，又将旗杆插入虹中。他到达了宇宙的东极少阳，又转而西行，将天上花园灵圉中的众神召集起来。五帝因此成为他的先导，众神之主太一驾驶着陵阳星跟随其后。他遍览八纮，游历四荒，渡过九江，穿越五河。

This part of the poem deliberately echoes the earlier *Rhapsody on the Shanglin Park*, and the heavenly "Magic Garden" mirrors Shanglin Park on earth. Indeed, up to this point, this composition is a new version of the old one; but instead of describing the physical appearance of an imaginary park, the poet focuses on the viewer's perception and imagination. In other words, if the subject of Xiangru's first work was a vision of Shanglin Park that had not yet been realized, the subject of his second work was an imaginary journey inside the park. During the two decades between these two works, his original vision had been turned into reality. The parallelism between these two rhapsodies, however, stops here. The Mighty one's heavenly journey culminates with his attainment of immortality:

> He gazes west to the hazy contours of Mount Kunlun,
> He gallops off to the Mountain of the Three Pinnacles.
> He opens the Changhe Gate of Heaven,
> Entering the palace of the Celestial Emperor,
> And bringing the Jade Maiden back home.[185]

It is said that these lines made Emperor Wu "ecstatic and feel as though he were whirling away over the clouds and wandering between Heaven and Earth."[186] The same lines also directly link the rhapsody to the new Jianzhang Palace, whose gate was also named Changhe and whose main hall was called Jade Palace (Yutang). The emperor thus once again followed the poet's steps to change the level of his discourse: he was no longer constructing an imaginary universe; he was now establishing a center, or his own "heavenly court," in this universe.

The Jianzhang Palace included two palatial halls called Jiaorao and Taidang, obscure names signifying the "loftiness" and "vastness" of paradise. There were also the Divine Terrace (Shenming tai) and a 46-meter-high bronze pillar upon which a sculptured immortal raised a plate above his head (Fig. 3.12). Sweet dew falling onto the

Fig. 3.12. Immortal receiving sweet dew. Bronze statue inspired by Emperor Wu's statue in the Jianzhang Palace. Qing dynasty. 18th century. Beihai Park, Beijing.

图 3.12 仙人承露。受武帝建章宫仙人像影响而建造的青铜像。清代，18 世纪。北京，北海公园。

《大人赋》的这一部分刻意与《上林赋》呼应，把天上的“灵圉”描写成现实世界中上林苑的镜像。确实，它可以被看成是旧赋的一个新版；但是作者不再着重描绘一座想象中苑囿的外观，而是集中于观者的感受和想象力。换言之，如果说相如第一篇赋的主题是尚未实现的上林苑的意象，那么这第二篇赋的主题就是在已建成的上林苑中幻想的旅行。在这两篇赋之间的二十年里，作者对这座皇家御园的原始意象已经变成现实。但是两篇赋的平行关系到此为止；大人的天上之旅以达到仙境而进入高潮：

> 西望昆仑之轧，沕荒忽兮，直径驰乎三危。
> 排阊阖而入帝宫兮，载玉女而与之归。[185]

据说这些词句使得武帝“飘飘有凌云之气，似游天地之间意”。[186] 这些句子也使得这篇赋和新造的建章宫发生了直接的联系：建章宫的门称作阊阖，其主要的建筑名曰玉堂。这样，汉武帝再次跟随着文学家的脚步转换了话语的平台：他不再致力于建造一个假想的宇宙，而是要在这个宇宙中建立一个中心，也就是他在天上的宫阙。

建章宫包括两座富丽堂皇的宫殿，一称嶕峣，一称骀荡，这两个晦涩的名字分别意味着天堂的“崇高”和“巨大”。宫内还有一座神明台和一具 46 米高的铜柱，柱顶饰有双手擎盘的仙人像［图 3.12］。

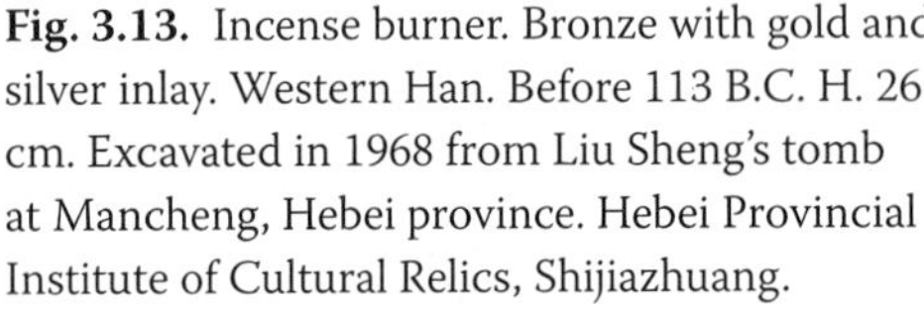

Fig. 3.13. Incense burner. Bronze with gold and silver inlay. Western Han. Before 113 B.C. H. 26 cm. Excavated in 1968 from Liu Sheng's tomb at Mancheng, Hebei province. Hebei Provincial Institute of Cultural Relics, Shijiazhuang.

图 3.13 博山炉。青铜嵌金、银。西汉，早于前113 年。1968 年河北满城刘胜墓出土。河北省文物研究所藏。

plate was mixed with powdered jade—a kind of elixir for spirits that was now served to the Mighty One. A large artificial lake was created and given the name of Cosmic Liquid (Taiye); the immortal island was duplicated in its center (Fig. 3.13), surrounded by sculptured fish and turtles.[187] But the central building of Jianzhang Palace was Jade Hall behind the heavenly Changhe Gate, both built of translucent white stone. The gate had three layers and was reportedly 60 meters tall (Fig. 3.14). Within it, a labyrinth with "a thousand doors and ten thousand windows" surrounded Jade Palace which soared over this architectural maze. More than one historian testified that this hall was so tall that it overlooked Gaozu's Weiyang Palace, and that its amazing height was further emphasized by a gilded phoenix on the roof, shining under the sun and turning in the wind.[188] The building was thus counterpoised to the old throne hall: standing side by side but separated by the city walls, Weiyang Palace was the heart of the administrative city; Jade Palace dominated the cosmic Shanglin Park.[189] Weiyang Palace was a wooden-framed structure heavily painted with bright colors; Jade Palace, with its pure marble walls and golden phoenix, must have appeared as a mirage in the sky. These

Fig. 3.14. The "Phoenix" Gate. Clay tile. Eastern Han. 2nd century A.D. H. 48 cm. W. 39 cm. Found in 1975 in vicinity of Chengdu, Sichuan province. Chengdu Museum.

图 3.14 "凤"阙。画像砖。东汉，2 世纪。高 48 厘米，宽 39 厘米。1975 年四川成都附近出土。成都市博物馆藏。

甘露降于盘中，调以玉屑，就成了大人所食的不死之药。宫内还开凿了一个人工湖，名曰太液池；池中央是一人造仙岛［图 3.13］，周围环绕着鱼和龟的雕像。[187] 但是，建章宫的主要建筑是阊阖门后的玉堂，门、堂均以晶莹的汉白玉筑成。阊阖门有三重，传说达 60 米高［图 3.14］。门内，一座"千门万户"的迷宫环绕着高耸入云的玉堂。不止一位历史学家说到这座宫殿的惊人高度，据他们的记载从玉堂甚至可以俯瞰高祖所建的未央宫。玉堂顶上站立着的一只镀金的凤凰，进一步突出了建筑的高度，金凤随风而转，在阳光下熠熠生辉。[188] 建章宫因此成为旧日朝堂未央宫的对立物：二者并列而立，但被城墙分隔；未央宫是行政性都城的中心，而玉堂主宰着微型宇宙般的上林苑；[189] 未央宫是一组以彩画装饰的木构建筑；玉堂的纯净白石墙和金凤使它看去犹如天上宫阙。这些对立的形象似

contrasting images seem to have been based on the opening lines in Sima Xiangru's rhapsody: although the Mighty One's imperial halls stretch 10,000 miles, saddened by the sordid press of the vulgar world, he takes his way aloft and soars far away.

Emperor Wu would remain on the throne for another eighteen years,
176 but Jianzhang Palace was the last major structure he built in Shanglin Park. With the completion of this project, the development of the emperor's fictional garden and his search for a monument of immortality had reached the end. Indeed, when fiction has become reality, there is no room left for further imagination; when immortality has been granted by architecture, no more building is necessary.

❺ Wang Mang's Bright Hall

The reconstruction of Chang'an's history has begun to reveal a dialectical process: new monumental forms were constantly modified by tradition, and again challenged and altered by innovation. The central determinant of this process was changes in notions of authority. When the Han was first established, its founder alone stood for the new ruling power; the imposing Weiyang Palace emerged as his personal monument, documenting his victory and symbolizing his mandate. The city of Chang'an was thus created by and for the One Man Under Heaven, and in this way epitomized China's historical transition into the new imperial era. Chang'an's symbolism, however, was substantially revised under the second Han ruler, Emperor Hui. Power once again became hereditary and imperial authority increasingly relied on autonomous political institutions backed by traditional ideology. The Confucian orthodox or "classical" city design prevailed: Gaozu's palace was integrated into a walled enclosure, becoming one of many elements of an institutionalized capital. This new Chang'an represented the supremacy of the state, and secondary monuments centered on individual mausoleums were established in the suburbs to commemorate the glory of dynastic rulers. The city as a whole thus documented the history of the dynasty within the Chinese political tradition. The construction of Chang'an again changed direction under Emperor Wu, an extraordinary figure who attempted to recreate himself as a mythical hero-sovereign. The city was expanded to include an even larger area, in which new religious monuments, with their dazzling

乎基于司马相如赋开头的词句：尽管大人的皇宫有万里之大，但他为世俗的迫隘而不快，仍要轻举远游。

武帝在位的时间还有 18 年，但是建章宫却是他在上林苑建造的最后一组重要建筑。随着这一工程的完结，这座"虚构"禁苑的发展以及武帝对"仙境纪念碑"的探求也走到尽头。的确，当虚幻成为现实，想象力也就没有了更多的空间去驰骋；当仙境已成为具体的建筑形象，也就再没必要建造更多的楼阁。

五、王莽的明堂

本章对长安历史的重构已经开始显示出一个辨证的过程：新的纪念碑形式不断被传统改造，同时也受到新观念的挑战和变更。这一过程的决定因素是变化中的"权力"概念。当汉朝建国之初，开国皇帝本人代表着新的统治力量，壮丽的未央宫以其个人纪念碑的形式出现，记载着他的成功，象征着他的指令。因此，长安既是由"天下一人"所创建的，也是为此人建设的，以这种方式成为中国历史进入新的帝国时代的缩影。然而，长安的象征意义在汉朝第二代统治者惠帝手中被改变。权力又一次成为世袭财产，皇帝的威信日益依赖于传统观念支持下的自为的官僚政治机构。儒家正统的或"经典性"的城市设计主宰了长安的建设：高祖的宫殿被并入城圈之内，成为行政制度化都城中的众多因素之一。新的长安代表着王朝至高无上的地位；同时，以单个陵墓为中心的第二级纪念碑在郊外建立起来，以纪念每个皇帝的往日荣光。通过这种方式，长安作为一个整体记录了中国政治传统中一个王朝的历史。长安的建设在武帝的手中再次发生转向。武帝是位非常独特、试图将自己再造为一位神化的英雄帝王的统治者。此时，长安的规模扩展到城外的广袤地区。在那里，新型的宗教性纪念碑以其令人眼花缭乱的形象和

images and astonishing scale, became counterparts of the administrative town. Sovereignty had to be immortalized; the enormous Ganquan
177 Palace and Shanglin Park resulted from the emperor's insistent pursuit of eternal life beyond his worldly domain.

A century later, at the beginning of the first century A.D., a new architectural fanaticism again seized Chang'an. Wang Mang (45 B.C.-A.D. 23), then regent, launched a new building campaign as an essential part of his political scheme to take over the dragon throne. Acting as the defender and restorer of traditional values, he destroyed Emperor Wu's magnificent Jianzhang Palace and many other structures in Shanglin Park.[190] Building materials gained from this destruction were reused to found a group of Confucian monuments. Of all the antagonisms between the "orthodox" and "heterodox" traditions in constructing the capital, this was the most violent.[191]

The central structure of this new monumental complex was Bright Hall (Mingtang), said to have been invented by sages of remote antiquity as the most authoritative symbol of sovereignty. According to Han Confucians, the ancient tradition of this monument had been largely "forgotten" after the Zhou and could only be "restored" with the aid of relevant passages scattered in ancient texts. Any person able to accomplish this historical mission would prove himself the legitimate successor of the former sage-kings. His success in rebuilding Bright Hall would be a definite sign of Heaven's approval of his ruling mandate. This "restoration" work—or rather the "creation" of the most important Confucian monument of imperial China—had begun during the Eastern Zhou and was finally realized in Wang Mang's Bright Hall.[192] The pursuit of this structure over a period of some two centuries was sustained by a profound political and intellectual movement with strong "scholastic" or "classic" tendencies. Unlike all previous monuments in Chinese history, Wang Mang's Bright Hall was based on a synthesis and exegesis of ancient texts.[193] Its manifold symbolism was governed by highly abstract elements such as measurement, direction, and geometrical shape—architectural references derived from the study of cosmology, astronomy, mathematics, geography, and musicology. Bright Hall was, on the one hand, a definite sign of the Confucian dominance in Han politics and, on the other, a political integration and interpretation of all branches of humanistic and scientific knowledge in early imperial China.

使人惊异的规模，成为行政性都市的对等物。其含义是：君权必须不朽；巨大的甘泉宫和上林苑产生于皇帝对超越尘世的永恒生命的追求。

又过了一个世纪，新一波的建筑狂热在公元 1 世纪初再次控制了长安。摄政的王莽（前 45—公元 23 年）发动了这个运动，将其作为他篡位夺权的一个实质性的组成部分。他以传统价值的卫道士和恢复者的面貌出现，摧毁了武帝华丽的建章宫以及上林苑中的许多建筑。[190] 破坏所获得的建筑材料被用来建造一组儒家的纪念碑。在长安的历史上，这是最为激烈的一次“正统”与“异端”间的对抗。[191]

王莽的新纪念碑群的中心建筑是明堂，据说它是由远古时期的圣贤发明的，是君权最权威的象征。根据汉儒的说法，周代以后的人们在很大程度上“忘却”了明堂的古老传统，只有依靠散见于古代典籍中的相关记载才能“修复”这个传统。如果某人能够完成这一历史使命，他便可以证明自己是上古圣王合法的继承者，因为重建明堂的成功是天授君权的明确标志。“修复”——或者不如说是“创造”——这尊中国古代最重要的纪念碑的工作在东周时期就已开始，最后在王莽明堂中得以完成。[192] 支持这个持续了大约两个世纪追求的，是一个具有强烈“经院式”或“古典主义”倾向的、影响深远的政治和文化运动。与先前中国历史上所有的纪念碑不同，王莽明堂的基础在于对古代典籍的综合和诠释，[193] 其多元的象征意义被一些高度抽象的元素所支配，包括尺度、方向，以及几何形体。这些元素来源于对宇宙哲学、天文学、数学、地理学和音乐学的研究，成为建设明堂的建筑基准。一方面，明堂是汉代在政治上独尊儒术的明确标志；另一方面，它又是早期中华帝国对人文和科学知识各个分支的一种政治性整合和诠释。

This monument was discovered in 1956 south of Chang'an almost directly facing the central gate on the city's southern wall.[194] The remaining foundation suggests an architectural complex of strict geometrical forms (Fig. 3.15a). In the center of this complex was Bright Hall, about 42 meters north-south and east-west, superimposed on an earthen core (Fig. 3.15b). This building can be tentatively reconstructed based on archaeological reports and ancient records (Fig. 3.16b).[195] On the third and top level, a single round room, called the Room of Communing with Heaven (Tongtian wu), stood directly above a square hall on the second level. This hall was surrounded by eight small free-standing halls radiating from the four corners,[196] and all nine chambers on the second story were erected on the solid "earthen core." On the first story, four rectangular halls stood against this "core" and faced the four directions. Each of these four halls was most likely divided into three sections with a central room flanked by two small ones. A covered portico extended outward from these halls and gave the building a stable look.

明堂遗址于 1956 年在长安南郊被发现，其位置几乎正对着长安南墙中门。[194] 残存的基址显示出这是一组具有严格的几何形式的建筑群［图 3.15a］。建筑群的中央为明堂，南北和东西各长约 42 米，中部有一逐级高起的夯土台［图 3.15b］。依据考古报告和文献，古建专家对该建筑做了试验性的复原［图 3.16b］。[195] 根据复原结果，顶部的第三层是一个单独的圆形房屋，称作通天屋，直接建在第二层的方形厅堂之上。这个厅堂四角带有八个小厅，[196] 连同主厅均建在坚实的夯土台上。建筑的第一层是夯土台周围面向四方的四个长方形的厅堂。每一厅堂很可能分为三间，中央一间较大，两边的较小。堂的外部有带檐的抱厦，在视觉上加强了整个建筑的稳定感。

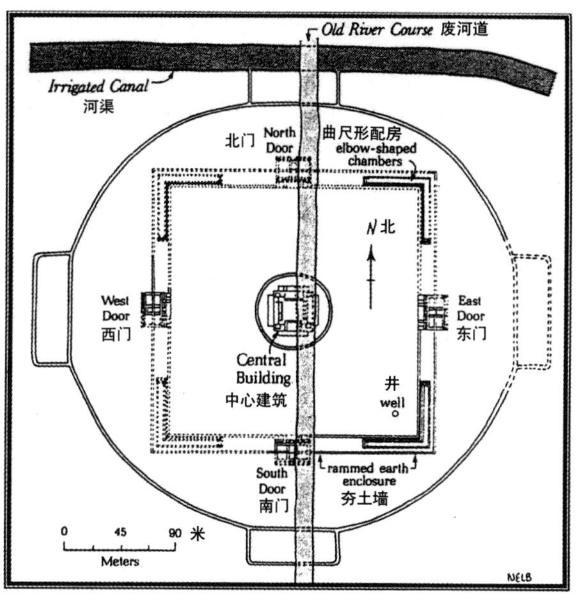

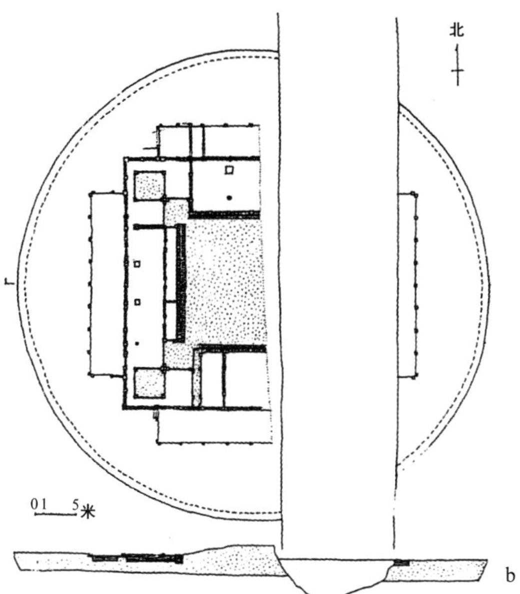

Fig. 3.15. (a) Floor plan of the ritual site of the Bright Hall and Piyong. Western Han. A.D. 4. Excavated in 1956 at Chang'an, Shaanxi province. (b) Floor plan of the Bright Hall.

图 3.15 （a）明堂辟雍遗址平面图。西汉，4 年。1956 年陕西长安出土。（b）明堂平、剖面图。

178 This central structure was founded on a circular platform about 62 meters in diameter (Fig. 3.16a), which was again raised by a large square platform, measuring 1.6 meters tall and 235 meters on each side. Walls originally surrounded this square platform, with two-storied gatehouses corresponding to the four compass points. Outside this walled courtyard was a large circle, formed by a ditch about 360 meters in diameter and 2 meters wide. Four rectangular areas, outlined by ditches, protruded from this circle at the four cardinal points. This network of ditches was connected with the Golden River (Jinshui) to the north, so that water could flow into it to make it a moat called the Piyong (the Jade Disk Moat).

The original plan of Wang Mang's Bright Hall has long been lost.[197] The most valuable textual reference is an essay of slightly later date, the Eastern Han scholar Cai Yong's "Treatise on Bright Hall and Monthly Observances" ("Mingtang yueling lun").[198] The section translated below highlights the three essential foci of Confucian discourse on Bright Hall: the hall as a synthesis of classical ritual structures, the hall as a symbol of the Universe, and the hall as a guide to rulership. The treatise begins with the following section on the hall's nomenclature:

> Bright Hall is the Great Temple [Tai miao] of the Son of Heaven, the place where the emperor pays respect to his ancestors in conjunction with worshipping the Lord on High. People of the Xia dynasty called this building the Chamber of Generations [Shishi]; people of the Shang named it the Layered House [Chongwu]; and people of the Zhou gave it the name Bright Hall. The east chamber is called Spring Shrine [Qingyang]; the south chamber is called Bright Hall; the chamber to the west is called Assembly of Decorations [Zongzhang]; the chamber to the north is called Somber Hall [Xuantang]: and the central chamber is called Great Hall [Taishi or Dashi]. The *Book of Changes* says: "Li means brightness";[199] this is a trigram referring to the south. The sage-king faces the south to administer the state and sits toward the sun-brightness to govern the world—the position of a human ruler cannot be more

upright than this. Thus, although there are five [major] chambers with different names, that of the south chamber, Bright Hall, is the principal 179
name [and is used for the whole building]. . . .

Bright Hall is the greatest thing among all things and possesses the deepest meaning of all meanings. People who are attracted by the appearance of its ancestral rituals call it Pure Temple [Qing miao]; those who cast their eyes on its central chamber call it Great Temple; those who focus on its loftiness call it Great Hall; those who favor its chambers call it Bright Hall; those who appreciate the schools in its four gatehouses call it Great Academy [Taixue]; and those who prefer the

这组中央建筑立于一个直径约 62 米的圆台上［图 3.16a］。圆台又建在一个高 1.6 米、边长 235 米的大方台上。方台四周原有围墙，四面中央各有一个双层门楼。一个直径约 360 米、深约 2 米的圜形水沟环绕这个带围墙的庭院，其正对四门部分的外侧各开有长方形的辅助水沟。这个名为辟雍的水沟系统在北部与金水河相接，将河水导入水沟，围绕明堂流转。

王莽明堂的原始设计久已失传。[197] 对研究其结构最有价值的是一篇年代略晚的文献，即东汉蔡邕的《明堂月令论》。[198] 下面所引的这段文字突出了儒家明堂理论的三个要点：明堂作为对古典礼仪结构的综合，明堂作为宇宙的象征，以及明堂作为统治的指南。文章首先解释了一系列关于明堂的术语：

> 明堂者，天子太庙，所以宗祀其祖，以配上帝者也。夏后氏曰世室，殷人曰重屋，周人曰明堂。东曰青阳，南曰明堂，西曰总章，北曰玄堂，中央曰太室。《易》曰：《离》也者，明也。[199] 南方之卦也。圣人南面而听天下，乡明而治，人君之位，莫正于此焉。故虽有五名，而主以明堂也……
>
> 故言明堂，事之大，义之深也。取其宗祀之貌，则曰清庙；取其正室之貌，则曰太庙；取其尊崇，则曰太室；取其乡明，则曰明堂；取其四门之学，则曰太学；取其

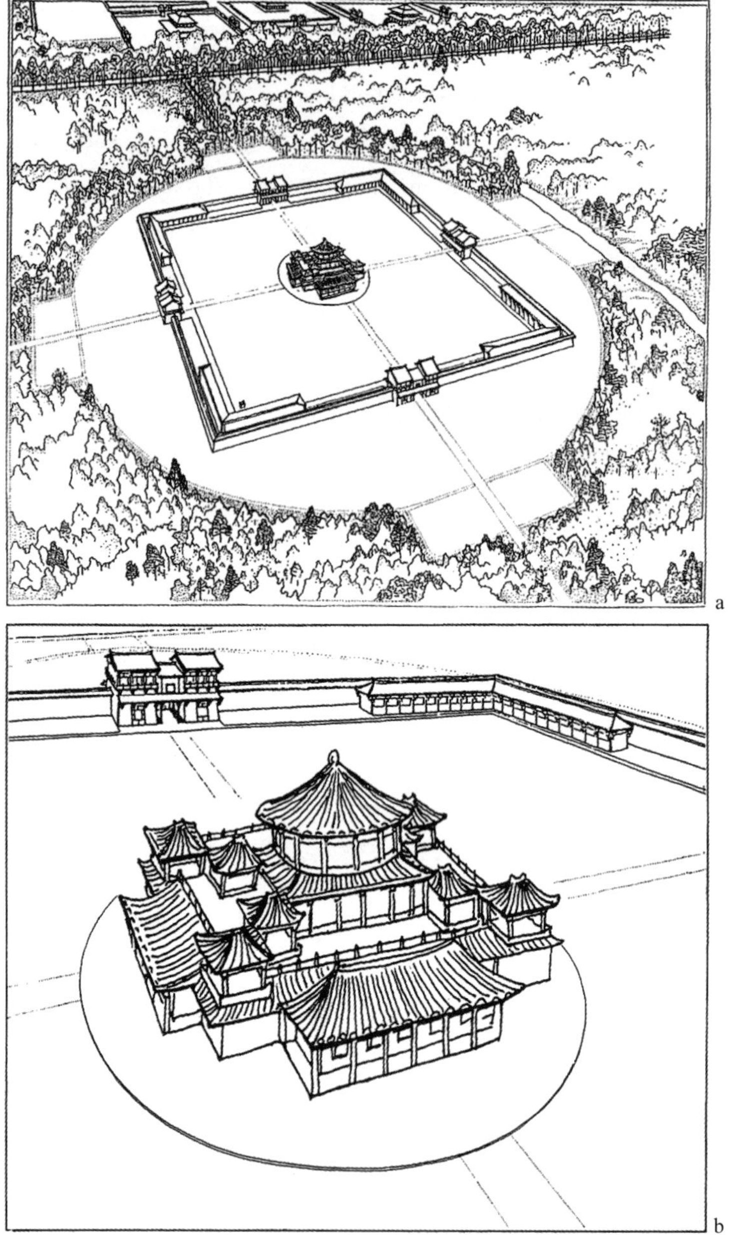

Fig. 3.16. (a) Reconstruction of Bright Hall. (b) Reconstruction of the ritual site of Bright Hall and Piyong.

图 3.16 （a）明堂复原图。（b）明堂辟雍复原图。

circular river surrounding it call it Jade Disk Moat. All these different names actually refer to the same building.

This last sentence encapsulates Cai Yong's central argument, which has become difficult for us moderns to grasp. "All these different names" given for Bright Hall are actually the names of ancient ritual structures recorded in the Confucian classics. These buildings, such as Great Temple, Pure Temple, Great Hall, and Piyong Moat, served various functions during the Three Dynasties. By arguing that all these names refer to Bright Hall—either to individual sections or to the entire building—Cai Yong could trace the tradition of Bright Hall back to the Golden Age in China's antiquity and could claim that this monument, as "the greatest thing among all things," ought to combine the forms and functions of all ancient ritual structures. Bright Hall was thus a religious center where gods and royal ancestors were worshipped, an administrative center where court audiences were held, and an educational center where history and moral principles were taught. Not coincidentally, these were exactly the three major functions of the emperor according to Han Confucianism, as Cai Yong documented in another passage:

四面之周水圆如璧，则曰辟雍。异名而同事，其实一也。

最后这句话浓缩了蔡邕的中心观点。这个观点对于现代人来说已经变得很难理解，即明堂的种种“异名”实际上是儒家经典所记载的各种古代礼仪建筑的名字。这些建筑，如太庙、清庙、太室和辟雍等，在三代时期有着不同的功能。蔡邕认为所有这些名称都是指明堂的组成部分或其整体。这样，他就将明堂的传统追溯到了中国上古的黄金时代，也就可以声言这个“事之大”的纪念碑能够将所有古代礼仪建筑的形式和功能综合于一身。明堂因此也就成为祭祀众神和皇家祖先的宗教中心、朝见群臣的行政中心、讲授历史和道德原则的教育中心。并非巧合的是，在汉代儒学中，这些内容恰是皇帝的三种主要职能。蔡邕在该文的另一段中说：

> [Bright Hall is constructed] for the emperor to observe Heaven and seasonal orders, to carry forward the virtuous ancestral rites, to confirm the contributions of royal predecessors and feudal lords, to declare the principles of honoring the old, and to promote the education of the young. Here, the emperor receives feudal lords and selects learned scholars in order to illuminate the regulations. Here, living people come to demonstrate their special skills, and the dead are offered various sacrifices according to their merits. Bright Hall is also the Palace of Great Learning, equipped completely with the four academies and all the government departments. It is like the North Pole, which stays in its own place while countless stars surround it and a myriad creations assist it. Bright Hall is thus the origin of administration and education, and the source of changes and transformations. It brings all things into its unifying light, and this is why it is called Bright Hall.

But it would be too simplistic to understand Bright Hall only in its exegetic and functional sense, since the meanings of this monument, according to all ancient writers, resided in the building's structure, form, and measurements. In other words, it is this monument that defines itself as the pivot of the world and the embodiment of Confucian principles. As Cai Yong stated clearly in the following section, this architectural symbolism is achieved through translating Confucian cosmology and ideology into a system of secret codes, which regulate the hall's design:

> The various sections of Bright Hall have their regulations. The whole building has a square floor plan of 144 *chi* on each side, a measurement determined by the numerical value assigned to Earth. The round roof is 216 *chi* in diameter, which is based on the numerical value assigned to Heaven. Great Temple [in the center] is three *zhang* on each side, and the Room of Communing with Heaven [above Great Temple] is nine *zhang* in diameter, because nine and six represent the transformation of *yin* and *yang*. [On the other hand,] to place the round room on top of the square chamber implies the reverse *yin-yang* transformation from

six to nine. The building's eight openings imply the eight trigrams [of the *Changes*]. The nine chambers [on the second floor] symbolize China's nine provinces. The twelve rooms [on the first floor] correspond to the twelve [zodiac] constellations. Each of the nine chambers has four doors and nine windows, so there are altogether 36 doors and 72 windows. The doors are all open outward and never close, meaning that there is nothing hidden. The Room of Communing with Heaven is 81 *chi* high, a measurement based on squaring the length of the Yellow Bell pitch pipe [*huangzhong*]. Twenty-eight columns are arranged along the four sides of the building; each group of seven columns symbolizes the seven stars [of

（皇帝以明堂）谨承天顺时之令，昭令德宗祀之礼，明前功百辟之劳，起尊老敬长之义，显教幼诲稚之学。朝诸侯选造士于其中，以明制度。生者乘其能而至，死者论其功而祭。故为大教之宫，而四学具焉，官司备焉。譬如北辰，居其所而众星拱之，万象翼之。政教之所由生，变化之所由来，明一统也，故言明堂。

但是，仅仅从明堂与经典的联系及其功能来理解它，未免过于简单化，因为根据所有的古代记载，这座纪念碑的意义存在于建筑的结构、形式和尺度中。换言之，是这座纪念碑将自己定义为天下的轴心和对儒家原则的体现。蔡邕在下面一段话中清楚地指出，这一建筑的象征意义是通过把儒家的宇宙观和思想转译为一个控制明堂设计的密码系统而获得的：

其制度之数，各有所依，堂方百四十四尺，坤之策也。屋圆屋径二百一十六尺，乾之策也。太庙明堂方三十六丈，通天屋径九丈，阴阳九六之变也。圆盖方载，六九之道也。八闼以象八卦，九室以象九州，十二宫以应十二辰。三十六户七十二牖，以四户八牖乘九室之数也。户皆外设而不闭，示天下不藏也。通天屋高八十一尺，黄钟九九之实也。二十八柱列于四方，亦七宿之象也。堂高三尺，

> the Big Dipper]. Each chamber is three *zhang* tall, a measurement based on the three realms [of Heaven, Earth, and Man]. The building has four sides and is painted with five colors; four and five are the numbers [of the four seasons and the Five Elements, which determine] the activities taking place there. The structure covers an area of 24 *zhang* on each side, a figure that echoes the 24 divisions of the year. It is surrounded by water, which symbolizes the four seas.

Not every section of Bright Hall mentioned here can be precisely identified, and to explore the various numerical systems would require a highly specialized study of Han cosmology, astronomy, musicology, and geography.[200] Generally speaking, the architectural complex is designed according to four major sets of codes: the *two* cosmic forces *yin* and *yang*, the four seasons (as well as the twelve months and 24 divisions of the year), the *Five* Elements of earth, wood, fire, metal, and water, and the *nine* provinces of China. Other systems, such as the *three* realms of Heaven, Earth, and Man, the *seven* stars of the Big Dipper, and the *nine cun* of the *huangzhong* pitch pipe, serve as secondary references. Based on *yin-yang* principles, the whole complex is designed as a series of alternating concentric circles and squares—two basic shapes symbolizing the two cosmic forces. The circular moat surrounds the square yard; the square yard encloses the round platform; the round platform supports the square hall; and on the summit of this hall is the round Room of Communing with Heaven. The repeated juxtapositions and alternations of these two shapes thus signify the three aspects of *yin-yang* cosmology: their opposition, interdependence, and transformation.

If a *yin-yang* pattern determines the overall design of the architectural complex, other systems govern the individual sections. Bright Hall in the center of the complex is said to have "nine chambers [*tang*] and twelve rooms [*shi*]." Cai Yong explains that the "nine chambers" on the second level symbolize China's nine provinces; the radiating pattern of these chambers seems to be based on a geometric map of the country in

ancient texts (Fig. 3.17).[201] Cai Yong also informs us that the twelve rooms on the first floor stood for the twelve months. These rooms are grouped into the four rectangular halls on the four sides of the building. While 181
corresponding to the four seasons and the four directions (Fig. 3.18), these four halls are also associated with the Great Temple in the center on the second floor to form a "Five Element" pattern (Fig. 3.19). This Great Temple, therefore, links all chambers and rooms in the building into a dynamic whole. Its focal location determines its multiple symbolism and extraordinary importance: it is the center of the Universe, the link with

以应三统。四乡五色者，象其行。外广二十四丈，应一岁二十四气。四周以水，象四海……

这里提到的明堂每个部分并非都能在遗址中准确地分辨出来。而且，要探讨这些数字系统也需要对汉代宇宙观、天文学、音乐学和地理学进行更深入的专门研究。[200]一般而言，这组建筑是根据四套主要的规则来设计的，包括（1）阴和阳这两种宇宙性，（2）四季（也包括十二个月和二十四节气），（3）五行（土、木、火、金、水），和（4）九州。其他如天、地、人三统，北斗七星，黄钟九寸等，构成第二级参考系数。根据阴阳学说，整个建筑被设计为若干象征着这两种宇宙性力量的同心圆形和方形：圆形水沟环绕着方形的庭院，方形庭院又环绕着圆台，圆台承托着方形的厅，厅的顶部是圆形的通天屋。圆、方两种形状如此重复地并置与交替，体现了阴阳宇宙观的三个方面，即二者之间的对立、依存和转化。

如果说阴阳模式决定了这组建筑的整体设计，那么其他的系统则统领着各个局部。中央的明堂据说有“九室十二宫”。蔡邕将位于第二层的“九室”解释为中国九州的象征；其放射状的布局似乎是基于古代文献中记载的一种几何形式的地图［图 3.17］。[201]蔡邕还告诉我们，第一层上的十二个厅堂代表了十二个月，被分为面向四个方向的四组，以与四季和四方相应［图 3.18］。这四组厅堂又与第二层中央的太庙共同形成了“五行”的格局［图 3.19］。太庙将所有的室和厅堂联结成一个动态的整体，其中心位置决定了它多重的象征意义和特殊重要性：它是这一宇宙系统的中心，是连接

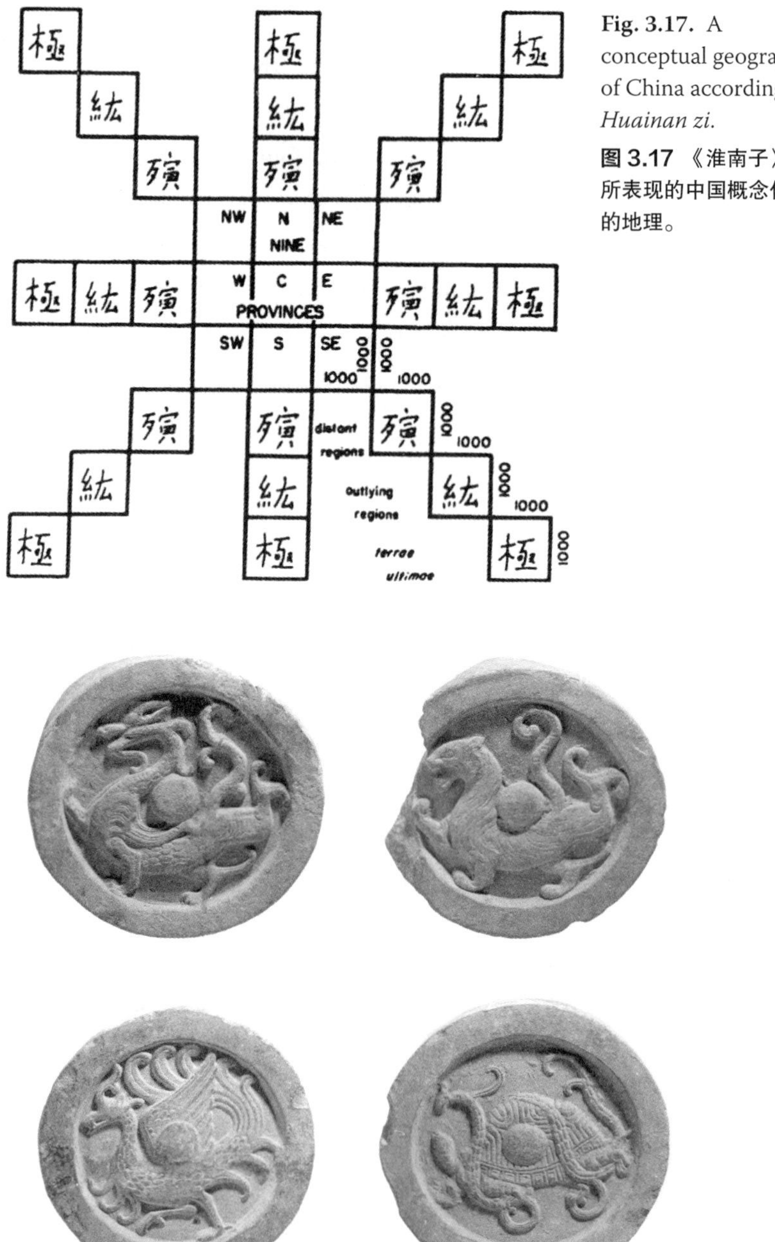

Fig. 3.17. A conceptual geography of China according to *Huainan zi*.

图 3.17 《淮南子》所表现的中国概念化的地理。

Fig. 3.18. Eave tiles decorated with the four directional animals and birds. Xin dynasty. A.D. 9-25. H. 17.2-19.3 cm. Found near the site of Bright Hall and Piyong.

图 3.18 四神瓦当。新，9—25 年。高 17.2—19.3 厘米。明堂、辟雍遗址附近出土。

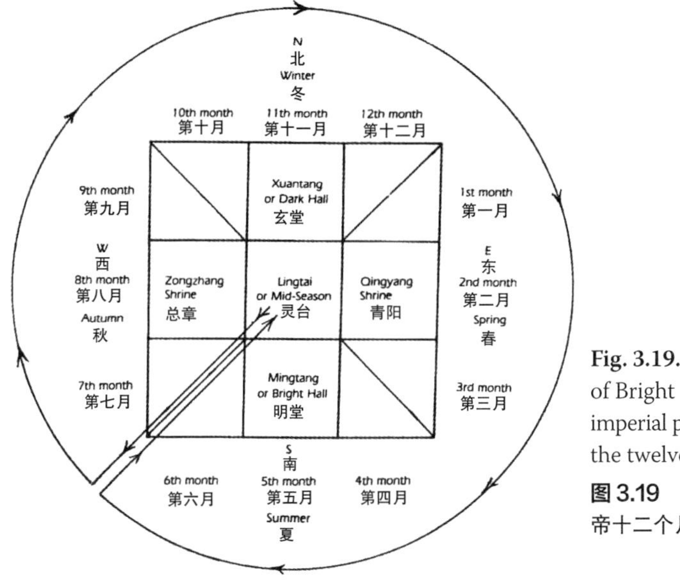

Fig. 3.19. Twelve rooms of Bright Hall and the imperial positions during the twelve months.

图 3.19　明堂十二宫和皇帝十二个月所在的位置 。

Heaven, the midpoint of the year, and the embodiment of Earth—the element associated with the Han dynasty.

Bright Hall thus presents a classification of cosmic elements as well as their transformation. Surrounding the Center, all the seasons and elements move in endless cycles. The building itself, however, does not move or change; the only movable element is its occupant. In other words, the hall's symbolism required the activities and movements of the emperor to complete it. Cai Yong suggests this most interesting aspect of Bright Hall in the following statement:[202]

上天的通道，是一年的中点，同时在五行系统中代表着与汉王朝相关的“土”。

明堂因而体现了宇宙中各种元素的分类及其转化。环绕着中心，季节和所有其他元素永无休止地运转。但是，这个建筑本身是静止不变的；不断移动着的只是其拥有者。换言之，明堂的象征意义要求由皇帝自己的行为和运转来完成。在下面这段文字中，蔡邕指出了明堂的这个最有趣的方面：[202]

> As for the great ceremonies of the emperor, it is stated in the "Monthly Observances" ["Yueling"] that human regulations must be
> 182 based on the rhythm of Heaven. In each month, the Son of Heaven should give different orders, make offerings to different deities, and assume different roles. This is called the "monthly observances," which enable the emperor to follow the movement of *yin* and *yang*, to obey the transformation of the four seasons, to modify his activities according to seasonal phenomena, and therefore to practice royal administration. Such regulations, which have been completed on the basis of monthly and yearly divisions, are concealed in Bright Hall. [By acting in accordance with these regulations,] the Son of Heaven demonstrates his succession to his ancestors' spirits and his ultimate respect [to Heaven].

The "Monthly Observances" mentioned here is a treatise in the *Book of Rites*,[203] which is based on a section in the third-century B.C. text *Master Lü's Spring and Autumn Annals*.[204] The treatise is rigidly divided into thirteen sections, corresponding to the twelve months plus the day in the middle of the year. Each section begins with a statement of the locations of the sun and stars, the god and spirit of the period, the month's corresponding creature, taste, smell, musical tone and pitch pipe, the position and object of the monthly sacrifice, and changes in the natural world. It then proceeds to regulate the king's position, costume, and utensils in Bright Hall. For example, we read in its first section: "[In the first Spring month,] the Son of Heaven occupies the left room of the Spring Shrine chamber; he rides in a carriage with phoenix decoration and drawn by azure-dragon horses; he carries a green flag; he wears green robes and jade ornaments of the same color; he eats wheat and mutton; his vessels have simple decor and imply the sense of 'openness.'"[205] Also in this month and in this particular chamber, the emperor gave orders to hold the ceremonies of the Inauguration of Spring and the Great Plowing, to reward his ministers, to perform certain songs and dances, and to offer certain victims to certain deities. He would also declare prohibitions in this month of growing, mainly against warfare, which implies "killing." The section ends with a severe warning against any disturbance of seasonal regulations: "No change in the ways of Heaven is allowed; nor any extinction of the principles of earth; nor any confounding of the bonds of men. . . . If the proceedings proper to autumn were carried out, there would be great pestilence among the people; boisterous winds would work their violence; and rain would descend in torrents."[206]

Figure 3.19 reconstructs the pattern of the emperor's movement in the hall, which also defines the basic structure of the ritual monument. The emperor would begin his year from "the left room of the Spring

王者之大礼也,《月令》篇名曰:因天时,制人事,天子发号施令。祀神受职,每月异礼,故谓之月令。所以顺阴阳,奉四时,效气物,行王政也。成法具备,各从时月,藏之明堂。所以示承祖考神明,明不敢泄渎之义。

此处提到的《月令》是《礼记》中的一篇,[203]其基础是公元前3世纪成书的《吕氏春秋》中的一章。[204]该文严整地分为十三个部分,与十二个月及年中的一日相应。每一部分的开头都提到太阳和星辰的方位,该月的帝与神,与月相应的动物、音、律、数、味、臭,祭祀的位置和牺牲,以及自然界的变化。接下来便是天子在明堂中的方位、服饰和所使用的器物。例如,我们在第一部分可以读到:"孟春之月……天子居青阳左个,乘鸾路,驾仓龙,载青旂,衣青衣,服仓玉,食麦与羊。其器疏以达。"[205]同样是在这个月,在这一特别的房间,皇帝要下令举行迎春和藉田的仪式,赏赐群臣,表演特定的歌舞,用特定的牺牲祭祀特定的神明。他还需要在这个万物生长的月份中禁止征伐,因为战争意味着"杀"。这一部分结尾的文字对扰乱季节性规则的行为提出了严厉的警告:"毋变天之道,毋绝地之理,毋乱人之纪……行秋令,则其民大疫,猋风暴雨总至。"[206]

图3.19重构了皇帝在明堂中移动的路线,这种移动最终完成了这一礼仪纪念碑的象征结构。皇帝的一年始于"青阳左个",

Shrine hall," or the north room on the east side where the *yang* ether rises. He would move clockwise in the hall; each month he would dwell in the proper room, dress in the proper color, eat the proper food, listen to the proper music, sacrifice to the proper deities, and attend to the proper affairs of state. The emperor thus literally becomes a moving hand on a big clock. It was understood that only his synchronous movement with Heaven and Earth would secure harmony between his rule and the natural world. In retrospect, we find that this structure, though called a Great Temple, differs fundamentally from a Three Dynasty temple in architectural form, and this difference implies a radical departure from traditional ritual and historiography. Unlike an archaic temple, which consisted of layers of halls and gates along a central axis (Figs. 2.7a, b), the sections of Bright Hall all surround a fixed center. In a Three Dynasties temple, members of a clan or lineage proceeded in a linear fashion to "return" to their Origin, but in Bright Hall it was the emperor who moved alone in endless cycles. History is no longer perceived as a linear progression with a definite beginning and end, but is remodeled into a circular movement constantly repeating itself. The chief function of this hall is to establish the absolute authority of the emperor through "scientific" means: the emperor's circular movement and his metamorphic appearance in different garb made him an integral part of the dynamic universe. His movement was interrupted regularly at the middle of the year when he ascended to the Great Temple. At that moment, he located himself in the center of the universe and proved himself the Son of Heaven.

The "Monthly Observances," which appeared toward the end of the
183 Zhou, signified a general interest in Bright Hall at the dawn of imperial China. But what it presented was a particular model of this monument promoted by the rising School of Five Elements. Encouraged by this school's strong interest in cosmology, the author of this text imagined Bright Hall as a cosmic mandala demonstrating the normal workings

of both the natural and human worlds. This plan, however, lacked a historical dimension and did not link the hall with former dynasties. Those who established such links were orthodox Confucians, whose social vision was largely modeled on an idealized past exemplified by the Western Zhou dynasty. Instead of stressing the cosmological significance of Bright Hall, these Confucians viewed it as a prime symbol of both

即“阳气”升起的东向厅堂北间。从这里开始，他将按照顺时针方向在明堂中移动，每个月在特定的房间中，穿着特定颜色的服装，吃着特定的食物，听着特定的音乐，祭祀着特定的神明，从事着特定的国事。皇帝因此变成一座大钟上的一根转动的指针。其含义是，只有与天地如此同步运行，皇帝才能保证他的统治与自然界协调。尽管明堂也被称作太庙，但如果我们回头将它与三代的庙比较一下，就会发现其建筑形式有着根本的差别，这种差别意味着与传统礼仪和历史观的一种根本性分离。旧时的庙由沿中轴线分布的重重厅堂和门构成［图 2.7］，而明堂的各部分则是围绕一个固定的中心。在一座三代的庙中，宗族或世系的成员按照一种线性形式“返回”其本源；但在明堂中，则是皇帝在独自无休止地循环运动。历史不再是一个有始有终的线性过程，而被重塑为一个圆周，在运动中不停地重复着自己。明堂的主要功能便是通过这种“科学的”手段确立皇帝绝对的权威：皇帝的循环移动以及他不停变换的外形，使自己成为生生不息地运转着的宇宙的一部分。只有在一年中间的一天，当他登临太庙时，其圆周式的移动才被有规律地打断。在这一刻，他置身于宇宙的核心，证明自己是上天之子。

成书于周代末年的《月令》表达了在帝国黎明之时人们对于明堂一种普遍的兴趣。但是，它所展现的是逐渐流行的五行学说影响下的一种明堂模式。受到五行说对于宇宙论强烈兴趣的激励，这篇文字的作者将明堂想象成一个能够演示自然界和人类社会运转常态的宇宙坛场。然而，这种设计缺乏历史维度，没有将明堂和以前的朝代联系起来。致力于建立这种联系的是正统儒学。儒家以西周为范例形成了一种理想化的历史，这是形成其社会观的主要基础。儒学的观点将明堂看作对理想化的过去和对光荣的未来的一种根本象征，

an idealized past and a glorious future. They frequently recalled a "lost" Zhou dynasty Bright Hall, which is reminiscent of a traditional Three Dynasties temple.[207] But their descriptions of this hall were "prophetic" rather than "reminiscential": to them, the construction of a new Bright Hall was synonymous with the founding of a unified political state governed by Confucian ideology. Thus, for example, a political proposal presented by the philosopher and politician Xunzi to a king of Qin:

> [As for good politics,] military domination should be restrained and civilian matters should be stressed. Gentlemen who are correct, sincere, trustworthy, and accomplished should be employed to govern the world. Your Majesty should collaborate with them in the administration of the state, should distinguish right and wrong, should separate the crooked and straight, and should adjudicate from your capital Xianyang. Those who are obedient should be rewarded with official posts; those who are not should be executed. If things are done in this way, then without sending the army outside the Pass, your commands will be followed by the whole world. *If things are done this way, then Bright Hall can be constructed, and you can hold court there to receive the feudal lords.*[208]

The pre-Han textual references to Bright Hall thus follow two separate traditions of discourse. On the one hand, Bright Hall was claimed to be an ageless symbol of ideal sovereignty and was used as a metaphor for the forthcoming Confucian state; on the other, it was required to demonstrate an understanding of the Universe and was taken as a cosmic symbol. These two trends began to intermingle during the Western Han. The *Master Huainan*, a text written by a number of authors during the second century B.C., contains a version of the "Monthly Observances,"[209] as well as passages that attribute the cosmic Bright Hall to various sage-kings in China's Golden Age:[210]

In the past, the Five Emperors and Three Kings based their administration and education on the codes "Three" and "Five." What do these two figures mean? "Three" means that they obtained their symbols from Heaven above, their measurements from Earth below, and their rules from Man in the middle. Thereupon they established their courts in [the five chambers of] Bright Hall and practiced the "observances" regulated by this hall. They were thus able to harmonize the *qi* ether of *yinyang* and to adjust the rhythm of the four seasons.[211]

而不强调明堂的宇宙观含义。当时的儒生们常常回忆起"消失"了的周代明堂；他们的文字使人想起传统的三代祖庙。[207] 但是，他们对明堂的描述与其说是"回忆性"的，倒不如说是"预言性"的：对这些儒生说来，新明堂的修建实际上意味着儒家思想统治下统一政体的建立。例如，哲学家和政治家荀子向秦王提出了如下建议：

> 节威反文。案用夫端诚信全之，君子治天下焉。因与之参国政，正是非，治曲直，听咸阳。顺者错之，不顺者而后诛之。若是，则兵不复出于塞外，而令行于天下矣。若是，则虽为之筑明堂于塞外，而朝诸侯殆可矣。[208]

汉代以前有关明堂的文献因此遵循着两种话语系统。根据一个系统，明堂被看作理想君权永恒的象征，是即将建立的儒家政体的隐喻；根据另一系统，明堂被看作宇宙的象征，必须涵盖当时对宇宙的理解。这两种趋向在西汉时期开始融和。公元前 2 世纪由多位作者合著的《淮南子》中包含了《月令》的另一个版本，[209] 以及将宇宙性明堂溯源到古代圣王的论述：[210]

> 昔者，五帝三王之莅政施教，必用参五。何谓参五？仰取象于天，俯取度于地，中取法于人，乃立明堂之朝，行明堂之令，以调阴阳之气，以和四时之节。[211]

In addition to integrating the two earlier discourses on Bright Hall, this text also reveals associations between the hall and new philosophical and political concepts such as the three realms of Heaven, Earth, and Man.[212] This elusive monument constantly attracted new concepts and was enriched by current thinking. Gradually, it was taken not only as a symbol of the Five Elements and sagehood, but also as a manifestation of *yin-yang* principles and the eight trigrams of the *Changes*.[213] It was linked with the idea of immortality; and later, when the virtue of filial piety prevailed, Bright Hall was again viewed as the embodiment of this most important moral standard.[214] Its impact on Han politics also increased: emperors attempted to construct this hall in order to demonstrate their mandate, and scholars insisted upon their right to interpret it. These scholars' specifications of the hall's design functioned as political propositions, with an unspoken premise that if a ruler wanted to build the monument, he had to accept the whole of their political plan.

Such exchanges between rulers and scholars, which had begun at the start of the Han dynasty,[215] heightened during Emperor Wu's reign. When this emperor ascended the throne, the first thing discussed in his court was the construction of Bright Hall. Sima Qian remarked that this intent clearly indicated the new ruler's favoring of Confucianism, and Ban
184 Gu also reported that the emperor sent a special envoy to Master Shen, a famous Confucian scholar in Shandong, to inquire about the hall's proper form.[216] This plan, however, ended with a violent court struggle: Empress Dowager Dou, a believer in Daoism, interfered and the scholars engaged in the project were forced to commit suicide.[217] Only thirty years later did Emperor Wu gain enough confidence to attempt the monument again. Interestingly, this time the design was supplied by a necromancer named Gongyu Dai, who produced a "Diagram of Bright Hall Transmitted from the Yellow Emperor." The proposed building seems to have pandered to the emperor's increasing desire for immortality: its central hall was called Kunlun, the symbol of eternity.[218]

Neither the location of this building (it was founded at the foot of Mount Tai, not in the capital) nor its association with Kunlun could convince Confucian scholars that this was an orthodox Bright Hall.[219] But it did force them to realize the absence of a precise design for this monument in their own arguments: pre-Han and early Han documents on Bright Hall were either too vague or self-contradictory, and even the plan in the "Monthly Observances" had become insufficient to illustrate

这段文字不仅综合了早期有关明堂的两种话语，也揭示了明堂与新的哲学和政治思想——如天、地、人三界的概念——的联系。[212] 这座变幻不定的纪念碑不断地吸取新的概念并被流行思想所丰富。逐渐地，它不但被看作五行和圣王的象征，同时也被看作阴阳和《易经》中八卦的体现。[213] 明堂又与升仙的观念联系起来；当孝的观念流行时，它进而被看作是这一最重要的道德标准的体现。[214] 它对汉代政治的影响也与日俱增：皇帝们为了证明君权天授屡屡试图建造明堂，学者们则坚守着他们对这座建筑的解释权。这些学者对明堂功能的规定也就是他们的政治纲领，其潜台词是，如果统治者想建造这座纪念碑，他就必须接受儒生们的政治主张。

统治者和儒生之间的这种对话在汉朝立国之初就已开始，[215] 至武帝时进一步升温。武帝登基后在朝廷上讨论的第一件事情就是建造明堂。司马迁认为这一意图清楚地表明新皇帝对于儒家学说的兴趣，班固也记载了武帝派遣特使访问山东的著名儒生申公，请教明堂正确的形式。[216] 但是，这个计划在激烈的朝廷斗争中夭折了：信奉黄老的窦太后对此加以干涉，参与此项计划的儒生们也被迫自杀。[217] 直到三十年之后，武帝才获得足够的信心，再次试图兴建这座纪念碑。有趣的是，这一次的方案是由方士公玉带提出的。他献上"黄帝时明堂图"，其中央的大殿称为昆仑，象征仙境。这一设计似乎正好迎合了皇帝日益增长的升仙热望。[218]

不管是该建筑的位置（它位于泰山脚下，而不是在都城），还是它与昆仑的联系，都无法使儒生们相信这是一座正宗的明堂。[219] 但是这件事也使他们意识到，他们对自己如此关心的这座纪念碑缺乏一个明确的设计：汉代以前和汉初文献中关于明堂的记载或过于模糊，或自相矛盾，即使是《月令》中的方案也不足以体现那些

the ideas increasingly associated with the hall. From the first century B.C. on, there appeared an effort to construct an up-to-date Bright Hall on paper. Following the old traditions, this effort was twofold and centered on the hall's cosmological and political significance. First, the hall was conceived to be a symbol of the universe demonstrating the systems of the Five Elements as well as other cosmic forces. This meant that the design of Bright Hall, instead of being determined by the teaching of a single school, had to synthesize various scholarly and philosophical traditions. Second, this hall was seen as a political statement of Confucian scholars, who by this time had concluded that the Han court had lost its mandate due to its corruption and unjust rule.[220] The result of this effort was the appearance of a series of texts entitled "The Yin-yang Principles of Bright Hall" ("Mingtang yinyang"),[221] which provided workable architectural designs for the monument.[222] Like their Eastern Zhou predecessors, the authors of these texts believed that Bright Hall possessed a prophetic significance: the monument they proposed could only be built by a future sage, a true Confucian comparable in virtue and conduct to ancient sages.[223] This is the point at which Wang Mang came on the scene.

Wang Mang was a relative of the Western Han royal house; his aunt Wang Zhengjun was the consort of Emperor Yuan (r. 48-33 B.C.) and the mother of Emperor Cheng (r. 32-7 B.C.). But this family association did not provide him with immediate political privileges, since a strict line separated the members of the Liu royal house from relatives by marriage, who had no right to become princes, not to mention the legitimate ruler. Moreover, Wang Mang's father died young and left him no noble rank or fief. It was his image as a learned Confucian scholar and virtuous man that opened his path to political power. The *History of the Former Han* records: "Wang Mang was a poor orphan, and he was even humbler in his behavior, always paying full respect to others. He first received instructions in ancient ritual canons, studying with Chen Can from Pei. He was diligent and acquired extensive learning. He wore the clothes of a scholar. He served his widowed mother and sister-in-law, and reared the orphaned son of his elder brother. His behavior was always extremely proper."[224] It is impossible in this short section even to outline the fascinating political campaign that finally led him to the throne; interested readers may consult his biography, which has been translated into English, as well as scholarly discussions.[225] My purpose here is to explore the role of Bright Hall in this dramatic moment in Chinese history.

不断加于明堂上的新概念。其结果是，从公元前 1 世纪开始，出现了一种在纸面上构建一座最新明堂的尝试。这些尝试遵循旧有的传统而具有双重性格，即明堂的宇宙性和政治性的意义。首先，人们相信这座明堂是宇宙的象征，体现了五行的系统和各种宇宙的力量。这意味着明堂的设计不可能为某种学说单独决定，而必须综合多种学术和哲学传统。再者，明堂继续被儒生们视为自己的政治宣言，但是这一时期的儒士认定当时的朝廷政令不公，腐化颓败，已失天祚。[220] 这两种趋势的结果是一系列题为《明堂阴阳录》的文章出现，[221] 为建设这座纪念碑提供了可行的建筑设计。[222] 与东周时期的哲学家一样，这些文章的作者相信明堂具有预言性：只有当一位圣贤出现，他们所提出的明堂方案才可能付诸实施。这位圣贤应该是一名真正的儒士，其道德和品行都可以与古代的圣贤相提并论。[223] 就是在这个节骨眼上，王莽出场了。

王莽出身外戚；他的姑母王政君是汉元帝（前 48—前 33 年在位）的皇后和成帝（前 32—前 7 年在位）的母亲。但是，这种家庭背景并不能为他带来直接的政治特权，因汉代制度中皇族和姻亲是有严格区别的，姻亲不能成为诸侯王，更不要说是合法的皇帝了。并且，王莽的父亲早逝，也没有给他留下任何贵族爵位或封地。王莽通过为自己塑造一个博学有德的儒生形象开启了通往政治权力的道路。根据《汉书》的记载，"莽独孤贫，因折节为恭俭。受《礼经》，师事沛郡陈参，勤身博学，被服如儒生。事母及寡嫂，养孤兄子，行甚敕备。"[224] 由于篇幅的限制，我们无法在这里详谈使他最终登上皇帝宝座的政治奋斗经历，有兴趣的读者可以读一读《汉书 · 王莽传》，这篇传记已被译为英文，并有许多学者进行了讨论。[225] 我在这里说起的目的，是探讨明堂在中国历史上这一戏剧性时刻所扮演的角色。

Broadly speaking, Wang Mang's political campaign consisted of two stages, before and after A.D. 4. His first goal was to become regent. He found his model in the Duke of Zhou, a Confucian sage who at the beginning of the Zhou dynasty had acted as regent during the minority of King Cheng. Once this goal was achieved, Wang Mang went one step further and replaced the Han emperor. This dynastic transition was based on a newly written Chinese history that predicted Wang Mang's mandate. Bright Hall, established in A.D. 4, served both purposes: the Duke of Zhou was said to have erected the Zhou dynasty Bright Hall, and the
185 pattern of history would be most concretely represented by Wang Mang's new monument.

Wang Mang's effort to link himself with the Duke of Zhou became evident in A.D. 1. In this year, a nine-year-old prince was brought to the throne (Emperor Ping, r. A.D. 1-5). A strange event immediately occurred. Some men identifying themselves as the people of Yueshang sent a tribute of a white pheasant to the Han court. An identical event recorded in the *Book of Documents* was recalled. When the Duke of Zhou was assisting King Cheng to rule the country, the Yueshang people had come to China to present the same kind of bird. When people asked the reason for their tribute, they replied: "In recent years there have been no harmful storms or violent winds in our kingdom; our elders determined that a sage must have appeared in the Central Kingdom and they sent us here to present the tribute." When this event recurred, a memorial was delivered to the young Emperor Ping:

> Wang Mang's virtues and accomplishments have led to the reappearance of the "white pheasant" omen of the Duke of Zhou and King Cheng, an omen that links our dynasty to the Zhou of a thousand years ago. According to the precepts of the sage-kings, if a minister has great merit, then he should have honorable titles. Of old the Duke of Zhou, while still alive, was given his title, which included the dynasty's name. Since Wang Mang has the great merit of having settled the country

and of having secured peace for the Han royal house, Your Majesty should bestow upon him the title of "Duke Protector of Han."[226]

This event reveals an important aspect of Wang Mang's political rhetoric: his constant use of historical allusions. Through these allusions, he established parallels between the present and the past and between himself and an ancient sage. This technique enabled him to collapse historical time, to recuperate antiquity, and to transform formulated

大体说来，王莽的政坛经历以公元 4 年为界分为两个阶段。第一个目标是成为摄政，他在此期间的榜样是周公，这是一位儒家历来推崇的先贤，曾在西周初年担任幼年成王的摄政。当这一目标达到后，王莽的下一步是进而取代汉朝皇帝。这一王朝更替的基础是一部新写的中国历史，预言王莽将承负天降大任，治理国家。公元 4 年建立的明堂同时为这两个目的服务：其一，据说周公也曾建造周代的明堂；其二，王莽建造的这座纪念碑最清晰地表明了王朝更替的历史图式。

王莽将自己与周公联系起来的意图在公元 1 年变得十分明显。在这一年，一位九岁的王子被送上皇帝的宝座（平帝，1—5 年在位）。一项奇异的事情立刻发生了：一些自称为"越裳人"的人向汉朝廷进献了一只白雉。这使人们回想起《尚书》中记载的一件类似的事：当周公辅佐成王统治国家时，越裳人就曾来到中国，进献了同样的鸟。当人们问起进献这种贡品的原因时，他们说："吾受命于吾国之黄发久矣，天之无烈风淫雨，意中国有圣人耶？有则盍朝之！"因此，当这件事在汉代再次发生时，群臣就奏请平帝，说：

> 莽功德致周成白雉之瑞，千载同符。圣王之法，臣有大功则生有美号，故周公及身在而托号于周。莽有定国安汉家之大功，宜赐号曰安汉公。[226]

这件事显示出王莽政治辩术的一个重要方式，即不断地运用历史隐喻于现在和过去、自己和古代圣贤之间建立起平行关系。这个方式使他得以混淆历史时间，复活古史中的章节，将程式化的

textual references into reality. Indeed, we may say that before A.D. 4, what Wang Mang had accomplished was to manipulate people's perception: his tireless uses of historical allusions actually transformed the present into a mirror image of the past. His training in the Classics allowed him to screen all historical records and to train public attention on a single focus: the Duke of Zhou.[227] He restaged all events relating to the ancient duke and reiterated all his speeches. During the five years from 1 B.C. to A.D. 3, more than 700 auspicious omens were reported as signs of Heaven's approval of Wang Mang's service. Many of them, like the "white pheasant omen," were originally associated with the Duke of Zhou. This manipulative process culminated in the construction of Bright Hall, which provided the final evidence for the rebirth of the Golden Age. The event was staged as a spontaneous act: more than a hundred thousand supporters of Wang Mang—scholars and commoners who had been convinced by his propaganda—gathered south of Chang'an and completed the hall in a mere twenty days.[228] Following this event, another memorial was presented to the throne:

> Formerly, when the Duke of Zhou accepted the duty of assisting the heir of the Zhou and occupied the honorable position of Superior Duke; yet only after more than seven years did the regulations of the dynasty become settled. Bright Hall and the Jade Disk Moat have been in disrepair and discarded for a thousand years, and no one has been able to restore them. . . . Indeed, even the achievements of former sages such as Tang [i.e., Yao], Yu [Shun], King Cheng, and the Duke of Zhou could not surpass what Wang Mang has done.[229]

But Emperor Ping would soon reach adulthood and would not need a regent; conveniently he fell ill right after the completion of Bright Hall.[230] Again imitating the Duke of Zhou, Wang Mang prayed to Heaven to let him die in place of the emperor, but for the first time Heaven ignored his petition.[231] The new ruler was selected from among 53 Liu royal family members: the youngest one, Liu Ying (Infant Liu), was chosen. The two-year-old emperor was called "Boy Ying" (Ruzi Ying), which reminded people of King Cheng's nickname, "Ruzi." Wang Mang was now not only regent but acting emperor. The first stage of his political campaign ended with his complete victory.[232]

文字化为真实的存在。确实，我们可以说在公元 4 年之前，王莽所完成的是操控人们的感知，他通过对历史隐喻无休止的运用，将现实转变为历史的一种镜像。由于对经典的娴熟，他得以筛选历史记载，将公众的全部注意力集中于一个焦点——周公。[227] 他重新上演了历史记载中有关周公的几乎所有事迹，反复申述周公的话语。在公元前 1 年到公元 3 年的四年中，超过 700 项祥瑞被作为上天降大任于王莽的征兆报告到朝廷。其中不少项，如上面提到的白雉，原来曾与周公或周代有关。明堂的修建是这一系列努力的顶点，为黄金时代的复生提供了最后的证据。这件事情被粉饰成一次自发行动：十万余名王莽的支持者——受到他的政治宣传蛊惑的儒生和庶民——齐集长安南郊，只用了 20 天的时间就完成了这一工程。[228] 在此之后，群臣又上奏于皇帝：

> 昔周公奉继体之嗣，据上公之尊，然犹七年制度乃定。夫明堂、辟雍，堕废千载莫能兴……唐虞发举，成周造业，诚亡以加。[229]

但是，平帝不久就要长大成人，不再需要摄政者。恰巧，在明堂建成后他就患病不起。[230] 王莽再次效法周公，向上天祈求，让自己代平帝死，但是上天第一次没有理睬他的请求。[231] 新皇帝是从 53 名皇族成员中挑选出来的，他便是其中最年轻的刘婴。这位两岁的皇帝被称为孺子婴，使人们回想起成王的乳名"孺子"。王莽现在不仅是名义上的摄政者，而且行使着皇帝之实。他政治战役的第一个阶段至此胜利完成。[232]

When the next stage of this campaign began, however, the Duke of
186 Zhou allusion could no longer support Wang Mang's further advance to the throne, since this ancient sage had finally yielded power to the adult Zhou king. New evidence had to be found to legitimate the dynastic transition. Once again, Bright Hall played a crucial role. This monument, according to the memorial submitted to the throne in A.D. 4, assumed a new function as the site of sacrifices to a "dynastic lineage."[233] A masterpiece in Chinese political historiography, this "dynastic lineage" was Wang Mang's most ambitious creation. All former dynasties, either legendary or real, were organized into a circular transmission pattern in accordance with the structure of Bright Hall.[234] The modern historian Gu Jiegang has reconstructed this pattern (Fig. 3.20), which predicted Wang Mang's Xin (New) dynasty.[235]

The fundamental premise of this pattern of history is that dynastic successions are predestined by Heaven and regulated by the internal movement of the universe. Each dynasty corresponds to one of the Five Elements and finds its position in a particular chamber in Bright Hall. To be sure, this theory was not Wang Mang's invention and had been associated with various cosmological models since the Eastern Zhou.[236]

但是，当这个政治战役的下一个阶段开始时，周公的隐喻已无法支撑王莽通往皇帝宝座的进程，因为这位贤人在成王长大后自动让出了权力。王莽必须寻找新的理由来使政权的更替合法化。明堂再次扮演了这个关键的角色。按照公元 4 年的上奏，这座纪念碑被赋予了祭祀“王朝世系”的新功能。[233] 作为中国政治史上的一项杰作，这个“王朝世系”是王莽最富有雄心的创造。以往所有的朝代，不管是传说上的，还是真实的，都被组织到与明堂结构相协调的一个呈圆周运转的模式中。[234] 顾颉刚对这一预言了王莽新朝的到来的模式进行了重构［图 3.20］和解释。[235]

这个历史模式的基本前提是，王朝的演替是由上天决定的，并被宇宙的内在运动所控制。每个朝代都与五行之一相对应，并且可以在明堂中找到其特定的位置。需要说明的是，这一理论并不是王莽的发明，而是自东周以来就与各种宇宙论的模型相联系的。[236]

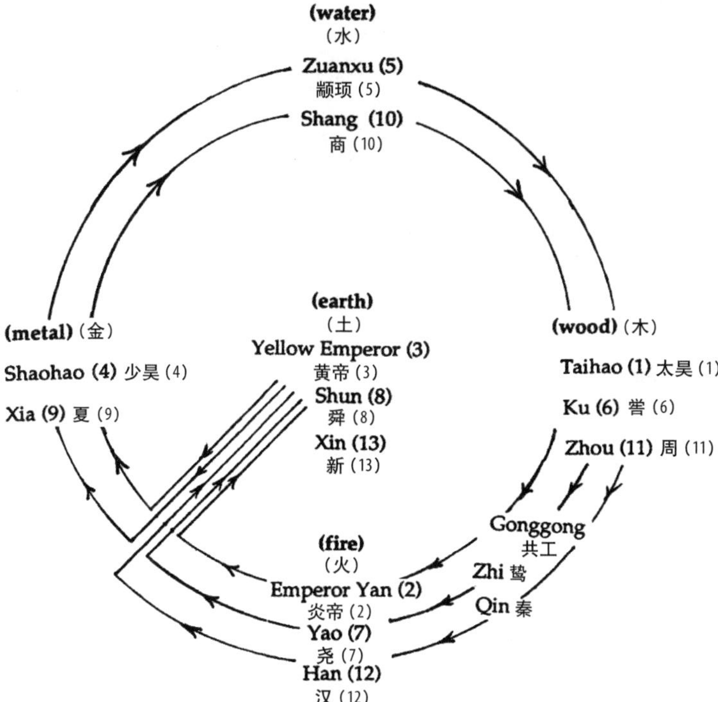

Fig. 3.20. Wang Mang's pattern of dynastic transmission.

图 3.20 王莽朝代更替理论的图示。

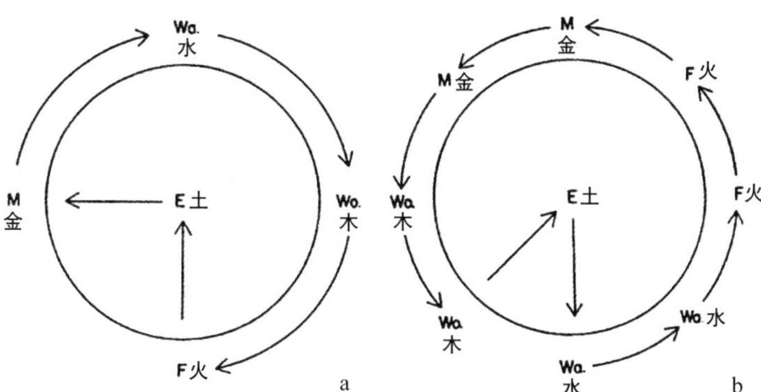

Fig. 3.21. (a) Cycle of the mutual production order of the Five Elements/Phases. (b) Cycle of the mutual overcoming order of the Five Elements/Phases.

图 3.21 （a）五行相生。（b）五行相克。

Fig. 3.22. Bronze tablet inscribed with Wang Mang's announcement of the founding of the Xin dynasty. A.D. 9. L. 25.3 cm. W. 25.6 cm. Excavated in 1982 at Dingxiang, Heshui, Gansu province. Gansu Provincial Museum, Lanzhou.

图 3.22 刻有王莽关于新朝建立诏令的铜牌。新，9 年。长 25.3 厘米，宽 25.6 厘米。1982 年甘肃合水定祥出土。甘肃省博物馆藏。

But Wang Mang's historiography had nothing to do with China's actual past. Rather, it was created to anticipate a future event—his takeover of the Han throne. Old patterns of history were thus deliberately altered to suit this specific need. Among other alternations, he changed the corresponding element of the Han dynasty from "earth" to "fire" and
187 claimed the element "earth" for his own dynasty. This change served a dual purpose: first, according to the "mutual production" order of the five elements (Fig. 3.21a) , "fire" naturally produces "earth." By taking "earth" as his element, Wang Mang could claim that his dynasty should naturally replace the Han through a peaceful transformation. Second, the element "earth" was represented by the central chamber of Bright Hall. By identifying himself with this element, Wang Mang located his dynasty in the center of the cosmic monument, directly under Heaven and as the pivot of the Universe.

This historical transformation from "fire" to "earth" finally took place in A.D. 9 (Fig. 3.22). Wang Mang, now the founder of the New dynasty, issued his first edict:

> I, unvirtuous one, as a descendent of my original imperial ancestor, the Yellow Emperor, as a descendent of my second imperial ancestor, Emperor Yu [i.e., Shun], and as a humble relative of the Grand Empress Dowager, have been abundantly protected by Heaven and Lord on High, which have given me the mandate for the continuation of the succession. The omens and symbols of authority, the "River Diagram" and the "Luo Writing," and the golden casket and the documents, all clearly indicate the divine commands entrusting to me all people under Heaven. The spirit of Emperor Gaozu of the Red (i.e., fire) lineage has received Heaven's order to transmit his kingdom to me through golden documents. Can I dare not accept this order with reverence?[237]

但是，王莽的历史观并非针对真实的过去，而是为一个未来事件的发生——他对汉朝的取代——而设计的。为了这个目的，往旧的历史模式被有意改造。如他把汉代的“土”德改变为“火”德，而将“土”德用于自己的王朝。这一改变有着双重目的。首先，根据五行“相生”的原则［图 3.21a］，“火”生“土”。以“土”作为与自己对应的五行因素，王莽就可以宣称他的新朝代通过和平的更替自然地取代汉朝。其次，“土”以明堂中央的厅堂来代表。一旦认定自己为“土”德，王莽就可以将其王朝置于这座宇宙性纪念碑的中心，成为直接位于上天之下的宇宙轴心。

从“火”到“土”的这一历史性转变发生在公元 9 年［图 3.22］。王莽，这位被称为“新”的朝代的缔造者，签署了他的第一个法令：

> 予以不德，托于皇初祖考黄帝之后，皇始祖考虞帝之苗裔，而太皇太后之末属。皇天上帝隆显大佑，成命统序，符契图文，金匮策书，神明诏告，属予以天下兆民。赤（即火——作者注）帝汉氏高皇帝之灵，承天命，传国金策之书，予甚祇畏，敢不钦受！[237]

This was the triumph, and the end, of Wang Mang's political campaign. In retrospect, we realize that his rhetorical means had changed from historical *allusions* to a historical *pattern*. Whereas allusions to the Duke of Zhou had helped him reorient people's mind toward the past, the "dynastic lineage" led people to anticipate an inevitable future. The allusions were derived from old texts and referred to concrete figures and events. When these events recurred, history was condensed into a single archetype represented by both remote and present sages. The "dynastic lineage," on the other hand, was an abstract linear pattern without tangible figures and events. It was constructed and perceived as a macrocosmic model of history, a chronology expanding on its own in accordance with the internal movement of the universe. There were no theoretical correlations between these two historical modes. In fact, Wang Mang's own practices demonstrated that he could never simultaneously employ both. Returning from his inauguration ceremony, he escorted the dismissed young emperor out of the capital. He held the boy's hands and wept: "In the past the Duke of Zhou made his master a great king. How unfortunate that I could not follow my heart's desire to follow his example, just because Heaven has demanded that I become the king."[238] The same logic can be applied to Bright Hall. This monument was first constructed to restage a historical event in order to complete Wang Mang's image as a reincarnation of the Duke of Zhou. But when his goal changed from imitating a past sage to becoming a future ruler, the monumentality of Bright Hall had to be altered according to this need: this monument, now the embodiment of "dynastic cycles," could not possibly be manufactured by any human being, neither by the Duke of Zhou nor by Wang Mang of the present day; it could only be created by Heaven, a mythical power that "demanded that Wang Mang become king."

这是王莽政治事业的最高峰，也是他政治战役的终结。综上所述，我们可以看到王莽辩术的核心已经从制造历史隐喻转移到创造历史模式。有关周公的隐喻曾经帮助他将人们的注意力引向过去，而“王朝世系”则使人们预见到一个必将发生的未来。隐喻来自古老的文献，所指涉的是具体的人物和事件。当这些事件再次发生，历史便被浓缩为由古今圣贤共同代表的单一原型。而“王朝世系”是一个没有切实人物和事件的抽象线性模式，被作为一个历史模型建造和感知的，是一个与宇宙内在运动协调的自身扩展的历时系统。在这两种历史构成之间并没有必然的联系。实际上，王莽自己的实践证明，他不可能同时使用这两种模式。从其称帝的就职典礼回来，他陪同着被赶下台的年轻皇帝离开都城。他拉着这个男孩的手，流着眼泪说：“昔周公摄位，终得复子明辟，今予独迫皇天威命，不得如意！”[238] 同样的逻辑也可以用在明堂上。这座纪念碑的修建起初是为了重现一个历史事件，以完成“再世周公”的王莽的形象。但是，当王莽的目标从仿效一位古代圣贤转移到成为一位未来君主，明堂的纪念碑性就必须根据这个需要做出调整：这座纪念碑现在成为“王朝循环”历史模式的体现。它不再出自任何人之手，既不是过去周公的发明，也不是现今王莽的营建，而只能是上天的创造，代表了要求王莽登上皇帝宝座的神秘力量。

Monumentality in Early Chinese Art and Architecture

英汉对照

中国古代艺术与建筑中的“纪念碑性”（下）

（美）巫鸿 著　李清泉 郑岩 等译

外语教学与研究出版社
FOREIGN LANGUAGE TEACHING AND RESEARCH PRESS
北京 BEIJING

图书在版编目（CIP）数据

中国古代艺术与建筑中的“纪念碑性”. 下 ：英汉对照 ／（美）巫鸿著 ；李清泉等译. -- 北京 ：外语教学与研究出版社，2024. 8. -- ISBN 978-7-5213-5366-2

I. J120.92；TU-092.2

中国国家版本馆 CIP 数据核字第 2024E2A324 号

出 版 人　王　芳
系列策划　吴　浩
责任编辑　仲志兰
责任校对　易　璐
封面设计　潘振宇
出版发行　外语教学与研究出版社
社　　址　北京市西三环北路 19 号（100089）
网　　址　https://www.fltrp.com
印　　刷　北京尚唐印装包装有限公司
开　　本　710×1000　1/16
印　　张　62
字　　数　1030 千字
版　　次　2024 年 8 月第 1 版
印　　次　2024 年 8 月第 1 次印刷
书　　号　ISBN 978-7-5213-5366-2
定　　价　258.00 元

如有图书采购需求，图书内容或印刷装订等问题，侵权、盗版书籍等线索，请拨打以下电话或关注官方服务号：
客服电话：400 898 7008
官方服务号：微信搜索并关注公众号“外研社官方服务号”
外研社购书网址：https://fltrp.tmall.com

物料号：353660001

CHAPTER FOUR VOICES OF FUNERARY MONUMENTS

189 How swiftly it dries,
The dew on the garlic-leaf,
The dew that dries so fast
Tomorrow will fall again.
But he whom we carry to the grave
Will never more return.

With its plain message, this Han folk song transports us from the urbane world of Chang'an to an ordinary graveyard.[1] I proposed in Chapter 2 that the funerary monuments of the Han resulted from a profound shift of the religious center in ancient China from temple to tomb, a shift paralleled in the movement of the political center from temple to palace seen in Chang'an. But rather than great emperors whose ambition and desire for power, glory, and immortality mobilized Chang'an's creation and expansion, the subjects of this chapter include people from lower social strata. My basic methodological premise, however, remains the same: we can comprehend the monumentality of Han mortuary structures—memorial stelae, offering shrines, and tombs—only when we reinstall their fragmented and silent remains into their original ritual and social environment.

Official Han histories and other texts record the series of ritual events that followed a person's death.[2] The primary descendent, usually the eldest son, announced the news to all clan members and associates of the deceased, including friends, colleagues, and students. Close members of the family traveling to or holding posts in remote areas were expected to hasten home to pay their final respects; those who failed to do so were punished by the government. Chen Tang, for example, was jailed because he did not rush home when his father died, and even his friend Marquis Zhang Bo, who had recommended him for an official post, was divested of part of his fief.[3] Friends and colleagues who offered their condolences in person were treated as honored guests and invited to feasts featuring musical and acrobatic performances. According to contemporary writers, some "shameless" people lived off such services: they traveled from one funeral to another, pretending to have been friends of the dead; they filled their stomachs with good food and wine and even demanded the company of dancers and singing girls.[4]

肆 丧葬纪念碑的声音

薤上露，
何易晞！
露晞明朝更复落，
人死一去何时归？

这段汉代民谣平实素朴，把我们从繁华的大都会长安带到了普通人的墓地。[1]笔者在第二章提出，汉代的丧葬纪念碑产生于中国古代宗教中心从宗庙到墓葬意义深远的转移过程。这一过程与政治中心从宗庙到宫殿的转移平行，后者的结果是产生了长安这样的政治中心。本章的主角不再是那些以其对权力、荣誉的追求和欲望来推动城市创建与拓展的帝王，而是那些处在社会较低层次的人们。但是，我的基本方法论前提并没有改变：只有将墓碑、祠堂和墓葬等零散的、无言的遗存复原到它们本来的礼仪与社会原境中去，我们才能够理解这些汉代丧葬建筑的纪念碑性。

汉代正史及其他文献记载了一个人死后随之而来的一系列礼仪行为。[2]通常，死者的长子，即其主要继承人，向家族成员以及死者的朋友、同僚和门生宣布噩耗。出游或任职于远方的近亲应立刻回家奔丧，以表达对死者最后的敬意；做不到这一点甚至会导致官府的惩罚。如陈汤就因为父亲死后没有回家奔丧而被治罪下狱，甚至推举他做官的朋友富平侯张勃也被削去部分领地。[3]当死者的朋友和同僚前来吊丧的时候，死者之家要飨之以酒肉，娱之以音乐百戏。据当时的记载，竟有一些无耻之徒赖此为生：他们冒充死者的朋友，奔走于各个丧家，大吃大喝，甚至与舞女歌伎胡闹。[4]

Diviners were hired to decide the location of the tomb and the time of the burial. An inauspicious place or date was thought capable of bringing misfortune to the family and perhaps even the extinction of the whole clan.[5] A possible consequence of such practices was the irregular interval between death and burial recorded in Han archives: the deceased
190 was sometimes buried soon after death, but often the corpse had to be preserved for months or years before it was finally buried in a permanent tomb.[6] Practical concerns, however, may also have caused delays. Unless a person had prepared his own tomb and funerary monuments before his death, his descendents needed a considerable period to build a graveyard. If these descendents were not wealthy, they had to save enough money before any serious mortuary construction could be undertaken. Indeed, such preparations sometimes took so long that a temporary tomb had to be built first and upgraded later.[7]

Once the family had prepared the tomb, memorial monuments, and other funerary paraphernalia, the burial ceremony was held. Friends, colleagues, and students of the deceased waited along the road for the hearse to pass and then accompanied the funerary procession to the graveyard. It was not rare for several thousand people to attend the funeral of a prominent official or Confucian master.[8] As part of their condolences to the deceased's family, these guests also established memorial monuments in the graveyard and inscribed long texts on these structures to commemorate the virtues of the deceased. After the burial, the direct descendents of the dead went into mourning for a long period. The cemetery, in most cases, was not closed to the public. People with good intentions were encouraged to visit the graveyard, so that the deceased's fame and his family's virtue could spread.[9]

This brief introduction to the public dimensions of Han funerary rites should not be entirely new to students of early Chinese art. A similar discussion is included in my 1989 monograph on the famous Wu Liang shrine.[10] Martin Powers, more than anyone else, has contributed to our understanding of the social, political, and economic aspects of Han mortuary art through a series of articles and his important *Art and Political Expression in Early China*, published in 1991. These two book-length studies of Han funerary art, however, are the products of diverse research strategies: *The Wu Liang Shrine* reconstructs a single monument and explores its political, religious, and intellectual implications; Powers's

丧家请来相地的冢师挑选墓地和入葬的吉日。人们认为不祥的地点和日期会带来厄运，甚至给整个家族带来灭顶之灾。[5] 这种观念的一个后果是死亡与下葬的间隔期长短不定，死者有时在咽气不久就被埋葬，而更常见的情况是，尸体在被葬入永久的墓葬之前往往要被保存几个月甚至几年。[6] 但是，现实问题也可能推延埋葬的时间：除非死者在世时就为自己建好了墓葬与祠堂，他的后人和家属常常需要相当长的一段时间来修建墓园。如果这些人并不富裕，那就更需要攒钱以便修建像样的丧葬建筑。的确，这种准备工作有时要花很长的时间，以至于人们有时会先修建一座临时的墓，以后再行增改。[7]

当丧家将墓葬、祠堂以及其他丧葬用具一一准备齐全，就可以举行公开的葬礼了。死者的朋友、同僚、门生分列在道路两边，注视着灵车通过，然后跟随着送葬队伍去往墓地。一位地方官员或儒生死后，前来送葬者多至数千人的例子并不少见。[8] 这些来宾有时在墓地中立碑，在上面铭刻长篇文字，以纪念死者的德行，表达对死者家属的慰问。葬礼结束后，死者的直系继承人要在相当长的一段时间内服丧。在大多数情况下，汉代的墓地对外界开放。死者家族鼓励善意的人们前来瞻仰，以使得死者的名声及其家庭的德行能够广为传播。[9]

以上关于汉代丧葬礼仪的简介，对于研究中国早期美术的学者来说并不陌生。我在 1989 年关于著名的武梁祠的研究中也已对此做过讨论。[10] 包华石曾就有关问题发表了大量文章，1991 年又出版了重要著作《早期中国的艺术与政治表达》，他在帮助我们了解汉代丧葬美术的社会、政治和经济诸方面背景所做的贡献比任何人都多。然而，这两项研究汉代丧葬美术的著作属于不同层面的作品。《武梁祠》一书着眼于重构一座单一的墓葬建筑并探索其政治、

work discusses issues against a broad social spectrum and shows how Han art and politics were shaped by the rise of the Confucian literati. The present study experiments with an "intermediate" level of interpretation: its organizing concept is neither a single structure nor the whole of society, but a "family graveyard"—a monumental complex consisting of multiple commemorative structures commissioned and constructed by several groups of people. This focus allows me to include a variety of monuments in a historical reconstruction and provides me with a definable ritual and architectural context, within which I hope to establish *direct* and *specific* links between monuments and their creators and audience.

Although no Eastern Han cemetery has survived intact, physical remains and textual records demonstrate a standard layout and a number of essential features (Fig. 4.1).[11] The boundary of the burial site is marked by a stone pillar-gate (Fig. 4.2), and the Spirit Path running through this gate determines the central axis of the graveyard. Flanking this path close to the gate stand pairs of sculptured stone animals and/or guardian figures (Fig. 4.3). At the end of this path is the tomb, whose earthen mound covers underground chambers. In front of the tumulus are sometimes built an offering shrine (Fig. 4.4) and memorial stela(e) (Fig. 4.5).

For the present discussion, what is most important is the multiple patrons responsible for the construction of such a cemetery. The three mortuary structures at the heart of the cemetery were the tomb, the shrine, and the stela(e). The tomb contained the physical remains of the dead and was thought to be the site of the deceased's earthly *po* soul; the shrine, the dwelling of the heavenly *hun* soul, housed offerings to the dead.[12] These two structures were in most cases established by the family who owned the graveyard, either purchased by the deceased during his lifetime or by his descendents. The stela, on the other hand, was in most cases erected by visitors. None of these patrons actually built these monuments, however; they were constructed by professional builders.

The establishment of a burial site, therefore, combined the efforts of at least four groups of people: the deceased, his family, his former friends, colleagues, and students, and the builders.

This recognition confirms that a Han cemetery represented a cross
section of society: it was not only a center of ancestor worship within the 192
family but also a focus of social relationships. Its monuments not only

宗教和思想含义，包氏的著作则从广泛的社会角度讨论问题，显示了随着儒家学者的兴起，汉代艺术与政治所发生的变化。本章中的研究试图在二者的“中间”层面上做试验性的探索，所使用的基本概念既不是一座单体建筑，也不是整个社会，而是“家族墓地”这个包括若干社会集团委托或建造的多项纪念性建筑物的综合体。从这一点出发，我试图通过在这些建筑物与其建造者和观者之间建立起直接的和具体的联系，在历史性重构的基础上对几组不同的建筑进行探讨，研究其特定的礼仪和建筑原境。

尽管没有任何一处东汉墓地完整地保存至今，但是考古发现和文献材料仍能大致显示出当时通行的墓地设计的基本特征［图 4.1］。[11] 墓地茔域的界限以一对石阙为标志［图 4.2］，阙门之间向内延伸的神道形成墓地的轴线。在靠近阙门的神道两侧有成对的石兽或石人［图 4.3］。神道尽头即是墓葬，地上有封土，地下有墓室。在封土前面有时还会建祠堂［图 4.4］，树墓碑［图 4.5］。

对于本章的讨论来说，最为重要的是墓地中各种建筑和不同赞助人的关系。墓葬、祠堂和墓碑构成一处墓地的三项中心设施。墓葬保存着死者的遗体，被认为是死后归于地下的“魄”的去处；而祠堂是死者接受祭品的地方，被看作是他的“魂”的居所。[12] 在大多数情况下，墓葬和祠堂由死者家庭建置，或由死者本人在生前购置，或由他的后人建筑。与此不同，墓碑则多由前来瞻仰的人们树立。然而，这两类赞助人都不是真正的建造者，这些墓葬建筑实际上出自专业的匠师之手。因此，墓地的营造至少是四种人努力的结果，包括死者本人，死者的家属，死者生前的朋友、同僚、门生，以及那些施工的工匠。

我们因此可以看到，一座汉代墓地是社会的一个交叉点：它不仅是家庭中祖先崇拜的中心，而且也是家庭之外社会关系的一个焦点。

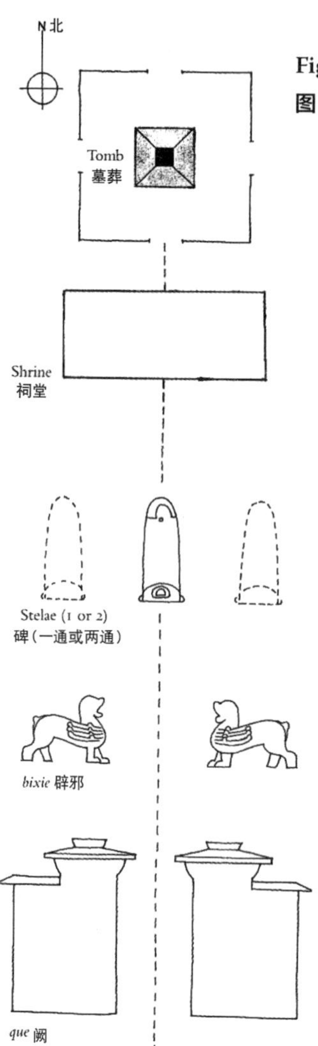

Fig. 4.1. Standard layout of an Eastern Han cemetery.
图 4.1 理想的东汉墓地平面图。

Fig. 4.2. Que pillar-gate of Gao Yi's graveyard. Late Eastern Han. A.D. 209. Ya'an, Sichuan province.
图 4.2 高颐阙。东汉晚期，209 年。四川雅安。

were the property of the dead but also bore witness to the concerns of patrons and builders. Rather than reiterating this general understanding, however, my purpose here is to test it—to uncover such relationships and concerns by reconstructing a number of "scenarios" based on existing funerary inscriptions and carvings. Such a study would ideally focus on a single family graveyard—by identifying its patrons and exploring their intentions, one could write a social history of this particular monumental complex. But since the available data are too scattered to support such a plan, my scenarios must utilize information from divergent sources. To

Fig. 4.3. Stone beast. Late Eastern Han. 2nd-3rd centuries A.D. H. 108 cm. L. 168 cm. Found in 1955 at Sunqitun, Luoyang, Henan province. Luoyang Stone Carving Museum.

图 4.3　石兽。东汉晚期，2—3 世纪。高 108 厘米，长 168 厘米。1955 年发现于河南洛阳孙旗屯。洛阳石刻博物馆藏。

emphasize that these scenarios represent complementary aspects of a Han funerary complex, I select my main examples from a single region in present-day western Shandong and eastern Henan and from a limited period between A.D. 150 and 170.

其中的建筑不仅是死者的财产，而且也汇聚了赞助人和建造者的思想。然而，这里我的目的不仅是要重复这个一般性的认识，而是要证实这个认识。证实的方法是，通过对现存丧葬铭文与雕刻的研究来建构若干具体“情节”，揭示出建造墓葬纪念碑的过程中人与人的关系以及相关的思想。在理想的情况下，这种研究最好集中于一个特殊的家庭墓地，通过对其赞助人及其意愿的研究，写出一部关于这个墓地的社会史。但是，由于现存材料过于零散，我不得不采用不同来源的多种信息以完成这一研究。为了强调这些“情节”表现了汉代丧葬系统互补的方面，我主要的例证均选自今鲁西豫东这一特定地区，时间则限定在公元 150 — 170 年间。

Fig. 4.4. Xiaotangshan Shrine. Early Eastern Han. *Ca.* mid-1st century A.D. H. 210 cm. W. 380 cm. Changqing, Shandong province.

图 4.4 孝堂山祠堂。东汉早期，约 1 世纪中叶。高 210 厘米，宽 380 厘米。山东济南长清。

Fig. 4.5. Gao Yi's memorial stela. A.D. 209. Ya'an, Sichuan province.

图 4.5 高颐碑。东汉晚期，209 年。四川雅安。

❶ The Family (1)

The troubled reign of Emperor Huan (A.D. 147-67) witnessed a heated struggle among scholar-officials, eunuchs, and royal relatives. Endless evil portents—earth-quakes, landslides, solar eclipses, floods, strange animals and birds—were reported to the throne as signs of Heaven's disapproval of current politics.[13] The emperor's biography in the *History of the Latter Han* is a litany of such disasters, along with apologies by the Son of Heaven. A single passage under the first year of the Yongxing reign period (153) reads: "Autumn, the seventh month: a plague of locusts spread over all 32 prefectures and principalities. The dike of the Yellow River is breached. As many as several hundred thousand hungry and destitute people are roaming the roads." A few months later, in early 154, an earthquake shook the capital, and the emperor issued an edict in response: "Stars and constellations move in disorder; the whole universe is shaking. So many inauspicious omens surely predict a future of misfortune." His prophecy came true: in June the Si River in southern Shandong suddenly flowed backward; in September a solar eclipse was
observed; and toward the end of the year a more fatal disaster took place: 193
a violent rebellion led by Gongsun Ju broke out in the Taishan area in

一、家庭（一）

桓帝统治时期（147—167 年）政局混乱，大臣、宦官和皇戚之间斗争激烈。地震、山崩、日食、洪水、怪鸟、异兽——有关这些不祥之兆的信息如流水般地汇集到朝廷，被视作上天对现行政治的不满。[13]《后汉书·孝桓帝纪》记录了这些灾难，并附有天子自责的言论。其中，永兴元年（153）的一段记载如下："秋七月，郡国三十二蝗。河水溢。百姓饥穷，流冗道路，至有数十万户。"几个月之后，即 154 年初，京师发生了地震，皇帝下诏说："比者星辰谬越，坤灵震动，灾异之降，必不空发。"他的预言随即变成现实：同年六月山东南部的泗水忽然倒流；九月日食出现；更致命的一次灾难发生于年底：山东中部泰山地区爆发了由公孙举领导的暴动，

central Shandong; the angry peasants killed the local governor.[14]

The Taishan area had special significance for the Han royal house. Taishan, or Mount Tai, was a sacred place where emperors received their mandate to rule from Heaven. Not far from this mountain was Qufu, the home town of Confucius, whose teachings had become the foundation of the Han state religion and ideology. South of Qufu was Pei, the origin of the Liu royal clan of the Han. To Emperor Huan, whose rule was already in trouble, nothing was worse than disturbances in this "holy land." He adopted two measures to put down the uprising: first, to prevent more people from joining the rebellion, he decreed tax relief for "those who had suffered from the disorders"; and second, he established a special military post at Taishan to deal with the riot. But the rebellion continued to spread. By 156, armed peasants had occupied three key districts in Shandong. Alarmed, Emperor Huan ordered his chief ministers to select a capable general to lead an expedition army. Duan Jiong, an officer with an impressive military record, was recommended to the throne and immediately set off to the region. His consequent success was largely due to the severe measure of massacring all troublemakers: by July 156, half of the 30,000 rebellious peasants had been beheaded.[15]

Records of this rebellion stop here in the official Han history.[16] But other sources suggest that the uprising continued at least to the end of the year. A funerary inscription found in 1980 in Jiaxiang, some 40 miles southwest of Taishan, is dedicated to a low-ranking officer in the government army named An Guo, who was sent to the center of the rebellion some time before 157 (Fig. 4.6). Falling ill or wounded, he fled and struggled home. Seven people in his family received him: his parents, three younger brothers, two sons, and also presumably his wife. All efforts to save An Guo's life were in vain, and he died at the beginning of 157 at age 34. During the following year the family was struck by further calamities: both An Guo's sons died, and the major branch of the family perished with them (since he was the eldest son of the family). Following tradition, his younger brothers carried out the funeral service: they built a tomb for their older brother and buried their nephews along the Spirit Path leading to the tomb. They also planted evergreen trees around the earthen tumulus and hired itinerant builders to construct a stone offering shrine in front of it. This took about a year, and upon the shrine's

愤怒的农民杀死了当地的官吏。[14]

对于汉朝廷来说，泰山地区具有特殊的意义。泰山是皇帝接受上天册命的圣地；距离泰山不远就是孔子的故乡曲阜，而孔子的学说是汉代国家宗教与思想的基础；由曲阜向南是汉朝皇室刘氏的发源地沛。对于政局已经陷入困境的桓帝来说，没有比在这一“圣地”发生动乱更糟的事了。他采取了两项措施来平息暴动。首先，他“诏太山、琅邪遇贼者，勿收租、赋”，以防止更多的人加入起义队伍；其次，他在泰山任命了新的军事官员来对付骚乱。但是，这些措施似乎功效甚微，暴乱仍继续扩大。156 年，武装的农民占领了山东的三个关键地区，桓帝急忙命令宰相挑选精兵强将，组成一支远征部队。一位名叫段颎的军功显赫的官员被举荐到朝廷，并被立刻派往泰山地区。段颎随后所取得的一连串胜利，在很大程度上是对暴动者残酷屠杀的结果。到 156 年七月，三万暴动农民中竟有半数被残酷杀戮。[15]

正史中关于这次暴动的记载到此结束。[16] 但其他资料表明，暴乱至少延续到 156 年年底。1980 年，在泰山西南大约 65 公里的嘉祥县发现了一段长篇丧葬铭文。这段文字是一位叫安国的下级军吏写的，他曾在 157 年之前的某时被派往这场暴动的中心地区［图 4.6］。因为生病或受伤，他离开战场并设法回到家中。家中迎接他的有七人，包括他的父母、三个弟弟、两个儿子，或者还有他的妻子。所有试图拯救他的措施都是徒劳，他于 157 年初辞世，年仅 34 岁。来年，这个家庭又受到了一连串灾祸的打击，安国的两个儿子相继死去，这个家庭的主支随之衰败了（因为安国是家庭的长子）。根据传统，安国的弟弟们为他操办了丧事，他们为兄长修建了墓葬，又在通往墓葬的神道旁安葬了两个侄子。他们还围绕着封土种植了柏树，雇用走方匠师在墓前建造了一座石祠。整个过程大约

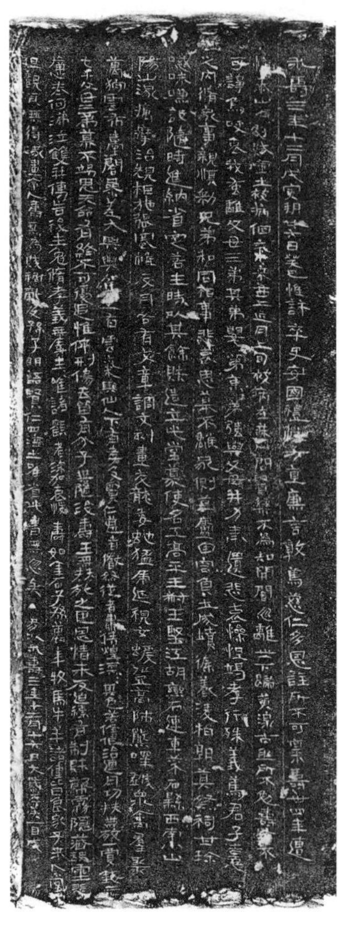

Fig. 4.6. Inscription on An Guo's shrine. A.D. 157. Excavated in 1980 at Songshan, Jiaxiang, Shandong province. Shandong Provincial Gallery of Stone Carvings.

图 4.6 安国祠堂题记。东汉晚期，157 年。1980 年山东嘉祥宋山出土。济南，山东省石刻艺术博物馆藏。拓片。

completion an inscription was engraved on it to record the family's devotion. Like many similar buildings, An Guo's shrine was destroyed in the third century during the iconoclastic movement mobilized by Cao Pi, and its stone slabs were reused for new tombs. This is why the inscribed stone, which may have formed the ceiling of An Guo's shrine, was discovered in a post Han burial.[17] Consisting of 490 characters, the inscription is not only the longest text from a Han offering shrine ever found but also the most vivid record of a funerary monument constructed for a deceased family member.[18] [This text is inscribed] on the sixteenth day of *guisi*, in the twelfth month of *wuyin*, in the third year of the Yongshou reign period [A.D. 157].

A military officer of the Xu district, An Guo, endowed with courteousness and uprightness, quietness and sincerity, kindness and generosity, met with calamity at age 34. Powerful robbers had arisen in the Taishan area. [Serving in the expedition army] as an officer, he fell ill. Hesitatingly, he went southwest [back home]. From the first ten days of the first month, he became seriously ill and could not leave his bed. Divination was sought, and medicines applied, but none was efficacious. Before long he passed away, returning to the Yellow Springs. [Death is a human destiny that] even the ancient sages could not avoid, and the allotted span of his life could not be extended. Alas! He died so early, leaving his parents and three younger brothers behind!

Melancholy and full of grief, An Guo's younger brothers, Ying, Dong, and Qiang, carried out the funeral service with their parents. Practicing filial piety to the utmost, engaging in outstanding conduct, and faithfully maintaining their integrity—all these are praised by people of excellence. They cultivate the household virtues, obediently

用了一年时间。祠堂建好后，他们在上面刻了一段文字，记载他们对死者的奉献。与许多同样的建筑相似，安国祠堂在 3 世纪曹丕发动的毁坏墓葬建筑的运动中被破坏，石板被用来建造新的墓葬。所以这段原来可能刻在安国祠堂顶部的题记，是在一座晚于汉代的墓葬中发现的。[17] 这段长达 490 字的题记是目前所见汉代最长的祠堂铭文，提供了为死去亲人修建墓祠的最为生动的记载。[18]

永寿三年十二月戊寅朔，廿六日癸巳，惟许卒史安国，礼性方直，廉言敦笃，慈仁多恩，注所不可。禀寿卅四年，遭□。泰山有剧贼，军士被病，徊气来西上。正月上旬，被病在床，卜问医药，不为知间，阉忽离世，下归黄淥，古聊所不勉，寿命不可诤。乌呼哀哉！蚤离父母三弟。

其弟婴、弟东、弟强与父母并力奉遗，悲哀惨怛。竭孝，行殊，义笃。君子熹之。内修家，事亲顺勅，兄弟

serving their parents and congenially associating with each other. They long for An Guo with deep sorrow and cannot bear to leave his tumulus. They erected a funerary shrine and transported soil on their
194 backs to make the tomb mound. They continuously plant lofty juniper trees. They make offerings every morning and night and present various delicious foods at all times, as if their older brother were still alive.

Exhausting their savings, they hired famous craftsmen of Gaoping [principality], named Wang Shu, Wang Jian, and Jiang Hu, to build this small [offering] hall. Tirelessly they carted unhewn stones from a small hill southwest of the county town, Yangshan. They cut, ground, and polished the slabs. They measured and built the hall. On the eaves and outer walls [?], they carved different designs. And [inside the hall] they engraved decorations and pictorial scenes: there are interlocking dragons and winding serpents; fierce tigers stretch forward their heads, gazing into the distance; black apes ascend heights; lions and bears roar, strewn everywhere like clouds. There are towers and pavilions of unequal heights; great processions of chariots set forth. Above, there are clouds and immortals; below, figures of filial piety, excellent virtue, and benevolence. Superiors are dignified, and their attendants, respectful. Inferiors are obedient and look agitated as well as joyous. Month by month, the craftsmen worked on this hall, expending tremendous effort. The hall cost 27,000 cash.

An Guo's parents and his three younger brothers cannot stop longing for him with all their hearts. Yet the span of our days is allotted by Heaven and cannot be regained. They are wan and sallow with broken hearts. But both life and death are predetermined by fate. How could An Guo's sons die so young in following their father? How could they forget their duty of carrying out their father's funeral and their gratitude to him? The funerary banners were made according to the regulations, and the furnishing goods were buried safely. The wandering soul grieves; the living are filled with sorrow.

Why shed bitter tears? We advise our descendents to lead honorable lives. You, observers, please offer your pity and sympathy. Then may your longevity be as gold and stone, and may your descendents extend your line for 10,000 years. You boys who herd horses and tend sheep and cows are all from good families. If you enter this hall, please just look and do not scribble [on the walls]. Then you will enjoy a long life. Please do not destroy the hall or make any trouble: this will cause disaster to your descendents. We are stating clearly to people of virtue and kindheartedness within the four seas: Please regard these words and do not ignore them.

[This text] was carved on the sixteenth day of the twelfth month, the third year of the Yongshou era. The planet Jupiter was in the position of *wu*.

和同相事。悲哀思慕，不离冢侧，草庐畲容，负土成坟。徐养淩柏，朝莫祭祠，甘珍嗞味嗛设，随时进纳，省定若生时。以其余财，造立此堂。募使名工高平王叔、王坚、江胡、栾石、连车，采石县西南小山阳山。涿疡瘵治，规柜施张，褰帷反月，各有文章。调文刻画，交龙委蛇，猛虎延视，玄蝯登高，陠熊嗥戏，众禽群聚，万狩云布，台阁参差，大兴舆驾，上有云气与仙人，下有孝及贤仁。遵者俨然，从者肃侍，煌煌濡濡，其色若偺。作治连月，功扶无亟，贾钱二万七千。

父母三弟，暮不竭思，天命有终，不可复追，惟倅刑伤，去留有分。子无随没寿，王无扶死之里，恩情未反，迫褾有制，财薛雾隐藏，魂灵悲痛夫！夫何涕泣双并，传告后生，勉修孝义，无辱生生。唯诸观者，深加哀怜，寿如金石，子孙万年。牧马牛羊诸僮，皆良家子，来入宅堂，但观耳，无得涿画，令人寿，无为贼祸，乱及子孙。明语贤仁四海士，唯省此书，无忽矣。易以永寿三年十二月十六日，太岁在矣，一目戊。

The following lines are inscribed on the other end of the slab:

> The elder son of An Guo, named Nan with the style name Boxiao, died at age six and was buried near the east road. Boxiao's younger brother, whose style name was Runde, also died at an early age. Both are following their father.

The inscription remains emotionally powerful almost two millennia later. Nevertheless, only a short segment describes the life of the deceased;
195 the focus of the text is clearly the patrons of the ritual building. It was these patrons—An Guo's three younger brothers—who in fulfilling their filial duty became "wan and sallow." It was they who "transported soil on their backs to make the tomb mound" and who "cannot bear to leave the tumulus."[19] Their devotion was not only spiritual but financial: the shrine exhausted their savings, 27,000 cash in all (this was the equivalent of three to four years' salary for a prefect of a county with 10,000 or more households). As we read through the inscription, we cannot help feeling that the brothers—the "narrators" of the text—were calling for the reader's sympathy not so much toward their departed brother as toward themselves. Indeed, the inscription was written for people who would appreciate their filial devotion; they ended with a strong appeal: "We are stating clearly to people of virtue and kindheartedness within the four seas: Please regard these words and do not ignore them."

Significant similarities link this funerary inscription with investiture inscriptions on Western Zhou ritual bronzes, which also focus on the virtues and achievements of living devotees rather than on the life and ambition of departed ancestors (see Chapter 1). In both the Western Zhou and Eastern Han cases, the mortuary or sacrificial texts seems to have been composed "to make oneself known," and in this way a consecrated object—a bronze vessel or a stone shrine—was readily understood as a monument established not only for the deceased but also for the donor. The most fundamental link between these two cases, however, is the moral code of *xiao*, or filial piety, which, though a product of the ancestor religion itself, stimulated and rationalized ancestral dedications, including Zhou ritual vessels and Han funerary structures.

It would be too simplistic to understand the concept and application of filial piety only in broad religious terms. During the Han, this virtue gained new social significance and a quasi-divine status. The *Classic of*

石板的另一端刻有另一段文字：

> 国子男，字伯孝，年適六岁，在东道边。孝有小弟，字闰得，俱去，皆随国。

近两千年过去了，读起这篇题记时我们仍会被它感动。但值得注意的是，文中只有一小节描述死者的生平；强调的重点明显是该礼仪建筑的赞助人。正是这些赞助人——安国的三个弟弟——为尽孝道而“惟倅刑（形）伤”，也正是他们“负土成坟”“不离冢侧”。[19]他们的奉献不仅是精神上的而且是物质上的：他们耗尽了所有的积蓄，花费了27000钱（相当于当时一个管辖一万户甚至更多人口的地方官员三至四年的收入）为他们的哥哥造墓。阅读这段文字，我们不禁感到这兄弟三人——即这段文字的“讲述者”——与其说是要唤起读者对死者的同情，倒不如说是要唤起人们对他们自己的同情。的确，铭文的结尾点明了这段题记是写给那些欣赏其孝行的人看的：“明语贤仁四海士，唯省此书，无忽矣。”

这段丧葬文字与西周青铜礼器上的册命铭文有着耐人寻味的共性，后者的重点也在于强调生者的德行与功绩，而不是已故祖先们的生平与雄心（见本书第一章的讨论）。无论是在西周还是在东汉，这些丧葬或祭祀文字似乎是为了“使自己扬名”而创作的。通过这些方式，奉献物——一件青铜器或一座祠堂——成为不仅为死者竖立，而且也为奉献者建造的纪念碑。而且，青铜器与祠堂都体现了“孝”这一道德准则。二者都是祖先崇拜的产品。通过它们，孝的观念刺激了对祖先的奉献并使之合理化。

但是，“孝”不是一个抽象的、超历史的概念，而是随着历史的发展不断地变化。在汉代，“孝”被赋予新的社会意义，有着近乎神性的地位。被汉代人高度重视的儒家经典《孝经》说：“夫孝，

Filial Piety (*Xiao jing*), a canonical Confucian text that enjoyed enormous popularity at the time, teaches that "filial piety is the foundation of all virtues and the root of civilization" and that "filial piety is the first principle of Heaven, the ultimate standard of Earth, and the norm of human conduct."[20] This doctrine was based on the Han notion that the father-son relation is the most fundamental of all human relations. It is not difficult to understand the historical origin of this emphasis: following China's transformation from a clan-lineage society to a family-oriented society, the principal subject of ancestor worship changed from a remote lineage ancestor to close family members, especially one's father. The important point here, however, is not so much social and religious change, but a new standard that this change brought about in political philosophy and rhetoric. The father-son relationship became analogous to relations between Heaven and ruler and between ruler and subject; the practice of filial piety was no longer a private family business but one's most important public duty. Thus, the *Classic of Filial Piety* teaches: "The superiority of the lord and father, the simplicity of the way of men, and the beginning of Heaven and Earth, all are contained in filial piety." During the Han the motto of rulership was "To govern the country with filial piety," and the *Classic of Filial Piety* was assigned to students in all schools throughout the nation. In the early Han, the government established a special official rank called "filial and uncorrupt." Local officials were responsible for recommending for this rank "filial sons, obedient grandsons, virtuous daughters, righteous wives, men who yielded property in order to relieve the distressed, and scholars who were a model to the people."[21] Not coincidentally, the posthumous titles of all Han emperors bear the prefix *xiao*, or "filial."

Filial piety, therefore, had multiple meanings and functions during the Han. These meanings and functions were reflected most directly in funerary practices. As Martin Powers has pointed out, filial piety mobilized the construction of funerary monuments and was expressed

by these monuments; it was recognized on public occasions such as a funeral, and such recognition was crucial for a person's political career.[22] In short, the practice of filial piety fulfilled moral obligations and helped win respect from others. Once recognized as a filial son, daughter, or brother, a person was automatically considered a reliable
member of his or her family and community, as well as a loyal subject 196
of the state. Such a reputation could lead to concrete gains: a person of

德之本也，教之所由生也；”“夫孝，天之经也，地之义也，民之行也。”[20] 这一学说的基础是，汉代人认为父子关系是所有社会关系中最基本的关系。这一观点的历史根源并不难以理解：在中国社会从宗族结构向家庭结构转变时，祖先祭祀的中心从远祖转向近亲，特别是父亲。然而，值得重视的并不只是社会和宗教的变化，我们还要注意到这一变化所带来的政治哲学与辩术中的新标准。父子关系为上天与统治者的关系、君与臣的关系提供了基本的比喻，履行孝道因此不再只是家庭中的私事，而是成了最重要的公共道义。因此，《孝经》中说：“天地之性，人为贵。人之行，莫大于孝。孝莫大于严父。严父莫大于配天。”汉代统治者的箴言是“以孝治天下”，《孝经》被指定为全国学校中必修的科目。自汉代初年，政府设置了一个称作“孝廉”的官职。地方官员负责举荐“孝子顺孙，贞女义妇，让财救患，及学士为民法式者”。[21] 并非巧合的是，所有汉代皇帝的谥号都缀有一“孝”字。

因此，“孝”在汉代具多种含义与功能，而这些含义与功能在丧葬活动中得到了最直接的体现。正如包华石所言，孝的观念推动了纪念性丧葬建筑的兴建，同时也被这些建筑所体现；葬礼之类的公众场合最能表现一个人的孝，而公众的认可对于一个人的政治生涯也至关重要。[22] 简言之，孝行是一个人道德责任的自我完成，同时也使其得到别人的尊重。一个人一旦被认为是尽孝的子女或兄弟，就自然地被看作一个对家庭、社会以及朝廷和国家具有责任心的人。这样的荣誉会带来实际的利益：一个至孝的人会得到地方

outstanding filial conduct might be rewarded by the local authorities or the central government. He or she might be exempted from taxation, and a filial son might even be recommended for an official post through the recommendation system, which had become a routine channel for entering the imperial bureaucracy.

A useful means of stabilizing the social organization, such encouragement of filial practices nevertheless produced a strong counter-reaction. Once a reputation for filial piety became indispensable for material and political benefits, the practitioner's question often shifted from fulfilling the moral duty to demonstrating the virtue. The *Classic of Filial Piety* defines five major filial practices: "The service that a filial son does his parents is as follows: in his general conduct to them, he manifests the utmost reverence; in nourishing them, he endeavors to give them the utmost pleasure; when they are ill, he feels the greatest anxiety; in mourning for them, he exhibits every demonstration of grief; in sacrificing to them, he displays the utmost solemnity."[23] Interestingly, a filial son had to "exhibit" his grief and "display" his solemnity in mourning and sacrifices. The first three filial practices were concerned with domestic affairs inside the family; only the last two took place on public occasions during the funerary rites. The first three practices were aimed at the comfort and security of parents; the last two practices were essentially a matter of a filial son's self-expression; the degree of his "grief" and "solemnity" had to be judged by the audience of his ritual performance.

It is not difficult to imagine that funerary services, including the erection of mortuary monuments and the composition of mortuary inscriptions, provided a filial son with the best chance "to make himself known." This tendency, which gradually grew into a fanatic exhibition of filial piety during the second century, led the scholar Huan Kuan to write the following bitter criticism:

> Nowadays when parents are alive their children do not show love and respect, but when they die their children elevate them to very lofty

positions through extravagant [spending]. Even though they have no sincere grief, they are nonetheless regarded as filial if they give [their parents] a lavish burial and spend a lot of money. *Therefore their names become prominent and their glory shines among the people*. Because of this, even the commoners emulate [these practices] to the extent that they sell their houses and property to do it.[24]

Huan Kuan offers an explanation for the hypocrisy behind lavish funerary monuments during the Eastern Han, but he also challenges us to detect the intention behind the construction of a specific monument.

官员或中央政府的奖赏；他被免除租赋；通过官吏选拔系统，孝子还有可能被举荐为官员，因此“行孝”也就成了当时进入官场的一个重要渠道。

鼓励尽孝是稳定社会的一种有效手段，但也会产生强烈的反作用。孝的荣誉一旦成为获得物质和政治利益的必要前提，实践者的问题就会从履行这一道德义务转向刻意证明其具有这样的德行。《孝经》提出五种孝行：“孝子之事亲也，居则致其敬，养则致其乐，病则致其尤，丧则致其哀，祭则致其严。”[23]值得注意的是，根据这个要求，孝子在葬礼和祭祀中必须充分表现其“哀”和“严”。前三种孝行是家庭内部的事情，后两种孝行则表现于丧葬和祭祀的公共场合中。前三种孝行旨在保障其父母的舒适与安全，后两种孝行从本质上说是孝子的表演；他所表达的“哀”和“严”的程度要由葬礼和祭礼中的观众们判断。

不难想象，葬礼仪式，包括修建丧葬建筑和书写丧葬文字，遂成为一个孝子扬名的最好机会。这种倾向在 2 世纪逐步发展成为对孝行的狂热宣示，当时的学者桓宽因而对此提出了严厉的批评：

> 今生不能致其爱敬，死以奢侈相高；虽无哀戚之心，而厚葬重币者，则称以为孝，显名立于世，光荣著于俗。故黎民相慕效，至于发屋卖业。[24]

桓宽的话揭示了东汉时期隐藏在豪华的丧葬建筑背后的伪善，同时也提醒我们去揭露隐藏在一座特别的纪念性建筑背后的真正意图。

Can we determine the meaning and function of an offering shrine—as an expression of a family's genuine filial devotion, as a convenient means of manipulating public opinion, or as a mixture of both? To what extent did a funerary monument demonstrate its meaning and function through its architecture and decoration? A number of difficulties prevent straightforward answers. First, most Han dynasty shrines were decorated with popular scenes illustrating virtuous men and women from Chinese history, as well as conventional images of banquets, chariot processions, immortals, and auspicious omens. In many cases these stereotypical motifs do not bear witness to the family's particular concerns. Second, since most Eastern Han shrines were destroyed after the dynasty's fall, the surviving slabs of a shrine rarely permit us to reconstruct its entire decorative program, which is often the key to understanding the meaning of its decoration.[25] Third, scholars have tried to explore the social and political implications of specific pictures on certain shrines. Because the owners of these buildings are often unknown, however, such speculations must perforce stop at a general level. This reflection implies that a comprehensive study of a funerary monument should be based on at least two groups of data: (1) an intact or reconstructible architectural structure and its decorative program, and (2) biographical sources of the patron and the deceased. To my knowledge, only two or three examples, all belonging to the Wu family from Jiaxiang in Shandong, meet these criteria; I discuss one of these in a later section. Fortunately, we have another important group of evidence consisting of some fourteen inscriptions written by patrons of funerary shrines; the An Guo inscription is the longest of these. Although the structures that originally
197 bore these texts can no longer be reconstructed, the inscriptions form a collective body of information, allowing us to observe the shifting focus and intention behind the construction of funerary monuments during the first and second centuries.[26]

The earliest inscription is also the simplest. Engraved on a stone column that may have been a central pillar of a funerary shrine are four characters, which can roughly be translated as "an offering shrine in a sacrificial park" (*shizhai ciyuan*) (Fig. 4.7).[27] Neither the deceased nor the donor are mentioned. The inscription simply identifies the ritual function of the building. Whereas the early date ascribed to this inscription is based largely on the pictorial style of its accompanying carvings,[28] a

但是，我们如何才能断定一座祠堂的真正意义和功能呢？如何知道它是一个家庭真正尽孝的结果，或是操纵公众舆论的简便手段，或二者兼而有之？一座丧葬纪念碑在多大程度上通过其建筑和装饰形式表达其意义和功能？几个方面的复杂事实使我们无法直接回答这些问题。首先，大多数汉代祠堂以流行题材装饰，这些题材包括历史上的贤人列女，还有司空见惯的宴饮、车马出行、神仙、祥瑞，等等。在通常的情况下，这些程式化的题材并不表达某个家庭的特殊思想。第二，因为大多数汉代祠堂在汉王朝终止时遭到了破坏，残存的石板很少能够被重构为原来的整体装饰程序，而这种整体程序是我们理解画像所含思想的关键。[25] 第三，学者们曾探讨过某些祠堂中特殊画面的社会和政治含义，但是，由于我们不知道这些建筑的主人，所以这种思考只能停留在一般性的层面上。以上这三点使我们认识到，对一座丧葬建筑进行全面研究至少需要两组信息，一是完整的或者可复原的建筑结构及装饰程序；二是赞助人和死者的传记材料。据我所知，只有山东嘉祥武氏家族的两或三个祠堂符合这些标准；我在下文中将讨论其中的一个。幸运的是，我们还有一组重要的材料，包括大约 14 条由祠堂赞助人撰写的题记；其中最长的是安国祠堂题记。尽管原来的建筑已经无法复原，但这些题记仍能构成一个信息集合体，使我们得以观察 1—2 世纪纪念性丧葬建筑背后焦点和目的的变化。[26]

年代最早的一条题记也是行文最简单的一条。这条题记刻在一石柱上，原来可能立在祠堂中央，上面只有"食斋祠园"四字［图 4.7］。[27] 题记既没有提到死者，也没有提到赞助人，只是简单地说明了建筑的礼仪功能。这条题记的年代是根据共存画像的风格来判断的。[28]

Fig. 4.7. "Shizhai ciyuan" carving and inscription. Late Western Han to early Eastern Han. 1st century B.C.—1st century A.D.

图 4.7 "食斋祠园"画像与题记。西汉晚期至东汉早期，公元前 1—公元 1 世纪。拓片。

second example, originally carved on an offering shrine at Wenshang in Shandong, bears the date of A.D. 16 (Fig. 4.8). The inscription, though still brief, includes a short introduction of the deceased. But a more crucial change is the narrative's voice: the construction of the ritual building is described by patrons who identify themselves at the end of the text. Labeled with this text, the funerary monument was no longer anonymous but devoted to a Confucian scholar by his filial brothers. "In the third year of the Tianfeng reign period [A.D. 16], we erected this offering hall for Gentleman Lu, who ceaselessly studied *Master Yan's Commentaries on the Spring and Autumn Annuals* [*Yanshi chunqiu*] On the tenth day of the second month, in the first year [eight characters missing]. Gentleman Lu's brothers."

This text remains the only decipherable shrine inscription written during the first century.[29] The next example, an inscription dated to A.D.

Fig. 4.8. Carving and inscription on Lugong's shrine. A.D. 16.

图 4.8　路公祠堂画像与题记。新，16 年。拓片。

106, demonstrates a dramatic shift in both content and style (Fig. 4.9). It records that a certain Marquis of Beixiang dedicated a shrine to his deceased father.[30] Upon completion of the building, he ordered his father's surname and honorable title, Yang sanlao (Thrice Venerable Yang), carved on it beside a far longer text describing his own filial devotion:

而另一条早期题记则有公元 16 年的纪年［图 4.8］。该题记刻在原立于山东汶上县的一座祠堂中，文为："□天凤三年（16）立食堂，路公治严氏春秋不踰，□□元年二月廿日□□□□□□□□□荆路公昆弟。"虽然行文仍很短，但这条题记对死者的情况进行了简单的介绍。更重要的一个变化是叙事者声音的出现——赞助人描述了祠堂的修建，并在最后题上了自己的名字。有了这段题记，这座祠堂不再属于无名氏，人们可以知道它是由两位有孝心的兄弟为儒生路公建造的。

这是写于 1 世纪的唯一可辨认的祠堂题记。[29] 下一个例子有公元 106 年的纪年，其内容和形式都有了很大的变化［图 4.9］。这条题记记载某一北乡侯为其父亲建造了一座祠堂，[30] 祠堂建成后，他将父亲的姓和尊称"阳三老"刻在题记顶部，下面的文字则记载了他本人的孝行：

Fig. 4.9. Inscription on Yangsanlao's shrine. A.D. 106. H. 51 cm. Found in the early 20th century at Qufu, Shandong province. Museum of Chinese History, Beijing.

图 4.9 阳三老祠堂题记。东汉中期，106 年。高 51 厘米。20 世纪初发现于山东曲阜。中国国家博物馆藏。拓片。

This stone hall was completed on the fourteenth day, in the twelfth month of *jiachen*, in the first year of the Yanping reign period [A.D. 106]. The planet Jupiter was
199 in the position of *bingwu*. I, the Marquis of Beixiang of the Lu principality, reflect that I am staying in my rural home in mourning, neither attending the imperial court nor pursuing Classical learning. I am bent on serving and worshipping [my deceased father]. I am grievous and sorrowful that I have not repaid [his favor] with filial piety. Wailing without end, I am afraid that soon I will be unable to keep myself alive. I make sacrifices every morning, and offer food at all times [several characters missing].

The inscription seems to deliberately echo the filial practices required by the *Classic of Filial Piety*: "in mourning for them [i.e., the deceased parents], he [the filial son] exhibits every demonstration of grief; in sacrificing to them, he displays the utmost solemnity." In fact, in composing the inscription, the marquis simply replaced the indefinitive subject and object of filial devotion in the *Classic of Filial*

Piety (an assumed filial son and his parents) with a definite subject and object (the marquis himself and his dead father). The inscription can thus be understood as an appropriation: "in mourning for my father, I am exhibiting every demonstration of grief; in sacrificing to him, I am displaying the utmost solemnity."

The focus of this commemorative text has thus shifted to the exhibition of the patron's filial devotion. The same tendency is also evident in another type of shrine inscription that appeared around the same time; it, however, demonstrates filial piety by providing the most calculable evidence—the amount of money a patron spent on a monument. The first such document is found on a large pictorial slab, originally installed on the back wall of a shrine belonging to a Dai family in Shandong (Fig. 4.10). The text on the left margin gives the names and

> 延平元年（106）十二月甲辰朔十四日石堂毕成，时太岁在丙午。鲁北乡侯……自思省居乡里，无画不在朝廷。又无经学，志在共养子道，未反……感切伤心，晨夜哭泣，恐身不全，朝半祠祭，随时进食……

这段题记似乎有意响应《孝经》中对于行孝的要求："（父母）丧则（孝子）致其哀，祭（父母）则（孝子）致其严。"北乡侯所做的只是将《孝经》中不确定的主体和客体（一位匿名的孝子及其父母）置换为确定的主体和客体（北乡侯及其已故的父亲）。因此，这篇题记可以被看作一种"挪用"："（吾父）丧则（吾）致其哀，祭（吾父）则（吾）致其严。"

这些纪念性文字的重点因此转移到展示赞助人的孝行上来。同一倾向也明显反映在大约同时期的另一类祠堂题记中；然而，这类题记是通过提供量化的证据——建造祠堂所花费钱财的数目——来证实赞助人的孝行。这类题记的第一个例子刻在一方较大的画像石上。该石原为山东戴氏祠堂的后壁［图 4.10］，石板左边的文字

Fig. 4.10. Carving and inscription on the Dai family shrine. A.D. 113. From Liangcheng, Weishan, Shandong province.

图 4.10 戴氏享堂画像与题记。东汉中期，113 年。山东微山两城出土。拓片。

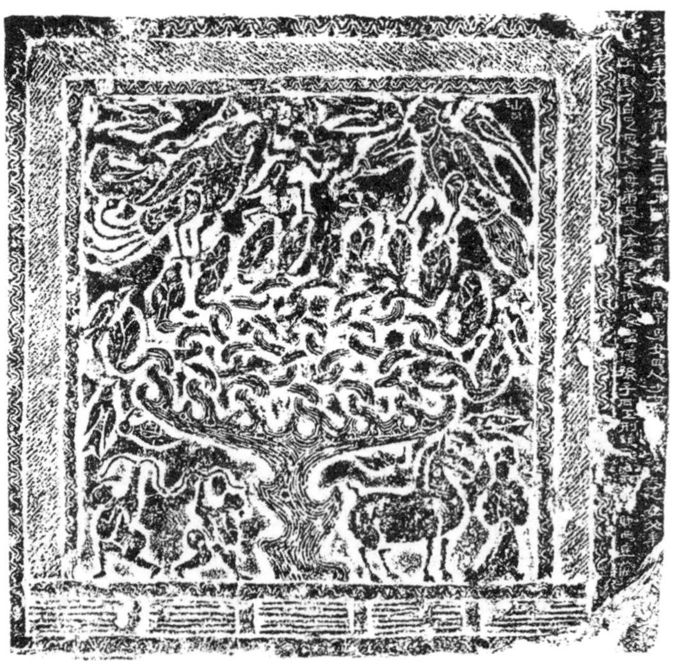

Fig. 4.11. Carving and inscription on the Yang family shrine. A.D. 137. From Liangcheng, Weishan, Shandong province. Now in the Confucian Temple in Qufu.

图 4.11 泱氏祠堂画像与题记。137 年。山东微山两城出土。山东曲阜孔庙藏。拓片。

death dates of the parents to whom the shrine was dedicated. The text to the right introduces the patrons and provides a detailed financial account:

> Dai Mu, whose style name is Kongdao, spent 5,000 cash to build this stone hall, and again spent 2,500 cash to make the *guobao* [carved ceiling?]. Two other sons of the Dai family, as well as Wu Zhu with the style name Chengchao, Yang Xun with the style name Bieqing, and Zhang Nian, together contributed 9,500 cash. [This shrine] was completed on the eighteenth day in the intercalary month of the seventh year in the Yongchu reign period [A.D. 113].

Martin Powers has associated this type of inscription with scholars and low-ranking officials from families of "middle to lower-middle income."[31] But in my opinion, the authors may have been commoners with little Classical education. The inscription on the Dai family shrine differs markedly from that written by the Marquis of Beixiang or by the brothers of Gentleman Lu. The deceased is not identified as a Confucian scholar, nor are the donors listed with official titles. A slightly later shrine was constructed in A.D. 137 by four brothers and sisters of a Yang family long after their parents' death (Fig. 4.11). They explained the reason

记录了赞助人父母的姓名和卒年，右边的文字则介绍了赞助人，并提供了所花钱财的详细数目：

> 戴□孔道建石宣（室？）五千，郭苞（疑指有雕刻的石室顶部）二千五百五，戴□、戴□、伍著承超、阳勋蒴卿、张年并九千五百，以永初七年（113）闰月十八日始立成。

包华石认为这类题记与出身于“中等和低等收入”家庭的文人和低级官吏有关。[31] 但我认为，戴氏祠堂题记的作者可能是没有受过多少教育的一般平民。与北乡侯、路公兄弟的题记明显不同，戴氏祠堂所纪念的死者不是一位儒家文人，赞助人也没有任何官衔。比这个祠堂年代略晚的一例，是公元 137 年泱氏兄弟姐妹四人为其已故多年的父母所建造的祠堂［图 4.11］。在题记中，他们解释了

for this delay: "As now we the brothers and sisters have accumulated sufficient money, we long for our parents and are full of sorrow; we upgraded their tombs and built a small offering hall. . . . The shrine cost 10,000 cash."[32] Their words remind us of Huan Kuan's statement: "Even the commoners emulate [the prevailing filial practices] to the extent that they sell their houses and property to do it." It is understandable that for the less well off the best means of demonstrating filial piety was the money they earned, saved, and finally spent to erect a funerary monument. The elaborate verbal displays of "grief" and "solemnity" may have been reserved for members of the elite such as the Marquis of Beixiang.

The inscription of the Marquis of Beixiang and that on the Dai family shrine, therefore, typify two kinds of funerary texts of the early second century; their differences may have been related to the differing social status and financial condition of the donors. These two literary modes, however, were soon integrated. Writers of shrine inscriptions from the mid-second century tried to employ every available means to stress their filial devotion. The result was the standardization as well as the inflation of texts. An inscription before this time rarely exceeded 50 characters, but the Xiang Tajun inscription of A.D. 154 (Fig. 4.12) consists of some 400 characters; the An Guo inscription of A.D. 157 has 490 characters (Fig. 4.6). Some sentences and phrases such as "transporting soil on one's back to build a tomb" and "planting pines and junipers in rows in a graveyard"
200 became formulas for expressing filial practices. A latecomer, however, always had the advantage of being able to synthesize new formulas. As a traditional Chinese proverb puts it, "When the river rises, the boat goes up"; filial piety had to be measured against the going rate. Thus as shrine inscriptions became inflated, the amount of money spent on a mortuary monument also increased. In 137 the descendents of the Yang family may have been proud of themselves for saving 10,000 cash to build their parents' shrine. But twenty years later, Xiang Tajun's brothers and

An Guo's brothers (both from ordinary families) had to donate 25,000 and 27,000 cash, respectively, to prove their sincerity. Rich families, understandably, had to spend even more: a pillar-gate erected in 147 by the four Wu brothers from a Shandong gentry family cost 190,000 cash (Fig. 4.13). In 182 Kong Dan, chancellor of a principality, enlarged his grandmother's cemetery and added a new offering shrine. Interestingly, we learn of this last instance not from an inscription on the shrine but from

他们延期修建祠堂的原因："昆弟男女四人，少□□□，复失慈母。父……时□有钱□自足，思念父母。弟兄悲哀，乃治冢作小食堂，传子孙……"[32] 虽然残缺，这些文字使我们回想起桓宽的评论："故黎民相慕效，至于发屋卖业。"不难理解，对于这些并不富裕的人们来说，表达孝行的最直接的方式就是，写明他们所积攒并最后用于建立丧葬纪念性建筑的钱数。"哀""严"之类的文雅辞藻只能出自像北乡侯那样的精英人物。

因此，北乡侯题记和戴氏祠堂题记代表了 2 世纪早期的两类丧葬文字，它们之间的差别与赞助人不同的社会身份和经济状况有关。但是，这两类文字不久就融合起来了。2 世纪中叶祠堂题记的作者，试图利用任何可能的手段来强调他们的孝行，其结果是产生了一种夸张的标准化的言辞。在此之前的祠堂题记很少超过 50 字，但是公元 154 年的芗他君祠堂题记长约 400 字［图 4.12］，公元 157 年的安国祠堂题记有 490 字［图 4.6］。有些语句如"负土成坟""徐养淩柏"成为表现孝行的套话；而后出的题记总是在综合新的格套方面更有优势。正如俗语所说的"水涨船高"，行孝的尺度也必须随着建造祠堂花费的增加而提升。这样，随着题记文辞不断的夸张，花在丧葬建筑上的钱的数目也日益增长。在公元 137 年，杨家的后人可以夸耀他们积攒了一万钱为父母建造祠堂，但是 20 年后，芗他君和安国的兄弟（均属一般家庭）就必须分别花上两万五千钱和两万七千钱来证明他们的诚心。富裕家庭的花费一定更多。一个例子是在 147 年，山东嘉祥大族武氏的四位兄弟花了十九万钱为已故的母亲建造了一对石阙［图 4.13］。梁相孔耽于 182 年扩建其祖母的墓地并增修了一座祠堂。有意思的是，我们并不是

Fig. 4.12. Carving and inscription on Xiang Tajun's shrine. A.D. 154. H. 120 cm. Found in 1934 at Dong'e, Shandong province. Palace Museum, Beijing.

图 4.12 芗他君祠堂画像与题记。东汉晚期，154 年。高 120 厘米。1934 年山东东阿出土。故宫博物院藏。拓片。

Fig. 4.13. Carvings and inscription on the Wu family pillar-gate. A.D. 147. Jiaxiang, Shandong province.

图 4.13 武氏阙画像与题记。东汉晚期，147 年。山东嘉祥。拓片。

the commemorative text on Kong Dan's own memorial stela (Fig. 4.14). This text, in fact Kong Dan's biography, recounts his outstanding filial practices in familiar sentences: "When he had managed his family estate to some extent, he longed for his grandmother and was engaged in building funerary structures to her memory. . . . He enlarged his ancestress's tomb, erected an offering hall, and increased the soil for planting juniper trees. His filial piety is indeed genuine."[33] The same text also records that the funerary structures Kong Dan built for himself cost 300,000 cash.

It would be misleading to conclude that all Eastern Han funerary monuments were motivated purely by their patrons' desires for fame and practical gain. Nevertheless, in an age when the rhetoric of filial piety was so prevalent, it is indeed difficult to distinguish genuine expressions of grief from fake and exaggerated ones. This is perhaps why the only truly moving funerary inscription to survive from this period is a eulogy dedicated to a child by his parents, which I discuss in the following section. Since filial piety was by nature an obligation of the young toward the old, it seems that only when this order was reversed could funerary
201 devotion free itself from the conventional rhetoric and gain a measure of authenticity. But as we will see, even in such cases, parents' "private love" toward their children still had to be cast in the light of "public duty."

从祠堂题记中，而是从孔耽本人墓碑上的纪念性文字中知道这最后的一个例子的［图 4.14］。这段文字——实际上是孔耽的传记——以我们所熟悉的套语罗列了他不凡的孝行："治产小有，追念祖母，故舞魂构……闿郭藏，造作堂宇，增土种柏，孝心达寳。"[33] 碑文提供的另一信息是，孔耽花了三十万钱为自己修造丧葬修筑。

当然，不可能所有的东汉丧葬建筑都是受赞助人追逐名利的热情所激发而建造的。但是，在一个风行以浮华言语粉饰孝行的时代，也确实难以将发自内心的哀痛与伪饰虚夸的感情区分开来。所以，2 世纪真正动人的一则丧葬题记，是一对父母悼念他们夭折的孩子的诔文，这也是我在下一节中将要讨论的内容。从本质上说，

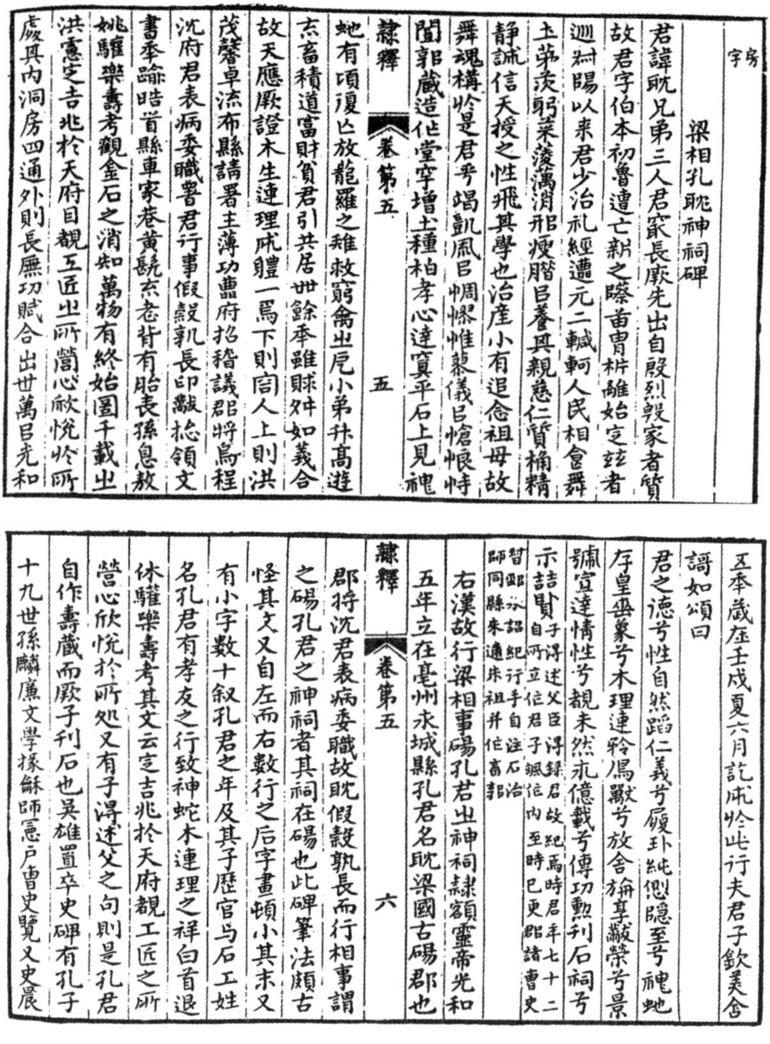

字房

梁相孔耽神祠碑

君諱耽兄弟三人君㝡長厥先出自殷烈殷家者質

故君字伯本初魯遭亡新之際苗胄析離始定玆者

廼紂賜以來君少治禮經遭元二轗軻人民相食舞

玉弟泼躬菜蔆滿消形瘦腊已養其親慈仁質榆精

靜誠信天授之性飛其學也治產小有退念祖母故

舞魂構於是君乃竭䘏凰吕惆悵帷幕儀吕愴悢恃

閭郭葳造作堂宇增土種柏孝心達寘平石上見䰟

隸釋 卷第五 五

虵有頃復亾放龍羅之難救窮禽出凥小弟升高遊

太畜積道富財貨君引共居卅餘年雖䝼舛如義合

故天應厥證木生連理戚體一焉下則冝人上則洪

茂馨卓流布縣請署主簿功曹府招稽議郡將烏程

沈府君表病委職署君行事假穀乳長印紱捻領文

書季踰晧首縣車家巷黃髮太耇皆有貽表孫息敖

姚驩樂壽考覩金石之消知萬物有終始圖千載出

洪惪定吉兆於天府目覩工匠出所嘗心欣悅於所

處其內洞房四通外則長廡功賦合出世萬已光和

五季歲在壬戌夏六月訖成於此行夫君子欽美舍

譌如頌曰

君之德兮性自然蹈仁義兮履玤純偲隱至兮䰟虵

存皇盎象兮木理連矜偶獻兮放舍旃享藏榮兮景

鵬宣達情性兮覩未然永億載兮傳功勲刊石祠兮

示詁賢 子孫得述父臣得錄君故紀焉時君年七十二 所立佐君子颯佐內至時已更郡諸曹史

習鄙郡功曹紀行手自注石治 師同縣朱通朱祖并佐高邦

右漢故行梁相事碭孔君出神祠隸額靈帝光和

五年立在亳州永城縣孔君名耽梁國古碭郡也

隸釋 卷第五 六

郡將沈君表病委職故耽假穀孰長而行相事謂

之碭孔君之神祠者其祠在碭也此碑筆法頗古

怪其文又自左而右數行之后字畫頓小其末又

有小字數十叙孔君之年及其子歷官与石工姓

名孔君有孝友之行致神蛇木連理之祥白首退

休驩樂壽考其文云定吉兆於天府覩工匠之所

營心欣悅於所処又有子得述父之句則是孔君

自作壽藏而厥子刊石也吳雄置卒史碑有孔子

十九世孫麟廉文學掾龢師悳戶曹史覽又史晨

Fig. 4.14. Hong Shi's record of the memorial inscription dedicated to Kong Dan (d. A.D. 182)

图 4.14 洪适著录的孔耽（卒于 182）碑碑文

“孝”表达的是幼者对长者的感情和责任。因此，似乎只有当这种秩序被颠倒，对死者的感情才能从套话的辞藻中解放出来，获得真实的价值。但是，正如我们将要看到，即使在这种情况下，父母对孩子的“私爱”仍然必须以“公义”的名义出现。

❷ The Family (2)

A child who died in A.D. 170 is portrayed on a stone relief, originally part of an offering shrine but reused in a later tomb (Fig. 4.15a).[34] The picture is divided into two registers; the child appears on the upper frieze, sitting on a dais in a dignified manner, and his name, Xu Aqu, is inscribed beside him. Three chubby boys are walking or running toward him; clad only in diapers, their tender age is also indicated by their *zongjiao* hairstyle: two round tufts protrude above their heads. Releasing a bird or pulling and driving a large turtledove, they seem to be amusing their young master. The theme of entertainment is continued on the lower register on a grander scale: two musicians are playing a *qin* zither and a windpipe; their music accompanies the performance of a male juggler and a female dancer. With her sleeves swirling, the dancer is jumping on top of large and small disc-drums, beating out varying rhythms with her steps.[35]

A eulogy in the Han poetic style called a *zan* is inscribed beside the relief (Fig. 4.15b).

> It is the Jianning era of the Han,
> The third year since our emperor
> [i.e., Emperor Ling] ascended the throne.
> In the third month of *wuwu*,
> On the fifteenth day of *jiayin*,
> We are expressing our grief and sorrow
> For Xu Aqu, our son.
>
> You were only five years old
> When you abandoned the glory of the living.
> You entered an endless night,
> Never to see the sun and stars again.
> Your spirit wanders alone
> In eternal darkness underground.
> You have left your home forever;

How can we still hope to glimpse your dear face?

Longing for you with all our hearts, 202
We came to pay an audience to our ancestors;
Three times we increased offerings and incense,
Mourning for our deceased kin.
But you did not even recognize your ancestors,
Only running east and west, crying and weeping.

二、家庭（二）

在南阳市东关李相公庄出土的一块画像石上，刻画了一位死于东汉建宁三年（170）的儿童的形象。这块石头原为一祠堂构件，后用于一座年代较晚的墓葬中［图 4.15a］。[34] 画面分为上下两栏，这位儿童出现在上栏，坐于榻上，显示出高贵的主人身份，其姓名“许阿瞿”刻于右侧。三名圆脸男孩或走或跑，来到许阿瞿跟前。三人皆穿兜肚，头上两个圆形的发髻应为“总角”，其服饰和发型具有明显的年龄特征。这三名儿童在主人面前戏耍娱乐，其一放出一鸟，随后一人牵鹅或鸠，第三人在后面驱赶。下栏中描绘一规模更大的乐舞场面，其中两乐师演奏琴与箫，一男性杂技师与一舞女和乐表演。舞女长袖翩跹，跳跃在大小不同的盘鼓上，击奏出高低不同的节拍。[35]

画像一侧是一段以赞体风格写成的诔文［图 4.15b］：

惟汉建宁，号政三年，
三月戊午，甲寅中旬。
痛哉可哀，许阿瞿身。
年甫五岁，去离世荣。
遂就长夜，不见日星。
神灵独处，下归窈冥。
永与家绝，岂复望颜？
谒见先祖，念子营营。
三增仗火，皆往吊亲。
瞿不识之，啼泣东西。

a

b

Fig. 4.15. (a) Carving and inscription on Xu Aqu's shrine. A.D. 170. Excavated in 1973 near Nanyang, Henan province. Nanyang Museum. (b) Inscription.

图 4.15 （a）许阿瞿祠堂画像与题记。东汉晚期，170 年。1973 年河南南阳附近出土。南阳市博物馆藏。（b）题记。拓片。

Finally you vanished with them,
While still turning back from time to time.

Deeply moved, we your father and mother. . . [inscription damaged]
To us all delicacies have become tasteless.
Wan and sallow,
We are exhausting our savings [to build your shrine and to make offerings],
Hoping your spirit will last forever
. . . . [inscription damaged]

You, the visitors,
When you come here and see dust on this grave,
Please sweep it without delay.
Your kindness will make the deceased happy.

This carving occupies a special position in Han art. Whereas most figurative images engraved on funerary monuments are part of illustrations of didactic stories from historical texts, this is a portrait of a real, contemporary child.[36] The parents of Xu Aqu ordered the carving made to express their grief, and in the eulogy they spoke directly to

久乃随逐（逝），当时复迁。

父之与母，感□□□。
父之与母，□王五月，
不□晚甘。羸劣瘦□。
投财连（联）篇（翩），冀子长哉。
□□□□。

□□□此，□□土尘，
立起□扫，以快往人。

这一画像在汉代艺术中有着特殊的地位。汉代丧葬建筑中大部分的人物画像出自历史文献中的说教性故事，但这一画像却是当时一位真实的儿童的“肖像”。[36] 许阿瞿的父母订做了该画像以表达

their son who tragically died so young. This eulogy, which assumes the parents' point of view, may be read together with a poem in a Han *yuefu* collection, in which an orphan appeals to his departed father and mother:

> To be an orphan,
> To be fated to be an orphan,
> How bitter is this lot!
> When my father and mother were alive
> I used to ride in a carriage
> With four fine horses.
> But when they both died,
> My brother and my sister-in-law
> Sent me out to be a merchant.
> . . .
> 203 I didn't get back till night-fall,
> My hands were all sore
> And I had no shoes.
> I walked the cold earth
> Treading on thorns and brambles.
> As I stopped to pull out the thorns,
> How bitter my heart was!
> My tears fell and fell
> And I went on sobbing and sobbing.
> In winter I have no great-coat;
> Nor in summer thin clothes.
> It is no pleasure to be alive.
> I had rather quickly leave the earth
> And go beneath the Yellow Springs.
> . . .
> I want to write a letter and send it
> To my mother and father under the earth,
> And tell them I can't go on any longer

Living with my brother and sister-in-law.[37]

In a broader sense, both poems—the Xu Aqu eulogy and the *yuefu* poem (which must have been written by an adult in imitation of a child's voice)—express a kind of intimate love and consequent fear: a child who had lost his parents' protection was extremely vulnerable. In the underground world, he (or his soul) would be surrounded by dangerous ghosts and spirits; in the human world he would be subject to ill-treatment and cruelty, especially from relatives with no direct blood relationship with him who were entitled to control his life. He would be

丧子的悲痛，诔文将这种悲痛用父母的口吻直接诉说给他们的儿子。传世的一首汉代乐府则是一名孤儿对已故父母的倾诉，可以与诔文对读：

孤儿生，孤子遇生，命当独苦！
父母在时，乘坚车，驾驷马。
父母已去，兄嫂令我行贾。
……
使我朝行汲，暮得水来归。
手为错，足下无菲。
怆怆履霜，中多蒺藜。
拔断蒺藜，肠中肉怆欲悲。
泪下渫渫，清涕累累。
冬无複襦，夏无单衣。
居生不乐，不如早去，下从地下黄泉。
……
愿与寄尺书，将与地下父母，兄嫂难与久居。[37]

从广义上讲，许阿瞿诔文与这首乐府（应是一位成年人模仿孩子的口气写成）都表达了一种对孩子的爱怜和由此而生的恐惧。一个失去父母保护的孩子，变得极易受到伤害。处于阴间，他（或他的灵魂）会被危险的鬼怪与精灵包围；身在人世，他会成为被虐待的对象。后者中，那些委托给没有直接血缘关系的亲属照顾的孩子

helpless and lonely, with neither the strength nor the ability to defend himself.

Such anxiety about the security of one's children, specifically one's male children, seems to have heightened during Han times (similar expressions are rare in pre-Han art and literature). We may attribute this psychological crisis to China's transformation into a family-oriented society. Textual and archaeological evidence reveals that the basic social unit increasingly became small "nuclear families" consisting of a married couple and their unmarried children.[38] Encouraged by the Qin and Western Han governments, this type of family soon became prevalent throughout
204 the newly united country.[39] Although the official policy was somewhat modified in the Eastern Han and the "extended family" was promoted as an ideal model, the result was a more integrated residential pattern, not the elimination of the "nuclear family" as the essential social element.[40] In fact, tension between individual families within a large household even increased; numerous instances of family struggles over property are reported in Eastern Han historical documents and reflected in art and literature.

From this social reality emerged the belief that the only reliable bond was that between parents and children; all other kin and non-kin relationships had to be treated with suspicion. But the problem was that the parent-child tie was inevitably challenged and conditioned by death. When a child died young, his soul would enter eternal darkness; to protect and nourish him, his parents had to rely on religious means. Thus Xu Aqu's father and mother constructed an offering shrine for their son and entrusted him to the family's ancestors. When parents were about to die, however, the problem would become far more serious and practical: Who would take care of their orphan in this dangerous world? The answer was not easy: they had to entrust their children to certain "agents," not ancestral spirits but living persons—a stepmother, relatives, friends, or servants—but were these agents dependable and trustworthy? As a solution to the problem, the responsibility of these agents to the orphan had to be cast as a serious "duty," and parents had to find some methods to keep reminding them of this duty. Not coincidentally, such concerns became an important theme in the decoration of a funerary monument: numerous pictures focus on the fate of the orphan, but unlike the Xu Aqu

将面临更大的威胁，他的生活会更加孤苦无助。

在汉代，人们对其子女安全的这种疑虑变得愈加强烈，尤其是对男性孤儿来说更是如此。汉代以前的艺术与文学中则很少见到类似的情况。我们可以认为，托孤于他人时的这种心理危机是中国社会向家庭结构转变时的一种共生现象。文献与考古学的资料表明，在这一时期，基本的社会单位变成数量迅速增长的小型“核心家庭”，这种家庭一般由一对夫妇和未婚子女组成。[38] 在秦与西汉政府的鼓励下，这种家庭类型不久就在刚刚统一的帝国中流行开来。[39] 尽管东汉时期官方的法规从某种意义上讲已比较宽松，“扩大家庭”也被当作理想的样板加以提倡，但其结果是形成了一种综合性的居民形态，核心家庭作为社会的基本单位并没有被废除。[40] 实际上，东汉的历史文献和文学作品记载了许多家庭成员为财产而争斗的事例，反映了大家庭内小家庭之间冲突的增长。

这一社会现实导致一种信念，即只有父母与亲子之间的关系才是牢固的，其他所有亲属和非亲属关系相对而言都靠不住。但问题是，父母与子女的关系也免不了会受到死亡的挑战和制约。当孩子夭亡了，他的灵魂将进入无尽的黑暗中，父母不得不借助宗教手段加以呵护。所以许阿瞿的父母为他们的亡子建立了祠堂，并把他委托给祖先来照顾。但当父母将要亡故，问题就会变得更为严重和实际：在这危机四伏的世界上，谁来照顾他们的孤儿？答案并不简单：一方面，父母不得不将他们的孩子托付给某一位特定的“代理人”，这位代理人不是祖先的亡灵，而是一位活着的人——继母、亲戚、朋友，或是仆人；但另一方面，这些代理人是不是那么地可靠和值得信任？解决这一矛盾的一个途径，是将监护人对孤儿的责任说成是一种严肃的社会“义务”，父母必须利用某种方式时时提醒他们这种义务的存在。并非巧合的是，这种努力成为丧葬建筑装饰中一个重要的主题。许多汉代画像表现了孤儿的命运，但与许阿瞿肖像

carving the emphasis of these pictures is on "public duty," not "private love."[41]

The hardship faced by the orphan described in the *yuefu* poem quoted earlier is reiterated in the story of Min Sun (style name Ziqian; Figs. 4.16a-c). The original tale is recorded in various versions of the *Biographies of Filial Sons* (*Xiaozi zhuan*). After Sun's mother died, his father remarried a woman who treated Sun with cruelty:

> Sun's winter clothes were all filled with reed catkins, but his stepmother's own son wore clothes filled with thick cotton. Sun's father asked him to drive. The winter day was cold, and Sun dropped the horsewhip. When the stepmother's son drove, he managed everything well. The father was angry and interrogated him, but Sun kept silent. Then his father looked at the two sons' clothing and understood the reason.[42]

Even worse, it was thought that once in a stepmother's evil clutches an orphan's life could be in great danger, especially once the child's father had also died. Such a calamity is the subject of pictures illustrating the story of Jiang Zhangxun.

> Jiang Zhangxun had the style name Yuanqing. He lived with his stepmother. . . who was an immoral woman and hated him. Zhangxun was aware of this and went to his father's tomb yard, where he built a thatched shack and planted many pine trees. The trees grew luxuriantly, and local people often rested in their shade. Even travelers stopped there to relax. Because of this his stepmother hated him even more. She put poison into wine that Zhangxun drank, but he did not die. She then attempted to kill Zhangxun with a knife at night, but Zhangxun was roused suddenly from sleep and again did not die. His stepmother then sighed, saying: "He must be protected by Heaven. It was a crime to intend to kill him."[43]

The underlying theme of both picture-stories was summarized by the sixth-century scholar Yan Zhitui in his famous *Family Instructions for the Yan Clan* (*Yanshi jiaxun*): "The second wife is certain to maltreat the son of the previous wife."[44] Ironically, in both stories an orphan's unconditioned obedience and submission to cruelty finally saved him. (Min Sun's obedience won back his father's love, and Jiang Zhangxun's piety moved and reformed his immoral stepmother.) The juxtaposition between a son and a stepmother highlights an important feature of Han didactic art: a human relationship, which by definition includes at least

不同的是，这些画像所强调的是"公义"而非"私爱"。[41]

闵损（字子骞）的故事重复了前文所引乐府诗中孤儿所面对的困境［图 4.16］。这个故事见于多种版本的《孝子传》，主要的一个情节是闵损在母亲去世后所遭到的继母的虐待：

> 损衣皆藁台木为絮，其子则绵纩重厚。父使损御，冬寒失后母辔。后母子御则不然。父怒诘之，损默然而已。后视二子衣，乃知其故。[42]

当孩子的父亲也去世后，继母会进一步威胁到孤儿的安危，这种危险是蒋章训故事的主题：

> 蒋章训，字元卿。与后母居，……后母无道，恒训为憎。训悉之，父墓边造草舍居。多栽松柏，其荫茂盛，乡里之人为休息，往还车马亦为息所。于是后母嫉妒甚于前时。以毒入酒，将来令饮。训饮不死。或夜持刀欲煞训，惊，不害。如之数度，遂不得害。爰后母叹曰："是有（天）护，吾欲加害，此吾过也。"[43]

这两例图画故事中所蕴含的主题，可以用 6 世纪学者颜之推所著《颜氏家训》中的一句话来概括："假继惨虐孤遗。"[44] 但具有反讽意味的是，在这两个故事中，正是由于孤儿对于恶行无条件的顺从屈服，才最终使自己得以解救。（闵损的屈从赢回了父爱，蒋章训的纯孝最终感动并改变了邪恶的继母。）这种解决方式引导我们注意到汉代说教艺术的一个重要特征：既然任何人际关系都必须由两个

Fig. 4.16. Story of Min Sun. (a, b) Wu Liang Shrine carving. A.D. 151. Jiaxiang, Shandong province. Ink rubbing and reconstruction. (c) Line engraving. Eastern Han. 2nd century A.D.

图 4.16 闵损故事。(a，b)武梁祠画像。东汉晚期，151 年。山东嘉祥。拓片与木版复制品。(c)线刻。东汉晚期，2 世纪。

two parties, must be approached from both angles; correspondingly, these pictorial stories provide alternative solutions to a given problem. (For example, many narratives and their illustrations on Han monuments propagate the virtue of ministers and assassins who carry out their masters' orders; other stories and illustrations emphasize rulers who pay respect to their subjects.)[45] In the case of an orphan, the potential destruction might be avoided through the child's own and often extremely painful effort; on the other hand, wouldn't it be far better if a stepmother were exceptionally virtuous and able to fulfill her assigned duty? Instead of being a destructive force, an ideal stepmother was supposed to protect the orphan, even at the cost of sacrificing her own son. In such a case she would be admired as an "exemplary woman," and her illustrated biography would be presented on mortuary monuments to the public. 205

One such example is the Righteous Stepmother of Qi (Qi yijimu; Figs. 4.17a, b). In the picture, a murdered man lies on the ground; an official on horseback has come to arrest the criminal, and the woman's two sons, one kneeling beside the corpse and the other standing behind it, are both

以上的社会个体组成，那么这种关系也必须从两个角度去看待。因此，汉代的绘画故事往往从多个视角阐述同一问题，提出多种处理办法。（例如，许多叙事性的文字和汉代建筑中与之相关的画面，宣扬了忠臣和不辱使命的刺客的义举，其他故事和图画则突出了明君礼贤下士的美德。）[45] 对于一个孤儿来说，他可能通过自己异乎寻常的痛苦努力来摆脱困境；但是从另一方面看，如果继母能够行善并履行辅助孤儿的义务岂不更好？这种理想的继母不再是害人的恶婆，而是一位努力去保护孤儿的慈母，有时为此目的她们甚至不惜牺牲自己的孩子。在这种情况下，继母就会被誉为“列女”，其事迹被以图画的形式描绘在纪念性丧葬建筑上向公众展示。

齐义继母的故事便是这样一个例子［图 4.17］。在画像中，一个被杀的人躺在地上，一位官吏来捉拿杀人罪犯。而这位妇人的两个儿子一个跪在尸体旁，另一个站在后面，都主动承认自己是凶手。

a

b

Fig. 4.17. Story of the Righteous Stepmother of Qi. Wu Liang Shrine carving. (a) Ink rubbing. (b) Reconstruction.

图 4.17 齐义继母故事。武梁祠画像。东汉晚期，151 年。（a）拓片。（b）木版复制品。

confessing to the murder. According to the story recorded in the *Biographies of Exemplary Women* (*Lienü zhuan*), the official could not decide which brother to arrest; the mother (portrayed in the picture at far left) was finally required to make the decision and surrender one of her sons.

> The mother wept sadly and replied: "Kill the younger one!" The minister heard her reply and asked: "The youngest son is usually the most beloved, but now you want him killed. Why is that?" The mother replied: "The younger son is my own; the older son is the previous wife's son. When his father took ill and lay dying, he ordered me raise him well and look after him, and I said, 'I promise.' Now, when you receive a trust from someone and you have accepted it with a promise, how can you forget such trust and be untrue to that promise? Moreover, to kill the older brother and let the younger brother live would be to cast aside a public duty for a private love; to make false one's words and to forget loyalty are to cheat the dead. If words are meaningless and promises are not distinguished [from non-promises], how can I dwell on this earth? Although I love my son, how shall I speak of righteousness?" Her tears fell, bedewing her robe, and the minister related her words to the king.[46]

据《列女传》记载，这位官吏无法决定逮捕兄弟中的哪一人，便要求该画面最左端的母亲做出判定，交出她的一个儿子。

> 其母泣而对曰："杀其少者。"相受其言，因而问之曰："夫少子者，人之所爱也。今欲杀之，何也？"其母对曰："少者，妾之子也；长者，前妻之子也。其父疾，且死之时，属之于妾曰：'善养视之。'妾曰：'诺。'今既受人之托，许人以诺，岂可以忘人之托，而不信其诺耶？且杀兄活弟，是以私爱废公义也；背言忘信，是欺死者也。夫言不约束，已诺不分，何以居于世哉？子虽痛乎，独谓行何？"泣下沾襟。相入言于王。[46]

Here we find the opposition between “private love” (*si ai*) and “public
206 duty” (*gong yi*): the stepmother was praised for her fulfillment of her “duty”—loyalty and righteousness—and she was given the honorific title “yi” (righteous). But in order to achieve this, she had to be ready to give up her own “love.” She was forced to choose one or the other, and her own example clearly indicated which was the right way.

In this sense a stepmother, though called a “mother,” was here not so different from an orphan’s relatives or even servants, whose responsibility toward an orphan, as we find in carvings on Han funerary monuments, also fell into the category of “public duty.” Two pictures illustrate such righteous relatives, one the Public-Spirited Aunt of Lu (Lu yiguzi) and the other the Virtuous Aunt of Liang (Liang jieguzi).[47] It is said that the Public-Spirited Aunt met an enemy when she and two boys were working in the fields. Being pursued by cavalrymen, she dropped one child while escaping with the other (Figs. 4.18a, b). When she was finally caught, the commander found out that the child she had cast aside was her own and the other was the son of her brother. The commander inquired:

> “A mother always loves her son, and her love is deep in her heart. Today, you put him from you and carried the son of your brother. How is that?”
>
> “To save my own son is a work of private love, but to save my brother’s child is a public duty. Now, if I had turned my back on a public duty and pursued my private love, and if I had abandoned my brother’s child to die to save my own child, even if by good fortune I should have escaped, still my sovereign would not tolerate me; the officials would not support me; and my compatriots would not live with me. If that were the case, then I should have no place to harbor my body and no ground for my tired feet to tread upon.”[48]

A new theme is introduced: not only did the aunt have to place “public duty” over her “private love,” but her sacrifice was based on a practical concern about her own livelihood. The lesson of the story appears to

mix both enticement and threat. Indeed, the unseen instructor of this lesson must have been the brother (or the social grouping the brother represented), who so successfully transplanted his own fear into his 208
relatives' hearts. We may condense his instructions into a simple form: those who failed to take care of his (orphaned) son would be held in

在这里，我们见到两个对立的概念——“私爱”与“公义”。齐义继母因为忠于她的“责任”而得到颂扬，并被誉以“义”名。但为了履行这种公共责任，她不得不牺牲掉自己的“私爱”。她必须选择其一，这一事例清楚地说明了什么是正确的选择。

从这种意义上说，一位继母虽被称作“母”，但实际上她与一位孤儿的关系和远亲，甚至和仆人相比，并没有多大的差别，因而她的责任心属于“公义”的范畴。我们在汉代丧葬建筑的雕刻中发现两幅画像描绘了具有这种高尚道德的亲属，其主人公一为鲁义姑姊，另一为梁节姑姊。[47] 前一个故事说，鲁义姑姊和两个男孩在田野中耕作时，遇上了敌军的骑兵。被敌兵所追，她无法带着两个孩子逃跑，只好抱起了一个男孩，而抛弃了另一个［图 4.18a，b］。当她最后被抓住时，敌军将领发现她所抛弃的竟是她自己的儿子。将领问曰：

> “子之与母，其亲爱也，痛甚于心，今释之，而反抱兄之子，何也？”
>
> “己之子，私爱也；兄之子，公义也。夫背公义而向私爱，亡兄子而存妾子，幸而得幸，则鲁君不吾畜，大夫不吾养，庶民国人不吾与也。夫如是，则胁肩无所容，而累足无所履也……”[48]

这里出现了一个新的主题：鲁义姑姊不仅把“公义”置于“私爱”之上，而且她的牺牲也基于对自身实实在在的关心。因此，这个故事的教义就显现出夹杂在其中的怂恿与胁迫。实际上，潜藏在这个教训背后不露面的训诫者，可能就是一位成功地将自己的忧虑转嫁到他的妹妹心中的兄长，或是他所代表的社会集团。我们可以将他的意图浓缩为一句话：不尽心抚养其（孤）子的人将受到天下

contempt by the whole world, whereas those who fulfilled "public duty" would not only live in peace but would be rewarded by the king. Thus, whereas one version of the picture story highlights the theme of sacrifice (Figs. 4.18a, b), another version represents its happy ending (Fig. 4.18c): two ministers come to present gold and silk to the Public-Spirited Aunt, and the woman kneels to thank them for the king's bounty. She is still holding her nephew in her arms, and her own son is jumping happily behind his glorious mother.

Fig. 4.18. Story of the Public-Spirited Aunt of Lu. (a, b) Wu Liang Shrine carving. Ink rubbing and reconstruction. (c) Carving on the Front Wu Family Shrine.

图 4.18 鲁义姑姊故事。(a,b)武梁祠画像。东汉晚期,151 年。拓片与木版复制品。(c)武氏祠前石室画像。东汉晚期，拓片。

The woman's frightened voice in this story becomes a scream in the tale of the Virtuous Aunt of Liang, another decorative motif of Eastern Han funerary monuments (Figs. 4.19a, b). The woman's house catches on fire with both her own son and her brother's son inside. She wants to rescue her nephew but in her haste she picks up her own son. In desperation she runs back into the fire and commits suicide. The following words are her final testament: "How can I tell every family in the state and let everyone know the truth?. . . I would like to cast my son into the fire, but this would violate a mother's love. In such a situation I cannot go on living." The official version of the story is concluded by the remark of a certain "Noble Gentleman" (*junzi*): "The Virtuous Aunt was pure and not debased. The *Book of Songs* says: 'That great gentleman would give his life rather than fail his lord.' This could be said of her."[49] In quoting the passage from the sacred Confucian text, the commentator compares the aunt's "public duty" toward her brother to that of a minister to his lord.

的蔑视，而履行此“公义”者不仅会生活安宁，而且会得到国君的奖赏。因此，上面谈到的表现这个故事的画面强调的是牺牲的主题［图 4.18a，b］，而描绘同一故事的另一个画面则表现了大团圆的结局［图 4.18c］：两位大臣前来向鲁义姑姊赏赐金帛，妇人跪谢国王的恩赐。她仍然怀抱着她的侄子以显示其“公义”，她自己的儿子则在这位光荣的母亲身后欢呼雀跃。

但鲁义姑姊恐惧的心声尚无法与梁节姑姊无助的悲鸣相比。后者是东汉丧葬画像中另一个故事的主角［图 4.19］。据说，当这位妇人家中失火时，她的儿子与侄子都在屋内，她试图救出她的侄子，却误将儿子救出。当发现这一错误后，她转身赴火，试图自杀。她的遗言是：“梁国岂可户告人晓也？……吾欲复投吾子，为失母之恩。吾势不可以生！”《列女传》对这一故事借用一“君子”之口加以总结：“君子谓节姑姊洁而不污。《诗》曰：‘彼其之子，舍命不渝。’此之谓也。”[49] 通过引证儒家经典，这位“君子”称赞姑姊对其兄的“公义”可以与臣对君的忠诚相提并论。

These illustrations seem to suggest that the selection of didactic stories for mortuary monuments reflected people's intense concerns about posthumous family affairs. These concerns included the chastity of widows and the relationship between family members, but the safety of their children was overwhelmingly important. It is misleading to simply attribute this concern to the selfishness of individuals. The Confucian sage Mencius had announced several hundred years earlier that "among the three sins of being unfilial, having no descendents is the greatest one,"[50] and filial piety, as explained in the *Classic of Filial Piety*, was the most fundamental virtue of humanity. If a person had no descendents, his family line was broken and his ancestors could no longer enjoy offerings. No disaster could be greater than this in a family-centered society.

As I explained earlier, a common method to express such concerns was to quote historical allusions from standard books. The analogues people drew did not necessarily (and could hardly completely) coincide with reality; hagiographic tales provided stereotypes, not real personages. A viewer of such pictures on a funerary monument was expected to discern the general parallels between himself or herself and a certain type. He or she would thus "identify" with this type and follow the moral lesson it embodied. In addition to virtuous stepmothers and relatives, another such type was the loyal servant. Understandably, a servant could play a considerable role in an orphan's life (and in fact some servants in a household were remote, poor relatives of the family).[51] The epitome of the loyal servant during the Han was a man named Li Shan, a veteran servant in the family of a certain Li Yuan. He saved his young master from other "evil servants" and helped him recover the family property.

> During the Jianwu era [A.D. 25-55], an epidemic broke out, and people in Yuan's family died one after the other. Only an orphan, who was named Xu and had been born only a few weeks earlier, survived. The family had property worth a million cash. The maids and a manservant plotted to murder Xu and then divide his property. Shan

was deeply sympathetic about the [bad fortune] of the Li family, but he could not control the situation singlehandedly. So he secretly carried Xu and fled, hiding in the territory of Xiaqiu in the Shanyang district. He nursed the child himself and fed him with raw cow's milk. He gave a dry place [to the child], while he himself stayed in a damp place. Although Xu was in his arms, he served the child as his elder master. Whenever something came up, he kneeled a long while before the child, reported on the matter, and then went to do it. The neighbors were inspired

这些画像可以支持这样一个论点：以这些说教性故事装饰丧葬建筑的做法，反映了当时人们对于死后家庭事务的强烈关心。这种关心包括遗孀的贞洁与家庭成员的和睦，但尚存人世的子女的安全是最为重要的一个主题。我们没有必要把这种对子孙的忧虑归因为纯粹个人的或自私的考虑。孟子已经说过："不孝有三，无后为大。"[50] 而《孝经》也将孝说成是人类最基本的品德。如果一个人没有子孙，其家庭的血脉就会中断，其祖先便无从得到祭祀。在一个以家庭为中心的社会中，还有比这更大的不幸吗？

如上文所述，表达对身后之事关心的共同方式，是从经典著作中援引一个可供比拟的道德故事。但所引故事并不一定（也很难完全）与所比拟的实际情况完全相合；这些理想化传记故事的目的，只是提供一些典型，而非描写真正的人物。通过发现自己与某种特定典型的大致平行，这类图画的观众将"认同"于这种典型，并遵循其体现的道德训诫。除了仁慈的继母及亲属以外，另一种典型是忠实的仆人。不难理解，在孤儿的生活中，一位仆人往往可以扮演举足轻重的角色（实际上，家仆常常是他为之服务的家庭的穷困远亲）。[51] 汉代忠仆的代表人物是李善。李善是李元家的一位老仆，他帮助年轻的主人从一群"恶奴"手中夺回了被剥夺的家财：

> 建武中疫疾，元家相继死没，惟孤儿续始生数旬，而赀财千万，诸奴婢私共计议，欲谋杀续，分其财产。善深伤李氏而力不能制，乃潜负续逃去，隐山阳瑕丘界中，亲自哺养，乳为生湩，推燥居湿，备尝艰勤。续虽在孩抱，奉之不异长君，有事辄长跪请白，然后行之。闾里感其行，

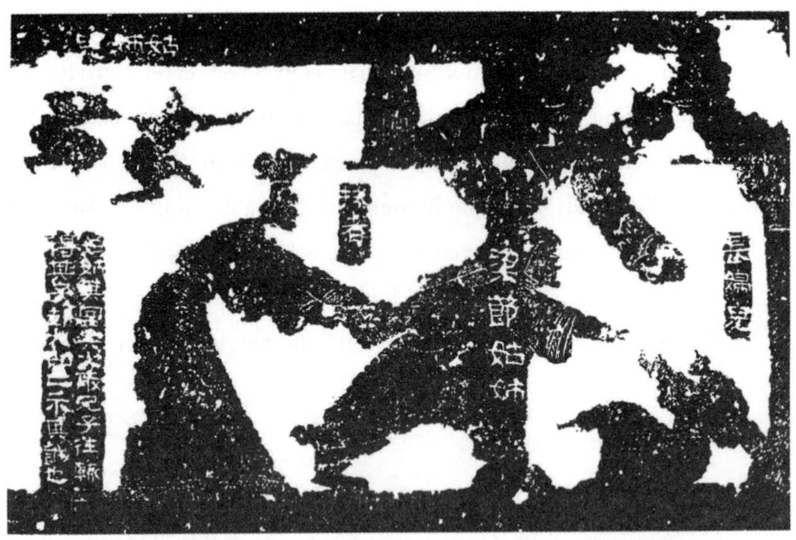

a

b

Fig. 4.19. Story of the Virtuous Aunt of Liang. Wu Liang Shrine carving. (a) Ink rubbing. (b) Reconstruction.

图 4.19 梁节姑姊故事。武梁祠画像。东汉晚期，151 年。（a）拓片。（b）木版复制品。

> by his behavior, and all started to cultivate righteousness. When Xu reached the age of ten, Shan returned to the county to rebuild the 209
> household. He brought a suit before the officials against the male and female servants, and all of them were arrested and put to death.[52]

This event must have created a sensation at the time: it was recorded in the chapter entitled "Distinctive Behavior" ("Duxing") in the Eastern Han official history, transformed into several folktale versions, and illustrated on funerary monuments. One of these illustrations is still extant. Its surviving portion shows an evil servant pulling the infant out of a basket (Fig. 4.20a). A nineteenth-century reproduction of the carving reconstructs the missing part (Fig. 4.20b): Li Shan kneels by the child and raises his arms in a gesture of reverence. This picture graphically highlights the opposition between the evil and the loyal servant, but the focus is still the orphan.

Although each of these stories has a happy ending, their depiction on funerary monuments reveals a deep suspicion toward the intended viewers of the pictures. The unspoken premise was that although "public duty" sounded glorious and might occasionally be carried out by relatives

> 皆相率修义。续年十岁，善与归本县，修理旧业。告奴婢于长吏，悉收杀之。[52]

这一事件在当时引起轰动，被记载在正史的“笃行”卷中，也见于有关当时风俗的其他几种文献，并且被刻画在丧葬建筑上。这些画像中有一幅幸存至今，画面残留的部分表现一名恶奴从一个筐子中拖拉那位婴儿［图 4.20a］。19 世纪的一个刻印本重构了残缺的部分，我们看到李善下跪拱手，一副恭敬的姿态［图 4.20b］。这一雕刻因此以图解的方式表现了两名奴仆的忠奸之别，但构图的焦点是在孤儿身上。

尽管这些故事都有圆满的结局，但是在丧葬建筑中刻画这类故事的做法本身反映出画像订购人对于画像观众的深深疑忌。其潜台词是：尽管“公义”听起来十分荣耀，而且也有可能被亲属奴仆履行，

or servants, it was preferable to rely on direct kin, primarily parents themselves, whenever possible. This understanding was formulated in A.D. 79 in an Eastern Han official document, the *Proceedings from the White Tiger Hall* (*Baihu tong*): the relationship between natural parents and children was considered one of the Three Bonds, but "paternal uncles, brothers, clan members, maternal uncles, teachers, and friends" were called the Six Strings (*liuji*): "The major relations are the Bonds, and the minor relations are the Strings."[53] Scholars have also proposed that during the Han, various kin relationships were classified into two distinct systems: the first was a linear patriline including the nine generations of a family from the great-great-grandfather to the great-great-grandson; the second included three indirect kin groups—paternal relatives, maternal relatives, and in-laws.[54] The last group was considered most distant and unreliable. The *Classic of Filial Piety* teaches that "the connecting link between serving one's father and serving one's mother is love."[55]
210 Correspondingly, the basic core in caring for one's children was also love, or in Mencius' words, "family feeling."[56]

Fig. 4.20. Story of Li Shan. Wu Liang Shrine carving. (a) Ink rubbing. (b) Reconstruction.

图 4.20 李善故事。武梁祠画像。东汉晚期，151 年。（a）拓片。（b）木版复制品。

The concept of "parents," however, is a generalization: a father and mother were from different families and, logically and practically, must have had divergent and even conflicting concerns. The old question about a child's security thus again surfaced, but this time posed by the father to the mother. More specifically, was a mother's love toward her (husband's) sons forever trustworthy? Had not many mothers in Chinese lore, from an empress to an ordinary housewife, betrayed their husband's family by bringing their own brothers and nephews (their own paternal relatives) to power? Such anxiety is reflected in a bitter letter by an Eastern Han gentleman named Feng Yan, in which he bitterly accused his wife of multiple crimes including having "destroyed the Way of a good family." It is interesting, however, that to Mr. Feng his personal tragedy was an

但如果可能，最好还是依靠直系的亲属，尤其是父母本人。这种思想在公元 79 年东汉官方文献《白虎通》中得到了系统的阐述。书中将父母与子女的关系作为主要社会关系的“三纲”之一，而“诸父、兄弟、族人、诸舅、师长、朋友”则被当作次要社会关系的“六纪”:“大者为纲，小者为纪”。[53] 有的学者指出，汉代各种亲属关系可以划分为两个系统，一是家族中从高祖父以降九代直线传承的父系，二是三种非直接的亲属集团，即父系的亲戚、母亲的亲戚及姻亲。[54] 最后一组被认为是最疏远和不可靠的。以孩子与双亲的关系而言，《孝经》云:“资于事父以事母，而爱同。”[55] 与之相应，父母对子女的关怀同样是基于爱，或如孟子所说的“亲爱”。[56]

但“双亲”的概念也是含混的，父亲和母亲来自不同的家庭，无论从逻辑还是实际讲，他们都可能有着不同的甚至是相悖的利害关系。因此孩子的安全这个老问题又浮现出来，不过这次是由父亲向母亲提出的。问题的关键是，一位母亲真的能永远令人信赖地爱她的（丈夫的）孩子吗？在历史记载中，从皇后到家庭主妇，将实权交给自己的兄弟或外甥（此等亲属都是她们自己娘家的人）而背叛其丈夫的例子难道不是屡见不鲜吗？东汉一位叫作冯衍的男子留下的一封信集中反映出这种不安。信中强烈谴责妻子的种种恶行，包括“家道崩坏”等等。但特别耐人寻味的是，在冯衍看来，他个人

example of a nightmare shared by all members of his sex: "Since antiquity it has always been considered a great disaster to have one's household dominated by a woman. Now this disaster has befallen me."[57]

To his contemporaries Feng's statement had a further implication, that a man's household, as well as his young children, would inevitably "be dominated by a woman" if his wife outlived him. Even worse, she could remarry and his children would be taken to another household. This worry must have had a solid basis: many passages in Han texts reveal that the parents of a widow would advise her or even force her to find another husband.[58] In these cases, the widow's paternal family relationship resurfaced and overpowered her marital relationship, which, in a sense, had been broken by the husband's death. To keep the widow in the husband's household to take care of *his* children, the time-honored rhetoric of "public duty" was again employed. In other words, her "private love" toward her children had to be reinterpreted as a "duty"—*xin* or "fidelity" to her deceased husband. Liang the Excellent, who destroyed her face to avoid the danger of remarrying, best exemplified this virtue of a widow (Figs. 4.21a, b). Remarking on her story translated below, the Noble Gentleman (*junzi*) says: "Liang was chaste, decorous, single-hearted, and pure. The *Book of Songs* states: 'You thought I had broken faith; I was true as the bright sun above.' This could be said of her."

> Gaoxing was a widow from the state of Liang. She was glorious in her beauty and praiseworthy in her conduct. Although her husband died, leaving her widowed early in life, she did not remarry. Many noblemen of Liang strove among themselves to marry her, but no one could win her. The King of Liang heard of this and sent his minister with betrothal gifts. Gaoxing said, "My husband unfortunately died early. I live in widowhood to raise his orphans, and [I am afraid that] I have not given them enough attention. Many honorable men have sought me, but I have fortunately succeeded in evading them. Today the king is seeking my hand. I have learned that the principle of a wife is that once having

gone forth to marry, she will not change over, and that she will keep all the rules of chastity and faithfulness. To forget the dead and to run to the living is not faithfulness; to be honored and forget the lowly is not chastity; and to abandon righteousness and follow gain is not worthy of a woman." Then she took up a mirror and knife, and cut off her nose, saying, "I have become a disfigured person. I did not commit suicide
because I could not bear to see my children orphaned a second time. 212
The king has sought me because of my beauty, but today, after having

的"不幸"不过是自古以来男子的共同经验："牝鸡司晨，唯家之索，古之大患，今始与衍。"[57]

对于和冯衍同时代的人来说，他的话有更深一层的含义，即当一个男人去世后，如果其妻子尚健在，那么他的家庭连同他的孩子不可避免地会遭遇"牝鸡司晨"。更糟糕的是，他的妻子可能会再嫁，把他的孩子带入另一个家庭。大量汉代文献记载，女子一旦寡居，她自己的父母常常会建议甚至强迫她再嫁。[58] 这一事实显然是造成丈夫们忧心的一个重要原因。在这种情况下，女子夫家的亲属关系因为丈夫的去世，在某种意义上说已经破裂，而女子娘家的亲戚就会站出来压服夫家的亲戚。为了保证遗孀留在夫家照顾他的孩子们，人们就搬出"公义"这个由来已久的辞藻。换言之，女子对其子女的"私爱"被重新诠释而成为其已故丈夫的"义"与"信"。寡妇梁高行为了避免再嫁的危险而自我毁容，就是这种品德的一个最好的例证［图 4.21］。《列女传》中说："君子谓高行节礼专精。《诗》云：'谓予不信，有如皎日。'此之谓也。"以下是对她事迹的记载：

> 高行者，梁之寡妇也。其为人荣于色而美于行。夫死早寡不嫁，梁贵人多争欲娶之者，不能得。梁王闻之，使相娉焉。高行曰："妾夫不幸早死，先狗马填沟壑。妾收养其幼孤，曾不得专意，贵人多求妾者，幸而得免。今王又重之。妾闻妇人之义，一往而不改，以全贞信之节。今忘死而趋生，是不信也；见贵而忘贱，是不贞也；弃义而从利，无以为人。"乃援镜持刃，以割其鼻，曰："妾已刑矣。所以不死者，不忍幼弱之重孤也。王之求妾者，以其色也，

Fig. 4.21. Story of Liang the Excellent. Wu Liang Shrine carving. (a) Ink rubbing. (b) Reconstruction.

图 4.21 梁高行故事。武梁祠画像。东汉晚期，151 年。(a) 拓片。(b) 木版复制品。

been disfigured, I may avoid the danger [of remarrying]." Thereupon, the minister made his report, and the king exalted her righteousness and praised her conduct. He exempted her from responsibility of labor or tax, and honored her with the title *Gaoxing*.[59]

Liang's statement that she must remain a widow to raise the orphans is reminiscent of the speech of the Righteous Stepmother of Qi, in which she likewise emphasizes the importance of keeping her "promise" to her deceased husband to raise his orphan. Indeed, once a wife had lost her husband, her conduct and morality were judged not on the grounds of her being a good mother but on the grounds of chastity and faithfulness. The difference between a widowed natural mother and a widowed stepmother thus largely disappeared: they both bore the liability of keeping their "promises" to their dead husband to bring up *his* son. In fact, a widowed mother was approached not that differently from relatives and servants, since the virtue they shared was classified as "loyalty." The Virtuous Aunt of Liang was praised for her faithfulness to her "lord," and Li Shan served the orphan "as his elder master." The moral presented to a widow was the same: "A loyal minister does not serve two lords, neither may a faithful widow marry a second husband."[60]

A widowed mother, however, differed from other guardian figures of an orphan: she was often forced to display some extreme proof of her fidelity such as self-disfigurement. Liang's example is not necessarily fictional; similar instances can be found in historical accounts.[61] Usually,

今刑余之人，殆可释矣。"于是相以报，王大其义，高其行，乃复其身，尊其号曰高行。[59]

梁高行声言要守寡养孤，齐义继母表明要信守对丈夫的"诺言"，抚养丈夫的遗孤，二人的言语十分相似。实际上，妻子一旦失去丈夫，评判其德行的标准就不再是她是否是一位良母，而要看她是否忠贞。因此，寡母与寡居的继母之间的差别就基本消失了，她们都要信守对亡夫的"诺言"，担当起将丈夫的孩子抚育成人的责任。事实上，寡母甚至与亲戚或仆人也没有很大的差别，他们共同具备的德行都能够用"忠"字一言以蔽之。我们已经谈到，梁节姑姊忠于她的兄长，将他视为"主人"，李善效忠于幼孤，"不异长君"。这些义举与寡妇对其亡夫的忠诚是一致的，即所谓"一仆不事二主，一女不嫁二夫"。[60]

然而，要证明自己的忠诚，一位寡妇与其他的道德卫护者相比又有不同，她往往必须做出一些如自残之类的超常之举，来显示其品德。梁高行的事迹不是刻意的虚构，在历史上可以找到许多相似的事例。[61]

the women who disfigured themselves (by cutting off their hair, ears, fingers, or noses) were widowed mothers being forced into remarriage by their parents or paternal relatives. Three such model widows named Peng Fei, Wang He, and Li Jin'e are presented in a single paragraph in the *Records of the Huayang Kingdom* (*Huayangguo zhi*), which ends with the sentence: "They all brought up their sons and fulfilled their public duty."[62]

Such behavior must be understood as a kind of symbolic self-immolation. Incidents of widows' suicide were not uncommon during the Han,[63] but, as Liang testified, she did not commit suicide because she had to care for her husband's children. Her self-execution had to be performed symbolically, since in actuality she had to remain functional as a mother. Women's self-disfigurement becomes even more alarming if we re-read Feng Yan's letter, in which he blamed his wife not only for her scandalous behavior but also for her slovenliness and lack of female refinement. But beauty or even a normal appearance would have become useless and even dangerous after the husband's death. By removing such useless and dangerous features, the widow became more "trustworthy" and "safe." (So Liang the Excellent said: "After having been disfigured, I may avoid the danger of remarrying.") Is it coincidence that the designer of her picture-story chose the moment of her "symbolic suicide" as the subject of illustration (Figs. 4.21a, b)? In the picture, a chariot drawn by four horses halts on the left, and the king's messenger stands beside the chariot waiting for Liang's answer. A female servant acts as an intermediary to present the king's betrothal gifts to the widow. The famous beauty is holding a knife in the left hand about to cut off her own nose; the mirror she holds in her right hand brings the theme of disfigurement into sharp focus.

In these pictures engraved on Han funerary monuments, we have gradually traced the vantage point from which these moral tales were told and from which the myth of "public duty" was created—this vantage point was set by the "father." Significantly, no father is depicted on Han funerary monuments as taking care of his son, nor is his responsibility to a motherless orphan referred to as a "public duty." The reason may be simple: he was the invisible instructor behind all these moral lessons. As T'ien Ju-K'ang has observed, "Throughout Chinese history, as a general rule morality has been vigorously propagated whenever immorality was actually prevailing."[64] The figures who devoted their lives to an orphan were virtuous widows, stepmothers, sisters-in-law, and loyal servants, because from the viewpoint of the husband-brother-master these were

自残（如割掉头发、耳朵、手指或鼻子）的妇女通常是被其父母或娘家的亲属逼迫再婚的寡母。《华阳国志》记载了三位这样的模范寡妇——彭非、王和、李进娥，她们在自残后"各养子终义"。[62]

寡妇的自残应理解为一种象征性的自殉。寡妇自杀的事件在汉代并不稀见，[63] 但正如梁高行所表明的，她不去自杀是因为她必须照顾其丈夫的孩子，因此她的自殉只能是象征性的。当我们再回头读冯衍的信时，妇女的自残就变得更为令人震惊。冯衍在信中指责他的妻子不但行为恶劣，而且邋遢粗俗。但丈夫死后，女人的美色便变得无用，甚至危险。毁掉了这种无用并且危险的容貌，她便变得更为"可靠"，可以安心守寡。（所以梁高行说："今刑余之人，殆可释矣！"）梁高行故事的画像也因为这个缘故而选择了"象征性自杀"的时刻作为主题［图 4.21］。画像中一辆马车停在左端，梁王的使者在马车旁等待梁高行的答复。一位女仆作为中间人正在向这位寡妇进献梁王的聘礼。而这位著名的美人左手执刀欲切掉自己的鼻子，她右手所持的镜子使自残的主题变得更为触目。

通过观察上述汉代丧葬建筑中的画像，我们逐渐发现孤儿抚养中所谓"公义"的神话必然产生于"父亲"的角度。耐人寻味的是，汉代丧葬建筑的装饰从未直接描绘父亲对儿子的关爱，也从未表现父亲对于失去母亲的孩子属于"公义"的责任。此中原因可能很简单：父亲是所有这些道德说教背后隐而不现的宣讲者。正如田汝康所言，"纵观中国历史，一个一般性的规律是：每当不道德行为高涨的时候，道德总要被大加宣扬。"[64] 为孤儿而献身的人物都是有德行的寡妇、继母、姑嫂及忠仆，因为从丈夫、兄弟或主人的

all untrustworthy: a widow naturally wished to find a second home; "the second wife is certain to maltreat the son of the previous wife";
213 "sisters-in-law are the cause of many quarrels";[65] and servants commonly schemed against their masters. The hagiographic stories were illustrated on funerary monuments to discourage these dangers, not to reward good individuals.

A maxim in the Confucian classic, *Master Zuo's Commentaries on the Spring and Autumn Annals*, typifies this anxiety: "If one be not of my kin, one is sure to have a different heart."[66] Who could be closer kin to a son than his father? The relationship between a son and his father differed radically from all other relationships, including the mother-son relationship: the son bore his father's surname and continued his father's family line. In other words, the father identified himself with his son and considered the son his incarnation. Moreover, in a patrilineal family the father-son relationship was repeated generation after generation (as indicated by the repetition of the family surname). A man was often simultaneously both a father and a son, a situation that again differed fundamentally from one's relations with mother, wife, relatives, friends, and servants (who all belonged to or came from "other families"). Such a patrilineal chain demanded and produced a specific moral code to sustain it—*xiao*, or filial piety. All male heroes represented in a family context on funerary monuments were therefore filial paragons.

Generally speaking, filial piety is the virtue of a child toward his parents: "The essence of this primal virtue is none other than to honor and obey one's parents while they are alive, to sacrifice to them reverently after their death, and to adhere to their guidance throughout one's whole life."[67] By practicing this virtue one thus identifies oneself as a child. This point requires a brief examination of the definition of *child*. Two different standards coexisted in early Imperial China. The first was based on age. Normally when a man reached twenty years old, he was considered an adult man; a special "capping ceremony" (*guanli*) was held to mark his coming-of-age. Before this age he was called a *tong* or *tongzi,* meaning "child."[68] The other definition of *child* is based not on age but on family relationships. As a popular saying goes: "As long as his parents are alive, a son is always a boy." This does not imply, as a modern person may imagine, that the son was treated by his parents as their "baby boy." Rather, it means that the son, though an adult, should remain a boy—to

观点来看，这些人物都是不可靠的：寡妇总想改嫁他人；"假继惨虐孤遗"；"娣姒者，多争之地也"；[65] 奴仆的本性是阴谋造反。丧葬建筑中理想化的传记故事，是为了避免这些威胁，而不是为了褒扬优秀人物而刻画。

儒家经典《左传》中的一句格言正可概括这种不安的心情："非我族类，其心必异。"[66] 对儿子来说，难道还有比父亲更亲近的吗？儿子与父亲的关系，与包括母子关系在内的其他亲属关系相比，有着根本的区别。儿子继承父姓，并延续着其父亲的家庭血统。换言之，父亲将儿子等同于自己，视儿子为自己的化身。进一步讲，在一个父系家庭中，父子关系（通过父姓的延续）代代重复。一个男人既是父亲又是儿子，这种情况和他与母亲、妻子、亲戚、朋友及仆人（均属于"其他家庭"）的关系，都有本质的区别。这种父系的链条决定并制造出一种特殊的道德准则来支撑它：孝。表现在丧葬建筑中的家庭结构内的男性主人公，便因此都是孝的典范。

一般来说，孝是孩子对其父母表现出的德行，"其本质是当父母在世时对他们尊敬照料，在父母去世后竭诚祭祀，并在一生中遵循父母的教诲。"[67] 孝道因此可以被称为是"孩子"的道德，但我们需要在这里对孩子这一概念做些解释。我们发现在中国帝国时代早期，"孩子"一词同时存在两种不同的含义。第一种基于年龄。一般说来，一个男子在 20 岁才算成人，这时要举行"冠礼"，表明他达到了这一年龄。在此之前，他被称作"童"或"童子"，意指"孩子"。[68] 另一种孩子的概念不基于年龄，而是基于家庭关系。正如一句中国俗语所言："父母在，不言老。"这种意义的"孩子"并不是像现代人想象的那样，指一个被其父母视作"小男孩"的儿子，而是指虽已成年，但仍视自己为孩子的人——就是说，他必须

behave as a child and cultivate the child's virtue of filial piety. The epitome of such "elderly boys" is Laizi, whose portrayal was a favorite motif on Han funerary monuments (Figs. 4.22a, b).

> Elder Laizi was a native of Chu. When he was 70 years old, his parents were still alive. With the ultimate filial piety, he often wore multicolored clothes to serve his parents food in the main hall. Once he hurt his feet. Afraid to sadden his parents, he made himself tumble stiffly to the ground and bawled like an infant. Confucius remarked: "One does not use the word 'old' when one's parents are getting old, because one fears this will make them grieve about their elderliness. A person like Elder Laizi can be called one who does not lose a child's heart."[69]

In Confucius' view, another famous "elderly boy" named Bo Yu, whose image also appears frequently on funerary monuments (Figs. 4.23a, b), would be less filial because he, though a paragon, let his mother realize her elderliness. Also 70 years old, Bo Yu was willing to be beaten by his mother whenever he made a mistake. But one day he wept, and his mother asked him: "I did not see you weep when I punished you before. Why do you cry today?" To his mother's surprise he answered: "Before, when I offended you and you beat me with the stick, I often felt pain. But today your weakness could not make me feel pain. That is why I am weeping."[70]

Logically speaking, if parents were not supposed to become "old," then the son had to be always "young," and this is exactly what the Laizi picture tells the viewer. This intention is manifested in the pictorial representations: the old Laizi is portrayed as a boy with a small frame, a plump body, and wearing a three-pointed baby hat; his aged parents (who in reality must have been close to a hundred years old) appear as a healthy young couple, the father wearing a gentleman's cap and the mother an elaborate headdress. What the artist tried to express seems to have been the moral implication of the story, not reality.

Thus, the images of these men-children are not "portraiture" at all, an artistic genre defined by Richard Delbrücl as "the representation, intending to be like, of a definite individual."[71] In these carvings, the 214
figures' physical likeness is vitiated to serve the moral content, and their identities as submissive "children" are shown in their juxtaposition with their parents. To understand this, we need only compare all nine filial

行为如孩子，遵循孩子所具有的孝的品质。这种“老男孩”的一个缩影是莱子，其形象是汉代丧葬画像中最受欢迎的主题［图4.22］：

> 老莱子者，楚人。行年七十，父母俱存，至孝蒸蒸。常着班兰之衣，为亲取饮。上堂脚跌，恐伤父母之（心），因僵仆为婴儿啼。孔子曰：“父母老，常言不称老，为其伤老也。若老莱子，可谓不失孺子之心矣。”[69]

另一个著名的“老男孩”的形象，是也经常出现在丧葬建筑上的伯榆［图4.23］。按照孔子上面的说法，尽管伯榆也是一个典范孝子，但却不如老莱子孝顺，因为他使自己的母亲意识到自己的年老。他的传记记载，伯榆70岁时仍顺从地在自己做错了事时挨母亲的打。但有一天他哭了起来。他的母亲问：“他日笞子，未尝见泣，今泣，何也？”令其母惊奇的是，伯榆说：“他日俞（榆）得罪，笞尝痛；今母之力衰，不能使痛，是以泣也。”[70]

如果不期望父母变“老”，儿子就必须永远“年轻”，而这正是莱子画像要告诉观众的：画像中老莱子被描绘成小而圆硕的男孩，戴一顶有三个尖角的婴儿帽。而他年迈的双亲（实际上应接近百岁）像是一对健康的中年人，父亲头戴一顶绅士的帽子，母亲头戴华美的头饰。艺术家所要表达的明显是故事的道德隐喻，而不是现实本身。

我们因此可以认为，这些“成年孩子”的画像完全不符合理查德·德尔布鲁斯为“肖像画”所下的定义，即肖像的目的是“尽量肖似地再现一个特定的人物”。[71]在这些汉代雕刻中，人物形象的形似让位于道德教化的目的。我们只需与著名的武梁祠中描绘的九幅

a

b

Fig. 4.22. Story of Laizi. Wu Liang Shrine carving. (a) Ink rubbing. (b) Reconstruction.

图 4.22 （上图）老莱子故事。武梁祠画像。东汉晚期，151 年。（a）拓片。（b）木版复制品。

sons "portrayed" on the famous Wu Liang Shrine. From textual sources we know that these men's ages range from 5 (Zhao Xun) to 70 (Laizi and Bo Yu), but their representations are by and large indistinguishable. Most of them kneel before their parents—a standard gesture of respect

a

b

Fig. 4.23. Story of Bo Yu. Wu Liang Shrine carving. (a) Ink rubbing. (b) Reconstruction.

图 4.23　伯榆故事。武梁祠画像。东汉晚期，151 年。(a) 拓片。(b) 木版复制品。

and submission. What these images represent is a particular species created by Han Confucian ideology, which we may call the "ageless child." A physically old filial son had to pretend to be young (and had to be represented as young); a filial son who was really young had to be mature enough to be insistently virtuous and morally unshakable. The former category is the "man-child" and the latter, the "child-man." The heroes'

孝子的“肖像”比较一下，就可以理解这种表现的方法。从文献中我们得知，这些孝子的年龄从 5 岁（如赵狗）到 70 岁（如莱子与伯榆）不等，但画像中的人物形象却几乎毫无差别。他们大部分以敬重与谦恭的标准姿势跪在父母身前。图像所描绘的人物因此是汉代儒家思想影响下产生出来的一种特殊形象，我们可以称之为“无年龄的孩子”。当一位实际上老迈年高的孝子不得不假装年轻时（同时也不得不被描绘得像位年轻人），真正年幼的孝子则是为人老成，他们有着崇高的品质和坚定的德行。前者是“成年的孩子”，后者是“年幼

individuality is entirely omitted—their "portraits" have become simply tokens of ideas. What remains is their morality, which, in the patrilineal society of Han China, was further promoted as the foundation of the whole universe. The *Classic of Filial Piety* teaches: "Filiality is the first principle of heaven, the ultimate standard of earth, the norm of conduct for the people."[72] It is hardly possible to imagine anything more "public" than the duty of filial piety, anything further removed from private family love.

Real children and "ageless children" are depicted in very different ways on Han funerary monuments. The former are mostly nameless creatures protected by virtuous mothers, stepmothers, relatives, and servants. The latter are famous paragons who nourished and protected their parents. This distinction further implies that a child labeled "filial," even if he were only five years old, had gained adulthood—he had become a symbol of the fundamental moral principle and an exemplar for the whole population. Once this idea prevailed, a whole group of child-men emerged in both fiction and reality. As mentioned earlier, from the early Western Han, the government regularly selected officials through a recruitment system. People with reputations for being "filial and uncorrupt" were recommended by local offices to the throne on a
215 regular basis. The chosen ones included young boys who were not only morally distinguished but also well versed in the Confucian classics. They were honored with a special title, *tongzi lang*, or "boy gentleman."[73]

Such Confucian prodigies were frequently represented in art. Xiang Tuo, a child of extraordinary wisdom and learning, was said to have been a teacher of Confucius himself, and his portrait regularly appears on funerary monuments between Confucius and Laozi (Figs. 4.24a, b): the small boy is holding a pull-toy, and the two masters are gazing at him instead of each other. Audrey Spiro has remarked on this image: "The child is meant to be seen, not as an opponent, but as a Confucian prodigy, ready to discourse on the highest subjects."[74] Martin Powers has further pointed out that Confucian scholars used the story as a political metaphor: it meant that "any man has a legitimate right to speak out if his words are righteous," and that "merit is to be determined by wisdom and intelligence, not by appearance, title, or pretense."[75] But once such a "metaphor"

的成人"。这些杰出人物的个性特征——例如他们不同的相貌体质——完全消失，而转变为一种单纯的意识符号。这些画像中保留下来的是说教，在中国汉代的父权社会中，这些说教进而发展成为整个天地万物的基础。《孝经》云："夫孝，天之经也，地之义也，民之行也。"[72] 确实，很难想象有比"孝"更为"公共"的义务，或任何更为彻底地从家庭私爱中抽绎出来的东西。

在汉代的丧葬建筑中，对真正的孩子与"无年龄的孩子"的描绘是十分不同的。前者几乎都是在有德行的母亲、继母、亲属及奴仆呵护下的不知名的角色，后者则被刻画成奉养保护其双亲的著名历史典范。进一步说，一个孩子一旦被冠以"孝"，哪怕他只有5岁，在某种意义上，他也已经长大成人。他会进入历史记载，变成道德准则的象征，成为全民的楷模。当这种意识形态一旦流布，一大批"具有孩子美德的成年人"就在故事或现实中出现了。例如，众所周知，从公元2世纪武帝时代起，汉代政府经常通过一种征召系统选拔任用官员，由地方官员将获得"孝廉"之名的人定期举荐到宫廷中。被举之人包括一些不但品质出众，而且熟通儒家经典的年轻男孩，他们被誉为"童子郎"。[73]

这些儒家神童经常出现在汉代艺术作品中。汉代丧葬建筑上经常刻画一位名叫项橐的男孩，据说他极为聪颖多才，甚至曾做过孔子的老师［图4.24］。在这类画像中，项橐手持一玩具车，身居孔子与老子之间，两位哲人并没有表现出对彼此的兴趣，而是都在注视着这位男孩。司白乐在讨论此图像时说："这名儿童不是被表现为一位对立者，而是一个正准备讨论高深问题的儒家神童。"[74] 包华石进一步指出，儒家学者把这些故事当作一种政治性隐喻，意味着"如果一个人的话是正确的，他就有合理的权利说出来"，"荣誉是由智慧和才华决定的，而不是来自外表、名头和矫饰。"[75] 但是，

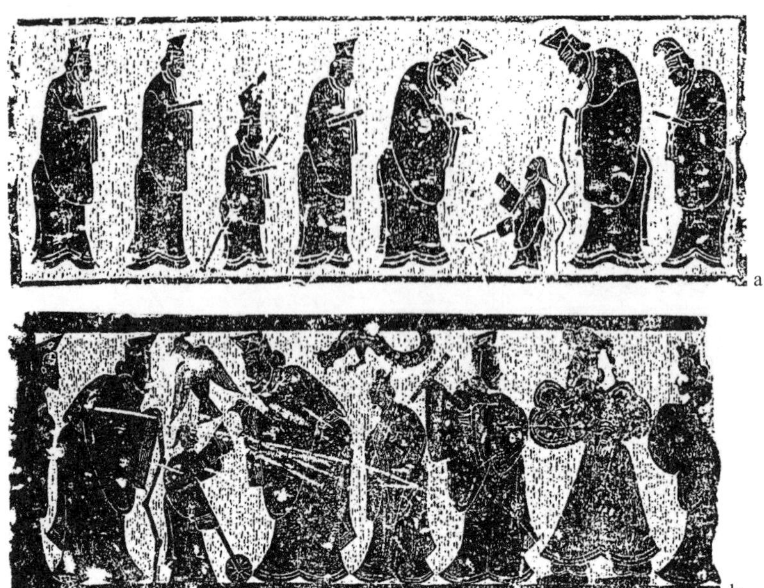

Fig. 4.24. Xiang Tuo with Confucius and Laozi. Eastern Han. 2nd century A.D. Excavated in 1978 at Songshan, Jiaxiang, Shandong province. Ink rubbings. (a) W. 66cm. (b) W. 68 cm.

图 4.24 项橐与孔子、老子。东汉晚期，2 世纪。1978 年山东嘉祥宋山出土。拓片。（a）宽 66 厘米。（b）宽 68 厘米。

prevailed, it was often taken literally. Michel Soymié, for example, has cited a tomb inscription (A.D. 179, Shandong), lamenting the premature death of a son from a certain Feng family. The child was described as having memorized the whole *Book of Songs* and the ritual canons. Indeed, so great was his learning that he was called a second Xiang Tuo.[76]

Then there were children who, rather than being specialists in the Confucian classics, were distinguished by their moral conduct. Zhao Xun (Fig. 4.25) had consistently demonstrated his filial piety since he was five years old and thus "became well known and his reputation spread far." He was finally promoted by the emperor himself to be a royal attendant.[77] The most interesting figure illustrated on Eastern Han funerary monuments, however, was the boy Yuan Gu (Figs. 4.26a, b), whose filial piety transformed his vicious father into a filial son.

When Yuan Gu's grandfather was old, his parents detested the old man and wanted to abandon him. Gu, who was fifteen years old, entreated them piteously with tears, but his parents did not listen to him. They made a carriage and carried the grandfather away and abandoned him. Gu brought the carriage back. His father asked him, "What are you going to do with this inauspicious thing?" Gu replied: "I am afraid that when you get old, I will not be able to make a new carriage, and so I have brought it back." His father was ashamed and carried the grandfather back and cared for him. He overcame his selfishness and criticized himself. He finally became a "purely filial son," and Gu became a "purely filial grandson."[78]

一旦这种"隐喻"流行开来，它便常常被从字面上去理解。例如，苏远鸣曾引用山东一座汉墓中的题记（179 年），这段题记哀悼一位逢姓的早夭男孩，铭文中称这位男孩能够背诵整部《诗经》及礼仪准则。他如此博学，因而被称为项橐再生。[76]

也有的孩子不是靠熟知儒家经典，而是靠德行而出人头地的。赵狗［图 4.25］在 5 岁时就已显示出他无可置疑的孝心，因而声名远扬，最后被皇帝提拔为宫廷的侍卫。[77] 在东汉丧葬画像中最耐人寻味的人物是一名叫原穀的男孩［图 4.26］，他的最大孝行在于将其不孝的父亲改变成一位孝子：

> 原穀者，不知何许人也，祖年老，父母厌患之，意欲弃之。穀年十五，涕泣苦谏，父母不从，乃作舆舁弃之。穀乃随收舆归。父谓之曰："尔焉用此凶具？"穀云："后父老不能更作得，是以取之耳。"父感悟愧惧，乃载祖归侍养，克己自责，更成纯孝，穀为纯孙。[78]

The characters in this story belong to three generations. Yuan Gu's father violates filial piety in his treatment of his own father; Yuan Gu demonstrates his extraordinary filial piety not only by rescuing his grandfather but, more important, by reforming his father. The moral of the illustrated story is twofold: Yuan Gu criticizes his father's behavior, but not directly. He employs a rhetorical method called *feng*, or remonstration, through metaphors and analogies. The key to his rhetoric is the carriage, which is depicted purposefully in the center of the scene. By bringing back the carriage the boy hints at the parallel between his own relation with his father and his father's relation with the grandfather; the implication is that although the father was now in control, in time he could well become a victim of his own model. In fact, Yuan Gu neither tries to prove the universality of filial piety nor advises his father to follow
216 this moral law. What he does is to appeal to his father's concerns about his own security and well-being. And he succeeds.

Fig. 4.25. Story of Zhao Xun. Wu Liang Shrine carving. Ink rubbing.

图 4.25 赵狗故事。武梁祠画像。东汉晚期，151年。拓片。

Fig. 4.26. Story of Yuan Gu. (a) Wu Liang Shrine carving. Ink rubbing. (b) Line engraving. Eastern Han. 2nd century A.D.

图 4.26　原穀故事。(a) 武梁祠画像。东汉晚期，151 年。拓片。(b) 线刻。东汉晚期，2 世纪。

这个故事中的角色包括三代人。原穀的父亲对祖父不孝，而原穀的至孝不仅表现在挽救了祖父，更重要的是他也改变了他的父亲。这一故事的道德说教有双重含义：父亲的行为应受到谴责；但原穀作为一名孝子，却不能坦言批评他的父亲。他巧妙地运用“讽”的方式，以隐喻和类比，委婉地表达了他的批评。这种巧言的关键是，画像中靠近原穀右手方向的舆被有意地置于画面正中。原穀将舆带回，暗示他和父亲的关系与父亲和祖父的关系是平行的。其中的含义十分明了：虽然他的父亲现在可以做主，但是他最终将受损于他自己树立的楷模。其实，原穀并未试图去证实孝的原理，也没有建议他的父亲遵循这一道德规范，他所做的只是让其父推想到自身的安全与幸福。因此，他成功了。

In this section I have tried to decipher the messages conveyed by the images of children depicted on Han funerary monuments. What we have found is an essential paradox in social attitudes and notions of responsibility toward a child. On the one hand, the concept of "private love" was often associated with a child's natural parents (especially the mother), whereas "public duty" was required from a child's stepmother, relatives, and servants. Upon closer investigation, however, we have seen that even one's relationship with one's own children or parents could become a social responsibility, determined by moral obligations assigned by society at large. Thus, although the desire for "private love" was sometimes murmured, the common themes represented on funerary monuments are "public duty"—the loyalty of a stepmother, aunt, friend, or servant; the fidelity and chastity of a widowed mother; and the filial piety of a son. Executed on a memorial shrine or pillar-gate, these pictures were exposed to the public, and their social function was again emphasized by inscriptions engraved alongside: "We are stating clearly to people of virtue and kindheartedness within the four seas: Please regard these [pictures and] words and do not ignore them."[79]

The general social and moral implication of these carvings contradict
217 and dismiss any artistic representation of individuality—an individual's distinctive features and personality. The images of children and other types of figures on funerary monuments are symbols—"a particular [that] represents the more general"[80] —that index people's mutual and conventional responsibilities in a community. Even the Xu Aqu carving (Fig. 4.15a)—the image of a "real" child—is not an exception: the "portrait" is based on a standard image of a male master receiving an audience and enjoying musical and dance performances (Fig. 4.27). Since the adult figures are replaced by children in this carving, Xu's "portrait" is again transformed into an idealized "public" image, as if the memory of the child could survive only in such a stereotype in a public art, as if his parents' love, so vividly expressed in their private appeal to their son in

the eulogy, could be expressed only in the generic language of funerary monuments.

❸ Friends and Colleagues

When the rebellion broke out in Taishan in 154, a few local officials, Confucian scholars for the most part, refused to carry out the severe

在本节中，我尝试着解释汉代丧葬建筑上儿童图像所反映出的问题。我们所发现的是一个带有本质性的悖理：表面看来，“私爱”的概念常常与孩子和其生身父母（特别是母亲）的关系相关，而“公义”则是对孩子的继母、亲戚、奴婢的要求。但进一步的观察表明，由于普遍地受到社会的制约，即使是某人与自己子女或父母之间的私人关系，最终也会变成一种受普遍道德准则控制的社会责任。因此，尽管“私爱”有时也会被人窃窃谈起，但丧葬建筑上的图画最为常见的主题总是那些与“公义”相关的人与事，包括继母、姑嫂、朋友或奴婢的忠诚，寡母的贞洁，以及儿子的孝顺。见诸祠堂或阙门上的这些图画，意在向公众展示题记中所强调的教化功能：“明语贤仁四海士，唯省此书，无忽矣。”[79]

这些画像的一般性社会与道德蕴意排斥任何对个性的艺术表现，其结果是人物形象鲜有表现个人的特征与性格。丧葬建筑中所见的儿童与其他人物的图画，便是这种“以特殊表现一般”的符号之一，[80]成为人们在社会中寻求其互相的、普遍的职责的索引。讨论至此，我们发现，即使是表现一名“真正”孩子的许阿瞿肖像［图4.15a］，也无法摆脱这种规范：这个“肖像”的造型来源于汉画中男主人接受拜见、欣赏乐舞表演的标准形式［图4.27］。在这一作品中，孩子的形象代替了成人，许阿瞿的“肖像”因此再次转化成一种理想化的“公共”图像。似乎对孩子的怀念只能寄托于约定俗成的公共艺术的公式才能得到表达，似乎赞文中显露的父母对儿子强烈的爱只能通过丧葬艺术的通行语言才能发出声音。

三、友人与同僚

当公元154年泰山的农民暴动爆发时，一些当地官员——其中

Fig. 4.27. Entertainment. Eastern Han. 2nd century A.D. Found in Nanyang region, Henan province.

图 4.27 乐舞百戏画像。东汉晚期，2 世纪。河南南阳出土。拓片。

measures adopted by the government to punish the rebels, for in their view the rebels were desperate people suffering from human and natural disasters. One such official was Han Shao, the prefect of a small county called Ying in central Shandong. According to the *History of the Latter Han*, instead of attacking the destitute peasants, he let them pour into his county. "He opened up the official granary, relieving them from hunger; more than 10,000 families received his aid. The county's financial officer tried to stop him, but he responded: 'If I shall be punished for rescuing these men and women from their graves, I will die with a smile on my face.'"[81]

Han Shao was not punished, but he was never promoted to a higher post. After he died in his county office, a group of people, including Li Ying (109-69), Du Mi (d. 169), Xun Yu (d. 169), and Chen Shi (103-87), paid him homage by erecting a stone stela in front of his tomb to commemorate his virtue.[82] The stela's inscription was never recorded; only its *establishment* is mentioned in the *History of the Latter Han*
218 at the conclusion of Han Shao's brief biography. Why was the act of constructing the stela considered so important and who were the men responsible? Surprisingly, there is no evidence of relations between Han Shao and the patrons of his memorial stela during his lifetime. Moreover, unlike Han Shao, who remained a low-ranking official in a

small county, the donors of the funerary monument were the nation's leading Confucians and famous statesmen at court. They also belonged to a single political group, and three of them—Li Ying, Du Mi, and Xun Yu—were later martyred in the struggles against the powerful eunuchs who dominated the Han court during most of Emperor Huan's and Emperor Ling's reigns. In Han society, a memorial stela dedicated by such renowned personages carried extraordinary weight:[83] it meant formal approval of the political agenda and moral deeds of the deceased; it indicated a kindred relationship between the donors and the deceased; and it gained the deceased national attention. It was Han Shao's memorial stela that brought posthumous fame and glory to this petty official and made him a model for other Confucians.

绝大多数是儒生——拒绝执行政府所推行的极端政策去镇压反叛者，因为在他们看来，造反者是遭受到天灾人祸之苦的绝望农民。这些官员中有一位名叫韩韶，是山东中部一个名为嬴的小县的县令。据《后汉书》记载，他没有率兵进攻那些赤贫的农民，而是让他们进入其县境。“乃开仓赈之，所禀赡万余户，主者争为不可，韶曰：‘长活沟壑之人，而以此伏罪，含笑入地矣。’”[81]

韩韶没有被治罪，但也因此从未被提拔。在他死后，一批人来到他的墓前，竖立了一座碑以赞颂他的德行。这些人包括李膺（109—169年）、杜密（？—169年）、荀昱（？—169年）和陈寔（103—187）。[82]《后汉书》中没有记载这篇碑文，只是在韩韶简短的传记最后提到了“立碑”这件事情。为什么此事被看得如此重要？这些为韩韶立碑的人到底是什么人？令人惊异的是，文献中并没有提到韩韶在世时与这些人有任何关系。与官居小小县令的韩韶不同，这几位立碑者是全国杰出的儒士和朝廷中著名的政治家。他们还属于一个独立的政治团体，其中的三人——李膺、杜密和荀昱——后来在桓、灵时期因反对掌控朝中大权的宦官时殉难。在汉代社会，一座由这些名人所竖立的碑有着特殊的分量：[83] 它意味着对死者政迹和德行的正式认可；它表明赞助人和死者有着志同道合的关系；它使死者获得全国性的关注。正是韩韶的碑为他带来了身后的声誉与荣耀，使他成为其他儒士的榜样。

The struggle between the scholar-officials and eunuchs surfaced shortly after 159. In this year, with the eunuchs' help, Emperor Huan dismissed Liang Ji, the brother of the empress dowager and the chief power in the state for eighteen years. Confucian courtiers resented the subsequent rise of eunuchs in state affairs, however, and formed a political faction to regain power from the "castrated evils." Their bravest leader was Li Ying.

Beginning his official career as a "filial and uncorrupt person," Li Ying finally attained the high office of grand commandant (*taiwei*).[84] Most of the activities recorded in his official biography are concerned with his tireless struggles against the eunuchs. He once enforced the law by executing a well-known tyrant who was the younger brother of the chief eunuch, Zhang Rang. Li Ying was thereupon interrogated by the emperor himself in a special court session. Later, he found out that an innocent man had been murdered, but no one dared to look into the case because the criminal's father, the popular necromancer Zhang Cheng, had intimate connections with eunuchs and even with the emperor. Li Ying managed to capture the murderer and beheaded him without reporting it to the throne. This event in 166 led to an explosion of the heightening tension between eunuchs and scholar-officials. Li Ying and more than 200 of his friends and followers were arrested. But this only increased his fame. Even before 166, more than a thousand young Confucians had studied with him; now he was honored as a national hero. Nevertheless, he maintained a high standard in choosing friends and students. We are told by his biographer that he never paid attention to the rich and the powerful, and that "those who received audiences from him were so proud that they called themselves 'the ones who had entered the Dragon Gate.'" In Confucian circles, he was considered a "model within the four seas" and one of the Eight Sterling Men (*bajun*).

Emperor Huan died in 167 and left no designated heir. The next ruler, Emperor Ling (r. 168-89), was a young boy brought to the throne

from the provinces. The Confucians and their allies saw this as a chance to seize power, and one of them even plotted a coup d'état to execute all eunuchs. But news of their plan leaked out, and their enemies got the upper hand. The persecution of Confucians, known as the Great Proscription (*danggu*), began in 168 and continued throughout Emperor Ling's reign. Li Ying bore the brunt: in 169 he and 600 other scholars were tortured to death. His wife was exiled to the frontier, and his relatives, 219
students, and subordinate officials were thrown into jail.

公元 159 年以后，儒士与宦官之间的斗争日异白热化。这一年，桓帝在宦官的帮助下将执掌朝政长达 18 年的太后的兄弟梁冀驱逐下台。但是，儒士们不满宦官权力的加强，他们组织了一个政治宗派，力图从“阉竖”手中夺回权力。他们之中最勇敢的领导者是李膺。

李膺的仕途从“孝廉”开始，一直走上太尉的高位。[84] 在记载其政绩的传记中，最精彩的是他对宦官们不懈抗争的事迹。他有一次坚持执法，处死了大宦官张让暴虐无道的弟弟张朔，以致皇帝特地诏他入殿，亲自诘问。166 年，李膺发现一位无辜的人被杀害，但是没有人敢过问此事，因为凶手的父亲是炙手可热的方士张成，而张成与宦官乃至皇帝的关系甚为密切。李膺先斩后奏，设法逮捕并处死了凶手。这一事件导致宦官与儒士的关系极度紧张，李膺及其两百多位友好和同党被捕，但此事更使得李膺声名大振。早在 166 年之前，就有千余名年轻的儒生问学于他的门下，而现在他被奉为一位英雄。此外，李膺又以其择友收徒的高标准而著称。我们从他的传记中知道，他无视财富与权势，“士有被其容接者，名为登龙门。”儒生们将李膺誉为“天下楷模”和“八俊”之一。

桓帝死于 167 年，死前没有指定继承人。其继任者灵帝是从郡国登上皇位的一个小男孩。儒士及其同党认为夺回权力的时机已到，他们当中的一位甚至密谋组织突袭，杀死所有当权宦官。但这一计划败露，他们的政敌先下了手。镇压儒士的行动在历史上称作“党锢”，从 168 年开始一直贯穿灵帝在位期间。李膺首当其冲，他与其他 600 位儒士被害于 169 年。他的妻子被流放，亲戚、门生和故吏被捕入狱。

Du Mi and Xun Yu, two other contributors to Han Shao's memorial stela, died together with Li Ying. The three men had known one another from childhood: they were from Yingchuan in southern Shandong, and Xun Yu's uncle Xun Shu had initiated Li Ying into Confucian learning. After Xun Shu passed away, Li Ying mourned him for three years—an act of ritual homage usually paid only to one's parents. The central factor uniting these three scholar-officials, however, was their common political goal. Du Mi, who held the lofty position of grand tutor in both Emperor Huan's and Emperor Ling's reigns, "would catch eunuchs' adherents and bring them to trial whenever they were found doing evil in office."[85] Xun Yu took even more extreme action: during his tenure of office in Pei, "he executed the followers and protégés of eunuchs in his county even when they had only committed a minor crime."[86] Like Li Ying, they headed the list of Eight Sterling Men.

The fourth person to take part in establishing Han Shao's memorial stela was Chen Shi.[87] A close friend of Li Ying and a member of the Confucian group, Chen Shi nevertheless tried to disengage himself from worldly affairs and to maintain his spiritual purity in reclusion. In this way, he became a representative of those "retired worthies" whose withdrawal from the corrupt court was itself a political gesture.[88] Chen Shi's growing reputation resulted not from his direct engagement in political struggles, but from the risks he took in maintaining a seemingly impartial position. Thus, when Li Ying was arrested in 166 and many scholars tried to flee, he went straight to prison and asked to be jailed along with his friend. But when the father of the chief eunuch Zhang Rang died, he was the only Confucian gentleman to attend the funeral held by Zhang Rang, one of the most hated men in the country and the engineer of the 166 trial. His seemingly unbiased position may have helped him escape the Great Proscription. After the tragic event, he continued to refuse any official assignment, even the highest post in the court. Chen Shi died in 187 at age 84. More than 30,000 people from all parts of the country attended his funeral; several hundred guests wore white mourning clothes; and a number of stone stelae were erected in front of his tomb to praise his virtues.

The scale of Chen Shi's funerary ceremony was not unique during the Han. According to historical records, more than 10,000 chariots accompanied the funeral of the famous scholar-official Kong Guang (65 B.C.-A.D. 5) to his burial ground, and when the Confucian master Zheng Xuan

参与为韩韶立碑的杜密和荀昱二人也与李膺一起被害。这三个人都是山东南部颍川人，自幼年起就彼此熟悉，荀昱的叔父荀淑还是李膺的启蒙老师。荀淑死后，李膺为之服丧三年——这是只有对父母才尽的礼数。但是，将这三位文人官员联系在一起的是其共同的政治目标。杜密在桓、灵时期担任泰山太守、北海相，“其宦官子弟为令长有奸恶者，辄捕案之。”[85] 荀昱的行为更为严厉，他在担任沛相时，“志除阉宦，其支党宾客有在二郡者，纤罪必诛。”[86] 像李膺一样，他们也都名列“八俊”。

参与为韩韶立碑的第四个人是陈寔。[87] 他是李膺的密友，也是儒士集团的中心成员。然而，他却脱离世事，以遁世来保全其精神的纯正。通过这种方式，他成为“隐士”的代表，对这派人来说，从腐败的朝廷中超脱出来本身就是一种政治姿态。[88] 陈寔日益增长的声望不是来自他在政治斗争中的直接表现，而是来自他在保持一种看似公正的姿态时所面临的风险。例如，当 166 年李膺被捕入狱，许多儒士试图逃匿时，他径直走进监狱要求与他的朋友一起坐牢。但是，当大宦官张让的父亲死后，他又是唯一参加其葬礼的儒士，而张让正是 166 年逮捕儒士一事的策划者，当时被举国上下所痛恨。他这种看似不偏不倚的姿态或可使他逃脱党锢之祸，但是当这场悲剧过后，他仍然拒绝担当任何官职，甚至包括朝中最高的职位。陈寔卒于 187 年，终年 84 岁。来自全国各地的三万多人参加了他的葬礼，数百位来宾为他穿白戴孝，一批颂扬其德行的石碑被竖立在了他的墓前。

陈寔葬礼的规模在汉代并不鲜见。根据史书记载，文官孔光（前 65—5 年）的葬礼有一万辆车参加，大儒郑玄（127—200 年）

(127-200) died, "all those who had studied with him, from those who held the official post of governor on down, put on their mourning robes to attend the funeral, over a thousand in all."[89] As Martin Powers has pointed out, many such funeral services served important social and political purposes.[90] The guests attended a service because they had or felt some specific connection with the deceased and because they wanted to stress that connection publicly. Since graveyards had become centers of social life during the Eastern Han, funerary ceremonies provided the most appropriate occasions for emotional and political expressions.

Han Shao's funeral was probably not a grand spectacle like the funerals held for Kong Guang, Zheng Xuan, and Chen Shi, but it served the same purpose. Li Ying, Du Mi, Xun Yu, and Chen Shi may have never had much contact with Han Shao, but this only made their tribute more significant. The stela they erected for Han Shao, in fact, expressed their spiritual relationship with this virtuous Confucian gentlemen, a relationship that transcended death. That these four men erected the stela together also emphasized their own comradeship. Moreover, their devotion to this humble scholar made it clear that status differences were irrelevant to the morals shared by true Confucians. Not coincidentally, we find that this stela was most likely established in 167 or 168, when Li Ying and Du Mi were forced to retire to their hometown in Shandong and Xun Yu held office in the same region.[91] During this period they as well as Chen Shi were active in the same area, teaching students and advocating Confucian virtues. The homage they paid to Han Shao was one such activity.

Han Shao's stela no longer exists, but another surviving example
221 allows us to speculate on the content and style of its inscription. This is the stela dedicated to a gentleman named Kong Zhou, who died in 163 at age 61 (Figs. 4.28a, b). The lives of Kong Zhou and Han Shao were surprisingly similar. They were contemporary scholar-officials who held office in adjacent counties. They were both involved in the

Taishan rebellion and took a similar strategy in dealing with the riot. The inscription on Kong Zhou's stela reads:

> THE STELA OF MASTER KONG,
> THE HAN CHIEF COMMANDANT OF TAISHAN
>
> Our lord's personal name was Zhou and his style name Jijiang. A nineteenth-generation descendent of Confucius, his heaven-endowed nature was pure and flawless, and he attained sagehood and reached the great Dao.

死后，"自郡守以下尝受业者，縗絰赴会千余人。"[89] 包华石指出，许多这样的葬礼有着社会和政治目的。[90] 来宾之所以参加葬礼，是因为他们与死者曾经有过或认为自己与死者有过特殊的关系，并希望把这种关系公开化。由于东汉时期墓地已变成社会生活的中心，因此葬礼就成了感情与政治表白的最佳场合。

韩韶的葬礼也许没有孔光、郑玄和陈寔的葬礼那样宏大壮观，但其目的是相同的。李膺、杜密、荀昱和陈寔或许从未与韩韶有过深交，但这使得他们的捐助更富有意味。实际上，为韩韶立碑一事表明他们与这位有德行的儒士之间具有精神上的、超越了死亡的联系。这四人一起立碑，也强调了他们之间志同道合的关系。不仅如此，他们对这位地位较低的儒士的奉献也清楚地说明，身份的差别并不影响真正的儒士们奉行共同的道德标准。并非巧合的是，我们发现这通石碑最有可能是在 167 年或 168 年树立的，也就是在这个时候，李膺和杜密去官回到山东老家，而荀昱也正在这一地区任职。[91] 在这个时期，这三人以及陈寔都活动在该地区，他们收徒授课，鼓吹儒家道德。为韩韶立碑以表达敬意，也是这些政治活动的一部分。

韩韶的石碑没有保存下来，但我们可以通过另一座幸存至今的石碑来观察这类碑文的内容和风格。该碑是为孔宙而立的［图 4.28］。孔宙死于 163 年，终年 61 岁，其生平事迹与韩韶惊人相似。二人当年在相邻的两个县任职，都被卷入泰山的农民暴动，而且采取了相同的策略对待农民暴动。孔宙碑正面碑文全文如下：

> 有汉泰山都尉孔君之铭
> 君讳宙，字季将，孔子十九世之孙也。天姿醇，齐圣达道。

Fig. 4.28. Inscriptions on Kong Zhou's memorial stela. A.D. 164. H. 2.45 m. Found in Qufu, Shandong province. (a) Front. (b) Back. Ink rubbing.

图 4.28 孔宙碑。东汉晚期，164 年。高 2.45 米。山东曲阜。拓片。(a) 碑阳。(b) 碑阴。

In his childhood he studied the doctrines of his great ancestor, and concentrated on *Master Yan's Commentaries on the Spring and Autumn Annals*. As his scholarship deepened and presaged a bright future, he behaved even more obediently in his family. His outstanding virtues became well known, and he was granted the title "Filial and Incorrupt." He became a Gentleman in the Palace [*langzhong*] and was then assigned to Duchang county as an officer. There he imparted widely the five principal Confucian teachings; he honored the virtuous, cared for the aged, and extended benevolence and magnanimity to all. Following the examples of Yu and Tang [the founders of the Xia and Shang dynasties], he was critical of himself. Thus he could carry forward honesty and sincerity when these virtues were vanishing [in his time] and could accomplish great exploits through simple practices. Based on his record during his first three years in office, the government promoted him to prefect of Yuancheng.

At that time gangs in the Eastern Mountain [Taishan] area rebelled against the central authority. Although the royal armies were sent to the region, the turmoil had not yet been suppressed. The government then assigned our lord to a military post [the chief commandant of Taishan], but [instead of resorting to force] he tried to cultivate people's civil virtues. Within a few months all the rebels took off their armor and admitted their guilt. They abandoned weapons in favor of agricultural implements. Desolate fields were cultivated, and merchants could travel safely even along dangerous routes. People could again welcome their guests by singing the ancient ode "The Deer's Cry," and the proper order between the old and the young was restored through the practice of peaceful rituals.

少习家训，治《严氏春秋》。缉熙之业既就，而闺阈之行允恭，德音孔昭。遂举孝廉，除郎中，都昌长。祗传五教，尊贤养老，躬忠恕以及人，兼禹汤之辠己，故能兴朴素于彫弊，济弘功于易简。三载考绩，迁元城令。是时，东岳黔首猾夏不共，衅鼓祠佽，遗畔未宁。乃擢君典戎，以文修之。旬月之间，莫不解甲服罪。载芟载耨，田畯喜于荒圃，商旅交乎险路，会鹿鸣于乐崩，复长幼于酬酢，

But our lord fell ill in that harmonious harvest year. He handed in his resignation and his appeal was granted. He died in the first month of *yiwei* in the sixth year of the Yanxi reign period [A.D. 163] at age 61. He had hoped that his dead body would decompose quickly so that his spirit could return to its true origin, and he had also admired the principles of simplicity and thrift. His tomb has no decoration, and no funerary goods are on display. People deeply revere his loftiness, and all hope to recount his merits. Thus we his students and subordinate officials traveled to famous mountains to find an auspicious stone, on which we have inscribed this text to show future generations an exemplar of virtue. Our praise goes:

O! Our glorious lord,
Your virtues were manifest.
Following your sage ancestor you chose the career of a scholar,
And you established yourself and made your name renowned.
As a Gentleman in the Palace,
You faithfully guarded the imperial domain.
Day and night you were at court,
And at court you were discriminating and intelligent.
You then restored peace in two counties,
Where commoners could thus prosper.
It was your hope to bring peace to the people,
A hope that guided you to pacify the region of Taishan.
You led those fierce rebels
Back to virtue and loyalty.
The fields in the south yielded abundant crops;
The roads through the Eastern Mountains were smooth again.
The year was good, and there was a bumper harvest of millet;
Everyone was happy and raised toasts in congratulation.
The emperor depended on your achievements;
People relied on your support.

When you fell ill you hoped to retire from office, 222
Leaving all worldly glory behind.
The court tried hard to persuade you to stay,
And finally granted your retirement only after repeated appeals.
You maintained the virtues of reverence and thrift till the end of
your life;
And even ritual vessels were not displayed during your funeral service.
Your reputation for loftiness had spread far during your lifetime,
And your eternal glory transcends your death.
We pledge to keep our loyalty to you, our lord,
All carrying out your teachings and advocating your name.

This stela was erected in the second month of *wuchen* in the seventh year of the Yanxi reign period [A.D. 164].

□□□稔，会遭笃病，告困致仕，得从所好。年六十一，延熹六年（163）正月乙未遂□卒疾。贵速朽之反真，慕宁俭之遗则，窀夕不华，明器不设，凡百仰高，德音靡述。于是故吏门人乃共陟名山，采嘉石，勒铭示后，俾有彝式。其辞曰：

于显我君，懿德惟光。绍圣作儒，身立名彰。
贡登圭室，阍阁是虔。夙夜匪懈，在公明明。
乃绥二县，黎仪以康。于天时雍，抚兹岱方。
帅彼凶人，覆俾□□。南亩孔馌，山有夷行。
丰年多黍，称彼兕觥。帝赖其勋，民斯是皇。
疾疢不复，乃委其荣。忠告殷勤，屡省乃听。
恭俭自终，簠簋不陈。生播高誉，殁垂令名。
永矢不刊，亿载扬声。

延熹七年（164）七月戊□造。

This text is a good example of the literary genre called *minglei* (eulogy and dirge). Even before the Han, Xunzi defined its basic function: "one's *minglei* and genealogy [*xishi*] spread one's 'name' in reverence."[92] Some 150 surviving Han dynasty *minglei* on funerary stelae are the results of this desire.[93] Writers engraved these words on stone, hoping that the "names" of their dead friends or colleagues would thus become eternal. As a form of historical and biographical writing, a *minglei* was required to stick to the facts[94] regarding both the deceased's family history and his personal conduct. It usually begins by recounting the genealogy of the dead (which could be either factual or based on a "legendary" family history).[95] The text then states his education, talents, virtues, official assignments, and achievements. In many cases a particular episode in his career (such as Kong Zhou's pacification of the Taishan rebellion) is singled out to highlight his life. This narrative would then lead to a pledge of loyalty by the donors. In the case of Kong Zhou's stela, the 62 people who contributed to this memorial included his direct students (*dizi*), indirect students (*mensheng*), boy-students (*mentong*), subordinate officials (*guli*), and a commoner under his administration (*gumin*). Their names, birthplaces, and relationships with Kong Zhou are inscribed on the back of the stela (Fig. 4.28b). An inscription always ends with a dirge, which paraphrases the preceding prose description in verse containing abundant quotations and allusions from the Confucian classics.

Such a text inscribed on a memorial stela by friends, students, and colleagues of the dead differs, therefore, from a text engraved by family members on an offering shrine. A stela inscription was supposed to be a formal and public document and follow a set of rigid and well-established rules. A shrine inscription, on the other hand, was essentially a private expression, and its content and style were far less formulaic. Stela inscriptions are modeled on "biographies" in historical writings; shrine inscriptions derive from a variety of sources, including poetry and even financial accounts. Stela inscriptions emphasize the public image of the dead and the donors' loyalty toward him; shrine inscriptions stress the patrons' filial piety. A stela is a memorial without other functions. A shrine is the dwelling of the *hun* soul of the deceased and the place where sacrifices are performed.

这段文字是“铭诔”文体的一个典型范例。早在汉代以前，荀子就界定了铭诔的基本功能:“其铭诔系世，敬传其名也。”[92] 保存至今的大约 150 篇刻在石碑上的汉代铭诔可说都是基于传名的目的而创作的。[93] 作者将文字刻在石头上，希望他们死去的友人或同事“声名”恒久。作为一种史传文体，铭诔要求忠于事实，[94] 写明死者家族的历史和个人的事迹。铭诔往往以死者的世系开篇（这种史系或是实在的，或是出自“传说的”家族史），[95] 接下来介绍死者的学业、才能、德行、官职以及事功。通常在谈到其事迹时要突出记述一段特别的事情（如孔宙调解泰山暴动）以为其生平增色。这一叙事最后引导出立碑者表示忠诚的誓言。以孔宙碑为例，为此碑出资的 62 个人包括弟子、门生、门童、故吏和故民。他们的名字、籍贯以及与孔宙的关系被铭刻在碑阴［图 4.28b］。碑文总是以一段大量征引儒家经典文辞的赞词结尾，总结前面的叙述。

这种由死者的朋友、学生和同事刻在碑上的文章因此与死者家人刻在祠堂上的文字迥然不同。碑文遵循着一套严格的既定规则，是一种正式和公开的文本；而祠堂题记基本上是一种私人话语，其内容和风格具有较少的规范化倾向。碑文模仿史书中“列传”的体例；而祠堂题记则有着多种来源，有歌谣，甚至还有账目。碑文强调死者的公众形象和立碑人对他的忠诚；而祠堂题记则着眼于建祠者的孝行。一座碑除了它的纪念意义外没有任何实际功能；而一座祠堂则是死者魂之所归并接受祭祀的场所。

These two kinds of funerary texts and structures attest to different concepts of monumentality that arise from divergent relationships with the deceased. Standing side by side in a graveyard, however, an offering shrine and a memorial stela(e) also formed a single cluster of monuments that communicated with each other. The subjects of this communication were again the two groups of patrons. The guests who attended a funeral ceremony paid their respects not only to the deceased but also to his family. Their homage not only brought posthumous fame to the dead but also offered a chance for his living descendents to exhibit their filial virtue. Interestingly, all three funerals mentioned in this section—those of Han Shao, Chen Shi, and Kong Zhou—had a profound impact on the descendents.

Chen Shi's grand funeral made his son, Chen Ji, a famous person: he cried to the point of spitting blood, and "even after the mourning period was over, he was still wan and sallow, almost going insane [in longing for his father]."[96] His filial conduct was reported to the throne and was
223 illustrated in pictures distributed throughout the country. He finally accepted the post of grand herald. As for Han Shao's son, Han Rong, his father's much-delayed glory nevertheless made him "prosper in his youth. All the five principal departments of the central government offered him positions. He finally attained the office of the grand tutor during Emperor Xian's reign [190-220]."[97]

Kong Zhou's son, Kong Rong, became even more famous in Chinese history.[98] In early childhood Kong Rong was an admirer of Li Ying. When he lost his father at age thirteen, according to the *History of the Latter Han*, "His excessive grief destroyed his physiognomy, and only with people's help could he sit up. His filial piety won the sympathy and admiration of all the people in his village and district." Later, when the warlord He Jin planned to assassinate him because of his brazen antagonism toward court eunuchs, the schemer was warned by one of his advisers: "Kong Rong has a famous name [*ming*]. If you make him your enemy, all the Confucian gentlemen in this country will leave you at once." In all these cases, the *ming* of the deceased, which had been spread far and wide by their friends and colleagues, seems to have been transmitted to their filial sons.

❹ The Deceased

The decoration of an Eastern Han funerary structure was not always determined by the descendents of the dead or his former associates. Some

这两种丧葬文本及建筑因此显示出两种纪念碑性的概念，其差异源于赞助人与死者不同的关系。但是，祠堂和墓碑又是肩并肩地矗立在墓地中，构成一组互相联系和交流的纪念性建筑。这种联系和交流的主体仍然是它们背后的两组赞助人。参加葬礼的来宾所表达的敬意，不仅献给死者，同时也是献给死者的家庭。他们的敬意不仅为死者带来了身后的名声，同时也为他的后人提供了一个表现其孝心的机会。无独有偶，本节所提到的三次葬礼——韩韶、陈寔、孔宙的葬礼——都对其后人产生了深刻的影响。

陈寔盛大的葬礼使他的儿子陈纪出了大名：他痛哭不已以至于吐血，甚至“虽衰服已除，而积毁消瘠，殆将灭性”。[96] 他的孝行被上报到朝廷，其画像被散布全国。最后，他官至大鸿胪。韩韶迟到的荣誉也使他的儿子韩融“声名甚盛，五府并辟。献帝（189—220年在位）初，至太仆”。[97]

孔宙的儿子孔融在中国历史上更为著名。[98] 孔融幼年即敬慕李膺。据《后汉书》记载，他 13 岁丧父，“哀悴过毁，扶而后起，州里归其孝。”后来，大将军何进因为孔融铁面无私地对抗朝中宦官，欲暗杀他，有人提醒何进说：“孔文举（孔融）有重名，将军若造怨此人，则四方之士引领而去矣。”在所有这些事例中，友人和同事所广为传播的死者的“名”，似乎也被转移到了他们的“孝子”身上。

四、死者

东汉丧葬建筑的装饰并不总是由死者的后人或故交来决定。有的

people may have participated in the planning process before their death in order to express their thoughts or feelings. They may have ordered favorite scenes and motifs to be depicted on their own (future) funerary monuments; in such cases they were the "designer" of the decorative program. One such person was Zhao Qi (alias Zhao Jia, d. 201).[99] As a young man, he gained a reputation as a learned scholar with high moral principles. He married a daughter of the head official scholar, Ma Rong (79-166), but refused to speak to his famous father-in-law because the latter lacked "a gentleman's integrity."[100] He fell ill before celebrating his fortieth birthday and was confined to his bed for seven years. When he finally decided that death was imminent, he summoned his nephew and told him his final wish:

> Although born into this world as a man of destiny, I cannot match Xu You in pursuing a reclusive life, nor can I compare myself to Yi Yin and Lü Shang in worldly achievements. Heaven has abandoned me—what can I say about it! Please place a stone in front of my tomb and inscribe it with the following words:
>
> There was a free man during the Han.
> His name was Zhao Jia.
> He had high aspirations but no fortune.
> Should such a fate be bestowed on him?

Zhao Qi did not die, however. After his recovery, he served in several official posts, until he incurred the enemy of powerful court eunuchs and was forced into hiding in 158. All his relatives were imprisoned and executed. He changed his name, wandered all over the country, and earned his living selling pancakes. One day he was recognized in a marketplace by a righteous man named Sun Song, who took him home and hid him inside a hollow wall. Only after the Great Proscription ended did Zhao Qi leave his living grave, where he had spent several years. He won respect from fellow Confucians and was finally promoted to a prominent office. But even during this period of glory, the idea of building a funerary monument for himself continued to occupy his mind. According to his biography in the *History of the Latter Han*, "He constructed his graveyard when he was still living. He painted four famous historical figures—Jizha, Zichan, Yan Ying, and Shuxiang—as guests flanking his self-portrait in the position of host. He also inscribed a eulogy alongside each image."[101] Zhao Qi's tomb still existed in the early sixth century, when the renowned geographer Li Daoyuan visited it and recorded its mural in his *Annotated Canon of Waterways*: "The tomb of Zhao Taiqing [Zhao Qi's style name] is [now] inside the city of Ying.

人在生前为了表达自己的思想或情感，也会参与设计，为自己（将来）的墓祠选择所钟爱的装饰主题与画面。从这种意义上讲，他们成了这些丧葬建筑装饰程序实际的“设计者”。赵岐（又名赵嘉，？—201 年）便是其中的一位。[99] 他年轻时便因为学问与德行而享盛名。他娶了当时的著名学者马融的女儿为妻，但却因为马融“不持士节”而不与之交往。[100] 在三十余岁时，赵岐患重疾卧床七年，他感到余日不多，便召来其侄子，留下了自己最终的愿望：

> 大丈夫生世，遁无箕山之操，仕无伊、吕之勋，天不我与，复何言哉？可立一员石于吾墓前，刻之曰：
>
> 汉有逸人，姓赵名嘉，有志无时，命也奈何？

然而赵岐并未死去，康复之后，他又担任了多种官职。158 年，赵岐受到朝廷中当权宦官的迫害而逃匿，其所有的亲属被捕入狱并处死。他变换姓名，浪迹乡野，以卖胡饼谋生。一日，义士孙嵩在市中认出了他，将他带回家，藏于复壁之中。直到数年之后，党锢结束，赵岐才得以复出。他受到儒生们的尊崇，升迁至显赫的官位。但即使在这段荣耀的时期，为自己建墓的计划仍萦绕于他心中。据《后汉书 · 赵岐传》记载：“（赵岐）先自为寿藏，图季札、子产、晏婴、叔向四像居宾位，又自画其像居主位，皆为赞颂。”[101] 赵岐的墓在 6 世纪初仍存在，地理学家郦道元曾寻访该墓，并在其所著《水经注》中记述了其壁画：“（郢）城中有赵台卿冢，岐平生

It was built by Zhao Qi himself when he was still alive. He painted a host with his guests to preserve his good feelings toward his friends and to express the values he had always admired."[102]

It is possible that Zhao Qi had the four ancient worthies painted in his tomb because he admired these men so highly that he wanted them to keep him company for eternity. Li Daoyuan's reading of the picture,
224 however, reveals a more specific meaning: these ancient figures stood for Zhao Qi's own friends who had helped save him during the years of trouble. By portraying these historical figures beside his self-portrait, Zhao Qi could express his deep gratitude toward his friends as well as his moral and political values. This design leads us to investigate once more the use of historical allusions. A check of historical records reveals that this trend developed into a standard mode of self-expression toward the end of the Western Han. Following this development came a massive effort to classify and catalogue all famous historical figures and events. Liu Xiang (77?-6 B.C.), for example, compiled three large works entitled the *Biographies of Exemplary Women*, the *Biographies of Exemplary Men* (*Lieshi zhuan*; also known as the *Biographies of Filial Sons*), and the *Biographies of Immortals* (*Liexian zhuan*), as well as a book entitled *A Garden of Talk* (*Shuo yuan*) whose 784 entries illuminate various political principles.[103] Another kind of catalogue contained various omens that conveyed Heaven's responses to human affairs.[104] These and other compilations formed a huge collection of classifications of historical knowledge and provided an enormous number of examples for anyone making a demonstration or argument. Some of these catalogues were illustrated, and their illustrations became the prototypes for the popular "pictorial allusions" used in decorating monuments.[105]

The comment that Zhao Qi "painted" the four ancient worthies in his tomb, therefore, does not necessarily imply that he created the images; models for these figures could have been found in illustrated biographies or "copybooks."[106] By selecting his own "heroes," however, Zhao Qi was able to make his personal ideas known. The same method was employed on a far greater scale by another Eastern Han Confucian scholar named Wu Liang (78-151) in designing his own funerary monument. We learn this, however, not from textual references as in the case of Zhao Qi, but from the coherent ideology reflected in the pictorial carvings on Wu Liang's memorial shrine, which I have thoroughly discussed in an earlier

自所营也，冢图宾主之容，用存情好，叙其宿尚矣。"[102]

赵岐把这四位古代高士的形象画在自己的墓中，自然是因为他对这几个人极为尊崇，以致希望与他们成为永恒的同伴。然而，郦道元对此画的解读揭示出另一层特殊含义：赵岐身边的四个古代贤人实际上象征着他的朋友，他们在赵岐陷入困境时曾给予他莫大的帮助。通过在自画像两侧图绘这些历史人物，赵岐既可以表达他对朋友的感激之情，又可抒发他在道义和政治上的价值观。这一例子引导我们再次去探索汉画中历史引喻的意义。从文献记载可知，历史引喻在西汉晚期发展成一种文学艺术表达的标准形式。在这一倾向的带动下，出现了一种对历史人物与事件进行大规模分类和编目的行动。例如刘向（前 77？—前 6 年）所编订的三部书《列女传》《列士传》（又名《孝子传》）和《列仙传》，以及采用 784 个人物事例来阐述各种政治原则的《说苑》，就都属于这类著作。[103] 另一种分类著作是符瑞目录，收集了上天向人间传达其意旨的各种祥瑞现象。[104] 这些鸿篇巨制的文献汇集梳理了大量历史知识，为人们引证和讨论种种问题提供了丰富的例证。这些著作有的带有插图，随即成为纪念性建筑上所流行的"图画引喻"的资源。[105]

当然，史书说赵岐在墓中"图"四位高士像，并不一定意味着他实际上创作了这些画像；这些人物形象的原形可能在带有插图的传记或"粉本"中找到。[106] 通过选择他心目中的英雄，赵岐得以抒发其个人情怀。这种手段被东汉时期另一位名叫武梁（78—151 年）的儒士在设计其墓祠时大量采用。我们并不是像了解赵岐那样通过文献，而是通过武梁祠堂中的画像雕刻来获知这一情况的，因为这些画像反映出只可能属于武梁本人的清晰有序的思想。[107] 武梁祠

monograph.[107] The following summary emphasizes the "intentionality" of the monument's design, clarifies some crucial arguments about the "authorship" and pictorial program of the design, and offers a new formulation of the narrative and symbolic structure of the decorative program.

A concise biography of Wu Liang can be found in the epitaph on his memorial stela:

> The late Han Attendant Wu had the personal name Liang and the style name Suizong. The attendant embodied the outstanding virtues of loyalty and filial piety. He studied the *Commentary of the Han School on the "Book of Songs"* [*Han shi*] and gave lectures [on this text]. He also mastered the "River [Chart]" and the "Luo [Writing]," as well as the works of the different schools. He studied widely and examined [the texts] in detail. He inquired into the roots of texts, and there was no book that he did not read. The departments of the prefecture and the district invited and summoned him [to official posts], but he declined on the grounds of illness. He contented himself with the poverty of his humble home and was pleased with the righteousness that he learned every morning. He never wearied of teaching people the great Dao. He felt ashamed of the [conventional] way in which people copied one another in the world, and he never even paid attention to those who wielded power. When he reached the age of 60, he followed only his mind, maintaining his inflexible purity without vacillation. Alas! He did not ascend to high official posts, but was instead hurt by public opinion. In the summer of the first year of the Yuanjia reign period [A.D. 151], at age 74, he fell ill and died.

This passage enables us to draw a general contour of Wu Liang's life and thought. In scholarship, he belonged to the New Text school, a scholastic tradition characterized by its emphasis on the exegesis of the Confucian classics and omen theories.[108] Politically, he was a "retired worthy," who escaped from the corrupt court dominated by royal relatives and eunuchs and sought spiritual purity in private learning and teaching.[109] In morality, he took the general Confucian principles of filial piety and loyalty as his guide. Wu Liang's epitaph singles out one particular event that summarizes his life: his declining of official posts offered by local authorities. Not coincidentally, this is also the only episode in his life portrayed on his memorial shrine. Illustrated in Fig. 4.29, this scene is identified by a cartouche as a "county official" paying respect to an invisible "retired gentlemen" in a humble ox-drawn carriage. 225

现存于山东省嘉祥县，是东汉武氏家族墓地中一组祠堂中的一座。我在以前的著作中对武梁祠做过系统的研究。本文将进一步探讨该祠堂设计的“意图”，澄清有关画像设计的“原作者”以及画像程序等一些关键性问题，并对其装饰的叙事性及象征性结构提出一些新的阐释。

在宋人著录的武梁碑碑文中，我们可以读到武梁简明的传记：

> 汉故从事武椽，椽讳梁，字绥宗。椽体德忠孝，岐嶷有异。治韩诗经，阙帻传讲，兼通河洛、诸子传记。广学甄彻，穷综典□，靡不□览。州郡请召，辞疾不就。安衡门之陋，乐朝闻之义。诲人以道，临川不倦。耻世雷同，不阒权门。年逾从心，执节抱分。始终不僓，弥弥益固。大位不济，为众所伤。年七十四，元嘉元年，季夏三日，遭疾陨灵。

这段文字勾画出了武梁生平与思想的一个大的轮廓。就学术方面讲，他属于以强调解释儒家经典和符瑞理论为特征的今文学派。[108] 从政治上看，他是一位从外戚和宦官所支配的腐败政坛逃离出来的“处士”，思想清素，专事私学与讲授。[109] 在道德上，他以儒家尽忠守孝的至理大道作为人生准则。碑文中记载武梁曾拒绝接受地方政府给他的官职，这个特殊事件综括了他一生的行迹。绝非偶然的是，该事件也是唯一刻画在祠堂中的武梁生活的片段。如图 4.29 所示，一位“县功曹”正在向隐于一辆卷棚牛车中的“处士”跪拜，该场面应即表现了这一事件。

Fig. 4.29. A county official paying his respects to a retired gentleman. Wu Liang Shrine carving. A.D. 151. Ink rubbing.

图 4.29　县功曹拜见处士。武梁祠画像。东汉晚期，151 年。拓片。

Like Zhao Qi's self-portrait, this scene denotes Wu Liang's presence in his memorial hall. The importance of this scene, however, lies not only in its content but also in its position on the shrine, which signifies the "authorship" of the whole decorative program. Engraved at the lower left corner on the left wall, it is the last scene in the whole decorative program (Fig. 4.30, no. 44).[110] This placement accords with a deeply rooted convention in Chinese historiography: as the observer of ongoing historical events, the historian actually "ends" history; by concluding his work with a "self-statement," he adopts a rhetorical form to consolidate this role. This convention had been firmly established in the first comprehensive Chinese history. Sima Qian (145-86 B.C.) of the Western Han ended his *Records of the Historian* with a chapter titled the "Self-statement of the Grand Historian."[111] His precedent was followed by Ban Gu (32-92) in compiling his *History of the Former Han* during the early Eastern Han. Their example was followed by Wu Liang in the second century. In all these cases, the "authors" come forth to conclude their historical observations—to identify themselves explicitly, to let their lives and ambitions be known, and to claim their works as their own lasting monuments.

This crucial parallel between the Wu Liang shrine and the *Records of the Historian* led to the discovery of other structural links between these two monumental works. As scholars have noted, advanced historical writings had appeared long before the Han.[112] But the *Records of the Historian*, in Burton Watson's words, "represents an entirely new departure in Chinese historiography" by initiating a coherent structure for a "general history" (*tongshi*).[113] Instead of following the year-by-year chronicle style popular during the Eastern Zhou period, Sima Qian divided his materials into a number of large "blocks." The "Treatises" ("Shu") deal with important subjects including "spirits and gods, [and] the relationships of heaven and man."[114] In most of the *Records of the*

和赵岐的自画像一样，这一画面意味着武梁本人在祠堂中的存在。该画面的重要性不仅在于其内容，还在于它在祠堂中的位置恰好标志着“设计者”与整套祠堂画像的关系。该画面刻在武梁祠左壁的左下角，是祠堂整个画像程序中的最后一幅［图 4.30，第 44］。[110] 据中国古代修史的一个基本惯例，作为一位对发展变化的历史事件的观察者，史家本人总把自己定位于所写历史的末端。通过一篇自传结束一部历史著作，史家就可以用反身自顾的方式来突出他作为捉笔者的角色。这种传统在中国第一部通史著作中便已牢固地确立了：司马迁以《太史公自序》来结束《史记》，首发其凡。[111] 班固（32—92 年）在东汉初年编订的《汉书》仍继其遗风。这种规范被 2 世纪的武梁承袭下来。在所有这些情况中，“作者”本人站出来总结他们对历史的观察，直述其生平与志向。通过这种方式，其著作便成了他们自己永恒的纪念碑。

武梁祠与《史记》这一共同点引导我们探寻这两部不朽作品之间更多结构上的联系。正如学者所指出的，中国在汉代以前已有了很久远的治史传统，[112] 但是用华兹生的话来说，《史记》一书是一部结构紧凑的“通史”，“确立了编修中国历史的一个全新的起点”。[113] 与东周时期流行的逐年纪事的编年体著作不同，司马迁将历史材料组织为若干宏大“版块”。一个“版块”是主题性的“书”，其内容涉及神明与上帝，“终始古今，深观时变。”[114] 另一“版块”包括了

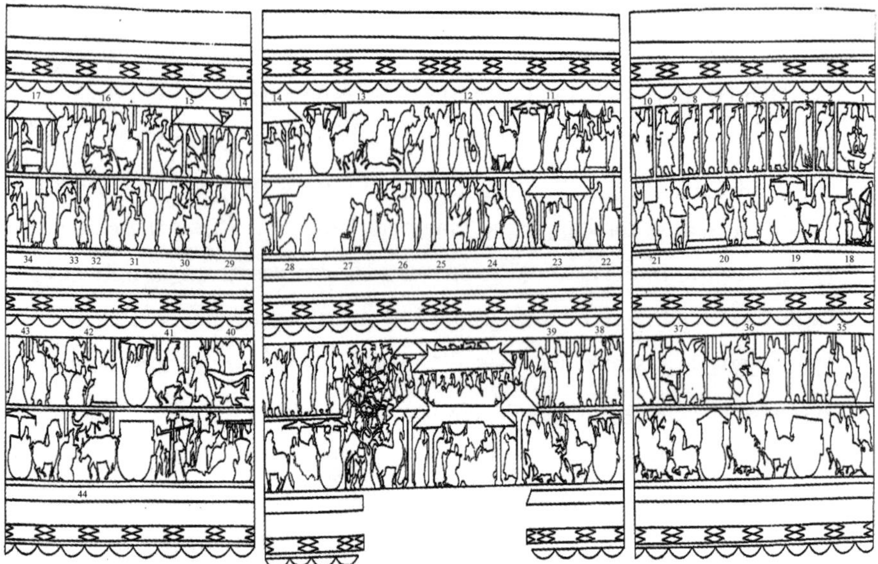

Fig. 4.30. The 44 scenes identified by cartouches on the walls of the Wu Liang Shrine. Drawing.

图 4.30 武梁祠中有榜题的 44 幅画像。东汉晚期，151 年。线图。

Historian, however, history as a whole is illustrated by the lives of selected individuals, who are grouped together by lineage, political ties, or by similar attributes and deeds. These groups are further classified into three lengthy sections: the "Basic Annals" ("Benji"), which narrates China's dynastic history from its beginning to the historian's time; the "Hereditary Houses" ("Shijia"), which describes noble lineages assisting their lords and rulers; and the "Memoirs" ("Liezhuan"), which records individuals of distinguished behavior.[115] Furthermore, the *Records of the Historian* includes the historian's judgments as an integral part of the history. Sima Qian ends most chapters with his own comments, introduced by the phrase "The Grand Historian remarks," and concludes the whole book with his "Self-statement."

226 The "designer" of the Wu Liang shrine adopted these general principles in decorating a three-dimensional structure. The ceiling of the shrine is covered with omen images representing "the relationship of heaven and man." Its two gables are decorated with "spirits and gods."

Forty-three "biographies" of men and women are illustrated on its three walls, representing the entire course of Chinese history up to Wu Liang's time. Eulogies inscribed beside pictures are the designer's comments, and the last scene echoes Sima Qian's "Self-statement." Created two and a half centuries after the *Records of the Historian*, however, these carvings also reflect new social, ethical, and religious currents, as well as a different compilation process. The omen images on the ceiling reflect the political values of the retired worthies, of which Wu Liang was a loyal member. The spirits and gods on the gables are represented by the Queen Mother of the West and the King Father of the East—two immortals who became extremely popular only from the second century.[116] The "biographies" of historical figures depicted on the walls are organized into a new structure

书中的大部分篇章，是从历史的总体着眼所选择记述的人物传记。这些人物被按照世系血统、政治关系或功业事迹进行分类。不同类型的人物进一步组成三个部分："本纪"记述了从历史开端至作者所处时代的中国王朝史，"世家"描写了辅佐君主的诸侯和贵族，"列传"记录了著名人物的功迹。[115] 不仅如此，史家本人的评判也被作为一个必不可少的部分包括在《史记》中。司马迁在大部分篇目的结尾用"太史公曰"的格式进行评论，又以《太史公自序》作为全书的结语。

武梁祠画像的"设计师"在装饰这座三维的建筑时采用了《史记》的总体结构。祠堂天顶上刻满了种种祥瑞图像，以再现"天人之际"。两个山墙的尖楣部分装饰了神灵和仙界。43 个不同人物的"传记"刻画在三面墙上，表现了武梁之前的全部中国历史。画像旁边的赞文是设计者的评论，最后一幅画像则模仿了司马迁的"自序"。当然，这些雕刻晚于《史记》两个半世纪，自然会反映新的社会、伦理和宗教潮流，以及一种不同的编纂程序。如屋顶的祥瑞画像反映了作为一个"隐逸儒士"的武梁的政治价值观。山墙尖楣上的仙界以西王母、东王公为中心，而这两位神明只是到了 2 世纪才得以流行。[116] 墙壁上的历史人物"列传"以"三纲"为基本结构，

determined by the Three Bonds (*sangang*; the relations between ruler and subject, father and son, husband and wife), a Confucian doctrine overwhelmingly emphasized during the Eastern Han period. Moreover, unlike Sima Qian who wrote the first general history in China, the designer of the Wu Liang shrine only selected his materials from existing catalogues—again a trend current in Wu Liang's time. Rather than inventing stories or scenes, this designer's creativity lay in his selection and organization of allusions for his own purpose.

As I have demonstrated elsewhere, the omen images on the ceiling and their explanatory cartouches are derived from annotated good-omen illustrations called *Ruitu*, which had appeared by the first century B.C. and gained increasing popularity among Confucian scholars during the first and second centuries A.D.[117] Ban Gu, for example, described his use of this text in a poem:

> I opened the *Spiritual Text*, and read the *Pictures of Auspicious Omens* [*Ruitu*].
> I found the [image of] the white pheasant, which resembles that of a pure crow.[118]

The rationalist Wang Chong, in his attacks on scholars of the New Text school, criticized such practices: "The scholars in their essays claim for themselves the faculty of knowing the phoenix and the unicorn when
227 they see them. They, of course, rely on the pictures of the phoenix and the unicorn."[119]

Neither Ban Gu's account nor Wang Chong's criticism, however, say much about the function of Wu Liang's omen images, since these images were not randomly copied from omen catalogues but were carefully selected to convey a specific political ideology. Whereas a Han omen catalogue must have contained hundreds of items related to all spheres of human life,[120] the much smaller number engraved on the Wu Liang Shrine had distinctive implications, explained by accompanying cartouches that identify the conditions for the omens' appearances:[121]

1. A manifestation of the *qilin* unicorn, the yellow dragon, the white tiger, or the intertwining trees admonishes the ruler to display virtues such as benevolence, righteousness, propriety, wisdom, and sincerity (Figs. 4.31a-d).

即"君为臣纲、父为子纲、夫为妻纲"，而三纲是东汉时期盛行的儒家学说。此外，与司马迁撰写的首部中国史不同，武梁祠画像是从已有的典籍和图录中选择材料，这是武梁所处时代的一种流行作法。画像设计师的工作在于根据自己的意图选择和编排这些已有的引喻材料，而不在于创作新的故事与画面。

我在他处已论证过，武梁祠内屋顶上的祥瑞图像以及榜题上的说明文字，均来源于一种叫作《瑞图》的带有说明文字的图解。《瑞图》至少在公元前1世纪已经出现，公元1—2世纪在儒家学者中十分流行。[117]例如，班固在一首诗中说道：

启灵篇兮披瑞图，获白雉兮效素乌。[118]

理性主义者王充在其驳斥今文经派的著作中有这样的批评："儒者之论，自说见凤皇、麒麟而知之。何则？案凤凰、麒麟之象。……考以图像，验以古今，则麒麟可得审也。"[119]

然而，无论是班固的叙述还是王充的批评，都未涉及武梁祠中所见的这类祥瑞图像的含义，因为这些图像并不是随便从《瑞图》中复制的，而是为了表达一种特定的政治思想而认真选取的。汉代符瑞目录中可能包括数以百计的与人类各方面生活相关的祥瑞，[120]但是武梁祠中所刻祥瑞的数量有限，有着特定的意义。下面所录的刻在图像一侧的榜题，规定了这些祥瑞出现的条件：[121]

1. 麟，不刳胎残少则至［图4.31a］。不漉池如渔，则黄龙游于池［图4.31b］。白虎，王者不暴虐，则白虎仁不害人［图4.31c］。木连理，王者德洽，八方为一家，则连理生［图4.31d］。

2. An appearance of the jade horse, the birds joined at the wing, the fish joined at the eye, the white horse with a red mane, or the red bear requires that the ruler honor and employ virtuous men and retired worthies, and exclude sycophants (Figs. 4.31e-i).

3. Three omens, the lake horse, the six-legged beast, and the beasts joined at the shoulder, demand that the ruler be concerned for ordinary people (Figs. 4.31j-l).

4. A sighting of the silver jar requires that the ruler practice "quiescence" and that punishments be properly applied (Fig. 4.31m).

5. The dark *gui* tablet, the jade *sheng* headdress, and the intertwining trees require that the country under the ruler's leadership be strong, peaceful, and unified (Figs. 4.31n, o).

6. A manifestation of the *bi* disk of glass requires that the ruler not dissemble his faults (Fig. 4.31p).

It is clear that these omens have nothing to do with popular beliefs in longevity and immortality. Rather, they dictate a series of demands on the ruler of the state: the ruler must be a model of Confucian virtues; he must employ Confucian worthies and take care of his subjects; his court should have no place for evil "sycophants"; his governance should be just; his country should be peaceful and strong; and, finally, he should criticize himself if he does not meet these criteria. The same ideas occur in the *Commentary of the Han School on the "Book of Songs,"* in which Wu Liang specialized: "By serving the old and nourishing the orphaned, the ruler transforms the people. By promoting the worthy and rewarding the meritorious, he encourages [people] to do good. By punishing the wicked and dismissing the negligent, he makes evil hateful."[122]

The omen images, therefore, reflected a general Confucian view of an ideal political state. On the other hand, they also voiced the Confucian criticism of the contemporary political scene, since all the ingredients of this state were absent in Emperor Huan's court. It was the unanimous view of Confucian scholars that this court was corrupt and controlled by sycophants—first by royal relatives and then by eunuchs. Virtuous men were forced into hiding or were brutally murdered. Commoners lived in an abyss of misery; wars and natural disasters were ceaseless. This situation, recorded in detail in various versions of the dynasty's written history, is summarized in the *History of the Latter Han*:

2.（玉）马，（王者）清明尊贤则至［图 4.31e］。比翼鸟，王者德及高远则至［图 4.31f］。比目鱼，王者德及幽隐则见［图 4.31g］。白马朱鬣，（王者任贤）良则见［图 4.31h］。赤熊，仁奸息［图 4.31i］。

3. 泽马，王者劳来（百姓）则（至）［图 4.31j］。六足兽，谋及众则至［图 4.31k］。（比肩兽，王）者德及鳏寡（则至）［图 4.31l］。

4. 银瓮，刑法得中（则）至［图 4.31m］。

5. 玄圭，水泉流通，四海会同则至［图 4.31n］。玉胜，王者……［图 4.31o］。

6. 璧流离，王者不隐过则至［图 4.31p］。

显而易见，这些祥瑞与当时流行的长寿与升仙的信仰并不相关，而是对一国之君做出一系列的指令：当权者必须成为儒家德行的榜样；他必须礼贤下士；在他的宫廷中不能有溜须拍马者的立足之地；他的统治必须公正；他的国家必须太平而强大。最后，在没能达到上述准则的时候，他必须有能力进行自我批评。武梁祠祥瑞画像中体现出的这些对皇帝的要求也见于武梁所专长的《韩诗》："事老养孤以化民，升贤赏功以劝善，惩奸绌失以丑恶。"[122]

这些祥瑞图像所反映的是儒家心目中一般性的理想政治体制。但由于桓帝时期的朝政每况愈下，越来越远离这些理想，这些图像也反映了儒生们对现实政治的批评。当时的儒者一致认为，朝廷先后为善于献媚的外戚与宦官所左右，已十分腐败。忠良之臣或被迫隐匿，或横遭残害。兵戎相继，天灾不绝，百姓挣扎于痛苦的深渊。各种汉代史书都对这种局面做了翔实的记载，《汉书·党锢列传》中总括云：

Fig. 4.31. Omen images carved on the ceiling of the Wu Liang Shrine. A.D. 151. (a) Qilin unicorn; (b) yellow dragon; (c) white tiger; (d) intertwining trees; (e) jade horse; (f) birds joined at the wing; (g) fish joined at the eye; (h) white horse with red mane; (i) red bear; (j) lake horse; (k) six-legged beast; (l) beasts joined at the shoulder; (m) silver jar; (n) black *gui* tablet; (o) jade *sheng* headdress; (p) glass *bi* disk. Reconstruction.

图 4.31 武梁祠顶部的祥瑞图。东汉晚期，151 年。木版复制品。（a）麒麟。（b）黄龙。（c）白虎。（d）木连理。（e）玉马。（f）比翼鸟。（g）比目鱼。（h）白马朱鬣。（i）赤熊。（j）泽马。（k）六足兽。（l）比肩兽。（m）银瓮。（n）玄圭。（o）玉胜。（p）璧流离。

During the reigns of Huan and Ling, the emperors were negligent, the government confused, and the fate of the empire rested with the eunuchs. Scholars were ashamed to be in league with these people and therefore there were those who went about voicing their grievances, and the retired scholars were liberal with their criticism. Consequently their reputations waxed high, and they mutually reviled or boasted about one another. They examined and evaluated all the high officials and criticized those who were in charge of the government. Thus the fashion of indignantly voicing criticism became widespread.[123]

Wu Liang's epitaph clearly identifies him as one of these "retired scholars." The selection and portrayal of specific omens on his memorial hall thus preserved and expressed his political ideals and criticisms. In fact, the two main themes implied in these images—the privilege of knowing Heaven's will and the glorification of virtuous retirement—are essential to the Han school teachings that Wu Liang had mastered. We read in a basic text of the school: "[The Confucian scholar] first understands the beginnings of disaster and good fortune, and his mind will be without illusions. For this reason the sages lived in retirement and reflected profoundly; they were unique in their apprehension and 229

逮桓、灵之间，主荒政缪，国命委于阉寺，士子羞与为伍，故匹夫抗愤，处士横议，遂乃激扬名声，互相题拂，品覈公卿，裁量执政，婞直之风，于斯行矣。[123]

武梁碑文清楚地说明，武梁本人即属于这类“处士”。祠堂内特殊祥瑞的选择与刻画明显地保存并表达了他的思想和他对当时政治的看法。实际上，这些图像所表现的两个原则，即对“天命”的特有重视和对独善其身的隐退之士的称赏，是《韩诗》学派的基本主张，也是武梁本人所秉持的信条。这一学派的基本文献《韩诗外传》声称：“（士）先知祸福之终始，而心无惑焉。故圣人隐居深念，

insight."[124] The third quality of a Confucian scholar, according to the same text, is his deep understanding of history and his effort to preserve correct human relationships.

In the thousand undertakings and the ten thousand transformations their Way is unexhausted—such are the Six Classics. Now as to appropriate relations between prince and subject, the love between father and son, the distinction between husband and wife, and precedence between friends—these are what the Confucian takes care to preserve; daily he "cuts and polishes" without ceasing. Though he live in a poor alley and in a wretched hut, not having enough to fill his emptiness or to clothe himself, and though he be without so much as an awl's point of territory, still his understanding is sufficient to control the empire.[125]

Wu Liang practiced this teaching wholeheartedly: "He inquired into the roots of texts, and there was no book that he did not read"; "he contented himself with the poverty of his humble home and was pleased with the righteousness that he learned every morning"; and "he never wearied of teaching people the great Dao." We are also told that "When he reached the age of 60, he followed only his mind, maintaining his inflexible purity without vacillation." From a Confucian approach, such a stage of mind represented the highest achievement of a scholar's learning and spiritual cultivation: historical patterns and essential human values would become crystal clear to him, and his personal existence would find its own justification in this macrocosmic universe. This approach underlies the wall carvings of the Wu Liang Shrine, the most ambitious representation of human history ever attempted in Chinese art.

This historical narrative begins with a series of ten archaic sovereigns (Fig. 4.30, nos. 1-10), a composition comparable to the "Basic Annals" in Sima Qian's *Records of the Historian*. The eulogy beside the image of Fu Xi, who, with his consort Nü Wa, initiates the sequence (Fig. 4.30, no. 1; Fig. 4.32), reads:

Fu Xi, the Black Spirit:

He initiated leadership;
He drew the Trigrams and made knotted cords,
To administer the land within the seas.[126]

Standing at the beginning of history, Fu Xi was thought to be an intermediary between divine and human spheres, and his greatness lay in his transmission of divine wisdom (symbolized by the Trigrams) to human knowledge. His unique role is represented by portraying him as a hybrid figure, half-human and half-serpent, holding a carpenter's square, which

独闻独见。"[124] 根据同一文献，深刻地理解历史，努力维护正确良好的人际关系，是儒家学者又一种重要品质：

> 千举万变，其道不穷，六经是也。若夫君臣之义，父子之亲，夫妇之别，朋友之序，此儒者之所谨守，日切磋而不舍也。虽居穷巷陋室之下，而内不足以充虚，外不足以盖形，无置锥之地，明察足以持天下。[125]

武梁全心全意地实践了这一学说："穷综典□，靡不□览"，"安衡门之陋，乐朝闻之义"，同时又"诲人以道，临川不倦"。我们还得知，他"年逾从心，执节抱分，始终不貮"。从儒家的眼光来看，这种思想境界表现了一个人学识与修养的最高成就：对他来说，历史的模式和人类的基本价值变得极为清晰，而他的个人存在也在宇宙的宏观存在中找到了价值。这种态度支撑着武梁祠三壁上画像的内容，这些画像可以说是中国艺术中对人类历史最宏大而系统的表现。

与司马迁《史记》中的"本纪"相对应，武梁祠画像对于历史的陈述从十位古代帝王开始［图 4.30，第 1—10］。这套画像的第一幅是伏羲与女娲［图 4.30，第 1；图 4.32］，伏羲画像左侧的赞文说：

> 伏戏苍精：初造王业，
> 画卦结绳，以理海内。[126]

屹立于历史的开端，伏羲是一位连接神界与人间的半神。他的伟大在于向人类传达了象征着神秘智慧的"八卦"。他特殊的历史位置以其半人半蛇的混合形体表现出来。他手持矩尺，表明他具有

Fig. 4.32. The Three Sovereigns. Wu Liang Shrine carvings. A.D. 151. Ink rubbing.
图 4.32 三皇。武梁祠画像。东汉晚期，151 年。拓片。

signifies his ability to "design" the world. He was thought to have instituted the laws of marriage—the most important rule of human society. This belief explains why he was depicted together with the goddess Nü Wa. From their union was born a child who, shown in the picture holding his parents with both hands, metaphorically represents the infant mankind.

Fu Xi and the two following figures, Zhu Rong and Shen Nong, are grouped together as the Three Sovereigns (*Sanhuang*) (Fig. 4.30, nos. 1-3; Fig. 4.32), who symbolize the first stage of human history, a utopian period of natural harmony and balance. This concept is revealed in cartouches as well as pictorial imagery: these figures wear short robes or shorts, with simple turbans to bind their hair. Their plain costumes form a sharp contrast with the elaborate crown and long robes of the next five figures (Fig. 4.30, nos. 4-8; Fig. 4.33) who belonged to the second stage of history, the period of the Five Emperors (*Wudi*).

230 The symbolism of these costumes is stated in the inscription beside the image of the Yellow Emperor, the first of the Five Emperors:

> The Yellow Emperor:
> He created and improved so much!
> He invented weapons and regulated fields;
> He had upper and lower garments hang down,
> And erected temples and palaces.

Fig. 4.33. The Five Emperors. Wu Liang Shrine carvings. A.D. 151. Ink rubbing.
图 4.33 五帝。武梁祠画像。东汉晚期，151 年。拓片。

The phrase "had upper and lower garments hang down" is commonly used in Chinese classical writings as an analogy for the creation of kingship and statecraft.[127] It was believed that at the end of the age of the Three Sovereigns the world had fallen into chaos and the Yellow Emperor

"设计"世界的能力。他司掌着人类社会最高的法则——婚姻的律条，这一观念解释了为何伏羲与女娲描绘在一起。画像中，这对神祇蛇体相缠，从二者的结合诞生出一位幼儿，他双手攀拉其父母，象征着童蒙时期的人类。

伏羲与其身后的祝融和神农共同组成"三皇"[图 4.30，第 1—3；图 4.32]，标志着人类历史的第一个阶段，即一个具有自然和谐与平衡的乌托邦时期。这个历史概念不仅仅由榜题揭示，同时也通过图像表现出来：这些人物身着短袍或短裤，以简单的头巾束发。他们朴素的装束与随后头戴华美王冠、身着长袍的五个人物形成鲜明的对比。接下去的这五个人物是属于第二个历史阶段的"五帝"[图 4.30，第 4—8；图 4.33]。其首领黄帝画像旁边的题记明确地说明了这种服饰的象征意义：

> 黄帝：
> 多所造作，造兵井田，垂衣裳，立宫宅。

中国古典文献常常用"垂衣裳而天下治"一语比喻国家的产生与王权的建立。[127] 根据这些文献，三皇时代结束时天下大乱，黄帝

established peace by using force: he defeated the troublemakers and became master within the four seas. The ages of the Three Sovereigns and the Five Emperors, therefore, are distinguished by oppositions such as "non-action" and "action," simplicity and refinement, equality and stratification; these distinctions are given visual forms in the carvings.

The period of the Five Emperors is again contrasted to the following historical stage in the manner of transmitting rulership. It was thought that political power was handed down among the Five Emperors according to the system called *shanrang*, meaning "to cede" or "to yield." Under this system, a ruler abdicated his throne to the worthiest man in the country regardless of origin or social class. The non-hereditary *shanrang* system, therefore, was based purely on virtue; as a logical consequence, all these rulers were cast as models of human excellence. The demolition of this system marked the beginning of dynastic history; political succession based on genealogy was established. History no longer proceeded in a peaceful linear fashion but began to follow a spiral pattern: each dynasty experienced a rise and decline. Each dynasty was founded by a virtuous king who was wise, benevolent, and hardworking, and each was terminated by an evil ruler who was corrupt, selfish, violent, and lustful. This new pattern, as well as the two opposing types of dynastic rulers, are represented by the portraits of Yu and Jie (Fig. 4.30, nos. 9-10, Fig. 4.34), the first and last rulers of the Xia dynasty. Like Sima Qian, Wu Liang's aim in portraying these archaic rulers was to "examine the deeds and events of the past and investigate the principles behind their success and failure, their rise and decay."[128]

These ancient sovereigns are embodiments of historical concepts, but the remaining three series of images on the shrine's walls—eminent wives, filial sons, and loyal subjects—are represented by dramatic events from their lives. The sources of motifs also vary: whereas descriptions of the ancient rulers are included in the *Records of the Historian* and other historical texts,[129] a close relationship exists between these three series

Fig. 4.34. Yu and Jie of the Xia dynasty. Wu Liang Shrine carvings. A.D. 151. Ink rubbing.

图 4.34　禹与桀。武梁祠画像。东汉晚期，151 年。拓片。

用武力重新确立起新的秩序，征服了作乱者，成为四海之主。因而，三皇与五帝代表了两个截然不同的历史时期，其对立的特征——“无为”与“有为”，简约与文雅，平等与等级——在武梁祠画像中以视觉形象表达出来。

五帝的时代与其后的历史时期又以统治权的传承方式相区别。古代历史学家认为，五帝时代的政治权力是通过“禅让”的制度来传递的。在这种体制下，退位的统治者将权力交给最有才智的一位贤者，而不考虑其出身与社会地位。由于这种非世袭的禅让制纯粹基于德行的优劣，因此从逻辑上讲，所有这一时期的统治者都是贤明的典范。这一系统的崩溃标志着王朝史的开端。政治权力的继承变成世袭，历史的演进不再以一成不变的和平面孔出现，而代之以螺旋形的模式。从此，每一个王朝都要历经勃兴与衰亡。每个王朝多由一位仁慈、明智、能干而富有德行的贤君建立，又由一位腐败、自私、残暴和淫邪的昏君断送。这两类截然相反的统治者的典型在武梁祠画像中分别由夏朝的首位和末位统治者禹和桀代表［图 4.30，第 9—10；图 4.34］。武梁描绘这些古代君王的目的与司马迁一样，在于“网罗天下放失旧闻，王迹所兴，原始察终，见盛观衰”。[128]

这些以单独肖像出现的古代君王体现了不同的历史观念，但是，祠堂墙壁上刻画的其他三组人物，即列女、孝子及忠臣刺客，则是通过戏剧化的叙事情节表现出其事迹和品德。这些画面的主题来源各不相同。

有关古代君王的素材主要来自《史记》和其他史书，[129] 但与这

and Liu Xiang's compilations of historical allusions (the *Biographies of Exemplary Women*, the *Biographies of Filial Sons*, and *A Garden of Talk*). But since Liu Xiang's books contain far more examples than a handful of
231 dynastic rulers, Wu Liang faced a severe challenge in selecting his motifs. An analysis of the pictorial stories on the Wu Liang Shrine suggests that at least three criteria were taken into account in motif selection. The first was chronology: following the archaic rulers from antiquity to the Xia, the eight virtuous women all lived during the Zhou; the series of filial sons begins with Zeng Shen of the Eastern Zhou and ends with two filial paragons who lived not long before Wu Liang's time. The second criterion was the basic Confucian virtues: these three series present, sequentially, chastity, filial piety, and loyalty. The third criterion was a certain personal preference; that is, particular messages pertaining to the wishes of the deceased.

Fig. 4.35. Chaste, obedient, and righteous women. Wu Liang Shrine carvings. A.D. 151. Ink rubbing.

图 4.35 列女。武梁祠画像。东汉晚期，151 年。拓片。

The emphasis on female chastity is disclosed in the selection of heroines from the *Biographies of Exemplary Women,* which records the lives of 105 famous women from antiquity in seven categories. None of the seven exemplary women depicted on the top register of the shrine walls (Fig. 4.30, nos. 11-17, Fig. 4.35) are chosen from Liu Xiang's categories of "reasoning and understanding," "virtuous and wise," and "benevolent and wise." All are from the two domestic types: "chaste and obedient" and "chaste and righteous."[130] This focus differs markedly from those in other surviving portraits of virtuous women: a screen from the tomb of Sima Jinlong (a relative of the Wei royal house) is painted with queens and palace ladies (Fig. 4.36),[131] and a handscroll painting attributed to Gu Kaizhi (*ca.* 345-406) portrays only "benevolent and wise" female figures (Fig. 4.37).[132]

三组人物具有密切关系的文献资料是刘向编订的三部历史著作——《列女传》《孝子传》和《说苑》。由于刘向著作中包括了大量人物，远比古帝王的数量多得多，武梁面对的一项重要挑战是从中挑选出对他最有意义的画像题材。对武梁祠故事画像的研究表明，武梁在选择题材时至少使用了三个标准。第一个是年代学：承接上古到夏代的古代帝王的是八位生活在周代的列女，随后的一系列孝子故事从东周的曾参开始，以生活在距武梁所处时代不远的两位孝子结束。第二个标准是儒家最基本的道德观念：这三组故事所表现的分别是节、孝、忠三种基本道德。第三个标准是死者的某些个人愿望，即他所希望传达给他的家属的特殊信息。

《列女传》七卷共记载了105位古代著名的妇女，武梁所挑选的例子明显地强调妇女的贞节。刻画在祠堂墙壁最上层的列女故事［图4.30，第11—17；图4.35］没有一幅是从《列女传》中“辩通”“贤明”“仁智”三卷中选出的，而都是出自记载“家庭类型”妇女的“贞顺”和“节义”两卷。[130]与此侧重点不同，北魏皇亲司马金龙墓出土的漆屏风上主要描绘了后妃的故事［图4.36］，[131]而传顾恺之（约345—406年）所作的手卷《列女仁智图》仅以“仁义”和“睿智”的女性为表现对象［图4.37］。[132]与这两个例子比较，更可以看出武梁祠画像列女图的特殊角度。

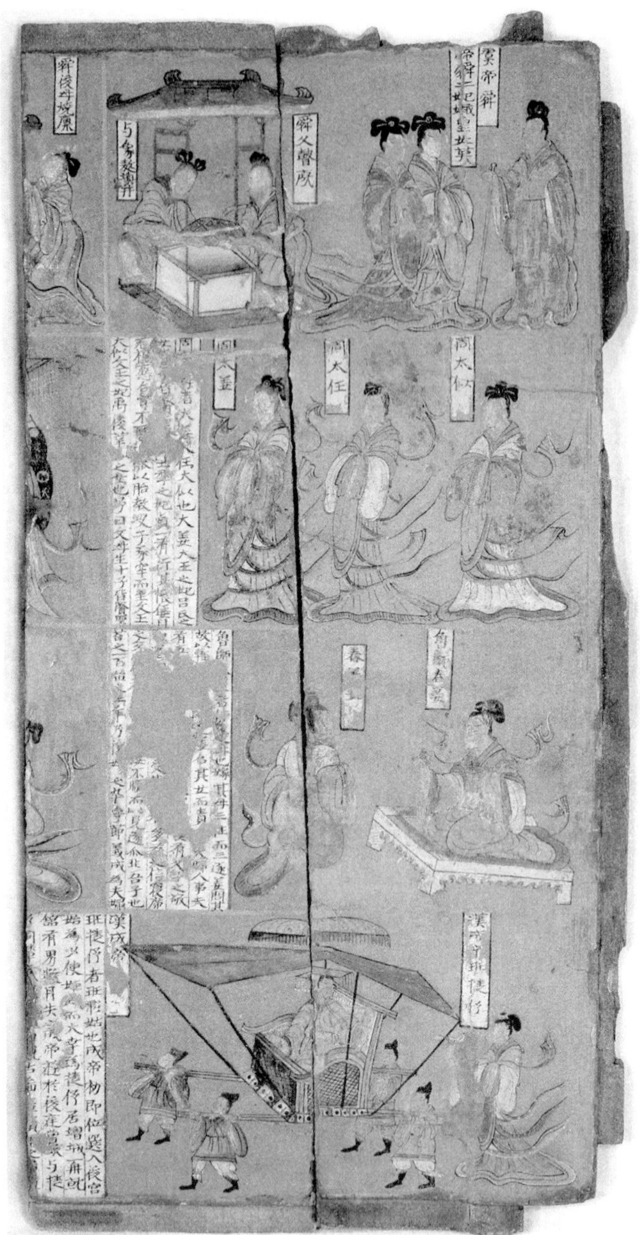

Fig. 4.36. Painted screen panel. Wood and lacquer. Northern Wei dynasty. Before A.D. 484. H. 80 cm. W. 20 cm. Excavated from Sima Jinlong's tomb at Datong, Shanxi province. Datong Museum.

图 4.36 画像屏风。木与漆。北魏，早于 484 年。高 80 厘米，宽 20 厘米。山西大同司马金龙墓出土。大同市博物馆藏。

Fig. 4.37. Girl from Qishi of Lu. Ink and color on silk. Detail of the "Portraits of Benevolent and Wise Women," attributed to Gu Kaizhi, but probably a 12th-century copy of a post-Han painting. Palace Museum, Beijing.

图 4.37　传顾恺之《列女仁智图》局部鲁漆室女。绢本，墨与彩。可能是 12 世纪摹本。故宫博物院藏。

Moreover, the selected historical allusions were reorganized in the shrine's decoration into a new sequence that placed special importance on its "title scene." This structure derives from the Han interpretation of the Confucian classics; for example, the poems initiating the four
chapters of the *Book of Songs* were called the Four Beginnings (*sishi*) 232
and were believed to imply a "secret code" for interpreting the whole classic. On the Wu Liang Shrine, the portrayal of eminent women begins with the story of Liang the Excellent (Fig. 4.30, no. 11; Figs. 4.21a, b). As mentioned earlier, Liang was a famous beauty; after her husband died,

我们也注意到，武梁祠堂装饰中对历史人物故事的排列特别重视每一系列的第一幅画像。这种结构是从汉代人对儒家经典的阐释中派生出的。例如《诗经》各卷的第一首诗称作“四始”，被认为含有解读整部经典的“密码”。武梁祠中的列女画像以梁高行故事开篇［图 4.30，第 11；图 4.21］。梁高行是一位美丽的女子，其丈夫

she was sought by noblemen including the king himself. To prevent the danger of remarriage, she disfigured herself by cutting off her nose. Of all the *Biographies of Exemplary Women*, this story demonstrates most dramatically the correct behavior for widows with sons, and the words attributed to her in her biography highlight the basic teaching of the scene engraved on the Wu Liang shrine: "My husband unfortunately died early, and I live in widowhood to raise his orphans; I have learned that the principle of a wife is that once having gone forth to marry, she will not change over, that she will keep all the rules of chastity and loyalty."[133]

As a counterpart of this story, the famous filial son Zeng Shen leads the group of seventeen virtuous men (Fig. 4.30, no. 18; Figs. 4.38a, b). It was widely believed during the Han that Zeng Shen's extraordinary filial piety led to a telepathic communication between him and his widowed mother. Once when Zeng Shen followed Confucius on a trip to the South, he suddenly felt a palpitation; he later learned that at that moment his mother had thought of him and bit her fingers. It is rather surprising, however, to find this story, which emphasizes the tie between a son and his (widowed) mother, given particular importance on the Wu Liang Shrine, since during the Han filial piety was primarily expressed in the father-son relationship.[134] It is even more surprising that among the five filial personages at the beginning of the series, four include a living mother who is served, amused, and protected by her son.[135] The exception is the story of Ding Lan, whose filial piety is directed toward his father, but in this case the father is dead. These pictures seemed to have been aimed at a particular audience—namely, Wu Liang's widow and orphaned sons—advising them to maintain harmonious relationships in the household and to be loyal and filial toward their deceased husband and father. In my opinion, only this hypothesis can explain the irregularities in the carvings: the designer of these carvings
235 deliberately changed the sex of some characters in the illustrated stories. For example, in most literary versions of the Ding Lan story, this filial son made a wooden statue in the likeness of his mother and worshipped it.

But on the Wu Liang Shrine the statue is an image of the deceased father. A similar transformation occurs in the picture depicting Jin Midi's filial conduct. Jin's biography in the *History of the Former Han* records that every time Jin saw his mother's portrait in the palace he would wail in pain. But the inscription accompanying the illustration on the Wu Liang Shrine identifies Jin as paying homage to his deceased father.[136] The last of the seventeen virtuous men is a "filial grandson"; not coincidentally, we learn from Wu Liang's epitaph that he had a grandson.

死后，许多贵族，包括国君本人，都在打她的主意。为了避免再婚的危险，她割鼻毁容。这个《列女传》中最富有戏剧性的故事表现的是有抚养孩子义务的寡妇的正确举措。梁高行传中所记录的她说的话，清楚地传达出祠堂中刻画这一故事的基本教化意义："妾夫不幸早死，先狗马填沟壑。妾守养其幼孤……妾闻妇人之义，一往而不改，以全贞信之节。"[133]

与这个故事相应，著名的孝子曾参则是 17 位有德行的男子的首位［图 4.30，第 18；图 4.38］。汉代人普遍相信，曾参的至孝使他与其守寡的母亲之间形成一种心灵感应。一次，曾参随孔子南游，突然感到心悸，不久他得知，当时曾母正因想念儿子而自咬手指。汉代的孝子故事主要强调父子之间的亲缘，但曾参的故事则重在表现（寡）母与子的联系，其在武梁祠中所占的重要地位值得我们特别重视。[134] 更引人注目的是，在孝子系列的前五个图像故事中，有四个讲述的是儿子侍奉、娱悦、保护其在世母亲的故事，[135] 唯一的例外是孝子丁兰向其父亲表达孝心，但他的父亲已经去世。这种观察使我们发现，这些故事似乎是针对着一种特殊的需要而选取的，即图像的设计者希望用这些历史故事教诲他的遗孀和孤儿，要求他们维护家庭的和睦，对死去的丈夫或父亲尽忠尽孝。在我看来，只有这种假设，才能解释画像设计者故意改变故事中一些角色的性别的不规范做法。例如，根据大多数文献，孝子丁兰以木头雕刻了已故母亲的肖像以事供奉，但在武梁祠中，这尊木雕却成了故去父亲的形象。金日磾的孝行画像中也有类似改变性别的现象。《汉书·金日磾》中记载金日磾每次在宫中见到亡母的画像，都禁不住痛哭。但武梁祠画像的榜题说明，画像中的金日磾是在对其亡父的画像表达敬意。[136] 这 17 个孝子故事的最后一幅表现的是一位"孝孙"的画像。无独有偶的是，我们从武梁碑获知武梁也有一个孙子。

Fig. 4.38. Story of Zengzi. Wu Liang Shrine carving. (a) Ink rubbing. (b) Reconstruction.

图 4.38 曾子故事。武梁祠画像。东汉晚期，151 年。（a）拓片。（b）木版复制品。

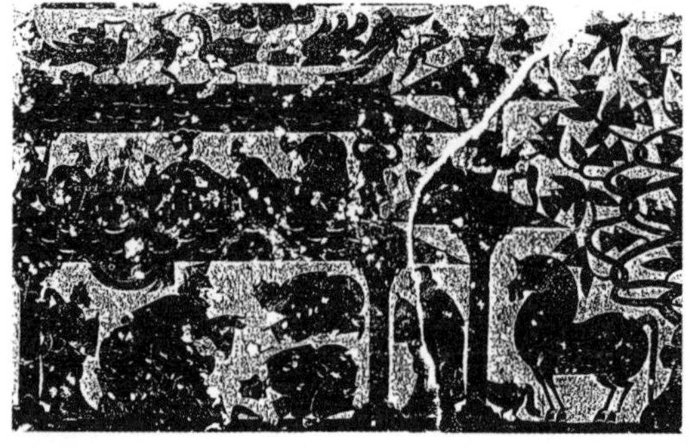

Fig. 4.39. Homage scenes from the Jiaxiang area. Late Eastern Han. 2nd half of the 2nd century A.D. (a) Carving on the Left Wu Family Shrine. Ink rubbing. (b) Excavated in 1978 at Songshan. Ink rubbing.

图 4.39 嘉祥地区楼阁画像。东汉晚期，2 世纪后半叶。（a）武氏祠左石室画像。拓片。（b）1978 年宋山出土画像。拓片。

The lower section of the shrine's walls follows a different compositional rule: here a grand pavilion at the center establishes a strong visual focus, so that the composition becomes symmetrical. The interior scene of the pavilion is damaged, but it can be easily reconstructed by consulting similar images widely copied in the Jiaxiang area (Figs. 4.39a, b): a figure of enormous size is receiving an audience in the main hall, and women with elaborate crowns are seated on the second floor. I have contended elsewhere that the central grand figure represents the concept of monarchy—an idealized ruler of the empire.[137] Some reviewers have found this opinion unacceptable because similar images portray the deceased in other Han dynasty funerary structures.[138] This rejection, however, is based on an erroneous methodological assumption, which I have tried to correct, that there is a rigid iconography in Han pictorial art and individual images with identical or similar features must possess the same meaning. I suggest the opposite: because there was no rigid iconography in Han pictorial art (comparable with the iconographic system in Christian or Buddhist art), people often employed similar images for different purposes. The precise

祠堂壁面下部画像的设计遵循了另一套构图法则。这里，画面中央矗立着一座巨大的楼阁，形成一个强烈的视觉焦点，并造成一种对称式的画面结构。楼阁中的物象已残，但根据嘉祥地区出现的同类图像，可以很容易地将这部分图像复原出来［图 4.39］：一位形体高大的人物在主厅接见来访者，头戴华冠的女子端坐在二楼中央。我曾提出，武梁祠中所画的这位形体高大的人物表现的是一种君主政体观念，即一位理想化的国君。[137] 一些研究者不同意这一看法，根据是在其他汉代墓葬建筑中，类似的图像常常表现死者。[138] 然而，这一反驳的前提恰恰是我试图纠正的一种方法论假说，即认为汉代画像艺术中存在着一套固定的图像志；具备同一或相近特征的个体图像必然表达相同的含义。我的观点是：与基督教或佛教艺术的图像系统相比较，汉代绘画艺术中并不存在一套固定的图像志，人们可以用类似的图像表达不同的内容和意图。一种图像的准确

content of an image is either identified by the accompanying inscription or is defined within its pictorial context.

My identification of the central pavilion in the Wu Liang Shrine as a symbolic representation of sovereignty is, therefore, not intended to offer a standard definition of all such scenes in Han art. Rather, this identification is based mainly on the scene's specific pictorial context—its relationship with the picture-stories flanking it. All nine heroes and heroines portrayed here are public and political figures. There are two wise ministers (Fig. 4.30, nos. 38, 39), six assassins who died serving their masters (Fig. 4.30, nos. 35-37, 40-42), and a virtuous queen who

a

b

Fig. 4.40. Story of Lin Xiangru. Wu Liang Shrine carving. (a) Ink rubbing. (b) Line engraving. Eastern Han. 2nd century A.D.

图 4.40 蔺相如故事。武梁祠画像。东汉晚期，151 年。(a) 拓片。(b) 木版复制品。

helped her husband rejuvenate the country (Fig. 4.30, no. 43). There is Lin Xiangru, who saved his state of Zhao from the fierce Qin (Figs. 4.40a, b), and Jing Ke who gave his life in his attempted assassination of Ying Zheng, the future First Emperor (Figs. 4.41a, b). Unlike the domestic men and women in the preceding series, these are political heroes whose virtues lay in their absolute loyalty to their sovereigns. Yao Li (Figs. 4.42a, b) was a commoner and physically weak; simply because a king trusted him, he decided to take on the task of assassinating the king's political enemy, Prince Qing Ji, a Herculean figure in Chinese history. Yao Li asked the king to kill his wife and children and to burn their bodies in the marketplace so that he could present himself to Qing Ji as a victim of the king's brutality, win the prince's trust, and find a chance to kill him. The carving on the Wu Liang Shrine represents the climax of the story: 237

内容，必须通过榜题或者根据图像之间的相互关系来判定。

我认为武梁祠正壁中央的楼阁图像是理想君主的象征，并不是希望为汉代艺术中所有这样的图像提供一个标准解读。这个论点是根据这个形象与其他相关画像之间的关系提出来的。整体地观察一下祠堂下部的画像，观者马上会发现画在中心楼阁两侧的九个故事表现的都是公共的、政治性的人物，包括两位贤明的宰相［图 4.30，第 38—39］，六位为其主人赴死的刺客［图 4.30，第 35—37、40—42］，以及一位助其夫君重振国威的王后［图 4.30，第 43］。这些人中有在强秦面前捍卫赵国利益的蔺相如［图 4.40］，也有试图刺杀秦王嬴政的荆轲［图 4.41］。与作为“家居人物”的列女和孝子不同，这些政治人物的德行表现为他们对君主的绝对忠诚。要离［图 4.42］是一位体弱无力的平民，势单力薄，只因为吴王对他的信任，便决定冒死行刺吴王的政敌庆忌，而庆忌是历史上一位大力神式的人物。要离请求国君杀死他的妻子儿女，焚其尸于市中，这样他便可以装扮成吴王暴行的受害者而取得庆忌的信任，以伺机杀死庆忌。武梁祠的画像表现了这个故事的高潮：要离的计划已成功，

a

b

Fig. 4.41. Story of Jing Ke. Wu Liang Shrine carving. (a) Ink rubbing. (b) Reconstruction.

图 4.41 荆轲故事。武梁祠画像。东汉晚期，151 年。（a）拓片。（b）木版复制品。

a

b

Fig. 4.42. Story of Yao Li. Wu Liang Shrine carving. (a) Ink rubbing. (b) Reconstruction.

图 4.42 要离故事。武梁祠画像。东汉晚期，151 年。（a）拓片。（b）木版复制品。

Yao Li's plan has succeeded, but the dying prince is still powerful enough to hurl him into a river. But he does not kill Yao Li, because, in Qing Ji's words, "the two bravest men in the world should not die on the same day." But a Han viewer of the picture would have known that in the end both men did die that day: after his victory, Yao Li denounced his three odious crimes of killing his wife, his children, and the new master who trusted him. He then "cut off his hands and feet, fell on his sword and died." With such exaggerated description of violence, this and similar stories place blind loyalty above all other ethical rules.

Although by no means complete, this survey of the Wu Liang Shrine carvings allows me to define the monumentality of this commemorative building by exploring the basic logic of its decoration, uncovering its intentions, and identifying the voice of the man responsible for the selection and compilation of the pictorial scenes. A number of internal and external factors have convinced me that this man was none other than Wu Liang himself.[139] Most important, the uniqueness of the pictorial program—its extraordinary sophistication and unusual coherence—implies a mastermind that could not possibly have belonged to Wei Gai, the named builder of the shrine.[140] As I discuss in the following section, the concerns of funerary monument builders differed from those of patrons, especially a politically minded Confucian scholar. It is also unlikely that Wu Liang's three sons and grandson were responsible for the pictorial program. They did append a short paragraph to Wu Liang's epitaph to specify their filial devotion in constructing the shrine, but this description is stereotypical and fails to mention anything about the shrine's extraordinary interior decoration. Possibly they did what they said they did—hire a "master workman" to erect their ancestor's monument. But it was the ancestor himself who planned his monument before his death.

To be sure, an intense concern with one's own mortuary monument emerged as soon as the tomb became the center of ancestor worship. As mentioned earlier, even in the fourth century B.C., a king of Zhongshan designed his funerary park and warned that anyone failing to complete it deserved execution. This tradition intensified during the Han, and it became conventional for a person to build his grave while still living. Kong Dan, for example, not only dedicated an offering shrine to his deceased grandmother but also built funerary structures for himself and commemorated this event on his memorial stela (Fig. 4.14):

但垂死的庆忌仍有力量将要离投入江中，但他并没有杀死要离，因为拿庆忌的话来说，“岂可一日而杀天下勇士二人哉！”但是，对于一位观看这幅画像的汉代人来说，他会知道要离和庆忌都在这一天死去了。要离在取得成功后，自责杀死妻儿、背叛新君、贪生弃行等种种非仁非义的罪恶，“乃自断手足，伏剑而死”。通过对于暴力如此夸张的描写，这些故事将忠君宣扬得高于其他一切伦理准则。

以上我概述了武梁祠画像的内容，尽管不是面面俱到，但是通过探索其基本逻辑，揭示其创作意图，分析设计者选择组织画面时的心态，我希望可以解释这座建筑的纪念碑性。许许多多内在和外在的证据使我相信，武梁祠的设计者不是别人，正是武梁本人。[139] 最重要的根据是，祠堂内整组画像超常的复杂和紧凑，说明其策划者不可能是碑中提到的“良匠卫改”。[140] 一般而言，艺术赞助人的目的和我在本书下节所讨论的丧葬建筑的建造者所关心的问题是大不一样的。而当赞助人是一位胸怀政治抱负的儒家学者时，情况就更是如此。武梁的三个儿子和一个孙子也不大可能设计这套图像。他们确实在武梁碑文结尾处说了一段话，表明他们修建祠堂的孝行，但这只是一堆套话，并无只言片语谈到祠堂内的装饰。可能正如他们自己所说的那样，他们只是去雇了一位“良匠”来修建亲人的丧葬纪念物，而这一纪念物的建筑和装饰计划则已由死者本人在生前决定了。

从历史发展的角度说，当墓葬成为祭祀祖先的中心后，人们便全心全意地关心其身后的墓葬。早在公元前 4 世纪，中山王就在生前为自己设计了茔园，并警告后人说，如不能完成这一计划，他们将受到惩罚。这一传统在汉代得以强化，生前建墓成为风气。如孔耽，不仅为其故去的祖母建立祠堂，同时还为自己造了墓，并立碑记载其事［图 4.14］：

> I realized that even gold and stone would erode and that everything in the world had its beginning and end. I then began to consider the great span of time after one's life, and settled on an auspicious posthumous home in the heavenly kingdom. As I looked at the structures which the craftsmen were fashioning, I rejoiced that I would abide there after this life. Inside there are chambers opening to the four cardinal directions; outside there are long corridors covered with roofs. The entire work cost 300,000 cash and was completed in the sixth month, in the summer of the fifth year of *renxu* in the Guanghe reign period [A.D. 182].[141]

It was only natural that some intellectuals, such as Zhao Qi and Wu Liang, would approach their own tomb and shrine as vehicles for expressing their ideas. In so doing they created a type of funerary monument that was truly "personal." True, nowhere can we find a written record about Wu Liang's choosing pictorial motifs for his shrine. But why can we not make such an inference based on a most unusual pictorial record? Wu Liang's voice—that of a scholar of the Confucian New Text
238 school, a member of the "retired worthies," a husband, and a father—cannot be confused with the voices of his family members, friends and colleagues, and builders. The important point is that we hear his distinct voice from the engravings on his memorial hall: the pictures of the heavenly omens, the chaste widows, and the filial descendents reveal a definite vantage point, from which these political images and domestic scenes were selected, revised, annotated, and compiled. This vantage point becomes most explicit in his "self-statement" at the end of an epic historical narrative. As I have argued, following an established Han historiographic convention, this scene concludes the Wu Liang Shrine carvings with the author's signature.

As a comprehensive presentation of Wu Liang's ideas and scholarship, the decoration on the shrine is a hierarchy consisting of four levels. On the first and most basic level, individual scenes depict stories or images of famous personages (Figs. 4.38, 40-42). The common themes and implications of the stories then lead to the second level of reading, where individual scenes constitute a series and are comprehended collectively as allusions to political and moral concepts (Figs. 4.32-35). The representation thus changes from narrative to abstraction. These series

……观金石之消，知万物有终始，图千载之洪宪，定吉兆于天府。目睹工匠之所营，心欣悦于所处。其内洞房四通，外则长庑切赋。合出卅万，以光和五年（182）岁在壬戌夏六月……[141]

在这个一般性的历史背景下，像赵岐、武梁这样的知识分子为自己修墓建祠，并以此作为媒介来抒发自己的思想，就是很自然的事情了。他们所设计的这类丧葬建筑可以说是地地道道"个人的"纪念建筑。虽然我们找不到武梁为自己的祠堂选择画像主题的文字记录，但是，我们为什么不能根据这些不寻常的图像本身作出如此的推理呢？作为一位今文学派的儒生，一位隐逸的"处士"，一位丈夫，一位父亲，武梁的声音是不能与其他人——他的家庭成员、朋友、同事以及建筑者——的声音混同在一起的。因此，对我们来说重要的是，从他的祠堂画像中倾听他特有的话语。这里，代表天意的祥瑞、贞洁的寡妇、孝顺的后人引导我们去发掘一个独特的视点。从这一视点出发，这些政治性的图像、家庭生活的情景被选取、修订、注解、编排。这个视点在这首长篇叙事史诗最后一章的"自叙"中得到最为明晰的表现。如前所述，根据汉代固定的史书撰写体例，这一画面，如同作者的签名，为整个武梁祠画像划上了一个句号。

作为武梁的思想与学术的综合表现，武梁祠画像是由四个层次构成的一个叙事和象征系统。在第一个，也是最基础的层次上，单独的图面表现了著名人物的形象或事迹［图 4.38，第 40—42］。若干形象和事迹的共同主题和含义把观者引向第二个层次。在这个层次上，若干单独画面构成一个系列，从总体上被理解为某种政治或道德概念的引喻（如忠、孝、节、义等）［图 4.32—图 4.35］。这样，画像便从叙事性的表现转换为抽象性的表现。若干系列进而成为

again become the elements of a larger narrative on the third level, which describes Chinese history from its beginning to the time of recording (Fig. 4.30). This historical narrative, however, is an element of an even larger abstraction. Depicted on the three walls, it is an integral part of a pictorial universe; the other two parts of this universe are Heaven (portrayed on the ceiling) and the immortal worlds (on the two gables; Fig. 4.43). On this fourth level, the whole decorative program achieves its final static form. It transforms the architectural structure that bears it into an everlasting symbol, a monument documenting Wu Liang's scholarship and ambition, and an offering hall where his descendents would come to place their sacrifices year after year, while listening to their father's teachings from the silent stones.

❺ Builders

Neither the deceased nor his descendents, friends, and colleagues actually built any shrine or stela. These funerary monuments were created by workers, including carvers, painters, masons, and presumably ordinary laborers. The existence of this group of people, whom I call collectively the "builders" of Han funerary monuments, is revealed in a number of inscriptions composed by the families of the dead, who hired such artisans to construct their family graveyards. An early set of evidence is related to the Wu family cemetery. In 147, the four sons of the family—Wu Shigong, Wu Liang, Wu Jingxing, and Wu Kaiming—employed the masons Meng Fu and Meng Mao to build a stone pillar-gate for their departed mother and hired a sculptor named Sun Zong to erect a pair of stone lions behind the pillar-gate (Fig. 4.13).[142] Four years later, in 151, the second son of the family, Wu Liang, passed away, and his three sons and a grandson "exhausted their savings" to build a memorial hall, probably according to the plan of their deceased ancestor. The result of their devotion was the famous Wu Liang Shrine discussed in the preceding section.

They [i.e., the builders] chose excellent stones from south of the southern mountains; they took those of perfect quality with flawless and unyellowed color. In front they established an altar; behind they erected an offering shrine. The master workman Wei Gai engraved the cartouches and carved the pictures in ordered sequences. He gave free rein to his talent, yet his gracious images exhibit perfect rules. This work will be transmitted to the sight of later generations and for 10,000 generations it will endure.[143]

第三个层次——从伏羲到武梁的一部宏大的中国历史——的结构元素［图 4.30］。然而，这个在三面墙壁上所描绘的历史叙事又是一个更大的抽象体系的一部分，与刻于屋顶的天界和刻于山墙上的仙界共同构成一宏观宇宙［图 4.43］。在这第四个，也是最高级的层次上，整个祠堂的装饰达到一种最终的静态表现。整个装饰程序把承载它的建筑转化为一个永恒的象征，一座记载了武梁学术与抱负的纪念碑。年复一年，武梁的后人来到这里陈设祭品，从无言的青石上聆听他的教诲。

五、建造者

真正亲手建造祠堂和雕刻墓碑的人既不是死者，也不是死者的后人、朋友和同僚。这些丧葬纪念物是由刻工、画师、石匠和另外一些普通工匠建造的。这一批人可以总称为汉代丧葬建筑的“建造者”。在由死者家人撰写的题记中，常提到他们雇用这些匠人来修建其家族墓地。其中一批早期的材料与武氏墓群有关：147 年，武家的四个儿子武始公、武梁、武景兴和武开明雇用了孟孚和孟卯为亡母建造石阙，又雇了石工孙宗雕刻一对石狮，立在阙门后面［图 4.13］。[142] 四年后，即 151 年，武家的第二子武梁亡故，他的三个儿子和一个孙子可能是根据了武梁本人的设计，“竭家所有”，为之建造了祠堂。其成果就是上文讨论的著名的武梁祠。武梁碑上对祠堂的建筑有以下记载：

> 选择名石，南山之阳，擢取妙好，色无斑黄。前设坛墠，后建祠堂。良匠卫改，雕文刻画，罗列成行，摅骋伎巧，委蛇有章。垂示后嗣，万世不亡。[143]

It is uncertain whether Wei Gai built and decorated the Wu Liang Shrine single-handedly or whether he was a contractor or the head of a group of workers. But the 157 inscription on An Guo's shrine (Fig. 4.6) makes it clear that a funerary monument was often a team result: An Guo's younger brothers hired three artisans—Wang Shu, Wang Jian, and Jiang Hu—from the nearby Gaoping principality, whose work was then recorded in the inscription that the family engraved on the shrine upon
239 its completion (see above). A third important reference to the builders of Han funerary monuments is found in a text originally carved on an offering hall at Dong'e, dedicated to the gentleman Xiang Tajun and his wife by their sons in 154 (Fig. 4.12):[144]

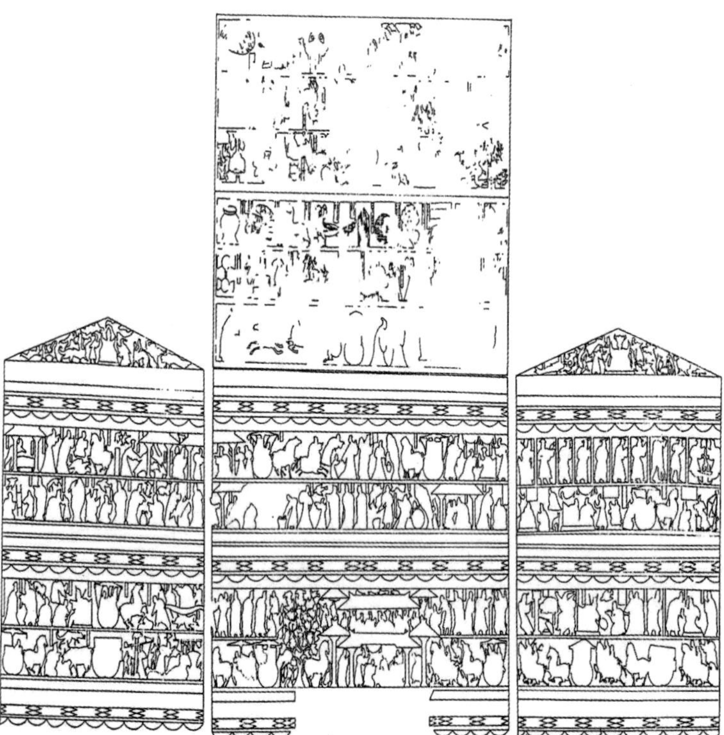

Fig. 4.43. The Wu Liang Shrine carvings. Drawing.
图 4.43 武梁祠画像。东汉晚期，151 年。线图。

> The shrine is small, but its construction took long. Its stones were quarried from southern hills. Only after two years of work is the hall now finally complete. We employed more than ten workers, including the craftsmen Cao Yi and Rong Bao from Xiaqiu in the Shanyang district, the painter Dai Sheng from Gaoping, and Shao Qiangsheng. The shrine cost 25,000 cash. We served these master workmen carefully morning and night, fearing to lose their favor and thus become unable to express our thanks to heaven and our gratitude to our parents.

Some generic features are easily observed in these passages, which were composed in the same decade by people who lived in adjacent areas. The stones for a shrine were always derived from "the southern hills," a vague designation that simply refers to the relative southern locations of the hills and their auspicious association with the *yang* force.

我们无法确定是卫改本人独自建造了这座祠堂，或者他仅仅是统领一批工匠的包工头。但是，在建于 157 年的安国祠堂的题记中［图 4.6］，可以很清楚地看到建祠工程通常是由一批人来实施的。安国的弟弟们从附近的高平县雇用了三个艺人，他们是王叔、王坚和江湖，在祠堂完工后，他们的工作被主人记录在祠堂的题记中（见上文）。第三个重要的例子是原坐落在山东东阿县的一座祠堂，是芗他君的儿子为其父母建造的［图 4.12］：[144]

> 堂虽小，经日甚久，取石南山，更逾二年，迄今成已。使师操义、山阳瑕丘荣保，画师高平代盛、邵强生等十余人。价钱二万五千。朝暮侍师，不敢失欢心。天恩不谢，父母恩不报。

这些题记出现在鲁西豫东地区，时间跨度不超过十年，从中可以看到一些明显的一般性特征。建造祠堂的石头都是采自“南山”，可能只是指大体上南边的，因此含有“阳”的吉祥寓意的某座山。

The builders' work is mentioned and admired, but both the description and praise appear to be stereotyped and impersonal.[145] The formulaic language repeated by the writers of these texts neither documents a monument's specific form and decor nor conveys a genuine appreciation of the workers' creative talent. Thus, although some art historians have suggested we take such references as direct evidence for the role of Han builders and their achievements,[146] I would argue that these words
240 represent not the voice of the people who created the monuments but that of the patrons who "bought" their services and benefited from them. The respect that the families paid to the builders was considered part of their filial devotion toward their ancestors, and they emphasized such respect in their inscriptions to demonstrate their piety. As Xiang Tajun's sons stated plainly: "We served these master workmen carefully morning and night, fearing to lose their favor and *thus become unable to express our thanks to heaven and our gratitude to our parents.*"

In fact, until 1973, all known funerary texts dating from the Han were written by patrons of mortuary structures; no composition by the builders themselves was identifiable.[147] But in 1973, Chinese archaeologists from the Shandong Provincial Museum discovered a long inscription in an ancient tomb that was, in all likelihood, from the hand of ordinary artisans. The tomb, located in western Cangshan county in southern Shandong, consists of two principal sections constructed of 60 stone slabs, ten of which are carved with pictorial scenes (Figs. 4.44a-c).[148] The rear section of the tomb is further divided into two narrow compartments by a partition wall, on which two "windows" are left open. The front section is a rectangular hall, whose facade is formed by three columns supporting a horizontal lintel. There is a shallow niche in the east wall of this "reception hall" (*tang*), and a tiny side chamber on the hall's west side. The facade of this side chamber is again constructed with a lintel and three supporting columns; the inscription appears on the central and right columns and consists of 238 characters (Fig. 4.45). The informal and irregular characters of the text make it difficult to read and interpret. My translation takes into consideration a number of readings by Chinese scholars,[149] and tries to relate the text with the pictorial scenes decorating the tomb.

题记中都提到建造者，并对他们表现出敬意，但行文和赞美都是程式化的，无甚个性可言。[145] 这些题记的撰写者不断地重复着这些相同的话语，它们既不记录建筑物的特殊形制和装饰，也没有传达出对工匠才华真正的赞赏。因此，尽管有的学者认为这些材料是反映汉代建造者作用及其成就的直接证据，[146] 但我认为这些文字并不直接传达创造这些纪念性建筑的人们的声音，而是“募使”这些工匠并从中受益的赞助人的声音。死者家庭对建造者表现出的敬意实际上是他们对于先人尽孝的一部分，在题记中强调这种敬意可以证明其虔敬的孝心。如芗他君的儿子们就清楚地说道：“朝暮侍师，不敢失欢心。天恩不谢，父母恩不报。”

在 1973 年以前，我们尚无法确认任何由建造者撰写的题记，所知汉代丧葬文字都是由丧葬建筑的赞助人写成的。[147] 但是在 1973 年，山东博物馆的考古工作者在一座古代墓葬中发现了一篇长篇题记，极有可能出自普通工匠之手。该墓位于鲁南的苍山县西部，分为前后室，以 60 块石块构筑而成，其中 10 块上刻有画像［图 4.44］。[148] 后室由一隔墙分为左右两间，隔墙上开有两扇“窗”。前室平面为长方形（题记中称之为“堂”），正面以三根立柱支撑一横梁，形成两个门洞。“堂”东壁开一龛，西壁开一侧室，侧室的正面也由三根立柱支撑一横梁形成两个门洞。一则 238 字的题记刻在侧室门洞中央和右边的立柱上［图 4.45］。题记中有不少别字，难以阅读和解释。已有不少中国学者撰文辨读这篇题记，我在他们研究的基础上将题记译为英文，[149] 并试图将这篇题记与墓中的画像联系起来。

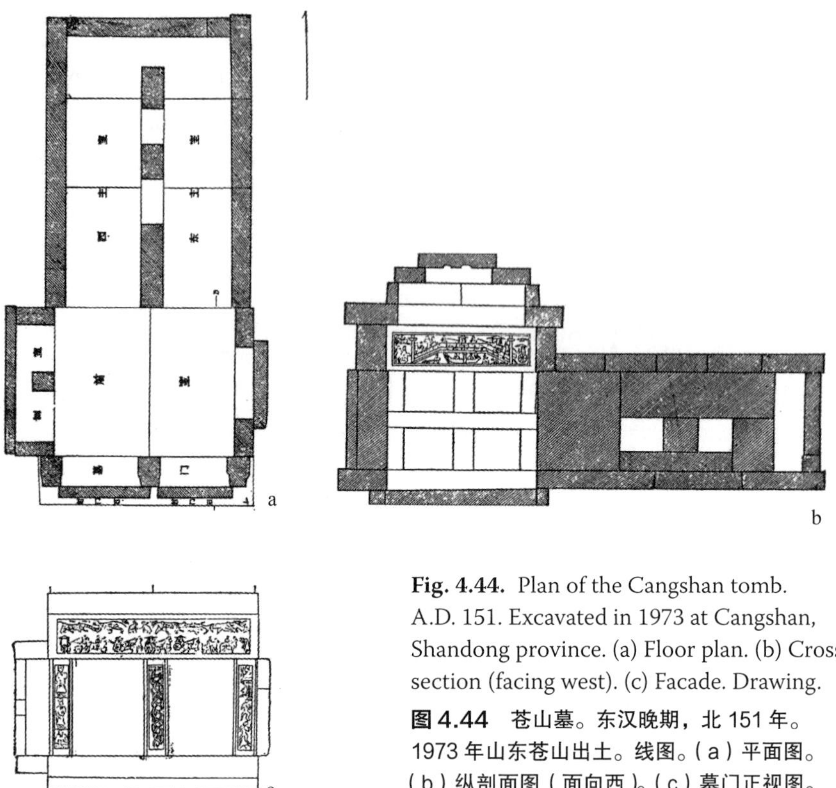

Fig. 4.44. Plan of the Cangshan tomb. A.D. 151. Excavated in 1973 at Cangshan, Shandong province. (a) Floor plan. (b) Cross section (facing west). (c) Facade. Drawing.

图 4.44 苍山墓。东汉晚期，北 151 年。1973 年山东苍山出土。线图。(a) 平面图。(b) 纵剖面图 (面向西)。(c) 墓门正视图。

On the twenty-fourth day of the eighth month, in the first year of
the Yuanjia reign period [A.D. 151],
We completed the construction of this tomb chamber, to send you,
241 the honorable member of the family, off on your journey.[150]
If your soul has consciousness, please take pity on your descendents,
Let them prosper in their livelihood and achieve longevity.
[Allow us] to list and explain the pictures inside the tomb.[151]
The rear wall [Fig. 4.46]:
The Red Bird encounters a roaming immortal.
Phoenixes trail after the White Tiger who is strolling in the middle.

The central column [in front of the rear section] [Fig. 4.47]:
Here a pair of intertwining dragons,
Guard the tomb's heart and ward off evil.[152]

The ceiling of the [rear] chamber:[153]
A *wuzi* carriage is followed by servant girls who are driving carps;
The chariot of the White Tiger and the Blue Dragon runs ahead [Fig. 4.48];
The Duke of Thunder on wheels brings up the rear;
And those pushing the vehicle are the assistants—foxes and mandarin ducks.

[The lintel above the west chamber] [Fig. 4.49]:
Ascending the bridge over the Wei River,
Here appear official chariots and horsemen.
The Head Clerk is in front,
And the Master of Records is behind.
Together with them are the Chief of a Commune,
The Assistant Commandant of Cavalry,
And a barbarian drawing his cross-bow.
Water flows under the bridge;
A crowd of people are fishing.

元嘉元年（151）八月廿四日，立郭（椁）毕成，以送贵亲。[150]魂灵有知，哀怜子孙，治生兴政，寿皆万年。薄踈（疏）郭（椁）内画观。[151]后当（后室后壁）[图 4.46]：朱爵（雀）对游栗（戏）扯（仙）人，中行白虎后凤皇（凰）。中直柱[图 4.47]：双结龙，主守中霤辟邪殃。[152]室上砄（后室顶）：[153]五子举，偅女随后驾鲤鱼。前有青龙白虎车[图 4.48]，后□被轮雷公君。从者推车，乎梩（狐狸）冤厨（鹓鸰）。（前室西侧室上方）[图 4.49]：上卫（渭）桥，尉车马，前者功曹后主簿，亭长骑佐胡使弩。下有深水多鱼

Servant boys are paddling a boat,
Ferrying [your] wives across the river.

[The lintel above the east niche] [Fig. 4.50]:
[The women] then sit in small *ping* carriages;[154]
243 Following one another they gallop to a *ting* station.[155]
The awaiting officer *youjiao*[156] pays them an audience,
And then apologizes for his departure.
Behind [the procession],
A ram-drawn carriage symbolizes a hearse;[157]
Above, divine birds are flying in drifting clouds.

The portrait inside [the east niche] [Fig. 4.51]:
Represents you, the member of the family.
The jade maidens are holding drinking vessels and serving boards—
How fine, how fragile, how delicate!

The face of the door lintel [Fig. 4.52]:
You are now taking a tour.
Chariots are guiding the retinue out,
While horsemen remain at home.
The *dudu*[158] is in front,
And the *zeicao*[159] is at the rear.
Above, tigers and dragons arrive with good fortune;
A hundred birds fly over bringing abundant wealth.

The back of the door lintel [Fig. 4.53]:
Here are the musicians and singing girls
Playing the wind-instruments of *sheng* and *yu* in harmony,
While the sound of a *lu* pipe strikes up.
Dragons and birds are driving evil away;
Cranes are poking at fish.

The three columns of the front hall [Fig. 4.54]:
In the middle, dragons ward off evil;
At the left, are the Jade Fairy and immortals;

And on the right column. . . [two characters missing],
The junior master is called upon,
And drink is served by his newly wedded wife.[160]
The ceiling of the front hall is decorated beautifully:
Surrounding a round protrusion, 244
Melon-leaf patterns embellish the center;
And fish patterns are added to the tips of the leaves.
[All these figures and animals,] when you eat and drink,
May you eat in the Great Granary,
And may you drink from the rivers and seas.
You who devote yourselves to learning,
May you be promoted to high rank and be awarded official seals and symbols.
You who devote yourselves to managing your livelihoods,
May your wealth increase 10,000-fold in a single day.
[But you, the deceased,] have entered the dark world,
Completely separated from the living.
After the tomb is sealed,
It will never be opened again.

（渔）者；从儿刺舟渡诸母。（前室东壁龛上方）[图 4.50]：使坐上，小车軿；[154] 驱驰相随到都亭，[155] 游徼 [156] 候见谢自便。后有羊车象其槥；[157] 上即圣鸟乘浮云。其中画（前室东壁龛内）[图 4.51]：橡（像）家亲，玉女执尊杯桉（案）柈（盘），局抹稳抗好弱貌。堂硖（央）外（墓门横梁外）[图 4.52]：君出游，车马导从骑吏留，都督 [158] 在前后贼曹 [159]。上有龙虎衔利来，百鸟共持至钱财。其硖内（墓门横梁内）[图 4.53]：有倡家，生（笙）汙（竽）相和，仳（比）吹庐（芦）。龙爵（雀）除央（殃），鳿噣（啄）鱼。堂三柱（墓门立柱）[图 4.54]：中直□龙非详；左有玉女与扯（仙）人，右柱□□请丞卿。新妇主待（侍）给水将（浆）。[160] 堂盖（前室顶）花好：中瓜叶□□包，未有盱（鱼）。其当饮食，就夫（太）仓，饮江海。学者高迁宜印绶，治生日进钱万倍。长就幽冥则决绝，闭旷之后不复发。

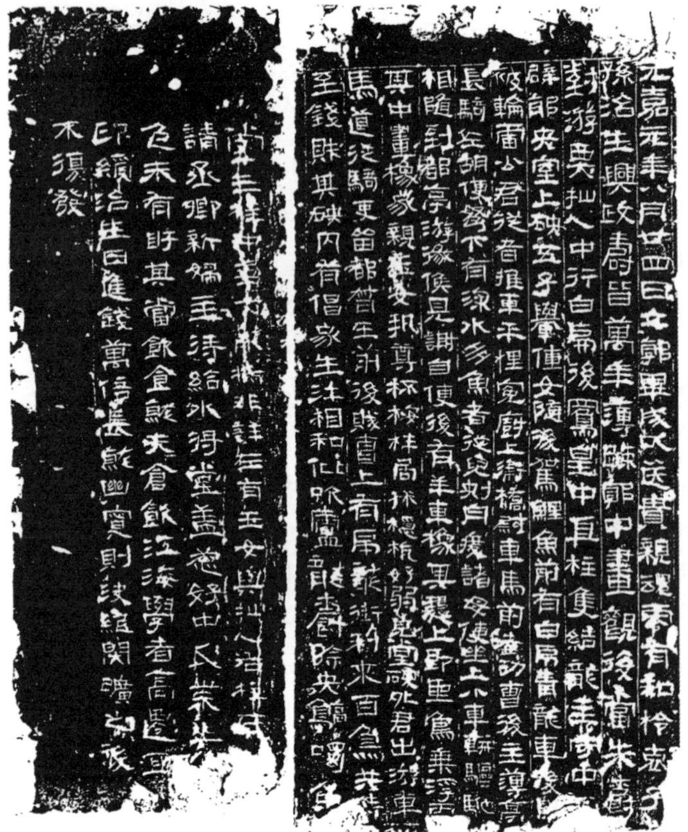

Fig. 4.45. Inscription in the Cangshan tomb. H. 44-45 cm. This and other engraved slabs from the tomb are preserved in the Cangshan County Cultural House. Ink rubbing.

图 4.45 苍山墓题记。东汉晚期。高 44—45 厘米。该石与墓内出土其他画像石均藏苍山县文化馆。拓片。

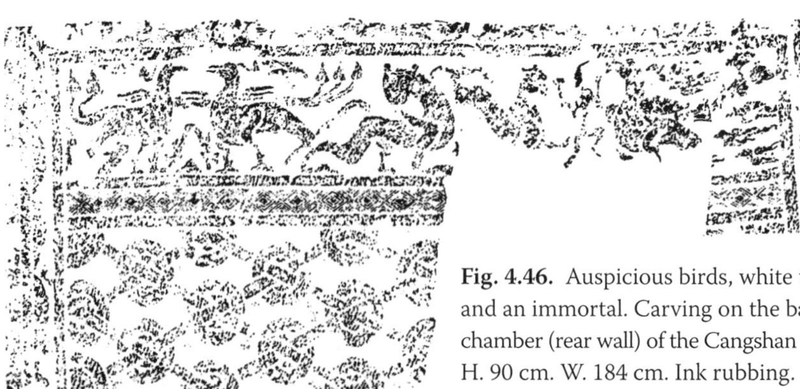

Fig. 4.46. Auspicious birds, white tiger, and an immortal. Carving on the back chamber (rear wall) of the Cangshan tomb. H. 90 cm. W. 184 cm. Ink rubbing.

图 4.46 瑞鸟、白虎、仙人。苍山墓后室后壁画像。高 90 厘米，东汉晚期。宽 184 厘米。拓片。

Fig. 4.47. Intertwining dragons. Carvings on the central column in the Cangshan tomb. H. 109.5 cm. W. 26.5 cm. Ink rubbing.

图 4.47 交龙。苍山墓后室入口处立柱画像。东汉晚期。高 109.5 厘米，宽 26.5 厘米。拓片。

Fig. 4.48. Blue dragon and white tiger. Carving in the back chamber (ceiling) of the Cangshan tomb. H. 52.5 cm. W. 124 cm. Ink rubbing.

图 4.48 青龙与白虎。苍山墓后室顶部画像。东汉晚期。高 52.5 厘米，宽 124 厘米。拓片。

Fig. 4.49. Crossing the Wei Bridge. Carvings in the central chamber (west wall) of the Cangshan tomb. H. 51.5 cm. W. 169 cm. Ink rubbing.

图 4.49 上渭桥。苍山墓前室西壁画像。东汉晚期。高 51.5 厘米，宽 169 厘米。拓片。

Fig. 4.50. Greeting the funerary procession. Carving in the central chamber (east wall) of the Cangshan tomb. H. 30 cm. W. 146 cm. Ink rubbing.

图 4.50 迎接送葬车马。苍山墓前室东壁画像。东汉晚期。高 30 厘米，宽 146 厘米。拓片。

Fig. 4.52. Chariot procession. Carving on the facade (lintel) of the Cangshan tomb. H. 51 cm. W. 246 cm. Ink rubbing.

图 4.52 车马行列。苍山墓墓门横梁正面画像。东汉晚期。高 51 厘米，宽 246 厘米。拓片。

Fig. 4.51. Portrait of the deceased. Carving in the central chamber (niche on the east wall) of the Cangshan tomb. H. 107.5 cm. W. 77 cm. Ink rubbing.

图 4.51 死者肖像。苍山墓前室东壁小龛内画像。东汉晚期。高 107.5 厘米，宽 77 厘米。拓片。

Fig. 4.53. Entertainment. Carving in the central chamber above the door of the Cangshan tomb. H. 50 cm. W. 242 cm. Ink rubbing.

图 4.53 乐舞百戏。苍山墓墓门横梁背面画像。东汉晚期。高 50 厘米，宽 242 厘米。拓片。

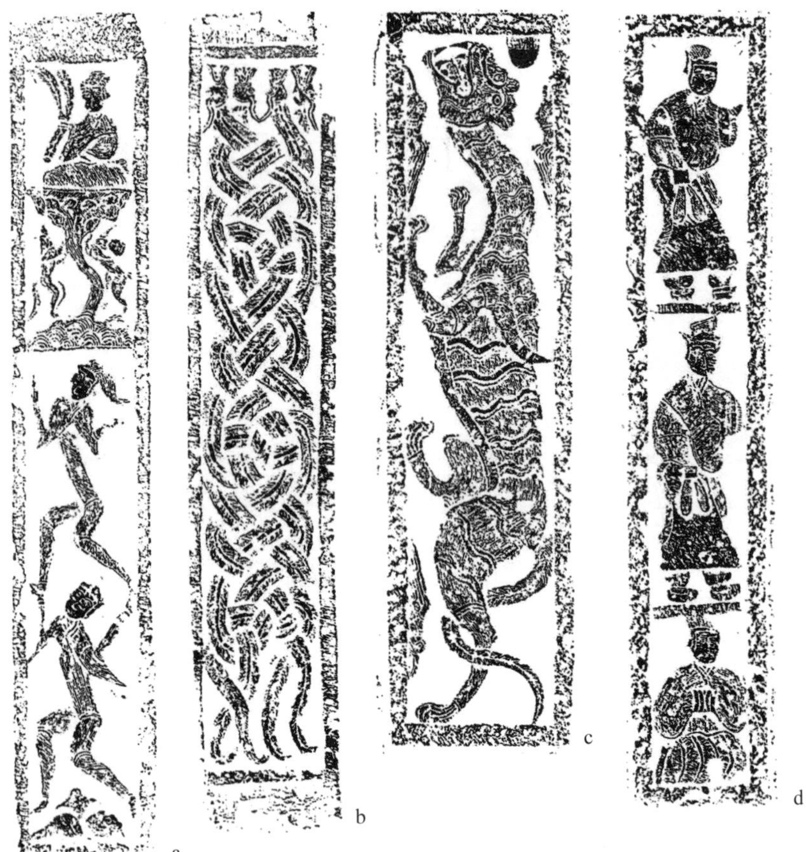

Fig. 4.54. Immortals, intertwining dragons, and the donors. Carvings on the facade of the Cangshan tomb. (a) Right column; (b) front of the central column; (c) back of the central column; (d) left column. H. 107.5-109.5. Ink rubbings.

图 4.54 仙人、交龙、死者后人。苍山墓墓门画像。东汉晚期。高 107.5—109.5 厘米。拓片。（a）右侧立柱。（b）中央立柱正面。（c）中央立柱背面。（d）左侧立柱。

A number of factors enable us to identify the writer of this text as the designer/builder of the tomb. In addition to many incorrect characters and homonyms in the text that suggest an ill-educated author,[161] the indefinite appellations of the deceased are an obvious clue. In two places the occupant of the tomb is addressed as *guiqin*, "an honorable member of the family," and *jiaqin*, "a member of the family." The writer's attitude toward the dead, therefore, differs fundamentally from that of the patrons of a funerary structure, who always first identified and introduced the dead in their devotional writings. All the information about the deceased usually provided in a stela inscription—his education, official career, and virtuous conduct—is absent here, and the text gives no account of the family's practices of filial piety as in a shrine inscription. In fact, the Cangshan text seems to have been composed by a writer who did not know the identity of the deceased. The writing could have been used in any tomb, since a dead person could always be referred to as "an honorable member of the family." 245

The modern Chinese scholar Li Falin has noticed this unusual feature of the Cangshan inscription. Unfortunately, his observation has led him to draw a misleading comparison: "This text does not record the name, official occupations, characteristics, virtues, achievements, and the family of the deceased, nor does it provide an elaborate dirge. From this point of view, it is inferior to the An Guo inscription and the Xiang Tajun inscription, which contain more detailed information in these

这篇文字的许多特征使我确信其作者是设计或建造该墓的工匠。除了文中的许多别字可以说明作者文化水平不高以外，[161] 最显著的线索是对死者称呼的不确定。墓主在文中被称作“贵亲”“家亲”。题记作者对死者的态度因此与丧葬建筑赞助人是根本不同的。如上所述，赞助人所撰的碑文中有关死者的信息非常详细，包括其世系、受教育的情况、官职、德行等各个方面，这些内容均不见于苍山墓题记；而这段题记中也没有祠堂题记中通常所见的对死者家人孝行的叙述。实际上，苍山墓题记的作者甚至不一定知道死者是谁，他所写的这篇文字可以适用于任何人的墓葬，因为任何一位死者都可以被称为“家亲”或“贵亲”。

中国当代学者李发林注意到了苍山墓题记的这些特征。但是，他随后进行的比较则值得商榷：“题记中没有墓主姓名、官职、品性、德行、事迹、家庭状况的记载和讴歌颂词。这一点是逊色于永寿三年石刻和芗他君石刻的，后二者在这方面记载较详。” [162] 这一比较

respects."[162] Li's mistake is to confuse two different kinds of funerary texts: those written by patrons and those written by builders. The absence of such information in the Cangshan inscription is not due to the author's failings or carelessness; rather, it indicates his different relationship with the dead, his different interest in composing the text, and his distinct cultural background.

We first recognize this writer's background in his language, which differs markedly from that used in both stela inscriptions and shrine inscriptions. Stylistically, the Cangshan text is a rhymed ballad, with most lines consisting of three, four, and seven characters.[163] This form is unknown in all other funerary inscriptions, which are often prose compositions sometimes followed by a dirge in uniform four-character lines.[164] In content, the Cangshan text does not allude to the Confucian classics or use filial formulas, which abound in inscriptions by patrons, either by the descendents or by friends and colleagues of the dead. This is not to say, however, that the writer of this inscription was free from cultural conventions. On the contrary, his language is likewise formulaic and stereotyped, but of a different sort. The text contains many popular sayings related to folk beliefs of the time. Many of its sentences and phrases are "auspicious words" (*jiyu*) in couplets, which one can also find on contemporary bronze mirrors and other objects of daily use: "Tigers and dragons arrive with good fortune; /A hundred birds fly over to bring abundant wealth"; "You who devote yourselves to learning, /May you be promoted to high rank and be awarded official seals and symbols. /You who devote yourselves to managing your livelihoods, /May your wealth
246 increase a 10,000-fold each day"; "In the middle, dragons ward off evil; /
At the left, are the Jade Fairy and immortals." Other formulas employed in the text include prayers, among which is the well-known expression: "All these figures and animals, when you eat and drink, /May you eat in the Grand Granary/And may you drink from the rivers and seas." The Grand Granary (*taicang*) refers to the Han state granary established by the

chief minister Xiao He in 200 B.C. During Han times, however, people used this term to symbolize the greatest grain depository, just as rivers and seas symbolized the greatest depository of water. By inscribing this sentence on a mortuary structure, the writer expressed the wish that the figures and animals depicted in the tomb would not seize food from the living but would eat and drink from greater natural sources.[165]

But more important, the Cangshan inscription reflects a different interest. Whereas the writers of shrine inscriptions and stela inscriptions were preoccupied with the desire to demonstrate their filial conduct or

值得商榷，因为它混淆了丧葬建筑上分别出自赞助人和建筑者的两种文字。苍山题记中缺少这些内容并不是由于作者的失误或粗心，而是由于作者与死者的特殊关系，其撰文时的特殊兴趣以及其特定的文化背景。

这段题记的行文与碑文和祠堂题记明显有别，从中我们可以看到作者的文化背景。从风格上看，苍山墓题记是韵文，每行大多由三、四或七字组成。[163] 而其他丧葬题记则以散文为主，配以四字句构成的赞辞。[164] 从内容上看，这篇题记没有使用任何儒家典故，也没有死者的后人、朋友、同僚常用的那些有关孝道的套话。当然，这并不是说其作者可以脱离文化传统的制约。实际上，其文辞仍然是程式化的，但只是属于另一类而已。如题记中有大量与当时民间信仰有关的习惯用语，包括不少工整上口的吉祥语，如"上有龙虎衔利来 / 百鸟共持至钱财"，"学者高迁宜印绶 / 治生日进钱万倍"，以及"中直□ / 龙非详 / 左有玉女与扯（仙）人"，等等。这些吉语也见于铜镜以及其他日常用品。此外，行文中的祝词也是程式化用语，包括一些常见的表达方式，如"其当饮食，/ 就夫（太）仓 / 饮江海"。这里所说的"太仓"指的西汉名相萧何在公元前 200 年建立的国家粮仓，被汉代人用来象征无穷的粮食储备，就像以江海象征无尽的水量。作者在墓中写这句话，意思是希望画像中的人物和动物向大自然获取饮食，而不与生者争夺食物。[165]

但最重要的是，苍山题记反映出一种特殊的兴趣。撰写祠堂或墓碑文字的人们热衷于证明他们的孝行或忠诚，而这篇题记的作者

loyalty, this text was written by someone who was interested in the tomb itself. Accordingly, most of the inscription documents this tomb or, more likely, its design.

This last statement contains an important proposal; namely, that prior to the construction of a mortuary structure, a Han builder would first have planned the general layout of its decoration and documented it in a written form. The possibility that the Cangshan inscription documented a design rather than the finished tomb is suggested by certain inconsistencies between the pictorial scenes as described and the actual tomb carvings. For example, most pictures found in the tomb accord with those mentioned in the text, but not those on the ceiling. According to the inscription, a group of vivid images—strange chariots, girls driving carps, foxes and mandarin ducks, and the Duke of Thunder on wheels—should have been depicted on the ceiling of the rear chamber. But in the Cangshan tomb only a tiger and a dragon appear in this position. The remaining images are missing and can only be observed on carved slabs from other sites. For example, two stone bas-reliefs from Honglou on the Shandong-Jiangsu border are filled with mythical images (Fig. 4.55), including chariots drawn by dragons and tigers, the bear-like Duke of Thunder beating drums, a fish with human feet, and an enormous mandarin duck. I have tried to reconstruct the original architectural form of these and other scattered slabs from Honglou and found that these two stones most likely formed the ceiling of a mortuary structure.[166] It is possible that in designing the Cangshan tomb, the builder recalled these scenes from his motif repertoire but was never able to realize his plan.

A similar fate befell the ceiling of the front chamber: its proposed decoration—melon leaves embellished with fish images—is likewise absent in the tomb. Again, carvings from other sites in Shandong prove that this pattern was not merely the writer's fantasy. In 1980, eight square or rectangular slabs with such a decor were discovered in Songshan (Fig. 4.56); one of them bears the An Guo inscription (Fig. 4.6). Their excavators proposed that these slabs must have come from several abandoned mortuary buildings, perhaps from their ceilings.[167] It is interesting to speculate why all the pictures on walls and columns described in the Cangshan text exist in the tomb, and only the ceiling designs are missing or incomplete. A possible explanation may be the building sequence of

兴趣却集中在墓葬本身，题记的大部分所描述的是墓葬或者其设计的情况。

最后的这个论点包含着一个重要的问题，即在修建一座丧葬建筑之前，汉代的建造者可能会对其装饰布局进行总体设计，并将其设计以文字形式记录下来。苍山题记所描述的画面内容与墓葬中实际的雕刻并不完全相合，因此这一题记所记录的很可能是原来预期的设计，而非已完成的墓葬中实有的装饰。例如，虽然墓葬中大多数画像与题记相符，但是墓室顶部则是例外。根据题记的文字，在后室顶部应当刻有一组十分生动的画面，包括奇异的车、女子驾鲤鱼、狐狸与鸳鸯、被轮雷公等。但是，在苍山墓中的这一部位，却仅刻有龙虎图像。然而，虽然题记所描写的这些画面不见于墓中，但其他地点发现的画像石却描绘了这些形象。例如，山东江苏交界处的徐州洪楼出土的两幅画像中表现了许多神话形象［图 4.55］，其中有龙虎拉车，外貌像熊的击鼓雷公，长有人脚的鱼，以及一个硕大的鸳鸯。我曾试图复原洪楼画像原有的建筑配置结构，发现这两幅画像原来可能位于建筑的顶部。[166] 也许在设计苍山墓的时候，建造者曾想到这类流行画像，并计划用在这个墓里，但最后却没有能够实现他的计划。

前室顶部也有类似的失误：题记中设计的图案是装饰着鱼纹的瓜叶，但墓葬中却没有发现这样的画像。同样，山东其他地区的发现证明这一图案并不是题记作者凭空的幻想。1980 年，嘉祥宋山发现了八块装饰着这种图案的方形和长方形画像石［图 4.56］，其中之一刻有著名的安国题记［图 4.6］。发掘者认为这些画像属于几座已经散乱的丧葬建筑，可能原来是建筑的顶部。[167] 值得思考的是，苍山墓题记对墙壁和柱子上画像的描述与墓中情况完全吻合，只是所描述的墓顶画像不存在或部分存在。一种可能的解释是，这一

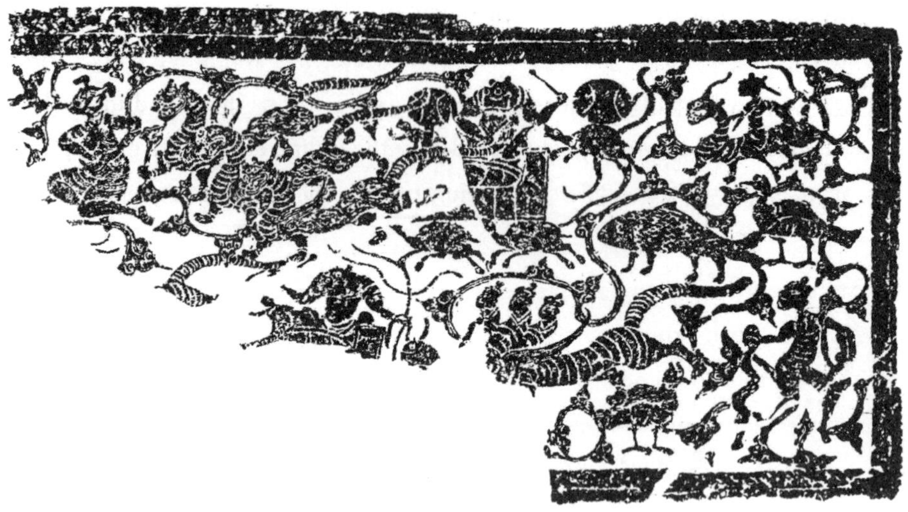

Fig. 4.55. Duke of Thunder and other fantastic creatures. Eastern Han. 2nd century A.D. H. 106 cm. W. 190 cm. Excavated at Honglou, Xuzhou, Jiangsu province. Ink rubbing.

图 4.55 雷公与其他神异动物。东汉晚期，2 世纪。高 106 厘米，宽 190 厘米。江苏徐州洪楼出土。拓片。

Fig. 4.56. “Melon leaf” pattern. Late Eastern Han. 2nd half of the 2nd century A.D. Excavated in 1978 at Songshan, Jiaxiang, Shandong province. Ink rubbing.

图 4.56 “瓜叶”图案。东汉晚期，2 世纪后半叶。1978 年山东嘉祥宋山出土。拓片。

the tomb: the construction of the ceiling, naturally the last step of the whole project, was for some reason hurriedly finished before the planned decoration could be completed.

We thus obtain another determinant for the authorship of the Cangshan inscription: only the builder could document the intended design; the patrons of the tomb could only describe (and would only wish to describe) its actual finished form. As an architectural design written in words, the inscription translates pictures planned for a three-dimensional structure into a linear narrative. This narrative begins from the scenes in the rear chamber—the sacred quarter of the burial that contained the coffin of the dead. All the images designed for this chamber were mystical in nature. Intertwining dragons would guard its entrance, and heavenly beasts and birds would be depicted on its ceiling and walls to transform the solid stone room into a world of wonder.

The builder then moves on to tell us his design for the front chamber,
which provided him with another enclosed space for the second part 248
of his pictorial program. Here, human figures would become the main

现象与墓葬的建筑次序有关：墓葬的顶部是最后完成的部分，出于某种原因，苍山墓的建造在其装饰计划完成之前草草结束了。

通过以上讨论，我们获得了判断苍山题记作者的又一决定性因素，即只有建造者才能记录设计的构思；墓葬的赞助人只能描述（也只希望描述）墓葬建造完成后的状况。题记中所叙述的建筑设计方案将一套为三维建筑而设计的图像转译成线性的叙述。叙述程序从放置死者遗体的后室开始，这是墓葬最神圣的部分，用来安放死者的棺。后室的画像皆属于神话内容：交龙守卫在后室的入口处，天界的鸟兽刻画在顶部和墙壁上，将坚硬的石室转换为一个神奇的世界。

接着，艺术家又向我们讲述了他对前室的设计，该室为图像程序的第二部分提供了一个闭合空间。这里，人物取代了神怪形象，

subject of depiction, and a funerary journey would be represented in two compositions on the east and west walls. The first picture above the west side chamber would show the procession crossing the Wei River Bridge. Two famous Han emperors, Jing and Wu, had built bridges across the Wei River north of Chang'an to link the capital with their own mausoleums; imperial guards of honor and hundreds of officials had accompanied their departed lords across these bridges. The Wei River must have become a general symbol of death.[168] Inspired by these royal precedents, the designer decided to label the riders in his picture with official titles, but he used only the local ranks that he knew. He also decided to draw the wives of the deceased, who were expected to accompany their husband to his burial ground. But the women had to take a boat across the river, since female (*yin*) had to be separated from male (*yang*) and since water embodied the *yin* principle.

Fig. 4.57. Detail of a tomb gate, with inscriptions identifying the standing figures as Tingzhang (innkeeper). Eastern Han. 2nd century A.D. Probably from Nanyang, Henan province. Art Institute of Chicago.

图 4.57 带有"亭长"题记的墓门画像细部。东汉，2 世纪。可能出土于河南南阳。芝加哥美术馆藏。

The second stage of the journey would be presented on the opposite east wall. Having crossed the River of Death, the women would get into special female carriages, escorting the hearse to a tomb prepared for the dead in the suburbs. The procession would arrive at a *ting* station and be greeted by officials in front of it. This *ting* station, which was in real life a public guesthouse for travelers, should be understood here as the symbol of the tomb, and the official who greets the procession should be identified as the tomb's guardian. The same idea is expressed by depicting the *tingzhang* (the officer at a *ting* station) on the gate of a tomb (Fig. 4.57) or by erecting stone statues in cemeteries with the title *tingzhang* inscribed on their chests (Fig. 4.58).[169] Moreover, we find that in the finished carving of this scene in the Cangshan tomb, the two doors of

成了主要的表现题材。东西两壁各刻画了一个丧葬车马行列。第一幅画像刻在西壁，表现一队车马从渭河桥上通过。汉代两位著名的皇帝景帝与武帝，先后都曾在渭河上修桥，以连接都城长安与城北的帝陵。西汉一代的大部分皇帝死后，其灵车在皇家殡葬队伍和数以百计官员的护送下通过这些桥梁去往陵区，渭河因此成为人们心目中死亡的象征。[168] 可能是遵循皇室的这种做法，苍山墓的建筑者也为其画像中的骑者标上官衔，但所标只是些他们所熟悉的地方官员的名称。他们还刻画出死者妻妾的形象：她们恭顺地陪伴着丈夫的灵柩去往墓地。但妇女必须乘船过河，因为男（阳）女（阴）有别，而水代表阴。

车马行列的第二部分被画在对面的东壁。死者的导从人员减少，只限于家庭中的近亲。此时他的妻妾已渡过象征生死界限的河，正乘坐着妇女专用的车——軿车——将丈夫的灵柩运至郊外。画面描绘了她们的送葬行列到达一座“亭”的前面，一位官员前来迎候。亭在汉代现实生活中是旅行者驻马歇脚的客栈，在这里则象征死者的坟墓；而迎候的官员应当是墓葬的守卫者。其他汉代墓地的“亭长”——墓门上的浮雕［图 4.57］或圆雕的墓前石人［图 4.58］——具有同样的含义。[169] 为了强调亭的这一特殊

Fig. 4.58. Tingzhang. Stone statue originally erected in the graveyard of Mr. Biao, the magistrate of Le'an in Shandong. H. 254 cm. Preserved in the Confucian Temple, Qufu, Shandong province.

图 4.58 乐安太守麃君亭长石人。东汉。高 254 厘米。山东曲阜孔庙藏。

the *ting* station are half open, and a figure emerges from the unknown interior behind each door. Holding the still closed door-leaf, he (or she) seems to be about to open it for the funerary procession. Very similar images can be found on stone sarcophagi (Figs. 4.59, 5.10). But in these cases, it is clearly the "gate" to the world inside the coffin, a universe of the deceased defined by motifs of immortality and cosmic symbols.[170]

In retrospect, we realize that these two pictures depict events prior to the burial of the deceased but in an overtly symbolic language. Stated plainly, in the first scene the deceased is sent off with a formal ceremonial

Fig. 4.59. Carving on a stone sarcophagus. Eastern Han. 2nd century A.D. From Xinjin, Sichuan province.

图 4.59　石棺画像。东汉，2 世纪。四川新津出土。

procession; in the second scene he is escorted by close family members to his graveyard. This funerary journey ends at his tomb—the building with the half-opened gate. Entering this gate signifies the burial of the dead. This is why the designer of the Cangshan tomb informs us, immediately after his description of these two scenes, that he will now portray the dead in the same front chamber, in a niche that functioned as a small shrine.

象征性，设计者将其门扉描绘为半闭半启，人物从门后看不见的地方探出身来，手扶门扉，似乎在为死者打开尚未关闭的半扇门。汉代石棺上可以见到与之非常相近的画像［图 4.59，图 5.10］，门后的空间明显是石棺内的世界——由仙界画像和宇宙象征所构成的死者的世界。[170]

反思一下，我们可以清楚地看到，苍山墓前室中的这两幅画像象征性地描绘了死者下葬之前所发生的事情。前一幅表现了当地官员在正式的葬礼中送别死者的过程，后一幅则反映了死者在亲属的陪伴下去往墓地的情景。送葬的队伍在门扉半启的亭前终止，进入这座建筑就意味着死者已得到安葬。这也就是为什么苍山墓的设计者接下来告诉我们，在这两幅画像之后，他所描绘的将是死者的形象，其位置则是一个祭祀用的壁龛。

249 In a more profound sense, this journey symbolizes the transition from death to rebirth followed in the designer's narrative. This narrative begins from the rear chamber, where the coffin concealing the corpse of the deceased is evidence of his former existence. The designer then describes the ritual process in which the coffin was transported to the graveyard—the otherworldly home of the deceased. Only after this step could the designer portray the deceased in his human form in the front tomb chamber—a definite indication of his rebirth in the underground world. It was understood that the dead, or his soul, was now *living* there with regained human desires. Logically, the third part of the tomb's decoration would illustrate the fulfillment of such desires. For the front side of the facade lintel, the designer planned a scene representing an outdoor tour; for the back of the same stone, he designed an elaborate musical performance. These two pictures, one facing out and the other in, epitomized the two main aspects of the leisurely life that the occupant of the Cangshan tomb would enjoy.

This analysis leads us to compare once more the Cangshan inscription with Han funerary texts composed by patrons. We find differences not only in their language and the degree of literacy but, more fundamentally, in their basic premises and points of view. First, the designer of the Cangshan tomb described his pictures in a sequence from death to rebirth and from the rear coffin chamber to the front reception hall. In a way, this designer was undergoing the (supposed) experiences of the dead: his corpse would be put into a coffin; his coffin would be carried out and transported to his tomb; he would be buried; and he would be reborn in a new home where he could again enjoy all sorts of entertainments. This series of experiences was depicted in a continuous pictorial narrative. The patron of a funerary monument, on the other hand, often assumed a visitor's viewpoint. As exemplified by the inscription on An Guo's shrine, the writer of the text approached the pictorial carvings as isolated images without obvious narrative links, and he described these images from exterior to interior, as though he were entering the building and recording what he saw as he went along. Unlike the designer, a patron would never have identified himself with the dead—his father, brother, former master, or friend. To him the whole significance of a devotional monument must have lain in the opposition between the deceased and himself—between the object of devotion and the devotee.

更为深刻的是，根据设计者的叙述，这一车马行列象征着从死亡到再生的转化。叙述从后室开始，那里安放着死者的遗体，代表着死亡的状态。接着，设计者描述了棺被运往墓地的礼仪过程，而墓地是死者在另一个世界的家。只是在这之后，死者才在前室以栩栩如生的形象出现，表现了他的再生。经过这种转化，死者或其灵魂因此得以“生活”在他的地下家园中，并重新获得了种种活人的欲望。墓葬下一部分的装饰因此顺理成章地描绘了满足死者欲望的各种内容。在墓葬入口横梁的正面，设计者安排了死者的出行活动，背面则刻画了盛大的乐舞表演。一幅向外，一幅向内，这两幅画像表现了墓主人在地下世界中闲适生活的两个主要方面。

上述分析引导我们再次将苍山题记与汉代丧葬建筑赞助人所写的文字进行比较。我们发现，二者的差别不仅表现在语言及文化修养上，更重要的是，二者具有截然不同的观念和前提。首先，苍山墓的设计者在描述墓中画像时遵循了从死亡到再生、从后室到前堂的顺序。可以说，设计者以这种方式体验了死者的（假想的）经历：他的遗体被放入棺中，他的棺被运往墓地，他被埋葬，他在新的家中再生并将享受各种娱乐。这一系列的经历被描绘为连续的叙事性图像。但对丧葬建筑的赞助人来说，他们总是从假定的参观者的角度来观看。例如，在安国祠堂题记中，作者提到的画像是一些彼此独立的，缺乏明显叙事性联系的图像。他描写这些图像的顺序是由外而内，就像他正在走进这个享堂，边走边记录他所看到的东西。赞助人与设计者不同，他们绝不会把自己设想为死者——他的父亲、兄弟或师友。对于他们来说，纪念性建筑的全部意义存在于死者和他们本人之间——奉献对象与奉献者之间的对立。

Second, the designer of the Cangshan tomb was guided by what I call the *primary or shared symbolism* of funerary art, in which images were
250 understood in light of a general interest in death, the transformation of the soul, and immortality. On this basic level of religious thinking, little attention was paid to the particularities of the deceased or to the social and political values of a funerary structure. The builder of the Cangshan tomb apparently had a strong fear of the dead tracing and haunting him, and so he ended his inscription with a prayer: "You, the deceased, have entered the dark world, /Completely separated from the living. /After the tomb is sealed, /It will never be opened again." Except for the payment agreed upon for his labor, he hoped to have nothing more to do with the departed soul.

The patron of a monument, on the other hand, was attracted by the *secondary or specific symbolism* of funerary art; he was often more inclined to read social and moral meanings into pictorial carvings. To him, the establishment of the mortuary monument was a moral and political event, and he expected that this monument would continue to exert influence on public opinion. His funerary inscription never explained the journey and life of the deceased in the underground world. Rather, he emphasized filial piety, loyalty, and other correct social norms. Understandably, the patron was himself a spectator of the carvings on the monument, and his description instructed other spectators how to comprehend these scenes. It is not strange, therefore, that during the Han, a patron's account of funerary art was often alarmingly similar to those visitors produced. An Guo's brothers urged "people of virtue and kindheartedness within the four seas" to pay attention to the "figures of filial piety, excellent virtue, and benevolence" depicted on their family shrine, and to scenes representing the "dignified superiors" and the "agitated yet joyous inferiors." Their words seem to echo Wang Yanshou's description of the mural in the Hall of Spiritual Light of the Lu principality (Lu Lingguang dian), which the poet visited at the beginning of the second century:

> From the later period of the Xia, Shang, and Zhou dynasties are shown the concubines who debauched their masters, loyal ministers and filial sons, noble knights and virtuous women. No detail of their wisdom or stupidity, successes or failures, is omitted from these records. Their evil deeds may serve to warn later generations; their good deeds may set an example for posterity.[171]

In both cases, the voice of the builders is obscured, if not entirely buried, by the patron's and visitor's ideological glorification of the monuments.

从另一个角度看，引导着苍山墓设计者的，是我所说的丧葬艺术原初的或共有的象征性。他对图像的兴趣集中于对死亡的一般性关注、灵魂的转化以及成仙。在这个宗教思维的基本层面上，人们所考虑的不是死者的特殊性或者丧葬建筑的社会和政治价值。苍山墓的建造者还表现出一种明显的忧虑，即死者会作祟，对他纠缠不放。所以在题记的最后，他祈求死者“长就幽冥则决绝，闭旷之后不复发”。他只希望拿到应得的工钱，而不希望与死者的灵魂有任何关系。

反之，吸引纪念性建筑赞助人的，常常是丧葬艺术次生的或特定的象征意义。他倾向于解读画像中的社会和道德含义。对他来说，丧葬纪念物的修建从根本上说是一个道德和政治的事件，他也希望所赞助的纪念物将对公众舆论产生影响。他的题记从不描写死者进入地下的旅程和在另一个世界中的生活，而是强调忠、孝和其他社会准则。可以理解，赞助人本身就是丧葬建筑雕刻的观者，他的描述也引导着其他观者去理解这些画面。因此，赞助人眼中的丧葬艺术与参观者所见往往惊人地相似。安国的兄弟提醒“贤仁四海士”去观看祠堂中对“孝及贤仁”和“遵者俨然，从者肃侍”的描绘。他们的话语与王延寿所描述的鲁灵光殿壁画相互呼应。这位诗人于2世纪初参观那座宫殿时写道：

> 下及三后，婬妃乱主。忠臣孝子，烈士贞女，贤愚成败，靡不载叙，恶以戒世，善以示后。[171]

在这两个例子中，赞助人和参观者对于纪念性建筑思想性的溢美之词即使没有彻底淹没，也是大大模糊了建筑者的声音。

CHAPTER FIVE THE TRANSPARENT STONE: THE END OF AN ERA

251 On foot I climbed up Beimang's slopes
and gazed afar on Luoyang's hills.
Luoyang, so silent and forlorn,
its halls and palaces all burned away.
Each wall has collapsed and crumbled,
briars and brambles stretch to sky.
I saw no old folks from times before,
in my eyes were only new young men.
I walked at an angle, there was no path,
fields had run wild, tilled no more.
Long had the traveler not returned,
he can no longer tell the boundary paths.
And the moors, so barren and bleak,
no hearth-fires seen for a thousand miles.
When I think on this place I used to live,
breath chokes within, I cannot speak.[1]

Composed by Cao Zhi in the early third century, this poem is an early example of the poetic genre *huai gu,* or "meditation on the past." Often inspired by the sight of ruins, such writings transform history into a site of lamentation. A broken stela, a collapsed palace, an abandoned city—old monuments no longer possess their original form; only their destruction and decay now arouse the spectator's sentiment and add another layer of meaning. It is fair to say the *huai gu* tradition depends on a particular notion of the past: separated by a huge gulf from the present, the past emerges as a distant image that one can gaze at and speculate on. Time alone can never create this gulf: Wu Liang of the Eastern Han felt an unbroken connection with paragons from bygone eras; Cao Zhi looked on Luoyang, the city where he used to live, and saw an infinitely remote territory.

Cao Zhi's Luoyang was a double, however: the past Luoyang in his *memory* and the current Luoyang in his *view*. These two sharply contradictory images intensified the tragedy shared by the poet and the city. Like the once glorious but now ruined capital, Cao Zhi belonged to both the past and the present and therefore to neither. He found no one of his own generation: "I saw no old folks from times before, /in my eyes were only new young men." No longer inside the city looking out,

伍 透明之石：一个时代的终结

步登北邙阪，遥望洛阳山。
洛阳何寂寞，宫室尽烧焚。
垣墙皆顿擗，荆棘上参天。
不见旧耆老，但睹新少年。
侧足无行径，荒畴不复田。
游子久不归，不识陌与阡。
中野何萧条，千里无人烟。
念我平常居，气结不能言。[1]

曹植作于 3 世纪初的这首诗是怀古诗的早期典范。这类诗歌通常从废墟景象获得灵感，将历史转换成一个哀悼的现场。残碑、败宫、废城——旧时纪念物的原貌不复存在，此时唯有其毁坏与衰败引起观者的一番感慨，从而赋予它们以另外一重意义。怀古传统取决于对过去的一种特别意识：与"现在"隔着一道鸿沟，"过去"显现为可被人凝望、思索的遥远映像。单单是时间本身并无可能造成这一鸿沟：东汉的武梁感到他和往古楷模之间具有一种不间断的联系；但当曹植望着自己昔日居住的洛阳，他所看到的却似乎是无限遥远的一片疆土。

然而，曹植的洛阳是一个双重影像：记忆中过去的洛阳和眼前当时的洛阳。这两个尖锐冲突的影像加深了诗人与这座古城共同经历的悲怆。如同这座一度辉煌但已成为废墟的故都，曹植既属于过去又属于现在，因而也就两者一无所属。他眼中所见的不是自己的同代人："不见旧耆老，但睹新少年。"他不再从城内向城外窥望，

he was now standing in the Beimang Hills and gazing at Luoyang. Stephen Owen, the English translator of Cao's poem, comments on this new point of view:

> One of the most durable openings of *yuefu* and the "old poems" was going out the gates of Luoyang, the Eastern Han capital, as in "Nineteen Old Poems" XIII. From the eastern gates could be seen the great cemetery in the Beimang Hills. In what seems to be a return poem, an ironic reversal occurs: Cao Zhi. . . climbs Beimang and looks back on Luoyang itself, in ruins, sacked by Dong Zhuo in 190 and now virtually deserted.[2]

Cao Zhi's reversal of the traditional way of describing Luoyang in literature indicated his own transformation from insider to outsider. The hills where he now stood symbolized the irrevocable nature of that shift: all Eastern Han Emperors were buried there, and the name Beimang had
252 become synonymous with death. The poet took the position of the dead, looking back to their (and his) former home, which was now nothing but a "ghost town." In the third century, social reality and one's personal experience caused this radical change in point of view. Two or three hundred years later, people would manipulate point of view to stimulate new experiences.

❶ Reversed Image and Inverted Vision

Near the modern city of Nanjing in eastern China, some ten mausoleums surviving from the early sixth century bear witness to the past glory of emperors and princes of the Liang dynasty (502-57).[3] The mausoleums share a general design (Fig. 5.1). Three pairs of stone monuments are usually erected in front of the tumulus: a pair of stone animals—lions or *qilin* unicorns according to the status of the dead are placed before a gate formed by two stone pillars; the name and title of the deceased appear on the flat panels beneath the pillars' capitals. Finally two opposing memorial stelae bear identical epitaphs recording the career and merits of the dead person. This sequence of paired stones defines a central axis or a ritual path leading to the tomb mound. As indicated by its ancient designation *shendao*, or "the spirit road," this path was built not for the living but for the departing soul, which, it was commonly

此时的曹植站在北邙山上，俯视着整个洛阳城。曹植这首诗的英译者宇文所安对这一新的视点做了如下评论：

> 正如《古诗十九首》之第十三首中所见，乐府和"古诗"中最为持久不变的一种开头，是步出洛阳这座东汉都城的城门。从城的东门可以看到北邙山上的大型坟地。而在这首看来为还乡主题的诗中，一种反讽式的逆转出现了：曹植……登上北邙，回望着废墟中的洛阳本身。经历了公元190年的董卓之乱，这座城此时实际已是一片荒芜。[2]

曹植对文学作品中描写洛阳的传统方式的逆转，暗示着他本人从内到外的转变。此时，他脚下的邙山象征着这种位移的不可逆转性：正是在这山丘上埋葬着东汉时期的所有帝王，而且北邙之名也已成为死亡的同义词。诗人因此选择了死者的视点，回望着他们（和自己）从前的家园——那座当时已不过是"鬼城"的家园。在3世纪，社会现实和个人的切身体验导致了这一视点上的根本转变。两三个世纪之后，人们将再次利用视点的改换来激发新的体验。

一、倒像与反视

今日的南京附近依然存留着不下十座建于6世纪初的陵墓，它们是梁代（502—557年）皇帝与太子们昔时辉煌的历史见证。[3]这些陵墓大致具有一套标准的规划［图5.1］，通常在封土前方立有三对石制纪念性雕刻：一对依墓主的身份或是麒麟或是天禄的石兽，安置在由一对石柱构成的阙门前方；柱头下方的长方形石板上分别刻有墓主人的名讳和头衔；最后是两座相对而立的石碑，其内容相同的碑文记述了墓主人的生平与业绩。这一对对石刻组成的序列界定出一条通向墓冢的中轴线，也就是被称作"神道"的礼仪通道。正如"神道"这一古老的名称所暗示，这条道路并非为活人，而是

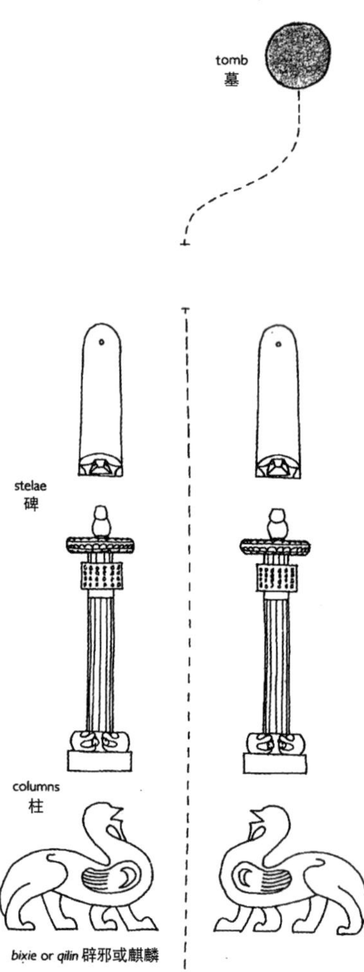

Fig. 5.1. Standard layout of a Liang royal tomb

图 5.1 梁朝皇陵的标准布局

believed, traveled along the path from its old home to its new abode, crossing the pillar-gate that marked out the boundary between these two worlds.[4]

Fifteen hundred years have passed, and these mausoleums have turned into ruins. The stone animals stand in rice fields; the stelae are cracked and their inscriptions blurred. Ann Paludan's photograph wonderfully captures the sentiments aroused by their decay (Fig. 5.2). But the "spirit road," which never takes a material form but is only defined by the shapes surrounding it, seems to have escaped the ravages of time. As long as the pairs of monuments—even their ruins—still exist *in situ*, a visitor recognizes this "path" and he, or his gaze, travels along it (Fig. 5.3). Like the ancients, he would first meet the twin stone animals, each with its body curving from crest to tail to form a smooth S-shaped contour. With their large round eyes and enormous gaping mouths, the mythical beasts seem to be in a state of alarm and amazement (Fig. 5.4). Compared to the bulky animal statues created three centuries earlier during the Han, these statues evince a new interest in psychology rather than in pure physique, in momentary expression rather than in permanent existence, in individuality rather than in anonymity, and in a complex combination of fantastic and human elements rather than in

Fig. 5.2. Qilin unicorn in Emperor Wu's (d. A.D. 494) An ling mausoleum. Qi dynasty. Danyang, Jiangsu province.

图 5.2　武帝（卒于 494）安陵石麒麟。齐。江苏丹阳。

uniformity. The vividness of the animals even seems at odds with the solemn atmosphere of a graveyard. Standing in front of the stone pillars, these strange creatures seem to have just emerged from the other side of the gate and are astonished by what they are confronting.

为了弃世而去的亡魂而建。当时的人们相信死者灵魂将沿着这条道路，穿过分隔生死两界的阙门，从生前故居来到死后新宅。[4]

一千五百余年过去了，这些陵墓已经变成了废墟。石兽伫立于稻田之中；碑碣残损，碑文斑驳模糊。帕鲁丹的照片准确地摄取了这些衰败陵墓引起的怀古情愫［图 5.2］。然而，不以物质形态呈现，仅仅由周边石刻界定出来的神道，则似乎摆脱了岁月的销蚀。只要那些成对的纪念物——哪怕是其残迹——依然存在于原位，来访者就能辨认出这条“路径”，他的脚步或视线也就会顺着这条路径延伸［图 5.3］。和古人一样，他将首先与那对石兽相遇，它们的整个身体弯曲成一个流畅的 S 形轮廓，圆睁的双目和呲咧的大口令人感到它们似乎正处于瞬间的惊诧之中［图 5.4］。和 3 世纪以前的汉代大型动物石雕相比，这些齐梁石刻不再是对体格和力量的表达，而更多地显现出对心理状态的新兴趣，它们所凸显的是瞬间的表情而非永恒的存在，是独特的个性而非匿名的共性，是幻想世界和人性的复杂综合而不是同一和统一。这些石兽栩栩如生的神态甚至似乎有违于墓地的肃穆气氛：伫立在阙门之前，它们仿佛刚刚从门内遽然出现，惊讶地面对着它们眼前的世界。

Fig. 5.3. Tomb of Prince Xiao Ji (d. A.D. 527). Liang dynasty. Jurong, Jiangsu province.

图 5.3 萧绩（卒于 527）墓。梁。江苏句容。

Fig. 5.4. The head of a *qilin* unicorn (detail of Fig. 5.2). A.D. 494. Danyang, Jiangsu province.

图 5.4 麒麟头部（图 5.2 局部）。齐，494 年。江苏丹阳。

人形灯，东周

Human-shaped lamp. Eastern Zhou (p. 208)

装饰画像的青铜壶，东周

Bronze *hu* vessel with pictorial decoration. Eastern Zhou (p. 206)

青铜铺首门环，东周晚期

Bronze door ring.
Late Eastern Zhou (p. 282)

塔楼模型，东周晚期

Miniature tower with figures and musicians inside. Late Eastern Zhou (p. 286)

乌纹空心砖，东周末至秦

Hollow tile with incised bird images.
Late Eastern Zhou to Qin (p. 290)

曾侯乙内棺，战国早期

Inner coffin of Marquis Yi of the state of Zeng.
Early Warring States period (p. 340)

彩陶俑，西汉

Painted clay figurines.
Western Han (p. 444)

霍去病墓前石雕“马踏匈奴”，西汉

“Horse trampling a barbarian.”
Stone statue at Huo Qubing’s tomb.
Western Han (p. 356)

博山炉，西汉

Incense burner.
Western Han (p. 484)

仙山熏炉，西汉

Incense burner.
Western Han (p. 342)

拜塔，出自巴尔胡特

Worshipping the stupa.
Bhārhut (p. 368)

四神瓦当，新

Eave tiles decorated with the
four directional animals and birds.
Xin dynasty (p. 500)

石棺画像，东汉

Carving on a stone sarcophagus.
Eastern Han (p. 683)

戴氏享堂画像与题记，东汉中期

Carving and inscription on the Dai family shrine.
Mid-Eastern Han (p. 552)

带有佛像的青铜摇钱树残片，东汉

Fragment of a bronze “money tree” with a Buddha’s image. Eastern Han (p. 379)

仙山摇钱树陶座，东汉晚期

Clay stand of a “money tree.”
Late Eastern Han (p. 342)

高颐阙，东汉晚期

Que pillar-gate of Gao Yi's graveyard. Late Eastern Han (p. 530)

高颐碑，东汉晚期

Gao Yi's memorial stela.
Late Eastern Han (p. 532)

宁懋石室，北魏

Shrine of Ning Mao.
Northern Wei dynasty (p. 722)

武帝安陵石麒麟，齐

Qilin unicorn in Emperor Wu's An ling mausoleum. Qi dynasty (p. 693)

The powerful imagery of these stone beasts must have contributed to the invention of abundant legends about them: people have repeatedly reported seeing them jumping up in the air.[5] In 546, the animals in front of the Jian ling mausoleum, the tomb of the dynastic founder's father, reportedly suddenly got up and began to dance. They then fought violently with a huge serpent under the pillar-gate, and one beast was even injured by the evil reptile.[6] This event must have created a great sensation at the time: it was recorded in the dynasty's official history, and the famous poet Yu Xin (513-81) incorporated it into his writings.[7] This and other tales, obviously originating from the statues' symbolic function of warding off evil and from the desire to explain their decay over time, nevertheless demanded and inspired further political interpretations. Thus when a similar event was later reported to the court, some ministers considered it a good omen, but the emperor feared it as an inauspicious indication of future rebellions—underlying both interpretations was the belief that the stone beasts carried divine messages to the living.[8]

这些石兽强有力的形象引发出许多传说：人们不断报道说看到它们腾飞至空中。[5] 一条记载说，梁朝建陵（也就是梁朝建立者萧衍父亲的陵墓）前的石辟邪于 546 年突然起舞，随后在阙门下和一条大蟒进行了一场激烈搏斗，其中一只石辟邪还为蟒蛇所伤。[6] 这件事在当时想必造成了很大反响，因为它不仅见载于《梁书》，还被著名诗人庾信（513—581 年）写入他的作品。[7] 诸如此类的故事显然出自石兽驱除邪恶的象征性功能，也来自人们试图解释它们为何经年受损的企图。不过，这类传说也不免引出带有政治色彩的解释。因此当一起类似的事件被上报到朝廷时，一些大臣以为是个好的兆头，而皇帝本人则担心不久将有反叛发生——两种解释的背后均隐含着石兽向人间传递天意这一根本观念。[8]

Having passed the animal statues, the visitor finds himself before the
254 stone pillars. As I mentioned a little earlier, these bear two panels with identical inscriptions. In the example illustrated in Fig. 5.5a, the passage reads: “The spirit road of Grand Supreme Emperor Wen,” the father of the founder of the Liang dynasty. There is nothing strange about the content of these inscriptions; what is puzzling is the way they are written: the inscription on the left panel is a piece of regular text, but the one on the right panel is reversed.[9]

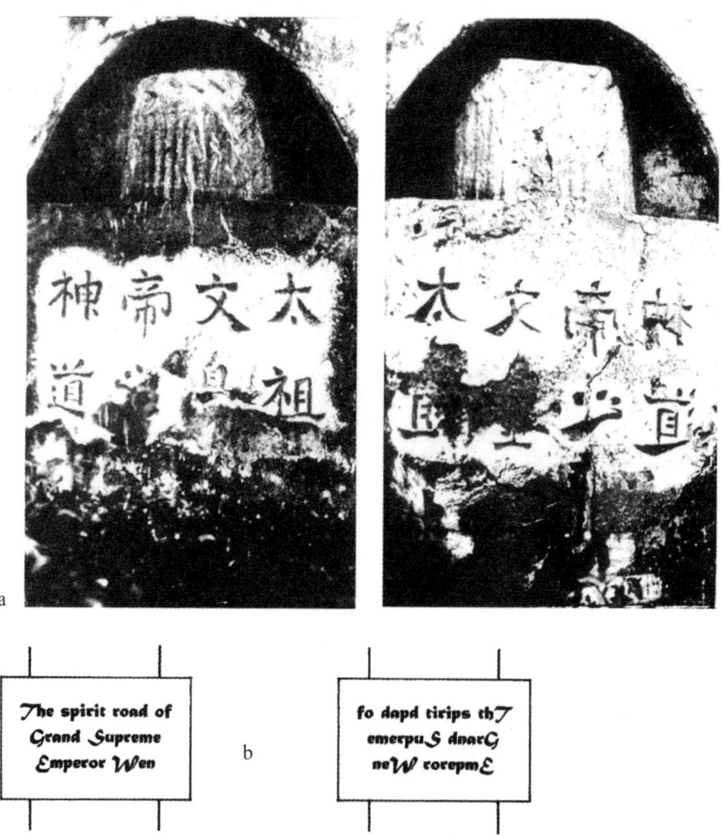

Fig. 5.5. (a) Mirror-image inscriptions on the stone pillars in Emperor Wen’s tomb. A.D. 502. H. 62.5 cm. W. 142 cm. Danyang, Jiangsu province. (b) English translation.

图 5.5 （a）文帝建陵前左右石柱上的镜像铭文。梁，502 年。高 62.5 厘米，宽 142 厘米。江苏丹阳。（b）英文翻译。

Readers unfamiliar with Chinese writing may gain some sense of the irony created by this juxtaposition from an English "translation" of the Chinese passages (Fig. 5.5b): although the content of the two inscriptions is identical, their effect is entirely different. The inscription on the left is as a series of words forming a coherent and readable text. But the inscription on the right, at first sight, consists of no more than individual and illegible signs. A temporal reading sequence is thus established: even though the two inscriptions would be *seen* simultaneously from the spirit path, they must be *comprehended* sequentially. It would not take more than a few seconds for a literate person to read the normal inscription on the left, but to understand the inscription on the right he would first need to find clues. Such clues are found *visually* in the physical relationship between the two inscriptions: both their symmetrical placement and echoing patterns suggest that the illegible text "mirrors" the legible one. Unconsciously, the visitor would have taken the normal text as his point of reference for the other's meaning.

越过石兽，观者就到了石柱的近前。如上文所言，两根石柱柱头下面都有一方刻着相同铭文的石板。图 5.5 所示的铭文为“太祖文皇帝之神道”，说明这是梁朝建立者梁武帝之父亲的神道。这段铭文在内容上毫无新奇之处，令人费解的是它们的书写方式：左边石板上的文字是正常的写法，但右边石板上的文字却是反书。[9]

尽管两段铭文的内容相同，但它们的视觉效果却大相径庭。左边的文字前后连贯，构成一个可读文本。而右边的文字乍一看去，不过是一系列孤立难认的符号。这个视觉反应产生了一个顺时的阅读顺序：尽管从神道上能够同时看到这两段铭文，但对它们的理解却有先后次序。对一个识字的人来说，阅读左边的正规铭文用不了几秒钟时间，但要理解右边的铭文，他首先需要找到线索。这个线索是以视觉方式从两段铭文的对应关系中发现的：它们位置上的对称和形式上的相互呼应，都表明那段难以辨读的铭文是可读铭文的“镜像”。不知不觉当中，观者已经以左边的正书铭文作为理解右边反书铭文的根据。

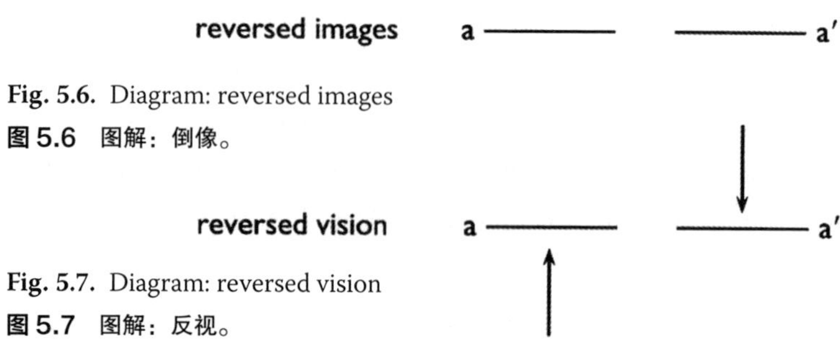

Fig. 5.6. Diagram: reversed images
图 5.6 图解：倒像。

Fig. 5.7. Diagram: reversed vision
图 5.7 图解：反视。

There would be no need to compare the individual characters of the two inscriptions: the problem no longer exists once the visitor realizes they are the *same*. The "illegible" inscription has become legible because he can read its mirror-image (Fig. 5.6). In other words, the mystery of its content has vanished: it is simply a reversed version of a regular piece of writing. What remains is the mystery of its reading: *it would become not only legible in content but normal in form if the reader could invert his own vision to read it from the "back" —from the other side of the column* (Fig. 5.7).[10] Once this inference is made, the reversed inscription changes from a subject to be deciphered to a stimulus of the imagination.[11] Controlled and deceived by the engraved signs, the visitor has mentally
255 transported himself to the other side of the gate. He has forgotten the solid and opaque stone material, which has now become "transparent."

All this may seem a psychological game and a quite subjective interpretation, but the perceptual transformation explored here is seen frequently in the funerary art and literature of the Six Dynasties. During a funerary rite, the "visitor" whom I have just described would have been a mourner; and as a mourner, his frame of mind would be focused on the function of a funerary ritual and the mortuary monuments framing it. Who was supposed to be in a position to read the reversed inscription "obversely"? In other words, who was thought to be on the other side of the stone column looking out? A gate always separates space into an interior and an exterior; in a cemetery these are commonly identified as the world of the dead and the world of the living. The pair of inscriptions on the twin pillars signifies the junction of these two worlds and the meeting point of two gazes projecting from the opposite sides of the gate (Fig. 5.7): the "natural" gaze of the mourner proceeding from the outside toward the burial ground (Fig. 5.8), and his "inverted" gaze, which is now attributed to the dead at the other end of the spirit road (where his body was buried and his life was recorded on memorial tablets).

一旦意识到这两件铭文的内容是相同的，观者也就没有必要对它们进行逐字比较了：通过阅读反书铭文的正书镜像，"不可读的"铭文已经变为可读［图 5.6］。换言之，反书铭文内容的神秘性已经消失了：它仅仅是一段正常文字的反像而已。所遗留下来的是"阅读"的神秘性：如果观者可以改变自己的视点，从"背面"——也就是从石柱的另一面——来阅读这段铭文的话，那它就不仅可读，而且其书写形式也将是正常的了［图 5.7］。[10] 一旦做出了这种推论，这一反书铭文就从有待译解的对象转变为对想象力的刺激。[11] 在这些镌刻符号的控制和诱导下，观者在想象中已经位移到门的另一边。他已忘却了石头材料的固体性和不透明性，冥冥之中建筑材料已经变成"透明"的了。

所有这一切或许像一个心理游戏或一种颇有主观色彩的解释，但我在这里所探究的此种知觉上的转换，在六朝时期的丧葬艺术和文学作品当中经常出现。在真实的葬礼当中，我所描述的"观者"通常是以送葬人的身份出现的；作为一位凭吊者，他的心绪势必聚焦在葬礼和那些构成葬礼的丧葬纪念物的功能上。是谁被假定为从"正面"的角度来阅读反书铭文呢？也就是说，是谁处在石柱门阙的另一边向外看呢？一道门总是把空间分成内外两个部分；在墓地当中，这两个空间分别是属于生者和死者的世界。石柱上的两方铭文所构成的，是这两个世界的临界线和从阙门内外相对发出视线的交汇点［图 5.7］：凭吊者的"正常"目光从外面投向墓地［图 5.8］，而他的"反视"的目光则归属于处于神道另一端的死者（他的尸体埋在那里，他的生平事迹也被铭刻在墓碑上）。

Fig. 5.8. A man kneels between two pillars and pays homage to a tomb mound. Stone carving. Northern Wei dynasty. Early 6th century A.D. H. 45.5 cm. From Luoyang, Henan province.

图 5.8　一人跪于双阙之间向坟丘礼拜。画像石。北魏，6 世纪初。高 45.5 厘米。河南洛阳出土。

The important point is that this reading/viewing process forces the mourner to go through a psychological dislocation from this world to the world beyond it. Confronted by the "illegible" inscription, his normal, mundane logic is disrupted and shaken. The discovery of the mirror relationship between the two inscriptions forges a powerful metaphor for the opposition between life and death. The sequential reading of the inscriptions creates a temporal shift from within to without; by mentally dislocating himself to the other side of the gate he identifies himself with the dead and assumes the viewpoint of the dead. The function of the gate is thus not merely to separate the two spaces and realms. As a static, physical boundary it can easily be crossed, but it is always *there*. More important, to completely fulfill the ritual transformation, the material existence of the gate has to be rejected. The underlying premise of this ritual transformation is that only when a living person accepts the otherworldly view can he enter the encircled graveyard without violating it, and only then can he not only pay respect to the dead but also speak for the dead.

In this light we can understand the progression traced by Lu Ji's (261-303) series of three mourning songs.[12] In the first song a funeral is narrated as if it were being watched by an anonymous but dispassionate observer:

> By divination an auspicious site is sought.
>
> . . .
>
> For early departure attendants and drivers are roused.
>
> . . .

重要的一点是，这一阅读或观看的过程使凭吊者在心理上经历了一次由此世界到彼世界的位移。面对着拒绝识读的反书铭文，他在日常生活中的正常逻辑被瓦解和动摇。对两种铭文之间的镜像关系的发现，则为生死的对立提供了一种强烈的隐喻，而对两段铭文的依次阅读则造成了从内到外的顺时移位。通过在心理上将自己移位到阙门内，他与死者保持认同并采取了死者的观点。阙门的功能因此不仅仅是区隔两个空间和两种领域。作为一种静态、物质的分界线，它容易被通过但永远存在于原地。更重要的是，礼仪的转化必须否定阙门的物质性存在。这种礼仪性转化的根本前提是，唯有生者接受了另一世界的视点，他才能进入到墓地里而不致对死者有所冒犯。只有这样他才能不但表示出对死者的尊敬，而且还能为死者代言。

由此，我们就可以理解陆机（261—303 年）所写的三首《挽歌》中对葬礼进程的陈述。[12] 第一首挽歌中对葬礼的描写，仿佛出自一个心平气和的匿名旁观者：

> 卜择考休贞，……
>
> 夙驾惊徒御。……

Life and death have different principles;
To carry out the coffin there must be a time.
A cup of wine is set before the two pillars;
The funeral is begun, and the sacred carriage advanced.

256 The funeral procession is still the focus of the second song, but the description becomes subjective and emotional. The poet speaks for the mourners and sees through their eyes:

Wandering, the thoughts of relatives and friends;
In their distress their spirits are uneasy.
...
The soul carriage is silent without sound;
Only to be seen are his cap and belt,
Objects of use represent his past life.
...
A mournful wind delays the moving wheels;
Lowering clouds bind the drifting mists.
We shake our whips and point to the sacred mound;
We yoke the horses and thereafter depart.

The point of view changes again as soon as the funeral procession finally departs toward the sacred mound. In the third and last song, it is the deceased who is seeing, hearing, and speaking in the first person. The poet now identifies not with the mourners but with the dead:

The piled-up hills, how they tower!
My dark hut skulks among them.
Wide stand the Four Limits;
High-arched spreads the azure skies.
By my side I hear the hidden river's flow;
On my back, I gaze at the sky roof suspended.
How lonely is the wide firmament!

When Prince Xiao Ziliang (459-94) went to Mount Zuxing, he gazed at his family tombs there and lamented: "Looking north there is my [dead] uncle; directly before me I see my [deceased] brother—if you have consciousness after your death, please let me be buried here in your land."[13] Ziliang was grieving for both his deceased kin and himself—as the survivor of the family he already saw himself buried in a dark tomb.

死生各异伦，祖载当有时。
舍爵两楹位，启殡进灵輀。

第二首挽歌所关注的焦点仍然是送葬的行列，但描述的口吻变得主观化和情绪化。诗人通过哀悼者的眼光来观察葬礼，并为哀悼者代言：

流离亲友思，惆怅神不泰。
……
魂舆寂无响，但见冠与带。
备物象平生，……
……
悲风徽行轨，倾云结流霭。
振策指灵丘，驾言从此逝。

当送葬的队伍最终离家走向神圣的墓地，诗人的视点再一次发生了变化。在第三首，也是最后一首挽歌中，诗人采取了死者的角度，以第一人称在看、听和叙说。此时他不再把自己与哀悼者等同，而是将自己视为死者化身：

重阜何崔嵬！玄庐窜其间。
磅礴立四极，穹隆放苍天。
侧听阴沟涌，卧观天井悬。
圹宵何寥廓！……

我们在史书中也读到，当萧子良（459—494 年）来到祖硎山，凝望着眼前的家族墓地，他哀伤地吟咏道："北瞻吾叔，前望吾兄，死而有知，请葬此地。"[13] 这里，子良同时在为死去的亲人和自己而感伤——作为家族的幸存者，他似乎已经看到自己被埋在黑暗的墓穴

Sentimental and self-pitying, he seems to have set an example for Xiao Yan (464-549), the founder of the Liang and a great patron of literature. Xiao Yan, or Emperor Wu of Liang, dedicated the Jian ling mausoleum to his deceased father, Xiao Shunzhi (444-94; his mirror inscriptions have been the focus of our discussion); he also had the Xiu ling mausoleum constructed for himself. During a trip in the third month of 544, he sacrificed at his father's graveyard and then visited his own tomb, where "he was deeply moved and began to cry."[14] One wonders what moved him to tears in this second mausoleum; the only possible answer is the vision of himself lying underground on the other side of the pillar-gate.

The concept of "mourner" thus needs to be redefined. A mourner was not only a living person who came to a graveyard to meet a deceased Other, but also possibly a person who visited his own tomb to mourn for himself as the Other. In the first case, the pillar-gate separated yet connected the dead and the living; in the second case, it separated and connected a man's split images that confronted each other. In the late third century, Lu Ji had tried to speak for both the mourners and the dead; in the fifth and sixth centuries people lamented for themselves as though they were dead.[15] From this second tradition emerged three great songs by Tao Qian (365-427), which chillingly observe the world from a dead person's silent perception:

How desolate the moorland lies,
The white poplars sough in the wind.
In the ninth month of sharp frost,
They escort me to the far suburbs.
There where no one dwells at all
The high grave mounds rear their heads.
The horses whinny to the sky,
The wind emits a mournful sound.
Once the dark house is closed
In a thousand years there will be no new dawn.

There will be no new dawn
And all man's wisdom helps not at all.
The people who have brought me here
Have now returned, each to his home.
My own family still feel grief—
The others are already singing.
What shall we say, we who are dead?
Your bodies too will lodge on the hill.[16]

中的情形。充满了善感与自怜，他的感慨为梁朝的创建者、酷爱文学的萧衍（464—549 年）做出前例。梁武帝萧衍为亡父萧顺之（444—494 年）修了建陵（这座陵墓前的正、反书铭文是我在上文中的讨论焦点），同时也为自己建了修陵。在公元 544 年三月的一次出行中，他祭奠过乃父的建陵后又视察了自己的陵墓，在那里"但增感恸"。[14] 究竟是什么使得梁武帝在自己的陵前如此伤感？唯一可能的答案是，他预见到了自己在阙门另一侧的地下长眠的情形。

因此，我们需要重新界定"凭吊者"这个概念：一个凭吊者不仅是来墓地凭吊他人的人，同时也可以是造访自己的墓葬，如凭吊他人一样凭吊自己的人。在第一种情况下，阙门分隔而联系着死者和生者；在第二种情况下，阙门区分和联系着一个人的分裂而对应的自身形像。3 世纪末的陆机试图为生、死两方代言；到了 5—6 世纪时，人们哀悼自己就好像自己已经死去了一般。[15] 从这后一种传统中产生出陶潜（365—427 年）三首不朽的《挽歌》；作者以死者无声的知觉冷冰冰地观察着周围的世界：

荒草何茫茫，白杨亦萧萧。
严霜九月中，送我出远郊。
四面无人居，高坟正嶕峣。
马为仰天鸣，风为自萧条。
幽室一已闭，千年不复朝。
千年不复朝，贤达无奈何。
向来相送人，各自还其家。
亲戚或余悲，他人亦已歌。
死去何所道，托体同山阿。[16]

Tao Qian must have been fascinated by the various possibilities
257 of "inverting" himself—observing and describing himself and his surroundings as though he had become a bodiless and transparent "gaze," moving along the funeral procession like a camera lens. He wrote *jiwen*—sacrificial eulogies—for his relatives, and in these pieces he presents himself as a living member of the family lamenting dead kin.[17] But he also composed a sacrificial eulogy for himself. Unlike the funeral song in which he (as a dead man) follows and watches the entire mortuary rite, in the short preface to his self-eulogy he placed himself in the shifting zone between life and death:

> The year is *dingmao* [A.D. 427] and the correspondence of the pitch pipe is *wuyi*. The weather is cold and the night is long. The atmosphere is mournful; the wild geese are on the move; plants and trees turn yellow and shed their leaves. Master Tao [i.e., Tao Qian himself] is about to take leave of the "traveler's inn" [life] to return forever to his eternal home [death]. His friends are sad in their grief for him; they will join in his funeral feast this very evening, make offering of fine vegetables and present libations of clear wine. The faces he sees already grow dim; the sounds he hears grow fainter.[18]

If life and death are separated by a pillar-gate, the experience described here must take place between the two pillars on the gate's threshold. Unlike Lu Ji, who narrated a funeral in distinct stages progressing from the living to the dead, Tao Qian assumes a position between the two. This suspended position was not completely Tao's invention, however; we find a classical example in Confucius' life:

> In the year *rensi* [479 B.C.], on the morning of the 11th of the 4th moon, Confucius arose, and then supporting himself with his walking stick in one hand while the other hand rested behind his back he advanced majestically to the front door of his apartment and began to chant the following words: "The mountain saint is going to disappear;

the main beam of the empire is going to be broken; the sage is going to die!" After the rhythmic recital of this solemn prediction he went and placed himself *in the center of the gate way*...After seven days, on the 18th day of the 4th moon, near mid-day, he expired at the age of seventy-three.[19]

陶潜想必是被各种"反观"自己的可能性所吸引——在观察和描述自己及其周围的事物时，他仿佛已化为一道无形、透彻的"目光"，就像一台电影摄像机沿着葬礼的行列推移。他常为亲友撰写祭文，在这类作品中作为活在世上的家族成员来哀悼死去的亲人。[17]但他也为自己写了祭文。与《挽歌》中将自己（作为一个死者）置身于并注视着葬礼的情形不同，在这篇《自祭文》的序言中，他把己身置于生死之间的中介地：

> 岁惟丁卯（427），律中无射。天寒夜长，风气萧索，鸿雁于征，草本黄落。陶子将辞逆旅之馆，永归于本宅。故人悽其相悲，同祖行于今夕。羞以嘉蔬，荐以清酌。候颜已冥，聆音愈漠。[18]

如果说生死两界是由一个阙门隔开，陶潜在这里所描述的体验当是发生在阙门两柱之间的门槛上。不同于陆机按照从生到死的不同阶段来描述葬礼，陶潜假定了一种介于生死之间的位置。但这种"悬浮"的位置并不是陶潜的发明；我们在孔子的生平里已经发现了一个经典的例子：

> 孔子蚤作，负手曳杖，消摇于门。歌曰："泰山其颓乎，梁木其坏乎，哲人其萎乎。"既歌而入，当户而坐。子贡闻之，曰："泰山其颓，则吾将安仰梁木其坏？哲人其萎，则吾将安放？夫子殆将病也。"遂趋而入。夫子曰："赐，尔来何迟也。夏后氏殡于东阶之上，则犹在阼也。殷人殡于两楹之间，则与宾主夹之也。周人殡于西阶之上，则犹宾之也。而丘也，殷人也。予畴昔之夜，梦坐奠于两楹之间。夫明王不兴，而天下其孰能宗予？予殆将死也，盖寝疾七日而没。"[19]

With this anecdote we return to the theme of the gate, but with a new interest in the elusive, two-dimensional plane between its two pillars rather than in the two spaces separated by it. Guided by this interest, our attention also shifts from the actual gates standing in a cemetery to their image depicted on flat stone. From the second century on, such images were often engraved on the frontal sides of sarcophagi.[20] In some cases an empty gate indicates the entrance to the other world (Fig. 5.9); in other cases horses or a rider guide the wandering soul through the gate (Fig. 5.10). A third variation offers a more complex illustration (Fig. 5.11), which would be repeated by artists as late as the Song dynasty (Fig. 5.12): a figure emerges from a half-opened gate, holding the still closed door-leaf. The gate is thus half-empty and half-solid; the empty space recedes into an unknown depth, while the solid door-leaf blocks the spectator's gaze from penetrating the hidden space. The figure crosses these two halves, both exposing himself against the empty space and concealing himself behind the closed door-leaf. It seems that he (or she) is about to vanish into the emptiness but is still grasping the door and looking at the world to which he once belonged.[21] Almost graphically, this image signifies an intermediary stage between life and death.

孔子的这段轶事再次把我们带回到关于门的主题，不过这次我们的兴趣不再是阙门所分隔的两个空间，而在于双阙之间难以捉摸的二维平面（也就是孔子梦见自己“坐奠于两楹之间”之处）。受此兴趣的引导，我们的注意力也从矗立在墓地前方的实际阙门转移到那些刻画在石头平面上的阙门图像。自 2 世纪起，这类图像经常出现在石棺的前挡上。[20] 在某些画面中，一扇敞开的空门象征着通向另一世界的入口［图 5.9］；而另外一些画面则描绘了马匹或骑者引导游魂进入大门［图 5.10］。第三种样式的形式更为复杂［图 5.11］，一直晚到宋、金仍被反复沿用［图 5.12］：一个人出现在半开半掩的门后，手扶着那扇依然关着的门扉。这种门是半虚半实的：虚的一边引导我们的视线向门内的未知空间延伸，而关着的门扉则把我们的视线阻挡在门的这一边。扶门的人跨越两界，既暴露在其身后虚幻的空间之前，又遮蔽于关闭的门扉之后。他（她）仿佛就要消失在身后的空间里，但仍然在抓住门扉，留恋地回望着外界。[21] 这种图像因此可以说是对生死之际的生动表现。

Fig. 5.9. Stone sarcophagus decorated with a *que* gate on the front end. Eastern Han. 2nd century A.D. L. 217.5 cm. H. 58.5 cm. From Shapingba, Chongqing, Sichuan province. Chongqing Museum.

图 5.9 前挡饰有阙门的石棺。东汉，2 世纪。重庆沙坪坝出土。重庆市博物馆藏。

Fig. 5.10. Que gate and a guardian. Carving on the front side of a stone sarcophagus from Xinjin, Sichuan province. Eastern Han. 2nd century A.D. Sichuan University Museum, Chengdu. Ink rubbing.

图 5.10 四川新津石棺前挡上的阙门与门吏画像。东汉，2 世纪。四川大学博物馆藏。拓本。

Fig. 5.11. Half-opened gate. Carving on the front side of the Wang Hui sarcophagus. A.D. 211. H. 83 cm. L. 101 cm. Found in 1942 at Lushan, Sichuan province. Lushan Museum. Ink rubbing.

图 5.11 王晖石棺前挡半启门画像。东汉晚期，211 年。高 83 厘米，长 101 厘米。1942 年四川芦山出土。芦山县博物馆藏。拓本。

Fig. 5.12. Half-opened gate. Mural in Song Tomb no. 2. Excavated in 1983 at Xin'an, Luoyang, Henan province. *Ca.* 12th century A.D. Luoyang Ancient Tomb Museum.

图 5.12 洛阳新安 2 号宋墓半启门壁画。北宋，约 12 世纪。洛阳古墓博物馆藏。

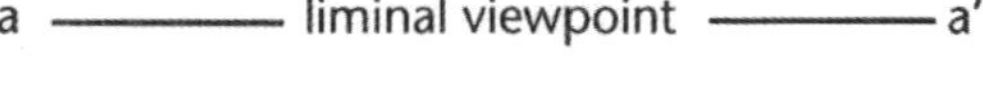

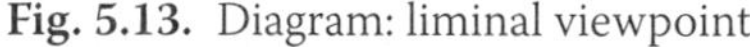

Fig. 5.13. Diagram: liminal viewpoint
图 5.13 图解：阈界视点

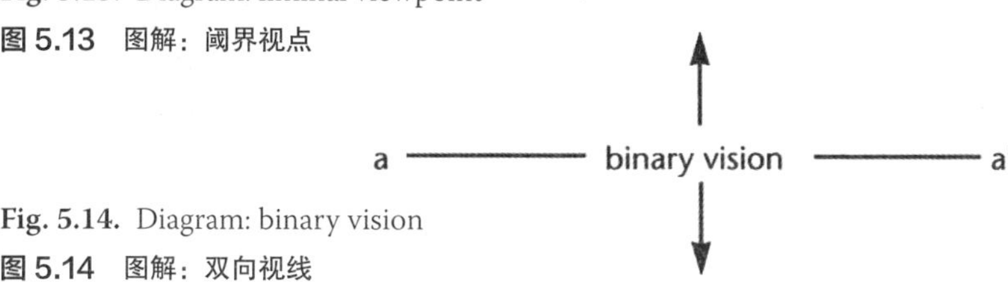

Fig. 5.14. Diagram: binary vision
图 5.14 图解：双向视线

We are reminded of Tao Qian's depiction of himself in his eulogy: 259
"Master Tao is about to take leave of the 'traveler's inn' to return forever to his eternal home. His friends are sad in their grief for him…The faces he sees already grow dim; the sounds he hears grow fainter." We can imagine that the same words could be murmured by the depicted figure who, with half of his or her body inside the dark sarcophagus, belongs to neither this world nor the world beyond it. Both the implied artist and the poet Tao Qian assume a "liminal position" on the threshold of the gate (Fig. 5.13). Their vision may be called a "binary vision" because they look in the two opposite directions of life and death at the same time (Fig. 5.14).

这一图像令我们回想起陶潜《自祭文》中的自我描写："陶子将辞逆旅之馆，永归于本宅。故人悽其相悲……候颜已冥，聆音愈漠。"我们可以想象，那个身体半掩于一片玄黑的石棺内部、灵魂游离于生死两界之间的人物形象可能会发出同样的感叹。创作这一图像的艺术家和诗人陶潜都采取了一种门槛上的"阈限位置"［图 5.13］。他们的视线可以被称为"双向视线"，因为他们同时朝着两个相对的方向审视生死［图 5.14］。

This mode of visualization is related to a general phenomenon during the Six Dynasties: many contemporary writers, painters, and calligraphers sought to see the "two facets of the universe" simultaneously. As we return to the "reversed inscriptions," the focus of this investigation shifts from the viewer's perception to the artist's ambition to create such inscriptions. But first, who was the artist? Usually we assume that an engraved stone inscription copies a piece of writing and reflects the original style of the calligrapher. But if a calligrapher wrote only a single "regular" text, which was then inscribed twice as both the front and back inscriptions on the two pillars, the calligrapher's work was essentially irrelevant to the final output; he can hardly be claimed as the writer of the "reversed" inscription. But if he had indeed created both versions of the text, it would be far more intriguing. This would mean that the mirror inscriptions directly reflected the artist's creativity and state of mind, for, as Emperor Wu of the Liang once stated himself, "the hand and mind [of a calligrapher] must work in correspondence."[22] This, in turn, would mean that the calligrapher had first tried to "reverse" himself; before there was any "transparent stone" he had to make himself transparent.

Two methods may enable us to solve this puzzle. We can check contemporary literary records for mentions of "reversed" or "inverted" writing. We can also try to find other clues from existing inscriptions. In an essay, the master calligrapher Yu Yuanwei (sixth century) introduces himself as a calligraphic acrobat who once inscribed a screen in a hundred different scripts, both in ink and in color. He lists all the fancy names of these scripts (such as "immortal script," "flower-and-grass script," "monkey script," "pig script," "tadpole script"). Toward the end of this long inventory appear two names: *daoshu* (reversed writing) and *fanzuoshu* (inverted and left writing).[23] Even more fascinating, in the same essay he identifies the origin of a type of reversed writing.

> During the Datong reign period [535-46], a scholar [named Kong Jingtong] working in the Eastern Palace could write cursive script

[*caoshu*] in a single stroke. His brush stroke, which broke only at the end of a line, was fluent, graceful, and restrained, and reflected his distinctive nature. Since then no one has been able to follow him. [Kong] also created the "left-and-right script" [*zuoyoushu*]. When people exchanged their writings at a gathering, no one could read his piece.[24]

这种视觉模式与六朝时期的一种普遍现象有关：这个时期的许多作家、画家和书法家都试图同时看到世界的两面。考虑到这个情况，当我们再一次考察包括正书和反书的铭文时，我们所关注的焦点就从观者的视觉感知转移到艺术家在创造这些铭文时的抱负。但我们首先要问，这里所说的艺术家是谁呢？我们通常认为，一篇石刻铭文是一篇书法作品的摹本，因此能够反映书家的原有风格。但是如果书家只是写了一篇"正常"的文字，之后被正反两次刻在石阙上，那么他的作品在本质上说与这最后的产品无甚关系；他基本上不能被看成是反书铭文的书写者。但是如果他真的创作了正、反两个不同版本的铭文，这其中就大有深意了。因为这意味着反书的铭文直接反映了作者的创造力和思想状态，也就是梁武帝所说的"心手相应"。[22] 这样的创作行为意味着书家首先要设法"反转"自我；在创造出"透明之石"之前，他必须首先在意识上穿透自己的实体。

有两种方法可以帮助我们解开有关反书作者的疑惑，即我们可以检索同时期有关反书的文献记载；或者设法从现存铭文资料中找到线索。根据文献，6 世纪的著名书法家庾元威在一篇论书法的文章中，称自己曾以百种不同的书体来书写一扇屏风，其中有墨书也有彩书。他列举了这些书体的奇怪名称，如"仙人篆""花草隶""猴书""豕书"和"蝌蚪书"等等。在这个名单的末尾出现了两个引人注意的名称："倒书"和"反左书"。[23] 更值得注意的是，在同一篇文章中，庾元威还说明了一种"左右书"的来源：

> （孔敬通，）梁大同中（535—546 年）东宫学士，能一笔草书，一笔一断，婉约流利，特出天性，顷出莫有继者。又创为左右书，座上酬答，无有识者。[24]

Yu Yuanwei's record offers at least three kinds of information. First, the term "left writing" (*zuoshu*) or "inverted and left writing" (*fanzuoshu*) should indicate completely inverted "mirror calligraphy," so that "no one could read" it at first sight. (As I explain below, the term *daoshu* or "reversed writing" probably refers to the method of writing a text in reverse order; the characters are not necessarily inverted.) Second, Kong Jingtong wrote both regular and inverted versions of a single text ("left-and-right writing") and exhibited them on a single occasion. As a gifted
260 and popular calligrapher, he must have first learned the conventional way of writing but later mastered the inverted style of calligraphy through a painful self-inversion. Third, Kong developed two different calligraphic styles: the first was the "cursive script" (*caoshu*) in a single fluent brush stroke; and the second was the "left-and-right" mirror texts. Both writing styles place "form" over "content."

To examine existing "inverted and left inscriptions," we can employ a simple method: turning over a rubbing of such an inscription and placing it against a light table, we should find standard calligraphy if the inscription was made by reversing a piece of regular writing. The best preserved "inverted inscription" is found in Prince Xiao Jing's tomb (Fig. 5.15; the counterpart "front" inscription was unfortunately lost long ago). Following the method suggested above, I have reversed this inverted inscription (Fig. 5.16a) to obtain the version shown in Fig. 5.16b. Any Chinese calligrapher of even an elementary level would immediately point out its weakness: the structure of several characters is unbalanced, and the horizontal strokes generally drop instead of rising as in normal writing. Both are typical symptoms of reversed writing or left-handed writing done by a right-handed person. This examination reveals that the term "left-and-right writing" may also mean that a calligrapher used both hands to write. From his right hand came a normal and readable text; from his left hand, reversed and illegible signs: Such ambidextrous skill seems almost supernatural. (Similar legends are still being created in modern Chinese literature. In a popular martial arts novel by the writer

Jin Yong, the heroine Little Dragon Girl [Xiaolongnü] has mastered the amazing skill of using her left and right hands simultaneously to fight in two entirely different yet complementary styles of swordplay. She thus combines two *gongfu* masters in one and, by making her moves incomprehensible even to a master opponent, becomes undefeatable.)

庾元威的记述至少提供了三种信息。第一，“左书”或“反左书”所指的可能是完全反转或“镜像”式的书体，以至于初看之下“无有识者”。（我在下文中将提及，“倒书”可能是指书写顺序的颠倒，写的字并不需要反过来。）第二，孔敬通能同时作“左右书”，即兴展示于友朋之间。作为一位有天赋、受欢迎的书法家，他肯定是首先精熟了传统的书写方式，而后经过一个艰苦的自我反转过程，才能掌握这种反常的书写技巧。第三，孔敬通发展了两种不同的书写体式：一为草书，一为左右书。值得注意的是，这两种书写风格都是对“形式”的重视超过对“内容”的关注。

要从现存的反书或“左书”铭文中寻找线索，我们可以借助一种简单的方法：将这样一篇铭文的拓片翻过来放在桌子上，如果该铭文是一篇正常书写文字的反像翻版的话，我们将会看到一篇以右手写就的标准书法。目前保存状况最为完好的反书铭文见于萧景墓［图 5.15］（不幸的是，与此相对的“正书”铭文早已佚失）。按照上面所说的方法将这篇反书的铭文［图 5.16a］翻转过来，我们得出了图 5.16b 所示的铭文。任何一位稍具书法常识的人都能立刻指出它的弊病：其中有几个字结构失衡，而且字的横划普遍向右下斜，而不是如正常书法那样将横划略微上挑。这都是一个习惯用右手书写的人在做反书或用左手书写时容易出现的问题。这一实验表明，所谓的“左右书”可能指一位书法家同时用双手书写。其右手所书是正常、可读的文本；左手所书则为“镜像”式的、一时不可辨识的符号。这种随意使用双手的技能表现出一种近乎超自然的能力，在中国当代文学作品中仍可见到类似的神话。如金庸在他的著名武侠小说中就塑造了能够双手同时使用不同剑法的小龙女。由于她能将两种功夫合而为一，出招变幻莫测，出神入化，因此成为天下无敌的武林高手。

Fig. 5.15. Reversed inscription on a stone pillar in the graveyard of Prince Xiao Jing (d. 523). Liang dynasty. Nanjing, Jiangsu province.
图 5.15 萧景（卒于 523）墓石柱上的倒书铭文。梁。江苏南京。

The inversion of an existing convention, however, may also create a new convention. Suppose that the "left-and-right scripts" were standardized and became a norm—they would lose their power to confuse readers, and the supernatural calligrapher would become merely a humble craftsman. Upon receiving such writing from Kong Jingtong, a guest would immediately lay bare his trick, and when a funeral procession proceeded toward a pillar-gate, no mourner would be intrigued by the pair of inscriptions because they would now be readily understandable. The stone columns would remain solid and opaque, and although the boundary marked out by the gate could be physically crossed, it would never be erased.

All seven surviving inscriptions on the pillar-gates of Liang tombs have been called *zhengfanshu* (front and reversed writing). But if we examine these inscriptions more closely, we find three distinctly different ways of "reversing" or "inverting" regular writing. The case that I discussed earlier (Fig. 5.5a) exemplifies one of these methods: regular writing is completely reversed to form a true mirror-image.[25] Another method, represented by the inscriptions reconstructed and "translated" in Figs. 5.16a-c, is to write the characters backward while keeping the standard right-to-left sequence of writing and reading (left-to-right 261
sequence in English).[26] The third way is again an inversion of the second method (Figs. 5.17a, b): the normal right-to-left sequence is changed to left-to-right (right-to-left in English), but all characters are written in their regular form.[27] This last script may be identified as *daoshu*, a type of reversed script found on Yu Yuanwei's list.

但对既有惯例的反转也可能导致一种新的惯例。一旦"左右书"变得标准化而且成为一种规范，它就会失去困惑读者的魔力，神乎其神的书家也就会沦落为不足一道的匠人。一个从孔敬通那里得到这类作品的客人将会一眼看穿他的把戏；而当丧葬的队伍行进到刻有正反书铭文的石柱前，也不再会有哀悼者对这些铭文产生特殊兴趣，因为它们已然变得豁然无疑。石柱将恢复到它们坚实、不可穿透的原始状态。虽然阙门所标定的界线可以被实际跨越，但这道界线却不会被抹除。

论者把梁朝陵墓石柱上现存的七件铭文一般地称作正反书。可是，如果我们对这些铭文做一番更为细致的检视，就会发现其中有三种不同的反书方式。我在前面谈到的是其中的一种形式［图5.5］：一通正常的铭文被整个反转过来形成全然的镜像。[25] 图 5.16 所示的是第二种形式：反刻每一个字，但是仍然保持正常的从右到左的书写和阅读次序。[26] 第三种方式则是第二种情况的再反转［图5.17］：将正常的从右到左的书写和阅读次序逆转为从左到右，但每个字都按正常格式书写。[27] 这最后一种书写形式也可能就是庾元威所列书体中的"倒书"。

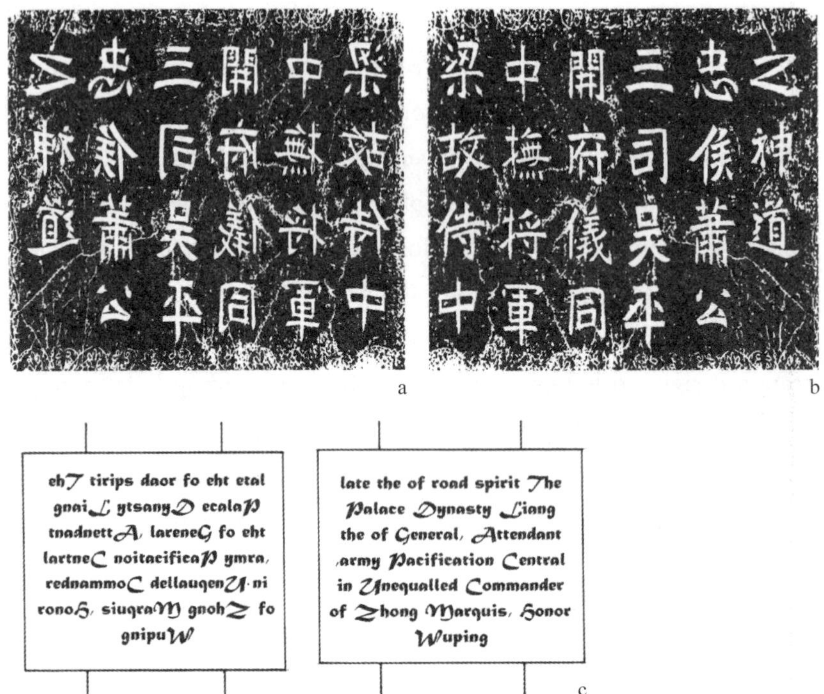

Fig. 5.16. (a, b) Reconstruction of the inscriptions on the pair of pillars in Prince Xiao Jing's graveyard. Ink rubbing. (c) English translation.

图 5.16 （a, b）萧景墓双石柱铭文复原。拓本。（c）英文翻译。

All inscriptions "inverted" according to these three methods were made during a short period of some 30 years. We must assume that some profound reason led to such interest in metamorphosis.[28] Such rapid changes can only testify to a deliberate effort to escape from a fixed pattern. The task is not easy since a regular inscription must be paired with an inverted one on the two pillars so that they can together define

这三种形式的"反书"铭文都大约出现于短短的三十余年间，可想而知必有某种深层原因导致了这种对变化书写形式的兴趣；[28] 这种迅速的变化只能表明人们对任何固定范式的刻意摆脱。这种努力并不是一件容易的事情，因为总的前提是，双柱上正常的铭文必须和一篇倒书铭文相匹配，才能界定出对立视线的

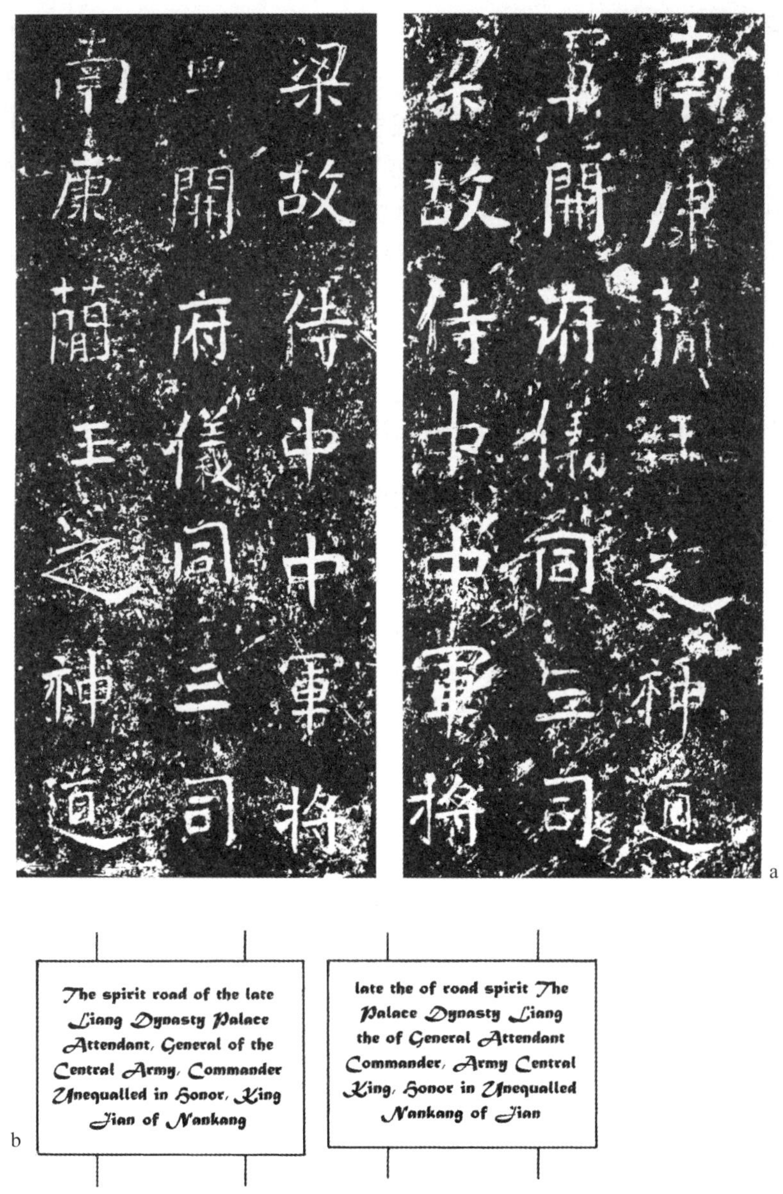

Fig. 5.17. (a) Inscriptions on the pair of pillars in Prince Xiao Ji's (d. 527) graveyard. Jurong, Jiangsu province. Ink rubbing. (b) English translation.

图 5.17 （a）萧绩（卒于 527）墓双石柱铭文。梁，江苏句容。拓本。（b）英文翻译。

the junction of two opposing views, yet any standardization would turn the inscriptions into static symbols without psychological power. It is probably no coincidence that only the earliest surviving examples of "front and back" writing—the pair of inscriptions dedicated to the father of the dynasty's founder—appear as true mirror-images. To avoid repeating the same imagery, later people either reversed the characters or reversed the writing (and reading) sequence. In fact, these three methods are the *only* possible ways to "reverse" a text. The Liang tried them all.

❷ "Binary" Imagery and the Birth of Pictorial Space

The period known as the Northern and Southern Dynasties (386-589; the Liang is one of the Southern Dynasties) is commonly recognized as a turning point in Chinese art history. Major developments during these two centuries include the construction of enormous Buddhist cave chapels, the emergence of great painters and calligraphers, and a profound change in visual perception and representation.[29] This last achievement has often been characterized as the discovery of pictorial space, meaning that the artist was finally able to turn an opaque canvas or stone slab into a transparent "window" open to an illusory reality. The assertion is not false, but it often attributes this development to some
262 master artists or views it as an independent evolution of pictorial forms. An alternative approach advanced here is that the new visual forms rebelled against traditional ritual art and monumentality. While old types of monuments—mortuary gate, shrine, and sarcophagus—continued, surface patterns—inscriptions and decorations—became independent. Although still ceremonial or didactic in content, an inscription or pictorial scene intrigued the eye and the mind. By transforming a monument into the sheer surface for pictures and writing, these forms allowed people to see things that had never been seen or represented before.

A number of stone funerary structures created at the beginning of the sixth century best demonstrate this transition. Dating from 529 (and thus contemporary with the reversed inscriptions), a small funerary shrine now in Boston's Museum of Fine Arts (Fig. 5.18) shows no major difference in form and structure from a Han shrine established some four centuries earlier (Fig. 4.4).[30] What distinguishes it from a Han

交汇点；然而，任何标准化倾向又不免会把一组对应铭文变成不具心理震撼力的静态符号。如此看来，现存最早的"正反"书——萧衍为其父亲做的那对铭文——之所以以真正的镜像形式出现，当非出自偶然。为了避免重复同样的图像，后来的人们不是颠倒铭文的字形，就是颠倒书写（和阅读）的顺序。事实上，上面提到的三种方式，也正是颠倒一篇铭文所有可能的三种方式。而梁朝人尝试了这仅有的三种方式。

二、"二元"图像与绘画空间的诞生

南北朝时期（386—589 年）通常被看作中国艺术史上的一个转折点。在这两个世纪中，中国艺术出现了一系列划时代的事件，包括大型佛教石窟群的兴建、杰出画家和书法家的出现，以及视觉感知和绘画表现的深刻变化。[29] 最后这项成就常常被描述为对绘画空间的发现，即画家终于能够通过绘画形象，将不透明的绢帛或石板转化为一扇通向虚幻世界的"窗口"。这个说法虽然不错，但问题在于，论者常把这个发展归功于某几位大艺术家，或是将其看成是图画形式本身的自然演进。这里我想提出的另一种可能的解释是，新的视觉形式通过对传统礼仪美术与纪念碑性的叛逆而导致了这一变革。当旧式纪念物（如墓门、祠堂、石棺和石碑等）仍被继续制造，其表面的形象，包括铭文和装饰却不断走向独立。尽管在内容上仍旧是礼仪性或劝诫性的，但是这些铭文和图像引起了人们在视觉与思维上新的兴趣。通过将一座纪念碑转变为承载图画和铭文的纯粹平面，这些形式使人们看到了先前从未见过或表现过的事物。

这一转变在创作于 6 世纪初的几座石构建筑上得到了最有力的证明。现藏波士顿美术馆的一件 529 年（与上述讨论的正反书铭文时间相当）的石享堂（或"石椁"）[图 5.18]，在形式和构造上与四个世纪前的汉代祠堂［图 4.4］并没有多大分别。[30] 它的新颖之处

Fig. 5.18. Shrine of Ning Mao (d. 527). Northern Wei dynasty. H. 138 cm. W. 200 cm. From Luoyang, Henan province. Museum of Fine Arts, Boston.

图 5.18 宁懋（卒于 527）石室。北魏。高 138 厘米，宽 200 厘米。河南洛阳出土。美国波士顿美术馆藏。

Fig. 5.19. Back wall of Ning Mao's shrine.

图 5.19 宁懋石室后壁画像。

ritual building are its engravings, especially those executed on the single stone panel that forms the shrine's rear wall (Figs. 5.19). Here, a faintly delineated architectural framework represents the timber facade of a building, a "frame" enclosing the portraits of three gentlemen. Attired in similar costumes and each accompanied by a female figure, the three men differ from one another mainly in age. The figure to the right is a younger man with a fleshy face and a strong torso; the one to the left is heavily bearded with an angular face and a slender body. Whereas these two figures, both shown in three-quarter view facing outward, appear vigorous and high-spirited, the third figure in the middle is a fragile older man retreating into an inner space. Slightly humpbacked and lowering his head, he concentrates on a lotus flower in his hand. The flower—a symbol of purity and wisdom—originated in Buddhism, which had rapidly spread among Chinese literati by the sixth century. Lost in deep contemplation, this focal figure is about to enter the wooden-framed building, leaving this world and us the viewers behind.

在于其表面所刻的图像，尤其是石室后壁上的线刻人物画像［图 5.19］。这幅画的背景部分隐约显现出建筑的构架，表现的应该是一座木构房屋的立面。这个构架犹如一系列“画框”，将三位男子的画像间隔开来。这三个人穿着同样的服饰，且身边皆有一少女相伴，不同之处主要是他们年纪上的差异。处于画面右侧的人物最为年轻，有着一副丰腴的面容和壮硕的身躯；画面左侧的人身态修长，清癯的面颊上生有浓密的胡须。这两个人都呈向外的半侧面，而且都显得精力充沛。位于中间的人物则是一位反身向内、体质虚弱的老者，他背部微驼，头部低垂，凝视着手中拿着的一朵莲花。作为纯净和智慧象征的莲花源于佛教，6 世纪时已经在中国士人当中广泛流行。画面中央这位陷入沉思的老人仿佛即将迈进那座木构建筑，离开他身后的世界和我们这些观众。

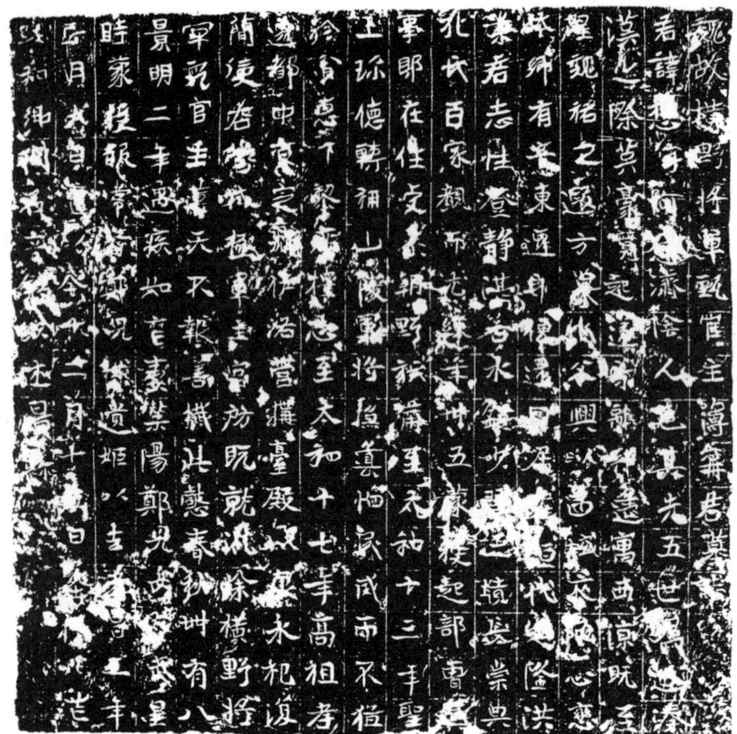

Fig. 5.20. Ning Mao's epitaph. Northern Wei dynasty. A.D. 529. W. 41 cm. L. 41 cm. From Luoyang, Henan province. Ink rubbing.

图 5.20 宁懋墓志。北魏，527 年。宽 41 厘米，长 41 厘米。河南洛阳出土。拓本。

The modern Chinese scholar Huang Minglan has offered an interesting reading of this composition. He suggested that all three images represent Ning Mao, to whom the mortuary shrine was
264 dedicated, and that these images together narrate the stages of Ning's life, from his vigorous youth to his final spiritual enlightenment.[31] Ning Mao's epitaph, which may still exist in China,[32] includes his biography (Fig. 5.20). It mentions three dated events: at the age of 35 (486) he became a clerk at the Ministry of the Imperial Cabinet. A few years later, in 489, he was promoted to general of the Imperial Mausoleum Guards in charge of ritual affairs. After the Northern Wei moved the capital to Luoyang in 494, he assumed the post of chief of the Construction Corps

in charge of building new palaces and temples. He was promoted to chief secretary of the Construction Office after the completion of the main palace, but soon fell ill and died in 501.[33] Although the three portraits on Ning's shrine do not necessarily coincide with these specific events, they do show the general contour of his life as described in the epitaph. His positions as ritual specialist and imperial architect must also explain the unusually high quality of the engravings on his memorial shrine. The sentiment conveyed by the portraits—transformation from engagement in worldly affairs to the internal pursuit of spiritual peace—was a favorite intellectual subject during the Northern and Southern Dynasties; Lu Ji and Tao Qian's poems quoted earlier describe similar experiences. But in the pictorial representation, the conflict between life and death, between worldly activities and internal peace, is crystallized in the "front and back" images. Again, we find that lived experience ends at the point where someone turns inward, about to penetrate the solid surface of the stone.

黄明兰曾为这幅画面提供过一个富有启发性的解释。他认为画中三个人像表现的都是石室所纪念的死者宁懋，分别反映了宁懋一生从朝气蓬勃的青年时期到最后精神升华的迟暮之年的三个不同阶段。[31] 目前可能仍存于国内的宁懋墓志[32] 记载了他一生的经历［图5.20］，其中提到三件有明确纪年的事件：一是三十五岁时（486）蒙获起部曹参事郎。二是在494年北魏迁都洛阳后任营戍极军、守卫营建台殿司，主管新宫和庙宇的建造。三是在新宫主殿完工后荐升为横野将军甄官主薄，但不久就因病于501年去世。[33] 尽管宁懋石室上的三幅画像并不一定和这几个具体事件吻合，但它们可能确实如墓志中所描述的那样，展现了宁懋生平的大致轮廓。由于宁懋担任过主管礼仪和宫廷建筑的职位，我们可以理解石室线刻图画的水平何以如此高超。这三幅人像所传达的心态——从入世转向出世——正是南北朝时期流行于士人当中的一个思想主题，上文所引陆机和陶潜的诗歌描写了类似的体验。但在绘画表达中，生与死、入世与出世之间的冲突，则是由“正反”的图像来体现的。这里，我们再次发现人生终结于转身向内、正要穿过石头表面的那一时刻。

Fig. 5.21. (a, b) The two long sides of a stone sarcophagus. Northern Wei dynasty. *Ca.* A.D. 525. H. 64 cm. L. 225 cm. From Luoyang, Henan province. Nelson-Atkins Museum of Art, Kansas City, Missouri.

图 5.21 （a，b）一具石棺两侧的画像。北魏，约 525 年。高 64 厘米，长 225 厘米。河南洛阳出土。美国堪萨斯市纳尔逊-阿特肯斯美术馆藏。

The juxtaposition of "front and back" images became a pictorial formula. In many cases this composition no longer possessed a specific ritual or philosophical implication, but was used as a standard device to increase the complexity of representation. Figure 5.21 reproduces the engravings on a famous Northern Wei sarcophagus now in the collection of the Nelson Gallery-Atkins Museum in Kansas City.[34] On the two long sides of the stone box, stories of filial paragons are delineated in a landscape setting. Compared with Han depictions of similar subjects (Figs. 4.16-26), these pictures signify many new developments, most
noticeably, a new sequential narrative mode and a three-dimensional 265
landscape setting. Framed by a patterned band, each composition seems a translucent "window" onto an elusive world.

The strong sense of three-dimensionality in these pictures has enticed scholars to interpret them in light of some standard criteria in a linear perspective system, such as overlapping forms and the technique of foreshortening.[35] In such an analysis the researcher, either consciously

这种并置的“正反”图像随即成为当时的一种一般性绘画模式，在很多情况下不再具有特定的礼仪或哲学含义，而是被当成增进绘画表现复杂性的一种通用策略。图 5.21 是现藏美国堪萨斯市纳尔逊 – 阿特肯斯美术馆的一具著名北魏石棺上的一组画像。[34] 该石棺的两个边板上描绘了一系列以山林为背景的孝子事迹。与汉代对同类题材的描绘相比［图 4.16—图 4.26］，这些画像在绘画表现上有了许多新的发展，最显著的是“连环画”式的叙述方式和三维空间的山水背景。以一道连续装饰带为外框，石棺每边的画面仿佛形成了通向虚幻世界的一扇透明的“窗户”。

由于这些画面强烈的三维感觉，一些学者以线性透视画法的概念，诸如重叠法和短缩法，来解释这件作品。[35] 在这类分析中，

or unconsciously, equates the Chinese example with post-Renaissance painting that employs linear perspective as the most powerful means to create pictorial illusions. But if we examine the pictures on the sarcophagus more carefully, we find some peculiar features that do not agree with the basic principles and purposes of linear perspective but fit perfectly well with the "binary" or "front-and-back" representational mode developed in fifth- and sixth-century China. In simplest terms, the single station-point assumption of linear perspective is that the artist's and viewer's gaze travels from a chosen vantage point to a fixed vanishing point (Fig. 5.22).[36] The "binary" mode, however, is based on the assumption that a form should be seen from both the front and the back; when a form is represented as such, it guides the viewer's gaze back and forth but never toward a real or implied vanishing point in the picture (Fig. 5.23).

A detail on the Nelson sarcophagus (Fig. 5.24) depicts the story of the famous Confucian paragon Wang Lin, who saved his brother from bandits. A tall tree in the middle divides the scene into two halves. Alexander Soper has boldly suggested that the images in both halves actually represent a single episode—the confrontation of Wang Lin and the bandits; the difference between the two scenes is that one is depicted from the front and the other from the rear.[37] It seems to me that in

研究者有意无意之间将中国的这种例子，与以线性透视为主要造型手段的后文艺复兴绘画等同起来。但如果我们更仔细地检视石棺上的图像，我们会发现许多有悖于线性透视基本原理和目的的特征，而这些特征却与 5—6 世纪中国所出现的“二元”或“正反”表现模式相吻合。概括地说，线性透视（即单点透视）意味着，画家和观者的视线从一个既定视点延伸到一个固定

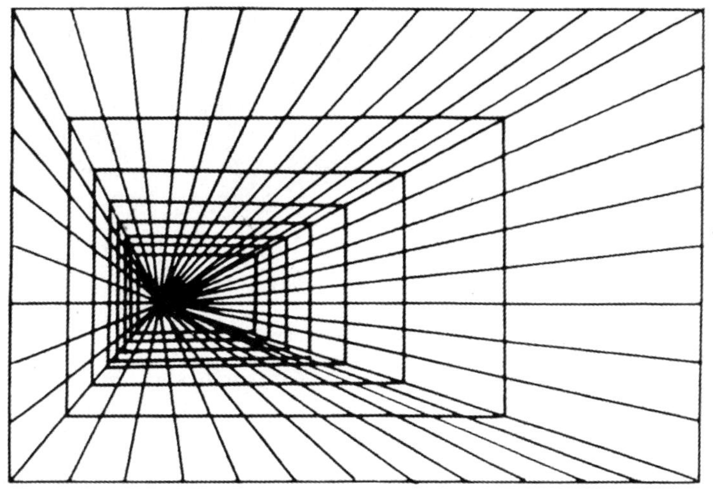

Fig. 5.22. Diagram: single-station perspective
图 5.22　图解：单点透视

Fig. 5.23. Diagram: binary composition
图 5.23　图解：二元透视

消逝点［图 5.22］。[36] 但是，“二元”模式则是基于一个形体应当同时从正反两面来观看的这样一种假定前提；当一个形体以“二元”模式呈现时，它引导观众的视线前后移动，但并不向画中的一个实在或隐含的消失点接近［图 5.23］。

纳尔逊美术馆石棺画像上的一个细节［图 5.24］所描绘的，是孝子王琳的故事，他从强盗手中救出了他的哥哥。一棵大树将画面一分为二。亚历山大·索柏曾大胆地提出，大树两边的画面实际表现了同一情节——即王琳与匪徒面对面时的情景；不同的是，一幅画面是从正面描绘的，另一幅则是从背面描绘的。[37] 在我看来，

Fig. 5.24. Story of Wang Lin. Carving on the Northern Wei sarcophagus in Nelson-Atkins Museum of Art, Kansas City, Missouri, detail. (a) Photograph. (b) Negative on ink rubbing showing line engravings.

图 5.24 王琳。北魏石棺画像局部。美国堪萨斯市纳尔逊-阿特肯斯美术馆藏。（a）拓本。（b）拓本的反相。

making this assertion Soper has gone too far. In the left-hand scene a rope is tied around Wang Lin's brother's neck, and Wang Lin has thrown himself on his knees in front of the bandits, begging them to take him instead of his brother. In the right-hand scene, both Wang Lin and his brother have been released. These two scenes, therefore, represent two consecutive episodes of the story in a temporal sequence.

This iconographic explanation, however, does not rule out Soper's basic observation regarding the different views of the two scenes. What is most important here is not which episode or episodes the picture stands for (since similar stories had been abundantly illustrated from the Han), but how these episodes are depicted and viewed. In the left scene we find that the bandits have just emerged from a deep valley and are meeting Wang Lin. (In a more general sense, they meet us the viewers.) In the next scene, Wang Lin and his brother are leading the bandits into another valley and the whole procession has turned away from us; all we can see are people's backs and the rear end of a horse: This composition once again reminds us of the reversed inscriptions, one confronting us and the other showing us its "back." But here our vision is controlled by the figures' motion. In viewing the left "frontal" scene our eyes take in

索柏在做这一推论时走得太远了。我们看到在左边的画面里，王琳哥哥的脖子上套着一根绳索，而王琳正跪在强盗面前，乞求以己身来代替哥哥。而在右边的画面里，王琳和他的哥哥都被释放了。由此可见，两个画面所反映的是故事发生过程中的两个连续情节。

不过这种解释并不排斥索柏有关两个画面不同视点的基本观察。实际上，这里最关键的问题并不在于画中描绘的是哪个或哪些故事情节（因为类似内容自从汉代以来屡见不鲜），而在于这些情节是如何被描绘和观看的。在左边的画面里，我们看到强盗刚从一个山谷中出现，与王琳相对（从看画者的感受来说，强人正在朝画外的我们走来）。在另一画面中，王琳和他的哥哥正带着强人走进另一个山谷。整个队列折转回头，离我们而去，我们所能看到的只是人的背影和马的臀尾。这种构图形式使我们再次回想起上文讨论过的"正反"铭文，一幅正对着观者，而另一幅则背向观者。但是在这里，画中人物的活动控制了我们的视线。在看左边的"正面"画面时，我们眼睛接收的是向我们走来的人物形象。而当我们将视线

the arriving figures, but when we turn to the next scene we cannot help but feel that we are abruptly and, in a way, very rudely abandoned and ignored. The figures are leaving us and about to vanish, and in an effort to catch them our gaze follows them into the deep valley.

This binary mode allows us to discover the compositional formula of another famous example of Northern and Southern Dynasties art: the celebrated handscroll "The Admonition of the Instructress to Palace Ladies" ("Nüshizhen tu") attributed to the master painter Gu Kaizhi (*ca.* 345-406).[38] This attribution is not secure: there is no pre-Tang reference for Gu's depiction of the subject; yet a newly discovered fifth-century screen bears a picture (Fig. 5.25a) almost identical in composition to one of the seven scenes on the "Admonition" scroll (Fig. 5.25b). Provided with this piece of evidence, we can view the scroll and the Nelson sarcophagus as approximately contemporary works. Not surprisingly, one of the most interesting features of the scroll is the binary composition, which, however, has been even further removed from its original ritual context to become a purely pictorial mode.

The painting illustrates the third-century poet Zhang Hua's composition of the same title. One of the scenes (Fig. 5.26) depicting Zhang's line—"Human beings know how to adorn their faces"—
268 demonstrates an extremely sophisticated use of the binary composition.
The scene is divided into two halves, each with an elegant palace lady

投向下一个画面时，我们不禁感到自己突然间被抛弃和忽视了：画中的人物正离我们而去，即将在我们眼前消逝。为了竭力留住这些形象，我们的视线追随着他们进入深谷。

对这种“二元”模式的理解也有助于我们探讨南北朝时期另一幅名作，即传为顾恺之所作的手卷《女史箴图》的构图方式。[38]《女史箴图》的作者问题并不确定，因为现在还没有唐代以前的资料能够证明顾恺之确实进行过这个题材的创作；然而，新近发现的一件5世纪的屏风上，有一个画面［图 5.25a］在构图上几乎与《女史箴

Fig. 5.25. Story of Ban Jieyu. (a) A scene on the Sima Jinlong screen from Datong, Shanxi province. Northern Wei dynasty. Before A.D. 484. Datong Museum. (b) A scene from the "Admonition of the Instructress to Palace Ladies." Scroll painting. Ink and color on silk. Attributed to Gu Kaizhi, but probably a Tang dynasty copy of a post-Han painting. British Museum.

图 5.25　班婕妤。（a）山西大同司马金龙墓出土彩漆屏风画像局部。北魏，不晚于 484 年。大同市博物馆藏。（b）《女史箴图》局部。绢本设色。传顾恺之作，或为唐代摹本。大英博物馆藏。

图》中的一段完全相同［图 5.26］。根据这一证据，我们大体可以认为《女史箴图》的创作时间与纳尔逊石棺接近。无独有偶的是，《女史箴图》最引人注意的特征之一是采取了“二元”或“正反”构图。只不过在这里，这种构图已经远离了原有的礼仪背景，变为一种纯粹的绘画模式。

《女史箴图》是根据 3 世纪诗人张华的同名文学作品而创作的。其中依张华“人咸知饰其容”一句而绘制的画面［图 5.26］，即显示出对“二元”构图法的娴熟运用。这一画面也是分为左右两个部分，

Fig. 5.26. Palace ladies. A scene from the "Admonition of the Instructress to Palace Ladies" (see Fig. 5.25).

图 5.26 宫女。《女史箴图》局部。

Fig. 5.27. Diagram: compositional scheme of Fig. 5.26

图 5.27 图解：图 5.26 的画面结构

looking at herself in a mirror. The lady on the right turns inward with her back toward us, and we see her face only in the mirror. The lady on the left faces us; her reflection in the mirror becomes implicit (only the mirror's patterned back is visible). The concept of a "mirror-image" is thus presented literally (Fig. 5.27): each group is itself a pair of mirror-images, and the two groups together again form a reflecting double. We may also imagine that this composition may be viewed from "both sides" of the scroll: an invisible viewer at the other side of the canvas would find the same picture as we do, but the images he sees would be reversed ones.

No picture like this existed before the Northern and Southern Dynasties. What we find on Han monuments are silhouette images "attached" to the pictorial plane: the virtuous widow Liang holding a mirror in her hand (Fig. 4.21) or the filial paragon Zengzi kneeling before his mother (Fig. 4.38). In viewing these pictures our eyes travel along the surface of stone slabs, whose striped patterns only make the medium even more impenetrable. Even pictures created during the fourth century do not substantially alter this traditional representational mode. It is true that the well-known portraits of the "Seven Worthies in the Bamboo Grove" ("Zhulin qixian") exhibit some new elements: more relaxed and varying poses, "spatial cells" formed by landscape elements, and an emphasis on fluent lines (Fig. 5.28). But the images are still largely attached to the two-dimensional picture surface, never guiding our eyes

每一部分中均有一位优雅的宫女对镜自鉴。右边的一位面内而坐，背朝画外，我们只能从镜子里面看到她的面孔。而左边的一位则是面朝画外，她在镜子里的面容成为隐含的（我们能够见到的只是镜子背面的花纹）。在这里，"镜像"的概念［图 5.27］得到了字面上的体现：画面的两半各包含一对镜像；而两个部分连在一起又构成了互为反照的一对。我们甚至可以设想这幅画能够从手卷的正背两面来看：一个假定的观者从画的背面会看到一幅同样构图的图画，但却刚好是我们所见画面的反像。

南北朝以前的绘画从未出现过这种构图形式。我们在汉代纪念性建筑物上见到的通常是"平贴"在石头表面上的剪影式画像。观看武梁祠上手执铜镜的梁高行画像［图 4.21］或跪在母亲面前的曾子画像［图 4.38］，我们的目光沿着画像石的表面移动，刻工留下的凿纹使石头这种介质变得更加实在。即便是创作于 4 世纪的画像也尚未全然扭转这一传统表现手法。的确，著名的"竹林七贤"画像中已经出现了某些新因素，诸如更放松和多样的人物姿态，以风景元素构成的空间单元，以及对流畅线条的注重等［图 5.28］（该图说明文字中所标注的年代是考古学界早年的看法，近年来的研究者多将该画像的年代定于南朝早期。——译者注）。但图像仍旧附于二维媒介的表面之上，尚未能引导观者的视线穿透负载画像的平面。

a

b

Fig. 5.28. "Seven Sages and Rong Qiqi." Brick relief. Western Jin dynasty. Late 4th-early 5th century A.D. H. 80 cm. L. 240 cm. Excavated in 1960 at Xishanqiao, Nanjing, Jiangsu province. Nanjing Museum. Ink rubbing.

图 5.28 《竹林七贤与荣启期》模印拼镶砖画。西晋，4 世纪末至 5 世纪初。高 80 厘米，长 240 厘米。1960 年江苏南京西善桥出土。南京博物院藏。拓本。

to penetrate it. The real revolution took place only in the fifth and sixth centuries: the figures in the Wang Lin picture seem to be coming and going of their own free will, and the ladies in the "Admonition" scroll stare at their own reflections and their gaze guides us to see them. In both cases our vision follows the pictured figures in and out, effortlessly crossing the transparent stone or canvas.

All these pictorial works—the engravings on the Ning Mao shrine and the Nelson sarcophagus, and the painted images on the "Admonition" scroll—testify to a desire to see things that had never been seen or represented before. The new points of view pursued by the artists, however, were not actual (or assumed) station points on earth. The mundane achievement of seeing and representing things “naturalistically” could hardly fulfill the artists’ high aspirations, for art, they claimed, should allow them to transcend observed reality with its temporal and spatial boundaries. The relationship between “seeing” and “imagining,” or between eyes and the mind, became a central topic of art criticism at the time. Sometimes the relationship was considered antithetical. Wang Wei (415-43), for example, criticized painters who relied only on their physical faculties and “focused on nothing but appearances and positioning.” When a good artist painted, he told his contemporaries, “it is not in order to record the boundaries of cities or to distinguish the locale of prefectures, to mark off mountains and hills or to demarcate floods and streams. For things which are rooted in form must be smelted with spiritual force, and that which activates the permutation is the heart-mind.”[39] His view may have represented an extreme; other critics 270

真正意义上的变革只是在5—6世纪才得以发生：在上文谈到的王琳画像中，人物似乎随心所欲地穿越一个三度空间；《女史箴图》里的仕女们注视着镜中的自己，而她们的视线引导我们欣赏她们。在这两幅画中，我们的视线随着画中人物进进出出，毫不费力地穿过那仿佛不复存在的石头或绢帛。

无论是宁懋石室画像、纳尔逊石棺画像，还是《女史箴图》中的“观镜”画面，所有这些绘画性作品都反映了一种试图发现和描绘前所未见、也不曾被描绘过的事物的愿望。但是，当时画家们所追求的新视点并不是现实中的一个实际（或假定）的观察点。以“自然”方式观察和表现事物似乎过于寻常，难于满足艺术家们的热望，因为对他们来说，“艺术”应该能够赋予他们超越现实世界及其时空限制的可能性。“观看”与“想象”，或者说眼睛与思维之间的关系，因此成为当时艺术评论中的一个中心话题。有时这种关系被认为是对立的，如王微（415—443年）就认为“图画非止艺行”，并且批评了当时一些画家“竟求容势而已”的艺术倾向，指出：“古人之作画也，非以案城域，辩方州，标镇阜，画浸流。本乎形者融灵，而动者变心。”[39]他的观点或许代表了一个极端，而另外

such as Xie He (*fl.* 500-535) considered both "physical likeness" (*yingwu xiangxing*) and "spirit resonance" (*qiyun shengdong*) necessary qualities of good art; nevertheless he placed the latter at the top of his "Six Laws" of painting.[40]

Simultaneously there appeared the notion of an ideal painter who could realize the artistic goals the new age demanded, and whose unrestrained imagination would make him an immortal:

> He moves along with the four seasons and sighs at their passing on,
> Peers on all the things of the world, broods on their profusion.
> ...
> Thus it begins: retraction of vision, reversion of listening,
> Absorbed in thought, seeking all around,
> [His] essence galloping to the world's eight bounds,
> [His] mind roaming ten thousand yards, up and down.
> He empties the limpid mind, fixes his thoughts,
> Fuses all his concerns together and makes words.
> He cages Heaven and Earth in fixed shape,
> Crushes all things beneath the brush's tip.
> At first it hesitates on his dry lips,
> But finally flows freely through the moist pen.[41]

Such description was not considered purely metaphorical; when Xie He came to rank painters based on artistic merit (thus giving himself the status of an authoritative viewer), he employed similar criteria and found his ideal artist in Lu Tanwei of the fifth century:

> He fathomed the principles [of the universe] and exhausted the nature [of man]. The matter is beyond the power of speech to describe. He embraced what went before him and gave birth to what succeeded him: from ancient times up till now he stands alone. Nor is he one whom even [the most] fervent enthusiasm could [adequately] praise. For is he not simply the pinnacle of all that is of highest value? He rises

beyond the highest grade, and that is all that there is to be said.[42]

Xie He seems to have felt short of words. Of an artist who has 274
fathomed the universe and exhausted human nature, there is indeed nothing one can say except to acknowledge his god-like existence. Such glorification gives us little sense of the actual masterpieces from that period (which have all long since disappeared), but the pictures on another sixth-century stone sarcophagus (created when Xie was compiling his classification of painters) may allow us to perceive the kind

一些评论家如谢赫（约500—535年）等人，则将“应物象形”和“气韵生动”视为一件优秀作品应该同时具备的品质；不过还是把“气韵生动”当成“六法”的首要准则。[40]

与此同时，理想化的艺术家的概念也出现了：这种“超人”能够实现新时代所要求的新的艺术目标，他们驰骋不羁的想象力将令他们永垂青史：

> 遵四时以叹逝，瞻万物而思纷……
> 其始也，皆收视反听，耽思傍讯，
> 精骛八极，心游万仞……
> 罄澄心以凝思，眇众虑而为言。
> 笼天地于形内，挫万物于笔端。[41]

这种描述在那个时代并不是纯粹抽象的隐喻。当谢赫按照艺术家的成就将其分等时（通过这种工作他也就获得了“权威”观者的身份），他使用了类似的标准，在5世纪的陆探微身上找到了他心目中的理想画家：在他看来，陆探微的画“穷理尽性，事绝言象。包前孕后，古今独立。非复激扬所能称赞，但价重之极乎上上品之外！无他寄言，故屈标第一等”。[42]

谢赫似乎感到难以用语言来表达他对陆探微的钦服：面对一个穷极宇宙和人类本性的艺术家，除了承认他的出神入化的天赐禀赋，论者的确是无法再说什么了。鉴于当时的绘画杰作早已散佚殆尽，我们很难从这种抽象的称誉中感知到它们的实际风貌。不过，刻在另外一件6世纪石棺上的画像（与谢赫著《古画品录》的时间

of art he had in mind. Like the Nelson sarcophagus, this example in the Minneapolis Institute of Art was unearthed at Luoyang, the capital of the Northern Wei after 494 (Fig. 5.29).[43] Again like the Nelson sarcophagus, both long sides of the sarcophagus are covered with a rich combination of pictorial and decorative images. At the bottom of each rectangular composition, a rolling hillock establishes a continuous foreground and further extends into the depths along the picture's vertical sides. Tall trees further divide this U-shaped picture frame into a number of subframes or "space cells" for depicting individual stories of famous filial paragons. Scholars have been astonished by the "naturalism" of these narrative scenes: well-proportioned figures—a series of famous filial sons from China's past—sit or kneel on a tilted ground or on platforms that recede into the depths (Fig. 5.30a). Behind them are a mountain range and floating clouds, whose greatly reduced size indicates their remoteness.

This coherent spatial representation serves symbolic purposes, however. It groups historical figures of different times and places into a synchronic setting; the rationale of this synthesis is that all these

相当），或许能让我们了解谢赫心目中的理想艺术。和纳尔逊石棺一样，这件现藏于美国明尼阿波利斯美术馆的石棺也出自494年以后的北魏都城洛阳［图5.29］。[43] 与纳尔逊石棺一样，这件石棺两侧刻满了融绘画和装饰于一体的画像。每一长方形画面的底部皆以连绵起伏的小丘构成连续的前景，小丘进而沿画面两边向纵深方向延伸，从而形成了一个U字形的“画框”。“画框”内部的空间被一些高树分割成若干部分或“空间单元”，用以表现单独的孝子故事。这些叙事性画面的写实主义风格常令学者们感到惊讶：身材比例匀称的古代孝子和其他历史人物，坐在斜坡地面或以透视法画出的榻上［图5.30a］。他们的身后是起伏的山峦和流云，其显著缩减的尺寸显现出其遥远的距离。

然而，这幅画中对连贯空间的表现所承担的是象征主义的功能。它把不同时间和不同地域的历史人物组合在同一个时间框架里，

Fig. 5.29. (a, b) The two long sides of a stone sarcophagus. Northern Wei dynasty. A.D. 524. From Luoyang, Henan province. Minneapolis Institute of Arts. Ink rubbing.

图 5.29 （a，b）一具石棺两侧的画像。北魏，524 年。河南洛阳出土。美国明尼阿波利斯美术馆藏。拓本。

Fig. 5.30. (a-c) Details of the stone sarcophagus in the Minneapolis Institute of Arts. Ink rubbing.

图 5.30 （a—c）石棺画像局部。北魏。拓本。美国明尼阿波利斯美术馆藏。

figures share the same virtue and their lives show a similar contour. The naturalism of the illustrations thus diminishes any vestige of historical reality. The figures belong neither to the past nor to the present; rather, they represent timeless Confucian paragons, who are again abstractions of history and human deeds. This may be why these virtuous men are positioned in the lower half of the pictures: they are still earth-bound, and so the naturalism of their portrayal attests to the trueness of the human principles they embody.

The historical Confucian figures, as well as the realistic pictorial style associated with them, disappear from the upper half of the composition, where we find fantastic and possibly Daoist images (Fig. 5.30b): an enormous dragon juxtaposed with a huge phoenix, beautiful fairies riding on clouds or exotic birds, fierce demons roaring against the wind. The decoration on the Minneapolis sarcophagus thus combines images of historical figures like those on the Kansas City sarcophagus with motifs of immortality—fairies and fantastic animals and birds—that embellish two other sarcophagi unearthed at Luoyang (Fig. 5.31).[44] This sarcophagus thus exhibits binary pictorial styles and spatial concepts.

而这种组合的前提是这些人所具有的共同道德和卓越品行。因此，这一看似具有自然主义风格的群像画面，实际上消解了任何历史真实的痕迹。画中人物既不属于过去，也不属于现在；他们所代表的是从历史和人类行为中抽象出来的、没有时限的儒家理想人格典范。由于这种意义，这些孝子贤人被安排在画像下半部：他们依然是地上的凡人，而他们画像的自然主义风格也证实了他们所体现的做人准则的真实性。

这些儒家历史人物，以及与其相关的自然主义绘画风格，在画面的上半部全然消失。我们在这里看到的是一些幻想的或道教的图像［图 5.30b］：一条巨龙与一只巨大的凤鸟并列，乘云驾鸟的美丽仙女应对着迎风咆哮的怪兽。这个石棺上的装饰因此综合了纳尔逊石棺上的历史人物图像与出土于洛阳的另外两件石棺上的仙女、异兽和灵鸟等升仙题材［图 5.31］，[44] 综合的结果是对二元图像和空间概念的呈现。

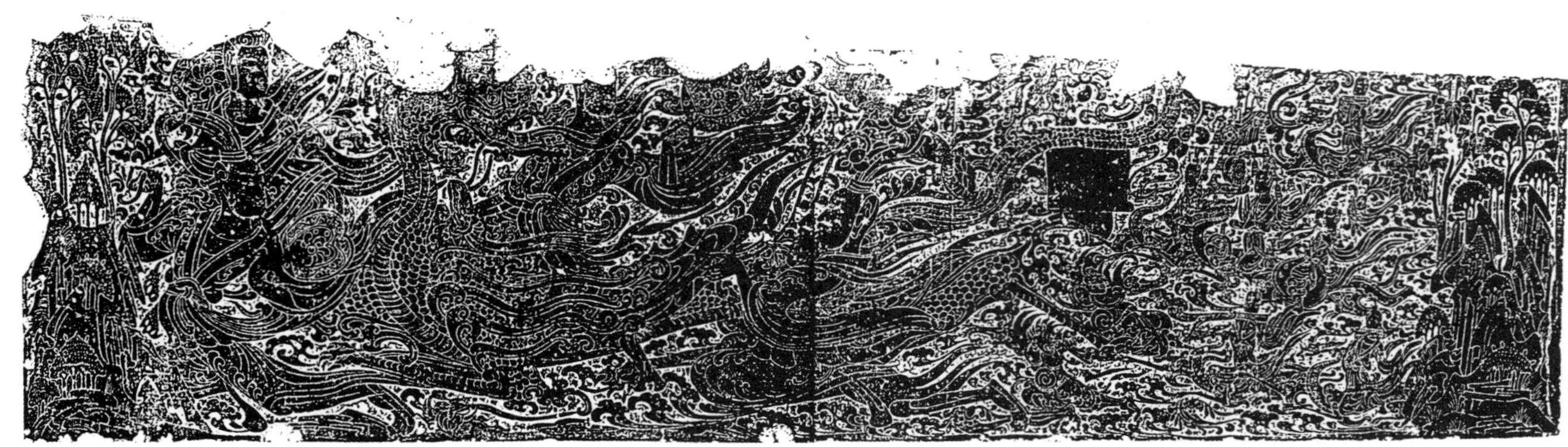

Fig. 5.31. Stone sarcophagus. Northern Wei dynasty. Early 6th century A.D. H. 102 cm. L. 246 cm. Excavated in 1977 at Shangyao, Luoyang, Henan province. Luoyang Ancient Stone Carving Museum. Ink rubbing.

图 5.31 石棺画像。北魏，6 世纪初。高 102 厘米，长 246 厘米。1977 年洛阳上窑出土。洛阳古代艺术馆藏。拓本。

Instead of being united by a three-dimensional landscape, these images are harmonized by the swelling, rhythmic lines that shape them. We may say that these fluent lines are themselves a metaphor of the vital energy of the universe,[45] from which all these images of the imagination—heavenly flowers, auspicious birds, mystical beasts, fairies, and demons—emerge. Floating and ever-changing, these line images seem to shift smoothly on the two-dimensional picture plane without penetrating it.

The design is further complicated by a focal image crossing the upper and lower halves—an animal mask with a ring hanging from its mouth (Fig. 5.30c). The model for this image is a sculptured mask made of gilded copper attached to a wooden coffin. Here it has been transformed into a flat silhouette on stone. A new layer of visual rhetoric is added: integrated into the overall two-dimensional pictorial representation, the mask seems suspended in air in front of the surrounding scenes, which recede and vanish behind it. Firm and unyielding, the mask reminds us of the stone surface and forces us to pull our gaze (and mind) back from

石棺上部所刻的图像并没有被纳入一个具有统一三维空间的山水环境，而是以行云流水一般富于节奏感的线条以取得视觉的和谐统一。我们也许可以说，这些流动的线条本身象征了充斥于宇宙的“气”。[45] 这里所有的图像，如天花、瑞鸟、异兽、仙女和鬼怪等，都从这包罗万象的“气”中生成和显现。这些线性图像仿佛是在二维平面上自由地浮动和变幻着，但从不企图穿越绘画的平面。

横跨画面上下两部分的焦点图像——衔环铺首［图 5.30c］——使整个画面的设计显得更加复杂。这个图像的原型是附加在木棺侧板上的鎏金铜铺首。它在这里演变为石棺画像中的一个平面图案。它的存在给整个画面设计增加了新的一重视觉辩术：纳入二维视觉表达系统中的铺首图像仿佛悬浮在半空，其后方的画面似乎在隐退和消逝。这个正面铺首图像既坚定又有力，不仅向观者提示着石头表面的存在，而且也迫使观者将目光（与思绪）

the distant and fantastic worlds, reasserting our own proximity to the solid sarcophagus. This image restores the surface of the picture plane but only to allow the artist to decompose and recompose it again. On either side of the mask, two windows, perfectly square, guide our gaze "into" the sarcophagus. Two figures stand inside each window and stare at us.[46] These windows, which allow us to see what is concealed *behind* the pictorial surface, thus reject any coherent system of pictorial illusion and any fixed spatial or temporal station.[47]

Viewing such a complex picture that integrates so many contradictory
276 elements, we feel that the artist is constantly challenging us with new modes of pictorial representation. Traveling through time and space, he leads us to confront different realms and states of beings—to "gallop to the world's eight bounds" and to "peer on all the things of the world, brood on their profusion." He creates and recreates tension between different images and between these images and the medium: whenever a scene is about to assume its independence and become "real," he brings in a conflicting image or style that dismisses any sense of illusionism and restocks the pictorial surface with new possibilities to further expand the visual field. Thus we find that the picture seems to ceaselessly rebel against itself— "reversing" itself and then balancing itself. The illusionist narrative-landscape scene is juxtaposed with the elusive, decorative immortal imagery; the "relief" animal mask is juxtaposed with the "sunken" windows. The first set of motifs transforms the pictorial surface into images and thus erases it; the second set restores the surface because the mask must be attached to it and the windows must be opened on it.[48] The structural key to understanding the creation of such a composition, therefore, is again the binary mode: the artist develops his imagery along opposite yet complementary paths. In making such an effort he breaks away from conventional representation and pushes the possibility of human perception to a new limit.

❸ Epilogue: The Gate

When Wang Ziya, the governor of Shu, died in the second century A.D., he left abundant wealth, three daughters, but no son. Longing for their father and thinking about his burial, the three daughters said to one another:

从遥远、虚幻的世界里拉回来，重新认识到自己与一具实实在在的石棺的关系。这个铺首图像的作用因此是“复原”画面的介质，但复原的结果是为了让画家能重新利用这一介质，再分解、重构画面。在铺首两侧分别刻有两扇正方形的“窗”，引导我们的视线“进入”石棺。每扇窗内各站两人，面向窗外的观者。[46] 似乎让我们看到画面背后掩藏的事物，这些窗户因此拒绝了任何视觉幻象的统一系统和任何固定的时空位置。[47]

面对这样一幅整合了如此之多矛盾元素的复杂画像，我们感到它的设计者在不停地以新的绘画表现方式向我们挑战。他引导我们跨越时空，面对不同的领域和不同的生命状态——就像陆机所说的那样“精骛八极”“瞻万物而思纷”。他在不同的图像之间，在图像与介质之间不断从事着对矛盾和张力的创造与再创造：当任何一个场景将要形成独立系统并变为“真实”的时候，他就引进一种与这个场景相冲突的图像或风格，来消解任何可能造成的“幻视”效应，通过重构画面的物质性以拓展新的视觉表现的可能。因此，我们发现这个画面似乎是为了自身的平衡而不停地对自身进行否定与逆转：写实风格的历史故事画与幻想和装饰性的线性形象相对；“凸起”的铺首与“凹陷”的窗户并列。前一对题材将石棺的表面转化为图像，因而消除了石棺的表面；后一对图像则还原了石棺的表面——因为铺首必须固定在这个表面上，窗户也必须在这个表面上打开。[48] 因此，理解这一构图的关键仍然是“二元”模式：艺术家沿着相反相成的方向发挥他的想象力，在这种努力中不断打破传统的艺术表现手法，将人类的感知推向一个新的境界。

三、尾声：门阙

卒于 2 世纪的蜀郡太守王子雅身后留下了丰厚的资财和三个女儿，可是没有儿子。女儿们思念父亲并考虑父亲的丧事，她们相互商议道：

> Now the spirit of our lord should dwell peacefully in an underground home where he would accompany the divine Master of Earth. But we do not have a brother to succeed him and make his virtue renowned. Let's take over a son's duty, each contributing five million cash. One of us will build his tomb and the other two will erect a *que* pillar-gate. In this way we may express our filial piety and longing.

Three centuries later, the famous geographer Li Daoyuan traveled to Wang Ziya's hometown of Xi'e in present-day Henan. He found two stone towers standing side by side, forming the entrance to an abandoned burial site. About eighteen *chi* high and five *chi* wide, the pillars were made of jade-like green stone, polished as smooth and shiny as a mirror. Imitating a wooden-framed tower, each pillar was exquisitely carved to represent a tiled roof, supported by complex brackets and sloping down on four sides. The late governor's name and official title were engraved on the pillars, followed by an inscription describing his daughters' filial devotion. Li Daoyuan recorded this group of funerary monuments in
277 his *Annotated Canon of Waterways* as a landmark that documented the region's bygone history.[49]

The Wang Ziya *que* have long since disappeared, but Li Daoyuan's record of its construction attests to the radically different concept of monumentality that separated a second-century gate from those established before and after the Han. A gate of the Three Dynasties, as discussed earlier in this book, was always an integral element of a larger architectural complex; it was never an independent "monument" like the Han example. Gates were absent in graveyards, and a series of gates along a temple's central axis created suspense and made the compound deep and inexhaustible. A free-standing earthen screen further blocked the temple's main entrance, concealing both the gates and the temple vessels behind it (Fig. 2.7). The "public" of this closed monumental complex were strictly insiders—the members of the clan or lineage to whom the temple and all its paraphernalia belonged. Only they could walk through the gates in ritual processions, and only they had access to the sacred vessels, which consolidated their social privilege, strengthened their mutual blood ties, and refreshed their shared memory of history. Underlying the whole architectural and ritual program was the notion that power resulted from secrecy.

> 先君生我姊妹，无男兄弟，今当安神玄宅，翳灵后土，冥冥绝后，何以彰吾君之德？各出钱五百万，一女筑墓，二女建楼，以表孝思。

三百年后，北魏著名地理学家郦道元来到今日河南的王子雅故乡西鄂，看到并列矗立的两座石阙（即以上引文中所说的“楼”）所构成的一座废弃墓地的入口。每座阙高约一丈七八，宽约五尺，石质青绿，光亮可鉴。仿效木构塔楼的形式，精心雕出的顶部作四阿式，其下有复杂的斗栱擎托。阙上镌刻着已故太守的名号与官职，名号之下又有记述其女儿孝行的题名。郦道元将这组丧葬纪念碑载录于《水经注》中，作为见证该地历史的地标。[49]

虽然王子雅阙早已湮灭不存，但郦道元对其营造的记载表明了 2 世纪墓阙的纪念碑性与汉代前后的阙门的本质不同。如前文所论，三代之阙门总是一个大型建筑群的内在组成部分，而不像汉阙那样被当作一座独立的“纪念碑”看待。三代墓地中不见阙门，而祖庙中轴线上设立的一道道门的目的在于造成心理上的悬念，加强建筑群体的幽深感觉。一堵独立的影壁进而建在祖庙正前方，将门和庙器都隐匿在它的背后［图 2.7］。这一封闭型纪念建筑群的“公众”仅限于内部人员——即拥有这个宗庙和其中一切礼器的宗族成员。只有他们才可以在举行礼仪的时候通过每一道门，也只有他们才有权使用那些巩固他们的社会特权、加强他们的血缘关系、恢复他们共同历史记忆的祭器。潜藏在这种建筑和礼仪程序之下的，是“权力来自秘密”的意识。

Changes took place during the late Zhou, when ambitious feudal lords were struggling for independence, and new political groups emerged and demanded a share of power. The old ritual system collapsed—at least on the surface—when an iron tripod bearing legal codes was displayed in a public space. The implication of this event, that power had to openly exhibit and demonstrate itself, was best signified by the transformation of the gate. Official documents began to be posted on the front gate of the palace. Both the gate and the documents were called *xiangwei*, meaning "legal codes" (*xiang*) and "loftiness" (*wei*).[50] The gate was then detached from its original architectural context to become a self-contained "monument" (Fig. 2.22). Almost graphically, this transformation symbolized the changing notion of political power—from keeping it secret to exhibiting it publicly. Some writers claimed that only the Son of Heaven could enjoy a *que* gate with a pair of flanking *guan* towers.[51] Others considered the height of the *guan* towers as well as the number of their "wings" measures of social privilege.[52] Gates not only dominated the facade of the palace but also marked the entrance to a mausoleum.[53] Ban Gu later summarized the new symbolism of the gate in the *Proceedings from the White Tiger Hall* (*Baihu tong*): "Why must a gate have [flanking] towers? This is because the towers 'embellish' a gate and distinguish the superior from the inferior."[54]

Ban Gu's words indicate the conceptual transformation of a gate. The original definition of a *que*, or a gate, was simply "a gap"—the empty space framed by some architectural forms.[55] This understanding corresponded to the archaic architectural program in which a gate provided an entrance into an enclosed space. The new social and political significance of an Eastern Zhou gate, however, had to be conveyed by the flanking *guan* towers, whose concrete shape and height could symbolize social status. A new definition was then coined to equate a gate with its towers; as the *Er ya* dictionary stated plainly: "*Guan* means a *que* gate."[56] Interestingly, the meaning of the word *guan* was "to look," which implied two alternative explanations of a tower. Standing in front of a palace, a gate's multistoried towers invited its owner to climb onto them and look out; a *guan* thus raised the viewpoint—it empowered a lord who could now "overlook" his kingdom and subjects.[57] But as a concrete symbol of authority, a *guan* was also an object of "looking"—its imposing appearance and intricate design inspired public awe.[58] When this wooden-framed tower was

这种情况到晚周时期开始发生变化。野心勃勃的封建领主们为独立而纷争，一些新兴政治集团也应时而起，要求分享政治权力。当一件铸有法典的铁鼎在公共场所出现，旧的礼仪体系随之崩溃了——至少在表面上是如此。这一事件意味着权力自身需要被公开展示和证明，而门的变化即是这一历史发展的最好体现。此时，官方的公文开始被张贴在宫殿正门，而宫殿大门和张贴的文书都被称作"象魏"，意即"法规"（象）和"崇高"（魏）。[50] 于是，门从其原先的建筑语境中分离了出来，成为自成一体的"纪念碑"［图 2.22］。几乎是以图解的方式，这个变化象征了政治权力意识的转变——从秘密地保持权力到公开地展示权力。当时有些著述主张唯有天子才可以享有两翼带"观"的阙门，[51] 另一些则将观的高度及翼的数目作为社会特权的衡量标准。[52] 阙门不仅建于宫殿的正面，同时也开始标志着一座陵墓的入口。[53] 班固后来在《白虎通》中概括道："门必有阙者何？阙者，所以饰门，别尊卑也。"[54]

班固的这句话指示对于阙的观念转变。阙的最初定义只不过是门两旁"缺然为道"的建筑（"阙"与"缺"同音）。[55] 这一理解与三代建筑中以门作为进入一个封闭空间的入口的概念相吻合。但门在东周时期的社会政治意义转而由两旁的"观"来传达，因为观的视觉形态及高度象征了所有者的社会地位。观等同于门的新定义于是出现了，如《尔雅》就明白地宣告："观谓之阙。"[56] 有趣的是，观的意义是"看"，而"看"又隐含了对观（塔楼）的两种交叉解释。矗立在宫殿前方，门侧的多层塔楼吸引宫殿的主人临观远眺；在这种意义上，"观"可以提高视点，使一个君主得以"俯瞰"自己的领地和属国。[57] 但是作为权威的具体象征，"观"同时也是"被看"的对象——它那突出的外观和复杂的设计令公众望而生畏。[58] 当木构

duplicated in stone in a Han cemetery, it lost its practical function and became a solid, sculptured pillar. It retained only the second significance of a *guan*, and here we return to the Wang Ziya *que*.

This gate obviously had an overwhelming importance for its patrons: Wang's daughters used most of their savings (ten million cash!) to build it, spending only half as much on their father's tomb, and nothing at all on other ritual buildings and sculptures. It seemed that the gate alone could make their virtue renowned. (Being an aboveground structure, the gate was a public monument; the underground tomb was the private domain of the deceased.) By imitating a timber structure in stone, the
278 gate signified the contemporary interest in the transformation from this life to the eternal afterlife. Its inscription, which followed the Eastern Zhou precedent of posting documents on a palace gate, best demonstrated the gate's social significance. Although the text must have begun with the name and official title of the dead father, its central theme was the daughters' filial devotion. Its content identifies it as a kind of "autobiographical" writing[59]—the daughters intimately describe their anxiety and fear, their conversation and decision. Exposed to travelers and local townsmen, both the gate and the inscription displayed the patrons' urgent desire for publicity: through images and words their reputation would spread far and wide.

About fifteen pillar gates surviving from the Eastern Han are examples of this type of monument (Fig. 4.2).[60] These are all sculptured, free-standing stone structures. In fact, one can hardly call them "gates"—without attached walls they retain only a symbolic function. Some of the pillars bear long inscriptions resembling the Wang Ziya eulogy.[61] Many have surface engravings (Fig. 4.13): galloping horses and official chariots, Confucius meeting the boy-genius Xiang Tuo, a host honoring his guests, a superior receiving his subordinates. The social and moral implications of these pictures accord with those of the pillar-gates; their forms—low reliefs in parallel registers—reinforce the gates' three-dimensionality and solidity.

Only in comparison with these Han examples do the Liang dynasty pillar gates show their true revolutionary nature (Fig. 5.32). The Liang works are not simply "forms that developed from Han gates," as some

塔楼以石头复制在汉代墓地之中，它失去了实际登临的功能，成为实心的、刻有纹饰的石柱，所保留下来的仅是观的第二重意义。这里，我们再次回到王子雅阙。

对于它的赞助人来说，这对阙显然具有极其重要的意义：王子雅的女儿们用了大部分的积蓄（动金千万！）来建这对阙。她们为父亲造墓的开销只是造阙的一半（三女"各出钱五百万，一女筑墓，二女建楼"，此处的"楼"指的就是双阙），而且只字未提其他的礼仪建筑与雕刻。似乎单单是这对门阙便可以让她们的孝行远播天下。（作为一种地上建筑，这对阙构成一座公共性纪念碑；地下的坟墓是死者的私人空间。）通过模仿木构建筑，这对石阙表达出当时人对从此生转换到永恒来世的兴趣。阙上的铭文效法东周宫阙上张贴公文的先例，有力地证明了这对阙的社会意义。尽管铭文必须以已故父亲的名字和官衔开头，但其主旨却是关乎女儿们的孝行。据其内容，这种铭文可以被看作是"自传体"的写作[59]——女儿们以私密的口吻表达她们的忧虑和担心，叙述她们的商谈与决定。呈现在路人与当地居民面前，这座阙门及其铭文都在向公众展示着造墓者的急切心愿：她们行孝的声誉将通过形象和话语广为传播。

留存至今的大约十五组东汉时期的阙大都是这种类型的纪念碑［图 4.2］。[60] 作为不具附墙的独立石构建筑，它们实际上不再发挥"门"的实际功能，而仅仅是保留着门的象征意义。与王子雅阙相似，这些石阙上有的也带有长长的题记，[61] 而大部分阙的表面都有浮雕图像［图 4.13］：奔马与轺车、孔子见神童项橐、主人待客、长者接见下属等。这些画像的社会道德含义与阙门的象征性相合；它们的形式——平行装饰区域内的浅浮雕图像——加强了阙的三维性与整体性。

唯有与这些汉阙相对照，梁朝的石柱阙门才能显示出它们真正的革命性［图 5.32］。这些建筑物并非仅仅如某些学者所称是"汉阙

Fig. 5.32. Stone pillar in the graveyard of Prince Xiao Jing (d. 523). Liang dynasty. Nanjing, Jiangsu province.

图 5.32 萧景（卒于 523）墓上的石柱。梁。江苏南京。

Fig. 5.33. Lion column. 243 B.C. Lauriyā Nandangarh, India.

图 5.33 坐狮石柱。前 243 年。印度劳利亚·南丹格尔。

scholars have claimed. What they signify is a historical challenge to the traditional concept of monumentality. Instead of imitating timber towers in the Chinese palace, these pillars derived their form from foreign Buddhist architecture (Fig. 5.33). Both the strategy and reference of the visual rhetoric have changed: a funerary gate no longer related itself to a counter-image in the living world and derived its meaning from this opposition; rather, it directly expressed the idea of transcendence and enlightenment. Confucian motifs and genre scenes no longer decorate the gate—fantastic creatures soaring in the sky have replaced these favorite Han themes (Fig. 5.34). Most important, the mirror inscriptions on the gate (Fig. 5.5) completely alter the relationship between a monument and its audience: instead of presenting readable texts confirming the shared values of filial piety, they "reverse" the conventional way of writing and challenge the viewer's perception, forcing him to reinterpret a funerary monument and to view it with fresh eyes. These engraved inscriptions have become independent of their bearers, and their independence destroys the sense of the monument's durability. The strange style of writing, invented by master calligraphers such as Kong Jingtong, is

形式的发展"，更为重要的是它们对传统的纪念碑性观念发起了历史性的挑战。这些石柱阙门不再模仿中国宫殿中的木构塔楼，而是从外来的佛教建筑当中吸取了形式外观［图 5.33］。它们在视觉表述的策略和参照上都发生了变化：墓地中的石阙不再与现实世界中的木构建筑形成一对，也不再从这一对立中界定自身的意义，而是直接表达超现实的经验。儒家题材和风俗场景不再用作阙的装饰；翱翔于空中的幻想动物取代了那些以往备受重视的汉代主题［图 5.34］。更根本的是，阙上的镜像铭文［图 5.5］完全改变了纪念碑与观众之间的关系：不再提供肯定孝道之公共价值的可读文本，它们"逆转"了传统的书写方式，挑战观者的感知，迫使他们重新解释丧葬纪念碑，并以新的眼光看待这些礼仪建筑。这些镌刻在石头表面上的铭文变得独立于它们的载体，而这种独立性破坏了纪念碑的永恒感。它们的奇特书写方式——可能由孔敬通这样的书法名家

Fig. 5.34. Fantastic beasts. Carvings on the side of the memorial stela to Prince Xiao Hong (d. 526). Liang dynasty. Nanjing, Jiangsu province.

图 5.34 异兽。刻在萧宏（卒于 526）墓碑边侧的画像。梁。江苏南京。

not aimed at the common reader but appeals to individuals like Tao Qian, whose refined mind would detect the subtle irony implied in the metamorphosis of words and images.

279 As I have shown, this rebellion against traditional monumental art was part of an effort to redefine art and artistic creation during the Northern and Southern Dynasties. This crucial period literally divides the course of Chinese art into two broad phases. The mainstream of earlier Chinese art from Neolithic times to the end of the Han can be characterized as a "ritual art tradition," in which political and religious concepts were transformed into material symbols. In this tradition, forms that we now call works of art were integral parts of larger monumental complexes such as temples and tombs, and their creators were anonymous craftsmen whose individual creativity was generally subordinated to larger cultural conventions. From the third and fourth
280 centuries on, however, there appeared a group of individuals—scholar-artists and art critics—who began to forge their own history. Although the construction of religious and political monuments never stopped,

these men of letters attempted to transform public art into their private possessions, either physically, artistically, or spiritually. They developed a strong sentiment toward ruins, accumulated collections of antiques, placed miniature monuments in their houses and gardens, and "refined" common calligraphy and painting idioms into individual styles. All the people mentioned by name in this chapter—Lu Ji, Tao Qian, Yu Yuanwei, Kong Jingtong, and Gu Kaizhi—belonged to this group. Their work, both literary and artistic, reflected their concern with abstract artistic elements—structure, brush line, and point of view—rather than with the general ritual function and symbolism of traditional public monumental art.

所发明——并非针对普通读者，而是对陶潜那种精英人物有着特殊的吸引。这些人物的文化教养使他们认识到暗含在镜像文字与图像中的微妙的逆转。

正如前面所讨论到的，这种对传统纪念性艺术的反叛是南北朝时期重新界定艺术和艺术创造的一种努力。这一关键历史时期将中国艺术的历程分作两个主要阶段。从新石器时代到汉代末，早期中国艺术的主流可以概括为“礼仪美术传统”。在这一美术传统中，政治与宗教的观念被转换成物质符号；我们今天称之为艺术品的物件，原本是诸如宗庙和陵墓等大型纪念性综合体的组成部分；其创作者是无名工匠，他们的个人创造力通常服从于更广阔的文化惯例。然而，从 3 世纪和 4 世纪开始，中国艺术中出现了一种个人化的群体，包括学者型艺术家和艺术批评家，这些人开始打造属于他们自己的历史。尽管宗教性和政治性纪念物的建构从未终止，这些精英人士还是试图在物质、艺术或精神的各个层面上，将公共艺术转化为他们的私有物品。他们对废墟产生了一种强烈的情感。他们收藏古物，在他们的住处和庭园当中设置个人的“微型纪念碑”，并将那些为人们司空见惯的书法和绘画格套“提炼”成具有鲜明个性的风格。本章当中提到名字的个人——陆机、陶潜、庾元威、孔敬通以及顾恺之——全都属于这一群体。他们的作品，无论是文学的还是美术的，所关心的不再是公共艺术品的一般礼仪功能和传统象征性，而是反映出对结构、用笔、视点等抽象艺术元素的关注。

What the reversed inscriptions symbolize, therefore, is a liminal point in Chinese art history. Although such a radical reversal of conventions might temporarily destroy traditional concepts of monumentality, it was not necessarily the last word. Recall that Kong Jingtong, said to be the inventor of "left-and-right writing," was also a master of cursive calligraphy: "His brush stroke, which broke only at the end of a line, was fluent, graceful, and restrained, and reflected his distinctive nature." Significantly, although both his calligraphic styles emphasize the form of calligraphy over the content of writing, only the cursive style survived and developed into a brilliant artistic genre (Fig. 5.35). His "negative" mirror writing soon died out. Similarly, although new pictorial images first appeared on shrines, gates, and sarcophagi, the ambitious scholar-artist could never conquer the territory of ritual art. He finally retreated and found more private media—the scroll and album—while continuing to interact with new forms of "popular" religious and political monuments.

因此，本章所讨论的反书铭文所标志的，是中国美术史上的一个阈限点。虽然这种铭文对习俗的极端逆转可能在短期内造成对传统纪念碑性观念的破坏，但这并不是最后的定论。让我们回想一下孔敬通——他不但发明了“左右书”，而且兼擅“一笔一断，婉约流利，特出天性”的草书。耐人寻味的是，虽然他的这两种书风都把对书写形式的强调置于书写内容之上，可是唯有草书这种艺术形式得到流传，被发展成一种绚丽多彩的艺术体裁［图 5.35］，而“左右书”则不久便灭绝于世。与之类似的是，尽管新的图画形象最先出现在墓葬中的享堂、门阙和石棺之上，可是抱负不凡的学者型画家却从没能够占领这个礼仪美术的领地。虽然从未中止自己与“流行”宗教和政治性纪念碑的互动，他们最终是在从这块公共领域的退出中，找到了更适合表现其个性化的艺术媒介——卷轴和册页。

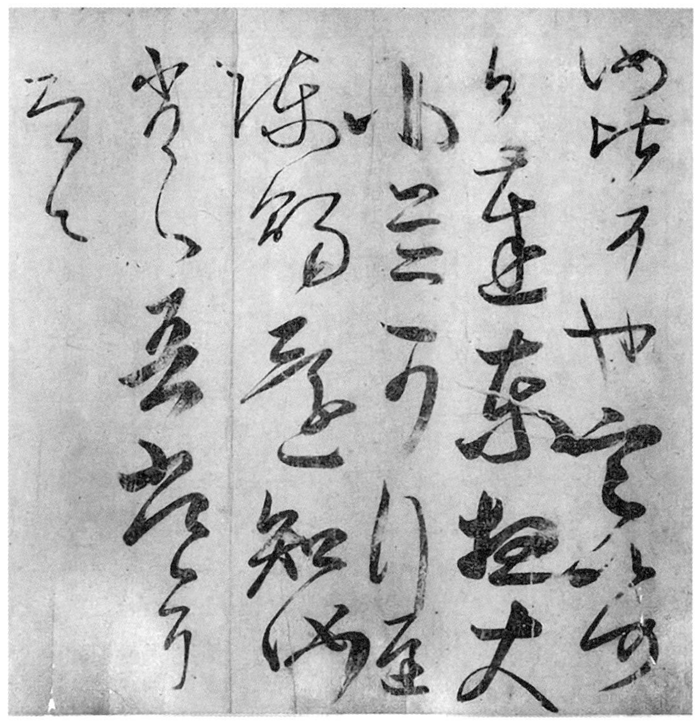

Fig. 5.35. Calligraphy by Wang Ci (451-91). Ink on paper. Qi dynasty. Liaoning Provincial Museum.

图 5.35 王慈（451—491 年）的“左书”。纸本。齐。辽宁省博物馆藏。

ILLUSTRATION CREDITS 插图出处

Fig. I.1b. Courtesy of Professor Zheng Yan. 图 I.1b 郑岩教授提供。

Fig. I.1c. Courtesy of Professor Zheng Yan. 图 I.1c 郑岩教授提供。

Fig. I.1d. Courtesy of Professor Zheng Yan. 图 I.1d 郑岩教授提供。

Fig. I.2. Courtesy of Professor Zheng Yan. 图 I.2 郑岩教授提供。

Fig. I.3. Courtesy of Professor Zheng Yan. 图 I.3 郑岩教授提供。

Fig. I.4. "Shi suo," 4.22. 图 I.4 "石索"，4.22。

Fig. I.5. *Huaxiangshi huaxiangzhuan*, pl. 70. 图 I.5《画像石画像砖》，插图 70。

Fig. I.6. Rawson, 1987: fig. 17; courtesy of the Trustees of the British Museum. 图 I.6 罗森，1987：图 17；大英博物馆授权使用图片。

Fig. I.7. Chavannes, 1913: vol. 2, no. 121. 图 I.7 沙畹，1913：卷 2，121 号。

Fig. 1.1. Tokyo National Museum, 1986: pl. 23. 图 1.1 东京国立博物馆，1986：插图 23。

Fig. 1.2. Seibu Museum, 1986: pl. 20. 图 1.2 西武美术馆，1986：插图 20。

Fig. 1.3. Shandong Provincial Cultural Relics Administration and Ji'nan City Museum, 1974: pls. 12, 17.4. 图 1.3 山东省文物管理委员会、济南市博物馆，1974：插图 12、17.4。

Fig. 1.4. Seibu Museum, 1986: pl. 8. 图 1.4 西武美术馆，1986：插图 8。

Fig. 1.5. Courtesy of Professor Zheng Yan. 图 1.5 郑岩教授提供。

Fig. 1.6. *Guyu tukao*, 55b-56a. 图 1.6《古玉图考》，55b—56a。

Fig. 1.7. Courtesy of Professor Zheng Yan. 图 1.7 郑岩教授提供。

Fig. 1.8. *Wenwu*, 1988.1: color pl. 2.2; p. 33, fig. 1. 图 1.8《文物》，1988.1：彩色插图 2.2；第 33 页，图 1。

Fig. 1.10. (a-c): Zhejiang Provincial Institute of Archaeology, 1989: pls. 156, 123, 221; (d): Childs-Johnson, 1988: fig. 19. 图 1.10（a—c）浙江省考古研究所，1989：插图 156、123、221；（d）蔡尔德–约翰逊,1988：图 19。

Fig. 1.11. (a) *Taoci, yi*, pl. 38. (b) *Kaogu xuebao*, 1978.1: 64. 图 1.11（a）《陶瓷》，一，插图 38；（b）《考古学报》，1978.1：第 64 页。

Fig. 1.12. Zhejiang Provincial Institute of Archaeology, 1989: pl. 164. 图 1.12 浙江省考古研究所，1989：插图 164。

Fig. 1.13. *Ibid.*, pls. 24, 25. 图 1.13 同上：插图 24、25。

Fig. 1.14. Han Wei, 1986: fig. 1. 图 1.14 韩伟，1986：图 1。

Fig. 1.15. Courtesy of Professor Zheng Yan. 图 1.15 郑岩教授提供。

Fig. 1.16. Courtesy of Professor Zheng Yan. 图 1.16 郑岩教授提供。

Fig. 1.17. Zhejiang Provincial Institute of Archaeology, 1989: pls. 237, 238. 图 1.17 浙江省考古研究所，1989：插图 237、238。

Fig. 1.18. *Ibid.*, pls. 6, 7. 图 1.18 同上，插图 6、7。

Fig. 1.19. *Ibid.*, pl. 71. 图 1.19 同上，插图 71。

Fig. 1.20. Murray, 1983: fig. 4. 图 1.20 孟久丽，1983：图 4。

Fig. 1.21. *Taoci, yi*, pl. 45. 图 1.21《陶瓷》，一，插图 45。

Fig. 1.22. (a-c) Shandong Provincial Cultural Relics Administration and Ji'nan City Museum, 1974: figs. 94.1, 2, 5; (d-f) Li Xueqin, 1987: figs. 3-5. 图 1.22（a—c）山东省文物管理委员会、济南市博物馆，1974：图 94.1、2、5；（d—f）李学勤，1987：图 3—5。

Fig. 1.23. Murray, 1983: figs. 6, 7. 图 1.23 孟久丽，1983：图 6、7。

Fig. 1.24. *Zhongguo yuqi quanji, yi*, pl. 190. 图 1.24《中国玉器全集》，一，插图 190。

Fig. 1.25. *Ibid.*, pls. 191, 192. 图 1.25 同上，插图 191、192。

Fig. 1.26. Deng Shuping, 1993: figs. 11.1b-2a. 图 1.26 邓淑苹，1993：图 11.1b—2a。

Fig. 1.27. *Zhongguo yuqi quanji, yi*, pl. 231. 图 1.27《中国玉器全集》，一，插图 231。

Fig. 1.28. Deng Shuping, 1993: fig. 2.1. 图 1.28 邓淑苹，1993：图 2.1。

Fig. 1.29. Based on *ibid.*, table 2. 图 1.29 据邓淑苹，1993：表 2。

Fig. 1.31. (a) *Taoci, yi*, pl. 51; (b) *Zhonghua renmin gongheguo chutu wenwu zhanlan zhanpin xuanji*, pl. 22. 图 1.31（a）《陶瓷》，一，插图 51；（b）《中华人民共和国出土文物展览展品选集》，插图 22。

Fig. 1.32. Photograph by the author. 图 1.32 作者摄影。

Fig. 1.33. *Zhongguo yuqi quanji*, pl. 18. 图 1.33《中国玉器全集》，一，插图 18。

Fig. 1.34. (a) *Qingtongqi, yi*, pl. 2; (b) *Kaogu*, 1978.4: 270, fig. 1.2. 图 1.34（a）《青铜器》，一，插图 2；（b）《考古》，1978.4：第 270 页，图 1、2。

Fig. 1.35. (a) *Yuqi*, pl. 49; (b) *Kaogu*, 1976.4: 262. 图 1.35（a）《玉器》，插图 49；（b）《考古》，1976.4：第 262 页。

Fig. 1.36. Based on W. Fong, 1980: fig. 1. 图 1.36 据方闻，1980：图 1。

Fig. 1.37. Courtesy of Professor Zheng Yan. 图 1.37 郑岩教授提供。

Fig. 1.38. K. C. Chang, The *Archaeology of Ancient China*, 4th ed. (Yale University Press, 1986), fig. 286, ©Yale University Press, 1986; reprinted by permission.

图 1.38 张光直，《古代中国考古学》第四版（耶鲁大学出版社，1986）图 286。耶鲁大学出版社，1986；授权复制。

Fig. 1.39. (a) Courtesy of Professor Zheng Yan; (b) *Shanghai hakubutsukan shutsudo bumbutsu seidōki tōjiki*, pl. 28. 图 1.39（a）郑岩教授提供；（b）《上海博物馆：出土文物 · 青铜器 · 陶瓷器》，插图 28。

Fig. 1.40. Courtesy of Professor Zheng Yan. 图 1.40 郑岩教授提供。

Fig. 1.41. Guo Baojun, 1956: pls. 13.6, 14.1-4; fig. 37. 图 1.41 郭宝钧，1956：插图 13.6、14.1—4；图 37。

Fig. 1.42. Henan Provincial Institute of Cultural Relics and Zhengzhou Museum, 1983: fig. 4. 图 1.42 河南省文物研究所、郑州市博物馆，1983：图 4。

Fig. 1.43. *Ibid.*, figs. 18, 19. 图 1.43 同上，图 18、19。

Fig. 1.44. *Ibid.*, figs. 12-15. 图 1.44 同上，图 12—15。

Fig. 1.45. Courtesy of Professor Zheng Yan. 图 1.45 郑岩教授提供。

Fig. 1.46. Courtesy of Professor Zheng Yan. 图 1.46 郑岩教授提供。

Fig. 1.47. Photograph courtesy of The Arthur M. Sackler Museum, Harvard University Art Museums, bequest of Grenville L. Winthrop. 图 1.47 哈佛大学赛克勒博物馆授权使用图片，格伦维尔 · L. 温思罗普捐赠品。

Fig. 1.48. Palace Museum in Taipei, 1989: pl. 26. 图 1.48 台北故宫博物院，1989：插图 26。

Fig. 1.49. (a) Courtesy of Professor Zheng Yan; (b) *Zhonghua renmin gongheguo chutu wenwu zhanlan zhanpin xuanji*, pl. 28. 图 1.49（a）郑岩教授提供；（b）《中华人民共和国出土文物展览展品选集》，插图 28。

Fig. 1.50. Institute of Archaeology, CASS, 1980: figs. 38.4, 25.2, 27.1. 图 1.50 中国社会科学院考古研究所，1980：图 38.4、25.2、27.1。

Fig. 1.51. *Henan chutu Shang Zhou qingtongqi*, pl. 377. 图 1.51《河南出土商周青铜器》，插图 377。

Fig. 1.52. Umehara, 1947: 1.18. 图 1.52 梅原末治，1947：1.18。

Fig. 1.53. (a) Courtesy of Professor Zheng Yan; (b) courtesy of The Saint Louis Art Museum. 图 1.53（a）郑岩教授提供；（b）圣路易斯美术馆授权使用图片。

Fig. 1.54. (a) Courtesy of Professor Zheng Yan; (b) *Henan chutu Shang Zhou qingtongqi*, pl. 321. 图 1.54（a）郑岩教授提供；（b）《河南出土商周青铜器》，插图 321。

Fig. 1.55. Bagley, 1987: fig. 103.12. 图 1.55 贝格利，1987：图 103.12。

Fig. 1.56. (a) Courtesy of Professor Zheng Yan; (b) Bagley, 1987: fig. 103.11. 图 1.56（a）郑岩教授提供；（b）贝格利，1987：图 103.11。

Fig. 1.57. W. Fong, 1980: pl. 59, fig. 82. 图 1.57 方闻，1980：插图 59，图 82。

Fig. 1.58. *Xuanhe bogu tulu*, 9.31. 图 1.58《宣和博古图录》，9.31。

Fig. 1.59. Pope et al., 1967: pl. 16. 图 1.59 波普等，1967：插图 16。

Fig. 1.60. *Ibid.*, pl. 49. 图 1.60 同上，插图 49。

Fig. 1.61. Courtesy of Professor Zheng Yan. 图 1.61 郑岩教授提供。

Fig. 1.62. Museum of Fine Arts, Boston, Anna Mitchell Richards Fund—photograph courtesy of the Museum of Fine Arts, Boston. 图 1.62 波士顿美术馆，安娜·米切尔·理查兹基金会——波士顿美术馆授权使用图片。

Fig. 1.63. Courtesy of Professor Zheng Yan. 图 1.63 郑岩教授提供。

Fig. 1.64. (a) Courtesy of Professor Zheng Yan; (b) W. Fong 1980: fig. 60. 图 1.64（a）郑岩教授提供；（b）方闻，1980：图 60。

Fig. 1.65. Photograph courtesy of the Harvard University Art Museums. 图 1.65 哈佛大学美术馆授权使用图片。

Fig. 1.66. Rong Geng and Zhang Weichi 1959: figs. 38, 55, 56, 87. 图 1.66 容庚、张维持，1959：图 38、55、56、87。

Fig. 1.67. *Gugong qingtongqi xuancui*, pl. 10, fig. 10. 图 1.67《故宫青铜器选粹》，插图 10、图 10。

Fig. 1.68. (a) *Qingtongqi, yi*, pl. 130; (b) courtesy of Professor Zheng Yan. 图 1.68（a）《青铜器》，一，插图 130；（b）郑岩教授提供。

Fig. 1.69. Guo Baojun 1963: pl. 2.2. 图 1.69 郭宝钧，1963：插图 2.2。

Fig. 1.70. Jiangxi Provincial Institute of Archaeology and Jiangxi Xin'gan Museum 1991: fig. 9. 图 1.70 江西省文物考古研究所、江西省新干县博物馆，1991：图 9。

Fig. 1.71. Photograph courtesy of The Arthur M. Sackler Museum, Harvard University Art Museums, bequest of Grenville L. Winthrop. 图 1.71 哈佛大学赛克勒博物馆授权使用图片，格伦维尔·L. 温思罗普捐赠品。

Fig. 1.72. *Sandai jijin wencun*, 20.49, 50. 图 1.72《三代吉金文存》，20.49、50。

Fig. 1.73. Li Xueqin 1984: figs. 147, 156. 图 1.73 李学勤，1984：图 147、156。

Fig. 1.74. Li Ji 1990: fig. 13. 图 1.74 李济，1990：图 13。

Fig. 1.75. Photograph courtesy of Freer Gallery of Art. 图 1.75 弗利尔美术馆授权使用图片。

Fig. 1.76. *Qingtongqi, yi*, pl. 26. 图 1.76《青铜器》，一，插图 26。

Fig. 1.77. (a) Courtesy of Professor Zheng Yan; (b) Pope et al., 1967: fig. 53b. 图 1.77（a）郑岩教授提供；（b）波普等，1967：图 53b。

Fig. 1.78. *Qingtongqi, er*, pl. 76. 图 1.78《青铜器》，二，插图 76。

Fig. 1.79. (a) Courtesy of Professor Zheng Yan; (b) Palace Museum, 1959: pl.

6b. 图 1.79（a）郑岩教授提供；（b）故宫博物院，1959：插图 6b。

Fig. 1.80. Courtesy of Professor Zheng Yan. 图 1.80 郑岩教授提供。

Fig. 2.2 *Gongshi kao*, as quoted in K. C. Chang, 1983: fig. 17. 图 2.2《宫室考》，转引自张光直，1983：图 17。

Fig. 2.3. J. H. An, 1986: fig. 9. 图 2.3 安金槐，1986：图 9。

Fig. 2.4. Li Xueqin, *Eastern Zhou and Qin Civilization* (Yale University Press, 1985), fig. 62, ©Yale University Press 1985; reprinted by permission. 图 2.4 李学勤，东周与秦代文明（耶鲁大学出版社，1985），图 62。耶鲁大学出版社，1985；授权复制。

Fig. 2.5. (a, b) *Kaogu*, 1974.4: 235; (c) Chinese Academy of Architecture, 1982: 24. 图 2.5（a, b）《考古》，1974.4：第 235 页；（c）中国建筑科学研究院，1982：第 24 页。

Fig. 2.6. *Kaogong ji tu*, 113. 图 2.6《考工记图》，第 113 页。

Fig. 2.7. (a) Steinhardt, 1990: fig. 35; (b) *Wenwu*, 1981.3: 25. 图 2.7（a）斯坦哈特，1990：图 35；（b）《文物》，1981.3：第 25 页。

Fig. 2.8. C. Y. Hsu and K. M. Linduff, *Western Zhou Civilization* (Yale University Press, 1988), tables 5.1, 5.2, ©Yale University Press, 1988; reprinted by permission. 图 2.8 许倬云、林嘉琳，西周史（耶鲁大学出版社，1988），表 5.1, 5.2。耶鲁大学出版社，1988；授权复制。

Fig. 2.9. Based on *Kaogu xuebao*, 1956.1: 110. 图 2.9 据《考古学报》，1956.1：110。

Fig. 2.10. (a) W. Fong, 1980: fig. 78; (b) Rawson, 1987: fig. 12; courtesy of the Trustees of the British Museum. 图 2.10（a）方闻，1980：图 78；（b）罗森，1987：图 12; 大英博物馆授权使用图片。

Fig. 2.11. (a) Courtesy of Professor Zheng Yan; (b) *Shaanxi chutu Shang Zhou qingtongqi*, fig. 15. 图 2.11（a）郑岩教授提供；（b）《陕西出土商周青铜器》，图 15。

Fig. 2.12. (a) Courtesy of Professor Zheng Yan; (b) *Shaanxi chutu Shang Zhou qingtongqi*, fig. 24. 图 2.12（a）郑岩教授提供；（b）《陕西出土商周青铜器》，图 24。

Fig. 2.13 (a) Courtesy of Professor Zheng Yan; (b) *Shaanxi chutu Shang Zhou qingtongqi*, fig. 27. 图 2.13（a）郑岩教授提供；（b）《陕西出土商周青铜器》，图 27。

Fig. 2.14 (a) Courtesy of Professor Zheng Yan; (b) *Shaanxi chutu Shang Zhou qingtongqi*, fig. 29. 图 2.14（a）郑岩教授提供；（b）《陕西出土商周青铜器》，图 29。

Fig. 2.15 (a) Courtesy of Professor Zheng Yan; (b) *Shaanxi chutu Shang Zhou qingtongqi*, fig. 31. 图 2.15（a）郑岩教授提供；（b）《陕西出土商周青铜器》，图 31。

Fig. 2.16. *Shaanxi chutu Shang Zhou qingtongqi*, fig. 54. 图 2.16《陕西出土商周青铜器》，图 54。

Fig. 2.17. *Ibid.*, fig. 59. 图 2.17 同上，图 59。

Fig. 2.18 (a) Courtesy of Professor Zheng Yan; (c) *Qingtongqi, er*, pl. 112; (b) Li Xueqin, Eastern Zhou and Qin Civilization (Yale University Press, 1985), fig. 48, ©Yale University Press, 1985; reprinted by permission. 图 2.18（a）郑岩教授提供；（c）《青铜器》，二，插图 112；（b）李学勤，东周与秦代文明（耶鲁大学出版社，1985），图 48。耶鲁大学出版社，1985；授权复制。

Fig. 2.19. Li Xueqin, *Eastern Zhou and Qin Civilization* (Yale University Press, 1985), fig. 55, ©Yale University Press, 1985; reprinted by permission. 图 2.19 李学勤，东周与秦代文明（耶鲁大学出版社，1985），图 55。耶鲁大学出版社，1985；授权复制。

Fig. 2.20. *Yongle dadian*, 9591. 图 2.20《永乐大典》，9591。

Fig. 2.21. Courtesy of Professor Zheng Yan. 图 2.21 郑岩教授提供。

Fig. 2.22. (a) Yang Hongxun, 1976*b*: fig. 6; (b) Chinese Academy of Architecture, 1982: 33. 图 2.22（a）杨鸿勋，1976b：图 6；（b））中国建筑科学研究院，1982: 33。

Fig. 2.23 Courtesy of Professor Zheng Yan. 图 2.23 郑岩教授提供。

Fig. 2.24 (a) Courtesy of Professor Zheng Yan; (b) *Yuanshi shehui zhi Nanbeichao huihua*, pl. 48. 图 2.24（a）郑岩教授提供；（b）《原始社会至南北朝绘画》，插图 48。

Fig. 2.25. Chinese Academy of Architecture, 1982: 30. 图 2.25 中国建筑科学研究院，1982: 30.

Fig. 2.26. (a) Institute of Archaeology, CASS 1980: fig. 2; (b) photograph courtesy of David Joel Cohen. 图 2.26（a）中国社会科学院考古研究所，1980：图 2；（b）戴维·乔尔·科恩授权使用图片。

Fig. 2.27. Institute of Archaeology, CASS, 1984: fig. 61. 图 2.27 中国社会科学院考古所，1984：图 61。

Fig. 2.28 (a) Yang Hongxun, 1980: fig. 5; (b) courtesy of Professor Zheng Yan. 图 2.28（a）杨鸿勋，1980：图 5；（b）郑岩教授提供。

Fig. 2.29. Fu Xinian, 1980: 110. 图 2.29 傅熹年，1980：第 110 页。

Fig. 2.30. Courtesy of Professor Zheng Yan. 图 2.30 郑岩教授提供。

Fig. 2.31. Thorp, 1983*a*: fig. 1. 图 2.31 杜朴，1983a：图 1。

Fig. 2.32. Courtesy of Professor Zheng Yan. 图 2.32 郑岩教授提供。

Fig. 2.33. Guo Baojun, 1956: fig. 118. 图 2.33 郭宝钧，1956：图 118。

Fig. 2.34. *Kaogu xuebao*, 1964.10: 110. 图 2.34《考古学报》,1964.10：第 110 页。

Fig. 2.35. Fairbank, 1942: fig. 15. 图 2.35 费正清，1942：图 15。

Fig. 2.36. *Yuanshi shehui zhi Nanbeichao huihua*, pl. 42. 图 2.36《原始社会至南北朝绘画》，插图 42。

Fig. 2.37. Tokyo National Museum, 1986: fig. 29. 图 2.37 东京国立博物馆，1986：图 29。

Fig. 2.38 (a) *Yuanshi shehui zhi Nanbeichao huihua*, pl. 40.3; (b) courtesy of Professor Zheng Yan. 图 2.38（a）《原始社会至南北朝绘画》，插图 40.3；（b）郑岩教授提供。

Fig. 2.39. (a, b) *Qingtongqi, er*, pls. 209, 210; (c) *Taoci, yi*, pl. 153. 图 2.39（a, b）《青铜器》，二，插图 209、210；（c）《陶瓷》，一，插图 153。

Fig. 2.40. Courtesy of Professor Zheng Yan. 图 2.40 郑岩教授提供。

Fig. 2.41. Rowland, 1967: figs. 192c, d. 图 2.41 罗兰，1967：图 192c, d.

Fig. 2.42 (a) Courtesy of Professor Zheng Yan; (b) *Qin Han diaosu*, pl. 36. 图 2.42（a）郑岩教授提供；（b）《秦汉雕塑》，插图 36。

Fig. 2.43. Y. D. Li, 1990: fig. 1. 图 2.43 李银德 , 1990：图 1。

Fig. 2.44. (a) Based on Institute of Archaeology, CASS, and Hebei Provincial Cultural Relics Administration, 1980: fig. 4; (b) W. Fong, 1980: fig. 112. 图 2.44（a）据中国社会科学院考古研究所、河北省文物管理处，1980：图 4；（b）方闻，1980：图 112。

Fig. 2.45. Institute of Archaeology, CASS, and Hebei Provincial Cultural Relics Administration, 1980: pl. 3. 图 2.45 中国社会科学院考古研究所、河北省文理管理处，1980：插图 3。

Fig. 2.46. *Ibid.*, figs. 112, 141. 图 2.46 同上，图 112、141。

Fig. 2.47. (a) *Ibid.*, fig. 6; (b) Rowland, 1967: fig. 6. 图 2.47（a）同上，图 6；（b）罗兰，1967：图 6。

Fig. 2.48. (a) Segalen et al., 1914-17: vol. 1, pl. 64; (b) Rudolph, 1951: fig. a. 图 2.48（a）谢阁兰等，1914—1917：卷 1，插图 64;（10）鲁道夫，1951：图 a。

Fig. 2.49. Chavannes, 1913: vol. 2, no. 116. 图 2.49 沙畹，1913：卷 2，116 号。

Fig. 2.50. Cunningham, 1879: pl. 31. 图 2.50 坎宁安，1879：插图 31。

Fig. 2.51. Shandong Provincial Museum and Shandong Cultural Relics and Archaeology Institute, 1982: pl. 184. 图 2.51 山东博物馆、山东省文物考古研究所，1982：插图 184。

Fig. 2.52. Inner Mongolia Museum, 1978: pl. 118. 图 2.52 内蒙古自治区博物馆，1978：插图 118。

Fig. 2.53. Fu Xihua, 1950: vol. 1, pl. 113. 图 2.53 傅惜华，1950：初编：插图 113。

Fig. 2.54. Chavannes, 1913: vol. 2, no. 81. 图 2.54 沙畹，1913：卷 2，81 号。

Fig. 2.55. (a) Shandong Provincial Museum and Shandong Cultural Relics and Archaeology Institute, 1982, pl. 187; (b) *Huaxiangshi, huaxiangzhuan*, pl. 248. 图 2.55（a）山东博物馆、山东省文物考古研究所 1982：插图 187；（b）《画像石画像砖》，插图 248。

Fig. 2.56. Lippe, 1970: pl. 14. 图 2.56 利佩，1970：插图 14。

Fig. 2.57. Zeng Zhaoyu et al., 1956: figs. 65-68. 图 2.57 曾昭燏等，1956：图 65-68。

Fig. 2.58 Courtesy of Professor Zheng Yan. 图 2.58 郑岩教授提供。

Fig. 2.59 Courtesy of Professor Zheng Yan. 图 2.59 郑岩教授提供。

Fig. 2.60. (a) *Qin Han diaosu*, pl. 127; (b) *Kaogu*, 1976.6: pl. 11.6. 图 2.60(a)《秦汉雕塑》，插图 127；(b)《考古》，1976.6：插图 11.6。

Fig. 3.1. *Shuijing zhu tu*, 630-31. 图 3.1《水经注图》，第 630—631 页。

Fig. 3.2. *Guanzhong shengji tukao*, "Xi'an fu," 23b, 24a. 图 3.2《关中胜迹图考》，"西安府"，23b、24a。

Fig. 3.3. *Chang'an zhi tu*, 1.5. 图 3.3《长安志图》，1.5。

Fig. 3.4. Wang Zhongshu, *Han Civilization* (Yale University Press, 1982) , fig. 30, ©Yale University Press, 1982; reprinted by permission. 图 3.4 王仲殊，《汉代考古学概说》(耶鲁大学出版社，1982)，图 30。耶鲁大学出版社，1982；授权复制。

Fig. 3.5. (a) Photograph courtesy of David Joel Cohen; (b) Bishop, 1938: 76. 图 3.5（a）戴维·乔尔·科恩授权使用图片；(b) 毕士博，1938: 76。

Fig. 3.6. Wheatley, 1971: fig. 26. 图 3.6 惠特利，1971：图 26。

Fig. 3.7. Le Jiazao, 1977: fig. 102. 图 3.7 乐嘉藻，1977：图 102。

Fig. 3.8. Courtesy of Professor Zheng Yan. 图 3.8 郑岩教授提供。

Fig. 3.9. Courtesy of Professor Zheng Yan. 图 3.9 郑岩教授提供。

Fig. 3.10. Courtesy of Professor Zheng Yan. 图 3.10 郑岩教授提供。

Fig. 3.11. *Qin Han diaosu*, pls. 34, 35. 图 3.11《秦汉雕塑》，插图 34、35。

Fig. 3.12. Photograph by the author. 图 3.12 作者摄影。

Fig. 3.13. Courtesy of Professor Zheng Yan. 图 3.13 郑岩教授提供。

Fig. 3.14. Courtesy of Professor Zheng Yan. 图 3.14 郑岩教授提供。

Fig. 3.15. (a) Wang Zhongshu, *Han Civilization* (Yale University Press, 1982), fig.

30, ©Yale University Press, 1982; reprinted by permission; (b) Tang Jinyu 1959. 图 3.15（a）王仲殊，《汉代考古学概说》（耶鲁大学出版社，1982），图 30。耶鲁大学出版社，1982；授权复制。（b）唐金裕，1959。

Fig. 3.16. Based on Liu Dunzhen, 1980: figs. 30.3, 30.4. 图 3.16 据刘敦桢，1980：图 30.3、30.4。

Fig. 3.17. Major, 1984: fig. 6. 图 3.17 马绛，1984：图 6。

Fig. 3.18. Courtesy of Professor Zheng Yan. 图 3.18 郑岩教授提供。

Fig. 3.19. Based on Steinhardt, 1984: pl. 3.5, courtesy of the China Institute Gallery. 图 3.19 据斯坦哈特，1984：插图 3.5，纽约华美协进社授权使用。

Fig. 3.20. Based on Gu Jiegang, 1982: 584. 图 3.20 据顾颉刚，1982：第 584 页。图 3.21 同上。

Fig. 3.22. *Qingtongqi, er*, pl. 235. 图 3.22 青铜器，二，插图 235。

Fig. 4.1. Based on A. Paludan, *The Chinese Spirit Road* (Yale University Press, 1991), chart 2a, ©Yale University Press, 1991; reprinted by permission. 图 4.1 据帕卢丹，《中国的神道》（耶鲁大学出版社，1991）表 2a。耶鲁大学出版社，1991；授权复制。

Fig. 4.2. Courtesy of Professor Zheng Yan. 图 4.2 郑岩教授提供。

Fig. 4.3. Courtesy of Professor Zheng Yan. 图 4.3 郑岩教授提供。

Fig. 4.4. Courtesy of Professor Zheng Yan. 图 4.4 郑岩教授提供。

Fig. 4.5. Courtesy of Professor Zheng Yan. 图 4.5 郑岩教授提供。

Fig. 4.6. Courtesy of Professor Zheng Yan. 图 4.6 郑岩教授提供。

Fig. 4.7. Chavannes, 1913: vol. 2, no. 180. 图 4.7 沙畹 ,1913：卷 2，180 号。

Fig. 4.8. Fu Xihua, 1950: pl. 120. 图 4.8 傅惜华，1950：插图 120。

Fig. 4.9. Beijing Library, 1989: 1.37. 图 4.9 北京图书馆，1989：1.37。

Fig. 4.10. Courtesy of Professor Zheng Yan. 图 4.10 郑岩教授提供。

Fig. 4.11. Shandong Provincial Museum and Shandong Cultural Relics and Archaeology Institute, 1982: pl. 32. 图 4.11 山东博物馆、山东省文物考古研究所，1982：插图 32。

Fig. 4.12. *Shang Zhou zhi Qin Han shufa*, pl. 75. 图 4.12《商周至秦汉书法》，插图 75。

Fig. 4.13. Sekino Tei, 1916: pls. 36, 37. 图 4.13 关野贞，1916：插图 36、37。

Fig. 4.14. *Li shi*, 5.5-6. 图 4.14《隶释》，5.5—6。

Fig. 4.15 (a) Courtesy of Professor Zheng Yan; (b) *Shang Zhou zhi Qin Han shufa*, pl. 89. 图 4.15（a）郑岩教授提供；（b）《商周至秦汉书法》，插图 89。

Fig. 4.16. (a, b) Rong Geng, 1936: 5b-6b; "Shi suo," 3.20-21. (c) Chavannes, 1914: pl. 4. 图 4.16（a, b）容庚，1936：5b—6b；"石索"，3.20—21。（c）沙畹，1914：插图 4。

Fig. 4.17. (a) Rong Geng, 1936: 19a-20a; (b) "Shi suo," 3.34-35. 图 4.17（a）容庚，1936：19a—20a；（b）"石索"，3.34—35。

Fig. 4.18. (a, b) Rong Geng, 1936: 17b-18b, and "Shi suo," 3.50-53; (c) Chavannes, 1913: vol. 2, no. 104. 图 4.18（a, b）容庚，1936：17b—18b，"石索"，3.50—53；（c）沙畹，1913：卷 2，104 号。

Fig. 4.19. (a) Rong Geng, 1936: 17b-18b; (b) "Shi suo," 3.32-33. 图 4.19（a）容庚，1936：17b—18b；（b）"石索"，3.32—33。

Fig. 4.20. (a) Rong Geng, 1936: 43ab; (b) "Shi suo," 3.61. 图 4.20（a）容庚，1936：43ab；（b）"石索"，3.61。

Fig. 4.21. (a) Rong Geng, 1936: 33a-35a; (b) "Shi suo," 3.46-47. 图 4.21（a）容庚，1936：33a—35a；（b）"石索"，3.46—47。

Fig. 4.22. (a) Rong Geng, 1936: 7a-8a; (b) "Shi suo," 3.22-23. 图 4.22（a）容庚，1936：7a—8a；（b）"石索"，3.22—23。

Fig. 4.23. (a) Rong Geng, 1936: 39ab; (b) "Shi suo," 3.57. 图 4.23（a）容庚，1936：39ab；（b）"石索"，3.57。

Fig. 4.24. Shandong Provincial Museum and Shandong Cultural Relics and Archaeology Institute, 1982: pls. 166, 168. 图 4.24 山东博物馆、山东省文物考古研究所，1982：插图 166、168。

Fig. 4.25. Rong Geng, 1936: 23b. 图 4.25 容庚，1936：23b。

Fig. 4.26. (a) Rong Geng, 1936: 24ab; (b) Chavannes, 1914: pl. 3. 图 4.26（a）容庚，1936：24ab；（b）沙畹，1914：插图 3。

Fig. 4.27. Zhang Wanfu, 1984: figs. 98, 100. 图 4.27 张万夫，1984：图 98、100。

Fig. 4.28. Beijing Library, 1989: 123, 124. 图 4.28 北京图书馆，1989：第 123、124 页。

Fig. 4.29. Rong Geng, 1936: 30b-32b. 图 4.29 容庚，1936：30b—32b。

Fig. 4.30. Based on Nagahiro Toshio, 1965: 62b. 图 4.30 据长广敏雄，1965：62b。

Fig. 4.31."Shi suo," 4.22-23. 图 4.31 "石索"，4.22—23。

Fig. 4.32. Rong Geng, 1936: 1a-2a. 图 4.32 容庚，1936：1a—2a。

Fig. 4.33. *Ibid.*, 2b-3b. 图 4.33 同上，2b—3b。

Fig. 4.34. *Ibid.*, 4ab. 图 4.34 同上，4ab。

Fig. 4.35. Chavannes, 1913: vol. 2, nos. 75-77. 图 4.35 沙畹，1913：卷 2，75—77 号。

Fig. 4.36. Courtesy of Professor Zheng Yan. 图 4.36 郑岩教授提供。

Fig. 4.37. Courtesy of Professor Zheng Yan. 图 4.37 郑岩教授提供。

Fig. 4.38. (a) Rong Geng, 1936: 5ab; (b) "Shi suo," 3.18-19. 图 4.38（a）容庚，1936：5ab；（b）"石索"，3.18—19。

Fig. 4.39. (a) Chavannes, 1913: vol. 2, no. 129; (b) *Wenwu*, 1982.5: 67, fig. 20. 图 4.39（a）沙畹，1913：卷 2，129 号；（b）《文物》，1982.5：第 67 页，图 20。

Fig. 4.40. (a) Rong Geng, 1936: 45ab; (b) Chavannes, 1914: pl. 3. 图 4.40（a）容庚，1936：45ab；（b）沙畹，1914：插图 3。

Fig. 4.41. (a) Rong Geng, 1936: 11b-12b; (b) "Shi suo," 3.30-31. 图 4.41（a）容庚，1936：11b—12b；（b）"石索"，3.30—31。

Fig. 4.42. (a) Rong Geng, 1936: 25ab; (b) "Shi suo," 3.39. 图 4.42（a）容庚，1936：25ab；（b）"石索"，3.39。

Fig. 4.44. Based on Shandong Provincial Museum and Cangshan Cultural House, 1975: fig. 1. 图 4.44 据山东博物馆、苍山县文化馆，1975：图 1。

Fig. 4.45. Shandong Provincial Museum and Shandong Cultural Relics and Archaeology Institute, 1982: pl. 403. 图 4.45 山东博物馆、山东省文物考古研究所，1982：插图 403。

Fig. 4.46. *Ibid.*, pl. 412. 图 4.46 同上，插图 412。

Fig. 4.47. *Ibid.*, pl. 413. 图 4.47 同上，插图 413。

Fig. 4.48. *Ibid.*, pl. 411. 图 4.48 同上，插图 411。

Fig. 4.49. *Ibid.*, pl. 407. 图 4.49 同上，插图 407。

Fig. 4.50. *Ibid.*, pl. 403. 图 4.50 同上，插图 403。

Fig. 4.51. *Ibid.*, pl. 410. 图 4.51 同上，插图 410。

Fig. 4.52. *Ibid.*, pl. 406. 图 4.52 同上，插图 406。

Fig. 4.53. *Ibid.*, pl. 409. 图 4.53 同上，插图 409。

Fig. 4.54. *Ibid.*, pls. 406-7, 414-15. 图 4.54 同上，插图 406、407、414、415。

Fig. 4.55. Jiangsu Provincial Administration of Cultural Relics, 1959: pl. 53. 图 4.55 江苏省文管会，1959：插图 53。

Fig. 4.56. Li Falin, 1982: pl. 18. 图 4.56 李发林，1982：插图 18。

Fig. 4.57. Courtesy of Professor Zheng Yan. 图 4.57 郑岩教授提供。

Fig. 4.58. Courtesy of Professor Zheng Yan. 图 4.58 郑岩教授提供。

Fig. 4.59. Courtesy of Professor Zheng Yan. 图 4.59 郑岩教授提供。

Fig. 5.1. A. Paludan, *The Chinese Spirit Road* (Yale University Press, 1991), chart 2b, ©Yale University Press, 1991; reprinted by permission. 图 5.1 据帕卢丹，《中国的神道》（耶鲁大学出版社，1991），表 2b。耶鲁大学出版社，1991；授权复制。

Fig. 5.2. Courtesy of Professor Zheng Yan. 图 5.2 郑岩教授提供。

Fig. 5.3. Courtesy of Professor Zheng Yan. 图 5.3 郑岩教授提供。

Fig. 5.4. Courtesy of Professor Zheng Yan. 图 5.4 郑岩教授提供。

Fig. 5.5. (a) Kanda Kiichirō, 1957-61: vol. 5, fig. 46. 图 5.5 神田喜一郎，1957—1961：卷 5，插图 46。

Fig. 5.8. Nagahiro Toshio, 1969: pl. 54. 图 5.8 长广敏雄，1969：插图 54。

Fig. 5.9. Courtesy of Professor Zheng Yan. 图 5.9 郑岩教授提供。

Fig. 5.10. Gao Wen, 1987b: 86. 图 5.10 高文，1987b：第 86 页。

Fig. 5.11. *Ibid*., 56. 图 5.11 同上，第 56 页。

Fig. 5.12. Courtesy of Professor Zheng Yan. 图 5.12 郑岩教授提供。

Fig. 5.15. Yao Qian and Gu Bing, 1981: fig. 284. 图 5.15 姚迁、古兵，1981：图 284。

Fig. 5.16. (a, b) Based on *ibid*., fig. 285. 图 5.16（a, b）同上，图 285。

Fig. 5.17. (a) Kanda Kiichirō, 1957-61: vol. 5, pls. 54, 55. 图 5.17 神田喜一郎，1957—1961：卷 5，插图 54、55。

Fig. 5.18. Courtesy of Professor Zheng Yan. 图 5.18 郑岩教授提供。

Fig. 5.19. Photograph courtesy of Zheng Yan. 图 5.19 郑岩绘图并授权使用。

Fig. 5.20. Beijing Library, 1989: 5.73. 图 5.20 北京图书馆，1989：5.73。

Fig. 5.21. Nelson-Atkins Museum of Art, Kansas City, Missouri (Purchase: Nelson Trust), 33-1543/1, 2—photographs courtesy of Nelson-Atkins Museum of Art. 图 5.21 纳尔逊–阿特肯斯美术馆（购买：纳尔逊信托），33-1543 / 1，2 ——纳尔逊–阿特肯斯美术馆授权使用图片。

Fig. 5.24. (a) Nelson-Atkins Museum of Art, Kansas City, Missouri (Purchase: Nelson Trust), 31-1543/2, detail—photograph courtesy of Nelson-Atkins Museum of Art; (b) Okumura Ikura, 1939: fig. 2. 图 5.24（a）纳尔逊–阿特肯斯美术馆（购买：纳尔逊信托），33-1543 / 2 ——纳尔逊–阿特肯斯美术馆授权使用图片局部。（b）奥村伊九良，1939：图 2。

Fig. 5.25 Courtesy of Professor Zheng Yan. 图 5.25郑岩教授提供。

Fig. 5.26. Courtesy of Professor Zheng Yan. 图 5.26 郑岩教授提供。

Fig. 5.28. Yao Qian and Gu Bing, 1981: figs. 162, 163. 图 5.28 姚迁、古兵，

1981：图 162、163。

Fig. 5.29. Okumura Ikura, 1939: 258. 图 5.29 奥村伊九良，1939：第 258 页。

Fig. 5.30. *Ibid.*, 258. 图 5.30 同上，第 258 页。

Fig. 5.31. *Kaogu*, 1980.3: 234-35. 图 5.31《考古》，1980.3：第 234—235 页。

Fig. 5.32. Courtesy of Professor Zheng Yan. 图 5.32 郑岩教授提供。

Fig. 5.33. Courtesy of Professor Zheng Yan. 图 5.33 郑岩教授提供。

Fig. 5.34. Courtesy of Professor Zheng Yan. 图 5.34 郑岩教授提供。

Fig. 5.35. Courtesy of Professor Zheng Yan. 图 5.35 郑岩教授提供。

NOTES 注释

DDLJ *Da Dai liji*

HHS *Hou Han shu*

HS *Han shu*

LJ *Li ji*

LNZ *Lienü zhuan*

SFHT *Sanfu huangtu*

SHJ *Shanhai jing*

SJ *Shiji*

SJZ *Shuijing zhu*

SW *Shuowen jiezi*

SZCZ *Song zhu Chang'an zhi*

TPYL *Taiping yulan*

WX *Wenxuan*

WXTK *Wenxian tongkao*

YWLJ *Yiwen leiju*

ZL *Zhou li*

ZZ *Chunqiu Zuozhuan*

The abbreviations above are used in the Notes and Works Cited.

Introduction The Nine Tripods and Traditional Chinese Concepts of Monumentality
导论 九鼎传说与中国古代的“纪念碑性”

1 This understanding is implied in Georges Bataille's description in his 1929 288
article "Architecture": "Thus great monuments are erected like dikes, opposing the logic and majesty of authority against all disturbing elements: it is in the form of cathedral or palace that Church or State speaks to the multitudes and imposes silence upon them" (see Hollier, 1992: 47). In the early 1940's, S. Giedion wrote articles criticizing what he called "pseudo monumentality" and promoting "new monuments" that would express "man's highest cultural needs." Both terms refer to architectural forms (Giedion, 1958: 22-39, 48-51). Two of the most recent studies on monuments also limit their focus to "monumental architecture," which, according to their authors, is "more or less monstrous exaggerations of the requirement that architecture be permanent" (Harbison, 1991: 37; Trigger, 1990: 119-20).

乔治·巴塔耶在其 1929 年论文《建筑》中的讨论已经隐含了这一理解：“因此宏伟的纪念碑如同堤坝般被建立，与权威的逻辑和高贵相抗，反对任何令人不安的因素。正是在大教堂或宫殿这样的建筑形式中，教会和国家对大众发话并使其沉默”（奥利耶，1992：第 47 页）。吉迪恩在 20 世纪 40 年代早期撰写了一系列文章批评他所认为的“伪纪念碑”，提倡能够表达“人类最高文化需要”的“新纪念碑”。他所用的这两个术语都意味着特殊的建筑形式（吉迪恩，1958：第 22—39、48—51 页）。对纪念碑的两项新近的研究也都将其注意力集中在“纪念碑建筑”上。根据其作者，这种建筑“或多或少地总是对使建筑得以永恒的条件极度夸张”（哈比森，1991：第 37 页；特里杰，1990：第 119—120 页）。

2 Quoted in Haskel, 1971: 59. For a related discussion, see Doezema and Hargrove, 1977: 9.
引文见哈斯克尔，1971: 第 59 页。有关讨论见多泽玛和哈格罗夫，1977：第 9 页。

3 Riegl, 1903. For discussions of Riegl's theory, see Forster, 1982a; Colquhoun, 1982.
李格尔，1903。关于对其理论的讨论，见福斯特，1982a；科洪，1982。

4 Jackson, 1980: 93, 91. 杰克逊，1980：第 91、93 页。

5 Conference program by Marian Sugano and Denyse Delcourt. The conference, sponsored by the Center for the Humanities of the University of Washington, was held in Seattle, Feb. 27—29, 1992.
见玛丽安・菅野和德尼斯・德尔古所撰会议介绍和程序。该会议由华盛顿大学人文研究中心主办，于 1992 年 2 月 27 日至 29 日在美国西雅图召开。

6 *Ibid*. 同上。

7 *Webster's New International Dictionary*, s. v. “monumentality.”
《新韦伯斯特国际英文词典》“纪念碑性”词条。

8 The original sentence is “King Cheng fixed the Tripods in Jiaru.” In Eastern Zhou texts, *Jiaru* refers to the locality of the Zhou capital and sometimes to the capital itself; see Tang Lan, 1979: 3-4.
“郏鄏”在周代文献中指周王室所在地或其首都，见唐兰，1979：第 3—4 页。

9 Trans. based on Legge, 1871: 5.292-93. 英译据理雅各，1871：5.292—293。

10 Riegl, 1903: 38. 李格尔，1903：第 38 页。

11 The largest extant bronze vessel, the Si Mu Wu tripod of the late Shang, is 52.4 inches tall and weighs 1,929 pounds.
目前发现的最大商代铜器司母戊鼎，高 133 厘米，重 875 公斤。

12 *LJ*, 1256; trans. based on Legge, 1967: 1.100. Different dates have been suggested for the *Book of Rites*. Most likely, this book was compiled during the early Han; see Legge, 1967: 1. xlvi. Since my discussion here concerns some general principles of early Chinese religion and art, *LJ* and other later documents are used as secondary sources complementing archaeological evidence.
《礼记》，第 1256 页。英译据理雅各，1967：1.100。学者对《礼记》的成书年代有不同意见。较可靠的说法认为，这本书是汉代初年编纂而成的；

见理雅各，1967：1. xlvi。我在此处进行的是关于中国古代宗教和艺术一般原理的讨论，《礼记》和其他晚出文献在这里作为辅助文献，配合考古材料使用。

13 *Mozi*, 256.《墨子》，第 256 页。

14 *Ruiying tu*, 10a. Sun Rouzhi, the author of this omen catalogue, lived in the post-Han era, but a similar inscription is found on the Wu Liang Shrine built in A.D. 151. See H. Wu, 1989: 236. For a longer discussion of the Nine Tripods legend, see *ibid.*, 92-96.
《瑞应图记》，第 10 页下。这本书的作者孙柔之生活于汉代以后，但建于 151 年的武梁祠中有一条非常相近的题记。见巫鸿，1989：第 236 页。另见同书第 92—96 页对九鼎传说的一个较为详尽的讨论。

15 Most inscribed bronze vessels from the Shang and Western Zhou were dedicated to deceased ancestors. As David N. Keightley (1978*b*: 217) has stated, the religion of the ancient Chinese was "primarily a cult of the ancestors concerned with the relationships between dead and living kin."
大部分商和西周的有铭铜器是奉献给先祖的。正如吉德炜（1978b：第 217 页）所言，古代中国的宗教“主要是祖先崇拜，关心的是生者和死者之间的关系问题”。

16 In addition to the two passages discussed below, other records about the feudal lords' desire for the Nine Tripods can be found in *Zhanguo ce*, 19, 21; *SJ*, 163. See Zhao Tiehan, 1975: 129-32.
除下面将讨论的两段文献外，其他诸侯问鼎的记载见于《战国策》，第 19、21 页；《史记》，第 163 页。参见赵铁寒，1975：第 129—132 页。

17 *SJ*, 2282.《史记》，第 2282 页。

18 *Zhanguo ce*, 22-23.《战国策》，第 22—23 页。

19 Rose, 1968: 83. 罗丝，1968：第 83 页。

20 *SJ*, 1365. But Sima Qian also offered a different account: the Nine Tripods were seized by the Qin during its attack on the Zhou in 256 B.C. (*SJ*, 169, 218, 1365). Ban Gu, however, dated this event to 327 B.C. (*HS*, 1200). See Zhao Tiehan, 1975: 135-36.
《史记》，第 1365 页。据司马迁提供的另一个说法，秦国于公元前 256 年在进攻周的时候获得了九鼎（《史记》，第 169、218、1365 页）。但班固把这个事件定于公元前 327 年（《汉书》，第 1200 页）。参见赵铁寒，1975：第 135—136 页。

21 For a concise explanation of these two principles, see Trigger, 1990: 122-28.
对这两个原则的简明解释，见特里杰，1990：第 122—128 页。

22 Veblen, 1899. 凡勃仑，1899。

23 Trigger, 1990: 119, 125. 特里杰，1990：第 119、125 页。

24 *SJ*, 248; *SJZ*, 327.《史记》，第 248 页；《水经注》，第 327 页。

25 K. C. Chang, 1983: 9-32. 张光直，1983：第 9—32 页。

26 *LJ*, 1439, 1441, 1595.《礼记》，第 1439、1441、1595 页。

27 Powers has discussed such issues in a number of articles; see especially his 1991 book on Han pictorial art.
包华石在一系列著作中讨论了这些问题，请特别参照包华石，1991。

Chapter One The Age of Ritual Art
㊀ 礼制艺术的时代

1 Liu Jie, 1941: 163-65.
刘节，1941：第 163—165 页。（原文见《诗经・大雅・烝民》，“天生烝民，有物有则，民之秉彝，好是懿德。”——译者注）

2 Legge, 1871: 4.541. 理雅各，1871：4.541。

3 See *Mengzi*, 2749; *Shi jing*, 568.《孟子》第 2749 页，《诗经》第 568 页。

4 Here Liu Jie followed Fu Sinian's (1936) interpretation of *wu*.
刘节在此沿用了傅斯年（1936）对于“物”字的解释。

5 Robert J. Sharer and Wendy Ashmore (1979: 278) add: "All societies maintain a kind of cultural classification or 'cognitive structure,' and different societies structure their world in different ways."
罗伯特・沙雷尔和温迪・阿什莫尔（1979：第 278 页）补充说：“所有社会都保持着一种文化分类或‘认知结构’，不同的社会构建世界的方式不同。”

6 The study of ancient objects in Europe followed a similar path. As Sharer and Ashmore (*ibid.* : 33) summarize: "Amassing a collection leads to attempts to bring order to the assembled material, resulting in the first efforts at *classification*."
欧洲的古器物研究也有着相似的方式。正如沙雷尔和阿什莫尔（1979：第 33 页）所总结的那样，“将藏品汇集起来，就要整理出这些收集品的序列，这就是分类的第一步尝试。”

7 Some Song antique catalogues contain both categories of *jin* and *shi*; others focus on one and exclude the other. The first major catalogue of antiques in Chinese history, for example, is entitled *Xian-Qin guqi ji* (Archaic bronze
289 vessels from pre-Qin periods). The most sophisticated Song antiques catalogue, *Xuanhe bogu tu* (Illustrated catalogue of various antiques in the Xuanhe imperial collection), records 839 bronzes in twenty formal-

functional types; objects belonging to a type are further classified into periods. The whole hierarchy of classification, therefore, consists of three levels based on medium, form and function, and chronology.

一些宋代的古物目录既包括“金”又包括“石”，有的则专注于一类而不及其余。例如，中国历史上第一部重要古物目录为《先秦古器集》。最成熟的宋代古物目录《宣和博古图》收录了 839 件铜器，这些铜器按照形态和功能被分为 20 类，每一类中的器物再分为不同的时期。因此，整个分类系统包含了材质、形态与功能、年代等三个层面。

8 Zhao Ruzhen, 1984. 赵汝珍，1984。

9 Bushell, 1910: 1.2. 卜士礼，1910: 1.2.

10 *Ibid.* 同上。

11 C. C. Liang, 1928: 456.
梁启超，1928：第 456 页。
（原文题为《中国考古学之过去及将来》，收入梁启超《饮冰室合集专集之卷一〇一，北京，中华书局，1989 年。——译者注）

12 Owen, 1985: 3. 欧文，1985：第 3 页。

13 See Sharer and Ashmore, 1979: 278.
沙雷尔和阿什莫尔，1979：第 278 页。

14 *LJ*, 1258.《礼记》，第 1258 页。

15 *LJ*, 1347; see Legge, 1967: 1.244.
同上，第 1347 页；英译据理雅各，1967: 1.244。

16 *LJ*, 1344. 同上，第 1344 页。

17 *ZL*, 757-71.《周礼》，第 757—771 页。

18 Quoted in Legge, 1967: 1.11. 转引自理雅各，1967: 1.11。

19 According to the *Book of Rites* (*LJ*, 1348) , “The six ceremonial observances were capping, marrying, mourning rites, sacrifices, feasts, and interviews” (trans. based on Legge, 1967: 1.248).
《礼记》（第 1348 页）：“六礼：冠、昏、丧、祭、乡、相见。”英译据理雅各，1967: 1.248。

20 A definite line between the secular and the sacred is, however, difficult to draw, as Noah Edward Fehl (1971: 3) has stated: “*Li* is an alternative to the specifically religious and the moral—an alternative so pervasive, persistent and successful in Chinese civilization that Chinese as well as western Sinologists can find no better word than ‘moral’ to define the perspective of Chinese philosophy and historiography.” Here I use *sacred* for relations

and communication between humans and supernatural beings and *secular* for relations and communication between people.
然而，世俗和宗教之间很难划出一条明确的界线，正如诺亚・爱德华・费尔（1971：第 3 页）所言："对于特定的宗教和道德来说，礼是另一种选择——这种选择在中华文明中如此普遍、持久和成功，以至于中国和西方的汉学家找不到比'道德'更好的词来解释他们对中国哲学和历史学的观察。"我在此使用"宗教"一词来指人类和超自然力量之间的联系和交流，用"世俗"一词来指人与人之间的关系和交流。"

21 Herbert Fingarette (1972: 16) remarks in his influential *Confucius: The Secular as Sacred*: "Rite brings out forcefully not only the harmony and beauty of social forms, the inherent and ultimate dignity of human intercourses; it brings out also the moral perfection implicit in achieving one's ends by dealing with others as beings of equal dignity, as free coparticipants in *li*. Furthermore, to act by ceremony is to be completely open to the others; for ceremony is public, shared, transparent; to act otherwise is to be secret, obscure and devious, or merely tyrannically coercive. It is in this beautiful and dignified, shared and open participation with others who are ultimately like oneself that man realizes himself. This perfect community of men—the Confucian analogue to Christian brotherhood—becomes an inextricable part, the chief aspect, of Divine worship—again an analogy with the central Law taught by Jesus."
赫伯特・芬加雷特（1972：第 16 页）在其颇有影响的著作《孔子：即凡而圣》中说："礼不仅有力地显示出社会形态的融洽与美好、人际交流固有的根本尊严，而且显示出人在达到其目的时所具有的道德上的完美，即将他人视为具有平等尊严的个体和礼的自由参与者。不仅如此，遵循礼仪行动就是完全地向他人开放；因为礼仪是公开的、共享的、透明的；不遵循礼仪行动就是隐秘的、晦涩的和迂回的，或者就是专横的、强制性的。正是在这种包含美好与尊严、共享与公开的参与中，使人实现了自我的意义，参与其中的他人也终和自己一样。这种完美的人类社会与基督教兄弟会相类似，成为儒家思想神圣崇拜的一个密不可分的部分和主要的方面。这种崇拜就像耶稣的重要的训诫一样。"

22 *LJ*, 1249.《礼记》，第 1249 页。

23 *LJ*, 1619; see Legge, 1967: 2.285.
同上，第 1619 页；英译据理雅各，1967：2.285。

24 Legge, 1967: 2.261. 同上，第 1611 页；英译据理雅各，1967：2.261。

25 See K. C. Chang, 1983: 9-32. 张光直，1983：第 9—32 页。

26 *LJ*, 1602; see Legge, 1967: 2.236.
《礼记》，第 1602 页；英译据理雅各，1967：2.236。

27 See K. C. Chang, 1983: 37-38. 张光直，1983：第 37—38 页。

28 *LJ*, 1416; trans. based on Legge, 1967: 1.369-70.
《礼记》，第 1416 页；英译据理雅各，1967：1.369—370。

29 *LJ*, 1416; see Legge, 1967: 1.369-70. Legge mistakenly translates the last sentence of the second paragraph of this passage as "In all these things we follow the example of that early time." My translation is based on Kong Yingda's commentary on the text (*LJ*, 1416) and is also determined by the textual context of the passage: in the following paragraph, forms of offerings and objects used in ancestral worship are all later inventions and not derived from "early times."
同上。理雅各将该节第二段的最后一句误译为 In all these things we follow the example of that early time。我根据孔颖达的疏（《礼记》，第 1416 页）和这一段的上下文对这个翻译做了修改。在接下来的一段中，祖庙中奉献的形式和对象全都是后世，而非"早年"的发明。

30 *LJ*, 1415; see Legge, 1967: 1.368.
同上，第 1415 页；英译据理雅各 1967：1.368。

31 The *shi* radical (a symbol for divinity) of the present character *li* was probably not added till the time of the Qin or Han; see Fehl, 1971: 4. Legge (1967: 1.10) explains: if according to the *Kangxi zidian* (Kangxi dictionary), the right part of the character "was anciently used alone for the present compound, still the spiritual significance would attach to it, and the addition of the *khih* [*shi*] to complete the character, whensoever it was made, shows that the makers considered the rites in which the vessel was used to possess in the first place a religious import."
"礼"字的"礻"旁（神性的符号）或许是晚到秦或汉才加上的；见费尔，1971：第 4 页。理雅各（1967: 1.10）解释说：如果根据《康熙字典》，礼字右边的部分"在古代可单独使用以表达字的意义，尽管如此，带有神性意味的'礻'仍被加上。这一附加，不论是什么时候完成的，表明了造字者认为使用器物的'礼'的场合从来就具有宗教意义。"

32 *SW*, 2; see Legge, 1967: 1.9.
《说文解字》，第 2 页；英译据理雅各，1967：1.9。

33 *LJ*, 1440; see Legge, 1967: 1.410.
《礼记》，第 1440 页；英译据理雅各，1967：1.410。

34 Quoted in Zhu Jianxin, 1940: 68-70. 转引自朱剑心，1940：第 68—70 页。

35 *SW*, 86. 《说文解字》，第 86 页。

36 *Ibid.* 同上。

37 The word *qi* is used extensively in *Huangdi neijing su wen* for human organs; see Guo Aichun et al., 1991: 949.
《黄帝内经·素问》中频繁地使用“器”字来指人体的器官，见郭霭春等，1991：第 949 页。

38 *Yi jing*, 83.《易经》，第 83 页。

39 *Zhuangzi*, 160.《庄子》，第 160 页。

40 *LJ*, 1530; see Legge, 1967: 2.100.《礼记》，第 1530 页；英译据理雅各，1967：2.100。

41 *Huainan zi*, 8.122.《淮南子》，卷八，第 122 页。

42 See Legge, 1967: 2.339, 344. 理雅各，1967：2.339，344。

43 *Yi jing*, 83; see Wilhelm, 1967: 323-24.
《易经》，第 83 页；英译据顾威廉，1967：第 323—324 页。

44 *Yi jing*, 81. 同上，第 81 页。

45 *LJ*, 1455; see Legge, 1967: 1.434-35.
《礼记》，第 1455 页；英译据理雅各，1967：1.434—435。

46 From a speech given at the dedication of the monument for the mother of George Washington at Mount Vernon; quoted in Jackson, 1980: 92.
出自献给位于弗农山庄的乔治·华盛顿母亲纪念碑的一篇讲话，转引自杰克逊，1980：第 92 页。

47 Quoted in Hollier, 1992: 47. 转引自奥利耶，1992：第 47 页。

48 Jackson, 1980: 94-95. 杰克逊，1980：第 94—95 页。

49 Summarized in Mothersill, 1984: 342.
有关概述见马瑟西尔，1984：第 342 页。

50 I follow David Keightley's (1987: 94) definition of the East Coast cultural
290 tradition: "Even though it is important to think, both first and last, in terms of a mosaic of Neolithic cultures whose edges blur and overlap, I believe that, for analytical purpose, one can—with all due allowance being taken for the crudity of the generalizations involved—still conceive of the Chinese Neolithic in terms of at least two major cultural complexes: that of Northwest China and the western part of the Central Plains, on the one hand, and that of the East Coast and the eastern part of Central Plains, on the other. I shall, for simplicity, refer to these two complexes, which should be regarded as ideal types, as those of the Northwest and the East Coast (or, more simply, East). There were numerous regional cultures within these two complexes. In the sixth and fifth millennia, for example, cultures like

Laoguantai, Dadiwan, and Banpo flourished in the Northwest; cultures like Hemudu, Qingliangang, and Majiabang arose in the area of the East Coast." See also K. C. Chang, 1977: 152-53. I discuss the Eastern coast tradition in a number of studies, including H. Wu, 1985, 1990a, b.

我同意吉德炜（1987：第 94 页）对东部沿海文化传统的界定："自始至终，中国的新石器时代文化都呈现出一种犬牙交错的分布状态，其边际模糊而交叠。认识到这一点很重要。尽管如此，我相信，从分析的目的来看，如果我们可以允许粗线条的概括，我们仍可以认为中国新石器时代至少有两个主要的文化系统：一个在中国西北和中原西部地区，另一个在东部沿海和中原东部地区。为了简单起见，我将这两个系统看作理想化的类型，分别称之为西北系统和东部沿海系统（或者更简单地说，东部系统）。两个系统中都包含有大量的区域性文化，例如，在距今 6000—5000 年间的西北地区有老官台文化、大地湾文化和半坡文化，东部沿海地区有河姆渡文化、青莲岗文化和马家浜文化。"又见张光直，1977：第 152—153 页。我在多项研究中曾讨论过东部沿海地区的文化传统，其中包括巫鸿，1985, 1990a, b。

51 As I have suggested elsewhere (H. Wu, 1985: 30-34), works dating before the Dawenkou period, especially ivory and jade carvings from the Hemudu and Hongshan cultures, are made of "precious materials." But to create an explicit "costly" impression is not the purpose of these works. These carvings represent vivid zoomorphic images. In such sculptured forms, a precious material is used as a "media" of representation; its value in color, texture, and hardness becomes secondary.

我在他处（巫鸿，1985：第 30—34 页）曾指出，早于大汶口阶段的一些作品，特别是河姆渡文化和红山文化的象牙制品和玉制品，也使用了"贵重材料"。但是这些作品的目的并不是要创造一种明确的"贵重性"。这些雕刻品表现了生动的动物形象。在这种雕刻形式中，一种贵重的材料被用作艺术表现的"媒介"；至于它在颜色、质地和硬度等方面的价值则是第二位的。

52 See Hansford, 1968: 26. In modern terminology, *yu* refers to two different minerals: "soft jade," or nephrite, a calcium and magnesium silicate with a fibrous structure; and "hard jade," or jadeite, a sodium and aluminium silicate with a crystalline structure. It was not until the eighteenth century that the Chinese began to use jadeite widely for carvings.

汉斯福德，1968：第 26 页。在现代术语中，玉指的是两种不同的矿石："软玉"，即具有纤维性结构的钙镁硅酸盐；"硬玉"，即具有晶体结构的钠铝硅酸盐。直至 18 世纪，中国人才开始广泛使用硬玉来雕刻。

53 See *ibid.*, 49. Different cultures in the ancient world shared this basic method; see Digby, 1972: 14-17.

同上，第 49 页。古代社会许多不同的文化都曾采用这种基本技术，见迪格比，1972：第 14—17 页。

54 One such example is Tomb no. 10 at Dawenkou. The deceased was buried in a carefully constructed wooden encasement and was covered with thick clothes. He wore an elaborate headdress of marble and turquoise, as well as a green jade bracelet. The corpse was surrounded by numerous articles, including more than 80 pottery vessels, 84 alligator scales, and two ivory tubes engraved with elaborate openwork patterns. A finely polished, dark-green jade axe was placed close to the waist of the deceased and was probably held in his hand. See Yu Zhonghang, 1976: 70.
其中一个例子是大汶口 10 号墓。死者穿着厚厚的衣物，安葬在精心打造的木质葬具中。他戴有大理石和绿松石制作的头饰、绿色的玉手镯。尸体周围有大量随葬品，包括 80 多件陶器，84 块鳄鱼鳞片，两件有精美的透雕图案的象牙筒。一件经过仔细抛光的墨绿色玉钺放置在他的腰部，或者原来被握在他的手中。见于中航，1976，第 70 页。

55 Some scholars have proposed that the graph for *father* in Chinese writing evolved from the image of an axe.
有的学者指出，“父”字即源于斧子的形象。

56 Dissanayake, 1988: 99.
迪萨纳亚克，1988：第 99 页。（这段文字采用了王睿的翻译。见郑岩、王睿编《礼仪中的美术——巫鸿中国古代美术史文编》，下卷，第 536 页，北京，三联书店，2005 年。——译者注）

57 For the unique aesthetics of such products in comparison with painted Yangshao pottery, see H. Wu, 1990b: 40-49.
关于这些作品与仰韶文化彩陶相比较所具有的独特美感，见巫鸿，1990b：第 40—49 页。

58 Wu Ruzuo, 1989: 40. 吴汝祚，1989：第 40 页。

59 *Ibid.*, 39-41. 同上，第 39—41 页。

60 *LJ*, 1455; see Legge, 1967: 1.434-35.
《礼记》，第 1455 页；英译据理雅各，1967：1.434—435。

61 *Guyu tukao* includes four *bi* disks (25a-26b), a tall *cong* (55b) , and a short *cong* (68a) identifiable as Liangzhu products.
在《古玉图考》中有四件璧（25a—26b）、一件高的琮（55b）和一件低的琮（68a）可以断定为良渚文化的遗物。

62 Shi Xingeng, 1938. 施昕更，1938。

63 See Wang Zunguo, 1984; Mou Yongkang et al., 1989: ii-iii.

汪遵国，1984；牟永抗等，1989：第 ii—iii 页。

64 For a summary of the excavations and research on the Liangzhu culture, see An Zhimin, 1988.
关于良渚文化发掘和研究的综述，见安志敏，1988。

65 Nanjing Museum, 1984. 南京博物院，1984。

66 Fanshan Excavation Team of the Zhejiang Provincial Institute of Archaeological and Cultural Relics 1988; Zhejiang Provincial Institute of Archaeology and Cultural Relics 1988. For an English summary of these two excavations, see James, 1991: 46-55.
浙江省文物考古研究所反山考古队，1988；浙江省文物考古研究所，1988。对于这两次发掘的英文综述，见詹姆斯，1991，第 46—55 页。

67 Zhejiang Provincial Institute of Archaeology, 1989: iv. *Zhongguo wenwu bao* no. 245, Aug. 11, 1991; no. 294, Aug. 2, 1992.
浙江省文物考古研究所，1989：第 iv 页。《中国文物报》，第 245 期，1991 年 8 月 11 日；第 294 期，1992 年 8 月 2 日。

68 *Zhongguo wenwu bao*, no. 370, Feb. 6, 1994.
《中国文物报》，第 370 期，1994 年 2 月 6 日。

69 Zhejiang Provincial Institute of Archaeology and Cultural Relics, 1988: 50-51; James, 1991: 47.
浙江省文物考古研究所，1988，第 50—51 页；詹姆斯，1991，第 47 页。

70 James, 1991: 46. 詹姆斯，1991，第 46 页。

71 Zhejiang Provincial Institute of Archaeology and Cultural Relics, 1988: 50.
浙江省文物考古研究所，1988：第 50 页。

72 Some Chinese scholars have attempted such an evolutionary sequence; see, e.g., Wang Wei, 1986; Liu Bin, 1990. Both authors make interesting proposals, but their classifications of Liangzhu *cong* differ markedly. Wang Wei bases his typology first on shape and size; Liu Bin considers decoration the primary feature. Both authors try to establish a linear, chronological sequence and neglect geographical factors important to the understanding of the development of *cong*.
有的中国学者曾尝试提出琮的发展顺序；见王巍，1986；刘斌，1990。这两位学者都提出了有趣的方案，但是他们对于良渚文化玉琮的分类却有所不同。王巍分类的根据首先是造型和大小；刘斌则将装饰作为首要的特征。两位学者都试图建立一种线性的、年代学的顺序，但却忽视了地域的因素，而这种因素是我们理解玉琮发展过程很重要的一点。

73 Schapiro, 1969: 224. 夏皮罗，1969，第 224 页。

74 See Gombrich, 1984: 33-62. 贡布里希，1984，第 33—62 页。

75 Grabar, 1992: 41. 格拉巴尔，1992，第 41 页。

76 Uspensky, 1975: 33. 乌司潘斯基，1975：第 33 页。

77 *Ibid.*, 38. 同上，第 38 页。

78 Zhang Minghua, 1990. 张明华，1990。

79 For a discussion of the iconic mode in later Chinese art, see H. Wu, 1989: 132-40.
对于后来中国艺术中这类图像样式的讨论，见巫鸿，1989：第 132—140 页。

80 Developing Lévi-Strauss's (1963: 245-68) observation of dualistic phenomena in ancient Chinese culture, K. C. Chang (1964; 1983: 77-78) has proposed that "the artistic dualism on Shang bronzes is merely one component, and
291 integral part, of a dualism that permeated Shang institutions and Shang thoughts." According to Chang, other Shang dualistic phenomena are found in the layout of the palaces and the royal cemetery, the composition of inscriptions on oracle bones, the ritual institutions of the Shang kings, and the two general styles of Shang bronzes.
张光直（1964; 1983: 77—78）发展了列维–施特劳斯（1963: 245—268）所提出的中国古代文化中的二元现象的理论，指出："二元现象弥漫在商的机制和思想中，商代青铜器艺术的二元现象只是其中一部分，是其整体中的一个局部。"根据张光直的观点，商文化中其他的二元现象见于宫殿和王室墓地的布局，甲骨卜辞的结构，商王的礼仪制度，以及商代青铜器两种普遍的风格之中。

81 The line between these two decorative modes is not absolute. As I discuss later in this section, it is only natural that they would influence each other and sometimes be employed in decorating a single object.
这两种装饰样式之间的界限不是绝对的。我在本节下文中指出，这二者之间彼此影响是很自然的，有时甚至用来装饰同一件器物。

82 Arnheim, 1982: 87. 阿恩海姆，1982：第 87 页。

83 Liu Bin, 1990: 33. 刘斌，1990：第 33 页。

84 Wang Wei, 1986: 1012, 1014. 王巍，1986：第 1012、1014 页。

85 James, 1991: 54. 詹姆斯，1991：第 54 页。

86 Salmony, 1963: pl. VII, 1-3. Julia K. Murray (1983) has found more details on these *bi* disks. According to her, "One of the *bi* is also incised on the narrow surface of its slightly concave rim. The rim design is organised in quadrants, with a flying bird seen from above and a fish skeleton alternating at the head of each quadrant. The space between the four emblems contains a

loose meander pattern resembling elongated *leiwen* [thunder patterns]."
苏蒙尼，1963 年，pl. VII, 第 1—3 页。孟久丽发现了这些玉璧上更多的细节，指出："在其中一件璧的狭窄并且微微凹入的边缘表面，也有着阴刻的细纹。边缘上的线刻纹被等分为四个部分，一只俯视的飞鸟和一条鱼的骨架交互装饰在每一部分的起始处。在这四个徽志之间是一个松散屈曲的图案，类似拉长的云雷纹。

87 As I discuss later in this section, the circular motif resembles graphs for the sun or "sun-brightness" in early Chinese writing.
我在本节还要谈到，圆形的图案代表太阳或中国早期文字中对"阳光"的表现。

88 Salmony, 1963: pl. VII, 3. 苏蒙尼，1963 年，插图 VII，3。

89 Salmony (1963: pl. VII, 1), however, did compare these images with some Shang dynasty bronzes published by C. Hentze that show a bird standing on a shrine. Based on Hentze's symbolic interpretation, he identified these motifs as symbols which "connect the soul with the stars of day and night."
但是，苏蒙尼（1963: 插图 VII, 1）将这些图像与亨兹所发表的一些商代青铜器上一只鸟栖落在一个祭坛上的图像进行了比较。根据亨兹解释，苏蒙尼认为这种图像象征着"灵魂与代表昼夜的星辰相连接"。

90 Hayashi Minao (1965) has hypothesized that these jars were ritual vessels.
林巳奈夫（1965）推测这种大口尊为礼器。

91 Chinese scholars have different explanations for this sign. Dominant opinion identifies it as the graph for "fire" (see Tang Lan, 1981: 80; Li Xueqin, 1987).
中国学者对这种符号有不同的解释。一个通行的观点认为，这一图形为象形的"火"字（见唐兰，1981：第 80 页；李学勤，1987）。

92 Wang Shuming, 1986; Li Xueqin, 1987. 王树明，1986；李学勤，1987。

93 Hayashi Minao, 1981: 22-23; Murray, 1983: 14-22; H. Wu, 1985.
林巳奈夫，1981：第 22—23 页；孟久丽，1983：第 14—22 页；巫鸿，1985。

94 Shi Zhilian, 1987; Hayashi Minao, 1991. 石志廉，1987；林巳奈夫，1991。

95 Li Xueqin, 1987: 78-79; Deng Shuping, 1993: 14.
李学勤，1987：第 78—79 页；邓淑苹，1993：第 14 页。

96 Mou Yongkang and Yun Xizheng, 1992: figs. 229-31.
牟永抗、云希正，1992：图 229—231。

97 Deng Shuping, 1993: 14. 邓淑苹，1993：第 14 页。

98 Rowley, 1959: 27. 罗丽，1959：第 27 页。

99 For an illustration, see Childs-Johnson, 1988: fig. 22a.
插图见江伊莉，1988：图 22a。

100 As I have suggested, the incisions on the three Freer *bi* seem to indicate a chronological development in style and a gradual "abstraction" of pictorial signs.
我曾经提出，弗利尔玉璧的刻纹似乎显示出一种风格发展的时间关系，以及画像符号逐步"抽象"的过程。

101 Friesen, 1969: 55. 弗里森，1969：第 55 页。

102 In a previous study (H. Wu, 1985: 40-41), I discuss the relationship between these motifs and ancient Chinese legends and propose an analytical method for studying and identifying such a relationship.
在以前的一项研究中（巫鸿，1985：第 40—41 页），我曾经讨论过这些母题与中国古代传说之间的关系，并提出了研究和界定这类关系的一种分析方法。

103 For various versions of this legend, see Xu Xusheng, 1960: 67-74.
关于这一传说的不同记载，见徐旭生，1960：第 67—74 页。

104 *SHJ*, 357. The phrase *jun ji* in the present version of the *Classic of Mountains and Seas* is difficult to understand. I suspect that the character *ji* is an error; the original character should be *zu* (clan).
《山海经》，第 357 页。《山海经》现存版本中"俊疾"二字的意思难以理解。我怀疑"疾"字有误；原字或为"族"。

105 See H. Wu, 1990a. 巫鸿，1990a.

106 See Legge, 1870: 3.108-11. 理雅各，1870: 3.108-111.

107 In a previous study (H. Wu, 1985: 35-36), I suggest that the three Freer *bi* were likely made in the Huai River region. After the publication of that paper, I learned that *bi* disks similar to the Freer examples in both shape and engraving had been discovered at Anxi in Yuhang county, Zhejiang; see Deng Shuping, 1993: 14; Y. S. Qiu and B. X. Hu, 1990: fig. 8.
在以前的研究中（巫鸿，1985：第 35—36 页），我认为弗利尔的三件璧可能出自淮河地区。文章发表后，我又获知浙江省余杭县安溪出土的玉璧在形制和雕刻上都与弗利尔璧十分相似；见邓淑苹，1993：第 14 页；Y. S. Qiu and B. X. Hu, 1990: 图 8。

108 Xu Xusheng, 1960: 73. 徐旭生，1960：第 73 页。

109 I have demonstrated elsewhere (H. Wu, 1985) that there was a long tradition in the lower Yangzi River region of presenting "birds" on ritual objects.
我在他处（巫鸿，1985）曾经论证，长江下游地区有着很久远的在礼器上描绘"鸟"的传统。

110 For the possible Longshan date of these jades, see H. Wu, 1979 and H. Wu, 1985.
这些玉器可能属于龙山时代，见巫鸿，1979 年；巫鸿，1985 年。

111 The historical identity of the Erlitou site (and Erlitou culture in general) has been the subject of a prolonged debate ever since its discovery. Some scholars believe that this site holds the remains of a late Xia capital; others identify it, or its upper strata, as an early Shang city. For a summary of this debate, see K. C. Chang, 1986: 307-16. The discovery of an early Shang city in 1983 seems to support the first opinion: it was founded later than the Erlitou settlement but predated the mid-Shang city at Zhengzhou. See Henan Provincial Institute of Cultural Relics, 1990: 178-79; Zhao Zhiquan, 1989. Here I follow the opinion accepted by most Chinese archaeologists, including the excavators of the Erlitou site.
二里头遗址（以及一般意义上的二里头文化）的历史属性自发现以后，引起了长期的争论。有的学者认为这一遗址中有夏都的遗存；有的将该遗址，或其上层视为早商城址。关于这些讨论的综述，见张光直，1986：第 307—316 页。1983 年所发现的商城似乎可以支持前一种看法，该城的年代晚于二里头遗址，而早于郑州商代中期的城址。见河南省文物研究所，1990：第 178—179 页；赵芝荃，1989。我赞同包括二里头遗址发掘者在内的大多数中国考古学家的意见。

112 Bagley in W. Fong, 1980: 74. 方闻引贝格利，1980：第 74 页。

113 Some Erlitou pottery shards are decorated with zoomorphic motifs such as animal masks and dragons. Although scholars have suggested that these designs imitate bronze decoration, this contention still needs to be proved, especially because it does not answer the question why all bronze vessels from Erlitou are plain or bear only simple decoration.
二里头陶片上曾见有兽面纹、龙纹等动物形象。有的学者认为这些图案是对青铜器装饰的模仿，但此说尚需更多证据，因为二里头所出土的青铜器多为素面或仅有很少装饰。

114 Two turquoise-inlaid plates excavated from Erlitou show "mask" motifs; seven similar plates exist in different collections. See Li Xueqin, 1991*a*: 292
2. Since these works are covered with precious stones, they cannot be considered pure bronze objects; rather, they are akin to jade or stone ornaments.
两件出土于二里头的镶嵌绿松石铜牌上有“兽面”纹；在各收藏者手中还有七件类似的铜牌。见李学勤，1991a：第 2 页。因为这些作品被松石片覆盖，所以不能看作单纯的青铜器；倒不如说它们与玉或石的装饰品更接近。

115 There are different opinions regarding the periodization of the Shang

dynasty. Some scholars who consider Erlitou a Xia site divide the Shang into two broad periods—the early Shang and the later Shang—represented by Erligang in Zhengzhou and Anyang, respectively. Other scholars periodize the Shang into three parts; the early Shang is represented by the two upper strata at Erlitou, the mid-Shang by the Erligang upper stratum at Zhengzhou, and the late Shang by Anyang. See K. C. Chang, 1986: 335-37; Soper, 1966: 5-38; Thorp, 1985: 8. Here I follow the second opinion, recently systematically stated in Institute of Archaeology, CASS, 1984: 211-48, 323-26.
关于商的分期有不同的意见。认为二里头为夏代遗址的学者将商分为两大期——以郑州二里岗为代表的早商和以安阳为代表的晚商。另有学者将商分为三期：早商以二里头上两层为代表，中商以二里岗上层为代表，晚商以安阳为代表。见张光直，1986：第335—337页；索柏，1966：第5—38页；杜朴，1985：第8页。本书跟从后一种意见，最近对这种意见的系统阐述，见中国社会科学院考古研究所，1984:第211—248，323—326页。

116 Langer, 1957: 98. 朗格，1957：第98页。

117 Consten, 1957: 300. 康时登，1957：第300页。

118 Paper, 1978: 20. 裴玄德，1978，第20页。

119 For discussions of the origins of the *taotie* mask, see Hayashi Minao, 1979; Rawson, 1980: 36-40, 70-79.
关于饕餮纹起源的讨论，见林巳奈夫，1979；罗森，1980：第36–40、70–79页。

120 An alternative interpretation is that the two types of mask in Liangzhu art—the frontal mask on a two-dimensional surface and the "split" mask along a corner of a *cong*—were inherited by the middle Shang people. This hypothesis, however, does not explain why two-dimensional *taotie* images on Shang bronzes are often shown as "split" ones. It is more logical to see such images as descendents of the "split" mask on Liangzhu *cong*.
另一种解释是，良渚文化艺术中的两种兽面——二维平面上装饰的正面兽面和沿着琮的转角处装饰的"分裂"的兽面——被商代中期的人们继承了下来。然而，这种假设并不能解释为什么商代青铜器上二维的饕餮形象常常表现出"分裂"的特征。将这种形象看作良渚玉琮上"分裂"式兽面的派生物似乎更合逻辑。

121 Quoted from Gombrich, 1969: 267. 转引自贡布里希，1969：第267页。

122 Loehr, 1953. 罗樾，1953。

123 These summaries can be found in W. Fong, 1980: 182; Rawson, 1980: 67; Soper, 1966: 37-38.
这些总结见于方闻，1980：第182页；罗森，1980：第67页；索柏，

1966：第 37—38 页。

124 Loehr, 1968: 13. 罗樾，1968：第 13 页。

125 As Robert Thorp (1985: 38) has pointed out, Loehr himself did not date his Style I, which was later placed at the beginning of the evolutional sequence of Shang bronze decoration.
杜朴（1985：38）指出，罗樾后来才将 I 式放置在商代青铜装饰演进序列的最前端，但他本人并没有讨论这种风格的年代问题。

126 To judge from excavated materials, bronzes decorated with zoomorphic motifs became popular only from the late part of the Zhengzhou period, or Upper Erligang phase, from 1400 to 1200 B.C. Bronzes from the earlier Lower Erligang phase are often undecorated or decorated only with simple geometric patterns; see Zhengzhou Museum, 1981: 97. Styles I-III characterize mid-Shang bronzes belonging to both the Upper Erligang phase and the "transitional period" defined by Thorp (1985: 37-51). Style IV decoration may have also appeared before the late Shang. As Robert Bagley has argued, "Tentative versions of Style IV are in evidence already among the bronzes, predominantly Style III, from the Taixicun, Gaocheng, site in Hebei Province; these may predate the Anyang period." (W. Fong 1980: 182) Such "tentative Style IV designs" may, however, still belong to the general category of Style III, since the motif-ground distinction is still far from mature. A more definite Style IV example is a *zun* found in 1954 in Huixian, Henan province (see *Henan chutu Shang-Zhou qingtongqi* 1: pl. 119). A detailed description of a stylistic development of Style IV can be found in Huber, 1981. Thorp (1988) discusses the chronological relationship between Styles IV and V. While agreeing that Style IV antedated Style V, he also emphasizes, quite correctly in my opinion, that these two styles should be "regarded as a single change in the way that Shang bronze designers created their art." (Thorp, 1988: 57) After the discovery of Fu Hao's tomb, most scholars have agreed that Style V must have been invented before 1200 B.C. when King Wu Ding, Fu Hao's consort, began his rule. As I discuss below, most bronze vessels from the tomb are decorated with mature Style V designs; this suggests that Style V must have been invented before Fu Hao's time.
从发掘材料来看，只是从郑州后期或者说二里岗上层阶段开始，即公元前 1400 年—前 1200 年，青铜装饰中才流行动物纹样。更早的二里岗下层阶段的青铜器通常没有装饰或只有简单的几何纹样；见郑州市博物馆，1981：第 97 页。商中期典型的 I—III 式属于二里岗上层和杜朴（1985：第 37—51 页）所说的"过渡阶段"。IV 式可能也出现在晚商之前。正如罗伯特·贝格利所言，"河北藁城台西村遗址出土的青铜器中，在 III 式占据支配地位之前，已经明显出现了 IV 式的试验性样式；它们可能早于安阳阶段”（方闻，1980：第 182 页）。但是，“IV 式的试验性样式”可能仍然属于总体分类中的 III 式，因为其主体纹样和地纹区分明显，仍与自然的形式有很大的距离。更为确定的 IV 式纹样见于 1954 年河南辉县出土的一件尊上（《河南出土商周青铜器 I》：插图 119）。关于 IV 式纹样风格发展过程的详细叙述，见胡博，1981。关于 IV 式和 V 式的年代序列关系，杜朴在承认 IV 式早于 V 式的同时，还强调这两种风格应被“看作商代青铜器设计者在艺术创作的道路上的同一次变化”（杜朴，1988：第 57 页）。这与我的看法十分相合。妇好墓发现以后，多数学者同意 V 式在公元前 1200 年——即妇好的丈夫武丁开始为王——之前已被发明。我在下文将谈到，该墓出土的大部分青铜器装饰有自然风格的 V 式纹样；这说明 V 式在妇好的时代之前已被发明。

127 Thorp (1985: 38, 41-42) has pointed out that “unfortunately, there has been little archaeological evidence, as opposed to theoretical logic, that would in fact assign absolute chronological priority to this technique [of placing Style I before Style II]. It has frequently been noted, for example, that both Styles I and II can be found on a single vessel, and some vessel types that appeared only well into the Upper Erligang Phase or in the Transitional Period have thin relief line decoration.” A number of *jue* and *jia* tripods, for example, share a decorative formula: the upper frieze is filled with thready, linear patterns, and the lower band is characterized by a pattern of flat relief ribbons. Even more telling, on a very complicated *you* vessel from a mid-Shang tomb at Zhengzhou, the main mask motif unmistakenly falls into the category of Style II, the sculptured handle required advanced precasting and cast-on techniques, and the shoulder is decorated with “primitive” Style I fine threads (see W. Fong, 1980: 107).

The following statistics on bronze from some excavated mid-Shang tombs in Henan demonstrates the wide coexistence of Style I and Style II vessels. (Style I: bronzes with pure Style I decor; Style Ia: bronzes with simple raised parallel lines; Style II: bronze with pure Style II decor; Style I+II: bronzes combining decorations of the two styles. The sites listed do not include those of the Transitional Period defined by Thorp. For sources, see Thorp, 1985: 60-62.

293

Sites	*Style I*	*Style Ia*	*Style II*	*Style I+II*
Minggonglu M2		3	3	
Minggonglu M4	1			1
Erqilu M1	1		4(?)	
Erqilu M2	1	2	1	
Liulige M110	1		2	
Liulige M148	1		1	
Lilou no. 1	1		2	

Objects from mid-Shang hoards exhibit similar mixtures. The thirteen bronzes from Xiangyang in Zhengzhou, for example, are decorated with Styles I and II patterns and with *taotie* classified by Loehr as Style III. High-relief images also appear on some vessels in this group (see Henan Provincial Institute of Cultural Relics and Zhengzhou Museum, 1983).
杜朴（1985：第 38，41–42 页）指出："不幸的是，与理论性的逻辑相反，我们尚缺乏考古学的证据，以确定 I 式在 II 式之前的年代学的绝对序列。例如，我们经常可以看到 I 式和 II 式往往出现在同一件器物上，恰恰是在二里岗上层阶段或过渡阶段的一些器物类型有着细凸线的装饰。"例如大量的爵和斝符合同一种装饰模式：上部装饰带上填充着单线状图案，下部装饰带上有扁平高起纹样。更能说明问题的是，郑州商代墓葬出土的一件十分复杂的中期卣上，主题的兽面纹无疑具有 II 式的风格，其立体的把手采用了单独铸造后再接铸的技术，其肩部装饰着"原始的" I 式细线（方闻，1980：第 107 页）。

以下河南部分商代中期墓葬出土青铜器的统计表显示出具有 I 式和 II 式装饰的器物大量并存的现象。（I 式：单纯装饰 I 式纹样的器物；Ia 式：装饰简单平行凸线的器物；II 式：单纯装饰 II 式纹样的器物；I+II 式：装饰两种纹样的器物。表中不包括杜朴所说的过渡阶段的地点。有关资料见杜朴，1985：第 60—62 页。）

地点	I 式	Ia 式	II 式	I+II 式
铭功路 M2		3	3	
铭功路 M4	1			1
二七路 M1	1		4（?）	
二七路 M2	1	2	1	
琉璃阁 M110	1		2	
琉璃阁 M148	1		1	
李楼 1 号	1		2	

商代中期窖藏中出土的器物也同样有混同性的特点。例如，郑州向阳回民食品厂出土的 13 件青铜器装饰有 I 式和 II 式图案，也有罗樾所划分的 III 式饕餮。这组器物上还有一些出现了高浮雕的图像（河南省文物研究所、郑州市博物馆，1983）。

128 For example, two of the four vessels from Tomb no. 110 in Huixian bear designs in fine relief lines (Style I), whereas similar motifs on other vessels are delivered in broad, ribbon-like bands (Style II) (see Guo Baojun, 1981: 10; pl. 4, nos. 1-2; pl. 5, no. 1). As I discuss below, the thirteen bronzes from a storage pit (H1) near Zhengzhou display combinations of various styles.
例如，辉县 110 号墓出土的四件青铜器中有两件装饰有凸起的细线图案（I 式），而同样的装饰母题在另外两件器物上则呈现为宽带状（II 式）（见郭宝钧，1981：第 10 页；插图 4，1-2；插图 5，1）。我在下文将谈到，郑州附近的一个窖藏（H1）出土的十三件青铜器上有不同风格的装饰结合在一起的例子。

129 For one such example, a *jia* vessel in the British Museum, see W. Watson, 1962: 53, pl. 8.
大英博物馆收藏的一件斝就是这样的一个例子，见华维廉，1962：第 53 页，插图 8。

130 In addition to Fu Hao's tomb, another example is Shang royal mausoleum no. 1400 at Anyang. See W. Watson, 1962: 53.
除了妇好墓，安阳侯家庄 1400 号商王陵提供了另一个例子，见华维廉，1962：第 53 页。

131 In an excellent study of Shang bronze styles, Huber (1981: 37) distinguishes "two new and diametrically opposed decorative styles [which] appear during the Late Anyang period": "on the one hand we find vessels decorated by narrow horizontal bands of purely geometric patterns, with the largest portion of the surface left plain; on the other, designs covering the entire surface in high relief, stark in effect, with minimal linear embellishment, and typically raised from a ground that is perfectly smooth."
胡博在一篇讨论商代青铜器风格的精彩论文中（1981：第 37 页），区分出"安阳晚期阶段新出现的两种完全相反的装饰风格"："一方面，我们发现有的器物饰有由纯粹几何图案构成的装饰带，而大部分的器表为素面；另一方面，有的器物表面以高浮雕覆盖，极少具有线性修饰，图案从平滑的器表上凸起，极富特色。"

132 In fact, Loehr (1953: 50) has noticed the coexistence of Style I and II designs on a single bronze: "It may be argued that this Chueh [i.e., a *jue* in the Sumitomo Collection] shows Styles I and II to be coeval; that they overlap; that they differ only technically. Secondly, the typological position of this Chueh has to be considered. A third inference would be this: the decor of the Chueh reveals that Style I lives on in the period of Style II without becoming obsolete. And indeed we shall have to reckon with a continually widening repertory of motifs: perpetuated older ones existed side by side with the new ones and did not necessarily recede as these later were invented." Although Loehr's speculation is very suggestive, he nevertheless considered that such a "hybrid" bronze, as he called it, combines "in its decoration elements of two successive styles, and on that account might be termed a 'transitional' specimen" (*ibid.*, 49).
实际上，罗樾（1953：第 50 页）已经注意到 I 式和 II 式纹样共存于同一件青铜器上的现象："可以认为这件爵（住友藏品）说明 I 式和 II 式的年代是相同的，它们部分地重叠，仅仅在技术上有所区别。其次，必须考虑到这件爵的类型学位置。第三种推测是：这个爵的装饰显示出在 II 式纹样流行的时代，I 式纹样仍然存在，并没有被遗忘。我们必须认识到青铜器装饰题材库持续扩大的现象，即持续存在的旧样式与新样式共存，并不因为新样式的发明而消失。”尽管罗樾的思考极富启发性，但他认为这种他所说的“混同式”青铜器“在装饰因素上结合了两种前后相继的样式，因此可以视作‘过渡’阶段的标本”（同前，第 49 页）。

133 Harrie A. Vanderstappen (Vanderstappen et al., 1989: 28) has noticed that "even granting overlaps and progressive and retrogressive steps in the process, Loehr's sequence is seriously challenged by the content of Tomb 5 of Fu Hao. Among the many bronze vessels found in the tomb [of Fu Hao], there is clear evidence establishing the contemporaneity of Loehr's styles III through V—instead of a chronological developmental sequence."
范德本（1989：第 28 页）曾经指出：“即使承认重叠的、进步的和退步的样式都在这一过程中，罗樾的序列仍受到妇好墓青铜器的严峻挑战。在该墓所见的许多青铜器中，有很明显的例证说明，罗樾的 III 式到 V 式应是一种共时关系，而不是历时的发展关系。”

134 Gombrich, 1984: 261. 贡布里希，1984：第 261 页。

135 *Huainan zi*, 8.123.《淮南子》，卷八，第 123 页。

136 Thorp (1985: 42) employs the concept of "mirror images" in describing the relationship between Style I and II motifs.
杜朴（1985：第 42 页）采用了“镜像”的概念来描述 I 式纹样和 II 式纹样母题之间的关系。

137 Loehr, 1968: 13. 罗樾，1968：第 13 页。

138 Thorp (1985: 42) rightly calls attention to the coexistence of Style I and Style II on bronzes from Erligang. His solution is to view these two styles not as a polarity but as variations of a "spectrum": "When many examples of Erligang Phase decoration are scrutinized, one finds many varieties of thick bands and thin lines and considerable free variation in the composition of the motifs."
杜朴（1985：第 42 页）正确地提醒我们，要注意到二里岗青铜器中 I 式和 II 式装饰并存的现象。他的办法是不能将这两种样式看作一种“谱系”中的极性元素，而应当看作变调：“仔细观察二里岗期青铜器装饰的许多例子，我们会发现其装饰母题极为不同，包括宽的带饰、细线纹以及相当自由的变化形式。”

139 Bagley, 1987: 20. 贝格利，1987：第 20 页。

140 Henan Provincial Institute of Cultural Relics and the Zhengzhou Museum,1983.
河南省文物研究所、郑州博物馆，1983。

141 Although these examples, especially the pair of square *ding*, have convinced me that their opposing decorative styles must have been deliberate, I do not want to suggest that this is a universal rule in mid-Shang bronze art. For example, a pair of *zun* from the same pit are basically identical in decorative style (Style I), although the lines on one vessel are slightly thicker than those on the other. Another pair of square *ding* discovered in 1974 in Zhengzhou are both embellished with Style I masks (see Henan Provincial Museum, 1975).
虽然这些例子，特别是那对方鼎，使我相信它们风格相反的装饰是有意为之，但是，我不认为这是商代中期青铜器艺术的一种普遍法则。例如，同一窖藏还出土一对尊，尽管其中一件的线条比另一件略粗，但两件的装饰基本上是相同的（I 式）。1974 年郑州出土的另一对方鼎也都装饰有 I 式的兽面（见河南省博物馆，1975）。

142 Chinese archaeologists periodize the late Shang into four phases and term them Yinxu I-IV. Yinxu I, which predates the Wu Ding period (*ca.* 1200-1180 B.C.), is represented by a series of tombs excavated both in Anyang and in other places. Bronzes from these sites differ markedly from those found in Fu Hao's tomb of the Wu Ding period, but basically continue the mid-Shang tradition while exhibiting some significant changes. See Zheng Zhenxiang and Chen Zhida, 1985: 39-45; Thorp, 1988: 48-49.
中国考古学家将晚商划分为四期，即殷墟 I—IV 期。殷墟 I 期早于武丁时期（约前 1200—前 1180 年），以安阳和其他地点出土的一系列墓葬为代表。这些地方出土的青铜器与武丁时期的妇好墓所出土的青铜器明显不同，但在显示出一些重要变化的同时，又基本延续了商代中期的传统。见郑振香、陈志达，1985：第 39—45 页；杜朴，1988：第 48—49 页。

143 Loehr, 1968: 12. 罗樾，1968：第 12 页。

144 W. Fong, 1980: 182. 方闻，1980：第 182 页。

294 145 Thorp (1988: 57) has made an important discovery related to my contention here. As he comments on the relationship between Style IV and V: "The two 'styles' bear a complementary relationship to each other. Differing in technique but not in function, they are perhaps better regarded as a single change in the way that Shang bronze designers created their art. In that respect, the situation is comparable to styles I and II of the Early Shang period, which again were different methods of rendering invoked in the service of a common goal. While I continue to refer to Loehr's styles as a five-part sequence, it may also be apt to think of the total development as a three-part evolution in which the first and third phases exhibit prominent alternative techniques. . . . It seems therefore that each phase of Shang decoration had its complementary aspects. This complementarity also

strikes one as a pervasive aspect of Shang culture as a whole."

杜朴（1988：第 57 页）有一项与我的论点相关的重要发现。他在讨论 IV 式和 V 式纹样的关系时说："这两种'风格'有一种彼此互补的关系。它们或许更应被看作商代青铜设计者在创作过程中的同一次变化，二者的技术不同，但功能无异。在这一点上，可以和商代早期 I 式和 II 式纹样相比较，后者同样运用了不同的表现方式服务于同样的目的。在继续把罗樾的风格划分看作一种五个阶段序列的同时，我也倾向于将整个发展过程看作三个阶段的演进，其中第一和第三阶段在技术上很明显地表现出了可选择性的特征……因此，商代装饰艺术的每一个阶段都有其补充性的方面。这种补充性也表明了商代文化作为一个整体的连贯性。"

146 Some scholars believe that instead of being Wu Ding's consort, the deceased named Fu Hao in this tomb belonged to a later period. This opinion has been rejected by most scholars. For the absolute date of Wu Ding's reign, see Keightley, 1978*a*: 203, table 14.

有的学者认为墓主妇好不是武丁的配偶，而属于更晚的阶段。这一观点为多数学者所反对。关于武丁时期的绝对年代，见吉德炜，1978a：第 203 页，表 14。

147 In Bagley's words, such an image "ceases to be synonymous with the pattern filling entire frieze units, and becomes instead a well-defined creature displayed against a background, in the frame provided by the frieze unit" (W. Fong, 1980: 179).

用贝格利的话来说，这种形象"不再是填充花纹带的图案，而变成了与地纹对立的完整意义上的物像，花纹带则成为这种物象的边框"。见方闻，1980：第 179 页。

148 Flanges are seen on a limited number of mid-Shang bronzes, such as those catalogued in *Henan chutu Shang-Zhou qingtongqi*, pls. 76, 126.

商代中期使用扉棱的青铜器数量有限，这类青铜器见《河南出土商周青铜器》，插图 76、126。

149 For a detailed discussion of "flanges," see Bagley, 1987: 1.4, 1.5; the decorative function of "flanges" is also pointed out in Rawson, 1990: 2a. 27.

关于"扉棱"的详细讨论，见贝格利，1987：1.4，1.5；"扉棱"装饰功能的讨论见罗森，1990：2a.27。

150 In analyzing a *lei* in the Shanghai Art Museum, Jessica Rawson (1990: 2a. 29) observes that "each of the surface compartments formed by its flanges and horizontal divisions encloses a different dragon or *taotie*. . . . It is highly unlikely that any of these designs was considered to represent a particular beast, whether natural or imaginary."

罗森（1990: 2a.29）在分析上海美术馆所藏罍时指出："器表由扉棱和水平

线构成的每一个单元内都有一条不同的龙或饕餮……这些形象极不可能表现了一种特殊的动物，或者是自然的，或者是想象中的。

151 Z. X. Zheng, 1986: 90. 郑振香，1986：第 90 页。

152 We know from archaeological excavations that marble sculptures representing mythical animals were arranged in Shang royal tombs, which were also painted with murals of similar images. Extant bronzes, jade, and ivory vessels, musical instruments, weapons, and chariot fittings are universally decorated with motifs from the same repertoire (see C. Li, 1977: 209-34).
从考古发掘得知，商代王室墓葬中有大理石雕刻的神异动物，同样的形象也见于壁面装饰中。现存的青铜器、玉器、象牙器、乐器、武器，以及车马器都普遍采用这些流行的装饰母题（李济，1977：第 209—234 页）。

153 See Gombrich, 1969: 258-61. 贡布里希，1969：第 258—261 页。

154 See Cao Shuqin, 1988. 曹淑琴，1988。

155 Kane, 1973. 凯恩，1973。

156 Keightley, 1991: 17. 吉德炜，1991：第 17 页。

157 A popular opinion considers "Mother Xin" Fu Hao's temple name. But Keightley (*ibid.*, 16-17) argues that this is impossible because Fu Hao's temple name could be decided only after her death. He thus proposed that the bronzes bearing the names "Queen Mother Xin" and "Queen Tu Mother Gui" must have been used by Fu Hao in her lifetime to worship these ancestresses and that these vessels were buried with her.
研究者普遍认为"母辛"为妇好的庙号。但是吉德炜（1991：第 16—17 页）认为此说不可能成立，因为妇好只有死后才会有庙号。因此他认为有"司母辛"和"司䍙母"铭文的铜器应是妇好生前用来祭祀其女性祖先的，这些器物在她死后成为其随葬品。

158 Keightley (*ibid.*) believes that a person's temple name was chosen by divination after his or her death and hence one could not possibly make a bronze with one's own temple name.
吉德炜（1991）认为，一个人的庙号要在其死后通过占卜来确定，所以此人不可能用自己的庙号来制作青铜器。

159 Keightley (*ibid.*, 16) speculates on this issue and reaches a different conclusion: "I assume that even in the case of the shortest inscriptions, which may consist of only two words, like 'Father Ji,' the full but unrecorded message was 'This is a vessel that I, the maker, made for my late Father [or Mother, Grandmother, etc.], whose temple name is Ji and who is to receive cult, on *ji* days, in this vessel.'" In my opinion, one of the distinct

features of such short inscriptions is their omission of the commissioner, or "I" in Keightley's reading. Only in later and longer inscriptions did a commissioner made him or herself known.
吉德炜（同上，第 16 页）对该问题进行了研究，他有不同的结论："我推测即使那些只有两个字的最简短的铭文，如'父己'，其没有被写出的完整意思应是'这是我（作器者）为已故的父亲（或母亲、祖母等）制作的铜器，其庙号为己，他（或她）在己日通过这件器物接受礼拜'。"我认为，这类简短铭文的一个鲜明的特征是省略了作器者（即吉德炜所说的"我"）的名字。只有在后来的长篇铭文中作器者才为人所知。

160 None of the 190 inscriptions on the bronzes from Fu Hao's tomb include the verb "to make." This suggests that the practice of including the verb in inscriptions must date to after the early thirteenth century B.C., when the tomb was constructed.
妇好墓所出土的 190 件带铭文的青铜器中，没有一件有动词"作"。这说明在铭文中出现这一动词的做法应晚于构建此墓的公元前 13 世纪早期。

161 These inscriptions have been gathered in Yetts, 1949; Chen Mengjia, 1954; Bagley, 1987: 525-30; Kane, 1973.
对这些铭文的汇集，见 Yetts, 1949；陈梦家，1954；贝格利，1987：第 525—530 页；凯恩，1973。

162 *ZZ*, 1911.《左传》，第 1911 页。

163 The inscriptions on one group of bronze vessels record a single place, perhaps the Shang royal temple, in which the award ceremonies were held. These include a *jiao* vessel in the Sumitomo Collection (20 *si* of Di Xin's reign; see Bagley, 1987: fig. 24.6), a *gui* vessel in the Guangdong Museum (see *ibid.*, fig. 103.13), the Shu Si Zi *ding* tripod (inscription translated in the text), and the Li *gui* (see Fig. 1.57) made at the beginning of the Western Zhou (see W. Fong, 1980: no. 41). Moreover, the inscription on the Si *gui* in the Sackler Art Museum in Washington, D.C., reads: "On the day *wuchen*, Bi Shi awarded me, Si, a sack of (large?) cowries from X-place, which I then used to make this precious vessel for [my deceased] father Yi. It was in the eleventh month, the king's twentieth *si*, a day in the *xie* sacrificial cycle, on the occasion when a pig was sacrificed to Ancestress Wu, King Wu Yi's consort. [Clan emblem]." It is clear that this vessel was also made after Si received an award while participating in a royal sacrifice. For a discussion 295
of this vessel, see Bagley, 1987: fig. 103 and interpretation.
一组青铜器上的铭文记载了举行册命典礼的一个地点，可能是商王的祖庙。其中包括住友藏品中的一件角（帝辛二十祀；见贝格利，1987：图 24.6）、广东省博物馆收藏的一件簋（同前，图 103.13）、叔嗣子鼎（铭文见正文），以及西周初年制作的盠簋［见图 1.57］（方闻，1980: no. 41）。

此外，华盛顿赛克勒美术馆收藏的簋的铭文为："戊辰弜师易（赐）𢦏贝，用乍（作）父乙宝彝。在十月一隹（维）王廿祀，劦日。遘于妣戊武乙奭豕一。（族徽）"（大意：在戊辰这一天，弜师在某地赏赐我——隹——一袋贝。我用来为我已故的父亲乙制作这件珍贵的礼器。这是在王进行第二十祀的第十一月劦日。在这时，还将一头猪献祭给了武王乙的配偶戊。）很明显，这件簋是𢦏在参加王室的祭祀并获得册命后制作的。关于这件器物的讨论，见贝格利，1987：图 103 及其解释。

164 This *ding* was excavated from a sacrificial pit in Hougang at Anyang; see Guo Moruo, 1960: 1-5; Bagley, 1987: fig. 103.14.
这件鼎出土于安阳后冈的一个祭祀坑；见郭沫若，1960：第 1—5 页；贝格利，1987：图 103.14。

165 These bronzes include a *you* vessel in the Hakutsuru Bijutsukan (see Bagley, 1987: fig. 71.4); a *yan* tripod in the Museum of Chinese History in Beijing (*ibid.*, fig. 103.12), a *gui* vessel, whose inscription is published in Luo Zhenyu, 1936: 8.33.2, and a rhinoceros *zun* vessel (see Fig. 1.56) in the Asian Art Museum of San Francisco (Bagley, 1987: fig. 103.11).
这些青铜器包括白鹤美术馆收藏的一件卣（贝格利，1987：图 71.4）、北京中国国家博物馆收藏的一件甗（同前，图 103.12）、罗振玉（1936：8.33.2）著录过铭文的一件簋，以及旧金山亚洲美术馆收藏的一件犀尊（见图 1.56，贝格利，1987：图 103.11）。

166 Some statements are general, as indicated by the inscription of the Zuoce Ban *yan* (inscription translated in the text). Others are more specific; for example, the Xiaozi X *you* in the Hakutsuru Bijutsukan first records a superior's command in the context of the military campaign: "On the day *yisi*, Zi ordered [me], Xiaozi X, to engage the Ren [Fang] at X-place. Zi awarded me, X, two strings of cowries. Zi said, 'The cowries are in recognition of your merits.' I, X, then used them to make this vessel for [my deceased] mother Xin. It was in the tenth month, when Zi issued the order to annihilate the chief [?] of the Ren Fang" (see Kane, 1973: 368n55).
如作册般甗铭文（见正文）所见，有些陈述是一般性的。有的则比较特别，例如白鹤美术馆所藏小子□卣就记载了征战中一位长官的命令："乙子（巳）子令（命）小子□先乓（以）人于堇。子光商（赏）□一贝二朋。子曰。贝隹（唯）蔑女（汝）䲨（曆）。□用乍（作）母辛彝。才（在）十月二。隹子曰。令侉（望）人方㣇。"（大意：在乙巳这天，子命令我小子□出兵进攻堇地的人方，子赏赐我二朋的贝。子说："这些贝是用来表彰你的功绩的。"我，□，于是用以为我故去的母亲辛制作了这件青铜器。时在十月二，子下令灭掉人方的将领［？］㣇。）（凯恩，1973：第 368 页，n55）。

167 *Ibid.* 同上。

168 For vessels related to these political events, see Rawson, 1990: 2a. 145. The earliest among them is a *gui* made by Li only seven days after the Zhou's conquest of the Shang. It follows the Shang narrative mode of first introducing the historical event; see W. Fong 1980: no. 41.
与这些政治事件有关的青铜器，见罗森，1990：2a. 145。其中年代最早的是盉在周征服商七天后所制作的一件簋。它的铭文遵循了商代的叙事模式，在起始处介绍了这一历史事件；见方闻，1980：no. 41。

169 One such example is a *zun* vessel made by He during the reign of King Cheng. Its inscription reads: "It was at the time when the king moved the Zhou capital to Chengzhou, and offered a *fu* sacrifice in the Hall of Heaven to {his deceased father} King Wu. In the fourth month, on the day *bingxu*, the king was in the Jing Hall and exhorted me, saying: 'In days past, your late ancestor Gong Shi was able to serve King Wen. King Wen accepted the great command, and King Wu carried out the conquest of the Great City of Shang, announcing it to Heaven with the words: "I must dwell in the center and from there rule the people." Now take heed! You must cherish the memory of the services that Gong Shi rendered to Heaven. Sacrifice to him with reverence!' Our king has indeed a virtuous character, compliant to Heaven, and is an inspiring example for my own feebleness. When the king had concluded, I, He, was given thirty strings of cowries, which I have used to make this vessel for sacrifices to Gong Shi. This happened in the king's fifth year." (based on Bagley's trans. in W. Fong, 1980: 198)
其中的一个例子是成王时的何尊。其铭文为："唯王初迁于成周，复禀武王礼。福自天。在四月丙戌。王诰宗小子于京室，曰：'昔在尔考公克逨文王。肆文王受兹大命。唯武王既克大邑商，则廷告于天，曰：余其宅兹中国，自兹乂民。乌虖！尔有唯小子无识，视于公氏，有劳于天，徹命。敬享哉！'唯王恭德裕天，顺我不敏。王咸诰。何赐贝卅朋，用作□公宝尊彝。唯王五祀。"（英译据贝格利的翻译，见方闻，1980：第198页）（大意：周成王开始迁都成周，还按照武王的礼，举行福祭，祭礼是从天室开始的。四月丙戌，成王在京室诰训"宗小子"们，说："过去你们的父亲能为文王效劳。文王接受了大命，武王战胜了'大邑商'，就向天卜告，说：'我要住在中央地区，从这里来治理民众。'鸣呼！你们或者还是小子，还有知识，要看公氏的样子，有功劳于天，完成使命，敬受享祀啊！"王是有恭德，能够顺天的，教训我们这些不聪敏的人。王的诰训讲完后，何被赏赐贝三十串，何用来做□公的祭器。这时是成王五年。）（据唐兰的译文，见唐兰《何尊铭文解释》，《文物》，1976年第1期，第60页——译者注）

170 Major studies of these inscriptions include Qi Sihe, 1947; Chen Mengjia, 1955-56, 1956; Huang Ranwei, 1978; Zhang Guangyu, 1979; Kane, 1982-83; Chen Hanping, 1986.

对这些铭文的研究主要有齐思和，1947；陈梦家，1955—1956、1956；黄然伟，1978；张光裕，1979；凯恩，1982—1983；陈汉平，1986。

171 Among the 80 examples Chen Hanping (1986: 21-25) lists, only three were from the early Zhou.
陈汉平（1986：第 21—25 页）所列举的 80 个例子中，只有三例属于周初。

172 Bagley's trans. in W. Fong, 1980: 246-47.
英译文见贝格利的翻译，方闻，1980：第 246—247 页。

173 "Anciently the intelligent rulers conferred rank on the virtuous, and emoluments on the meritorious; and the rule was that this should take place in the Grand Temple, to show that they did not dare to do it on their own private motion. Therefore, on the day of sacrifice, after the first presenting [of the cup to the representative], the ruler descended and stood on the south of the steps on the east, with his face to the south, while those who were to receive their appointments stood facing the north. The recorder was on the right of the ruler, holding the tablets on which the appointments were written. He read these, and [each man] bowed twice, with his head to the ground, received the writing, returned [home], and presented it in his [own] ancestral temple:—such was the way in which rank and reward were given" (*LJ*, 1605; trans. from Legge, 1967: 2.247). For other ancient records of the "investiture" ceremony, see Chen Hanping, 1986: 12-20.
"古者明君，爵有德而禄有功，必赐爵禄于大庙，示不敢专也。故祭之日，一献，君降立于阼阶之南，南乡，所命北面。史由君右，执策命之。再拜稽首，受书以归，而舍奠于其庙。此爵赏之施也。"《礼记》，第 1605 页；英译据理雅各，1967：2.247。其他文献中对于"册命"仪式的记载，见陈汉平，1986：第 12—20 页。

174 Trans. based on Legge 1967: 2.251. The same idea is stated elsewhere in the text: "In this way the superior men of antiquity panegyrised the excellent qualities of their ancestors, and clearly exhibited them to future generations, thereby having the opportunity to introduce their own personality and magnify their states" (*ibid.*, 253).
英译据理雅各，1967：2.251。同样的思想还见于该文另一处："古之君子，论撰其先祖之美，而明著之后世者也，以比其身，以重其国家如此。"同前，第 253 页。

175 *Ibid.* 同上。

176 Huber, 1981: 33. 胡博，1981：第 33 页。

177 To my knowledge, this style was first defined in Kane, 1970: 76-78.
据我所知，凯恩首先对这种风格进行了界定。见凯恩，1970：第 76—78 页。

178 Huber, 1981: 35. 胡博，1981：第 35 页。

179 Quoted in *ibid.*, 33. 转引自胡博，1981：第 33 页。

180 Allan, 1991. 艾兰，1991。

181 For an excellent description of this development, see Rawson, 1980: 103-23; 1987: 33-45; and 1990.
对这一发展过程的精彩描述，见罗森，1980：第 103—123 页；1987：第 33—45 页；1990。

182 The Chinese archaeologist Guo Baojun (1959: 13) was the first to study such "vessel sets" and invented the term *lieding* (a series of *ding*). He concluded: "During the Zhou from King Xuan and King Li on, rich nobles often used groups of *lieding* consisting of 3, 5, 7, or 9 bronzes in decreasing size as tomb furnishings." Other studies of such groups of bronzes include Yu Weichao and Gao Ming, 1978-79; Yu Weichao, 1985; Wang Shimin, 1987.
中国考古学家郭宝钧（1959:第 13 页）首先对这种"器物群"进行了研究，并使用了"列鼎"一词。他指出:"周自厉宣以降，统治阶级中的一些阔绰者，都爱用三、五、七、九成组的大小相次的列鼎随葬。"其他关于这种青铜器群的研究包括俞伟超、高明，1978—1979;俞伟超，1985;王世民，1987。

183 See Guo Baojun, 1963: 16. 郭宝钧，1963：第 16 页。

184 Lucretius wrote in his poem *De Rerum Natura*: "The earliest weapons were
the hands, nails, and teeth; then came stone and clubs. These were followed 296
by iron and bronze, but bronze came first, the use of iron not being known until later" (MacCurdy, 1933: 1.9). In interpreting objects from burial mounds, Johann von Eckart asserted that there must have been an age prior to the invention of metal tools and that this era (Stone Age) was followed by a Bronze Age and finally an Age of Iron (see Sharer and Ashmore, 1979: 52).
卢克莱修在其《物性论》一诗中说:"最早的工具是手、指甲和牙齿；然后是石块和棍棒。再接下来是铁和青铜，但青铜首先出现，铁在后来才被认识。"见麦柯迪，1933：1.9。在解释坟墓中出土的器物时，约翰·冯·艾科特指出，一定有一个时代早于金属工具的发明，这个时代（石器时代）的后继者是青铜时代，最后是铁器时代。见沙雷尔、阿什莫尔，1979：第 52 页。

185 See Daniel, 1967: 93-95. 丹尼尔，1967：第 93—95 页 .

186 See *ibid.*; McNairn, 1980: 74-77. 同上；麦克奈恩，1980：第 74—77 页。

187 K. C. Chang, 1980*b*: 35-36. 张光直，1980b：第 35—36 页 .

188 Orenstein's word; quoted in *ibid.*, 202. 此为奥瑞斯坦因的话，转引自上书第 202 页。

189 For some scholars' opinions, see Lei Haizong, 1957; Yu Xingwu, 1957, 1958; Chen Mengjia, 1956.
有关这些学者的观点，见雷海宗，1957；于省吾，1957、1958；陈梦家，1956。

190 K. C. Chang, 1980*b*: 45. 张光直，1980b：第 45 页。

191 *Ibid.*, 35, 45. 同上，第 35、45 页。

192 The Shang royal army was equipped with bronze weapons and chariots (see Zou Heng, 1979: 75-82).
关于商王军队装备有青铜兵器和马车的讨论，见邹衡，1979：第 75—82 页。

193 Hu Houxuan's estimate, in Guo Baojun, 1963: 21.
关于胡厚宣对这一数量的估计，见郭宝钧，1963：第 21 页。

194 An Zhimin, 1954: 91; *Zhengzhou Erligang*, 37.
安志敏，1954：第 91 页；《郑州二里岗》，第 37 页。

195 Guo Baojun, 1963: 21. 郭宝钧，1963：第 21 页。

196 Jiangxi Provincial Institute of Archaeology and Jiangxi Xin'gan Museum, 1991; esp. 8-10.
江西省考古研究所、江西省新干县博物馆，1991；特别是第 8—10 页。

197 For the positions of the tomb furnishings, see *ibid.*, 2-4.
关于这些随葬品的摆放位置，见江西省考古研究所、江西省新干县博物馆，1991：第 2—4 页。

198 The most important agricultural ritual in Bronze Age China was the plowing ceremony (see Yang Kuan, 1965: 218-33). Interestingly, among the "tools" from the Xin'gan tomb are three large bronze plows decorated with *taotie* masks.
中国青铜时代最重要的农业礼仪是"籍礼"。有关讨论见杨宽，1965：第 218—233 页。有趣的是，在新干墓葬出"农具"中，有三件装饰有饕餮纹的大型青铜犁。

199 *Renmin ribao*, May 13, 1961; see also Gao Zhixi, 1963: 648; Institute of Archaeology, CASS, 1984: 242.
《人民日报》，1961 年 5 月 13 日；又见高至喜，1963：第 648 页；中国社会科学院考古研究所，1984：第 242 页。

200 Gao Zhixi, 1963: 646-48; Hunan Provincial Museum, 1972; see also Wenwu Press, 1979: 311.

高至喜，1963：第 646—648 页；湖南省博物馆，1972；文物出版社，1979：第 311 页。

201 See Guo Baojun, 1963: 20.
郭宝钧，1963：第 20 页。

202 For a summary of these finds, see Institute of Archaeology, CASS, 1984: 218.
关于这些发现的综述，见中国社会科学院考古研究所，1984：第 218 页。

203 Shi Zhangru, 1933; An Zhimin, 1947. 石璋如，1933；安志敏，1947。

204 Lei Haizong, 1957: 42. 雷海宗，1957：第 42 页。

205 Yu Xingwu, 1957, 1958. 于省吾，1957、1958。

206 Chen Mengjia, 1956: 541-42. 陈梦家，1956：第 541—542 页。

207 For discussions about the relationship between Childe's ideas and Marxist historical materialism, see McNairn, 1980: chap. 6; Thomas, 1982.
关于柴尔德思想与马克思历史唯物主义的关系的讨论，见麦克奈恩，1980：第 6 章；托马斯，1982。

208 Tang Lan, 1960. Tang's opinion has been repeated, "confirmed," and elaborated by some recent authors, see Chen Zhenzhong, 1982; Ma Chengyuan et al., 1991: 24-44; Li Xueqin, 1991*b*: 36. Among these scholars, Chen Zhenzhong "updated" Tang Lan's study by collecting more examples of Shang-Zhou "tools." He provided an impressive inventory of 207 such examples. This list, however, includes very few excavated Shang and Western Zhou objects. There are only two "hoes" (6.2 cm and 4 cm wide, respectively) and seventeen "spades" (seven from Fu Hao's tomb) from this period. Methodologically, Chen also accepted all the assumptions Tang Lan made more than thirty years ago. His study is therefore not reviewed here in the text.
唐兰，1960。唐兰的观点新近被有些学者重复、"证实"和阐发，见陈振中，1982；马承源等，1991：第 24—44 页；李学勤，1991b：第 36 页。在这些学者中，陈振中收集了更多商周"工具"的例子，因此扩充了唐兰的研究。他所提供的一个详细目录包括 207 个例子，给人印象深刻。然而，这个目录中几乎没有出土的商周遗物。只有这一时期的两件"锄"（分别宽 6.2 厘米和 4 厘米）和 17 件"铲"（其中 7 件出自妇好墓）。从方法论上讲，陈振中仍然接受了三十多年前唐兰的设想。所以他的研究不再在这部分的正文中加以评论。

209 Among these finds, for example, the 1,928 objects found in Fu Hao's tomb include 468 bronzes, weighing 1,625 kg. The excavators have identified some of these bronzes as "tools," but these are chisels with relief *taotie* masks, knives with intricate open work designs, and spades with fragile hooked

shoulders. It is apparent that these objects could hardly have been used in real productive activities (see Institute of Archaeology, CASS, 1980: 15, 100-103). Two years after the excavation of the Fu Hao tomb, some 140 bronzes were found in the tomb of Marquis Yi of the Eastern Zhou state of Zeng; a set of bronze bells from this tomb alone weighed 2,500 kg. Archaeologists failed to find even a single bronze implement from the tomb that could have been used in production (see Hubei Provincial Museum, 1980: 1-2).
例如，在这些发现中，妇好墓出土器物达1928件，其中468件青铜器，重达1625千克。发掘者从中确定有些青铜器为“工具”，但它们实际上是铸有饕餮纹的凿子，具有复杂的透雕图案的刀，以及具有脆弱的钩状肩的铲子。很清楚，这些物品几乎不可能用于真正的生产活动。（见中国社会科学院考古研究所，1980：第15页、第100—103页）。妇好墓发掘两年后，东周时期的曾侯乙墓又出土了大约140件青铜器，仅是其中的一套编钟就重达2500千克。但是发掘者没有在该墓中发现一件可能用于生产的青铜工具。见湖北省博物馆，1980：第1—2页。

210 Tang Lan, 1960: 20-22. 唐兰，1960：第20—22页。

211 This argument is made in Chen Mengjia, 1956: 541-42. It might be argued that tools were probably not buried in tombs, but this contention is again rejected by archaeology: thousands of stone tools were discovered in Shang royal tombs, and virtually no bronze implements have been found in excavated Shang-Zhou village sites.
关于这个论点，见陈梦家，1956：第541—542页。论者或可提出工具不用于随葬，但这一观点同样得不到考古学的支持：在商王室的墓葬中曾出土数以千计的石质工具，而在商周村落遗址的发掘中也未发现过青铜工具。

212 *Yuejue shu*, 50. 《越绝书》，第50页。

213 For the “achievements” and historical symbolism of the Yellow Emperor, see H. Wu, 1989: 158-59.
关于黄帝的“功绩”及历史象征意义的讨论，见巫鸿，1989：第158—159页。

214 See, e.g., *Guo yu* (“Qi yu”) and *Guanzi*, 156.
例如《国语》（“齐语”）和《管子》，第156页。

215 Clarke et al., 1985: 12. 克拉克等，1985：第12页。

216 *Ibid.*, 5; see also Althusser, 1971; Poulantzas, 1973: 99-105.
克拉克等，1985：第5页；阿尔都塞，197；普兰查斯，1973：第99—105页。

217 Miller and Tilley, 1984: 5. 米勒、蒂利，1984：第5页。

218 Foucault, 1981: 94; see also Foucault, 1977, 1980; Miller and Tilley, 1984: 5-9.
福柯，1981：第94页；福柯，1977, 1980；米勒、蒂利，1984；第5—9页。

219 For criticism of Foucault's interpretation of power, see Miller and Tilley, 1984: 7.
对福柯有关权力解释的评论，见米勒、蒂利，1984：第 7 页。

220 K. C. Chang, 1980*b*: 45; quotation from *ZZ*, 1911.
张光直，1980b：第 45 页；语出《左传》，第 1911 页。

221 Benton, 1981. 本顿，1981。

222 This interpretation is given in Miller and Tilley, 1984: 7.
这种解释见米勒、蒂利，1984：第 7 页。

223 *Ibid.* 同上。

224 K. C. Chang, 1983: 9-16. 张光直，1983：第 9—16 页。

225 See Luo Kun, 1982: 178-91. Military conquests were not, however, the only means of accumulating wealth. Progress in production was achieved during the Shang-Zhou period through other means, including the development 297
of irrigation systems, new technology, and the organization of labor. For example, it is commonly believed that the establishment of the Xia was a consequence of a grand water project directed by the dynastic founder, Yu, and the Zhou developed the famous *jingtian* (well-field) system.
罗焜，1982：第 178—191 页。然而，军事征伐并不是积累财富的唯一手段。商周时期生产的进步还可以通过其他的手段取得，包括灌溉系统、新技术和劳动组织方式等方面的发展。例如，人们普遍相信夏的建立就是其开创者禹所率领的治水工程的结果，周则发展了著名的井田制。

226 The flourishing of the Shang during this period is best reflected in the abundant furnishings of Fu Hao's tomb, among which many objects are from remote regions. More than 300 inscriptions on oracle bones record Wu Ding's military expeditions against the Gong Fang; over 70 inscriptions pertain to the wars with the Tu Fang. Some of these expeditions were led by Fu Hao.
妇好墓丰富的随葬品反映了这一时期商的繁荣，其中有的物品来自远方。有 300 多条卜辞记载了武丁军队对工方的征伐；70 多条与对土方的战争有关。这些战役有些是由妇好指挥的。

227 I discuss the social and political significance of Western Zhou investitures in Chapter 2, second section, "From Temple to Palace."
我将在第二章的第二节"从宗庙到宫殿"中讨论西周册命礼的社会和政治意义。

228 *LJ*, 1348; Legge, 1967: 1.248.
《礼记》，第 1348 页；英译据理雅各，1967：1.248。

229 In Foucault's words (1981: 93), "it is the moving substrata of force relations, which by virtue of their inequality, constantly engender states of power."
用福柯（1981:93）的话说，"正是权力关系底层由于不平等所产生的动荡，才不断地形成了权力的状态"。

230 Clarke et al., 1985: 4-6. 克拉克等，1985：第4—6页。

231 The original passage in *Yi Zhou shu*, 53, states that King Wu obtained "the Nine Tripods and *sanwu* (three shamans)." In the *SJ* account of the same episode, the term *sanwu* is replaced by *baoyu* (precious jades). Because the characters for *sanwu* and *baoyu* are similar in shape, Tang Lan (1979: 3) has suggested that the correct term should be *baoyu*, *sanwu* being a copyist's mistake. The present version of *Yi Zhou shu* includes documents of different dates and schools. According to Jiang Shanguo (1988: 440), only ten articles in this collection, including "Ke Yin," "Shi fu," "Shang shi," "Du yi," and "Zuo Luo," are authentic works of the Shang and Zhou period and comparable with the *Book of Documents* in historical value. In this study, I draw evidence only from these five documents.
《逸周书》（第53页）的一段原文记载了武王获取了"九鼎"和"三巫"。在《史记》对此事的记载中，"三巫"一词被替换为"宝玉"。因为"三巫"和"宝玉"的字形相近，唐兰（1979:第3页）认为原文应为"宝玉"，"三巫"系抄本之误。现存的《逸周书》版本包括了不同时代和不同流派的文字。据蒋善国（1988：第440页）的看法，只有其中十篇属于商周时期的作品，其历史价值可以与《尚书》相比，这些篇章包括"克殷解""世俘解""商誓解""都邑解"和"作雒解"等。在此，我只从这五篇中选取材料。

232 *ZZ*, 1743. 《左传》，第1743页。

233 *Yi jing*, 96. 《易经》，第96页。

234 According to Sima Qian (*SJ*, 133), King Cheng ordered the Duke of Zhou and the Duke of Shao to determine the location of the capital, or the "dwelling of the Tripods through divination." Li Daoyuan (*SJZ*, 210) recorded that "Jiashan is the name of a town in Ru. After a divination was made, the Tripods were located at this place, which was also the king's eastern capital. It was called the New Capital and was used by the king as his own city. The southeastern [gate] of the city was called the Gate of Tripods."
据司马迁（《史记》，第133页）记载，成王命周公和召公去决定都城的位置，"卜申视""居九鼎"。郦道元（《水经注》，第210页）记载"郏，山名，鄏，地邑也。十年定鼎为王之东都，谓之新邑，是为王城。其城东南，名曰鼎门"。

235 One of these vessels is a *zun* made by He whose inscription begins with the sentence: "It is the time when King Cheng first moved to the capital Chengzhou" (see W. Fong, 1980: no. 42).
这类器物中，有一件是"何"所作的尊，其铭文的开头说："维王初迁宅于成周。"见本章注 169。

236 Yu Weichao (1985: 68-69) and Gao Ming argue that this represents the Western Zhou system, which was then changed during the Eastern Zhou when feudal princes began to use nine *ding*. Sima Qian (*SJ*, 1734) called the Nine Tripods "Three *he* and Six *yi*." According to Sima Zhen, the *li* is a type of tripod with baggy legs, and the *yi* is another type of tripod with handles attached to its outer walls. Bronzes of the first type appeared during the mid-Shang, and those of the second type appeared during the Western Zhou and became popular during the Eastern Zhou.
俞伟超（1985：第 68—69 页）和高明认为这属于西周的制度，东周以后诸侯王开始使用九鼎，使这一制度受到挑战。司马迁（《史记》，第 1734 页）称九鼎为"三翮六翼"。据司马贞《索隐》，翮是一种空足的鼎，翼是另一种外壁有把手的鼎。第一种类型的鼎出现于商中期，第二种类型的鼎出现于西周、流行于东周。

237 Clarke et al. 1985: 38. 克拉克等，1985：第 38 页。

238 John Ruskin (1904: 11.6-7) defines "luxuriance" or "extravagance" in artistic taste as "that character of extravagance in the ornament itself which shows that it was addressed to jaded faculties; a violence and coarseness in curvature, a depth of shadow, a lusciousness in arrangement of lines, evidently arriving out of an incapability of feeling the true beauty of chaste form and restrained power." See also Gombrich, 1969: 42-46; Powers, 1986; 1991: 74-82.
拉斯金（1904：11.6—7）将艺术趣味中的"繁茂"和"奢靡"定义为"装饰本身中奢靡的特征表现为专注于厌腻的才能、其弯曲部分强烈而粗糙、阴影过深、线条布局俗恶，有了这些特征，显然就无法再感受由朴素的形式和有限度的力量所构成的真正美感。"见贡布里希，1969：第 42—46 页；包华石，1986；1991：第 74—82 页。

239 *ZZ*, 2124-25. 《左传》，第 2124—2125 页。

240 This is not to say that *liqi* were completely abolished in the late Eastern Zhou. But ritual vessels and luxury goods produced during this period seem very different in form and function. The bronzes from the famous Zhongshan mausoleums in Pingshan, Hebei province, can be classified into two large groups; one group consists of inlaid objects used in palaces, and the other of commemorative bronzes bearing long inscriptions and fashioned in traditional styles.

这并不是说礼器在东周晚期就彻底消亡了。但这时期所制作的礼器在形式和功能上与奢侈品的确不同。河北平山中山王墓出土的青铜器可以分为两大类，一类包括在宫殿中使用的镶嵌华美的器物，另一类纪念性的青铜器则具有长篇的铭文并沿袭着传统风格。

Chapter Two Temple, Palace, and Tomb
㊁ 宗庙、宫殿与墓葬

1 Such studies are often sociological reconstructions and interpretations of *li*; for two representative studies, see Yang Kuan, 1965; Chen Shuguo, 1991.
这类研究通常为社会重构与礼的解说；具有代表性的成果，见杨宽，1965；陈戍国，1991。

2 See Hollier, 1992: 46-47. 奥利耶，1992：第 46—47 页。

3 According to the poem "Gong Liu" in the *Book of Songs* (*Shi jing*, 542), Gong Liu, a Zhou ancestor preceding Tan Fu, had built houses at Xu and Bin. But as Cho-yun Hsu (C. Y. Hsu and Linduff, 1988: 62) has pointed out, Gong Liu only constructed a temporary settlement, whereas "Tan Fu engaged in large-scale construction in order to build a capital. The endeavors differed not only in scale, but also in intent."
据《诗经·大雅·公刘》。早于亶父的周人祖先公刘，已在许、豳安家。但是如许倬云（许倬云、林嘉琳，1988：第 62 页）业已指出的那样，公刘只是建了个临时的居处，而"亶父则建了一座城，从事的是大型的建筑活动，二者不仅表现为规模的不同，而且还表现为动机的不同"。

4 Jing was originally the name of the site where Tan Fu built his town, but later this term came to mean "capital." The character *gong* means temple (see Tang Lan, 1962: 27-28).
京，本为亶父所建之城的名称，而后来演化为"都城"之意。"宫"字意为庙（唐兰，1962：第 27—28 页）。

298 5 Waley's translation quoted in K. C. Chang, 1980*a*: 159-60.
张光直，1980a：第 159—160 页所引韦利的译文。

6 *ZZ*, 1782.《春秋左传》，第 1782 页。

7 *LJ*, 1589, 1258.《礼记》，第 1589、1258 页。

8 *LJ*, 1258; trans. based on Legge 1967: 1.103-4. Legge translated the character *jia* as "clan," but the corresponding Chinese term for "clan" is *zu* (see *LJ*, 1508). Here the character *jia* means "lineage" or "extended family."
同上，第 1258 页。

9 See C. Y. Hsu and Linduff, 1988: 68-93. 许倬云、林嘉琳，1988：第 68—93 页。

10 *Shi jing*, 615; trans. based on Waley, 1978: 270.

《诗经》，第 615 页；英译据韦利，1978：第 270 页。

11 *Shi jing*, 526; trans. from Waley, 1978: 263.
《诗经》，第 526 页；英译据韦利，1978：第 263 页。

12 Here I follow Tang Lan's (1962: 18) interpretation.
此从唐兰（1962：第 18 页）的解释。

13 See Wang Guowei, "Zhou fengjian kao" (On the Zhou dynasty *fengjian*), in *Guantang jilin*, *juan* 12.
见王国维《周封建考》，《观堂集林》卷十二。

14 *Shi jing*, 597; trans. from Waley, 1978: 232.
《诗经》，第 597 页；英译据韦利，1978：第 232 页。

15 *Yi Zhou shu*, 52-53; *SJ*, 125-26. Li Xueqin (1959: 9) suggests that since at the time King Wu was far from his homeland, these rituals must have been held in a temporary or "borrowed" ritual site.
《逸周书》，第 52—53 页；《史记》，第 125—126 页。李学勤（1959：第 9 页）提出，既然当时武王远离故土，这些仪式应该是在一个临时的或者"借来"的场所里举行的。

16 *Yi Zhou shu*, 54.《逸周书》，第 54 页。

17 *Ibid.*, 55; *Lüshi chunqiu*, 53.《逸周书》，第 55 页；《吕氏春秋》，第 53 页。

18 For a brief introduction to King Cheng's reign, see C. Y. Hsu and Linduff, 1988: 123-28.
有关成王统治时期的简要介绍，见许倬云、林嘉琳，1988：第 123-128 页。

19 According to *SJ* (128-29) and the "Du yi" (Planning the city) in *Yi Zhou shu*, King Wu first decided to establish a capital in the Luo area. Wei Tingsheng (1970: 68-70) suggests that the construction of Chengzhou during King Cheng's reign followed and realized King Wu's original plan. Scholars usually focus on the political and military significance of Chengzhou: since trouble most frequently arose from the east where the Shang's old base lay, the "eastern capital" Chengzhou was founded in response. Chengzhou, however, was not simply a strategic town but *the* capital of dynastic Zhou. As discussed later in this section, this significance is most clearly revealed by the building of a new dynastic temple in Chengzhou and by placing the Nine Tripods in this city.
据《史记》（第 128—129 页）和《逸周书·度邑》，武王最先确定建都于洛。卫挺生（1970：第 68—70 页）认为，成王时期成周的建立是遵照武王的原计划实施的。学者们的注意力通常集中于成周的政治、军事地位：由于纷争多自商的古老本部所居的东部而起，故以"东都"成周的建造为回应。然而，成周不仅仅是座战略意义上的城，同时也是周王朝的都城。

如本章下文所论，这一意义通过成周一座新的王朝宗庙建筑及安放在城中的九鼎被揭示得极为清楚。

20 Chengzhou's construction is most carefully recorded in "Shao gao" (The announcement of the Duke of Shao) and "Luo gao" (The announcement concerning Luo) in the *Book of Documents*, and in "Zuo Luo jie" (On the construction of Luo) in *Yi Zhou shu*.
成周的建筑结构在《尚书·召诰》《尚书·洛诰》和《逸周书·作雒解》中有详细记载。

21 *Shang shu*, 211; trans. based on Karlgren, 1950*a*: 48.
《尚书》，第 211 页；英译据高本汉，1950a：第 48 页。

22 In "The Announcement Concerning Luo," the Duke of Zhou described his activities in the first person: "On the day *yimao*, in the morning I came to [the intended] capital Luo. I prognosticated about [the region of] the Li River north of the He; I then prognosticated about [the region] east of the Chen River; but again, it was [the region of] Luo that was ordered. I have sent a messenger [to the king] to bring a map and to present the oracles" (trans. based on Karlgren, 1950*a*: 48).
在《洛诰》中，周公对他的活动做了如下描述："乙卯，朝至于洛师，我卜河朔黎水，我乃卜涧水东，瀍水西，惟洛食。我又卜瀍水东，亦惟洛食。伻来以图，及献卜。"英译据高本汉，1950a：第 48 页。

23 Trans. based on Legge, 1871: 3.451-52; and Karlgren, 1950*a*: 53-55.
参见理雅各，1871：3.451—452；高本汉，1950a：第 53—55 页。

24 Jiaxu *ding*, a Western Zhou bronze vessel, bears an inscription that identifies the temple in Chengzhou as Jingzong or Jinggong (*Xi-Qing xujian jiabian*, 1.36).
一件带有铭文的西周鼎——甲戌鼎，证明成周的庙即是京宗或京宫（《西清续鉴甲编》，1.36）。

25 *Yi Zhou shu*, 55.《逸周书》，第 55 页。

26 *Shi jing*, 525.《诗经》，第 525 页。

27 *Yi Zhou shu*, 78.《逸周书》，第 78 页。

28 The "Methods of Sacrifices" ("Ji fa") section of the *Book of Rites* describes this organization: "Thus the king made for himself seven ancestral temples. . . the temples were—his father's; his grandfather's; his great-grandfather's; his great-great-grandfather's; and the temple of the [High] ancestor. At all of these a sacrifice was offered every month. The temples of the more remote ancestors formed the receptacles for the tablets as they were displaced; they were two, and at these only the seasonal sacrifices were offered" (*LJ*,

1589; trans. from Legge, 1967: 2.204). Zheng Xuan identified these two "more remote ancestors" as King Wen and King Wu; see *ZL*, 753, 784. A somewhat different record is found in the "Royal Regulations" ("Wang zhi") section of the *Book of Rites*: "[The ancestral temple of] the son of Heaven embraced seven fanes [or smaller temples]; three on the left and three on the right, and that of his great ancestor [fronting the south]" (*LJ*, 1335; Legge, 1967: 1.223). Wang Su of the Wei dynasty argued that all six side shrines belonged to the direct ancestors of the living king and did not include the *tiao*. For a brief discussion of these different opinions, see Tang Lan, 1962: 25-26.
《礼记 · 祭法》中记述了这种组织形式："是故，王立七庙……曰考庙，曰王考庙，曰皇考庙，曰显考庙，曰祖考庙，皆月祭之。远庙为祧，有二祧，享尝乃止。"(《礼记》，第 1589 页；英译据理雅各 , 1967：2.204)。郑玄即认为这两位"远祖"是文王和武王；见《周礼》，第 753、784 页。《礼记 · 王制》中的记载有所不同："天子七庙，三昭三穆，与太祖之庙而七。"(《礼记》，第 1335 页；英译据理雅各，1967：1.223）三国魏经学家王肃则认为，所有六个族系祠堂归属于在位之王的直系先祖，其中并不包括"祧"。对上述不同论点的简要讨论，见唐兰，1962：第 25—26 页。

29 Only during King Gong's reign could the four *zhao* and *mu* shrines be fully occupied by dynastic kings (Cheng, Kang, Zhao, and Mu). Tang Lan (1962: 26), however, argued that the organization of the Zhou royal temple must have undergone an important change after King Kang's death, as indicated by the posthumous titles of the two following kings, Zhao and Mu. According to the old sequence of temple worship, King Zhao should have belonged to the *mu* sequence and King Mu should have belonged to the *zhao* sequence. The positions of these two kings in the new system seem to have been reversed.
只有在恭王在位时期，四个昭穆祠堂才全部祭祀四王，即成王、康王、昭王、穆王。但是，唐兰（1962：第 26 页）认为，康王后继两王的谥号分别为昭王、穆王，因此周的王庙在康王死后一定经过了重要的调整。根据庙祭原有的次序，昭王应属于"穆"的一列，而穆王应属于"昭"的一列。在新的系统中，两王的位置似乎被颠倒。

30 *ZL*, 784.《周礼》，第 784 页。

31 According to Wei Tingsheng (1970: 93-101), after King Zhao, Chengzhou was called Zongzhou—the seat of the Zhou lineage.
根据卫挺生的研究（1970：第 93—101 页），昭王以后，成周也被称作宗周——周宗室的所在地。

32 *Ibid.* 同上。

33 *ZZ*, 1743.《春秋左传》，第 1743 页。

34 *SJ*, 133.《史记》，第 133 页。

299 35 This vessel, a *zun* commissioned by He, was found in 1963 in Baoji (Shaanxi). Here I follow Tang Lan's (1976) interpretation of its inscription, which has been supported by a number of scholars, including Wang Rencong (1990) and Chen Changyuan (1982). For a summary of different opinions, see Wang Rencong, 1990.
该器即何尊，1963 年发现于陕西宝鸡。我在本文中采用了唐兰（1976）对何尊铭文的解释，这一解释已为王人聪（1990）、陈昌远（1982）等多位学者所认同。有关不同观点的综述性文字，见王人聪，1990。

36 *LJ*, 1439, 1441, 1595.《礼记》，第 1439、1441、1595 页。

37 *SJ*, 528-32, 622-27; Waley, 1978: 239-80; see also K. C. Chang, 1983: 10-15.
《诗经》，第 528—532 页、第 622—627 页；韦利，1978：第 239—280 页；张光直，1983：第 10—15 页。

38 *SJ*, 528; trans. based on Waley, 1978: 241.
《诗经》，第 528 页；英译据韦利，1978：第 241 页。

39 *SJ*, 614; trans. from Waley, 1978: 269.
同上，第 614 页；英译据韦利，1978：第 269 页。

40 *SJ*, 528; trans. from Waley, 1978: 241.
同上，第 528 页；英译据韦利，1978：第 241 页。

41 *SJ*, 532; trans. from Waley, 1978: 243.
同上，第 532 页；英译据韦利，1978：第 243 页。

42 K. C. Chang, 1980a: 272-283, 297-306.
张光直，1980a：第 272—283 页、第 297—306 页。

43 For preliminary excavations of Qufu by Japanese scholars in the early 1940's, see Komai Kazuchika, 1950. Later excavations are reported in Shandong Team of the Institute of Archaeology, CASS, and the Qufu County Cultural Relics Administration 1965. For a summary of these excavations, see Steinhardt, 1990: 46-47.
20 世纪 40 年代初日本学者对曲阜的初步发掘，见驹井和爱，1950。之后的发掘成果，见中国社会科学院考古研究所山东工作队、曲阜县文物管理委员会，1965。对上述发掘资料的综述，见斯坦哈特，1990：第 46—47 页。

44 Thorp, 1983b: 22-26. 杜朴，1983b：第 22—26 页。

45 *Kaogong ji tu*, 104-7, 113. Zou Heng (1979: 27) first noted similarities in the architectural plan of the Erlitou buildings and a Three Dynasties ancestral temple reconstructed by Dai Zhen. He also contended that the Erlitou

buildings were royal temples during the late Xia dynasty.
《考工记图》，第 104—107、113 页。邹衡（1979：第 27 页）最先注意到二里头两处建筑方案与戴震复原的三代明堂之间的相似点，并且坚定地认为二里头的两处建筑遗址是夏代晚期的王室明堂。

46 Arnheim, 1986: 83. 阿恩海姆，1986：第 83 页。

47 These structures were built inside a "palace town," a walled area at the center of the early Shang city at Shixianggou in Yanshi. Excavation reports of this site include Work Team at the Han-Wei Capital Site in Luoyang, Institute of Archaeology, CASS, 1984; Henan Work Team No. 2 of the Institute of Archaeology, CASS, 1984, 1985, 1988.
这些建筑物建在位于偃师尸乡沟早期商城中央带有围墙的“宫城”之内。该遗址的发掘报道见中国社会科学院考古研究所洛阳汉魏城址工作队，1984；中国社会科学院考古研究所河南第二工作队，1984、1985、1988。

48 Thorp, 1983b: 26-31. A number of Chinese scholars have discussed the date, function, and identification of this building. For an up-to-date discussion, which includes a summary of different opinions, see Chen Quanfang, 1988: 37-69.
杜朴，1983b：第 26—31 页。部分中国学者已经讨论过这座建筑的年代、功能与性质问题，其中包含对不同观点综述的最新讨论，见陈全方，1988：第 37—69 页。

49 *LJ*, 1416; trans. based on Legge, 1967: 1.370-71.
《礼记》，第 1416 页；英译据理雅各，1967：1.370—371。

50 *SJ*, 510-11; see Chang, 1980a: 159-60; trans. slightly modified.
《诗经》，第 510—511 页；张光直，1980a：第 159—160 页；英译文略有调整。

51 *SJ*, 614; trans. based on Waley, 1978: 269.
《诗经》，第 614 页；英译据韦利，1978：第 269 页。

52 *SJ*, 583; trans. based on Waley, 1978: 226.
同上，第 583 页；英译据韦利，1978：第 226 页。

53 I suggest in Chapter 1 that ritual bronzes were not the subject of ancestral worship. As sacrificial vessels, they were instruments of this worship. Although their zoomorphic decorative motifs have often been viewed as representations of deities and even the Lord on High, these are not self-contained icons but are surface elements of ritual objects. In fact, Chinese art before the Eastern Zhou was essentially non-iconic. Spirits and deities remained shapeless, and this is why ancestral deities, the most important subjects of religious worship in ancient China, were represented merely by plain wooden tablets. K. C. Chang (1983: 56-80) contends

that ritual bronzes, as well as their decoration, were a means of religious communication between man and divinities. It is likely that ritual bronzes served such a religious function through metamorphic animal images.
我在第一章里提到青铜礼器不是祖先崇拜的主体，作为祭祀用具，它们是这一礼拜活动的道具。尽管它们的动物装饰母题常常被视为对神甚至对上帝的表现，但这些装饰图像并不是独立完整的偶像，而不过是礼器的表面元素。事实上，在东周以前，中国艺术本质上是非偶像式的，灵与神皆处于无形的阶段，这就是为什么祖先神这一中国古代宗教中最为重要的崇拜对象仅仅以木牌来表示的原因。张光直（1983：第 56—80 页）论到，青铜礼器及其装饰，是人与神之间宗教交流的一种凭借。青铜礼器极有可能是通过变形的动物形象来体现这样一种礼仪功能的。

54 Although many buildings and sacrificial sites have been discovered in Anyang, the site of the last Shang capital, their identities and functions are still the subject of speculation. For discussions, see Shi Zhangru, 1959: 326; 1960. Very limited records about the Shang temple system exist. In this chapter, I focus on the Western Zhou temple, whose structure and ritual activities are described in transmitted texts and bronze inscriptions.
尽管在安阳殷墟发现了很多建筑和祭祀遗址，然而它们的性质与功能，迄今仍是待解的课题。相关的讨论，见石璋如，1959：第 326 页；1960。现存有关商代宗庙的记载极其有限，我于本章集中讨论西周宗庙，其建筑结构与礼仪活动，俱见之于传抄文献与青铜器铭文。

55 Creel, 1937: 336. For a more detailed discussion of the political functions of the royal temple during the Three Dynasties, see Yang Kuan, 1965: 167-74.
顾立雅，1937：第 336 页。有关三代王室宗庙政治功能的详细讨论，见杨宽，1965：第 167—174 页。

56 *LJ*, 1588; see also K. C. Chang, 1983: 15-16.
《礼记》，第 1588 页；张光直，1983：第 15—16 页。

57 *ZZ*, 2134-35; trans. based on Legge, 1871: 5.754.
《春秋左传》，第 2134 页；英译据理雅各，1871：5.754。

58 Legge, 1871: 5.754. The investiture of Kangshu is also recorded in the "Kang gao" (The announcement of Kangshu) in the *Book of Documents*; see Legge, 1871: 3.386-91.
理雅各，1871：5.754。康叔封之事《尚书・康诰》中有载，理雅各，1871：3.386—391。

59 *Xunzi*, 73. Ancient authors attributed the establishment of these vassal states to the Duke of Zhou. But as Cho-yun Hsu (C. Y. Hsu and Linduff 1988: 127) has pointed out, "There was. . . no actual disparity between the activities of kings Ch'eng and K'ang and those of the duke. The regency

of the Duke of Chou and the reign of King Ch'eng overlapped; the duke is simply taken historically as the symbol of the early reigns of the dynasty."
《荀子》，第 73 页。古人往往将这些诸侯国的建立归之于周公，但正如许倬云所指出："……成王、康王与周公的作为并无实际分别，周公摄政时期与成王统治期重叠；周公只是被当作周代早期统治的历史性象征。"见许倬云、林嘉琳，1988：第 127 页。

60 For a detailed discussion of this segmentation process, see C. Y. Hsu and Linduff, 1988: 153-85.
有关这一分化过程的详细讨论，见许倬云、林嘉琳，1988：第 153—185 页。

61 *Ibid.*, 177. 同上，1988：第 177 页。

62 *LJ*, 1611. 《礼记》，第 1611 页。

63 *LJ*, 1335. 《礼记》，第 1335 页。

64 According to Zheng Xuan's commentary on the *Rites of Zhou*, "*Ce* means to record the king's order on bamboo splints" (*ZL*, 820).
据郑玄对《周礼》的注释，"策（册）谓以简策书王命"。(《周礼》，第 820 页)

65 For reconstructions of a Western Zhou investiture ceremony, see Chen Mengjia, 1956: 109-10; Chen Hanping, 1986: 101-30.
有关西周分封仪式的复原，见陈梦家，1956：第 109—110 页；陈汉平，1986：第 101—130 页。

66 Chen Mengjia, 1956: 110. 陈梦家，1956：第 110 页。

67 Sometimes the king announced the order himself, but such examples are very rare; see Chen Hanping, 1986: 119.
有时王亲自宣布诏书，但这种例子极其鲜见；见陈汉平，1986：第 119 页。

68 For textual records of Western Zhou investiture ceremonies, see Chen 300
Hanping, 1986: 12-20. For a list of Western Zhou bronzes bearing investiture inscriptions, see *ibid.*, 21-25.
西周册命仪式的文献记载，见陈汉平，1986：第 12—20 页；带有册命铭文的青铜器，见同书第 21—25 页。

69 Chen Hanping (1986: 29-31) actually classified investiture ceremonies into six types. The last type was not held in the Zhou royal temple, however, and was never recorded in bronze inscriptions. It is called *zhuiming*, or a "posthumous order" given to a deceased minister or relative. Usually the Zhou king sent an official to the home state of the deceased to conduct this ritual.
陈汉平实际将册命仪式分成六种类型。然而，最后一种在周先王庙中并没有出现，也不曾见于青铜器铭文，这种类型称为“追命”，是为已故大臣或宗亲而设的。通常，周王会委派朝中命官前往死者故国举行这类仪式。见陈汉平，1986：第 29—31 页。

70 In a poem from the *Book of Songs* (*SJ*, 565-68; see Legge, 1871: 4.536-39), the Zhou king ordered the Lord of Shen to continue the services of his forebears.
《诗经》中即有一首诗，记周天子命申伯继任其先祖之职。《诗经》，第 565—568 页；理雅各，1871：4.536—539。

71 For examples of these two kinds of investiture, see Chen Hanping, 1986: 30.
有关这两种册命的事例，见陈汉平，1986：第 30 页。

72 *Ibid.*, 30. In fact, Sima Qian (*SJ*, 127) recorded that it was King Wu who enfeoffed the Duke of Zhou and his other brothers. If this record is reliable, then the orders King Cheng gave to his uncles belonged to the type of investiture called *chongming*.
同上，第 30 页。实际上，据司马迁（《史记》，第 127 页）记载，册封周公及其兄弟的是武王。如此说可足取信，成王给予其叔父的册命，当属“重命”。

73 *Baihu tong*, “Jue.” Similar statements are found in the “Ji tong” (“Tradition of sacrifices”) and “Ji yi” (“Meaning of sacrifices”) sections in the *Book of Rites*; see Chen Hanping, 1986: 65.
《白虎通疏证》，卷一“爵”。类似的表述见之于《礼记》“祭统”与“祭义”；参见陈汉平，1986：第 65 页。

74 An archaeological complex discovered at Majiazhuang village in Fengxiang (Shaanxi) may be identified as the remains of the temple of a Zhou lord. But this group of ritual buildings, presumably the ancestral temple of the state of Qin, was constructed during the Spring and Autumn period after the Western Zhou; see Yongcheng Archaeological Team of Shaanxi Province 1985; Han Wei, 1985. I therefore exclude this example from my discussion.
位于陕西凤翔马家庄的一处遗址似可确认为一位周贵族的庙址，但这组建筑可能是秦国先祖之庙，建于西周之后的春秋时期（陕西省雍城考古队，1985；韩伟，1985），故这里不拟纳入讨论。

75 Luo Xizhang, 1988. According to an inventory list included in Luo’s article, 454 bronzes have been found in Western Zhou “storage pits” since 1949. But the number of articles from four hoards discovered before 1949 are unclear. To my knowledge, three of these four hoards (the Liangqi group from Renjiacun, the Hanhuangfu and Baixian group from Kangjiacun, and the group from Qishan including the famous Maogong *ding* and Dafeng *gui*) yielded hundreds of bronzes.

罗西章，1988。根据收录于罗西章文中的一项统计，1949 年以来已有 454 件铜器被发现于西周“窖藏”，但 1949 年前发现的四个窖藏中的器物数目不详。就我所知，四个窖藏中有三个（任家村的梁其组、康家村的函皇父和白鲜组以及岐山组，包括著名的毛公鼎和大丰簋在内）出土青铜器达数百件之多。

76 Huang Shengzhang, 1978: 199-20. 黄盛璋，1978：第 199—200 页。

77 Guo Moruo, 1963: 5. 郭沫若，1963：第 5 页。

78 Luo Xizhang, 1988: 44. 罗西章，1988：第 44 页。

79 For example, members of the Ta lineage and Baigong Fu's descendents buried their ritual bronzes in at least two hoards, respectively; see *ibid.*, 43.
例如“它”族成员和白公父的后代至少在两个窖藏中分别埋有他们的礼器；同上，第 43 页。

80 For a concise report on this excavation, see Zhouyuan Archaeological Team, 1978.
有关这一发掘的准确报道，见周原考古队，1978。

81 Rawson, 1990: 2a. 19. 罗森，1990：2a. 19。

82 Li Xueqin, 1978: 157. 李学勤，1978：第 157 页。

83 Falkenhausen, 1988: 985n55. Falkenhausen interprets this phenomenon in terms of the Wei clan's fission, which, according to traditional texts, would occur regularly every five generations. For this custom, see K. C. Chang, 1976: 72-74.
罗泰，1988：第 985 页，n55。罗泰将这种现象解释为微氏家族的分裂，因为根据传统文献的记载，这样的分裂每五代会发生一次。关于这种习俗的讨论，见张光直，1976：第 72—74 页。

84 As mentioned earlier, this hoard yielded bronzes dated back to the late Shang or early Zhou based on their shape and decoration. But their inscribed commissioners were probably not members of the Wei clan. One of them, named Shang, may have belonged to the Ji royal clan of the Zhou. It is possible that the Wei clan acquired such bronzes through marriage. See Tang Lan, 1978: 21; Falkenhausen, 1988: 985.
如前文提及，根据形制与纹饰，这些出土于窖藏的铜器，年代可以断在晚商至西周初。但是其中留名的史官有可能不是微氏成员，其中一个名字叫“商”的，或许属于周王室的姬姓氏族。微氏也可能通过联姻的方式得到了这些铜器。见唐兰，1978：第 21 页；罗泰，1988：第 985 页。

85 For illustrations and inscriptions of these bronzes, see *Shaanxi chutu Shang Zhou qingtongqi* 2.28-42; and Zhouyuan Archaelogical Team, 1978: 3-4.

这些铜器的插图和拓片资料，见《陕西出土商周青铜器》，卷二，第28—42页；周原考古队，1978：第3—4页。

86 The following English rendering of the inscription is based on C. Y. Hsu and Linduff, 1988: 115, and a manuscript that Falkenhausen kindly provided to this author. For discussion of this inscription, see Tang Lan, 1978; Li Zhongcao, 1978; Qiu Xigui, 1978; Xu Zhongshu, 1978; Li Xueqin, 1978; Chen Shihui, 1980.
接下来这段铭文的英译主要根据许倬云、林嘉琳，1988：第115页，同时也参考了罗泰热心提供给我的他的一份手稿中的译文。关于这段铭文的讨论，参见唐兰，1978；李仲操，1978；裘锡圭，1978；徐仲舒，1978；李学勤，1978；陈世辉，1980。

87 As Falkenhausen (1988: 981) has pointed out, the first paragraph of this new inscription is derived from the Shi Qiang *pan* inscription: "They quote two short passages of 24 characters each that are separated by 109 characters in the much longer *pan* inscription."
正如罗泰（1988：981）所指出的那样，这篇新铭文的首段源自史墙盘铭文："它们援引了各有24字的两段短文，内容比更长的史墙盘铭文少109字。"

88 A group of bronzes from the hoard, commissioned by a certain Bo Xian Fu, can be dated to the late Western Zhou according to their formal attributes. It is unclear whether Bo Xian Fu is another of Xing's names or the name of Xing's son. See Li Xueqin, 1979: 30.
窖藏中由某位伯先父所铸的一组铜器，据其形式特征，可以断为西周晚期，伯先父是瘐的另一名称还是瘐的儿子的名称尚不清楚；见李学勤，1979：第30页。

89 *Lidai zhongding yiqi kuanzhi*, 10.88ab; see Tang Lan, 1978: 19. This also suggests that the Wei lineage may have buried their temple bronzes in more than one pit.
《历代钟鼎彝器款识》，卷十，第88页；唐兰，1978：第19页。这也意味着微氏家族可能不只在一个窖藏中埋葬了他们祖庙的铜器。

90 Some authors date this bronze to King Yi's reign. Here I follow Li Xueqin's (1979: 35) opinion.
有学者将这件铜器定为夷王时期，这里，笔者采纳李学勤（1979：第35页）的观点。

91 Trans. partially from Falkenhausen, 1988: 976-78.
英译部分取自罗泰，1988：第976—978页。

92 Trans. based on *ibid.*, 967-71. 英译部分取自罗泰，1988：第967—971页。

93 Gernet, 1972: 58. 谢和耐，1972：第58页。

94 *Ibid.*, 62. 同上，第 62 页。

95 For a concise summary of these excavations, see Steinhardt, 1990: 46-53.
有关这些发现的简述，见斯坦哈特，1990：第 46—53 页。

96 For a discussion of the Western Zhou regulations on city planning, see He Yeju, 1983: 200-201.
有关西周对城市规划之规定的讨论，见贺业钜，1983：第 200—201 页。

97 *ZZ*, 1716.《春秋左传》，第 1716 页。

98 According to recent surveys, the Royal Capital (Wang cheng) at Luoyang
was square in shape, with a north wall 2,890 meters long; the length of the 301
entire city wall was thus about 12,500 meters. Qufu, the capital of Lu, had a 12,000-meter wall. The wall of Linzi, the capital of Qi, was about 15,000 meters. The outer city of Xinzheng, the capital of Zheng, was about 16,000 meters in circumference. The walls of Yan's Lower Capital were over 27,000 meters, including the partition wall between its eastern and western cities (see Ye Xiaojun, 1988: 61-76).
根据最近的调查，洛阳王城呈方形，北城墙长 2890 米，因而其整个城墙的全长当在 12500 米左右。曲阜的鲁国都城有一围 12000 米的城墙，齐国故都临淄的城墙长约 15000 米，郑国都城新郑的外城周长 16000 米，燕下都城墙含东西两城之间的隔墙在内 27000 余米（叶骁军，1988：第 61—76 页）。

99 Cultural Relics Work Team of the Hebei Provincial Cultural Bureau, 1965.
河北省文化局文物工作队，1965。

100 *Kaogong ji tu*, 102; see Steinhardt, 1990: 33. Scholars commonly consider the *Kaogongji* an independent treatise written during the Warring States period by Confucians from the state of Qin. After it was integrated into the *Rites of Zhou* during the Han, this treatise was canonized, and the "state capital" described in the text was believed to be the Zhou royal capital. But the text does not provide this identification.
《考工记图》，第 102 页；斯坦哈特，1990：第 33 页。学者们一般认为，《考工记》是战国时期秦国儒家学者所著的一本独立的著作，汉代并入《周礼》后被打上了经书的烙印，而且文中所述之"国"，也被误认为是周的王城。但文献本身并不足以证明这一观点。

101 Shandong Provincial Cultural Relics Administration, 1961; Qun Li, 1972; Liu Dunyuan, 1981; Zhang Longhai and Zhu Yude, 1988.
山东省文物局，1961；群力，1972；刘敦愿，1981；张龙海、朱玉德，1988。

102 *Xin yu*, 134.《新语》，第 134 页。

103 See *TPYL*, 861-64.《太平御览》，第 861—864 页。

104 *Hanzi* (The writing of Hanzi), quoted in *ibid*., 862.
《太平御览》，第 862 页引《韩子》。

105 *SJ*, quoted in *TPYL*, 861.《太平御览》，第 861 页引《史记》。

106 *Shuo yuan*, quoted in *TPYL*, 863.《太平御览》，第 863 页引《说苑》。

107 *SJ*, 192.《史记》，第 192 页。

108 *Xin xu*, quoted in *TPYL*, 863.《太平御览》，第 863 页引《新序》。

109 Precisely speaking, Shang Yang moved the Qin capital from Liyang to Xianyang. But Liyang was only one of several temporary capitals of the kingdom; before the establishment of Xianyang, Yong had been the Qin's chief political and religious center. Sima Qian (*SJ*, 2232) thus stated that "Lord Shang moved the capital from Yong to Xianyang."
确切地说，商鞅是由郦阳移秦宫至咸阳的，但郦阳只是当时秦王国的几个都城之一；建都咸阳之前，雍一直是秦最主要的政治、宗教中心，所以司马迁说："宫庭于咸阳，秦自雍徙都之。"（《史记》，第 2232 页）

110 *Ibid*.《史记》，第 2232 页。

111 Wang Xueli, 1985: 18. 王学理，1985：第 18 页。

112 Sima Zhen's commentary at *SJ*, 2232.《史记》，第 2232 页司马贞的注疏。

113 Sun Yirang's commentary at *ZL*, 648; see also *Lüshi chunqiu*, 281.
见《周礼》，第 648 页孙诒让的注释；又见《吕氏春秋》，第 281 页。

114 Archaeological Station at the Qin Capital Xianyang 1976. The authors of this and some other articles initially identified the buildings as part of the Xianyang Palace of the First Emperor. But other scholars have argued, quite convincingly in my opinion, that they were actually founded by Shang Yang and were later enlarged by the First Emperor; see Wang Xueli et al., 1979; WangXueli, 1982.
秦都咸阳考古站，1976。该文的作者和其他一些学者最初将这一建筑认定为秦始皇咸阳宫的一部分。我同意另外学者的看法，即认为这一建筑实际上是由商鞅创建的，后来被秦始皇加以扩大；见王学理等，1979；王学理，1982。

115 Yang Hongxun, 1976b. 杨鸿勋，1976b。

116 Yang Kuan, 1965. 杨宽，1965。

117 According to Yang Hongxun's (1987: 72, 100) reconstruction, both the Shang temple at Erlitou and the Western Zhou temple at Fengchu had a foundation of about 1 meter high.

根据杨鸿勋（1987：第 72、100 页）的复原，偃师商庙和凤雏的西周庙皆有一约一米高的台基。

118 For a statement of this theory, see *ibid.*, 82.
关于这一说法，见杨鸿勋，1987：第 82 页。

119 *Ibid.*, 155. I will discuss the *guan* in greater detail in the final section of this book.
同上，第 155 页。关于这里提到的“观”，我将在本书的末尾一章详加讨论。

120 *SFHT*, 3-4. For an inventory of these palaces, see Wang Xueli, 1985: 38-54.
《三辅皇图》，第 3—4 页。关于这些宫殿的详目，见王学理，1985：第 38—54 页。

121 *Miao ji* (A record of temples), quoted in Zhang Shoujie's commentary in *SJ*, 241.
《庙记》，引自张守节正义。《史记》，第 241 页。

122 *SJ*, 239; trans. based on H. Y. Yang and G. Yang, 1979: 168.
《史记》，第 239 页；英译据杨宪益、戴乃迭，1979：第 168 页。

123 *Ibid.* 《史记》，第 239 页。

124 I discuss the symbolism of the Nine Tripods in the Introduction to this book.
关于九鼎象征性的讨论，见本书导论。

125 *SJ*, 256; trans. based on H. Y. Yang and G. Yang, 1979: 179.
《史记》，第 256 页；英译据杨宪益、戴乃迭，1979：第 179 页。

126 Keightley, 1978b: 217. 吉德炜，1978b：第 217 页。

127 See *LJ*, 1605-7. 《礼记》，第 1605—1607 页。

128 *LJ*, 1495, 1508, 1589; see also K. C. Chang, 1983: 37-41.
同上，第 1495、1508、1589 页；张光直，1983：第 37—41 页。

129 Institute of Archaeology, CASS 1980: 4-6. Remains of aboveground mortuary houses from the later Shang dynasty have also been found in Dasikong village; see Ma Dezhi et al., 1953: 20.
中国社会科学院考古研究所，1980：第 4—6 页。商代晚期地上丧葬性建筑的遗迹还见于大司空村，见马得志等，1953：第 20 页。

130 K. C. Chang, 1980a: 119-24. 张光直，1980a：第 119—124 页。

131 *ZL*, 757-59. 《周礼》，第 757—759 页。

132 *LJ*, 1595-96. 《礼记》，第 1595—1596 页。

133 It is important to distinguish "funerary rituals" (*sangli*) from "grave

sacrifices" (*muji*) in ancient Chinese ritual practices. The former were carried out immediately following a death; the latter refer to rituals practiced routinely in graveyards. The Three Ritual Canons describe the "funerary ritual" at great length but make no mention of the "grave sacrifice."
将古代中国礼仪活动中的“丧礼”与“墓祭”区分开来是十分重要的，前者的实施紧接着死亡；后者指的是墓地中的例行仪式。三礼对“丧礼”有很长的记述，但对“墓祭”却未置一词。

134 The origin of "grave sacrifices" has been the focus of a debate among Chinese scholars for some 2,000 years. Scholars of the Eastern Han held similar opinions on this issue. Wang Chong provided a typical statement (Lun heng, 469): "Ancient people held ancestral sacrifices in temples; nowadays people have the custom of sacrificing in graveyards." Similar statements also appear in the writings of two distinguished Eastern Han historians, Ying Shao and Cai Yong. Ying Shao reported: "In ancient times the ritual of 'grave sacrifices' did not exist. . . . Emperors [of the present] hold ceremonies in the first month of the year at the Yuan ling Mausoleum" (quoted in *HHS*, 99). The same idea was expressed even more categorically in a statement by Cai Yong quoted in note 168 below.

Confusion about the origin of grave sacrifices first appeared during the Jin dynasty. Sima Biao's statement that "the mausoleum sacrifice had been
302 practiced during the Western Han" (*HHS*, 3103) contradicted the belief of Eastern Han historians that the ceremony had not existed until Emperor Ming created it. Going even further, Sima Biao argued that the "grave sacrifice" had actually been initiated during the Qin dynasty: "In ancient times the ritual of the 'grave sacrifice' did not exist. The Han mausoleums all contained a *qin* hall because the Han followed the regulation of the Qin" (*HHS*, 3199-200).

This issue became a favorite topic in the Qing dynasty. Some scholars, such as Xu Qianxue and Gu Yanwu disagreed with Sima Biao and returned to the view of Han historians (Duli tongkao, 94.1b; Rizhi lu, 15.1-3). Other scholars represented by Yan Ruoju (Yan Ruoju et al., 1967: 20.14ab) derived their evidence from historical writings and the Confucian classics to prove that the ritual of the "grave sacrifice" not only had existed during the Qin and Western Han but had actually been practiced by disciples of Confucius and even by King Wu of the Zhou dynasty.

This debate has been renewed during recent years. In 1982, Yang Hongxun (1982: 403) declared that the ritual practice of the grave sacrifice can be traced back as far as the Shang dynasty. He provided archaeological evidence including the sacrificial ground discovered at the Shang royal cemetery, the remains of Shang-Zhou aboveground mortuary houses, and the "design of the royal cemetery of the Zhongshan kingdom." Opposing him was the noted historian Yang Kuan (1982: 31; 1983: 636-40), who based his entire argument on the argument built by Gu Yanwu and Xu Qianxue, and concluded that the pre-Han funerary structures found in archaeological excavations "could only be *qin* halls—the 'retiring room' for the soul of the deceased, rather than 'offering halls' in which people held ritual sacrifices to their ancestors." A third scholar, Wang Shimin (1981: 465), returned to Sima Biao's opinion, saying that the official "grave sacrifice" was initiated by the First Emperor.

In my opinion, this debate has been caused by different understandings and uses of the term *muji*, or "grave sacrifice." Yan Ruoju and Yang Hongxun understood the word in its general, broad sense as any kind of ritual held in a graveyard; Sima Biao and Wang Shimin understood it in a narrower sense as the imperial sacrifices held in mausoleums; the Han dynasty scholars, as well as Gu Yanwu, Xu Qianxue, and Yang Kuan, used the term in a specific sense to mean the most important official ancestral sacrifice held in the royal mausoleums in the first month of the year—that is, the *shangling* ceremony initiated by Emperor Ming of the Eastern Han in A.D. 58.

In short, these scholars have focused on two different historical problems: one is the origin of the ritual practice of grave sacrifices; the other is the formulation of the official "mausoleum sacrifice." Both kinds of ritual are important for our understanding of the development of ancestor worship in ancient China.

大约 2000 年间，“墓祭”的起源问题一直是中国学者争论的焦点。东汉人对这一问题的见解大体一致，王充曾提出过一个比较有代表性的说法（《论衡》，第 469 页）：“古礼庙祭，今俗墓祀。”类似说法也在应劭和蔡邕这两位东汉著名史学家的著述中出现。应劭说：“古不墓祭。……天子 以正月上原陵。”（应劭《汉官仪》，《后汉书 · 明帝纪》李贤注引，见《后汉书》，第 99 页）。同样的观点在本章注 168 所引蔡邕的一段陈述中表达得更为直截了当。

对墓祭起源的疑惑最早出现于晋代。司马彪“西都旧有上陵”的说法（《后汉书》，第 3103 页）与东汉史学家认为明帝确立上陵礼之前不存在这种礼仪的见解相左。司马彪甚至认为“墓祭”实际在秦代已经产生：“古不墓祭，汉诸陵皆有园寝，承秦所为也。”（《后汉书》，第 3199—3200 页）。

这一论点在清朝成了一个热门话题。一些学者如徐乾学、顾炎武不同意司马彪的观点，而认同汉代史家的看法（《读礼通考》，卷九十四，第 1 页；《日知录》，卷十五，第 1—3 页）。以阎若璩为代表的部分学者（《读礼丛钞》，卷二十，第 14 页）从历史文献和儒家经典中寻求依据，证明“墓祭”礼仪不仅秦汉时代存在，而且已为孔子的门徒乃至周武王所实践。

这一争论近些年来再度展开。1982 年，杨鸿勋（1982：第 403 页）称墓祭行为可以上溯到商代，他提出的考古学依据，包括了发现于商王室墓地的祭台，商周时期建于地上的停尸房遗迹，以及“中山王陵兆域图”。不同意这种看法的是著名历史学家杨宽（1982：第 31 页；1983：第 636—640 页），他的主要论据建立在顾炎武与徐乾学的论点基础之上，并推断出考古发现的汉代以前的殡葬结构（墓上建筑）“只能是‘寝’而不是享堂，是用来作为死者灵魂起居的，并非祭祀先祖”。第三种观点来自学者王世民（1981：第 465 页），他遵循司马彪的观点，认为官方“墓祭”制度建立于秦始皇时期。

在我看来，这些争论是由对“墓祭”一词的理解与应用所存在的差异而引起的。阎若璩与杨鸿勋所理解的为广义上的“墓祭”一词，它只是所有在墓地上举行的仪式礼制之一；司马彪与王世民所理解的为狭义上的“墓祭”一词，特指在陵寝上举行的帝王祭礼；汉代学者们与顾炎武、徐乾学和杨宽一样，把“墓祭”一词理解为每年元月于皇陵上举行的盛大的皇家祭祖仪式，即公元 58 年东汉明帝时确立的“上陵礼”。

简单来说，这些学者把目光集中在了两种不同的历史问题上：一为于墓地上祭祀这种礼制的起源；另一为皇家“上陵礼”制度的定则。这两种礼制对于我们理解古代中国祖先崇拜仪式的发展都至关重要。

135 *LJ*, 1275.《礼记》，第 1275 页。

136 *Ibid.*, 1292. 同上，第 1292 页。

137 For two reconstruction plans of the Zhongshan mausoleum, see Yang Hongxun 1980 and Fu Xinian, 1980. In addition to the plan of the Zhongshan mausoleum, an important Warring States mausoleum excavated in Guweicun, Hebei, has been identified as a royal burial of the state of Wei. The plan of the mausoleum is similar to that of the Zhongshan mausoleum; the square funerary park, encircled by double walls, was centered on three individual sacrificial structures built in a row on a terrace (see Yang Hongxun, 1980: 131-32).
关于两种中山王陵的复原图样，参见杨鸿勋，1980；傅熹年，1980。此外，在河北省发掘的战国陵墓，已被确认为魏国的王陵（参见杨鸿勋，1980：第 131—132 页）。魏王陵的复原图样与中山王陵相似；两圈城环绕的方形陵园位于露台上成排建造的三组独立祭祀建筑的正中。

138 *ZL*, 786. This passage records that the *zhongren*, or the officer in charge of tombs, was “to regulate the measurement of the tumuli and the number of trees [planted in the graveyards] according to the rank of the deceased.” For a specific study on the Qin funerary system, see Ma Zhenzhi, 1989.
《周礼》，第 786 页。这段文献记载看守墓地的冢人，“以爵等为丘封之度，与其树数”。关于秦陵寝制度的研究，见马振智，1989。

139 *Shangjun shu*, 74.《商君书》，第 74 页。

140 *Lüshi chunqiu*, 98.《吕氏春秋》，第 98 页。

141 General excavation reports and studies on the Lishan Mausoleum include Shaanxi Provincial Cultural Relics Administration, 1962: 407-11; Thorp, 1983a; Yang Kuan, 1985: 183-201.
有关骊山陵的发掘与研究，见陕西省文物管理局，1962：第 407—411 页；杜朴，1983a；杨宽，1985。

142 *SJ*, 265.《史记》，第 265 页。

143 See note 53 to this chapter. 见本章注 53。

144 Han Wei, 1983; Shaanxi Provincial Archaeological Institute, 1987.
韩伟，1983；陕西省考古研究所，1987。

145 Lishan xuehui 1987. My discussion does not follow the Lishan xuehui's suggestion that the Lishan mausoleum was one of the Lintong Qin royal tombs.
骊山学会，1987。骊山学会认为骊山陵是临潼秦王室墓葬的一部分，我的观点与此并不相同。

146 Remains of buildings have been found between the two walls of the funerary park. Pottery vessels unearthed there are stamped with inscriptions such as *Lishanyuan* (Lishan mausoleum) and *Lishan shiguan* (the sacrificial officer of the Lishan mausoleum), and thus identify these buildings as departments of ritual affairs (see Zhao Kangmin, 1980; Wang Xueli, 1989).
陵园内外墙之间发现了建筑遗迹，那里出土的陶器印有“骊山园”与“骊山食官”的标记，进一步证明了这些建筑是礼仪活动的一个组成部分。见赵康民，1980；王学理，1989。

147 This architectural complex consisted of four individual buildings arranged in an east-west row. The largest was about 20 meters long and 3.4 meters wide, with an elaborate limestone doorway. Its walls were constructed of plastered stone and the walkways were paved with stones. Other remains, including postholes, large bricks, and decorated tiles, suggest that these buildings were wooden-framed structures with tiled roofs (Zhao Kangmin, 1979).
这组风格化的建筑群，由东西向排列的四个独立建筑物组成。其中最大的建筑长 20 米，宽 3.4 米，出入口由精细的石灰岩制成，墙体由熟石膏石建造，人行道以石铺就。包括柱洞、巨型砖、瓦当在内的其他遗迹表明，这组建筑物是瓦顶木架结构的（赵康民，1979）。

148 *Du duan*, 20; see Yang Kuan, 1985: 638.《独断》，第 20 页；杨宽，1985：第 638 页。

149 Lishan xuehui, 89. 骊山学会，1987：第 89 页。

303 150 *HHS*, 3199.《后汉书》，第 3199 页。

151 Important archaeological reports regarding excavations in the outer district of the Lishan mausoleum include Archaeological Team of the Qin Terracotta Army, 1975; 1978; 1979; 1980a; 1980b; 1982a; 1982b.
有关骊山陵外围的重要考古发掘报告，参见秦俑坑考古队，1975；1978；1979；1980a；1980b；1982a；1982b。

152 The pre-dynastic Qin temple system is not clear. According to *SJ* 266, the most important royal temples were located in the two capitals, Yong and Xianyang. Other records, however, suggest that from King Zhao's reign on a temple was built near a deceased ruler's mausoleum; see Yang Kuan, 1985: 24.
秦朝建立之前的宗庙系统并不清晰，据《史记》（第 266 页）的记载，最重要的王室宗庙设在雍与咸阳两座城内，但是其他记载却表明自昭王始，王陵附近就有一座庙；见杨宽，1985：第 24 页。

153 *SJ*, 241.《史记》，第 241 页。

154 *Ibid.*, 266. 同上，第 266 页。

155 *LJ*, 1292; trans. based on Legge, 1967: 1.155-56.
《礼记》，第 1292 页；英译据理雅各，1967：1.115—156 页。

156 Z. S. Wang, 1982: 175-79. 王仲殊，1982：第 175—179 页。

157 Luo Fuyi, 1960. 罗福颐，1960。

158 *Li shi*, 6806.《隶释》，第 6806 页。

159 Quoted in Zhu Kongyang, 1937, 13.5a. 转引自朱孔阳，1937：卷十三，第 5 页。

160 *LJ*, 1589: "The mass of ordinary officers and the common people had no ancestral temple. Their dead were left in their ghostly state" (trans. Legge, 1967: 2.206).
《礼记》，第 1589 页："庶士庶人无庙，死曰鬼。"（英译据理雅各，1967：2.206）

161 According to the biography of Wei Xuancheng (*HS*, 99), a Western Han mausoleum contained four major architectural units: the *qin* or "retiring hall," the *biandian* or "side hall," the *yeting* or place for concubines, and the imperial offices.
根据韦玄成的传记资料（《汉书》，第 99 页），西汉陵墓包含四个主要的建筑形式：寝，即"隐宫"；便殿，即"旁宫"；"掖廷"，也就是妾妃居住的后宫；还有皇帝办公的处所。

162 According to textual evidence, free-standing sculptures of the Qin, such as the famous Twelve Golden Men, were erected above ground only in

the imperial palace (see *SJ*, 239). From the epoch of Emperor Wu of the Western Han, large stone figures for funerary purposes began to be placed on the ground in front of mausoleums. Remains of such statues were repeatedly found in front of Emperor Wu's tomb, flanking the Spirit Path (see Xie Mincong, 1979: 58). The stone statues in front of Huo Qubing's tomb may support the authenticity of this report. Huo was a famous general under Emperor Wu, and his tomb was one of the satellite burials near the emperor's mausoleum.

As I discuss in Chapter 3, in the early Han dynasty, a satellite burial system was established. In this system, an emperor's tomb was the focal point of the mausoleum complex and surrounded by the tombs of his concubines, relatives, and meritorious ministers and generals. The scale of such burials is astonishing. According to archaeological surveys, at least 175 satellite burials surrounded Emperor Gaozu's tomb, 34 surrounded Emperor Jing's, and 59 surrounded Emperor Xuan's (see Liu Qingzhu and Li Yufang, 1982; Yang Kuan, 1985: app. 1).

有关文献表明，类似十二金人这类秦代单体雕塑，仅仅是放置在皇宫之内的（《史记》，第 239 页）。自西汉武帝时起，丧葬用大型石雕开始置于陵墓前方的空地上。类似的石雕遗迹就反复出现于武帝茂陵的前方，夹护在神道的两旁（谢敏聪，1979：第 58 页）。霍去病墓前的石雕，便是这种记载的明证。霍为武帝名将，他的墓即是武帝茂陵周围的陪葬墓之一。

正如我在第三章所论，西汉前期，陪葬制度已经确立。在这一制度中，帝王墓是陵墓群体的焦点，其周围为嫔妃、亲属及功臣骁将的墓葬所环绕。这些墓葬的规模是十分惊人的。据一些考古勘察，汉高祖陵墓周围至少有陪葬墓 175 座，景帝陵墓周围至少有 34 座，宣帝陵墓周围不少于 59 座（刘庆柱、李毓芳，1982；杨宽，1985：附表 1）。

163 *SJ*, 2725-26.《史记》，第 2725 — 2726 页。

164 Wang Pizhong et al., 1980; Li Hongtao and Wang Pizhong, 1980. It is also reported that a large architectural foundation, 51 meters long and 29.6 meters wide, was found southeast of Emperor Xuan's mausoleum. The reporter identified this building as a *qin* hall, but since the foundation was located outside the funerary park, it was more probably the remains of a *miao* (see Archaeological Team of the Du Mausoleum, 1984).

王丕忠等，1980；李宏涛、王丕忠，1980。据报道，宣帝陵东南方发现一处长 51 米，宽 29.6 米的建筑基址，报告者确认该建筑系一寝殿。但鉴于该建筑基址位于陵园之外，它很可能是一处庙的遗址（杜陵考古队，1984）。

165 *HS*, 2130.《汉书》，第 2130 页。

166 For example, we read in texts that King Wuling of Zhao passed on the

throne to his younger son in the Zhao ancestral temple; that Ying Zheng, the future emperor of Qin, stayed overnight in the Qin ancestral temple at Yong before becoming the heir; and that all the emperors of the Western Han designated their crown princes in the Great Ancestral Temple dedicated to the founder of the dynasty (see *SJ*, 1812; *SFHT*, 43). Again, according to *HS* (3115-16), only daily meals were offered to a deceased emperor in his *qin*; the more important monthly sacrifices were held in his *miao*.
举例来说，史书记载，赵武灵王于祖庙传位幼子；秦王嬴政继位之前夜守雍地祖庙；而且西汉所有皇帝都会遣派王位继承人去高祖庙祭拜汉朝的创立者（《史记》，第 1812 页；《三辅黄图》，第 43 页）。根据《汉书》（第 3115—3116 页），日供先王于寝，月祭先王于庙，后者更加重要。

167 *HHS*, 99.《后汉书》，第 99 页。

168 For example, Cai Yong stated in A.D. 172 after attending the "mausoleum sacrifice" that year: "I heard that the ancients did not sacrifice to their ancestors in graveyards, and I had wondered about the necessity of the ritual of the 'mausoleum sacrifice' practiced by the present court. Only after I witnessed the dignified manner of the ceremony today did I begin to realize its original motivation. Now I understand the complete filial piety and sincerity of Emperor Filial Ming [who initiated the ritual]. It would be improper to replace this ritual with the old custom" (*HHS*, 3103).
举例来说，蔡邕于公元 172 年参加“上陵礼”时向同座说道：“闻古不墓祭，朝廷有上陵之礼，始谓可损，今见其仪，察其本意，乃知孝明皇帝至孝恻隐，不可易旧。”（《后汉书》，第 3103 页）

169 *Ibid.*, 27-28, 3194-95.《后汉书》，第 27—28 页，第 3194—3195 页。

170 *Ibid.*, 3193. 同上，第 3193 页。

171 *Ibid.*, 1-87. 同上，第 1—87 页。

172 *Rizhi lu*, 15.2-3.《日知录》，卷十五，第 2—3 页。

173 *HHS*, 123-24.《后汉书》，第 123—124 页。

174 Zhao Yi, 1960: 32ab. 赵翼，1960：第 32 页。

175 See Powers, 1984. 包华石，1984。

176 During the Eastern Han, the funerary shrine of a family was open to the public. This is most clearly indicated by the An Guo inscription translated in Chapter 4; see Li Falin, 1982: 101.
东汉时期，一个家族的墓上祠堂是可以向公众开放的，这一点在第四章的安国祠堂铭文中表达得最为清晰；见李发林，1982：第 101 页。

177 *Sanguo zhi*, 81; Jin shu, 634. 《三国志》，第 81 页；《晋书》，第 634 页。

178 For a discussion of these archaeological finds and their implications, see Wu Hong, 1989. Some Chinese archaeologists have tried to explain why Han pictorial carvings were reused in constructing these Wei-Jin tombs. For example, Li Falin (1982: 50) suggested that the custom of making funerary pictorial carvings ceased around the end of the Eastern Han and considered that this change was caused by the Yellow Turban rebellion in the Shandong
region, which "smashed local feudal despots and landlords so that they 304
could not continue this sort of extravagant funerary services, which wasted a great amount of time, manpower, and material." In my opinion, this interpretation is too vague to explain the destruction of funerary shrines on a nationwide scale.

有关这些考古发现及其意义的讨论，见巫鸿，1989。一些中国考古学家试图解释为何汉代的画像石构件在这些魏晋墓地中被重复利用。例如，李发林（1982：第 50 页）曾推测制作丧葬画像石刻的习俗大约在东汉末停歇，并且认为引起这一变动的原因是黄巾军在山东的起义，这次起义"打击了封建豪强地主的势力，使他们无力去维持这种浪费人力、物力和时间的厚葬陋俗"。在我看来，这种说法太过含糊，无法解释墓上祠堂在全国范围内的大规模解体。

179 G. D. Su, 1964: 203; cited in Li Yunshuo, 1982: 29.
徐敬直，1964：第 203 页；引自李允鉌，1982：第 29 页。

180 Liu Zhiping, 1957a: 22. 刘致平，1957a：第 22 页。

181 Needham, 1954-88: IV. 3.90. 李约瑟，1954—1988：IV. 3.90。

182 Patterned bronze panels and joints were used in some elaborate Eastern Zhou palatial structures. But this technique never developed into a prevalent architectural convention. In fact, understood in the Eastern Zhou social context, this way of using bronze reflected the decline of traditional ritual art and the growing importance of architectural monuments.

东周时期有些精致考究的宫殿建筑，应用了饰有图案的青铜嵌板与连接件，但这种技术绝不会进入普通建筑的传统惯例当中。事实上，从东周时期的社会背景着眼，这种使用青铜的方式，反映了传统礼制艺术的衰退以及建筑纪念物之重要性的增长。

183 To my knowledge, the only pre-Han funerary stone inscription is found in the mausoleum of a Zhongshan king. But since the stone retains its natural shape and the inscription has nothing to do with the deceased, it is difficult to identify it as a memorial stela (see Hebei Cultural Relics Administration, 1979; Fan Bangjin, 1990: 52).

据我所知，西汉以前唯一的丧葬石刻题铭发现于某一代中山王陵。但是由于石头保持着自然的形态，且石刻的内容也没有涉及死者，因此很难将其指认为纪念性石碑（河北省文物管理处，1979；范邦瑾，1990：第 52 页）。

184 Passage from the inscription on Wu Liang's memorial stela; see H. Wu, 1989: 25. A similar statement is found in a long inscription from Songshan, Shandong, discussed later in this chapter.
这段文字录自武梁碑，见巫鸿，1989：第 25 页。发现于山东嘉祥宋山的一段长篇铭文，其中也有类似的表述。稍后将于本章中讨论。

185 As mentioned earlier in this book, the ancient Chinese distinguished jade from stone and gave jade a special symbolism. Likewise, the exquisite marble carvings found in great Shang royal tombs, including imitations of bronze ritual vessels and large and small sculptures, must also be distinguished from ordinary stone products. Some texts record the construction of certain stone buildings before the Qin-Han period. For example, it is said that King Zhao of Yan honored the philosopher Zou Yan with a "stone palace" (*SJ*, 2345). But such instances are extremely rare.
正如本书前文所述，古代中国人从石头当中辨别出玉，并赋予玉以特殊的象征意义。同样，发现于商王大墓中的那些精美的大理石雕刻，包括仿制的青铜礼器和大小不等的雕塑作品，也必定是与普通石制品有所区别的。某些秦汉之前的石制建筑在文献当中有所记载，例如燕昭王曾以"石宫"赐邹衍（《史记》，第 2345 页），不过这种情况十分罕见。

186 In addition to a "stone chamber" of the Queen Mother of the West recorded in *SJ*, 3163-64, extant stone structures dedicated to gods and immortals include pillar-gates at Dengfeng in Henan, one forming the entrance to the sacred mountain Shaoshi and the other belonging to the temple of a legendary figure Qimu (the Mother of Qi; see Chen Mingda, 1961: 10-11).
《史记》（第 3163—3164 页）记载了西王母的"石室"，此外，现存为诸神和仙人而做的石构建筑，有河南登封的两对石阙，一对作为少室山的入口，另一对属于传说中的启母庙；见陈明达，1961：第 10—11 页。

187 Loewe, 1982: 25. 鲁惟一，1982：第 25 页。

188 Gu Jiegang, 1935: 16. 顾颉刚，1935：第 16 页。

189 Trans. from Watson 1968b: 33. Ying-shih Yü (1987: 387) remarks: "The only difference between the *hun* [soul] and the *hsien* [*xian*; immortal] is that while the former leaves the body at death the latter obtains its total freedom by transforming the body into something purely ethereal, that is, the heavenly *ch'i* [*qi*; breath, ether, etc.]."
华兹生，1968b：第 33 页。余英时（1987：第 387 页）解释道："魂与仙的唯一区别，在于前者死后离开身体，后者则经过身体向某种纯粹、轻灵的物质——即‘气’的转变，从而获得身体与灵魂的完全自由。”

190 See my discussion of the relationship between Emperor Wu and necromancers in Chapter 3.
见我在第三章所论武帝与方士的关系。

191 Y. S. Yü, 1987: 378. 余英时，1987：第 378 页。

192 This understanding is most clearly stated in Xunzi, 231-51.
这种理解在《荀子》（第 231—251 页）中表述得最为明确。

193 Mori, 1943. A recent archaeological discovery indicates that even during the early Western Han, the underground bureaucracy was still modeled upon the social hierarchy: Mawangdui Tomb no. 3 yielded a wooden tablet on which an inscription, written by the "family retainer" (*jiachen*) of the deceased, informs the assistant master of funerary goods (*zhucang langzhong*) that a complete collection of burial goods (*cangwu*) had been transmitted to the lord administrator of funerary goods (*zhucangjun*; Hunan Provincial Museum and Institute of Archaeology, CASS, 1974: 43).
森三树三郎，1943。最近的一项考古发现表明，即使在西汉初期，死者在地下的等级地位仍旧照搬着地上的社会等级制度：马王堆 3 号汉墓出土一块木简，其上有死者“家臣”所刻的一段文字，内容为告知“主藏郎中”全部“藏物”已转交“主藏君”。见湖南省博物馆、中国社会科学院考古研究所，1974：第 43 页。

194 During Emperor Wu's time, Penglai was often associated with a divine master named Anqi Sheng, who was originally a necromancer of pre-Qin times (*SJ*, 453-55; Watson, 1958: 2.38-40). Another legendary figure, Xiwangmu or the Queen Mother of the West, was first among a number of personages who, according to Zhuangzi, had succeeded in attaining immortality (see Legge, 1891: 293). This figure became associated with Mount Kunlun during the Han (H. Wu, 1989: 117-26).
武帝时期，蓬莱通常与一位名叫安期生的神人联系在一起。安是先秦时期的一位术士（《史记》，第 453—455 页；华兹生，1958：2.38—40）。另一位神人西王母，起初是《庄子》所列得以成仙的一组人物之一（理雅各，1891:第 293 页）。到了汉代，这一人物形象开始与昆仑山相连（巫鸿，1989：第 117—126 页）。

195 *SJ*, 1388.《史记》，第 1388 页。

196 For a sociological explanation of the development of Han funerary art, see H. Wu, 1988.
有关汉代丧葬美术发展的社会学解释，见巫鸿，1988。

197 *Baopu zi*, 2.6. This record is an elaborate version of a passage in *SJ*, 1386.

《抱朴子》，卷二，第 6 页。这段记载是《史记》（第 1386 页）一段文字更详尽的版本。

198 *SJ*, 1396.《史记》，第 1396 页。

199 Quoted in *Baopu zi*, 2.6.《抱朴子》，卷二，第 6 页。

200 *SJ*, 434.《史记》，第 434 页。

201 Sima Qian only stated that Ba ling was a rock-cut burial but said nothing about its internal structure. We find an interesting record in the *Yong da ji* (Record of the greater Yong area) by He Jingming of the Ming dynasty: “In the autumn of the *xinmao* year during the Zhiyuan reign period [1291], the flood of the Ba River broke up Ba ling’s outer gate. More than 500 stone slabs were washed out [from the rock-cut tomb].” It seems that stone structures may have been originally built inside the tomb—an assumption supported by excavated rock-cut Western Han tombs at Mancheng and other places. According to the *SJ*, before his death Emperor Wen ordered that only clay objects be buried in his tomb and that no gold and silver decoration should be used. But when the tomb was looted in A.D. 315, grave robbers found that the burial chamber was filled with “shining gold and
305 jades” (see Lin Liming and Sun Zhongjia, 1984: 28-29).
司马迁仅仅记述霸陵为崖墓，并未提及其内部构造。我们在明代人何景明的《雍大记》中，发现了一处有趣的记载：“至元辛卯年（1291）秋，灞水冲开霸陵外羡门，冲出石板五百余片。”由此可见，墓内原本似乎还有石构筑——这一猜测可以满城等地西汉崖墓的考古发现为支撑。据《史记》，文帝死前下诏说，他的陵内唯以土制器物随葬，金银装饰皆不得用。但是，该墓于公元 315 年被盗时，盗墓者发现墓室内充斥着大量耀眼的金玉（林利明、孙仲嘉，1984：第 28—29 页）。

202 *SJ*, 2753. Author’s supplementary note: In 2021, Chinese archaeologists finally located Baling in Bailuyuan near Xi’an, which differs from the traditional understanding of the tomb’s location. Preliminary surveys reveal that this is an ultra-large tomb containing a wooden *guo* casket. It did not have a tumulus but a “stone enclosure.”
《史记》，第 2753 页。作者加注：中国考古人员于 2021 年最后确定了霸陵坐落在西安市白鹿原，与传统认为的地点不同。根据初步调查，此墓为一个特大型木椁墓，无封土但有一个“石围界”。

203 Bauer, 1976: 95-100. 鲍吾刚，1976：第 95—100 页。

204 Gu Jiegang, 1935: 15-17. 顾颉刚，1935：第 15—17 页。

205 *SJ*, 3166; Watson, 1958: 280.《史记》，第 3166 页；华兹生，1958：第 280 页。

206 Sickman and Soper, 1956: 21. 史克门、索柏，1956：第 21 页。

207 See Said, 1979: 49-73. For Said, Orientalism was a specific historical phenomenon in European culture. But his analysis may help explain the Han fascination with the idea of a mysterious alien space.
在萨义德（1979：第 49—73 页）看来，东方主义在欧洲文化中是一种特殊的历史现象，但他的分析或许可以帮助解释汉代人对那种神秘的异域观念的兴趣。

208 These places are identified in Watson, 1958: 274-75.
有关这些地方的确定，见华兹生，1958：第 274—275 页。

209 For example, Zhang Qian told the emperor that "the coins of Anxi [Persia] are made of silver and bear the face of the king. When the king dies, the currency is immediately changed and new coins issued with the face of his successor" (*SJ*, 3162; trans. based on Watson, 1958: 278).
例如，张骞曾谓武帝曰："（安息）以银为钱，钱如其王面，王死辄更钱，效王面焉。"（《史记》，第 3162 页，英译据华兹生，1958：第 278 页）

210 "The old men of Anxi say they have heard that in Tiaozhi are to be found the River of Weak Water and the Queen Mother of the West" (*SJ*, 3163-64; trans. based on Watson, 1958: 278). Some scholars have identified the Weak Water as being near the Persian Gulf; see Loewe, 1979: 150n51.
"安息长老传闻条枝有弱水、西王母。"（《史记》，第 3163—3164 页；英译据华兹生，1958：第 278 页）一些学者已经确认弱水紧临波斯湾。见鲁惟一，1979：第 150 页，n51。

211 Bachelard, 1964: 183-231. 巴什拉，1964：第 183—231 页。

212 Said, 1979: 54, 72, 70. 萨义德，1979：第 54、72、70 页。

213 It is said that winged heavenly horses were found in the third year of the Yuanshou era (120 B.C.) and again in the fourth year of the Taichu era (101 B.C.). In celebrating these events, Emperor Wu wrote two poems: ". . . The horse of Heaven has come. /Open the far gates, /Raise up my body, /I go to Kunlun"; and "The horse of Heaven has come. /Mediator for the dragon, / He travels to the gates of Heaven, /And looks on the Terrace of Jade" (*HS* 176, 202, 1060). The same emperor also wrote a poem for a tribute elephant: "The elephant, white like jade /Came here from the West. . . /It reveals Heaven's will, /Bringing happiness to human beings" (*HS*, 176, 1069).
据记载，元狩三年（公元前 120 年）曾有翼马发现，太初四年（公元前 101 年）再次发现。为了庆祝这些时刻，武帝赋诗二首："……天马徕，开远门。竦予身，逝昆仑"；"天马徕，龙之媒。游阊阖，观玉台。"（《汉书》：第 176、202、1061 页）。武帝也为贡象赋诗一首："象载瑜，白集西，食甘露，饮荣泉。赤雁集，六纷员，殊瓮杂，五采文。神所见，施祉福，登蓬莱，结无极。"（《汉书》：第 176、1069 页）。

214 H. Wu, 1984: 43. 巫鸿，1984：第 43 页。

215 "After Zhang Qian achieved honor and position by opening up communications with the lands of the West, all the officials and soldiers who had accompanied him vied with one another in submitting reports to the emperor telling of the wonders and profits to be gained in foreign lands and requesting to become envoys. The emperor considered that, since the lands of the West were so far away, no man would choose to make the journey simply for his own pleasure, and so when he had listened to their stories he immediately presented them with the credentials of an envoy. In addition he called for volunteers from among the people and fitted out with attendants and dispatched anyone who came forward, without inquiring into his background, in an effort to broaden the area that had been opened to communication." Some of these envoys indeed reached the West, but others spent the emperor's money somewhere else. "All of them," said Sima Qian who lived in that age, "would in turn start at once enthusiastically describing the wealth to be found in the foreign nations; those who told the most impressive tales were granted the seals of an envoy, while those who spoke more modestly were made assistants. As a result all sorts of worthless men hurried forward with wild tales to imitate their examples" (*SJ*, 3171; trans. based on Watson, 1958: 286).
"自博望侯开外国道以尊贵，其后从吏卒皆争上书言外国奇怪利害，求使。天子为其绝远，非人所乐往，听其言，予节，募吏民毋问所从来，为具备人众遣之，以广其道。"其中的一些使节的确到达了西域，但是其他人却把军需用在了不相干的地方。"其吏卒，"司马迁曰，"亦辄复盛推外国所有，言大者予节，言小者为副，故妄言无行之徒皆争效之。"（《史记》，第 3171 页；英译据华兹生，1958：第 286 页）

216 Waley, 1955. 韦利，1955。

217 Anthony F. P. Hulsewé rejects Waley's interpretation as unproved, and puts forward two other suggestions: either the horses were sought for Emperor Wu's stables, or they were prized as a means of improving the Chinese breed of horses (Loewe and Hulsewé, 1979: 134n332).
何四维认为韦利的阐述未经证实，因而拒绝接受；同时他又提出了另外两种假设：对这些马的寻求，不是为了补充武帝的马厩，就是因为它们被看作改良中国马种的途径（鲁惟一、何四维，1979：134，n332）。

218 For a detailed discussion of the development of the Kunlun myth and the belief in the Queen Mother of the West, see H. Wu, 1989: 110-41, esp. 117-26.
关于昆仑神话与西王母信仰发展的详细讨论，见巫鸿，1989：第 110—141 页，特别是第 117—126 页。

219 *Huainan zi*, 4.13.《淮南子》，卷四，第 13 页。

220 *HS*, 2596; trans. from Dubs, 1942: 232.
《汉书》，第 2596 页；英译据德效骞，1942：第 232 页。

221 *HS*, 1611; see Dubs, 1942: 233; Loewe, 1979: 96.
《汉书》，第 1611 页；德效骞，1942：第 233 页；鲁惟一，1979：第 96 页。

222 For photos and descriptions of these stone works, see Paludan, 1991: 17-27. It is tempting to link these sculptured works with a statue that Huo Qubing seized during his expedition to the northwest. The records of this event, however, remain open to doubt. In the earliest sources the statue was named "the golden man [used by] the king of the Xiutu in sacrificing to Heaven." Another version of the story is found in the *Han Wu gushi* (The tale of Emperor Wu of the Han): "After the king of Kunxie killed the king of Xiutu, he surrendered his tribe to [the Han court]. He obtained the divine golden men [from Xiutu], and [after these statues were presented to the Han court], they were placed in the Ganquan Palace. These golden men were all more than ten *chi* high. No cows or sheep were used in sacrifices to them, and only incense was burned and people worshipped." Based on the description of the ritual, Liu Xiaobiao (462-521 A.D.) suspected that these were actually Buddhist images. This interpretation is unreliable because even Indians did not make anthropomorphic images of the Buddha during the second century B.C. For discussions of records related to the statue, see Ren Jiyu, 1981: 61-62; Zürcher, 1959: 21.
关于这些石雕作品的图像与描述，见帕鲁丹，1991：第 17—27 页。作者将这些雕塑作品与霍去病西征时所得的一件雕像相联系，是十分引人入胜的。而事实上，关于此事的记载值得怀疑。在早期的文献里，这件雕像被命名为"休屠王祭天金人"。关于这个传说的另一版本见《汉武故事》："昆邪王杀休屠王，以其众降。得金人之神，上置甘泉宫。金人皆长丈余。其祭不用牛羊，惟烧香礼拜。"基于对此仪式的描述，刘孝标（462—521 年）推测这些金人实际为佛教形象。这一阐述是不可信的，因为在公元前 2 世纪，即便是印度人，也没有创造出佛陀的拟人化形象。对有关该雕像文献记载的讨论，见任继愈，1981：第 61—62 页；许理和，1959：第 21 页。

223 For excavation reports and discussions of these rock-cut tombs, see
Shandong Provincial Museum, 1972; Xuzhou Museum et al., 1988; Li Yinde, 306
1990. Nanjing Museum and Tongshan Cultural House, 1985; Nanjing Museum, 1973; Xuzhou Museum, 1984; Thorp, 1987, 1991.
关于这些崖墓的发掘报告和讨论，见山东博物馆，1972；徐州市博物馆等，1988；李银德，1990；南京博物院、铜山县文化馆，1985；南京博物院，1973；徐州市博物馆，1984；杜朴，1987, 1991。

224 Institute of Archaeology, CASS, and Hebei Provincial Cultural Relics Administration, 1980. For an English introduction to the tombs, see Thorp, 1991.
中国社会科学院考古研究所、河北省文物管理局，1980。关于这些墓葬的英文介绍，见杜朴，1991。

225 *SJ*, 256.《史记》，第 256 页。

226 Nails with traces of wood were found in the rear chamber. The excavators hypothesized that in order to secure the stone panels, pieces of wood may have been inserted into the gaps between these panels (Institute of Archaeology, CASS, and Hebei Provincial Cultural Relics Administration, 1980: 1.22). This method, however, could not possibly secure the stone ceiling without the support of beams and lintels.
后室发现有铁钉和朽木残迹。据考古工作者推测，这是为了保证石板不致坠落，因而在石板之间的缝隙里嵌入了大量木条（中国社会科学院考古研究所、河北省文物管理局，1980:1.22）。然而，没有横梁和立柱的支撑，这种方法并不能保障石天花板的安全。

227 *Ibid.* 同上。

228 It is said that Zhang Qian, after staying in the Western Territories (Xiyu) from 138 to 126 B.C., "reported on Indian Buddhism" to the emperor on his return. For discussions of this episode and related historical records, see Ren Jiyu, 1981: 59-60; Zürcher, 1959: 20-21. According to another tradition, a Chinese envoy named Jing Lu was instructed in the teachings of Buddhist sutras by the Yuezhi prince in the year 2 B.C. This story occurs first in the *Wei lue* (A brief history of Wei), compiled around the mid-third century by Yu Huan; see *Sanguo zhi*, 858.
据说张骞自公元前 138—前 126 年滞留西域，返汉后向武帝禀报"天竺浮屠之教"的事。有关这段情节之相关历史记载的讨论，见任继愈，1981：第 59—60 页；许理和，1959：第 20—21 页。根据另一种传说，一个叫景卢的中国使臣，曾于公元前 2 年由月氏王传授讲解佛经。该说法最早见于《魏略》，大约在公元 3 世纪中叶，又经过了鱼豢的编辑加工；见《三国志》，第 858 页。

229 The Eastern Han text *Gujin zhu* (Commentaries on past and present events) by Fu Wuji records architectural plans of the mausoleums of the twelve Eastern Han emperors. According to this record, five Eastern Han imperial cemeteries shared the same design, and each contained a "stone palace." The earliest one belonged to Emperor Ming (*HHS*, 3149).
东汉伏无忌所撰《古今注》，记载了东汉十二帝陵的修筑计划。按此书记载，五个东汉皇家墓地采用了相同的设计，每一墓地都包含一个"石室"，其中建筑最早的是明帝陵。(《后汉书》，第 3149 页)。

230 *Luoyang qielan ji*, 196, records: "Upon the emperor's death, [a model of] Jetavana Garden was built on his tomb. Thereafter stupas were sometimes constructed [even] on the graves of the common people" (trans. based on Y. T. Wang, 1984: 173). *Lihuo lun* also records that Emperor Ming's tomb bore an image of the Buddha; quoted in *Luoyang qielan ji*, 198.
《洛阳伽蓝记》，第 196 页："明帝崩，起祇洹于陵上。自此以后，百姓冢上，或作浮图焉。"（英译据王伊同，1984：第 173 页）《理惑论》亦言明帝陵上有浮图（《洛阳伽蓝记》，第 198 页）。

231 Based on archaeological finds, old texts, and inscriptions, I have identified 33 stone shrines. All these examples were built during the 150 years from the mid-first century to the end of the second century. A study of the 23 Han imperial funerary shrines further confirms that the change in building material from wood to stone occurred in the mid-first century A.D. According to archaeological surveys, the offering shrines of all Western Han emperors were wooden-framed structures covered with tile roofs. Remains of large foundations, roof tiles, and pillar bases have been observed in the funerary parks of five Western Han rulers, namely, Emperors Jing, Wu, Zhao, Xuan, and Yuan. As mentioned earlier, the first imperial stone shrine was built for Emperor Ming soon after A.D. 58 (see H. Wu, 1987a: 426-504).
根据古代文献、碑刻及考古发现的有关资料，我已经汇集了 33 处石祠堂的材料；这些祠堂都建于公元 1 世纪中叶至 2 世纪末的 150 年间。有关汉代 23 处帝王墓祠的一项研究进一步证实，祠堂建筑材料由木到石的变化发生于公元 1 世纪中叶。根据考古勘测，西汉帝王的享堂都属瓦顶木架结构。经测定，西汉帝王陵园内的所有庞大地基、瓦顶、石阙遗迹，分别属于景帝、武帝、昭帝、宣帝、元帝。正如先前所述，第一处石构祠堂，是公元 58 年之后不久为明帝而建的（巫鸿，1987a：第 426—504 页）。

232 A pillar-gate at Zitong in Sichuan has been attributed to Li Ye, who died in A.D. 36. Although this gate lacks an original inscription, two other early stone gates that bear inscribed dates are the Huang Shengqing gate and the Gongcao gate, both located at Pingyi in Shandong. The Huang Shengqing gate was built in A.D. 86, and the Gongcao gate in A.D. 87 (see Chen Mingda, 1961: 11).
位于四川省梓潼的一座阙门，据说属于卒于公元 36 年的李业。该阙不见铭文资料。另外两座年代更早的纪年石阙——皇圣卿阙和功曹阙，皆在山东平邑。皇圣卿阙建于公元 86 年，功曹阙建于公元 87 年（陈明达，1961：第 11 页）。

233 Some Western Han stone tablets have been found, but their inscriptions are short and usually only document the construction of burial structures. These early examples differ from Eastern Han stelae, which recorded the life and merit of the deceased (see Yang Kuan, 1985: 154-56).

目前已有部分西汉石碑被发现，其铭文简短，通常只是作为墓葬建构的标识。这些早期石碑记录了墓主的行状，与东汉石碑有所不同（杨宽，1985：第 154—156 页）。

234 According to *SJZ*, 294, stone horses and elephants were erected along the Spirit Road at the mausoleum of Emperor Guangwu, the founder of the Eastern Han. But according to *Dongguan Han ji*, 13, the construction of this mausoleum only began in A.D. 50 (see Lin Liming and Sun Zhongjia, 1984: 37). For a general introduction to Eastern Han mortuary statues, see Yang Guan, 1985: 150-51.
据《水经注》（第 294 页），东汉创建者光武帝陵前的石马和石象是沿神道而立的。但是据《东观汉记》（第 13 页），该陵墓的建造只是在公元 50 年才刚刚开始（林利明、孙仲嘉，1984：第 37 页）。有关东汉丧葬雕刻的基本介绍，见杨宽，1985：第 150—151 页。

235 For discussions of Eastern Han rock-cut tombs in Sichuan, see T. K. Cheng, 1957: 139-54; Fairbank, 1972: 19-28; H. Wu, 1987a: 459-64.
有关四川地区东汉崖墓的讨论，见郑德坤，1957：第 139—154 页；费慰梅，1972：第 19—28 页；巫鸿，1987a：第 459—464 页。

236 For the history and textural resources of this temple, see Ren Jiyu, 1981: 101-3.
关于此庙的历史文献资料，见任继愈，1981：第 101—103 页。

237 *HHS* 1428-29. Evidence for Liu Ying's worship of the Buddha can also be found in an edict issued by Emperor Ming: "The Prince of Chu recites the subtle words of Huanglao, and respectfully performs the gentle sacrifices to the Buddha. After three months of purification and fasting, he has made a solemn covenant (or a vow) with the spirits. What dislike or suspicion (from Our part) could there be, that he must repent (for his sins)? Let [the silk which he sent for] redemption be sent back, in order thereby to contribute to the lavish entertainment of the upasakas and śramanas" (*HHS* 1429; trans. based on Zürcher, 1959: 1.27). Emperor Ming and Liu Ying grew up together, and they remained close. *HHS* (102, 109, 110, 114) records that after Liu Ying became prince of Chu in A.D. 41, he met the emperor in Luoyang at least four times, in 56, 59, 63, and 68.
《后汉书》，第 1428—1429 页。刘英兼祠浮图事，亦见之于明帝的一份诏书："楚王诵黄老之微言，尚浮屠之仁祠，洁斋三月，与神为誓，何嫌何疑，当有悔吝，其还赎，以助伊蒲塞桑门之盛馔。"（《后汉书》，第 1429 页；英译据许理和，1959：1.27）明帝与刘英一起长大，他们保持着亲密的关系。《后汉书》（第 102、109、110、114 页）记载，刘英于公元 41 年成为楚王后，分别于公元 56、59、63 和 68 年，在洛阳与明帝至少有过四次会晤。

238 Zürcher, 1959: 1.26. 许理和，1959：1.26。

239 *Ibid.*, 1.30. 同上，1.30。

240 *HHS* 1082, 2922. See Tang Yongtong, 1938: 56. I have proposed elsewhere that the emperor sacrificed to the Buddha as part of his Daoist worship (H. 307
Wu, 1986: 300-301).
《后汉书》，第1082、2922页。见汤用彤，1938：第56页。桓帝祠佛，是其道教信仰的一部分，这个观点我已经在别处提及（巫鸿，1986：第300—301页）。

241 *HHS*, 1075.《后汉书》，第1075页。

242 The original record reads: "He erected a large Buddhist temple. From bronze he had a human [effigy] made, the body of which was gilded and dressed in silk and brocade. [At the top of the building] nine layers of bronze scales were suspended, and below there was a building of several stories with covered ways, which could contain more than 3,000 people, who all studied and read Buddhist scriptures. He ordered the Buddhist devotees from the region [under his supervision] and from the adjacent prefectures to listen and to accept the doctrine. [Those people] he exempted from the other statutory labor duties in order to attract them. Those who on account of this from near and afar came to [the monastery] numbered more than 5,000. Whenever there was [the ceremony of] 'bathing the Buddha,' he had always great quantities of wine and food set out [for distribution], and mats were spread along the roads over a distance of several tens of *li*. [On these occasions] some 10,000 people came to enjoy the spectacle and the food. The expenses [of such a ceremony] amounted to many millions [of cash]" (*HHS* 2368; *Sanguo zhi*, 1185; trans. based on Zürcher, 1959: 1.28).
最初的记载是这样的："（笮融）大起浮屠寺。上累金盘，下为重楼，又堂阁周回，可容三千许人，作黄金涂像，衣以锦采……每浴佛，辄多设饮饭，布席于路，其有就食及观者且万余人。"（《后汉书》，第2368页；《三国志》，第1185页；英译据许理和，1959：1.28）。

243 H. Wu, 1986: 297-303. 巫鸿，1986：第297—303页。

244 Sima Qian recorded that when Zhang Qian visited Daxia, he saw bamboo canes from Qiong and cloth made in Sichuan, which were imported to Daxia via India. He therefore speculated that a direct route must have connected India and southwest China. Upon receiving this report, Emperor Wu sent troops to attempt to reopen this route (*SJ*, 3166). In a previous study I have examined some 50 motifs and artworks that show Indian influences. Only those from Sichuan imitate Indian prototypes in a quite

literal manner; those from eastern China are free interpretations of Indian works (H. Wu, 1986: 266-73).
据司马迁所记，张骞出使大夏时，见有经由印度传入大夏的邛竹杖、蜀布。张骞据此推测必有连接印度与中国西南部的一条直接通道。武帝接到报告后，遂遣军前往，试图再度打通这个通道（《史记》，第 3166 页）。我在先前的研究中分析过大约 50 种带有印度影响的艺术题材和艺术作品，其中，只有出自四川的作品对其印度原型的仿效几近于翻制；而那些出自中国东部的艺术品，则对其印度原型做了自由的发挥（巫鸿，1986：第 266—273 页）。

245 *Luoyang qielan ji*; quoted in Zhu Kongyang, 1937: 13.10a.
《洛阳伽蓝记》，引自朱孔阳，1937：卷十三，第 10 页。

246 *Chu sanzang ji*, 42-43. Zürcher (1959: 1.29-30) believes that the *Sutra in Forty-two Sections* was written during the late first or early second century.
《出三藏记集》，第 42—43 页。许理和（1959：1.29—30）认为，《四十二章经》著于 1 世纪末或 2 世纪初。

247 *Fayuan zhulin, juan* 13.《法苑珠林》，卷十三。

248 *Hou Han ji, juan* 10, 122.《后汉纪》，卷十，第 122 页。

249 See Tang Yongtong, 1938: 3-4. There are many conflicting opinions concerning the authenticity of the *Lihuo lun*. Some leading scholars, e.g., Hu Yinling, Liang Qichao, Tokiwa Daijo, and Lü Zheng, have considered this treatise a spurious work. Others, more numerous, e.g., Sun Yirang, Hu Shi, Tang Yongtong, Henri Maspero, and Paul Pelliot, regard it as an invaluable source of information on the earliest history of Chinese Buddhism. Fukui Kojun (1952) reexamines most of these opinions in his extensive study on this work. He concluded that the treatise was written around the middle of the third century (see also Zürcher, 1959: 1.13-15).
汤用彤，1938：第 3—4 页。学界关于《理惑论》的真伪问题，观点颇不一致。一些著名学者当中，如胡应麟、梁启超、常盘大定、吕澂等，认为该书系伪书；而更多学者如孙诒让、胡适、汤用彤、马伯乐、伯希和等，认为该书并没有为中国早期佛教史提供有价值的信息。福井康顺（1952）在对该书进行过深入研究后，对上述各家观点作了进一步检视，他推断该书成于公元 3 世纪中叶左右（又见许理和，1959：1.13—15）。

250 I have found a number of mirrors bearing Buddha images, but these were all created after the second century. Buddhist images have also been found on a cliff near Lianyungang in Jiangsu, but these may have been created after the second century. For a discussion of these works. see H. Wu, 1986: 273-302.
我已发现了相当部分带有佛像的铜镜资料，但它们全都制作于公元 2 世纪后。佛教图像在江苏连云港附近的一处摩崖上也有发现，但它们或许也是公元 2 世纪后的作品。关于这些作品的讨论，见巫鸿，1986：第 273—302 页。

251 For a more detailed discussion of these motifs and their contexts, see *ibid.*, 268-73.
有关这些题材及与其相关背景问题的详细讨论，见巫鸿，1986：第 268—273 页。

252 H. Wu, 1989: 132-40. 巫鸿，1989：第 132—140 页。

253 H. Wu, 1986: 266-69. 巫鸿，1986：第 266—269 页。

254 These are lines from the Han folk song, "Buchu Ximen xing" (Strolling out the western gate).
选自汉代民谣《步出西门行》。

255 Translation from Birrell, 1988: 75. 英译据比勒尔，1988：第 75 页。

Chapter Three The Monumental City Chang'an
㊂ 纪念碑式城市——长安

1 My quotation of the poem is based on the trans. in Graham, 1965: 106.
这首诗的英译据葛瑞汉，1965：第 106 页。

2 *HS*, 4193.《汉书》，第 4193 页。

3 Schorske, 1963. 舒尔斯克，1963。

4 For a concise and critical introduction to these two approaches, see Kostof, 1991: 43-45. Some scholars have consciously tried to employ these two views as alternative methods in their reconstruction of a city. Thus, the first and second chapters in Anselm L. Strauss's (1961: 5-31) popular book, *Images of the American City*, focus on the spatial and temporal aspects of a city, respectively.
关于这两种观察方法的简介和评论，见科斯托夫，1991：第 43—45 页。有的学者在关于重构城市历史的研究中已经有意识地将这两种观点作为不同的方法进行探讨。安塞姆·L. 施特劳斯在其论美国城市形象的通俗著作的第一章和第二章（1961：第 5—31 页）中，分别集中讨论了城市的空间性和时间性。

5 For a discussion of the literary genre of *fu*, see Knechtges, 1976: 12-43.
关于"赋"这一文体的讨论，见康达维，1976：第 12—43 页。

6 *WX*, 1.21-22; trans. based on Knechtges, 1982: 99.
《文选》，卷一，第 21—22 页；英译据康达维，1982：第 99 页。

7 *SJ*, 2715-17; *HS*, 58, 2119-21; trans. based on Watson, 1958: 1.218.
《史记》，第 2715—2717 页；《汉书》，第 58、2119—2121 页；英译据华兹生，

1958：1.218。

8 *WX*, 1.46; trans. from Knechtges, 1982: 103.
《文选》，卷一，第 46 页；英译据康达维，1982：第 103 页。

9 *WX* 1.151-53; trans. from Knechtges, 1982: 143-44.
《文选》，卷一，第 151—153 页；英译据康达维，1982：第 143—144 页。

10 Zhang Heng wrote his two rhapsodies on the Eastern and Western capitals when he served as master of documents in Nanyang some time between A.D. 100 and 108.
大约公元 100 年至 108 年间，张衡在任南阳主簿时写了《东京赋》和《西京赋》。

11 *YWLJ*, 1098.《艺文类聚》，第 1098 页。

12 In this discussion I focus only on the beginnings of the two rhapsodies. Knechtges (1982: 28) compares the two works on a larger scale: "Zhang Heng, who must have been dissatisfied with Ban Gu's treatment of the subject, wrote two much longer rhapsodies on the Han capitals. In his treatment of
308 Chang'an, Zhang pokes fun at the Former Han emperor's obsession with material comfort, his futile efforts to discover the 'secret of immortality,' and his infatuation with pretty young consorts. In his Luoyang rhapsody, Zhang describes in detail many of the important Eastern Han rituals, that were either omitted or only casually mentioned in Ban Gu's *fu*."
在此我只集中讨论两赋的开头部分。康达维（1982：第 28 页）在更大范围内对两篇作品进行了比较："张衡不满意班固的作品，他为汉代都城写了两篇更长的赋。在关于长安的赋中，张衡取笑西汉皇帝沉迷于物质享乐，为追求神秘的仙境所做的各种无用事情，以及他对女色的迷恋。在关于洛阳的赋中，张衡对东汉重要的礼仪活动进行了详细的描述，这些内容在班固的赋中或者被忽略，或者一带而过。"

13 *WX*, 1.268-73; trans. based on Knechtges, 1982: 185-86.
《文选》，卷一，第 268—273 页；英译据康达维，1982：第 185—186 页。

14 *WX*, 1.488-90; trans. from Knechtges, 1982: 241.
同上，第 488—490 页；英译据康达维，1982：第 241 页。

15 *HS*, 1755; trans. based on Knechtges, 1976: 12-13.
《汉书》，第 1755 页；英译据康达维，1976：第 12—13 页。

16 Lowenthal, 1975: 28. 鲁文思，1975：第 28 页。

17 For an excellent discussion of the rhetorical tradition of *fu*, see Knechtges, 1976: 21-25.
关于赋的历史的精彩论述，见康达维，1976：第 21—25 页。

18 Ban Gu wrote in the preface to his two rhapsodies on the western and eastern capitals: "Even though this matter is inconsequential, the old patterns of former statesmen and the good deeds bequeathed by the reigning house cannot be forgotten. I humbly observe the area within the sea is calm and peaceful and the court has no problems. At the capital they have built palaces and halls, dredged moats and ditches, erected parks and enclosures in order to complete the institutions. Aged men from the western territory, all harboring resentment and hoping for a kind glance from the emperor, lavishly praise the old institutions of Chang'an and hold the opinion that Luoyang is a shabby place. Therefore. I have written the 'Two Capitals Rhapsody' in order to present an exhaustive account of the things that daze and dazzle the Chang'an multitudes and rebut them by means of the patterns and institutions of the present" (*WX*, 1.18-21; trans. from Knechtges, 1982: 99).
班固在《两都赋》序中写道："斯事虽细，然先臣之旧式，国家之遗美，不可阙也。臣窃见海内清平，朝廷无事，京师脩宫室，浚城隍，起苑囿，以备制度。西土耆老，咸怀怨思，冀上之眷顾，而盛称长安旧制，有陋雒邑之议。故臣作两都赋，以极众人之所眩曜，折以今之法度。"《文选》，卷一，第 18—21 页；英译据康达维，1982：第 99 页。

19 Zhang Heng's biography records that he "comprehended all the Five Classics." Although he was given the position of grand historian, he never wrote a historical work and later became an attendant (*shizhong*) of Emperor Shun (*HHS*, 1897-951).
见《张衡传》。尽管他被迁为太史令，但他并没有写过任何历史著作，后来在顺帝时又升迁为侍中。《后汉书》，第 1897—1951 页。

20 *WX*, 1.274-75; trans. based on Knechtges, 1982: 187.
《文选》，卷一，第 274—275 页；英译据康达维，1982：第 187 页。

21 Trans. from Wheatley, 1971: 430. 英译据惠特利，1971：第 430 页。

22 *Shijing*, 315; trans. from Waley, 1978: 281.
《诗经》，第 315 页；英译据韦利，1978：第 281 页。

23 *SJ*, 510; trans. from Karlgren, 1950b: 189-90. There are other similar descriptions in the Classic. For example, the poem "Wen Wang you sheng" (*SJ*, 526-27) records the first Zhou king's construction of his capital Feng: "King Wen made a city in Feng. . . . / The wall he built was moated. . . . /The walls of Feng were where the four quarters came together; /the royal ruler was their support" (Karlgren, 1950b: 198-99).
同上，第 510 页；英译据高本汉，1950b：第 189—190 页。文献中还有其他类似的表述。例如，《文王有声》篇（《诗经》，第 526—527 页）记载了第一代周王营建其都城丰的历史："作邑于丰……/筑城伊淢……/维丰之垣。四方攸同，/王后维翰。"英译见高本汉，1950b：第198—199页。

24 For a concise introduction to these Classics and the growth of classical scholarship, see Twitchett and Loewe, 1986: 754-64.
关于这些经典以及经学发展的历史简要介绍，见杜希德、鲁惟一，1986：第754—764页。

25 Trans. based on Steinhardt, 1990: 33. 英译据斯坦哈特，1990：第33页。

26 It should be noted that this "classical" model has also offered possibilities for different interpretations. In some works, mostly those completed shortly after the Han but also including modern reconstructions, the Confucian classical tradition is adapted in a literal sense. Chang'an is thought of as a well-planned metropolis "60 *li* on each side," its shape modeled on stars and constellations, and its streets forming a rigid grid as in the "Records of Workmanship" plan. In many other cases, especially in works done from the Song dynasty on, historical information is increasingly integrated into a general reconstruction plan.
需要说明的是，这种"经典性"模式同样为不同的解释提供了可能性。在一些很可能成文于汉代稍后的作品中（但也包括现代的一些重构计划），传统儒家经典被按照字面的意义进行解释。比如，长安被看作一座"每面六十里长"的大都会，其形状模仿了星宿，其街道按照《考工记》的规划交错为严格的网格，等等。在其他一些例子中，特别是在宋代以后的作品中，历史信息被日益综合进总体性的重构方案。

27 During recent years the "classical" tradition has begun to lose its grip. Encouraged by extensive archaeological excavations of Chang'an, some Chinese scholars have begun to shift their focus to the complex history of the city. But such works have just begun and a reconstruction of Chang'an's development is often blurred by generalizations based on references from various periods. The excellent work on Chang'an by Liu Yunyong (1982), for example, roughly follows the city's history from its birth to its flourishing and fall. But chapters within this framework are devoted to various aspects of this city and synthesize early and late historical records.
近年来，"经典性"的传统开始失去控制力。受到不断积累的长安考古发掘的启发，有的中国学者开始将其考虑点转移到该城的复杂的历史。但是，这类研究还只是刚刚开始出现，对长安历史发展的重构仍常常被基于不同时代材料的一般性描述所模糊。例如，刘运勇（1982）在其关于长安的一篇精彩文章中勾勒了该城诞生、繁荣和衰落的历史，但是这一叙事框架中的各部分陷入了对该城不同方面的论述，并且综合了早期和晚期的各种历史记载。

28 *HS*, 22-23. From the time when Gaozu was forced by Xiang Yu to leave Xianyang until 202 B.C., he conquered several places in southern Shaanxi, including Yong (*HS*, 31) and Shaan (*HS*, 33), and established a temporary capital in Yueyang (*HS*, 33). There is no record that he went back to Xianyang before 202 B.C.
《汉书》，第 22—23 页。公元前 202 年之前，高祖为项羽所迫，撤离咸阳，此后，他攻下了陕西的许多个地方，包括雍（《汉书》，第 31 页）和陕（《汉书》，第 33 页），在栎阳建立了临时的都城（《汉书》，第 33 页）。史书中未记载他在公元前 202 年之前再回过咸阳。

29 In 202 B.C., following his visit to Xianyang in the fifth month, Gaozu attacked the King of Yan and Li Ji in Yingchuan (*HS*, 58; *SJ*, 381).
公元前 202 年五月高祖重访咸阳之后，又击破了燕王和颍川的利机（《史记》，第 381 页；《汉书》，第 58 页）。

30 *Chang'an ji* records: "The Xingle Palace was built by the First Emperor, and was repaired and redecorated during the Han" (quoted in *SZCZ*, 2.12b). For Xiao He's activities during this period, see *HS*, 2007-11.
《长安记》记载，兴乐宫是秦始皇所建，在汉代被重新修整和装饰（转引自《宋注长安志》，卷二，第 12 页）。关于这一时期萧何的事迹，见《汉书》，第 2007—2011 页。

31 It is said that the construction began in the ninth month of 202 B.C. and was completed in the second month of 200 B.C. (see Liu Yunyong, 1982: 5).
据说这一重建工程开始于公元前 202 年九月，完成于公元前 200 年二月。见刘运勇 1982：第 5 页。

32 *Guanzhong ji* (A record of the Guanzhong region) states that the whole complex was more than 20 *li* in circumference and had fourteen halls (quoted in *SZCZ*, 3.12b). A Han *li* equals 417.5 meters. The names of some of these halls are recorded in *SFHT*, 13.
据《关中记》记载，这组宫殿周长 20 多里，有 14 座宫殿（转引自《宋注长安志》，3.12b）。汉代一里折合 417.5 米。这些宫殿的名字见于《三辅黄图》，第 13 页。

33 *SFHT* (13) states that the hall was 49 *zhang* and 7 *chi* east and west. A Han *chi* equals 23.1 cm.
《三辅黄图》（第 13 页）记载，该殿东西长四十九丈七尺。汉代的一尺折合 23.1 厘米。

34 According to *SFHT*, quoted in *SZCZ*, 3.13a, it is unclear whether these figures were the Qin emperor's Twelve Golden Men.
根据《宋注长安志》，卷三，第 13 页引《三辅黄图》。我们无法确定这些雕像是否一定是秦始皇所铸的十二金人。

35 See Liu Yunyong, 1982: 7. 刘运勇，1982：第 7 页。

36 According to *Miao ji* (A record of temples) quoted in *SZCZ*, 3.5a.
《三辅黄图》引《庙记》。

37 See *SFHT*, 13, 14.《三辅黄图》，第 13、14 页。

38 *HS*, 64; *SJ*, 385.《史记》，第 385 页；《汉书》，第 64 页。

39 Sima Qian's record of this event is rather confusing: under the eighth year of Gaozu (199 B.C.) he stated that the emperor saw the Weiyang Palace and complained about its extravagance. But he also relates that the palace was not completed until the ninth year (198 B.C.). Ban Gu redated this event to the seventh year (200 B.C.) and partially resolves the problem: it can be inferred that the emperor saw the unfinished Weiyang Palace when he went to Chang'an to hold the ceremony marking the completion of the Changle Palace (*SJ*, 385-86; *HS*, 64).
司马迁对这一事件的记述相当混乱。如他说在高祖八年（前 199），皇帝看到未央宫，抱怨过分奢华。但他又说到九年（前 198）九月，该宫尚未竣工。班固把该宫殿的修建定为高祖七年（前 200），部分地解决了这一问题。据此我们可以推测，当皇帝在公元前 199 年到长安时，见到的是没有完全竣工的未央宫。(《史记》，第 385—386 页；《汉书》，第 64 页。)

40 *HS*, 65-66.《汉书》，第 65—66 页。

41 *SJ*, 2723; *HS*, 2127-28.
《史记》，第 2723 页；《汉书》，第 2127—2128 页。

42 Both *SJ* and *HS* contain biographies of Shusun Tong (*SJ*, 2720-26; *HS*, 2124-31). The translations of the following quotations from the *SJ* biography are based on Watson, 1958: 222-29.
《史记》和《汉书》都有叔孙通传（《史记》，第 2720—2726 页；《汉书》，第 2124—2131 页）。以下所引《史记》中的文字，英译据华兹生，1958：第 222—229 页。

43 *SJ*, 2722; *HS*, 2126; trans. from Watson, 1958: 224.
《史记》，第 2722 页；《汉书》，第 2126 页；英译据华兹生，1958：第 224 页。

44 Different dates of this ceremony are given in *SJ* and *HS*. Whereas Gaozu's biographies in both books record that the Changle Palace was completed in the second month of the seventh year and the emperor went there on that occasion (*SJ*, 385; *HS*, 64), it is stated in the biographies of Shusun Tong that these events took place in the tenth month of the year. This second record is suspicious, because according to Ban Gu, in the tenth month Gaozu was leading an expeditionary army to attack the rebellious general Han Xin (*HS*, 63). It is possible that the ceremony, actually held in the

second month, was later assigned a new date because in the Han calender the tenth month marked the beginning of the new year.
《史记》和《汉书》所记载的这次典礼的时间不同。两书中高祖的传记都记载长乐宫竣工于七年二月，当时皇帝出席了竣工典礼（《史记》，第 385 页；《汉书》，第 64 页），而叔孙通传记载这些事件发生在该年十月。第二种记载颇值得怀疑，因为根据《汉书》记载，十月高祖率军攻打韩信的叛乱（《汉书》，第 63 页）。实际上典礼很可能举行在二月，后来按以十月为正月的历法改记。

45 *SJ*, 2723; *HS*, 2126; trans. from Watson, 1958: 224.
《史记》，第 2723 页；《汉书》，第 2126 页；英译据华兹生，1958：第 224 页。

46 *SJ*, 385. Ban Gu gives a different date, see note 39 above.
《史记》，第 385 页。班固所记载的时间不同，见本章注 39。

47 *WX*, 1.42-45; trans. based on Knechtges, 1982: 103.
《文选》，卷一，第 42—45 页；英译据康达维，1982：第 103 页。

48 *SJZ*, 241.《水经注》，第 241 页。

49 *HS*, 1210.《汉书》，第 1210 页。

50 *HS*, 2098. 同上，第 2098 页。

51 This measurement is given in Z. S. Wang, 1982: 4. Other measurements and descriptions of this site can be found in Bishop, 1938: 68-78; Adachi Kiroku, 1933; Liu Dunzhen, 1932.
这一数据取自王仲殊，1982：第 4 页。关于这一遗址的其他数据和描述见毕士博，1938：第 68—78 页；足立喜六，1933；刘敦桢，1932。

52 See Wang Yi, 1990: 36. The *Zuo zhuan* (1783, 2149) records that Duke Zhuang of Lu built three *tai* in a single year, and that even ministers constructed similar buildings.
王毅，1990：第 36 页。《左传》（第 1783、2149 页）记载鲁庄公在一年内修建了三座台，甚至大臣也修建这类建筑。

53 *SJ*, 385-86; trans. based on Watson, 1958: 137. The same passage is also given in *HS*, 64.
《史记》，第 385—386 页；英译据华兹生，1958：第 137 页。同样的文字还见《汉书》，第 64 页。

54 *SJ*, 2015; *HS*, 2008; trans. based on Watson, 1958: 151-52. This event and the tension between military generals and civil officers are also recorded in *HS*, 2031-32.
《史记》，第 2015 页；《汉书》，第 2008 页；英译据华兹生，1958：第 151—152 页。这一事件以及将领和文官的紧张关系的记载，也见于《汉书》，第

2031—2032 页。

55 *SJ*, 2627; *HS*, 1876; trans. from Watson, 1958: 197.
《史记》，第 2627 页；《汉书》，第 1876 页；英译据华兹生，1958：第 197 页。

56 *SJ*, 981-82. For Yang Chengyan's role in Chang'an's early construction, see Ma Xianxing, 1976: 233-34.
《史记》，第 981—982 页。关于阳成延在长安早期建造史中地位的讨论，见马先醒，1976：第 233—234 页。

57 *SJ*, 385; *HS*, 64. It is also said that Xiao He built two pavilions, one called Tianlu ge and the other Qilin ge, to house official documents. But this record is from a much later text and is not supported by Sima Qian and Ban Gu's writings; see *SZCZ*, 3.9b.
《史记》，第 385 页；《汉书》，第 64 页。据说萧何建造了两座阁来保存官方的档案，一曰天禄阁，一曰麒麟阁。但是这一记载出自晚期文献，在司马迁和班固的著作中找不到证据；见《宋注长安志》，卷三，第 9 页。

58 See Yan Shigu's commentary in *HS*, 64. 见《汉书》，第 64 页颜师古注。

59 *HS*, 67, records a formal audience at the beginning of the tenth year, but according to *SJ*, 387, it was held in the Changle Palace.
《汉书》第 67 页记载了十年年初的一次正式的宫廷会议，但是根据《史记》第 387 页来看，这次会议是在长乐宫举行的。

60 *SJ*, 386-87; *HS*, 66. 《史记》，第 386—387 页；《汉书》，第 66 页。

61 The arsenal and granary were built by Xiao He in the seventh or eighth year of Gaozu's reign (*HS*, 64; *SJ*, 385). The market was probably established in the sixth year; see *Shi ji dashiji* (A *Shi ji* chronicle), quoted in Wang Yizhi, 1937: 17.
萧何在高祖七年或八年建造武库和太仓（《史记》，第 385 页；《汉书》，第 64 页）。大市可能建于六年；见王益之，1937：第 17 页引《史记大事记》

62 Karlgren, 1950b: 198. 高本汉，1950b：第 198 页。

63 *LJ*, 1588-1589. 《礼记》，第 1588—1589 页。

64 *ZZ* cited in *SZCZ*, 2.2a. 《宋注长安志》卷二，第 2 页，引《左传》。

65 *Shi ming*, 2.10b. 《释名》，卷二，第 10 页。

66 Gaozu's father died in the seventh month of 197 B.C. and was immediately buried. His tomb should have been prepared before his death (*SJ*, 387; *HS*, 67).
高祖的父亲卒于公元前 197 年七月，立刻被下葬。可以想象他的墓葬应在其死前就已经准备好了。《史记》，第 387 页；《汉书》，第 67 页。

67 *SJ*, 392; *HS*, 79-80. Gaozu died on the *jiachen* day in the fourth month and was buried 23 days later on the *bingyin* day in the fifth month.
《史记》，第 392 页；《汉书》，第 79—80 页。高祖卒于四月甲辰，于 23 天后，五月丙寅下葬。

68 The tradition of the "mausoleum town" can be traced back to the Qin dynasty. It had been noted as early as in the first century A.D. that "the [subsequent] flourishing of 'mausoleum towns' originated from the powerful Qin" (*HHS*, 1437). Not long after the future First Emperor started to construct his Lishan mausoleum, a small town called Li Yi, or the Town of Li(shan), was established near the site in 231 B.C.; and it was further expanded in 221 B.C., when he claimed the title of emperor. The purpose of this Qin town, however, was to house and administer the large number of workers, and thus differed essentially from that of the Han dynasty mausoleum towns, which functioned both "to serve the dead" and "to strengthen the root [i.e., the capital area] of the dynasty" (*HS*, 2123). See Liu Qingzhu and Li Yufang, 1987: 224.
设立"陵邑"的传统至少可以追溯到秦代。文献提到，早在公元 1 世纪的人就说过："臣愚以园邑之兴，始自强秦。"（《后汉书》，第 1437 页）公元前 231 年，未来的始皇帝开始修建骊山陵不久后，就在附近营建了骊邑。公元前 221 年嬴政称皇帝后，该城进一步扩大。但是，开始修建这座城的目的在于容纳并管理数量庞大的工匠；而汉代陵邑的功能则在于为死者服务，并且是"强本（都城地区）弱末（其他地区）之术"（《汉书》，第 2123 页）。因此，二者仍有根本的差别。见刘庆柱、李毓芳，1987：第 224 页。

69 According to a passage from *Kuodi zhi* (A geographic record), cited in a 310
commentary in *SJ*, 387.
据《史记》（第 387 页）正义引《括地志》。

70 For a general introduction to this mausoleum, see Liu Qingzhu and Li Yufang, 1987: 126-31.
对于该陵墓的总体介绍，见刘庆柱、李毓芳，1987：第 126—131 页。

71 According *SFHT*, 51, a section of this city was separated as the mausoleum town of Gaozu's father and was named Wannian Xian (County of 10,000 Years). But two modern archaeologists, Liu Qingzhu and Li Yufang (1987: 130), have argued that Wannian Xian was simply another name for Yueyang.
根据《三辅黄图》，第 51 页，该城的一部分划分出来当作高祖父亲的陵邑，称为万年县。但是刘庆柱和李毓芳（1987：第 130 页）认为万年县只是栎阳的别名。

72 *Han jiuyi* (Old ceremonies of the Han) cited in *WXTK*, *juan* 124, *kao* 1115.
《文献通考》，卷一二四引《汉旧仪》。

73 Upon Gaozu's death his heir and ministers held a ceremony in this temple (*HS*, 80). It thus must have been built during Gaozu's reign.
高祖去世时，他的继承者和大臣在该庙举行了葬礼（《汉书》，第 80 页）。因此该庙应建于高祖时期。

74 It is unclear when Gaozu began to built his tomb. According to Han ritual codes, each emperor began to construct his own tomb on ascending the throne. But this rule was probably put into practice after Gaozu's reign. It is possible that Gaozu started the construction of his tomb after he moved his capital to Chang'an in 200 B.C.
高祖开始修建其墓葬的时间不详。根据汉朝的礼法，每一位皇帝在登基时即开始建造自己的陵墓。但是，这个规则也许是在高祖之后开始实行的。有可能高祖在公元前 200 年迁都到长安之后就开始建造他的陵墓。

75 For an up-to-date introduction to Gaozu's mausoleum, see Liu Qingzhu and Li Yufang, 1987: 3-24.
关于高祖陵墓最新的介绍，见刘庆柱、李毓芳，1987：第 3—24 页。

76 Ban Gu provides two contradictory dates for the founding of Chang Ling Town: in the "Geography" chapter of *HS* he states that it was founded during Gaozu's reign (*HS*, 1545), but in the "Biography of Empress Lü" he records that it was established in 182 B.C., thirteen years after the emperor's death (*HS*, 99). The second date is confirmed by Liu Qingzhu and Li Yufang, 1987: 21.
班固所记建造长陵邑的两个时间彼此矛盾。《汉书・地理志》称建于高祖时期（《汉书》，第 1545 页），但是《高后纪》称建于高祖死后 13 年的公元前 182 年（《汉书》，第 99 页）。刘庆柱、李毓芳证实了后一种说法（1987：第 21 页）。

77 *HS*, 59.《汉书》，第 59 页。

78 *Yong lu, juan* 2.《雍录》，卷二。

79 Z. S. Wang, 1982: 4. The same author also states that the base of the later Chang'an city wall was 12 to 16 meters in width (*ibid.*, 2).
王仲殊，1982：第 4 页。同一作者也提到后期长安城墙的基础厚 12—16 米（同前，第 2 页）。

80 *SJ*, 1122.《史记》，第 1122 页。

81 *SJ*, 398. 同上，第 398 页。

82 *HS*, 88-91.《汉书》，第 88—91 页。

83 *HS*, 1543. 同上，第 1543 页。

84 Ma Xianxing (1976: 226-32) has reached a similar conclusion regarding the

building of the Chang'an wall. He also suggests that the second *SJ* passage cited may have been miscopied during the book's transmission and that the original text should have read: "In the fifth year it was completed; and in the sixth year feudal princes came to a court audience, celebrating [its inauguration] in the tenth month."
关于长安城墙的修建问题，马先醒（1976：第226—232页）也有同样的结论。他还指出此处所引《史记》的第二段可能在流传过程中有抄写错误，原文应为："五年城就。六年诸侯来会。十月朝贺。"

85 *SJ*, 399.《史记》，第399页。

86 Z. S. Wang, 1982: 2; I have made minor changes based on the Chinese version of his book (Wang Zhongshu, 1984: 4-5).
王仲殊，1984：第4—5页；参见王仲殊，1982：第2页。

87 Ma Xianxing, 1976: 229. 马先醒，1976：第229页。

88 According to historical records, the population of the Guanzhong area was reduced by two-thirds during the war. Gaozu had tried to increase this population by moving a large number of households from the provinces to the capital area. These immigrants, as many scholars have suggested, settled down north of the Wei River in the mausoleum district.
根据历史记载，关中地区的人口数量在战争期间减少了三分之二。高祖曾从地方向都城地区大量移民，以求扩大该地区的人口数量。许多学者曾指出，这些移民定居在渭河以北的陵区。

89 Loewe, 1982: 144. 鲁惟一，1982：第144页。

90 *SJ*, 2699; *HS*, 2113; trans. based on Watson, 1958: 210-11.
《史记》，第2699页；《汉书》，第2113页；英译据华兹生，1958：第210—211页。

91 The information about Shusun Tong is derived from his biographies in *SJ* and *HS*, and from the *HS* chapter on ritual and music (1043-44). For a trans. of Shusun's biography, see Watson, 1958: 222-29.
叔孙通的资料取自《史记》和《汉书》的叔孙通传，以及《汉书·礼乐志》（第1043—1044页）。关于叔孙通传的英译文，见华兹生，1958：第222—229页。

92 Watson's trans. of the relevant passage (1958: 227) creates the erroneous impression that Shusun Tong was criticized by the new ruler: "After Kao-tsu had passed away, and Emperor Hui had come to the throne, he sent for Shu-sun T'ung. 'None of the officials know what sort of ceremonies should be performed at the funerary park and temple of the former emperor,' he complained, and transferred Shu-sun T'ung back to the position of master

of ritual." The original text and commentaries, however, do not suggest any such criticism. In fact, the rest of the biography focuses on Shusun's authority over the emperor.
华兹生对相关段落的翻译（1958：第 227 页）会给读者造成一个不正确的印象，即叔孙通受到了新统治者的批评。但是其原文和注释并没有明显批评的意思。（原文为："高帝崩，孝惠即位，乃谓叔孙生曰：'先帝园陵寝庙，群臣莫能习。' 徙为太常，定宗庙仪法。"——译者注）实际上，传记的其余部分突出表现了叔孙通在礼法上比皇帝更具权威。

93 *HS*, 2129. 见《汉书》，第 2129 页。

94 *Lun yu*, 56.《论语》，第 56 页。

95 The capping ceremony is a major Confucian rite. The *Book of Rites*, compiled during the Han based on old materials, says that the ritual should be held when a man reaches age 20. The *Yi li* states that the proper age for the ceremony is 19. Emperor Hui was born in the 37th year of the First Emperor (210 B.C.) and was 19 *sui* in 192 B.C. The date of his "capping ceremony" agrees with the *Yi li* regulation.
冠礼是一种重要的儒家礼法。在汉代根据旧材料编订的《礼记》说，男子 20 岁举行冠礼。《仪礼》说举行冠礼的合适年龄是 19 岁。惠帝生于高祖三十七年（前 210），公元前 192 年时 19 岁。这与《仪礼》的说法相一致。

96 *HS*, 90.《汉书》，第 90 页。

97 See *SFHT*, 91; Jin Zhuo's commentary in *HS*, 2130. When Hui came to the throne, the inauguration ceremony was held in the temple of Gaozu's father; only from Emperor Wen were such ceremonies held in Gaozu's temple. This implies that this temple was constructed during Hui's reign (see *HS*, 80, 110).
《三辅黄图》，第 91 页；《汉书》，第 2130 页晋灼注。惠帝登基的典礼在太上皇庙举行；只是到了文帝之后，登基典礼才在高庙举行。这说明高庙建于惠帝时期。《汉书》，第 80、110 页。

98 *ZL*, 671.《周礼》，第 671 页。

99 Traditional Chinese scholars considered a tomb east of Gaozu's Chang ling to be the mausoleum of Emperor Hui. Based on both textual and archaeological evidence, some modern scholars have pointed out that this is
311 a misidentification, and that the real An ling should be a large tomb in the present-day Baimiao village (see Liu Qingzhu and Li Yufang, 1987: 26).
传统学者们认为，惠帝的陵墓在高祖长陵以东。当代学者根据文献和考古材料判断，这一看法是错误的，真正的安陵是今白庙村的一座大墓。刘庆柱、李毓芳，1987：第 26 页。

100 *ZL*, 786.《周礼》，第 786 页。

101 See Institute of Archaeology, CASS, 1962. 中国社会科学院考古研究所，1962。

102 See Liu Yunyong, 1982: 20-22. 刘运勇，1982：第 20—22 页。

103 See Yang Kuan, 1985: 190-92; Liu Qingzhu and Li Yufang, 1987: 176-77.
杨宽，1985：第 190—192 页；刘庆柱、李毓芳，1987：第 176—177 页。

104 Arnheim, 1986: 83. 阿恩海姆，1986：第 83 页。

105 *WX*, 1.47-51; trans. from Knechtges, 1982: 104-5.
《文选》，卷一，第 47—51 页；英译据康达维，1982：第 104—105 页。

106 *HS*, 2130; trans. from Watson, 1958: 228.
《汉书》，第 2130 页；英译据华兹生，1958：第 228 页。

107 See Liu Qingzhu and Li Yufang, 1987: 12. 刘庆柱、李毓芳，1987：第 12 页。

108 Liu Qingzhu and Li Yufang (*ibid.*) suggest that Zhang Er, the king of the state of Zhao, was also buried near Chang ling. But this is quite impossible: not only had Zhang Er died in 202 B.C., even before Gaozu's death, but his tomb has been found in Hebei province, far from Chang'an (see Shijiazhuang Library, 1980).
刘庆柱和李毓芳（同上）认为赵王张耳也葬于长陵附近。但是，这一看法似有问题，张耳死于公元前 202 年，早于高祖去世的时间，并且他的墓葬已在远离长安的河北发现。见石家庄图书馆，1980。

109 The first two persons buried there were Gaozu's daughter Princess Luyang (d. 187 B.C.) and her husband, Zhang Ao (d. 182 B.C.). They belonged to Emperor Hui's generation, and their tombs thus flanked the mausoleum of this second Han ruler. This genealogical pattern, however, seems to have been applied only to members of the royal house. Zhang Cang (d. 152 B.C.), the occupant of another satellite burial near An ling, was the prime minister of the next ruler, Emperor Wen (r. 179-157 B.C.), and it was Wen's son, Emperor Jing (r. 156-141 B.C.), who honored him with a burial ground near Emperor Hui's funerary park. A third situation is represented by Emperor Jing's Great Ceremonialist Yuan Ang (d. 148 B.C.). The Yuan family had dwelled in the mausoleum town of An Ling Yi since the early Han, and so Yuan Ang's tomb was located not only near the emperor's mausoleum, but also close to his home.
首先陪葬在帝陵区的是高祖的女儿鲁阳公主（卒于前 187）和她的丈夫张敖（卒于前 182）。他们都与惠帝同辈，所以他们的墓葬都在惠帝的陵墓附近。但是，这种按照家族排列的方式似乎只限于皇室成员。陪葬于安陵的张苍（卒于前 152）是下一位皇帝文帝（前 179—前 157 年在位）时的丞相，文帝的儿子景帝（前 156—前 141 年在位）赐给他陪葬于惠帝陵园的荣誉。第三种情况以景帝时期的太常爰盎（卒于前 148）为代表。爰氏从汉初起就居住在安陵邑，所以爰盎的墓葬不仅在帝陵附近，而且也靠近他的家。

110 Zhan Li et al., 1977. See Liu Qingzhu and Li Yufang, 1987: 15-21; Z. S. Wang, 1982: 209.
展力等，1977；刘庆柱、李毓芳，1987：第 15—21 页；王仲殊，1982：第 209 页。

111 *HS*, 99.《汉书》，第 99 页。

112 Liu Qingzhu and Li Yufang, 1987: 23. According to ancient texts, this town had only north, south and west walls. See *Guanzhong ji* quoted in *SZCZ, juan* 13, 86. This record seems to be confirmed by archaeological surveys.
刘庆柱、李毓芳，1987：第 23 页。根据古代文献记载，长陵邑只有北、南和西墙。见《宋注长安志》，卷十三，第 86 页引《关中记》。这一记载似乎可以得到考古调查的支持。

113 Liu Qingzhu and Li Yufang, 1987: 31. 刘庆柱、李毓芳，1987：第 31 页。

114 *Ibid.*, 24, 32, 225. 同上，第 24、32、225 页。

115 *SJ*, 2720; *HS*, 2123; trans. based on Watson, 1958: 221.
《史记》，第 2720 页；《汉书》，第 2123 页；英译据华兹生，1958：第 221 页。

116 These were the seven mausoleum towns of the Western Han emperors from Gaozu to Emperor Xuan, as well as those of Gaozu's father, Empress Dowager Bo (Emperor Wen's natural mother), Empress Dowager Gouyi (Emperor Zhao's natural mother), and Emperor Xuan's parents.
西汉从高祖到宣帝有 7 处陵邑，此外太上皇、薄太后（文帝的生母）、钩弋太后（昭帝的生母）以及宣帝的父母也有陵邑。

117 *HS*, 1545, 1547.《汉书》，第 1545、1547 页。

118 Liu Qingzhu and Li Yufang, 1987: 68, 102.
刘庆柱、李毓芳，1987：第 68、102 页。

119 *HS*, 1543.《汉书》，第 1543 页。

120 *HS*, 170, 205; *SFHT*, 53. 同上，第 170、205 页；《三辅黄图》，第 53 页。

121 *SJ*, 3187-88.《史记》，第 3187—3188 页。

122 See Liu Qingzhu and Li Yufang, 1987: 67. 刘庆柱、李毓芳，1987：第 67 页。

123 *WX*, 1.55-59; Knechtges, 1982: 107-9.
《文选》，卷一，第 55—59 页；康达维，1982：第 107—109 页。

124 *SJ*, 3319; trans. based on Watson in de Bary 1960: 1.232-33. Sima Qian wrote these sentences to summarize the chapters on "Hereditary Houses" ("Shijia"). I have argued elsewhere that this statement reflects a Han idea of the political relationship between the ruler and the feudal lords and ministers under him (H. Wu, 1989: 151-52).

《史记》，第 3319 页；英译据狄百瑞引用华兹生，1960：1.232—233。司马迁以这些句子结束了"世家"。我在他处曾指出，这些话反映了汉代关于统治者和诸侯以及其臣属之间政治关系的一种观念。见巫鸿，1989：第 151—152 页。

125 Many historians have pointed to the tax reduction as a major reform of the Wen-Jing period; as Loewe (Twitchett and Loewe, 1986: 150) has summarized: "In 168 B.C. the standard rate of the tax on produce was reduced from one-fifteenth to one-thirtieth part; in the following year it was abolished altogether. When it was reintroduced in 156 B.C., the levy was kept at the lower rate of one thirtieth, which remained standard throughout the Han period."

许多史学家指出，减少税收是文景时期一项重要的改革措施；正如鲁惟一（1986: 150）归纳说："公元前 168 年，农产品的标准税率从十五税一减少到三十税一；过了几年又全部减免。公元前 156 年再次征税时，税率保持在三十税一的低水平，这一比例成为后来汉代通行的标准。"

126 *SJ*, 433; *HS*, 134; trans. based on Watson, 1961: 1.362.

《史记》，第 433 页；《汉书》，第 134 页；英译据华兹生，1961：1.362。

127 Yi Feng, a famous official scholar under Emperor Yuan, once recalled in a memorial that during Emperor Wen's reign the Weiyang Palace included the Anterior Hall, two terraces called Qu tai and Jian tai, and three palatial halls called Xuanshi, Wenshi, and Chengming (*HS*, 3175). The Anterior Hall is the only one of these buildings mentioned in the historical records as existing before Emperor Wen's reign. But generally speaking, Chang'an witnessed no dramatic changes during the 40 years of the Wen-Jing period. The city grew almost biologically: each emperor left a royal tomb with a tumulus, funerary park, shrine, and mausoleum town, and when a prominent minister or royal relative died, his or her tomb joined the satellite burials around an imperial mausoleum. Besides these mortuary structures, the only significant addition is an altar that Emperor Wen dedicated to the Five Supreme Powers in 164 B.C. northeast of Chang'an (*SJ*, 430; *HS*, 127). This altar, however, was soon abandoned; the emperor discovered that its designer, the necromancer Xin Yuanping, was a swindler and executed him (*SJ*, 1383).

元帝手下一位叫作翼奉的著名学者有次上疏说，文帝时期的未央宫包括前殿、曲台、渐台和叫作宣室、温室、承明的三个室（《汉书》，第3175页）。前殿是文献中提到的文帝以前唯一存留的建筑。但是总的来说，长安在文景统治的40年间并没有引人注目的变化。在这一时期内，这座城市的成长几乎是“生物性”的：每一位皇帝留下一组高大的坟冢、陵园、祠堂和陵邑，当一位显赫的大臣或皇室成员去世后，其墓葬又围绕着帝陵陪葬。除了这些丧葬建筑，其他重要的建筑只有公元前164年文帝在长安东北修建的五帝庙（《史记》，第430页；《汉书》，第127页）。但是该庙不久就被废弃了，文帝发现其设计者方士新垣平是一名骗子并处死了他（《史记》，第1383页）。

128 *SJ*, 433-34; *HS*, 131-32; trans. from Watson, 1961: 1.363.
《史记》，第433—434页；《汉书》，第131—132页；英译据华兹生，1961：1.363。

129 *SJ*, 434; *HS*, 132; see Watson, 1961: 1.364.
《史记》，第434页；《汉书》，第132页；英译据华兹生，1961：1.364。

130 We are told that when he came to the throne “the granaries in the cities and the countryside were full and the government treasuries were running over
312 with wealth. In the capital the strings of cash had been stacked up by the hundreds of millions until the cords that bound them had rotted away and they could no longer be counted. In the central granary of the government, new grain was heaped on top of the old until the building was full and the grain overflowed and piled up outside, where it spoiled and became unfit to eat” (*SJ*, 1420; trans. from Watson, 1961: 2.81).
当武帝登基时，“都鄙廪庾皆满，而府库余货财。京师之钱累巨万，贯朽而不可校。大仓之粟陈陈相因，充溢露积于外，至腐败不可食。”《史记》，第1420页；英译据华兹生，1961：2.81。

131 *SFHT*, 14-15; *Taiping huanyu ji* (A record of the peaceful universe) cited in *SZCZ*, 3.13a.
《三辅黄图》，第14—15页；《宋注长安志》，卷三，第13页引《太平寰宇记》。

132 For information regarding these three palaces, see *SFHT*, 16-17, 23, 28.
关于这三组宫殿的情况，见《三辅黄图》，第16—17、23、28页。

133 *Ibid.*, 17. 同上，第17页。

134 For information regarding Emperor Wu’s tomb, see Liu Qingzhu and Li Yufang, 1987: 47-68.
关于武帝陵墓的情况，见刘庆柱、李毓芳，1987：第47—68页。

135 See Twitchett and Loewe, 1986: 153; Grousset, 1964: 54.
杜希德、鲁惟一，1986：第153页；格鲁塞，1964：第54页。

136 For a more detailed discussion of the term and especially the key character *fang*, see DeWoskin, 1983: 1-2.
关于“方士”这一名称更详细的讨论，特别是对“方”字的研究，见杜志豪，1983：第1—2页。

137 “Song Wuji, Zhengbo Qiao, Chong Shang, Xianmen Zigao, and Zui Hou were all men of Yan who practiced magic and followed the way of the immortals, discarding their mortal forms and changing into spiritual beings by means of supernatural aid. Zou Yan won fame among the feudal lords for his theories of *yin* and *yang* and the succession of the Five Elements, but the magicians who lived along the seacoast of Qi and Yan, though they claimed to transmit his teachings, were unable to understand them. Thus from time to time there appeared a host of men, too numerous to mention, who expounded all sorts of weird and fantastic theories and went to any lengths to flatter the rulers of the day and ingratiate themselves with them” (*SJ*, 1368-69; trans. based on Watson, 1961: 2.25-26). For an excellent discussion of the *fangshi* tradition, see DeWoskin, 1983: 1-42.
“而宋毋忌、正伯侨、充尚、羡门子高、最后皆燕人，为方仙道，形解销化，依于鬼神之事。驺衍以阴阳主运显于诸侯，而燕齐海上之方士传其术不能通，然则怪迂阿谀苟合之徒自此兴，不可胜数也。”（《史记》，第1368—1369页；英译据华兹生，1961：2.25–26）关于方士的精彩论述，见杜志豪，1983：第1—42页。

138 DeWoskin, 1983: 3. 杜志豪，1983：第3页。

139 For information regarding Li Shaojun, see *SJ*, 453-55; Watson, 1961: 2.38-40.
关于李少君的情况，见《史记》，第453—455页；华兹生，1961：2.38–40。（下文所说的李夫人，《史记》第1389页作王夫人，《汉书》第3952页作李夫人——译者注）

140 *SJ*, 455-56; Watson, 1961: 2.40.
《史记》，第455—456页；华兹生，1961：2.40。

141 For information about Shao Weng, see *SJ*, 458-59; Watson, 1961: 2.41-42.
关于少翁的情况，见《史记》，第458—459页；华兹生，1961：2.41–42。

142 *SJ*, 1388; trans. based on Watson, 1961: 2.42.
《史记》，第1388页；英译据华兹生，1961：2.42。

143 *SJ*, 1392; Watson, 1961: 2.48.《史记》，第1392页；华兹生，1961：2.48。

144 *SJ*, 1394; Watson, 1961: 2.52. For the religious context of this new altar, see Bilsky, 1975: 2.315-18.
同上，第1394页；华兹生，1961：2.52。关于这类新出现的坛的宗教背景，见毕士基，1975：2.315—318。

145 *SJ*, 1400; see Watson, 1961: 2.63. 同上，第 1400 页；华兹生，1961：2.63。

146 *SJ*, 1400; see Watson, 1961: 2.63. 同上。

147 *SFHT*, 38. The rituals held there are also described in *SJ*, 1178.
《三辅黄图》，第 38 页。关于再次举行的礼仪的描写也见《史记》，第 1178 页。

148 *SJ*, 1400; trans. based on Watson, 1961: 2.63.
《史记》，第 1400 页；英译据华兹生，1961：2.63。

149 *SJ*, 1396; Watson, 1961: 2.54.
同上，第 1396 页；英译据华兹生，1961：2.54。

150 *SJ*, 1390; trans. based on Watson, 1961: 2.46.
《史记》，第 1390 页；英译据华兹生，1961：2.46。

151 *SJ*, 1369-70; Watson, 1961: 2.26.
同上，第 1369—1370 页；英译据华兹生，1961：2.26。

152 DeWoskin (1983: 3, 21) has proposed that such tales were "the stuff of early hagiography, remote-land geography, and miracle lore, and this put *fangshi* at the center of important developments in early fiction." He also noticed that a well-known *fangshi* named Dongfang Shuo often entertained Emperor Wu with stories of exotic places and at imperial request compiled the *Account of Ten Continents* (*Shizhou ji*). A number of post-Han collections of strange tales followed this tradition and included Zhang Hua's *Records of the Widely Diverse Things* (*Bowu zhi*) and Gan Bao's *In Search of the Supernatural* (*Soushen ji*).
杜志豪（1983：第 3、21 页）曾指出，这类故事成为"早期的圣者传、远土地理志和奇迹故事的素材，这些故事将方士置于早期小说发展过程的中心地位"。他还注意到著名方士东方朔经常以异域故事取悦皇帝，并受皇帝之命编写了《十洲记》一书。大量汉代以后的传奇故事都继承了这一传统，包括张华《博物志》和干宝《搜神记》。

153 *SJ*, 1396; trans. from Watson, 1961: 2.55.
《史记》，第 1396 页；英译据华兹生，1961：2.55。

154 Walton, 1990: 41. 沃尔顿，1990：第 41 页。

155 *Ibid.*, 39. 同上，第 39 页。

156 *WX*, 4.1622-1710; Knechtges, 1987: 53-71.
《文选》，卷四，第 1622—1710 页；康达维，1987：第 53—71 页。

157 Wangshi Gong literally means "Master it is not." Knechtges translates the name as "Lord No-such"; Watson as "Master Not-real."
"亡是公"字面的意思是"并不存在的先生"。康达维将该名译作 Lord No-such；华兹生译作 Master Not-real。

158 For this rhapsody, see *WX*, 4.1711-881; unless noted, trans. based on Watson, 1961: 2.307-21.
《文选》，卷四，第 1711—1881 页；除注明外，英译据华兹生，1961：2.307—321。

159 Trans. from Knechtges, 1987: 75. 英译据康达维，1987：第 75 页。

160 See commentaries in *WX*, 4.1719. 见《文选》，卷四，第 1719 页注释。

161 *SHJ*, 1.9a, 3.3b.《山海经》，卷一，第 9 页；卷三，第 3 页。

162 *SJ*, 3043; trans. based on Watson, 1961: 2.321.
《史记》，第 3043 页；英译据华兹生，1961：2.321。

163 Many scholars, for example, have argued that the poem's initial definition of the park's boundary is realistic, and that all the four place names—Verdant Parasol, Western Limits, Cinnabar River, and Purple Gulf—refer to real places near Chang'an (see commentaries in *WX*, 4.1719-22; Knechtges, 1987: 74). Art historians and architectural historians also frequently quote the poem in studies of Han garden designs.
例如，许多学者认为该赋对上林边界的界定是真实的，苍梧、西极、丹水、紫渊都是长安附近真实的地名。见《文选》，卷四，第 1719—1722 页注；康达维，1987：第 74 页。美术史家和建筑史家在研究汉代园林设计时也经常引用这段文献。

164 *Yan fanlu, juan* 11.《演繁露》，卷十一。

165 *Yong lu*, 9.7a.《雍录》，卷九，第 7 页。

166 *HS*, 2011.《汉书》，第 2011 页。

167 *HS*, 2847. 同上，第 2847 页。

168 For example, a lengthy section in the rhapsody describes an imperial hunting party: among the captured animals and birds are sagacious stags, spiritual apes, white tigers, albino deer, peacocks, and phoenixes. In pursuing such strange creatures, the emperor is said to "transcend the mundane realm" (*WX*, 4.1834; Knechtges, 1987: 101). But the emperor's hunting party in 138 B.C. ended with a dispute, and all he killed were a few foxes and rabbits. Moreover, Sima Xiangru relates that after the hunt Emperor Wu returns to worldly business: he changes the calender, regulates
rituals and court costumes, and holds a grand ceremony in Bright Hall. In 313
real history, however, these events took place some thirty years later in 109 B.C. and 104 B.C. (*SJ*, 1401).
例如，赋中有一大段描写了皇帝的校猎活动：在捕获的禽兽中，有白虎、白鹿、孔鸾、凤凰等。在射猎中，皇帝"追怪物，出宇宙"。(《文选》，卷四，第1834页；康达维，1987：第101页）。但是实际上，汉武帝公元前138年的校猎却以争执告终，所获猎物也只有狐狸和兔子。不仅如此，司马相如还描述了皇帝校猎归来后的一系列活动：他更改了历法，调整了礼仪和朝服，在明堂中举行了盛大的典礼。在真实的历史中，这些事情发生在大约30年后的公元前109和前104年（《史记》，第1401页）。

169 *SFHT*, 29.《三辅黄图》，第29页。

170 *Ibid.*, 35. 同上，第35页。

171 *Ibid.*, 29-30. 同上，第29—30页。

172 These include 10 Rangoon creepers, 12 giant banana trees, 100 cassia-bark trees, and 100 honey-scented flowering balsams, as well as lichi, longan, palm, canary, and sweet tangerine trees, and a kind of vine producing fruits called "seeds of a thousand years" (*ibid.*, 26-27).
其中有"菖蒲百本、山姜十本、甘蕉十二本、留求子十本，皆百本，密香指甲花百本，龙眼、荔枝、槟榔、橄榄、千岁子、柑橘，皆百余本"。同上，第26—27页。

173 *WX*, 1.75.《文选》，卷二，第75页。

174 *HS*, 176.《汉书》，第176页。

175 *HS*, 1069. Emperor Wu wrote this poem in 94 B.C., but its contents clearly refer to the earlier elephant tribute.
同上，第1069页。武帝此诗作于公元前94年，但其内容显然指的是时间更早的进贡大象的事。

176 *SFHT*, 30. *Guanzhong ji* quoted in *SZCZ*, 4.7ab.
《三辅黄图》，第30页。《宋注长安志》，卷四，第7页引《关中记》。

177 The two meanings are given in two Han dictionaries, respectively. *SW* (408) defines *guan* as "viewing and gazing," and *Shi ming* (5.18a) interprets the terms as "viewing from a lofty spot."
"观"在汉代的两部辞书中有不同的解释。《说文解字》（第408页）："观，谛视也。"《释名》（卷五，第18页）："观，观也，于上观望也。"

178 For the relationship between "props" and "imagination," see Walton, 1990: 35-43.
关于"道具"和"想象"之间的关系的讨论，见沃尔顿，1990：第35—43页。

179 *WX*, 4.1781-84; 1815; trans. from Watson, 1961: 2.312, 314.
《文选》，卷四，第1781—1784页、第1815页；英译据华兹生，1961：2.312，314。

180 *SFHT*, 29.《三辅黄图》，第29页。

181 Quoted in *SZCZ*, 4.6b, 8a.
转引自《宋注长安志》，卷四，第 6 页、第 8 页。

182 According to *Guanfu guyu* (Ancient dialogues about the capital area) and *Sanfu gushi* (Stories about the three capital districts) quoted in *SFHT*, 32.
据《三辅黄图》，第 32 页所引《关辅古语》和《三辅故事》。

183 Earlier that year the Terrace of Cypress Beams (Bailiang tai) in Weiyang Palace reportedly caught fire and was destroyed. A shaman from Yue advised the emperor to erect a taller building "in order to overcome evil influences" (*SJ*, 1402; Watson, 1961: 2.65-66). In that year, the emperor also changed the dynasty's calender and symbolic systems and named the new reign period the "Great Beginning" (Taichu). The new palace was possibly related to this important reform, which had been brewing for a hundred years (*SJ*, 1402; Watson, 1961: 2.66-67). This reform had been advocated by Gongsun Chen, a Confucian from Lu, during Emperor Wen's reign (*SJ*, 1381). These two factors, however, are still insufficient to explain the new palace, especially the reason it was built as part of Shanglin Park.
传说在这一年之前，未央宫的柏梁台失火被毁。来自越的一名巫师建议皇帝建造一处更高大的建筑"用胜服之"(《史记》，第 1402 页；华兹生，1961：2.65—66)。就在这一年，皇帝改历法，色尚黄，年号改为"太初"。新宫殿的建立或许与这一酝酿了百年的重要改革有关(《史记》，第 1402 页；华兹生，1961：2.66—67)。文帝时期，来自鲁的儒生公孙臣就鼓吹这一改革(《史记》，第 1381 页)。但是，这两点还不足以构成建立新宫殿的缘由，特别是无法说明为何这一宫殿成了上林苑的一部分。

184 *SJ*, 3056; *HS*, 2592; trans. from Watson, 1961: 2.332.
《史记》，第 3056 页；《汉书》，第 2592 页；英译据华兹生，1961：2.332。

185 *HS*, 2596; trans. based on Watson, 1961: 2.334.
《汉书》，第 2596 页；英译据华兹生，1961：2.334。

186 *SJ*, 3063.《史记》，第 3063 页。

187 A bronze censer was discovered in 1968 in the tomb of Liu Sheng, the prince of Zhongshan and one of Emperor Wu's brothers. The censer has layers of soaring peaks on top to form the contour of a conical mountain, which emerges from an ocean indicated by the inlaid wave patterns on the bowl-shaped base. Small human and animal figures among the mountain peaks include celestial beasts and an archer chasing animals—motifs related to scenes and activities in Shanglin Park.
1968 年，在武帝的兄弟中山王刘胜墓中出土的一件铜博山炉，底盘上嵌有波浪纹，上部为圆锥形的重峦叠嶂，看似大海中升起的一座仙山。山峦中所雕刻的细小的人物及动物中有神兽和射猎的场面，与上林苑中的景色和活动十分相近。

188 See *SZCZ*, 3.11a.《宋注长安志》，卷三，第 11 页。

189 The western location of Jianzhang Palace may have been associated with the magical mountain Kunlun in the west, which Sima Xiangru identified in his poem as the foundation of the heavenly court. Perhaps for the same reason Emperor Wu also founded his tomb, Mao ling, directly west of Chang'an.
建章宫位于长安西部，这一位置可能和西方的神山昆仑有联系，司马相如在赋中就将昆仑看作天庭之基。武帝将自己的陵墓建在长安正西，或许出于同样的原因。

190 *HS*, 4161-62.《汉书》，第 4161—4162 页。

191 The establishment of Bright Hall (Mingtang) was part of Wang Mang's restoration of the Confucian tradition. Ban Gu records its historical context: "That year [A.D. 4] Wang Mang proposed to construct Bright Hall, the Jade Disk Moat [Piyong], the Spiritual Terrace [Lingtai], and ten thousand residences for scholars. He also built a marketplace and equalizing granaries [*changman cang*]. The regulations were exceedingly elaborate. He established the *Canon of Music* [as a Confucian Classic], increased the number of Imperial Doctors to five for each of the Classics, and sought throughout the empire persons who possessed ability in any of the [Six] Arts who had taught groups of eleven men and more, together with those who comprehended the ideas of the *Lost Ritual Canons* [*Yili*], the Old Text version of the *Documents*, the *Songs* with Master Mao's commentaries, the *Institutes of Zhou* [*Zhou guan*], the *Er ya* dictionary, and texts on astronomy, divination, musical pitches, monthly observances, the art of war, and historiography" (*HS*, 4069; trans. based on Sargent, 1947: 125-26).
通过班固的记载，我们可以更全面地了解明堂的建立是王莽重建儒家传统的一部分："是岁（公元 4 年），莽奏起明堂、辟雍、灵台，为学者筑舍万区，作市、常满仓，制度甚盛。立《乐经》，益博士员，经各五人。征天下通一艺教授十一人以上，及有《逸礼》、古《书》、《毛诗》、《周官》、《尔雅》、天文、图谶、钟律、月令、兵法、《史篇》文字，通知其意者，皆诣公车。"《汉书》，第 4069 页；英译据萨进德，1947：第 125—126 页。

192 As I discuss later in this section, the Bright Hall built by Emperor Wu beneath Mount Tai was not based on a synthesis of the Confucian classics and thus differed fundamentally from the one constructed by Wang Mang.
我在本章中将谈到，武帝在泰山下所建造的明堂并不是依照对于儒家经典的某个综合体，因此它与王莽的明堂有着根本的差别。

193 Because Bright Hall synthesized and reinterpreted ancient texts, it differed from structures such as Emperor Hui's Chang'an walls, which were more

strictly based on a single classic.
王莽的明堂是对古典文献的综合和重新诠释，而诸如惠帝所修建的长安城墙等工程，则是更为严格地遵循单一的文献，因此二者并不相同。

194 For reports of the excavation, see Liu Zhiping, 1957b; Wang Shiren, 1957; Qi Yingtao, 1957; Luo Zhongru, 1957; Han City Excavation Team, Institute of Archaeology, 1960; Tang Jinyu, 1959. For a discussion and reconstruction of Wang Mang's Bright Hall, see Huang Zhanyue, 1960; Wang Shiren, 1963; Xu Daolin and Liu Zhiping, 1959; Steinhardt, 1984: 70-77; Yang Hongxun, 1987: 169-200.
考古发掘报告，见刘致平，1957b；王世仁，1957；祁英涛，1957；雒忠如，1957；考古研究所汉城发掘队，1960；唐金裕，1959。有关王莽明堂的讨论和复原，见黄展岳，1960；王世仁，1963；许道麟、刘致平，1959；斯坦哈特，1984：70—77；杨鸿勋，1987：第 169—200 页。

195 Among various reconstruction plans, those proposed by Wang Shiren (1963)
and Yang Hongxun (1987) have been widely cited by scholars of Chinese 314
architectural history. It must be realized, however, that the archaeological reports provide little evidence for reconstructing the aboveground part of Bright Hall, and that Yang and Wang's plans are largely based on their own visions of this monument. My reconstruction differs in some major points from both plans. For example, the round "Room of Communing with Heaven" recorded in all ancient texts is missing from Wang Shiren's reconstruction, and the number of chambers reconstructed by Yang Hongxun differ from those documented by ancient writers.
在不同的复原方案中，王世仁（1963）和杨鸿勋（1987）的方案被研究中国建筑史的学者引用最多。但是必须意识到，考古发掘为复原明堂地上部分提供的信息很少，王和杨对地上部分复原的方案在很大程度上基于他们自己对这一纪念碑的想象。我的复原在一些主要的点上与这两个方案都有所不同。例如，王世仁的方案中未提到所有文献中都记载了的“通天屋”，杨鸿勋复原的房间的数量也与文献记载不同。

196 Wang Shiren (1963: 504-5) has reconstructed four of these halls. Yang Hongxun (1987: 185), however, suggests that there was only a central hall on the top floor.
王世仁（1963：第 504—505 页）复原了其中的四个小厅。但是，杨鸿勋（1987：第 185 页）认为顶层只有一个中央大厅。

197 The existence of such designs is revealed in *HHS*, 1196: When Zhang Chun proposed to establish another Bright Hall at the beginning of the Eastern Han, he presented to the emperor, among other documents, "the conference records of Emperor Ping's [Bright Hall]" and a "diagram of Bright Hall" established by Wang Mang.

其原始设计存在的依据见于《后汉书》，第 1196 页。当东汉初年张纯建议建造另一座明堂时，他向皇帝提供了很多资料，其中包括王莽明堂的“平帝时议”和“明堂图”。

198 “Mingtang yueling lun.” Wang Shiren (1963: 503) believes that the subject of this treatise is the Eastern Han Bright Hall in Luoyang, which was modeled on Wang Mang’s Bright Hall. He also suggests that before writing this essay Cai Yong had visited Chang’an and possibly also investigated Wang Mang’s building.
《明堂月令论》。王世仁（1963：第 503 页）相信这篇文章所谈的是东汉雒阳的明堂，这一建筑是对王莽明堂的模仿。他还认为在写作这篇文章之前，蔡邕曾经到过长安，可能还考察过明堂。

199 See Wilhelm, 1967: 118. 英译据卫礼贤，1967：第 118 页。

200 Readers interested in these issues may consult Tjan Tjoe Som’s translation and discussion of *Baihu tong* (Proceedings from the White Tiger Hall), the most important official theological text of the Eastern Han.
对这些问题感兴趣的读者，可以参考曾珠森翻译的《白虎通》，这是东汉时期最重要的官方儒学文献。

201 For an interesting discussion of such geometric maps, see Major, 1984.
对于这种几何式地图的讨论，见马绛，1984。

202 Another passage in Cai Yong’s essay suggests a similar movement: “It is stated in the ‘Great Origin’ [‘Taichu’] chapter of the ‘Great Commentary’ [‘Dazhuan’] to the *Book of Changes*: ‘In the early morning the Son of Heaven goes to [study in] the eastern academy; during the day he goes to [study in] the southern academy; in the evening he goes to [study in] the western academy; the Great Academy is in the center and the place of the Son of Heaven, where he studies by himself.’ The ‘Grand Tutors’ (‘Baofu’) chapter of the *Book of Rites* says: ‘The emperor goes to the eastern academy in order to honor his kin and praise righteousness; he goes to the western academy in order to honor virtuous men and praise goodness; he goes to the southern academy in order to honor elder men and praise faith; he goes to the northern academy in order to honor noble men and praise the ranks; and he goes to the Great Academy in order to seek for the Dao from masters.’ This record agrees with that in the ‘Great Commentary.’” (“Mingtang yueling lun,” 2b-3a).
蔡邕文章中另一段文字提到一种相似的运转：“《易传·太初篇》曰：‘天子旦入东学，昼入南学，暮入西学。太学在中央，天子之所自学也。’《礼记·保傅篇》曰：‘帝入东学，尚亲而贵仁；入西学，尚贤而贵德；入南学，尚齿而贵信；入北学，尚贵而尊爵；入太学，承师而问道。’与《易传》同。”《明堂月令论》，第 2—3 页。

203 *LJ*, 1352-88; Legge, 1967: 1.236-310.
《礼记》，第 1352—1388 页；理雅各，1967：1.236—1.310。

204 *Lüshi chunqiu*, 1-3, 12-14, 23-25, 34-35, 44-46, 54-56, 65-66, 75-77, 84-86, 94-96, 104-6, 114-5.
《吕氏春秋》，第 1—3、12—14、23—25、34—35、44—46、54—56、65—66、75—77、84—86、94—96、104—106、114—115 页。

205 *LJ*, 1352-55; trans. based on Legge, 1967: 1.249-52.
《礼记》，第 1352—1355 页；英译据理雅各，1967：1.249—252。

206 *LJ*, 1357; trans. from Legge, 1967: 1.257.
《礼记》，第 1357 页；英译据理雅各，1967：1.257。

207 This Zhou dynasty Bright Hall is documented in the "Places in Bright Hall" ("Mingtang wei"), a treatise later incorporated into the *Book of Rites*, and in the "Regulations of Workmanship," which then became a chapter of the *Rites of Zhou*. The author of the "Places in Bright Hall" states that this hall functioned "to differentiate the ranks of feudal lords," a definition testifying to a strong Confucian interest in political organization and hierarchy. This political organization gained its most idealized and concrete form in a court audience held by the Duke of Zhou in this legendary Bright Hall: "Formerly, when the Duke of Zhou gave an audience to the feudal princes in their several places in Bright Hall, the Son of Heaven stood with his back to the axe-embroidered screen and faced the south. The three dukes were in front of the steps. . . . The places of the marquises were located east of the eastern steps. . . . The lords of the earldoms were west of the western steps. . . . The counts were east of the gate, facing north···. The barons were west of the gate. . . . The chiefs of the nine Yi tribes were outside the eastern door. . . . The chiefs of the eight Man tribes were outside the southern door. . . . The chiefs of the six Rong tribes were outside the western door. . . . The chiefs of the five Di tribes were outside the northern door. . . . The chiefs of the nine Cai areas were outside the Ying Gate" (*LJ*, 1487-89; see Legge, 1967: 2.29-31). A reconstruction of this ceremony suggests that the Zhou Bright Hall was centered on a south-facing building inside a courtyard; the architectural complex has nothing to do with the ritual structure implied in the "Monthly Observances," but resembles the traditional temple-palace compound found in Shang-Zhou sites and recorded in ancient texts. The specific ritual function of this Bright Hall is also indicated in two other places in the *Book of Rites* (*LJ*, 1543, 1600): "The purpose of holding sacrifices in Bright Hall is to instruct the feudal lords on the virtue of filial piety"; and "The king sacrifices in Bright Hall, thus his subject can

realize [the importance] of filial piety." According to the "Regulations of Workmanship" (*ZL*, 927-8), the Zhou Bright Hall, which derived its form from the Chamber of Generations of the Xia and the Layered House of the Shang, was 81 *chi* east-west, 63 *chi* south-north, and consisted of five
315 chambers. It is obvious that this rectangular building does not fit the Five Element diagram, which requires a square chamber in the center. Yang Hongxun (1987: 78-79) has also suggested a close relationship between this type of building and the Three Dynasty temple-palace structure excavated at Erlitou.

这座周代明堂记载于《明堂位》一文，该文后来收入《礼记》，也见于《周礼·考工记》。《明堂位》的作者说，明堂的功能在于"明诸侯之尊卑也"，这一定义包含着儒家对于政治体制和等级的一种强烈的兴趣。在传说的明堂中，周公举行的朝会使这种政治体制被最大程度地理想化，并获得了最具体的形式："昔者，周公朝诸侯于明堂之位，天子负斧依南乡而立。三公，中阶之前……诸侯之位，阼阶之东……诸伯之国，西阶之西……诸子之国，门东……诸男之国，门西……九夷之国，东门之外……八蛮之国，南门之外……六戎之国，西门之外……五狄之国，北门之外……九采之国，应门之外……"（《礼记》，第1487—1489页；英译据理雅各，1967：2.29—31）。对这一仪式的复原显示，周明堂是以庭院中一座南向的建筑为中心的；其建筑组合与《月令》所记载的礼仪结构毫无关系，而更像商周遗址和文献中所见的传统祖庙和宫殿。该明堂的礼仪功能也见于《礼记》另外两处文字中（《礼记》，第1543、1600页）："揔明堂，而民知孝。""祀乎明堂，所以教诸侯之孝也。"根据《考工记》（《周礼》，第927—928页），周明堂的形式来源于夏后氏世室和殷人重屋，面阔81尺，深63尺，有五室。五行的图式要求中央有一方形的室，周明堂长方形的建筑显然与之不合。杨鸿勋（1987：第78—79页）也指出这种类型的建筑与二里头发掘的三代宫庙有密切的关系。

208 *Xunzi*, 201-2; trans. based on Knoblock, 1989: 1.246. My translation of the last sentence is based on an original comment in the Chinese text. Mencius makes a similar political statement in his conversation with an Eastern Zhou prince: "King Xuan of Qi said: 'People all tell me to pull down Bright Hall. Shall I pull it down, or stop the movement for that object?' Mencius replied, 'Bright Hall is a hall appropriate to the sovereigns. If Your Majesty wishes to practice true royal government, then do not pull it down.'" He then proceeded to instruct the king on "the true royal government." A third reference to Bright Hall along the same lines can be found in *Master Zuo's Commentaries on the Spring and Autumn Annals*: "It is said in one of the histories of Zhou: 'The violent man who killed his superior shall have no place in Bright Hall'" (Legge, 1871: 6.231).

《荀子》，第201—202页；英译据王志民，1989：1.246。我对最后一句的翻译根据的是原文的注释。孟子在与东周齐宣王的对话中表达了相似的政治观点："齐宣王问曰：'人皆谓我毁明堂。毁诸？已乎？' 孟子对曰：'夫明堂者，王者之堂也。王欲行王政，则勿毁之矣。'" 他接下来便教导齐宣王如何"行王政"。第三条关于明堂的文献也遵循了同样的思路，《左传》："周志有之：'勇则害上，不登于明堂。'" 英译见理雅各，1871：6.231。

209 Important changes in this version of the "Monthly Observances" concern the names of different chambers. Unlike the earlier *Lüshi chunqiu* version, the name "Great Temple" refers to the central room in each of the four main chambers, and the central chamber is called the Central Palace (*Huainan zi*, 69-87).
这个版本的《月令》中一个重要的变化是提到了不同室的名称。与更早的《吕氏春秋》的版本不同，"太庙"指的是每面四个堂正中的一间，中央的堂则称"中宫"。见《淮南子》，第 69—87 页。

210 *Ibid.*, 127-28, 149, 351. 同上，第 127—128、149、351 页。

211 *Ibid.*, 351. 同上，第 351 页。

212 For a discussion of this concept, see Fung, 1948-53: 2.46-55.
关于这一概念的讨论，见冯友兰，1948—1953：2.46—55。

213 The *History of the Former Han* (*HS*, 3139) records that in the early first century B.C., the Confucian scholar Wei Xiang (? -59 B.C.) proposed a plan to the throne based on "a combination of the *Changes*, *yin-yang*, and the 'Monthly Observances' in Bright Hall." Fung Yu-lan and D. Bodde (Y. L. Fung, 1953: 2.8) have outlined the integration of these philosophical schools: "During the fourth and third century B.C. the Yin-yang school and the School of the Five Elements seem to have existed quite separately from one another, but during the Han dynasty, in accordance with the eclectic trend of the time, they coalesced. The resulting amalgam was in turn taken over by that particular brand of Confucianism represented by the New Text school." Again, "This correlation of the eight trigrams with the eight compass points and with the seasonal fluctuations of the *yin* and *yang* is of later date than that based on the Five Elements. Once promulgated, however, it had the advantage of being readily understandable, and therefore soon gained wide currency, even though the earlier correlation of the Five Elements with the phases of the year also enjoyed continued popularity" (*ibid.*, 2.104).
《汉书》（第 3139 页）记载，在公元前 1 世纪初，儒士魏相（？—前 59 年）"又数表采《易》《阴阳》及《明堂月令》奏之"。冯友兰和卜德（1953: 2.8）概括了这些哲学派别的融合情况："在公元前 4—前 3 世纪，阴阳学派和五行学派似乎彼此保持着相当的距离，但是到了汉代，与当时折中主义的倾向相一致，这些学派接合在了一起。其接合的结果反过来又被以今文经派为代表的儒家派别所接受。”另外，“八卦和八极以及阴阳的季节变换之间的联系要比基于五行的联系出现得晚，但是，一旦有关这种联系的思想传布开来，它就因为其明白易懂的优势而得到流行。尽管如此，更早的五行与时节相关的思想仍持续流通。”同前，2.104。

214 See *Mingtang dadao lu*, 1.18.《明堂大道录》，卷一，第 18 页。

215 For the influences of the "Monthly Observances" on the rules of Emperors Gaozu and Wen, see *HS*, 3140.
关于《月令》对高祖和文帝的影响，见《汉书》，第 3140 页。

216 *SJ*, 452; *HS*, 157.《史记》，第 452 页；《汉书》，第 157 页。

217 *SJ*, 452.《史记》，第 452 页。

218 *Ibid.*, 1401. 同上，第 1401 页。

219 Some texts suggest that Emperor Wu also built a Bright Hall south of Chang'an. But as many scholars have pointed out, these records do not have a substantial historical basis. See Yang Hongxun, 1987: 169-70.
有的文献提到，武帝也曾在长安南郊建造过一座明堂。但是正如许多学者所指出的，这些记载缺乏坚实的历史基础。见杨鸿勋，1987：第 169—170 页。

220 Such criticism became unmistakable during the later years of Emperor Wu. Wei Xiang frequently pointed out in his memorials the problems in the state administration and related them to the "disharmony of *yin* and *yang*." His advice to the emperor to follow the "Monthly Observances" ends with a warning: "I consider that Your Majesty has much fortune, yet the noxious influences have not yet been eradicated. I am afraid that not all your edicts and orders are in accordance with the seasonal orders" (*HS*, 3139-40).
这种责难在武帝后期已经表现得十分明显。魏相在其奏折中经常指出朝政中的问题，并且将这些问题与阴阳不顺联系在一起。如他根据《月令》上奏皇帝，最后警告说："臣相伏念陛下恩泽甚厚，然而灾气未息，窃恐诏令有未合当时者也。"《汉书》，第 3139—3140 页。

221 *HS*, 1709. One important piece of writing belonging to this category is Dai De's (active 48-33 B.C.) *Elder Dai's Book of Rites* (*Da Dai liji*). See *HS*, 3615; *DDLJ*, 4-7; Yang Hongxun, 1987: 200n30. Titles of Han texts on Bright Hall can be found in the biography of Niu Hong in *Sui shu*, 1302.
《汉书》，第 1709 页。戴德（活跃于前 48—前 33 年）的《大戴礼记》是这类著作中较重要者。见《汉书》，第 3615 页；《大戴礼记》，第 4—7 页；杨鸿勋，1987：第 200 页。汉代关于明堂的著作的题目见于《隋书·牛弘传》，第 1302 页。

222 A surviving fragment of "The Yin-yang Principles of Bright Hall" reads: "The regulation of the Bright Hall compound is as follows: it is surrounded by water that flows counterclockwise to symbolize the sky. Its central chamber is called the Great Hall [Taishi], which stands for Zigong; its south chamber, which shares the name of the whole building [Mingtang], symbolizes the Taiwei [stars in Virgo, Coma Berenices, and Leo], its western chamber, called Zongzhang, symbolizes the Wuhuang; its northern chamber, Yuantang, symbolizes the Yingshi, and its eastern chamber, Qingyang, symbolizes the Tianshi. The God on High and the four seasons govern these five spaces as their palaces; the sovereign, who follows Heaven to rule the world, holds audiences of state affairs in corresponding directions" (*TPYL*, 2418). A more detailed plan in the *Elder Dai's Book of Rites* is too long and complex to be translated and discussed here; see *DDLJ*, 149-52.
《明堂阴阳录》现存的片段中说："明堂之制，周旋以水，水行左旋以象天。内有太室，象紫宫；南出明堂，象太微；西出总章，象五潢；北出玄堂，象营室；东出青阳，象天市。上帝四时各治其宫。王者承天统物，亦于其方以听国事。"见《太平御览》，第 2418 页。《大戴礼记》对明堂的格局有更为详细的描述，但篇幅较长，行文复杂，难以在此进行翻译和讨论；见《大戴礼记》，第 149—152 页。

223 "Whenever people are sick, epidemic diseases spread among six kinds of livestock, and natural disasters fall upon the five kinds of crops, the reason must be found in Heaven. The disharmony of Heaven is caused by the neglect of Bright Hall" (*DDLJ*, 143). Emperor Yuan's reign (when this text is 316
thought to have been written) was full of such disasters. Epidemic diseases, natural disasters, and rebellions were reported almost every year, and a great shortage of food forced people to cannibalism. There were also endless evil portents—eclipses, fires, earthquakes, irregular movements of stars, frost in the summer, and rain in the winter. The author of the text attributed such cosmological and political disorders to the ruler's disobedience of Confucian principles, symbolically stated as his "neglect of Bright Hall."
"凡人民疾、六畜疫、五谷灾者，生于天；天道不顺，生于明堂不饰。"《大戴礼记》，第 243 页。元帝时期（估计就是这些文字写作的时期）充斥着这类灾难。几乎时时都有瘟疫、自然灾害和暴乱发生，粮食严重短缺以至于人相残食。此外，还有无数灾异出现——日食、火灾、地震、星辰不规则的运转、夏寒冬雨。作者将自然界和政治的失衡归结于对儒家原则的背离，其象征性的表达就是"明堂不饰"。

224 *HS*, 4039; see Sargent, 1947: 48.
《汉书》，第 4039 页；萨进德，1947：第 48 页。

225 Sargent, 1947. See also Bielenstein's discussion of Wang Mang in Twitchett and Loewe, 1986: 223-40.
萨进德，1947. 又见毕汉斯对王莽的讨论，转引自杜希德、鲁惟一，1986：第 223—240 页。

226 *HS*, 4046; see Sargent, 1947: 79.《汉书》，第 4046 页；英译据萨进德，1947：第 79 页。

227 For Wang Mang's screening and forging of ancient texts, see Gu Jiegang, 1982: 5.450-613.
有关王莽对古典文献的筛选和伪造的论述，见顾颉刚，1982：第 5 章，第 450—613 页。

228 The construction of Wang Mang's Bright Hall is only briefly mentioned in a memorial included in the *History of the Former Han*: "At present the Duke Protector of Han has arisen among royal relatives and assisted Your Majesty for a period of four years. His accomplishments and virtue have been brilliant. The Duke, in the eighth month at the beginning of the waxing moon, on the *gengzi* day, received documents from the court authorizing the conscription of labor and the construction of the monuments. On the next day [*xinchou*], scholars and citizens held a great assembly, and 100,000 persons gathered together. They worked zealously for twenty days, and the great work was completed" (*HS*, 4069; trans. based on Sargent, 1947: 128).
《汉书》所记载的一份群臣上奏中只简单地提及王莽建造明堂一事："今安汉公起于第家，辅翼陛下，四年于兹，功德烂然。公以八月载生魄庚子奉使朝，用书临赋营筑，越若翊辛丑，诸生、庶民大和会，十万众并集，平作二旬，大功毕成。"《汉书》，第 4069 页；英译据萨进德，1947：第 128 页。

229 *HS*, 4069; trans. based on Sargent, 1947: 128.
同上，第 4069 页；英译据萨进德，1947：第 128 页。

230 Both Emperors Ling and Xian had married when they were fifteen years old. Emperor Ping died when he was fourteen.
灵帝和献帝都在 15 岁时结婚。平帝 14 岁时去世。

231 *HS*, 4078. According to Yan Shigu (*HS*, 360), Emperor Ping was murdered by Wang Mang.
《汉书》，第 4078 页。据颜师古（《汉书》，第 360 页）的说法，平帝为王莽谋杀。

232 An important memorial preceded this event: "When the Duke of Zhou held audiences with the feudal lords in Bright Hall, using the royal screen of the Son of Heaven and facing south, he stood like the Son of Heaven. This is to say that the Duke of Zhou occupied the position of the Son of Heaven

for six years, during which he gave audiences to feudal nobles, established the ceremonies, and arranged the ritual music; and the empire completely submitted. . . . We, your courtiers, request that the Duke Protector of Han act as regent and occupy the throne, and that he wear the imperial robes and crown. At his back he shall have the imperial screen between the doors and windows. He shall face south and receive the courtiers in audience and hear the affairs of the court. His carriage and costume shall indicate his imperial authority; and when he goes out or enters the palace, the people shall retire from the streets. The populace and courtiers shall call themselves vassal subjects. Everything shall be according to the regulations for the Son of Heaven. When he performs the suburban sacrifices to Heaven and Earth, the Dynastic Lineage Sacrifices in Bright Hall, when he sacrifices in the Ancestral Temples, and when he sacrifices to the various spirits, the master of ceremonies shall proclaim: 'The Acting Emperor.'" (*HS*, 4080-81; trans. based on Sargent,1947: 149-50).
在此之前有一个重要的奏议："《礼记·明堂位》曰：'周公朝诸侯于明堂，天子负斧依南面而立。'谓'周公践天子位，六年朝诸侯，制礼作乐，而天下大服'也……臣请安汉公居摄践祚，服天子韨冕，背斧依于户牖之间，南面朝群臣，听政事。车服出入警跸，民臣称臣妾，皆如天子之制。郊祀天地，宗祀明堂，共祀宗庙，享祭群神，赞曰'假皇帝'……"《汉书》，第4080—4081页；英译据萨进德，1947：第149—150页。

233 See the memorial cited in the previous note. 见本章注232所引奏议。

234 An important figure who helped Wang Mang create this system was the Confucian scholar Liu Xin, who also played a central role in designing Bright Hall; see *HS*, 359, 4045-46, 4077; Gu Jiegang, 1982: 5.450-613.
帮助王莽创建该系统的一个重要人物是儒士刘歆，他也在明堂的设计中扮演了中心角色。《汉书》，第359、4045—4046、4077页；顾颉刚，1982：第5章，第450—613页。

235 Gu Jiegang, 1982: 5.583. For the complex history of this new historical system, see *ibid.*, 554-617.
顾颉刚，1982：第5章，第583页。关于这一新历史体系错综复杂的历史，见该书第554—627页。

236 See Gu Jiegang, 1982: 5.417-25, 441-50. 同上，第5章，第417—425、442—450页。

237 *HS*, 4095; trans. based on Sargent, 1947: 178.
《汉书》，第4095页；英译据萨进德，1947：第178页。

238 *HS*, 4100. 《汉书》，第4100页。

Chapter Four Voices of Funerary Monuments
肆 丧葬纪念碑的声音

1 "Xie lu" (Dew on the garlic-leaf); trans. from Waley, 1982: 49.
《薤露》；译文见韦利，1982：第 49 页 。

2 For textual information about Han funerary practices, see Yang Shuda, 1933: 72-289.
有关汉代丧葬的文献，见杨树达，1933：第 72—289 页。

3 *HS*, 3007.《汉书》，第 3007 页。

4 *Yantie lun*, 6.48.《盐铁论》，卷六，第 48 页。

5 See *HHS*, 1546. For conventions for selecting burial sites and dates, see *Lun heng*, 477-81.
《后汉书》，第 1546 页。有关选择葬地和日期的习俗，见《论衡》，第 477—481 页。

6 See Yang Shuda, 1933: 132-44. 杨树达，1933：第 132—144 页。

7 The inscription on the An Guo shrine contains the sentence: "Exhausting their savings, they hired famous craftsmen of Gaoping kingdom [to construct the shrine]." The patron of the Yan family shrine mentioned that "since now the brothers and sisters have sufficient money, they long for their parents and are full of sorrow. They upgraded the tomb mound and built a small offering hall that will be transmitted to future generations" (Shandong Provincial Museum and Shandong Cultural Relics and Archaeology Institute, 1982: 15-16).
安国祠堂的题记中有"以其余财，造立此堂，募使名工高平王叔……"等句子；山东微山永和二年（137）祠堂的题记中有"昆弟男女四人少□□□复失慈母父年……时经（？）有钱刀（？）自足思念父母弟兄悲哀乃治冢作小食堂传孙子"。山东博物馆、山东省文物考古研究所，1982：第 15—16 页。

8 See H. Wu, 1989: 225. 巫鸿，1989：第 225 页。

9 This is suggested by a number of texts engraved on funerary monuments.
317 For example, the patrons of the An Guo shrine advise visitors "to offer their pity and sympathy" and "to regard" their inscription. The inscription on the Xiang Tajun shrine ends with a similar appeal. For a discussion of these two inscriptions, see H. Wu, 1987a: 496-99.
丧葬纪念碑中的许多题记都反映出这一点。例如，安国祠堂的赞助人提醒观者"深加哀怜"并且要"省"这些题记。芗他君石祠堂题记的结尾也有类似的内容。关于这两条题记的讨论，见巫鸿，1987a：第 496—499 页。

10 H. Wu, 1989: 225-28. 巫鸿，1989：第 225—228 页。

11 For a discussion of the structures of Eastern Han cemeteries, see H. Wu, 1989: 30-37. The layout described here is based on Yin Jian's graveyard recorded in *SJZ*, 391.
关于东汉墓地结构的讨论，见巫鸿，1989：第 30—37 页。这里所描述的设计基于《水经注》第 391 页所记载的尹俭墓地的情况。

12 As I explain in Chapter 2, some inscriptions on Han mortuary structures disclose the belief that the tomb and shrine housed the *po* and *hun*, respectively. But many textual sources also reveal that people of the Han did not always distinguish the two clearly. Terms such as *hun*, *po*, and *hunpo* were often used interchangeably. Sometimes we are told that the soul resided in a tomb.
我在第二章已讨论，有些汉代丧葬建筑的题记透露，人们相信墓葬和祠堂分别容纳魂和魄。但是，有的文献也反映出汉代人并不总是十分清楚地将魂与魄划分开来。魂、魄、魂魄等字眼常常可以交替使用。有时我们被告知魂魄居留在墓葬中。

13 For a concise introduction to the political situation during Emperor Huan's reign, see Twitchett and Loewe, 1986: 311-16.
关于桓帝时期政治局势的简要介绍，见杜希德、鲁惟一，1986：第 311—316 页。

14 *HHS*, 298-300.《后汉书》，第 298—300 页。

15 *Ibid.*, 301-2, 2145-46.《后汉书》，第 301—302、2145—2146 页。

16 After an interval of a decade, the rebellion resurfaced in A.D. 170; see *ibid.*, 307.
间隔 10 年后，公元 170 年，暴动再次爆发；同上，第 307 页。

17 Jining Cultural Relics Group and Jiaxiang Cultural Relics Administration, 1982.
济宁市文物局、嘉祥县文物管理所，1982。

18 Several scholars have tried to punctuate, transcribe, and interpret this inscription. My translation is based on *ibid.*; Li Falin, 1982: 101-8; idem, 1984; Feng Zhou, 1983: 98-100.
有多位学者曾对这一题记进行断句、释文和解释。我的翻译根据济宁市文物局、嘉祥县文物管理所，1982；李发林，1982：第 101—108 页；李发林，1984；丰州，1983：第 98—100 页，等多项成果。

19 Such descriptions had become conventional during the Eastern Han and may have been copied from standard books. This becomes clear if we compare this inscription with a passage from the Xiang Tajun Shrine

inscription: "[The second son,] Wuhuan, is carrying on the family line. He deeply bears in mind his parents' bounty and remembers constantly the mournfulness and grief [which he felt at his parents' death]. He and his younger brother worked in the open air in their parents' graveyard, even in the early morning or the heat of summer. They transported soil on their backs to build the tumulus, and planted pine and juniper trees in rows. They erected a stone shrine, hoping that the *hun* souls of their parents would have a place to abide." This inscription is engraved on the frontal side of a stone column now in the collection of the Palace Museum, Beijing (Luo Fuyi, 1960).
这种题记在东汉时期已经变成一种套话，其来源可能是某些标准的抄本。如果我们将这条题记与芗他君祠堂的题记加以比较，这种情况就十分清楚："无患（死者第二子的名字）奉宗。克念父母之恩，思念忉怛悲楚之情。兄弟暴露在冢，不辟晨夏，负土成墓，列种松柏，起立石祠堂，冀二亲魂零（灵）有所依止。"这条题记刻在一个石柱的正面，实物现存故宫博物院。见罗福颐，1960。

20 Trans. based on Makra, 1961: 2-3, 15. 英译据马克拉，1961：第 2—3、15 页。

21 See T. T. Ch'u, 1972: 205-6. 瞿同祖，1972：第 205—206 页。

22 Powers, 1991: 42-43. 包华石，1991；第 42—43 页。

23 Trans. based on Legge, 1881: 10.72. 英译据理雅各，1881：10.72。

24 *Yantie lun*, 6.48; trans. based on Powers, 1984: 148.
《盐铁论》，卷六，第 48 页；英译据包华石，1984：第 148 页。

25 See H. Wu, 1989: 69-70. Only two complete Han dynasty shrines have survived; one is Wu Liang's shrine and the other is the Xiaotang Shan shrine, both in Shandong. I discuss their pictorial programs in *ibid.*, 73-230.
见巫鸿，1989：第 69—70 页。汉代的祠堂只有两组完整地保留至今；这两组祠堂都在山东，其一为武梁祠，另一座为孝堂山祠堂。我对其图像程序的讨论，见上引书，第 73—230 页。

26 These include the inscriptions from the following funerary shrines: (1) the "Shizhai ciyuan" (early 1st century A.D.), (2) the Lugong shrine (A.D. 16), (3) the "Yongyuan eighth year" shrine (A.D. 96), (4) the Yang sanlao shrine (A.D. 106), (5) the Boshuang shrine (A.D. 109), (6) the Dai family shrine (A.D. 113), (7) the "Yongjian fifth year" shrine (A.D. 130), (8) the Yang family shrine (A.D. 137), (9) the Huan Sangzhong shrine (A.D. 141), (10) the Wen Shuyang shrine (A.D. 144), (11) the Wu Liang shrine (A.D. 151), (12) the Xiang Tajun shrine (A.D. 154), (13) the An Guo shrine (A.D. 158), (14) the Kong Dan shrine (A.D. 182). For sources and translations of these inscriptions, see H. Wu, 1987a: 484-507.

刻有这些题记的祠堂包括：①“食斋祠园”（1世纪早期），②路公祠（16），③“永元八年”祠（96），④阳三老祠（106），⑤伯爽祠（109），⑥戴氏享堂（113），⑦“永建五年”祠（130），⑧杨氏祠（137），⑨桓桑终祠（141），⑩叔阳食堂（144），⑪武梁祠（151），⑫芗他君祠（154），⑬安国祠（157），⑭孔耽祠（182）。关于这些题记的出处和翻译，见巫鸿，1987a：第484—507页。

27 Xin Lixiang, 1982: 47. But in my opinion, the slab seems too short to be such a pillar and more likely was an individual tablet erected in a graveyard, possibly in front of an offering shrine.
信立祥，1982：第47页。但我认为，该石用作祠堂的柱子似乎太短，它更像是竖立在墓地里或立在一座祠堂前面的一块独立石刻。

28 A guardian figure in frontal view is executed rather naively in simple sunken lines on the unpolished surface of the stone. Similar images and carving technique are observable on two other slabs dated to this period: one from Baozhaishan (80-75 B.C.) and the other from Pingyi (A.D. 26); see Li Falin, 1982: 45-46.
在没有打磨的石面上有用简单的阴线条刻出的一正面而立的武士，其风格十分拙朴。有着相似形象和雕刻技术的石刻见于沂水鲍宅山石刻（前80—前75年）和平邑麃孝禹碑。见李发林，1982：第45—46页。

29 A pictorial stone from Yutai in Shandong bears an inscription on its right margin. Most of the text has been obscured beyond recognition, and only four or five characters at the beginning of the inscription can be read as “the eighth year of the Yongyuan era” (A.D. 96) (see Shandong Provincial Museum and Shandong Cultural Relics and Archaeology Institute, 1982: 2).
山东鱼台出土的一块画像石的右边有题记。其大多数文字已不可辨认，但最开端的四五个字可辨为“永元八年”（96）等。见山东博物馆、山东省文物考古研究所，1982：第2页。

30 This slab was unearthed around 1888 in Qufu. The inscription is recorded only in Fang Ruo, 1923: 1.5ab. According to Fang, originally there were pictorial designs on the stone but these had completely “peeled off” by the time of discovery. The noble rank, Marquis of Beixiang, was established in the Western Han for members of the royal house. Only during the Eastern Han was the title also assigned to ministers. The *History of the Latter Han* records three persons who held this title; none of them, however, had the surname Yang and could be identified as the man who commissioned this shrine.
该石大约在1888年出土于曲阜。题记仅著录于方若，1923：卷一，第5页。根据方若的观点，该石原有画像，但发现时已全部剥泐。北乡侯的爵位设于西汉，当时只授予皇室贵族。只有到了东汉时期，其他大臣才能被授予这一爵位。《后汉书》记载有三人有此爵位，但其中没有阳姓的，因此都不是出资修建该祠堂的人。

31 Powers, 1991: 135. 包华石，1991：第 135 页。

32 Shandong Provincial Museum and Shandong Cultural Relics and Archaeology Institute, 1982: 15-16.
山东博物馆、山东省文物考古研究所，1982：第 15—16 页。

33 *Li shi*, 6806. As I discuss below, Kong Dan also constructed his own funerary structures.
《隶释》，第 6806 页。如下文所述，孔耽也为自己建造了丧葬建筑。

318 34 Nanyang Museum, 1974. As the excavators have demonstrated, the tomb is not Xu Aqu's grave; the carving was reused as a building stone by fourth-century builders. For the practice of reusing early stone carvings in later tombs, see H. Wu, 1989.
南阳市博物馆，1974。发掘者认为，该墓不是许阿瞿的墓葬，而是 4 世纪的人重新利用了这些石材建造的墓葬。关于对于早期画像石再利用现象的讨论，见巫鸿，1989。

35 Such entertainment scenes are common in Eastern Han pictorial art; for a discussion, see DeWoskin, 1987.
此类乐舞百戏的画面在东汉极为常见；有关讨论见杜志豪，1987。

36 For a discussion of the definition of *portrait* in the Chinese context, see Spiro, 1990: 1-11. In this study I use the term in a stricter sense, not for fictional or mythological figures based on texts (which I call "illustration"), but only for images representing real personages.
关于中国文化中"肖像画"定义的讨论，见司白乐 , 1990: 1–11。我在此处使用的"肖像"一词意义要严格一些，只指一个真实存在的人的像，而不包括文献中虚构的或神话中的人物（我称这类为"画像"）。

37 Trans. from Waley, 1982: 44-45. 英译据韦利，1982：第 44—45 页。

38 For textual information, see T. T. Ch'u, 1972: 5, 8-9. Unlike pre-Qin cemeteries, which usually belonged to large clans or lineages, Western Han funerary sites were small and often included tombs for members of an individual family. A representative of this type of cemetery is the famous Mawangdui site whose three graves belonged to the first Marquis Dai (Li Cang), his wife, and one of their sons; the second Marquis Dai was not buried in this cemetery. Another product of the same social transformation was the "single-pit tomb" containing the corpses of a deceased couple, which became popular during the Western Han (see Institute of Archaeology, CASS, 1984: 413-15; Z. S. Wang, 1982: 175-77).

有关文献见瞿同祖，1972：第5、8—9页。先秦墓地往往为一个氏族或家族共有；与之不同，西汉墓地规模较小，常包括一个核心家庭内各成员的墓葬。这种类型的墓地可以举著名的马王堆墓地为例，其中包括三座墓，分别属于第一代轪侯利仓、利仓夫人及利仓的一个儿子，第二代轪侯并未葬在这一墓地中。这一社会转变的另一产物是西汉十分普遍的夫妇“同穴”埋葬现象。见中国社会科学院考古研究所，1984：第413—415页；王仲殊，1982：第175—177页。

39 During the Qin-Western Han period a law required families with two or more adult sons living at home to pay double taxes. For textual sources and the impact of this law, see T. T. Ch'u, 1972: 8-9.
根据秦与西汉时期的法律，有两名以上成年儿子的家庭须付双倍的税。有关文献见瞿同祖，1972：第8—9页。

40 The Eastern Han periodically established models of such "extended families" based on Confucian morality: in one place a scholar who lived with his paternal relatives and whose whole family held its property in common for three generations was highly praised (see T. T. Ch'u, 1972: 301; H. Wu, 1989: 32-37).
基于儒家的伦理观念，东汉统治者在一定时期内推崇“扩大家庭”模式。在某些情况下，一位儒士与父系的亲属及整个家庭共同生活、三代人共同拥有财产的做法，受到了极高的推崇。见瞿同祖，1972：第301页；巫鸿，1989：第32—37页。

41 The public/private issue is one of the major themes in Martin Powers's works (esp. 1986, 1991). Whereas Powers discusses this problem mainly in its large social and political context, I observe the issue in a family context and hope to explore the significance of funerary structures within local communities.
公、私的问题是包华石所研究的主要问题之一（特别是包华石，1986、1991）。他主要是在广泛的社会和政治的语境中讨论这一问题。与之不同，我对这一问题的观察主要限于家庭的语境，更希望探讨丧葬建筑对地方上的家庭和社团的意义。

42 A version of the story is quoted in *YWLJ*, 369. The present translation is based on another version in Shi Jueshou's *Biographies of Filial Sons*. For a full discussion of the story, see H. Wu, 1989: 278-80.
该故事的另一个版本见于《艺文类聚》，第369页。此处的引文见《太平御览》卷四一三引师觉授《孝子传》。关于这个故事详细的讨论，见巫鸿，1989：第278—280页。

43 This story is recorded in a version of the *Biographies of Filial Sons* housed in Tokyo University. For a full English translation and discussion, see H. Wu, 1989: 291-92.

该故事见于京都大学所藏《孝子传》版本，完整的英译文和更详细的讨论见巫鸿，1989：第 291—292 页。

44 Trans. from S. Y. Teng, 1968: 13. 英译据邓嗣禹，1968：第 13 页。

45 See H. Wu, 1989: 167-85. 巫鸿，1989：第 167—185 页。

46 *LNZ*, 70; O'Hara 1945: 147. For a full discussion and translation of the story, see H. Wu, 1989: 264-66.
《列女传》，第 70 页；郝继隆，1945: 147。更详细论述见巫鸿，1989：第 264—266 页。

47 The story of the Public-Spirited Aunt of Lu is illustrated on the Wu Liang Shrine and, according to textual information, also on Li Gang's shrine, which is no longer extant. The story of the Virtuous Aunt of Liang is depicted on the Wu Liang Shrine and on the Front Shrine in the Wu family cemetery (see H. Wu, 1989: 256-58, 262-64).
鲁义姑姊画像见于武梁祠。据文献记载，也见于现已不存的李刚祠中。梁节姑姊画像见于武梁祠和武氏祠前石室。见巫鸿，1989：第 256—258，262—264 页。

48 *LNZ*, 65; O'Hara, 1945: 138. For a full discussion and translation of the story, see H. Wu, 1989: 256-58.
《列女传》，第 65 页；郝继隆，1945：第 138 页。有关该故事更详细的论述和完整的英译文，见巫鸿，1989：第 256—258 页。

49 *LNZ*, 70; O'Hara, 1945: 147. For a full discussion and translation of the story, see H. Wu, 1989: 262-64.
《列女传》，第 70 页；郝继隆，1945：第 147 面。有关该故事更详细的讨论和完整的英译文，见巫鸿，1989：第 262—264 页。

50 *Mengzi*, 2723.《孟子》，第 2723 页。

51 Besides the loyal servant Li Shan discussed below, a wet nurse is praised in the *Biographies of Exemplary Women* because she became a martyr in protecting the orphaned heir of the state of Wei (*LNZ*, 69).
除了下文要提到的忠仆李善，《列女传》还赞扬了一位乳母，她不愿出卖已失去父亲的魏国公子，从而毅然捐躯。《列女传》，第 69 页。

52 *HHS*, 2679; see H. Wu, 1989: 295.
《后汉书》，第 2679 页；见巫鸿，1989：第 295 页。

53 *Baihu tong*, 7.15ab; see D. L. Hsü, 1970-71: 30.
《白虎通》，卷七，第 15 页；见徐道邻，1970—1971：第 30 页。

54 See Lang, 1946: chaps. 2 and 14; H. Y. Feng, 1948.
朗，1946：第 2、14 章；冯汉骥，1948。

55 Trans. from Makra, 1961: IX. 英译据马克拉，1961：IX。

56 Ware, 1960: 72. 魏鲁南，1960：第 72 页。

57 *HHS*, 1003-4; trans. from Ebrey, 1981: 34-35.
《后汉书》，第 1003—1004 页；英译据伊沛霞，1981：第 34—35 页。

58 See Yang Shuda, 1933: 53-64. 杨树达，1933：第 53—64 页。

59 *LNZ*, 58; O'Hara, 1945: 122-24. See H. Wu, 1989: 253-54.
《列女传》，第 58 页；郝继隆，1945：第 122—124 页；见巫鸿，1989：第 253—254 页。

60 See J. K. T'ien, 1988: 17. 田汝康，1988：第 17 页。

61 For examples, see Yang Shuda, 1933: 56-57.
有关的事例见杨树达，1933：第 56—57 页。

62 *Huayangguo zhi*, 10.86; see Yang Shuda, 1933: 56-57.
《华阳国志》，卷十，第 86 页；见杨树达，1933：第 56—57 页。

63 Yang Shuda, 1933: 57-62. 杨树达，1933：第 57—62 页。

64 J. K. T'ien, 1988: 17. 田汝康，1988：第 17 页。

65 S. Y. Teng, 1968: 13, 10. 邓嗣禹，1968：第 13、10 页。

66 Legge, 1871: 5.355. 理雅各，1871：5.355。

67 J. K. T'ien, 1988: 149. 田汝康，1988：第 149 页。

68 Some texts further separate *you* from *tong*. For example, the *Book of Rites* records: "During the first ten years in life one is called *you*. After this age one begins to study" (*LJ*, 1232).
有的文献进一步将"幼"与"童"区分开来。例如《礼记》中说："人生十年曰幼，学。"《礼记》，第 1232 页。

69 *TPYL*, 1907-8; see Huang Renheng, 1925: 11b. Another version of the story quoted in *Chuxue ji* contains one more detail: "At age seventy he. . . played with a nesting chick beside his parents" (Huang Renheng, 1925: 11b). This image is also found in Han pictorial carvings. For a fuller discussion of the Laizi story and pictorial illustrations, see H. Wu, 1989: 280-81.
《太平御览》，第 1907—1908 页；见黄任恒，1925：第 11 页。《初学记》所录该故事的另一版本包括 70 岁的老莱子在父母旁边玩鸟的细节。这一形象也见于汉画像石中。有关老莱子故事的详细讨论，见巫鸿，1989：第 280—281 页。

70 *Shuo yuan*, 3. For a fuller discussion of the story, see H. Wu, 1989: 286-87.
《说苑》，卷三。有关该故事的详细讨论，见巫鸿，1989：第 286—287 页。

71 Quoted in Breckenridge, 1968: 7. This definition is by no means final or
319 universal. Spiro (1990: 1-11) has demonstrated the necessity of redefining the art of portraiture in the context of ancient Chinese art.
转引自布雷肯里奇，1968：第 7 页。这并非最终的或普遍性的定义。如司白乐认为，中国古代艺术中肖像画的概念需要重新界定。司白乐，1990：第 1—11 页。

72 Makra, 1961: 15. 马克拉，1961：第 15 页。

73 *HHS*, 2020-21; see also *WXTK* 35, "Xuanju" ("Election"), and 8, "Tong ke" ("Children").
《后汉书》，第 2020—2021 页；又见《文献通考》卷三十五"选举"，卷八"童科"。

74 Spiro, 1990: 31. 司白乐，1990：第 31 页。

75 Powers, 1991: 205. 包华石，1991：第 205 页。

76 Soymié, 1954: 378.
苏远鸣，1954：第 378 页。（这条材料应指《隶释》卷十所著录的《童子逢盛碑》。据《隶释》所言，该碑原在山东昌邑。其纪年应为光和四年，即 181 年，而不是苏远鸣所说的 179 年。——译者注）

77 *TPYL*, 1909; see Huang Renheng, 1925: 13b. For a fuller discussion of this story, see H. Wu, 1989: 303-4.
《太平御览》，第 1909 页；见黄任恒，1925：第 13 页。关于这一故事更详细的讨论，见巫鸿，1989：第 303—304 页。

78 *TPYL*, 2360; see Huang Renheng, 1925: 28ab. For a fuller discussion of the story, see H. Wu, 1989: 304-5.
《太平御览》，第 2360 页；见黄任恒，1925：第 28 页。关于这一故事更详细的讨论，见巫鸿，1989：第 304—305 页。

79 This passage is from the inscription on the An Guo shrine, which also describes scenes on the memorial hall, including "personages of filial piety, excellent virtue, and benevolence."
这段文字摘自安国祠堂的题记。据此题记，该祠堂中也刻画了包括"孝及贤仁"在内的主题。

80 Wellek, 1955: 1.211. 韦勒克，1955：1.211。

81 *HHS*, 2063.《后汉书》，第 2063 页。

82 *Ibid*. The *History of the Latter Han* gives the name Xun Shu instead of Xun Yu. This is obviously a mistake because Xun Shu died in 149, some ten years before Han Shao's death. Moreover, since Xun Shu was the teacher of Li Ying, it is quite impossible that his name would be listed last and following

that of his student. It is very possible that the person who joined Li Ying and others to erect the stela was Xun Yu, a nephew of Xun Shu. At the time, Xun Yu was the governor of Pei county in Shandong; he and Han Shao were both from Yingchuan; and he was a radical member of the Confucian faction to which the other three commissioners of the stela belonged.
同上。《后汉书》中荀昱作荀淑。这很明显是一个错误，因为荀淑在公元149年已经去世，比韩韶之死大约早十年。此外，因为荀淑是李膺的老师，所以他的名字不可能放在他学生的名字的后面。与李膺和其他人一起参加立碑活动的人更有可能是荀淑的侄子荀昱。当时，荀昱是沛县的县令，他和韩韶都来自颍川，他也是其他参加立碑人所属的儒家集团的激进分子。

83 See Ebrey, 1980. 伊沛霞，1980。

84 The following introduction to Li Ying's life is based mainly on *HHS*, *juan* 67 (2183-218), which includes his biography. Dates of his persecution and death are given in *HHS*, 318, 330-31. For the struggle between different political factions during the reigns of Emperors Huan and Ling, see Twitchett and Loewe, 1986: 286-90, 311-30.
下文对于李膺生平的介绍主要依据《后汉书》卷六十七“李膺传”（第2183—2218页）。《后汉书》第318、330—331页记载了他受迫害和死亡的时间。关于桓、灵时期不同政治派别争斗的情况，见杜希德、鲁惟一，1986：第286—290、311—330页。

85 *HHS*, 2198.《后汉书》，第2198页。

86 *Ibid.*, 2050. 同上，第2050页。

87 The following introduction to Chen Shi's life is based on his biography in *ibid.*, 2065-67.
下文关于陈寔生平的介绍，依据是《后汉书》第2065—2067页“陈寔传”。

88 See Powers, 1983: 8-11; C. Y. Chen, 1975: 19-20.
包华石，1983：第8—11页；陈启云，1975：第19—20页。

89 *HS*, 3364; *HHS*, 1211.
《汉书》，第3364页；《后汉书》，第1211页。

90 For an excellent discussion of this subject, see Powers, 1984: 142-54.
关于这一问题的精彩讨论，见包华石，1984：第142—154页。

91 The *History of the Latter Han* does not provide the date of Han Shao's death and the time of the stela's establishment is thus uncertain. During the Han, such a dedication required the donors to be at the funerary ceremony. According to *HHS* (2066, 2195, 2198), after being released from jail in 167, Li Ying and Du Mi returned home to Shandong. Du Mi was reinstated

before Emperor Huan's death in 167, and Li Ying returned to the court shortly afterward. Both men died in 169. In 167 Chen Shi, after a brief incarceration, returned to his hometown, Yingchuan (*HHS*, 2066). Only Xun Yu seemed to have kept his official post in Pei (*HHS*, 2050).
《后汉书》并没有记载韩韶去世的时间，因此立碑的时间也就不得而知。在汉代，这种贡献要求贡献者亲临葬礼现场。根据《后汉书》(第 2066、2195、2198 页)，李膺和杜密于 167 年获释并回到老家山东。在 167 年桓帝去世之前，杜密已经复职，李膺也在稍后回到朝廷。这两人都死于 169 年。陈寔经过短暂的牢狱之灾后，于 167 年回到故乡颍川(《后汉书》，第 2066 页)。似乎只有荀昱继续担任他在沛县的官职(《后汉书》，第 2050 页)。

92 *Xunzi*, 246.《荀子》，第 246 页。

93 For a useful index to these inscriptions, see Yang Dianxun, 1940. For a brief introduction to Han epitaphs and other types of inscriptions, see Ebrey, 1980.
杨殿珣(1940)提供了有用的碑刻索引。关于对汉代墓志和其他类型铭刻的简要介绍，见伊沛霞，1980。

94 Cao Pi wrote in his "Dian lun" (Authoritative discourses): "Though all writing is essentially the same, the specific forms differ. Thus memorials [*zou*] and deliberations [*yi*] should be decorous; letters [*shu*] and essays [*lun*] should be logical; inscriptions [*ming*] and dirges [*lei*] should stick to the facts; poetry [*shi*] and rhymeprose [*fu*] should be ornate" (trans. from Hightower, 1957: 513). For discussions of this subject, see Holzman, 1978; R. Miao, 1972: 1025; Watson, 1968a; and Kinney, 1990: 21-22.
曹丕在其《典论》中写道："夫文，本同而末异，盖奏、议宜雅，书、论宜理，铭、诔尚实，诗、赋欲丽。"(英译据海陶玮，1957: 513)对此文的研究，见侯思孟，1978；缪文杰，1972：第 1025 页；华兹生，1968a；司马安，1990：第 21—22 页。

95 Such cases are numerous; for example, a member of the Wu family in Jiaxiang identified his remote ancestor as King Wu Ding of the Shang, though Wu Ding's surname was not even Wu. Another famous stela dedicated to Zhang Qian records that Zhang's ancestors include Zhang Zhong of the Zhou, and three famous Western Han figures: Zhang Liang, Zhang Shizhi, and another Zhang Qian. None was actually related to Zhang Qian, however.
这种例子数量极多。例如，嘉祥武氏家族中的一人就认定他的远祖是商王武丁，尽管武丁并不姓武。著名的张迁碑记载张的祖先有周代的张仲，以及西汉时期三个著名的人物张良、张释之、张骞。但是，这些人与张迁并没有直接亲属关系。

96 *HHS*, 2067-68.《后汉书》，第 2067—2068 页。

97 *Ibid.*, 2063. 同上，第 2063 页。

98 The following information about Kong Rong is from his biography in *ibid.*, 2261-63.
孔融的生平见《后汉书·孔融传》，第 2261—2263 页。

99 Unless noted, information about Zhao Qi is from his biography in *ibid.*, 2121-25.
除特别注明外，关于赵岐生平的记载，均据《后汉书·赵岐传》，第 2121—2125 页。

100 *Sanfu juelu* (Records of the Sanfu area reexamined); cited in *HHS*, 2121.
《后汉书》，第 2121 页引《三辅决录》。

101 *HHS*, 2124.《后汉书》，第 2124 页。

102 See Shi Zhecun, 1987: 405. 施蛰存，1987：第 405 页。

103 For a brief discussion of these works, see H. Wu, 1989: 188-89, 252-53, 272-75.
有关这些文献的简要讨论，见巫鸿，1989：第 188—189、252—253、272—275 页。

104 For a discussion of Han omen catalogues, see H. Wu, 1989: 76-92.
有关汉代祥瑞目录的讨论，同上，第 76—92 页。

105 According to historical records, such illustrated texts included the *Biographies of Exemplary Women*, the *Annotated Good-Omen Illustrations*, and the *Classic of Mountains and Seas*; see H. Wu, 1989: 76-95, 171-73.
根据史书记载，这些有插图的文献包括《列女传》《瑞图》和《山海经》等，同上，第 76—95，第 171—173 页。

106 One such copybook recorded in the "Bibliography" chapter of the *History of the Former Han* is called *The Method of Painting Confucius' Disciples* (*Kongzi* 320
turen huafa) (*HS*, 1717).
《汉书·艺文志》记载了一种粉本，题为《孔子徒人图法》。《汉书》，第 1717 页。

107 H. Wu, 1989: 73-230, esp. 96-107, 173-80, 182-86.
巫鸿，1989：第 73—230 页；特别是第 96—107、173—180、182—186 页。

108 For a discussion of these characteristics of the New Text school, see *ibid.*, 97-101.
有关今文学派特征的讨论，同上，第 97—101 页。

109 For Wu Liang's relationship with the "retired worthies," see *ibid.*, 102-7.
有关武梁与"隐士"的关系问题的讨论，同上，第 102—107 页。

110 This argument is based on (1), as I will demonstrate later, the historical narrative depicted on the shrine's walls develops from right to left and from top to bottom; and (2) traditional Chinese writing, painting, and reading always followed this order.
这一论点的根据是：一，我将在下文证明，祠堂墙面上历史性画面的叙述顺序是从右到左，从上到下；二，中国传统的书写、绘画、阅读，总是遵循这一顺序。

111 Part of this chapter is translated in Watson, 1958: 42-57.
该卷部分的英译文见华兹生，1958：第 42—57 页。

112 *Ibid.*, 70-100. 同上，第 70—100 页。

113 *Ibid.*, 92. 同上，第 92 页。

114 Sima Qian's own words, in reference to the "Treatise on Heavenly Signs" ("Tianguan shu") and the "Treatise on the Feng and Shan Sacrifices" ("Fengshan shu"); see *ibid.*, 115.
司马迁的原文见"天官书"和"封禅书"；同上，第 115 页。

115 For discussions of the structure of the *Historical Records*, see Watson, 1958: 101-34; H. Wu, 1989: 151-52.
有关《史记》结构的讨论，见华兹生，1958：第 101—134 页；巫鸿，1989：第 151—152 页。

116 For the development of the Queen Mother myth and iconography, see H. Wu, 1989: 108-41.
有关西王母神话与形象演化的讨论，见巫鸿，1989：第 108—141 页。

117 *Ibid.*, 76-80, 234-35. 同上，第 76—80、234—235 页。

118 *HHS*, 1373.《后汉书》，第 1373 页。

119 Forke, 1962: 259. 佛尔克，1962：第 259 页。

120 Extant omen catalogues date to post-Han periods, but as I have argued elsewhere, these later works are very likely based, partially or entirely, on Han examples (H. Wu, 1989: 234-35).
现存祥瑞目录的年代晚于汉代，但我曾讨论过，这些文献的部分或全部，与汉代的作品非常相似。巫鸿，1989：第 234—235 页。

121 For translations of these cartouches and their textual sources, see *ibid.*, 235-43.
关于这些题榜的翻译及其文字出处的讨论，同上，第 235—243 页。

122 Trans. based on Hightower, 1952: 265-66. 英译据海陶玮，1952：第 265—266 页。

123 *HHS*, 2185; trans. based on Powers, 1983: 7.
《后汉书》，第 2185 页；英译据包华石，1983：第 7 页。

124 Trans. based on Hightower, 1952: 229. 英译据海陶玮，1952：第 229 页。

125 *Ibid*., 173.《后汉书》，第 173 页；英译据海陶玮，1952：第 173 页。

126 The source of this inscription is the "Xi ci" section of the *Book of Changes*: "When in early antiquity Fu Xi ruled the world, he looked upward and contemplated the images in Heaven; he looked downward and contemplated the patterns on earth. He contemplated the markings of birds and beasts and the adaptations to the regions. He proceeded directly from himself and indirectly from objects. Thus he invented the eight trigrams in order to enter into the wisdom of the gods and to regulate the conditions of all beings. He made knotted cords and used them for nets and baskets in hunting and fishing" (trans. based on Wilhelm, 1967: 328-29).
这一榜题的文字出自《易·系辞》:"古者包犧氏之王天下也，仰则观象于天，俯则观法于地，观鸟兽之文，与地之宜，近取诸身，远取诸物。于是始作八卦，以通神明之德，以类万物之情，作结绳以为网罟，以佃以渔，盖取诸离。"英译据卫礼贤，1967：第 328—329 页。

127 A passage from *Fengsu tongyi* (1.9) reads: "The Yellow Emperor invented the royal crown, and had upper and lower garments hang down." A similar expression appears in the "Xi ci": "The Yellow Emperor. . . had upper and lower garments hang down, so the world was in order" (trans. based on Wilhelm, 1976: 332).
《风俗通义·皇霸》:"黄帝始制冠冕，垂衣裳。"《易·系辞》:"黄帝……垂衣裳而天下治。"英译据卫礼贤，1967：第 332 页。

128 *SJ*, 3319.《史记》，第 3319 页。

129 H. Wu, 1989: 244-45. 巫鸿，1989：第 244—245 页。

130 An exception is the story of Zhongli Chun, which is included in the sixth chapter of the *Biographies of Exemplary Women*, "Reasoning and Understanding." On the Wu Liang shrine, this picture is separated from other female images and is placed in the lower section. As I have argued elsewhere, this position emphasizes the figure's loyalty toward the ruler (H. Wu, 1989: 191).
《列女传》卷六"辩通传"所载钟离春的故事是一个例外。在武梁祠中，这个故事与其他妇女的形象分开，位于墙壁下部。我在他处曾讨论过，这一位置强调了儒家伦理中对君主的忠。巫鸿，1989：第 191 页。

131 Datong Museum, 1972. 山西省大同市博物馆、山西省文物工作委员会，1972。

132 Palace Museum, 1978: figs. 20-32. 故宫博物院，1978：图 20—32。

133 *LNZ*, 4.58.《列女传》，卷四，第 58 页。

134 For example, it was said that Confucius once claimed: "Of all the actions of man, there is none greater than filial piety and in filial piety there is nothing greater than the reverential awe of one's father." The *Xiaojing*, or *Classic of Filial Piety*, state in the first chapter that in practicing filial piety one should extend the love of one's father to one's mother.
例如，据说孔子曾讲："人之行，莫大于孝，孝莫大于严父。""资于事父以事母，而爱同。"《孝经》，卷一。

135 These are the stories of Zeng Shen, Min Ziqian, Elder Laizi, and Han Boyu.
这些故事包括曾参、闵子骞、老莱子和韩伯榆的故事。

136 See H. Wu, 1989: 296-98. 巫鸿，1989：第 296—298 页。

137 *Ibid.*, 193-213. 同上，第 193—213 页。

138 Berger, 1990: 231-34. 白瑞霞，1990：第 231—234 页。

139 See H. Wu, 1989: 222-23. 巫鸿，1989：第 222—223 页。

140 For a different view, see Hay, 1993: 171.
我不同的观点，见乔迅，1993：第 171 页。

141 The stela, called "Tablet of the Divine Shrine of the Late Chancellor of Liang, Kong Dan," is now missing; only its inscription is recorded by Hong Shi (*Li shi*, 6806). According to Hong, the stela was originally located in Yongcheng near Xuzhou. A passage at the end of the inscription identifies its author as Kong Dan's son, who wrote the text when his father was still alive.
该碑名为《梁相孔耽神祠碑》，已佚，洪适《隶释》（第 6806 页）著录其文。据《隶释》记载，该碑原立于亳州永城县。据碑文最后一段，此文为孔耽的儿子在孔耽尚在世时撰写。

142 For information about these monuments and their inscriptions, see *ibid.*, 5-9, 24-25.
关于这些纪念碑及其铭文的情况，见洪适《隶释》，第 5—9、24—25 页。

143 Trans. partially based on Fairbank, 1941: 8. 英译文部分地依据费慰梅，1941：第 8 页。

144 The inscription is engraved on the front side of a stone column, now in the collection of the Palace Museum in Beijing. According to Luo Fuyi (1960), this column was found in 193 on a small hill called Tietoushan about 22 kms west of Dong'e county in present-day Shandong. It consists of two connected sections, a four-sided shaft and a lion base. Human figures,

mythical animals, and geometric patterns in low relief appear on the front, the right side, and the back of the shaft. The left side is plain. Luo Fuyi thought that this column was originally a central pillar located in the entrance of a tomb. Based on the inscription and the decorative features of the column, Nagahiro Toshio (1965: 46-47) has argued, rightly in my opinion, that it may have been a pillar standing in the facade of a shrine and attached to the left wall. I discuss and translate this inscription in H. Wu, 1987a: 496-99.

这段文字刻在一根石柱的正面，原石现存故宫博物院。根据罗福颐（1960）的介绍，该石柱 1934 年发现于今山东东阿县西约 22 公里处一座名为铁头山的小山上。它包括两个相连的部分，一个方形柱身和一个狮形的柱础。柱身前面、右侧和背面刻有人物、神异动物和几何纹样。左侧素面。罗福颐认为该柱原是一座墓葬入口中央的立柱。长广敏雄根据柱子的铭文和装饰特征认为这应是一座祠堂正面靠近左壁的立柱（1965：第 46—47 页）。我赞同这一看法。我对其题记的讨论和翻译，见巫鸿，1987a：第 496—499 页。

145 As I discuss later in this section, the inscription on the An Guo shrine is a rare Han funerary text that describes the shrine's decoration. But even in this case the writer only mentions the most common scenes in Han art and offers no information about the shrine's specific decoration. We also find interesting parallels between the An Guo inscription and Wang Yanshou's "Rhapsody on the Hall of Spiritual Light of the Lu" (translated in Bush and Shih, 1985: 26). Both texts seem to follow a standard literary formula at the time.

我在这一章稍后将讨论到，安国祠堂的题记是一则罕见的描述祠堂装饰的汉代丧葬文字。但即使在这一例子中，写作者也只是提到了汉代艺术中最为常见的画面，并没有涉及该祠堂特别的装饰。我们可以看到安国祠堂与王延寿《鲁灵光殿赋》（英译文见卜寿珊、时学颜，1985：第 26 页）有趣的相似点，二者似乎遵循了当时一种标准的写作程式。

146 Hay, 1993: 171. 乔迅，1993：第 171 页。

147 These patrons could be the family members of the deceased, the former associates of the deceased, and the deceased himself. Workers' signatures and marks inscribed inside tombs were known, but these can hardly be considered "texts."

这些赞助人可能是死者家庭的成员、死者生前的同僚，或者死者本人。虽然有的墓葬中曾发现工匠的署名和记号，但这些刻铭难以被看作"文章"。

148 Shandong Provincial Museum and Cangshan Cultural House, 1975. The date of the Cangshan tomb has been the focus of a scholarly debate, primarily because the date on its inscription is ambiguous: "the first year of the

Yuanjia reign period" could be either A.D. 151 or 424. The excavators first dated the tomb to 424, but most scholars have been rejected their opinion (see Li Falin, 1982: 68-77).
山东博物馆、苍山县文化馆，1975。该墓的年代问题曾引起争论，原报告认为画像题记中的"元嘉元年"为南朝刘宋文帝元嘉元年，即 424 年，而多数学者则主张这一纪年为东汉桓帝元嘉元年，即 151 年。见李发林，1982：第 68—77 页。

149 A rough transliteration of the text appeared in the excavation report, and some passages were quoted as iconographic sources for the pictures engraved in the tomb. The authors of the report, however, cautiously avoided punctuating and interpreting the whole text. Five years after the publication of the report in *Kaogu*, a short publisher's note appeared in the magazine, saying that the editorial board had received several articles criticizing the transliteration and interpretation of the inscription as provided in the report. Since then, three articles on the inscription, two by Li Falin (1982、1985) and the other by Fang Pengjun and Zhang Xunliao (1980), have been published, laying a foundation for a more comprehensive study of the text. In addition, Jiang Yingju and Wu Wenqi proposed another reading in a catalogue of Shandong pictorial carvings in 1982 (Shandong Provincial Museum and Shandong Cultural Relics and Archaeology Institute, 1982: 42).

Li Falin's two articles exhibit only minor differences. His basic method is to discover references for individual words and phrases and then to find the relationships between these units. Fang Pengjun and Zhang Xunliao, on the other hand, first focused on phonology and punctuation. They found that the whole text is actually a rhymed composition. After a careful phonological study, the two authors concluded that "the recognition of (these rhyming rules) is the key to interpreting the text" (1980: 271).

These studies provide the present author with important clues. My identification of characters takes into consideration the different opinions. Fang Pengjun and Zhang Xunliao's punctuation differs markedly from that proposed by Li Falin and, in my opinion, is more convincing. Except for one place, I accept it as the basis for my punctuation of the text. On the other hand, Li Falin has provided many literary sources important for our understanding of the text. Unless noted, I follow his interpretations of words and phrases.
发掘报告对于这篇题记做了大致的释读，有的段落被用作对墓中画像进行图像学解释的材料，但没有对整篇文字做标点和解释。《考古》杂志在发表这篇发掘报告 5 年之后，于 1980 年第 3 期第 271 页刊发编者按语，称编辑部收到多篇文章对原报告的释读提出异议。此后，若干篇文章对这一题记进行讨论，其中两篇是李发林的文章（1982、1985），另一篇的作者为方鹏均和张勋燎（1980）。这些文章为更全面地理解这篇题记提供了基础。此外，1982 年蒋英炬、吴文祺等在山东汉画像石的图录中提出了另一种释读方案。见山东博物馆、山东省文物考古研究所，1982：第 42 页。

李发林的两篇文章差别不大。他基本的方法是逐字逐句论证题记中的字、词与文献的对应关系。方鹏均和张勋燎则着力于音韵和句读，因此发现题记是一篇韵文。通过对读音的研究，他们认为“掌握上述这一特点，是正确理解题记释文和整个断代问题的关键”。（1980：第 271 页）

这些研究为我们理解这篇题记提供了不少线索。我对文字的认读考虑到了以上不同的观点。方鹏均、张勋燎与李发林的句读不同，我个人认为更有说服力。除了一处以外，我接受了他们的方案作为我断句的基础。但是，李发林的文章也为我们理解题记中的一些用语提供了重要的文献资料。除特别注明外，我接受他对于字句的解释。

150 Li Falin (1982: 96) interpreted the character *song* as "to present" or "to donate" and the sentence as "we completed the construction of this tomb chamber and presented it to you, the honorable member of a family." The latter parts of the inscription, however, clearly suggest that this tomb was a vehicle to transport the dead to the other world. The character *song* can thus be more properly translated as "to send off" or "to send away."
李发林（1982：第 96 页）对“送”字的解释是“送给”，全句的意思是“……石室全部修建成功了。这是用来送给尊贵的亲人的”。但是，题记后半部分很明显是将墓室看作死者去往彼世界的交通工具，因此“送”字应更准确地被理解为“送出”“送走”。

151 Li Falin provided two different interpretations for the terms *boshu* and *huaguan*. In 1982: 96, he explained *boshu* as "simple and coarse," and *huaguan* as "rooms decorated with pictures." The sentence would then read: "Chambers decorated with pictures are inside the simple and coarse tomb." In 1985: 72, he explained *boshu* as "decoration and carving," and *huaguan* as "paintings people can view and enjoy." The sentence would then be interpreted as: "In the decorated and engraved tomb chambers are pictures people can see and enjoy." My understanding of this sentence differs. In Han literature the character *bo* and *bu* are interchangeable; the latter means "a list" or "to list." The meaning of *shu* is close to *bu* and can be translated in certain contexts as "to list," "to explain," or "to propose" (see *HS*, 2128). As defined in *SW* (408), the original meaning of *guan* is "to see." Its secondary meanings include "to show," "to appear," or "appearance." The word *huaguan* thus means "the appearance of the pictures" or simply "the pictures."
李发林对“薄疏”和“画观”提出了两种解释。在 1982 年（第 96 页），他认为“薄疏”意指“绵薄粗疏”，“画观”意指“有画的楼观，这儿当即指墓室”，因此全句的意思是“绵薄粗疏的椁室中有画观”。在 1985 年（第 72 页），他将“薄疏”解释为“装饰”和“刻镂”，将“画观”解释为“可观赏的画幅”，全句的意思是，“在装饰仙刻（原文如此——译者）的墓室中，刻着一幅可观赏的画。”我的理解与李发林不同。在汉代文献中，“薄”通“簿”，“簿”的意思是“名单”或“列出”；“疎”即“疏”，意思与“薄”相近，在文中可释作“列出”、“解释”或“列举”（《汉书》，第 2128 页》)。《说文解字》释“观”为“谛视也”（第 408 页）。其衍生的意义有“展示”“呈现”或“出现”。因此，“画观”的意义可释为“展示其画像”，或简单地理解为“画像”。

152 A commentary to the “Yueling” chapter in *LJ* (1372) reads: “*Zhongliu* means the central chamber. The element ‘earth’ governs the center, and its spirit is in the chamber.”
《礼记》“月令”（第 1372 页）郑玄注云：“中霤，犹中室也。土主中央而神在室。”

153 Li Falin (1982: 96) misidentifies the character *yang* as *jia* and reads *jiashi* together to mean the tomb’s side chamber. Two factors lead me to identify
322 the supposed placement of these scenes (hence the meaning of the phrase *shishangyang*) as the ceiling of the rear chamber: (1) the location of the images of the Blue Dragon and the White Tiger in the present tomb, and (2) the narrative sequence of the inscription, which describes the pictures in the tomb from the rear to the front section.
李发林误将“砄”释为“夹”，认为“夹室”即墓葬的耳室（1982 年，第 96 页）。我认为这幅画像的位置应在后室的顶部（即题记所谓“室上”），原因有二：首先，墓室内该位置现存的画像为青龙白虎，与题记所述一致；二，题记叙事的顺序是从后室到前室。

154 A *ping* is a type of carriage used by women. According to *Shi ming* (364-65), “*Ping* means ‘to shield.’ A *ping* chariot is covered on all four sides; it is an ox-drawn carriage for female transportation.”
軿车是一种妇女乘坐的车。《释名》（第 364—365 页）：“軿车，軿，屏蔽也，四面屏蔽，妇人所乘牛车也。”

155 *Fengsu tongyi* defines a *ting* as “the inn where travelers rest” (see Li Falin, 1982: 98). Yan Shigu’s commentary on *HS*, 3 reads: “*Ting* means ‘to stop’; it is the inn where travelers rest and dine.”
《风俗通义》：“亭，留也，盖行旅宿舍之所馆。”见李发林，1982：第 98 页。《汉书》颜师古注曰：“亭谓停留，行旅宿食之馆。”（第 3 页）

156 *Youjiao* is a low official rank in an administrative body called a *xiang* (a large village). His principal duty was to maintain public order and to catch thieves and robbers. *Xu Han shu*, “Baiguan zhi” (A record of official ranks) records that “in every *xiang* district there is a *youjiao* who is in charge of the prohibition against stealing and robbing” (see Li Falin, 1982: 98).
“游徼”是乡一级的官员，其主要职责是维持公共秩序，捉捕盗贼。《续汉书·百官志》注云："游徼掌循、禁司歼盗。"见李发林，1982年：第98页。

157 According to *SW* (270) and *HS* (310-11), the character *hui* in the inscription means "coffin" or "small coffin." A hearse carrying a coffin is thus called a *hui* carriage.
根据《说文解字》（第27页）和《汉书》（第310—311页），题记中的"槥"意思是"棺"或"小棺"，因此运送棺的车称为"槥车"。

158 The title *dudu* does not appear in Han official documents but can be found in several Eastern Han inscriptions. On the "Stela of the Divine Master White Stone," donors' names are listed in order of their official ranks. Two persons entitled *dudu* are listed after those who held the post *jijiu* (official in charge of ceremonies) but before those entitled *zhubu* (the chief of records). Li Falin (1982: 71) thus suggests that *dudu* was a relatively low official rank during the Eastern Han.
文献中对于汉代官职的记载不见"都督"一职，但是该职见于东汉石刻文字中。《白石神君碑》按官职刻赞助人姓名，有两个官位为都督的人名列于祭酒与主簿之间。李发林认为都督是东汉地位较为低下的官职(1982：第71页)。

159 According to the "Baiguan zhi" in *Xu Han shu*, "The responsibility of a *zeicao* is to guard against robbery" (quoted in Li Falin, 1982: 99).
《续汉书·百官志》注云："贼曹主盗贼事。"转引自李发林，1982：第99页。

160 Li Falin (1982: 99) interprets the term *chengqing* as "favorite official assistant." Indeed, the character *cheng* was usually used in official titles to mean "assistant" or "junior." *Qing* is not a Han official post, however, but is sometimes used as *gongzi*, meaning "young master." The term *chengqing*, therefore, can be understood in the context of the inscription as the "junior master"—the son of the deceased—who stands at the entrance of the reception hall to greet guests, while the *xinfu*, his bride, is serving drink to guests. The term *xinfu* was used in Han times for either a "daughter-in-law" or a "bride." This reading is further supported by an Eastern Han carving from Xinjin in Sichuan. Three figures are portrayed on two door leaves of a tomb. According to the accompanying cartouches, the woman is "a filial daughter-in-law" and the two men are Zhao Mai and his son Zhao Chuan (see Wen Yu, 1956: interpretations of pls. 21, 22; Rudolph, 1951: 30). It is not difficult to find parallels between this carving and the Cangshan images both in terms of decorative position and subject matter.
李发林释"丞"为"辅助官员"，"卿"为爱称。(1982：第99页）诚然，"丞"字常与官职联系在一起，意为助手或地位较低者。但"卿"并不是汉代的官职，而有时用来指"公子"。因此题记中的"丞卿"可理解为死者的儿子。“右柱□□请丞卿”大意是死者之子站在客厅的门旁迎接客人。“新妇”即新娘正在进献水浆。“新妇”一词在汉代可指儿媳。这一解释可从四川新津东汉一幅崖墓画像中得到支持。根据榜题可知，画像中的妇人是赵买的儿媳妇，两男子分别是赵买和他的儿子赵椽。见闻宥，1956：插图 21、22 的解释；鲁德福，1951：30。在装饰位置和主题两方面，我们不难看出新津画像与苍山墓门画像的共同之处。

161 For a listing of these characters, see Li Falin, 1982: 100; Fang Pengjun and Zhang Xunliao, 1980: 273-74.
对于这些字的汇集，见李发林，1982：第 100 页；方鹏钧、张勋燎，1980：第 273—274 页。

162 Li Falin, 1982: 100. 李发林，1982：第 100 页。

163 According to Fang Pengjun and Zhang Xunliao (1980: 271), the beginning and ending sections of this text both consist of four-character lines, with rhymes on odd-numbered lines. The rest of the inscription is composed of three-character, four-character, and seven-character lines. All seven-character sentences are rhymed, whereas rhyming words only end the second three-character line if there is a pair. These two authors also suggest that "except for the character *jun*, the remaining 45 rhymes in the inscription are all consistent with those in Han literature" (1980: 273).
根据方鹏钧、张勋燎的看法（1980：第 271 页），这篇题记的开头和结尾由四个字的句子组成，在奇数行押韵。题记的其他部分由三字、四字和七字的句子组成。所有的七字句都押韵，如果三字句成对出现，则只在其第二句押韵。这两位学者还认为“除‘君’字一字出韵外，其余四十五个字也都符合汉代用韵的特点”。（1980：第 273 页）

164 This literary form, which is most commonly seen in stela inscriptions, is sometimes imitated by the family members of the dead in their devotional texts. One such example is the inscription composed by Wu Liang's descendents, which begins with a prose narrative and ends with a paragraph consisting of rhymed four-character lines (see H. Wu, 1989: 25).
这种文学形式在碑铭中最为常见，有时被死者家人的挽词模仿。武梁后人所作的一篇题记就是这样一个例子，其开篇为散文形式的叙事，结尾的段落是四字句组成的韵文。参见巫鸿，1989：第 25 页。

165 For a discussion of this expression, see Chen Zhi, 1962.
关于这种意义的讨论，见陈直，1962。

166 H. Wu, 1987a: 446-53. 巫鸿，1987a：第 446—453 页。

167 Jining Area Cultural Relics Group and Jiaxiang Cultural Relics Administration, 1982: 70.
济宁地区文物组、嘉祥文管所，1982：第 70 页。

168 Li Falin (1982: 97) identifies the bridge mentioned here as one of the three Wei Bridges outside the Western Han capital Chang'an. He thus infers that the person buried in the Cangshan tomb must have held an official post in the capital before his death. In my opinion, the inscription uses *Wei Bridge* in a general and symbolic sense. The first or Middle Wei Bridge was built by the First Emperor to connect the Xianyang Palace and the Changle Palace, which were separated by the Wei River. The second or East Wei Bridge was constructed by Emperor Jing of the Han to connect the capital and his tomb. The third or West Bridge built by Emperor Wu linked the capital with his tomb. The two bridges built during the Han were both part of imperial funerary constructions. By connecting the capital and imperial tombs, they made it possible for ritual processions to cross the river to the imperial mausoleums.
李发林（1982：第 97 页）认为此处的渭桥是指西汉长安西郊渭水上的桥梁，因此他认为苍山墓的墓主生前曾在都城做过官。我认为渭桥在此处的意义是一般性和象征性的。第一座渭桥，即中渭桥，是由秦始皇修建的，用以连接咸阳宫和长乐宫；第二座渭桥，即东渭桥，是由汉景帝修建的，用以连接都城和皇帝的陵墓；第三座渭桥，即西渭桥，是由汉武帝修建的，用以连接都城和他自己的陵墓。汉代修建的两座渭桥都是皇帝陵墓工程的一部分。渭桥将都城和墓地连起来，送葬的行列才能跨过渭水去往帝陵。

169 For such figures, see Omura Seigai, 1915: 1.143-45.
关于这种石人，见大村西崖，1915：卷一，第 143—145 页。

170 For the iconography and symbolism of the Wang Hui sarcophagus, see H. Wu, 1987a: 75.
关于王晖石棺图像和象征意义的讨论，见巫鸿，1987a：第 75 页。

171 Trans. based on Bush and Shih, 1985: 26.
英译据卜寿珊、时学颜，1985：第 26 页。

Chapter Five The Transparent Stone: The End of an Era
㈤ 透明之石：一个时代的终结

1 Trans. from Stephen Owen, *An Anthology of Chinese Poems*. Cambridge, Mass.: Harvard University Press, forthcoming (romanization altered). 323
曹植，《送应氏二首》，《曹子建集》，卷五。英译据宇文所安，*An Anthology of Chinese Poems*. 剑桥马萨诸塞，剑桥大学出版社，即将出版。

2 *Ibid*. (romanization altered). 同上（拼音有所变化）。

3 According to the recent inventory in Yao Qian and Gu Bing, 1981, altogether eleven Liang mausoleums have been found: (1) Jian ling (of Emperor Wen, Xiao Shunzhi; probably built in 535), (2) Xiu ling (of Emperor

Wu, Xiao Yan; built before 549 when the emperor died), (3) Zhuang ling (of Emperor Jianwen, Xiao Gang; built before 552), (4) tombs of eight Liang princes—Xiao Hong (d. 526), Xiao Xiu (d. 518), Xiao Hui (d. 527), Xiao Dan (d. 522), Xiao Jing (d. 523), Xiao Ji (d. 529), Xiao Zhengli (d. before 548), and Xiao Ying (d. 544). The remains of the Zhuang ling of Emperor Jianwen, however, are buried and cannot be seen. The relationship between the deceased is shown in the following table (the tombs of those whose names are in parentheses have not been found) :

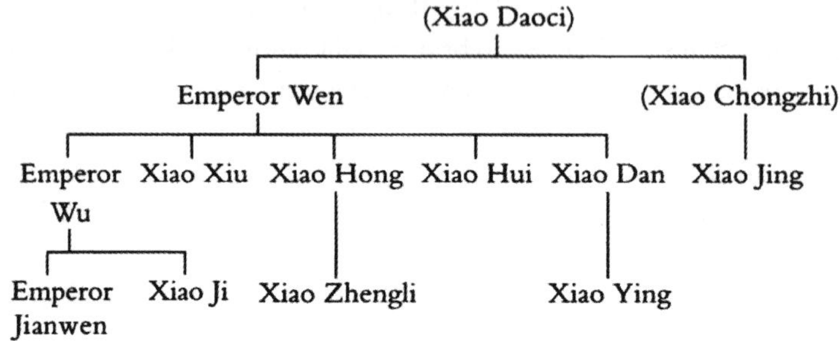

The Liang tombs and other mausoleums of the Southern Dynasties in the Nanjing area have been recorded since Tang times (for traditional sources, see Zhu Xizu et al., 1935: 2-4). Important investigation reports and synthetic studies by modern scholars include H. Chang (14 mausoleums of the Six Dynasties are recorded); Zhu Xizu et al., 1935 (28 mausoleums are recorded, and Chang's mistakes are corrected) ; Zhu Xie, 1936, 1957; Jin Qi, 1959; Kanda Kiichir ō et al., 1957; Yao Qian and Gu Bing, 1981 (31 mausoleums are recorded).

据姚迁、古兵，1981，迄今发现的梁朝陵墓共有 11 座，分别是：①文帝的建陵（可能建于 535 年）；②武帝的修陵（修建于 549 年即武帝卒年前）；③简文帝庄陵（552 年前修建）；④ 八位梁朝皇子的墓，其中包括萧宏墓（526）、萧秀墓（518）、萧恢墓（527）、萧憺墓（522）、萧景墓（523）、萧绩墓（529）、萧正立墓（548 年前）、萧暎墓（544）。但是，简文帝庄陵遗迹已不可见。死者之间的关系见下表（名字在括号中者墓葬尚未发现）：

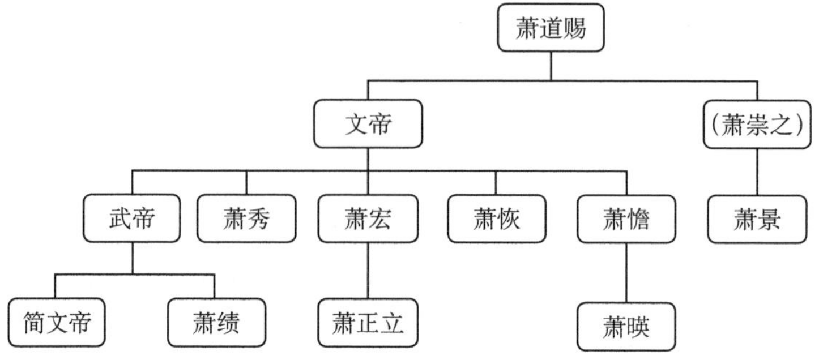

南京地区的南朝陵墓自唐代就开始见于记载（这类传统资料，见朱希祖等，1935：第 2—4 页）。当代学者所作的重要调查报告和综合性研究，有张璜（记录了 14 座六朝陵墓）；朱希祖等，1935（记录了 28 座陵墓，并纠正了张璜的错误）；朱偰，1936、1957；金琦，1959；神田喜一郎等，1957；姚迁、古兵，1981（记录了 31 座陵墓）。

4 The terms *shendao* and *suidao* denote the path extending from the pillar-gate to the tomb; see Zhu Xizu et al., 1935: 100, 202. This is why the word *shendao* is always inscribed on the pillar-gate.
神道和隧道皆指从阙门至陵墓的通道；见朱希祖等，1935：第 100、202 页。这也正是神道一词为什么总被刻在阙门上的原因。

5 Zhu Xizu et al., 1935: 23. 朱希祖等，1935：第 23 页。

6 *Jiankang shilu*, 17.19b. I interpret the word *suitou*, which means literally "the opening of a *suidao* path," as the place under the pillar-gate. As Zhu Xizu has explained, the term *suidao* or *sui* indicates the path extending from the pillar-gate to the tomb mound; see note 4 to this chapter.
《建康实录》，卷十七，第 19 页。我将"隧头"一词解释为"在阙门下"。因为如朱希祖所说，"隧道"或"隧"是指从阙门到陵前的通道，见本章注 4。

7 *Liang shu,* 90; Yu Xin's "Ai Jiangnan fu" quoted in Zhu Xie, 1936: 24.
《梁书》，第 90 页；朱偰，1936：第 24 页引庾信《哀江南赋》。

8 *Yudi zhi* (A geographical record) cited in *Danyangxian zhi* (A gazetteer of Danyang county); see Zhu Xie, 1936: 23.
《丹阳县志》引《舆地志》，见朱偰，1936：第 23 页。

9 Here I assume a visitor's view. Chinese and Japanese authors usually describe the pillars from the position of the tomb mound (i.e., from the position of the deceased), thus the "right pillar" in their writings is the left one in mine and vice versa.
我在这里采取了一个观者的视角，而中国和日本学者通常是从墓冢所在的位置来描述石柱的（如从死者的角度来看），因此他们文章中所说的右边石柱则是本文中的左石柱，反之亦然。

10 Most inscriptions on the pillar-gates in the Liang mausoleums face outward; the only exception are those on Emperor Wen's gates, which face each other and form a pair of true mirror images. My analysis here focuses on the majority cases.
绝大多数梁朝陵墓石柱上的铭文是朝外的，唯一的例外是文帝陵前的铭文，它们刚好相对，形成一组真正的镜像。这里我主要讨论多数情形。

11 In other words, the binary inscriptions first appeared as something external to and independent of the visitor; they then became something to be visualized and comprehended and finally become the stimulus for an imagined vision or visualization. For a concise discussion of images and imagination, see Frazer, 1960. Here I also borrow ideas from P. Yu, 1987: 3-19.
换句话来说，这种二元的铭文，首先是独立于观者的外在的东西，然后才成为一种可视的、可被理解的东西，最后才成为图像视觉的刺激物。对于图像和幻象的简要讨论，可参看弗雷泽，1960。这里我还参考了余宝琳，1987：3–19。

12 *Lu Shiheng ji*, 7.3b-4a; trans. from Davis, 1983: 1.168-70.
《陆士衡集》，卷七，第 36—41 页；英译据戴伟士，1983：1.168—170。

13 *Nan Qi shu*, 701.《南齐书》，第 701 页。

14 *Liang shu*, 88.《梁书》，第 88 页。

15 As scholars have noted, writing funeral songs in the voice of the dead was not Tao Qian's invention; Lu Ji and Miao Xi (186-245) wrote a number of such works (see Davis, 1983: 1.167-68). This tradition may be even traced back to the Han; the author of the *yuefu* poem "Battle South of the City" ("Zhan chengnan") assumes the view of a dead soldier. But only Tao Qian wrote funeral songs for himself.
正如许多学者们所指出的那样，从死者的角度来写挽歌并非是陶潜的首创；陆机和缪袭（186—245 年）都曾写过这样的作品（戴伟士，1983：1.167—168）。在我看来，这一传统至少可以追溯到汉代，乐府诗《战城南》的作者就是从一个牺牲的战士的角度来写的。但是，只有陶渊明为他自己写过挽歌。

16 This is the third of the three songs. *Tao Yuanming ji,* 142; trans. based on Hightower, 1970: 248.
这是第三首挽歌，见《陶渊明集》，第 142 页；英译据海陶玮，1970：第 248 页。

17 *Tao Yuanming ji,* 191-96.《陶渊明集》，第 191—196 页。

18 *Ibid.*, 196-97; trans. based on Davis, 1983: 1.240-41.
同上，第 196—197 页；英译据戴伟士，1983：1.240–241。

19 Doré, 1938: 8.89. 禄是遒，1938：8.89。

20 For the decorative programs of such sarcophagi and the symbolism of the "gate" motif, see H. Wu, 1987b.
有关此类石棺的装饰题材和"阙门"的表现形式，参看巫鸿，1987b。

21 In an earlier article (*ibid.*, 75-77), I suggested that this figure stands at the entrance of the other world to receive the dead. Although this interpretation is not impossible, my present discussion offers an alternative understanding. Supported by Tao Qian's writings and other literary evidence, this interpretation focuses on changes in perception after the Han.
在我先前的一篇文章中（巫鸿，1987b：第75—77页），曾经认为站在门口的这个人是另一世界里来迎接死者的人。虽然这种解释并非没有可能，但我现在还是提出了另一种说法。据陶潜和其他人的作品，这种新说法可能反映了汉代以后观念的变化。

22 Quoted in *TPYL*, 3315. 引自《太平御览》，第3315页。

23 "Master" is based on Yu Yuanwei's self-introduction. In fact, we know nothing about Yu and his works except for this piece of writing which, moreover, is preserved only as fragments in *TPYL*, 3318.
实际上，除了《太平御览》第3318页中的这条片段材料以外，我们对庾元威本人及其作品一无所知。

24 Quoted in *Zhongguo meishujia renming cidian*, 27. 324
引自《中国美术家人名辞典》，第27页。

25 The only existing example of this type of inscription is found in Emperor Wen's mausoleum.
现存这种铭文类型的唯一例子，见于梁文帝的建陵。

26 An example of such an inscription is found on a surviving pillar in Xiao Jing's (Emperor Wen's nephew) tomb. Only two "reversed" characters in the inscription dedicated to Xiao Xiu have survived. According to Mo Youzhi, the original inscription was also written in the regular right-to-left order; see Zhu Xizu et al., 1935: 57.
在文帝之侄萧景墓前的一根石柱上还可见到这样的一篇铭文，而萧秀墓前石柱上的铭文仅存两个反刻的字。据莫友芝，萧景神道石柱上的铭文是反刻顺读的；见朱希祖等，1935：第57页。

27 Examples of this type of inscription has been found in tombs of Xiao Hong (Emperor Wen's son), and Xiao Ying, Xiao Zhengli, and Xiao Ji (Emperor Wen's grandsons).
这种类型的铭文见于萧宏（文帝之子）、萧暎、萧正立和萧绩（文帝之孙）之墓。

28 According to *Yudi zhi*, the stone animals in front of the Jian ling Mausoleum (and perhaps other stone carvings as well) were made in 535; quoted in *Danyangxian zhi*; see Zhu Xie, 1936: 23.
据《舆地志》，建陵前的石兽（也可能包括其他石雕）是535年雕刻而成的。引自《丹阳县志》；见朱偰，1936：第23页。

29 Bachhofer, 1931; Soper, 1948. 巴赫霍夫，1931；索柏，1948。

30 For introductions to the Boston shrine, see K. Tomita, 1942; Guo Jianbang, 1980. Here I follow Tomita's dating of the shrine. For the structure of the Zhu Wei Shrine, see Fairbank, 1942.
有关波士顿美术馆所藏石享堂的介绍，可参看田幸次郎，1942；郭建邦，1980。在本文中，我采纳了前者所定的年代。有关朱鲔石室，可参看费慰梅，1942。

31 *Zhongguo meishu quanji* 1, pt. 19; interpretation of fig. 5.
《中国美术全集》，卷一，插图 19；图 5 的说明。

32 Laurence Sickman first saw the stone shrine in Kaifeng in 1933. Later, he came upon a complete set of rubbings in Beijing, including both the engravings on the shrine and an epitaph on a separate stone; see K. Tomita, 1942: 109n1.
史克门最早于 1933 年在开封见到此石室，后来他在北京偶然得到一套完整的拓片。见田幸次郎，1942：第 109 页，n1。

33 See *ibid.*, 109-10. 同上，第 109—110 页。

34 This sarcophagus was probably made for Lady Yuan in 522. It has been repeatedly studied by scholars; for references, see Cleveland Museum of Art, 1980: 5-6.
这件石棺可能是 522 年为元氏所作。已经有众多的学者对其进行过研究，可参看克利夫兰艺术博物馆，1980：第 5—6 页。

35 One such study is Soper, 1948; for his discussion of the Nelson sarcophagus, see 180-85.
这类研究见索柏，1948；有关纳尔逊石棺的讨论部分，见该文第 180—185 页。

36 There are numerous studies of the history and principles of the linear perspective system. For a recent discussion, see Hagen, 1986: 142-65. For discussions on the Wang Lin scene, see Siren, 1956: 1.58; Soper, 1941: 159-60.
有关线状透视法的研究很多，而最近的研究则有哈根，1986：第 142—165 页。有关王琳故事的研究，见喜仁龙，1956：1.58；索柏，1941：第 159—160 页。

37 Soper, 1941: 159-60. 索柏，1941：第 159—160 页。

38 This painting has been repeatedly published and discussed. For references, see Cahill, 1980: 12-13.
这幅画被多次地出版和讨论过。可参看高居翰，1980：第 12—13 页。

39 See Bush and Shih, 1985: 38-39. 卜寿珊、时学颜，1985：第 38—39 页。

40 *Ibid.*, 36-40. 同上，第 36—40 页。

41 *Lu Shiheng ji*, 1.1a-4b; trans. based on Owen, 1992: 90-110. See P. Yu, 1987: 33, 35. Owen (1992: 96) comments on the expression *shoushi fanting* ("retraction of vision, reversion of listening"), which is intimately related to the "reversed perception" discussed in this section: "Most Chinese exegeses. . . interpret this passage as a cutting off of sense perceptions, taking *shou* [retract] in a common usage as 'cease,' and apparently taking *fan* [revert] as the attention of listening 'reverting' to non-attention. Chinese theorists often spoke of the necessity of cutting oneself off from the determinations of the lived world in order to write."
《陆士衡集》，卷一，第 1—4 页；英文译文见宇文所安，1992：第 90—110 页。又见余宝琳，1987：第 33、35 页。宇文所安（1992：第 96 页）对这一节中和"反悟"紧密联系的"收视反听"是这样评论的："绝大多数中文注释将这段话解释为中断知觉，将'收'解释为平常的'停止'，而把'反'解释作将对听的注意状态'转化'为不注意的状态。为了写作，中国的理论家经常谈到从现实世界超脱出来的必要性。"

42 Translation based on Acker, 1954: 1.6-7. 英译见艾维廉，1954：1.6—7。

43 For a stylistic study of the sarcophagus's engravings, see Okumara Ikura, 1939: 359-82. This sarcophagus has been dated to 524 as part of a larger group of funerary paraphernalia of a Northern Wei prince (Minneapolis Institute of Arts, 1948). Nagahiro Toshio (1969: 173-218) discussed it and the Kansas City sarcophagus, along with other Northern Wei stone engravings dating from the early sixth century. The Chinese scholar Wang Shucun (1986: 11) recently reported that more than ten such "pictorial sarcophagi" have been found in the Luoyang area.
有关该石棺画像的风格研究，见奥村伊九良，1939：第 359—382 页。这件石棺作为一位北魏王储随葬品的一个组成部分，其年代被确定为 524 年（明尼阿波利斯美术馆，1984）。长广敏雄（1969：第 173—218 页）也曾将这件石棺与纳尔逊石棺以及其他年代定为 6 世纪初的北魏石刻一起讨论过。中国学者王树村（1986：第 11 页）最近介绍说，洛阳附近目前发现的这类石棺已经不下十件。

44 See Huang Minglan, 1987: 117-18, figs. 13-34.
黄明兰，1987：第 117—118 页，图 13—34。

45 I explore this idea at greater length in H. Wu, 1984: 46-48.
我在先前的著述中曾对这一概念做过更详细的探讨。见巫鸿，1984：第 46—48 页。

46 These figures may represent servants of the deceased: another Northern Wei sarcophagus discovered in 1973 in Guyuan is decorated on two sides

with similar windows and figures, and the deceased is portrayed on the front side of the coffin (Guyuan Cultural Relics Work Station, 1984).
这些人物形象表现的可能是墓主的仆从：1973 年发现于固原的一件漆棺，其两侧也画有这样的窗户和人物，而墓主像则出现在漆棺的前挡上（固原文物工作站，1984）。

47 There are interesting parallels—both superficial and profound—between this picture and Velasquez's famed painting "Las Meninas," which also employs sets of (seemingly) disconnected images to extend the visual field. In particular, directly facing the spectator in the background, a framed rectangular mirror holds in its glow two standing figures who are staring at the spectator. In Foucault's words, this mirror "shows us nothing of what is represented in the picture itself. Its motionless gaze extends out in front of the picture, into that necessary invisible region which forms its exterior face, to apprehend the figures arranged in that space. Instead of surrounding visible objects, this mirror cuts straight through the whole field of the representation, ignoring all it might apprehend within that field, and restores visibility to that which resides outside all view" (Foucault, 1973: 7-8). This mirror-imagery is thus comparable with the window imagery on the sarcophagus.
这件石棺线画和委拉斯贵支的名画《宫娥图》之间有着很多表面和深层的相似，后者也采用了一系列的（似乎）互不联系的形象来扩大视野。尤其是用作背景、直接面对观众的一面长方形镜子里，也有两个直视观众的人物。用福柯的话来说："它并没有向我们展现画本身所要表现的东西，它的无目的视线向画的前方延伸，直至不可视的最远处，在这里形成了它的外在的表面并表现这一空间里的人物。"（福柯，1973：第 7—8 页）这面镜子里的人物形象因而可以和石棺窗户里的画像相比较。

48 Norman Bryson (1983: 92, 94) has compared Western painting and Chinese painting in terms of their different notions and treatments of the pictorial plane: "Through much of the Western tradition oil paint is treated primarily as an erasive medium. What it must first erase is the surface of the picture plane: visibility of the surface would threaten the coherence of the fundamental technique through which the Western representational image classically works the trace, of ground-to-figure relations: 'ground,'
325 the absence of figure, is never accorded parity, is always a *subtractive* term. . . . The individual history of the oil-painting is therefore largely irretrievable, for although the visible surface has been worked, and worked as a total expanse, the viewer cannot ascertain the degree to which other surfaces lie concealed beneath the planar display: the image that suppresses deixis has no interest in its own genesis or past, except to bury it in a palimpsest of which only the final version shows through, above an indeterminable debris

of revisions." In Chinese painting, on the other hand, "Everything that is marked on the surface remains visible, save for those preliminaries or errors that are not considered part of the image." A Chinese painting "cannot be taken in all at once, *tota simul*, since it has itself unfolded within the duree of process; it consists serially, in the somatic time of its construction." The engraving on the sarcophagus, however, also show these two modes of representation in a single composition: some scenes erase the surface and other images restore the surface.

诺曼·布列逊（1983：第92、94页）曾经比较了中西方绘画对画面的不同意识和不同处理方法："从西方绘画的大致传统来看，油画颜料主要是被处理成一种'可以涂改的媒材'。首先要涂改的就是画的表面：表面的可视性将会严重影响到基本技巧间的联系，正是通过平面上的技巧联系，西方具象派肖像画才产生了从背景到人物的关系的古典主义痕迹：'底子'，人物形象不在之处，绝不会与人物等量齐观，它永远是一个负面的术语……所以油画自身的历史在很大程度上是无法复原的，因为尽管可见的表面被当作一个完整的空间制作了出来，观者还是无法判断其他表面被最外面一层覆盖的程度：抑制着指示功能的图像，总是在不断修正和掩盖原有的图像痕迹，直到在不确定的修改碎片上形成最后的版本，除此之外并不关心其自身的渊源和过去。"而在中国画中，"除了那些并不作为画的一部分的草稿和错误，其他画在画面上的任何东西都是看得到的"。看一幅中国画，是"不可能一目了然的，因为它是呈现在持续的过程中的；它连续地存在于自身的时间结构当中"。然而，石棺上的画像却将两种表现方式融进同一个画面：有的场景消除了石棺的表面，而另一些形象又使石棺的表面得以恢复。

49 *SJZ*, 373-94.《水经注》，第373—394页。

50 *ZL*, 648; Guo yu, 223, 225n17.《周礼》，第648页；《国语》，第223、225页。

51 According to *Gongyang's Commentaries on the Spring and Autumn Annals* (Chunqiu Gongyang zhuan, 473), only the Son of Heaven could enjoy a pair of *guan* towers. For similar regulations, see *LJ*, 1433 and 1448.
根据《春秋公羊传》，第473页，只有天子才可以享有观。类似的规定，见《礼记》，第1433、1448页。

52 In the *Book of Rites*, a *que* is called a *taimen* (terrace gate)—"the taller the more honorable" (*LJ*, 1433).
《礼记》当中，阙被称作"台门"——"此以高为贵也。"《礼记》，第1433页。

53 We know that at least from the second century B.C., the elite began to erect *que* in graveyards to distinguish the ranks and status of the deceased. For example, Huo Guang's wife built imperial *que* with "three wings" (*sanchu*) to honor her dead husband, and this practice was viewed as an omen presaging the fall of the Huo family (*HS*, 2950-51). It is possible that

que gates had already appeared in Eastern Zhou graveyards. *Zuo zhuan* (ZZ, 1773, 1886) records a kind of building called *diehuang*, or "funerary *huang*," which the Jin dynasty commentator Du Yu identified as *que* pillars in front of cemeteries. Some scholars also believe that *que* gates originally marked the entrances of the Lishan mausoleum of the First Emperor.
我们知道，至晚于公元前 2 世纪，上层社会开始在墓地上建阙，以表明死者的等级和身份。例如，霍光死后，其夫人为之起"三出阙"，以显其尊。这一行为在当时被看作霍光家族走向衰落的征兆（《汉书》，第 2950—2951 页）。阙门很可能在东周墓地当中已经出现了，《左传》（第 1773、1886 页）中记载了一种称作"绖皇"的建筑，被晋代注疏家杜预注为墓前的阙。有学者认为，骊山始皇陵前方的入口原本即有阙。

54 Quoted in *SJZ*, 215. 引自《水经注》，第 215 页。

55 *Shi ming* (5.17b): "Que means *que*—'short of.' It stands at either side of a gate; the gap in the middle is a path."
《释名》（卷五，第 17 页）："阙，在门两旁，中央缺然为道也。"

56 *Er ya*, 171. Similarly, *SW* (588a): "A *que* is the *guan* at a gate."
《尔雅》，第 171 页。与其相似，《说文》（第 588 页）也说："阙门，观也。"

57 *Shi ming* (5.18): "Guan means 'to see.' On its top one observes." *LJ* (1413): "In the past, Confucius attended a *la* ritual. Upon the completion of the ceremony he came out, strolled on top of a *guan* terrace, and sighed. What he sighed for was the state of Lu." The Han commentator Zheng Xuan explained: "*Guan* means *que*."
《释名》（卷五，第 18 页）："观，观也，于上观望也。"《礼记》（第 1413 页）："昔者，仲尼与于蜡宾，事毕，出游于观之上，喟然而叹。仲尼之叹，盖叹鲁也。"郑玄注曰："观，阙也。"

58 Sun Yan wrote: "[*Que* is called *guan* because] in the past, legal documents were hung on the pair of *que* in front of the palace. It thus became the place people always looked at" (quoted in Kong Yingda's commentary to *LJ*, 1413).
孙炎云："宫门双阙者，旧县法象使民观之处，因谓之阙。"（引自《礼记》，第 1413 页孔颖达疏）

59 As exemplified by Sima Qian's "Self-statement of the Grand Historian" ("Taishigong zixu"), it is an established convention in ancient China to write an autobiography in third person.
正如司马迁的附在《史记》之后的《太史公自序》那样，以第三人称形式写自传，在古代中国是一种惯例。

60 These inscriptions can be classified into four types. Type 1 identifies the pillars as forming the gate to a cemetery. Thus, the inscriptions on Huang

Shengqing *que* (A.D. 86) reads: "The main gate [*damen*] to the tomb of Huang Shengqing from Pingyi in South Wuyang, who [died] in the third year of the Yuanhe reign period [A.D. 86]." Type 2, which identifies the pillars as *que,* includes Wang Zhizi *que* (A.D. 105), the Wu Family *que* (A.D. 147; Jiaxiang, Shandong), Li Ye *que* (A.D. 36, Zitong, Sichuan). Type 3, which identifies a pillar gate as the beginning point of the spirit road, includes Pingyang Fujun *que* and Shangyongzhang *que* (respectively in Mianyang and Deyang, Sichuan; second century A.D.), Feng Huan *que* (A.D. 121, Quxian, Sichuan), Shen Fujun *que* (Quxian, Sichuan; second century A.D.), and Er Yang *que* (Sichuan; second century A.D.). Pillars belonging to Type 4 bear only the name and title of the deceased; an example is the Gao Yi *que* (A.D. 209, Sichuan).
这些题记可以分为四种类型。第一种类型将阙视为墓地前方的大门。如此，皇圣卿阙（86）上的题记写道："南武阳平邑皇圣卿冢之大门，卿以元和三年（86）（卒）。"第二种类型直呼为阙，其中有王稚子阙（105）、武氏阙（147，山东嘉祥）、李业阙（36，四川梓潼）。第三种类型将阙门看作神道的起点，其中有平阳府君阙和上庸长阙（2 世纪，分别在四川的绵阳和德阳）、冯焕阙（121，四川渠县）、沈府君阙（2 世纪，四川渠县）和二杨阙（2 世纪，四川）。属于第四种类型的阙，仅刻具了死者的名讳和官衔，可以高颐阙为例（209，四川）。

61 One such example is the gate of the Wu Family cemetery at Jiaxiang in Shandong; see H. Wu, 1989: 25.
这类阙的一个例子是山东嘉祥武氏墓地的阙门；见巫鸿，1989：第 25 页。

WORKS CITED 参考文献

WESTERN-LANGUAGE REFERENCES

Acker, W. R. B. 1954. *Some T'ang and Pre-T'ang Texts on Chinese Painting.* 2 vols. Leiden: E. J. Brill.

Allan, S. 1991. *The Shape of the Turtle: Myth, Art, and Cosmos in Early China.* Albany: State University of New York Press.

Althusser, L. 1971. *Lenin and Philosophy and Other Essays.* London: New Left Books.

An, J. H. (An Chin-huai). 1986: "The Shang City at Chengchou." In K. C. Chang, ed., *Studies of Shang Archaeology.* New Haven: Yale University Press, 15-48.

Arnheim, R. 1982. *The Power of the Center.* Berkeley: University of California Press.

—. 1986. *New Essays on the Psychology of Art.* Berkeley: University of California Press.

Bachelard, G. 1964. *The Poetics of Space.* Trans. Maria Jolas. New York: Orion Press.

Bachhofer, L. 1931. "Die Raumdarstellung in der chinesischen Malerei desersten Jahrtausends n. Chr" (The representation of space in Chinese paintings of the first millennium A.D.). In *Münchher Jahrbuch derBildenden Kunst* (Munich yearbook of pictorial arts), vol. 3. Trans. H. Joachim into English. MS in the Rübel Art Library, Harvard University.

Bagley, R. W. 1987. *Shang Ritual Bronzes in the Arthur M. Sackler Collection.* Washington, D.C., and Cambridge, Mass.: A. M. Sackler Foundation and A. M. Sackler Museum.

Bamard, N. 1980-81. "Wrought Metal-Working Prior to Middle Shang (?): A Problem in Archaeological and Art Historical Research Approaches." *Early China*, 6: 4-30.

Bauer, W. 1976. *China and the Search for Happiness.* Trans. M. Shaw. New York: Seabury Press.

Benton, T. 1981. "'Objective' Interests and the Sociology of Power." *Sociology* 15.2: 161-84.

Berger, P. 1990. "An Ideology of One: The Offering Shrine of Wu Liang." *Early China*, 15: 223-35.

Bielenstein, H. 1980. *The Bureaucracy of Han Times.* Cambridge, Eng.: Cambridge University Press.

Bilsky, L. J. 1975. *The State Religion of Ancient China.* 2 vols. Taibei: Asian Folklore and Social Life Monographs Series.

Birrell, A. 1988. *Popular Songs and Ballads of Han China.* London: Unwin Hyman.

Bishop, C. W. 1938. "An Ancient Chinese Capital, Earthworks at Old Ch'ang-an." *Antiquity*, 13: 68-78.

Breckenridge, J: D. 1968. Likeness: *A Conceptual History of Ancient Portraiture*. Evanston, Ill.: Northwestern University Press.

Bryson, N. 1983. *Vision and Painting: The Logic of the Gaze*. New Haven: Yale University Press.

Bush, S., and H. Y. Shih. 1985. *Early Chinese Texts on Painting*. Cambridge, Mass.: Harvard University Press.

Bushell, S. W. 1910. *Chinese Art*. 2 vols. London: Board of Education.

Cahill, J. 1980. *An Index of Early Chinese Painters and Paintings*. Berkeley: University of California Press.

Chang Huang. 1912. "Tombeau des Liang." *Variétés sinologiques*, 33.

Chang, K. C. 1964. "Some Dualistic Phenomena in Shang Society." *Journal of Asian Studies*, 24: 45-61. Reprinted in Chang, 1976: 93-114.

—. 1976. *Early Chinese Civilization: Anthropological Perspectives*. Cambridge, Mass.: Harvard University.

—. 1977. *Archaeology of Ancient China*. 3rd ed. New Haven: Yale University Press.

—. 1980a. *Shang Civilization*. New Haven: Yale University Press.

—. 1980b. "The Chinese Bronze Age: A Modern Synthesis." In W. Fong, 1980: 35-36.

—. 1981. "In Search of China's Beginnings: New Light on an Old Civilization." *American Scientist*, 69.2: 30-41.

—. 1983. *Art, Myth, and Ritual*. Cambridge, Mass.: Harvard University Press.

—. 1986. *The Archaeology of Ancient China*. 4th ed. New Haven: Yale University Press.

Chavannes, E. 1913. *Mission archéologique dans la Chine septentrionale* (An archaeological mission to northern China). 13 vols. Paris: lmprimerie nationale.

—. 1914. *Six monuments de la sculpture chinoise*. Paris: Librairie d'art et d'histoire.

Chen, C. Y. 1975. *Hsün Yüen: The Life and Reflections of an Early Medieval Confucian*. London: Cambridge University Press.

Cheng Te-k'un. 1957. *Archaeological Studies in Szechwan*. Cambridge, Mass.: Harvard University Press.

Childs-Johnson, E. 1988. "Dragons, Masks, Axes and Blades from Four Newly-Documented Jade-Producing Cultures of Ancient China." *Orientations*, 19.4: 30-41.

Chinese Academy of Architecture. 1982. *Ancient Chinese Architecture*. Beijing: China Building Industry Press.

Ch'u, T. T. 1972. *Han Social Structure*. Ed. J. L. Dull. Seattle: University of

Washington Press.

Clarke, D. V., T. G. Cowie, and A. Foxon. *Symbols of Power at the Time of Stonehenge*. Edinburgh: National Museum of Antiquities of Scotland.

Cleveland Museum of Art. 1980. Eight Dynasties of Chinese Painting: *The Collections of the Nelson Gallery-Atkins Museum, Kansas City, and the Cleveland Museum of Art*. Cleveland: Cleveland Museum of Art.

Colquhoun, A. 1982. "Thought on Riegl." In Forster, 1982b: 79-83.

Costen Erdberg, E. yon. 1957, 1958. "A Terminology of Chinese Bronze Decoration." 2 parts. *Monumenta Serica*, 16: 287-314; 18: 208-54.

Creel, H. G. 1937. *The Birth of China: A Study of the Formative Period of Chinese Civilization*. New York: Reynal & Hitchcock.

Cunningham, A. 1879. *Stupa of Bharhut*. London: Secretary of State for India in Council.

Daniel, G. 1967. *The Origins and Growth of Archaeology*. Harmonds worth, Eng.: Penguin.

D'Argencé. R. L. *Ancient Chinese Bronzes in the Avery Brundage Collection*. San Francisco: M. H. de Young Memorial Museum.

Davis, A. R. 1983. *T'ao Yüan-ming: His Works and Their Meaning*. 2 vols. Cambridge, Eng.: Cambridge University Press.

de Bary, W. T., ed. 1960. *Sources of Chinese Tradition*. 2 vols. New York: Columbia University Press.

DeWoskin, K. J. 1983. *Doctors, Diviners, and Magicians: Biographies of Fang-shi*. New York: Columbia University Press.

—. 1987. "Music and Voices from the Han Tombs: Music, Dance, and Entertainments During the Han." In Lim, 1987: 64-71.

Digby, A. 1972. *Maya Jades*. London: British Museum.

Dissanayake, E. 1988. *What Is Art For?* Seattle: University of Washington Press.

Doezema, M., and J. Hargrove. 1977. *The Public Monument and Its Audience*. Cleveland: Cleveland Museum of Art.

Doré, H. 1938. *Researches into Chinese Superstitions*, vol. 8. Trans. M. Kennelly. Shanghai: T'usewe Printing Press.

Dubs, H. H. 1938. *Pan Ku: The History of the Former Han Dynasty*. 3 vols. Baltimore: Waverly Press.

—. 1942. "An Ancient Chinese Mystery Cult." *Harvard Theological Review*, 35: 221-40.

Ebrey, P. B. 1980. "Later Han Stone Inscriptions." *Harvard Journal of Asiatic Studies*, 40.2: 325-53.

—. 1983. "Patron-Client Relations in the Late Han." *Journal of the American Oriental Society*, 103.3: 533-42.

Ebrey, P. B., ed. 1981. *Chinese Civilization and Society: A Sourcebook*. New York: Free Press.

Ekman, P. 1969. "The Repertoire of Nonverbal Behavior: Categories, Origins, Usage, and Coding." *Semiotica*, 1.1: 49-98.

Fairbank, W. 1941. "The Offering Shrines of 'Wu Liang Tz'u.'" *Harvard Journal of Asiatic Studies*, 6.1: 1-36. Reprinted in Fairbank, 1972: 43-86.

—. 1942. "A Structural Key to Han Mural Art." *Harvard Journal of Asiatic Studies*, 7.1: 52-88. Reprinted in Fairbank, 1972: 89-140.

—. 1972. *Adventures in Retrieval*. Harvard-Yenching Institute Studies, 28. Cambridge, Mass.: Harvard University Press.

Falkenhausen, L. von. 1988. "Ritual Music in Bronze Age China: An Archaeological Perspective." Ph.D. dissertation. Harvard University.

Fehl, N. E. 1971. *Rites and Propriety in Literature and Life*. Hong Kong: Chinese University of Hong Kong.

Feng Han-yi. 1948. *The Chinese Kinship System*. Cambridge, Mass.: Harvard University Press.

Fingarette, H. 1972. *Confucius: The Secular as Sacred*. New York: Harper & Row.

Fong, Wen, ed. 1980. *The Great Bronze Age of China*. New York: Metropolitan Museum of Art.

Forke, A. 1962. *Lun-Heng: Philosophical Essays by Wang Ch'ung*. 2 vols. New York: Paragon.

Forster, K. W. 1982a. "Monument/Memory and the Morality of Architecture." In Forster, 1982b: 2-19.

Forster, K. W., ed. 1982b. *Monument/Memory. Oppositions* special issue, 25.

Foucault, M. 1973. *The Order of Things: An Archaeology of the Human Sciences*. New York: Vintage Books.

—. 1977. *Discipline and Punish*. New York: Vintage Books.

—. 1980. *Power/Knowledge*. Ed. C. Gordon. Hassocks, Eng.: Harvester.

—. 1981. *The History of Sexuality*. Harmondsworth, Eng.: Penguin.

Frazer, R. 1960. "The Origin of the Term 'Image.'" ELH 27: 149-61.

Fung Yu-lan. 1948, 1953. *History of Chinese Philosophy*. 2 vols. Trans. and comm. D. Bodde. Princeton: Princeton University Press.

Gernet, J. 1972. *A History of Chinese Civilization*. Cambridge, Eng.: Cambridge University Press.

Giedion, S. 1958. *Architecture, You and Me*. Cambridge, Mass.: Harvard University Press.

Gilson, E. 1968. "Aesthetic Existence." In Lee A. Jacobus, ed. *Aesthetics and the Arts*. New York: McGraw-Hill.

Gombrich, E. H. 1969. *Art and Illusion: A Study in the Psychology of Pictorial Representation*. 2nd ed. Princeton: Princeton University Press.

—. 1984. *The Sense of Order*. 2nd ed. Ithaca, N. Y.: Cornell University Press.

Grabar, O. 1992. *The Mediations of Ornament*. Princeton: Princeton University Press.

Graham, A. C. 1965. *Poems of the Late T'ang*. Harmondsworth, Eng.: Penguin.

Grousset, R. 1964. *The Rise and Splendour of the Chinese Empire*. Berkeley: University of California Press.

Hagen, M. A. 1986. *Varieties of Realism: Geometries of Representational Art*. Cambridge, Eng.: Cambridge University Press.

Hansford, H. 1968. *Chinese Carved Jades*. London: Faber & Faber.

Harbison, R. 1991. *The Built, the Unbuilt and the Unbuildable: In Pursuit of Architectural Meaning*. Cambridge, Mass.: MIT Press.

Haskel, B. 1971. *Claes Oldenburg: Object into Monument*. Pasadena, Calif.

Hay, J. 1993. "Review: Wu Hung, *The Wu Liang Shrine: The Ideology of Early Chinese Pictorial Art* and Martin J. Powers, *Art and Political Expression in Early China*." *Art Bulletin*, 75.1: 169-74.

Hightower, J. R. 1952. *Han Shih Wai Chuan*. Cambridge, Mass.: Harvard University Press.

—. 1957. "*The Wen Hsüan* and Genre Theory." *Harvard Journal of Asiatic Studies*, 20: 512-33.

—. 1970. *The Poetry of T'ao Ch'ien*. Oxford: Clarendon Press.

Hollier, D. 1992. *Against Architecture: The Writings of Georges Bataille*. Cambridge, Mass.: MIT Press.

Holzman, D. 1978. "Literary Criticism in China in the Early Third Century A.D." *Asiatische Studien*, 28.2: 113-49.

Hsu, C. Y., and K. M. Linduff. 1988. *Western Zhou Civilization*. New Haven: Yale University Press.

Hsü, D. L. 1970-71. "The Myth of the 'Five Relations' of Confucius." *Monumenta Serica*, 29: 27-37.

Huber, L. G. F. 1981. "Some Anyang Royal Bronzes: Remarks on Shang Bronze Decor." In G. Kuwayama, ed., *The Great Bronze Age of China*. Los Angeles: Los Angeles County Museum of Art, 16-43.

Jackson, J. B. 1980. *The Necessity for Ruins*. Amherst: University of Massachusetts Press.

James, J. 1991. "Images of Power: Masks of the Liangzhu Culture." *Orientations*, 22.6: 46-55.

Kane, V. C. 1970. "Chinese Bronzes of the Shang and Western Chou Period." Ph.D dissertation, Harvard University.

—. 1973. "The Chronological Significance of the Inscribed Ancestor Dedication in the Periodization of Shang Dynasty Bronze Vessels." *Artibus Asiae*, 35: 335-70.

—. 1982-83. "Aspects of Western Chou Appointment Inscriptions: The Charge, the Gifts, the Response." *Early China*, 8: 14-28.

Karlgren, B. 1950a. "The Book of Documents." *Bulletin of the Museum of Far Eastern Antiquities*, 22: 1-81.

——. 1950b. *The Book of Odes*. Stockholm: Museum of Far Eastern Antiquities.

Keightley, D. N. 1978a. *Sources of Shang History: The Oracle Bone Inscriptions of Bronze Age China*. Berkeley: University of California Press.

——. 1978b. "The Religious Commitment: Shang Theology and the Genesis of Chinese Political Culture." *History of Religions*, 17.3-4: 211-25.

——. 1987. "Archaeology and Mentality: The Making of China." *Representations*, 18: 91-128.

——. 1991. "The Quest for Eternity in Ancient China: The Dead, Their Gifts, Their Names." In Kuwayama, 1991: 12-25.

Kinney, A. B. 1990. *The Art of the Han Essay: "Wang Fu's Ch'ien-fu Lun."* Tempe: Arizona State University, Center for Asian Studies.

Kleinbauer, W. E. 1971. *Modern Perspectives in Art History*. New York: Holt, Rinehart & Winston.

Knechtges, D. R. 1976. *The Han Rhapsody*. Cambridge, Eng.: Cambridge University Press.

——. 1982, 1987. *Wen Xuan, or Selections of Refined Literature*. 2 vols. Princeton: Princeton University Press.

Knoblock, J. 1989-90. *Xunzi*. 2 vols. Stanford: Stanford University Press.

Kostof, S. 1991. *The City Shaped: Urban Patterns and Meanings Through History*. Boston: Little, Brown.

Kuwayama, G., ed. 1991. *Ancient Mortuary Traditions of China*. Los Angeles: Los Angeles County Museum of Art, Far Eastern Art Council.

Lang, O. 1946. *Chinese Family and Society*. New Haven: Yale University Press.

Langer, S. K. 1957. *Problems of Art*. New York: Charles Scribner's Sons.

Legge, J. 1871. *The Chinese Classics*. 5 vols. Vol. 1: *Confucian Analects, The Great Learning, and the Doctrine of the Mean*; vol. 2: *The Works of Mencius*; vol. 3: *The Shoo King or the Book of Historical Documents*; vol. 4: *The She King or the Book of Poetry*; vol. 5: *The Ch'un Ts'ew, with the Tso Chuen*. Oxford: Clarendon Press.

——. 1881. *The Religions of China*. New York: Chades Scribner's Sons.

——. 1891. *The Tao Te Ching, the Writings of Chuang-tzu, the Tai-shan*. In *Sacred Books of the East*, vols. 39-40. London: Oxford University Press.

——. 1967 [1885]. *Li Chi: Book of Rites*. 2 vols. New York: University Books.

Lévi-Strauss, Claude. 1963. *Structural Anthropology*. New York: Basic Books.

Li Chi (Li Ji). 1977. *Anyang*. Seattle: University of Washington Press.

Li Xueqin. 1985. *Eastern Zhou and Qin Civilizations*. Trans. K. C. Chang. New Haven: Yale University Press.

Li Yinde. 1990. "The 'Underground Palace' of a Chu Prince at Beidongshan." *Orientations*, 21.10: 57-61.

Liang Ch'i-ch'ao (Liang Qichao). 1928. "Archaeology in China." *Smithsonian Report for 1927*. Washington, D.C.: Smithsonian Institution, 453-66.

Lim, L., ed. 1987. *Stories from China's Past.* San Francisco: Chinese Cultural Center.

Lippe, A. 1970. *The Freer Indian Sculptures.* Washington, D.C.: Smithsonian Institution.

Loehr, M. 1953. "Bronze Styles of the Anyang Period." *Archives of the Chinese Art Society of America,* 7: 42-53.

—. 1968. *Ritual Vessels of Bronze Age China.* New York: Asia Society.

Loewe, M. 1979. *Ways to Paradise: The Chinese Quest for Immortality.* London: George Allen & Unwin.

—. 1982. *Chinese Ideas of Life and Death.* London: George Allen & Unwin.

Loewe, M., and A. F. P. Hulsewé. 1979. *China in Central Asia: The Early Stage, 125 B.C.-A.D. 23. Annotated Translation of Chapters 61 and 96 of the History of the Former Han Dynasty.* Sinica Leidensia, 14. Leiden: Brill.

Lowenthal, D. 1975. "Past Time, Present Place: Landscape and Memory." *Geographical Review,* 65.1: 1-36.

MacCurdy, G. G. 1933. *Human Origins.* New York: Appleton Century.

Major, J. 1984. "The Five Phases, Magic Squares, and Schematic Cosmology." In H. Rosemont, Jr., ed. *Explorations in Early Chinese Cosmology.* Thematic Studies of the *Journal of the American Academy of Religion* 50.2. Chico, Calif.: Scholars Press, 133-46.

Makra, M. L. 1961. *The Hsiao Ching.* Washington, D.C.: St. John's University Press.

McNairn, B. 1980. *The Method and Theory of V. Gordon Childe.* Edinburgh: Edinburgh University Press.

Miao, R. 1972. "Literary Criticism at the End of the Eastern Han." *Literature East and West,* 16.3: 1013-34.

Miller, D., and C. Tilley, eds. 1984. *Ideology, Power and Prehistory.* Cambridge, Eng. : Cambridge University Press.

Minneapolis Institute of Arts. 1948. "A Stone Sarcophagus of the Wei Dynasty." *Bulletin of the Minneapolis Institute of Arts,* 37.23: 110-16.

Mothersill, M. 1984. *Beauty Restored.* Oxford: Clarendon Press.

Murray, J. K. 1983. "Neolithic Chinese Jades." *Orientations,* 14.11: 14-22.

Needham, J. 1954-88. *Science and Civilization in China.* 6 vols. in multiple parts. Cambridge, Eng.: Cambridge University Press.

O'Hara, A. R. 1945. *The Position of Women in Early China.* Washington, D.C.: Catholic University of American Press.

Oldenburg, C. 1969. *Proposals for Monuments and Buildings,* 1965-69. Chicago: Big Table Publishing Company.

Owen, S. 1985. *Remembrances: The Experience of the Past in Classical Chinese Literature.* Cambridge, Mass.: Harvard University Press.

—. 1992. *Readings in Chinese Literary Thought.* Cambridge, Mass.: Harvard

University Press.
Paludan, A. 1991. *The Chinese Spirit Road.* New Haven: Yale University Press.
Paper, J. 1978. "The Meaning of the 'T'ao-t'ie. ...*History of Religions,* 18.1: 18-41.
Pirazzoli-t'serstevens, M. 1982. *The Han Dynasty.* Trans. J. Seligrnan. New York: Rizzoli.
Pope, J. A., et al. 1967. *The Freer Chinese Bronzes,* vol. 1. Washington, D.C.: Smithsonian Institution.
Poulantzas, N. 1973. *Political Power and Social Classes.* London: New Left Books.
Powers, M. J. 1983. "Hybrid Omens and Public Issues in Early Imperial China." *Bulletin of the Museum of Far Eastern Antiquities,* 55: 1-55.
—. 1984. "Pictorial Art and Its Public Issues in Early Imperial China." *Art History,* 7.2: 135-63.
—. 1986. "Artistic Taste, the Economy and the Social Order in Former Han China." *Art History,* 9.3: 285-305.
—. 1991. *Art and Political Expression in Early China.* New Haven: Yale University Press.
Qiu Yongsheng and Hu Baoxi. 1990."Highlights of the Huating Neolithic Site." *Orientations,* 20.10: 54-56.
Rawson, J. 1980. *Ancient China, Art and Archaeology.* London: British Museum.
—. 1987. *Chinese Bronzes: Art and Ritual.* London: British Museum.
—. 1990. *Western Zhou Ritual Bronzes from the Arthur M. Sackler Collections.* 2 vols. Washington, D.C.: Arthur M. Sackler Foundation.
Riegl, A. 1903. "The Modern Cult of Monuments: Its Character and Its Origin." Trans. K. W. Forster and D. Chirardo. In Forster, 1982a: 20-51.
Rose, B. 1968. "Blow Up: The Problem of Scale in Sculpture." *Art in America,* 56: 80-91.
Rowland, B. 1967. *The Art and Architecture of India.* 3rd ed. Baltimore.
Rowley, G. 1959. *Principles of Chinese Painting.* 2nd ed. Princeton: Princeton University Press.
Rudolph, R. C. 1951. *Han Tomb Art of West China.* Berkeley: University of California Press.
Ruskin, J. 1904. *The Works of John Ruskin.* 39 vols. Eds. E. T. Cook and A. Wedderburn. London.
Said, E. W. 1979. *Orientalism.* New York: Vintage Books.
Salmony, A. 1963. *Chinese Jade Through the Wei Dynasty.* New York: Ronald.
Sargent, C. B. 1947. *Wang Mang.* Shanghai: Graphic Art.
Schapiro, M. 1969. "On Some Problems in the Semiotics of Visual Art: Field and Vehicle in Image-Signs." *Semiotica,* 1.3: 223-42.
Schorske, C. E. 1963. "The Idea of the City in European Thought: Voltaire to Spengler." In O. Handlin and J. Burchard, eds., *The Historian and the City.* Cambridge, Mass.: MIT Press, 95-114.

Segalen, V. G., et al. 1914-17. *Mission archéologique en Chine* (Archaeological mission to China). Paris: Geuthner.

Sharer, R. J., and W. Ashmore. 1979. *Fundamentals of Archaeology*. Menlo Park, Calif. : Benjamin/Cummings.

Sickman, L., and A. Soper. 1956. *The Art and Architecture of China*. Harmondsworth, Eng. : Penguin.

Sirén, O. 1956. *Chinese Painting: Leading Masters and Principles*. 5 vols. New York: Ronald.

Soper, A. C. 1941. "Early Chinese Landscape Painting." *Art Bulletin*, 23: 159-60.

——. 1948. "Life-Motion and the Sense of Space in Early Chinese Representational Art." *Art Bulletin*, 30: 167-86.

——. 1966. "Early, Middle, and Late Shang: A Note." *Artibus Asiae*, 28: 5-38.

Soymie, M. 1954. "L'Entrevue de Confucius et de Hiang T'o." *Journal asiatique* 242: 311-92.

Spiro, A. 1990. *Contemplating the Ancient*. Berkeley: University of California Press.

Steinhardt, N. S. 1984. *Chinese Traditional Architecture*. New York: China Institute.

——. 1990. *Chinese Imperial City Planning*. Honolulu: University of Hawaii Press.

Strauss, A. L. 1961. *Images of the American City*. New York: Free Press.

Su, Gin Djih. 1964. *Chinese Architecture, Past and Contemporary*. Hong Kong.

Teng Ssu-yü. 1968. *Family Instructions for the Yen Clan*. Leiden: E. J. Brill.

Thomas, N. 1982. "Childe, Marxism, and Archaeology." *Dialectical Anthropology*, 6.3: 245-52.

Thorp, R. L. 1983a. "An Archaeological Reconstruction of the Lishan Necropolis." In G. Kuwayama, ed., *The Great Bronze Age of China: A Symposium*. Los Angeles: Los Angeles County Museum of Art, 72-83.

——. 1983b. "Origins of Chinese Architectural Style: The Earliest Plans and Building Types." *Archives of Asian Art*, 36: 22-26.

——. 1985. "The Growth of Early Shang Civilization: New Data from Ritual Vessels." *Harvard Journal of Asiatic Studies*, 45.1: 5-67.

——. 1987. "The Qin and Han Imperial Tombs and the Development of Mortuary Architecture." In Los Angeles County Museum of Art, *The Quest for Eternity: Chinese Ceramic Sculpture from the People's Republic of China*. San Francisco: Chronicle Books, 17-37.

——. 1988. "The Archaeology of Style at Anyang: Tomb 5 in Context." *Archives of Asian Art*, 41: 47-69.

——. 1991. "Mountain Tombs and Jade Burial Suits: Preparations for Eternity in the Western Han." In Kuwayama, 1991: 26-39.

T'ien Ju-k'ang. 1988. *Male Anxiety and Female Chastity*. Leiden: E. J. Brill.

Tjan Tjoe Som. 1949, 1952. *Po Hu T'ung: The Comprehensive Discussions in the*

White Tiger Hall. 2 vols. Leiden: E. J. Brill.

Tomita, Kojiro. 1942. "A Chinese Sacrificial Stone House of the Sixth Century A.D." *Bulletin of the Museum of Fine Arts* (Boston) 40.242: 98-110.

Trigger, B. G. 1990. "Monumental Architecture: A Thermodynamic Explanation of Symbolic Behaviour." In R. Bradley, ed., *Monuments and the Monumental. World Archaeology* special issue, 22.2: 119-32.

Twitchett, D., and M. Loewe, eds. 1986. *The Cambridge History of China*, vol. 1, *The Ch'in and Han Empires*. Cambridge, Eng.: Cambridge University Press.

Uspensky, B. A. 1975. "'Left' and 'Right' in Icon Painting." *Semiotica*, 13.1: 34-39.

Vanderstappen, H. A., et al. eds. 1989. *Ritual and Reverence: Chinese Art at the University of Chicago*. Chicago: David and Alfred Smart Gallery.

Veblen, T. 1899. *The Theory of Leisure Class*. New York: Macmillan.

Waley, A. 1955. "The Heavenly Horses of Ferghana: A New View." *History Today*, 5.2: 95-103.

——. 1978. *The Book of Songs*. New York: Grove Press.

——. 1982. *Chinese Poems*. London: Unwin.

Walton, K. L. 1990. *Mimesis as Make-Believe*. Cambridge, Mass.: Harvard University Press.

Wang, Yi-t'ung. 1984. *A Record of Buddhist Monasteries in Luoyang*. Princeton: Princeton University Press.

Wang Zhongshu. 1982. *Han Civilization*. Trans. K. C. Chang. New Haven: Yale University Press.

Ware, J. R. 1960. *The Sayings of Mencius*. New York: New American Library.

Watson, B. 1958. *Ssu-ma Ch'ien, Grand Historian of China*. New York: Columbia University Press.

——. 1961. *Records of the Grand Historian of China*. 2 vols. New York: Columbia University Press.

——. 1963. *Basic Writings of Mo Tsu, Hsün Tzu, and Han Fei Tzu*. New York: Columbia University Press.

——. 1968a. "Literary Theory in the Eastern Han." In *Yoshikawa hakase taikyū kinen Chūgoku bungaku ronshū*. Tokyo: Chikuma Shobō, 1968, 1-13.

——. 1968b. *The Complete Works of Chuang Tzu*. New York: Columbia University Press.

Watson, W. 1962. *Ancient Chinese Bronzes*. London: Faber & Faber.

Weber, C. D. 1968. *Chinese Pictorial Bronze Vessels of the Late Chou Period*. Ascona, Switz.: Artibus Asiae.

Webster's New International Dictionary of the English Language. 1934. Springfield, Mass.: G. & C. Merriam Co.

Wellek, R. 1955. *A History of Modern Criticism*. New Haven: Yale University Press.

Wheatley, P. 1971. *Pivot of the Four Quarters*. Edinburgh: Edinburgh University

Press.

Wilhelm, R. 1967. *The I Ching*. 3rd ed. Princeton: Princeton University Press.

Wu Hung. 1984. "A Sanpan Shan Chariot Ornament and the Xiangrui Design in Western Han Art." *Archive of Asian Art*, 37: 38-59.

—. 1985. "Bird Motifs in Eastern Yi Art." *Orientations*, 16.10: 30-41.

—. 1986. "Buddhist Elements in Early Chinese Art (2nd and 3rd centuries A.D.)." *Artibus Asiae*, 47: 263-376.

—. 1987a. "The Wu Liang Ci and Eastern Han Offering Shrines." Ph.D. dissertation, Harvard University.

—. 1987b. "Myths and Legends in Han Funerary Art: Their Pictorial Structure and Symbolic Meanings as Reflected in Carvings on Sichuan Sarcophagi." In Lim, 1987: 72-81.

—. 1988. "From Temple to Tomb: Ancient Chinese Art and Religion in Transition." *Early China*, 13: 78-115.

—. 1989. *The Wu Liang Shrine: The Ideology of Early Chinese Pictorial Art*. Stanford: Stanford University Press.

—. 1990a. "A Great Beginning: Ancient Chinese Jades and the Origin of Ritual Art." In Wu Hung and B. Morgan, *Chinese Jades from the Mu-Fai Collection*. London: Bluett & Sons.

—. 1990b. "The Art of Xuzhou: A Regional Approach." *Orientations*, 21.10: 40-49.

Yang Hsien-yi and Gladys Yang, trans. 1979. *Selections from Records of the Historian*. Beijing: Foreign Languages Press.

Yetts, P. 1949. "A Datable Shang-Yin Inscription." 2 parts. *Asia Major* (London), n.s. 1: 74-98, 275-77.

Yu, P. 1987. *The Reading of Imagery in the Chinese Poetic Tradition*. Princeton: Princeton University Press.

Yü, Ying-shih. 1987. "'O Soul, Come Back!' A Study in the Changing Conceptions of the Soul and Afterlife in Pre-Buddhist China." *Harvard Journal of Asiatic Studies*, 47.2: 363-95.

Zheng Zhenxiang (Cheng Chen-hsiang). 1986. "A Study of the Bronze with the 'Su T'u Mu' Inscriptions Excavated from the Fu Hao Tomb." In K. C. Chang, ed., *Studies of Shang Archaeology*. New Haven: Yale University Press.

Zürcher, E. 1959. *The Buddhist Conquest of China*. 2 vols. Leiden: E. J. Brill.

中文文献

安志敏，1947 年，《殷墟的石刀》，《燕京学报》第 33 期，第 77—94 页。

——. 1954 年，《一九五二年秋季郑州二里岗发掘记》，《考古学报》第 8 期，第 109—126 页。

——. 1988 年，《关于良渚文化的若干问题》，《考古》第 3 期，第 236—245 页。

《白虎通》，班固，收入《丛书集成》，第 238—239 号。

《抱朴子》，葛洪，收入《诸子集成》，第 8 册。

北京图书馆，1989 年，《北京图书馆藏历代石刻拓本汇编》（全 10 册），郑州，中州古籍出版社。

编辑委员会，1985 年，《南阳汉代画像石》，北京，文物出版社。

曹淑琴，1988 年，《商代中期有铭铜器初探》，《考古》第 3 期，第 246—257 页。

《长安志图》，李好文，收入毕沅编《经训堂丛书》，台北，台湾商务印书馆，1978 年重印。

《朝庙宫室考》，任启运，收入王先谦编《皇清经解续编》，出版地不详，南菁书院，1888 年。

陈昌远，1982 年，《有关何尊的几个问题》，《中原文物》第 2 期，第 52—57 页。

陈汉平，1986 年，《西周册命制度研究》，上海，学林出版社。

陈梦家，1954 年，《殷代铜器》，《考古学报》第 7 期，第 15—59 页。

——. 1955—1956 年，《西周铜器断代》，《考古学报》1955 年第 9 期，第 137—176 页；第 10 期，第 69—142 页；1956 年第 1 期，第 65—114 页；第 2 期，第 85—94 页；第 3 期，第 105—127 页；第 4 期，第 85—122 页。

——. 1956 年，《殷墟卜辞综述》，北京，科学出版社。

陈明达，1961 年，《汉代的石阙》，《文物》第 12 期，第 9—23 页。

陈全方，1988 年，《周原与周文化》，上海，上海人民出版社。

陈世辉，1980 年，《墙盘铭文图解说》，《考古》第 5 期，第 433—435 页。

陈戍国，1991 年，《先秦礼制研究》，长沙，湖南教育出版社。

陈振中，1982 年，《殷周的钱镈：青铜铲和锄》，《考古》第 3 期，第 289—299 页。

陈直，1962 年，《望都汉墓壁画题字通释》，《考古》第 3 期，第 161—164 页。

《初学记》，徐坚，北京，中华书局，1962 年。

《春秋公羊传》，收入杜预等《春秋三传》，上海，上海古籍出版社，1987 年。

《春秋左传》，见孔颖达《春秋左传正义》，收入《十三经注疏》，第 1697—2188 页。

《大戴礼记》，戴德，王聘珍《大戴礼记解诂》，北京，中华书局，1983 年。

大同博物馆，1972 年，《山西大同石家寨北魏司马金龙墓》，《文物》第 3 期，第 20—33 页。

邓淑苹，1984 年，《玉器篇 · 一》，《中华五千年文物集刊》，台北，中华五千年文物集刊编辑委员会。
——. 1993 年，《中国新石器时代玉器上的神秘符号》，《故宫学术季刊》卷 10，第 3 号，第 1—50 页。
《东观汉记》，刘珍，吴树平《东观汉记校注》（全 2 册），郑州，中州古籍出版社，1987 年。
《独断》，蔡邕，收入程荣编《汉魏丛书》，明万历壬辰（1592）序，新安程序刊本，卷十四。
《读礼通考》，徐乾学，1696 年编，哈佛大学，哈佛燕京图书馆。
杜陵考古队，1984 年，《一九八二——一九八三年西汉杜陵的考古工作收获》，《考古》第 10 期，第 887—894 页。
《法苑珠林》，道释，上海，商务印书馆，1929 年。
范邦瑾，1990 年，《东汉墓碑溯源》，邹振亚等《汉碑研究》，第 49—63 页，济南，齐鲁书社。
方鹏钧、张勋燎，1980 年，《山东苍山元嘉元年画像石题记的时代和有关问题的讨论》，《考古》第 3 期，第 271—278 页。
方若，1923 年，《校碑随笔》，东京，朋友书店。
丰州，1983 年，《考古杂记，二》，《考古与文物》第 3 期，第 96—103 页。
《风俗通》，应劭，收入《四部丛刊》，第 100 种。
傅斯年，1936 年，跋陈槃《春秋公射于棠说》，《历史语言研究所集刊》，卷 7，2 号。
傅惜华，1950 年，《汉代画像全集》（全 2 编），北京，中法汉学研究所。
傅熹年，1980 年，《战国中山王厝墓出土兆域图及其陵园规制的研究》，《考古学报》第 1 期，第 97—119 页。
高文，1987 年 a，《四川汉代画像砖》，上海，上海人民美术出版社。
——. 1987 年 b，《四川汉代画像石》，成都，巴蜀书社。
高至喜，1963 年，《湖南宁乡黄材发现商代铜器和遗址》，《考古》第 12 期，第 646—648 页。
《古诗源》，沈德潜、汪莼父《古诗源笺注》，台北，华正书局，1983 年。
《古玉图考》，吴大澂，上海，同文书局，1889 年。
固原县文物工作站，1984 年，《宁夏固原北魏墓清理简报》，《文物》第 6 期，第 46—56 页。
故宫博物院，1959 年，《历代艺术馆》，北京，北京故宫博物院。
——. 1978 年，《中国历代绘画：故宫博物院藏画集 · 一》，北京，人民美术出版社。
《故宫铜器选粹》，台北，台北故宫博物院，1974 年。
顾颉刚，1935 年，《汉代学术史略》，上海，亚细亚书局。
——. 1982 年，《五德终始说下的政治和历史》，顾颉刚编《古史辨》（全 7 册），第 5 册，第 404—617 页，上海，上海古籍出版社，重印。
《关中胜迹图考》，毕沅，1776 年。
《管子》，戴望《管子校正》，收入《诸子集成》，第 5 册。

郭霭春等，1991 年，《黄帝内经词典》，天津，天津科学技术出版社。
郭宝钧，1956 年，《辉县发掘报告》，北京，科学出版社。
——. 1959 年，《山彪镇与琉璃阁》，北京，科学出版社。
——. 1963 年，《中国青铜器时代》，北京，三联书店。
——. 1981 年，《商周铜器群综合研究》，北京，文物出版社。
郭建邦，1980 年，《北魏宁懋石室和墓》，《河南文博通讯》第 1 期，第 22—40 页。
郭沫若，1960 年，《安阳圆坑墓中鼎铭考释》，《考古学报》第 1 期，第 1—5 页。
——. 1963 年《扶风齐家村青铜器群》，北京，文物出版社。
《国语》，上海，上海古籍出版社，1988 年。
韩伟，1983 年，《凤翔秦公陵园钻探与试掘简报》，《文物》第 7 期，第 30—37 页。
——. 1985 年，《马家庄秦宗庙建筑制度研究》，《文物》第 2 期，第 30—38 页。
《汉书》，班固，北京，中华书局，1962 年。
河北省文化局文物处，1959 年，《郑州二里岗》，北京，科学出版社。
河北省文化局文物工作队，1965 年，《河北易县燕下都故城勘察和试掘》，《考古学报》第 1 期，第 83—106 页。
河北省文物管理处，1979 年，《河北省平山县战国时期中山国墓葬发掘简报》，《文物》第 1 期，第 1—31 页。
《河南出土商周青铜器》，北京，文物出版社，1981 年。
河南省博物馆，1975 年，《郑州新出土的商代前期大铜鼎》，《文物》第 6 期，第 64—68 页。
河南省文物研究所，1990 年，《近十年河南文物工作的新进展》，文物编辑委员会《文物考古工作十年》，第 176—191 页，北京，文物出版社。
河南省文物研究所、郑州市博物馆，1983 年，《郑州新发现商代窖藏青铜器》，《文物》第 3 期，第 49—59 页。
贺业钜，1983 年，《试论周代两次城市建设高潮》，李润海编《中国建筑史论文选集》，台北，明文书局。
《后汉纪》，袁宏，上海，商务印书馆，1937 年。
《后汉书》，范晔，北京，中华书局，1965 年。
湖北省博物馆，1980 年，《随县曾侯乙墓》(全 2 册)，北京，文物出版社。
湖南省博物馆，1972 年，湖南省工农兵热爱祖国文化遗产，《文物》第 1 期，第 6—7 页。
湖南省博物馆、中国社会科学院考古研究所，1974 年，《长沙马王堆二、三号汉墓发掘简报》，《文物》第 7 期，第 39—48 页。
《画像石画像砖》，《中国美术全集》，上海，上海人民美术出版社，1988 年。
《华阳国志》，收入《四部丛刊》，第 85 种。
《淮南子》，刘安，收入《诸子集成》，第 7 册。
《黄帝内经 · 素问》，王冰《补注黄帝内经素问》。

黄明兰，1987 年，《洛阳北魏世俗石刻线画集》，北京，人民美术出版社。
黄然伟，1978 年，《殷周青铜器赏赐铭文研究》，香港，龙门书局。
黄任恒，1925 年，《古孝汇传》，广州，聚珍印务局。
黄盛璋，1978 年，《西周微氏家窖藏群初步研究》，《社会科学战线》第 3 期，第 194—206 页。
黄展岳，1960 年，《汉长安城南郊礼制建筑的位置及其有关问题》，《考古》第 9 期，第 53—58 页。
济宁地区文物组、嘉祥文管所，1982 年，《山东嘉祥宋山一九八零年出土的汉画像石》，《文物》第 5 期，第 60—69 页。
《建康实录》，北京，中华书局，1984 年。
江苏省文管会，1959 年，《江苏徐州汉画像石》，北京，科学出版社。
江西省文物考古研究所、江西省新干县博物馆，1991 年，《江西新干大洋洲商墓发掘简报》，《文物》第 10 期，第 1—23 页。
蒋善国，1988 年，《尚书综述》，上海，上海古籍出版社。
金琦，1959 年，《南京附近六朝陵墓石刻整修纪要》，《文物》第 4 期，第 26—31 页。
《晋书》，房玄龄，北京，中华书局，1974 年。
《考工记图》，戴震，上海，商务印书馆，1955 年。
考古研究所汉城发掘队，1960 年，《汉长安城南郊礼制建筑遗址群发掘简报》，《考古》第 7 期，第 36—39 页。
乐嘉藻，1977 年（1933），《中国建筑史》，台北，华世出版社。
雷海宗，1957 年，《世界史分期与上古中古史中的一些问题》，《历史教学》第 7 期，第 41—47 页。
骊山学会，1987 年，《秦东陵探查初议》，《考古与文物》第 4 期，第 86—88 页。
《礼记》，孔颖达《礼记正义》，收入《十三经注疏》，第 1221—1696 页。
李发林，1982 年，《山东汉画像石研究》，济南，齐鲁书社。
——. 1984 年，《关于"嘉祥宋山安国墓祠题记释读"的意见》，《考古与文物》第 6 期，第 105—106 页。
——. 1985 年，《山东苍山元嘉元年画像石墓题记试释》，《中原文物》第 1 期，第 72—75 页。
李辅耀，1967 年，《读礼丛钞》，台北，文海出版社。
李宏涛、王丕忠，1980 年，《汉元帝渭陵调察记》，《考古与文物》第 1 期，第 40—41 页。
李济，1990 年（1951），《殷墟有刃石图说》，张光直、李光谟编《李济考古学论文选集》，第 373—453 页，北京，文物出版社。
李学勤，1959 年，《殷代地理简论》，北京，科学出版社。
——. 1978 年，《论史墙盘及其意义》，《考古学报》第 2 期，第 149—158 页。
——. 1979 年，《西周中期青铜器的重要标尺：周原庄白、强家两处青铜器窖藏的综合研究》，《中国历史博物馆馆刊》第 1 期，第 29—36 页。
——. 1984 年，《东周与秦代文明》，北京，文物出版社。

——. 1987 年,《论新出土的大汶口文化陶器符号》,《文物》第 12 期，第 75—80 页。
——. 1991 年 a,《论二里头文化的饕餮纹》,《中国文物报》10 月 20 日。
——. 1991 年 b,《新干大洋洲商墓的若干问题》,《文物》第 10 期，第 33—38 页。
李允鉌，1982 年,《华夏意匠：中国古典建筑设计原理分析》，香港，广角镜出版社。
李仲操，1978 年,《史墙盘铭文试释》,《文物》第 3 期，第 33—34 页。
《历代钟鼎彝器疑识法帖》，薛尚功，海城于氏，1935 年。
《隶释》，洪适,《石刻史料新编》，第 9 册，第 6747—7042 页，台北，新文丰出版公司。
《梁书》，姚思廉，北京，中华书局，1973 年。
《列女传》，刘向，收入《四部丛刊》，第 60 种。
林利明、孙仲嘉，1984 年,《中国历代陵寝纪略》，哈尔滨，黑龙江人民出版社。
《陵墓建筑》,《中国美术全集》，北京，中国建筑工业出版社，1988 年。
刘斌，1990 年,《良渚文化玉琮初探》,《文物》第 2 期，第 30—37 页。
刘敦愿，1981 年,《春秋时期齐国故城的复原与城市布局》,《历史地理》第 1 期，第 148—159 页。
刘敦桢，1932 年,《汉代长安城及未央宫》,《中国营造学社会刊》，卷 3，3 号，第 147—169 页。
——. 1980 年,《中国古代建筑史》，北京，中国建筑工业出版社。
刘节，1941 年,《说彝》,《图书季刊》3.3/4，重印于刘节《古史考存》，第 163—173 页，北京，人民出版社，1958 年。
刘庆柱、李毓芳，1982 年,《西汉诸陵调查与研究》,《文物参考资料》第 6 辑，第 1—15 页。
——. 1987 年,《西汉十一陵》，西安，陕西人民出版社。
刘运勇，1982 年,《西汉长安》，北京，中华书局。
刘致平，1957 年 a,《中国建筑类型与结构》，北京，建筑工程出版社。
——. 1957 年 b,《西安西北郊古代建筑遗址勘察初记》,《文物参考资料》第 3 期，第 5—12 页。
《陆士衡集》，陆机，收入《四部备要》，上海，中华书局，1930 年。
《论语》，刘宝楠《论语正义》，收入《诸子集成》，第 1 册。
《论衡》，王充，见刘盼遂《论衡集解》，北京，古籍出版社，1957 年。
罗福颐，1960 年,《芗他君石祠堂题字解释》,《故宫博物院院刊》第 2 期，第 178—180 页。
罗焜，1982 年,《商代人祭及相关问题》，胡厚宣主编《甲骨探史录》，第 112—191 页，北京，三联书店。
罗西章，1988 年,《周原青铜器窖藏及其有关问题的探讨》,《考古》第 2 期，第 40—47 页。
罗振玉，1936 年,《三代吉金文存》，东京，上虞罗氏。

《洛阳伽蓝记》，杨衒之，见范祥雍《洛阳伽蓝记校注》，上海，上海古籍出版社，1978年。
雒忠如，1957年，《西安西郊发现汉代建筑遗址》，《考古通讯》第6期，第26—30页。
《吕氏春秋》，收入《诸子集成》第6册。
马承源等，1991年，《中国青铜器》，上海，上海古籍出版社。
马得志等，1953年，《一九五三年秋安阳大司空村发掘报告》，《考古学报》第9期，第25—40页。
马先醒，1976年，《汉简与汉代城市》，台北，简牍社。
马振智，1989年，《试论泰国陵寝制度的形成发展及特点》，《考古》第5期，第110—116页。
《梦溪笔谈》，沈括，《元刊梦溪笔谈》，1975年，据1305年版本影印，北京，文物出版社。
《孟子》，孙奭《孟子注疏》，收入《十三经注疏》，第2659—2782页。
《明堂大道录》，惠栋，共二卷，收入《丛书集成》，第1035—1036种，上海，商务印书馆，1937年。
《明堂月令论》，蔡邕，《蔡中郎文集》，卷十，第1—6页，上海，涵芬楼，1931年。
《墨子》，孙诒让《墨子闲诂》，收入《诸子集成》，第4册。
牟永抗、云希正，1992年，《中国玉器全集·原始社会》，石家庄，河北美术出版社。
牟永抗等，1989年，《良渚文化玉器》，北京，文物出版社。
南京博物院，1973年，《铜山小龟山西汉崖洞墓》，《文物》第4期，第21—35页。
——. 1984年，《一九八二年江苏武进寺墩遗址的发掘》，《考古》第2期，第109—129页。
南京博物院、铜山县文化馆，1985年，《铜山龟山二号西汉崖洞墓》，《考古学报》第1期，第119—133页。
《南齐书》，萧子显，北京，中华书局1972年。
南阳市博物馆，1974年，《南阳发现东汉许阿瞿墓志画像石》，《文物》第8期，第73—75页。
内蒙古自治区博物馆，1978年，《和林格尔汉墓壁画》，北京，文物出版社。
《漆器》，《中国美术全集》，北京，文物出版社，1989年。
齐思和，1947年，《周代锡命礼考》，《燕京学报》第32期，第197—226页。
祁英涛，1957年，《西安的几处汉代建筑遗址》，《文物参考资料》第5期，第57—58页。
秦都咸阳考古站，1976年，《秦都咸阳第一号宫殿建筑遗址简报》，《文物》第11期，第12—24页。
《秦汉雕塑》，《中国美术全集》，北京，人民美术出版社，1985年。
秦俑坑考古队，1975年，《临潼县秦俑坑试掘第一号简报》，《文物》第11期，第1—18页。

——. 1978 年,《秦始皇陵东侧第二号兵马俑坑钻探试掘简报》,《文物》第 5 期，第 1—19 页。
——. 1979 年,《秦始皇陵东侧第三号兵马俑坑清理简报》,《文物》第 12 期，第 1—12 页。
——. 1980 年 a,《临潼上焦村秦墓清理简报》,《考古与文物》第 2 期，第 42—50 页。
——. 1980 年 b,《秦始皇陵东侧马厩坑钻探清理简报》,《考古与文物》第 4 期，第 31—41 页。
——. 1982 年 a,《秦始皇陵西侧赵家背户村秦刑徒墓》,《文物》第 3 期，第 1—11 页。
——. 1982 年 b,《秦始皇陵园陪葬坑钻探清理简报》,《考古与文物》第 1 期，第 25—29 页。
《青铜器 · 一、二》(全 2 册),《中国美术全集》，北京，文物出版社，1985、1986 年。
裘锡圭，1978 年,《史墙盘铭解释》,《文物》第 3 期，第 25—32 页。
群力，1972 年,《临淄齐国故城勘探纪要》,《文物》第 5 期，第 45—54 页。
《人民日报》。
任继愈，1981 年,《中国佛教史》，北京，中国社会科学出版社。
《日知录》，顾炎武，见黄汝成《日知录集释》，收入《四部备要》，上海，中华书局，1927 年。
容庚，1936 年,《汉武梁祠画像录》，北平，北平考古学社。
容庚、张维持，1958 年,《殷周彝器通考》，北京，科学出版社。
《瑞应图记》，孙柔之，叶德辉《观古堂所著书》，湘潭叶氏，1902 年。
《三代吉金文存》，罗振玉，北京，中华书局，1983 年重印。
《三辅黄图》，见张宗祥《校正三辅黄图》，北京，古典文学出版社，1958 年。
《三国志》，陈寿，中华书局，1959 年。
山东博物馆，1972 年,《曲阜九龙山汉墓发掘简报》,《文物》第 5 期，第 39—44 页。
山东博物馆、苍山县文化馆,《山东苍山元嘉元年画像石墓》,《考古》第 2 期，第 124—134 页。
山东博物馆、山东省文物考古研究所, 1982 年,《山东汉画像石选集》，济南，齐鲁书社。
山东省文管会、济南市博物馆，1974 年,《大汶口》，北京，文物出版社。
山东省文物管理处，1961 年,《山东临淄齐故域试掘简报》,《考古》第 6 期，第 289—297 页。
《陕西出土商周青铜器》(全三册)，北京，文物出版社，1980 年。
陕西省考古研究所，1987 年,《秦东陵第一号陵园勘察记》,《考古》第 4 期，第 19—28 页。
陕西省雍城考古队，1985 年,《凤翔马家庄一号建筑群遗址发掘简报》,《文物》第 2 期，第 1—29 页。
陕西文物管理委员会，1962 年,《秦始皇陵调察简报》,《考古》第 8 期，第

407—411 页。
陕西周原考古队，1978 年，《陕西扶风庄白一号西周青铜器窖藏发掘简报》，《文物》第 3 期，第 1—8 页。《商君书》，见朱师辙《商君书解诂定本》，北京，古籍出版社，1956 年。
《商周青铜酒器特展图录》，台北，台北故宫博物院，1989 年。
《商周至秦汉书法》，《中国美术全集》，北京，人民美术出版社，1987 年。
《尚书》，见孔颖达《尚书正义》，收入《十三经注疏》，第 109—258 页。
《诗经》，见孔颖达《毛诗正义》，收入《十三经注疏》，第 259—629 页。
施昕更，1938 年，《良渚：杭县第二区黑陶文化遗址初步报告》，浙江教育厅。
施蛰存，1987 年，《水经注碑录》，天津，天津古籍出版社。
《十三经注疏》，阮元编，北京，中华书局，1980 年。
石家庄图书馆，1980 年，《河北石家庄北郊西汉墓发掘报告》，《考古》第 1 期，第 52—55 页。
《石索》，冯云鹏、冯云鹓《金石索》，上海，商务印书馆，重印。
石璋如，1933 年，第七次殷墟发掘，《安阳发掘报告》4，第 709—728 页。
——. 1959 年，《小屯第一本：遗址的发现与发掘乙编：殷墟建筑遗存》，台北，“中央研究院”历史语言研究所。
——. 1960 年，河南安阳小屯殷代的三组基址，《大陆杂志》，卷 21，1/2 期，第 19—26 页。
石志廉，1987 年，《最大最古的刻纹玉琮》，《中国文物报》10 月 1 日。
《释名》，刘熙，见王先谦《释名疏证补》，上海，上海古籍出版社，1984 年。
《山海经》，见袁珂《山海经校注》，上海，上海古籍出版社，1980 年。
《史记》，司马迁，北京，中华书局，1959 年。
《水经注》，郦道元，上海，世界书局，1936 年。
《水经注图》，杨守敬，台北，文海出版社，1966 年，重印。
《说文解字》，许慎，见段玉裁《说文解字注》，上海，上海古籍出版社，1981 年。
《说苑》，刘向，见卢元骏《说苑今注今译》，天津，天津古籍出版社，1988 年。
《宋书》，沈约，北京，中华书局，1974 年。
《宋注长安志》，阮元编，长安县志局。
《隋纪》，收入吴楚材《纲鉴易知录》，台北，华联出版社，1964 年。
《隋书》，魏征，北京，中华书局，1973 年。
孙诒让，《周礼正义》，收入《四部备要》，上海，中华书局，1934 年。
《太平御览》，李昉编，北京，中华书局，1960 年。
汤用彤，1938 年，《汉魏两晋南北朝佛教史》上海，商务印书馆。
唐金裕，1959 年，《西安西郊汉代建筑遗址发掘报告》，《考古学报》第 2 期，第 45—54 页。
唐兰，1960 年，《中国古代社会使用青铜农器问题的初步研究》，《故宫博物院院刊》第 2 期，第 10—34 页。
——. 1962 年，《西周铜器断代中的康宫问题》，《考古学报》第 1 期，第 15—

48 页。
——. 1976 年,《何尊铭文解释》,《文物》第 1 期，第 60—63 页。
——. 1978 年,《略论西周微氏家族窖藏铜器群的重要意义》,《文物》第 3 期，第 19—24 页。
——. 1979 年,《关于〈夏鼎〉》,《文史》第 7 期，第 1—8 页。
——. 1981 年,《从大汶口文化的陶器文字看我国最早文化的年代》,《大汶口文化讨论文集》，第 79—84 页，济南，齐鲁书社。
《陶瓷 · 一》,《中国美术全集》，上海，上海人民美术出版社，1980 年。
《陶渊明集》，陶潜，北京，中华书局，1979 年。
汪遵国，1984 年,《良渚文化玉敛葬述略》,《文物》第 2 期，第 23—35 页。
王国维，1961 年,《观堂集林》，台北，世界书局。
王丕忠等, 1980 年,《汉景帝阳陵调察简报》,《考古》第 1 期，第 36—37 页。
王人聪，1990 年,《何尊铭文解释与成王迁都问题》,《考古》第 3 期，第 47—51 页。
王世民，1981 年,《中国春秋战国时代的冢墓》,《考古》第 5 期，第 459—466 页。
——. 1987 年,《关于西周春秋高级贵族礼器制度的一些看法》,《文物考古论集》，北京，文物出版社。
王世仁，1957 年,《西安市西郊工地的汉代建筑遗址》,《文物参考资料》第 3 期，第 11—12 页。
——. 1963 年,《汉长安城南郊礼制建筑原状的推测》,《考古》第 9 期，第 501—515 页。
王树村，1986 年,《中国石刻线画略史》,《中国美术全集》，第 19 册。
王树明，1986 年,《陵阳河与大朱村出土陶尊上的文字》,《山东史前文化论文集》，济南，齐鲁书社。
王巍，1986 年,《良渚文化玉琮刍议》,《考古》第 11 期，第 1009—1016 页。
王学理，1982 年,《秦都咸阳与咸阳宫辨正》,《考古与文物》第 2 期，第 67—71 页。
——. 1985 年《秦都咸阳》，西安，陕西人民出版社。
——. 1989 年,《"丽山食官"（东段）复原的构想》,《考古》第 5 期，第 125—129 页。
王学理等，1979 年,《秦都咸阳发掘报导的若干补充意见》,《文物》第 2 期，第 85—86 页。
王益之，1937 年,《西汉年纪》，收入《国学基本丛书》，第 17 种，上海，商务印书馆。
王毅，1990 年,《园林与中国文化》，上海，上海人民出版社。
王仲殊，1957 年,《汉长安城考古工作的初步收获》,《考古通讯》第 5 期，第 102—104 页。
——. 1984 年,《汉代考古学概说》，北京，中华书局。
卫挺生，1970 年,《周自穆王都洛考》，台北，台湾中华学术院。
《魏晋南北朝书法》，北京，人民美术出版社，1987 年。

文物出版社，1979 年，《文物考古工作三十年》，北京，文物出版社。
《文献通考》，马端临，台北，台湾商务印书馆，1983 年。
《文选》，萧统，见高步瀛《文选李注义疏》(全四册)，北京，中华书局，1985 年。
闻宥，1956 年，《四川汉代画像选集》，北京，中国古典艺术出版社。
巫鸿，1979 年，《一组早期的玉石雕刻》，《美术研究》第 1 期，第 64—70 页。
——. 1989 年，《汉明、魏文的礼制改革与汉代画像艺术之盛衰》，《九州学刊》卷三，第 2 期，第 31—44 页。
吴汝祚，1989 年，《从黑陶杯看大汶口—龙山文化发展的阶段性及其中心范围》，苏秉琦主编《考古学文化论集》第 2 集，第 31—43 页。
《西清续鉴甲编》，王杰等，北京，1910 年。
谢敏聪，1979 年，《中国历代帝陵考略》，台北，中正书局。
《新序》，刘向，见卢元骏《新序今注今释》，天津，天津古籍出版社，1987 年。
《新语》，陆贾，见王利器《新语校注》，北京，中华书局，1986 年。
信立祥，1982 年，《汉画像石的分区和分期》，北京大学硕士论文。
徐旭生，1960 年，《中国古史的传说时代》，北京，科学出版社。
徐中舒，1978 年，《西周墙盘铭文笺释》，《考古学报》第 2 期，第 139—148 页。
徐州博物馆，1984 年，《徐州石桥汉墓清理报告》，《文物》第 11 期，第 22—40 页。
徐州博物馆等，1988 年，《徐州北洞山西汉墓发掘简报》，《文物》第 2 期，第 2—18 页。
许道龄、刘致平，1959 年，《关于西安西郊发现的汉代建筑遗址是明堂或辟雍的讨论》，《考古》第 4 期，第 193—196 页。
《宣和博古图录》，王黼，1603 年，哈佛燕京图书馆，哈佛大学。
《荀子》，见王先谦《荀子集解》，收入《诸子集成》，第 2 册。
《盐铁论》，桓宽，收入《四部丛刊》，第 14 种，上海，商务印书馆。
《演繁露》，程大昌，上海，商务印书馆，1936 年。
杨殿珣，1940 年，《石刻题跋索引》，上海，上海商务印书馆，1990 年，重印。
杨鸿勋 (陶复)，1976 年 a，《从盘龙城商代宫殿遗址谈中国宫廷建筑的几个问题》，《文物》第 2 期，第 16—25 页；收入杨鸿勋，1987 年，第 81—93 页。
——. 1976 年 b，《秦咸阳宫第一号遗址复原问题的初步探讨》，《文物》第 11 期，第 31—41 页；收入杨鸿勋，1987 年，第 153—168 页。
——. 1980 年，《战国中山王陵及兆域图研究》，《考古学报》第 1 期，第 119—137 页；收入杨鸿勋，1987 年，第 120—142 页。
——. 1981 年，《西周岐邑建筑遗址初步考察》，《文物》第 3 期，第 23—33 页；收入杨鸿勋，1987 年，第 94—109 页。
——. 1982 年，《关于秦代以前墓上建筑的问题》，《考古》第 4 期，第 402—406 页；收入杨鸿勋，1987 年，第 143—149 页。

——. 1987 年，《建筑考古学论文集》，北京，文物出版社。
杨宽，1965 年，《古史新探》，北京，中华书局。
——. 1982 年，《先秦墓上建筑和陵寝制度》，《文物》第 1 期，第 31—37 页。
——. 1983 年，《先秦墓上建筑问题的再探讨》，《考古》第 7 期，第 636—640 页；收入杨宽，1985 年，第 211—218 页。
——. 1985 年，《中国古代陵寝制度研究》，上海，上海古籍出版社。
杨树达，1933 年，《汉代婚丧礼俗考》，上海，商务印书馆。
姚迁、古兵，1981 年，《六朝艺术》，北京，文物出版社。
叶骁军，1988 年，《中国都城发展史》，西安，陕西人民出版社。
《仪礼》，见贾公彦《仪礼疏》，收入《十三经注疏》，第 941—1220 页。
《艺文类聚》，欧阳询编，上海，上海古籍出版社，1965 年。
《易经》，见孔颖达《周易正义》，收入《十三经注疏》，第 5—108 页。
《逸周书》，见朱右曾《逸周书集训校释》，收入《国学基本丛书》，长沙，商务印书馆，1940 年。
《殷墟青铜器》，北京，文物出版社。
《雍录》，程大昌，收入吴管《古今逸史》，卷 22—26，上海，涵芬楼，1937 年。
《永乐大典》，解缙等编，上海，中华书局重印本，1960 年。
于省吾，1957 年，《从甲骨文看商代社会性质》，《吉林大学社会科学学报》第 2/3 期，第 97—136 页。
——. 1958 年，《斥唐兰先生关于商代社会性质的讨论》，《历史研究》第 8 期。第 59—71 页。
于中航，1976 年，《大汶口文化和原始社会的解体》，《文物》第 5 期，第 64—73 页。
俞伟超，1985 年，《先秦两汉考古学论集》，北京，文物出版社。
俞伟超、高明，1978—1979 年，《周代用鼎制度研究》，《北京大学学报（人文科学）》，1978 年第 1/2 期，第 84—98 页；1979 年第 1 期，第 83—96 页；修订稿见俞伟超 1985 年，第 62—114 页。
《原始社会至南北朝绘画》，《中国美术全集》，北京，人民美术出版社，1986 年。
《越绝书》，袁康，收入《四部丛刊》，第 64 种。
曾昭燏等，《沂南古画像石墓发掘报告》，北京，文化部文物事业管理局，1956 年。
展力等，1977 年，《试谈杨家湾汉墓骑兵俑》，《文物》第 10 期，第 22—26 页。
《战国策》，刘向，收入《四部丛刊》。
张光裕，1979 年，《金文中册命之典》，《香港中文大学中国文化研究所学报》，10b。
张龙海、朱玉德，1988 年，《临淄齐国古城的排水系统》，《考古》第 9 期，第 784—787 页。
张明华，1990 年，《良渚玉符试探》，《文物》第 12 期，第 32—36 页。

张万夫，1984 年，《汉画选》，天津，天津人民美术出版社。
赵康民，1979 年，《秦始皇秦陵北二、三、四号建筑遗址》，《文物》第 12 期，第 13—6 页。
——. 1980 年，《秦始皇陵原名骊山》，《考古与文物》第 3 期，第 34—38 页。
赵汝珍，1984 年，《古玩指南》，北京，中国书店。
赵铁寒，1975 年，《说九鼎》，《古史考述》，台北，中正书局。
赵翼，1960 年，《陔余丛考》，台北，世界书局。
赵芝荃，1989 年，《二里头遗址与偃师商城》，《考古与文物》第 2 期，第 76—83 页。
浙江考古研究所，1989 年，《良渚文化玉器》，北京，文物出版社。
浙江省文物考古研究所，1988 年，《余杭瑶山良渚文化祭坛遗址发掘简报》，《文物》第 1 期，第 32—51 页。
浙江省文物考古研究所反山考古队，1988 年，《浙江余杭反山良渚墓地发掘简报》，《文物》第 1 期，第 1—31 页。
郑振香、陈志达，1985 年，《殷墟青铜器的分期与年代》，中国社会科学院考古研究所《殷墟青铜器》，第 2—75 页，北京，文物出版社。
《郑州二里岗》，北京，科学出版社，1959 年。
郑州市博物馆，1981 年，《河南荥阳西史村遗址试掘简报》，《文物资料丛刊》第 5 期，第 84—102 页。
《中华人民共和国出土文物展览展品选集》，北京，文物出版社，1973 年。
《中国美术家人名辞典》，上海，上海人民美术出版社，1981 年。
《中国美术全集》(全 60 卷)，多家出版社，1985—1989 年。
中国社会科学院考古研究所，1956 年，《辉县发掘报告》，北京，科学出版社。
——. 1962 年，《中国科学院考古研究所一九六一年田野工作的主要收获》，《考古》第 5 期，第 272—274 页。
——. 1980 年，《殷墟妇好墓》，北京，文物出版社。
——. 1984 年，《新中国的考古发现和研究》，北京，文物出版社。
中国社会科学院考古研究所、河北省文物管理处，1980 年，《满城汉墓发掘报告》，北京，文物出版社。
中国社会科学院考古研究所、洛阳汉魏故城工作队，《偃师商城的初步勘探和发掘》，《考古》第 6 期，第 488—504 页。
中国社会科学院考古研究所河南第二工作队，1984 年，《一九八三年秋季河南偃师商城发掘简报》，《考古》第 10 期，第 872—879 页。
中国社会科学院考古研究所山东工作队、曲阜县文物管理委员会，1965 年，《山东曲阜考古调察试掘简报》，《考古》第 12 期，第 599—613 页。
——. 1985 年，《一九八四年春偃师尸乡沟商城宫殿遗址发掘简报》，《考古》第 4 期，第 322—35 页。
——. 1988 年，《河南偃师尸乡沟商城第五号宫殿遗址发掘简报》，《考古》第 2 期，第 128—140 页。
《中国文物报》，北京，国家文物局。
《中国文物精华》，北京，文物出版社，1992 年。

《中国玉器全集·一》，石家庄，河北美术出版社，1992年。
朱剑心，1940年，《金石学》，上海，商务印书馆。
朱孔阳，1937年，《历代陵寝备考》，上海，申报馆。
朱希祖等，1935年，《六朝陵墓调察报告》，南京，中央古物保管委员会。
朱偰，1936年，《建康兰陵六朝陵墓图考》，上海，商务印书馆。
——. 1957年，《修复南京六朝陵墓古迹中重要的发现》，《文物参考资料》第3期，第44—45页。
《诸子集成》(全8册)，北京，中华书局，1986年。
《庄子》，见郭庆藩《庄子集释》，收入《诸子集成》，第3册。
《周礼》，见贾公彦《周礼注疏》，收入《十三经注疏》，第631—940页。
《总目录》，《中国美术全集》，北京，人民美术出版社，1989年。
邹衡，1979年，《商周考古》，北京，文物出版社。

日文文献

奥村伊九良，1947 年，《瓜茄》，東京，瓜茄研究所。
長広敏雄，1965 年，《漢代画象の研究》，東京，中央公論美術出版。
大村西崖，1915、1920 年，《支那美術史雕塑篇》（全 2 巻），東京，佛書刊行會圖像部。
東京国立博物館，1986 年，《黄河文明展》，東京，中日新聞社。
福井康順，1952 年，《道教の基礎的研究》，東京，理想社。
関野貞，1916 年，《支那山東省に於ける漢代墳墓の表飾》，東京，東京帝国大学。
駒井和愛，1950 年，《曲阜魯城の遺蹟》，東京，東京大学文学部考古学研究室。
林巳奈夫，1965 年，《中国古代の酒甕》，《考古学雜誌》第 65 巻第 2 期，第 1—22 页。
——. 1979 年，《先殷式の玉器文化》，*Museum* 第 334 期，第 4—16 页。
——. 1981 年，《良渚文化の玉器若干をめぐって》，*Museum* 第 360 期，第 22—33 页。
——. 1990 年，《良渚文化と大汶口文化の図象記号》，《史林》第 73 巻第 5 期，第 116—134 页。
——. 1991 年，《中国古代における日の暈と神話的図像》，《史林》第 74 巻第 4 期，第 96—121 页。
梅原末治，1947 年，《冠斝樓吉金圖》，京都。
森三樹三郎，1943 年，《支那の神々の官僚的性格》，《支那学》第 11 巻第 1 期，第 49—81 页。
僧祐，《出三藏記集》，高楠顺次郎、渡边海旭編《大正新脩大藏經》収録，東京，大正一切経刊行会，1922—1924 年，No.2145。
——. 1969 年，《六朝時代美術の研究》，東京，美術出版社。
上海博物館，1976 年，《上海博物館：出土文物・青銅器・陶磁器》，東京，平凡社。
神田喜一郎，1957—1961 年，《書道全集》（全 25 巻），東京，平凡社。
西武美術館，1986 年，《大黄河文明の流れ：山東省文物展》，東京，西武美術館、朝日新聞社。
足立喜六，1933 年，《長安史蹟の研究》第 2 巻，東京，東洋文庫。

INDEX 索引

（索引页码为原英文书页码，即本书边码。）

In this index an "f" after a number indicates a separate reference on the next page, and an "ff" indicates separate references on the next two pages. A continuous discussion over two or more pages is indicated by a span of page numbers, e.g., "57-59." *Passim* is used for a cluster of references in close but not consecutive sequence. Entries are alphabetized letter by letter, ignoring word breaks, hyphens, and accents.

在本索引中，数字后的 f 表示该条也见于下一页，ff 表示该条也见于下两页。连续两页以上的论述则用连续的页码表示，例如：57—59。标有 Passim 者表示一组相关但不连续的出处。所有的条目按照字母排列，而不考虑词语的断分、连字符和重音等。

CHRONOLOGIES 年表

Hemudu culture 河姆渡文化	*ca*. 5000—3300 B.C.
Dawenkou culture 大汶口文化	*ca*. 4300—2600
Liangzhu culture 良渚文化	*ca*. 3300—2300
Longshan culture 龙山文化	*ca*. 2600—2000
Xia dynasty (unconfirmed) 夏代（不确定）	*ca*. 2070—1600
Shang dynasty 商代	*ca*. 1600—1046
Western Zhou 西周	*ca*. 1046—771
Eastern Zhou 东周	770—256
Spring and Autumn period 春秋	770—476
Warring States period 战国	475—256
Qin dynasty 秦	221—206
Western Han dynasty 西汉	206 B.C.—A.D. 8
Xin dynasty 新	9—23
Eastern Han dynasty 东汉	25—220
Three Kingdoms period 三国	220—280
Western Jin dynasty 西晋	265—317
Eastern Jin dynasty 东晋	317—420
Southern dynasties 南朝	420—589
Song 宋	420—479
Qi 齐	479—502
Liang 梁	502—557
Chen 陈	557—589

Appropriate dates of the late Shang kings
晚商诸王在位大致时间

Wu Ding 武丁	1250—1192 B.C.
Zu Geng 祖庚	1191—
Zu Jia 祖甲	
Lin Xin and/or Kang Ding 廪辛和/或康丁	1148
Wu Yi 武乙	1147—1113
Wen Ding 文丁	1112—1102
Di Yi 帝乙	1101—1076
Di Xin 帝辛	1075—1046

Periodization of the Western Zhou and appropriate dates of dynastic rulers
西周分期与诸王在位大致时间

Early Western Zhou 西周早期	1046—973 B.C.
Wu 武王	1046—1043

Cheng 成王	1042—1021
Kang 康王	1020—996
Zhao 昭王	995—977
Middle Western Zhou 西周中期	976—886
Mu 穆王	976—922
Gong 共王	922—900
Yi 懿王	899—892
Xiao 孝王	891—886
Late Western Zhou 西周晚期	885—771
Yi 夷王	885—878
Li 厉王	877—841
Gonghe 共和	841—828
Xuan 宣王	827—782
You 幽王	781—771

Emperors of the Western Han, Xin and Eastern Han dynasties
西汉、新、东汉诸皇帝在位时间

Western Han 西汉	206 B.C.—A.D. 8
Gaozu 高祖	206—195 B.C.
Hui 惠帝	195—188
Empress Dowager Lv 吕后	187—180
Wen 文帝	180—157
Jing 景帝	157—141
Wu 武帝	141—87
Zhao 昭帝	87—74
Xuan 宣帝	74—49
Yuan 元帝	49—33
Cheng 成帝	33—7
Ai 哀帝	7—1
Ping 平帝	1 B.C.—A.D. 5
Ruzi Ying 孺子婴	6—8
Xin 新	8—23
Wang Mang 王莽	8—23
Eastern Han 东汉	25—220
Guangwu 光武帝	25—57
Ming 明帝	57—75
Zhang 章帝	75—88
He 和帝	88—105
Shang 殇帝	105—106
An 安帝	106—125

Shun 顺帝	125—144
Chong 冲帝	144—145
Zhi 质帝	145—146
Huan 桓帝	146—167
Ling 灵帝	167—188
Shao 少帝	189—190
Xian 献帝	190—220

Emperors of the Liang dynasty
梁诸皇帝在位时间

Wu 武帝	502—549
Jianwen 简文帝	549—551
Yuan 元帝	552—554
Jing 敬帝	555—557

译者后记

本书的翻译分工如下：导论，孙庆伟、巫鸿译；第一章，郑岩译；第二章，李清泉译；第三章，郑岩译；第四章，郑岩译；第五章，李清泉译；鸣谢、年表、索引等，郑岩译。对于原文中少数技术性错误，译文进行了修改，未一一注出。

在翻译过程中，承韩国翰林大学金秉骏教授惠赠他所翻译的该书韩文本。韩文本将书中所引大部分中文文献原文列出，使我们得以按图索骥，加快了工作进度。特此向金教授致谢！

承原作者审读修改全部译稿，特此鸣谢！

译者

2007 年 6 月 5 日